COLLINS GEM

GERMAN DICTIONARY

GERMAN • ENGLISH
ENGLISH • GERMAN

HarperCollins*Publishers*

first published in this edition 1978
second edition 1988
third edition 1993

© William Collins Sons & Co. Ltd. 1978, 1988
© HarperCollins Publishers 1993

ISBN 0 00 458976-9

editors / Text
Veronika Calderwood-Schnorr
Ute Nicol, Peter Terrell

contributors / Mitarbeiter
Helga Holtkamp, Horst Kopleck,
Eva Vennebusch, John Whitlam

editorial staff / Manuskriptbearbeitung
Joyce Littlejohn, Anne Dickinson
Val McNulty

A catalogue record for this book is
available from the British Library

Typeset by Morton Word Processing Ltd, Scarborough

Printed in Great Britain by
HarperCollins Manufacturing, Glasgow

INHALT

CONTENTS

EINLEITUNG

Wir freuen uns, daß Sie sich zum Kauf dieses Collins Gem German Wörterbuchs entschlossen haben und hoffen, daß es Ihnen in der Schule, zu Hause, im Urlaub oder im Büro nützlich ist und Freude macht.

Diese Einleitung enthält Tips, wie Sie das Beste aus ihrem Wörterbuch herausholen können — nicht nur aus der umfangreichen Wortliste, sondern auch aus den Informationen, die in jedem Artikel stehen. Das wird Ihnen dabei helfen, modernes Englisch zu lesen und zu verstehen, und sich auf Englisch auszudrücken und zu verständigen.

Vorne in diesem Wörterbuch steht eine Liste der im Text verwendeten Abkürzungen und eine Erläuterung der Symbole der Lautschrift. Hinten finden Sie deutsche Verbtabellen und englische unregelmäßige Verben, und abschließend einen Abschnitt über Zahlen und Uhrzeit.

ZUM GEBRAUCH IHRES COLLINS GEM WÖRTERBUCHS

Das Wörterbuch enthält eine Fülle von Informationen, die mit Hilfe von unterschiedlichen Schriften und Schriftgrößen, Symbolen, Abkürzungen und Klammern vermittelt werden. Die dabei verwendeten Regeln und Symbole werden in den folgenden Abschnitten erklärt.

Stichwörter

Die Wörter, die Sie im Wörterbuch nachschlagen — „Stichwörter" — sind alphabetisch geordnet. Sie sind **fett** gedruckt, damit man sie schnell erkennt. Die beiden Stichwörter oben an jeder Seite geben das erste und letzte Wort an, das auf der betreffenden Seite behandelt wird.

Informationen zur Verwendung oder zur Form bestimmter Stichwörter stehen in Klammern hinter der Lautschrift. Sie erscheinen meist in abgekürzter Form und sind *kursiv* gedruckt (z.B. *(fam, (COMM))*.

Wo es angebracht ist, werden mit dem Stichwort verwandte Wörter im selben Artikel behandelt (z.B. **accept, acceptance**). Sie sind wie das Stichwort fett, aber etwas kleiner gedruckt.
Häufig verwendete Ausdrücke, in denen das Stichwort vorkommt (z.B. **to be cold**), sind in einer anderen Schrift halbfett gedruckt.

Lautschrift

Die Lautschrift für jedes Stichwort (zur Angabe seiner Aussprache) steht in eckigen Klammern direkt hinter dem Stichwort (z.B. **Quark** |kvark|; **knead** |ni:d|). Die Symbole der Lautschrift sind auf Seite xi erklärt.

Übersetzungen

Die Übersetzungen des Stichworts sind normal gedruckt. Wenn es mehr als eine Bedeutung oder Verwendung des Stichworts gibt, sind diese durch ein Semikolon voneinander getrennt. Vor den Übersetzungen stehen oft andere, *kursiv* gedruckte Wörter in Klammern. Sie geben an, in welchem Zusammenhang das Stichwort erscheinen könnte (z.B. **rough** *(voice)* oder *(weather)*), oder sie sind Synonyme (z.B. **rough** *(violent)*).

Schlüsselwörter

Besonders behandelt werden bestimmte deutsche und englische Wörter, die man als „Schlüsselwörter" der jeweiligen Sprache betrachten kann. Diese Wörter kommen beispielsweise sehr häufig vor oder werden unterschiedlich verwendet (z.B. **sein, auch; get, that**). Mit Hilfe von Rauten und Ziffern können Sie die verschiedenen Wortarten und Verwendungen unterscheiden. Weitere nützliche Hinweise finden Sie kursiv und in Klammern in der jeweiligen Sprache des Benutzers.

Grammatische Informationen

Wortarten stehen in abgekürzter Form *kursiv* gedruckt hinter der Aussprache des Stichworts (z.B. *vt, adv, conj*).

Die unregelmäßigen Formen englischer Substantiven und Verben stehen in Klammern vor der Wortart (z.B. **man** (*pl* **men**) *n*, **give** (*pt* **gave**, *pp* **given**) *vt*).

INTRODUCTION

We are delighted you have decided to buy the Collins Gem German Dictionary and hope you will enjoy and benefit from using it at school, at home, on holiday or at work.

This introduction gives you a few tips on how to get the most out of your dictionary — not simply from its comprehensive wordlist but also from the information provided in each entry. This will help you to read and understand modern German, as well as communicate and express yourself in the language.

The Collins Gem German Dictionary begins by listing the abbreviations used in the text and illustrating the sounds shown by the phonetic symbols. You will find German verb tables and English irregular verbs at the back, followed by a final section on numbers and time expressions.

USING YOUR COLLINS GEM DICTIONARY

A wealth of information is presented in the dictionary, using various typefaces, sizes of type, symbols, abbreviations and brackets. The conventions and symbols used are explained in the following sections.

Headwords
The words you look up in a dictionary — "headwords" — are listed alphabetically. They are printed in **bold type** for rapid identification. The two headwords appearing at the top of each page indicate the first and last word dealt with on the page in question.

Information about the usage or form of certain headwords is given in brackets after the phonetic spelling. This usually appears in abbreviated form and in italics (e.g. (*ung*), (*COMM*)).

Where appropriate, words related to headwords are grouped in the same entry (**Glück, glücken**) in a slightly smaller bold type than the headword.

Common expressions in which the headword appears are shown in a different bold roman type (e.g. **Glück haben**).

Phonetic spellings

The phonetic spelling of each headword (indicating its pronunciation) is given in square brackets immediately after the headword (e.g. **Quark** |kvark|). A list of these symbols is given on page xi.

Meanings

Headword translations are given in ordinary type and, where more than one meaning or usage exists, these are separated by a semicolon. You will often find other words in italics in brackets before the translations. These offer suggested contexts in which the headword might appear (e.g. **eng** (*Kleidung*) or (*Freundschaft*)) or provide synonyms (e.g. **eng** (*fig: Horizont*)).

"Key" words

Special status is given to certain German and English words which are considered as "key" words in each language. They may, for example, occur very frequently or have several types of usage (e.g. **sein, auch; get, that**). A combination of lozenges and numbers helps you to distinguish different parts of speech and different meanings. Further helpful information is provided in brackets and in italics in the relevant language for the user.

Grammatical information

Parts of speech are given in abbreviated form in italics after the phonetic spellings of headwords (e.g. *vt, av, konj*).

Genders of German nouns are indicated as follows: m for a masculine and f for a feminine and nt for a neuter noun. The genitive and plural forms of regular nouns are shown on the table on page x. Nouns which do not follow these rules have the genitive and plural in brackets immediately preceding the gender (e.g. **Spaß**, (**-es, -̈e**), *m*).

Adjectives are normally shown in their basic form (e.g. **groß** *adj*), but where they are only used attributively (i.e. before a noun) feminine and neuter endings follow in brackets (**hohe (r, s)** *adj attrib*).

ABKÜRZUNGEN

ABBREVIATIONS

Abkürzung	**abk, abbr**	abbreviation
Adjektiv	**adj**	adjective
Akkusativ	**acc**	accusative
Adverb	**adv**	adverb
Landwirtschaft	**AGR**	agriculture
Akkusativ	**akk**	accusative
Anatomie	**ANAT**	anatomy
Architektur	**ARCHIT**	architecture
Astrologie	**ASTROL**	astrology
Astronomie	**ASTRON**	astronomy
attributiv	**attrib**	attributive
Kraftfahrzeuge	**AUT**	automobiles
Hilfsverb	**aux**	auxiliary
Luftfahrt	**AVIAT**	aviation
besonders	**bes**	especially
Biologie	**BIOL**	biology
Botanik	**BOT**	botany
britisch	**BRIT**	British
Chemie	**CHEM**	chemistry
Film	**CINE**	cinema
Konjunktion	**conj**	conjunction
Handel	**COMM**	commerce
Komparativ	**compar**	comparative
Computer	**COMPUT**	computing
Kochen und Backen	**COOK**	cooking
zusammengesetztes Wort	**cpd**	compound
Dativ	**dat**	dative
kirchlich	**ECCL**	ecclesiastical
Eisenbahn	**EISENB**	railways
Elektrizität	**ELEK, ELEC**	electricity
besonders	**esp**	especially
und so weiter	**etc**	et cetera
etwas	**etw**	something
Euphemismus, Hüllwort	**euph**	euphemism
Femininum	**f**	feminine
übertragen	**fig**	figurative
Finanzwesen	**FIN**	finance
Genitiv	**gen**	genitive
Geographie	**GEOG**	geography
Geologie	**GEOL**	geology
Grammatik	**GRAM**	grammar
Geschichte	**HIST**	history
unpersönlich	**impers**	impersonal
unbestimmt	**indef**	indefinite
umgangssprachlich (! vulgär)	**inf**	informal (! particularly offensive)

ABKÜRZUNGEN

ABBREVIATIONS

nicht getrennt gebraucht	insep	inseparable
Interjektion, Ausruf	interj	interjection
interrogativ, fragend	interrog	interrogative
unveränderlich	inv	invariable
unregelmäßig	irreg	irregular
jemand	jd	somebody
jemandem	jdm	(to) somebody
jemanden	jdn	somebody
jemandes	jds	somebody's
Rechtswesen	JUR	law
Konjunktion	konj	conjunction
Kochen und Backen	KOCH	cooking
Komparativ	komp	comparative
Sprachwissenschaft	LING	linguistics
literarisch	liter	literary
Literatur	LITER	of literature
Maskulinum	m	masculine
Mathematik	MATH	mathematics
Medizin	MED	medicine
Meteorologie	MET	meteorology
militärisch	MIL	military
Bergbau	MIN	mining
Musik	MUS	music
Substantiv, Hauptwort	n	noun
nautisch, Seefahrt	NAUT	nautical, naval
Nominativ	nom	nominative
Neutrum	nt	neuter
Zahlwort	num	numeral
Objekt	obj	object
oder	od	or
sich	o.s.	oneself
Parlament	PARL	parliament
abschätzig	pej	pejorative
Photographie	PHOT	photography
Physik	PHYS	physics
Plural	pl	plural
Politik	POL	politics
besitzanzeigend	poss	possessive
Präfix, Vorsilbe	pp	prefix
Präposition	präp, prep	preposition
Typographie	PRINT	printing
Pronomen, Fürwort	pron	pronoun
Psychologie	PSYCH	psychology

ABKÜRZUNGEN

ABBREVIATIONS

1. Vergangenheit, Imperfekt	**pt**	past tense
Partizip Perfekt	**pp**	past participle
Radio	**RADIO**	radio
Eisenbahn	**RAIL**	railways
Relativ-	**rel**	relative
Religion	**REL**	religion
jemand (-en, -em)	**sb**	someone, somebody
Schulwesen	**SCH**	school
Naturwissenschaft	**SCI**	science
schottisch	**Scot**	Scottish
Singular, Einzahl	**sg**	singular
etwas	**sth**	something
Suffix, Nachsilbe	**subj**	suffix
Superlativ	**superl**	superlative
Technik	**TECH**	technology
Nachrichtentechnik	**TEL**	telecommunications
Theater	**THEAT**	theatre
Fernsehen	**TV**	television
Typographie	**TYP**	printing
umgangssprachlich (! vulgär)	**umg(!)**	colloquial (! particularly offensive)
Hochschulwesen	**UNIV**	university
unpersönlich	**unpers**	impersonal
unregelmäßig	**unreg**	irregular
(nord)amerikanisch	**US**	(North) America
gewöhnlich	**usu**	usually
Verb	**vb**	verb
intransitives Verb	**vi**	intransitive verb
reflexives Verb	**vr**	reflexive verb
transitives Verb	**vt**	transitive verb
Zoologie	**ZOOL**	zoology
zusammengesetztes Wort	**zW**	compound
zwischen zwei Sprechern		change of speaker
ungefähre Entsprechung	≈	cultural equivalent
eingetragenes Warenzeichen	®	registered trademark

REGULAR GERMAN NOUN ENDINGS

nom		*gen*	*pl*
-ant	*m*	-anten	-anten
-anz	*f*	-anz	-anzen
-ar	*m*	-ar(e)s	-are
-chen	*nt*	-chens	-chen
-e	*f*	-	-n
-ei	*f*	-ei	-eien
-elle	*f*	-elle	-ellen
-ent	*m*	-enten	-enten
-enz	*f*	-enz	-enzen
-ette	*f*	-ette	-etten
-eur	*m*	-eurs	-eure
-euse	*f*	-euse	-eusen
-heit	*f*	-heit	-heiten
-ie	*f*	-ie	-ien
-ik	*f*	-ik	-iken
-in	*f*	-in	-innen
-ine	*f*	-ine	-inen
-ion	*f*	-ion	-ionen
-ist	*m*	-isten	-isten
-ium	*nt*	-iums	-ien
-ius	*m*	-ius	-iusse
-ive	*f*	-ive	-iven
-keit	*f*	-keit	-keiten
-lein	*nt*	-leins	-lein
-ling	*m*	-lings	-linge
-ment	*nt*	-ments	-mente
-mus	*m*	-mus	-men
-schaft	*f*	-schaft	-schaften
-tät	*f*	-tät	-täten
-tor	*m*	-tors	-toren
-ung	*f*	-ung	-ungen
-ur	*f*	-ur	-uren

PHONETIC SYMBOLS / LAUTSCHRIFT

[ː] *length mark* *Längezeichen* ['] *stress mark* *Betonung*
['] *glottal stop* *Knacklaut*

all vowel sounds are approximate only
alle Vokallaute sind nur ungefähre Entsprechungen

lie	[aɪ]	weit	day	[eɪ]	
now	[aʊ]	Haut	girl	[ɜː]	
above	[ə]	bitte	board	[ɔː]	
green	[iː]	viel	root	[uː]	Hut
pity	[ɪ]	Bischof	come	[ʌ]	Butler
rot	[ɒ,ɔ]	Post	salon	[ɔ̃]	Champignon
full	[ʊ]	Pult	avant (garde)	[ɑ̃]	Ensemble
			fair	[eə]	mehr
bet	[b]	Ball	beer	[ɪə]	Bier
dim	[d]	dann	toy	[ɔɪ]	Heu
face	[f]	Faß	pure	[ʊə]	
go	[g]	Gast	wine	[w]	
hit	[h]	Herr	thin	[θ]	
you	[j]	ja	this	[ð]	
cat	[k]	kalt			
lick	[l]	Last	Hast	[a]	mash
must	[m]	Mast	Ensemble	[ã]	avant (garde)
nut	[n]	Nuß	Metall	[e]	meths
bang	[ŋ]	lang	häßlich	[ɛ]	
pepper	[p]	Pakt	Cousin	[ɛ̃]	
sit	[s]	rasse	vital	[i]	
shame	[ʃ]	Schal	Moral	[o]	
tell	[t]	Tal	Champignon	[õ]	salon
vine	[v]	was	ökonomisch	[ø]	
loch	[x]	Bach	gönnen	[œ]	
zero	[z]	Hase	Heu	[ɔy]	toy
leisure	[ʒ]	Genie	kulant	[u]	
			physisch	[y]	
bat	[æ]		Müll	[ʏ]	
farm	[ɑː]	Bahn	ich	[ç]	
set	[e]	Kette			
	[*]	r can be pronounced before a vowel; Bindungs-R			

xi

DEUTSCH - ENGLISCH
GERMAN - ENGLISH

A

Aal [aːl] (-(e)s, -e) *m* eel

Aas [aːs] (-es, -e *od* **Äser**) *nt* carrion; **~geier** *m* vulture

ab [ap] *präp +dat* from; **Kinder ab 12 Jahren** children from the age of 12; **ab morgen** from tomorrow; **ab sofort** as of now

♦ *adv* **1** off; **links ab** to the left; **der Knopf ist ab** the button has come off; **ab nach Hause!** off you go home

2 (*zeitlich*): **von da ab** from then on; **von heute ab** from today, as of today

3 (*auf Fahrplänen*): **München ab 12.20** leaving Munich 12.20

4: **ab und zu** *od* **an** now and then *od* again

Abänderung ['apˈɛndərʊŋ] *f* alteration

Abbau ['apbau] (-(e)s) *m* (+*gen*) dismantling; (*Verminderung*) reduction (in); (*Verfall*) decline (in); (MIN) mining; quarrying; (CHEM) decomposition; **a~en** *vt* to dismantle; (MIN) to mine; to quarry; (*verringern*) to reduce; (CHEM) to break down

abbeißen ['apbaɪsən] (*unreg*) *vt* to bite off

abbekommen ['apbəkɔmən] (*unreg*) *vt* (*Deckel, Schraube, Band*) to loosen; **etwas ~** (*beschädigt werden*) to get damaged; (*: Person*) to get injured

abbestellen ['apbəʃtɛlən] *vt* to cancel

abbezahlen ['apbətsaːlən] *vt* to pay off

abbiegen ['apbiːgən] (*unreg*) *vi* to turn off; (*Straße*) to bend ♦ *vt* to

bend; (*verhindern*) to ward off

abbilden ['apbɪldən] *vt* to portray

Abbildung *f* illustration

abblenden ['apblɛndən] *vt*, *vi* (AUT) to dip (BRIT), to dim (US)

Abblendlicht *nt* dipped (BRIT) *od* dimmed (US) headlights *pl*

abbrechen ['apbrɛçən] (*unreg*) *vt*, *vi* to break off; (*Gebäude*) to pull down; (*Zelt*) to take down; (*aufhören*) to stop; (COMPUT) to abort

abbrennen ['apbrɛnən] (*unreg*) *vt* to burn off; (*Feuerwerk*) to let off ♦ *vi* (*aux sein*) to burn down

abbringen ['apbrɪŋən] (*unreg*) *vt*: **jdn von etw ~** to dissuade sb from sth; **jdn vom Weg ~** to divert sb

abbröckeln ['apbrœkəln] *vt*, *vi* to crumble off *od* away

Abbruch ['apbrʊx] *m* (*von Verhandlungen etc*) breaking off; (*von Haus*) demolition; **jdm/etw ~ tun** to harm sb/sth; **a~reif** *adj* only fit for demolition

abbrühen ['apbryːən] *vt* to scald; **abgebrüht** (*umg*) hard-boiled

abbuchen ['apbuːxən] *vt* to debit

abbürsten ['apbyrstən] *vt* to brush off

abdanken ['apdaŋkən] *vi* to resign; (*König*) to abdicate

Abdankung *f* resignation; abdication

abdecken ['apdɛkən] *vt* to uncover; (*Tisch*) to clear; (*Loch*) to cover

abdichten ['apdɪçtən] *vt* to seal; (NAUT) to caulk

abdrehen ['apdreːən] *vt* (*Gas*) to turn off; (*Licht*) to switch off; (*Film*) to shoot ♦ *vi* (*Schiff*) to change course

Abdruck ['apdrʊk] *m* (*Nachdrucken*) reprinting; (*Gedrucktes*) reprint; (*Gips~*, *Wachs~*) impression;

(*Finger~*) print; **a~en** vt to print, to publish

abdrücken ['apdrʏkən] vt (*Waffe*) to fire; (*Person*) to hug, to squeeze

Abend ['a:bənt] (-s, -e) m evening; **guten ~** good evening; **zu ~ essen** to have dinner or supper; **a~** adv; **heute a~** this evening; **~brot** nt supper; **~essen** nt supper; **~kasse** f box office; **~kleid** nt evening dress; **~kurs** m evening classes pl; **~land** nt (*Europa*) West; **a~lich** adj evening; **~mahl** nt Holy Communion; **~rot** nt sunset; **a~s** adv in the evening

Abenteuer ['a:bəntɔyər] (-s, -) nt adventure; **a~lich** adj adventurous

Abenteurer (-s, -) m adventurer; **~in** f adventuress

aber ['a:bər] konj but; (*jedoch*) however ♦ adv: **tausend und ~ tausend** thousands upon thousands; **das ist ~ schön** that's really nice; **nun ist ~ Schluß!** now that's enough!; **vielen Dank — ~ bitte!** thanks a lot — you're welcome; **A~glaube** m superstition; **a~gläubisch** adj superstitious

aberkennen ['ap'ɛrkɛnən] (unreg) vt (*JUR*): **jdm etw ~** to deprive sb of sth, to take sth (away) from sb

abermals ['a:bərma:ls] adv once again

Abf. abk (= *Abfahrt*) dep.

abfahren ['apfa:rən] (unreg) vi to leave, to depart ♦ vt to take off cart away; (*Strecke*) to drive; (*Reifen*) to wear; (*Fahrkarte*) to use

Abfahrt ['apfa:rt] f departure; (*SKI*) descent; (*Piste*) run; **~slauf** m (*SKI*) descent, run down; **~szeit** f departure time

Abfall ['apfal] m waste; (*von Speisen etc*) rubbish (*BRIT*), garbage (*US*); (*Neigung*) slope; (*Verschlechterung*) decline; **~eimer** m rubbish bin (*BRIT*), garbage can (*US*); **a~en** (unreg) vi (*auch fig*) to fall or drop off; (*POL, vom Glauben*) to break away; (*sich neigen*) to fall or drop

abfällig ['apfɛlɪç] adj disparaging, deprecatory

abfangen ['apfaŋən] (unreg) vt to intercept; (*Person*) to catch; (*unter Kontrolle bringen*) to check

abfärben ['apfɛrbən] vi to lose its colour; (*Wäsche*) to run; (*fig*) to rub off

abfassen ['apfasən] vt to write, to draft

abfertigen ['apfɛrtɪgən] vt to prepare for dispatch, to process; (*an der Grenze*) to clear; (*Kundschaft*) to attend to

abfeuern ['apfɔyərn] vt to fire

abfinden ['apfɪndən] (unreg) vt to pay off ♦ vr to come to terms; **sich mit jdm ~/nicht ~** to put up with /not get on with sb

Abfindung f (von *Gläubigern*) payment; (*Geld*) sum in settlement

abflauen ['apflauən] vi (*Wind, Erregung*) to die away, to subside; (*Nachfrage, Geschäft*) to fall or drop off

abfliegen ['apfli:gən] (unreg) vi (*Flugzeug*) to take off; (*Passagier auch*) to fly ♦ vt (*Gebiet*) to fly over

abfließen ['apfli:sən] (unreg) vi to drain away

Abflug ['apflu:k] m departure; (*Start*) take-off; **~zeit** f departure time

Abfluß ['apflʊs] m draining away; (*Öffnung*) outlet

Abflußrohr nt drain pipe; (*von sanitären Anlagen auch*) waste pipe

abfragen ['apfra:gən] vt (*bes SCH*) to test orally (on)

Abfuhr ['apfu:r] f (-, -en) f removal; (*fig*) snub, rebuff

abführen ['apfy:rən] vt to lead away; (*Gelder, Steuern*) to pay ♦ vi (*MED*) to have a laxative effect

Abführmittel ['apfy:rmɪtəl] nt laxative, purgative

abfüllen ['apfʏlən] vt to draw off; (*in Flaschen*) to bottle

Abgabe ['apga:bə] f handing in; (*von*

Ball) pass; (*Steuer*) tax; (*eines Amtes*) giving up; (*einer Erklärung*) giving

Abgang ['apgaŋ] *m* (*von Schule*) leaving; (*THEAT*) exit; (*MED: Ausscheiden*) passing; (: *Fehlgeburt*) miscarriage; (*Abfahrt*) departure; (*der Post, von Waren*) dispatch

Abgas ['apga:s] *nt* waste gas; (*AUT*) exhaust

abgeben ['apge:bən] (*unreg*) *vt* (*Gegenstand*) to hand od give in; (*Ball*) to pass; (*Wärme*) to give off; (*Amt*) to hand over; (*Schuß*) to fire; (*Erklärung, Urteil*) to make ♦ *vr*: **sich mit jdm /etw ~** to associate with sb/bother with sth; **jdm etw ~** (*überlassen*) to let sb have sth

abgebrüht ['apgəbry:t] (*umg*) *adj* (*skrupellos*) hard-boiled

abgehen ['apge:ən] (*unreg*) *vi* to go away, to leave; (*THEAT*) to exit; (*Baby*) to be aborted; (*Knopf etc*) to come off; (*abgezogen werden*) to be taken off; (*Straße*) to branch off ♦ *vt* (*Strecke*) to go od walk along; **etw geht jdm ab** (*fehlt*) sb lacks sth

abgelegen ['apgəle:gən] *adj* remote

abgemacht ['apgəmaxt] *adj* fixed; **~!** done!

abgeneigt ['apgənaɪkt] *adj* disinclined

Abgeordnete(r) ['apgə'ɔrdnətə(r)] *mf* member of parliament; elected representative

abgeschlossen ['apgəʃlɔsən] *adj attrib* (*Wohnung*) self-contained

abgeschmackt ['apgəʃmakt] *adj* tasteless

abgesehen ['apgəze:ən] *adj*: **es auf jdn/etw ~ haben** to be after sb/sth; **~ von ...** apart from ...

abgespannt ['apgəʃpant] *adj* tired out

abgestanden ['apgəʃtandən] *adj* stale; (*Bier auch*) flat

abgestorben ['apgəʃtɔrbən] *adj* numb; (*BIOL, MED*) dead

abgetragen ['apgətra:gən] *adj* shab-

by, worn out

abgewinnen ['apgəvɪnən] (*unreg*) *vt*: **etw etw /Geschmack ~** to get sth/pleasure from sth

abgewöhnen ['apgəvø:nən] *vt*: **jdm/sich etw ~** to cure sb of sth /give sth up

abgleiten ['apglaɪtən] (*unreg*) *vi* to slip, slide

abgöttisch ['apgœtɪʃ] *adj*: **~ lieben** to idolize

abgrenzen ['apgrentsən] *vt* (*auch fig*) to mark off; to fence off

Abgrund ['apgrʊnt] *m* (*auch fig*) abyss

abhacken ['aphakən] *vt* to chop off

abhaken ['apha:kən] *vt* (*auf Papier*) to tick off

abhalten ['aphaltən] (*unreg*) *vt* (*Versammlung*) to hold; **jdn von etw ~** (*fernhalten*) to keep sb away from sth; (*hindern*) to keep sb from sth

abhanden [ap'handən] *adj*: **~ kommen** to get lost

Abhandlung ['aphandluŋ] *f* treatise, discourse

Abhang ['aphaŋ] *m* slope

abhängen ['aphɛŋən] *vt* (*Bild*) to take down; (*Anhänger*) to uncouple; (*Verfolger*) to shake off ♦ *vi* (*unreg*: *Fleisch*) to hang; **von jdm/etw ~** to depend on sb/sth

abhängig ['aphɛŋɪç] *adj*: **~ (von)** dependent (on); **A~keit** *f*: **A~keit (von)** dependence (on)

abhärten ['aphɛrtən] *vt, vr* to toughen (o.s.) up; **sich gegen etw ~** to inure o.s. to sth

abhauen ['aphaʊən] (*unreg*) *vt* to cut off; (*Baum*) to cut down ♦ *vi* (*umg*) to clear off od out

abheben ['aphe:bən] (*unreg*) *vt* to lift (up); (*Karten*) to cut; (*Masche*) to slip; (*Geld*) to withdraw, to take out ♦ *vi* (*Flugzeug*) to take off; (*Rakete*) to lift off; (*KARTEN*) to cut ♦ *vr* to stand out

abheften ['apheftən] *vt* (*Rechnungen etc*) to file away

abhetzen ['aphɛtsən] *vr* to wear od

tire o.s. out

Abhilfe ['aphɪlfə] f remedy; ~ **schaffen** to put things right

abholen ['apho:lən] vt (Gegenstand) to fetch, to collect; (Person) to call for; (am Bahnhof etc) to pick up, to meet

abholzen ['aphɔltsən] vt (Wald) to clear

abhorchen ['aphɔrçən] vt (MED) to listen to a patient's chest

abhören ['aphø:rən] vt (Vokabeln) to test; (Telefongespräch) to tap; (Tonband etc) to listen to

Abhörgerät nt bug

Abitur [abi'tu:r] (-s, -e) nt German school-leaving examination; ~**ient(-in)** m(f) candidate for school-leaving certificate

Abk. abk (= Abkürzung) abbr.

abkapseln ['apkapsəln] vr to shut od cut o.s. off

abkaufen ['apkaofən] vt: **jdm etw ~** (auch fig) to buy sth from sb

abkehren ['apke:rən] vt (Blick) to avert, to turn away ♦ vr to turn away

abklingen ['apklɪŋən] (unreg) vi to die away; (Radio) to fade out

abknöpfen ['apknœpfən] vt to unbutton; **jdm etw ~** (umg) to get sth off sb

abkochen ['apkɔxən] vt to boil

abkommen ['apkɔmən] (unreg) vi to get away; **A~** (-s, -) nt agreement; **von der Straße/von einem Plan ~** to leave the road/give up a plan

abkömmlich ['apkœmlɪç] adj available, free

abkratzen ['apkratsən] vt to scrape off ♦ vi (umg) to kick the bucket

abkühlen ['apky:lən] vt to cool down ♦ vr (Mensch) to cool down od off; (Wetter) to get cool; (Zuneigung) to cool

abkürzen ['apkvrtsən] vt to shorten; (Wort auch) to abbreviate; **den Weg ~** to take a short cut

Abkürzung f (Wort) abbreviation;

(Weg) short cut

abladen ['apla:dən] (unreg) vt to unload

Ablage ['apla:gə] f (für Akten) tray; (für Kleider) cloakroom

ablassen ['aplasən] (unreg) vt (Wasser, Dampf) to let off; (vom Preis) to knock off ♦ vi: **von etw ~** to give sth up, to abandon sth

Ablauf ['aplauf] m (Abfluß) drain; (von Ereignissen) course; (einer Frist, Zeit) expiry (BRIT), expiration (US); **a~en** (unreg) vi (abfließen) to drain away; (Ereignisse) to happen; (Frist, Zeit, Paß) to expire ♦ vt (Sohlen) to wear (down od out)

ablegen ['aple:gən] vt to put od lay down; (Kleider) to take off; (Gewohnheit) to get rid of; (Prüfung) to take, to sit; (Zeugnis) to give

Ableger (-s, -) m layer; (fig) branch, offshoot

ablehnen ['aple:nən] vt to reject; (Einladung) to decline, to refuse ♦ vi to decline, to refuse

ablehnend adj (Haltung, Antwort) negative; (Geste) disapproving; **ein ~er Bescheid** a rejection

Ablehnung f rejection; refusal

ableiten ['aplaitən] vt (Wasser) to divert; (deduzieren) to deduce; (Wort) to derive

Ableitung f diversion; deduction; derivation; (Wort) derivative

ablenken ['aplɛŋkən] vt to turn away, to deflect; (zerstreuen) to distract ♦ vi to change the subject

Ablenkung f distraction

ablesen ['aple:zən] vt to read out; (Meßgeräte) to read

abliefern ['apli:fərn] vt to deliver; **etw bei jdm/einer Dienststelle ~** to hand sth over to sb/in at an office

Ablieferung f delivery

abliegen ['apli:gən] (unreg) vi to be some distance away; (fig) to be far removed

ablösen ['aplø:zən] vt (abtrennen) to take off, to remove; (in Amt) to take over from; (Wache) to relieve

Ablösung f removal; relieving

abmachen ['apmaxən] vt to take off; (vereinbaren) to agree

Abmachung f agreement

abmagern ['apma:gərn] vi to get thinner

Abmagerungskur f diet; eine ~ machen to go on a diet

Abmarsch ['apmarʃ] m departure

abmelden ['apmɛldən] vt (Zeitungen) to cancel; (Auto) to take off the road ♦ vr to give notice of one's departure; (im Hotel) to check out; jdn bei der Polizei ~ to register sb's departure with the police

abmessen (unreg) vt to measure

Abmessung f measurement

abmontieren ['apmonti:rən] vt to take off

abmühen ['apmy:ən] vr to wear o.s. out

Abnahme ['apna:mə] f (+gen) removal; (COMM) buying; (Verringerung) decrease (in)

abnehmen ['apne:mən] (unreg) vt to take off, to remove; (Führerschein) to take away; (Prüfung) to hold; (Maschen) to decrease ♦ vi to decrease; (schlanker werden) to lose weight; (jdm) etw ~ (Geld) to get sth (out of sb); (kaufen, umg: glauben) to buy sth (from sb); jdm Arbeit ~ to take work off sb's shoulders

Abnehmer (-s, -) m purchaser, customer

Abneigung ['apnaigʊŋ] f aversion, dislike

abnorm [ap'nɔrm] adj abnormal

abnutzen ['apnutsən] vt to wear out

Abnutzung f wear (and tear)

Abonnement [abɔn(ə)'mã:] (-s, -s) nt subscription

Abonnent(in) [abɔ'nɛnt(ɪn)] m(f) subscriber

abonnieren [abɔ'ni:rən] vt to subscribe to

Abordnung ['ap'ɔrdnʊŋ] f delegation

abpacken ['appakən] vt to pack

abpassen ['appasən] vt (Person, Gelegenheit) to wait for; (in Größe: Stoff etc) to adjust

abpfeifen ['appfaifən] (unreg) vt, vi (SPORT): (das Spiel) ~ to blow the whistle (for the end of the game)

Abpfiff ['appfif] m final whistle

abplagen ['appla:gən] vr to wear o.s. out

abprallen ['apprallən] vi to bounce off; to ricochet

abputzen ['apputsən] vt to clean

abraten ['apra:tən] (unreg) vt: jdm von etw ~ to advise sb against sth, to warn sb against sth

abräumen ['aprɔymən] vt to clear up od away

abreagieren ['apreagi:rən] vt: seinen Zorn (an jdm/etw) ~ to work one's anger off (on sb/sth) ♦ vr to calm down

abrechnen ['aprɛçnən] vt to deduct, to take off ♦ vi to settle up; (fig) to get even

Abrechnung f settlement; (Rechnung) bill

Abrede ['apre:də] f: etw in ~ stellen to deny od dispute sth

abregen ['apre:gən] (umg) vr to calm od cool down

Abreise ['apraizə] f departure; a~n vi to leave, to set off

abreißen ['apraisən] (unreg) vt (Haus) to tear down; (Blatt) to tear off

abrichten ['apriçtən] vt to train

abriegeln ['apri:gəln] vt (Tür) to bolt; (Straße, Gebiet) to seal off

Abriß ['apris] (-sses, -sse) m (Übersicht) outline

Abruf ['apru:f] m: auf ~ on call; a~en (unreg) vt (Mensch) to call away; (COMM: Ware) to request delivery of

abrunden ['aprundən] vt to round off

abrüsten ['aprystən] vi to disarm

Abrüstung f disarmament

abrutschen ['aprutʃən] vi to slip; (AVIAT) to sideslip

Abs. abk (= Absender) sender, from

Absage ['apza:gə] f refusal; **a~n** vt to cancel, to call off; (Einladung) to turn down ♦ vi to cry off; (ablehnen) to decline

absägen ['apzɛːgən] vt to saw off

absahnen ['apza:nən] vt to skim

Absatz ['apzats] m (COMM) sales pl; (Bodensatz) deposit; (neuer Abschnitt) paragraph; (Treppen~) landing; (Schuh~) heel; **~gebiet** nt (COMM) market

abschaben ['apʃa:bən] vt to scrape off; (Möhren) to scrape

abschaffen ['apʃafən] vt to abolish, to do away with

Abschaffung f abolition

abschalten ['apʃaltən] vt, vi (auch umg) to switch off

abschätzen ['apʃɛtsən] vt to estimate; (Lage) to assess; (Person) to size up

abschätzig ['apʃɛtsɪç] adj disparaging, derogatory

Abschaum ['apʃaum] (-(e)s) m scum

Abscheu ['apʃɔy] (-(e)s) m loathing, repugnance; **a~erregend** adj repulsive, loathsome; **a~lich** [ap'ʃɔylɪç] adj abominable

abschicken ['apʃɪkən] vt to send off

abschieben ['apʃi:bən] (unreg) vt to push away; (Person) to pack off; (; POL) to deport

Abschied ['apʃi:t] (-(e)s, -e) m parting; (von Armee) discharge; (von jdm) ~ nehmen to say goodbye (to sb), to take one's leave (of sb); seinen ~ nehmen (MIL) to apply for discharge; **~sbrief** m farewell letter; **~sfeier** f farewell party

abschießen ['apʃi:sən] (unreg) vt (Flugzeug) to shoot down; (Geschoß) to fire; (umg: Minister) to get rid of

abschirmen ['apʃɪrmən] vt to screen

abschlagen ['apʃla:gən] (unreg) vt (abhacken, COMM) to knock off; (ablehnen) to refuse; (MIL) to repel

abschlägig ['apʃlɛːgɪç] adj negative

Abschlagszahlung f interim payment

abschleifen ['apʃlaɪfən] (unreg) vt to grind down; (Rost) to polish off ♦ vr to wear off

Abschlepp- ['apʃlɛp] zW: **~dienst** m (AUT) breakdown service (BRIT), towing company (US); **a~en** vt to take in tow; **~seil** nt towrope

abschließen ['apʃli:sən] (unreg) vt (Tür) to lock; (beenden) to conclude, to finish; (Vertrag, Handel) to conclude ♦ vr (sich isolieren) to cut o.s. off; **~d** adj concluding

Abschluß ['apʃlus] m (Beendigung) close, conclusion; (COMM: Bilanz) balancing; (von Vertrag, Handel) conclusion; **zum ~** in conclusion; **~feier** f (SCH) end-of-term party; **~prüfung** f final exam

abschmieren ['apʃmi:rən] vt (AUT) to grease, to lubricate

abschneiden ['apʃnaɪdən] (unreg) vt to cut off ♦ vi to do, to come off

Abschnitt ['apʃnɪt] m section; (MIL) sector; (Kontroll~) counterfoil; (MATH) segment; (Zeit~) period

abschöpfen ['apʃœpfən] vt to skim off

abschrauben ['apʃraubən] vt to unscrew

abschrecken ['apʃrɛkən] vt to deter, to put off; (mit kaltem Wasser) to plunge in cold water; **~d** adj deterrent; **~des Beispiel** warning

abschreiben ['apʃraɪbən] (unreg) vt to copy; (verlorengeben) to write off; (COMM) to deduct

Abschrift ['apʃrɪft] f copy

Abschuß ['apʃus] m (eines Geschützes) firing; (Herunterschießen) shooting down; (Tötung) shooting

abschüssig ['apʃʏsɪç] adj steep

abschütteln ['apʃʏtəln] vt to shake off

abschwächen ['apʃvɛçən] vt to lessen; (Behauptung, Kritik) to tone down ♦ vr to lessen

Abschweifung ['apʃvaɪfuŋ] f digression

abschwellen ['apʃvɛlən] (unreg) vi (Geschwulst) to go down; (Lärm) to die down

abschwören ['apʃvøːrən] vi (+dat) to renounce

absehbar adj foreseeable; **in ~er Zeit** in the foreseeable future; **das Ende ist ~** the end is in sight

absehen ['apzeːən] (unreg) vt (Ende, Folgen) to foresee ♦ vi: **von etw ~** to refrain from sth; (nicht berücksichtigen) to leave sth out of consideration

abseilen ['apzaɪlən] vr (Bergsteiger) to abseil (down)

abseits ['apzaɪts] adv out of the way ♦ präp +gen away from; **A~ nt** (SPORT) offside

Absend- ['apzɛnd-] zW: **a~en** (unreg) vt to send off, to dispatch; **~er (-s, -)** m sender

absetzen ['apzɛtsən] vt (niederstellen, aussteigen lassen) to put down; (abnehmen) to take off; (COMM: verkaufen) to sell; (FIN: abziehen) to deduct; (entlassen) to dismiss; (König) to depose; (streichen) to drop; (hervorheben) to pick out ♦ vr (sich entfernen) to clear off; (sich ablagern) to be deposited

Absetzung f (FIN: Abzug) deduction; (Entlassung) dismissal; (von König) deposing; (Streichung) dropping

absichern ['apzɪçərn] vt to make safe; (schützen) to safeguard ♦ vr to protect o.s.

Absicht ['apzɪçt] f intention; **mit ~** on purpose; **a~lich** adj intentional, deliberate

absinken ['apzɪŋkən] (unreg) vi to sink; (Temperatur, Geschwindigkeit) to decrease

absitzen ['apzɪtsən] (unreg) vi to dismount ♦ vt (Strafe) to serve

absolut [apzo'luːt] adj absolute; **A~ismus** [-'tɪsmʊs] m absolutism

absolvieren [apzɔl'viːrən] vt (SCH) to complete

absonder- ['apzɔndər-] zW: **~lich** adj

odd, strange; **~n** vt to separate; (ausscheiden) to give off, to secrete ♦ vr to cut o.s. off; **A~ung** f separation; (MED) secretion

abspalten ['apʃpaltən] vt to split off

abspannen [apʃpanən] vt (Pferde) to unhitch; (Wagen) to uncouple

abspeisen ['apʃpaɪzən] vt (fig) to fob off

abspenstig ['apʃpɛnstɪç] adj: (jdm) **~ machen** to lure away (from sb)

absperren [apʃpɛrən] vt to block or close off; (Tür) to lock

Absperrung f (Vorgang) blocking or closing off; (Sperre) barricade

abspielen ['apʃpiːlən] vt (Platte, Tonband) to play; (SPORT: Ball) to pass ♦ vr to happen

absplittern [apʃplɪtərn] vt to chip off

Absprache ['apʃpraːxə] f arrangement

absprechen ['apʃprɛçən] (unreg) vt (vereinbaren) to arrange; **jdm etw ~** to deny sb sth

abspringen ['apʃprɪŋən] (unreg) vi to jump down/off; (Farbe, Lack) to flake off; (AVIAT) to bale out; (sich distanzieren) to back out

Absprung ['apʃprʊŋ] m jump

abspülen ['apʃpyːlən] vt to rinse; (Geschirr) to wash up

abstammen ['apʃtamən] vi to be descended; (Wort) to be derived

Abstammung f descent; derivation

Abstand ['apʃtant] m distance; (zeitlich) interval; **davon ~ nehmen, etw zu tun** to refrain from doing sth; **~ halten** (AUT) to keep one's distance; **mit ~ der beste** by far the best

abstatten ['apʃtatən] vt (Dank) to give; (Besuch) to pay

abstauben ['apʃtaʊbən] vt, vi to dust; (umg: stehlen) to pinch; (: schnorren) to scrounge

Abstecher ['apʃtɛçər] (-s, -) m detour

abstehen ['apʃteːən] (unreg) vi (Ohren, Haare) to stick out; (entfernsein) to stand away

absteigen ['apʃtaɪɡən] (unreg) vi (vom Rad etc) to get off, to dismount; **in einem Gasthof ~** to put up at an inn; **(in die zweite Liga) ~** to be relegated (to the second division)

abstellen ['apʃtɛlən] vt (niederstellen) to put down; (entfernt stellen) to pull out; (hinstellen: Auto) to park; (ausschalten) to turn od switch off; (Mißstand, Unsitte) to stop; (ausrichten): **~ auf +akk** to gear to

Abstellgleis nt siding

Abstellkammer f boxroom

Abstellraum m storage room

abstempeln ['apʃtɛmpəln] vt to stamp

absterben ['apʃtɛrbən] (unreg) vi to die; (Körperteil) to go numb

Abstieg ['apʃtiːk] (-(e)s, -e) m descent; (SPORT) relegation; (fig) decline

abstimmen ['apʃtɪmən] vi to vote ♦ vt: **~ (auf +akk)** (Instrument) to tune (to); (Interessen) to match (with); (Termine, Ziele) to fit in (with) ♦ vr to agree

Abstimmung f vote

Abstinenz [apstiˈnɛnts] f abstinence; teetotalism; **~ler(in)** (-s, -) m(f) teetotaller

abstoßen ['apʃtoːsən] (unreg) vt to push off od away; (verkaufen) to unload; (anekeln) to repel, to repulse; **~d** adj repulsive

abstrakt [ap'strakt] adj abstract ♦ adv abstractly, in the abstract

abstreiten ['apʃtraɪtən] (unreg) vt to deny

Abstrich ['apʃtrɪç] m (Abzug) cut; (MED) smear; **~e machen** to lower one's sights

abstufen ['apʃtuːfən] vt (Hang) to terrace; (Farben) to shade; (Gehälter) to grade

abstumpfen ['apʃtumpfən] vt (auch fig) to dull, to blunt ♦ vi to become dulled

Absturz ['apʃturts] m fall; (AVIAT) crash

abstürzen ['apʃtʏrtsən] vi to fall; (AVIAT) to crash

absuchen ['apzuːxən] vt to scour, to search

absurd [ap'zurt] adj absurd

Abszeß [aps'tsɛs] (-sses, -sse) m abscess

Abt [apt] (-(e)s, ⁀e) m abbot

Abt. abk (= Abteilung) dept.

abtasten ['aptastən] vt to feel, to probe

abtauen ['aptaʊən] vt, vi to thaw

Abtei [ap'taɪ] (-, -en) f abbey

Abteil [ap'taɪl] (-(e)s, -e) nt compartment; **'a~en** vt to divide up; (abtrennen) to divide off; **~ung** f (in Firma, Kaufhaus) department; (in Krankenhaus) section; (MIL) unit

abtippen ['aptɪpən] vt (Text) to type up

abtransportieren ['aptransportiːrən] vt to take away, to remove

abtreiben ['aptraɪbən] (unreg) vt (Boot, Flugzeug) to drive off course; (Kind) to abort ♦ vi to be driven off course; to abort

Abtreibung f abortion

abtrennen ['aptrɛnən] vt (lostrennen) to detach; (entfernen) to take off; (abteilen) to separate off

abtreten ['aptreːtən] (unreg) vt to wear out; (überlassen) to hand over, to cede ♦ vi to go off; (zurücktreten) to step down

Abtritt ['aptrɪt] m resignation

abtrocknen ['aptrɔknən] vt, vi to dry

abtun ['aptuːn] (unreg) vt to take off; (Gewohnheit) to give up; (fig) to dismiss

abwägen ['apvɛːɡən] (unreg) vt to weigh up

abwälzen ['apvɛltsən] vt (Schuld, Verantwortung): **~ (auf +acc)** to shift (onto)

abwandeln ['apvandəln] vt to adapt

abwandern ['apvandərn] vi to move away; (FIN) to be transferred

abwarten ['apvartən] vt to wait for

♦ *vi* to wait

abwärts ['apvɛrts] *adv* down

Abwasch ['apvaʃ] (-(e)s) *m* washing-up; **a~en** (*unreg*) *vt* (*Schmutz*) to wash off; (*Geschirr*) to wash (up)

Abwasser ['apvasər] (-s, -wässer) *nt* sewage

abwechseln ['apvɛksəln] *vi, vr* to alternate; (*Personen*) to take turns; **~d** *adj* alternate

Abwechslung *f* change

abwegig ['apve:giç] *adj* wrong

Abwehr ['apve:r] (-) *f* defence; (*Schutz*) protection; (~*dienst*) counterintelligence (service); **a~en** *vt* to ward off; (*Ball*) to stop

abweichen ['apvaiçən] (*unreg*) *vi* to deviate; (*Meinung*) to differ

abweisen ['apvaizən] (*unreg*) *vt* to turn away; (*Antrag*) to turn down; **~d** *adj* (*Haltung*) cold

abwenden ['apvɛndən] (*unreg*) *vt* to avert ♦ *vr* to turn away

abwerfen ['apvɛrfən] (*unreg*) *vt* to throw off; (*Profit*) to yield; (*aus Flugzeug*) to drop; (*Spielkarte*) to discard

abwerten ['apve:rtən] *vt* (*FIN*) to devalue

abwertend *adj* (*Worte, Sinn*) pejorative

abwesend ['apve:zənt] *adj* absent

Abwesenheit ['apve:zənhait] *f* absence

abwickeln ['apvikəln] *vt* to unwind; (*Geschäft*) to wind up

abwimmeln ['apvimǝln] (*umg*) *vt* (*Menschen*) to get shot of

abwischen ['apviʃən] *vt* to wipe off *od* away; (*putzen*) to wipe

Abwurf ['apvʊrf] *m* throwing off; (*von Bomben etc*) dropping; (*von Reiter, SPORT*) throw

abwürgen ['apvyrgən] (*umg*) *vt* to scotch; (*Motor*) to stall

abzahlen ['aptsa:lən] *vt* to pay off

abzählen ['aptsɛ:lən] *vt, vi* to count (up)

Abzahlung *f* repayment; **auf ~**

kaufen to buy on hire purchase

abzapfen ['aptsapfən] *vt* to draw off; **jdm Blut ~** to take blood from sb

abzäunen ['aptsɔynən] *vt* to fence off

Abzeichen ['aptsaiçən] *nt* badge; (*Orden*) decoration

abzeichnen ['aptsaiçnən] *vt* to draw, to copy; (*Dokument*) to initial ♦ *vr* to stand out; (*fig: bevorstehen*) to loom

Abziehbild *nt* transfer

abziehen ['aptsi:ən] (*unreg*) *vt* to take off; (*Tier*) to skin; (*Bett*) to strip; (*Truppen*) to withdraw; (*subtrahieren*) to take away, to subtract; (*kopieren*) to run off ♦ *vi* to go away; (*Truppen*) to withdraw

abzielen ['aptsi:lən] *vi*: **~ auf** +*akk* to be aimed at

Abzug ['aptsu:k] *m* departure; (*von Truppen*) withdrawal; (*Kopie*) copy; (*Subtraktion*) subtraction; (*Betrag*) deduction; (*Rauch~*) flue; (*von Waffen*) trigger

abzüglich ['aptsy:kliç] *präp* +*gen* less

abzweigen ['aptsvaigən] *vi* to branch off ♦ *vt* to set aside

Abzweigung *f* junction

ach [ax] *excl* oh; **~ ja!** (oh) yes; **~ so!** I see; **mit Ach und Krach** by the skin of one's teeth

Achse ['aksə] *f* axis; (*AUT*) axle

Achsel ['aksəl] (-, -n) *f* shoulder; **~höhle** *f* armpit

acht [axt] *num* eight; **~ Tage** a week; **A~** *f* -, **-en** eight; (*beim Eislaufen etc*) figure (of) eight; **~e(r, s)** *adj* eighth; **A~el** *num* eighth

Acht *f* -, **-en**: **sich in ~ nehmen** (vor +*dat*) to be careful (of), to watch out (for); **etw außer ~ lassen** to disregard sth; **a~bar** *adj* worthy; **a~en** *vt* to respect ♦ *vi*: **a~en (auf** +*akk*) to pay attention (to); **a~en, daß ...** to be careful that ...

ächten ['ɛçtən] *vt* to outlaw, to ban

Achterbahn ['axtər-] *f* roller coaster

Achterdeck *nt* (*NAUT*) afterdeck

acht- *zW:* **~fach** *adj* eightfold; **~geben** (*unreg*) *vi:* **~geben (auf** +*akk*) to pay attention (to); **~hundert** *num* eight hundred; **~los** *adj* careless; **~mal** *adv* eight times; **~sam** *adj* attentive

Achtung ['axtʊŋ] *f* attention; (*Ehrfurcht*) respect ♦ *excl* look out!; (*MIL*) attention!; **alle ~!** good for you/him *etc*

achtzehn *num* eighteen

achtzig *num* eighty

ächzen ['ɛçtsən] *vi* to groan

Acker ['akər] (-s, ⁻) *m* field; **~bau** *m* agriculture; **a~n** *vt, vi* to plough; (*umg*) to slog away

ADAC [a:de:ʔa:tse:] *abk* (= *Allgemeiner Deutscher Automobil-Club*) ≈ AA, RAC

addieren [a'di:rən] *vt* to add (up)

Addition [aditsi'o:n] *f* addition

ade [a'de:] *interj* bye!

Adel ['a:dəl] (-s) *m* nobility; **a~ig** *adj* noble

adeln *vt* to raise to the peerage

Ader ['a:dər] (-, -n) *f* vein

Adjektiv ['atjɛkti:f] (-s, -e) *nt* adjective

Adler ['a:dlər] (-s, -) *m* eagle

adlig *adj* noble

Admiral [atmi'ra:l] (-s, -e) *m* admiral

Adopt- *zW:* **a~ieren** [adɔp'ti:rən] *vt* to adopt; **~ion** [adɔptsi'o:n] *f* adoption; **~iveltern** [adɔp'ti:f-] *pl* adoptive parents; **~ivkind** *nt* adopted child

Adress- [adrɛ'sant] *zW:* **~buch** *nt* directory; (*privat*) address book; **~e** [a'drɛsə] *f* address; **a~ieren** [adrɛ'si:rən] (an +*akk*) to address (to)

Adria ['a:dria] (-) *f* Adriatic

Advent [at'vɛnt] (-(e)s, -e) *m* Advent; **~skalender** *m* Advent calendar; **~skranz** *m* Advent wreath

Adverb [at'vɛrp] *nt* adverb

aero- [aero] *präfix* aero-

Aerobic [ae'rɔbɪk] *nt* aerobics *sg*

Affäre [a'fɛːrə] *f* affair

Affe ['afə] (-n, -n) *m* monkey

affektiert [afɛk'ti:rt] *adj* affected

Affen- *zW:* **a~artig** *adj* like a monkey; **mit a~artiger Geschwindigkeit** like a flash; **~hitze** (*umg*) *f* incredible heat; **~schande** (*umg*) *f* crying shame

affig ['afɪç] *adj* affected

Afrika ['a:frika] (-s) *nt* Africa; **~ner(in)** [-'ka:nər(ın)] (-s, -) *m(f)* African; **a~nisch** *adj* African

After ['aftər] (-s, -) *m* anus

AG [a:'ge:] *abk* (= *Aktiengesellschaft*) ≈ Ltd. (*BRIT*); ≈ Inc. (*US*)

Agent [a'gɛnt] *m* agent; **~ur** *f* agency

Aggregat [agre'ga:t] (-(e)s, -e) *nt* aggregate; (*TECH*) unit

Aggress- *zW:* **~ion** [agrɛsi'o:n] *f* aggression; **a~iv** [agrɛ'si:f] *adj* aggressive; **~ivität** [agrɛsivi'tɛ:t] *f* aggressiveness

Agrarpolitik [a'gra:r-] *f* agricultural policy

Ägypt- *zW:* **~en** (-s) *nt* Egypt; **~er(in)** (-s, -) *m(f)* Egyptian; **ä~isch**, **ä~isch** *adj* Egyptian

ah [a:] *excl* ah

aha [a'ha:] *excl* aha

ähneln ['ɛ:nəln] *vi* +*dat* to be like, to resemble ♦ *vr* to be alike *od* similar

ahnen ['a:nən] *vt* to suspect; (*Tod, Gefahr*) to have a presentiment of

ähnlich ['ɛ:nlɪç] *adj* +*dat* similar (to); **A~keit** *f* similarity

Ahnung ['a:nʊŋ] *f* idea, suspicion; presentiment; **a~slos** *adj* unsuspecting

Ahorn ['a:hɔrn] (-s, -e) *m* maple

Ähre ['ɛ:rə] *f* ear

Aids [e:dz] *nt* AIDS *sg*

Akademie [akade'mi:] *f* academy

Akademiker(in) [aka'de:mikər(ın)] (-s, -) *m(f)* university graduate

akademisch *adj* academic

akklimatisieren [aklimati'zi:rən] *vr* to become acclimatized

Akkord [a'kɔrt] (-(e)s, -e) *nt* (*MUS*) chord; **im ~ arbeiten** to do piecework

Akkordeon [a'kɔrdeɔn] (-s, -s) nt accordion

Akkusativ ['akuzati:f] (-s, -e) m accusative

Akne ['aknə] f acne

Akrobat [akro'ba:t(in)] (-en, -en) m(f) acrobat

Akt [akt] (-(e)s, -e) m act; (KUNST) nude

Akte ['aktə] f file; ~**nkoffer** m attaché case; ~**nkundig** adj on the files; ~**nschrank** m filing cabinet; ~**ntasche** f briefcase

Aktie ['aktsjə] f share

Aktien- zW: ~**gesellschaft** f joint-stock company; ~**index** (-(es), -e od -indices) m share index; ~**kurs** m share price

Aktion [aktsi'on] f campaign; (Polizei~, Such~) action; ~**är** [-'nɛ:r] (-s, -e) m shareholder

aktiv [ak'ti:f] adj active; (MIL) regular; ~**ieren** [-'vi:rən] vt to activate; **A~ität** f activity

Aktualität [aktuali'tɛ:t] f topicality; (einer Mode) up-to-dateness

aktuell [aktu'el] adj topical; up-to-date

Akupunktur [akupuŋk'tu:ər] f acupuncture

Akustik [a'kustik] f acoustics pl

akut [a'ku:t] adj acute

Akzent [ak'tsɛnt] m accent; (Betonung) stress

akzeptieren [aktsep'ti:rən] vt to accept

Alarm [a'larm] (-(e)s, -e) m alarm; ~**anlage** f alarm system; a~**bereit** adj readiness for action; ~**bereitschaft** f stand-by; a~**ieren** [-'mi:rən] vt to alarm

Alban- [al'ba:n] zW: ~**er(in)** [al'ba:nər(m)] (-s, -) m(f) (GEOG) Albanian; ~**ien** (-s) nt Albania; a~**isch** adj Albanian

albern ['albərn] adj silly

Album ['album] (-s, Alben) nt album

Alge ['algə] f algae

Algebra ['algebra] (-) f algebra

Alger- [al'ge:r] zW: ~**ien** (-s) nt Algeria; ~**ier(in)** (-s, -) m(f) Algerian; a~**isch** adj Algerian

alias ['a:lias] adv alias

Alibi ['a:libi] (-s, -s) nt alibi

Alimente [ali'mentə] pl alimony sg

Alkohol ['alkoho:l] (-s, -e) m alcohol; a~**frei** adj non-alcoholic; ~**iker(in)** [alko'ho:likər(in)] (-s, -) m(f) alcoholic; a~**isch** adj alcoholic; ~**verbot** nt ban on alcohol

All [al] (-s) nt universe; a~**abendlich** adj every evening; 'a~**bekannt** adj universally known

<hr>

SCHLÜSSELWORT

alle(r, s) ['alə(r, s)] adj **1** (sämtliche) all; wir alle all of us; alle Kinder waren da all the children were there; alle Kinder mögen ... all children like ...; alle beide both of us/them; sie kamen alle they all came; alles Gute all the best; alles in allem all in all

2 (mit Zeit- oder Maßangaben) every; alle vier Jahre every four years; alle fünf Meter every five metres

♦ pron everything; alles was er sagt everything he says, all that he says

♦ adv (zu Ende, aufgebraucht) finished; die Milch ist alle the milk's all gone, there's no milk left; etw alle machen to finish sth up

Allee [a'le:] f avenue

allein [a'lam] adv alone; (ohne Hilfe) on one's own, by oneself ♦ konj but, only; nicht ~ (nicht nur) not only; **A~erziehende(r)** mf single parent; **A~gang** m: im **A~gang** on one's own; ~**stehend** adj single

allemal ['alə'ma:l] adv (jedesmal) always; (ohne weiteres) with no bother; ein für ~ once and for all

allenfalls ['alnfals] adv at all events; (höchstens) at most

aller- ['alər] zW: ~**beste(r, s)** adj very best; ~**dings** adv (zwar)

mittedly; *(gewiß)* certainly
Allergie [alɛr'giː] *f* allergy; **allergisch** *adj* allergic
aller- *zW:* ~**hand** *(umg) adj inv* all sorts of; das ist doch ~hand! that's a bit much; ~**hand!** *(lobend)* good show!; **A**~**heiligen** *nt* All Saints' Day; ~**höchstens** *adv* at the very most; ~**lei** *adj inv* all sorts of; ~**letzte(r, s)** *adj* very last; ~**seits** *adv* on all sides; prost ~**seits!** cheers everyone!
Allerwelts- *in zW (Durchschnitts-)* common; *(nichtssagend)* commonplace
alles *pron* everything; ~ in allem all in all; ~ Gute! all the best!
Alleskleber [ˈaləsˌkleːbər] (*-s, -*) *m* multi-purpose glue
allgemein [ˈalgəˈmaɪn] *adj* general; im ~**en** in general; ~**gültig** *adj* generally accepted
Allgemeinwissen *nt* general knowledge
Alliierte(r) [aliˈiːrtə(r)] *m* ally
all- *zW:* ~**jährlich** *adj* annual; ~**mählich** *adj* gradual; **A**~**tag** *m* everyday life; ~**täglich** *adj, adv* daily; *(gewöhnlich)* commonplace; ~**tags** *adv* on weekdays; ~**wissend** *adj* omniscient; ~**zu** *adv* all too; ~**zuoft** *adv* all too often; ~**zuviel** *adv* too much
Allzweck- [ˈaltsvɛk-] *in zW* multi-purpose
Alm [alm] (*-, -en*) *f* alpine pasture
Almosen [ˈalmoːzən] (*-s, -*) *nt* alms *pl*
Alpen [ˈalpən] *pl* Alps
Alphabet [alfaˈbeːt] (*-(e)s, -e*) *nt* alphabet; **a**~**isch** *adj* alphabetical
Alptraum *m* nightmare

als [als] *konj* **1** *(zeitlich)* when; *(gleichzeitig)* as; damals, als ... (in the days) when ...; gerade, als ... just as ...
2 *(in der Eigenschaft)* than; als Antwort as an answer; als Kind as

a child
3 *(bei Vergleichen)* than; ich kam später als er I came later than he (did) *od* later than him; lieber ... als ... rather ... than ...; nichts als Ärger nothing but trouble
4: als ob/wenn as if

also [ˈalzo] *konj* so; *(folglich)* therefore; ~ gut *od* schön! okay then; ~, so was! well really!; na ~! there you are then!
alt [alt] (*-s, -e*) *m* (*MUS*) alto
alt *adj* old; alles beim ~en lassen to leave everything as it was
Altar [alˈtaːr] (*-(e)s, -äre*) *m* altar
Altbau *m* old building
altbekannt *adj* long-known
Alt'eisen *nt* scrap iron
Alten(wohn)heim *nt* old people's home
Alter [ˈaltɐ] (*-s, -*) *nt* age; *(hohes)* old age; im ~ von at the age of; **a**~**n** *vi* to grow old, to age
Alternativ- [altɛrnaˈtiːf] *in zW* alternative; ~**e** *f* alternative
Alters- *zW:* ~**grenze** *f* age limit; ~**heim** *nt* old people's home; ~**rente** *f* old age pension; ~**schwach** *adj* *(Mensch)* frail; ~**versorgung** *f* old age pension
Altertum *nt* antiquity
alt- *zW:* **A**~**glas** *nt* glass for recycling; **A**~**glascontainer** *m* bottle bank; ~**klug** *adj* precocious; ~**modisch** *adj* old-fashioned; **A**~**papier** *nt* waste paper; **A**~**stadt** *f* old town
Alufolie [ˈaːluˌfoːliə] *f* aluminium foil
Aluminium [aluˈmiːniʊm] (*-s*) *nt* aluminium, aluminum (*US*); ~**folie** *f* tinfoil
Alzheimer-Krankheit [ˈæltshaɪmɐ-] *f* Alzheimer's (disease)
am [am] = **an dem**; ~ Schlafen *(umg)* sleeping; ~ 15. März on March 15th; ~ besten/schönsten best/most beautiful
Amateur [amaˈtøːr] *m* amateur
Amboß [ˈambɔs] (*-sses, -sse*) *m* anvil

ambulant [ambu'lant] *adj* outpatient

Ambulanz [ambu'lants] *f* outpatients *sg*

Ameise ['a:maizə] *f* ant

Ameisenhaufen *m* ant hill

Amerika [a'me:rika] (-s) *nt* America; **~ner(in)** [-'ka:nər(in)] (-s, -) *m(f)* American; **a~nisch** [-'ka:nɪʃ] *adj* American

Amnestie [amnɛs'ti:] *f* amnesty

Ampel ['ampəl] (-, -n) *f* traffic lights *pl*

amputieren [ampu'ti:rən] *vt* to amputate

Amsel ['amzəl] (-, -n) *f* blackbird

Amt [amt] (-(e)s, ∺er) *nt* office; (*Pflicht*) duty; (*TEL*) exchange; **a~ieren** [am'ti:rən] *vi* to hold office; **a~lich** *adj* official

Amts- *zW*: **~richter** *m* district judge; **~stunden** *pl* office hours; **~zeit** *f* period of office

amüsant [amy'zant] *adj* amusing

amüsieren [amy'zi:rən] *vt* to amuse ♦ *vr* to enjoy o.s.

SCHLÜSSELWORT

an [an] *präp +dat* **1** (*räumlich: wo?*) at; (*auf, bei*) on; (*nahe bei*) near; **an diesem Ort** at this place; **an der Wand** on the wall; **zu nahe an etw** too near to sth; **unten am Fluß** down by the river; **Köln liegt am Rhein** Cologne is on the Rhine

2 (*zeitlich: wann?*) on; **an diesem Tag** on this day; **an Ostern** at Easter

3: **arm an Fett** low in fat; **an etw sterben** to die of sth; **an (und für) sich** actually

♦ *präp +akk* **1** (*räumlich: wohin?*) to; **er ging ans Fenster** he went (over) to the window; **etw an die Wand hängen/schreiben** to hang /write sth on the wall

2 (*zeitlich: woran?*): **an etw denken** to think of sth

3 (*gerichtet an*) to); **ein Gruß/eine Frage an dich** greetings/a question to you

♦ *adv* **1** (*ungefähr*) about; **an die hundert** about a hundred

2 (*auf Fahrplänen*): **Frankfurt an 18.30** arriving Frankfurt 18.30

3 (*ab*): **von dort/heute an** from there/today onwards

4 (*angeschaltet, angezogen*) on; **das Licht ist an** the light is on; **ohne etwas an sein** with nothing on; *siehe auch* **am**

---

analog [ana'lo:k] *adj* analogous; **A~ie** [-'gi:] *f* analogy

Analyse [ana'ly:zə] *f* analysis

analysieren [analy'zi:rən] *vt* to analyse

Ananas ['ananas] (-, - *od* -se) *f* pineapple

Anarchie [anar'çi:] *f* anarchy

Anatomie [anato'mi:] *f* anatomy

anbahnen ['anba:nən] *vt, vr* to open up

Anbau ['anbau] *m* (*AGR*) cultivation; (*Gebäude*) extension; **a~en** *vt* (*AGR*) to cultivate; (*Gebäudeteil*) to build on

anbehalten ['anbəhaltən] (*unreg*) *vt* to keep on

anbei [an'bai] *adv* enclosed

anbeißen ['anbaisən] (*unreg*) *vt* to bite into ♦ *vi* to bite; (*fig*) to swallow the bait; **zum A~** (*umg*) good enough to eat

anbelangen ['anbəlaŋən] *vt* to concern; **was mich anbelangt** as far as I am concerned

anbeten ['anbe:tən] *vt* to worship

Anbetracht ['anbətraxt] *m*: **in ~** +*gen* in view of

anbiedern ['anbi:dərn] *vr*: **sich ~ (bei)** to make up (to)

anbieten ['anbi:tən] (*unreg*) *vt* to offer ♦ *vr* to volunteer

anbinden ['anbindən] (*unreg*) *vt* to tie up; **kurz angebunden** (*fig*) curt

Anblick ['anblik] *m* sight; **a~en** *vt* to look at

anbrechen ['anbrɛçən] (*unreg*) *vt* to start; (*Vorräte*) to break into ♦ *vi* to start; (*Tag*) to break; (*Nacht*) to fall

anbrennen ['anbrɛnən] (unreg) vi to
catch fire; (KOCH) to burn

anbringen ['anbrɪŋən] (unreg) vt to
bring; (Ware) to sell; (festmachen)
to fasten

Anbruch ['anbrʊx] m beginning; ~
des Tages/der Nacht dawn/nightfall

anbrüllen ['anbrʏlən] vt to roar at

Andacht ['andaxt] (-, -en) f devotion; (Gottesdienst) prayers pl

andächtig ['andɛçtɪç] adj devout

andauern ['andauərn] vi to last, to
go on; **~d** adj continual

Anden ['andən] pl Andes

Andenken ['andɛŋkən] (-s, -) nt
memory; souvenir

andere(r, s) ['andərə(r, s)] adj
other; (verschieden) different; ein
~s Mal another time; kein ~r nobody else; von etw ~m sprechen to
talk about something else; **~rseits**
adv on the other hand

andermal adv: ein ~ some other
time

ändern ['ɛndərn] vt to alter, to
change ♦ vr to change

andernfalls ['andərnfals] adv otherwise

anders ['andərs] adv: ~ (als) differ-
ently (from); **wer ~?** who else?;
jd/irgendwo ~ sb/somewhere else;
~ aussehen/klingen to look/sound
different; **~artig** adj different; **~her-
um** adv the other way round; **~wo**
adv somewhere else; **~woher** adv
from somewhere else

anderthalb ['andərt'halp] adj one
and a half

Änderung ['ɛndərʊŋ] f alteration,
change

anderweitig ['andər'vaitɪç] adj other
♦ adv otherwise; (anderswo) elsewhere

andeuten ['andɔytən] vt to indicate;
(Wink geben) to hint at

Andeutung f indication; hint

Andrang ['andraŋ] m crush

andrehen ['andre:ən] vt to turn od
switch on; **jdm etw ~** (umg) to unload sth onto sb

androhen ['andro:ən] vt: **jdm etw
~** to threaten sb with sth

aneignen ['an'aignən] vt: **sich dat
etw ~** to acquire sth; (widerrechtlich) to appropriate sth

aneinander [an'ai'nandər] adv at
/on/to etc one another od each other;
~geraten (unreg) vi to clash

Anekdote [anɛk'do:tə] f anecdote

anekeln ['an'e:kəln] vt to disgust

Anemone [ane'mo:nə] f anemone

anerkannt ['an'ɛrkant] adj recog-
nized, acknowledged

anerkennen ['an'ɛrkɛnən] (unreg)
vt to recognize, to acknowledge;
(würdigen) to appreciate; **~d** adj appreciative

Anerkennung f recognition, acknowledgement; appreciation

anfachen ['anfaxən] vt to fan into
flame; (fig) to kindle

anfahren ['anfa:rən] (unreg) vt to
deliver; (fahren gegen) to hit; (Hafen) to put into; (fig) to bawl out ♦
vi to drive up; (losfahren) to drive
off

Anfahrt ['anfa:rt] f (Anfahrtsweg,
Anfahrtszeit) departure

Anfall ['anfal] m (MED) attack;
a~en (unreg) vt to attack; (fig) to
overcome ♦ vi (Arbeit) to come up;
(Produkt) to be obtained

anfällig ['anfɛlɪç] adj delicate; **~ für
etw** prone to sth

Anfang ['anfaŋ] m (-(e)s, -fänge) m
beginning, start; **von ~ an** right
from the beginning; **zu ~** at the beginning; **~ Mai** at the beginning of
May; **a~en** (unreg) vt, vi to begin,
to start; (machen) to do

Anfänger(in) ['anfɛŋər(ɪn)] (-s, -)
m(f) beginner

anfänglich ['anfɛŋlɪç] adj initial

anfangs adv at first; **A~buchstabe**
m initial od first letter

anfassen ['anfasən] vt to handle;
(berühren) to touch ♦ vi to lend a
hand ♦ vr to feel

anfechten ['anfɛçtən] (unreg) vt to
dispute; (beunruhigen) to trouble

anfertigen ['anfɛrtɪgən] vt to make

anfeuern ['anfɔyərn] vt (fig) to spur on

anflehen ['anfle:ən] vt to implore

anfliegen ['anfli:gən] (unreg) vt to fly to

Anflug ['anflu:k] m (AVIAT) approach; (Spur) trace

anfordern ['anfɔrdərn] vt to demand; (COMM) to requisition

Anforderung f (+gen) demand (for)

Anfrage ['anfra:gə] f inquiry; **a~n** vi to inquire

anfreunden ['anfrɔyndən] vr to make friends

anfügen ['anfy:gən] vt to add; (beifügen) to enclose

anfühlen ['anfy:lən] vt, vr to feel

anführen ['anfy:rən] vt (leiten; (zitieren) to quote; (umg: betrügen) to lead up the garden path

Anführer m leader

Anführung f leadership; (Zitat) quotation; **~szeichen** pl quotation marks, inverted commas

Angabe ['anga:bə] f statement; (TECH) specification; (umg: Prahlerei) boasting; (SPORT) service

angeben ['ange:bən] (unreg) vt to give; (anzeigen) to inform on; (bestimmen) to set ♦ vi (umg) to boast; (SPORT) to serve

Angeber (-s, -; umg) m show-off; **Angebe'rei** (umg) f showing off

angeblich ['ange:plɪç] adj alleged

angeboren ['angəbo:rən] adj inborn, innate

Angebot ['angəbo:t] nt offer; ~ (an +dat) (COMM) supply (of)

angebracht ['angəbraxt] adj appropriate, in order

angegriffen ['angəgrɪfən] adj exhausted

angeheitert ['angəhaɪtərt] adj tipsy

angehen ['ange:ən] (unreg) vt to concern; (angreifen) to attack; (bitten): **jdn ~ (um)** to approach sb (for) ♦ vi (Feuer) to light; (umg: beginnen) to begin; **~d** adj prospec-tive

Angehörige(r) mf relative

Angeklagte(r) ['angəkla:ktə(r)] mf accused

Angel ['aŋəl] (-, -n) f fishing rod; (Tür~) hinge

Angelegenheit ['angəle:gənhaɪt] f affair, matter

Angel- zW: **~haken** m fish hook; **a~n** vt to catch ♦ vi to fish; **~n** (-s) nt angling, fishing; **~rute** f fishing rod

angemessen ['angəmesən] adj appropriate, suitable

angenehm ['angəne:m] adj pleasant; **~!** (bei Vorstellung) pleased to meet you

angeregt ['angəre:kt] adj animated, lively

angesehen ['angəze:ən] adj respected

angesichts ['angəzɪçts] präp +gen in view of, considering

angespannt ['angəʃpant] adj (Aufmerksamkeit) close; (Arbeit) hard

Angestellte(r) ['angəʃtɛltə(r)] mf employee

angetan ['angəta:n] adj: **von jdm/etw ~ sein** to be impressed by sb/sth; **es jdm ~ haben** to appeal to sb

angetrunken ['angətruŋkən] adj tipsy

angewiesen ['angəvi:zən] adj: **auf jdn/etw ~ sein** to be dependent on sb/sth

angewöhnen ['angəvø:nən] vt: **jdm/sich etw ~** to get sb/become accustomed to sth

Angewohnheit ['angəvo:nhaɪt] f habit

angleichen ['anglaɪçən] (unreg) vt, vr to adjust

Angler ['aŋlər] (-s, -) m angler

angreifen ['angraɪfən] (unreg) vt to attack; (anfassen) to touch; (Arbeit) to tackle; (beschädigen) to damage

Angreifer (-s, -) m attacker

Angriff ['angrɪf] m attack; **etw in ~ nehmen** to make a start on sth

Angst [aŋst] (-, ⸚e) f fear; **jdm ist**

a~ sb is afraid *od* scared; ~ **haben (vor** +*dat*) to be afraid *od* scared (of); ~ **haben um** jdn/etw to be worried about sb/sth; jdn etw **machen** to scare sb; **~hase** (*umg*) *m* chicken, scaredy-cat

ängst- ['ɛŋst] *zW:* **~igen** *vt* to frighten ♦ *vr:* **sich ~igen** (*vor* +*dat od* **um**) to worry (o.s.) (about); **~lich** *adj* nervous; (*besorgt*) worried; **Ä~lichkeit** *f* nervousness

anhaben ['anha:bən] (*unreg*) *vt* to have on; **er kann mir nichts ~** he can't hurt me

anhalt- ['anhalt] *zW:* **~en** (*unreg*) *vt* to stop ♦ *vi* to stop; (*andauern*) to persist; (jdm) **etw ~** to hold sth up (against sb); jdn **zur Arbeit/ Höflichkeit ~en** to make sb work/be polite; **~end** *adj* persistent; **A~er (-s, -)** *m* hitch-hiker; **per A~er fahren** to hitch-hike; **A~spunkt** *m* clue

anhand [an'hant] *präp* +*gen* with

Anhang ['anhaŋ] *m* appendix; (*Leute*) family; supporters *pl*

anhäng- ['anhɛŋ] *zW:* **~en** (*unreg*) *vt* to hang up; (*Wagen*) to couple up; (*Zusatz*) to add (on); **A~er (-s, -)** *m* supporter; (*AUT*) trailer; (*am Koffer*) tag; (*Schmuck*) pendant; **E~erschaft** *f* supporters *pl*; **~lich** *adj* devoted; **A~lichkeit** *f* devotion; **A~sel (-s, -)** *nt* appendage

Anhäufung ['anhɔyfʊŋ] *f* accumulation

anheben ['anhe:bən] (*unreg*) *vt* to lift up; (*Preise*) to raise

anheizen ['anhaitsən] *vt* (*Stimmung*) to lift; (*Morale*) to boost

Anhieb ['anhi:b] *m:* **auf ~** at the very first go; (*kurz entschlossen*) on the spur of the moment

Anhöhe ['anhø:ə] *f* hill

anhören ['anhø:rən] *vt* to listen to; (*anmerken*) to hear ♦ *vr* to sound

animieren [ani'mi:rən] *vt* to encourage, to urge on

Anis [a'ni:s] (**-es, -e**) *m* aniseed

Ank. *abk* (= *Ankunft*) arr.

Ankauf ['ankauf] *m* (*von Wertpapier-*

en, Devisen, Waren) purchase

ankaufen ['ankaufən] *vt* to purchase, to buy

Anker ['aŋkər] (**-s, -**) *m* anchor; **vor ~ gehen** to drop anchor; **a~n** *vt, vi* to anchor

Anklage ['ankla:gə] *f* accusation; (*JUR*) charge; **~bank** *f* dock; jdn **a~n** *vt* to accuse; jdn (*eines Verbrechens*) **a~n** (*JUR*) to charge sb (with a crime)

Ankläger ['anklɛ:gər] *m* accuser

Anklang ['anklaŋ] *m:* **bei jdm ~ finden** to meet with sb's approval

Ankleidekabine *f* changing cubicle

ankleiden ['anklaidən] *vt, vr* to dress

anklopfen ['anklɔpfən] *vi* to knock

anknüpfen ['anknʏpfən] *vt* to fasten *od* tie on; (*fig*) to start ♦ *vi* (*anschließen*): **~ an** +*akk* to refer to

ankommen ['ankɔmən] (*unreg*) *vi* to arrive; (*näherkommen*) to approach; (*Anklang finden*): **bei jdm (gut) ~** to go down well with sb; **es kommt darauf an it** depends; (*wichtig sein*) that (is what) matters; **es darauf ~ lassen** to let things take their course; **gegen jdn/etw ~** to cope with sb/sth; **bei jdm schlecht ~** to go down badly with sb

ankreuzen ['ankrɔytsən] *vt* to mark with a cross; (*hervorheben*) to highlight

ankündigen ['ankʏndɪgən] *vt* to announce

Ankündigung *f* announcement

Ankunft ['ankʊnft] (**-, -künfte**) *f* arrival; **~szeit** *f* time of arrival

ankurbeln ['ankʊrbəln] *vt* (*AUT*) to crank; (*fig*) to boost

Anlage ['anla:gə] *f* disposition; (*Begabung*) talent; (*Park*) gardens *pl*; (*Beilage*) enclosure; (*TECH*) plant; (*FIN*) investment; (*Entwurf*) layout

Anlaß ['anlas] (**-sses, -lässe**) *m:* **~ (zu)** cause (for); (*Ereignis*) occasion; **aus ~** +*gen* on the occasion of; **~ zu etw geben** to give rise to sth; **etw zum ~ nehmen** to take the opportunity of sth

anlassen (unreg) vt to leave on; (Motor) to start ♦ vr (umg) to start off

Anlasser (-s, -) m (AUT) starter

anläßlich ['anlɛslɪç] präp +gen on the occasion of

Anlauf ['anlauf] m run-up; (unreg) vi to begin; (neuer Film) to show; (SPORT) to run up; (Fenster) to mist up; (Metall) to tarnish ♦ vt to call at; rot a~en to blush; angelaufen kommen to come running up

anlegen ['anleːgən] vt to put; (anziehen) to put on; (gestalten) to lay out; (Geld) to invest ♦ vi (Schiff) to berth; etw an etw akk ~ to put sth against od on sth; ein Gewehr ~ (auf +akk) to aim a weapon (at); es auf etw akk ~ to be out for sth/to do sth; sich mit jdm ~ (umg) to quarrel with sb

Anlegestelle f landing place

anlehnen ['anleːnən] vt to lean; (Tür) to leave ajar; (sich) an etw akk ~ to lean on/against sth

Anleihe ['anlaɪə] f (FINANZ) loan

anleiten ['anlaɪtən] vt to instruct

Anleitung f instructions pl

anlernen ['anlɛrnən] vt to teach, to instruct

anliegen ['anliːgən] (unreg) vi (Kleidung) to cling; A~ (-s, -) nt matter; (Wunsch) wish; ~d adj adjacent; (beigefügt) enclosed

Anlieger ['anliːgɐ] m resident; ~frei "residents only"

anmachen ['anmaxən] vt to attach; (Elektrisches) to put on; (Zigarette) to light; (Salat) to dress

anmaßen ['anmaːsən] vt: sich dat etw ~ (Recht) to lay claim to sth; ~d adj arrogant

Anmaßung f presumption

anmelden ['anmɛldən] vt to announce ♦ vr (sich ankündigen) to make an appointment; (polizeilich, für Kurs etc) to register

Anmeldung f announcement; appointment; registration

anmerken ['anmɛrkən] vt to observe; (anstreichen) to mark; sich dat nichts ~ lassen to not give anything away

Anmerkung f note

Anmut ['anmuːt] (-) f grace; a~en vt to give a feeling; a~ig adj charming

annähen ['anneːən] vt to sew on

annähern ['anneːɐn] vr to get closer; ~d adj approximate

Annäherung f approach; ~sversuch m advances pl

Annahme ['annaːmə] f acceptance; (Vermutung) assumption

annehm- ['anneːm] zW: ~bar adj acceptable; ~en (unreg) vt to accept; (Namen) to take; (Kind) to adopt; (vermuten) to suppose, to assume ♦ vr (+gen) to take care (of); A~lichkeit f comfort

Annonce [a'nõːsə] f advertisement

annoncieren [anõ'siːrən] vt, vi to advertise

annullieren [anʊ'liːrən] vt to annul

Anode [a'noːdə] f anode

anonym [ano'nyːm] adj anonymous

Anorak ['anorak] (-s, -s) m anorak

anordnen ['anʔɔrdnən] vt to arrange; (befehlen) to order

Anordnung f arrangement; order

anorganisch ['anʔɔrɡaːnɪʃ] adj inorganic

anpacken ['anpakən] vt to grasp; (fig) to tackle; mit ~ to lend a hand

anpassen ['anpasən] vt: (jdm) ~ to fit (on sb); (fig) to adapt ♦ vr to adapt

anpassungsfähig adj adaptable

Anpfiff ['anpfɪf] m (SPORT) (starting) whistle; kick-off; (umg) rocket

anprallen ['anpralən] vi: ~ (gegen od an +akk) to collide (with)

anprangern ['anpraŋɐn] vt to denounce

anpreisen ['anpraɪzən] (unreg) vt to extol

Anprobe ['anproːbə] f trying on

anprobieren ['anprobiːrən] vt to try on

anrechnen ['anrɛçnən] vt to charge; (fig) to count; **jdm etw hoch ~** to value sb's sth greatly

Anrecht ['anrɛçt] nt: **~ (auf +akk)** right (to)

Anrede ['anreːdə] f form of address; **a~n** vt to address; (belästigen) to accost

anregen ['anreːgən] vt to stimulate; **angeregte Unterhaltung** lively discussion; **~d** adj stimulating

Anregung f stimulation; (Vorschlag) suggestion

anreichern ['anraɪçɐn] vt to enrich

Anreise ['anraɪzə] f journey; **a~n** vi to arrive

Anreiz ['anraɪts] m incentive

Anrichte ['anrɪçtə] f sideboard; **a~n** vt to serve up; **Unheil a~n** to make mischief

anrüchig ['anrʏçɪç] adj dubious

anrücken ['anrʏkən] vi to approach; (MIL) to advance

Anruf ['anruːf] m call; **a~en** (unreg) vt to call out to; (bitten) to call on; (TEL) to ring up, to phone, to call

ans [ans] **= an das**

Ansage ['anzaːgə] f announcement; **a~n** vt to announce ♦ vr to say one will come; **~r(in)** (-s, -) m(f) announcer

ansammeln ['anzaməln] vt (Reichtümer) to amass ♦ vr (Menschen) to gather, to assemble (Wasser) to collect

Ansammlung f collection; (Leute) crowd

ansässig ['anzɛsɪç] adj resident

Ansatz ['anzats] m start; (Haar~) hairline; (Hals~) base; (Verlängerungsstück) extension; (Veranschlagung) estimate; **~punkt** m starting point

anschaffen ['anʃafən] vt to buy, to purchase

Anschaffung f purchase

anschalten ['anʃaltən] vt to switch on

anschau- ['anʃao] zW: **~en** vt to look at; **~lich** adj illustrative;

A~ung f (Meinung) view; **aus eigener A~ung** from one's own experience

Anschein ['anʃaɪn] m appearance; **allem ~ nach** to all appearances; **den ~ haben** to seem, to appear; **a~end** adj apparent

Anschlag ['anʃlaːk] m notice; (Attentat) attack; (COMM) estimate; (auf Klavier) touch; (Schreibmaschine) character; **a~en** ['anʃlaːgən] (unreg) vt to put up; (beschädigen) to chip; (Akkord) to strike; (Kosten) to estimate ♦ vi to hit; (wirken) to have an effect; (Glocke) to ring; (Hund) to bark; **an etw akk a~en** to hit against sth

anschließen ['anʃliːsən] (unreg) vt to connect up; (Sender) to link up ♦ vi: **an etw akk ~** to adjoin sth; (zeitlich) to follow sth; **sich jdm/etw ~** to join sb/sth; (beipflichten) to agree with sb/sth; **sich an etw akk ~** to adjoin sth; **~d** adj adjacent; (zeitlich) subsequent ♦ adv afterwards

Anschluß ['anʃlʊs] m (ELEK, EISENB) connection; (von Wasser etc) supply; **im ~ an +akk** following; **~ finden** to make friends

anschmiegsam ['anʃmiːkzaːm] adj affectionate

anschnallen ['anʃnalən] vt to buckle on ♦ vr to fasten one's seat belt

anschneiden ['anʃnaɪdən] (unreg) vt to cut into; (Thema) to introduce

anschreiben ['anʃraɪbən] (unreg) vt to write (up); (COMM) to charge up; (benachrichtigen) to write to

anschreien ['anʃraɪən] (unreg) vt to shout at

Anschrift ['anʃrɪft] f address

Anschuldigung ['anʃʊldɪgʊŋ] f accusation

anschwellen ['anʃvɛlən] (unreg) vi to swell (up)

anschwindeln ['anʃvɪndəln] vt to lie to

ansehen ['anzeːən] (unreg) vt to look at; **A~** (-s) nt respect; (Ruf) re-

putation; **jdm etw ~ to see** sth
(from sb's face); **jdn/etw als etw ~**
to look on sb/sth as sth; **~ für** to consider

ansehnlich ['anzeːnlɪç] *adj* fine-
looking; (*beträchtlich*) considerable

ansetzen ['anzɛtsən] *vt* (*festlegen*)
to fix; (*entwickeln*) to develop;
(*Fett*) to put on; (*Blätter*) to grow;
(*zubereiten*) to prepare ♦ *vi* (*anfangen*) to start, to begin; (*Entwicklung*) to set in; (*dick werden*) to put
on weight ♦ *vr* (*Rost etc*) to start to
develop; **~ an** *+akk* (*anfügen*) to
put on to; (*anlegen, an Mund etc*) to put
to

Ansicht ['anzɪçt] *f* (*Anblick*) sight;
(*Meinung*) view, opinion; **zur ~** on
approval; **meiner ~ nach** in my opinion; **~skarte** *f* picture postcard;
~ssache *f* matter of opinion

anspannen ['anʃpanən] *vt* to harness; (*Muskel*) to strain

Anspannung *f* strain

anspielen ['anʃpiːlən] *vi* (*SPORT*) to
start play; **auf etw akk ~** to refer
od allude to sth

Anspielung *f*: **~** (**auf** *+akk*) reference (to), allusion (to)

Ansporn ['anʃpɔrn] (**-(e)s**) *m* incentive

Ansprache ['anʃpraːxə] *f* address

ansprechen ['anʃprɛçən] (*unreg*) *vt*
to speak to; (*bitten, gefallen*) to appeal to ♦ *vi*: (**auf etw akk**) **~** to react (to sth); **jdn auf etw akk** (**hin**)
~ to ask sb about sth; **~d** *adj* attractive

anspringen ['anʃprɪŋən] (*unreg*) *vi*
(*AUT*) to start ♦ *vt* to jump at

Anspruch ['anʃprʊx] *m* (*Recht*): **~**
(**auf** *+akk*) claim (to); **hohe Ansprüche stellen/haben** to demand
/expect a lot; **jdn/etw in ~ nehmen**
to occupy sb/take up sb's time; **a~slos**
adj undemanding; **a~svoll** *adj* demand-
ing

anstacheln ['anʃtaxəln] *vt* to spur on

Anstalt ['anʃtalt] (**-, -en**) *f* institution; **~en machen, etw zu tun** to

prepare to do sth

Anstand ['anʃtant] *m* decency

anständig ['anʃtɛndɪç] *adj* decent;
(*umg*) proper; (*groß*) considerable

anstandslos *adv* without any ado

anstarren ['anʃtarən] *vt* to stare at

anstatt [an'ʃtat] *präp +gen* instead
of ♦ *konj*: **~ etw zu tun** instead of
doing sth

Ansteck- ['anʃtɛk] *zW*: **a~en** *vt* to
pin on; (*MED*) to infect; (*Pfeife*) to
light; (*Haus*) to set fire to ♦ *vr*: **ich
habe mich bei ihm angesteckt** I
caught it from him ♦ *vi* to be
infectious; **a~end** *adj* infectious;
~ung *f* infection

anstehen ['anʃteːən] (*unreg*) *vi* to
queue (*BRIT*), to line up (*US*)

ansteigen ['anʃtaɪgən] *vi* (*Straße*) to
climb; (*Gelände, Temperatur,
Preise*) to rise

anstelle [an'ʃtɛlə] *präp +gen* in
place of; **~n** [an-] *vt* (*einschalten*) to
turn on; (*Arbeit geben*) to employ;
(*machen*) to do ♦ *vr* to queue (up)
(*BRIT*), to line up (*US*); (*umg*) to
act

Anstellung *f* employment; (*Posten*)
post, position

Anstieg ['anʃtiːk] (**-(e)s, -e**) *m*
(*+gen*) climb; (*fig: von Preisen etc*)
increase (in)

anstiften ['anʃtɪftən] *vt* (*Unglück*) to
cause; **jdn zu etw ~** to put sb up to

Anstifter (**-s, -**) *m* instigator

anstimmen ['anʃtɪmən] *vt* (*Lied*) to
strike up with; (*Geschrei*) to set up

Anstoß ['anʃtoːs] *m* impetus;
(*Ärgernis*) offence; (*SPORT*) kick-
off; **der erste ~** the initiative; **~
nehmen an** *+dat* to take offence at;
a~en (*unreg*) *vt* to push; (*mit Fuß*)
to kick ♦ *vi* to knock, to bump; (*mit
der Zunge*) to lisp; (*mit Gläsern*):
a~en (**auf** *+akk*) to drink (to), to
drink a toast to

anstößig ['anʃtøːsɪç] *adj* offensive,
indecent

anstreichen ['anʃtraɪçən] (*unreg*)

to paint

Anstreicher (-s, -) m painter

anstrengen ['anʃtrɛŋən] vt to strain; (JUR) to bring ♦ vr to make an effort; **angestrengt** adv as hard as one can; **~d** adj tiring

Anstrengung f effort

Anstrich ['anʃtrɪç] m coat of paint

Ansturm ['anʃtʊrm] m rush; (MIL) attack

Antarktis [ant'arktɪs] (-) f Antarctic

antasten ['antastən] vt to touch; (Recht) to infringe upon; (Ehre) to question

Anteil ['antaɪl] (-s, -e) m share; (Mitgefühl) sympathy; **~ nehmen an** +dat to share in; (sich interessieren) to take an interest in; **~nahme** (-) f sympathy

Antenne [an'tɛnə] f aerial

Anti- [anti] in zW anti; **~alkoholiker** m teetotaller; **a~autoritär** adj anti-authoritarian; **~biotikum** [antibi'oːtikʊm] (-s, -ka) nt antibiotic

antik [an'tiːk] adj antique; **A~e** f (Zeitalter) ancient world; (Kunstgegenstand) antique

Antilope [anti'loːpə] f antelope

Antiquariat [antikvari'aːt] (-(e)s, -e) nt secondhand bookshop

Antiquitäten [antikvi'tɛːtən] pl antiques; **~händler** m antique dealer

antiseptisch ['zɛptɪʃ] adj antiseptic

Antrag ['antraːk] (-(e)s, -träge) m proposal; (PARL) motion; (Gesuch) application

antreffen ['antrɛfən] (unreg) vt to meet

antreiben ['antraɪbən] (unreg) vt to drive on; (Motor) to drive; (anschwemmen) to wash up ♦ vi to be washed up

antreten ['antreːtən] (unreg) vt (Amt) to take up; (Erbschaft) to come into; (Beweis) to offer; (Reise) to start, to begin ♦ vi (MIL) to fall in; (SPORT) to line up; **gegen jdn ~** to play/fight (against) sb

Antrieb ['antriːp] m (auch fig) drive;

aus eigenem **~** of one's own accord

antrinken ['antrɪŋkən] (unreg) vt (Flasche, Glas) to start to drink from; sich dat Mut/einen Rausch **~** to give o.s. Dutch courage/get drunk; **angetrunken sein** to be tipsy

Antritt ['antrɪt] m beginning, commencement; (eines Amts) taking up

antun ['antuːn] (unreg) vt: **jdm etw ~** to do sth to sb; **jdm Zwang ~** to force o.s.; **sich dat etwas ~** (try to) take one's own life

Antwort ['antvɔrt] (-, -en) f answer, reply; **a~en** vi to answer, to reply

anvertrauen ['anfɛrtrauən] vt: **jdm etw ~** to entrust sb with sth; **sich jdm ~** to confide in sb

anwachsen ['anvaksən] (unreg) vi to grow; (Pflanze) to take root

Anwalt ['anvalt] (-(e)s, -wälte) m solicitor; lawyer; (fig) champion

Anwältin ['anvɛltɪn] f siehe Anwalt

Anwärter ['anvɛrtər] m candidate

anweisen ['anvaɪzən] (unreg) vt to instruct; (zuteilen) to assign

Anweisung f instruction; (COMM) remittance; (Post-, Zahlungs~) money order

anwend- ['anvɛnd] zW: **~bar** ['anvɛnt-] adj practicable, applicable; **~en** (unreg) vt to use, to employ; (Gesetz, Regel) to apply; **A~ung** f use; application

anwesend ['anveːzənt] adj present; **die A~en** those present

Anwesenheit f presence

anwidern ['anviːdərn] vt to disgust

Anwohner(in) ['anvoːnər(m)] (-s, -) m(f) neighbour

Anzahl ['antsaːl] f: **~ (an** +dat) number (of); **a~en** vt to pay on account; **~ung** f deposit, payment on account

Anzeichen ['antsaɪçən] nt sign, indication

Anzeige ['antsaɪgə] f (Zeitungs~) announcement; (Werbung) advertisement; (bei Polizei) report; **~ erstatten gegen jdn** to report sb (to the police); **a~n** vt (zu erkennen geben)

to show; (*bekanntgeben*) to announce; (*bei Polizei*) to report

anziehen ['antsi:ən] (*unreg*) *vt* to attract; (*Kleidung*) to put on; (*Mensch*) to dress; (*Seil*) to pull tight; (*Schraube*) to tighten; (*Knie*) to draw up; (*Feuchtigkeit*) to absorb ♦ *vr* to get dressed; **~d** *adj* attractive

Anziehung *f* (*Reiz*) attraction; **~skraft** *f* power of attraction; (*PHYS*) force of gravitation

Anzug ['antsu:k] *m* suit; (*Herankommen*): **im ~ sein** to be approaching

anzüglich ['antsy:klıç] *adj* personal; (*anstößig*) offensive; **A~keit** *f* offensiveness; (*Bemerkung*) personal remark

anzünden ['antsʏndən] *vt* to light

Anzünder *m* lighter

anzweifeln ['antsvaɪfəln] *vt* to doubt

apathisch [a'pa:tıʃ] *adj* apathetic

Apfel ['apfəl] (*-s, -*) *m* apple; **~saft** *m* apple juice; **~sine** [-'zi:nə] *f* orange

Apostel [a'pɔstəl] (*-s, -*) *m* apostle

Apotheke [apo'te:kə] *f* chemist's (shop), drugstore (*US*); **~r(in)** (*-s, -*) *m(f)* chemist, druggist (*US*)

Apparat [apa'ra:t] (*-(e)s, -e*) *m* piece of apparatus; camera; telephone; (*RADIO, TV*) set; **am ~!** speaking!; **~ur** [-'tu:r] *f* apparatus

Appartement [apartə'mã:] (*-s, -s*) *nt* flat

appellieren [ape'li:rən] *vi*: **~** (**an** +*akk*) to appeal (to)

Appetit [ape'ti:t] (*-(e)s, -e*) *m* appetite; **guten ~** enjoy your meal; **a~lich** *adj* appetizing; **~losigkeit** *f* lack of appetite

Applaus [a'plaʊs] (*-es, -e*) *m* applause

Aprikose [apri'ko:zə] *f* apricot

April [a'prıl] (*-(s), -e*) *m* April

Aquarell [akva'rɛl] (*-s, -e*) *nt* watercolour

Aquarium [a'kva:riʊm] *nt* aquarium

Äquator [ɛ'kva:tɔr] (*-s*) *m* equator

Arab- ['arab] *zW*: **~er(in)** (*-s, -*) *m(f)*

Arab-; **~ien** [a'ra:biən] (*-s*) *nt* Arabia; **a~isch** [a'ra:bıʃ] *adj* Arabian

Arbeit ['arbaɪt] (*-, -en*) *f* work *no art*; (*Stelle*) job; (*Erzeugnis*) piece of work; (*wissenschaftliche*) dissertation; (*Klassen~*) test; **das war eine ~** that was a hard job; **a~en** *vi* to work ♦ *vt* to work, to make; **~er(in)** (*-s, -*) *m(f)* worker; (*ungelernt*) labourer; **~erschaft** *f* workers *pl*, labour force; **~geber** (*-s, -*) *m* employer; **~nehmer** (*-s, -*) *m* employee

Arbeits- *zW*: **a~am** *adj* industrious; **~amt** *nt* employment exchange; **~erlaubnis** *f* work permit; **a~fähig** *adj* fit for work, able-bodied; **~gang** *m* operation; **~kräfte** *pl* (*Mitarbeiter*) workforce; **a~los** *adj* unemployed, out-of-work; **~lose(r)** *f(m)* unemployed person; **~losigkeit** *f* unemployment; **~markt** *m* job market; **~platz** *m* job; place of work; (*Großraumbüro*) workstation; **a~scheu** *adj* work-shy; **~tag** *m* working(day); **a~unfähig** *adj* unfit for work; **~zeit** *f* working hours *pl*

Archäologe [arçɛo'lo:gə] (*-n, -n*) *m* archaeologist

Architekt(in) [arçi'tɛkt(ın)] (*-en, -en*) *m(f)* architect; **~ur** [-'tu:r] *f* architecture

Archiv [ar'çi:f] (*-s, -e*) *nt* archive

arg [ark] *adj* bad, awful ♦ *adv* awfully, very

Argentin- [argɛn'ti:n] *zW*: **~ien** (*-s*) *nt* Argentina, the Argentine; **~ier(in)** (*-s, -*) *m(f)* Argentinian; **a~isch** *adj* Argentinian

Ärger ['ɛrgər] (*-s*) *m* (*Wut*) anger; (*Unannehmlichkeit*) trouble; **ä~lich** *adj* (*zornig*) angry; (*lästig*) annoying, aggravating; **ä~n** *vt* to annoy ♦ *vr* to get annoyed

arg- *zW*: **~listig** *adj* cunning, insidious; **~los** *adj* guileless, innocent

Argument [argu'mɛnt] *nt* argument

argwöhnisch *adj* suspicious

Arie ['a:riə] *f* aria

Aristokrat [arısto'kra:t] (*-en, -en*) *m* aristocrat; **~ie** ['ti:] *f* aristocracy

Arktis ['arktɪs] (-) f Arctic

Arm [arm] (-(e)s, -e) m arm; (Fluß~) branch

arm adj poor

Armatur [arma'tuːr] f (ELEK) armature; ~enbrett nt instrument panel; (AUT) dashboard

Armband nt bracelet; ~uhr f (wrist) watch

Arme(r) mf poor man(woman); die ~n the poor

Armee [ar'meː] f army

Ärmel ['ɛrməl] (-s, -) m sleeve; etw aus dem ~ schütteln (fig) to produce sth just like that; ~kanal m English Channel

ärmlich ['ɛrmlɪç] adj poor

armselig adj wretched, miserable

Armut ['armuːt] (-) f poverty

Aroma [a'roːma] (-s, Aromen) nt aroma; a~tisch [aro'maːtɪʃ] adj aromatic

arrangieren [arãˈʒiːrən] vt to arrange ♦ vr to come to an arrangement

Arrest [a'rɛst] (-(e)s, -e) m detention

arrogant [aro'gant] adj arrogant

Arsch [arʃ] (-es, ²e; umg!) m arse (BRIT!), ass (US!)

Art [aːrt] (-, -en) f (Weise) way; (Sorte) kind, sort; (BIOL) species; eine ~ (von) Frucht a kind of fruit; Häuser aller ~ houses of all kinds; es ist nicht seine ~, das zu tun it's not like him to do that; ich mache das auf meine ~ I do that my (own) way

Arterie [ar'teːriə] f artery; ~nverkalkung f arteriosclerosis

artig ['aːrtɪç] adj good, well-behaved

Artikel [ar'tiːkəl] (-s, -) m article

Artillerie [artɪlə'riː] f artillery

Artischocke [artɪ'ʃɔka] f artichoke

Arznei [aːrts'naɪ] f medicine; ~mittel nt medicine, medicament

Arzt [aːrtst] (-es, ²e) m doctor

Ärztin ['ɛːrtstɪn] f doctor

ärztlich ['ɛːrtstlɪç] adj medical

As [as] (-ses, -se) nt ace

Asche ['aʃə] f (-, -n) ash, cinder; ~nbahn f cinder track; ~nbecher m ashtray; ~rmittwoch m Ash Wednesday

Äser ['ɛːzər] pl von Aas

Asi- ['aːzi] zW: ~en (-s) nt Asia; ~at(in) [azi'aːt(ɪn)] (-en, -en) m(f) Asian; a~atisch [-'aːtɪʃ] adj Asian

asozial ['azotsiaːl] adj antisocial; (Familien) asocial

Aspekt [as'pɛkt] (-(e)s, -e) m aspect

Asphalt [as'falt] (-(e)s, -e) m asphalt; a~ieren [asfal'tiːrən] to asphalt

aß etc [as] vb siehe essen

Asse ['asə] pl von Aß

Assistent(in) [asɪs'tɛnt(ɪn)] m(f) assistant

Assoziation [asotsiatsi'oːn] f association

Ast [ast] (-(e)s, ²e) m bough, branch

ästhetisch [ɛs'teːtɪʃ] adj aesthetic

Asthma ['astma] (-s) nt asthma; ~tiker(in) [ast'maːtikər(ɪn)] (-s, -) m(f) asthmatic

Astro- [astro] zW: ~loge (-n, -n) m astrologer; ~lo'gie f astrology; ~'naut (-en, -en) m astronaut; ~'nom (-en, -en) m astronomer; ~no'mie f astronomy

Asyl [a'zyːl] (-s, -e) nt asylum; (Heim) home; (Obdachlosen~) shelter

Atelier [atəli'eː] (-s, -e) nt studio

Atem ['aːtəm] (-s) m breath; den ~ anhalten to hold one's breath; außer ~ out of breath; a~beraubend adj breath-taking; a~los adj breathless; ~pause f breather; ~zug m breath

Atheismus [ate'ɪsmʊs] m atheism

Atheist m atheist; a~isch adj atheistic

Athen [a'teːn] (-s) nt Athens

Äther ['ɛːtər] (-s, -) m ether

Äthiopien [ɛti'oːpiən] (-s) nt Ethiopia

Athlet [at'leːt] (-en, -en) m athlete

Atlantik [at'lantɪk] (-s) m Atlantic (Ocean)

atlantisch adj Atlantic

Atlas ['atlas] (- od -ses, -se od Atlanten) m atlas

atmen ['a:tmən] vt, vi to breathe

Atmosphäre [atmo'sfɛ:rə] f atmosphere

atmosphärisch adj atmospheric

Atmung ['a:tmʊŋ] f respiration

Atom [a'to:m] (-s, -e) nt atom; **a~ar** [ato'ma:r] adj atomic; **~bombe** f atom bomb; **~energie** f atomic od nuclear energy; **~kern** m atomic nucleus; **~kraftwerk** nt atomic power station; **~krieg** m nuclear od atomic war; **~müll** m atomic waste; **~strom** m (electricity generated by) nuclear power; **~versuch** m atomic test; **~waffen** pl atomic weapons; **a~waffenfrei** adj nuclear-free; **~zeitalter** nt atomic age

Attentat ['atənta:t] (-(e)s, -e) nt: ~ (**auf** +akk) (attempted) assassination (of)

Attentäter ['atəntɛ:tər] m (would-be) assassin

Attest [a'tɛst] (-(e)s, -e) nt certificate

Attraktion [atrak'tsio:n] f (Tourismus, Zirkus) attraction

attraktiv [atrak'ti:f] adj attractive

Attrappe [a'trapə] f dummy

Attribut [atri'bu:t] (-(e)s, -e) nt (GRAM) attribute

ätzen ['ɛtsən] vi to be caustic

ätzend adj (Säure) corrosive; (fig: Spott) cutting

au [au] excl ouch!; ~ **ja!** oh yes!

─── SCHLÜSSELWORT ───

auch [aux] adv **1** (ebenfalls) also, too, as well; **das ist auch schön** that's nice too od as well; **er kommt - ich auch** he's coming - so am I, me too; **auch nicht nicht** ... either; **ich auch nicht** nor I, me neither; **oder auch** or; **auch das noch!** not that as well!

2 (selbst, sogar) even; **auch wenn das Wetter schlecht ist** even if the weather is bad; **ohne auch nur zu fragen** without even asking

3 (wirklich) really; **du siehst müde**

aus - bin ich auch you look tired - (so) I am; **so sieht es auch aus** it looks like it too

4 (auch immer): **wer auch whoever; was auch** whatever; **wie dem auch sei** be that as it may; **wie sehr er sich auch bemühte** however much he tried

─── SCHLÜSSELWORT ───

auf [auf] präp +dat (wo?) on; **auf dem Tisch** on the table; **auf der Reise** on the way; **auf der Post /dem Fest** at the post office/party; **auf der Straße** on the road; **auf dem Land/der ganzen Welt** in the country/the whole world

♦ präp +akk **1** (wohin?) on(to); **auf den Tisch** on(to) the table; **auf die Post gehen** go to the post office; **auf das Land** into the country; **etw auf einen Zettel schreiben** to write sth on a piece of paper

2: **auf deutsch** in German; **auf Lebenszeit** for my/his lifetime; **bis auf ihn** except for him; **auf einmal** at once; **auf seinen Vorschlag (hin)** at his suggestion

♦ adv **1** (offen) open; **das Fenster ist auf** the window is open

2 (hinauf) up; **auf und ab up and down**; **auf und davon** up and away; **auf!** (los!) come on!

3 (aufgestanden) up; **ist er schon auf?** is he up?

♦ konj: **auf daß** (so) that

aufatmen ['aufʔa:tmən] vi to heave a sigh of relief

aufbahren ['aufba:rən] vt to lay out

Aufbau ['aufbau] m (Bauen) building, construction; (Struktur) structure; (aufgebautes Teil) superstructure; **a~en** vt to erect, to build (up); (Existenz) to make; (gestalten) to construct; **a~en** (auf +dat) (gründen) to found od base (on)

aufbauschen ['aufbauʃən] vt to puff out; (fig) to exaggerate

aufbekommen ['aufbəkɔmən] (*unreg*) *vt* (*öffnen*) to get open; (*Hausaufgaben*) to be given

aufbessern ['aufbɛsərn] *vt* (*Gehalt*) to increase

aufbewahren ['aufbəva:rən] *vt* to keep; (*Gepäck*) to put in the left-luggage office (*BRIT*) *od* baggage check (*US*)

Aufbewahrung *f* (safe)keeping; (*Gepäck~*) left-luggage office (*BRIT*), baggage check (*US*)

aufbieten ['aufbi:tən] (*unreg*) *vt* (*Kraft*) to summon (up); (*Armee, Polizei*) to mobilize; (*Brautpaar*) to publish the banns of

aufblasen ['aufbla:zən] (*unreg*) *vt* to blow up, to inflate ♦ *vr* (*umg*) to become big-headed

aufbleiben ['aufblaibən] (*unreg*) *vi* (*Laden*) to remain open; (*Person*) to stay up

aufblenden ['aufblɛndən] *vt* (*Scheinwerfer*) to switch on full beam ♦ *vi* (*Fahrer*) to have the lights on full beam; (*AUT: Scheinwerfer*) to be on full beam

aufblicken ['aufblikən] *vi* to look up; ~ **zu** to look up at; (*fig*) to look up to

aufblühen ['aufbly:ən] *vi* to blossom, to flourish

aufbrauchen ['aufbrauxən] *vt* to use up

aufbrausen ['aufbrauzən] *vi* (*fig*) to flare up; **~d** *adj* hot-tempered

aufbrechen ['aufbrɛçən] (*unreg*) *vt* to break *od* prise (*BRIT*) open ♦ *vi* to burst open; (*gehen*) to start, to set off

aufbringen ['aufbriŋən] (*unreg*) *vt* (*öffnen*) to open; (*in Mode*) to bring into fashion; (*beschaffen*) to procure; (*FIN*) to raise; (*ärgern*) to irritate; **Verständnis für etw ~** to be able to understand sth

Aufbruch ['aufbrux] *m* departure

aufbrühen ['aufbry:ən] *vt* (*Tee*) to make

aufbürden ['aufbyrdən] *vt*: **jdm etw ~** to burden sb with sth

aufdecken ['aufdɛkən] *vt* to uncover

aufdrängen ['aufdrɛŋən] *vt*: **jdm etw ~** to force sth on sb ♦ *vr* (*Mensch*): **sich jdm ~** to intrude on sb

aufdrehen ['aufdre:ən] *vt* (*Wasserhahn etc*) to turn on; (*Ventil*) to open up

aufdringlich ['aufdriŋliç] *adj* pushy

aufeinander [auf ai'nandər] *adv* on top of each other; (*schießen*) at each other; (*vertrauen*) each other; **~folgen** *vi* to follow one another; **~folgend** *adj* consecutive; **~prallen** *vi* to hit one another

Aufenthalt ['aufɛnthalt] *m* stay; (*Verzögerung*) delay; (*EISENB*: *Halten*) stop; (*Ort*) haunt

Aufenthaltserlaubnis *f* residence permit

auferlegen ['auf ɛrle:gən] *vt*: (**jdm**) **~** to impose (upon sb)

Auferstehung ['auf ɛrʃte:uŋ] *f* resurrection

aufessen ['auf ɛsən] (*unreg*) *vt* to eat up

auffahr- ['auffa:r] *zW*: **~en** (*unreg*) *vi* (*herankommen*) to draw up; (*hochfahren*) to jump up; (*wütend werden*) to flare up; (*in den Himmel*) to ascend ♦ *vt* (*Kanonen, Geschütz*) to bring up; **~en auf** *+akk* (*stoßen*) to run *od* crash into; **~end** *adj* hot-tempered; **A~t** *f* (*Hausauffahrt*) drive; (*Autobahnauffahrt*) slip road (*BRIT*), (*freeway*) entrance (*US*); **A~unfall** *m* pile-up

auffallen ['auffalən] (*unreg*) *vi* to be noticeable; **jdm ~** to strike sb; **~d** *adj* striking

auffällig ['auffɛliç] *adj* conspicuous, striking

auffangen ['auffaŋən] (*unreg*) *vt* to catch; (*Funkspruch*) to intercept; (*Preise*) to peg

auffassen ['auffasən] *vt* to understand, to comprehend; (*auslegen*) to see, to view

Auffassung *f* (*Meinung*) opinion; (*Auslegung*) view, concept; (*auch:*

Auffassungsgabe) grasp

auffindbar ['aʊffɪntbaːr] adj to be found

auffordern ['aʊffɔrdərn] vt (*befehlen*) to call upon, to order; (*bitten*) to ask

Aufforderung f (*Befehl*) order; (*Einladung*) invitation

auffrischen ['aʊffrɪʃən] vt to freshen up; (*Kenntnisse*) to brush up; (*Erinnerungen*) to reawaken ♦ vi (*Wind*) to freshen

aufführen ['aʊffyːrən] vt (*THEAT*) to perform; (*in einem Verzeichnis*) to list, to specify ♦ vr (*sich benehmen*) to behave

Aufführung f (*THEAT*) performance; (*Liste*) specification

Aufgabe f ['aʊfgaːbə] f task; (*SCH*) exercise; (*Haus~*) homework; (*Verzicht*) giving up; (*von Gepäck*) registration; (*von Post*) posting; (*von Inserat*) insertion

Aufgang m ['aʊfgaŋ] ascent; (*Sonnen~*) rise; (*Treppe*) staircase

aufgeben ['aʊfgeːbən] (*unreg*) vt (*verzichten*) to give up; (*Paket*) to send, to post; (*Gepäck*) to register; (*Bestellung*) to give; (*Inserat*) to insert; (*Rätsel, Problem*) to set ♦ vi to give up

Aufgebot ['aʊfgəboːt] nt supply; (*Ehe~*) banns pl

aufgedunsen ['aʊfgədʊnzən] adj swollen, puffed up

aufgehen ['aʊfgeːən] (*unreg*) vi (*Sonne, Teig*) to rise; (*sich öffnen*) to open; (*klarwerden*) to become clear; (*MATH*) to come out exactly; ~ (*in +dat*) (*sich widmen*) to be absorbed (in); **in Rauch/Flammen** ~ to go up in smoke/flames

aufgelegt ['aʊfgəleːkt] adj: **gut/schlecht** ~ **sein** to be in a good/bad mood; **zu etw** ~ **sein** to be in the mood for sth

aufgeregt ['aʊfgəreːkt] adj excited

aufgeschlossen ['aʊfgəʃlɔsən] adj open, open-minded

aufgeweckt ['aʊfgəvɛkt] adj bright, intelligent

aufgießen ['aʊfgiːsən] (*unreg*) vt (*Wasser*) to pour over; (*Tee*) to infuse

aufgreifen ['aʊfgraɪfən] (*unreg*) vt (*Thema*) to take up; (*Verdächtige*) to pick up, to seize

aufgrund [aʊf'grʊnt] präp +gen on the basis of; (*wegen*) because of

aufhaben ['aʊfhaːbən] (*unreg*) vt to have on; (*Arbeit*) to have to do

aufhalsen ['aʊfhalzən] vt: **jdm etw** ~ to saddle od lumber sb with sth

aufhalten ['aʊfhaltən] (*unreg*) vt (*Person*) to detain; (*Entwicklung*) to check; (*Tür, Hand*) to hold open; (*Augen*) to keep open ♦ vr (*sich aufhalten*) (*wohnen*) to live; (*bleiben*) to stay; **sich mit etw** ~ to waste time over sth

aufhängen ['aʊfhɛŋən] (*unreg*) vt (*Wäsche*) to hang up; (*Menschen*) to hang ♦ vr to hang o.s.

Aufhänger ['aʊfhɛŋər] (-s, -) m (*am Mantel*) loop; (*fig*) peg

aufheben ['aʊfheːbən] (*unreg*) vt (*hochheben*) to raise, to lift; (*Sitzung*) to wind up; (*Urteil*) to annul; (*Gesetz*) to repeal, to abolish; (*aufbewahren*) to keep open ♦ vr to cancel itself out; **bei jdm gut aufgehoben sein** to be well looked after at sb's; **viel A~(s) machen** (*von*) to make a fuss (about)

aufheitern ['aʊfhaɪtərn] vt, vr (*Himmel, Miene*) to brighten; (*Mensch*) to cheer up

aufhellen ['aʊfhɛlən] vt, vr to clear up; (*Farbe, Haare*) to lighten

aufhetzen ['aʊfhɛtsən] vt to stir up

aufholen ['aʊfhoːlən] vt to make up ♦ vi to catch up

aufhorchen ['aʊfhɔrçən] vi to prick up one's ears

aufhören ['aʊfhøːrən] vi to stop; ~, **etw zu tun** to stop doing sth

aufklappen ['aʊfklapən] vt to open up

aufklären ['aʊfklɛːrən] vt (*Geheimnis etc*) to clear up; (*Person*) to enlighten; (*sexuell*) to tell the facts of

Aufklärung f (von Geheimnis) clearing up; (Unterrichtung, Zeitalter) enlightenment; (sexuell) sex education; (MIL, AVIAT) reconnaissance

aufkleben ['aufkle:bən] vt to stick on

Aufkleber (-s, -) m sticker

aufknöpfen ['aufknœpfən] vt to unbutton

aufkommen ['aufkɔmən] (unreg) vi (Wind) to come up; (Zweifel, Gefühl) to arise; (Mode) to start; **für etw/jetw ~** to be liable od responsible for sb/sth

aufladen ['aufla:dən] (unreg) vt to load

Auflage ['aufla:gə] f edition; (Zeitung) circulation; (Bedingung) condition; **jdm etw zur ~ machen** to make sth a condition for sb

auflassen ['auflasən] (unreg) vt (offen) to leave open; (aufgesetzt) to leave on

auflauern ['auflauərn] vi: **jdm ~** to lie in wait for sb

Auflauf ['auflauf] m (KOCH) pudding; (Menschen~) crowd

aufleben ['aufle:bən] vi (Mensch, Gespräch) to liven up; (Interesse) to revive

auflegen ['aufle:gən] vt to put on; (Telefon) to hang up; (TYP) to print

auflehnen ['aufle:nən] vt to lean on ♦ vr to rebel

Auflehnung f rebellion

auflesen ['aufle:zən] (unreg) vt to pick up

aufleuchten ['auflɔyçtən] vi to light up

auflockern ['auflɔkərn] vt to loosen; (fig: Eintönigkeit etc) to liven up

auflösen ['auflø:zən] vt to dissolve; (Haare etc) to loosen; (Mißverständnis) to sort out ♦ vr to dissolve; (Problem, Widerspruch) to be resolved; (in Tränen) **aufgelöst sein** to be in tears

Auflösung f dissolving; (fig) solution

aufmachen ['aufmaxən] vt to open; (Kleidung) to undo; (zurechtmachen) to do up ♦ vr to set out

Aufmachung f (Kleidung) outfit, get-up; (Gestaltung) format

aufmerksam ['aufmɛrkza:m] adj attentive; **jdn auf etw akk ~ machen** to point sth out to sb; **A~keit** f attention, attentiveness

aufmuntern ['aufmuntərn] vt (ermutigen) to encourage; (erheitern) to cheer up

Aufnahme ['aufna:mə] f reception; (Beginn) beginning; (in Verein etc) admission; (in Liste etc) inclusion; (Notieren) taking down; (PHOT) shot; (auf Tonband etc) recording; **a~fähig** adj receptive; **~prüfung** f entrance test

aufnehmen ['aufne:mən] (unreg) vt to receive; (hochheben) to pick up; (beginnen) to take up; (in Verein etc) to admit; (in Liste etc) to include; (fassen) to hold; (notieren) to take down; (fotografieren) to photograph; (auf Tonband, Platte) to record; (FIN: leihen) to take out; **es mit jdm ~ können** to be able to compete with sb

aufopfern ['auf?ɔpfərn] vt, vr to sacrifice; **~d** adj selfless

aufpassen ['aufpasən] vi (aufmerksam sein) to pay attention; **auf jdn/etw ~** to look after od watch sb/sth; **aufgepaßt!** look out!

Aufprall ['aufpral] (-s, -e) m impact; **a~en** vi to hit, to strike

Aufpreis ['aufprais] m extra charge

aufpumpen ['aufpumpən] vt to pump up

aufräumen ['aufrɔymən] vt, vi (Dinge) to clear away; (Zimmer) to tidy up

aufrecht ['aufrɛçt] adj (auch fig) upright; **~erhalten** (unreg) vt to maintain

aufreg- ['aufre:g] zW: **~en** vt to excite ♦ vr; to get excited; **~end** adj exciting; **A~ung** f excitement

aufreibend ['aufraɪbənt] adj strenuous

aufreißen ['aufraɪsən] (unreg) vt (Umschlag) to tear open; (Augen) to open wide; (Tür) to throw open; (Straße) to take up

aufreizen ['aufraɪtsən] vt to incite, to stir up; **~d** exciting, stimulating

aufrichten ['aufrɪçtən] vt to put up, to erect; (moralisch) to console ♦ vr to rise; (moralisch): **sich ~** (an +dat) to take heart (from)

aufrichtig ['aufrɪçtɪç] adj sincere, honest; **A~keit** f sincerity

aufrücken ['aufrʏkən] vi to move up; (beruflich) to be promoted

Aufruf ['aufruːf] m summons; (zur Hilfe) call; (des Namens) calling out; **a~en** (unreg) vt (Namen) to call out; (auffordern): **jdn a~en (zu)** to call upon sb (to)

Aufruhr ['aufruːr] (-(e)s, -e) m uprising, revolt

aufrührerisch ['aufryːrərɪʃ] adj rebellious

aufrunden ['aufrundən] vt (Summe) to round up

Aufrüstung ['aufrʏstʊŋ] f rearmament

aufrütteln ['aufrʏtəln] vt (auch fig) to shake up

aufs [aufs] = **auf das**

aufsagen ['aufzaːgən] vt (Gedicht) to recite

aufsammeln ['aufzaməln] vt to gather up

aufsässig ['aufzɛsɪç] adj rebellious

Aufsatz ['aufzats] m (Geschriebenes) essay; (auf Schrank etc) top

aufsaugen ['aufzaugən] (unreg) vt to soak up

aufschauen ['aufʃauən] vi to look up

aufscheuchen ['aufʃɔʏçən] vt to scare od frighten away

aufschieben ['aufʃiːbən] (unreg) vt to push open; (verzögern) to put off, to postpone

Aufschlag ['aufʃlaːk] m (Ärmel~) cuff; (Jacken~) lapel; (Hosen~)

turn-up; (Aufprall) impact; (Preis~) surcharge; (Tennis) service; **a~en** [-gən] (unreg) vt (öffnen) to open; (verwunden) to cut; (hochschlagen) to turn up; (aufbauen: Zelt, Lager) to pitch, to erect; (Wohnsitz) to take up ♦ vi (aufprallen) to hit; (teurer werden) to go up; (Tennis) to serve

aufschließen ['aufʃliːsən] (unreg) vt to open up, to unlock ♦ vi (aufrücken) to close up

Aufschluß ['aufʃlus] m information; **a~reich** adj informative, illuminating

aufschnappen ['aufʃnapən] vt (umg) to pick up ♦ vi to fly open

aufschneiden ['aufʃnaɪdən] (unreg) vt (Geschwür) to cut open; (Brot) to cut up; (MED) to lance ♦ vi to brag

Aufschneider (-s, -) m boaster, braggart

Aufschnitt ['aufʃnɪt] m (slices of) cold meat

aufschrauben ['aufʃraubən] vt (fest~) to screw on; (lösen) to unscrew

aufschrecken ['aufʃrɛkən] vt to startle ♦ vi (unreg) to start up

aufschreiben ['aufʃraɪbən] (unreg) vt to write down

aufschreien ['aufʃraɪən] (unreg) vi to cry out

Aufschrift ['aufʃrɪft] f (Inschrift) inscription; (auf Etikett) label

Aufschub ['aufʃuːp] (-(e)s, -schübe) m delay, postponement

Aufschwung ['aufʃvʊŋ] m (Elan) boost ♦ nt; (wirtschaftlich) upturn, boom; (SPORT) circle

Aufsehen ['aufzeːən] (-s) nt sensation, stir

aufsehen (unreg) vi to look up; **~ zu** to look up to; (fig) to look up to

aufsehenerregend adj sensational

Aufseher(in) (-s, -) m(f) guard; (im Betrieb) supervisor; (Museums~) attendant; (Park~) keeper

aufsein ['aufzaɪn] (unreg, umg) vi (Tür, Geschäft etc) to be open; (Mensch) to be up

aufsetzen ['aufzɛtsən] vt to put on;

(Flugzeug) to put down; (Dokument) to draw up ♦ vr to sit up(right) ♦ vi (Flugzeug) to touch down

Aufsicht ['aufzɪçt] f supervision; die ~ haben to be in charge

aufsitzen ['aufzɪtsən] (unreg) vi (aufrecht hinsitzen) to sit up; (aufs Pferd, Motorrad) to mount, to get on; (Schiff) to run aground; jdm ~ (umg) to be taken in by sb

aufsparen ['aufʃpaːrən] vt to save (up)

aufsperren ['aufʃpɛrən] vt to unlock; (Mund) to open wide

aufspielen ['aufʃpiːlən] vr to show off

aufspießen ['aufʃpiːsən] vt to spear

aufspringen ['aufʃprɪŋən] (unreg) vi (hochspringen) to jump up; (sich öffnen) to spring open; (Hände, Lippen) to become chapped; auf etw akk ~ to jump onto sth

aufspüren ['aufʃpyːrən] vt to track down, to trace

aufstacheln ['aufʃtaxəln] vt to incite

Aufstand ['aufʃtant] m insurrection, rebellion

aufständisch ['aufʃtɛndɪʃ] adj rebellious, mutinous

aufstecken ['aufʃtɛkən] vt to stick on, to pin up; (umg) to give up

aufstehen ['aufʃteːən] (unreg) vi to get up; (Tür) to be open

aufsteigen ['aufʃtaɪgən] (unreg) vi (hochsteigen) to climb; (Rauch) to rise; auf etw akk ~ to get on sth

aufstellen ['aufʃtɛlən] vt (aufrecht stellen) to put up; (aufreihen) to line up; (nominieren) to nominate; (formulieren: Programm etc) to draw up; (leisten: Rekord) to set up

Aufstellung f (SPORT) line-up; (Liste) list

Aufstieg ['aufʃtiːk] (-(e)s, -e) m (auf Berg) ascent; (Fortschritt) rise; (beruflich, SPORT) promotion

aufstoßen ['aufʃtoːsən] (unreg) vt to push open ♦ vi to belch

aufstützen ['aufʃtʏtsən] vt (Körperteil) to prop, to lean; (Person) to

prop up ♦ vr: sich auf etw akk ~ to lean on sth

aufsuchen ['aufzuːxən] vt (besuchen) to visit; (konsultieren) to consult

Auftakt ['auftakt] m (MUS) upbeat; (fig) prelude

auftanken ['auftaŋkən] vi to get petrol (BRIT) od gas (US) ♦ vt to refuel

auftauchen ['auftauxən] vi to appear; (aus Wasser etc) to emerge; (U-Boot) to surface; (Zweifel) to arise

auftauen ['auftauən] vt to thaw ♦ vi to thaw; (fig) to relax

aufteilen ['auftailən] vt to divide up; (Raum) to partition

Aufteilung f division; partition

Auftrag ['auftraːk] (-(e)s, -träge) m order; (Anweisung) commission; (Aufgabe) mission; im ~ von on behalf of; a~en [-gən] (unreg) vt (Essen) to serve; (Farbe) to put on; (Kleidung) to wear out; jdm etw a~en to tell sb sth; dick a~en (fig) to exaggerate; ~geber (-s, -) m (COMM) purchaser, customer

auftreiben ['auftraibən] (unreg) vt (umg: beschaffen) to raise

auftreten ['auftreːtən] (unreg) vt to kick open ♦ vi to appear; (mit Füßen) to tread; (sich verhalten) to behave; A~ (-s) nt (Vorkommen) appearance; (Benehmen) behaviour

Auftrieb ['auftriːp] m (PHYS) buoyancy, lift; (fig) impetus

Auftritt ['auftrɪt] m (des Schauspielers) entrance; (Szene: auch fig) scene

auftun ['auftuːn] (unreg) vt to open ♦ vr to open up

aufwachen ['aufvaxən] vi to wake up

aufwachsen ['aufvaksən] (unreg) vi to grow up

Aufwand ['aufvant] (-(e)s) m expenditure; (Kosten auch) expense; (Luxus) show

aufwärmen ['aufvɛrmən] vt to

warm up; (alte Geschichten) to rake up

aufwärts ['aʊfvɛrts] adv upwards; A~entwicklung f upward trend

Aufwasch m washing-up

aufwecken ['aʊfvɛkən] vt to wake up, to waken up

aufweisen ['aʊfvaɪzən] (unreg) vt to show

aufwenden ['aʊfvɛndən] (unreg) vt to expend; (Geld) to spend; (Sorgfalt) to devote

aufwendig adj costly

aufwerfen ['aʊfvɛrfən] (unreg) vt (Fenster etc) to throw open; (Probleme) to throw up, to raise

aufwerten ['aʊfveːrtən] vt (FIN) to revalue; (fig) to raise in value

aufwickeln ['aʊfvɪkəln] vt (aufrollen) to roll up; (umg: Haar) to put in curlers

aufwiegen ['aʊfviːgən] (unreg) vt to make up for

Aufwind ['aʊfvɪnt] m up-current

aufwirbeln ['aʊfvɪrbəln] vt to whirl up; Staub ~ (fig) to create a stir

aufwischen ['aʊfvɪʃən] vt to wipe up

aufzählen ['aʊftsɛːlən] vt to list

aufzeichnen ['aʊftsaɪçnən] vt to sketch; (schriftlich) to jot down; (auf Band) to record

Aufzeichnung f (schriftlich) note; (Tonband~) recording; (Film~) record

aufzeigen ['aʊftsaɪgən] vt to show, to demonstrate

aufziehen ['aʊftsiːən] (unreg) vt (hochziehen) to raise, to draw up; (öffnen) to pull open; (Uhr) to wind; (umg: necken) to tease; (großziehen: Kinder) to raise, to bring up; (Tiere) to rear

Aufzug ['aʊftsuːk] m (Fahrstuhl) lift, elevator; (Aufmarsch) procession, parade; (Kleidung) get-up; (THEAT) act

aufzwingen ['aʊftsvɪŋən] (unreg) vt: jdm etw ~ to force sth upon sb

Augapfel m eyeball; (fig) apple of one's eye

Auge ['aʊgə] (-s, -n) nt eye; (Fett~) globule of fat; **unter vier ~n** in private

Augen- zW: **~blick** m moment; **im ~blick** at the moment; **a~blicklich** adj (sofort) instantaneous; (gegenwärtig) present; **~braue** f eyebrow; **~weide** f sight for sore eyes; **~zeuge** m eye witness

August [aʊˈgʊst] (-(e)s od -, -e) m August

Auktion [aʊktsˈioːn] f auction

Aula ['aʊla] (-, Aulen od -s) f assembly hall

SCHLÜSSELWORT

aus [aʊs] präp +dat **1** (räumlich) out of; (von … her) from; **er ist aus Berlin** he's from Berlin; **aus dem Fenster** out of the window

2 (gemacht/hergestellt aus) made of; **ein Herz aus Stein** a heart of stone

3 (auf Ursache deutend) out of; **aus Mitleid** out of sympathy; **aus Erfahrung** from experience; **aus Spaß** for fun

4: aus ihm wird nie etwas she'll never get anywhere

♦ adv **1** (zu Ende) finished, over; **aus und vorbei** over and done with

2 (ausgeschaltet, ausgezogen) out; (Aufschrift an Geräten) off; **Licht aus!** lights out!

3 (in Verbindung mit von): **von Rom** as from Rome; **vom Fenster aus** out of the window; **von sich aus** (selbständig) of one's own accord; **von ihm aus** as far as he's concerned

ausarbeiten ['aʊsʔarbaɪtən] vt to work out

ausarten ['aʊsʔartən] vi to degenerate; (Kind) to become overexcited

ausatmen ['aʊsʔaːtmən] vi to breathe out

ausbaden ['aʊsbaːdən] (umg) vt: **etw ~ müssen** to carry the can for sth

Ausbau ['aʊsbaʊ] m extension, expansion; removal; **a~en** vt to extend, to expand; (herausnehmen) to take out, to remove; **a~fähig** adj (fig) worth developing

ausbessern ['ausbɛsərn] vt to mend, to repair

ausbeulen ['ausbɔylən] vt to beat out

Ausbeute ['ausbɔytə] f yield; (Fische) catch; **a~n** vt to exploit; (MIN) to work

ausbild- ['ausbild-] zW: **~en** vt to educate; (Lehrling, Soldat) to instruct, to train; (Fähigkeiten) to develop; (Geschmack) to cultivate; **A~er** (-s, -) m instructor; **A~ung** f education; training, instruction; development; cultivation

ausbleiben ['ausblaɪbən] (unreg) vi (Personen) to stay away, not to come; (Ereignisse) to fail to happen, not to happen

Ausblick ['ausblɪk] m (auch fig) prospect (lit, fig), outlook, view

ausbrechen ['ausbrɛçən] (unreg) vi to break out ♦ vt to break off; in Tränen/Gelächter ~ to burst into tears/out laughing

ausbreiten ['ausbraɪtən] vt to spread (out); (Arme) to stretch out ♦ vr to spread; **sich über ein Thema ~** to expand od enlarge on a topic

ausbrennen ['ausbrɛnən] (unreg) vt to scorch; (Wunde) to cauterize ♦ vi to burn out

Ausbruch ['ausbrʊx] m outbreak; (von Vulkan) eruption; (Gefühls~) outburst; (von Gefangenen) escape

ausbrüten ['ausbry:tən] vt (auch fig) to hatch

Ausdauer ['ausdauər] f perseverance, stamina; **a~nd** adj persevering

ausdehnen ['ausde:nən] vt, vr (räumlich) to expand; (zeitlich, auch Gummi) to stretch; (Nebel, fig: Macht) to extend

ausdenken ['ausdɛŋkən] (unreg) vt: **sich etw ~** to think sth up

Ausdruck ['ausdrʊk] m expression, phrase; (Kundgabe, Gesichts~) ex-

pression; (COMPUT) print-out, hard copy; **a~en** vt (COMPUT) to print out

ausdrücken ['ausdrykən] vt (auch vr: formulieren, zeigen) to express; (Zigarette) to put out; (Zitrone) to squeeze

ausdrücklich adj express, explicit

ausdrucks- zW: **~los** adj expressionless, blank; **~voll** adj expressive; **A~weise** f mode of expression

auseinander [aus'aɪ'nandər] adv (getrennt) apart; ~ **schreiben** to write as separate words; **~bringen** (unreg) vt to separate; **~fallen** (unreg) vi to fall apart; **~gehen** (unreg) vi (Menschen) to separate; (Meinungen) to differ; (Gegenstand) to fall apart; (umg: dick werden) to put on weight; **~halten** (unreg) vt to tell apart; **~nehmen** (unreg) vt to take to pieces, to dismantle; **~setzen** vt (erklären) to set forth, to explain ♦ vr (sich verständigen) to come to terms, to settle; (sich befassen) to concern o.s.; **A~setzung** f argument

ausfahren ['ausfa:rən] (unreg) vi (spazierenfahren: im Auto) to take for a drive; (: im Kinderwagen) to take for a walk; (Weg) to bring

Ausfahrt ['ausfa:rt] f (des Zuges etc) leaving, departure; (Autobahn~) exit; (Garagen~ etc) exit, way out; (Spazierfahrt) drive, excursion

Ausfall ['ausfal] m loss; (Nichtstattfinden) cancellation; (MIL) sortie; (Fechten) lunge; (radioaktiv) fall-out; **a~en** (unreg) vi (Zähne, Haare) to fall od come out; (nicht stattfinden) to be cancelled; (wegbleiben) to be omitted; (Person) to drop out; (Lohn) to be stopped; (nicht funktionieren) to break down; (Resultat haben) to turn out; **~straße** f arterial road

ausfertigen ['ausfertigən] vt (förmlich: Urkunde, Paß) to draw up; (Rechnung) to make out

Ausfertigung ['ausfertigʊŋ] f drawing up; making out; (Exemplar)

copy

ausfindig ['ausfɪndɪç] adj: ~ **machen** to discover

ausfließen ['ausfliːsən] (unreg) vi (herausfließen): ~ **(aus)** to flow out (of); (auslaufen: Öl etc): ~ **(aus)** to leak (out of)

Ausflucht ['ausfluxt] (-, -flüchte) f excuse

Ausflug ['ausfluːk] m excursion, outing

Ausflügler ['ausflyːklər] (-s, -) m tripper

Ausfluß ['ausflus] m outlet; (MED) discharge

ausfragen ['ausfraːgən] vt to interrogate, to question

ausfressen ['ausfresən] (unreg) vt to eat up; (aushöhlen) to corrode; (umg: anstellen) to be up to

Ausfuhr ['ausfuːr] (-, -en) f export, exportation ♦ in zW export

ausführ- ['ausfyːr] zW: ~**en** vt (verwirklichen) to carry out; (Person) to take out; (Hund) to take for a walk; (COMM) to export; (erklären) to give details of; ~**lich** adj detailed ♦ adv in detail; A~**lichkeit** f detail; A~**ung** f execution, performance; (Durchführung) completion; (Herstellungsart) version; (Erklärung) explanation

ausfüllen ['ausfʏlən] vt to fill up; (Fragebogen etc) to fill in; (Beruf) to be fulfilling for

Ausgabe ['ausgaːbə] f (Geld) expenditure, outlay; (Aushändigung) giving out; (Gepäck~) left-luggage office; (Buch) edition; (Nummer) issue; (COMPUT) output

Ausgang ['ausgaŋ] m way out, exit; (Ende) end; (Ausgangspunkt) starting point; (Ergebnis) result; (Ausgehtag) free time, time off; **kein** ~ no exit

Ausgangspunkt m starting point; ~**sperre** f curfew

ausgeben ['ausgeːbən] (unreg) vt (Geld) to spend; (austeilen) to issue, to distribute ♦ vr: **sich für etw/jdn**

~ **to pass o.s. off as sth/sb**

ausgebucht ['ausgaːbuːxt] adj (Vorstellung, Flug, Maschine) fully booked

ausgedient ['ausgədiːnt] adj (Soldat) discharged; (verbraucht) no longer in use; ~ **haben** to have done good service

ausgefallen ['ausgəfalən] adj (ungewöhnlich) exceptional

ausgeglichen ['ausgəglɪçən] adj (well-)balanced; A~**heit** f balance; (von Mensch) even-temperedness

ausgehen ['ausgeːən] (unreg) vi to go out; (zu Ende gehen) to come to an end; (Benzin) to run out; (Haare, Zähne) to fall od come out; (Feuer, Ofen, Licht) to go out; (Strom) to go off; (Resultat haben) to turn out; **mir ging das Benzin aus** I ran out of petrol (BRIT) od gas (US); **auf etw** akk ~ to aim at sth; **von etw** ~ (wegführen) to lead away from sth; (herrühren) to come from sth; (zugrunde legen) to proceed from sth; **wir können davon ..., daß ...** we can take as our starting point that ...; **leer** ~ to get nothing; **schlecht** ~ to turn out badly

Ausgehverbot nt curfew

ausgelassen ['ausgəlasən] adj boisterous, high-spirited

ausgelastet ['ausgəlastət] adj fully occupied

ausgelernt ['ausgəlɛrnt] adj trained, qualified

ausgemacht ['ausgəmaxt] adj settled; (umg: Dummkopf etc) out-and-out; (downright; **es war eine** ~**e Sache, daß ...** it was a foregone conclusion that ...

ausgenommen ['ausgənɔmən] präp +gen except ♦ konj except; **Anwesende sind** ~ present company excepted

ausgeprägt ['ausgəprɛːkt] adj distinct

ausgerechnet ['ausgərɛçnət] adv just, precisely; ~ **du/heute** you of all people/today of all days

ausgeschlossen ['ausgəʃlɔsən] adj (unmöglich) impossible, out of the question

ausgeschnitten ['ausgəʃnɪtən] adj (Kleid) low-necked

ausgesprochen ['ausgəʃprɔxən] adj (Faulheit, Lüge etc) out-and-out; (unverkennbar) marked ♦ adv decidedly

ausgezeichnet ['ausgətsaɪçnət] adj excellent

ausgiebig ['ausgiːbɪç] adj (Gebrauch) thorough, good; (Essen) generous, lavish; ~ **schlafen** to have a good sleep

Ausgleich ['ausglaɪç] (-(e)s, -e) m balance; (Vermittlung) reconciliation; (SPORT) equalization; **zum ~ einer Sache** gen in order to offset sth; **a~en** (unreg) vt to balance (out); to reconcile; (Höhe) to even up ♦ vi (SPORT) to equalize

ausgraben ['ausgraːbən] (unreg) vt to dig up; (Leichen) to exhume; (fig) to unearth

Ausgrabung f excavation; (Ausgraben auch) digging up

Ausguß ['ausgus] m (Spüle) sink; (Abfluß) outlet; (Tülle) spout

aushalten ['aushaltən] (unreg) vt to bear, to stand; (Geliebte) to keep ♦ vi to hold out; **das ist nicht zum A~** that is unbearable

aushandeln ['aushandəln] vt to negotiate

aushändigen ['aushɛndɪgən] vt: **jdm etw ~** to hand sth over to sb

Aushang ['aushaŋ] m notice

aushängen ['aushɛŋən] (unreg) vt (Meldung) to put up; (Fenster) to take off its hinges ♦ vi to be displayed ♦ vr to hang out

ausharren ['ausharən] vi to hold out

ausheben ['aushɛːbən] (unreg) vt (Erde) to lift out; (Grube) to hollow out; (Tür) to take off its hinges; (Diebesnest) to clear out; (MIL) to enlist

aushecken ['aushɛkən] (umg) vt to cook up

aushelfen ['aushɛlfən] (unreg) vi:

jdm ~ to help sb out

Aushilfe ['aushɪlfə] f help, assistance; (Person) (temporary) worker

Aushilfskraft f temporary worker

aushilfsweise adv temporarily, as a stopgap

ausholen ['aushoːlən] vi to swing one's arm back; (zur Ohrfeige) to raise one's hand; (beim Gehen) to take long strides; **weit ~** (fig) to be expansive

aushorchen ['aushɔrçən] vt to sound out, to pump

aushungern ['aushuŋərn] vt to starve out

auskennen ['auskɛnən] (unreg) vr to know a lot; (an einem Ort) to know one's way about; (in Fragen etc) to be knowledgeable

Ausklang ['ausklaŋ] m end

auskleiden ['ausklaɪdən] vr to undress ♦ vt (Wand) to line

ausklingen ['ausklɪŋən] (unreg) vi (Ton, Lied) to die away; (Fest) to peter out

ausklopfen ['ausklɔpfən] vt (Teppich) to beat; (Pfeife) to knock out

auskochen ['auskɔxən] vt to boil; (MED) to sterilize; **ausgekocht** (fig) out-and-out

Auskommen ['auskɔmən] (-s) nt: **sein ~ haben** to have a regular income; **a~** (unreg) vi: **mit jdm ~** to get on with sb; **mit etw a~** to get by with sth

auskosten ['auskɔstən] vt to enjoy to the full

auskundschaften ['auskuntʃaftən] vt to spy out; (Gebiet) to reconnoitre

Auskunft ['auskunft] (-, -künfte) f information; (nähere) details pl, particulars pl; (Stelle) information office; (TEL) directory inquiries sg

auslachen ['auslaxən] vt to laugh at, to mock

ausladen ['auslaːdən] (unreg) vt to unload; (umg: Gäste) to cancel an invitation to

Auslage ['auslaːgə] f shop window (display); **~n** pl (Ausgabe) outlay sg

Ausland ['auslant] nt foreign countries pl; im ~ abroad; ins ~ abroad
Ausländer(in) ['auslɛndər(ɪn)] (-s, -) m(f) foreigner
ausländisch adj foreign
Auslandsgespräch nt international call; ~reise f trip abroad
auslassen ['auslasən] (unreg) vt to leave out; (Wort etc auch) to omit; (Kleidungsstück) to let out ♦ vr: sich über etw akk ~ to speak one's mind about sth; seine Wut etc an jdm ~ to vent one's rage etc on sb
Auslassung f omission
Auslauf ['auslauf] m (für Tiere) run; (Ausfluß) outflow, outlet; a~en (unreg) vi to run out; (Behälter) to leak; (NAUT) to put out (to sea); (langsam aufhören) to run down
Ausläufer ['auslɔyfər] m (von Gebirge) spur; (Pflanze) runner; (MET: von Hoch) ridge; (: von Tief) trough
ausleeren ['auslerən] vt to empty
auslegen ['auslegən] vt (Waren) to lay out; (Köder) to put down; (Geld) to lend; (bedecken) to cover; (Text etc) to interpret
Auslegung f interpretation
ausleiern ['auslaɪərn] vi (Gummi) to wear out
Ausleihe ['auslaɪə] f issuing; (Stelle) issue desk; a~n (unreg) vt (verleihen) to lend; sich dat etw a~n to borrow sth
Auslese ['auslezə] f selection; (Elite) elite; (Wein) choice wine; a~n (unreg) vt to select; (umg: zu Ende lesen) to finish
ausliefern ['auslifərn] vt to deliver (up), to hand over; (COMM) to deliver; jdm/etw ausgeliefert sein to be at the mercy of sb/sth
auslöschen ['auslœʃən] vt to extinguish; (fig) to wipe out, to obliterate
auslosen ['auslozən] vt to draw lots for
auslösen ['ausløzən] vt (Explosion, Schuß) to set off; (hervorrufen) to

cause, to produce; (Gefangene) to ransom; (Pfand) to redeem
Auslöser (-s, -) m (PHOT) release
ausmachen ['ausmaxən] vt (Licht, Radio) to turn off; (Feuer) to put out; (entdecken) to make out; (vereinbaren) to agree; (beilegen) to settle; (Anteil darstellen, betragen) to represent; (bedeuten) to matter; macht es Ihnen etwas aus, wenn ...? would you mind if ...?
ausmalen ['ausmalən] vt to paint; (fig) to describe; sich dat etw ~ to imagine sth
Ausmaß ['ausmaːs] nt dimension; (fig auch) scale
ausmessen ['ausmɛsən] (unreg) vt to measure
Ausnahme ['ausnaːmə] f exception; ~fall m exceptional case; ~zustand m state of emergency
ausnahmslos adv without exception
ausnahmsweise adv by way of exception, for once
ausnehmen ['ausneːmən] (unreg) vt to take out, to remove; (Tier) to gut; (Nest) to rob; (umg: Geld abnehmen) to clean out; (ausschließen) to make an exception of ♦ vr to look, to appear; ~d adj exceptional
ausnützen ['ausnytsən] vt (Zeit, Gelegenheit) to use, to turn to good account; (Einfluß) to use; (Mensch, Gutmütigkeit) to exploit
auspacken ['auspakən] vt to unpack
auspfeifen ['auspfaɪfən] (unreg) vt to hiss/boo at
ausplaudern ['ausplaudərn] vt (Geheimnis) to blab
ausprobieren ['ausprobiːrən] vt to try (out)
Auspuff ['auspuf] (-(e)s, -e) m (TECH) exhaust; ~rohr nt exhaust (pipe); ~topf m (AUT) silencer
ausradieren ['ausradiːrən] vt to erase, to rub out; (fig) to annihilate
ausrangieren ['ausrãʒiːrən] (umg) vt to chuck out
ausrauben ['ausraubən] vt to rob
ausräumen ['ausrɔymən] vt (Dinge)

to clear away; (Schrank, Zimmer) to empty; (Bedenken) to dispel

ausrechnen ['ausrɛçnən] vt to calculate, to reckon

Ausrede ['ausreːdə] f excuse; **a~n** vi to have one's say ♦ vi: **jdm eine a~n** to talk sb out of sth

ausreichen ['ausraiçən] vi to suffice, to be enough; **~d** adj sufficient, adequate; (SCH) adequate

Ausreise ['ausraizə] f departure; **bei der ~** when leaving the country; **~erlaubnis** f exit visa; **a~n** vi to leave the country

ausreißen ['ausraisən] (unreg) vt to tear od pull out ♦ vi (Riß bekommen) to tear; (umg) to make off, to scram

ausrenken ['ausrɛŋkən] vt to dislocate

ausrichten ['ausriçtən] vt (Botschaft) to deliver; (Gruß) to pass on; (Hochzeit etc) to arrange; (in gerade Linie bringen) to get in a straight line; (angleichen) to bring into line; (TYP) to justify; **ich werde es ihm ~** I'll tell him; **etwas /nichts bei jdm ~** to get somewhere/nowhere with sb

ausrotten ['ausrotən] vt to stamp out, to exterminate

ausrücken ['ausrykən] vi (MIL) to move off; (Feuerwehr, Polizei) to be called out; (umg: weglaufen) to run away

Ausruf ['ausruːf] m (Schrei) cry, exclamation; (Bekanntmachung) proclamation; **a~en** (unreg) vt to cry out, to exclaim; to call out; **~ezeichen** nt exclamation mark

ausruhen ['ausruːən] vt, vr to rest

ausrüsten ['ausrystən] vt to equip, to fit out

Ausrüstung f equipment

ausrutschen ['ausrutʃən] vi to slip

Aussage ['auszaːgə] f (JUR) statement; **a~n** vt to say, to state ♦ vi (JUR) to give evidence

ausschalten ['ausʃaltən] vt to switch off; (fig) to eliminate

Ausschank ['ausʃaŋk] (-(e)s, -schänke) m dispensing, pouring out; (COMM) selling; (Theke) bar

Ausschau ['ausʃau] f: **~ halten (nach)** to look out (for), to watch (for); **a~en** vi: **~ (nach)** to look out (for), to be on the look-out (for)

ausscheiden ['ausʃaidən] (unreg) vt to take out; (MED) to secrete ♦ vi: **~ (aus)** to leave; (SPORT) to be eliminated (from) od knocked out (of)

Ausscheidung f separation; secretion; elimination; (aus Amt) retirement

ausschenken ['ausʃɛŋkən] vt (Alkohol, Kaffee) to pour out; (COMM) to sell

ausschildern ['ausʃildərn] vt to signpost

ausschimpfen ['ausʃimpfən] vt to scold, to tell off

ausschlafen ['ausʃlaːfən] (unreg) vi, vr to have a good sleep ♦ vt to sleep off; **ich bin nicht ausgeschlafen** I didn't have od get enough sleep

Ausschlag ['ausʃlaːk] m (MED) rash; (Pendel~) swing; (Nadel~) deflection; **den ~ geben** (fig) to tip the balance; **a~en** [-gən] (unreg) vt to knock out; (auskleiden) to deck out; (verweigern) to decline ♦ vi (Pferd) to kick out; (BOT) to sprout; **a~gebend** adj decisive

ausschließen ['ausʃliːsən] (unreg) vt to shut od lock out; to exclude

ausschließlich adj exclusive ♦ adv exclusively ♦ präp +gen exclusive of, excluding

Ausschluß ['ausʃlos] m exclusion

ausschmücken ['ausʃmʏkən] vt to decorate; (fig) to embellish

ausschneiden ['ausʃnaidən] (unreg) vt to cut out; (Büsche) to trim

Ausschnitt ['ausʃnit] m (Teil) section; (von Kleid) neckline; (Zeitungs~) cutting; (aus Film etc) excerpt

ausschreiben ['ausʃraibən] (unreg)

vt (ganz schreiben) to write out (in full); *(ausstellen)* to write (out); *(Stelle, Wettbewerb etc)* to announce, to advertise

Ausschreitung ['aʊsʃraɪtʊŋ] *f (usu pl)* riot

Ausschuß ['aʊsʃʊs] *m* committee, board; *(Abfall)* waste, scraps *pl*; *(COMM: auch: ~ware f)* reject

ausschütten ['aʊsʃʏtən] *vt* to pour out; *(Einer)* to empty; *(Geld)* to pay ♦ *vr* to shake (with laughter)

ausschweifend ['aʊsʃvaɪfənt] *adj (Leben)* dissipated, debauched; *(Phantasie)* extravagant

aussehen ['aʊszeːən] *(unreg) vi* to look; **A~** (-s) *nt* appearance; *es sieht nach Regen aus* it looks like rain; *es sieht schlecht aus* things look bad

aussein ['aʊszaɪn] *(unreg; umg) vi (zu Ende sein)* to be over; *(nicht zu Hause sein)* to be out; *(nicht brennen)* to be out; *(abgeschaltet sein: Radio, Herd)* to be off

außen ['aʊsən] *adv outside; (nach ~)* outwards; *~ ist es rot* it's red (on the) outside

Außen- *zW:* **~bordmotor** *m* outboard motor; **~dienst** *m: im ~dienst sein* to work outside the office; **~handel** *m* foreign trade; **~minister** *m* foreign minister; **~ministerium** *nt* foreign office; **~politik** *f* foreign policy; **a~politisch** *adj (Entwicklung, Lage)* foreign; **~seite** *f* outside; **~seiter** (-s, -) *m* outsider; **~stehende(r)** *f(m)* outsider; **~welt** *f* outside world

außer ['aʊsər] *präp +dat (räumlich)* out of; *(abgesehen von)* except ♦ *konj (ausgenommen)* except; **~ Gefahr** out of danger; **~ Zweifel** beyond any doubt; **~ Betrieb** out of order; **~ Dienst** retired; **~ Landes** abroad; **~ sich dat sein** to be beside o.s.; **~ sich akk geraten** to go wild; **~ wenn** unless; **~ daß** except; **~dem** *konj* besides, in addition

äußere(r, s) ['ɔʏsərə(r, s)] *adj* outer, external

außergewöhnlich *adj* unusual

außerhalb *präp +gen* outside ♦ *adv* outside

äußerlich *adj* external

äußern *vt* to utter, to express; *(zeigen)* to show ♦ *vr* to give one's opinion; *(Krankheit etc)* to show itself

außerordentlich *adj* extraordinary

außerplanmäßig *adj* unscheduled

äußerst ['ɔʏsərst] *adv* extremely, most; **~e(r, s)** *adj* utmost; *(räumlich)* farthest; *(Termin)* last possible; *(Preis)* highest

Äußerung(r) *f* remark, comment

aussetzen ['aʊszɛtsən] *vt (Kind, Tier)* to abandon; *(Boote)* to lower; *(Belohnung)* to offer; *(Urteil, Verfahren)* to postpone ♦ *vi (aufhören)* to stop; *(Pause machen)* to have a break; **jdm etw ausgesetzt sein** to be exposed to sb/sth; **an jdm/etw etwas ~** to find fault with sb/sth

Aussicht ['aʊszɪçt] *f* view; *(in Zukunft)* prospect; **etw in ~ haben** to have sth in view

Aussichts- *zW:* **a~los** *adj* hopeless; **~punkt** *m* viewpoint; **a~reich** *adj* promising; **~turm** *m* observation tower

aussöhnen ['aʊszøːnən] *vt* to reconcile ♦ *vr* to reconcile o.s., to become reconciled

aussondern ['aʊszɔndərn] *vt* to separate, to select

aussortieren ['aʊszɔrtiːrən] *vt* to sort out

ausspannen ['aʊsʃpanən] *vt* to spread out & stretch out; *(Pferd)* to unharness; *(umg: Mädchen)* **jdm jdn ~** to steal sb (from sb) ♦ *vi* to relax

aussperren ['aʊsʃpɛrən] *vt* to lock out

ausspielen ['aʊsʃpiːlən] *vt (Karte)* to lead; *(Geldprämie)* to offer as a prize ♦ *vi (KARTEN)* to lead; **jdn gegen jdn ~** to play sb off against sb; **ausgespielt haben** to be finished

Aussprache ['aʊsʃpraːxə] *f* pronunciation; (Unterredung) (frank) discussion

aussprechen ['aʊsʃprɛçən] (unreg) vt to pronounce; (äußern) to say, to express ♦ vr (sich äußern): **sich** ~ (über +akk) to speak (about); (sich anvertrauen) to unburden o.s. (about od on); (diskutieren) to discuss ♦ vi (zu Ende sprechen) to finish speaking

Ausspruch ['aʊsʃprʊx] m saying, remark

ausspülen ['aʊsʃpyːlən] vt to wash out; (Mund) to rinse

Ausstand ['aʊsʃtant] m strike; **in den ~ treten** to go on strike

ausstatten ['aʊsʃtatən] vt (Zimmer etc) to furnish; (Person) to equip, to kit out

Ausstattung f (Ausstatten) provision; (Kleidung) outfit; (Aussteuer) dowry; (Aufmachung) make-up; (Einrichtung) furnishing

ausstechen ['aʊsʃtɛçən] (unreg) vt (Augen, Rasen, Graben) to dig out; (Kekse) to cut out; (übertreffen) to outshine

ausstehen ['aʊsʃteːən] (unreg) vt to stand, to endure ♦ vi (noch nicht dasein) to be outstanding

aussteigen ['aʊsʃtaɪgən] (unreg) vi to get out, to alight

ausstellen ['aʊsʃtɛlən] vt to exhibit, to display; (umg: ausschalten) to switch off; (Rechnung etc) to make out; (Paß, Zeugnis) to issue

Ausstellung f exhibition; (FIN) drawing up; (einer Rechnung) making out; (eines Passes etc) issuing

aussterben ['aʊsʃtɛrbən] (unreg) vi to die out

Aussteuer ['aʊsʃtɔʏər] f dowry

Ausstieg ['aʊsʃtiːk] (-(e)s, -e) m exit

ausstopfen ['aʊsʃtɔpfən] vt to stuff

ausstoßen ['aʊsʃtoːsən] (unreg) vt (Luft, Rauch) to give off, to emit; (aus Verein etc) to expel, to exclude; (Auge) to poke out

ausstrahlen ['aʊsʃtraːlən] vt, vi to radiate; (RADIO) to broadcast

Ausstrahlung f radiation; (fig) charisma

ausstrecken ['aʊsʃtrɛkən] vt, vr to stretch out

ausstreichen ['aʊsʃtraɪçən] (unreg) vt to cross out; (glätten) to smooth (out)

ausströmen ['aʊsʃtrøːmən] vi (Gas) to pour out, to escape ♦ vt to give off; (fig) to radiate

aussuchen ['aʊszuːxən] vt to select, to pick out

Austausch ['aʊstaʊʃ] m exchange; **a~bar** adj exchangeable; **a~en** vt to exchange, to swap; **~motor** m reconditioned engine

austeilen ['aʊstaɪlən] vt to distribute, to give out

Auster ['aʊstər] (-, -n) f oyster

austoben ['aʊstoːbən] vr (Kind) to run wild; (Erwachsene) to sow one's wild oats

austragen ['aʊstraːgən] (unreg) vt (Post) to deliver; (Streit etc) to decide; (Wettkämpfe) to hold

Australien [aʊsˈtraːliən] (-s) nt Australia

Australier(in) (-s, -) m(f) Australian

australisch adj Australian

austreiben ['aʊstraɪbən] (unreg) vt to drive out, to expel; (Geister) to exorcize

austreten ['aʊstreːtən] (unreg) vi (zur Toilette) to be excused ♦ vt (Feuer) to tread out, to trample; (Schuhe) to wear out; (Treppe) to wear down; **aus etw** ~ to leave sth

austrinken ['aʊstrɪŋkən] (unreg) vt (Glas) to drain; (Getränk) to drink up ♦ vi to finish one's drink, to drink up

Austritt ['aʊstrɪt] m emission; (aus Verein, Partei etc) retirement, withdrawal

austrocknen ['aʊstrɔknən] vt, vi to dry up

ausüben ['aʊsʔyːbən] vt (Beruf) to practise, to carry out; (Funktion) to perform; (Einfluß) to exert; **einen**

Reiz auf jdn ~ to hold an attraction for sb; **eine Wirkung auf jdn ~** to have an effect on sb

Ausverkauf ['ausfɛrkauf] *m* sale; **a~en** *vt* to sell out; (*Geschäft*) to sell up; **a~t** *adj* (*Karten, Artikel*) sold out; (*THEAT: Haus*) full

Auswahl ['ausva:l] *f:* **eine ~** (an +*dat*) a selection (of), a choice (of)

auswählen ['ausvɛːlən] *vt* to select, to choose

Auswander- ['ausvandər] *zW:* **~er** *m* emigrant; **a~n** *vi* to emigrate; **~ung** *f* emigration

auswärtig ['ausvɛrtɪç] *adj* (*nicht am Wohnort*) out-of-town; (*ausländisch*) foreign

auswärts ['ausvɛrts] *adv* outside; (*nach außen*) outwards; **~ essen** to eat out; **A~spiel** ['ausvɛrtsʃpiːl] *nt* away game

auswechseln ['ausvɛksəln] *vt* to change, to substitute

Ausweg ['ausveːk] *m* way out; **a~los** *adj* hopeless

ausweichen ['ausvaiçən] (*unreg*) *vi:* **jdm/etw ~** to move aside *od* make way for sb /sth; (*fig*) to side-step sb/ sth; **~d** *adj* evasive

ausweinen ['ausvainən] *vr* to have a (good) cry

Ausweis ['ausvais] (**-es, -e**) *m* identity card; passport; (*Mitglieds-, Bibliotheks- etc*) card; **a~en** [-'zən] (*unreg*) *vt* to expel, to banish ♦ *vr* to prove one's identity; **~papiere** *pl* identity papers; **~ung** *f* expulsion

ausweiten ['ausvaitən] *vt* to stretch

auswendig ['ausvɛndɪç] *adv* by heart; **~ lernen** to learn by heart

auswerten ['ausveːrtən] *vt* to evaluate

Auswertung *f* evaluation, analysis; (*Nutzung*) utilization

auswirken ['ausvɪrkən] *vr* to have an effect

Auswirkung *f* effect

auswischen ['ausvɪʃən] *vt* to wipe out; **jdm eins ~** (*umg*) to put one over on sb

Auswuchs ['ausvuːks] *m* (out-) growth; (*fig*) product

auswuchten ['ausvuxtən] *vt* (*AUT*) to balance

auszahlen ['austsaːlən] *vt* (*Lohn, Summe*) to pay out; (*Arbeiter*) to pay off; (*Miterbe*) to buy out ♦ *vr* (*sich lohnen*) to pay

auszählen ['austsɛːlən] *vt* (*Stimmen*) to count; (*BOXEN*) to count out

auszeichnen ['austsaiçnən] *vt* to honour; (*MIL*) to decorate; (*COMM*) to price ♦ *vr* to distinguish o.s.

Auszeichnung *f* distinction; (*COMM*) pricing; (*Ehrung*) awarding of decoration; (*Ehre*) honour; (*Orden*) decoration; **mit ~** with distinction

ausziehen ['austsiːən] (*unreg*) *vt* (*Kleidung*) to take off; (*Haare, Zähne, Tisch etc*) to pull out; (*nachmalen*) to trace ♦ *vr* to undress ♦ *vi* (*aufbrechen*) to leave; (*aus Wohnung*) to move out

Auszug ['austsuːk] *m* (*aus Wohnung*) removal; (*aus Buch etc*) extract; (*Konto-*) statement; (*Ausmarsch*) departure

Auto ['auto] (**-s, -s**) *nt* (motor-)car; **~ fahren** to drive; **~atlas** *m* road atlas; **~bahn** *f* motorway; **~bahndreieck** *nt* motorway junction; **~bahnkreuz** *nt* motorway intersection; **~bus** *m* bus; **~fahrer(in)** *m(f)* motorist, driver; **~fahrt** *f* drive; **a~gen** ['gɛːn] *adj* autogenous; **~gramm** *nt* autograph; **~mat** (**-en, -en**) *m* machine; **~matik** [auto'maːtɪk] *f* (*AUT*) automatic; **a~matisch** *adj* automatic; **a~nom** ['noːm] *adj* autonomous

Autor(in) ['autor, au'toːrɪn, *pl* -'toːrən] (**-s, -en**) *m(f)* author

Auto- *zW:* **~radio** *nt* car radio; **~reifen** *m* car tyre; **~reisezug** *m* motorail train; **~rennen** *nt* motor racing

autoritär [autori'tɛːr] *adj* authoritarian

Autorität f authority

Auto- zW: ~**stopp** m to hitch-hike; ~**telefon** nt car phone; ~**unfall** m car od motor accident; ~**verleih** m car hire (BRIT) od rental (US); ~**wäsche** f car wash

Axt [akst] (-, ˝e) f axe

B

Baby ['be:bi] (-s, -s) nt baby; ~**nahrung** f baby food; ~**sitter** ['be:bɪzɪtɐ] (-s, -) m baby-sitter

Bach [bax] (-(e)s, ˝e) m stream, brook

Backbord (-(e)s, -e) nt (NAUT) port

Backe ['bakə] f cheek

backen (unreg) vt, vi to bake

Backenzahn m molar

Bäcker ['bɛkɐ] (-s, -) m baker; ~**ei** f bakery; (~laden) baker's (shop)

Backform f baking tin

Back- zW: ~**obst** nt dried fruit; ~**ofen** m oven; ~**pflaume** f prune; ~**pulver** nt baking powder; ~**stein** m brick

Bad [ba:t] (-(e)s, ˝er) nt bath; (Schwimmen) bathe; (Ort) spa

Bade- ['ba:də] zW: ~**anstalt** f (swimming) baths pl; ~**anzug** m bathing suit; ~**hose** f bathing od swimming trunks pl; ~**mantel** m bath(ing) robe; ~**meister** m baths attendant; ~**mütze** f bathing cap; ~**n** vi to bathe, to have a bath ♦ vt to bath; ~**ort** m spa; ~**tuch** nt bath towel; ~**wanne** f bath (tub); ~**zimmer** nt bathroom

Bagatelle [baga'tɛlə] f trifle

Bagger ['bagɐ] (-s, -) m excavator; (NAUT) dredger; **b~n** vt, vi to excavate; to dredge

Bahn [ba:n] (-, -en) f railway, railroad (US); (Weg) road, way; (Spur) lane; (Renn~) track; (ASTRON) orbit; (Stoff~) length; **b~brechend** adj pioneering; ~**damm** m railway embankment; **b~en** vt: sich/jdm einen Weg b~en to clear a way/a way for sb; **b~fahrt** f railway journey; ~**hof** m station; auf dem ~**hof** at the station; ~**hofshalle** f station concourse; ~**hofsvorsteher** m station-master; ~**linie** f (railway) line; ~**steig** m platform; ~**übergang** m level crossing, grade crossing (US); ~**wärter** m signalman

Bahre ['ba:rə] f stretcher

Bakterien [bak'te:riən] pl bacteria pl

Balance [ba'lã:sə] f balance, equilibrium

balan'cieren vt, vi to balance

bald [balt] adv (zeitlich) soon; (beinahe) almost; ~**ig** ['baldɪç] adj early, speedy

Baldrian ['baldria:n] (-s, -e) m valerian

Balkan ['balka:n] (-s) m: der ~ the Balkans pl

Balken ['balkən] (-s, -) m beam; (Trag~) girder; (Stütz~) prop

Balkon [bal'kõ:] (-s, -s od -e) m balcony; (THEAT) (dress) circle

Ball [bal] (-(e)s, ˝e) m ball; (Tanz) dance, ball

Ballast ['balast] (-(e)s, -e) m ballast; (fig) weight, burden

Ballen ['balən] (-s, -) m bale; (ANAT) ball; **b~** vt (formen) to make into a ball; (Faust) to clench ♦ vr (Wolken etc) to build up; (Menschen) to gather

Ballett [ba'lɛt] (-(e)s, -e) nt ballet

Ballkleid nt evening dress

Ballon [ba'lõ:] (-s, -s od -e) m balloon

Ballspiel nt ball game

Ballungsgebiet ['baluŋsgəbi:t] nt conurbation

Baltikum ['baltikum] (-s) nt (GEO): das ~ the Baltic States

Bambus ['bambus] (-ses, -se) m bamboo; ~**rohr** nt bamboo cane

Banane [ba'na:nə] f banana

Band¹ [bant] (-(e)s, ˝e) m (Buch~) volume

Band² (-(e)s, ˝er) nt (Stoff~) ribbon, tape; (Fließ~) production line;

(Faß~) hoop; (Ton~) tape; (ANAT)
ligament; etw auf Band aufnehmen to tape sth; am laufenden
Band (umg) non-stop
Band³ (-(e)s, -e) nt (Freund-
schafts~ etc) bond
Band⁴ [bɛnt] (-, -s) f band, group
band vb siehe binden
Bandage [ban'daːʒə] f bandage
banda'gieren vt to bandage
Bande ['bandə] f band; (Straßen~)
gang
bändigen ['bɛndɪgən] vt (Tier) to
tame; (Trieb, Leidenschaft) to control, to restrain
Bandit [ban'diːt] (-en, -en) m bandit
Band- zW: **~nudel** f (KOCH: gew
pl) ribbon noodles (pl); **~scheibe** f
(ANAT) disc; **~wurm** m tapeworm
bange ['baŋə] adj scared; (besorgt)
anxious; jdm wird es ~ sb is be-
coming scared; jdm ~ machen to
scare sb; **~n** vi: um jdn/etw ~n to
be anxious od worried about sb/sth
Banjo ['banjo, 'bɛndʒo] (-s, -s) nt
banjo
Bank¹ [baŋk] (-, -e) f (Sitz~) bench;
(Sand~ etc) (sand)bank, (sand)bar
Bank² (-, -en) f (Geld~) bank
Bankanweisung f banker's order
Bankett [baŋ'kɛt] (-(e)s, -e) nt (Essen) banquet; (Straßenrand) verge
(BRIT), shoulder (US); **~e** f verge
(BRIT), shoulder (US)
Bankier [baŋki'eː] (-s, -s) m banker
Bank- zW: **~konto** nt bank account;
~leitzahl f bank sort code number;
~note f banknote; **~raub** m bank
robbery
Bankrott [baŋ'krɔt] (-(e)s, -e) m
bankruptcy; **b~** adj bankrupt; **~**
machen to go bankrupt
Bann [ban] (-(e)s, -e) m (HIST)
ban; (Kirchen~) excommunication;
(fig: Zauber) spell; **b~en** vt (Geister) to exorcise; (Gefahr) to avert;
(bezaubern) to enchant; (HIST) to
banish
Banner (-s, -) nt banner, flag
Bar (-, -s) f bar

bar [baːr] adj (+gen) (unbedeckt)
bare; (frei von) lacking in; (offenkundig) utter, sheer; **~(e)s** Geld
cash; etw (in) **~** bezahlen to pay
sth (in) cash; etw für **~e** Münze
nehmen (fig) to take sth at its face
value
Bär [bɛːr] (-en, -en) m bear
Baracke [ba'rakə] f hut
barbarisch [bar'baːrɪʃ] adj barbaric,
barbarous
Bar- zW: **b~fuß** adj barefoot;
~geld nt cash, ready money;
b~geldlos adj non-cash
Barhocker m bar stool
Barkauf m cash purchase
Barkeeper ['baːrkiːpər] (-s, -) m
barman, bartender
barmherzig [barm'hɛrtsɪç] adj merciful, compassionate
Barometer [baro'meːtər] (-s, -) nt
barometer
Baron [ba'roːn] (-s, -e) m baron;
~in f baroness
Barren ['barən] (-s, -) m parallel
bars pl; (Gold~) ingot
Barriere [bari'ɛːrə] f barrier
Barrikade [bari'kaːdə] f barricade
Barsch [barʃ] (-(e)s, -e) m perch
barsch adj brusque, gruff
Barschaft f ready money
Barscheck m open od uncrossed
cheque (BRIT), open check (US)
Bart [baːrt] (-(e)s, -e) m beard;
(Schlüssel~) bit
bärtig ['bɛːrtɪç] adj bearded
Barzahlung f cash payment
Base ['baːzə] f (CHEM) base; (Ku-
sine) cousin
Basel ['baːzəl] nt Basle
Basen pl von Base; Basis
BASIC ['beːsɪk] nt (COMPUT) BASIC
basieren [ba'ziːrən] vt to base ♦ vi
to be based
Basis ['baːzɪs] (-, Basen) f basis
Baß [bas] (Basses, Bässe) m bass
Bassin [ba'sɛ̃ː] (-s, -s) nt pool
Baßstimme f bass voice
Bast [bast] (-(e)s, -e) m raffia
basteln vt to make ♦ vi to do handi-

crafts
bat *etc vb siehe* **bitten**
Bataillon [batal'joːn] (-s, -e) *nt* battalion
Batik ['baːtik] *f* (*Verfahren*) batik
Batist [ba'tist] (-(e)s, -e) *m* batiste
Batterie [batə'riː] *f* battery
Bau [bau] (-(e)s) *m* (*Bauen*) building, construction; (*Aufbau*) structure; (*Körper~*) frame; (*~stelle*) building site; *(pl* Baue: *Tier~*) hole, burrow; (: MIN working(s); *(pl* Bauten: *Gebäude*) building; **sich im ~ befinden** to be under construction; **~arbeiter** *m* building worker
Bauch [baux] (-(e)s, **Bäuche**) *m* belly; (ANAT *auch*) stomach, abdomen; **~fell** *nt* peritoneum; **~ig** *adj* bulbous; **~nabel** *m* navel; **~redner** *m* ventriloquist; **~schmerzen** *pl* stomach-ache; **~tanz** *m* belly dance; belly dancing; **~weh** *nt* stomach-ache
bauen ['bauən] *vt, vi* to build; (TECH) to construct; **auf jdn/etw ~** to depend *od* count upon sb/sth
Bauer¹ ['bauər] (-n *od* -s, -n) *m* farmer; (*Schach*) pawn
Bauer² (-s, -) *nt od m* (*bird-*)cage
Bäuerin ['bɔyərin] *f* farmer; (*Frau des Bauers*) farmer's wife
bäuerlich *adj* rustic
Bauern- *zW:* **~haus** *nt* farmhouse; **~hof** *m* farm(yard)
Bau- *zW:* **b~fällig** *adj* dilapidated; **~gelände** *nt* building site; **~genehmigung** *f* building permit; **~herr** *m* purchaser; **~kasten** *m* box of bricks; **~land** *nt* building land; **b~lich** *adj* structural
Baum [baum] (-(e)s, **Bäume**) *m* tree
baumeln ['baumǝln] *vi* to dangle
bäumen ['bɔymǝn] *vr* to rear (up)
Baum- *zW:* **~schule** *f* nursery; **~stamm** *m* tree trunk; **~stumpf** *m* tree stump; **~wolle** *f* cotton
Bau- *zW:* **~plan** *m* architect's plan; **~platz** *m* building site
bausparen *vi* to save with a build-

ing society
Bausparkasse *f* building society
Bausparvertrag *m* building society savings agreement
Bau *zW:* **~stein** *m* building stone, freestone; **~stelle** *f* building site; **~teil** *nt* prefabricated part (of building); **~ten** *pl von* **Bau;** **~weise** *f* (*method*) of construction; **~werk** *nt* building; **~zaun** *m* hoarding
Bayer(in) ['baiər(in)] *m(f)* Bavarian
Bayern ['baiərn] *nt* Bavaria
bayrisch ['bairiʃ] *adj* Bavarian
Bazillus [ba'tsilus] (-, **Bazillen**) *m* bacillus
beabsichtigen [bə'apziçtigən] *vt* to intend
beachten [bə'axtən] *vt* to take note of; (*Vorschrift*) to obey; (*Vorfahrt*) to observe
beachtlich *adj* considerable
Beachtung *f* notice, attention, observation
Beamte(r) [bə'amtə(r)] (-n, -n) *m* official; (*Staats-*) civil servant; (*Bank-* etc) employee
Beamtin *f siehe* **Beamte(r)**
beängstigend [bə'ɛŋstigənd] *adj* alarming
beanspruchen [bə'anʃpruxən] *vt* to claim; (*Zeit, Platz*) to take up, to occupy; **jdn ~** to take up sb's time
beanstanden [bə'anʃtandən] *vt* to complain about, to object to
beantragen [bə'antraːgən] *vt* to apply for, to ask for
beantworten [bə'antvɔrtən] *vt* to answer
Beantwortung *f* (+*gen*) reply (to)
bearbeiten [bə'arbaitən] *vt* to work; (*Material*) to process; (*Thema*) to deal with; (*Land*) to cultivate; (CHEM) to treat; (*Buch*) to revise; (*umg: beeinflussen wollen*) to work on
Bearbeitung *f* processing; cultivation; treatment; revision
Beatmung [bə'aːtmuŋ] *f* respiration
beaufsichtigen [bə'aufziçtigən] *vt*

to supervise

Beaufsichtigung f supervision

beauftragen [bə'auftra:gən] vt to instruct; **jdn mit etw ~** to entrust sb with sth

Beauftragte(r) f(m) (dekl wie adj) representative

bebauen [bə'bauən] vt to build on; (AGR) to cultivate

beben ['be:bən] vi to tremble, to shake; **B~ (-s, -)** nt earthquake

Becher ['bɛçər] (-s, -) m mug; (ohne Henkel) tumbler

Becken ['bɛkən] (-s, -) nt basin; (MUS) cymbal; (ANAT) pelvis

bedacht [bə'daxt] adj thoughtful, careful; **auf etw** akk **~ sein** to be concerned about sth

bedächtig [bə'dɛçtɪç] adj (umsichtig) thoughtful, reflective; (langsam) slow, deliberate

bedanken [bə'daŋkən] vr: **sich (bei jdm) ~** to say thank you (to sb)

Bedarf [bə'darf] (-(e)s) m need, requirement; (COMM) demand; **je nach ~** according to demand; **bei ~** if necessary; **~ an etw** dat **haben** to be in need of sth

Bedarfsfall m case of need

Bedarfshaltestelle f request stop

bedauerlich [bə'dauərlɪç] adj regrettable

bedauern [bə'dauərn] vt to be sorry for; (bemitleiden) to pity; **B~ (-s)** nt regret; **~swert** adj (Zustände) regrettable; (Mensch) pitiable, unfortunate

bedecken [bə'dɛkən] vt to cover

bedeckt adj covered; (Himmel) overcast

Bedenken (-s, -) nt (Überlegen) consideration

bedenken [bə'dɛŋkən] (unreg) vt to think over, to consider; **B~ (-s, -)** nt; (Zweifel) doubt; (Skrupel) scruple

bedenklich adj doubtful; (bedrohlich) dangerous, risky

Bedenkzeit f time to think

bedeuten [bə'dɔytən] vt to mean; to

signify; (wichtig sein) to be of importance; (wichtig sein) to be of importance; **~d** adj important; (beträchtlich) considerable

bedeutsam adj (wichtig) significant

Bedeutung f meaning; significance; (Wichtigkeit) importance; **b~slos** adj insignificant, unimportant; **b~svoll** adj momentous, significant

bedienen [bə'di:nən] vt to serve; (Maschine) to work, to operate ♦ vr (beim Essen) to help o.s.; **sich jds/ einer Sache ~** to make use of sb/sth

Bedienung f service; (Kellnerin) waitress; (Verkäuferin) shop assistant; (Zuschlag) service (charge)

bedingen [bə'dɪŋən] vt (verursachen) to cause

bedingt adj (Richtigkeit, Tauglichkeit) limited; (Zusage, Annahme) conditional

Bedingung f condition; (Voraussetzung) stipulation; **b~slos** adj unconditional

bedrängen [bə'drɛŋən] vt to pester, to harass

bedrohen [bə'dro:ən] vt to threaten

Bedrohung f threat, menace

bedrücken [bə'drʏkən] vt to oppress, to trouble

bedürf- [bə'dʏrf] zW: **~en** (unreg) vt +gen to need, to require; **B~nis** (-ses, -se) nt need; **B~nisanstalt** f public convenience, comfort station (US); **~tig** adj in need, poor, needy

beeilen [bə'aɪlən] vr to hurry

beeindrucken [bə'aɪndrʊkən] vt to impress, to make an impression on

beeinflussen [bə'aɪnflʊsən] vt to influence

beeinträchtigen [bə'aɪntrɛçtɪgən] vt to affect adversely; (Freiheit) to infringe upon

beend(ig)en [bə'ɛnd(ɪg)ən] vt to end, to finish, to terminate

beengen [bə'ɛŋən] vt to cramp; (fig) to hamper, to oppress

beerben [bə'ɛrbən] vt: **jdn ~** to inherit from sb

beerdigen [bə'e:rdɪgən] vt to bury

Beerdigung f funeral, burial; **~sin-**

stitut nt funeral director's

Beere ['be:rə] f berry; (Trauben~) grape

Beet [be:t] (-(e)s, -e) nt bed

befähigen [bə'fɛ:ɪgən] vt to enable

befähigt adj (begabt) talented; ~ (für) (fähig) capable (of)

Befähigung f capability; (Begabung) talent, aptitude

befahrbar [bə'fa:rba:r] adj passable; (NAUT) navigable

befahren [bə'fa:rən] (unreg) vt to use, to drive over; (NAUT) to navigate ♦ adj used

befallen [bə'falən] (unreg) vt to come over

befangen [bə'faŋən] adj (schüchtern) shy, self-conscious; (voreingenommen) biased

befassen [bə'fasən] vr to concern o.s.

Befehl [bə'fe:l] (-(e)s, -e) m command, order; b~en (unreg) vt to order ♦ vi to give orders; jdm etw b~en to order sb to do sth; ~sverweigerung f insubordination

befestigen [bə'fɛstɪgən] vt to fasten; (stärken) to strengthen; (MIL) to fortify; ~ an +dat to fasten to

Befestigung f fastening; strengthening; (MIL) fortification

befeuchten [bə'fɔyçtən] vt to damp(en), to moisten

befinden [bə'fɪndən] (unreg) vr to be; (sich fühlen) to feel ♦ vt: jdn/ etw für od als etw ~ to deem sb/sth to be sth ♦ vi: ~ (über +akk) to decide (on), to adjudicate (on); B~ (-s) nt health, condition; (Meinung) view, opinion

befolgen [bə'fɔlgən] vt to comply with, to follow

befördern [bə'fœrdərn] vt (senden) to transport, to send; (beruflich) to promote

Beförderung f transport; promotion

befragen [bə'fra:gən] vt to question

befreien [bə'fraɪən] vt to set free; (erlassen) to exempt

Befreier (-s, -) m liberator

Befreiung f liberation, release; (Erlassen) exemption

befremden [bə'frɛmdən] vt to surprise, to disturb; B~ (-s) nt surprise, astonishment

befreunden [bə'frɔyndən] vr to make friends; (mit Idee etc) to acquaint o.s.

befreundet adj friendly

befriedigen [bə'fri:dɪgən] vt to satisfy; ~d adj satisfactory

Befriedigung f satisfaction, gratification

befristet [bə'frɪstət] adj limited

befruchten [bə'fruxtən] vt to fertilize; (fig) to stimulate

Befruchtung f: künstliche ~ artificial insemination

Befugnis [bə'fu:knɪs] (-, -se) f authorization, powers pl

befugt adj authorized, entitled

Befund [bə'funt] (-(e)s, -e) m findings pl; (MED) diagnosis

befürchten [bə'fyrçtən] vt to fear

Befürchtung f fear, apprehension

befürworten [bə'fy:rvɔrtən] vt to support, to speak in favour of

Befürworter (-s, -) m supporter, advocate

begabt [bə'ga:pt] adj gifted

Begabung [bə'ga:bʊŋ] f talent, gift

begann etc [bə'gan] vb siehe beginnen

begeben [bə'ge:bən] (unreg) vr (gehen) to betake o.s.; (geschehen) to occur; sich ~ nach od zu to proceed to(wards); B~heit f occurrence

begegnen [bə'ge:gnən] vi: jdm ~ to meet sb; (behandeln) to treat sb; einer Sache dat ~ to meet with sth

Begegnung f meeting

begehen [bə'ge:ən] (unreg) vt (Straftat) to commit; (abschreiten) to cover; (Straße etc) to use, to negotiate; (Feier) to celebrate

begehren [bə'ge:rən] vt to desire

begehrt adj in demand; (Junggeselle) eligible

begeistern [bə'gaɪstərn] vt to fill with enthusiasm, to inspire ♦ vr:

sich für etw ~ to get enthusiastic about sth

begeistert adj enthusiastic

Begierde [bəˈgiːrdə] f desire, passion

begierig [bəˈgiːrɪç] adj eager, keen

begießen [bəˈgiːsən] (unreg) vt to water; (mit Alkohol) to drink to

Beginn [bəˈgɪn] m (-(e)s) m beginning; **zu** ~ at the beginning; **b~en** (unreg) vt, vi to start, to begin

beglaubigen [bəˈglaubɪgən] vt to countersign

Beglaubigung f countersignature

begleichen [bəˈglaɪçən] (unreg) vt to settle, to pay

Begleit- [bəˈglaɪt] zW: **b~en** vt to accompany; (MIL) to escort; **~er** (-s, -) m companion; (Freund) escort; (MUS) accompanist; **~schreiben** nt covering letter; **~umstände** pl concomitant circumstances; **~ung** f company; (MIL) escort; (MUS) accompaniment

beglücken [bəˈglʏkən] vt to make happy, to delight

beglückwünschen [bəˈglʏkvʏnʃən] vt: ~ (zu) to congratulate (on)

begnadigen [bəˈgnaːdɪgən] vt to pardon

Begnadigung f pardon, amnesty

begnügen [bəˈgnyːgən] vr to be satisfied, to content o.s.

Begonie [bəˈgoːniə] f begonia

begonnen [bəˈgɔnən] vb siehe beginnen

begraben [bəˈgraːbən] (unreg) vt to bury

Begräbnis [bəˈgrɛːpnɪs] (-ses, -se) nt burial, funeral

begreifen [bəˈgraɪfən] (unreg) vt to understand, to comprehend

begreiflich [bəˈgraɪflɪç] adj understandable

Begrenztheit [bəˈgrɛntsthaɪt] f limitation, restriction; (fig) narrowness

Begriff [bəˈgrɪf] (-(e)s, -e) m concept, idea; **im** ~ **sein**, etw zu tun to be about to do sth; **schwer von** ~ (umg) slow, dense; **b~sstutzig** adj slow, dense

begründ- [bəˈgrʏnd] zW: **~en** vt (Gründe geben) to justify; **~et** adj well-founded, justified; **B~ung** f justification, reason

begrüßen [bəˈgryːsən] vt to greet, to welcome

Begrüßung f greeting, welcome

begünstigen [bəˈgʏnstɪgən] vt (Person) to favour; (Sache) to further, to promote

begutachten [bəˈguːtˌaxtən] vt to assess

begütert [bəˈgyːtərt] adj wealthy, well-to-do

behaart [bəˈhaːrt] adj hairy

behäbig [bəˈhɛːbɪç] adj (dick) portly, stout; (geruhsam) comfortable

behagen [bəˈhaːgən] vi: das behagt ihm nicht he does not like it; **B~** (-s) nt comfort, ease

behaglich [bəˈhaːklɪç] adj comfortable, cosy; **B~keit** f comfort, cosiness

behalten [bəˈhaltən] (unreg) vt to keep, to retain; (im Gedächtnis) to remember

Behälter [bəˈhɛltər] (-s, -) m container, receptacle

behandeln [bəˈhandəln] vt to treat; (Thema) to deal with; (Maschine) to handle

Behandlung f treatment; (von Maschine) handling

beharren [bəˈharən] vi: auf etw dat ~ to stick od keep to sth

beharrlich [bəˈharlɪç] adj (ausdauernd) steadfast, unwavering; (hartnäckig) tenacious, dogged; **B~keit** f steadfastness; tenacity

behaupten [bəˈhauptən] vt to claim, to assert, to maintain; (sein Recht) to defend ♦ vr to assert o.s.

Behauptung f claim, assertion

beheben [bəˈheːbən] (unreg) vt to remove

beheizen [bəˈhaɪtsən] vt to heat

behelfen [bəˈhɛlfən] (unreg) vr: sich mit etw ~ to make do with sth

behelfsmäßig adj improvised,

makeshift; *(vorübergehend)* temporary

behelligen [bə'hɛlɪɡən] *vt* to trouble, to bother

beherbergen [bə'hɛrbɛrɡən] *vt* to put up, to house

beherrschen [bə'hɛrʃən] *vt (Volk)* to rule, to govern; *(Situation)* to control; *(Sprache, Gefühle)* to master ♦ *vr* to control o.s.

beherrscht *adj* controlled

Beherrschung *f* rule; control; mastery

beherzigen [bə'hɛrtsɪɡən] *vt* to take to heart

beherzt *adj* courageous, brave

behilflich [bə'hɪlflɪç] *adj* helpful; jdm ~ sein *(bei)* to help sb *(with)*

behindern [bə'hɪndərn] *vt* to hinder, to impede

Behinderte(r) *mf* disabled person

Behinderung *f* hindrance; *(Körper~)* handicap

Behörde [bə'høːrdə] *f (auch pl)* authorities *pl*

behördlich [bə'høːrtlɪç] *adj* official

behüten [bə'hyːtən] *vt* to guard; jdn vor etw *dat* ~ to preserve sb from sth

behutsam [bə'huːtzaːm] *adj* cautious, careful; B~keit *f* caution, carefulness

bei [baɪ] *präp +dat* **1** *(nahe bei)* near; *(zum Aufenthalt)* at, with; *(unter, zwischen)* among; **bei München** near Munich; **bei uns** at our place; **beim Friseur** at the hairdresser's; **bei seinen Eltern wohnen** to live with one's parents; **bei einer Firma arbeiten** to work for a firm; **etw bei sich haben** to have sth on one; **jdn bei sich haben** to have sb with one; **bei Goethe** in Goethe; **beim Militär** in the army

2 *(zeitlich)* at, on; *(während)* during; *(Zustand, Umstand)* in; **bei Nacht** at night; **bei Nebel** in fog; **bei Regen** if it rains; **bei solcher Hitze** in such heat; **bei meiner Ankunft** on my arrival; **bei der Arbeit** when I'm *etc* working; **beim Fahren** while driving

beibehalten ['baɪbəhaltən] *(unreg) vt* to keep, to retain

beibringen ['baɪbrɪŋən] *(unreg) vt (Beweis, Zeugen)* to bring forward; *(Gründe)* to adduce; **jdm etw ~** *(lehren)* to teach sb sth; *(zu verstehen geben)* to make sb understand sth; *(zufügen)* to inflict sth on sb

Beichte ['baɪçtə] *f* confession; b~n *vt* to confess ♦ *vi* to go to confession

Beichtstuhl *m* confessional

beide(s) ['baɪdə(s)] *pron, adj* both; meine ~n Brüder my two brothers, both my brothers; die ersten ~n the first two; wir ~ we two; einer von ~n one of the two; alles ~s both (of them)

beider- ['baɪdər] *zW:* ~lei *adj inv* of both; ~seitig *adj* mutual, reciprocal; ~seits *adv* mutually ♦ *präp +gen* on both sides of

beieinander [baɪaɪ'nandər] *adv* together

Beifahrer ['baɪfaːrər] *m* passenger; ~sitz *m* passenger seat

Beifall ['baɪfal] *(-(e)s) m* applause; *(Zustimmung)* approval

beifällig ['baɪfɛlɪç] *adj* approving; *(Kommentar)* favourable

beifügen ['baɪfyːɡən] *vt* to enclose

beige ['beːʒə] *adj* beige, fawn

beigeben ['baɪɡeːbən] *(unreg) vt (zufügen)* to add; *(mitgeben)* to give ♦ *vi (nachgeben)* to give in

Beihilfe ['baɪhɪlfə] *f* aid, assistance; *(Studien~)* grant; *(JUR)* aiding and abetting

beikommen ['baɪkɔmən] *(unreg) vi +dat* to get at; *(einem Problem)* to deal with

Beil [baɪl] *(-(e)s, -e) nt* axe, hatchet

Beilage ['baɪlaːɡə] *f (Buch~ etc)* supplement; *(KOCH)* vegetables and potatoes *pl*

beiläufig ['baɪlɔyfɪç] *adj* casual, incidental ♦ adv casually, by the way

beilegen ['baile:gən] vt (hinzufügen) to enclose, to add; (beimessen) to attribute, to ascribe; (Streit) to settle

Beileid ['bailait] nt condolence, sympathy; **herzliches ~** deepest sympathy

beiliegend ['baili:gənt] adj (COMM) enclosed

beim [baim] = **bei dem**

beimessen ['baimesən] (unreg) vt (+dat) to attribute (to), to ascribe (to)

Bein [bain] (-(e)s, -e) nt leg

beinah(e) ['baina:(ə)] adv almost, nearly

Beinbruch m fracture of the leg

beinhalten [bə'inhaltən] vt to contain

beipflichten ['baipflictən] vi: **jdm/etw ~** to agree with sb/sth

beisammen [bai'zamən] adv together; **B~sein** (-s) nt get-together

Beischlaf ['baiʃla:f] m sexual intercourse

Beisein ['baizain] (-s) nt presence

beiseite [bai'zaitə] adv to one side, aside; (stehen) to one side, aside; **etw ~ legen** (sparen) to put sth by; **jdn/etw ~ schaffen** to put sb/get sth out of the way

beisetzen ['baizɛtsən] vt to bury

Beisetzung f funeral

Beisitzer ['baizitsər] (-s, -) m (bei Prüfung) assessor

Beispiel ['baiʃpi:l] (-(e)s, -e) nt example; **sich** (+dat) **an jdm ein** example; **sich** (+dat) **an jdm ein example; **zum ~ for** example; **b~haft** adj exemplary; **b~los** adj unprecedented; **b~sweise** adv for instance or example

beißen ['baisən] (unreg) vt, vi to bite; (stechen: Rauch, Säure) to sting ♦ vr (Farben) to clash; **~d** adj biting, caustic; (fig auch) sarcastic

Beistand ['baiʃtant] (-(e)s, -e) m support, help; (JUR) adviser

beistehen ['baiʃte:ən] (unreg) vi: **jdm ~** to stand by sb

beisteuern ['baiʃtɔyərn] vt to contribute

beistimmen ['baiʃtimən] vi +dat to agree with

Beitrag ['baitra:k] (-(e)s, -e) m contribution; (Zahlung) fee, subscription; (Versicherungs~) premium; **beitragen** ['baitra:gən] (unreg) vt, vi: **b~ (zu)** to contribute (to); (mithelfen) to help (with)

beitreten ['baitre:tən] (unreg) vi +dat to join

Beitritt ['baitrit] m joining, membership

Beiwagen m (Motorrad~) sidecar

Beize ['baitsə] f (Holz~) stain; (KOCH) marinade

beizeiten [bai'tsaitən] adv in time

bejahen [bə'ja:ən] vt (Frage) to say yes to, to answer in the affirmative; (gutheißen) to agree with

bejahrt [bə'ja:rt] adj aged, elderly

bekämpfen [bə'kɛmpfən] vt (Gegner) to fight; (Seuche) to combat ♦ vr to fight

Bekämpfung f fight, struggle

bekannt [bə'kant] adj (well-)known; (nicht fremd) familiar; **mit jdm ~ sein** to know sb; **jdn mit jdm ~ machen** to introduce sb to sb; **das ist mir ~** I know that; **es/sie kommt mir ~ vor** it/she seems familiar; **B~e(r)** mf acquaintance; friend; **B~enkreis** m circle of friends; **~geben** (unreg) vt to announce publicly; **~lich** adv as is well known, as you know; **~machen** vt to announce; **B~machung** f publication; announcement; **B~schaft** f acquaintance

bekehren [bə'ke:rən] vt to convert ♦ vr to become converted

Bekehrung f conversion

bekennen [bə'kɛnən] (unreg) vt to confess; (Glauben) to profess; **Farbe ~ (umg)** to show where one stands

Bekenntnis [bə'kɛntnis] (-ses, -se) nt admission, confession; (Religion) confession, denomination

beklagen [bə'kla:gən] vt to deplore,

to lament ♦ vr to complain; ~swert adj lamentable, pathetic

bekleiden [bəˈklaɪdən] vt to clothe; (Amt) to occupy, to fill

Bekleidung f clothing

beklemmen [bəˈklɛmən] vt to oppress

beklommen [bəˈklɔmən] adj anxious, uneasy; B~heit f anxiety, uneasiness

bekommen [bəˈkɔmən] (unreg) vt to get, to receive; (Kind) to have; (Zug) to catch, to get ♦ vi: jdm ~ to agree with sb

bekömmlich [bəˈkœmlɪç] adj easily digestible

bekräftigen [bəˈkrɛftɪɡən] vt to confirm, to corroborate

bekreuzigen [bəˈkrɔʏtsɪɡən] vr to cross o.s.

bekümmern [bəˈkʏmərn] vt to worry, to trouble

bekunden [bəˈkʊndən] vt (sagen) to state; (zeigen) to show

belächeln [bəˈlɛçəln] vt to laugh at

beladen [bəˈlaːdən] (unreg) vt to load

Belag [bəˈlaːk] (-(e)s, -e) m covering, coating; (Brot~) spread; (Zahn~) tartar; (auf Zunge) fur; (Brems~) lining

belagern [bəˈlaːɡərn] vt to besiege

Belagerung f siege

Belang [bəˈlaŋ] (-(e)s) m importance; ~e pl (Interessen) interests, concerns; b~los adj trivial, unimportant

belassen [bəˈlasən] (unreg) vt (in Zustand, Glauben) to leave; (in Stellung) to retain

belasten [bəˈlastən] vt to burden; (fig: bedrücken) to trouble, to worry; (COMM: Konto) to debit; (JUR) to incriminate ♦ vr to weigh o.s. down; (JUR) to incriminate o.s.; ~d adj (JUR) incriminating

belästigen [bəˈlɛstɪɡən] vt to annoy, to pester

Belästigung f annoyance, pestering

Belastung [bəˈlastʊŋ] f load; (fig:

Sorge etc) weight; (COMM) charge, debit(ing); (JUR) incriminatory evidence

belaufen [bəˈlaʊfən] (unreg) vr: sich ~ auf +akk to amount to

beleben [bəˈleːbən] vt (anregen) to liven up; (Konjunktur, jds Hoffnungen) to stimulate ♦ vr (Augen) to light up; (Stadt) to come to life

belebt [bəˈleːpt] adj (Straße) busy

Beleg [bəˈleːk] (-(e)s, -e) m (COMM) receipt; (Beweis) documentary evidence, proof; (Beispiel) example; b~en [bəˈleːɡən] vt to cover; (Kuchen, Brot) to spread; (Platz) to reserve, to book; (Kurs, Vorlesung) to register for; (beweisen) to verify, to prove; (MIL: mit Bomben) to bomb; ~schaft f personnel, staff; b~t adj: b~tes Brot open sandwich

belehren [bəˈleːrən] vt to instruct, to teach

Belehrung f instruction

beleibt [bəˈlaɪpt] adj stout, corpulent

beleidigen [bəˈlaɪdɪɡən] vt to insult, to offend

Beleidigung f insult; (JUR) slander; libel

belesen [bəˈleːzən] adj well-read

beleuchten [bəˈlɔʏçtən] vt to light, to illuminate; (fig) to throw light on

Beleuchtung f lighting, illumination

Belgien [ˈbɛlɡiən] nt Belgium; **Belgier(in)** m(f) Belgian; **belgisch** adj Belgian

belichten [bəˈlɪçtən] vt to expose

Belichtung f exposure; ~smesser m exposure meter

Belieben [bəˈliːbən] nt: (ganz) nach ~ (just) as you wish

beliebig [bəˈliːbɪç] adj any you like ♦ adv as you like; ein ~es Thema any subject you like od want; ~ viel/viele as much/many as you like

beliebt [bəˈliːpt] adj popular; sich bei jdm ~ machen to make o.s. popular with sb; B~heit f popularity

beliefern [bəˈliːfərn] vt to supply

bellen [ˈbɛlən] vi to bark

belohnen [bəˈloːnən] vt to reward

Belohnung f reward

belügen [bə'ly:gən] (unreg) vt to lie to, to deceive

belustigen [bə'lʊstɪgən] vt to amuse

Belustigung f amusement

bemalen [bə'ma:lən] vt to paint

bemängeln [bə'mɛŋəln] vt to criticize

bemerk- [bə'mɛrk] zW: **~bar** adj perceptible, noticeable; **sich ~bar machen** (Person) to make od get o.s. noticed; (Unruhe) to become noticeable; **~en** vt (wahrnehmen) to notice, to observe; (sagen) to say, to mention; **~enswert** adj remarkable, noteworthy; **B~ung** f remark; (schriftlich auch) note

bemitleiden [bə'mɪtlaɪdən] vt to pity

bemühen [bə'my:ən] vr to take trouble od pains

Bemühung f trouble, pains pl, effort

ber achbart [bə'naxba:rt] adj neighbouring

benachrichtigen [bə'na:xrɪçtɪgən] vt to inform

Benachrichtigung f notification, information

benachteiligen [bə'na:xtaɪlɪgən] vt to put at a disadvantage; to victimize

benehmen [bə'ne:mən] (unreg) vr to behave; **B~** (-s) nt behaviour

beneiden [bə'naɪdən] vt to envy; **~swert** adj enviable

benennen [bə'nɛnən] (unreg) vt to name

Bengel ['bɛŋəl] (-s, -) m (little) rascal od rogue

benommen [bə'nɔmən] adj dazed

benoten [bə'no:tən] vt to mark

benötigen [bə'nø:tɪgən] vt to need

benutzen [bə'nʊtsən] vt to use

benützen [bə'nʏtsən] vt to use

Benutzer (-s, -) m user

Benutzung f utilization, use

Benzin [bɛn'tsi:n] (-s, -e) nt (AUT) petrol (BRIT), gas(oline) (US); **~kanister** m petrol (BRIT) od gas (US) can; **~tank** m petrol tank (BRIT),

gas tank (US); **~uhr** f petrol (BRIT) od gas (US) gauge

beobachten [bə'o:baxtən] vt to observe; **Beobachter** (-s, -) m observer; (eines Unfalls) witness; (PRESSE, TV) correspondent; **Beobachtung** f observation

bepacken [bə'pakən] vt to load, to pack

bequem [bə'kve:m] adj comfortable; (Ausrede) convenient; (Person) lazy, indolent; **~en** vr: **sich ~en(, etw zu tun)** to condescend (to do sth); **B~lichkeit** [-lɪçkaɪt] f convenience, comfort; (Faulheit) laziness, indolence

beraten [bə'ra:tən] (unreg) vt to advise; (besprechen) to discuss, to debate ♦ vr to consult; **gut/schlecht ~ sein** to be well/ill advised; **sich ~ lassen** to get advice

Berater (-s, -) m adviser

Beratung f advice; (Besprechung) consultation; **~stelle** f advice centre

berauben [bə'raʊbən] vt to rob

berechenbar [bə'rɛçənba:r] adj calculable

berechnen [bə'rɛçnən] vt to calculate; (COMM: anrechnen) to charge; **~d** adj (Mensch) calculating, scheming

Berechnung f calculation; (COMM) charge

berechtigen [bə'rɛçtɪgən] vt to entitle; (bevollmächtigen) to authorize; (fig) to justify

berechtigt [bə'rɛçtɪçt] adj justifiable, justified

Berechtigung f authorization; (fig) justification

bereden [bə're:dən] vt (besprechen) to discuss; (überreden) to persuade ♦ vr to discuss

Bereich [bə'raɪç] (-(e)s, -e) m (Bezirk) area; (PHYS) range; (Ressort, Gebiet) sphere

bereichern [bə'raɪçərn] vt to enrich ♦ vr to get rich

bereinigen [bə'raɪnɪgən] vt to settle

bereisen [bə'raɪzən] vt (Land) to travel through

bereit [bəˈraɪt] *adj* ready, prepared; **zu** ~ **sein** to be ready for sth; **sich** ~ **erklären** to declare o.s. willing; **~en** *vt* to prepare, to make ready; (*Kummer, Freude*) to cause; **~halten** (*unreg*) *vt* to keep in readiness; **~legen** *vt* to lay out; **~machen** *vt*, *vr* to prepare, to get ready; **~s** *adv* already; **B~schaft** *f* readiness; (*Polizei*) alert; **B~schaftsdienst** *m* emergency service; **~stehen** (*unreg*) *vi* (*Person*) to be prepared; (*Ding*) to be ready; **~stellen** *vt* (*Kisten, Pakete etc*) to put ready; (*Geld etc*) to make available; (*Truppen, Maschinen*) to put at the ready; **~willig** *adj* willing, ready; **B~willigkeit** *f* willingness, readiness

bereuen [bəˈrɔʏən] *vt* to regret

Berg [bɛrk] (-(e)s, -e) *m* mountain; hill; **b~ab** *adv* downhill; **~arbeiter** *m* miner; **b~auf** *adv* uphill; **~bahn** *f* mountain railway; **~bau** *m* mining

bergen [ˈbɛrɡən] (*unreg*) *vt* (*retten*) to rescue; (*Ladung*) to salvage; (*enthalten*) to contain

Berg- *zW:* **~führer** *m* mountain guide; **~gipfel** *m* peak, summit; **b~ig** [ˈbɛrɡɪç] *adj* mountainous, hilly; **~kamm** *m* ridge, crest; **~kette** *f* mountain range; **~mann** *pl* **Bergleute**) *m* miner; **~rettungsdienst** *m* mountain rescue team; **~rutsch** *m* landslide; **~steigen** *nt* mountaineering; **~steiger(in)** (-s, -) *m(f)* mountaineer, climber

Bergung [ˈbɛrɡʊŋ] *f* (*von Menschen*) rescue; (*von Material*) recovery; (*NAUT*) salvage

Bergwacht *f* mountain rescue service

Bergwerk *nt* mine

Bericht [bəˈrɪçt] (-(e)s, -e) *m* report, account; **b~en** *vt*, *vi* to report; **~erstatter** (-s, -) *m* reporter; (*newspaper*) correspondent

berichtigen [bəˈrɪçtɪɡən] *vt* to correct

Berichtigung *f* correction

Bernstein [ˈbɛrnʃtaɪn] *m* amber

bersten [ˈbɛrstən] (*unreg*) *vi* to burst, to split

berüchtigt [bəˈryçtɪçt] *adj* notorious, infamous

berücksichtigen [bəˈrʏkzɪçtɪɡən] *vt* to consider, to bear in mind

Berücksichtigung *f* consideration

Beruf [bəˈruːf] (-(e)s, -e) *m* occupation, profession; (*Gewerbe*) trade; **b~en** (*unreg*) *vt:* **b~en zu** to appoint to ♦ *vr:* **sich auf jdn/etw b~en** to refer od appeal to sb/sth ♦ *adj* competent, qualified; **b~lich** *adj* professional

Berufs- *zW:* **~ausbildung** *f* job training; **~berater** *m* careers adviser; **~beratung** *f* vocational guidance; **~geheimnis** *nt* professional secret; **~leben** *nt* professional life; **b~mäßig** [-mɛːsɪç] *adj* professional; **~schule** *f* vocational od trade school; **~sportler** [-ʃpɔrtlər] *m* professional (sportsman); **b~tätig** *adj* employed; **b~unfähig** *adj* unfit for work; **~verkehr** *m* rush-hour traffic

Berufung *f* vocation, calling; (*Ernennung*) appointment; (*JUR*) appeal; **~ einlegen** to appeal

beruhen [bəˈruːən] *vi:* **auf etw dat ~** to be based on sth; **etw auf sich ~ lassen** to leave sth at that

beruhigen [bəˈruːɪɡən] *vt* to calm, to pacify, to soothe ♦ *vr* (*Mensch*) to calm (o.s.) down; (*Situation*) to calm down

Beruhigung *f* soothing; (*der Nerven*) calming; **zu jds ~** (in order) to reassure sb; **~smittel** *nt* sedative

berühmt [bəˈryːmt] *adj* famous; **B~heit** *f* (*Ruf*) fame; (*Mensch*) celebrity

berühren [bəˈryːrən] *vt* to touch; (*gefühlsmäßig bewegen*) to affect; (*flüchtig erwähnen*) to mention, to touch on ♦ *vr* to meet, to touch

Berührung *f* contact

besagen [bəˈzaːɡən] *vt* to mean

besagt *adj* (*Tag etc*) said

besänftigen vt to soothe, to calm

Besatz [bəˈzats] (-es, ₊e) m trimming, edging

Besatzung f garrison; (NAUT, AVIAT) crew; **~smacht** f occupying power

beschädigen [bəˈʃɛːdɪgən] vt to damage; **Beschädigung** f damage; (Stelle) damaged spot

beschaffen [bəˈʃafən] vt to get, to acquire ♦ adj: das ist so ~, daß that is such that; **B~heit** f (von Mensch) constitution, nature

Beschaffung f acquisition

beschäftigen [bəˈʃɛftɪgən] vt to occupy; (beruflich) to employ ♦ vr to occupy od concern o.s.

beschäftigt adj busy, occupied

Beschäftigung f (Beruf) employment; (Tätigkeit) occupation; (Befassen) concern

beschämen [bəˈʃɛːmən] vt to put to shame; **~d** adj shameful; (Hilfsbereitschaft) shaming

beschämt adj ashamed

beschatten [bəˈʃatən] vt to shade; (Verdächtige) to shadow

Bescheid [bəˈʃaɪt] (-(e)s, -e) m information; (Weisung) directions pl; ~ **wissen** (über +akk) to be well-informed (about); **ich weiß** ~ I know; **jdm** ~ **geben** od **sagen** to let sb know

bescheiden [bəˈʃaɪdən] (unreg) vr to content o.s. ♦ adj modest; **B~heit** f modesty

bescheinen [bəˈʃaɪnən] (unreg) vt to shine on

bescheinigen [bəˈʃaɪnɪgən] vt to certify; (bestätigen) to acknowledge

Bescheinigung f certificate; (Quittung) receipt

beschenken [bəˈʃɛŋkən] vt: **jdn mit etw** ~ to give sb sth as a present

bescheren [bəˈʃeːrən] vt: **jdm etw** ~ to give sb sth as a Christmas present; **jdm** ~ to give Christmas presents to sb

Bescherung f giving of Christmas

presents; (umg) mess

beschildern [bəˈʃɪldərn] vt to put signs/a sign on

beschimpfen [bəˈʃɪmpfən] vt to abuse

Beschimpfung f abuse; insult

Beschlag [bəˈʃlaːk] (-(e)s, ₊e) m (Metallband) fitting; (auf Fenster) condensation; (auf Metall) tarnish; finish; (Hufeisen) horseshoe; **jdn in** ~ **nehmen** od **mit** ~ **belegen** to monopolize sb/sth; **b~en** [bəˈʃlaːgən] (unreg) vt to cover; (Pferd) to shoe ♦ vi (Fenster etc) to mist over; **b~en sein** (in od auf +dat) to be well versed (in); **b~nahmen** vt to seize, to confiscate; to requisition; **~nahmung** f confiscation, sequestration

beschleunigen [bəˈʃlɔʏnɪgən] vt to accelerate, to speed up ♦ vi (AUT) to accelerate

Beschleunigung f acceleration

beschließen [bəˈʃliːsən] (unreg) vt to decide on; (beenden) to end, to close

Beschluß [bəˈʃlʊs] (-sses, ₊sse) m decision, conclusion; (Ende) conclusion, end

beschmutzen [bəˈʃmʊtsən] vt to dirty, to soil

beschönigen [bəˈʃøːnɪgən] vt to gloss over

beschränken [bəˈʃrɛŋkən] vt, vr: **(sich)** ~ **(auf** +akk) to limit od restrict (o.s.) (to)

beschränk- 2W: **~t** adj confined, restricted; (Mensch) limited, narrow-minded; **B~ung** f limitation

beschreiben [bəˈʃraɪbən] (unreg) vt to describe; (Papier) to write on

Beschreibung f description

beschriften [bəˈʃrɪftən] vt to mark, to label

Beschriftung f lettering

beschuldigen [bəˈʃʊldɪgən] vt to accuse

Beschuldigung f accusation

Beschuß m: **jdn/etw unter** ~ **nehmen** (MIL) to open fire on sb/sth

beschützen [bəˈʃʏtsən] vt: ~ (vor +dat) to protect (from); **Beschützer** (-s, -) m protector

Beschwerde [bəˈʃveːrdə] f complaint; (Mühe) hardship; ~n pl (Leiden) trouble

beschweren [bəˈʃveːrən] vt to weight down; (fig) to burden ♦ vr to complain

beschwerlich adj tiring, exhausting

beschwichtigen [bəˈʃvɪçtɪɡən] vt to soothe, to pacify

beschwindeln [bəˈʃvɪndəln] vt (betrügen) to cheat; (belügen) to fib to

beschwingt [bəˈʃvɪŋt] adj in high spirits

beschwipst [bəˈʃvɪpst] (umg) adj tipsy

beschwören [bəˈʃvøːrən] (unreg) vt (Aussage) to swear to; (anflehen) to implore; (Geister) to conjure up

beseitigen [bəˈzaɪtɪɡən] vt to remove

Beseitigung f removal

Besen [ˈbeːzən] (-s, -) m broom; ~stiel m broomstick

besessen [bəˈzɛsən] adj possessed

besetz- [bəˈzɛts] zW: ~en vt (Haus, Land) to occupy; (Platz) to take, to fill; (Posten) to fill; (Rolle) to cast; (mit Edelsteinen) to set; ~t adj (Platz) taken; (TEL) engaged, busy; (WC) engaged; **B~tzeichen** nt engaged tone; **B~ung** f occupation; filling; (von Rolle) casting; (die Schauspieler) cast

besichtigen [bəˈzɪçtɪɡən] vt to visit, to have a look at

Besichtigung f visit

Besied(e)lung [bəˈziːd(ə)lʊŋ] f population

besiegen [bəˈziːɡən] vt to defeat, to overcome

besinnen [bəˈzɪnən] (unreg) vr (nachdenken) to think, to reflect; (erinnern) to remember; **sich anders ~** to change one's mind

besinnlich adj contemplative

Besinnung f consciousness; **zur ~**

kommen to recover consciousness; (fig) to come to one's senses; **b~slos** adj unconscious

Besitz [bəˈzɪts] (-es) m possession; (Eigentum) property; **b~en** (unreg) vt to possess, to own; (Eigenschaft) to have; **~er(in)** (-s, -) m(f) owner, proprietor; **~ergreifung** f occupation, seizure

besoffen [bəˈzɔfən] (umg) adj drunk, stoned

besohlen [bəˈzoːlən] vt to sole

Besoldung [bəˈzɔldʊŋ] f salary, pay

besonder(r, s) [bəˈzɔndərə(r, s)] adj special; (eigen) particular; (gesondert) separate; (eigentümlich) peculiar

Besonderheit [bəˈzɔndərhaɪt] f peculiarity

besonders [bəˈzɔndərs] adv especially, particularly; (getrennt) separately

besonnen [bəˈzɔnən] adj sensible, level-headed

besorg- [bəˈzɔrg] zW: ~en vt (beschaffen) to acquire; (kaufen auch) to purchase; (erledigen: Geschäfte) to deal with; (sich kümmern um) to take care of; **B~nis** (-, -se) f anxiety, concern; ~t adj [bəˈzɔrçt] anxious, worried; **B~theit** f anxiety, worry; **B~ung** f acquisition; (Kauf) purchase

bespielen [bəˈʃpiːlən] vt to record

bespitzeln [bəˈʃpɪtsəln] vt to spy on

besprechen [bəˈʃprɛçən] (unreg) vt to discuss; (Tonband etc) to record, to speak onto; (Buch) to review ♦ vr to discuss, to consult

Besprechung f meeting, discussion; (von Buch) review

besser [ˈbɛsər] adj better; **~gehen** (unreg) vi unpers: **es geht ihm besser**, he is feeling better; **~n** vt to make better, to improve ♦ vr to improve; (Menschen) to reform; **B~ung** f improvement; **gute Besserung!** get well soon!; **B~wisser** (-s, -) m know-all

Bestand [bəˈʃtant] (-(e)s, ¨e)

(Fortbestehen) duration, stability; *(Kassen~)* amount, balance; *(Vorrat)* stock; ~ **haben, von** ~ **sein** to last long, to endure

beständig [bəˈʃtɛndɪç] *adj (ausdauernd: auch fig)* constant; *(Wetter)* settled; *(Stoffe)* resistant; *(Klagen etc)* continual

Bestandsaufnahme [bəˈʃtantsaufnaːmə] *f* stocktaking

Bestandteil *m* part, component; *(Zutat)* ingredient

bestärken [bəˈʃtɛrkən] *vt*: **jdn in etw** *dat* ~ to strengthen od confirm sb in sth

bestätigen [bəˈʃtɛːtɪɡən] *vt* to confirm; *(anerkennen, COMM)* to acknowledge

Bestätigung *f* confirmation; acknowledgement

bestatten [bəˈʃtatən] *vt* to bury; **B~ung** *f* funeral

Bestattungsinstitut *nt* funeral director's

bestaunen [bəˈʃtaunən] *vt* to marvel at, gaze at in wonder

beste(r, s) [ˈbɛstə(r, s)] *adj* best; **so ist es am** ~**n** it's best that way; **am** ~**n gehst du gleich** you'd better go at once; **jdn zum** ~**n haben** to pull sb's leg; **einen Witz** *etc* **zum** ~**n geben** to tell a joke etc; **aufs** ~ in the best possible way; **zu jds B~n** for the benefit of sb

bestechen [bəˈʃtɛçən] *(unreg) vt* to bribe

bestechlich *adj* corruptible

Bestechung *f* bribery, corruption

Besteck [bəˈʃtɛk] *(-(e)s, -e) nt* knife, fork and spoon, cutlery; *(MED)* set of instruments

bestehen [bəˈʃteːən] *(unreg) vi* to be; to exist; *(andauern)* to last ♦ *vt (Kampf, Probe, Prüfung)* to pass; ~ **auf** +*dat* to insist on; ~ **aus** to consist of

bestehlen [bəˈʃteːlən] *(unreg) vt*: **jdn (um etw)** ~ to rob sb (of sth)

besteigen [bəˈʃtaɪɡən] *(unreg) vt* to climb, to ascend; *(Pferd)* to mount;

(Thron) to ascend

Bestell- [bəˈʃtɛl] *zW*: ~**buch** *nt* order book; **b~en** *vt* to order; *(kommen lassen)* to arrange to see; *(nominieren)* to name; *(Acker)* to cultivate; *(Grüße, Auftrag)* to pass; ~**ung** *f (COMM)* order; *(Bestellen)* ordering

bestenfalls [ˈbɛstənˈfals] *adv* at best

bestens [ˈbɛstəns] *adv* very well

besteuern [bəˈʃtɔyərn] *vt (jdn, Waren)* to tax

Bestie [ˈbɛstjə] *f (auch fig)* beast

bestimm- [bəˈʃtɪm] *zW*: ~**en** *vt (Regeln)* to lay down; *(Tag, Ort)* to fix; *(beherrschen)* to characterize; *(vorsehen)* to mean; *(ernennen)* to appoint; *(definieren)* to define; *(veranlassen)* to induce; ~**t** *adj (entschlossen)* firm; *(gewiß)* certain, definite; *(Artikel)* definite ♦ *adv (gewiß)* definitely, for sure; **suchen Sie etwas B~tes?** are you looking for something in particular?; **B~theit** *f* firmness; certainty; **B~ung** *f (Verordnung)* regulation; *(Festsetzen)* determining; *(Verwendungszweck)* purpose; *(Schicksal)* fate; *(Definition)* definition

Bestleistung *f* best performance

bestmöglich *adj* best possible

bestrafen [bəˈʃtraːfən] *vt* to punish

Bestrafung *f* punishment

bestrahlen [bəˈʃtraːlən] *vt* to shine on; *(MED)* to treat with X-rays

Bestrahlung *f (MED)* X-ray treatment, radiotherapy

Bestreben [bəˈʃtreːbən] *(-s) nt* endeavour, effort

bestreichen [bəˈʃtraɪçən] *(unreg) vt (Brot)* to spread

bestreiten [bəˈʃtraɪtən] *(unreg) vt (abstreiten)* to dispute; *(finanzieren)* to pay for, to finance

bestreuen [bəˈʃtrɔyən] *vt* to sprinkle, to dust; *(Straße)* to grit

bestürmen [bəˈʃtʏrmən] *vt (mit Fragen, Bitten etc)* to overwhelm, to swamp

bestürzend [bəˈʃtʏrtsənd] *adj (Na-*

chrichten) disturbing

bestürzt [bəˈʃtʏrtst] adj dismayed

Bestürzung f consternation

Besuch [bəˈzuːx] (-(e)s, -e) m visit; (Person) visitor; **einen ~ machen bei jdm** to pay sb a visit od call; ~ **haben** to have visitors; **bei jdm auf od zu ~ sein** to be visiting sb; **b~t** to visit; (SCH etc) to attend; **gut b~t** well-attended; **~er(in)** (-s, -) m(f) visitor, guest; **~zeit** f visiting hours pl

betätigen [bəˈtɛːtɪgən] vt (bedienen) to work, to operate ♦ vr to involve o.s.; **sich als etw ~** to work as sth

Betätigung f activity; (beruflich) occupation; (TECH) operation

betäuben [bəˈtɔʏbən] vt to stun; (fig: Gewissen) to still; (MED) to anaesthetize

Betäubung f (Narkose): **örtliche ~** local anaesthetic

Betäubungsmittel nt anaesthetic

Bete [ˈbeːtə] f: **rote ~** beetroot (BRIT), beet (US)

beteiligen [bəˈtaɪlɪgən] vr: **sich ~ (an +dat)** to take part (in), to participate (in), to share (in); (an Geschäft: finanziell) to have a share (in); **jdn ~ (an +dat)** to give sb a share od interest in

Beteiligte(r) f(m) (Mitwirkender) partner; (finanziell) shareholder

Beteiligung f participation; (Anteil) share, interest; (Besucherzahl) attendance

beten [ˈbeːtən] vt, vi to pray

beteuern [bəˈtɔʏərn] vt to assert; (Unschuld) to protest

Beteuerung f assertion; protestation; assurance

Beton [beˈtɔ̃] (-s, -s) m concrete

betonen [bəˈtoːnən] vt to stress

betonieren [betoˈniːrən] vt to concrete

Betonung f stress, emphasis

betören [bəˈtøːrən] vt to beguile

betr. abk (= betrifft) re

Betracht [bəˈtraxt] m: **in ~ kommen** to be considered od relevant;

etw in ~ ziehen to take sth into consideration; **außer ~ bleiben** not to be considered; **b~en** vt to look at; (fig) to look at, to consider; **~er(in)** (-s, -) m(f) observer

beträchtlich [bəˈtrɛçtlɪç] adj considerable

Betrachtung f (Ansehen) examination; (Erwägung) consideration

Betrag [bəˈtraːk] (-(e)s, **e**) m amount; **b~en** [bəˈtraːgən] (unreg) vt to amount to ♦ vr to behave; **~en** (-s) nt behaviour

Betreff m: **Ihr Schreiben vom ...** re your letter of ...

betreffen [bəˈtrɛfən] (unreg) vt to concern, to affect; **was mich betrifft** as for me; **~d** adj relevant, in question

betreffs [bəˈtrɛfs] präp +gen concerning, regarding; (COMM) re

betreiben [bəˈtraɪbən] (unreg) vt (ausüben) to practise; (Politik) to follow; (Studien) to pursue; (vorantreiben) to push ahead; (TECH: antreiben) to drive

betreten [bəˈtreːtən] (unreg) vt to enter; (Bühne etc) to step onto ♦ adj embarrassed; **B~ verboten** keep off/out

Betreuer(in) [bəˈtrɔʏər] (-s, -) m(f) (einer Person) minder; (eines Gebäude, Arbeitsgebiet) caretaker; (SPORT) coach

Betreuung f care

Betrieb [bəˈtriːp] (-(e)s, -e) m (Firma) firm, concern; (Anlage) plant; (Tätigkeit) operation; (Treiben) traffic; **außer ~ sein** to be out of order; **in ~ sein** to be working

Betriebs- zW: **~ausflug** m works outing; **b~fähig** adj in working order; **~ferien** pl company holidays (BRIT), company vacation sg (US); **~klima** nt (working) atmosphere; **~kosten** pl running costs; **~rat** m workers' council; **b~sicher** adj safe (to operate); **~störung** f breakdown; **~system** nt (COMPUT) operating system; **~unfall** m industrial acci-

dent; ~**wirtschaft** f economics
betrinken [bə'trıŋkən] (unreg) vr to
get drunk
betroffen [bə'trɔfən] adj (bestürzt)
full of consternation; **von etw** ~
werden od sein to be affected by sth
betrüben [bə'try:bən] vt to grieve
betrübt [bə'try:pt] adj sorrowful,
grieved
Betrug [bə'tru:k] (-(e)s) m deception; (JUR) fraud
betrügen [bə'try:gən] (unreg) vt to
cheat; (JUR) to defraud; (Ehepart-
ner) to be unfaithful to ♦ vr to deceive o.s.
Betrüger (-s, -) m cheat, deceiver;
b~isch adj deceitful; (JUR) fraudulent
betrunken [bə'trʊŋkən] adj drunk
Bett [bɛt] (-(e)s, -en) nt bed; **ins od
zu** ~ **gehen** to go to bed; ~**bezug** m
duvet cover; ~**decke** f blanket;
(Daunen~) quilt; (Überwurf) bed-
spread
Bettel- ['bɛtəl] zW: **b~arm** adj very
poor, destitute; ~**ei** [bɛtə'laı] f beg-
ging; **b~n** vi to beg
bettlägerig ['bɛtlɛːgərıç] adj bedrid-
den
Bettlaken nt sheet
Bettler(in) ['bɛtlər(ın)] (-s, -) m(f)
beggar
Bett- zW: ~**(t)uch** nt sheet; ~**vorle-
ger** m bedside rug; ~**wäsche** f bed
linen; ~**zeug** nt bedlinen pl
beugen ['bɔygən] vt to bend;
(GRAM) to inflect ♦ vr (sich fügen)
to bow
Beule ['bɔylə] f bump, swelling
beunruhigen [bə'ʊnru:ıgən] vt to
disturb, to alarm ♦ vr to become
worried
Beunruhigung f worry, alarm
beurlauben [bə'u:rlaʊbən] vt to
give leave of a holiday to (BRIT); to
grant vacation time to (US)
beurteilen [bə'ʊrtaılən] vt to judge;
(Buch etc) to review
Beurteilung f judgement; review;
(Note) mark

Beute ['bɔytə] (-) f booty, loot
Beutel (-s, -) m bag; (Geld~) purse;
(Tabak~) pouch
Bevölkerung [bə'fœlkərʊŋ] f population
bevollmächtigen [bə'fɔlmɛçtıgən]
vt to authorize
Bevollmächtigte(r) mf authorized
agent
bevor [bə'fo:r] konj before; ~**mun-
den** vt insep to treat like a child;
~**stehen** (unreg) vi: (jdm) ~**stehen**
to be in store (for sb); ~**stehend** adj
imminent, approaching; ~**zugen** vt
insep to prefer
bewachen [bə'vaxən] vt to watch, to
guard
Bewachung f (Bewachen) guard-
ing; (Leute) guard, watch
bewaffnen [bə'vafnən] vt to arm
Bewaffnung f (Vorgang) arming;
(Ausrüstung) armament, arms pl
bewahren [bə'va:rən] vt to keep;
jdn vor jdm/etw ~ to save sb from
sth/sb
bewähren [bə'vɛːrən] vr to prove
o.s.; (Maschine) to prove its worth
bewahrheiten [bə'va:rhaıtən] vr to
come true
bewährt adj reliable
Bewährung f (JUR) probation
bewältigen [bə'vɛltıgən] vt to overcome; (Arbeit) to finish; (Portion) to
manage
bewandert [bə'vandərt] adj expert,
knowledgeable
bewässern [bə'vɛsərn] vt to irrigate
Bewässerung f irrigation
bewegen [bə've:gən] vt, vr to move;
jdn zu etw ~ to induce sb to do sth;
~**d** adj touching, moving
Beweg- [bə've:k] zW: ~**grund** m
motive; **b~lich** adj movable, mobile;
(flink) quick; **b~t** adj (Leben) eventful; (Meer) rough; (ergriffen)
touched
Bewegung f movement, motion;
(innere) emotion; (körperlich) exercise; ~**sfreiheit** f freedom of movement; (fig) freedom of action;

b~slos adj motionless

Beweis [bəˈvaɪs] (-es, -e) m proof; (Zeichen) sign; b~en (unreg) vt to prove; (zeigen) to show; ~mittel nt evidence

Bewerb- [bəˈvɛrb] zW: b~en (unreg) vr to apply (for); ~er(in) (-s, -) m(f) applicant; ~ung f application

bewerkstelligen [bəˈvɛrkʃtɛlɪɡən] vt to manage, to accomplish

bewerten [bəˈvɛːrtən] vt to assess

bewilligen [bəˈvɪlɪɡən] vt to grant, to allow

Bewilligung f granting

bewirken [bəˈvɪrkən] vt to cause, to bring about

bewirten [bəˈvɪrtən] vt to feed, to entertain (to a meal)

bewirtschaften [bəˈvɪrtʃaftən] vt to manage

Bewirtung f hospitality

bewog etc [bəˈvoːk] v siehe bewegen

bewohn- [bəˈvoːn] zW: ~bar adj habitable; ~en vt to inhabit, to live in; B~er(in) (-s, -) m(f) inhabitant; (von Haus) resident

bewölkt [bəˈvœlkt] adj cloudy, overcast

Bewölkung f clouds pl

Bewunder- [bəˈvʊndər] zW: ~er (-s, -) m admirer; b~n vt to admire; b~nswert adj admirable, wonderful; ~ung f admiration

bewußt [bəˈvʊst] adj conscious; (absichtlich) deliberate; sich dat einer Sache gen ~ sein to be aware of sth; ~los adj unconscious; B~losigkeit f unconsciousness; B~sein nt consciousness; bei B~sein conscious

bezahlen [bəˈtsaːlən] vt to pay for

Bezahlung f payment

bezaubern [bəˈtsaʊbərn] vt to enchant, to charm

bezeichnen [bəˈtsaɪçnən] vt (kennzeichnen) to mark; (nennen) to call; (beschreiben) to describe; (zeigen) to show, to indicate; ~d adj: ~d (für) characteristic (of), typical (of)

Bezeichnung f (Zeichen) mark, sign; (Beschreibung) description

bezeugen [bəˈtsɔʏɡən] vt to testify to

Bezichtigung [bəˈtsɪçtɪɡʊŋ] f accusation

beziehen [bəˈtsiːən] (unreg) vt (mit Überzug) to cover; (Bett) to make; (Haus, Position) to move into; (Standpunkt) to take up; (erhalten) to receive; (Zeitung) to subscribe to, to take ↓ vr (Himmel) to cloud over; etw auf jdn/etw ~ to relate sth to sb/sth; sich ~ auf +akk to refer to

Beziehung f (Verbindung) connection; (Zusammenhang) relation; (Verhältnis) relationship; (Hinsicht) respect; ~en haben (vorteilhaft) to have connections or contacts; b~sweise adv or; (genauer gesagt auch) that is, or rather

Bezirk [bəˈtsɪrk] (-(e)s, -e) m district

Bezug [bəˈtsuːk] (-(e)s, -e) m (Hülle) covering; (COMM) ordering; (Gehalt) income, salary; (Beziehung) ~ (zu) relation(ship) (to); in b~ auf +akk with reference to; ~ nehmen auf +akk to refer to

bezüglich [bəˈtsyːklɪç] präp +gen concerning, referring to ↓ adj (GRAM) relative; auf etw akk ~ relating to sth

bezwecken [bəˈtsvɛkən] vt to aim at

bezweifeln [bəˈtsvaɪfəln] vt to doubt, to query

BH m abk von Büstenhalter

Bhf. abk (= Bahnhof) station

Bibel [ˈbiːbəl] (-, -n) f Bible

Biber [ˈbiːbər] (-s, -) m beaver

Biblio- [biblio] zW: ~graphie [-graˈfiː] f bibliography; ~thek [-ˈteːk] (-, -en) f library; ~thekar(in) [-teˈkaːr(ɪn)] (-s, -e) m(f) librarian

biblisch [ˈbiːblɪʃ] adj biblical

bieder [ˈbiːdər] adj upright, worthy; (Kleid etc) plain

bieg- [ˈbiːk] zW: ~en (unreg) vt, vr to bend ↓ vi to turn; ~sam [ˈbiːk-] adj flexible; B~ung f bend, curve

Biene ['biːnə] f bee

Bienenhonig m honey

Bienenwachs nt beeswax

Bier [biːr] (-(e)s, -e) nt beer; **~deckel** m beer mat; **~krug** m beer mug

Biest [biːst] (-s, -er umg: pej) nt (Tier) beast, creature; (Mensch) beast

bieten ['biːtən] (unreg) vt to offer; (bei Versteigerung) to bid ♦ vr (Gelegenheit): **sich jdm ~** to present itself to sb; **sich** dat **etw ~ lassen** to put up with sth

Bikini [bi'kiːni] (-s, -s) m bikini

Bilanz [bi'lants] f balance; (fig) outcome; **~ ziehen (aus)** to take stock (of)

Bild [bɪlt] (-(e)s, -er) nt (auch fig) picture; photo; (Spiegel~) reflection; **~bericht** m photographic report

bilden ['bɪldən] vt to form; (erziehen) to educate; (ausmachen) to constitute ♦ vr to arise; (erziehen) to educate o.s.

Bilderbuch nt picture book

Bilderrahmen m picture frame

Bild- zW: **~fläche** f screen; (fig) scene; **~hauer** (-s, -) m sculptor; **b~hübsch** adj lovely, pretty as a picture; **b~lich** adj figurative; pictorial; **~schirm** m television screen; (COMPUT) monitor; **b~schön** adj lovely; **~ung** [-dʊŋ] f formation; (Wissen, Benehmen) education

Billard ['bɪljart] (-s, -e) nt billiards sg; **~kugel** f billiard ball

billig ['bɪlɪç] adj cheap; (gerecht) fair, reasonable; **~en** ['bɪlɪgən] vt to approve of

Binde ['bɪndə] f bandage; (Arm~) band; (MED) sanitary towel; **~gewebe** nt connective tissue; **~glied** nt connecting link; **b~n** (unreg) vt to bind, to tie; **~strich** m hyphen; **~wort** nt conjunction

Bindfaden m string

Bindung f bond, tie; (Ski~) binding

binnen ['bɪnən] präp (+dat od gen) within; **B~hafen** m river port; **B~handel** m internal trade

Binse ['bɪnzə] f rush, reed; **~nwahrheit** f truism

Bio- [bio] in zW bio-; **~chemie** f biochemistry; **~graphie** [-gra'fiː] f biography; **~loge** [-'loːgə] (-n, -n) m biologist; **~logie** [-lo'giː] f biology; **b~logisch** [-'loːgɪʃ] adj biological; **~top** m od nt biotope

Birke ['bɪrkə] f birch

Birnbaum m pear tree

Birne ['bɪrnə] f pear; (ELEK) (light) bulb

SCHLÜSSELWORT

bis [bɪs] präp +akk, adv **1** (zeitlich) till, until; (bis spätestens) by; **Sie haben bis Dienstag Zeit** you have until od till Tuesday; **bis Dienstag muß es fertig sein** it must be ready by Tuesday; **bis auf weiteres** until further notice; **bis in die Nacht** into the night; **bis bald/gleich** see you later/soon

2 (räumlich) (up) to; **ich fahre bis Köln** I'm going to od I'm going as far as Cologne; **bis an unser Grundstück** (right od up) to our plot; **bis hierher** this far

3 (bei Zahlen) up to; **bis zu** up to

4: **bis auf etw** akk (außer) except sth; (einschließlich) including sth

♦ konj **1** (mit Zahlen) 10 bis 20 10 to 20

2 (zeitlich) till, until; **bis es dunkel wird** till od until it gets dark; **von ... bis ...** from ... to ...

Bischof ['bɪʃɔf] (-s, -e) m bishop

bischöflich ['bɪʃøːflɪç] adj episcopal

bisher [bɪs'heːr] adv till now, hitherto; **~ig** adj till now

Biskuit [bɪs'kviːt] (-(e)s, -s od -e) m od nt (fatless) sponge

Biß [bɪs] (-sses, -sse) m bite

biß etc vb siehe **beißen**

bißchen ['bɪsçən] adj, adv bit

Bissen ['bɪsən] (-s, -) m bite, morsel

bissig ['bɪsɪç] adj (Hund) snappy; (Bemerkung) cutting, biting

bist [bɪst] vb siehe **sein**

bisweilen ['bɪs'vaɪlən] *adv* at times, occasionally

Bit [bɪt] *nt* (*COMPUT*) bit

Bitte ['bɪtə] *f* request; **b~** *excl* please; (*wie b~?*) (I beg your) pardon? ♦ *interj;* (*als Antwort auf Dank*) you're welcome; **darf ich? – aber b~!** may I? – please do; **b~ schön!** it was a pleasure; **b~n** (*unreg*) *vt, vi:* **b~n (um)** to ask (for); **b~nd** *adj* pleading, imploring

bitter ['bɪtər] *adj* bitter; **~böse** *adj* very angry; **B~keit** *f* bitterness; **~lich** *adj* bitter

Blähungen ['blɛːʊŋən] *pl* (*MED*) wind *sg*

blamabel [bla'maːbəl] *adj* disgraceful

Blamage [bla'maːʒə] *f* disgrace

blamieren [bla'miːrən] *vr* to make a fool of o.s., to disgrace o.s. ♦ *vt* to let down, to disgrace

blank [blaŋk] *adj* bright; (*unbedeckt*) bare; (*sauber*) clean, polished; (*umg: ohne Geld*) broke; (*offensichtlich*) blatant

blanko ['blaŋko] *adv* blank; **B~scheck** *m* blank cheque

Bläschen ['blɛːsçən] *nt* bubble; (*MED*) (small) blister

Blase ['blaːzə] *f* bubble; (*MED*) blister; (*ANAT*) bladder; **~balg** (-(e)s, -bälge) *m* bellows *pl;* **b~n** (*unreg*) *vt, vi* to blow

Blas- ['blaːs] *zW:* **~instrument** *nt* wind instrument; **~kapelle** *f* brass band

blaß [blas] *adj* pale

Blässe ['blɛsə] (-) *f* paleness, pallor

Blatt [blat] (-(e)s, ̈er) *nt* leaf; (*von Papier*) sheet; (*Zeitung*) newspaper; (*KARTEN*) hand

blättern ['blɛtərn] *vi:* **in etw** *dat* **~** to leaf through sth

Blätterteig *m* flaky *od* puff pastry

blau [blaʊ] *adj* blue; (*umg*) drunk, stoned; (*KOCH*) boiled; (*Auge*) black; **~er Fleck** bruise; **Fahrt ins B~e** mystery tour; **~äugig** *adj* blue-eyed

Blech [blɛç] (-(e)s, -e) *nt* tin, sheet metal; (*Back~*) baking tray; **~büchse** *f* tin, can; **~dose** *f* tin, can; **b~en** (*umg*) *vt, vi* to fork out; **~schaden** *m* (*AUT*) damage to bodywork

Blei [blaɪ] (-(e)s, -e) *nt* lead

Bleibe ['blaɪbə] *f* roof over one's head; **b~n** (*unreg*) *vi* to stay, to remain; **b~nd** *adj* (*Erinnerung*) lasting (*Schaden*) permanent; **b~nlassen** (*unreg*) *vt* to leave (alone)

bleich [blaɪç] *adj* faded, pale; **~en** *vt* to bleach

Blei- *zW:* **b~ern** *adj* leaden; **b~frei** *adj* (*Benzin*) lead-free; **~stift** *m* pencil; **~stiftspitzer** *m* pencil sharpener

Blende ['blɛndə] *f* (*PHOT*) aperture; **b~n** *vt* to blind, to dazzle; (*fig*) to hoodwink; **b~nd** (*umg*) *adj* grand; **b~nd aussehen** to look smashing

Blick [blɪk] (-(e)s, -e) *m* (*kurz*) glance, glimpse; (*Anschauen*) look; (*Aussicht*) view; **b~en** *vi* to look; **sich b~en lassen** to put in an appearance; **~fang** *m* eye-catcher

blieb *etc* [bliːp] *vb siehe* **bleiben**

blind [blɪnt] *adj* blind; (*Glas etc*) dull; **~er Passagier** stowaway; **B~darm** *m* appendix; **B~darmentzündung** *f* appendicitis; **B~enschrift** ['blɪndən-] *f* braille; **B~heit** *f* blindness; **~lings** *adv* blindly; **B~schleiche** *f* slow worm

blinken ['blɪŋkən] *vi* to twinkle, to sparkle; (*Licht*) to flash, to signal; (*AUT*) to indicate ♦ *vt* to flash, to signal

Blinker (-s, -) *m* (*AUT*) indicator

Blinklicht *nt* (*AUT*) indicator; (*an Bahnübergangen usw*) flashing light

blinzeln ['blɪntsəln] *vi* to blink, to wink

Blitz [blɪts] (-es, -e) *m* (*flash of*) lightning; **~ableiter** *m* lightning conductor; **b~en** *vi* (*aufleuchten*) to flash, to sparkle; **es b~t** (*MET*) there's a flash of lightning; **~licht** *nt* flashlight; **b~schnell** *adj* lightning *adv* (as) quick as a flash

Block [blɔk] (-(e)s, ≈e) *m* block; (*von Papier*) pad; **~ade** [blɔ'ka:də] *f* blockade; **~flöte** *f* recorder; **b~frei** *adj* (*POL*) unaligned; **b~ieren** [blɔ'ki:rən] *vt* to block ♦ *vi* (*Räder*) to jam; **~schrift** *f* block letters *pl*

blöd [blø:t] *adj* silly, stupid; **~eln** ['blø:dəln] (*umg*) *vi* to act the goat (*fam*), to fool around; **B~sinn** *m* nonsense; **b~sinnig** *adj* silly, idiotic

blond [blɔnt] *adj* blonde, fair-haired

bloß [blo:s] *adj* **1** (*unbedeckt*) bare; (*nackt*) naked; **mit der bloßen Hand** with one's bare hand; **mit bloßem Auge** with the naked eye
2 (*alleinig, nur*) mere; **der bloße Gedanke** the very thought; **bloßer Neid** sheer envy
♦ *adv* only, merely; **laß das bloß!** just don't do that!; **wie ist das bloß passiert?** how on earth did that happen?

Blöße ['blø:sə] *f* bareness; nakedness; (*fig*) weakness

bloßlegen *vt* to expose

bloßstellen *vt* to show up

blühen ['bly:ən] *vi* to bloom (*lit*), to be in bloom; (*fig*) to flourish

blühend *adj* (*Pflanze*) blooming; (*Aussehen*) blooming, radiant; (*Handel*) thriving, booming

Blume ['blu:mə] *f* flower; (*von Wein*) bouquet; **~nkohl** *m* cauliflower; **~ntopf** *m* flowerpot; **~nzwiebel** *f* bulb

Bluse ['blu:zə] *f* blouse

Blut [blu:t] (-(e)s) *nt* blood; **b~arm** *adj* anaemic; (*fig*) penniless; **b~befleckt** *adj* bloodstained; **~druck** *m* blood pressure

Blüte ['bly:tə] *f* blossom; (*fig*) prime

Blutegel *m* leech

bluten *vi* to bleed

Bluter *m* (*MED*) haemophiliac

Bluterguß *m* haemorrhage; (*auf Haut*) bruise

Blütezeit *f* flowering period; (*fig*) prime

Blut- *zW*: **~gruppe** *f* blood group; **b~ig** *adj* bloody; **b~jung** *adj* very young; **~probe** *f* blood test; **~spender** *m* blood donor; **~transfusion** *f* (*MED*) blood transfusion; **~ung** *f* bleeding, haemorrhage; **~vergiftung** *f* blood poisoning; **~wurst** *f* black pudding

Bö [bø:] (-, -en) *f* squall

Bock [bɔk] (-(e)s, ≈e) *m* buck, ram; (*Gestell*) trestle, support; (*SPORT*) buck; **~wurst** *f* type of pork sausage

Boden ['bo:dən] (-s, ≈) *m* ground; (*Fuß~*) floor; (*Meeres~, Faß~*) bottom; (*Speicher*) attic; **b~los** *adj* bottomless; (*umg*) incredible; **~schätze** *pl* mineral resources; **~see** *m*: **der ~see** Lake Constance; **~turnen** *nt* floor exercises *pl*

Böe ['bø:ə] *f* squall

Bogen ['bo:gən] (-s, -) *m* (*Biegung*) curve; (*ARCHIT*) arch; (*Waffe, MUS*) bow; (*Papier*) sheet

Bohle ['bo:lə] *f* plank

Bohne ['bo:nə] *f* bean

bohnern *vt* to wax, to polish

Bohnerwachs *nt* floor polish

Bohr- ['bo:r] *zW*: **b~en** *vt* to bore; **~er** (-s, -) *m* drill; **~insel** *f* oil rig; **~maschine** *f* drill; **~turm** *m* derrick

Boje ['bo:jə] *f* buoy

Bolivien [bo'li:viən] *nt* Bolivia

Bolzen ['bɔltsən] (-s, -) *m* bolt

bombardieren [bɔmbar'di:rən] *vt* to bombard; (*aus der Luft*) to bomb

Bombe ['bɔmbə] *f* bomb

Bombenangriff *m* bombing raid

Bombenerfolg (*umg*) *m* smash hit

Bon (-s, -s) *m* voucher, chit

Bonbon [bõ'bõ:] (-s, -s) *nt od nt* sweet

Boot [bo:t] (-(e)s, -e) *nt* boat

Bord [bɔrt] (-(e)s, -e) *m* (*AVIAT, NAUT*) board; *nt* (*Brett*) shelf; **an ~** on board

Bordell [bɔr'dɛl] (-s, -e) *nt* brothel

Bordstein *m* kerb(stone)

borgen ['bɔrgən] *vt* to borrow; jdm

etw ~ to lend sb sth

Borke ['bɔrkə] f (BOT) bark

borniert [bɔr'niːrt] adj narrow-minded

Börse ['bœrzə] f stock exchange; (Geld~) purse; **~nmakler** m stockbroker

Borste ['bɔrstə] f bristle

Borte ['bɔrtə] f edging; (Band) trimming

bös [bøːs] adj = böse

bösartig ['bøːsaːrtiç] adj malicious

Böschung ['bœʃuŋ] f slope; (Ufer etc) embankment

böse ['bøːzə] adj bad, evil; (zornig) angry

boshaft ['bɔshaft] adj malicious, spiteful

Bosheit f malice, spite

Bosnien und Herzegowina ['bɔsniən, hɛrtseˈgoːvina] nt Bosnia (and) Herzegovina

böswillig ['bøːsvɪliç] adj malicious

bot etc [boːt] vb siehe **bieten**

Botanik [boˈtaːnɪk] f botany

botanisch [boˈtaːnɪʃ] adj botanical

Bot- [boːt] zW: **~e** (-n, -n) m messenger; **~schaft** f message, news; (POL) embassy; **~schafter** (-s, -) m ambassador

Bottich ['bɔtiç] (-(e)s, -e) m vat, tub

Bouillon [buˈljõː] (-, -s) f consommé

Bowle ['boːlə] f punch

Box- ['bɔks] zW: **b~en** vi to box; **~er** (-s, -) m boxer; **~handschuh** m boxing glove; **~kampf** m boxing match

boykottieren [bɔykɔˈtiːrən] vt to boycott

brach etc [braːx] vb siehe **brechen**

brachte etc ['braxtə] vb siehe **bringen**

Branche ['brãːʃə] f line of business; **~nverzeichnis** nt yellow pages pl

Brand [brant] (-(e)s, ≈e) m fire; (MED) gangrene; **b~en** ['brandən] vi to surge; (Meer) to break; **b~marken** vt to brand; (fig) to stigmatize; **~salbe** f ointment for burns; **~stifter** [-ʃtɪftər] m arsonist, fireraiser; **~stiftung** f arson; **~ung** f surf

Branntwein ['brantvain] m brandy

Brasilien [braˈziːliən] nt Brazil

Brat- ['braːt] zW: **~apfel** m baked apple; **b~en** (unreg) vt to roast; to fry; **~en** (-s, -) m roast; joint; **~hähnchen** nt roast chicken; **~huhn** nt roast chicken; **~kartoffeln** pl fried od roast potatoes; **~pfanne** f frying pan

Bratsche ['braːtʃə] f viola

Bratspieß m spit

Bratwurst f grilled/fried sausage

Brauch [braux] (-(e)s, Bräuche) m custom; **b~bar** adj usable, serviceable; (Person) capable; **b~en** vt (bedürfen) to need; (müssen) to have to; (inf: verwenden) to use

Braue ['brauə] f brow

brauen vt to brew

Braue'rei f brewery

braun [braun] adj brown; (von Sonne auch) tanned

Bräune ['brɔynə] (-) f brownness; (Sonnen~) tan; **b~n** vt to make brown; (Sonne) to tan

braungebrannt adj tanned

Brause ['brauzə] f shower bath; (von Gießkanne) rose; (Getränk) lemonade; **b~n** vi to roar; (auch vr: duschen) to take a shower

Braut [braut] (-, Bräute) f bride; (Verlobte) fiancée

Bräutigam ['brɔytigam] (-s, -e) m bridegroom; fiancé

Brautpaar nt bride and (bride)groom, bridal pair

brav [braːf] adj (artig) good; (ehrenhaft) worthy, honest

bravo ['braːvo] excl well done

BRD ['beːˈʔɛr'deː] f abk = **Bundesrepublik Deutschland**

Brech- ['brɛç] zW: **~eisen** nt crowbar; **b~en** (unreg) vt, vi to break; (Licht) to refract; (fig: Mensch) to crush; (speien) to vomit; **~reiz** m nausea, retching

Brei [brai] (-(e)s, -e) m (Masse) pulp; (KOCH) gruel; (Hafer~) porridge

breit [braɪt] *adj* wide, broad; **B~e** *f* width; (*esp bei Maßangaben*) breadth; (*GEOG*) latitude; ~en vt: etw über etw *akk* ~en to spread sth over sth; **B~engrad** *m* degree of latitude; ~machen *vr* to spread o.s. out; ~treten (*unreg; umg*) *vt* to go on about

Brems- [brems] *zW:* ~belag *m* brake lining; ~e [-zə] *f* brake; (*ZOOL*) horsefly; **b~en** [-zən] *vi* to brake ♦ *vt* (*Auto*) to brake; (*fig*) to slow down; ~flüssigkeit *f* brake fluid; ~licht *nt* brake light; ~pedal *nt* brake pedal; ~spur *f* skid mark(s *pl*); ~weg *m* braking distance

Brenn- [bren] *zW:* ~bar *adj* inflammable; **b~en** (*unreg*) *vi* to burn, to be on fire; (*Licht, Kerze etc*) to burn ♦ *vt* (*Holz etc*) to burn; (*Ziegel, Ton*) to fire; (*Kaffee*) to roast; **darauf b~en, etw zu tun** to be dying to do sth; ~(n)essel *f* stinging nettle; ~punkt *m* (*PHYS*) focal point; (*Mittelpunkt*) focus; ~spiritus *m* methylated spirits; ~stoff *m* fuel

brenzlig ['brentslɪç] *adj* precarious

Brett [bret] (-(e)s, -er) *nt* board, plank; (*Bord*) shelf; (*Spiel~*) board; ~er *pl* (*SKI*) skis; (*THEAT*) boards; **Schwarze(s)** ~ notice board; ~erzaun *m* wooden fence; ~spiel *nt* board game

Brezel ['bre:tsəl] (-, -n) *f* pretzel

brichst *vb siehe* **brechen**

Brief [bri:f] (-(e)s, -e) *m* letter; ~freund(in) *m(f)* pen friend; ~kasten *m* letterbox; **b~lich** *adj, adv* by letter; ~marke *f* (postage) stamp; ~öffner *m* letter opener; ~papier *nt* notepaper; ~tasche *f* wallet; ~träger *m* postman; ~umschlag *m* envelope; ~waage *f* letter scales; ~wechsel *m* correspondence

briet *etc vb siehe* **braten**

Brikett [bri'kɛt] (-s, -s) *nt* briquette

brillant [brɪl'jant] *adj* (*fig*) brilliant; **B~** (-en, -en) *m* brilliant, diamond

Brille ['brɪlə] *f* spectacles *pl*; (*Schutz~*) goggles *pl*; (*Toiletten~*) (toilet) seat; ~ngestell *nt* (spectacle) frames

bringen ['brɪŋən] (*unreg*) *vt* to bring; (*mitnehmen, begleiten*) to take; (*einbringen: Profit*) to bring in; (*veröffentlichen*) to publish; (*THEAT, CINE*) to show; (*RADIO, TV*) to broadcast; (*in einen Zustand versetzen*) to get; (*umg: tun können*) to manage; **jdn dazu** ~, etw zu tun to make sb do sth; **jdn nach Hause** ~ to take sb home; **jdn um etw** ~ to make sb lose sth; **jdn auf eine Idee** ~ to give sb an idea

Brise ['bri:zə] *f* breeze

Brit- ['brɪt] *zW:* ~e *m* Briton; ~in *f* Briton; **b~isch** *adj* British

bröckelig ['brœkəlɪç] *adj* crumbly

Brocken ['brɔkən] (-s, -) *m* piece, bit; (*Fels~*) lump of rock

brodeln ['bro:dəln] *vi* to bubble

Brokat [bro'ka:t] (-(e)s, -e) *m* brocade

Brokkoli ['brɔkoli] *pl* (*BOT*) broccoli

Brombeere ['brɔmbe:rə] *f* blackberry, bramble (*BRIT*)

Bronchien ['brɔnçiən] *pl* bronchia(l tubes) *pl*

Bronchitis (-) *f* bronchitis

Bronze ['brɔ:sə] *f* bronze

Brosche ['brɔʃə] *f* brooch

Broschüre [brɔ'ʃy:rə] *f* pamphlet

Brot [bro:t] (-(e)s, -e) *nt* bread; (*Laib*) loaf

Brötchen ['brø:tçən] *nt* roll

Bruch [brux] (-(e)s, ⸚e) *m* breakage; (*zerbrochene Stelle*) break; (*fig*) split, breach; (*MED: Eingeweide~*) rupture, hernia; (*Bein~ etc*) fracture; (*MATH*) fraction

brüchig ['bryçɪç] *adj* brittle, fragile; (*Haus*) dilapidated

Bruch- *zW:* ~landung *f* crash landing; ~strich *m* (*MATH*) line; ~stück *nt* fragment; ~teil *m* fraction; ~zahl [bruxtsa:l] *f* (*MATH*) fraction

Brücke ['brykə] *f* bridge; (*Teppich*)

rug

Bruder ['bruːdər] (-s, ꞏꞏ) m brother

brüderlich ['bryːdərlɪç] adj brotherly

Brühe ['bryːə] f broth, stock; (pej) muck; **Brühwürfel** m (KOCH) stock cube

brüllen ['brʏlən] vi to bellow, to roar

brummen ['brʊmən] vi (Bär, Mensch etc) to growl; (Insekt) to buzz; (Motoren) to roar; (murren) to grumble ♦ vt to growl

brünett [bry'nɛt] adj brunette, dark-haired

Brunnen ['brʊnən] (-s, -) m fountain; (tief) well; (natürlich) spring

brüsk [brʏsk] adj abrupt, brusque

Brust [brʊst] (-, ꞏe) f breast; (Männer-) chest

brüsten ['brʏstən] vr to boast

Brust- zW: **~fellentzündung** f pleurisy; **~kasten** m chest; **~schwimmen** nt breast-stroke

Brüstung ['brʏstʊŋ] f parapet

Brut [bruːt] (-, -en) f brood; (Brüten) hatching

brutal [bru'taːl] adj brutal; **B~i'tät** f brutality

brüten ['bryːtən] vi (auch fig) to brood

Brutkasten m incubator

brutto ['brʊto] adv gross; **B~einkommen** nt gross salary; **B~gehalt** nt gross salary; **B~gewicht** nt gross weight; **B~lohn** m gross wages pl; **B~sozialprodukt** nt gross national product

Bube ['buːbə] (-n, -n) m (Schurke) rogue; (KARTEN) jack

Buch [buːx] (-(e)s, ꞏer) nt book; (COMM) account book; **~binder** m bookbinder; **~drucker** m printer

Buche f beech tree

buchen vt to book; (Betrag) to enter

Bücher- ['byːçər] zW: **~brett** nt bookshelf; **~ei** [-'raɪ] f library; **~regal** nt bookshelves pl, bookcase; **~schrank** m bookcase

Buch- zW: **~fink** m chaffinch; **~führung** f book-keeping, accounting; **~halter(in)** (-s, -) m(f) book-

keeper; **~handel** m book trade; **~händler(in)** m(f) bookseller; **~handlung** f bookshop

Büchse ['bʏksə] f tin, can; (Holz-) box; (Gewehr) rifle; **~nfleisch** nt tinned meat; **~nmilch** f (KOCH) evaporated milk, tinned milk; **~nöffner** m tin od can opener

Buch- zW: **~stabe** ['buːxʃtaːbə] (-ns, -n) m letter (of the alphabet); **b~stabieren** [buːxʃta'biːrən] vt to spell; **b~stäblich** ['buːxʃtɛːplɪç] adj literal

Bucht [bʊxt] (-, -en) f bay

Buchung ['buːxʊŋ] f booking; (COMM) entry

Buckel ['bʊkəl] (-s, -) m hump

bücken ['bʏkən] vr to bend

Bückling ['bʏklɪŋ] m (Fisch) kipper; (Verbeugung) bow

Bude ['buːdə] f booth, stall; (umg) digs pl (BRIT)

Büfett [bʏ'feː] (-s, -s) nt (Anrichte) sideboard; (Geschirrschrank) dresser; **kaltes ~** cold buffet

Büffel ['bʏfəl] (-s, -) m buffalo

Bug [buːk] (-(e)s, -e) m (NAUT) bow; (AVIAT) nose

Bügel ['byːgəl] (-s, -) m (Kleider-) hanger; (Steig-) stirrup; (Brillen-) arm; **~brett** nt ironing board; **~eisen** nt iron; **~falte** f crease; **b~frei** adj crease-resistant, noniron; **b~n** vt, vi to iron

Bühne ['byːnə] f stage; **~nbild** nt set, scenery

Buhruf ['buːruːf] m boo

buk etc [buːk] vb siehe backen

Bulgarien [bʊl'gaːriən] nt Bulgaria

Bullauge nt (NAUT) porthole

Bull- [bʊl] zW: **~dogge** f bulldog; **~dozer** ['bʊldoːzər] (-s, -) m bulldozer; **~e** (-n, -n) m bull

Bumerang ['buːmeraŋ] (-s, -e) m boomerang

Bummel ['bʊməl] (-s, -) m stroll; (Schaufenster-) window-shopping; **~ant** [-'lant] m slowcoach; **~ei** f wandering; dawdling; skiving; **b~n** vi to wander, to stroll; (trödeln)

dawdle; *(faulenzen)* to skive, to loaf around; **~streik** [ˈbʊndʃtraɪk] *m* go-slow

Bund¹ [bʊnt] (-(e)s, ⸚e) *m (Freundschafts~ etc)* bond; *(Organisation)* union; *(POL)* confederacy; *(Hosen~, Rock~)* waistband

Bund² (-(e)s, -e) *nt* bunch; *(Stroh~)* bundle

Bündel [ˈbʏndəl] (-s, -) *nt* bundle, bale; **b~n** *vt* to bundle

Bundes- [ˈbʊndəs] *in zW* Federal *(bes West German)*; **~bahn** *f* Federal Railways *pl*; **~bürger** *m* West German citizen; **~hauptstadt** *f* Federal capital; **~kanzler** *m* Federal Chancellor; **~land** *nt* Land; **~liga** *f* football league; **~präsident** *m* Federal President; **~rat** *m* upper house of West German Parliament; **~regierung** *f* Federal government; **~republik** *f* Federal Republic (of West Germany); **~staat** *m* Federal state; **~tag** *m* West German Parliament; **~wehr** *f* West German Armed Forces *pl*

bündig *adj (kurz)* concise

Bündnis (-ses, -se) *nt* alliance

Bunker [ˈbʊŋkar] (-s, -) *m* bunker

bunt [bʊnt] *adj* coloured; *(gemischt)* mixed; **jdm wird es zu ~** it's getting too much for sb; **B~stift** *m* coloured pencil, crayon

Burg [bʊrk] (-, -en) *f* castle, fort

Bürge [ˈbʏrgə] (-n, -n) *m* guarantor; **b~n** *vi:* **b~n für** to vouch for

Bürger(in) [ˈbʏrgar(ɪn)] (-s, -) *m(f)* citizen; member of the middle class; **~krieg** *m* civil war; **b~lich** *adj (Rechte)* civil; *(Klasse)* middle-class; *(pej)* bourgeois; **~meister** *m* mayor; **~recht** *nt* civil rights *pl*; **~schaft** *f* population, citizens *pl*; **~steig** *m* pavement

Bürgschaft *f* surety; **~ leisten** to give security

Büro [byˈroː] (-s, -s) *nt* office; **~angestellte(r)** *mf* office worker; **~klammer** *f* paper clip; **~kra'tie** *f* bureaucracy; **b~'kratisch** *adj* bur-

eaucratic; **~schluß** *m* office closing time

Bursch (-en, -en) *m* = **Bursche**

Bursche [ˈbʊrʃə] (-n, -n) *m* lad, fellow; *(Diener)* servant

Bürste [ˈbʏrstə] *f* brush; **b~n** *vt* to brush

Bus [bʊs] (-ses, -se) *m* bus

Busch [bʊʃ] (-(e)s, ⸚e) *m* bush, shrub

Büschel [ˈbʏʃəl] (-s, -) *nt* tuft

buschig *adj* bushy

Busen [ˈbuːzən] (-s, -) *m* bosom; *(Meer~)* inlet, bay

Buße [ˈbuːsə] *f* atonement, penance; *(Geld)* fine

büßen [ˈbyːsən] *vi* to do penance, to atone ♦ *vt* to do penance for, to atone for

Bußgeld [ˈbuːsgɛlt] *nt* fine

Büste [ˈbʏstə] *f* bust; **~nhalter** *m* bra

Butter [ˈbʊtər] (-) *f* butter; **~blume** *f* buttercup; **~brot** *nt* (piece of) bread and butter; *(umg)* sandwich; **~brotpapier** *nt* greaseproof paper; **~dose** *f* butter dish; **b~weich** [ˈbʊtərvaɪç] *adj* soft as butter; *(fig, umg)* soft

b.w. *abk (= bitte wenden)* p.t.o.

bzgl. *abk (= bezüglich)* re

bzw. *abk* = **beziehungsweise**

C

ca. *abk (= circa)* approx.

Café [kaˈfeː] (-s, -s) *nt* café

Cafeteria [kafeteˈriːa] (-, -s) *f* cafeteria

Camp- [kɛmp] *zW:* **c~en** *vi* to camp; **~er** (-s, -) *m* camper; **~ing** (-s) *nt* camping; **~ingkocher** *m* camping stove; **~ingplatz** *m* camp(ing) site

CD *f abk (disc)* CD; **~-Spieler** *m* CD (player)

Cellist [tʃɛˈlɪst] *m* cellist

Cello [ˈtʃɛlo] (-s, -s *od* Celli) *nt* cello

Celsius [ˈtsɛlzius] (-) *nt* Celsius

Chamäleon [ka'mɛːleon] (-s, -e) nt chameleon

Champagner [ʃam'panjər] (-s, -) m champagne

Champignon ['ʃampinjõ] (-s, -s) m button mushroom

Chance ['ʃãːs(ə)] f chance, opportunity

Chaos ['kaːɔs] (-, -) nt chaos

chaotisch [ka'oːtiʃ] adj chaotic

Charakter [ka'raktər, pl karak'teːrə] (-s, -e) m character; **c~fest** adj of firm character, strong; **c~i'sieren** vt to characterize; **c~istisch**
c~istisch (für) [karak-teːristiʃ] adj: characteristic, typical (of); **c~los** adj unprincipled; **~losigkeit** f lack of principle; **~schwäche** f weakness of character; **~stärke** f strength of character; **~zug** m characteristic, trait

charmant [ʃar'mant] adj charming

Charme [ʃarm] (-s) m charm

Charterflug ['(t)ʃartərfluːk] m charter flight

Chauffeur [ʃo'føːr] m chauffeur

Chauvinist [ʃovi'nist] m chauvinist, jingoist

Chef [ʃɛf] (-s, -s) m head; (umg) boss; (~arzt m senior consultant; **~in** (umg) f boss

Chemie [çe'miː] (-) f chemistry; **~faser** f man-made fibre

Chemikalie [çemi'kaːliə] f chemical

Chemiker(in) ['çeːmikər(ın)] (-s, -) m (industrial) chemist

chemisch ['çeːmiʃ] adj chemical; **~e Reinigung** dry cleaning

Chicorée [ʃiko'reː] m od f chicory

Chiffre ['ʃifrə] f (Geheimzeichen) cipher; (in Zeitung) box number

Chile ['çiːlə, 'tʃiːlə] nt Chile

Chin- ['çiːn] zW: **~a** nt China; **~akohl** m Chinese leaves; **~ese** [çi-'neːzə] m Chinese; **~esin** f Chinese; **c~esisch** adj Chinese

Chirurg [çi'rʊrk] (-en, -en) m surgeon; **~ie** [-'giː] f surgery; **c~isch** adj surgical

Chlor [kloːr] (-s) nt chlorine; **~o'form** (-s) nt chloroform

Cholera ['koːlera] (-) f cholera

cholerisch [ko'leːrıʃ] adj choleric

Chor [koːr] (-(e)s, -e) m choir; (Musikstück, THEAT) chorus; **~al** [ko'raːl] (-s, -äle) m chorale

Choreograph [koreo'graːf] (-en, -en) m choreographer

Christ [krıst] (-en, -en) m Christian; **~baum** m Christmas tree; **~enheit** f Christendom; **~entum** nt Christianity; **~in** f Christian; **~kind** nt ~ Father Christmas; (Jesus) baby Jesus; **c~lich** adj Christian; **~us** (-) m Christ

Chrom [kroːm] (-s) nt (CHEM) chromium; chrome

Chron- ['kroːn] zW: **~ik** f chronicle; **c~isch** adj chronic; **c~ologisch** [-o'loːgıʃ] adj chronological

Chrysantheme [kryzan'teːmə] f chrysanthemum

circa ['tsırka] adv about, approximately

Clown [klaʊn] (-s, -s) m clown

Cocktail ['kɔkteːl] (-s, -s) m cocktail

Cola ['koːla] (-, -s) f Coke (®)

Computer [kɔm'pjuːtər] (-s, -) m computer; **~spiel** nt computer game

Conférencier [kõferãsi'eː] (-s, -s) m compère

Cord [kɔrt] (-s) m cord, corduroy

Couch [kaʊtʃ] (-, -es od -en) f couch

Coupé [ku'peː] (-s, -s) nt (AUT) coupé, sports version

Coupon [ku'põ] (-s, -s) m coupon; (Stoff~) length of cloth

Cousin [ku'zɛ̃] (-s, -s) m cousin; **~e** [ku'ziːnə] f cousin

Creme [krɛːm] (-, -s) f cream; (Schuh~) polish; (Zahn~) paste; (KOCH) mousse; **c~farben** adj cream(-coloured)

cremig adj creamy

Curry ['kœri] (-s) m od nt curry powder; **~pulver** nt curry powder

Cursor ['kœrsər] m cursor

Cutter ['katər(ın)] (-s, -) m (CINE) editor

D

SCHLÜSSELWORT
---

da [daː] *adv* **1** (*örtlich*) there; (*hier*) here; **da draußen** out there; **da bin ich** here I am; **da, wo** where; **ist noch Milch da?** is there any milk left?

2 (*zeitlich*) then; (*folglich*) so

3: **da haben wir Glück gehabt** we were lucky there; **da kann man nichts machen** nothing can be done about it

♦ *konj* (*weil*) as, since

dabehalten (*unreg*) *vt* to keep

dabei [daˈbaɪ] *adv* (*räumlich*) close to it; (*noch dazu*) besides; (*zusammen mit*) with them; (*zeitlich*) during this; (*obwohl doch*) but, however; **was ist schon ~?** what of it?; **es ist doch nichts ~, wenn ...** it doesn't matter if ...; **bleiben wir ~** let's leave it at that; **es bleibt ~** that's settled; **das Dumme /Schwierige ~** the stupid/difficult part of it; **er war gerade ~, zu gehen** he was just leaving; ~**sein** (*unreg*) *vi* (*anwesend*) to be present; (*beteiligt*) to be involved; ~**stehen** (*unreg*) *vi* to stand around

Dach [dax] (-(e)s, ¨er) *nt* roof; ~**boden** *m* attic, loft; ~**decker** (-s, -) *m* slater, tiler; ~**fenster** *nt* skylight; ~**luke** *f* skylight; ~**pappe** *f* roofing felt; ~**rinne** *f* gutter

Dachs [daks] (-es, -e) *m* badger

dachte *etc* [ˈdaxtə] *vb siehe* **denken**

Dackel [ˈdakəl] (-s, -) *m* dachshund

dadurch [daˈdʊrç] *adv* (*räumlich*) through it; (*durch diesen Umstand*) thereby, in that way; (*deshalb*) because of that, for that reason ♦ *konj*: ~, **daß** because

dafür [daˈfyːr] *adv* for it; (*anstatt*) instead; **er kann nichts ~** he can't

help it; **er ist bekannt ~** he is well-known for that; **was bekomme ich ~?** what will I get for it?

dafürkönnen *unreg* (*vt*): **er kann nichts dafür** he can't help it

dagegen [daˈgeːgən] *adv* against it; (*im Vergleich damit*) in comparison with it; (*bei Tausch*) for it/them ♦ *konj* however; **ich habe nichts ~** I don't mind; **ich war ~** I was against it; ~ **kann man nichts tun** one can't do anything about it; ~**halten** (*unreg*) *vt* (*vergleichen*) to compare with it; (*entgegnen*) to object to it; ~**sprechen** (*unreg*) *vi*: **es spricht nichts ~** there's no reason why not

daheim [daˈhaɪm] *adv* at home; **D~** (-s) *nt* home

daher [daˈheːr] *adv* (*räumlich*) from there; (*Ursache*) from that ♦ *konj* (*deshalb*) that's why

dahin [daˈhɪn] *adv* (*räumlich*) there; (*zeitlich*) then; (*vergangen*) gone; ~**gegen** *konj* on the other hand; ~**gehend** *adv* on this matter; ~**gestellt** *adv*: ~**gestellt bleiben** to remain to be seen; ~**gestellt sein lassen** to leave open od undecided

dahinten [daˈhɪntən] *adv* over there

dahinter [daˈhɪntər] *adv* behind it; ~**kommen** (*unreg*) *vi* to get to the bottom of it

Dahlie [ˈdaːliə] *f* dahlia

dalli [ˈdali] (*umg*) *adv* chop chop

damalig [ˈdaːmaːlɪç] *adj* of that time, then

damals [ˈdaːmaːls] *adv* at that time, then

Damast [daˈmast] (-(e)s, -e) *m* damask

Dame [ˈdaːmə] *f* lady; (*SCHACH, KARTEN*) queen; (*Spiel*) draughts sg; **d~nhaft** *adj* ladylike; ~**nwahl** *f* ladies' excuse-me

damit [daˈmɪt] *adv* with it; (*begründend*) by that ♦ *konj* in order that, in order to; **was meint er ~?** what does he mean by that?; **genug ~!** that's enough!; ~ **eilt es nicht** there's no hurry

dämlich ['dɛ:mlɪç] (*umg*) *adj* silly, stupid

Damm [dam] (-(e)s, ⁀e) *m* dyke; (*Stau~*) dam; (*Hafen~*) mole; (*Bahn~, Straßen~*) embankment

dämmen ['dɛmən] *vt* (*Wasser*) to dam up; (*Schmerzen*) to keep back

dämmer- *zW*: **~ig** *adj* dim, faint; **~n** *vi* (*Tag*) to dawn; (*Abend*) to fall; **D~ung** *f* twilight; (*Morgen~*) dawn; (*Abend~*) dusk

dämonisch [dɛ'mo:nɪʃ] *adj* demoniacal

Dampf [dampf] (-(e)s, ⁀e) *m* steam; (*Dunst*) vapour; **d~en** *vi* to steam

dämpfen ['dɛmpfən] *vt* (*KOCH*) to steam; (*bügeln*) to iron with a damp cloth; (*fig*) to dampen, to subdue

Dampf- *zW*: **~kochtopf** *m* pressure cooker; **~schiff** *nt* steamship; **~walze** *f* steamroller

danach [da'na:x] *adv* after that; (*zeitlich*) after that, afterwards; (*gemäß*) accordingly; according to which; according to that; **er sieht ~ aus** he looks it

Däne (-n, -n) *m* Dane

daneben [da'ne:bən] *adv* beside it; (*im Vergleich*) in comparison; **~benehmen** (*unreg*) *vr* to misbehave; **~gehen** (*unreg*) *vi* to miss; (*Plan*) to fail

Dän- ['dɛ:n] *zW*: **~emark** *nt* Denmark; **~in** *f* Dane; **d~isch** *adj* Danish

Dank [daŋk] (-(e)s, -e) *m* thanks *pl*; **d~** *präp* (+*dat od gen*) thanks to; **vielen** *od* **schönen ~** many thanks; **jdm ~ sagen** to thank sb; **d~bar** *adj* grateful; (*Aufgabe*) rewarding; **~barkeit** *f* gratitude; **d~e** *excl* thank you, thanks; **d~en** *vi* +*dat* to thank; **d~enswert** *adj* (*Arbeit*) worthwhile; rewarding; (*Bemühung*) kind; **d~sagen** *vi* to express one's thanks

dann [dan] *adv* then; **~ und wann** now and then

daran [da'ran] *adv* on it; (*stoßen*) against it; **es liegt ~, daß ...** the cause of it is that ...; **gut/schlecht ~**

sein to be well-/badly off; **das Beste/Dümmste ~** the best/ stupidest thing about it; **ich war nahe ~, ...** I was on the point of ...; **er ist ~ gestorben** he died from it *od* of it; **~gehen** (*unreg*) *vi* to start; **~setzen** *vt* to stake; **er hat alles ~gesetzt, von Glasgow wegzukommen** he has done his utmost to get away from Glasgow

darauf [da'rauf] *adv* (*räumlich*) on it; (*zielgerichtet*) towards it; (*danach*) afterwards; **es kommt ganz ~ an, ob ...** it depends whether ...; **die Tage ~** the days following *od* thereafter; **am Tag ~** the next day; **~folgend** *adj* (*Tag, Jahr*) next, following; **~legen** *vt* to lay *od* put on top

daraus [da'raus] *adv* from it; **was ist ~ geworden?** what became of it?; **~ geht hervor, daß ...** this means that ...

Darbietung ['da:rbi:tuŋ] *f* performance

darf *etc* [darf] *vb siehe* **dürfen**

darin [da'rɪn] *adv* in (there), in it

Dar- ['da:r] *zW*: **~legen** *vt* to explain, to expound, to set forth; **~legung** *f* explanation; **~leh(e)n** (-s, -) *nt* loan

Darm [darm] (-(e)s, ⁀e) *m* intestine; (*Wurst~*) skin; **~grippe** *f* (*MED*) gastric influenza *od* 'flu; **~saite** *f* gut string

darstellen ['da:rʃtɛlən] *vt* (*abbilden, bedeuten*) to represent; (*THEAT*) to act; (*beschreiben*) to describe ♦ *vr* to appear to be

Darsteller(in) (-s, -) *m(f)* actor(actress)

Darstellung *f* portrayal, depiction

darüber [da'ry:bər] *adv* (*räumlich*) over it, above it; (*fahren*) over it; (*mehr*) more; (*währenddessen*) meanwhile; (*sprechen, streiten*) about it; **~ geht nichts** there's nothing like it

darum [da'rum] *adv* (*räumlich*) round it ♦ *konj* that's why; **er bittet**

~ he is pleading for it; es geht ~, daß ... the thing is that ...; er würde viel ~ geben, wenn ... he would give a lot to ...; ich tue es ~, weil ... I am doing it because ...

darunter [da'rɔntər] adv (räumlich) under it; (dazwischen) among them; (weniger) less; ein Stockwerk ~ one floor below (it); was verstehen Sie ~? what do you understand by that?

das [das] def art the ♦ pron that

Dasein ['daːzaɪn] (-s) nt (Leben) life; (Anwesenheit) presence; (Bestehen) existence

dasein (unreg) vi to be there

daß [das] konj that

dasselbe [das'zɛlbə] ,art, pron the same

dastehen ['daːʃteːən] (unreg) vi to stand there

Datei [da'taɪ] f file

Datenbank ['daːtənbaŋk] f data base

Datensichtgerät nt visual display unit, VDU

Datenverarbeitung f data processing

datieren [da'tiːrən] vt to date

Dativ ['daːtiːf] (-s, -e) m dative (case)

Dattel ['datəl] (-, -n) f date

Datum ['daːtʊm] (-s, Daten nt) date; Daten pl (Angaben) data pl

Dauer ['dauər] f duration; (gewisse Zeitspanne) length; (Bestand, Fortbestehen) permanence; es war nur von kurzer ~ it didn't last long; auf die ~ in the long run; (auf längere Zeit) indefinitely; ~auftrag m standing order; d~haft adj lasting, durable; ~karte f season ticket; ~lauf m jog(ging); d~n vi to last; es hat sehr lang gedauert, bis er ... it took him a long time to ...; d~nd adj constant; ~welle f perm, permanent wave; ~wurst f German salami; ~zustand m permanent condition

Daumen ['daumən] (-s, -) m thumb

Daune ['daunə] f down; ~ndecke f

down duvet, down quilt

davon [da'fɔn] adv of it; (räumlich) away; (weg von) from it; (Grund) because of it; das kommt ~! that's what you get; ~ abgesehen apart from that; ~ sprechen/wissen to talk/know of od about it; was habe ich ~? what's the point?; ~kommen (unreg) vi to escape; ~laufen (unreg) vi to run away

davor [da'foːr] adv (räumlich) in front of it; (zeitlich) before (that); ~ warnen to warn about it

dazu [da'tsuː] adv (legen, stellen) by it; (essen, singen) with it; und ~ noch and in addition; ein Beispiel/seine Gedanken ~ one example for/his thoughts on this; wie komme ich denn ~? why should I?; ~ fähig sein to be capable of it; sich ~ äußern to say something on it; ~gehören vi to belong to it; ~kommen (unreg) vi (Ereignisse) to happen too; (an einen Ort) to come along

dazwischen [da'tsvɪʃən] adv between; (räumlich auch) between (them); (zusammen mit) among them; der Unterschied ~ the difference between them; ~kommen (unreg) vi (hineingeraten) to get caught in it; es ist etwas ~gekommen something cropped up; ~reden vi (unterbrechen) to interrupt; (sich einmischen) to interfere; ~treten (unreg) vi to intervene

Debatte [de'batə] f debate

Deck [dɛk] (-(e)s, -s od -e) nt deck; an ~ gehen to go on deck

Decke f cover; (Bett~) blanket; (Tisch~) tablecloth; (Zimmer~) ceiling; unter einer ~ stecken to be hand in glove; ~l (-s, -) m lid; d~n vt to cover ♦ vi to coincide

Deckung f (Schützen) covering; (Schutz) cover; (SPORT) defence; (Übereinstimmen) agreement; d~sgleich adj congruent

Defekt [de'fɛkt] (-(e)s, -e) m fault, defect; d~ adj faulty

defensiv [defɛn'siːf] adj defensive

definieren [defi'niːrən] vt to define

Definition [definitsi'oːn] f definition

Defizit ['deːfitsɪt] (-s, -e) nt deficit

deftig ['dɛftɪç] adj (Essen) large; (Witz) coarse

Degen ['deːgən] (-s, -) m sword

degenerieren [degene'riːrən] vi to degenerate

dehnbar [deːnbaːr] adj elastic; (fig: Begriff) loose

dehnen vt, vr to stretch

Deich [daɪç] (-(e)s, -e) m dyke, dike

Deichsel ['daɪksəl] (-, -n) f shaft

deichseln (umg) vt (fig) to wangle

dein(e) [daɪn(ə)] adj (D~ in Briefen) your; **~e(r, s)** pron yours; **~er** (gen von du) pron of you; **~erseits** adv on your part; **~esgleichen** pron people like you; **~etwegen** adv (für dich) for your sake; (wegen dir) on your account; **~etwillen** adv: um **~etwillen** = um deinetwegen; **~ige** pron: der/die/das ~ige yours

dekadent [deka'dɛnt] adj decadent

Deklination [deklinatsi'oːn] f declension

deklinieren [dekli'niːrən] vt to decline

Dekolleté [dekɔl'teː] (-s, -s) nt low neckline

Deko- [deko] zW: **~rateur** [-ra'tøːr] m window dresser; **~ration** [-ratsi'oːn] f decoration; (in Laden) window dressing; **d~rativ** [-ra'tiːf] adj decorative; **d~rieren** [-'riːrən] vt to decorate; (Schaufenster) to dress

Delegation [delegatsi'oːn] f delegation

delegieren [dele'giːrən] vt: **~ an** +akk (Aufgaben) to delegate to

delikat [deli'kaːt] adj (zart, heikel) delicate; (köstlich) delicious

Delikatesse [delika'tɛsə] f delicacy; **~n** pl (Feinkost) delicatessen food; **~ngeschäft** nt delicatessen

Delikt [de'lɪkt] (-(e)s, -e) nt (JUR) offence

Delle ['dɛlə] (umg) f dent

Delphin [dɛl'fiːn] (-s, -e) m dolphin

dem [deː(ə)m] art dat von **der**

Demagoge [dema'goːgə] (-n, -n) m demagogue

dementieren [demɛn'tiːrən] vt to deny

dem- zW: **~gemäß** adv accordingly; **~nach** adv accordingly; **~nächst** adv shortly

Demokrat [demo'kraːt] (-en, -en) m democrat; **~ie** [-'tiː] f democracy; **d~isch** adj democratic; **d~isieren** [-i'ziːrən] vt to democratize

demolieren [demo'liːrən] vt to demolish

Demon- [demɔn] zW: **~strant(in)** [-'strant(ɪn)] m(f) demonstrator; **~stration** [-stratsi'oːn] f demonstration; **d~strativ** [-stra'tiːf] adj demonstrative; (Protest) pointed; **d~strieren** [-'striːrən] vt, vi to demonstrate

Demoskopie [demosko'piː] f public opinion research

Demut [de'muːt] (-) f humility

demütig [de'myːtɪç] adj humble; **~en** [de'myːtɪgən] vt to humiliate; **D~ung** f humiliation

demzufolge ['deːmtsu'fɔlgə] adv accordingly

den [deː(ə)n] art akk von **der**

denen [deːnən] pron (dat pl) der; die; das

Denk- [dɛŋk] zW: **d~bar** adj conceivable; **~en** (-s) nt thinking; **d~en** (unreg) vt, vi to think; **d~faul** adj lazy; **~fehler** m logical error; **~mal** (-s, -er) nt monument; **d~würdig** adj memorable; **~zettel** m: jdm einen **~zettel** verpassen to teach sb a lesson

denn [dɛn] konj for ♦ adv then; (nach Komparativ) than; **warum ~?** why?

dennoch ['dɛnɔx] konj nevertheless

Denunziant [denuntsi'ant] m informer

deponieren [depo'niːrən] vt (COMM) to deposit

Depot [de'poː] (-s, -s) nt warehouse; (Bus~, EISENB) depot; (Bank~) strongroom, safe (US)

Depression [depresi'o:n] f depression

depressiv adj depressive

deprimieren [depri'mi:rən] vt to depress

SCHLÜSSELWORT

der [de:r] (f die, nt das, gen des, der, des, dat dem, der, dem, akk dendef art) def art the; **der Rhein** the Rhine; **der Klaus** (umg) Klaus; **die Frau** (im allgemeinen) women; **der Tod/das Leben** death/life; **der Fuß des Berges** the foot of the hill; **gib es der Frau** give it to the woman; **er hat sich die Hand verletzt** he has hurt his hand

♦ relativ pron (bei Menschen) who, that; (bei Tieren, Sachen) which, that; **der Mann, den ich gesehen habe** the man who od whom od that I saw

♦ demonstrativ pron he/she/it; (jener, dieser) that; (pl) those; **der/die war es** it was him/her; **der mit der Brille** the one with glasses; **ich will den** (da) I want that one

derart ['de:r'?a:rt] adv so; (solcher Art) such; **~ig** adj such, this sort of

derb [dɛrp] adj sturdy; (Kost) solid; (grob) coarse

der- zW: **~gleichen** pron such; **~jenige** pron he; she; it; the one who; (das Ding) that (which); (das welche) that; **~maßen** adv to such an extent, so; **~selbe** art, pron the same; **~weil(en)** adv in the meantime; **~zeitig** adj present, current; (damalig) then

des [dɛs] art gen von der

desertieren [dezer'ti:rən] vi to desert

desgleichen ['dɛs'glaɪçən] adv likewise, also

deshalb ['dɛs'halp] adv therefore, that's why

Desinfektion [dɛzinfɛktsi'o:n] f disinfection; **~smittel** nt disinfectant

desinfizieren [dɛzinfi'tsi:rən] vt to disinfect

dessen ['dɛsən] pron gen von der; das; **~ungeachtet** adv nevertheless, regardless

Dessert [dɛ'se:r] (-s, -s) nt dessert

destillieren [dɛsti'li:rən] vt to distil

desto ['dɛsto] adv all the, so much the; **~ besser** all the better

deswegen ['dɛs've:gən] konj therefore, hence

Detail [de'taɪ] (-s, -s) nt detail

Detektiv [detɛk'ti:f] (-s, -e) m detective

deut- ['dɔyt] zW: **~en** vt to interpret, to explain ♦ vi: **~en** (auf +akk) to point to od at); **~lich** adj clear; (Unterschied) distinct; **D~lichkeit** f clarity; distinctness

Deutsch [dɔytʃ] nt German

deutsch adj German; **auf ~** in German; **D~e Demokratische Republik** German Democratic Republic, East Germany; **~es Beefsteak** = hamburger; **D~e** f German; **D~er** m German; **ich bin D~er** I am German; **D~land** nt Germany

Devise [de'vi:zə] f motto, device; **~n** pl (FIN) foreign currency, foreign exchange

Dezember [de'tsɛmbər] (-s, -) m December

dezent [de'tsɛnt] adj discreet

dezimal [detsi'ma:l] adj decimal; **D~bruch** m decimal (fraction); **D~system** nt decimal system

d.h. abk (= das heißt) i.e.

Dia ['di:a] (-s, -s) nt (PHOT) slide, transparency

Diabetes [dia'be:tɛs] (-, -) m (MED) diabetes

Diagnose [dia'gno:zə] f diagnosis

diagonal [diago'na:l] adj diagonal; **D~e** f diagonal

Dialekt [dia'lɛkt] (-(e)s, -e) m dialect; **d~isch** adj dialectal; (Logik) dialectical

Dialog [dia'lo:k] (-(e)s, -e) m dialogue

Diamant [dia'mant] m diamond

Diaprojektor ['di:aprojɛktɔr] m slide projector

Diät [dɪ'ɛ:t] (-, -en) f diet
dich [dɪç] (akk von **du**) pron you;
yourself
dicht [dɪçt] adj dense; (Nebel) thick;
(Gewebe) close; (undurchlässig)
(water)tight; (fig) concise ♦ adv ~
an/bei close to; **~bevölkert** adj den-
sely od heavily populated; **D~e** f
density; thickness; closeness; (water)tightness; (fig) conciseness; **~en**
vt (dicht machen) to make water-
tight; to seal; (NAUT) to caulk; (LI-
TER) to compose, to write ♦ vi to
compose, to write; **D~er(in)** (-s, -)
m(f) poet; (Autor) writer; **~erisch**
adj poetical; **~halten** (unreg; umg)
vi to keep one's mouth shut; **D~ung**
f (TECH) washer; (AUT) gasket;
(Gedichte) poetry; (Prosa) (piece of
writing
dick [dɪk] adj thick; (fett) fat; durch
~ und dünn through thick and thin;
D~darm m (ANAT) colon; **D~e** f
thickness; fatness; **~flüssig** adj viscous; **D~icht** (-s, -e) nt thicket;
D~kopf m mule; **D~milch** f soured
milk
die [di:] def art siehe **der**
Dieb(in) [di:p, 'di:bɪn] (-(e)s, -e)
m(f) thief; **d~isch** adj thieving;
(umg) immense; **~stahl** [-s, -s, ⸚e]
m theft
Diele ['di:lə] f (Brett) board; (Flur)
hall, lobby
dienen ['di:nən] vi: (jdm) ~ to
serve (sb)
Diener (-s, -) m servant; **~in** f
(maid)servant; **~schaft** f servants pl
Dienst [di:nst] (-(e)s, -e) m service;
außer ~ retired; ~ **haben** to be on
duty
Dienstag ['di:nsta:k] m Tuesday;
d~s adv on Tuesdays
Dienst- zW: **~bote** m servant; **~ge-**
heimnis nt official secret; **~ge-**
spräch nt business call; **d~habend**
adj (Arzt) on duty; **~leistung** f service;
d~lich adj official; **~mädchen**
nt (house)maid; **~reise** f business
trip; **~stelle** f office; **~vorschrift** f

official regulations pl; **~weg** m official channels pl; **~zeit** f working
hours pl; (MIL) period of service
dies ['di:s] pron (demonstrativ: sg)
this; (: pl) these; **~bezüglich** adj
(Frage) on the matter; **~e(r, s)**
['di:zə(r, s)] pron this (one)
Diesel ['di:zəl] m (Kraftstoff) diesel
dieselbe [di:'zɛlbə] pron, art the
same
Dieselöl ['di:zəl'ø:l] nt diesel oil
diesig ['di:zɪç] adj drizzly
dies- zW: **~jährig** adj this year's;
~mal adv this time; **~seits** präp
+gen on this side; **D~seits** (-) nt this
life
Dietrich ['di:trɪç] (-s, -e) m picklock
diffamieren [dɪfa'mi:rən] (pej) vt to
defame
differential [dɪferentsi'a:l] adj differential; **D~rechnung** f differential
calculus
Differenz [dɪfe'rɛnts] (-, -en) f (Unterschied) difference; **~en** pl (geh.
Meinungsverschiedenheit) difference
(of opinion)
differenzieren [dɪferɛn'tsi:rən] vt to
make distinctions in; **differenziert**
adj (Mensch etc) complex
digital [digi'ta:l] adj digital
Dikt- [dɪkt] zW: **~aphon** [-a'fo:n] nt
dictaphone; **~at** [-'ta:t] (-(e)s, -e) nt
dictation; **~ator** [-'ta:tɔr] m dictator;
d~atorisch [-a'to:rɪʃ] adj dictatorial;
~atur [-a'tu:r] f dictatorship;
d~ieren [-'ti:rən] vt to dictate
Dilemma [di'lɛma] (-s, -s od -ta) nt
dilemma
Dilettant [dile'tant] m dilettante,
amateur; **d~isch** adj amateurish, dilettante
Dimension [dimenzi'o:n] f dimension
Ding [dɪŋ] (-(e)s, -e) nt thing, object; **d~lich** adj real, concrete;
~s(bums) ['dɪŋks(bums)] (-; umg) nt
thingummybob
Diphtherie [dɪfte'ri:] f diphtheria
Diplom [di'plo:m] (-(e)s, -e) nt diploma, certificate; **~at** [-'ma:t] (-en, -

Reich; **D~l** (-s, -e) *nt* third; **~ns** *adv* thirdly

droben ['dro:bən] *adv* above, up there

Droge ['dro:gə] *f* drug; **d~nabhängig** *adj* addicted to drugs; **~nhändler** *m* drug pedlar, pusher; **~rie** [dro:gə'ri:] *f* chemist's shop

Drogist [dro'gɪst] *m* pharmacist, chemist

drohen ['dro:ən] *vi:* **(jdm)** ~ to threaten (sb)

dröhnen ['drø:nən] *vi* (*Motor*) to roar; (*Stimme, Musik*) to ring, to resound

Drohung ['dro:ʊŋ] *f* threat

drollig ['drɔlɪç] *adj* droll

Drossel ['drɔsəl] (-, -n) *f* thrush

drüben ['dry:bən] *adv* over there, on the other side

drüber ['dry:bər] (*umg*) *adv* = darüber

Druck [drʊk] (-(e)s, -e) *m* (*PHYS, Zwang*) pressure; (*TYP: Vorgang*) printing; (: *Produkt*) print; (*fig: Belastung*) burden, weight; **~buchstabe** *m* block letter

drücken ['drʏkən] *vt* (*Knopf, Hand*) to press; (*zu eng sein*) to pinch; (*fig: Preise*) to keep down; (: *belasten*) to oppress, to weigh down ♦ *vi* to press; to pinch ♦ *vr:* **sich vor etw dat ~** to get out of (doing) sth; **~d** *adj* oppressive

Drucker (-s, -) *m* printer

Drücker (-s, -) *m* button; (*Tür~*) handle; (*Gewehr~*) trigger

Druck- *zW:* **~erei** *f* printing works, press; **~erschwärze** *f* printer's ink; **~fehler** *m* misprint; **~knopf** *m* press stud, snap fastener; **~sache** *f* printed matter; **~schrift** *f* block od printed letters *pl*

drum [drʊm] (*umg*) *adv* = darum

drunten ['drʊntən] *adv* below, down there

Drüse ['dry:zə] *f* gland

Dschungel ['dʒʊŋəl] *m* jungle

du [du:] (*nom*) *pron* (**D~** *in Briefen*)

you; **D~ sagen = duzen**

Dübel ['dy:bəl] (-s, -) *m* Rawlplug (®)

ducken ['dʊkən] *vt* (*Kopf, Person*) to duck; (*fig*) to take down a peg or two ♦ *vr* to duck

Duckmäuser ['dʊkmɔʏzər] (-s, -) *m* yes-man

Dudelsack ['du:dəlzak] *m* bagpipes *pl*

Duell [du'ɛl] (-s, -e) *nt* duel

Duft [dʊft] (-(e)s, ⁼e) *m* scent, odour; **d~en** *vi* to smell, to be fragrant; **d~ig** *adj* (*Stoff, Kleid*) delicate, diaphanous

dulden ['dʊldən] *vt* to suffer; (*zulassen*) to tolerate ♦ *vi* to suffer

duldsam *adj* tolerant

dumm [dʊm] *adj* stupid; (*ärgerlich*) annoying; **der D~e sein** to be the loser; **~erweise** *adv* stupidly; **D~heit** *f* stupidity; (*Tat*) blunder, stupid mistake; **D~kopf** *m* blockhead

dumpf [dʊmpf] *adj* (*Ton*) hollow, dull; (*Luft*) musty; (*Erinnerung, Schmerz*) vague

Düne ['dy:nə] *f* dune

düngen ['dʏŋən] *vt* to manure

Dünger (-s, -) *m* dung, manure; (*künstlich*) fertilizer

dunkel ['dʊŋkəl] *adj* dark; (*Stimme*) deep; (*Ahnung*) vague; (*rätselhaft*) obscure; (*verdächtig*) dubious, shady; **im ~n tappen** (*fig*) to grope in the dark

Dunkel- *zW:* **~heit** *f* darkness; (*fig*) obscurity; **~kammer** *f* (*PHOT*) dark room; **d~n** *vi unpers* to grow dark; **~ziffer** *f* estimated number of unreported cases

dünn [dʏn] *adj* thin; **~flüssig** *adj* watery, thin

Dunst [dʊnst] (-es, ⁼e) *m* vapour; (*Wetter*) haze

dünsten ['dʏnstən] *vt* to steam

dunstig ['dʊnstɪç] *adj* vaporous; (*Wetter*) hazy, misty

Duplikat [dupli'ka:t] (-(e)s, -e) *nt* duplicate

Dur [du:r] (-, -) *nt* (*MUS*) major

durch [dʊrç] *präp +akk* **1** (*hindurch*) through; **durch den Urwald** through the jungle; **die ganze Welt reisen** to travel all over the world
2 (*mittels*) through, by (means of); (*aufgrund*) due to, owing to; **Tod durch Herzschlag/den Strang** death from a heart attack/by hanging; **durch die Post** by post; **durch seine Bemühungen** through his efforts

♦ *adv* **1** (*hindurch*) through; **die ganze Nacht durch** all through the night; **den Sommer durch** during the summer; **8 Uhr durch** past 8 o'clock; **durch und durch** completely
2 (*durchgebraten etc*): (**gut**) **durch** well-done

durch- *zW:* **~arbeiten** *vt, vi* to work through ♦ *vr* to work one's way through; **~aus** *adv* completely; (*unbedingt*) definitely; **~aus nicht** absolutely not; **~blättern** *vt* to leaf through
Durchblick ['dʊrçblɪk] *m* view; (*fig*) comprehension; **d~en** *vi* to look through; (*umg: verstehen*): (**bei etw**) **d~en** to understand (sth); **etw d~en lassen** (*fig*) to hint at sth
durchbrechen [dʊrç'brɛçən] (*unreg*) *vt, vi* to break; **durch'brechen** (*unreg*) *vt* insep to break through; (*Schallmauer*) to break; (*Gewohnheit*) to break free from
durchbrennen [dʊrçbrɛnən] *vi* (*Draht, Sicherung*) to burn through; (*umg*) to run away
durchbringen (*unreg*) *vt* (*Kranken*) to pull through; (*unreg, umg: Familie*) to support; (*durchsetzen: Antrag, Kandidat*) to get through; (*vergeuden: Geld*) to get through, to squander
Durchbruch ['-brʊx] *m* (*Öffnung*) opening; (*MIL*) breach; (*von Gefühlen etc*) eruption; (*der Zähne*) cut-

ting; (*fig*) breakthrough; **zum ~ kommen** to break through

durch- *zW:* **~dacht** [-'daxt] *adj* well thought-out; **~denken** (*unreg*) *vt* to think out; **~drehen** *vt* (*Fleisch*) to mince ♦ *vi* (*umg*) to crack up
durcheinander [dʊrçaɪ'nandər] *adv* in a mess, in confusion; (*umg: verwirrt*) confused; **~ trinken** to mix one's drinks; **D~** (**-s**) *nt* (*Verwirrung*) confusion; (*Unordnung*) mess; **~bringen** (*unreg*) *vt* to mess up; (*verwirren*) to confuse; **~reden** *vi* to talk at the same time
durch- *zW:* **~fahren** (*unreg*) *vi* (*durch Tunnel usw*) to drive through; (*ohne Unterbrechung*) to drive straight through; (*ohne anzuhalten*): **der Zug fährt bis Hamburg ~** the train runs direct to Hamburg; (*ohne Umsteigen*): **können wir ~fahren?** can we go direct?, can we go nonstop?; **D~fahrt** *f* transit; (*Verkehr*) thoroughfare; **D~fall** *m* (*MED*) diarrhoea; **~fallen** (*unreg*) *vi* to fall through; (*in Prüfung*) to fail; **~finden** (*unreg*) *vr* to find one's way through; **~forschen** *vt* insep to explore; **~fragen** *vr* to find one's way by asking
durchführ- *zW:* **~bar** *adj* feasible, practicable; **~en** *vt* to carry out; **D~ung** *f* execution, performance
Durchgang ['-gaŋ] *m* passage(way); (*bei Produktion, Versuch*) run; (*SPORT*) round; (*bei Wahl*) ballot; **„~ verboten"** "no thoroughfare"
Durchgangslager *nt* transit camp
Durchgangsverkehr *m* through traffic
durchgefroren [dʊrçgəfroːrən] *adj* (*Mensch*) frozen stiff
durchgehen ['dʊrçgeːən] (*unreg*) *vt* (*behandeln*) to go over ♦ *vi* to go through; (*ausreißen: Pferd*) to break loose; (*Mensch*) to run away; **mein Temperament ging mit mir durch** my temper got the better of me; **jdm etw ~ lassen** to let sb get away with

sth; **~d** adj (Zug) through; (Öffnungszeiten) continuous

durch- zW: **~greifen** (unreg) vi to take strong action; **~halten** (unreg) vi to last out ♦ vt to keep up; **~kommen** (unreg) vi to get through; (überleben) to pull through

durch'kreuzen vt insep to thwart, to frustrate

durch- zW: **~lassen** (unreg) vt (Person) to let through; (Wasser) to let in; **'durchlesen** (unreg) vt to read through; **'durchleuchten** vt insep to X-ray; **'durchmachen** vt to go through; **die Nacht ~machen** to make a night of it: **D~marsch** m march through

Durchmesser (-s, -) m diameter

durch- zW: **~nässen** vt insep to soak (through); **~nehmen** (unreg) vt to go over; **~numerieren** vt to number consecutively; **~queren** [durç'kve:rən] vt insep to cross; **~reiche** f (serving) hatch; **D~reise** f transit; **auf der D~reise** passing through; (Güter) in transit; **~ringen** (unreg) vr to reach a decision after a long struggle; **~rosten** vi to rust through

durchs [durçs] = durch das

Durchsage ['durçza:gə] f intercom od radio announcement

durchschauen ['durçʃauən] vt to look od see through (Person, Lüge) to see through

durchscheinen ['durçʃaɪnən] (unreg) vi to shine through; **~d** adj translucent

Durchschlag ['durçʃla:k] m (Doppel) carbon copy; (Sieb) strainer; **d~en** (unreg) vt (entzweischlagen) to split (in two); (sieben) to sieve ♦ vi (zum Vorschein kommen) to emerge, to come out ♦ vr to get by; **d~end** adj resounding

durchschneiden ['durçʃnaɪdən] (unreg) vt to cut through

Durchschnitt ['durçʃnɪt] m (Mittelwert) average; **über/unter dem ~** above/below average; **im ~** on av-

erage; **d~lich** adj average ♦ adv on average

Durchschnittsgeschwindigkeit f average speed

Durchschnittswert m average

durch- zW: **D~schrift** f copy; **~sehen** (unreg) vt to look through; **~setzen** vt to enforce ♦ vr (Erfolg haben) to succeed; (sich behaupten) to get one's way; **seinen Kopf ~setzen** to get one's way to mix

Durchsicht ['durçzɪçt] f looking through, checking; **d~ig** adj transparent

durch- zW: **~sprechen** (unreg) vt to talk over; **~stehen** (unreg) vt to live through; **~stöbern** (auch untr) vt (Kisten) to rummage through, to rifle through; (Haus, Wohnung) to ransack; **~streichen** (unreg) vt to cross out; **~suchen** vt insep to search; **D~suchung** f search; **~trieben** [~'tri:bən] adj cunning, wily; **~wachsen** adj (Speck) streaky; (fig: mittelmäßig) so-so; **D~wahl** f (TEL) direct dialling; **~weg** adv throughout, completely; **~ziehen** (unreg) vt (Faden) to draw through ♦ vi to pass through; **D~zug** m (Luft) draught; (von Truppen, Vögeln) passage

---

dürfen ['dYrfən] (unreg) vi **1** (Erlaubnis haben) to be allowed to; **ich darf das?** am I allowed to (do this)? **darf ich?** may I?; **darf ich ins Kino?** can od may I go to the cinema?; **es darf geraucht werden** you may smoke

2 (in Verneinungen): **er darf das nicht** he's not allowed to (do that); **das darf nicht geschehen** that must not happen; **da darf sie sich nicht wundern** that shouldn't surprise her

3 (in Höflichkeitsformeln): **darf ich Sie bitten, das zu tun?** may od could I ask you to do that?; **was darf es sein?** what can I do for you?

4 (*können*): das dürfen Sie mir glauben you can believe me
5 (*Möglichkeit*): das dürfte genug sein that should be enough; es dürfte Ihnen bekannt sein, daß ... as you will probably know ...

dürftig ['dʏrftɪç] *adj* (*ärmlich*) needy, poor; (*unzulänglich*) inadequate
dürr [dʏr] *adj* dried-up; (*Land*) arid; (*mager*) skinny, gaunt; **D~e** *f* aridity; (*Zeit*) drought; (*Magerkeit*) skinniness

Durst [dʊrst] (-(e)s) *m* thirst; ~ **haben** to be thirsty; **d~ig** *adj* thirsty
Dusche ['dʊʃə] *f* shower to have a shower
Düse ['dy:zə] *f* nozzle; (*Flugzeug~*) jet
Düsen- *zW*: ~**antrieb** *m* jet propulsion; ~**flugzeug** *nt* jet (plane); ~**jäger** *m* jet fighter
Dussel ['dʊsəl] (-s, -; *umg*) *m* twit
düster ['dy:stər] *adj* dark; (*Gedanken, Zukunft*) gloomy
Dutzend ['dʊtsənt] (-s, -e) *nt* dozen; **d~(e)mal** *adv* a dozen times; **d~weise** *adv* by the dozen
duzen ['du:tsən] *vt*: (jdn) ~ to use the familiar form of address "du" (*to od* with sb)

Dynamik [dy'na:mɪk] *f* (*PHYS*) dynamics *sg*; (*fig: Schwung*) momentum; (*von Mensch*) dynamism
dynamisch [dy'na:mɪʃ] *adj* (*auch fig*) dynamic
Dynamit [dyna'mi:t] (-s) *nt* dynamite
Dynamo [dy'na:mo] (-s, -s) *m* dynamo
D-Zug ['de:tsu:k] *m* through train

E

Ebbe ['ɛbə] *f* low tide
eben ['e:bən] *adj* level, flat; (*glatt*) smooth ♦ *adv* just; (*bestätigend*) exactly; ~ **deswegen** just because of that; ~**bürtig** *adj*: jdm ~**bürtig**

sein to be sb's equal; **E~e** *f* plain; (*fig*) level; ~**falls** *adv* likewise; ~ *adv* just as
Eber ['e:bər] (-s, -) *m* boar; ~**esche** *f* mountain ash, rowan
ebnen ['e:bnən] *vt* to level
Echo ['ɛço] (-s, -s) *nt* echo
echt [ɛçt] *adj* genuine; (*typisch*) typical; **E~heit** *f* genuineness
Eck- *zW*: ~**ball** *m* corner (kick); ~**e** *f* corner; (*MATH*) angle; **e~ig** *adj* angular; ~**zahn** *m* eye tooth
ECU (-, -s) *m* (*FINANZ*) ECU
edel ['e:dəl] *adj* noble; **E~metall** *nt* rare metal; **E~stein** *m* precious stone
EDV [e:de:'fau] (-) *f abk* (= *elektronische Datenverarbeitung*) electronic data processing
Efeu ['e:fɔy] (-s) *m* ivy
Effekt [ɛ'fɛkt] (-s, -e) *m* effect
Effekten [ɛ'fɛktən] *pl* stocks
effektiv [ɛfɛk'ti:f] *adj* effective, actual
EG ['e:'ge:] *f abk* (= *Europäische Gemeinschaft*) EC
egal [e'ga:l] *adj* all the same
Ego- *zW*: ~**ismus** *m* [-'ɪsmʊs] egoism; ~**ist** [-'ɪst] *m* egoist; **e~istisch** *adj* selfish, egoistic
Ehe ['e:ə] *f* marriage
ehe *konj* before
Ehe- *zW*: ~**beratung** *f* marriage guidance (counselling); ~**bruch** *m* adultery; ~**frau** *f* married woman; wife; ~**leute** *pl* married people; **e~lich** *adj* matrimonial; (*Kind*) legitimate
ehemalig *adj* former
ehemals *adv* formerly
Ehemann *m* married man; husband
Ehepaar *nt* married couple
eher ['e:ər] *adv* (*früher*) sooner; (*lieber*) rather, sooner; (*mehr*) more
Ehering *m* wedding ring
Eheschließung *f* marriage ceremony
ehestе(r, s) ['e:əstə(r, s)] *adj* (*früheste*) first, earliest; **am ~n** (*liebsten*) soonest; (*meist*) mostly

(wahrscheinlichst) most probably

Ehr- ['eːr] *zW:* **e~bar** *adj* honourable, respectable; **~e** *f* honour; **e~en** *vt* to honour

Ehren- ['eːrən] *zW:* **~gast** *m* guest of honour; **~haft** *adj* honourable; **~platz** *m* place of honour *od US* honor; **~runde** *f* lap of honour; **~sache** *f* point of honour; **e~voll** *adj* honourable; **~wort** *nt* word of honour

Ehr- *zW:* **~furcht** *f* awe, deep respect; **e~fürchtig** *adj* reverent; **~gefühl** *nt* sense of honour; **~geiz** *m* ambition; **e~geizig** *adj* ambitious; **e~lich** *adj* honest; **~lichkeit** *f* honesty; **e~los** *adj* dishonourable; **~ung** *f* honour(ing); **e~würdig** *adj* venerable

Ei [ai] (-(e)s, **-er**) *nt* egg

ei *excl* well, well

Eich- *zW:* **~e** ['aiçə] *f* oak (tree); **~el** (-, -n) *f* acorn; **~hörnchen** *nt* squirrel; **~maß** *nt* standard

Eid [ait] (-(e)s, **-e**) *m* oath

Eidechse ['aidɛksə] *f* lizard

eidesstattlich *adj:* **~e Erklärung** affidavit

Eidgenosse *m* Swiss

Eidotter ['aidɔtər] *nt* egg yolk

Eier- *zW:* **~becher** *m* eggcup; **~kuchen** *m* omelette; pancake; **~likör** *m* advocaat; **~schale** *f* eggshell; **~stock** *m* ovary; **~uhr** *f* egg timer

Eifer ['aifər] (-s) *m* zeal, enthusiasm; **~sucht** *f* jealousy; **e~süchtig** *adj:* **e~süchtig (auf** +*akk)* jealous (of)

eifrig ['aifrɪç] *adj* zealous, enthusiastic

Eigelb ['aigɛlp] (-(e)s) *nt* egg yolk

eigen ['aigən] *adj* own; (*~artig*) peculiar; **mit der/dem ihm ~en ...** with that ... peculiar to him; **sich** *dat* **etw zu ~ machen** to make sth one's own; **E~art** *f* peculiarity; characteristic; **~artig** *adj* peculiar; **E~bedarf** *m:* **zum E~bedarf** for (one's own) personal use/domestic requirements; **der Vermieter machte E~bedarf geltend** the landlord showed he needed the house/flat for himself; **~händig** *adj* with one's own hand; **E~heim** *nt* owner-occupied house; **E~heit** *f* peculiarity; **~mächtig** *adj* high-handed; **E~name** *m* proper name; **~s** *adv* expressly, on purpose; **E~schaft** *f* quality, property, attribute; **E~schaftswort** *nt* adjective; **E~sinn** *m* obstinacy; **~sinnig** *adj* obstinate; **~tlich** *adj* actual, real ♦ *adv* actually, really; **E~tor** *nt* own goal; **E~tum** *nt* property; **E~tümer(in)** (-s, -) *m(f)* owner, proprietor; **~tümlich** *adj* peculiar; **E~tümlichkeit** *f* peculiarity; **E~tumswohnung** *f* freehold flat

eignen ['aignən] *vr* to be suited

Eignung *f* suitability

Eil- ['ail] *zW:* **~bote** *m* courier; **~brief** *m* express letter; **~e** *f* haste; **es hat keine ~e** there's no hurry; **e~en** *vi* (*Mensch*) to hurry; (*dringend sein*) to be urgent; **e~ends** *adv* hastily; **~gut** *nt* express goods *pl*, fast freight (*US*); **e~ig** *adj* hasty, hurried; (*dringlich*) urgent; **es ~ig haben** to be in a hurry; **~zug** *m* semi-fast train, limited stop train

Eimer ['aimər] (-s, -) *m* bucket, pail

ein [ain] *adv:* **nicht ~ noch aus wissen** not to know what to do

ein(e) *num one* ♦ *indef art* a, an

einander [ai'nandər] *pron* one another, each other

einarbeiten ['ainarbaitən] *vt* to train ♦ *vr:* **sich in etw** *akk* **~** to familiarize o.s. with sth

einatmen ['aina:tmən] *vt, vi* to inhale, to breathe in

Einbahnstraße ['ainba:nʃtra:sə] *f* one-way street

Einband ['ainbant] *m* binding, cover

einbauen ['ainbauən] *vt* to build in; (*Motor*) to install, to fit

Einbaumöbel *pl* built-in furniture *sg*

einbegriffen *adj* included

einberufen ['ainbəru:fən] (*unreg*) *vt* to convene; (*MIL*) to call up

einbeziehen ['ainbətsi:ən] (*unreg*) *vt* to include

einbiegen ['ainbi:gən] (*unreg*) *vt* to

turn

einbilden ['aɪnbɪldən] *vt*: **sich** *dat* **etw ~ to** imagine sth

Einbildung *f* imagination; (*Dünkel*) conceit; **~skraft** *f* imagination

Einblick ['aɪnblɪk] *m* insight

einbrechen ['aɪnbrɛçən] (*unreg*) *vi* (*in Haus*) to break in; (*Nacht*) to fall; (*Winter*) to set in; (*durchbrechen*) to break; **~ in** +*akk* (*MIL*) to invade

Einbrecher (-**s**, -) *m* burglar

einbringen ['aɪnbrɪŋən] (*unreg*) *vt* to bring in; (*Geld, Vorteil*) to yield; (*mitbringen*) to contribute

Einbruch ['aɪnbrʊx] *m* (*Haus~*) break-in, burglary; (*Eindringen*) invasion; (*des Winters*) onset; (*Durchbrechen*) break; (*MET*) approach; (*MIL*) penetration; **bei/vor ~ der Nacht** at/before nightfall; **e~ssicher** *adj* burglar-proof

einbürgern ['aɪnbʏrgərn] *vt* to naturalize ♦ *vr* to become adopted

Einbuße ['aɪnbuːsə] *f* loss, forfeiture

einbüßen ['aɪnbyːsən] *vt* to lose, to forfeit

einchecken ['aɪntʃɛkən] *vt, vi* to check in

eincremen ['aɪnkreːmən] *vt* to put cream on

eindecken ['aɪndɛkən] *vr*: **sich (mit etw) ~ to** lay in stocks (of sth); to stock up (with sth)

eindeutig ['aɪndɔʏtɪç] *adj* unequivocal

eindringen ['aɪndrɪŋən] (*unreg*) *vi*: **~ (in** +*akk*) to force one's way in(to); (*unreg*) (*in Haus*) to break in(to); (*in Land*) to invade; (*Gas, Wasser*) to penetrate; (*auf jdn*) ~ (*mit Bitten*) to press (sb)

eindringlich *adj* forcible, urgent

Eindringling *m* intruder

Eindruck ['aɪndrʊk] *m* impression

eindrücken ['aɪndrʏkən] *vt* to press in

eindrucksvoll *adj* impressive

eine(r, s) *pron* one; (*jemand*) someone

eineiig ['aɪn'aɪɪç] *adj* (*Zwillinge*) identical

eineinhalb ['aɪn'aɪn'halp] *num* one and a half

einengen ['aɪn'ɛŋən] *vt* to confine, to restrict

einer- ['aɪnər] *zW*: **'E~'lei** (-**s**) *nt* sameness; '~**lei** *adj* (*gleichartig*) the same kind of; **es ist mir ~lei** it is all the same to me; ~**seits** *adv* on the one hand

einfach ['aɪnfax] *adj* simple; (*nicht mehrfach*) single ♦ *adv* simply; **E~heit** *f* simplicity

einfädeln ['aɪnfɛːdəln] *vt* (*Nadel, Faden*) to thread; (*fig*) to contrive

einfahren ['aɪnfaːrən] (*unreg*) *vt* to bring in; (*Barriere*) to knock down; (*Auto*) to run in ♦ *vi* (*unreg*) to drive in; (*Zug*) to pull in; (*MIN*) to go down

Einfahrt *f* (*Vorgang*) driving in, pulling in; (*MIN*) descent; (*Ort*) entrance

Einfall ['aɪnfal] *m* (*Idee*) idea, notion; (*Licht~*) incidence; (*MIL*) raid; **e~en** (*unreg*) *vi* (*Licht*) to fall; (*MIL*) to raid; (*einstürzen*) to fall in, to collapse; (*einstimmen*): **(in etw** *akk*) **e~en** to join in (with sth); **etw fällt jdm ein** sth occurs to sb; **das fällt mir gar nicht ein** I wouldn't dream of it; **sich** *dat* **etwas e~en lassen** to have a good idea

einfältig ['aɪnfɛltɪç] *adj* simple(-minded)

Einfamilienhaus [aɪnfa'miːliənhaʊs] *nt* detached house

einfarbig ['aɪnfarbɪç] *adj* all one colour; (*Stoff etc*) self-coloured

einfetten ['aɪnfɛtən] *vt* to grease

einfließen ['aɪnfliːsən] (*unreg*) *vi* to flow in

einflößen ['aɪnfløːsən] *vt*: **jdm etw ~ to** give sb sth; (*fig*) to instil sth in sb

Einfluß ['aɪnflʊs] *m* influence; **~bereich** *m* sphere of influence

einförmig ['aɪnfœrmɪç] *adj* uniform; **E~keit** *f* uniformity

einfrieren ['aɪnfriːrən] (*unreg*) *vi* to freeze in ♦ *vt* to freeze

einfügen ['ainfy:gən] vt to fit in; (zusätzlich) to add

Einfuhr ['ainfu:r] (-) f import

einführen ['ainfy:rən] vt to bring in; (Mensch, Sitten) to introduce; (Ware) to import

Einführung f introduction

Eingabe ['ainga:bə] f petition; (COMPUT) input

Eingang ['aingaŋ] m entrance; (COMM: Ankunft) arrival; (Erhalt) receipt; **e~s** adv at the outset ♦ präp +gen at the outset of

eingeben ['ainge:bən] (unreg) vt (Arznei) to give; (Daten etc) to enter

eingebildet ['aingəbildət] adj imaginary; (eitel) conceited

Eingeborene(r) ['aingəbo:rənə(r)] mf native

Eingebung f inspiration

eingedenk ['aingədeŋk] präp +gen bearing in mind

eingefleischt ['aingəflaiʃt] adj (Gewohnheit, Vorurteile) deep-rooted

eingehen ['ainge:ən] (unreg) vi (Aufnahme finden) to come in; (Sendung, Geld) to be received; (Tier, Pflanze) to die; (Firma) to fold; (schrumpfen) to shrink ♦ vt to enter into; (Wette) to make; **auf etw akk ~** to go into sth; **auf jdn ~** to respond to sb; **jdm ~** (verständlich sein) to be comprehensible to sb; **~d** adj exhaustive, thorough

Eingemachte(s) ['aingəmaxtə(s)] nt preserves pl

eingenommen ['aingənɔmən] adj: **~ (von)** fond (of), partial (to); **~ (gegen)** prejudiced (against)

eingeschrieben ['aingəʃri:bən] adj registered

eingespielt ['aingəʃpi:lt] adj: **aufeinander ~ sein** to be in tune with each other

Eingeständnis ['aingəʃtɛntnis] (-ses, -se) nt admission, confession

eingestehen ['aingəʃte:ən] (unreg) vt to confess

eingestellt ['amgəʃtɛlt] adj: **auf etw ~ sein** to be prepared for sth

eingetragen ['aingətra:gən] adj (COMM) registered

Eingeweide ['aingəwaidə] (-s, -) nt innards pl, intestines pl

Eingeweihte(r) ['aingəwaitə(r)] mf initiate

eingewöhnen ['aingəvø:nən] vr: **sich ~ in** +akk to settle (down) in

eingleisig ['ainglaiziç] adj single-track

eingreifen ['aingraifən] (unreg) vi to intervene, to interfere; (Zahnrad) to mesh

Eingriff ['aingrif] m intervention, interference; (Operation) operation

einhaken ['ainha:kən] vt to hook in ♦ vr: **sich bei jdm ~** to link arms with sb ♦ vi (sich einmischen) to intervene

Einhalt ['ainhalt] m: **~ gebieten** +dat to put a stop to; **e~en** (unreg) vt (Regel) to keep ♦ vi to stop

einhändigen ['ainhɛndigən] vt to hand in

einhängen ['ainhɛŋən] vt to hang; (Telefon) to hang up ♦ vi (TEL) to hang up; **sich bei jdm ~** to link arms with sb

einheimisch ['ainhaimiʃ] adj native; **E~e(r)** f(m) local

Einheit ['ainhait] f unity; (Maß, MIL) unit; **e~lich** adj uniform; **~spreis** m standard price

einholen ['ainho:lən] vt (Tau) to haul in; (Fahne, Segel) to lower; (Vorsprung aufholen) to catch up with; (Verspätung) to make up; (Rat, Erlaubnis) to ask ♦ vi (einkaufen) to shop

Einhorn ['ainhɔrn] nt unicorn

einhüllen ['ainhylən] vt to wrap up

einhundert num one hundred, a hundred

einig ['ainiç] adj (vereint) united; **sich dat ~ sein** to be in agreement; **~ werden** to agree

einige(r, s) ['ainigə(r, s)] adj, pron some ♦ pl some; (mehrere) several; **~mal** adv a few times; **~n** vt to unite ♦ vr: **sich ~n (auf** +akk to agree (on)

einigermaßen adv somewhat; (leidlich) reasonably

einig- zW: **~gehen** (unreg) vi to agree; **E~keit** f unity; (Übereinstimmung) agreement; **E~ung** f agreement; (Vereinigung) unification

einkalkulieren ['aınkalkuliːrən] vt to take into account, to allow for

Einkauf ['aınkauf] m purchase; **e~en** vt to buy ♦ vi to shop; **e~en gehen** to go shopping

Einkaufs- zW: **~bummel** m shopping spree; **~korb** m shopping basket; **~wagen** m shopping trolley; **~zentrum** nt shopping centre

einklammern ['aınklamərn] vt to put in brackets, to bracket

Einklang ['aınklaŋ] m harmony

einklemmen ['aınklɛmən] vt to jam

einkochen ['aınkɔxən] vt to boil down; (Obst) to preserve, to bottle

Einkommen ['aınkɔmən] (-s, -) nt income; **~(s)steuer** f income tax

Einkünfte ['aınkʏnftə] pl income sg, revenue sg

einladen ['aınlaːdən] (unreg) vt (Person) to invite; (Gegenstände) to load; **jdn ins Kino ~** to take sb to the cinema

Einladung f invitation

Einlage ['aınlaːgə] f (Programm~) interlude; (Spar~) deposit; (Schuh~) insole; (Fußstütze) support; (Zahn~) temporary filling; (KOCH) noodles pl, vegetables pl etc in soup

einlagern vt to store

Einlaß ['aınlas] (-sses, -lässe) m (Zutritt) admission

einlassen ['aınlasən] (unreg) vt to let in; (einsetzen) to set in ♦ vr: **sich mit jdm/auf etw akk ~** to get involved with sb/sth

Einlauf ['aınlauf] m arrival; (von Pferden) finish; (MED) enema; **e~en** (unreg) vi to arrive, to come in; (in Hafen) to enter; (SPORT) to finish; (Wasser) to run in; (Stoff) to shrink ♦ vt (Schuhe) to break in ♦ vr (SPORT) to warm up; (Motor,

Maschine) to run in; **jdm das Haus e~en** to invade sb's house

einleben ['aınleːbən] vr to settle down

einlegen ['aınleːgən] vt (einfügen: Blatt, Sohle) to insert; (KOCH) to pickle; (Pause) to have; (Protest) to make; (Veto) to use; (Berufung) to lodge; (AUT: Gang) to engage

einleiten ['aınlaıtən] vt to introduce, to start; (Geburt) to induce

Einleitung f introduction; induction

einleuchten ['aınlɔʏçtən] vi: (jdm) **~** to be clear od evident (to sb); **~d** adj clear

einliefern ['aınliːfərn] vt: **~ (in** +akk) to take (into)

Einliegerwohnung ['aınliːgərvoːnuŋ] f self-contained flat; (für Eltern, Großeltern) granny flat

einlösen ['aınløːzən] vt (Scheck) to cash; (Schuldschein, Pfand) to redeem; (Versprechen) to keep

einmachen ['aınmaxən] vt to preserve

einmal ['aınmaːl] adv once; (erstens) first; (zukünftig) sometime; **nehmen wir ~** an just let's suppose; **noch ~** once more; **nicht ~** not even; **auf ~** all at once; **es war ~** once upon a time there was/were; **E~eins** nt multiplication tables pl; **~ig** adj unique; (nur einmal erforderlich) single; (prima) fantastic

Einmarsch ['aınmarʃ] m entry; (MIL) invasion; **e~ieren** vi to march in

einmischen ['aınmıʃən] vr: **sich ~ (in** +akk) to interfere (with)

einmütig ['aınmyːtıç] adj unanimous

Einnahme ['aınnaːmə] f (von Medizin) taking; (MIL) capture, taking; **~n** pl (Geld) takings, revenue sg; **~quelle** f source of income

einnehmen ['aınneːmən] (unreg) vt to take; (Stellung, Raum) to take up; **~ für/gegen** to persuade in favour of/against; **~d** adj charming

Einöde ['aınʔøːdə] f desert, wilderness

einordnen ['aɪn'ɔrdnən] vt to arrange, to fit in ♦ vr to adapt; (AUT) to get into lane

einpacken ['aɪnpakən] vt to pack (up)

einparken ['aɪnparkən] vt to park

einpendeln ['aɪnpɛndəln] vr to even out

einpflanzen ['aɪnpflantsən] vt to plant; (MED) to implant

einplanen ['aɪnplaːnən] vt to plan for

einprägen ['aɪnprɛːgən] vt to impress, to imprint; (beibringen): (jdm) ~ to impress (on sb); sich dat etw ~ to memorize sth

einrahmen ['aɪnraːmən] vt to frame

einräumen ['aɪnrɔʏmən] vt (ordnend) to put away; (überlassen: Platz) to give up; (zugestehen) to admit, to concede

einreden ['aɪnreːdən] vt: jdm/sich etw ~ to talk sb/o.s. into believing sth

einreiben ['aɪnraɪbən] (unreg) vt to rub in

einreichen ['aɪnraɪçən] vt to hand in; (Antrag) to submit

Einreise ['aɪnraɪzə] f entry; ~bestimmungen pl entry regulations; ~erlaubnis f entry permit; ~genehmigung f entry permit; e~n vi: (in ein Land) e~n to enter (a country)

einrichten ['aɪnrɪçtən] vt (Haus) to furnish; (schaffen) to establish, to set up; (arrangieren) to arrange; (möglich machen) to manage ♦ vr (in Haus) to furnish one's house; sich ~ (auf +akk) (sich vorbereiten) to prepare o.s. (for); (sich anpassen) to adapt to

Einrichtung f (Wohnungs~) furnishings pl; (öffentliche Anstalt) organization; (Dienste) service

einrosten ['aɪnrɔstən] vi to get rusty

einrücken ['aɪnrʏkən] vi (MIL: in Land) to move in

Eins [aɪns] (-, -en) f one; e~ num one; es ist mir alles e~ it's all one to me

einsam ['aɪnzaːm] adj lonely, solitary; E~keit f loneliness, solitude

einsammeln f ['aɪnzaməln] vt to collect

Einsatz ['aɪnzats] m (Teil) inset; (an Kleid) insertion; (Verwendung) use, employment; (Spiel~) stake; (Risiko) risk; (MIL) operation; (MUS) entry; im ~ in action; e~bereit adj ready for action

einschalten ['aɪnʃaltən] vt (einfügen) to insert; (Pause) to make; (ELEK) to switch on; (Anwalt) to bring in ♦ vr (dazwischentreten) to intervene

einschärfen ['aɪnʃɛrfən] vt: jdm etw ~ to impress sth (up)on sb

einschätzen ['aɪnʃɛtsən] vt to estimate, to assess ♦ vr to rate o.s.

einschenken ['aɪnʃɛŋkən] vt to pour out

einschicken ['aɪnʃɪkən] vt to send in

einschl. abk (= einschließlich) incl.

einschlafen ['aɪnʃlaːfən] (unreg) vi to fall asleep, to go to sleep

einschläfernd ['aɪnʃlɛːfərnt] adj (MED) soporific; (langweilig) boring; (Stimme) lulling

Einschlag ['aɪnʃlaːk] m impact; (fig: Beimischung) touch, hint; e~en (unreg) vt to knock in; (Fenster) to smash, to break; (Zähne, Schädel) to smash in; (AUT: Räder) to turn; (kürzer machen) to take up; (Ware) to pack, to wrap up; (Weg, Richtung) to take ♦ vi to hit; (sich einigen) to agree; (Anklang finden) to work, to succeed; in etw akk/auf jdn e~en to hit sb/sth

einschlägig ['aɪnʃlɛːgɪç] adj relevant

einschließen ['aɪnʃliːsən] (unreg) vt (Kind) to lock in; (Häftling) to lock up; (Gegenstand) to lock away; (Bergleute) to cut off; (umgeben) to surround; (MIL) to encircle; (fig) to include, to comprise ♦ vr to lock o.s. in

einschließlich adv inclusive ♦ präp +gen inclusive of, including

einschmeicheln ['aɪnʃmaɪçəln] vr: sich ~ (bei) to ingratiate o.s. (with)

einschnappen ['aɪnʃnapən] vi (Tür) to click to; (fig) to be touchy; **eingeschnappt sein** to be in a huff

einschneidend ['aɪnʃnaɪdənt] adj drastic

Einschnitt ['aɪnʃnɪt] m cutting; (MED) incision; (Ereignis) decisive point

einschränken ['aɪnʃrɛŋkən] vt to limit, to restrict; (Kosten) to cut down, to reduce ♦ vr to cut down (on expenditure)

Einschränkung f restriction, limitation; reduction; (von Behauptung) qualification

Einschreib- zW: **~(e)brief** m recorded delivery letter; **e~en** (unreg) vt to write in; (Post) to send recorded delivery ♦ vr to register; (UNIV) to enrol; **~en** nt recorded delivery letter

einschreiten ['aɪnʃraɪtən] (unreg) vi to step in, to intervene; **~ gegen** to take action against

einschüchtern ['aɪnʃʏçtərn] vt to intimidate

einschulen ['aɪnʃuːlən] vt: **eingeschult werden** (Kind) to start school

einsehen ['aɪnzeːən] (unreg) vt (hineinsehen in) to realize; (Akten) to have a look at; (verstehen) to see; **E~** (-s) nt understanding; **ein E~ haben** to show understanding

einseitig ['aɪnzaɪtɪç] adj one-sided

Einsend- ['aɪnzɛnd] zW: **~en** (unreg) vt to send in; **~er** (-s, -) m sender, contributor; **~ung** f sending in

einsetzen ['aɪnzɛtsən] vt to put (in); (in Amt) to appoint, to install; (Geld) to stake; (verwenden) to use; (MIL) to employ ♦ vi (beginnen) to set in; (MUS) to enter, to come in ♦ vr to work hard; **sich für jdn/etw ~** to support sb/sth

Einsicht ['aɪnzɪçt] f insight; (in Akten) look, inspection; **zu der ~ kommen** to come to the conclusion that ...; **e~ig** adj (Mensch) judicious; **e~slos** adj unreasonable;

e~svoll adj understanding

Einsiedler ['aɪnziːdlər] m hermit

einsilbig ['aɪnzɪlbɪç] adj (auch fig) monosyllabic; (Mensch) uncommunicative

einspannen ['aɪnʃpanən] vt (Papier) to insert; (Pferde) to harness; (umg: Person) to rope in

Einsparung ['aɪnʃpaːrʊŋ] f economy, saving

einsperren ['aɪnʃpɛrən] vt to lock up

einspielen ['aɪnʃpiːlən] vr (SPORT) to warm up ♦ vt (Film: Geld) to bring in; (Instrument) to play in; **sich aufeinander ~** to become attuned to each other; **gut eingespielt** running smoothly

einsprachig ['aɪnʃpraːxɪç] adj monolingual

einspringen ['aɪnʃprɪŋən] (unreg) vi (aushelfen) to help out, to step into the breach

Einspruch ['aɪnʃprʊx] m protest, objection; **~srecht** nt veto

einspurig ['aɪnʃpuːrɪç] adj (EISENB) single-track; (AUT) single-lane

einst [aɪnst] adv once; (zukünftig) one day, some day

Einstand ['aɪnʃtant] m (TENNIS) deuce; (Antritt) entrance (to office)

einstecken ['aɪnʃtɛkən] vt to stick in, to insert; (Brief) to post; (ELEK: Stecker) to plug in; (Geld) to pocket; (mitnehmen) to take; (überlegen sein) to put in the shade; (hinnehmen) to swallow

einstehen ['aɪnʃteːən] (unreg) vi: **für jdn/etw ~** to guarantee sb/sth; (verantworten): **für etw ~** to answer for sth

einsteigen ['aɪnʃtaɪgən] (unreg) vi to get in od on; (in Schiff) to go on board; (sich beteiligen) to come in; (hineinklettern) to climb in

einstellen ['aɪnʃtɛlən] vt (aufhören) to stop; (Geräte) to adjust; (Kamera etc) to focus; (Sender, Radio) to tune in; (unterstellen) to put; (in Firma) to employ, to take on ♦ vi (Firma:

take on staff/workers ♦ *vr* (*anfangen*) to set in; (*kommen*) to arrive; **sich auf jdn ~** to adapt to sb; **sich auf etw** *akk* **~** to prepare o.s. for sth

Einstellung *f* (*Aufhören*) suspension, cessation; adjustment; focusing; (*von Arbeiter etc*) appointment; (*Haltung*) attitude

Einstieg ['aɪnʃtiːk] (-(e)s, -e) *m* entry; (*fig*) approach

einstig ['aɪnstɪç] *adj* former

einstimmig ['aɪnʃtɪmɪç] *adj* unanimous; (*MUS*) for one voice

einstmalig ['aɪnstmaːlɪç] *adj* former

einstmals *adv* once, formerly

einstöckig ['aɪnʃtœkɪç] *adj* twostoreyed

Einsturz ['aɪnʃtʊrts] *m* collapse

einstürzen ['aɪnʃtʏrtsən] *vi* to fall in, to collapse

einstweilen *adv* meanwhile; (*vorläufig*) temporarily, for the time being

einstweilig *adj* temporary

eintägig ['aɪntɛːgɪç] *adj* one-day

eintasten ['aɪntastən] *vt* to key (in)

eintauschen ['aɪntaʊʃən] *vt*: **~** (**gegen** *od* **für**) to exchange (for)

eintausend ['aɪn'taʊzənt] *num* one thousand

einteilen ['aɪntaɪlən] *vt* (*in Teile*) to divide (up); (*Menschen*) to assign

einteilig *adj* one-piece

eintönig ['aɪntøːnɪç] *adj* monotonous

Eintopf ['aɪntɔpf] *m* stew; **~gericht** *nt* stew

Eintracht ['aɪntraxt] (-) *f* concord, harmony

einträchtig ['aɪntrɛçtɪç] *adj* harmonious

Eintrag ['aɪntraːk] (-(e)s, -e) *m* entry; **amtlicher ~** entry in the register; **e~en** (*unreg*) *vt* (*in Buch*) to enter; (*Profit*) to yield ♦ *vr* to put one's name down; **jdm etw e~en** to bring sth to sb

einträglich ['aɪntrɛːklɪç] *adj* profitable

eintreffen ['aɪntrɛfən] (*unreg*) *vi* to

happen; (*ankommen*) to arrive

eintreten ['aɪntreːtən] *vi* to occur; (*sich einsetzen*) to intercede ♦ *vt* (*Tür*) to kick open; **~ in** +*akk* to enter; (*in Club, Partei*) to join

Eintritt ['aɪntrɪt] *m* (*Betreten*) entrance; (*Anfang*) commencement; (*in Club etc*) joining

Eintritts- *zW*: **~geld** *nt* admission charge; **~karte** *f* (admission) ticket; **~preis** *m* admission charge

einüben ['aɪn'yːbən] *vt* to practise

Einvernehmen ['aɪnfɛrneːmən] (-s, -) *nt* agreement, harmony

einverstanden ['aɪnfɛrʃtandən] *excl* agreed, okay ♦ *adj*: **~ sein** to agree, to be agreed

Einverständnis ['aɪnfɛrʃtɛntnɪs] *nt* understanding; (*gleiche Meinung*) agreement

Einwand ['aɪnvant] (-(e)s, -e) *m* objection

Einwanderer ['aɪnvandərər] *m* immigrant

einwandern *vi* to immigrate

Einwanderung *f* immigration

einwandfrei *adj* perfect ♦ *adv* absolutely

Einwegflasche ['aɪnveːgflaʃə] *f* nodeposit bottle

Einwegspritze *f* disposable syringe

einweichen ['aɪnvaɪçən] *vt* to soak

einweihen ['aɪnvaɪən] *vt* (*Kirche*) to consecrate; (*Brücke*) to open; (*Gebäude*) to inaugurate; (**~ in** +*akk*) (*Person*) to initiate (in)

Einweihung *f* consecration; opening; inauguration; initiation

einweisen ['aɪnvaɪzən] (*unreg*) *vt* (*in Amt*) to install; (*in Arbeit*) to introduce; (*in Anstalt*) to send

einwenden ['aɪnvɛndən] (*unreg*) *vt*: **etwas ~ gegen** to object to, to oppose

einwerfen ['aɪnvɛrfən] (*unreg*) *vt* to throw in; (*Brief*) to post; (*Geld*) to put in, to insert; (*Fenster*) to smash; (*äußern*) to interpose

einwickeln ['aɪnvɪkəln] *vt* to wrap up; (*fig: umg*) to outsmart

einwilligen ['aɪnvɪlɪgən] vi: ~ (in +akk) to consent (to), to agree (to)

Einwilligung f consent

einwirken ['aɪnvɪrkən] vi: auf jdn/ etw ~ to influence sb/sth

Einwohner ['aɪnvoːnər] (-s, -) m inhabitant; ~**meldeamt** nt registration office; ~**schaft** f population, inhabitants pl

Einwurf ['aɪnvʊrf] m (Öffnung) slot; (von Münze) insertion; (von Brief) posting; (Einwand) objection; (SPORT) throw-in

Einzahl ['aɪntsaːl] f singular; **e~en** vt to pay in; ~**ung** f paying in

einzäunen ['aɪntsɔʏnən] vt to fence in

Einzel ['aɪntsəl] (-s, -) nt (TENNIS) singles; ~**fahrschein** m one-way ticket; ~**fall** m single instance, individual case; ~**handel** m retail trade; ~**handelspreis** m retail price; ~**heit** f particular, detail; **e~n** adj single; (vereinzelt) the odd ◆ adv singly; **e~n angeben** to specify; **der/die e~ne** the individual; **das e~ne** the particular; **ins e~ne gehen** to go into detail; ~**teil** nt component (part); ~**zimmer** nt single room

einziehen ['aɪntsiːən] (unreg) vt to draw in, to take in; (Kopf) to duck; (Fühler, Antenne, Fahrgestell) to retract; (Steuern, Erkundigungen) to collect; (MIL) to draft, to call up; (aus dem Verkehr ziehen) to withdraw; (konfiszieren) to confiscate ◆ vi to move in; (Friede, Ruhe) to come; (Flüssigkeit) to penetrate

einzig ['aɪntsɪç] adj only; (ohnegleichen) unique; **das ~e** the only thing; **der/die ~e** the only one; ~**artig** adj unique

Einzug ['aɪntsuːk] m entry, moving in

Eis [aɪs] (-es, -) nt ice; (Speise-) ice cream; ~**bahn** f ice od skating rink; ~**bär** m polar bear; ~**becher** m sundae; ~**bein** nt pig's trotters pl; ~**berg** m iceberg; ~**café** nt ice-cream parlour (BRIT) or parlor

(US); ~**decke** f sheet of ice; ~**diele** f ice-cream parlour

Eisen ['aɪzən] (-s, -) nt iron

Eisenbahn f railway, railroad (US); ~**abteil** nt railway compartment; ~**er** (-s, -) m railwayman, railway employee, railroader (US); ~**schaffner** m railway guard; ~**wagen** m railway carriage

Eisenerz nt iron ore

eisern ['aɪzərn] adj iron; (Gesundheit) robust; (Energie) unrelenting; (Reserve) emergency

Eis- [aɪs] zW: **e~frei** adj clear of ice; ~**hockey** nt ice hockey; **e~ig** ['aɪzɪç] adj icy; **e~kalt** adj icy cold; ~**kunstlauf** m figure skating; ~**laufen** nt ice skating; ~**pickel** m ice-axe; ~**schießen** nt ≈ curling; ~**schrank** m fridge, ice-box (US); ~**würfel** m ice cube; ~**zapfen** m icicle; ~**zeit** f ice age

eitel ['aɪtəl] adj vain; **E~keit** f vanity

Eiter ['aɪtər] (-s) m pus; **e~ig** adj suppurating; **e~n** vi to suppurate

Eiweiß (-es, -e) nt white of an egg; (CHEM) protein

Ekel¹ ['eːkəl] (-s) m nausea, disgust

Ekel² (-s, -) nt (umg: Mensch) nauseating person

ekelerregend adj nauseating, disgusting

ekelhaft adj nauseating, disgusting

ekelig adj nauseating, disgusting

ekeln vt to disgust ◆ vr: **sich ~** (vor +dat) to loathe, to be disgusted (at); **es ekelt jdn** od **jdm** sb is disgusted

eklig adj nauseating, disgusting

Ekstase [ɛk'staːzə] f ecstasy

Ekzem [ɛk'tseːm] (-s, -e) nt (MED) eczema

Elan [e'laːn] (-s) m elan

elastisch [e'lastɪʃ] adj elastic

Elastizität [elastitsi'tɛːt] f elasticity

Elch [ɛlç] (-(e)s, -e) m elk

Elefant [ele'fant] m elephant

elegant [ele'gant] adj elegant

Eleganz [ele'gants] f elegance

Elek- [e'leːk] zW: ~**triker** [-trikər] (-s,

-) *m* electrician; **e~trisch** [-trɪʃ] *adj*
electric; **e~trisieren** [-tri'zi:rən] *vt*
(*auch fig*) to electrify; (*Mensch*) to
give an electric shock to ♦ *vi* to get
an electric shock; **~trizität**
[-tritsi'tɛːt] *f* electricity; **~trizi-**
tätswerk *nt* power station; (*Gesellschaft*) electric power company

Elektro- [e'lɛktro] *zW*: **~de** [-'tro:də]
f electrode; **~herd** *m* electric cooker; **~n** (-s, -en) *nt* electron; **~nen-**
rechner *m* computer; **~nik** *f* electron-
ics *sg*; **e~nisch** *adj* electronic;
e~nische Post electronic mail;
e~nischer Briefkasten electronic
mailbox; **~rasierer** *m* electric razor

Elektrotechnik *f* electrical engineering

Element [ele'mɛnt] (-s, -e) *nt* element; (*ELEK*) cell, battery; **e~ar**
[-'taːr] *adj* elementary; (*naturhaft*)
elemental

Elend ['eːlɛnt] (-(e)s) *nt* misery; **e~**
adj miserable; **~sviertel** *nt* slum

elf [ɛlf] *num* eleven; **E~** (-, -en) *f*
(*SPORT*) eleven

Elfe *f* elf

Elfenbein *nt* ivory

Elfmeter *m* (*SPORT*) penalty (kick)

Elite [e'liːtə] *f* elite

Elixier [eli'ksiːr] (-s, -e) *nt* elixir

Ellbogen *m* elbow

Elle ['ɛlə] *f* ell; (*Maß*) yard

Ellenbogen *m* elbow

Ell(en)bogenfreiheit *f* (*fig*) elbow
room

Ellipse [ɛ'lɪpsə] *f* ellipse

Elsaß ['ɛlzas] (- od -sses) *nt*: **das ~**
Alsace

Elster ['ɛlstər] (-, -n) *f* magpie

Eltern ['ɛltərn] *pl* parents; **~beirat** *m*
(*SCH*) ≈ PTA (*BRIT*), parents' council; **~haus** *nt* home; **e~los** *adj* par-
entless

Email [e'maːi] (-s, -s) *nt* enamel;
e~lieren [ema'jiːrən] *vt* to enamel

Emanzipation [emantsipatsi'oːn] *f*
emancipation

emanzi'pieren *vt* to emancipate

Embryo ['ɛmbryo] (-s, -s *od* Em-

bryonen) *m* embryo

Emi- *zW*: **~grant(in)** *m(f)* emigrant;
~gration [emigratsi'oːn] *f* emigration; **e~grieren** [-'griːrən] *vi* to emigrate

Emissionen [emisi'oːnən] *fpl* emis-
sions

Empfang [ɛm'pfaŋ] (-(e)s, **ᴂ**) *m* reception; (*Erhalten*) receipt; **in ~**
nehmen to receive; **e~en** (*unreg*) *vt*
to receive ♦ *vi* (*unreg*) (*schwanger
werden*) to conceive

Empfäng- [ɛm'pfɛŋ] *zW*: **~er** (-s, -)
m receiver; (*COMM*) addressee, con-
signee; **e~lich** *adj* receptive, susceptible; **~nis** (-, -se) *f* conception;
~nisverhütung *f* contraception

Empfangs- *zW*: **~bestätigung** *f*
acknowledgement; **~dame** *f* receptionist; **~schein** *m* receipt; **~zim-**
mer *nt* reception room

empfehlen [ɛm'pfeːlən] (*unreg*) *vt*
to recommend ♦ *vr* to take one's
leave; **~swert** *adj* recommendable

Empfehlung *f* recommendation

empfiehlst *etc* [ɛm'pfiːlst] *vb siehe*
empfehlen

empfind- [ɛm'pfɪnt] *zW*: **~en** [-dən]
(*unreg*) *vt* to feel; **~lich** *adj* sensitive; (*Stelle*) sore; (*reizbar*) touchy;
~sam *adj* sentimental; **E~ung** *f*
feeling, sentiment

empfohlen *etc* [ɛm'pfoːlən] *vb siehe*
empfehlen

empor [ɛm'poːr] *adv* up, upwards

empören [ɛm'pøːrən] *vt* to make indignant; to shock ♦ *vr* to become indignant; **~d** *adj* outrageous

Emporkömmling [ɛm'poːrkœmlɪŋ]
m upstart, parvenu

Empörung *f* indignation

emsig ['ɛmzɪç] *adj* diligent, busy

End- ['ɛnd] *m zW* final; **~e** (-s, -n) *nt*
end; **am ~e** at the end; (*schließlich*)
in the end; **am ~e sein** to be at the
end of one's tether; **~e Dezember**
at the end of December; **zu ~e sein**
to be finished; **e~en** *vi* to end;
e~gültig *adj* final, definite

Endivie [ɛn'diːviə] *f* endive

End- zW: **e~lich** adj final; (MATH) finite ♦ adv finally; **e~lich!** at last!; **komm e~lich!** come on!; **e~los** adj endless, infinite; **~spiel** nt final(s); **~spurt** m (SPORT) final spurt; **~station** f terminus; nt ending

Energie [ɛnɛr'giː] f energy; **~bedarf** m energy requirement; **e~los** adj lacking in energy, weak; **~versorgung** f supply of energy; **~wirtschaft** f energy industry

energisch [e'nɛrgɪʃ] adj energetic

eng [ɛŋ] adj narrow; (Kleidung) tight; (fig: Horizont) narrow, limited; (Freundschaft, Verhältnis) close; **~ an etw** dat close to sth

Engagement [ãgaʒə'mãː] (-s, -s) nt engagement; (Verpflichtung) commitment

engagieren [ãga'ʒiːrən] vt to engage ♦ vr to commit o.s.; **ein engagierter Schriftsteller** a committed writer

Enge ['ɛŋə] f (auch fig) narrowness; (Land~) defile; (Meer~) straits pl; **jdn in die ~ treiben** to drive sb into a corner

Engel ['ɛŋəl] (-s, -) m angel; **e~haft** adj angelic

engherzig adj petty

England nt England

Engländer(in) m(f) Englishman-(woman)

englisch adj English

Engpaß m defile, pass; (fig, Verkehr) bottleneck

en gros [ã'groː] adv wholesale

engstirnig ['ɛnʃtɪrnɪç] adj narrow-minded

Enkel ['ɛŋkəl] (-s, -) m grandson; **~in** f granddaughter

Enkelkind nt grandchild

enorm [e'nɔrm] adj enormous

Ensemble [ã'sãbəl] (-s, -s) nt company, ensemble

entbehren [ɛnt'beːrən] vt to do without, to dispense with

entbehrlich adj superfluous

Entbehrung f deprivation

entbinden [ɛnt'bɪndən] (unreg) vt

(+gen) to release (from); (MED) to deliver ♦ vi to give birth

Entbindung f release; (MED) confinement; **~sheim** nt maternity hospital

entdeck- [ɛnt'dɛk] zW: **~en** vt to discover; **E~er** (-s, -) m discoverer; **E~ung** f discovery

Ente ['ɛntə] f duck; (fig) canard, false report

enteignen [ɛnt'aignən] vt to expropriate; (Besitzer) to dispossess

enterben [ɛnt'ɛrbən] vt to disinherit

entfallen [ɛnt'falən] (unreg) vi to drop, to fall; (wegfallen) to be dropped; **jdm ~** (vergessen) to slip sb's memory; **auf jdn ~** to be allotted to sb

entfalten [ɛnt'faltən] vt to unfold; (Talente) to develop ♦ vr to open; (Mensch) to develop one's potential

Entfaltung f unfolding; (von Talenten) development

entfern- [ɛnt'fɛrn] zW: **~en** vt to remove; (hinauswerfen) to expel ♦ vr to go away, to withdraw; **~t** adj distant; **weit davon ~t sein, etw zu tun** to be far from doing sth; **E~ung** f distance; (Wegschaffen) removal; **E~ungsmesser** (-s, -) m (PHOT) rangefinder

entfremden [ɛnt'frɛmdən] vt to estrange, to alienate

Entfremdung f alienation, estrangement

entfrosten [ɛnt'frɔstən] vt to defrost

Entfroster (-s, -) m (AUT) defroster

entführ- [ɛnt'fyːr] zW: **~en** vt to carry off, to abduct; to kidnap; **E~er** m kidnapper; **E~ung** f abduction, kidnapping

entgegen [ɛnt'geːgən] präp +dat contrary to, against ♦ adv towards; **~bringen** (unreg) vt to bring; **jdm etw ~bringen** (fig) to show sb sth; **~gehen** (unreg) vi +dat to go to meet, to go towards; **~gesetzt** adj opposite; (widersprechend) opposed; **~halten** (unreg) vt (fig) to object;

E~kommen nt obligingness; **~kommen** (unreg) vi +dat to approach; to meet; (fig) to accommodate; **~kommend** adj obliging; **~nehmen** (unreg) vt to receive; to accept; **~sehen** (unreg) vt +dat to await; **~setzen** vt to oppose; **~treten** (unreg) vi +dat to step up to; (fig) to oppose, to counter; **~wirken** vi +dat to counteract

entgegnen [ɛnt'ge:gnən] vt to reply, to retort

entgehen [ɛnt'ge:ən] (unreg) vi (fig): **jdm ~** to escape sb's notice; **sich** dat **etw ~** lassen to miss sth

entgeistert [ɛnt'gaɪstərt] adj thunderstruck

Entgelt [ɛnt'gɛlt] (-(e)s, -e) nt compensation, remuneration

entgleisen [ɛnt'glaɪzən] vi (EISENB) to be derailed; (fig: Person) to misbehave; **~ lassen** to derail

entgräten [ɛnt'grɛ:tən] vt to fillet, to bone

Enthaarungscreme [ɛnt'ha:rʊŋs-] f hair-removing cream

enthalten [ɛnt'haltən] (unreg) vt to contain ♦ vr: **sich (von etw) ~** to abstain (from sth), to refrain (from sth)

enthaltsam [ɛnt'haltza:m] adj abstinent, abstemious

enthemmen [ɛnt'hɛmən] vt: **jdn ~** to free sb from his inhibitions

enthüllen [ɛnt'hʏlən] vt to reveal, to unveil

Enthusiasmus [ɛntuzi'asmʊs] m enthusiasm

entkommen [ɛnt'kɔmən] (unreg) vi: **~ (aus** od **+dat)** to get away (from), to escape (from)

entkräften [ɛnt'krɛftən] vt to weaken, to exhaust; (Argument) to refute

entladen [ɛnt'la:dən] (unreg) vt to unload; (ELEK) to discharge ♦ vr (ELEK, Gewehr) to discharge; (Ärger etc) to vent itself

entlang [ɛnt'laŋ] adv along; **entlang dem Fluß**, **den Fluß entlang** along the river; **~gehen** (unreg) vi to walk along

entlarven [ɛnt'larfən] vt to unmask, to expose

entlassen [ɛnt'lasən] (unreg) vt to discharge; (Arbeiter) to dismiss

Entlassung f discharge; dismissal

entlasten [ɛnt'lastən] vt to relieve; (Achse) to relieve the load on; (Angeklagten) to exonerate; (Konto) to clear

Entlastung f relief; (COMM) crediting

entlegen [ɛnt'le:gən] adj remote

entlocken [ɛnt'lɔkən] vt: **jdm etw ~** to elicit (sth from sb)

entmündigen [ɛnt'mʏndɪgən] vt to certify

entmutigen [ɛnt'mu:tɪgən] vt to discourage

entnehmen [ɛnt'ne:mən] (unreg) vt (+dat) to take out (of), to take (from); (folgern) to infer (from)

entrahmen [ɛnt'ra:mən] vt to skim

entreißen [ɛnt'raɪsən] (unreg) vt: **jdm etw ~** to snatch sth (away) from sb

entrichten [ɛnt'rɪçtən] vt to pay

entrosten [ɛnt'rɔstən] vt to derust

entrüst- [ɛnt'rʏst] zW: **~en** vt to incense, to outrage ♦ vr to be filled with indignation; **~et** adj indignant, outraged; **E~ung** f indignation

entrümpeln vt to clear out

entschädigen [ɛnt'ʃɛ:dɪgən] vt to compensate

Entschädigung f compensation

entschärfen [ɛnt'ʃɛrfən] vt to defuse; (Kritik) to tone down

Entscheid [ɛnt'ʃaɪt] (-(e)s, -e) m decision; **e~en** (unreg) vt, vi, vr to decide; **e~end** adj decisive; (Stimme) casting; **~ung** f decision

entschieden [ɛnt'ʃi:dən] adj decided; (entschlossen) resolute; **E~heit** f firmness, determination

entschließen [ɛnt'ʃli:sən] (unreg) vr to decide

entschlossen [ɛnt'ʃlɔsən] adj determined, resolute; **E~heit** f determination

Entschluß [ɛnt'ʃlʊs] m decision;

e~**freudig** adj decisive; ~**kraft** f determination, decisiveness

entschuldigen [ɛnt'ʃʊldɪgən] vt to excuse ♦ vr to apologize; **jdn um ~ bitten** to apologize to sb; **~!** excuse me; (Verzeihung) sorry

Entschuldigung f apology; (Grund) excuse; **jdn um ~ bitten** to apologize to sb; **~!** excuse me; (Verzeihung) sorry

entsetz- [ɛnt'zɛts] zW: ~**en** vt to horrify; (MIL) to relieve ♦ vr to be horrified od appalled; **E~en** (-s) nt horror, dismay; **~lich** adj dreadful, appalling; **~t** adj horrified

Entsorgung [ɛnt'zɔrgʊŋ] f (von Kraftwerken, Chemikalien) (waste) disposal

entspannen [ɛnt'ʃpanən] vt, vr (Körper) to relax; (POL: Lage) to ease

Entspannung f relaxation, rest; (POL) détente; ~**spolitik** f policy of détente

entsprechen [ɛnt'ʃprɛçən] (unreg) vi +dat to correspond to; (Anforderungen, Wünschen) to meet, to comply with; ~**d** adj appropriate ♦ adv accordingly

entspringen [ɛnt'ʃprɪŋən] (unreg) vi (+dat) to spring (from)

entstehen [ɛnt'ʃteːən] (unreg) vi: ~ (aus od durch) to arise (from), to result (from)

Entstehung f genesis, origin

entstellen [ɛnt'ʃtɛlən] vt to disfigure; (Wahrheit) to distort

entstören [ɛnt'ʃtøːrən] vt (RADIO) to eliminate interference from; (AUT) to suppress

enttäuschen [ɛnt'tɔʏʃən] vt to disappoint

Enttäuschung f disappointment

entwaffnen [ɛnt'vafnən] vt (lit, fig) to disarm

entwässern [ɛnt'vɛsərn] vt to drain

Entwässerung f drainage

entweder ['ɛntveːdər] konj either

entwenden [ɛnt'vɛndən] (unreg) vt to purloin, to steal

entwerfen [ɛnt'vɛrfən] (unreg) vt (Zeichnung) to sketch; (Modell) to

design; (Vortrag, Gesetz etc) to draft

entwerten [ɛnt'veːrtən] vt to devalue; (stempeln) to cancel

Entwerter (-s, -) m ticket punching machine

entwickeln [ɛnt'vɪkəln] vt, vr (auch PHOT) to develop; (Mut, Energie) to show (o.s.), to display (o.s.)

Entwicklung [ɛnt'vɪklʊŋ] f development; (PHOT) developing

Entwicklungs- zW: ~**hilfe** f aid for developing countries; ~**jahre** pl adolescence sg; ~**land** nt developing country

entwöhnen [ɛnt'vøːnən] vt to wean; (Süchtige) to cure (of sth); (einer Sache dat od von etw) ~ to cure (of sth)

Entwöhnung f weaning; cure, curing

entwürdigend [ɛnt'vʏrdɪgənt] adj degrading

Entwurf [ɛnt'vʊrf] m outline, design; (Vertrags~, Konzept) draft

entziehen [ɛnt'tsiːən] (unreg) vt (+dat) to withdraw (from), to take away (from); (Flüssigkeit) to draw (from), to extract (from) ♦ vr (+dat) to escape (from); (jds Kenntnis) to be outside od beyond; (der Pflicht) to shirk (from)

Entziehung f withdrawal; ~**sanstalt** f drug addiction/alcoholism treatment centre; ~**skur** f treatment for drug addiction/alcoholism

entziffern [ɛnt'tsɪfərn] vt to decipher; to decode

entzücken [ɛnt'tsʏkən] vt to delight; **E~** (-s) nt delight; ~**d** adj delightful, charming

entzünden [ɛnt'tsʏndən] vt to light, to set light to; (fig, MED) to inflame; (Streit) to spark off ♦ vr (auch fig) to catch fire; (Streit) to start; (MED) to become inflamed

Entzündung f (MED) inflammation

entzwei [ɛnt'tsvaɪ] adv broken; in two; ~**brechen** (unreg) vt, vi to break in two; ~**en** vt to set at odds ♦ vr to fall out; ~**gehen** (unreg) vi to break (in two)

Enzian ['ɛntsiaːn] (-s, -e) m gentian

Epidemie [epide'miː] f epidemic

Epilepsie [epile'psiː] f epilepsy

Episode [epi'zoːdə] f episode

Epoche [e'pɔxə] f epoch; **e~machend** adj epoch-making

Epos ['eːpɔs] (-, Epen) nt epic (poem)

er [eːɐ] (nom) pron he; it

erarbeiten [ɛr''arbaitən] vt to work for, to acquire; (Theorie) to work out

erbarmen vr (+gen) to have pity od mercy (on); **E~** (-s) nt pity

erbärmlich [ɛr'bɛrmlɪç] adj wretched, pitiful; **E~keit** f wretchedness

erbarmungslos [ɛr'barmuŋsloːs] adj pitiless, merciless

erbau- [ɛr'bau] zW: **~en** vt to build, to erect; (fig) to edify; **E~er** (-s, -) m builder; **~lich** adj edifying

Erbe¹ ['ɛrbə] (-n, -n) m heir

Erbe² nt inheritance; (fig) heritage

erben vt to inherit

erbeuten [ɛr'bɔytən] vt to carry off, (MIL) to capture

Erb- [ɛrb] zW: **~faktor** m gene; **~folge** f (line of) succession; **~in** f heiress

erbittern [ɛr'bɪtərn] vt to embitter; (erzürnen) to incense

erbittert [ɛr'bɪtərt] adj (Kampf) fierce, bitter

erblassen [ɛr'blasən] vi to (turn) pale

erbleichen [ɛr'blaiçən] (unreg) vi to (turn) pale

erblich ['ɛrplɪç] adj hereditary

erblinden [ɛr'blɪndən] vi to go blind

erbosen [ɛr'boːzən] vt to anger ♦ vr to grow angry

erbrechen [ɛr'brɛçən] (unreg) vt, vr to vomit

Erbschaft f inheritance, legacy

Erbse ['ɛrpsə] f pea

Erbstück nt heirloom

Erd- ['eːɐd] zW: **~achse** f earth's axis; **~atmosphäre** f earth's atmosphere; **~beben** nt earthquake; **~beere** f strawberry; **~boden** m

ground; **~e** f earth; **zu ebener ~e** at ground level; **e~en** vt (ELEK) to earth

erdenklich [ɛr'dɛŋklɪç] adj conceivable

Erd- zW: **~gas** nt natural gas; **~geschoß** nt ground floor; **~kunde** f geography; **~nuß** f peanut; **~öl** nt (mineral) oil

erdrosseln [ɛr'drɔsəln] vt to strangle, to throttle

erdrücken [ɛr'drykən] vt to crush

Erdrutsch m landslide

Erdteil m continent

erdulden [ɛr'dʊldən] vt to endure, to suffer

ereifern [ɛr''aifərn] vr to get excited

ereignen [ɛr''aignən] vr to happen

Ereignis [ɛr''aignɪs] (-ses, -se) nt event; **e~los** adj uneventful; **e~reich** adj eventful

ererbt [ɛr''ɛrpt] adj (Haus) inherited, (Krankheit) hereditary

erfahren [ɛr'faːrən] (unreg) vt to learn, to find out; (erleben) to experience ♦ adj experienced

Erfahrung f experience; **e~sgemäß** adv according to experience

erfassen [ɛr'fasən] vt to seize; (fig: einbeziehen) to include, to register; (verstehen) to grasp

erfind- [ɛr'fɪnd] zW: **~en** (unreg) vt to invent; **E~er** (-s, -) m inventor; **~erisch** adj inventive; **E~ung** f invention

Erfolg [ɛr'fɔlk] (-(e)s, -e) m success; (Folge) result; **e~en** vi to follow; (sich ergeben) to result; (stattfinden) to take place; (Zahlung) to be effected; **e~los** adj unsuccessful; **~losigkeit** f lack of success; **e~reich** adj successful; **e~versprechend** adj promising

erforderlich adj requisite, necessary

erfordern [ɛr'fɔrdərn] vt to require, to demand

erforschen [ɛr'fɔrʃən] vt (Land) to explore; (Problem) to investigate; (Gewissen) to search

Erforschung f exploration; investigation; searching

erfreuen [ɛr'frɔYən] *vr:* sich ~ an +*dat* to enjoy ♦ *vt* to delight; sich einer Sache *gen* ~ to enjoy sth

erfreulich [ɛr'frɔYlɪç] *adj* pleasing, gratifying; **~erweise** *adv* happily, luckily

erfrieren [ɛr'friːrən] (*unreg*) *vi* to freeze (to death); (*Glieder*) to get frostbitten; (*Pflanzen*) to be killed by frost

erfrischen [ɛr'frɪʃən] *vt* to refresh

Erfrischung *f* refreshment; **~sgetränk** *nt* (liquid) refreshment; **~sraum** *m* snack bar, cafeteria

erfüllen [ɛr'fYlən] *vt* (*Raum etc*) to fill; (*fig: Bitte etc*) to fulfil ♦ *vr* to come true

ergänzen [ɛr'gɛntsən] *vt* to supplement, to complete ♦ *vr* to complement one another

Ergänzung *f* completion; (*Zusatz*) supplement

ergeben [ɛr'geːbən] (*unreg*) *vt* to yield, to produce ♦ *vr* to surrender; (*folgen*) to result ♦ *adj* devoted, humble; sich etw *dat* ~ (*sich hingeben*) to give o.s. up to sth, to yield to sth; dem Trunk ~ addicted to drink

Ergebnis [ɛr'geːpnɪs] (*-ses, -se*) *nt* result; **e~los** *adj* without result, fruitless

ergehen [ɛr'geːən] (*unreg*) *vi* to be issued, to go out ♦ *vr unpers:* es ergeht ihm gut/schlecht he's faring *od* getting on well/badly ♦ *vr:* sich in etw *dat* ~ to indulge in sth; etw über sich ~ lassen to put up with sth

ergiebig [ɛr'giːbɪç] *adj* productive

Ergonomie [ɛrgonoˈmiː] *f* ergonomics

Ergonomik *f* = Ergonomie

ergreifen [ɛr'graYfən] (*unreg*) *vt* (*auch fig*) to seize; (*Beruf*) to take up; (*Maßnahmen*) to resort to; (*rühren*) to move; **~d** *adj* moving, touching

ergriffen [ɛr'grɪfən] *adj* deeply moved

Erguß [ɛr'gʊs] *m* discharge; (*fig*) outpouring, effusion

erhaben [ɛr'haːbən] *adj* raised, embossed; (*fig*) exalted, lofty; über etw *akk* ~ sein to be above sth

erhalten [ɛr'haltən] (*unreg*) *vt* to receive; (*bewahren*) to preserve, to maintain; gut ~ in good condition

erhältlich [ɛr'hɛltlɪç] *adj* obtainable, available

Erhaltung *f* maintenance, preservation

erhärten [ɛr'hɛrtən] *vt* to harden; (*These*) to substantiate, to corroborate

erheben [ɛr'heːbən] (*unreg*) *vt* to raise; (*Protest, Forderungen*) to make; (*Fakten*) to ascertain, to establish ♦ *vr* to rise (up); sich über etw *akk* ~ to rise above sth

erheblich [ɛr'heːplɪç] *adj* considerable

erheitern [ɛr'haYtərn] *vt* to amuse, to cheer (up)

Erheiterung *f* exhilaration; zur allgemeinen ~ to everybody's amusement

erhitzen [ɛr'hɪtsən] *vt* to heat ♦ *vr* to heat up; (*fig*) to become heated

erhoffen [ɛr'hɔfən] *vt* to hope for

erhöhen [ɛr'høːən] *vt* to raise; (*verstärken*) to increase

erhol- [ɛr'hoːl] *zW:* **~en** *vr* to recover; (*entspannen*) to have a rest; **~sam** *adj* restful; **E~ung** *f* recovery; relaxation, rest; **~ungsbedürftig** *adj* in need of a rest, rundown; **E~ungsgebiet** *nt* ~ holiday area; **E~ungsheim** *nt* convalescent/ rest home

erhören [ɛr'høːrən] *vt* (*Gebet etc*) to hear; (*Bitte etc*) to grant

erinnern [ɛr'ɪnərn] *vt:* ~ (an +*akk*) to remind (of) ♦ *vr:* sich (an *akk* etw) ~ to remember (sth)

Erinnerung *f* memory; (*Andenken*) reminder

erkältet [ɛr'kɛltət] *adj* with a cold; ~ sein to have a cold

Erkältung *f* cold

erkennbar adj recognizable

erkennen [ɛrˈkɛnən] (unreg) vt to recognize; (sehen, verstehen) to see

erkennt- zW: **~lich** adj: **sich ~lich zeigen;** to show one's appreciation; **E~lichkeit** f gratitude; (Geschenk) token of one's gratitude; **E~nis** (-, -se) f knowledge; (das Erkennen) recognition; (Einsicht) insight; **zur E~nis kommen** to realize

Erkennung f recognition

Erkennungszeichen nt identification

Erker [ˈɛrkər] (-s, -) m bay; **~fenster** nt bay window

erklär- [ɛrˈklɛːr] zW: **~bar** adj explicable; **~en** vt to explain; **~lich** adj explicable; (verständlich) understandable; **E~ung** f explanation; (Aussage) declaration

erkranken [ɛrˈkraŋkən] vi to fall ill

Erkrankung f illness

erkund- [ɛrˈkʊnd] zW: **~en** vt to find out, to ascertain; (bes MIL) to reconnoitre, to scout; **~igen** vr: **sich ~igen (nach)** to inquire (about); **E~igung** f inquiry; **E~ung** f reconnaissance, scouting

erlahmen [ɛrˈlaːmən] vi to tire; (nachlassen) to flag, to wane

erlangen [ɛrˈlaŋən] vt to attain, to achieve

Erlaß [ɛrˈlas] (-sses, -lässe) m decree; (Aufhebung) remission

erlassen (unreg) vt (Verfügung) to issue; (Gesetz) to enact; (Strafe) to remit; **jdm etw ~** to release sb from sth

erlauben [ɛrˈlaʊbən] vt: (jdm etw) **~** to allow od permit (sb (to do) sth) ♦ vr to permit o.s., to venture

Erlaubnis [ɛrˈlaʊpnɪs] (-, -se) f permission; (Schriftstück) permit

erläutern [ɛrˈlɔytərn] vt to explain

Erläuterung f explanation

Erle [ˈɛrlə] f alder

erleben [ɛrˈleːbən] vt to experience; (Zeit) to live through; (mit~) to witness; (noch mit~) to live to see

Erlebnis [ɛrˈleːpnɪs] (-ses, -se) nt experience

erledigen [ɛrˈleːdɪgən] vt to take care of, to deal with; (Antrag etc) to process; (umg: erschöpfen) to wear out; (: ruinieren) to finish; (: umbringen) to do in

erleichtern vt to make easier; (fig: Last) to lighten; (lindern, beruhigen) to relieve

Erleichterung f facilitation; lightening; relief

erleiden [ɛrˈlaɪdən] (unreg) vt to suffer, to endure

erlernen [ɛrˈlɛrnən] vt to learn, to acquire

erlesen [ɛrˈleːzən] adj select, choice

erleuchten [ɛrˈlɔʏçtən] vt to illuminate; (fig) to inspire

Erleuchtung f (Einfall) inspiration

Erlös [ɛrˈløːs] (-es, -e) m proceeds pl

erlösen [ɛrˈløːzən] vt to redeem, to save

Erlösung f release; (REL) redemption

ermächtigen [ɛrˈmɛçtɪgən] vt to authorize, to empower

Ermächtigung f authorization; authority

ermahnen [ɛrˈmaːnən] vt to exhort, to admonish

Ermahnung f admonition, exhortation

ermäßigen [ɛrˈmɛːsɪgən] vt to reduce

Ermäßigung f reduction

ermessen [ɛrˈmɛsən] (unreg) vt to estimate; **E~** (-s) nt estimation

Ermessen (unreg) vt, to gauge; discretion; **in jds E~ liegen** to lie within sb's discretion

ermitteln [ɛrˈmɪtəln] vt to determine; (Täter) to trace ♦ vi: **gegen jdn ~** to investigate sb

Ermittlung [ɛrˈmɪtlʊŋ] f determination; (Polizei~) investigation

ermöglichen [ɛrˈmøːklɪçən] vt (+dat) to make possible (for)

ermorden [ɛrˈmɔrdən] vt to murder

Ermordung f murder

ermüden [ɛrˈmyːdən] vt, vi to tire;

(TECH) to fatigue; **~d** adj tiring; *(fig)* wearisome

Ermüdung f fatigue; **~serscheinung** f sign of fatigue

ermutigen [ɛrˈmuːtɪgən] vt to encourage

ernähr- [ɛrˈnɛːr] zW: **~en** vt to feed, to nourish; *(Familie)* to support ♦ vr to support o.s., to earn a living; **sich ~en von** to live on; **E~er (-s, -)** m breadwinner; **E~ung** f nourishment; nutrition; *(Unterhalt)* maintenance

ernennen [ɛrˈnɛnən] *(unreg)* vt to appoint

Ernennung f appointment

erneu- [ɛrˈnɔʏ] zW: **~ern** vt to renew; to restore; to renovate; **E~erung** f renewal; restoration; renovation; **~t** adj renewed, fresh ♦ adv once more

ernst [ɛrnst] adj serious; **E~ (-es)** m seriousness; **das ist mein E~** I'm quite serious; **im E~** in earnest; **E~machen mit etw** to put sth into practice; **E~fall** m emergency; **~gemeint** adj meant in earnest, serious; **~haft** adj serious; **E~haftigkeit** f seriousness; **~lich** adj serious

Ernte [ˈɛrntə] f harvest; **e~n** vt to harvest; *(Lob etc)* to earn

ernüchtern [ɛrˈnʏçtərn] vt to sober up; *(fig)* to bring down to earth

Erober- [ɛrˈʔoːbər] zW: **~er (-s, -)** m conqueror; **e~n** vt to conquer; **~ung** f conquest

eröffnen [ɛrˈʔœfnən] vt to open ♦ vr to present itself; **jdm etw ~** to disclose sth to sb

Eröffnung f opening

erörtern [ɛrˈʔœrtərn] vt to discuss

Erotik [eˈroːtɪk] f eroticism

erotisch adj erotic

erpress- [ɛrˈprɛs] zW: **~en** vt *(Geld etc)* to extort; *(Mensch)* to blackmail; **E~er (-s, -)** m blackmailer; **E~ung** f extortion; blackmail

erprobt [ɛrˈprɔpt] adj *(Gerät, Medikamente)* proven, tested

erraten [ɛrˈraːtən] *(unreg)* vt to guess

erreg- [ɛrˈreːg] zW: **~en** vt to excite; *(ärgern)* to infuriate; *(hervorrufen)* to arouse, to provoke ♦ vr to get excited od worked up; **E~er (-s, -)** m causative agent; **E~ung** f excitement

erreichbar adj accessible, within reach

erreichen [ɛrˈraɪçən] vt to reach; *(Zweck)* to achieve; *(Zug)* to catch

errichten [ɛrˈrɪçtən] vt to erect, to put up; *(gründen)* to establish, to set up

erringen [ɛrˈrɪŋən] *(unreg)* vt to gain, to win

erröten [ɛrˈrøːtən] vi to blush, to flush

Errungenschaft [ɛrˈrʊŋənʃaft] f achievement; *(umg: Anschaffung)* acquisition

Ersatz [ɛrˈzats] **(-es)** m substitute; replacement; *(Schaden)* compensation; *(MIL)* reinforcements pl; **~dienst** m *(MIL)* alternative service; **~reifen** m *(AUT)* spare tyre; **~teil** nt spare (part)

erschaffen [ɛrˈʃafən] *(unreg)* vt to create

erscheinen [ɛrˈʃaɪnən] *(unreg)* vi to appear

Erscheinung f appearance; *(Geist)* apparition; *(Gegebenheit)* phenomenon; *(Gestalt)* figure

erschießen [ɛrˈʃiːsən] *(unreg)* vt to shoot (dead)

erschlagen [ɛrˈʃlaːgən] *(unreg)* vt to strike dead

erschöpf- [ɛrˈʃœpf] zW: **~en** vt to exhaust; *(fig)* exhaustive, thorough; **E~ung** f exhaustion

erschrecken [ɛrˈʃrɛkən] vt to startle, to frighten ♦ vi to be frightened od startled; **~d** adj alarming, frightening

erschrocken [ɛrˈʃrɔkən] adj frightened, startled

erschüttern [ɛrˈʃʏtərn] vt to shake; *(fig)* to move deeply

Erschütterung f shaking; shock

erschweren [ɛrˈʃveːrən] vt to complicate

erschwinglich adj within one's means

ersetzen [ɛrˈzɛtsən] vt to replace; **jdm Unkosten** etc ~ to pay sb's expenses etc

ersichtlich [ɛrˈzɪçtlɪç] adj evident, obvious

ersparen [ɛrˈʃpaːrən] vt (Ärger etc) to spare; (Geld) to save

Ersparnis (-, -se) f saving

erst [eːrst] adv 1 first; **mach erst mal die Arbeit fertig** finish your work first; **wenn du das erst mal hinter dir hast** once you've got that behind you

2 (nicht früher als, nur) only; (nicht bis) not till; **erst gestern** only yesterday; **erst morgen** not until tomorrow; **erst als** only when, not until; **wir fahren erst später** we're not going until later; **er ist (gerade) erst angekommen** he's only just arrived

3: **wäre er doch erst zurück!** if only he were back!

erstatten [ɛrˈʃtatən] vt (Kosten) to (re)pay; **Anzeige** etc **gegen jdn** ~ to report sb; **Bericht** ~ to make a report

Erstaufführung [ˈeːrstʔaʊffyːrʊŋ] f first performance

erstaunen [ɛrˈʃtaʊnən] vt to astonish ♦ vi to be astonished; **E~** (-s) nt astonishment

erstaunlich adj astonishing

erst- [ˈeːrst] zW: **E~ausgabe** f first edition; **~beste(r, s)** adj first that comes along; **~e(r, s)** adj first

erstechen [ɛrˈʃtɛçən] (unreg) vt to stab (to death)

erstehen [ɛrˈʃteːən] (unreg) vt to buy ♦ vi to (a)rise

erstens [ˈeːrstəns] adv firstly, in the first place

ersticken [ɛrˈʃtɪkən] vt (auch fig) to stifle; (Mensch) to suffocate; (Flammen) to smother ♦ vi (Mensch) to

suffocate; (Feuer) to be smothered; **in Arbeit** ~ to be snowed under with work

erst- zW: **~klassig** adj first-class; **E~kommunion** f first communion; **~malig** adj first; **~mals** adv for the first time

erstrebenswert [ɛrˈʃtreːbənsveːrt] adj desirable, worthwhile

erstrecken [ɛrˈʃtrɛkən] vr to extend, to stretch

ersuchen [ɛrˈzuːxən] vt to request

ertappen [ɛrˈtapən] vt to catch, to detect

erteilen [ɛrˈtaɪlən] vt to give

Ertrag [ɛrˈtraːk] (-(e)s, -̈e) m yield; (Gewinn) proceeds pl

ertragen (unreg) vt to bear, to stand

erträglich [ɛrˈtrɛːklɪç] adj tolerable, bearable

ertrinken [ɛrˈtrɪŋkən] (unreg) vi to drown; **E~** (-s) nt drowning

erübrigen [ɛrˈyːbrɪɡən] vt to spare ♦ vr to be unnecessary

erwachen [ɛrˈvaxən] vi to awake

erwachsen [ɛrˈvaksən] adj grown-up; **E~e(r)** mf adult; **E~enbildung** f adult education

erwägen [ɛrˈvɛːɡən] (unreg) vt to consider

Erwägung f consideration

erwähn- [ɛrˈvɛːn] zW: **~en** vt to mention; **~enswert** adj worth mentioning; **E~ung** f mention

erwärmen [ɛrˈvɛrmən] vt to warm, to heat ♦ vr to get warm, to warm up; **sich** ~ **für** to warm to

Erwarten nt: **über meinen/unseren usw** ~ beyond my/our etc expectations; **wider** ~ contrary to expectations

erwarten [ɛrˈvartən] vt to expect; (warten auf) to wait for; **etw kaum** ~ **können** to be hardly able to wait for sth

Erwartung f expectation; **e~sgemäß** adv as expected; **e~svoll** adj expectant

erwecken [ɛrˈvɛkən] vt to rouse, to awake; **den Anschein** ~ to give the impression

Erweis [ɛr'vaɪs] (-es, -e) m proof;
e~en (unreg) vt to prove ♦ vr: **sich
e~en** (als) to prove (to be); **jdm
einen Gefallen/Dienst e~en** to do
sb a favour/service

Erwerb [ɛr'vɛrp] (-(e)s, -e) m acquisition; (Beruf) trade; **e~en** (unreg)
vt to acquire

erwerbs- zW: **~los** adj unemployed;
E~quelle f source of income; **~tätig**
adj (gainfully) employed

erwidern [ɛr'viːdərn] vt to reply;
(vergelten) to return

erwischen [ɛr'vɪʃən] (umg) vt to
catch, to get

erwünscht [ɛr'vʏnʃt] adj desired

erwürgen [ɛr'vʏrgən] vt to strangle

Erz [eːrts] (-es, -e) nt ore

erzähl- [ɛr'tsɛːl] zW: **~en** vt to tell ♦
vi: **sie kann gut ~en** she's a good
story-teller; **E~er** (-s, -) m narrator;
E~ung f story, tale

Erzbischof m archbishop

erzeug- [ɛr'tsɔʏg] zW: **~en** vt to produce; (Strom) to generate; **E~nis** (-
ses, -se) nt product, produce;
E~ung f production; generation

erziehen [ɛr'tsiːən] (unreg) vt to
bring up; (bilden) to educate, to train

Erzieher(in) (-s, -) m(f) (Berufsbe-
zeichnung) teacher

Erziehung f bringing up; (Bildung)
education

Erziehungsbeihilfe f educational
grant

Erziehungsberechtigte(r) mf
parent; guardian

erzielen [ɛr'tsiːlən] vt to achieve, to
obtain; (Tor) to score

erzwingen [ɛr'tsvɪŋən] (unreg) vt to
force, to obtain by force

es [ɛs] (nom, akk) pron it

Esche ['ɛʃə] f ash

Esel ['eːzəl] (-s, -) m donkey, ass

Eskalation [ɛskalatsi̯o:n] f escalation

Eskimo ['ɛskimo] (-s, -s) m eskimo

eßbar ['ɛsbaːr] adj eatable, edible

Eßbesteck nt knife, fork and spoon

Eßecke f dining area

essen ['ɛsən] (unreg) vt, vi to eat;
E~ (-s, -) nt meal; food

Essig ['ɛsɪç] (-s, -e) m vinegar;
~gurke f gherkin

Eß- ['ɛs] zW: **~kastanie** f sweet chestnut; **~löffel** m tablespoon; **~tisch** m
dining table; **~waren** pl foodstuffs, provisions; **~zimmer** nt dining room

etablieren [eta'bliːrən] vr to become
established; to set up in business

Etage [e'taːʒə] f floor, storey; **~nbet-
ten** pl bunk beds; **~nwohnung** f flat

Etappe [e'tapə] f stage

Etat [e'ta:] (-s, -s) m budget

etc abk (= et cetera) etc

etepetete [e:təpe'te:tə] (umg) adj
fussy

Ethik ['e:tɪk] f ethics sg

ethisch ['e:tɪʃ] adj ethical

Etikett [eti'kɛt] (-(e)s, -e) nt label;
tag; **~e** f etiquette, manners pl

etliche ['ɛtlɪçə] pron pl some, quite a
few

etliches pron a thing or two

Etui [ɛt'viː] (-s, -s) nt case

etwa ['ɛtva] adv (ungefähr) about;
(vielleicht) perhaps; (beispielsweise)
for instance; **nicht ~** by no means;
~ig ['ɛtvaɪç] adj possible

etwas pron something; anything;
(ein wenig) a little ♦ adv a little

euch [ɔʏç] pron (akk von ihr) you;
yourselves; (dat von ihr) (to) you

euer ['ɔʏər] pron (gen von ihr) of you
♦ possessiv (gen) your

Eule ['ɔʏlə] f owl; **eure** ['ɔʏrə(r, s)]
adj f siehe **euer**

eure(r, s) pron yours; **~rseits** adv
on your part; **~s** adj nt siehe **euer**;
~sgleichen pron people like you;
~twegen adv (für euch) for your
sakes; (wegen euch) on your account; **~twillen** adv: **um ~twillen**
= euretwegen

eurige ['ɔʏrɪgə] pron: **der/die/das ~**
yours

Euro- zW: **~pa** [ɔʏ'roːpa] nt Europe;
~päer(in) [ɔʏro'pɛːər(ɪn)] mf European; **e~päisch** adj European;

~**pameister** [ɔʏˈrɔːpəː-] m European
champion; ~**scheck** m (FINANZ)
eurocheque

Euter [ˈɔʏtɐ] (-s, -) nt udder

ev. abk = **evangelisch**

evakuieren [evakuˈiːrən] vt to
evacuate

evangelisch [evaŋˈɡeːlɪʃ] adj Protestant

Evangelium [evaŋˈɡeːliʊm] nt gospel

eventuell [eventuˈɛl] adj possible ♦
adv possibly, perhaps

evtl. abk = **eventuell**

EWG [eːveːˈɡeː] (-) f abk (= Europäische Wirtschaftsgemeinschaft)
EEC, Common Market

ewig [ˈeːvɪç] adj eternal; ~**keit** f
eternity

exakt [ɛˈksakt] adj exact

Examen [ɛˈksaːmən] (-s, - od Ex-
amina) nt examination

Exemplar [ɛksɛmˈplaːr] (-s, -e) nt
specimen; (Buch~) copy; e~**isch** adj
exemplary

exerzieren [ɛksɛrˈtsiːrən] vi to drill

Exil [ɛˈksiːl] (-s, -e) nt exile

Existenz [ɛksɪsˈtɛnts] f existence;
(Unterhalt) livelihood, living; (pej:
Mensch) character; ~**minimum** [-s]
nt subsistence level

existieren [ɛksɪsˈtiːrən] vi to exist

exklusiv [ɛkskluˈziːf] adj exclusive;
~**e** [-ˈziːvə] adv exclusive of, not including ♦ präp ~gen exclusive of, not
including

exotisch [ɛˈksoːtɪʃ] adj exotic

Expedition [ɛkspeditsiˈoːn] f expedition

Experiment [ɛksperiˈmɛnt] nt experiment; e~**ell** adj experimental;
e~**ieren** vi to experiment

Experte [ɛksˈpɛrtə] (-n, -n) m expert, specialist

Expertin f expert, specialist

explo- [ɛksploˈ-] zW: ~**dieren**
[-ˈdiːrən] vi to explode; E~**sion** [-
ziˈoːn] f explosion; ~**siv** adj explosive

Export [ɛksˈpɔrt] (-(e)s, -e) m export; ~**eur** [-ˈtøːr] m exporter;
~**handel** m export trade; e~**ieren**

[-ˈtiːrən] vt to export; ~**land** nt ex-
porting country

Expreßgut [ɛksˈprɛs-] nt express
goods pl, express freight

Expreßzug m express (train)

extra [ˈɛkstra] adj inv (umg: gesondert) separate; (besondere) extra ♦
adv (gesondert) separately; (speziell) specially; (absichtlich) on purpose; (vor Adjektiven, zusätzlich)
extra; E~ (-s, -s) nt extra; E~**ausgabe** f special edition; E~**blatt** nt
special edition

Extrakt [ɛksˈtrakt] (-(e)s, -e) m
extract

extravagant adj extravagant

extrem [ɛksˈtreːm] adj extreme;
~**istisch** [-ˈmɪstɪʃ] adj (POL) extrem-
ist; E~**itäten** [-ˈtɛːtən] extremities

exzentrisch [ɛksˈtsɛntrɪʃ] adj eccentric

Exzeß [ɛksˈtsɛs] (-sses, -sse) m excess

F

Fa. abk (= Firma) firm; (in Briefen)
Messrs

Fabel [ˈfaːbəl] (-, -n) f fable; f~**haft**
adj fabulous, marvellous

Fabrik [faˈbriːk] f factory; ~**ant**
[-ˈkant] m (Hersteller) manufacturer;
(Besitzer) industrialist; ~**arbeiter** m
factory worker; ~**at** [-ˈkaːt] (-(e)s,
-e) nt manufacture, product; ~**gelände** nt factory site

Fach [fax] (-(e)s, ᵉer) nt compartment; (Sachgebiet) subject; **ein
Mann vom** ~ an expert; ~**arbeiter**
m skilled worker; ~**arzt** m (medical)
specialist; ~**ausdruck** m technical
term

Fächer [ˈfɛçɐ] (-s, -) m fan

Fach- zW: ~**geschäft** nt specialist
shop; ~**hochschule** f ≈ technical college; ~**kraft** f skilled worker, trained
employee; ~**kundig** adj expert, skilled;
~**lich** adj professional; expert; ~**mann** (pl -**leute**) m special-

ist; f~männisch adj professional;
~schule f technical college;
f~simpeln vi to talk shop; ~werk nt
timber frame
Fackel ['fakəl] (-, -n) f torch
fad(e) [fa:t, 'fa:də] adj insipid; (langweilig) dull
Faden ['fa:dən] (-s, ⁺) m thread;
f~scheinig adj (auch fig) thread-
bare
fähig ['fɛ:ɪç] adj: ~ (zu od +gen)
capable (of); able (to); F~keit f ability
fahnden ['fa:ndən] vi: ~ nach to
search for
Fahndung f search; ~sliste f list of
wanted criminals, wanted list
Fahne ['fa:nə] f flag, standard; eine
~ haben (umg) to smell of drink;
~nflucht f desertion
Fahrausweis m ticket
Fahrbahn f carriageway (BRIT),
roadway
Fähre ['fɛ:rə] f ferry
fahren ['fa:rən] (unreg) vt to drive;
(Rad) to ride; (befördern) to drive,
to take; (Rennen) to drive in ♦ vi
(sich bewegen) to go; (Schiff) to
sail; (abfahren) to leave; mit dem
Auto/Zug ~ to go od travel by car/
train; mit der Hand ~ über +akk
to pass one's hand over
Fahr- zW: ~er(in) (-s, -) m(f) driver; ~erflucht f hit-and-run; ~gast
m passenger; ~geld nt fare; ~karte
f ticket; ~kartenausgabe f ticket
office; ~kartenautomat m ticket
machine; ~kartenschalter m ticket
office; f~lässig adj negligent;
f~lässige Tötung manslaughter;
~lehrer m driving instructor; ~plan
m timetable; f~planmäßig adj scheduled; ~preis m fare; ~prüfung f
driving test; ~rad nt bicycle; ~rad-
weg m cycle lane; ~schein m ticket; ~scheinentwerter m (automatic)
ticket stamping machine
Fährschule ['fɛ:rʃi] nt ferry(-boat)
Fahrschule f driving school
Fahrstuhl m lift (BRIT), elevator

(US)
Fahrt [fa:rt] (-, -en) f journey; (kurz)
trip; (AUT) drive; (Geschwindigkeit)
speed; gute ~! have a good journey
Fährte ['fɛ:rtə] f track, trail
Fahrtkosten pl travelling expenses
Fahrtrichtung f course, direction
Fahrzeug nt vehicle; ~brief m log
book
fair [fe:r] adj fair
Fakten pl von Faktum
Faktor ['faktɔr] m factor
Fakultät [fakul'tɛ:t] f faculty
Falke ['falkə] (-n, -n) m falcon
Fall [fal] (-(e)s, ⁺e) m (Sturz) fall;
(Sachverhalt, JUR, GRAM) case;
auf jeden ~, auf alle Fälle in any
case; (bestimmt) definitely; auf keinen ~! no way!; ~e f trap; f~en
(unreg) vi to fall; etw f~en lassen
to drop sth
fällen ['fɛlən] vt (Baum) to fell; (Urteil) to pass
fallenlassen (unreg) vt (Bemerkung) to make; (Plan) to abandon, to
drop
fällig ['fɛlɪç] adj due
falls [fals] adv in case, if
Fallschirm m parachute; ~springer
m parachutist
falsch [falʃ] adj false; (unrichtig)
wrong
fälschen ['fɛlʃən] vt to forge
fälsch- zW: ~lich adj false; ~licher-
weise adv mistakenly; F~ung f for-
gery
Falte ['faltə] f (Knick) fold, crease;
(Haut~) wrinkle; (Rock~) pleat;
f~n vt to fold; (Stirn) to wrinkle
faltig adj (Hände, Haut) wrinkled;
(zerknittert: Rock) creased
familiär [famili'ɛ:r] adj familiar
Familie [fa'mi:liə] f family
Familien- zW: ~betrieb m family
business; ~kreis m family circle;
~mitglied nt member of the family;
~name m surname; ~stand m marital status
Fan (-s, -s) m fan
Fanatiker [fa'na:tikər] (-s, -) m fana-

tic

fanatisch adj fanatical

fand etc [fant] vb siehe **finden**

Fang [faŋ] (-(e)s, -e) m catch; (Jagen) hunting; (Kralle) talon, claw; f~en (unreg) vt to catch ♦ vr to get caught; (Flugzeug) to level out; (Mensch: nicht fallen) to steady o.s.; (fig) to compose o.s.; (in Leistung) to get back on form

Farb- ['farb] zW: ~abzug m colour print; ~aufnahme f colour photograph; ~band m typewriter ribbon; ~dia nt colour slide; ~e f (zum Malen etc) paint; (Stoffarbe) dye; f~echt adj colourfast

färben ['fɛrbən] vt to colour; (Stoff, Haar) to dye

farben- ['farbən-] zW: ~blind adj colour-blind; ~freudig adj colourful; ~froh adj colourful, gay

Farb- zW: ~fernsehen nt colour television; ~film m colour film; ~foto nt colour photograph; f~ig adj coloured; ~ige(r) mf coloured (person); ~kasten m paintbox; f~lich adj colour; f~los adj colourless; ~stift m coloured pencil; ~stoff m dye; ~ton m hue, tone

Färbung ['fɛrbʊŋ] f colouring; (Tendenz) bias

Farn [farn] (-(e)s, -e) m fern; bracken

Fasan [fa'za:n] (-(e)s, -e(n)) m pheasant

Fasching ['faʃɪŋ] (-s, -e od -s) m carnival

Faschismus [fa'ʃɪsmʊs] m fascism

Faschist m fascist

Faser ['fa:zər] (-, -n) f fibre; f~n vi to fray

Faß [fas] (-sses, Fässer) nt vat, barrel; (für Öl) drum; **Bier vom** ~ draught beer

Fassade [fa'sa:də] f façade

fassen ['fasən] vt (ergreifen) to grasp, to take; (inhaltlich) to hold; (Entschluß etc) to take; (verstehen) to understand; (Ring etc) to set; (formulieren) to formulate, to phrase ♦ vr to calm down; **nicht zu ~** unbelievable

Fassung ['fasʊŋ] f (Umrahmung) mounting; (Lampen-) socket; (Wortlaut) version; (Beherrschung) composure; **jdn aus der ~ bringen** to upset sb; f~slos adj speechless

fast [fast] adv almost, nearly

fasten ['fastən] vi to fast; F~zeit f Lent

Fastnacht f Shrove Tuesday; carnival

faszinieren [fastsi'ni:rən] vt to fascinate

fatal [fa'ta:l] adj fatal; (peinlich) embarrassing

faul [faul] adj rotten; (Person) lazy; (Ausreden) lame; **daran ist etwas ~** there's something fishy about it; f~en vi to rot; f~enzen vi to idle; F~enzer (-s, -) m idler, loafer; F~heit f laziness; f~ig adj putrid

Faust [faust] (-, Fäuste) f fist; **auf eigene ~** off one's own bat; ~handschuh m mitten

Favorit [favo'ri:t] (-en, -en) m favourite

faxen ['faksən] vt to fax; **jdm etw ~** to fax sth to sb

FCKW m abk (= Fluorchlorkohlenwasserstoff) CFC

FDP [ɛfde:'pe:] (-) f abk (= Freie Demokratische Partei) Free Democratic Party

Februar ['fe:brua:r] (-(s), -e) m February

fechten ['fɛçtən] (unreg) vi to fence

Feder ['fe:dər] (-, -n) f feather; (Schreib-) pen nib; (TECH) spring; ~ball m shuttlecock; ~bett nt continental quilt; ~halter m penholder, pen; f~leicht adj light as a feather; f~n vi (nachgeben) to be springy; (sich bewegen) to bounce ♦ vt to spring; ~ung f (AUT) suspension

Fee [fe:] f fairy

Fegefeuer nt purgatory

fegen ['fe:gən] vt to sweep

fehl [fe:l] adj: ~ **am Platz** od **Ort** out of place; ~en vi to be wanting od missing; (*abwesend sein*) to be absent; **etw ~t jdm** sb lacks sth; **du ~st mir** I miss you; **was ~t ihm?** what's wrong with him? **F~er** (-s, -) *m* mistake, error; (*Mangel, Schwäche*) fault; **~erfrei** *adj* faultless; without any mistakes; **~erhaft** *adj* incorrect; faulty; **~erlos** *adj* flawless, perfect; **F~geburt** *f* miscarriage; **~gehen** (*unreg*) *vi* to go astray; **F~griff** *m* blunder; **F~konstruktion** *f* badly designed thing; **~schlagen** (*unreg*) *vi* to fail; **F~start** *m* (*SPORT*) false start; **~zündung** *f* (*AUT*) misfire, backfire

Feier ['faɪər] (-, -n) *f* celebration; **~abend** *m* time to stop work; **~abend machen** to stop, to knock off; **jetzt ist ~abend!** that's enough!; **f~lich** *adj* solemn; **~lichkeit** *f* solemnity; **~lichkeiten** *pl* (*Veranstaltungen*) festivities; **f~n** *vt, vi* to celebrate; **~tag** *m* holiday

feig(e) ['faɪg(ə)] *adj* cowardly
Feige *f* fig
Feigheit *f* cowardice
Feigling *m* coward
Feile [faɪlə] *f* file
feilschen *vi* to haggle
fein [faɪn] *adj* fine; (*vornehm*) refined; (*Gehör etc*) keen; **~! great!**
Feind [faɪnt] (-(e)s, -e) *m* enemy; **f~lich** *adj* hostile; **~schaft** *f* enmity; **f~selig** *adj* hostile; **~seligkeit** *f* hostility

Fein- *zW:* **f~fühlig** *adj* sensitive; **~gefühl** *nt* delicacy, tact; **~heit** *f* fineness; refinement; keenness; **~kostgeschäft** *nt* delicatessen (shop); **~schmecker** (-s, -) *m* gourmet

Feinwäsche *f* delicate clothing (*when washing*)

Feld [fɛlt] (-(e)s, -er) *nt* field; (*SCHACH*) square; (*SPORT*) pitch; **~herr** *m* commander; **~stecher** (-s, -) *m* binoculars *pl*; **~weg** *m* path
Feldzug *m* (*fig*) campaign
Felge ['fɛlgə] *f* (wheel) rim

Fell [fɛl] (-(e)s, -e) *nt* fur; coat; (*von Schaf*) fleece; (*von toten Tieren*) skin
Fels [fɛls] (-en, -en) *m* rock; (*Klippe*) cliff
Felsen ['fɛlzən] (-s, -) *m* = **Fels**; **f~fest** *adj* firm
feminin [femi'ni:n] *adj* feminine; (*pej*) effeminate
Fenster ['fɛnstər] (-s, -) *nt* window; **~bank** *f* windowsill; **~laden** *m* shutter; **~leder** *nt* chamois (leather); **~platz** *m* window seat; **~scheibe** *f* windowpane

Ferien ['fe:riən] *pl* holidays, vacation *sg* (*US*); **~ haben** to be on holiday; **~kurs** *m* holiday course; **~lager** *nt* holiday camp; **~reise** *f* holiday; **~wohnung** *f* holiday apartment

Ferkel ['fɛrkəl] (-s, -) *nt* piglet

fern [fɛrn] *adj, adv* far-off, distant; **~ von hier** a long way (away) from here; **der F~e Osten** the Far East; **F~amt** *nt* (*TEL*) exchange; **F~bedienung** *f* remote control; **F~e** *f* distance; **~er** *adj* further ♦ *adv* further; (*weiterhin*) in future; **F~gespräch** *nt* trunk call; **F~glas** *nt* binoculars *pl*; **~halten** (*unreg*) *vt, vr* to keep away; **F~licht** *nt* (*AUT*) full beam; **F~meldeamt** *nt* international exchange; **F~rohr** *nt* telescope; **F~ruf** *m* (*förmlich*) telephone number; **F~schreiben** *nt* telex; **F~sehapparat** *m* television set; **F~sehen** (-s) *nt* television; **im F~sehen** on television; **~sehen** (*unreg*) *vi* to watch television; **F~seher** *m* television; **F~sprecher** *m* telephone; **F~sprechzelle** *f* telephone box od booth (*US*); **F~steuerung** *f* remote control; **F~straße** *f* ≈ 'A' road (*BRIT*), highway (*US*); **F~verkehr** *m* long-distance traffic

Ferse ['fɛrzə] *f* heel

fertig ['fɛrtɪç] *adj* (*bereit*) ready; (*beendet*) finished; (*gebrauchs-*) ready-made; **~bringen** (*unreg*) *vt* (*fähig sein*) to be capable of; **F~gericht** *nt* precooked meal; **F~haus** *nt* kit house, prefab; **F~keit**

f skill; ~**machen** *vt* (*beenden*) to finish; (*umg*: *Person*) to finish; (: *körperlich*) to exhaust; (: *moralisch*) to get down ♦ *vr* to get ready; ~**stellen** *vt* to complete

Fessel ['fɛsəl] (-, -**n**) *f* fetter; ~**n** *vt* to bind; (*mit Fesseln*) to fetter; (*fig*) to spellbind; **f~nd** *adj* fascinating, captivating

Fest (-(**e**)**s**, -**e**) *nt* party; festival; **frohes ~!** Happy Christmas!

fest [fɛst] *adj* firm; (*Nahrung*) solid; (*Gehalt*) regular ♦ *adv* (*schlafen*) soundly; (: *Kosten*) fixed cost; ~**angestellt** *adj* permanently employed; ~**binden** (*unreg*) *vt* to tie, to fasten; ~**bleiben** (*unreg*) *vi* to stand firm; **F~essen** *nt* banquet; ~**halten** (*unreg*) *vt* to seize, to hold fast; (*Ereignis*) to record ♦ *vr*: **sich ~halten (an** +*dat*) to hold on (to); ~**igen** *vt* to strengthen; **F~igkeit** *f* strength; ~**ival** ['fɛstival] (-**s**, -**s**) *nt* festival; ~**land** *nt* mainland; ~**legen** *vt* to fix ♦ *vr* to commit o.s.; ~**lich** *adj* festive; ~**liegen** (*unreg*) *vi* (*feststehen*: *Termin*) to be confirmed, be fixed; ~**machen** *vt* to fasten; (*Termin etc*) to fix; **F~nahme** *f* arrest; ~**nehmen** (*unreg*) *vt* to arrest; **F~rede** *f* address; ~**setzen** *vt* to fix, to settle; **F~spiele** *pl* (*Veranstaltung*) festival *sg*; ~**stehen** (*unreg*) *vi* to be certain; ~**stellen** *vt* to establish; (*sagen*) to remark; **F~tag** *m* feast day, holiday; **F~ung** *f* fortress; **F~wochen** *pl* festival *sg*

Fett [fɛt] (-(**e**)**s**, -**e**) *nt* fat, grease **fett** *adj* fat; (*Essen etc*) greasy; (*TYP*) bold; ~**arm** *adj* low fat; ~**en** *vt* to grease; **F~fleck** *m* grease stain; ~**ig** *adj* greasy, fatty

Fetzen ['fɛtsən] (-**s**, -) *m* scrap **feucht** [fɔʏçt] *adj* damp; (*Luft*) humid; **F~igkeit** *f* dampness; humidity

Feuer ['fɔʏɐ] (-**s**, -) *nt* fire; (*zum Rauchen*) a light; (*fig*: *Schwung*) spirit; ~**alarm** *m* fire alarm; **f~fest** *adj* fireproof; ~**gefahr** *f* danger of fire; **f~gefährlich** *adj* inflammable;

f ~**leiter** *f* fire escape ladder; ~**löscher** (-**s**, -) *m* fire extinguisher; ~**melder** (-**s**, -) *m* fire alarm; **f~n** *vt*, *vi* (*auch fig*) to fire; ~**stein** *m* flint; ~**treppe** *f* fire escape; ~**wehr** (-, -**en**) *f* fire brigade; ~**wehrauto** *nt* fire engine; ~**wehrmann** *m* fireman; ~**werk** *nt* fireworks *pl*; ~**zeug** *nt* (cigarette) lighter

Fichte ['fɪçtə] *f* spruce, pine

Fieber ['fiːbɐ] (-**s**, -) *nt* fever, temperature; **f~haft** *adj* feverish; ~**thermometer** *nt* thermometer; **fieberig** *adj* (*Erkältung*) feverish

fiel *etc* [fiːl] *vb siehe* **fallen**

fies [fiːs] (*umg*) *adj* nasty

Figur [fi'guːɐ] (-, -**en**) *f* figure; (*Schach*~) chessman, chess piece

Filet [fi'leː] (-**s**, -**s**) *nt* (*KOCH*) fillet

Filiale [fi'liaːlə] *f* (*COMM*) branch

Film [fɪlm] (-(**e**)**s**, -**e**) *m* film; ~**aufnahme** *f* shooting; **f~en** *vt*, *vi* to film; ~**kamera** *f* cine-camera

Filter ['fɪltɐ] (-**s**, -) *m* filter; **f~n** *vt* to filter; ~**papier** *nt* filter paper; ~**zigarette** *f* tipped cigarette

Filz [fɪlts] (-**es**, -**e**) *m* felt; **f~en** *vt* (*umg*) to frisk ♦ *vi* (*Wolle*) to mat; ~**stift** *m* felt-tip pen

Finale [fi'naːlə] (-**s**, -(**s**)) *nt* finale; (*SPORT*) final(s)

Finanz [fi'nants] *f* finance; ~**amt** *nt* Inland Revenue Office; ~**beamte(r)** *m* revenue officer; **f~iell** [-tsi'ɛl] *adj* financial; ~**ieren** [-'tsiːrən] *vt* to finance; **f~kräftig** *adj* financially strong; ~**minister** *m* Chancellor of the Exchequer (*BRIT*), Minister of Finance

Find- [ˈfɪnd] *zW*: **f~en** (*unreg*) *vt* to find; (*meinen*) to think ♦ *vr* to be (found); (*sich fassen*) to compose o.s.; **ich f~e nichts dabei, wenn ...** I don't see what's wrong if ...; **das wird sich f~en** things will work out; ~**er** (-**s**, -) *m* finder; ~**erlohn** *m* reward (*for sb who finds sth*); **f~ig** *adj* resourceful

fing *etc* [fɪŋ] *vb siehe* **fangen**

Finger ['fɪŋɐ] (-**s**, -) *m* finger; ~**ab-**

druck m fingerprint; **~hut** m thimble; (BOT) foxglove; **~nagel** m fingernail; **~spitze** f fingertip
fingiert adj made-up, fictitious
Fink [fɪŋk] (-en, -en) m finch
Finn- [fɪn] zW: **~e** (-n, -n) m Finn; **~in** f Finn; **f~isch** adj Finnish; **~land** nt Finland
finster ['fɪnstər] adj dark, gloomy; (verdächtig) dubious; (verdrossen) grim; (Gedanke) dark; **F~nis** (-) f darkness, gloom
Firma ['fɪrma] (-, -men) f firm
Firmen- ['fɪrmən] zW: **~inhaber** m owner of firm; **~schild** nt (shop) sign; **~zeichen** nt trademark
Firnis ['fɪrnɪs] (-ses, -se) m varnish
Fisch [fɪʃ] (-(e)s, -e) m fish; **~e** pl (ASTROL) Pisces sg; **f~en** vt, vi to fish; **~er** (-s, -) m fisherman; **~erei** f fishing, fishery; **~fang** m fishing; **~geschäft** nt fishmonger's (shop); **~gräte** f fishbone
fit [fɪt] adj fit
Fitneß ['fɪtnəs] (-, -) f (physical) fitness
fix [fɪks] adj fixed; (Person) alert, smart; **~ und fertig** finished; (erschöpft) done in; **~ieren** [fi'ksiːrən] vt to fix; (anstarren) to stare at
flach [flax] adj flat; (Gefäß) shallow
Fläche ['flɛçə] f area; (Ober~) surface
Flachland nt lowland
flackern ['flakərn] vi to flare, to flicker
Flagge ['flagə] f flag
flaggen vi to fly a flag
Flamingo [fla'mɪŋgo] (-s, -s) m (ZOOL) flamingo
flämisch ['flɛːmɪʃ] adj (LING) Flemish
Flamme ['flamə] f flame
Flandern ['flandərn] nt Flanders
Flanell [fla'nɛl] (-s, -e) m flannel
Flanke ['flaŋkə] f flank; (SPORT: Seite) wing
Flasche ['flaʃə] f bottle; (umg: Versager) wash-out

Flaschen- zW: **~bier** nt bottled beer; **~öffner** m bottle opener; **~zug** m pulley
flatterhaft adj flighty, fickle
flattern ['flatərn] vi to flutter
flau [flau] adj weak, listless; (Nachfrage) slack; **jdm ist ~** sb feels queasy
Flaum [flaum] (-(e)s) m (Feder) down; (Haare) fluff
flauschig ['flauʃɪç] adj fluffy
Flaute ['flautə] f calm; (COMM) recession
Flechte ['flɛçtə] f plait; (MED) dry scab; (BOT) lichen; **f~n** (unreg) vt to plait; (Kranz) to twine
Fleck [flɛk] (-(e)s, -e) m spot; (Schmutz~) stain; (Stoff~) patch; (Makel) blemish; **nicht vom ~ kommen** (auch fig) not to get any further; **vom ~ weg** straight away
Flecken (-s, -) m = Fleck; **f~los** adj spotless; **f~mittel** nt stain remover; **~wasser** nt stain remover
fleckig adj spotted; stained
Fledermaus ['fleːdərmaus] f bat
Flegel ['fleːgəl] (-s, -) m (Mensch) lout; **f~haft** adj loutish, unmannerly; **~jahre** pl adolescence sg
flehen ['fleːən] vi to implore; **~tlich** adj imploring
Fleisch [flaɪʃ] (-(e)s) nt flesh; (Essen) meat; **~brühe** f beef tea, meat stock; **~er** (-s, -) m butcher; **~erei** f butcher's (shop); **f~ig** adj fleshy; **f~los** adj meatless, vegetarian
Fleiß [flaɪs] (-es) m diligence, industry; **f~ig** adj diligent, industrious
fletschen ['flɛtʃən] vt (Zähne) to show
flexibel [flɛ'ksiːbəl] adj flexible
Flicken ['flɪkən] (-s, -) m patch; **f~** vt to mend
Flieder ['fliːdər] (-s, -) m lilac
Fliege ['fliːgə] f fly; (Kleidung) bow tie; **f~n** (unreg) vt, vi to fly; **auf jdn/etw f~n** (umg) to be mad about sb/sth; **~npilz** m toadstool; **~r** (-s, -) m flier, airman
fliehen ['fliːən] (unreg) vi to flee
Fliese ['fliːzə] f tile

Fließ- ['fliːs] zW: **~band** nt production od assembly line; **f~en** (unreg) vi to flow; **f~end** adj flowing; (Rede, Deutsch) fluent; (Übergänge) smooth

flimmern ['flɪmərn] vi to glimmer

flink [flɪŋk] adj nimble, lively

Flinte ['flɪntə] f rifle; shotgun

Flitterwochen pl honeymoon sg

flitzen ['flɪtsən] vi to flit

Flocke ['flɔkə] f flake

flog etc [floːk] vb siehe **fliegen**

Floh [floː] (-(e)s, ⁓e) m flea; **~markt** m flea market

florieren [flo'riːrən] vi to flourish

Floskel ['flɔskəl] (-, -n) f set phrase

Floß [floːs] (-es, ⁓e) nt raft, float

floß etc vb siehe **fließen**

Flosse ['flɔsə] f fin

Flöte ['fløːtə] f flute; (Block~) recorder

Flötist(in) [fløː'tɪst(ɪn)] m(f) flautist

flott [flɔt] adj lively; (elegant) smart; (NAUT) afloat; **F~e** f fleet, navy

Fluch [fluːx] (-(e)s, ⁓e) m curse; **f~en** vi to curse, to swear

Flucht [flʊxt] (-, -en) f flight; (Fenster~) row; (Zimmer~) suite; **f~artig** adj hasty

flücht- ['flʏçt] zW: **~en** vi, vr to flee, to escape; **~ig** adj fugitive; (vergänglich) transitory; (oberflächlich) superficial; (eilig) fleeting; **F~igkeitsfehler** m careless slip; **F~ling** m fugitive, refugee

Flug [fluːk] (-(e)s, ⁓e) m flight; im ~ airborne, in flight; **~blatt** nt pamphlet

Flügel ['flyːgəl] (-s, -) m wing; (MUS) grand piano

Fluggast m airline passenger

flügge ['flʏgə] adj (full-)fledged

Flug- zW: **~gesellschaft** f airline (company); **~hafen** m airport; **~lärm** m aircraft noise; **~linie** f airline; **~plan** m flight schedule; **~platz** m airport; (klein) airfield; **~verkehr** m air traffic; **~zeug** nt (aero)plane, airplane (US); **~zeugentführung** f hijacking of a plane; **~zeughalle** f hangar; **~zeugträger** (-, -n) m aircraft carrier

Flunder ['flʊndər] (-, -n) f flounder

flunkern ['flʊŋkərn] vi to fib, to tell stories

Fluor ['fluːɔr] (-s) nt fluorine

Flur ['fluːr] (-(e)s, -e) m hall; (Treppen~) staircase

Fluß [flʊs] (-sses, ⁓sse) m river; (Fließen) flow; im ~ sein (fig) to be in a state of flux

flüssig ['flʏsɪç] adj liquid; **F~keit** f liquid; (Zustand) liquidity; **~machen** vt (Geld) to make available

flüstern ['flʏstərn] vt, vi to whisper

Flut [fluːt] (-, -en) f (auch fig) flood; (Gezeiten) high tide; **f~en** vi to flood; **~licht** nt floodlight

Fohlen ['foːlən] (-s, -) nt foal

Föhn [føːn] (-(e)s, -e) m (warmer Fallwind) föhn

Föhre ['føːrə] f Scots pine

Folge ['fɔlgə] f series, sequence; (Fortsetzung) instalment; (-, -n) (Auswirkung) result; in rascher ~ in quick succession; etw zur ~ haben to result in sth; **~n haben** to have consequences; **f~n** vi (+dat) (zeitlich) to follow; **~n leisten** to comply with sth; **f~n** vi +dat to follow; (gehorchen) to obey; jdm **f~n können** (fig) to follow od understand sb; **f~nd** adj following; **f~ndermaßen** adv as follows, in the following way; **f~rn** vt: **f~rn (aus)** to conclude (from); **~rung** f conclusion

folglich adv consequently

folgsam adj obedient

Folie ['foːliə] f foil

Folklore ['fɔlkloːrə] f folklore

Folter ['fɔltər] (-, -n) f torture; (Gerät) rack; **f~n** vt to torture

Fön [føːn] (-(e)s, -e; ®) m hairdryer

Fondue [fõ'dyː] (-s, -s od -, -s) nt od f (KOCH) fondue

fönen vt to (blow) dry

Fönfrisur f blow-dry hairstyle

Fontäne [fɔn'tɛːnə] f fountain

Förder- ['fœrdər] zW: **~band** nt conveyor belt; **~korb** m pit cage; **f~lich** adj beneficial

fordern ['fɔrdərn] vt to demand

fördern ['fœrdərn] vt to promote; (unterstützen) to help; (Kohle) to extract; **Förderung** f promotion; help; extraction

Forderung ['fɔrdəruŋ] f demand

Forelle [fo'rɛlə] f trout

Form [fɔrm] (-, -en) f shape; (Gestaltung) form; (Guß~) mould; (Back~) baking tin; **in ~ sein** to be in good form od shape; **in ~ von** in the shape of

Formali'tät f formality

Format [fɔr'maːt] (-(e)s, -e) nt format; (fig) distinction

formbar adj malleable

Formel (-, -n) f formula

formell [fɔr'mɛl] adj formal

formen vt to form, to shape

Formfehler m faux-pas, gaffe; (JUR) irregularity

formieren [-'miːrən] vr to form ♦ vr to form up

förmlich ['fœrmlɪç] adj formal; (umg) real; **F~keit** f formality

formlos adj shapeless; (Benehmen etc) informal

Formu'lar (-s, -e) nt form

formu'lieren vt to formulate

forsch [fɔrʃ] adj energetic, vigorous

forschen vi: **~ (nach)** to search (for); (wissenschaftlich) to (do) research; **~d** adj searching

Forscher (-s, -) m research scientist; (Natur~) explorer

Forschung ['fɔrʃuŋ] f research

Forst [fɔrst] (-(e)s, -e) m forest

Förster ['fœrstər] (-s, -) m forester; (für Wild) gamekeeper

fort [fɔrt] adv away; (verschwunden) gone; (vorwärts) on; **und so ~** and so on; **in einem ~** on and on; **~be-stehen** (unreg) vi to survive; **~be-wegen** vt, vr to move away; **~bil-den** vr to continue one's education; **~bleiben** (unreg) vi to stay away;

F~dauer f continuance; **~fahren** (unreg) vi to depart; (fortsetzen) to go on, to continue; **~führen** vt to continue, to carry on; **~gehen** (unreg) vi to go away; **~geschritten** adj advanced; **~müssen** (unreg) vi to have to go; **~pflanzen** vr to reproduce; **F~pflanzung** f reproduction

fortschaffen vt to remove

fortschreiten (unreg) vi to advance

Fortschritt ['fɔrtʃrɪt] m advance; **~e machen** to make progress; **f~lich** adj progressive

fort- zW: **~setzen** vt to continue; **F~setzung** f continuation; (folgender Teil) instalment; **F~setzung folgt** to be continued; **~während** adj incessant, continual

Foto ['foːto] (-s, -s) nt photo(graph); **~apparat** m camera; **~'graf** m photographer; **~gra'fie** f photography; (Bild) photograph; **f~gra-fieren** vt to photograph ♦ vi to take photographs; **~kopie** f photocopy

Fr. abk (= Frau) Mrs, Ms

Fracht [fraxt] (-, -en) f freight; (NAUT) cargo; (Preis) carriage; **~ zahlt Empfänger** (COMM) carriage forward; **~er** (-s, -) m freighter, cargo boat; **~gut** nt freight

Frack [frak] (-(e)s, -e) m tails pl

Frage ['fraːgə] (-, -n) f question; **eine ~ stellen** to question sth; **jdm eine ~ stellen** to ask sb a question, to put a question to sb; **nicht in ~ kommen** to be out of the question; **~bogen** m questionnaire; **f~n** vt, vi to ask; **~zeichen** nt question mark

fraglich adj questionable, doubtful

fraglos adv unquestionably

Fragment [fra'gmɛnt] nt fragment

fragwürdig ['fraːkvʏrdɪç] adj questionable, dubious

Fraktion [fraktsi'oːn] f parliamentary party

frankieren [fraŋ'kiːrən] vt to stamp, to frank

franko ['fraŋko] adv post-paid; carriage paid

Frankreich ['fraŋkraɪç] (-s) nt

France
Franse ['franzə] f fringe
Franzose [fran'tsozə] m Frenchman
Französin [fran'tsøːzɪn] f Frenchwoman
französisch adj French
fraß etc [fras] vb siehe **fressen**
Fratze ['fratsə] f grimace
Frau [frau] f (-, -en) woman; (Ehe~) wife; (Anrede) Mrs, Ms; ~ Doktor Doctor; ~**enarzt** m gynaecologist; ~**enbewegung** f feminist movement; ~**enzimmer** nt female, broad (US)
Fräulein ['frɔylain] nt young lady; (Anrede) Miss, Ms
fraulich ['fraulɪç] adj womanly
frech [frɛç] adj cheeky, impudent; F~**heit** f cheek, impudence
frei [frai] adj free; (Stelle, Sitzplatz) free, vacant; (Mitarbeiter) freelance; (unbekleidet) bare; **sich** dat **einen Tag ~ nehmen** to take a day off; **von etw ~ sein** to be free of sth; **im F~en** in the open air; **~ sprechen** to talk without notes; ~ **Haus** (COMM) carriage paid; ~**er Wettbewerb** fair/open competition; F~**bad** nt open-air swimming pool; ~**bekommen** (unreg) vt: **jdn ~bekommen** to get sb freed; **einen Tag ~bekommen** to get a day off; ~**gebig** adj generous; ~**halten** (unreg) vt to keep free; ~**händig** adv (fahren) with no hands; F~**heit** f freedom; ~**heitlich** adj liberal; F~**heitsstrafe** f prison sentence; F~**karte** f free ticket; ~**lassen** (unreg) vt to (set) free; ~**legen** vt to expose; ~**lich** adv certainly, admittedly; **ja ~lich** yes of course; F~**lichtbühne** f open-air theatre; F~**lichtmuseum** nt open-air museum; ~**machen** vt (Post) to frank ♦ vr to arrange to be free; (entkleiden) to undress; **Tage ~machen** to take days off; ~**sprechen** (unreg) vt: ~**sprechen (von)** to acquit (of); F~**spruch** m acquittal; F~**stehen** (unreg) vi: **es steht dir ~, das zu tun** you're free to do that ♦ vt (leerstehen: Wohnung,

Haus) to lie/stand empty; ~**stellen** vt: **jdm etw ~stellen** to leave sth (up) to sb; F~**stoß** m free kick
Freitag m Friday; f~**s** adv on Fridays
frei- zW: ~**willig** adj voluntary; F~**zeit** f spare od free time; F~**zeitzentrum** nt leisure centre; ~**zügig** adj liberal, broad-minded; (mit Geld) generous
fremd [frɛmt] adj (unvertraut) strange; (ausländisch) foreign; (nicht eigen) someone else's; **etw ist jdm ~** sth is foreign to sb; ~**artig** adj strange; F~**enführer** m (tourist) guide; F~**enverkehr** m tourism; F~**enzimmer** nt guest room; F~**körper** m foreign body; ~**ländisch** adj foreign; F~**sprache** f foreign language; F~**wort** nt foreign od loan word
Frequenz [fre'kvɛnts] f (RAD) frequency
fressen ['frɛsən] (unreg) vt, vi to eat
Freude ['frɔydə] f joy, delight
freudig adj joyful, happy
freuen ['frɔyən] vt unpers to make happy od pleased ♦ vr to be glad od happy; **freut mich!** pleased to meet you; **sich auf etw** akk ~ to look forward to sth; **sich über etw** akk ~ to be pleased about sth
Freund [frɔynt] m (-(e)s, -e) m friend; boyfriend; f~**in** [-dɪn] f friend; girlfriend; f~**lich** adj kind, friendly; f~**licherweise** adv kindly; ~**lichkeit** f friendliness, kindness; ~**schaft** f friendship; f~**schaftlich** adj friendly
Frieden ['friːdən] m (-s, -) m peace; **im ~** in peacetime
Friedens- zW: ~**schluß** m peace agreement; ~**vertrag** m peace treaty; ~**zeit** f peacetime
fried- ['friːt] zW: ~**fertig** adj peaceable; F~**hof** m cemetery; ~**lich** adj peaceful
frieren ['friːrən] (unreg) vt, vi to freeze; **ich friere, es friert mich** I'm freezing, I'm cold
Friesland nt Friesland

frigid(e) [fri'giːt, fri'giːdə] *adj* frigid

Frikadelle [frika'dɛlə] *f* rissole

Frikassee [frika'seː] (-s, -s) *nt* (KOCH) fricassee

frisch [frɪʃ] *adj* fresh; (*lebhaft*) lively; ~ **gestrichen!** wet paint!; **sich** ~ **machen** to freshen (o.s.) up; **F~e** *f* freshness; liveliness

Friseur [fri'zøːr] *m* hairdresser

Friseuse [fri'zøːzə] *f* hairdresser

frisieren [fri'ziːrən] *vt* to do (one's hair); (*fig: Abrechnung*) to fiddle, to doctor ♦ *vr* to do one's hair

Frisiersalon *m* hairdressing salon

frißt *etc* [frɪst] *vb siehe* **fressen**

Frist (-, -en) *f* period; (*Termin*) deadline; **f~gerecht** *adj* within the stipulated time or period; **f~los** *adj* (*Entlassung*) instant

Frisur [fri'zuːr] *f* hairdo, hairstyle

frivol [fri'voːl] *adj* frivolous

froh [froː] *adj* happy, cheerful; **ich bin ~, daß ...** I'm glad that ...

fröhlich ['frøːlɪç] *adj* merry, happy; **F~keit** *f* merriness, gaiety

fromm [frɔm] *adj* pious, good; (*Wunsch*) idle

Frömmigkeit ['frœmɪçkaɪt] *f* piety

Fronleichnam [froːn'laɪçnaːm] (-(e)s) *m* Corpus Christi

Front [frɔnt] (-, -en) *f* front; **f~al** [frɔn'taːl] *adj* frontal

fror *etc* [froːr] *vb siehe* **frieren**

Frosch [frɔʃ] (-(e)s, ̈e) *m* frog; (*Feuerwerk*) squib; **~mann** *m* frogman; **~schenkel** *m* frog's leg

Frost [frɔst] (-(e)s, ̈e) *m* frost; **~beule** *f* chilblain

frösteln ['frœstəln] *vi* to shiver

frostig *adj* frosty

Frostschutzmittel *nt* anti-freeze

Frottee [frɔ'teː] (-(s), -s) *nt or m* toweling

Frottier(hand)tuch [frɔ'tiːr(hant)tuːx] *nt* towel

Frucht [fruxt] (-, ̈e) *f* (*auch fig*) fruit; (*Getreide*) corn; **f~bar** *adj* fruitful, fertile; **~barkeit** *f* fertility; **f~ig** *adj* (*Geschmack*) fruity; **f~los** *adj* fruitless; **~saft** *m* fruit juice

früh [fryː] *adj, adv* early; **heute** ~ this morning; **F~aufsteher** (-s, -) *m* early riser; **F~e** *f* early morning; **~er** *adj* earlier; (*ehemalig*) former ♦ *adv* formerly; **~er war das anders** that used to be different; **~estens** *adv* at the earliest; **F~jahr** *nt* spring; **F~ling** *m* spring; **~reif** *adj* precocious; **F~stück** *nt* breakfast; **~stücken** *vi* to have breakfast; **F~stücksbüfett** *nt* breakfast buffet; **~zeitig** *adj* early; (*pej*) untimely

frustrieren [frʊs'triːrən] *vt* to frustrate

Fuchs [fʊks] (-es, ̈e) *m* fox

fuchsen (*umg*) *vt* to rile, to annoy

fuchsteufelswild *adj* hopping mad

fuchteln ['fʊxtəln] *vi* to gesticulate wildly

Fuge ['fuːgə] *f* joint; (*MUS*) fugue

fügen ['fyːgən] *vt* to place, to join ♦ *vr*: **sich** ~ (**in** +*dat*) to be obedient (to); (*anpassen*) to adapt oneself (to) ♦ *vr* (*unpers*) to happen

fügsam ['fyːkzaːm] *adj* obedient

fühl- *zW*: **~bar** *adj* perceptible, noticeable; **~en** *vt, vi, vr* to feel; **F~er** (-s, -) *m* feeler

fuhr *etc* [fuːr] *vb siehe* **fahren**

führen ['fyːrən] *vt* to lead; (*Geschäft*) to run; (*Name*) to bear; (*Buch*) to keep ♦ *vi* to lead ♦ *vr* to behave

Führer ['fyːrər] (-s, -) *m* leader; (*Fremden~*) guide; **~schein** *m* driving licence

Führung ['fyːrʊŋ] *f* leadership; (*eines Unternehmens*) management; (*MIL*) command; (*Benehmen*) conduct; (*Museums~*) conducted tour; **~szeugnis** *nt* certificate of good conduct

Fülle ['fylə] *f* wealth, abundance; **f~n** *vt* to fill; (KOCH) to stuff ♦ *vr* to fill (up)

Füllen (-s, -) *nt* foal

Füller (-s, -) *m* fountain pen

Füllfederhalter *m* fountain pen

Füllung *f* filling; (*Holz~*) panel

fummeln ['fʊməln] (umg) vi to fumble

Fund [fʊnt] (-(e)s, -e) m find

Fundament [-da'ment] nt foundation; **fundamen'tal** adj fundamental

Fundbüro nt lost property office, lost and found (US)

Fundgrube f (fig) treasure trove

fundiert [fun'di:rt] adj sound

fünf [fynf] num five; ~**hundert** num five hundred; **F~kampf** m pentathlon; ~**te(r, s)** adj fifth; **F~tel** (-s, -) nt fifth; ~**zehn** num fifteen; ~**zig** num fifty

Funk [fʊŋk] (-s) m radio, wireless; ~**e** (-ns, -n) m (auch fig) spark; **f~eln** vi to sparkle; ~**en** (-s, -) m (auch fig) spark; **f~en** vi (durch Funk) to signal, to radio; (umg: richtig funktionieren) to work ♦ vt (Funken sprühen) to shower with sparks; **endlich hat es bei ihr gef~t** (umg) the penny has finally dropped, he's finally got it; ~**er** (-s, -) m radio operator; ~**gerät** nt radio set; ~**rufempfänger** m pager, paging device; ~**streife** f police radio patrol; ~**telefon** nt cellphone

Funktion [fʊŋktsi'o:n] f function; **f~ieren** [-'ni:rən] vi to work, to function

für [fy:r] präp +akk for; **was ~** what kind of sort of; **das F~ und Wider** the pros and cons pl; **Schritt ~ Schritt** step by step; **F~bitte** f intercession

Furche ['fʊrçə] f furrow

Furcht [fʊrçt] f fear; **f~bar** adj terrible, frightful

fürchten ['fʏrçtən] vt to be afraid of, to fear ♦ vr: **sich ~ (vor** +dat) to be afraid of)

fürchterlich adj awful

furchtlos adj fearless

furchtsam adj timid

füreinander [fy:r'ar'nandər] adv for each other

Furnier [fur'ni:r] (-s, -e) nt veneer

fürs [fy:rs] = **für das**

Fürsorge ['fy:rzɔrgə] f care; (So-

zial~) welfare; ~**r(in)** (-s, -) m(f) welfare worker; ~**unterstützung** f social security, welfare benefit (US)

fürsorglich adj attentive, caring

Fürsprache f recommendation; (um Gnade) intercession

Fürsprecher m advocate

Fürst [fʏrst] (-en, -en) m prince; ~**entum** nt principality; ~**in** f princess; **f~lich** adj princely

Furunkel [fu'rʊŋkəl] (-s, -) nt od m (MED) boil

Fuß [fu:s] (-es, -e) m foot; (von Glas, Säule etc) base; (von Möbel) leg; **zu ~** on foot; ~**ball** m football; ~**ballplatz** m football pitch; ~**ballspiel** nt football match; ~**ballspieler** m footballer; ~**boden** m floor; ~**bremse** f (AUT) footbrake; ~**ende** nt foot; ~**gänger(in)** (-s, -) m(f) pedestrian; ~**gängerzone** f pedestrian precinct; ~**nagel** m toenail; ~**note** f footnote; ~**spur** f footprint; ~**tritt** m kick; (Spur) footstep; ~**weg** m footpath

Futter ['fʊtər] (-s, -) nt fodder, feed; (Stoff) lining; ~**al** [-'ra:l] (-s, -e) nt case

füttern ['fʏtərn] vt to feed; (Kleidung) to line

Futur [fu'tu:r] (-s, -e) nt future

G

g abk = Gramm

gab [ga:p] vb siehe **geben**

Gabe ['ga:bə] f gift

Gabel ['ga:bəl] (-, -n) f fork; ~**ung** f fork

gackern ['gakərn] vi to cackle

gaffen ['gafən] vi to gape

Gage ['ga:ʒə] f fee; salary

gähnen ['gɛ:nən] vi to yawn

Galerie [galə'ri:] f gallery

Galgen ['galgən] (-s, -) m gallows sg; ~**frist** f respite; ~**humor** m macabre humour

Galle ['galə] f gall; (Organ) gallbladder; ~**nstein** m gallstone

Galopp [ga'lɔp] (-s, -s od -e) m gal-

lop; **g~ieren** [-'giːrən] vi to gallop
Gamasche [ga'maʃə] f gaiter; (kurz) spat

gammeln ['gaməln] (umg) vi to bum around

Gammler(in) (-s, -; pej) m(f) layabout, loafer (inf)

Gang [gaŋ] (-(e)s, ⁼e) m walk; (Boten~) errand; (~art) gait; (Abschnitt eines Vorgangs) operation; (Essens~, Ablauf) course; (Flur etc) corridor; (Durch~) passage; (TECH) gear; **in ~ bringen** to start up; (fig) to get off the ground; **in ~ sein** to be in operation; (fig) to be under way

gang adj: **~ und gäbe** usual, normal

gängig ['gɛŋɪç] adj common, current; (Ware) in demand, selling well

Ganove [ga'noːvə] (-n, -n; umg) m crook

Gans [gans] (-, ⁼e) f goose

Gänse- ['gɛnzə] zW: **~blümchen** nt daisy; **~füßchen** (umg) pl (Anführungszeichen) inverted commas; **~haut** f goose pimples pl; **~marsch** m: **im ~marsch** in single file; **~rich** (-s, -e) m gander

ganz [gants] adj whole; (vollständig) complete ♦ adv quite; (völlig) completely; **~ Europa** all Europe; **sein ~es Geld** all his money; **~ und gar nicht** not at all; **es sieht ~ so aus** it really looks like it; **aufs G~e gehen** to go for the lot

gänzlich ['gɛntslɪç] adj complete, entire ♦ adv completely, entirely

Ganztagsschule f all-day school

gar [gaːr] adj cooked, done ♦ adv quite; **~ nicht/nichts/keiner** not/ nothing/nobody at all; **~ nicht schlecht** not bad at all

Garage [ga'raːʒə] f garage

Garantie [garan'tiː] f guarantee; **g~ren** vt to guarantee; **er kommt g~rt** he's guaranteed to come

Garbe ['garbə] f sheaf; (MIL) burst

Garde f guard

Garderobe [gardə'roːbə] f wardrobe; (Abgabe) cloakroom; **~nfrau** f cloakroom attendant

Gardine [gar'diːnə] f curtain

garen ['gaːrən] vt, vi to cook

gären ['gɛːrən] (unreg) vi to ferment

Garn [garn] (-(e)s, -e) nt thread; yarn (auch fig)

Garnele [gar'neːlə] f shrimp, prawn

garnieren [gar'niːrən] vt to decorate; (Speisen, fig) to garnish

Garnison [garni'zoːn] (-, -en) f garrison

Garnitur [garni'tuːr] f (Satz) set; (Unterwäsche) set of (matching) underwear; **erste ~** (fig) top rank; **zweite ~** second rate

garstig ['garstɪç] adj nasty, horrid

Garten ['gartən] (-s, ⁼) m garden; **~arbeit** f gardening; **~gerät** nt gardening tool; **~lokal** nt beer garden; **~schere** f pruning shears pl; **~tür** f garden gate

Gärtner(in) ['gɛrtnər(ɪn)] (-s, -) m(f) gardener; **~ei** [-'rai] f nursery; (Gemüse~) market garden (BRIT), truck farm (US)

Gärung ['gɛːrʊŋ] f fermentation

Gas [gaːs] (-es, -e) nt gas; **~ geben** (AUT) to accelerate, to step on the gas; **~hahn** m gas tap; **~herd** m gas cooker; **~kocher** m gas cooker; **~leitung** f gas pipe; **~pedal** nt accelerator, gas pedal

Gasse ['gasə] f lane, alley

Gast [gast] (-es, ⁼e) m guest; (in Lokal) patron; **bei jdm zu ~ sein** to be sb's guest; **~arbeiter(in)** m(f) foreign worker

Gästebuch ['gɛstəbuːx] nt visitors' book, guest book

Gast- zW: **g~freundlich** adj hospitable; **~geber** (-s, -) m host; **~geberin** f hostess; **~haus** nt hotel, inn; **~hof** m hotel, inn; **g~ieren** [-'iːrən] vi (THEAT) to (appear as a) guest; **g~lich** adj hospitable; **~rolle** f guest role; **~spiel** nt (THEAT) guest performance; **~stätte** f restaurant; pub; **~wirt** m innkeeper; **~wirtschaft** f hotel, inn; **~zimmer**

(guest) room

Gaswerk nt gasworks sg

Gaszähler m gas meter

Gatte ['gatə] m (-n, -n) m husband, spouse

Gatter ['gatər] (-s, -) nt railing, grating; (Eingang) gate

Gattin f wife, spouse

Gattung f ['gatʊŋ] f genus; kind

Gaudi ['gaʊdi] (umg; SÜDD, ÖSTERR) m od f fun

Gaul [gaʊl] (-(e)s, Gäule) m horse; nag

Gaumen ['gaʊmən] (-s, -) m palate

Gauner ['gaʊnər] (-s, -) m rogue; ~ei [-'raɪ] f swindle

Gaze ['gaːzə] f gauze

geb. abk = geboren

Gebäck [gə'bɛk] (-(e)s, -e) nt pastry

gebacken [gə'bakən] adj baked; (gebraten) fried

Gebälk [gə'bɛlk] (-(e)s) nt timberwork

Gebärde [gə'bɛːrdə] f gesture; g~n vr to behave

gebären [gə'bɛːrən] (unreg) vt to give birth to, to bear

Gebärmutter f uterus, womb

Gebäude [gə'bɔʏdə] (-s, -) nt building; ~komplex m (building) complex

Gebell [gə'bɛl] (-(e)s) nt barking

geben ['geːbən] (unreg) vt, vi to give; (Karten) to deal ♦ vb unpers: es gibt there is/are; there will be (sich verhalten) to behave, to act; (aufhören) to abate; jdm etw ~ to give sb sth od sth to sb; ein Wort gab das andere one angry word led to another; was gibt's? what's up?; was gibt es im Kino? what's on at the cinema?; sich geschlagen ~ to admit defeat; das wird sich schon ~ that'll soon sort itself out

Gebet [gə'beːt] (-(e)s, -e) nt prayer

gebeten vb siehe bitten

Gebiet [gə'biːt] (-(e)s, -e) nt area; (Hoheits~) territory; (fig) field; g~en (unreg) vt to command, to demand; g~erisch adj imperious

Gebilde [gə'bɪldə] (-s, -) nt object

gebildet adj cultured, educated

Gebirge [gə'bɪrgə] (-s, -) nt mountain chain

Gebiß [gə'bɪs] (-sses, -sse) nt teeth pl; (künstlich) dentures pl

gebissen vb siehe beißen

geblieben [gə'bliːbən] vb siehe bleiben

geblümt [gə'blyːmt] adj (Kleid, Stoff, Tapete) floral

geboren [gə'boːrən] adj born; (Frau) née

geborgen [gə'bɔrgən] adj secure, safe

Gebot [gə'boːt] (-(e)s, -e) nt command; (REL) commandment; (bei Auktion) bid

geboten vb siehe bieten

Gebr. abk (= Gebrüder) Bros.

gebracht [gə'braxt] vb siehe bringen

gebraten [gə'braːtən] adj fried

Gebräu [gə'brɔʏ] (-(e)s, -e) nt concoction

Gebrauch [gə'braʊx] (-(e)s, Gebräuche) m use; (Sitte) custom; g~en vt to use

gebräuchlich [gə'brɔʏçlɪç] adj usual, customary

Gebrauchs- zW: ~anweisung f directions pl for use; g~fertig adj ready for use; ~gegenstand m commodity

gebraucht [gə'braʊxt] adj used; G~wagen m secondhand od used car

gebrechlich [gə'brɛçlɪç] adj frail

gebrochen [gə'brɔxən] adj broken

Gebrüder [gə'bryːdər] pl brothers

Gebrüll [gə'brʏl] (-(e)s) nt roaring

Gebühr [gə'byːr] (-, -en) f charge, fee; nach ~ fittingly; über ~ unduly; g~en vi: jdm ~en to be sb's due od that is due to sb ♦ vr to be fitting; g~end adj fitting, appropriate ♦ adv fittingly, appropriately

Gebühren- zW: ~einheit f (TEL) unit; ~erlaß m remission of fees; ~ermäßigung f reduction of fees; g~frei adj free of charge; g~pflichtig adj subject to a charge

gebunden [gəˈbʊndən] vb siehe **binden**

Geburt [gəˈbuːrt] (-, -en) f birth

Geburtenkontrolle f birth control

Geburtenregelung f birth control

gebürtig [gəˈbʏrtɪç] adj born in, native of; **~e Schweizerin** native of Switzerland

Geburts- zW: **~anzeige** f birth notice; **~datum** nt date of birth; **~jahr** nt year of birth; **~ort** m birthplace; **~tag** m birthday; **~urkunde** f birth certificate

Gebüsch [gəˈbʏʃ] (-(e)s, -e) nt bushes pl

gedacht [gəˈdaxt] vb siehe **denken**

Gedächtnis [gəˈdɛçtnɪs] (-ses, -se) nt memory; **~feier** f commemoration

Gedanke [gəˈdaŋkə] (-ns, -n) m thought; **sich über etw** akk **~n machen** to think about sth

Gedanken- zW: **~austausch** m exchange of ideas; **g~los** adj thoughtless; **~strich** m dash; **~übertragung** f thought transference, telepathy

Gedeck [gəˈdɛk] (-(e)s, -e) nt cover(ing); (Speisenfolge) menu; **ein ~ auflegen** to lay a place

gedeihen [gəˈdaɪən] (unreg) vi to thrive, to prosper

Gedenken nt: **zum ~ an jdn** in memory of sb; **g~** [gəˈdɛŋkən] (unreg) vi +gen: (beabsichtigen) to intend; **~: nt: zum ~ an jdn** in memory of sb

gedenken (unreg) vi +gen (sich erinnern) to remember

Gedenk- zW: **~feier** f commemoration; **~minute** f minute's silence; **~tag** m remembrance day

Gedicht [gəˈdɪçt] (-(e)s, -e) nt poem

gediegen [gəˈdiːɡən] adj (good) quality; (Mensch) reliable, honest

Gedränge [gəˈdrɛŋə] (-s) nt crush, crowd; **ins ~ kommen** (fig) to get into difficulties

gedrängt adj compressed; **~ voll** packed

gedrückt adj (deprimiert) low, depressed

gedrungen [gəˈdrʊŋən] adj thickset, stocky

Geduld [gəˈdʊlt] f patience; **g~en** [gəˈdʊldən] vr to be patient; **g~ig** adj patient, forbearing; **~sprobe** f trial of one's patience

gedurft [gəˈdʊrft] vb siehe **dürfen**

geehrt [gəˈeːrt] adj: **Sehr ~e Frau X! Dear Mrs X**

geeignet [gəˈaɪɡnət] adj suitable

Gefahr [gəˈfaːr] (-, -en) f danger; **~ laufen, etw zu tun** to run the risk of doing sth; **auf eigene ~** at one's own risk

gefährden [gəˈfɛːrdən] vt to endanger

Gefahrenquelle f source of danger

Gefahrenzulage f danger money

gefährlich [gəˈfɛːrlɪç] adj dangerous

Gefährte [gəˈfɛːrtə] (-n, -n) m companion; (Lebenspartner) partner

Gefährtin [gəˈfɛːrtɪn] (female) companion; (Lebenspartner) (female) partner

Gefälle [gəˈfɛlə] (-s, -) nt gradient, incline

Gefallen¹ [gəˈfalən] (-s, -) m favour

Gefallen² (-s) nt pleasure; **an etw** dat **Gefallen finden** to derive pleasure from sth

gefallen pp von **fallen ♦** vi: **jdm ~** to please sb; **er/es gefällt mir** I like him/it; **das gefällt mir an ihm** that's one thing I like about him; **sich** dat **etw ~ lassen** to put up with sth

gefällig [gəˈfɛlɪç] adj (hilfsbereit) obliging; (erfreulich) pleasant; **G~keit** f favour; helpfulness; **etw aus G~keit tun** to do sth out of the goodness of one's heart

gefälligst adv kindly

gefangen [gəˈfaŋən] adj captured; (fig) captivated; **G~e(r)** m(f) prisoner, captive; **g~halten** (unreg) vt to keep prisoner; **g~nehmen** (unreg) vt to take prisoner; **G~schaft** f captivity

Gefängnis [gəˈfɛŋnɪs] (-ses, -se) nt prison; **~strafe** f prison sentence;

~**wärter** m prison warder; ~**zelle** f prison cell

Gefäß [gə'fɛːs] (-es, -e) nt vessel (auch ANAT), container

gefaßt [gə'fast] adj composed, calm; **auf etw** akk ~ **sein** to be prepared od ready for sth

Gefecht [gə'fɛçt] (-(e)s, -e) nt fight; (MIL) engagement

Gefieder [gə'fiːdər] (-s, -) nt plumage, feathers pl

gefleckt [gə'flɛkt] adj spotted, mottled

geflogen [gə'floːgən] vb siehe **fliegen**

geflossen [gə'flɔsən] vb siehe **fließen**

Geflügel [gə'flyːgəl] (-s) nt poultry

Gefolge [gə'fɔlgə] (-s, -) nt retinue

Gefolgschaft f following

gefragt [gə'fraːkt] adj in demand

gefräßig [gə'frɛːsɪç] adj voracious

Gefreite(r) [gə'fraitə(r)] m lance corporal; (NAUT) able seaman; (AVIAT) aircraftman

gefrieren [gə'friːrən] (unreg) vi to freeze

Gefrier- zW: ~**fach** nt icebox; ~**fleisch** nt frozen meat; **g~getrocknet** [-gətrɔknət] adj freezedried; ~**punkt** m freezing point; ~**schutzmittel** nt antifreeze; ~**truhe** f deep-freeze

gefroren [gə'froːrən] vb siehe **frieren**

Gefühl [gə'fyːl] (-(e)s, -e) nt feeling; **etw im** ~ **haben** to have a feel for sth; ~**los** adj unfeeling

gefühls- [-duːʦlaɪ] zW: ~**betont** adj emotional; **G~duselei** [-duːʦlaɪ] f over-sentimentality; ~**mäßig** adj instinctive

gefüllt [gə'fʏlt] adj (KOCH) stuffed

gefunden [gə'fʊndən] vb siehe **finden**

gegangen [gə'gaŋən] vb siehe **gehen**

gegeben [gə'geːbən] vb siehe **geben** ♦ adj given; **zu** ~**er Zeit** in good time

gegebenenfalls [gə'geːbənənfals] adv if need be

gegen ['geːgən] präp +akk **1** against; **nichts gegen jdn haben** to have nothing against sb; **X gegen Y** (SPORT, JUR) X versus Y; **ein Mittel gegen Schnupfen** something for colds

2 (in Richtung auf) towards; **gegen Osten** to(wards) the east; **gegen Abend** towards evening; **gegen einen Baum fahren** to drive into a tree

3 (ungefähr) round about; **gegen 3 Uhr** around 3 o'clock

4 (gegenüber) towards; (ungefähr) around; **gerecht gegen alle** fair to all

5 (im Austausch für) for; **gegen bar** for cash; **gegen Quittung** against a receipt

6 (verglichen mit) compared with

Gegenangriff m counter-attack

Gegenbeweis m counter-evidence

Gegend [geːgənt] (-, -en) f area, district

Gegen- zW: **g~ei'nander** adv against one another; ~**fahrbahn** f oncoming carriageway; ~**frage** f counter-question; ~**gewicht** nt counterbalance; ~**gift** nt antidote; ~**leistung** f service in return; ~**mittel** nt antidote, cure; ~**satz** m contrast; ~**sätze überbrücken** to overcome differences; **g~sätzlich** adj contrary, opposite; (widersprüchlich) contradictory; **g~seitig** adj mutual, reciprocal; **sich g~seitig helfen** to help each other; ~**spieler** m opponent; ~**stand** m object; ~**stimme** f vote against; ~**stoß** m counterblow; ~**stück** nt counterpart; ~**teil** nt opposite; **im** ~**teil** on the contrary; **g~teilig** adj opposite, contrary

gegenüber [geːgən'yːbər] präp +dat opposite; (zu) to(wards); (angesichts) in the face of ♦ adv opposite; **G~** (-s, -) nt person opposite; ~**liegen** (unreg) vr to face each other; ~**stehen** (unreg) vr to be opposed (to each other); ~**stellen** vt to confront; (fig) to contrast; **G~stellung** f confrontation; (fig) contrast; ~**treten** (unreg) vi +dat to face

Gegen- zW: ~**verkehr** m oncoming traffic; ~**vorschlag** m counterproposal; ~**wart** f present; **g~wärtig** adj present ♦ adv at present; **das ist mir nicht mehr g~wärtig** that has slipped my mind; ~**wert** m equivalent; ~**wind** m headwind; **g~zeichnen** vt, vi to countersign

gegessen [gə'gɛsən] vb siehe **essen**

Gegner ['gɛgnər] (-s, -) m opponent; **g~isch** adj opposing; ~**schaft** f opposition

gegr. abk (= gegründet) est.

gegrillt [gə'grɪlt] adj grilled

Gehackte(s) [gə'haktə(s)] nt mince(d meat)

Gehalt¹ [gə'halt] (-(e)s, -e) m content

Gehalt² (-(e)s, -er) nt salary

Gehalts- zW: ~**empfänger** m salary earner; ~**erhöhung** f salary increase; ~**zulage** f salary increment

gehaltvoll adj (nahrhaft) nutritious

gehässig [gə'hɛsɪç] adj spiteful, nasty

Gehäuse [gə'hɔʏzə] (-s, -) nt case; casing; (von Apfel etc) core

Gehege [gə'he:gə] (-s, -) nt reserve; (im Zoo) enclosure

geheim [gə'haɪm] adj secret; **G~dienst** m secret service, intelligence service; ~**halten** (unreg) vt to keep secret; **G~nis** (-ses, -se) nt secret; mystery; ~**nisvoll** adj mysterious; **G~nummer** f (TEL) secret number; **G~polizei** f secret police

gehemmt [gə'hɛmt] adj inhibited, self-conscious

gehen ['ge:ən] (unreg) vt, vi to go; (zu Fuß ~) to walk ♦ vb unpers: **wie geht es (dir)?** how are you od how do things?; ~ **nach** (Fenster) to face; **mir/ihm geht es gut** I'm/he's (doing) fine; **geht das?** is that possible?; **geht's noch?** can you manage?; **es geht** not too bad, O.K.; **das**

geht nicht that's not on; **es geht um etw** sth is concerned, it's about sth

gehenlassen (unreg) vr (unbeherrscht sein) to lose control (of o.s.) ♦ vt to let/leave alone; **laß mich gehen!** leave me alone!

geheuer [gə'hɔʏər] adj: **nicht ~** eerie; (fragwürdig) dubious

Gehilfe [gə'hɪlfə] (-n, -n) m assistant

Gehilfin f assistant

Gehirn [gə'hɪrn] (-(e)s, -e) nt brain; ~**erschütterung** f concussion; ~**wäsche** f brainwashing

gehoben [gə'ho:bən] pp ♦ adj (Position) elevated; high

geholfen vb siehe **helfen**

Gehör [gə'hø:r] (-(e)s) nt hearing; **musikalisches ~** ear; ~ **finden** to gain a hearing; **jdm ~ schenken** to give sb a hearing

gehorchen [gə'hɔrçən] vi +dat to obey

gehören [gə'hø:rən] vi to belong ♦ vr unpers to be right od proper

gehörig adj proper; ~ **zu** od +dat belonging to; part of

gehorsam [gə'ho:rzam] adj obedient; **G~** (-s) m obedience

Gehsteig ['ge:ʃtaɪk] m pavement, sidewalk (US)

Gehweg ['ge:ve:k] m pavement, sidewalk (US)

Geier ['gaɪər] (-s, -) m vulture

Geige ['gaɪgə] f violin

Geiger (-s, -) m violinist

Geigerzähler m geiger counter

geil [gaɪl] adj randy (BRIT), horny (US)

Geisel ['gaɪzəl] (-, -n) f hostage

Geist [gaɪst] (-(e)s, -er) m spirit; (Gespenst) ghost; (Verstand) mind

geisterhaft adj ghostly

Geistes- zW: **g~abwesend** adj absent-minded; ~**blitz** m brainwave; ~**gegenwart** f presence of mind; **g~krank** adj mentally ill; ~**kranke(r)** mf mentally ill person; ~**krankheit** f mental illness; ~**wissenschaften** pl the arts; ~**zustand**

m state of mind

geist- *zW:* **~ig** *adj* intellectual; mental; (*Getränke*) alcoholic; **~ig behindert** mentally handicapped; **~lich** *adj* spiritual, religious; clerical; **G~liche(r)** *m* clergyman; **G~lichkeit** *f* clergy; **~los** *adj* uninspired, dull; **~reich** *adj* clever; witty; **~voll** *adj* intellectual; (*weise*) wise

Geiz [gaits] (**-es**) *m* miserliness, meanness; **~en** *vi* to be miserly; **~hals** *m* miser; **~ig** *adj* miserly, mean; **~kragen** *m* miser

gekannt [gə'kant] *vb siehe* **kennen**

geknickt [gə'knıkt] *adj* (*fig*) dejected

gekonnt [gə'kɔnt] *adj* skilful ♦ *vb siehe* **können**

Gekritzel [gə'krıtsəl] (**-s**) *nt* scrawl, scribble

gekünstelt [gə'kynstəlt] *adj* artificial, affected

Gel [geːl] (**-s, -e**) *nt* gel

Gelächter [gə'lɛçtər] (**-s, -**) *nt* laughter

geladen [gə'laːdən] *adj* loaded; (*ELEK*) live; (*fig*) furious

Gelage [gə'laːgə] (**-s, -**) *nt* banquet

gelähmt [gə'lɛːmt] *adj* paralysed

Gelände [gə'lɛndə] (**-s, -**) *nt* land, terrain; (*von Fabrik, Sport*~) grounds *pl*; (*Bau*~) site; **~lauf** *m* cross-country race

Geländer [gə'lɛndər] (**-s, -**) *nt* railing; (*Treppen*~) banister(s)

gelangen [gə'laŋən] *vi:* **~ (an** +*akk od* **zu)** to reach; (*erwerben*) to attain; **in jds Besitz ~** to come into sb's possession

gelangweilt [gə'laŋvailt] *adj* bored

gelassen [gə'lasən] *adj* calm, composed; **G~heit** *f* calmness, composure

Gelatine [ʒela'tiːnə] *f* gelatine

geläufig [gə'lɔyfıç] *adj* (*üblich*) common; **das ist mir nicht ~** I'm not familiar with that

gelaunt [gə'launt] *adj:* **schlecht/gut ~** in a bad/good mood; **wie ist er ~?** what sort of mood is he in?

gelb [gɛlp] *adj* yellow; (*Ampellicht*) amber; **~lich** *adj* yellowish; **G~sucht** *f* jaundice

Geld [gɛlt] (**-(e)s, -er**) *nt* money; **etw zu ~ machen** to sell sth off; **~anlage** *f* investment; **~automat** *m* cash dispenser; **~beutel** *m* purse; **~börse** *f* purse; **~geber (-s, -)** *m* financial backer; **g~gierig** *adj* avaricious; **~schein** *m* banknote; **~schrank** *m* safe, strongbox; **~strafe** *f* fine; **~stück** *nt* coin; **~wechsel** *m* exchange (of money)

Gelee [ʒe'leː] (**-s, -s**) *nt od m* jelly

gelegen [gə'leːgən] *adj* situated; (*passend*) convenient, opportune ♦ *vb siehe* **liegen**; **etw kommt jdm ~** sth is convenient for sb

Gelegenheit [gə'leːgənhait] *f* opportunity; (*Anlaß*) occasion; **bei jeder ~** at every opportunity; **~sarbeit** *f* casual work; **~skauf** *m* bargain

gelegentlich [gə'leːgəntlıç] *adj* occasional ♦ *adv* occasionally; (*bei Gelegenheit*) some time (or other) ♦ *präp* +*gen* on the occasion of

gelehrt [gə'leːrt] *adj* learned; **G~e(r)** *mf* scholar; **G~heit** *f* scholarliness

Geleise [gə'laizə] (**-s, -**) *nt* = **Gleis**

Geleit [gə'lait] (**-(e)s, -e**) *nt* escort; **g~en** *vt* to escort

Gelenk [gə'lɛŋk] (**-(e)s, -e**) *nt* joint; **g~ig** *adj* supple

gelernt [gə'lɛrnt] *adj* skilled

Geliebte(r) [gə'liːptə(r)] *mf* sweetheart, beloved

geliehen *vb siehe* **leihen**

gelind(e) [gə'lınt, gə'lındə] *adj* mild, light; (*fig: Wut*) fierce; **gelinde gesagt** to put it mildly

gelingen [gə'lıŋən] (*unreg*) *vi* to succeed; **es ist mir gelungen, etw zu tun** I succeeded in doing sth

gell [gɛl] *excl* isn't it?; aren't you? *etc*

geloben [gə'loːbən] *vt, vi* to vow, to swear

gelten [gɛltən] (*unreg*) *vt* (*wert sein*) to be worth ♦ *vi* (*gültig sein*) to be valid; (*erlaubt sein*) to be allowed ♦ *vb unpers:* **es gilt, etw zu tun** it is necessary to do sth; **jdm viel/ wenig ~** to mean a lot/not much to sb; **was gilt die Wette?** what do you bet?; **jdm ~ (betreffen) sein auf)** to be meant for **od** aimed at sb; **etw ~ lassen** to accept sth; **als od für etw ~** to be considered to be sth; **jdm od für jdn ~ (betreffen)** to apply to **od** for sb; **~d** adj prevailing; **etw ~d machen** to assert sth; **sich ~d machen** to make itself/o.s. felt

Geltung ['gɛltʊŋ] f: **~ haben** to have validity; **sich/etw dat ~ verschaffen** to establish one's position/ the position of sth; **etw zur ~ bringen** to show sth to its best advantage; **zur ~ kommen** to be seen/ heard etc to its best advantage

Geltungsbedürfnis nt desire for admiration

Gelübde [gə'lʏpdə] (-s, -) nt vow

gelungen [gə'lʊŋən] adj successful

gemächlich [gə'mɛːçlɪç] adj leisurely

Gemahl [gə'maːl] (-(e)s, -e) m husband; **~in** f wife

Gemälde [gə'mɛːldə] (-s, -) nt picture, painting

gemäß [gə'mɛːs] präp +dat in accordance with ♦ adj (+dat) appropriate (to)

gemäßigt adj moderate; (Klima) temperate

gemein [gə'maɪn] adj common; (niederträchtig) mean; **etw ~ haben (mit)** to have sth in common (with)

Gemeinde [gə'maɪndə] f district, community; (Pfarr~) parish; (Kirchen~) congregation; **~steuer** f local rates pl; **~verwaltung** f local administration; **~wahl** f local election

Gemein- zW: **g~gefährlich** adj dangerous to the public; **~heit** f commonness; mean thing to do/to say; **~platz** m commonplace, platitude; **g~sam** adj joint, common (auch MATH) ♦ adv together, jointly; **g~same Sache mit jdm machen** to be in cahoots with sb; **etw g~sam**

haben to have sth in common; **~samkeit** f community, having in common; **~schaft** f community; **in ~schaft** mit jointly od together with; **g~schaftlich** adj = gemeinsam; **~schaftsarbeit** f teamwork; team effort; **~sinn** m public spirit

Gemenge [gə'mɛŋə] (-s, -) nt mixture; (Hand~) scuffle

gemessen [gə'mɛsən] adj measured

Gemetzel [gə'mɛtsəl] (-s, -) nt slaughter, carnage, butchery

Gemisch [gə'mɪʃ] (-es, -e) nt mixture; **g~t** adj mixed

gemocht [gə'mɔxt] vb siehe **mögen**

Gemse ['gɛmzə] f chamois

Gemurmel [gə'mʊrməl] (-s) nt murmur(ing)

Gemüse [gə'myːzə] (-s, -) nt vegetables pl; **~garten** m vegetable garden; **~händler** m greengrocer

gemußt vb siehe **müssen**

gemustert [gə'mʊstərt] adj patterned

Gemüt [gə'myːt] (-(e)s, -er) nt disposition, nature; person; **sich dat etw zu ~e führen** (umg) to indulge in sth; **die ~er erregen** to arouse strong feelings; **g~lich** adj comfortable, cosy; (Person) good-natured; **~lichkeit** f comfortableness, cosiness; amiability

Gemüts- zW: **~mensch** m sentimental person; **~ruhe** f composure; **~zustand** m state of mind

gemütvoll adj warm, tender

Gen [geːn] (-s, -e) nt gene

genannt [gə'nant] vb siehe **nennen**

genau [gə'nau] adj exact, precise ♦ adv exactly, precisely; **etw ~ nehmen** to take sth seriously; **g~genommen** adv strictly speaking; **G~igkeit** f exactness, accuracy; **~so** adv just the same; **~so gut** just as good

genehm [gə'neːm] adj agreeable, acceptable; **~igen** vt to approve, to authorize; **sich dat etw ~igen** to indulge in sth; **G~igung** f (Schriftstück) permit

General [gene'raːl] (-s, -e od ≃e) m

general; **~direktor** *m* director general; **~konsulat** *nt* consulate general; **~probe** *f* dress rehearsal; **~streik** *m* general strike; **g~überholen** *vt* to overhaul thoroughly; **~versammlung** *f* general meeting

Generation [generatsi'o:n] *f* generation

Generator [gene'ra:tɔr] *m* generator, dynamo

generell [genə'rɛl] *adj* general

genesen [gə'ne:zən] (*unreg*) *vi* to convalesce, to recover

Genesung *f* recovery, convalescence

genetisch [ge'ne:tɪʃ] *adj* genetic

Genf [ɡɛnf] *nt* Geneva (*GEOG*) Geneva; **der ~er See** Lake Geneva

genial [geni'a:l] *adj* brilliant

Genick [gə'nɪk] (-(e)s, -e) *nt* (back of the) neck

Genie [ʒe'ni:] (-s, -s) *nt* genius

genieren [ʒe'ni:rən] *vt* to bother • *vr* to feel awkward *od* self-conscious; **geniert es Sie, wenn ...?** do you mind if ...?

genießbar *adj* edible; drinkable

genießen [gə'ni:sən] (*unreg*) *vt* to enjoy; to eat; to drink

Genießer (-s, -) *m* epicure; pleasure lover; **g~isch** *adj* appreciative • *adv* with relish

genommen *vb siehe* **nehmen**

Genosse [gə'nɔsə] (-n, -n) *m* (*bes POL*) comrade, companion; **~nschaft** *f* cooperative (association)

Genossin *f* (*bes POL*) comrade, companion

Gentechnologie ['ge:ntɛçnoloɡi:] *f* genetic engineering

genug [gə'nu:k] *adv* enough

Genüge [gə'ny:ɡə] *f*: **jdm/etw ~ tun** *od* **leisten** to satisfy sb/sth; **g~n** *vi* (+*dat*) to be enough (for); **g~nd** *adj* sufficient

genügsam [gə'ny:kza:m] *adj* modest, easily satisfied; **G~keit** *f* undemandingness

Genugtuung [gə'nu:ktu:ʊŋ] *f* satisfaction

Genuß [gə'nʊs] (-sses, -sse) *m* pleasure; (*Zustimmung*) consumption; **in den ~ von etw kommen** to receive the benefit of sth

genüßlich [gə'nʏslɪç] *adv* with relish

Genußmittel *pl* (semi-)luxury items

geöffnet [ɡə'œfnət] *adj* open

Geograph [geo'ɡra:f] (-en, -en) *m* geographer; **Geogra'phie** *f* geography; **g~isch** *adj* geographical

Geologe [geo'lo:ɡə] (-n, -n) *m* geologist; **Geolo'gie** *f* geology

Geometrie [geome'tri:] *f* geometry

Gepäck [gə'pɛk] (-(e)s) *nt* luggage, baggage; **~abfertigung** *f* luggage office; **~annahme** *f* luggage office; **~aufbewahrung** *f* left-luggage office (*BRIT*), baggage check (*US*); **~aufgabe** *f* luggage office; **~ausgabe** *f* luggage office; **~netz** *nt* luggage-rack; **~träger** *m* porter; (*Fahrrad*) carrier; **~wagen** *m* luggage van (*BRIT*), baggage car (*US*)

gepflegt [gə'pfle:kt] *adj* well-groomed; (*Park etc*) well looked after

---

SCHLÜSSELWORT

gerade [ɡə'ra:də] *adj* straight; (*aufrecht*) upright; **eine gerade Zahl** an even number
♦ *adv* **1** (*genau*) just, exactly; (*speziell*) especially; **gerade deshalb** that's just *od* exactly why; **das ist es ja gerade!** that's just it!; **gerade du** you especially; **warum gerade ich?** why me (of all people)?; **jetzt gerade nicht!** not now!; **gerade neben** right next to
2 (*eben, soeben*) just; **er wollte gerade aufstehen** he was just about to get up; **gerade erst** only just; **gerade noch** (only) just

Gerade *f* straight line; **g~aus** *adv* straight ahead; **g~heraus** *adv* straight out, bluntly; **g~stehen**: **für jdn/etw g~stehen** to be answerable for sb('s actions)/sth; **g~wegs** *adv* direct, straight; **g~zu** adv (beinahe) virtually, almost

gerannt [gəˈrant] vb siehe rennen

Gerät [gəˈrɛːt] (-(e)s, -e) nt device; (Werkzeug) tool; (SPORT) apparatus; (Zubehör) equipment no pl

geraten [gəˈraːtən] (unreg) vi (gedeihen) to thrive; (gelingen): (jdm) ~ to turn out well (for sb); gut/ schlecht ~ to turn out well/badly; an jdn ~ to come across sb; in etw akk ~ to get into sth; in Angst ~ to get frightened; nach jdm ~ to take after sb

Geratewohl [gəraːtəˈvoːl] nt: aufs ~ on the off chance; (bei Wahl) at random

geräuchert [gəˈrɔʏçərt] adj smoked

geräumig [gəˈrɔʏmɪç] adj roomy

Geräusch [gəˈrɔʏʃ] (-(e)s, -e) nt sound, noise; **g~los** adj silent

gerben [ˈgɛrbən] vt to tan

gerecht [gəˈrɛçt] adj just, fair; jdm/ etw ~ werden to do justice to sb/ sth; **G~igkeit** f justice, fairness

Gerede [gəˈreːdə] (-s) nt talk, gossip

geregelt [gəˈreːgəlt] adj (Arbeit) steady, regular; (Mahlzeiten) regular, set

gereizt [gəˈraɪtst] adj irritable; **G~heit** f irritation

Gericht [gəˈrɪçt] (-(e)s, -e) nt court; (Essen) dish; mit jdm ins ~ gehen (fig) to judge sb harshly; das Jüngste ~ the Last Judgement; **g~lich** adj judicial, legal ♦ adv judicially, legally

Gerichts- zW: **~barkeit** f jurisdiction; **~hof** m court (of law); **~kosten** pl (legal) costs; **~saal** m courtroom; **~verfahren** nt legal proceedings pl; **~verhandlung** f trial; **~vollzieher** m bailiff

gerieben [gəˈriːbən] adj grated; (umg: schlau) smart, wily ♦ vb siehe reiben

gering [gəˈrɪŋ] adj slight, small; (niedrig) low; (Zeit) short; **~fügig** adj slight, trivial; **~schätzig** adj dis-

paraging

geringste(r, s) adj slightest, least; **~nfalls** adv at the very least

gerinnen [gəˈrɪnən] vi to congeal; (Blut) to clot; (Milch) to curdle

Gerippe [gəˈrɪpə] (-s, -) nt skeleton

gerissen [gəˈrɪsən] adj wily, smart

geritten [gəˈrɪtən] vb siehe reiten

gern(e) [ˈgɛrn(ə)] adv willingly, gladly; ~(e) haben, ~(e) mögen to like; etwas ~(e) tun to like doing something; ich möchte ~(e) ... I'd like ...; ja, ~(e) yes, please; yes, I'd like to; ~(e) geschehen it's a pleasure

gerochen [gəˈrɔxən] vb siehe riechen

Geröll [gəˈrœl] (-(e)s, -e) nt scree

Gerste [ˈgɛrstə] f barley; **~nkorn** nt (im Auge) stye

Geruch [gəˈrux] (-(e)s, ⁓e) m smell, odour; **g~los** adj odourless

Gerücht [gəˈrʏçt] (-(e)s, -e) nt rumour

geruhen [gəˈruːən] vi to deign

geruhsam adj (Leben) peaceful; (Nacht, Zeit) peaceful, restful; (langsam: Arbeitsweise, Spaziergang) leisurely

Gerümpel [gəˈrʏmpəl] (-s) nt junk

Gerüst [gəˈrʏst] (-(e)s, -e) nt (Bau~) scaffold(ing); frame

gesalzen [gəˈzaltsən] pp von salzen ♦ adj (umg: Preis, Rechnung) steep

gesamt [gəˈzamt] adj whole, entire; (Kosten) total; (Werke) complete; im ~en all in all; **~deutsch** adj all-German; **G~eindruck** m general impression; **G~heit** f totality, whole; **G~schule** f comprehensive school

gesandt [gəˈzant] vb siehe senden

Gesandte(r) m envoy

Gesandtschaft f legation

Gesang [gəˈzaŋ] (-(e)s, ⁓e) m song; (Singen) singing; **~buch** nt (REL) hymn book

Gesangverein m choral society

Gesäß [gəˈzɛːs] (-es, -e) nt seat, bottom

Geschäft [gəˈʃɛft] (-(e)s, -e) nt business; (*Laden*) shop; (~sabschluß) deal; **g~ig** adj active, busy; (*pej*) officious; **g~lich** adj commercial ♦ adv on business

Geschäfts- zW: **~bericht** m financial report; **~führer** m manager; (*Klub*) secretary; **~geheimnis** nt trade secret; **~jahr** nt financial year; **~lage** f business conditions pl; **~mann** m businessman; **g~mäßig** adj businesslike; **~partner** m business partner; **~reise** f business trip; **~schluß** m closing time; **~stelle** f office, place of business; **g~tüchtig** adj business-minded; **G~viertel** nt business quarter; shopping centre; **~wagen** m company car; **~zeit** f business hours

geschehen [gəˈʃeːən] (*unreg*) vi to happen; **es war um ihn ~** that was the end of him

gescheit [gəˈʃaɪt] adj clever

Geschenk [gəˈʃɛŋk] (-(e)s, -e) nt present, gift

Geschichte [gəˈʃɪçtə] f story; (*Sache*) affair; (*Historie*) history

geschichtlich adj historical

Geschick [gəˈʃɪk] (-(e)s, -e) nt aptitude; (*Schicksal*) fate; **~lichkeit** f skill, dexterity; **g~t** adj skilful

geschieden [gəˈʃiːdən] adj divorced

geschienen [gəˈʃiːnən] vb siehe **scheinen**

Geschirr [gəˈʃɪr] (-(e)s, -e) nt crockery; pots and pans pl; (*Pferde~*) harness; **~spülmaschine** f dishwasher; **~tuch** nt dish cloth

Geschlecht [gəˈʃlɛçt] (-(e)s, -er) nt sex; (*GRAM*) gender; (*Gattung*) race; family; **g~lich** adj sexual

Geschlechts- zW: **~krankheit** f venereal disease; **~teil** nt genitals pl; **~verkehr** m sexual intercourse

geschlossen [gəˈʃlɔsən] adj shut ♦ vb siehe **schließen**

sth; **g~los** adj tasteless; (*fig*) in bad taste; **~(s)sache** f matter of taste; **~ssinn** m sense of taste; **g~voll** adj tasteful

geschmeidig [gəˈʃmaɪdɪç] adj supple; (*formbar*) malleable

Geschnetzelte(s) [gəˈʃnɛtsəltə(s)] nt (*KOCH*) strips of meat stewed to produce a thick sauce

geschnitten [gəˈʃnɪtən] vb siehe **schneiden**

Geschöpf [gəˈʃœpf] (-(e)s, -e) nt creature

Geschoß [gəˈʃɔs] (-sses, -sse) nt (*MIL*) projectile, missile; (*Stockwerk*) floor

geschossen vb siehe **schießen**

geschraubt [gəˈʃraʊpt] adj stilted, artificial

Geschrei [gəˈʃraɪ] (-s) nt cries pl, shouting; (*fig: Aufheben*) noise, fuss

geschrieben [gəˈʃriːbən] vb siehe **schreiben**

Geschütz [gəˈʃʏts] (-es, -e) nt gun, cannon; **ein schweres ~ auffahren** (*fig*) to bring out the big guns; **~feuer** nt artillery fire, gunfire

geschützt adj protected

Geschw. abk siehe **Geschwister**

Geschwafel [gəˈʃvaːfəl] (-s) nt silly talk

Geschwätz [gəˈʃvɛts] (-es) nt chatter, gossip; **g~ig** adj talkative

geschweige [gəˈʃvaɪgə] adv: ~ (denn) let alone, not to mention

geschwind [gəˈʃvɪnt] adj quick, swift; **G~igkeit** [-dɪçkaɪt] f speed, velocity; **G~igkeitsbeschränkung** f speed limit; **G~igkeitsüberschreitung** f exceeding the speed limit

Geschwister [gəˈʃvɪstər] pl brothers and sisters

geschwollen [gəˈʃvɔlən] adj pompous

geschwommen [gəˈʃvɔmən] vb siehe **schwimmen**

Geschworene(r) [gəˈʃvoːrənə(r)] mf juror; **~n** pl jury

Geschwulst [gəˈʃvʊlst] (-, ⁀e) f

swelling; growth, tumour

geschwungen [gə'ʃvʊŋən] pp von schwingen ♦ adj curved, arched

Geschwür [gə'ʃvyːr] (-(e)s, -e) nt ulcer

Gesell- [gə'zɛl] zW: **~e** (-n, -n) m fellow; (Handwerk~) journeyman; **g~ig** adj sociable; **~igkeit** f sociability; **~schaft** f society; (Begleitung, COMM) company; (Abendgesellschaft etc) party; **g~schaftlich** adj social; **~schaftsordnung** f social structure; **~schaftsschicht** f social stratum; **~schaftsspiel** nt party game

gesessen [gə'zɛsən] vb siehe sitzen

Gesetz [gə'zɛts] (-es, -e) nt law

gesetz adj: **G~buch** nt statute book; **G~gebung** f legislation; **~lich** adj legal, lawful statutory holiday; **~los** adj lawless; **~mäßig** adj lawful; **~t** adj (Mensch) sedate; **~widrig** adj illegal, unlawful

Gesicht [gə'zɪçt] (-(e)s, -er) nt face; das zweite **~** second sight; das ist mir nie zu **~** gekommen I've never laid eyes on that

Gesichts- zW: **~ausdruck** m (facial) expression; **~farbe** f complexion; **~punkt** m point of view; **~züge** pl features

Gesindel [gə'zɪndəl] (-s) nt rabble

gesinnt [gə'zɪnt] adj disposed, minded

Gesinnung [gə'zɪnʊŋ] f disposition; (Ansicht) views pl

gesittet [gə'zɪtət] adj well-mannered

Gespann [gə'ʃpan] (-(e)s, -e) nt team; (umg) couple

gespannt [gə'ʃpant] adj tense, strained; (begierig) eager; **ich bin ~, ob** I wonder if od whether; **auf jdn/etw ~ sein** to look forward to sth/meeting sb

Gespenst [gə'ʃpɛnst] (-(e)s, -er) nt ghost, spectre

gesperrt [gə'ʃpɛrt] adj closed off

Gespött [gə'ʃpœt] (-(e)s) nt mockery; **zum ~ werden** to become a laughing stock

Gespräch [gə'ʃprɛːç] (-(e)s, -e) nt

conversation; discussion(s); (Anruf) call; **g~ig** adj talkative

gesprochen [gə'ʃprɔxən] vb siehe sprechen

gesprungen [gə'ʃprʊŋən] vb siehe springen

Gespür [gə'ʃpyːr] (-s) nt feeling

Gestalt [gə'ʃtalt] (-, -en) f form, shape; (Person) figure; **in ~ von** in the form of; **~ annehmen** to take shape; **g~en** vt (formen) to shape, to form; (organisieren) to arrange, to organize ♦ vr: **sich g~en (zu)** to turn out (to be); **~ung** f formation; organization

gestanden [gə'ʃtandən] vb siehe stehen

Geständnis [gə'ʃtɛntnɪs] (-ses, -se) nt confession

Gestank [gə'ʃtaŋk] (-(e)s) m stench

gestatten [gə'ʃtatən] vt to permit, to allow; **~ Sie?** may I?; **sich** dat **~, etw zu tun** to take the liberty of doing sth

Geste ['gɛstə] f gesture

gestehen [gə'ʃteːən] (unreg) vt to confess

Gestein [gə'ʃtaɪn] (-(e)s, -e) nt rock

Gestell [gə'ʃtɛl] (-(e)s, -e) nt frame; (Regal) rack, stand

gestern ['gɛstərn] adv yesterday; **~ abend/morgen** yesterday evening /morning

Gestirn [gə'ʃtɪrn] (-(e)s, -e) nt star; (Sternbild) constellation

gestohlen [gə'ʃtoːlən] vb siehe stehlen

gestorben [gə'ʃtɔrbən] vb siehe sterben

gestört [gə'ʃtøːrt] adj disturbed

gestreift [gə'ʃtraɪft] adj striped

gestrichen [gə'ʃtrɪçən] adj cancelled

gestrig ['gɛstrɪç] adj yesterday's

Gestrüpp [gə'ʃtrʏp] (-(e)s, -e) nt undergrowth

Gestüt [gə'ʃtyːt] (-(e)s, -e) nt stud farm

Gesuch [gə'zuːx] (-(e)s, -e) nt petition; (Antrag) application; **g~t** adj (COMM) in demand; wanted; (fig) contrived

gesund [gə'zʊnt] adj healthy; **wieder ~ werden** to get better; **G~heit** f health(iness); **G~heit!** bless you!; **~heitlich** adj health attrib, physical ♦ adv: **wie geht es Ihnen ~heitlich?** how's your health?; **~heitsschädlich** adj unhealthy; **G~heitswesen** nt health service; **G~heitszustand** m state of health

gesungen [gə'zʊŋən] vb siehe **singen**

getan [gə'ta:n] vb siehe **tun**

Getöse [gə'tø:zə] (-s) nt din, racket

Getränk [gə'trɛŋk] (-(e)s, -e) nt drink; **~ekarte** f wine list

getrauen [gə'trauən] vr to dare, to venture

Getreide [gə'traidə] (-s, -) nt cereals pl, grain; **~speicher** m granary

getrennt [gə'trɛnt] adj separate

Getriebe [gə'tri:bə] (-s, -) nt (Leute) bustle; (AUT) gearbox

getrieben [gə'tri:bən] vb siehe **treiben**

getroffen [gə'trɔfən] vb siehe **treffen**

getrost [gə'tro:st] adv without any bother

getrunken [gə'trʊŋkən] vb siehe **trinken**

Getue [gə'tu:ə] (-s) nt fuss

geübt [gə'y:pt] adj experienced

Gewächs [gə'vɛks] (-es, -e) nt growth; (Pflanze) plant

gewachsen [gə'vaksən] adj: **jdm /etw ~ sein** to be sb's equal/equal to sth

Gewächshaus nt greenhouse

gewagt [gə'va:kt] adj daring, risky

gewählt [gə've:lt] adj (Sprache) refined, elegant

Gewähr [gə've:r] (-) f guarantee; **keine ~ übernehmen für** to accept no responsibility for; **g~en** vt to grant; (geben) to provide; **g~leisten** vt to guarantee

Gewahrsam [gə'va:rza:m] (-s, -e) m safekeeping; (Polizei~) custody

Gewährsmann m informant, source

Gewalt [gə'valt] (-, -en) f power;

(große Kraft) force; (~taten) violence; **mit aller ~** with all one's might; **~anwendung** f use of force; **g~ig** adj tremendous; (Irrtum) huge; **~marsch** m forced march; **g~sam** adj forcible; **g~tätig** adj violent

Gewand [gə'vant] (-(e)s, ⁻er) nt gown, robe

gewandt [gə'vant] adj deft, skilful; (erfahren) experienced; **G~heit** f dexterity, skill

gewann etc vb siehe **gewinnen**

Gewässer [gə'vɛsər] (-s, -) nt waters pl

Gewebe [gə've:bə] (-s, -) nt (Stoff) fabric; (BIOL) tissue

Gewehr [gə've:r] (-(e)s, -e) nt gun; rifle; **~lauf** m rifle barrel

Geweih [gə'vai] (-(e)s, -e) nt antlers pl

Gewerb- [gə'vɛrb] zW: **~e** (-s, -) nt trade, occupation; **Handel und ~e** trade and industry; **~eschule** f technical school; **~szweig** m line of trade

Gewerkschaft [gə'vɛrkʃaft] f trade union; **~ler** (-s, -) m trade unionist; **~sbund** m trade unions federation

gewesen [gə'vezən] pp von **sein**

Gewicht [gə'viçt] (-(e)s, -e) nt weight; (fig) importance

gewieft [gə'vi:ft] adj shrewd, cunning

gewillt [gə'vɪlt] adj willing, prepared

Gewimmel [gə'vɪml] (-s) nt swarm

Gewinde [gə'vɪndə] (-s, -) nt (Kranz) wreath; (von Schraube) thread

Gewinn [gə'vɪn] (-(e)s, -e) m profit; (bei Spiel) winnings pl; **etw mit ~ verkaufen** to sell sth at a profit; **~und Verlustrechnung** (COMM) profit and loss account; **~beteiligung** f profit-sharing; **g~bringend** adj profitable; **g~en** (unreg) vt to win; (erwerben) to gain; (Kohle, Öl) to extract ♦ vi to win; (profitieren) to gain; **an etw** dat **g~en** to gain (in) sth; **g~end** adj (Lächeln, Aussehen) winning, charming; **~er(in)** (-s, -) *m(f)* winner; **g~end** *adj* (*Lächeln, Aussehen*) winning, charming; **~panne** *f* profit margin; **~ung** *f* winning; gaining; (*von Kohle etc*) extraction

Gewirr [gə'vɪr] (-(e)s, -e) *nt* tangle; (*von Straßen*) maze

gewiß [gə'vɪs] *adj* certain ♦ *adv* certainly

Gewissen [gə'vɪsən] (-s, -) *nt* conscience; **g~haft** *adj* conscientious; **g~los** *adj* unscrupulous

Gewissens- zW: **~bisse** *pl* pangs of conscience, qualms; **~frage** *f* matter of conscience; **~freiheit** *f* freedom of conscience; **~konflikt** *m* moral conflict

gewissermaßen [gəvɪsər'ma:sən] *adv* more or less, in a way

Gewißheit [gə'vɪshait] *f* certainty

Gewitter [gə'vɪtər] (-s, -) *nt* thunderstorm; **g~n** *vi unpers*: es g~t there's a thunderstorm

gewitzt [gə'vɪtst] *adj* shrewd, cunning

gewogen [gə'vo:gən] *adj* (+*dat*) well-disposed (towards)

gewöhnen [gə'vø:nən] *vt*: **jdn an etw** *akk* ~ to accustom sb to sth; (*erziehen zu*) to teach sb sth; **sich an etw** *akk* ~ to get used *od* accustomed to sth

Gewohnheit [gə'vo:nhait] *f* habit; (*Brauch*) custom; **aus** ~ from habit; **zur** ~ **werden** to become a habit

Gewohnheitsmensch *m* creature of habit

Gewohnheitsrecht *nt* common law

gewöhnlich [gə'vø:nlɪç] *adj* usual; ordinary; (*pej*) common; **wie** ~ as usual

gewohnt [gə'vo:nt] *adj* usual; etw ~ sein to be used to sth

Gewöhnung *f*: ~ (**an** +*akk*) getting accustomed (to)

Gewölbe [gə'vœlbə] (-s, -) *nt* vault

gewollt *adj* affected, artificial

gewonnen [gə'vɔnən] *vb siehe* gewinnen

geworden [gə'vɔrdən] *vb siehe* werden

geworfen [gə'vɔrfən] *vb siehe* werfen

Gewühl [gə'vy:l] (-(e)s) *nt* throng

Gewürz [gə'vʏrts] (-es, -e) *nt* spice, seasoning; **~nelke** *f* clove; **g~t** *adj* spiced

gewußt [gə'vʊst] *vb siehe* wissen

Gezeiten [gə'tsaitən] *pl* tides

gezielt [gə'tsi:lt] *adj* with a particular aim in mind, purposeful; (*Kritik*) pointed

geziert [gə'tsi:rt] *adj* affected

gezogen [gə'tso:gən] *vb siehe* ziehen

Gezwitscher [gə'tsvɪtʃər] (-s) *nt* twitter(ing), chirping

gezwungen [gə'tsvʊŋən] *adj* forced; **~ermaßen** *adv* of necessity

ggf *abk* von **gegebenenfalls**

gibst *etc vb siehe* **geben**

Gicht [gɪçt] (-) *f* gout; **g~isch** *adj* gouty

Giebel ['gi:bəl] (-s, -) *m* gable; **~dach** *nt* gable(d) roof; **~fenster** *nt* gable window

Gier [gi:r] (-) *f* greed; **g~ig** *adj* greedy

gießen ['gi:sən] (*unreg*) *vt* to pour; (*Blumen*) to water; (*Metall*) to cast; (*Wachs*) to mould

Gießkanne *f* watering can

Gift [gɪft] (-(e)s, -e) *nt* poison; **g~ig** *adj* poisonous; (*fig: boshaft*) venomous; **~müll** *m* toxic waste; **~stoff** *m* toxic substance; **~zahn** *m* fang

ging *etc vb siehe* **gehen**

Ginster ['gɪnstər] (-s, -) *m* broom

Gipfel ['gɪpfəl] (-s, -) *m* summit, peak; (*fig: Höhepunkt*) height; **g~n** *vi* to culminate; **~treffen** *nt* summit (meeting)

Gips [gɪps] (-es, -e) *m* plaster; (*MED*) plaster (of Paris); **~abdruck** *m* plaster cast; **g~en** *vt* to plaster; **~verband** *m* plaster (cast)

Giraffe [gi'rafə] *f* giraffe

Girlande [gɪr'landə] *f* garland

Giro ['ʒi:ro] (-s, -s) *nt* giro; **~konto** *nt* current account

Gischt [gɪʃt] (-e)s, -e) m spray
Gitarre [gi'tarə] f guitar
Gitter ['gɪtər] (-s, -) nt grating, bars pl; (für Pflanzen) trellis; (Zaun) railing(s); ~**bett** nt cot; ~**fenster** nt barred window; ~**zaun** m railing(s)
Glacéhandschuh [gla'se:hantʃu:] m kid glove
Glanz [glants] (-es) m shine, lustre, (fig) splendour
glänzen ['glɛntsən] vi to shine (also fig), to gleam ♦ vt to polish; ~**d** adj shining; (fig) brilliant
Glanz- zW: ~**leistung** f brilliant achievement; ~**los** adj dull; ~**zeit** f heyday
Glas [gla:s] (-es, -er) nt glass; ~**er** (-s, -) m glazier; ~**faser** f fibreglass; **g~ieren** [gla'zi:rən] vt to glaze; **g~ig** adj glassy; ~**scheibe** f pane; ~**ur** [gla'zu:r] f glaze; (KOCH) icing
glatt [glat] adj smooth; (rutschig) slippery; (Absage) flat; (Lüge) downright
Glätte ['glɛtə] f smoothness; slipperiness
Glatteis nt (black) ice; **jdn aufs ~ führen** (fig) to take sb for a ride
glätten vt to smooth out
Glatze ['glatsə] f bald head; **eine ~ bekommen** to go bald
Glaube ['glaubə] (-ns, -n) m: ~ (an +akk) faith (in); belief (in); **g~n** vt, vi to believe; to think; **jdm g~n** to believe sb; **an etw akk g~n** to believe in sth; **daran g~n müssen** (umg) to creep for it; ~**nsbekenntnis** nt creed
glaubhaft ['glauphaft] adj credible
gläubig ['glɔybɪç] adj (REL) devout; (vertrauensvoll) trustful; **G~e(r)** mf believer; **die G~en** the faithful; **G~er** (-s, -) m creditor
glaubwürdig ['glaubvʏrdɪç] adj credible; (Mensch) trustworthy; **G~keit** f credibility; trustworthiness
gleich [glaɪç] adj equal; (identisch) (the) same, identical ♦ adv equally; (sofort) straight away; (bald) in a minute; **es ist mir ~** it's all the

same to me; **2 mal 2 ~ 4** 2 times 2 is od equals 4; ~ **groß** the same size; ~ **nach/an** right after/at; ~**alt-rig** adj of the same age; ~**artig** adj similar; ~**bedeutend** adj synonymous; **G~berechtigung** f equal rights pl; ~**bleibend** adj constant; ~**en** (unreg) vi: **jdm/etw ~en** to be like sb/sth ♦ vr to be alike; ~**falls** adv likewise; **danke ~falls!** the same to you; **G~förmigkeit** f uniformity; (eintönig) like-minded; **G~gesinnt** adj like-minded; **G~gewicht** nt equilibrium, balance; ~**gültig** adj indifferent; (unbedeutend) unimportant; **G~gültigkeit** f indifference; **G~heit** f equality; ~**kommen** (unreg) vi +dat to be equal to; ~**mäßig** adj even, equal; **G~nis** (-ses, -se) nt parable; ~**sam** adv as it were; **G~schritt** m: **im G~schritt gehen** to walk in step; ~**stellen** vt (rechtlich etc) to treat as (an) equal; ~**strom** m (ELEK) direct current; ~**tun** (unreg) vi: **jdm ~tun** to match sb; **G~ung** f equation; ~**viel** adv no matter; ~**wertig** adj (Geld) of the same value; (Gegner) evenly-matched; ~**zei-tig** adj simultaneous
Gleis [glaɪs] (-es, -e) nt track, rails pl; (Bahnsteig) platform
gleiten ['glaɪtən] (unreg) vi to glide; (rutschen) to slide
Gletscher ['glɛtʃər] (-s, -) m glacier; ~**spalte** f crevasse
Glied [gli:t] (-(e)s, -er) nt member; (Arm, Bein) limb; (von Kette) link; (MIL) rank(s); **g~ern** vt to organize, to structure; ~**erung** f structure, organization
glimmen ['glɪmən] (unreg) vi to glow, to gleam
glimpflich ['glɪmpflɪç] adj mild, lenient; ~ **davonkommen** to get off lightly
glitschig ['glɪtʃɪç] adj (Fisch, Weg) slippery
glitzern ['glɪtsərn] vi to glitter; to twinkle
global [glo'ba:l] adj global

Globus ['glo:bus] (- od -ses, Globen od -se) m globe

Glocke ['glɔkə] f bell; etw an die große ~ hängen (fig) to shout sth from the rooftops

Glockenblume f bellflower

Glocken- zW: ~geläut nt peal of bells; ~spiel nt chime(s); (MUS) glockenspiel; ~turm m bell tower

Glosse ['glɔsə] f comment

glotzen ['glɔtsən] (umg) vi to stare

Glück [glʏk] (-(e)s) nt luck, fortune; (Freude) happiness; ~ haben to be lucky; viel ~! good luck!; zum ~ fortunately; zum ~ fortunately; g~en vi to succeed; es g~te ihm, zu bekommen he succeeded in getting it

gluckern ['glukərn] vi to glug

Glück- zW: ~lich adj fortunate; (froh) happy; g~licherweise adv fortunately; g~selig adj blissful

Glücks- zW: ~fall m stroke of luck; ~kind nt lucky person; ~sache f matter of luck; ~spiel nt game of chance

Glückwunsch m congratulations pl, best wishes pl

Glüh- ['gly:] zW: ~birne f light bulb; g~en vi to glow; ~wein m mulled wine; ~würmchen nt glow-worm

Glut [glu:t] (-, -en) f (Röte) glow; (Feuers~) fire; (Hitze) heat; (fig) ardour

Glyzerin [glytsə'ri:n] nt glycerine

Gnade ['gna:də] f (Gunst) favour; (Erbarmen) mercy; (Milde) clemency

Gnaden- zW: ~frist f reprieve, respite; g~los adj merciless; ~stoß m coup de grâce

gnädig ['gnɛ:dɪç] adj gracious; (voll Erbarmen) merciful

Gold [gɔlt] (-(e)s) nt gold; g~en adj golden; ~fisch m goldfish; ~grube f goldmine; g~ig (umg) adj (fig: allerliebst) sweet, adorable; ~regen m laburnum; G~schmied m goldsmith

Golf¹ [gɔlf] (-(e)s, -e) m gulf

Golf² (-s) nt golf; ~platz m golf course; ~schläger m golf club

Golfstrom m Gulf Stream

Gondel ['gɔndəl] (-, -n) f gondola; (Seilbahn) cable-car

gönnen ['gœnən] vt: jdm etw ~ not to begrudge sb sth; sich dat etw ~ to allow o.s. sth

Gönner (-s, -) m patron; g~haft adj patronizing

Gosse ['gɔsə] f gutter

Gott [gɔt] (-(e)s, ¨er) m god; mein ~! for heaven's sake!; um ~es Willen! for heaven's sake!; grüß ~! hello; ~ sei Dank! thank God!; ~heit f deity

Göttin ['gœtɪn] f goddess

göttlich adj divine

gottlos adj godless

Götze ['gœtsə] (-n, -n) m idol

Grab [gra:p] (-(e)s, ¨er) nt grave; g~en ['gra:bən] (unreg) vt to dig; ~en (-s, ¨) m ditch; (MIL) trench; ~stein m gravestone

Grad [gra:t] (-(e)s, -e) m degree; ~einteilung f graduation

Graf [gra:f] (-en, -en) m count, earl

Gram [gra:m] (-(e)s) m grief, sorrow

grämen ['grɛ:mən] vr to grieve

Gramm [gram] (-s, -e) nt gram(me)

Grammatik [gra'matɪk] f grammar

Grammophon [gramo'fo:n] (-s, -e) nt gramophone

Granat [gra'na:t] (-(e)s, -e) m (Stein) garnet

Granate f (MIL) shell; (Hand~) grenade

Granit [gra'ni:t] (-s, -e) m granite

Graphiker(in) ['gra:fikər(ɪn)] (-s, -) m(f) graphic designer

graphisch ['gra:fɪʃ] adj graphic

Gras [gra:s] (-es, ¨er) nt grass; g~en vi to graze; ~halm m blade of grass

grassieren [gra'si:rən] vi to be rampant, to rage

gräßlich ['grɛslɪç] adj horrible

Grat [gra:t] (-(e)s, -e) m ridge

Gräte ['grɛ:tə] f fishbone

gratis ['gra:tɪs] adj, adv free of charge; G~probe f free sample

Gratulation [gratulatsi'o:n] f congra-

tulation(s)
gratulieren [gratu'li:rən] vi: **jdm ~ (zu etw) to** congratulate sb (on sth); **(ich) gratuliere!** congratulations!
grau [grau] adj grey
Grauen (-s) nt horror; **g~** vi unpers: **es graut jdm vor etw sb** dreads sth, sb is afraid of sth: **sich g~ vor to dread, to have a horror of; g~haft** adj horrible
grauhaarig adj grey-haired
grausam ['grauzam] adj cruel; **G~keit** f cruelty
Grausen ['grauzən] (-s) nt horror; **g~** vb = **grauen**
gravieren [gra'vi:rən] vt to engrave; **~d** adj grave
graziös [gratsi'ø:s] adj graceful
greifbar adj tangible, concrete; in **~er Nähe** within reach
greifen ['graifən] (unreg) vt to seize; to grip; **nach etw ~ to reach for** sth; **um sich ~** (fig) to spread; **zu etw ~ to turn to sth**
Greis [grais] (-es, -e) m old man; **g~enhaft** adj senile; **~in** f old woman
grell [grɛl] adj harsh
Grenz- ['grɛnts] zW: **~beamte(r)** m frontier official; **~e** f boundary; (Staats~) frontier; (Schranke) limit; **g~en** vi: **g~en (an +akk)** to border (on); **g~enlos** adj boundless; **~fall** m borderline case; **~übergang** m frontier crossing
Greuel ['grɔyəl] (-s, -) m horror, revulsion; **etw ist jdm ein ~ sb** loathes sth
greulich ['grɔyliç] adj horrible
Griech- ['gri:ç] zW: **~e** (-n, -n) m Greek; **~enland** nt Greece; **~in** f Greek; **g~isch** adj Greek
griesgrämig ['gri:sgrɛːmiç] adj grumpy
Grieß [gri:s] (-es, -e) m (KOCH) semolina
Griff [grif] (-(e)s, -e) m grip; (Vorrichtung) handle; **g~bereit** adj handy
Grill [gril] m grill; **~e** f cricket

g~en vt to grill
Grimasse [gri'masə] f grimace
grimmig ['grimiç] adj furious; (heftig) fierce, severe
grinsen ['grinzən] vi to grin
Grippe ['gripə] f influenza, flu
grob [grɔp] adj coarse, gross; (Fehler, Verstoß) gross; **G~heit** f coarseness; coarse expression
grölen ['grø:lən] (pej) vt to bawl, to bellow
Groll [grɔl] (-(e)s) m resentment; **g~en** vi (Donner) to rumble; **g~en (mit od +dat)** to bear ill will (towards)
groß [gro:s] adj big, large; (hoch) tall; (fig) great ♦ adv greatly; **im ~en und ganzen** on the whole; **~artig** adj great, splendid; **G~aufnahme** f (CINE) close-up; **G~britannien** nt Great Britain
Größe ['grø:sə] f size; (Höhe) height; (fig) greatness
Groß- zW: **~einkauf** m bulk purchase; **~eltern** pl grandparents; **g~enteils** adv mostly
Groß- zW: **~format** nt large size; **~handel** m wholesale trade; **~händler** m wholesaler; **~macht** f great power; **g~mütig** adj magnanimous; **~mutter** f grandmother; **~rechner** m mainframe (computer); **g~schreiben** (unreg) vt to write in block capitals; **bei jdm g~schreiben werden to be high on** sb's list of priorities; **g~spurig** adj pompous; **~stadt** f city, large town
größte(r, s) [grø:stə(r, s)] adj superl von **groß**; **~nteils** adv for the most part
Groß- zW: **g~tun** (unreg) vi to boast; **~vater** m grandfather; **g~ziehen** (unreg) vt to raise; **g~zügig** adj generous; (Planung) on a large scale
grotesk [gro'tɛsk] adj grotesque
Grotte ['grɔtə] f grotto
Grübchen ['gry:pçən] nt dimple
Grube ['gru:bə] f pit; mine
grübeln ['gry:bəln] vi to brood

Grubengas nt firedamp

Gruft [gruft] (-, -e) f tomb, vault

grün [gry:n] adj green; **G~anlage** f park

Grund [grunt] (-(e)s, -e) m ground; (von See, Gefäß) bottom; (fig) reason; **im ~e genommen** basically; **~ausbildung** f basic training; **~besitz** m land(ed property), real estate; **~buch** nt land register

gründen ['gryndən] vt to found ♦ vr: **sich ~ (auf** +dat) to be based (on); **~ auf** +akk to base on

Gründer (-s, -) m founder

Grund- zW: **~gebühr** f basic charge; **~gesetz** nt constitution; **~lage** f foundation; **g~legend** adj fundamental

gründlich adj thorough

Grund- zW: **g~los** adj groundless; **~regel** f basic rule; **~riß** m plan; (fig) outline; **~satz** m principle; **g~sätzlich** adj fundamental; (Frage) of principle ♦ adv fundamentally; (prinzipiell) on principle; **~schule** f elementary school; **~stein** m foundation stone; **~stück** nt estate; plot

Grundwasser nt ground water

Grünen pl (POL): **die ~** the Greens

Grünspan m verdigris

Grünstreifen m central reservation

grunzen ['gruntsən] vi to grunt

Gruppe ['grupə] f group; **g~nweise** adv in groups

gruppieren [gru'pi:rən] vt, vr to group

gruselig adj creepy

gruseln ['gru:zəln] vi unpers: **es gruselt jdm vor etw** sth gives sb the creeps ♦ vr to have the creeps

Gruß [gru:s] (-es, -e) m greeting; (MIL) salute; **viele Grüße** best wishes; **mit freundlichen Grüßen** yours sincerely; **Grüße an** +akk regards to

grüßen ['gry:sən] vt to greet; (MIL) to salute; **jdn von jdm ~** to give sb sb's regards; **jdn ~ lassen** to send sb one's regards

gucken ['gukən] vi to look

gültig ['gyltıç] adj valid; **G~keit** f validity

Gummi ['gumi] (-s, -s) nt od m rubber; (~harze) gum; **~band** nt rubber od elastic band; (Hosen~) elastic; **~bärchen** f jelly baby (BRIT); **~baum** m rubber plant; **g~eren** [gu'mi:rən] vt to gum; **~knüppel** m rubber truncheon; **~strumpf** m elastic stocking

günstig ['gynstıç] adj convenient; (Gelegenheit) favourable; **das habe ich ~ bekommen** it was a bargain

Gurgel ['gurgəl] (-, -n) f throat; **g~n** vi to gurgle; (im Mund) to gargle

Gurke ['gurkə] f cucumber; **saure ~** pickled cucumber, gherkin

Gurt [gurt] (-(e)s, -e) m belt

Gürtel ['gyrtəl] (-s, -) m belt; (GEOG) zone; **~reifen** m radial tyre

GUS f abk (= Gemeinschaft unabhängiger Staaten) CIS

Guß [gus] (-sses, Güsse) m casting; (Regen~) downpour; (KOCH) glazing; **~eisen** nt cast iron

gut [gu:t] adj good; **alles Gute** all the best; **also gut** all right then ♦ adv well; **gut schmecken** to taste good; **gut, aber ...** OK, but ...; (na) **gut, ich komme ja** all right, I'll come; **gut drei Stunden** a good three hours; **das kann gut sein** that may well be; **laß es gut sein** that'll do

Gut [gu:t] (-(e)s, -er) nt (Besitz) possession; **Güter** pl (Waren) goods; **~achten** (-s, -) nt (expert) opinion; **~achter** (-s, -) m expert; **g~artig** adj good-natured; (MED) benign; **g~bürgerlich** adj (Küche) (good) plain; **~dünken** nt: **nach ~dünken** at one's discretion

Güte ['gy:tə] f goodness, kindness; (Qualität) quality

Güter- zW: **~abfertigung** f (EISENB) goods office; **~bahnhof** m goods station; **~wagen** m goods waggon (BRIT), freight car (US);

~**zug** m goods train (BRIT), freight train (US)

Gütezeichen nt quality mark, ≈ kite mark

gut- zW: ~**gehen** (unreg) vi unpers to work, to come off; **es geht jdm ~** sb's doing fine; ~**gemeint** adj well meant; ~**gläubig** adj trusting; **G~haben** (-s) nt credit; ~**heißen** (unreg) vt to approve (of)

gütig ['gy:tɪç] adj kind

Gut- zW: **g~mütig** adj good-natured; ~**mütigkeit** f good nature; ~**schein** m voucher; **g~schreiben** (unreg) vt to credit; **g~tun** (unreg) vi: **jdm g~tun** to do sb good; **g~willig** adj willing

Gymnasium [gym'na:zium] nt grammar school (BRIT), high school (US)

Gymnastik [gym'nastɪk] f exercises pl, keep fit

H

Haag [ha:g] m: **Den ~ the Hague**

Haar [ha:r] (-(e)s, -e) nt hair; **um ein ~** nearly; **an den ~en herbeigezogen** (umg: Vergleich) very farfetched; ~**bürste** f hairbrush; **h~en** vi, vr to lose hair; ~**esbreite** f: **um ~esbreite by a hair's-breadth**; **h~genau** adv precisely; **(fig) nasty**; ~**klammer** f hairgrip; ~**klemme** f hair grip; ~**nadel** f hairpin; **h~scharf** adv (beobachten) very sharply; (daneben) by a hair's breadth; ~**schnitt** m haircut; ~**spange** f hair slide; **h~sträubend** adj hair-raising; ~**teil** nt hairpiece; ~**waschmittel** nt shampoo

Habe ['ha:bə] (-) f property

haben ['ha:bən] (unreg) vt, vb aux to have; **Hunger/Angst ~** to be hungry/afraid; **woher hast du das?** where did you get that from?; **was hast du denn?** what's the matter (with you?); **du hast zu schweigen** you're to be quiet; **ich hätte gern I would like**; **H~** (-s, -) nt credit

Habgier f avarice; **h~ig** adj avaricious

Habicht ['ha:bɪçt] (-s, -e) m hawk

Habseligkeiten pl belongings

Hachse ['haksə] f (KOCH) knuckle

Hacke ['hakə] f hoe; (Ferse) heel; **h~n** vt to hack, to chop; (Erde) to hoe

Hackfleisch nt mince, minced meat

Hafen ['ha:fən] (-s, ⁻) m harbour, port; ~**arbeiter** m docker; ~**stadt** f port

Hafer ['ha:fər] (-s, -) m oats pl; ~**flocken** pl rolled oats; ~**schleim** m gruel

Haft [haft] (-) f custody; **h~bar** adj liable, responsible; ~**befehl** m warrant (for arrest); **h~en** vi to stick, to cling; **h~en für** to be liable od responsible for; ~**enbleiben** (unreg) vi: ~**enbleiben (an +dat)** to stick (to); ~**fläng** adj prisoner; ~**pflicht** f liability; ~**pflichtversicherung** f (AUT) third party insurance; ~**schalen** pl contact lenses; ~**ung** f liability

Hagebutte ['ha:gəbutə] f rose hip

Hagel ['ha:gəl] (-s) m hail; **h~n** vi unpers to hail

hager ['ha:gər] adj gaunt

Hahn [ha:n] (-(e)s, ⁻e) m cock; (Wasser~) tap, faucet (US)

Hähnchen ['he:nçən] nt cockerel; (KOCH) chicken

Hai(fisch) ['haɪ(fɪʃ)] (-(e)s, -e) m shark

häkeln ['hɛ:kəln] vt to crochet

Häkelnadel f crochet hook

Haken ['ha:kən] (-s, -) m hook; (fig) catch; ~**kreuz** nt swastika; ~**nase** f hooked nose

halb [halp] adj half; ~ **eins** half past twelve; **ein ~es Dutzend** half a dozen; **H~dunkel** nt semi-darkness

halber ['halbər] präp +gen (wegen) on account of; (für) for the sake of

Halb- zW: ~**heit** f half-measure; **h~ieren** vt to halve; ~**insel** f peninsula; ~**jahr** nt six months; (auch: Komm) half-year; **h~jährlich** adj half-yearly; ~**kreis** m semicircle; ~**leiter** m semiconductor; ~**links** (-, -) m (SPORT) inside left; ~**mond** m half-moon; (fig) crescent; **h**~**offen** adj half-open; ~**pension** f half-board; ~**rechts** (-, -) m (SPORT) inside right; ~**schuh** m shoe; ~**tags** adv: **h**~**tags arbeiten** to work part-time, to work mornings/afternoons; **h**~**wegs** adv half-way; halfways besser more or less better; ~**zeit** f (SPORT) half; (Pause) half-time

Halde ['haldə] f (Kohlen) heap

half [half] vb siehe **helfen**

Hälfte ['hɛlftə] f half

Halfter¹ ['halftər] m od nt (für Tiere) halter

Halfter² (-, -) f od nt (Pistolen~) holster

Halle ['halə] f hall; (AVIAT) hangar; **h**~**n** vi to echo, to resound; ~**nbad** nt indoor swimming pool

hallo [ha'lo] excl hello

Halluzination [halutsinatsi'o:n] f hallucination

Halm [halm] (-(e)s, -e) m blade; stalk

Hals [hals] (-es, ⸗e) m neck; (Kehle) throat; ~ **über Kopf** in a rush; ~**band** nt (von Hund) collar; ~**kette** f necklace; ~-**Nasen-Ohren-Arzt** m ear, nose and throat specialist; ~**schmerzen** pl sore throat sg; ~**tuch** nt scarf

Halt [halt] (-(e)s, -e) m stop; (fester ~) hold; (innerer ~) stability; **h**~ excl stop!, halt!; **h**~**bar** adj durable; (Lebensmittel) non-perishable; (MIL, fig) tenable; ~**barkeit** f durability; (non-)perishability

halten ['haltən] (unreg) vt to keep; (fest~) to hold ♦ vi to hold; (frisch bleiben) to keep; (stoppen) to stop ♦ vr (frisch bleiben) to keep; (sich behaupten) to hold out; ~ **für** to regard as; ~ **von** to think of; an sich ~ to restrain o.s.; **sich rechts/links** ~ to keep to the right/left

Haltestelle f stop

Halteverbot nt: **hier ist** ~ there's

no waiting here

Halt- zW: **h**~**los** adj unstable; **h**~**machen** vi to stop; ~**ung** f posture; (fig) attitude; (Selbstbeherrschung) composure

Halunke [ha'loŋkə] (-n, -n) m rascal

hämisch ['hɛːmɪʃ] adj malicious

Hammel ['haməl] (-s, ⸗ od -) m wether; ~**fleisch** nt mutton

Hammer ['hamər] (-s, ⸗) m hammer

hämmern ['hɛmərn] vt, vi to hammer

Hämorrhoiden [hɛmɔro'i:dən] pl haemorrhoids

Hampelmann ['hampəlman] m (auch fig) puppet

Hamster ['hamstər] (-s, -) m hamster; ~**ei** [-'rai] f hoarding; **h**~**n** vi to hoard

Hand [hant] (-, ⸗e) f hand; ~**arbeit** f manual work; (Nadelarbeit) needlework; ~**ball** m (SPORT) handball; ~**bremse** f handbrake; ~**buch** nt handbook, manual; ~**creme** f handcream

Händedruck ['hɛndədrʊk] m handshake

Handel ['handəl] (-s) m trade; (Geschäft) transaction

Handeln ['handəln] (-s) nt action

handeln ['handəln] vi to trade; (agieren) to act ♦ vr unpers: **sich** ~ **um** to be a question of, to be about; ~ **von** to be about

Handels- zW: ~**bilanz** f balance of trade; ~**kammer** f chamber of commerce; ~**reisende(r)** m commercial traveller; ~**schule** f business school; **h**~**üblich** adj customary; (Preis) going attrib; ~**vertreter** m sales representative

Hand- zW: ~**feger** m hand-brush; **h**~**fest** adj hefty; **h**~**gearbeitet** adj handmade; ~**gemenge** nt scuffle; ~**gepäck** nt hand-luggage; **h**~**geschrieben** adj hand-written; **h**~**greiflich** adj palpable; **h**~**greiflich werden** to become violent; ~**granate** f hand grenade; ~**griff** m flick of the wrist; **h**~**haben**

vt insep to handle

Händler ['hɛndlər] (-s, -) *m* trader, dealer

handlich ['hantlɪç] *adj* handy

Handlung ['handluŋ] *f* action(s); (*in Buch*) plot; (*Geschäft*) shop

Hand- *zW:* **~pflege** *f* manicure; **~schelle** *f* handcuff; **~schrift** *f* handwriting; (*Text*) manuscript; **~schuh** *m* glove; **~stand** *m* (SPORT) handstand; **~tasche** *f* handbag; **~tuch** *nt* towel; **~umdrehen** *nt:* **im ~umdrehen** in the twinkling of an eye; **~werk** *nt* trade, craft; **~werker** (-s, -) *m* craftsman, artisan; **~werkzeug** *nt* tools *pl*

Hanf [hanf] (-(e)s) *m* hemp

Hang [haŋ] (-(e)s, -e) *m* inclination; (*Ab~*) slope

Hänge- ['hɛŋə] *in zW* hanging; **~brücke** *f* suspension bridge; **~matte** *f* hammock

hängen ['hɛŋən] *vi (unreg)* to hang ♦ *vt:* **etw** (**an etw** *akk*) **~** to hang sth (on sth); **~ an** *+dat* (*fig*) to be attached to; **sich ~ an** *+akk* to hang on to, to cling to; **~bleiben** (*unreg*) *vi* to be caught; (*fig*) to remain, to stick; **~bleiben an** *+dat* to catch *od* get caught on; **~lassen** (*unreg*) *vt* (*vergessen*) to leave; **den Kopf ~lassen** to get downhearted

Hannover [ha'noːfər] (-s) *nt* Hannover

hänseln ['hɛnzəln] *vt* to tease

Hansestadt ['hanzəʃtat] *f* Hanse town

hantieren [han'tiːrən] *vi* to work, to be busy; **mit etw ~** to handle sth

hapern ['haːpərn] *vi unpers:* **es hapert an etw** *dat* there is a lack of sth

Happen ['hapən] (-s, -) *m* mouthful

Harfe ['harfə] *f* harp

Harke ['harkə] *f* rake; **h~n** *vt, vi* to rake

harmlos ['harmloːs] *adj* harmless; **H~igkeit** *f* harmlessness

Harmonie [harmo'niː] *f* harmony; **h~ren** *vi* to harmonize

Harmonika [har'moːnika] (-, -s) *f* (*Zieh~*) concertina

harmonisch [har'moːnɪʃ] *adj* harmonious

Harmonium [har'moːniʊm] (-s, -nien *od* -s) *nt* harmonium

Harn [harn] (-(e)s, -e) *m* urine; **~blase** *f* bladder

Harpune [har'puːnə] *f* harpoon

harren ['harən] *vi:* **~ (auf** *+akk*) to wait (for)

hart [hart] *adj* hard; (*fig*) harsh

Härte ['hɛrtə] *f* hardness; (*fig*) harshness

hart- *zW:* **~gekocht** *adj* hard-boiled; **~herzig** *adj* hard-hearted; **~näckig** *adj* stubborn; **H~näckigkeit** *f* stubbornness; **H~platte** *f* hard disk

Harz [harts] (-es, -e) *nt* resin

Haschee [ha'ʃeː] (-s, -s) *nt* hash

Haschisch ['haʃɪʃ] (-) *nt* hashish

Hase ['haːzə] (-n, -n) *m* hare

Haselnuß ['haːzəlnʊs] *f* hazelnut

Hasenfuß *m* coward

Hasenscharte *f* harelip

Haß [has] (-sses) *m* hate, hatred

hassen ['hasən] *vt* to hate

häßlich ['hɛslɪç] *adj* ugly; (*gemein*) nasty; **H~keit** *f* ugliness; nastiness

Hast [hast] *f* haste

hast *vb siehe* **haben**

hasten *vi* to rush

hastig *adj* hasty

hat [hat] *vb siehe* **haben**

hatte *etc* ['hatə] *vb siehe* **haben**

Haube ['haubə] *f* hood; (*Mütze*) cap; (AUT) bonnet, hood (US)

Hauch [haux] (-(e)s, -e) *m* breath; (*Luft~*) breeze; (*fig*) trace; **h~dünn** *adj* extremely thin; **h~en** *vi* to breathe

Haue ['hauə] *f* hoe, pick; (*umg*) hiding; **h~n** (*unreg*) *vt* to hew, to cut; (*umg*) to thrash

Haufen ['haufən] (-s, -) *m* heap; (*Leute*) crowd; **ein ~ (x)** (*umg*) loads *od* a lot of (x); **auf einem ~** in one heap

häufen ['hɔyfən] *vt* to pile up ♦ *vr* to accumulate

haufenweise adv in heaps; in droves; etw ~ **haben** to have piles of sth

häufig ['hɔyfıç] adj frequent ♦ adv frequently; **H~keit** f frequency

Haupt [haupt] (-(e)s, Häupter) nt head; (Ober~) chief ♦ in zW main; **~bahnhof** m central station; **h~beruflich** adv as one's main occupation; **~darsteller(in)** m(f) leading actor(actress); **~eingang** m main entrance; **~fach** nt (SCH, UNIV) main subject, major (US); **~film** m main film; **~gericht** nt (KOCH) main course

Häuptling ['hɔyptlıŋ] m chief(tain)

Haupt- zW: **~mann** (pl -leute) m (MIL) captain; **~person** f central figure; **~quartier** nt headquarters pl; **~rolle** f leading part; **~sache** f main thing; **h~sächlich** adj chief ♦ adv chiefly; **~saison** f high season, peak season; **~schule** f ≈ secondary school; **~stadt** f capital; **~straße** f main street; **~verkehrszeit** f rush-hour, peak traffic hours pl; **~wort** nt noun

Haus [haus] (-es, Häuser) nt house; **nach ~e** home; **zu ~e** at home; **~angestellte** f domestic servant; **~apotheke** f medicine cabinet; **~arbeit** f housework; (SCH) homework; **~arzt** m family doctor; **~aufgabe** f (SCH) homework; **~besitzer(in)** m(f) house-owner; **~besuch** m (von Arzt) house call

Häuserblock ['hɔyzərblɔk] m block (of houses)

Häusermakler ['hɔyzər-] m estate agent (BRIT), real estate agent (US)

Haus- zW: **~frau** f housewife; **~flur** m hallway; **h~gemacht** adj home-made; **~halt** m household; (POL) budget; **h~halten** (unreg) vi (sparen) to economize; **~hälterin** f housekeeper; **~haltsgeld** nt housekeeping (money); **~haltsgerät** nt domestic appliance; **~herr** m host; (Vermieter) landlord; **h~hoch** adv: **h~hoch verlieren** to lose by a mile

hausieren [hau'ziːrən] vi to peddle

Hausierer (-s, -) m peddlar

häuslich ['hɔyslıç] adj domestic

Haus- zW: **~meister** m caretaker, janitor; **~nummer** f street number; **~ordnung** f house rules pl; **~putz** m house cleaning; **~schlüssel** m front-door key; **~schuh** m slipper; **~suchung** f police raid; **~tier** nt pet; **~tür** f front door; **~wirt** m landlord; **~wirtschaft** f domestic science

Haut [haut] (-, Häute) f skin; (Tier~) hide; **~creme** f skin cream; **h~eng** adj skin-tight; **~farbe** f complexion; **~krebs** m skin cancer

Haxe ['haksə] f = Hachse

Hbf abk = Hauptbahnhof

Hebamme ['heːp'amə] f midwife

Hebel ['heːbəl] (-s, -) m lever

heben ['heːbən] (unreg) vt to raise, to lift

Hecht [hɛçt] (-(e)s, -e) m pike

Heck [hɛk] (-(e)s, -e) nt stern; (von Auto) rear

Hecke ['hɛkə] f hedge

Heckenrose f dog rose

Heckenschütze m sniper

Heer [heːr] (-(e)s, -e) nt army

Hefe ['heːfə] f yeast

Heft [hɛft] (-(e)s, -e) nt exercise book; (Zeitschrift) number; (von Messer) haft

heften vt: ~ **(an** +akk) to fasten (to); (nähen) to tack ((on) to); etw an etw akk ~ to fasten sth to sth

Hefter (-s, -) m folder

heftig adj fierce, violent; **H~keit** f fierceness, violence

Heft- zW: **~klammer** f paper clip; **~maschine** f stapling machine; **~pflaster** nt sticking plaster; **~zwecke** f drawing pin

hegen ['heːgən] vt (Wild, Bäume) to care for, to tend; (fig, geh: empfinden: Wunsch) to cherish; (: Mißtrauen) to feel

Hehl [heːl] m od nt: **kein(en) ~ aus etw machen** to make no secret of sth; **~er** (-s, -) m receiver of (stolen goods), fence

Heide¹ ['haɪdə] f heath, moor; (~kraut) heather

Heide² (-n, -n) m heathen, pagan

Heidekraut nt heather

Heidelbeere f bilberry

Heidentum nt paganism

Heidin f heathen, pagan

heikel ['haɪkəl] adj awkward, thorny; (wählerisch) fussy

Heil (haɪl] (-(e)s) nt well-being; (Seelen~) salvation; h~ adj in one piece, intact; ~and (-(e)s, -e) m saviour; h~bar adj curable; h~en vt to cure ♦ vi to heal; h~froh adj very relieved

heilig ['haɪlɪç] adj holy; H~abend m Christmas Eve; H~e(r) mf saint; ~en vt to sanctify, to hallow; H~enschein m halo; H~keit f holiness; ~sprechen (unreg) vt to canonize; H~tum nt shrine; (Gegenstand) relic

Heil- zW: h~los adj unholy; (fig) hopeless; ~mittel nt remedy; ~praktiker(in) m(f) non-medical practitioner; h~sam adj (fig) salutary; ~sarmee f Salvation Army; ~ung f cure

Heim [haɪm] (-(e)s, -e) nt home; h~ adv home

Heimat ['haɪmaːt] (-, -en) f home (town/country etc); ~land nt homeland; h~lich adj native, home attrib; (Gefühle) nostalgic; h~los adj homeless; ~ort m home town/area; ~vertriebene(r) mf displaced person

Heim- zW: ~computer m home computer; h~elig adj cosy; h~fahren (unreg) vi to drive home; ~fahrt f journey home; h~gehen (unreg) vi to go home; (sterben) to pass away; h~isch adj (gebürtig) native; sich h~isch fühlen to feel at home; ~kehr (-, -en) f homecoming; h~kehren vi to return home; h~lich adj secret; ~lichkeit f secrecy; ~reise f journey home; ~spiel nt (SPORT) home game; h~suchen vt to afflict; (Geist) to haunt; ~trainer m exercise bike;

h~tückisch adj malicious; ~weg m way home; ~weh nt homesickness; ~zahlen vt: jdm etw h~zahlen to pay sb back for sth

Heirat ['haɪraːt] (-, -en) f marriage; h~en vt to marry ♦ vi to marry, to get married ♦ vr to get married; ~santrag m proposal

heiser ['haɪzər] adj hoarse; H~keit f hoarseness

heiß [haɪs] adj hot; ~e(s) Eisen (umg) hot potato; h~blütig adj hot-blooded

heißen ['haɪsən] (unreg) vi to be called; (bedeuten) to mean ♦ vt to command; (nennen) to name ♦ vi unpers: es heißt it says; it is said; das heißt that is (to say)

Heißhunger m ravenous hunger

heißlaufen (unreg) vi, vr to overheat

Heißmangel f rotary iron

heiter ['haɪtər] adj cheerful; (Wetter) bright; H~keit f cheerfulness; (Belustigung) amusement

Heiz- ['haɪts] zW: h~bar adj heated; (Raum) with heating; h~en vt to heat; ~er (-s, -) m stoker; ~körper m radiator; ~öl nt fuel oil; ~sonne f electric fire; ~ung f heating; ~ungsanlage f heating system

hektisch ['hɛktɪʃ] adj hectic

Held [hɛlt] (-en, -en) m hero; h~enhaft adj heroic; ~in f heroine

helfen ['hɛlfən] (unreg) vi to help; (nützen) to be of use ♦ vb unpers: es hilft nichts, du mußt ... it's no use, you'll have to ...; jdm (bei etw) ~ to help sb (with sth); sich dat zu ~ wissen to be resourceful

Helfer (-s, -) m helper, assistant; **Helfershelfer** m accomplice

hell [hɛl] adj clear, bright; (Farbe, Bier) light; ~blau adj light blue; ~blond adj ash-blond; H~e (-) f clearness, brightness; h~hörig adj (Wand) paper-thin; h~hörig werden (fig) to prick up one's ears; H~seher m clairvoyant; ~wach adj wide-awake

Helm [hɛlm] (-(e)s, -e) m (auf Kopf) helmet

Hemd [hɛmt] (-(e)s, -en) nt shirt; (Unter~) vest; (~bluse) f blouse

hemmen ['hɛmən] vt to check, to hold up; gehemmt sein to be inhibited

Hemmung f check; (PSYCH) inhibition; **h~slos** adj unrestrained, without restraint

Hengst [hɛŋst] (-es, -e) m stallion

Henkel ['hɛŋkəl] (-s, -) m handle

Henker (-s, -) m hangman

Henne ['hɛnə] f hen

her [heːr] adv 1 (Richtung): komm her zu mir come here (to me); von England her from England; von weit her from a long way away; von damit! hand it over!; wo hat er das her? where did he get that from?

2 (Blickpunkt): von der Form her as far as the form is concerned

3 (zeitlich): das ist 5 Jahre her that was 5 years ago; wo bist du her? where do you come from?; ich kenne ihn von früher her I know him from before

herab [hɛ'rap] adv down(ward)s; **~hängen** (unreg) vi to hang down; **~lassen** (unreg) vt to let down ♦ vr to condescend; **~lassend** adj condescending; **~setzen** vt to lower, to reduce; (fig) to belittle, to disparage

heran [hɛ'ran] adv näher ~! come up closer!; ~ zu mir! come up to me!; **~bringen** (unreg) vt: **~bringen** (an +akk) to bring up (to); **~fahren** (unreg) vi: **~fahren** (an +akk) to drive up (to); **~kommen** (unreg) vi: (an jdn/etw) **~kommen** to approach (sb/sth), to come near (to sb/sth); **~machen** vr: sich an jdn **~machen** to approach sb; **~treten** (unreg) vi: mit etw an jdn **~treten** to approach sb with sth; **~wachsen** (unreg) vi to grow up;

~ziehen (unreg) vt to pull nearer; (aufziehen) to raise; (ausbilden) to train; jdn zu etw **~ziehen** to call upon sb to help in sth

herauf [hɛ'rauf] adv up(ward(s)); **~beschwören** (unreg) vt to conjure up, to evoke; **~bringen** (unreg) vt to bring up; **~setzen** vt (Preise, Miete) to raise, put up

heraus [hɛ'raus] adv out; **~bekommen** (unreg) vt to get out; (fig) to find out figure out; **~bringen** (unreg) vt to bring out; (Geheimnis) to elicit; **~finden** (unreg) vt to find out; **~fordern** vt to challenge; **H~forderung** f challenge; provocation; **~geben** (unreg) vt to hand over; to surrender; (zurückgeben) to give back; (Buch) to edit; (veröffentlichen) to publish; **H~geber** (-s, -) m editor; (Verleger) publisher; **~gehen** (unreg) vi: aus sich **~gehen** to come out of one's shell; **~halten** (unreg) vr: sich aus etw **~halten** to keep out of sth; **~hängen¹** vt to hang out; **~hängen²** (unreg) vi to hang out; **~holen** vt: **~holen** (aus) to get out (of); **~kommen** (unreg) vi to come out; dabei kommt nichts **~** nothing will come of it; **~nehmen** (unreg) vt to remove (from), take out (of); sich etw **~nehmen** to take liberties; **~reißen** (unreg) vt to tear out; to pull out; **~rücken** vt (Geld) to fork out, to hand over; mit etw **~rücken** (fig) to come out with sth; **~stellen** vr: sich **~stellen** (als) to turn out (to be); **~suchen** vt: sich etw/jdn **~suchen** to pick sb/sth out; **~ziehen** (unreg) vt to pull out, to extract

herb [hɛrp] adj (slightly) bitter, acid; (Wein) dry; (fig: schmerzlich) bitter; (: streng) stern, austere

herbei [hɛr'bai] adv (over) here; **~führen** vt to bring about; **~schaffen** vt to procure

herbemühen ['hɛːrbəmyːən] vr to take the trouble to come

Herberge ['hɛrbɛrgə] f shelter; hos-

tel, inn
Herbergsmutter f warden
Herbergsvater m warden
herbitten (unreg) vt to ask to come (here)
herbringen (unreg) vt to bring here
Herbst [hɛrpst] (-(e)s, -e) m autumn, fall (US); **h~lich** adj autumnal
Herd [heːrt] (-(e)s, -e) m cooker; (fig, MED) focus, centre
Herde [ˈheːrdə] f herd; (Schaf~) flock
herein [hɛˈraɪn] adv in (here), here; ~! come in!; ~**bitten** (unreg) vt to ask in; ~**brechen** (unreg) vi to set in; ~**bringen** (unreg) vt to bring in; ~**fallen** (unreg) vi to be caught, to be taken in; ~**fallen auf** +akk to fall for; ~**kommen** (unreg) vi to come in; ~**lassen** (unreg) vt to admit; ~**legen** vt: jdn ~**legen** to take sb in; ~**platzen** (umg) vi to burst in
Her- zW: ~**fahrt** f journey here; **h~fallen** (unreg) vi: **h~fallen über** +akk to fall upon; ~**gang** m course of events; **h~geben** (unreg) vt to give, to hand (over); **sich zu etw h~geben** to lend one's name to sth; **h~gehen** (unreg) vi: **hinter jdm h~gehen** to follow sb; **es geht hoch h~** there are a lot of goings-on; **h~halten** (unreg) vt to hold out; **h~halten müssen** (unreg) vi to have to suffer; **h~hören** vi to listen
Hering [ˈheːrɪŋ] (-s, -e) m herring
her- [heːr] zW: ~**kommen** (unreg) vi to come; **komm mal ~!** come here!; ~**kömmlich** adj traditional; **H~kunft** f (-, -künfte) f origin; ~**laufen** (unreg) vi: ~**laufen hinter** +dat to run after
Hermelin [hɛrməˈliːn] (-s, -e) m od nt ermine
hermetisch [hɛˈmeːtɪʃ] adj hermetic
♦ adv hermetically
her'nach adv afterwards
Heroin [heroˈiːn] (-s) nt heroin
Herr [hɛr] (-(e)n, -en) m master; (Mann) gentleman; (REL) Lord; (vor Namen) Mr.; **mein ~!** sir!;

meine ~en! gentlemen!; ~**endoppel** nt men's doubles; ~**einzel** nt men's singles; ~**enhaus** nt mansion; ~**enkonfektion** f menswear; **h~enlos** adj ownerless
herrichten [ˈheːrrɪçtən] vt to prepare
Herr- zW: ~**in** f mistress; **h~isch** adj domineering; **h~lich** adj marvellous, splendid; ~**lichkeit** f splendour, magnificence; ~**schaft** f power, rule; (Herr und Herrin) master and mistress; **meine ~schaften!** ladies and gentlemen!
herrschen [ˈhɛrʃən] vi to rule; (bestehen) to prevail, to be
Herrscher(in) (-s, -) m(f) ruler
her- zW: ~**rühren** vi to arise, to originate; ~**sagen** vt to recite; ~**stellen** vt to make, to manufacture; **H~steller** (-s, -) m manufacturer; **H~stellung** f manufacture
herüber [hɛˈryːbər] adv over (here), across
herum [hɛˈrʊm] adv about, (a)round; **um etw ~** around sth; ~**führen** vt to show around; ~**gehen** vt to walk about; **um etw ~gehen** to walk od go round sth; ~**kommen** (unreg) vi (um Kurve etc) to come round, to turn (round); ~**kriegen** (umg) vt to bring od talk around; ~**lungern** (umg) vi to hang about od around; ~**sprechen** (unreg) vr to get around, to be spread; ~**treiben** vi, vr to drift about; ~**ziehen** vi, vr to wander about
herunter [hɛˈrʊntər] adv downward(s), down (there); ~**gekommen** adj run-down; ~**kommen** (unreg) vi to come down; (fig) to come down in the world; ~**machen** vt to take down; (schimpfen) to have a go at
hervor [hɛrˈfoːr] adv out, forth; ~**bringen** (unreg) vt to produce; (Wort) to utter; ~**gehen** (unreg) vi to emerge, to result; ~**heben** (unreg) vt to stress; (als Kontrast) to set off; ~**ragend** adj (fig) excellent; ~**rufen** (unreg) vt to cause, to give rise to; ~**treten** (unreg) vi to come

out (from behind/between/below);
(Adern) to be prominent

Herz [hɛrts] (-ens, -en) nt heart;
(KARTEN) hearts pl; ~anfall m
heart attack; ~enslust f: nach
~enslust to one's heart's content;
~fehler m heart defect; h~haft adj
hearty

herziehen ['hɛːrtsiːən] (unreg) vi:
über jdn/etw ~ (umg: auch: fig) to
pull sb/sth to pieces (inf)

Herz- zW: ~infarkt m heart attack;
~klopfen nt palpitation; h~lich adj
cordial; h~lichen Glückwunsch
congratulations pl; h~liche Grüße
best wishes; h~los adj heartless

Herzog ['hɛrtsɔk] (-(e)s, ⁺e) m
duke; ~tum nt duchy

Herzschlag m heartbeat; (MED)
heart attack

herzzerreißend adj heartrending

Hessen ['hɛsən] (-s) nt Hesse

hessisch adj Hessian

Hetze ['hɛtsə] f (Eile) rush; h~n vt
to hunt; (verfolgen) to chase ♦ vi
(eilen) to rush; jdn/etw auf jdn/etw
h~n to set sb/sth on sb/sth; h~n
gegen to stir up feeling against;
h~n zu to agitate for; ~rei f agita-
tion; (Eile) rush

Heu [hɔy] (-(e)s) nt hay; Geld wie
~ stacks of money; ~boden m hay-
loft

Heuchelei [hɔyçə'laɪ] f hypocrisy

heucheln ['hɔyçəln] vt to pretend, to
feign ♦ vi to be hypocritical

Heuchler(in) ['hɔyçlər(ɪn)] (-s, -)
m(f) hypocrite; h~isch adj hypocritical

heulen ['hɔylən] vi to howl; to cry;
das ~de Elend bekommen to get
the blues

Heurige(r) ['hɔyrɪgə] m new wine

Heuschnupfen m hay fever

Heuschrecke ['hɔyʃrɛkə] f grasshop-
per; locust

heute ['hɔytə] adv today; ~ abend/
früh this evening/morning

heutig ['hɔytɪç] adj today's

heutzutage ['hɔyttsuːtaːgə] adv no-

wadays

Hexe ['hɛksə] f witch; h~n vi to
practise witchcraft; ich kann doch
nicht h~n I can't work miracles;
~nschuß m lumbago; ~rei f witchcraft

Hieb [hiːp] (-(e)s, ⁺e) m blow;
(Wunde) cut, gash; (Stichelei) cutting remark; ~e bekommen to get
a thrashing

hielt etc [hiːlt] vb siehe halten

hier [hiːr] adv here; h~auf adv there-
upon; (danach) after that; ~behal-
ten (unreg) vt to keep here; ~bei
adv herewith, enclosed; ~bleiben
(unreg) vi to stay here; ~durch adv
by this means; (örtlich) through
here; ~her adv this way, here; ~in
adv here; ~lassen (unreg) vt to
leave here; ~mit adv hereby; ~nach
adv hereafter; ~von adv about this,
hereof; ~zulande adv in this country

hiesig ['hiːzɪç] adj of this place, local

hieß etc [hiːs] vb siehe heißen

Hilfe ['hɪlfə] f help; aid; Erste ~
first aid; ~! help!

Hilf- zW: h~los adj helpless; ~losig-
keit f helplessness; h~reich adj helpful

Hilfs- zW: ~arbeiter m labourer;
h~bedürftig adj needy; h~bereit
adj ready to help; ~kraft f assistant,
helper

hilfst [hɪlfst] vb siehe helfen

Himbeere ['hɪmbeːrə] f raspberry

Himmel ['hɪməl] (-s, -) m sky;
(REL, liter) heaven; ~bett nt four-
poster bed; h~blau adj sky-blue;
~fahrt f Ascension; ~srichtung f
direction

himmlisch ['hɪmlɪʃ] adj heavenly

hin [hɪn] adv 1 (Richtung): hin und
zurück there and back; hin und her
to and fro; bis zur Mauer hin up to
the wall; wo ist er hin? where has
he gone?; Geld hin, Geld her
money or no money

2 (auf ... hin): auf meine Bitte hin

at my request; **auf seinen Rat hin** on the basis of his advice

3: mein Glück ist hin my happiness has gone

hinab [hɪ'nap] *adv* down; **~gehen** (*unreg*) *vi* to go down; **~sehen** (*unreg*) *vi* to look down

hinauf [hɪ'nauf] *adv* up; **~arbeiten** *vr* to work one's way up; **~steigen** (*unreg*) *vi* to climb

hinaus [hɪ'naus] *adv* out; **~gehen** (*unreg*) *vi* to go out; **~gehen über** +*akk* to exceed; **~laufen** (*unreg*) *vi* to run out; **~laufen auf** +*akk* to come to, to amount to; **~schieben** (*unreg*) *vt* to put off, to postpone; **~werfen** (*unreg*) *vt* (*Gegenstand, Person*) to throw out; **~wollen** *vi* to want to go out; **~wollen auf** +*akk* to drive at, to get at

Hinblick ['hɪnblɪk] *m*: **in od im ~ auf** +*akk* in view of

hinder- ['hɪndər] *zW*: **~lich** *adj* to be a hindrance *od* nuisance; **~n** *vt* to hinder, to hamper; **jdn an etw** *dat* **~n** to prevent sb from doing sth; **H~nis** (**-ses**, **-se**) *nt* obstacle; **H~nisrennen** *nt* steeplechase

hindeuten ['hɪndɔytən] *vi*: **~ auf** +*akk* to point to

hindurch [hɪn'dʊrç] *adv* through; across; (*zeitlich*) through(out)

hinein [hɪ'naɪn] *adv* in; **~fallen** (*unreg*) *vi* to fall in; **~fallen in** +*akk* to fall into; **~gehen** (*unreg*) *vi* to go in; **~gehen in** +*akk* to go into, to enter; **~geraten** (*unreg*) *vi*: **~geraten in** +*akk* to get into; **~passen** *vi* to fit in; **~passen in** +*akk* to fit into; (*fig*) to fit in with; **~steigern** *vr*: **sich ~versetzen in** +*akk* to put o.s. in the position of; **~ziehen** (*unreg*) *vt* to pull in **▶** *vi* to go in

hin- ['hɪn] *zW*: **~fahren** (*unreg*) *vi* to go; to drive; **~fahrt** *f* way there; to drive; **H~fahrt** *f* journey there; **~fallen** (*unreg*) *vi* to fall (down); **~fällig** *adj*: **fig**: **ungültig**) invalid; **H~flug**

m outward flight; **~gabe** *f* devotion; **~geben** (*unreg*) *vr* +*dat* to give o.s. up to, to devote o.s. to; **~gehen** (*unreg*) *vi* to go; (*Zeit*) to pass; **~halten** (*unreg*) *vt* to hold out; (*warten lassen*) to put off, to stall

hinken ['hɪŋkən] *vi* to limp; (*Vergleich*) to be unconvincing

hinkommen (*unreg*) *vi* (*an Ort*) to arrive

hin- ['hɪn] *zW*: **~legen** *vt* to put down **▶** *vr* to lie down; **~nehmen** (*unreg*) *vt* (*fig*) to put up with, to take; **H~reise** *f* journey out; **~reißen** (*unreg*) *vt* to carry away, to enrapture; **sich ~reißen lassen, etw zu tun** to get carried away and do sth; **~richten** *vt* to execute; **H~richtung** *f* execution; **~setzen** *vt* to put down **▶** *vr* to sit down; **~sichtlich** *präp* +*gen* with regard to; **~stellen** *vt* to put (down) **▶** *vr* to place o.s.

hinstellen [hɪnt'ʃtɛlən] *vt* (*fig*) to ignore

hinten ['hɪntən] *adv* at the back; behind; **~herum** *adv* round the back; (*fig*) secretly

hinter ['hɪntər] *präp* (+*dat od akk*) behind; (*: nach*) after; **~ jdm hersein** to be after sb; **H~achse** *f* rear axle; **H~bliebene(r)** *mf* surviving relative; **~e(r, s)** *adj* rear, back; **~einander** *adv* one after the other; **H~gedanke** *m* ulterior motive; **~gehen** (*unreg*) *vt* to deceive; **H~grund** *m* background; **H~halt** *m* ambush; **~hältig** *adj* underhand, sneaky; **~her** *adv* afterwards, after; **H~hof** *m* backyard; **H~kopf** *m* back of one's head; **~lassen** (*unreg*) *vt* to leave; **~legen** *vt* to deposit; **H~list** *f* cunning, trickery; (*Handlung*) trick, dodge; **~listig** *adj* cunning, crafty; **H~mann** *m* person behind; **H~rad** *nt* back wheel; **H~radantrieb** *m* (*AUT*) rear wheel drive; **~rücks** *adv* from behind; **H~tür** *f* back door; (*fig*: *Ausweg*) loophole; **~ziehen** (*unreg*) *vt* (*Steuern*) to evade

hinüber [hɪ'nyːbər] *adv* across, over;

~**gehen** (unreg) vi to go over od across

hinunter [hɪ'nʊntər] adv down; ~**bringen** (unreg) vt to take down; ~**schlucken** vt (auch fig) to swallow; ~**steigen** (unreg) vi to descend

Hinweg ['hɪnveːk] m journey out

hinweghelfen [hɪn'vɛk-] (unreg) vi: jdm über etw akk ~ to help sb to get over sth

hinwegsetzen [hɪn'vɛk-] vr: sich ~ über +akk to disregard

hin- ['hɪn] zW: **H~weis** (-es, -e) m (Andeutung) hint; (Anweisung) instruction; (Verweis) reference; ~**weisen** (unreg) vi: ~**weisen auf** +akk (anzeigen) to point to; (sagen) to point out, to refer to; ~**werfen** (unreg) vt to throw down; ~**ziehen** (unreg) vr (fig) to drag on

hinzu [hɪn'tsuː] adv in addition; ~**fügen** vt to add; ~**kommen** (unreg) vi (Mensch) to arrive, to turn up; (Umstand) to ensue

Hirn [hɪrn] (-(e)s, -e) nt brain(s); ~**gespinst** (-(e)s, -e) nt fantasy

Hirsch [hɪrʃ] (-(e)s, -e) m stag

Hirse ['hɪrzə] f millet

Hirt [hɪrt] (-en, -en) m herdsman; (Schaf~, fig) shepherd

Hirte (-n, -n) m stag

hissen ['hɪsən] vt to hoist

Historiker [hɪs'toːrikər] (-s, -) m historian

historisch [hɪs'toːrɪʃ] adj historical

Hitze ['hɪtsə] (-) f heat; h~**beständig** adj heat-resistant; **h~frei** adj: **h~frei haben** to have time off school because of excessively hot weather; ~**welle** f heat wave

hitzig ['hɪtsɪç] adj hot-tempered; (Debatte) heated

Hitzkopf m hothead; **Hitzschlag** m heatstroke

hl. abk von heilig

hm [(h)m] excl hm

Hobby ['hɔbi] nt hobby

Hobel ['hoːbəl] (-s, -) m plane; ~**bank** f carpenter's bench; **h~n** vt, vi to plane; ~**späne** pl wood shav-

ings

Hoch (-s, -s) nt (Ruf) cheer; (MET) anticyclone

hoch [hoːx] (attrib hohe(r, s)) adj high; ~**achten** vt to respect; **H~achtung** f respect, esteem; ~**achtungsvoll** adv yours faithfully; **H~amt** nt high mass; ~**arbeiten** vr to work one's way up; ~**begabt** adj extremely gifted; ~**betrieb** m intense activity; (COMM) peak time; ~**burg** f stronghold; **H~deutsch** nt High German; ~**dotiert** adj highly paid; ~**druck** m high pressure; ~**ebene** f plateau; **H~form** f top form; **H~glanz** m (PHOT) high gloss print; etw auf **H~glanz bringen** to make sth sparkle like new; ~**halten** (unreg) vt to hold up; (fig) to uphold, to cherish; **H~haus** nt multi-storey building; ~**heben** (unreg) vt to lift (up); **H~konjunktur** f boom; **H~land** nt highlands pl; ~**leben** vi: jdn ~**leben lassen** to give sb three cheers; **H~mut** m pride; ~**mütig** adj proud, haughty; ~**näsig** adj stuck-up, snooty; **H~ofen** m blast furnace; ~**prozentig** adj (Alkohol) strong; ~**rechnung** f projection; **H~saison** f high season; **H~schule** f college; university; **H~sommer** m middle of summer; **H~spannung** f high tension; **H~sprung** m high jump

höchst [høːçst] adv highly, extremely

Hochstapler ['hoːxʃtaːplər] (-s, -) m swindler

höchste(r, s) adj highest; (äußerste) extreme

Höchst- zW: **h~ens** adv at the most; ~**geschwindigkeit** f maximum speed; **h~persönlich** adv in person; ~**preis** m maximum price; **h~wahrscheinlich** adv most probably

Hoch- zW: ~**verrat** m high treason; ~**wasser** nt high water; (Überschwemmung) floods pl; ~**zahl** f (MATH) exponent

Hochzeit ['hɔxtsaɪt] (-, -en) f wedding; ~**sreise** f honeymoon

hocken ['hɔkən] *vi, vr* to squat, to crouch

Hocker (-s, -) *m* stool

Höcker ['hœkər] (-s, -) *m* hump

Hoden ['ho:dən] (-s, -) *m* testicle

Hof [ho:f] (-(e)s, ˙e) *m* (Hinter~) yard; (Bauern~) farm; (Königs~) court

hoffen ['hɔfən] *vi:* ~ (auf +akk) to hope (for)

hoffentlich ['hɔfəntliç] *adv* I hope, hopefully

Hoffnung ['hɔfnuŋ] *f* hope

Hoffnungs- *zW:* **h~los** *adj* hopeless; **~losigkeit** *f* hopelessness; **~schimmer** *m* glimmer of hope; **h~voll** *adj* hopeful

höflich ['hø:fliç] *adj* polite, courteous; **H~keit** *f* courtesy, politeness

hohe(r, s) ['ho:ə(r, s)] *adj attrib siehe* **hoch**

Höhe ['hø:ə] *f* height; (An~) hill

Hoheit ['ho:hait] *f* (POL) sovereignty; (Titel) Highness

Hoheitsgebiet *nt* sovereign territory

Hoheitsgewässer *nt* territorial waters *pl*

Höhen- ['hø:ən] *zW:* **~luft** *f* mountain air; **~messer** (-s, -) *m* altimeter; **~sonne** *f* sun lamp; **~unterschied** *m* difference in altitude

Höhepunkt *m* climax

höher *adj, adv* higher

hohl [ho:l] *adj* hollow

Höhle ['hø:lə] *f* cave, hole; (Mund~) cavity; (fig, ZOOL) den

Hohlmaß *nt* measure of volume

Hohn [ho:n] (-(e)s) *m* scorn

höhnisch *adj* scornful, taunting

holen ['ho:lən] *vt* to get, to fetch; (Atem) to take; **jdn/etw** ~ **lassen** to send for sb/sth

Holland ['hɔlant] *nt* Holland; **Holländer** ['hɔlɛndər] *m* Dutchman

holländisch ['hɔlɛndɪʃ] *adj* Dutch

Hölle ['hœlə] *f* hell

höllisch ['hœlɪʃ] *adj* hellish, infernal

holperig ['hɔlpəriç] *adj* rough, bumpy

Holunder [ho'lundər] (-s, -) *m* elder

Holz [hɔlts] (-es, ˙er) *nt* wood

hölzern ['hœltsərn] *adj* (auch fig) wooden

Holz- *zW:* **~fäller** (-s, -) *m* lumberjack, woodcutter; **h~ig** *adj* woody; **~kohle** *f* charcoal; **~scheit** *nt* log; **~schuh** *m* clog; **~weg** *m* (fig) wrong track; **~wolle** *f* fine wood shavings *pl*

Homöopathie [homøopa'ti:] *f* homeopathy

homosexuell [homozɛksu'ɛl] *adj* homosexual

Honig ['ho:niç] (-s, -e) *m* honey; **~melone** *f* (BOT, KOCH) honeydew melon; **~wabe** *f* honeycomb

Honorar [hono'ra:r] (-s, -e) *nt* fee

Hopfen ['hɔpfən] (-s, -) *m* hops *pl*

hopsen ['hɔpsən] *vi* to hop

Hörapparat *m* hearing aid

hörbar *adj* audible

horchen ['hɔrçən] *vi* to listen; (pej) to eavesdrop

Horde ['hɔrdə] *f* horde

hören ['hø:rən] *vt, vi* to hear; **Musik/Radio** ~ to listen to music/the radio

Hörer (-s, -) *m* hearer; (RADIO) listener; (UNIV) student; (Telefon~) receiver

Hörfunk (-s) *m* radio

Horizont [hori'tsɔnt] (-(e)s, -e) *m* horizon; **h~al** [-'ta:l] *adj* horizontal

Hormon [hɔr'mo:n] (-s, -e) *nt* hormone

Hörmuschel *f* (TEL) earpiece

Horn [hɔrn] (-(e)s, ˙er) *nt* horn; **~haut** *f* horny skin

Hornisse [hɔr'nisə] *f* hornet

Horoskop [horo'sko:p] (-s, -e) *nt* horoscope

Hörspiel *nt* radio play

Hort [hɔrt] (-(e)s, -e) *m* (SCH) day centre for school children whose parents are at work

horten ['hɔrtən] *vt* to hoard

Hose ['ho:zə] *f* trousers *pl*, pants *pl* (US)

Hosen- *zW:* **~anzug** *m* trouser suit; **~rock** *m* culottes *pl;* **~tasche** *f* (trouser) pocket; **~träger** *m* braces *pl (BRIT),* suspenders *pl (US)*

Hostie ['hɔstiə] *f (REL)* host

Hotel [ho'tɛl] **(-s, -s)** *nt* hotel

Hotelier [hoteli'e:] **(-s, -s)** *m* hotel-keeper, hotelier

Hubraum ['hu:p-] *m (AUT)* cubic capacity

hübsch [hypʃ] *adj* pretty, nice

Hubschrauber ['hu:pʃraubər] **(-s, -)** *m* helicopter

Huf [hu:f] **(-(e)s, -e)** *m* hoof; **~eisen** *nt* horseshoe

Hüft- ['hyft] *zW:* **~e** *f* hip; **~gürtel** *m* girdle; **~halter** **(-s, -)** *m* girdle

Hügel ['hy:gəl] **(-s, -)** *m* hill; **h~ig** *adj* hilly

Huhn [hu:n] **(-(e)s, ⁻er)** *nt* hen; *(KOCH)* chicken

Hühnerauge ['hy:nər-] *nt* corn

Hühnerbrühe ['hy:nər-] *f* chicken broth

Hülle ['hylə] *f* cover(ing), wrapping; in **~ und Fülle** galore; **h~n** *vt:* **h~n** (in +*akk*) to cover (with); to wrap (in)

Hülse ['hylzə] *f* husk, shell; **~nfrucht** *f* pulse

human [hu'ma:n] *adj* humane; **~itär** *adj* humanitarian; **H~ität** *f* humanity

Hummel ['huməl] **(-, -n)** *f* bumble-bee

Hummer ['humər] **(-s, -)** *m* lobster

Humor [hu'mo:r] **(-s, -e)** *m* humour; **~ haben** to have a sense of humour; **~ist** [-'rist] *m* humorist; **h~istisch** *adj* humorous; **h~voll** *adj* humorous

humpeln ['humpəln] *vi* to hobble

Humpen ['humpən] **(-s, -)** *m* tankard

Hund [hunt] **(-(e)s, -e)** *m* dog

Hunde- ['hundə] *zW:* **~hütte** *f (dog)* kennel; **~kuchen** *m* dog biscuit; **h~müde** *(umg) adj* dog-tired

hundert ['hundərt] *num* hundred; **H~jahrfeier** *f* centenary; **~prozentig** *adj, adv* one hundred per cent

Hundesteuer *f* dog licence fee

Hündin ['hyndɪn] *f* bitch

Hunger ['huŋər] **(-s)** *m* hunger; **~ haben** to be hungry; **h~n** *vi* to starve; **~snot** *f* famine; **~streik** *m* hunger strike

hungrig ['huŋrɪç] *adj* hungry

Hupe ['hu:pə] *f* horn; **h~n** *vi* to hoot, to sound one's horn

hüpfen ['hypfən] *vi* to hop; to jump

Hürde ['hyrdə] *f* hurdle; *(für Schafe)* pen; **~nlauf** *m* hurdling

Hure ['hu:rə] *f* whore

hurtig ['hurtɪç] *adj* brisk, quick ♦ *adv* briskly, quickly

huschen ['huʃən] *vi* to flit; to scurry

Husten ['hu:stən] **(-s)** *m* cough; **h~** *vi* to cough; **~anfall** *m* coughing fit; **~bonbon** *m od nt* cough drop; **~saft** *m* cough mixture

Hut[1] [hu:t] **(-(e)s, ⁻e)** *m* hat

Hut[2] *f (-)* care; **auf der Hut sein** to be on one's guard

hüten ['hy:tən] *vt* to guard ♦ *vr* to watch out; **sich ~, zu** to take care not to; **sich ~ (vor)** to beware (of), to be on one's guard (against)

Hütte ['hytə] *f* hut; cottage; *(Eisen~)* forge

Hüttenkäse *m (KOCH)* cottage cheese

Hüttenschuh *m* slipper-sock

Hyäne [hy'ɛ:nə] *f* hyena

Hyazinthe [hya'tsɪntə] *f* hyacinth

Hydrant [hy'drant] *m* hydrant

hydraulisch [hy'draulɪʃ] *adj* hydraulic

Hygiene [hygi'e:nə] *(-)* *f* hygiene

hygienisch [hygi'e:nɪʃ] *adj* hygienic

Hymne ['hymnə] *f* hymn; anthem

hyper- ['hypər] *präfix* hyper-

Hypno- [hyp'no:] *zW:* **~se** *f* hypnosis; **h~tisch** *adj* hypnotic; **~tiseur** [-'tizø:r] *m* hypnotist; **h~tisieren** *vt* to hypnotize

Hypothek [hypo'te:k] **(-, -en)** *f* mortgage

Hypothese [hypo'te:zə] *f* hypothesis

Hysterie [hyste'ri:] *f* hysteria

hysterisch [hys'te:rɪʃ] *adj* hysterical

I

Ich (-(s), -(s)) *nt* self; (*PSYCH*) ego
ich [ɪç] *pron* I; ~ **bin's!** it's me!
Ideal [ide'a:l] (-s, -e) *nt* ideal; **i~** *adj*
ideal; **i~istisch** [-'lɪstɪʃ] *adj* idealistic
Idee [i'de:, *pl* i'de:ən] *f* idea
identifizieren [i'dɛntifi'tsi:rən] *vt* to
identify
identisch [i'dɛntɪʃ] *adj* identical
Identität [idɛnti'tɛːt] *f* identity
Ideo- [ideo] *zW:* **~loge** [-'lo:gə] (-n,
-n) *m* ideologist; **~logie** [-lo'gi:] *f*
ideology; **~logisch** [-'lo:gɪʃ] *adj* ideo-
logical
Idiot [idi'o:t] (-en, -en) *m* idiot;
i~isch *adj* idiotic
idyllisch [i'dylɪʃ] *adj* idyllic
Igel ['i:gəl] (-s, -) *m* hedgehog
ignorieren [ɪgno'ri:rən] *vt* to ignore
ihm [i:m] (*dat von* **er, es**) *pron* (to)
him; (to) it
ihn [i:n] (*akk von* **er**) *pron* him; it;
~en (*dat von* **sie** *pl*) *pron* (to) them;
I~en (*dat von* **Sie** *pl*) *pron* (to) you

SCHLÜSSELWORT

ihr [i:r] *pron* **1** (*nom pl*) you; **ihr seid**
es it's you
2 (*dat von* **sie**) to her; **gib es ihr**
give it to her; **er steht neben ihr** he
is standing beside her
♦ *possessiv pron* **1** (*sg*) her; (*bei*
Tieren, Dingen); its; **ihr Mann** her
husband
2 (*pl*) their; **die Bäume und ihre**
Blätter the trees and their leaves

ihr(e) *adj* (*sg*) her; its; (*pl*) their;
I~(e) *adj* your
ihre(r, s) *pron* (*sg*) hers; its; (*pl*)
theirs; **I~(r, s)** *pron* yours; **~ (gen**
von **sie** *sg/pl*) *pron* of her/them; **I~r**
(*gen von* **Sie**) *pron* yours; **~rseits**
adv for her/their part; **~sgleichen**
pron people like her/them; (*von Din-*
gen) others like it; **~twegen** *adv*
(*für sie*) for her/its/their sake; (*we-*

gen ihr) on her/its/their account;
~twillen *adv:* **um ~twillen = um**
~wegen
ihrige *pron:* **der/die/das ~** hers; its;
theirs
illegal ['ɪlega:l] *adj* illegal
Illusion [ɪluzi'o:n] *f* illusion
illusorisch [ɪlu'zo:rɪʃ] *adj* illusory
illustrieren [ɪlʊs'tri:rən] *vt* to illustrate
Illustrierte *f* magazine
Iltis ['ɪltɪs] (-ses, -se) *m* polecat
im [ɪm] = **in dem**
Imbiß ['ɪmbɪs] (-sses, -sse) *m*
snack; **~halle** *f* snack bar; **~stube** *f*
snack bar
imitieren [ɪmi'ti:rən] *vt* to imitate
Imker ['ɪmkər] (-s, -) *m* beekeeper
immatrikulieren [ɪmatriku'li:rən]
vi, vr to register
immer ['ɪmər] *adv* always; ~ **wie-**
der again and again; ~ **noch** still;
~ **noch nicht** still not; **für** ~ forever; ~ **wenn ich ...** every time I
...; ~ **schöner/trauriger** more and
more beautiful/sadder and sadder;
was/wer (auch) ~ whatever/who-
ever; **~hin** *adv* all the same; **~zu**
adv all the time
Immobilien [ɪmo'bi:liən] *pl* real estate *sg*
immun [ɪ'mu:n] *adj* immune; **I~ität**
[-i'tɛːt] *f* immunity; **I~system** *nt* immune system
Imperfekt ['ɪmpɛrfɛkt] (-s, -e) *nt*
imperfect (tense)
Impf- ['ɪmpf] *zW:* **i~en** *vt* to vaccinate; **~stoff** *m* vaccine, serum;
~ung *f* vaccination
imponieren [ɪmpo'ni:rən] *vi* +*dat* to
impress
Import [ɪm'pɔrt] (-(e)s, -e) *m* import; **~eur** *m* importer; **i~ieren** *vt*
to import
imposant [ɪmpo'zant] *adj* imposing
impotent ['ɪmpotɛnt] *adj* impotent
imprägnieren [ɪmprɛ'gni:rən] *vt* to
(water)proof
improvisieren [ɪmprovi'zi:rən] *vt, vi*
to improvize

Impuls [ɪm'pʊls] (-es, -e) *m* impulse; **i~iv** [-'zi:f] *adj* impulsive

imstande [ɪm'ʃtandə] *adj*: ~ **sein** to be in a position; *(fähig)* to be able

---

SCHLÜSSELWORT

in [ɪn] *präp +akk* **1** *(räumlich: wohin?)* in, into; **in die Stadt** into town; **in die Schule gehen** to go to school

2 *(zeitlich)*: **bis ins 20. Jahrhundert** into *od* up to the 20th century ♦ *präp +dat*

♦ *präp +dat* **1** *(räumlich: wo?)* in; **in der Stadt** in town; **in der Schule sein** to be at school

2 *(zeitlich: wann)*: **in diesem Jahr** this year; *(in jenem Jahr)* in that year; **heute in zwei Wochen** two weeks today

---

Inanspruchnahme [ɪn'anʃpruːxna:mə] *f (+gen)* demands *pl* (on)

Inbegriff ['ɪnbəgrɪf] *m* embodiment, personification; **i~en** *adv* included

indem [ɪn'de:m] *konj* while; ~ **man etw macht** *(dadurch)* by doing sth

Inder(in) ['ɪndər(ɪn)] *m(f)* Indian

indes(sen) [ɪn'dɛs(ən)] *adv* however; *(inzwischen)* meanwhile ♦ *Konj* while

Indianer(in) [ɪndi'a:nər(ɪn)] (-s, -) *m(f)* American Indian, native American

indianisch *adj* Red Indian

Indien ['ɪndiən] *nt* India

indirekt ['ɪndirɛkt] *adj* indirect

indisch ['ɪndɪʃ] *adj* Indian

indiskret ['ɪndɪskre:t] *adj* indiscreet

indiskutabel ['ɪndɪsku'ta:bəl] *adj* out of the question

individuell [ɪndividu'ɛl] *adj* individual

Individuum [ɪndi'vi:duʊm] (-s, -en) *nt* individual

Indiz [ɪn'di:ts] (-es, -ien) *nt* (JUR) clue; ~ *(für)* sign *(of)*

industrialisieren [ɪndʊstriali'zi:rən] *vt* to industrialize

Industrie [ɪndʊs'tri:] *f* industry ♦ *in zW* industrial; **~gebiet** *nt* industrial area; **~zweig** *m* branch of industry

ineinander [ɪnʔaɪ'nandər] *adv* in(to) one another *od* each other

Infarkt [ɪn'farkt] (-(e)s, -e) *m* coronary (thrombosis)

Infektion [ɪnfɛktsi'o:n] *f* infection; **~skrankheit** *f* infectious disease

Infinitiv ['ɪnfiniti:f] (-s, -e) *m* infinitive

infizieren [ɪnfi'tsi:rən] *vt* to infect ♦ *vr*: **sich (bei jdm)** ~ to be infected (by sb)

Inflation [ɪnflatsi'o:n] *f* inflation

inflationär [ɪnflatsio'nɛ:r] *adj* inflationary

infolge [-'dɛsən] *präp +gen* as a result of, owing to; **~dessen** [-'dɛsən] *adv* consequently

Informatik [ɪnfɔr'ma:tik] *f* information studies *pl*

Information [ɪnfɔrmatsi'o:n] *f* information *no pl*

informieren [ɪnfɔr'mi:rən] *vt* to inform ♦ *vr*: **sich ~ (über +akk)** to find out (about)

Infusion [ɪnfuzi'o:n] *f* infusion

Ingenieur [ɪnʒeni'ø:r] *m* engineer; **~schule** *f* school of engineering

Ingwer ['ɪŋvər] (-s) *m* ginger

Inh. *abk (= Inhaber)* prop.; (= *Inhalt*) contents

Inhaber(in) ['ɪnha:bər(ɪn)] (-s, -) *m(f)* owner; *(Haus~)* occupier; *(Lizenz~)* licensee, holder; *(FIN)* bearer

inhaftieren *vt* to take into custody

inhalieren [ɪnha'li:rən] *vt, vi* to inhale

Inhalt ['ɪnhalt] (-(e)s, -e) *m* contents *pl*; *(eines Buchs etc)* content; *(MATH)* area; volume; **i~lich** *adj* as regards content

Inhalts- *zW*: **~angabe** *f* summary; **~verzeichnis** *nt* table of contents

inhuman ['ɪnhuman] *adj* inhuman

Initiative [initsia'ti:və] *f* initiative

Injektion [ɪnjɛktsi'o:n] *f* injection

inklusive [ɪnklu'zi:və] *präp +gen* inclusive of ♦ adv inclusive

inkognito [ɪn'kɔɡnito] adv incognito

Inkrafttreten [ɪn'krafttreːtən] (-s) nt coming into force

Inland ['ɪnlant] (-(e)s) nt (GEOG) inland; (POL, COMM) home (country)

inmitten [ɪn'mɪtən] präp +gen in the middle of; ~ **von** amongst

innehaben ['ɪnəhaːbən] (unreg) vt to hold

innen ['ɪnən] adv inside; **I~architekt** m interior designer; **I~einrichtung** f (interior) furnishings pl; **I~hof** m inner courtyard; **I~minister** m minister of the interior, Home Secretary (BRIT); **I~politik** f domestic policy; **~politisch** adj (Entwicklung, Lage) internal, domestic; **I~stadt** f town/city centre

inner- ['ɪnər] zW: **~e(r, s)** adj inner; (im Körper, inländisch) internal; **I~e(s)** nt inside; (Mitte) centre; (fig) heart; **~eien** [-'raɪən] pl innards; **~halb** adv within; (räumlich) inside ♦ präp +gen within; inside; **~lich** adj internal; (geistig) inward; **~ste(r, s)** adj innermost; **I~ste(s)** nt heart

innig adj (Freundschaft) close

inoffiziell ['ɪn'ɔfitsiɛl] adj unofficial

ins [ɪns] = in das

Insasse ['ɪnzasə] (-n, -n) m (Anstalt) inmate; (AUT) passenger

insbesondere [ɪnsbə'zɔndərə] adv (e)specially

Inschrift ['ɪnʃrɪft] f inscription

Insekt [ɪn'zɛkt] (-(e)s, -en) nt insect

Insel ['ɪnzəl] (-, -n) f island

Inser- [ɪnze'raːt] zW: **~at** [ɪnze'raːt] (-(e)s, -e) nt advertisement; **~ent** [ɪnze'rɛnt] m advertiser; **i~ieren** [ɪnze'riːrən] vt, vi to advertise

insgeheim [ɪnsɡə'haɪm] adv secretly

insgesamt [ɪnsɡə'zamt] adv altogether, all in all

insofern ['ɪnzo'fɛrn] adv in this respect ♦ konj if; (deshalb) (and) so; **~ als** in so far as

insoweit ['ɪnzo'vaɪt] = **insofern**

Installateur [ɪnstala'tøːr] m electrician; plumber

Instandhaltung [ɪn'ʃtant-] f maintenance

inständig [ɪn'ʃtɛndɪç] adj urgent

Instandsetzung [ɪn'ʃtant-] f overhaul; (eines Gebäudes) restoration

Instanz [ɪn'stants] f authority; (JUR) court

Instinkt [ɪn'stɪŋkt] (-(e)s, -e) m instinct; **i~iv** [-'tiːf] adj instinctive

Institut [ɪnsti'tuːt] (-(e)s, -e) nt institute

Instrument [ɪnstru'mɛnt] nt instrument

Intell- [ɪntɛl] zW: **i~ektuell** [-ɛktu'ɛl] adj intellectual; **i~igent** [-i'ɡɛnt] adj intelligent; **I~igenz** [-i'ɡɛnts] f intelligence; (Leute) intelligentsia pl

Intendant [ɪntɛn'dant] m director

intensiv [ɪntɛn'ziːf] adj intensive

Interess- zW: **i~ant** [ɪntərɛ'sant] adj interesting; **i~anterweise** adv interestingly enough; **~e** [ɪntə'rɛsə] (-s, -n) nt interest; **~e haben an** +dat to be interested in; **~ent** [ɪntərɛ'sɛnt] m interested party; **i~ieren** [ɪntərɛ'siːrən] vt to interest ♦ vr: **sich i~ieren für** to be interested in

intern adj (Angelegenheiten, Regelung) internal; (Besprechung) private

Internat [ɪntɛr'naːt] (-(e)s, -e) nt boarding school

inter- [ɪntɛr] zW: **~national** [-natsio'naːl] adj international; **~pretieren** [-pre'tiːrən] vt to interpret; **I~vall** [-'val] (-s, -e) nt interval; **I~view** [-'vjuː] (-s, -s) nt interview; **~viewen** [-'vjuːən] vt to interview

intim [ɪn'tiːm] adj intimate; **I~ität** f intimacy

intolerant ['ɪntolerant] adj intolerant

intransitiv ['ɪntranzitiːf] adj (GRAM) intransitive

Intrige [ɪn'triːɡə] f intrigue, plot

Invasion [ɪnvazi'oːn] f invasion

Inventar [ɪnvɛn'taːr] (-s, -e) nt inventory

Inventur [ɪnvɛn'tuːr] f stocktaking:

~ **machen** to stocktake

investieren [ɪnvɛsˈtiːrən] *vt* to invest

inwiefern [ɪnviˈfɛrn] *adv* how far, to what extent

inwieweit [ɪnviˈvaɪt] *adv* how far, to what extent

inzwischen [ɪnˈtsvɪʃən] *adv* meanwhile

Irak [iˈrɑːk] (-s) *m:* **der** ~ Iraq; **i~isch** *adj* Iraqi

Iran [iˈrɑːn] (-s) *m:* **der** ~ Iran; **i~isch** *adj* Iranian

irdisch [ˈɪrdɪʃ] *adj* earthly

Ire [ˈiːrə] (-n, -n) *m* Irishman

irgend [ˈɪrɡənt] *adv* at all; **wann/ was/wer** ~ whenever/whatever/whoever; ~ **jemand/etwas** somebody/ something; anybody/anything; ~**ein(e, s)** *adj* some, any; ~**einmal** *adv* sometime or other; *(fragend)* ever; ~**wann** *adv* sometime; ~**wie** *adv* somehow; ~**wo** *adv* somewhere; anywhere; ~**wohin** *adv* somewhere; anywhere

Irin [ˈiːrɪn] *f* Irishwoman

Irland [ˈiːrlant] (-s) *nt* Ireland

Ironie [iroˈniː] *f* irony

ironisch [iˈroːnɪʃ] *adj* ironic(al)

irre [ˈɪrə] *adj* crazy, mad; **i~(r)** *mf* lunatic; ~**führen** *vt* to mislead; ~**machen** *vt* to confuse; ~**n** *vi* to be mistaken; *(umherirren)* to wander, to stray ♦ *vr* to be mistaken; **i~nanstalt** *f* lunatic asylum

Irrgarten *m* maze

irrig [ˈɪrɪç] *adj* incorrect, wrong

irritieren [ɪriˈtiːrən] *vt* (*verwirren*) to confuse; (*ärgern*) to irritate; (*stören*) to annoy

Irr- *zW:* **i~sinnig** *adj* mad, crazy; (*umg*) terrific; ~**tum** (-s, -**tümer**) *m* mistake, error; **i~tümlich** *adj* mistaken

Islam [ˈɪslam] (-s) *m* Islam

Island [ˈiːslant] (-s) *nt* Iceland

Isolation [izolatsiˈoːn] *f* isolation; (*ELEK*) insulation

Isolier- [izoˈliːr] *zW:* ~**band** *nt* insulating tape; **i~en** *vt* to isolate;

(*ELEK*) to insulate; ~**station** *f* (*MED*) isolation ward; ~**ung** *f* isolation; (*ELEK*) insulation

Israel [ˈɪsraːɛl] (-s) *nt* Israel; ~**i** (-s, -s) *m* Israeli; **i~isch** *adj* Israeli

ißt [ɪst] *vb siehe* **essen**

ist [ɪst] *vb siehe* **sein**

Italien [iˈtaːliən] (-s) *nt* Italy; ~**er(in)** *m(f)* Italian; **i~isch** *adj* Italian

i.V. *abk* = **in Vertretung**

J

ja [jaː] *adv* 1 yes; **haben Sie das gesehen? - ja** did you see it? - yes(, I did); **ich glaube ja** (yes) I think so 2 (*fragend*) really?; **ich habe gekündigt - ja?** I've quit - have you?; **du kommst, ja?** you're coming, aren't you?

3: **sei ja vorsichtig** do be careful; **Sie wissen ja, daß ...** as you know, ...; **tu das ja nicht!** don't do that!; **ich habe es ja gewußt** I just knew it; **ja, also ...** well you see ...

Jacht [jaxt] (-, -en) *f* yacht

Jacke [ˈjakə] *f* jacket; (*Woll~*) cardigan

Jackett [ʒaˈkɛt] (-s, -s *od* -e) *nt* jacket

Jagd [jaːkt] (-, -en) *f* hunt; (*Jagen*) hunting; ~**beute** *f* kill; ~**flugzeug** *nt* fighter; ~**gewehr** *nt* sporting gun; ~**hund** *m* hunting dog

jagen [ˈjaːɡən] *vi* to hunt; (*eilen*) to race ♦ *vt* to hunt; (*weg~*) to drive (off); (*verfolgen*) to chase

Jäger [ˈjɛːɡər] (-s, -) *m* hunter

Jägerschnitzel *nt* (*KOCH*) pork in a spicy sauce with mushrooms

jäh [jɛː] *adj* sudden, abrupt; (*steil*) steep, precipitous

Jahr [jaːr] (-(e)s, -e) *nt* year; ~**elang** *adv* for years

Jahres- *zW:* ~**abonnement** *nt* annual subscription; **~abschluß** m end of the year; (COMM) annual statement of account; **~beitrag** m annual subscription; **~karte** f yearly days ticket; **~tag** m anniversary; **~wechsel** m turn of the year; **~zahl** f date; year; **~zeit** f season

Jahrgang m age group; (von Wein) vintage

Jahr'hundert (-s, -e) nt century

jährlich ['jɛːrlɪç] adj, adv yearly

Jahrmarkt m fair

Jahrtausend nt millenium

Jahr'zehnt nt decade

Jähzorn m sudden anger; hot temper; **j~ig** adj hot-tempered

Jalousie [ʒaluˈziː] f venetian blind

Jammer ['jamər] (-s) m misery; es ist ein ~, daß ... it is a crying shame that ...

jämmerlich ['jɛmɐlɪç] adj wretched, pathetic

jammern vi to wail ♦ vt unpers: es jammert jdn it makes sb feel sorry

jammerschade adj: es ist ~ it is a crying shame

Januar ['januaːr] (-(s), -e) m January

Japan ['jaːpan] (-s) nt Japan; **~er(in)** [-ˈpaːnər(ɪn)] (-s) m(f) Japanese; **j~isch** adj Japanese

Jargon [ʒarˈgõː] (-s, -s) m jargon

jäten ['jɛːtən] vt: Unkraut ~ to weed

jauchzen ['jaʊxtsən] vi to rejoice, to shout (with joy)

jaulen ['jaʊlən] vi to howl

jawohl [jaˈvoːl] adv yes (of course)

Jawort ['jaːvɔrt] nt consent

Jazz [dʒɛs] (-) m Jazz

je [jeː] adv 1 (jemals) ever; hast du so was je gesehen? did you ever see anything like it?

2 (jeweils) every, each; sie zahlten je 3 Mark they paid 3 marks each ♦ konj 1: je nach depending on; je nachdem it depends; je nachdem, ob ... depending on whether ...

2: je eher, desto od um so besser the sooner the better

Jeans [dʒiːnz] pl jeans

jede(r, s) ['jeːdə(r, s)] adj every, each ♦ pron everybody; (~ einzelne) each; ohne ~ x without any x

jedenfalls adv in any case

jedermann pron everyone

jederzeit adv at any time

jedesmal adv every time, each time

jedoch [jeˈdɔx] adv however

jeher ['jeːheːr] adv: von/seit ~ always

jemals ['jeːmaːls] adv ever

jemand ['jeːmant] pron somebody; anybody

jene(r, s) ['jeːnə(r, s)] adj that ♦ pron that one

jenseits ['jeːnzaɪts] adv on the other side ♦ präp +gen on the other side of, beyond

Jenseits nt: das ~ the hereafter, the beyond

jetzig ['jɛtsɪç] adj present

jetzt [jɛtst] adv now

jeweilig adj respective

jeweils adv: ~ zwei zusammen two at a time; zu ~ 5 DM at 5 marks each; ~ das erste the first each time

Jh. abk = Jahrhundert

Jockei ['dʒɔke] (-s, -s) m jockey

Jod [joːt] (-(e)s) nt iodine

jodeln ['joːdəln] vi to yodel

joggen ['dʒɔgən] vi to jog

Joghurt ['joːgʊrt] (-s, -s) m od nt yogurt

Johannisbeere [joˈhanɪsbeːrə] f redcurrant; **schwarze ~** blackcurrant

johlen ['joːlən] vi to yell

jonglieren [ʒõˈgliːrən] vi to juggle

Journal [ʒurˈnaːl] zW: **~ismus** [-ˈlɪsmʊs] m journalism; **~ist(in)** [-ˈlɪst(ɪn)] m(f) journalist; **journa'listisch** adj journalistic

Jubel ['juːbəl] (-s) m rejoicing; **j~n** vi to rejoice

Jubiläum [jubiˈlɛːʊm] (-s, Jubiläen)

nt anniversary; jubilee

jucken ['jʊkən] *vi* to itch ♦ *vt*: es juckt mich am Arm my arm is itching; **das juckt mich** that's itchy

Juckreiz ['jʊkraɪts] *m* itch

Jude ['juːdə] (-n, -n) *m* Jew

Judentum (-) *nt* Judaism; Jewry

Judenverfolgung *f* persecution of the Jews

Jüdin ['jyːdɪn] *f* Jewess

jüdisch ['jyːdɪʃ] *adj* Jewish

Judo ['juːdo] (-(s)) *nt* judo

Jugend ['juːɡənt] (-) *f* youth; **j~frei** *adj* (CINE) (f (BRIT), G (US)), suitable for children; **~herberge** *f* youth hostel; **j~lich** *adj* youthful; **J~liche(r)** *mf* teenager, young person

Jugoslaw- [jugo'slaːv-] *zW*: **~e** *m* Yugoslavian; **~ien** (-s) *nt* Yugoslavia; **~in** *f* Yugoslavian; **j~isch** *adj* Yugoslavian

Juli ['juːli] (-(s), -s) *m* July

jun. *abk* (= junior) jr.

jung [jʊŋ] *adj* young; **J~e** (-n, -n) *m* boy, lad; **J~e(s)** *nt* young animal; **J~en** *pl* (von Tier) young *pl*

Jünger ['jyŋər] (-s, -) *m* disciple

jünger *adj* younger

Jung- *zW*: **~frau** *f* virgin; (ASTROL) Virgo; **~geselle** *m* bachelor; **~gesellin** *f* unmarried woman; **Jüngling** *m* youth

jüngst [jʏŋst] *adv* lately, recently; **~e(r, s)** *adj* youngest; (neueste) latest

Juni ['juːni] (-(s), -s) *m* June

Junior ['juːniɔr, pl -'oːrən] (-s, -en) *m* junior

Jurist [ju'rɪst] *m* jurist, lawyer; **j~isch** *adj* legal

Justiz [jus'tiːts] (-) *f* justice; **~beamte(r)** *m* judicial officer; **~irrtum** *m* miscarriage of justice; **~minister** *m* ≈ Lord (High) Chancellor (BRIT); ≈ Attorney General (US)

Juwel [ju'veːl] (-s, -en) *nt od m* jewel

Juwelier [juve'liːr] (-s, -e) *m* jeweller; **~geschäft** *nt* jeweller's (shop)

Jux [jʊks] (-es, -e) *m* joke, lark

K

Kabarett [kaba'rɛt] (-s, -e od -s) *nt* cabaret; **~ist** [-'tɪst] *m* cabaret artiste

Kabel ['kaːbəl] (-s, -) *nt* (ELEK) wire; (stark) cable; **~fernsehen** *nt* cable television

Kabeljau ['kaːbəljau] (-s, -e od -s) *m* cod

kabeln *vt, vi* to cable

Kabine [ka'biːnə] *f* cabin; (Zelle) cubicle

Kabinett [kabi'nɛt] (-s, -e) *nt* (POL) cabinet

Kachel ['kaxəl] (-, -n) *f* tile; **k~n** *vt* to tile; **~ofen** *m* tiled stove

Käfer ['kɛːfər] (-s, -) *m* beetle

Kaffee ['kafe] (-s, -s) *m* coffee; **~kanne** *f* coffeepot; **~löffel** *m* coffee spoon

Käfig ['kɛːfɪç] (-s, -e) *m* cage

kahl [kaːl] *adj* bald; **~geschoren** *adj* shaven, shorn; **~köpfig** *adj* bald-headed

Kahn [kaːn] (-(e)s, -e) *m* boat, barge

Kai [kaɪ] (-s, -e od -s) *m* quay

Kaiser ['kaɪzər] (-s, -) *m* emperor; **~in** *f* empress; **k~lich** *adj* imperial; **~reich** *nt* empire; **~schnitt** *m* (MED) Caesarian (section)

Kajak ['kaːjak] (-s, -s) *m* (SPORT) kayak

Kakao [ka'kao] (-s, -s) *m* cocoa

Kaktee [kak'teː(ə)] (-, -n) *f* cactus

Kaktus ['kaktʊs] (-, -teen) *m* cactus

Kalb [kalp] (-(e)s, -er) *nt* calf; **k~en** ['kalbən] *vi* to calve; **~fleisch** *nt* veal; **~sleder** *nt* calf(skin)

Kalender [ka'lɛndər] (-s, -) *m* calendar; (Taschen~) diary

Kaliber [ka'liːbər] (-s, -) *nt* (auch fig) calibre

Kalk [kalk] (-(e)s, -e) *m* lime; (BIOL) calcium; **~stein** *m* limestone

kalkulieren [kalku'liːrən] *vt* to calculate

Kalorie [kalo'ri:] f calorie

kalt [kalt] adj cold; **mir ist (es)** ~ I am cold; ~**bleiben** (unreg) vi to remain unmoved; ~**blütig** adj coldblooded; (ruhig) cool

Kälte ['kɛltə] (-) f cold; coldness; ~**grad** m degree of frost od below zero; ~**welle** f cold spell

kalt- zW: ~**herzig** adj cold-hearted; ~**schnäuzig** adj cold, unfeeling; ~**stellen** vt to chill; (fig) to leave out in the cold

kam etc vb siehe **kommen**

Kamel [ka'me:l] (-(e)s, -e) nt camel

Kamera ['kamera] (-, -s) f camera

Kamerad [kamə'ra:t] (-en, -en) m comrade, friend; ~**schaft** f comradeship; **k**~**schaftlich** adj comradely

Kameramann (-(e)s, -männer) m cameraman

Kamille [ka'mɪlə] f camomile; ~**ntee** m camomile tea

Kamin [ka'mi:n] (-s, -e) m (außen) chimney; (innen) fireside, fireplace; ~**feger** (-s, -) m chimney sweep; ~**kehrer** (-s, -) m chimney sweep

Kamm [kam] (-(e)s, ᵂe) m comb; (Berg~) ridge; (Hahnen~) crest

kämmen ['kɛmən] vt to comb ♦ vr to comb one's hair

Kammer ['kamər] (-, -n) f chamber; small bedroom; ~**diener** m valet

Kampagne [kam'panjə] f campaign

Kampf [kampf] (-(e)s, ᵂe) m fight, battle; (Wettbewerb) contest; (fig: Anstrengung) struggle; **k**~**bereit** adj ready for action

kämpfen ['kɛmpfən] vi to fight

Kämpfer (-s, -) m fighter, combatant

Kampf- zW: ~**handlung** f action; **k**~**los** adj without a fight; ~**richter** m (SPORT) referee; (TENNIS) umpire; ~**stoff** m: **chemischer/ biologischer** ~**stoff** chemical/ biological weapon

Kanada ['kanada] (-s) nt Canada

Kanadier(in) [ka'na:diər(ɪn)] (-s, -) m(f) Canadian

kanadisch [ka'na:dɪʃ] adj Canadian

Kanal [ka'na:l] (-s, Kanäle) m (Fluß) canal; (Rinne, Ärmel~) channel; (für Abfluß) drain; ~**inseln** pl Channel Islands; ~**isation** [-izatsi'o:n] f sewage system

Kanarienvogel [ka'na:rɪənfo:gəl] m canary

kanarisch [ka'na:rɪʃ] adj: **K**~**e Inseln** Canary Islands, Canaries

Kandi- [kandi] zW: ~**dat** [-'da:t] (-en, -en) m candidate; ~**datur** [-da'tu:r] f candidature, candidacy; **k**~**dieren** [-'di:rən] vi to stand, to run

Kandis(zucker) ['kandɪs(tsʊkɐ)] (-) m candy

Känguruh ['kɛnguru] (-s, -s) nt kangaroo

Kaninchen [ka'ni:nçən] nt rabbit

Kanister [ka'nɪstər] (-s, -) m can, canister

Kännchen [kɛnçən] nt pot

Kanne ['kanə] f (Krug) jug; (Kaffee~) pot; (Milch~) churn; (Gieß~) can

kannst etc vb siehe **können**

Kanon ['ka:nɔn] (-s, -s) m canon

Kanone [ka'no:nə] f gun; (HIST) cannon; (fig: Mensch) ace

Kantate [kan'ta:tə] f cantata

Kante ['kantə] f edge

Kantine [kan'ti:nə] f canteen

Kanu ['ka:nu] (-s, -s) nt canoe

Kanzel [kantsəl] (-, -n) f pulpit

Kanzler ['kantslər] (-s, -) m chancellor

Kap [kap] (-s, -s) nt cape (GEOG); ~ **der Guten Hoffnung** Cape of Good Hope

Kapazität [kapatsi'tɛ:t] f capacity; (Fachmann) authority

Kapelle [ka'pɛlə] f (Gebäude) chapel; (MUS) band

kapieren [ka'pi:rən] (umg) vt, vi to get, to understand

Kapital [kapi'ta:l] (-s, -e od -ien) nt capital; ~**anlage** f investment; ~**ismus** [-'lɪsmʊs] m capitalism; ~**ist** [-'lɪst] m capitalist; **k**~**istisch** adj capitalist

Kapitän [kapiˈtɛːn] (-s, -e) m captain

Kapitel [kaˈpɪtəl] (-s, -) nt chapter

Kapitulation [kapitulatsiˈoːn] f capitulation

kapitulieren [kapituˈliːrən] vi to capitulate

Kaplan [kaˈplaːn] (-s, **Kapläne**) m chaplain

Kappe [ˈkapə] f cap; (Kapuze) hood

kappen vt to cut

Kapsel [ˈkapsəl] (-, -n) f capsule

kaputt [kaˈput] (umg) adj kaput, broken; (Person) exhausted, finished; **am Auto ist etwas ~** there's something wrong with the car; **~gehen** (unreg) vi to break; (Schuhe) to fall apart; (Firma) to go bust; (Stoff) to wear out; (sterben) to cop it (umg); **~machen** vt to break; (Mensch) to exhaust, to wear out

Kapuze [kaˈpuːtsə] f hood

Karaffe [kaˈrafə] f carafe; (geschliffen) decanter

Karamel [karaˈmɛl] (-s) m caramel; **~bonbon** m od nt toffee

Karat [kaˈraːt] (-(e)s, -e) nt carat

Karate [kaˈraːtə] (-s) nt karate

Karawane [karaˈvaːnə] f caravan

Kardinal [kardiˈnaːl] (-s, **Kardinäle**) m cardinal; **~zahl** f cardinal number

Karfreitag [kaːrˈfraɪtaːk] m Good Friday

karg [kark] adj (Landschaft, Boden) barren; (Lohn) meagre

kärglich [ˈkɛrklɪç] adj poor, scanty

Karibik [kaˈriːbɪk] (-) f: **die ~** the Caribbean

karibisch [kaˈriːbɪʃ] adj: **K~e Inseln** Caribbean Islands

kariert [kaˈriːrt] adj (Stoff) checked; (Papier) squared

Karies [ˈkaːriɛs] (-) f caries

Karikatur [karikaˈtuːr] f caricature; **~ist** [-ˈrɪst] m cartoonist

Karneval [ˈkarnəval] (-s, -e od -s) m carnival

Karo [ˈkaːro] (-s, -s) nt square; (KARTEN) diamonds; **~-As** nt ace of diamonds

Karosserie [karɔsəˈriː] f (AUT) body(work)

Karotte [kaˈrɔtə] f carrot

Karpfen [ˈkarpfən] (-s, -) m carp

Karre [ˈkarə] f cart, barrow

Karren (-s, -) m cart, barrow

Karriere [kariˈɛːrə] f career; **~ machen** to get on, to get to the top; **~macher** (-s, -) m careerist

Karte [ˈkartə] f card; (Land~) map; (Speise~) menu; (Eintritts~, Fahr~) ticket; **alles auf eine ~ setzen** to put all one's eggs in one basket

Kartei [karˈtaɪ] f card index; **~karte** f index card

Kartell [karˈtɛl] (-s, -e) nt cartel

Kartenspiel nt card game; pack of cards

Kartoffel [karˈtɔfəl] (-, -n) f potato; **~brei** m mashed potatoes pl; **~mus** nt mashed potatoes pl; **~püree** nt mashed potatoes pl; **~salat** m potato salad

Karton [karˈtõː] (-s, -s) m cardboard; (Schachtel) cardboard box; **k~iert** adj hardback

Karussell [karuˈsɛl] (-s, -s) nt roundabout (BRIT), merry-go-round

Karwoche [ˈkaːrvɔxə] f Holy Week

Käse [ˈkɛːzə] (-s, -) m cheese; **~glocke** f cheese(-plate) cover; **~kuchen** m cheesecake

Kaserne [kaˈzɛrnə] f barracks pl; **~nhof** m parade ground

Kasino [kaˈziːno] (-s, -s) nt club; (MIL) officers' mess; (Spiel~) casino

Kasper [ˈkaspər] (-s, -) m Punch; (fig) fool

Kasse [ˈkasə] f (Geldkasten) cashbox; (in Geschäft) till, cash register; cash desk, checkout; (Kino-, Theater- etc) box office; ticket office; (Kranken~) health insurance; (Spar~) savings bank; **~ machen** to count the money; **getrennte ~ führen** to pay separately; **an der ~** (in Geschäft) at the desk; **gut bei ~ sein** to be in the money

Kassen- zW: **~arzt** m panel doctor (BRIT); **~bestand** m cash balance;

~**patient** m panel patient (BRIT);
~**prüfung** f audit; (~**sturz** m:
~**sturz machen** to check one's
money; ~**zettel** m receipt
Kassette [ka'sɛtə] f small box; (Tonband, PHOT) cassette; (Bücher-)
case
Kassettenrecorder (-s, -) m cassette recorder
kassieren [ka'si:rən] vt to take ♦ vi:
darf ich ~? would you like to pay
now?
Kassierer [ka'si:rər] (-s, -) m cashier; (von Klub) treasurer
Kastanie [kas'ta:niə] f chestnut;
(Baum) chestnut tree
Kasten ['kastən] (-s, ⸚) m (auch
SPORT) box; case; (Truhe) chest;
~**wagen** m van
kastrieren [kas'tri:rən] vt to castrate
Katalog [kata'lo:k] (-(e)s, -e) m catalogue
Katalysator [kataly'za:tɔr] m catalyst; (AUT) catalytic convertor
Katarrh [ka'tar] (-s, -e) m catarrh
katastrophal [katastro'fa:l] adj cata-
strophic
Katastrophe [kata'stro:fə] f cata-
strophe, disaster
Kat-Auto ['kat'auto] n car fitted with
a catalytic converter
Kategorie [katego'ri:] f category
kategorisch [kate'go:rɪʃ] adj cate-
gorical
Kater ['ka:tər] (-s, -) m tomcat;
(umg) hangover
kath. abk (= katholisch) Cath.
Kathedrale [kate'dra:lə] f cathedral
Kathode [ka'to:də] f cathode
Katholik [kato'li:k] (-en, -en) m
Catholic
katholisch [ka'to:lɪʃ] adj Catholic
Kätzchen ['kɛtsçən] nt kitten
Katze ['katsə] f cat; **für die Katz**
(umg) in vain, for nothing
Katzen- zW: ~**auge** nt cat's eye;
(Fahrrad) rear light; ~**jammer**
(umg) m hangover; ~**sprung** (umg)
m stone's throw; short journey
Kauderwelsch ['kaudərvɛlʃ] (-(s))

nt jargon; (umg) double Dutch
kauen ['kauən] vt, vi to chew
kauern ['kauərn] vi to crouch down;
(furchtlich) to cower
Kauf [kauf] (-(e)s, Käufe) m
purchase, buy; (Kaufen) buying; **ein
guter ~** a bargain; **etw in ~ nehmen** to put up with sth; **k~en** vt to
buy
Käufer(in) ['kɔyfər(ɪn)] (-s, -) m(f)
buyer
Kauffrau f businesswoman
Kaufhaus nt department store
Kaufkraft f purchasing power
käuflich ['kɔyflɪç] adj purchasable,
for sale; (pej) venal ♦ adv: ~ erwerben to purchase
Kauf- zW: **k~lustig** adj interested in
buying; ~**mann** (pl -leute) m businessman; shopkeeper; **k~männisch**
adj commercial; **k~männischer
Angestellter** office worker
Kaugummi ['kaugumi] m chewing
gum
Kaulquappe ['kaulkvapə] f tadpole
kaum [kaum] adv hardly, scarcely
Kaution [kautsi'o:n] f deposit; (JUR)
bail
Kauz [kauts] (-es, Käuze) m owl;
(fig) queer fellow
Kavalier [kava'li:r] (-s, -e) m gentleman, cavalier; ~**sdelikt** nt peccadil-
lo
Kaviar ['ka:viar] m caviar
keck [kɛk] adj daring, bold; **K~heit** f
daring, boldness
Kegel ['ke:gəl] (-s, -) m skittle;
(MATH) cone; ~**bahn** f skittle alley;
bowling alley; **k~n** vi to play skittles
Kehle ['ke:lə] f throat
Kehlkopf m larynx
Kehre ['ke:rə] f turn(ing), bend; **k~n**
vt, vi (wenden) to turn; (mit Besen)
to sweep; **sich an etw dat nicht
k~n** not to heed sth
Kehricht ['ke:rɪçt] (-s) m sweepings
pl
Kehrmaschine f sweeper
Kehrseite f reverse, other side;
wrong side; bad side

kehrtmachen vi to turn about, to about-turn

keifen ['kaifən] vi to scold, to nag

Keil [kail] (-(e)s, -e) m wedge; **~riemen** m (AUT) fan belt

Keim [kaim] (-(e)s, -e) m bud; (MED, fig) germ; **k~en** vi to germinate; **k~frei** adj sterile; **~zelle** f (fig) nucleus

kein [kain] adj no, not ... any; **~e(r, s)** pron no one, nobody; none; **~erlei** adj attrib no ... whatsoever

keinesfalls adv on no account

keineswegs adv by no means

keinmal adv not once

Keks [ke:ks] (-es, -e) m od nt biscuit

Kelch [kɛlç] (-(e)s, -e) m cup, goblet, chalice

Kelle ['kɛlə] f (Suppen~) ladle; (Maurer~) trowel

Keller ['kɛlər] (-s, -) m cellar

Kellner(in) ['kɛlnər(in)] (-s, -) m(f) waiter(tress)

keltern ['kɛltərn] vt to press

kennen ['kɛnən] (unreg) vt to know; **~lernen** vt to get to know; sich **~lernen** to get to know each other; (zum erstenmal) to meet

Kenner (-s, -) m connoisseur

kenntlich adj distinguishable, discernible; etw **~ machen** to mark sth

Kenntnis (-, -se) f knowledge no pl; etw zur **~ nehmen** to note sth; von etw **~ nehmen** to take notice of sth; jdn in **~ setzen** to inform sb

Kenn- zW: **~zeichen** nt mark, characteristic; **k~zeichnen** vt insep to characterize; **~ziffer** f reference number

kentern ['kɛntərn] vi to capsize

Keramik [ke'ra:mik] (-, -en) f ceramics pl, pottery

Kerbe ['kɛrbə] f notch, groove

Kerker ['kɛrkər] (-s, -) m prison

Kerl [kɛrl] (-s, -e) m chap, bloke (BRIT); guy; sie ist ein netter **~** she's a good sort

Kern [kɛrn] (-(e)s, -e) m (Obst~)

pip, stone; (Nuß~) kernel; (Atom~) nucleus; (fig) heart, core; **~energie** f nuclear energy; **~forschung** f nuclear research; **~frage** f central issue; **k~gesund** adj thoroughly healthy, fit as a fiddle; **k~ig** adj (kraftvoll) robust; (Ausspruch) pithy; **~kraftwerk** nt nuclear power station; **k~los** adj seedless, pipless; **~physik** f nuclear physics sg; **~spaltung** f nuclear fission; **~waffen** pl nuclear weapons

Kerze ['kɛrtsə] f candle; (Zünd~) plug; **k~ngerade** adj straight as a die; **~nständer** m candle holder

keß [kɛs] adj saucy

Kessel ['kɛsəl] (-s, -) m kettle; (von Lokomotive etc) boiler; (GEOG) depression; (MIL) encirclement

Kette ['kɛtə] f chain; **k~n** vt to chain

Ketten- zW: **~laden** m chain store; **~rauchen** nt chain smoking; **~reaktion** f chain reaction

Ketzer ['kɛtsər] (-s, -) m heretic

keuchen ['kɔyçən] vi to pant, to gasp

Keuchhusten m whooping cough

Keule ['kɔylə] f club; (KOCH) leg

keusch [kɔyʃ] adj chaste; **K~heit** f chastity

kfm. abk = kaufmännisch

KG [ka:'ge:] (-, -s) f abk (= Kommanditgesellschaft) limited partnership

kg abk = Kilogramm

kichern ['kiçərn] vi to giggle

kidnappen ['kidnɛpən] vt to kidnap

Kiefer[1] ['ki:fər] (-s, -) m jaw

Kiefer[2] (-, -n) f pine; Kieferzapfen m pine cone

Kiel [ki:l] (-(e)s, -e) m (Feder~) quill; (NAUT) keel

Kieme ['ki:mə] f gill

Kies [ki:s] (-es, -e) m gravel

Kilo ['ki:lo] nt kilo; **~gramm** [kilo'gram] nt kilogram; **~meter** [kilo'me:tər] nt kilometre; **~meterzähler** m = milometer

Kind [kint] (-(e)s, -er) nt child; von **~ auf** from childhood

Kinder- ['kindər] zW: **~ei** f childishness; **~garten** m nursery school,

klipp und klar ['klɪp'ʊntklaːr] adj clear and concise

klirren ['klɪrən] vi to clank, to jangle; (Gläser) to clink; (Kälte) biting cold

Klischee [klɪ'ʃeː] (-s, -s) nt (Druckplatte) plate, block; (fig) cliché; ~vorstellung f stereotyped idea

Klo [kloː] (-s, -s) nt (umg) nt loo (BRIT), john (US)

Kloake [klo'aːkə] f sewer

klobig ['kloːbɪç] adj clumsy

Klopapier (umg) nt loo paper (BRIT)

klopfen ['klɔpfən] vi to knock; (Herz) to thump ♦ vt to beat; es klopft somebody's knocking; jdm auf die Schulter ~ to tap sb on the shoulder

Klopfer (-s, -) m (Teppich~) beater; (Tür~) knocker

Klops [klɔps] (-es, -e) m meatball

Klosett [klo'zɛt] (-s, -e od -s) nt lavatory, toilet; ~papier nt toilet paper

Kloß [kloːs] (-es, -e) m (im Hals) lump; (KOCH) dumpling

Kloster ['kloːstər] (-s, -) nt (Männer-) monastery; (Frauen~) convent

klösterlich ['kløːstərlɪç] adj monastic; convent cpd

Klotz [klɔts] (-es, -e) m log; (Hack~) block; ein ~ am Bein (fig) a drag, a millstone round (sb's) neck

Klub [klʊp] (-s, -s) m club; ~sessel m easy chair

Kluft [klʊft] (-, -e) f cleft, gap; (GEOG) gorge, chasm

klug [kluːk] adj clever, intelligent; K~heit f cleverness, intelligence

Klumpen ['klʊmpən] (-s, -) m (Erd~) clod; (Blut~) clot; (Gold~) nugget; (KOCH) lump; k~ vi to go lumpy; to clot

km abk = Kilometer

knabbern ['knabərn] vt, vi to nibble

Knabe ['knaːbə] (-n, -n) m boy; k~nhaft adj boyish

Knäckebrot ['knɛkəbroːt] nt crispbread

knacken ['knakən] vt, vi (auch fig) to crack

Knacks [knaks] (-es, -e) m crack; (fig) defect

Knall [knal] (-(e)s, -e) m bang; (Peitschen~) crack; ~ und Fall (umg) unexpectedly; ~bonbon nt cracker; k~en vi to bang; to crack; k~rot adj bright red

knapp [knap] adj tight; (Geld) scarce; (Sprache) concise; eine ~e Stunde just under an hour; ~ unter/neben just under/by; ~halten (unreg) vt: jdn (mit etw) ~halten to keep sb short of sth; K~heit f tightness; scarcity; conciseness

knarren ['knarən] vi to creak

Knast [knast] (-(e)s, -e) m (Haftstrafe) porridge (inf), time (inf); (Gefängnis) slammer (inf), clink (inf)

knattern ['knatərn] vi to rattle; (Maschinengewehr) to chatter

Knäuel ['knɔyəl] (-s, -) m od nt (Woll~) ball; (Menschen~) knot

Knauf [knauf] (-(e)s, Knäufe) m knob; (Schwert~) pommel

knautschen ['knautʃən] vt, vi to crumple

Knebel ['kneːbəl] (-s, -) m gag; k~n vt to gag; (NAUT) to fasten

kneifen ['knaɪfən] (unreg) vt to pinch ♦ vi to pinch; (sich drücken) to back out; vor etw ~ to dodge sth

Kneipe ['knaɪpə] (umg) f pub

kneten ['kneːtən] vt to knead; (Wachs) to mould

Knick [knɪk] (-(e)s, -e) m (Sprung) crack; (Kurve) bend; (Falte) fold; k~en vt, vi (springen) to crack; (brechen) to break; (Papier) to fold; gek~t sein to be downcast

Knicks [knɪks] (-es, -e) m curtsey; k~en vi to curtsey

Knie [kniː] (-s, -) nt knee; ~beuge f knee bend; ~bundhose f knee breeches; ~gelenk nt knee joint; ~kehle f back of the knee; k~n vi to kneel; ~scheibe f

~**strumpf** m knee-length sock
Kniff [knɪf] (-(e)s, -e) m (fig) trick, knack; **k~elig** adj tricky
knipsen ['knɪpsən] vt (Fahrkarte) to punch; (PHOT) to take a snap of, to snap ♦ vi to take a snap od snaps
Knirps [knɪrps] (-es, -e) m little chap; (®: Schirm) telescopic umbrella
knirschen ['knɪrʃən] vi to crunch; **mit den Zähnen ~** to grind one's teeth
knistern ['knɪstərn] vi to crackle
Knitter- ['knɪtər] zW: ~**falte** f crease; **k~frei** adj non-crease; **k~n** vi to crease
Knoblauch ['kno:plaux] (-(e)s) m garlic
Knoblauchzehe f (KOCH) clove of garlic
Knöchel ['knœçəl] (-s, -) m knuckle; (Fuß~) ankle
Knochen ['knɔxən] (-s, -) m bone; ~**bruch** m fracture; ~**gerüst** nt skeleton
knöchern ['knœçərn] adj bone
knochig ['knɔxɪç] adj bony
Knödel ['knø:dəl] (-s, -) m dumpling
Knolle ['knɔlə] f tuber
Knopf [knɔpf] (-(e)s, ᵉe) m button; (Kragen~) stud
knöpfen ['knœpfən] vt to button
Knopfloch nt buttonhole buttonhole
Knorpel ['knɔrpəl] (-s, -) m cartilage, gristle; **k~ig** adj gristly
Knospe ['knɔspə] f bud
Knoten ['kno:tən] (-s, -) m knot; (BOT) node; (MED) lump; **k~** vt to knot; ~**punkt** m junction
Knüller ['knʏlər] (-s, -; umg) m hit; (Reportage) scoop
knüpfen ['knʏpfən] vt to tie; (Teppich) to knot; (Freundschaft) to form
Knüppel ['knʏpəl] (-s, -) m cudgel; (Polizei~) baton, truncheon; (AVIAT) (joy)stick; ~**schaltung** f (AUT) floor-mounted gear change
knurren ['knʊrən] vi (Hund) to snarl; to growl; (Magen) to rumble; (Mensch) to mutter

knusperig ['knʊspərɪç] adj crisp; (Keks) crunchy
k.o. [ka:'o:] adj knocked out; (fig) exhausted
Koalition [koalitsi'o:n] f coalition
Kobalt ['ko:balt] (-s) nt cobalt
Kobold ['ko:bɔlt] (-(e)s, -e) m goblin, imp
Kobra ['ko:bra] (-, -s) f cobra
Koch [kɔx] (-(e)s, ᵉe) m cook; ~**buch** nt cook(ery) book; **k~en** vt, vi to cook; (Wasser) to boil; ~**er** (-s, -) m stove, cooker
Köcher ['kœçər] (-s, -) m quiver
Kochgelegenheit ['kɔxgəle:gənhaɪt] f cooking facilities pl
Köchin ['kœçɪn] f cook
Koch- ['kɔx] zW: ~**löffel** m kitchen spoon; ~**nische** f kitchenette; ~**platte** f hotplate; ~**salz** nt cooking salt; ~**topf** m saucepan, pot
Köder ['kø:dər] (-s, -) m bait, lure
ködern vt (Tier) to trap with bait; (Person) to entice, to tempt
Koexistenz [ko:ɛksɪs'tɛnts] f coexistence
Koffein [kɔfe'i:n] (-s) nt caffeine; **k~frei** adj decaffeinated
Koffer ['kɔfər] (-s, -) m suitcase; (Schrank~) trunk; ~**radio** nt portable radio; ~**raum** m (AUT) boot (BRIT), trunk (US)
Kognak ['kɔnjak] (-s, -s) m brandy, cognac
Kohl [ko:l] (-(e)s, -e) m cabbage
Kohle ['ko:lə] f (Holz~) charcoal; (CHEM) carbon; (MIN) coal; ~**(e)s, -e)** nt carbohydrate
Kohlen- zW: ~**dioxyd** (-(e)s, -e) nt carbon dioxide; ~**händler** m coal merchant, coalman; ~**säure** f carbon dioxide; ~**stoff** m carbon
Kohlepapier nt carbon paper
Koje ['ko:jə] f cabin; (Bett) bunk
Kokain [koka'i:n] (-s) nt cocaine
kokett [ko'kɛt] adj coquettish, flirtatious
Kokosnuß ['ko:kɔsnʊs] f coconut
Koks [ko:ks] (-es, -e) m coke
Kolben ['kɔlbən] (-s, -) m (Ge-

wehr~) rifle butt; *'(Keule)* club; *(CHEM)* flask; *(TECH)* piston; *(Mais~)* cob

Kolchose [kɔl'çoːzə] f collective farm

Kolik ['koːlɪk] f colic, the gripes pl

Kollaps [kɔ'laps] (-es, -e) m collapse

Kolleg [kɔ'leːk] (-s, -s od -ien) nt lecture course; **~e** [kɔ'leːgə] (-n, -n) m colleague; *~in f colleague;* **~ium** nt working party; *(SCH)* staff

Kollekte [kɔ'lɛktə] f *(REL)* collection

kollektiv [kɔlɛk'tiːf] adj collective

Köln [kœln] (-s) nt Cologne

Kolonie [kolo'niː] f colony

kolonisieren [koloni'ziːrən] vt to colonize

Kolonne [ko'lɔnə] f column; *(von Fahrzeugen)* convoy

Koloß [ko'lɔs] *(-sses, -sse)* m colossus

kolossal [kolɔ'saːl] adj colossal

Kombi- ['kɔmbi] zW: **~nation** [-natsi'oːn] f combination; *(Vermutung)* conjecture; *(Hemdhose)* combinations pl; **~nationsschloß** nt combination lock; **k~nieren** [-'niːrən] vt to combine ♦ vi to deduce, to work out; *(vermuten)* to guess; **~wagen** m station wagon; **~zange** f (pair of) pliers pl

Komet [ko'meːt] (-en, -en) m comet

Komfort [kɔm'foːr] (-s) m luxury

Komik ['koːmɪk] f humour, comedy; **~er** (-s, -) m comedian

komisch ['koːmɪʃ] adj funny

Komitee [komi'teː] (-s, -s) nt committee

Komma ['kɔma] (-s, -s od -ta) nt comma; 2 ~ 3 2 point 3

Kommand- [kɔ'mand] zW: **~ant** [-'dant] m commander, commanding officer; **k~ieren** [-'diːrən] vt, vi to command; **~o** (-s, -s) nt command, order; *(Truppe)* detachment, squad; **auf ~o** to order

kommen ['kɔmən] *(unreg)* vi to come; *(näher~)* to approach; *(pas-*

sieren) to happen; *(gelangen, geraten)* to get; *(Blumen, Zähne, Tränen etc)* to appear; *(in die Schule, das Zuchthaus etc)* to go; ~ **lassen** to send for; **das kommt in den Schrank** that goes in the cupboard; **zu sich ~** to come round od to; **zu etw ~** to acquire sth; **um etw ~** to lose sth; **nichts auf jdn/etw ~ lassen** to have nothing said against sb/ sth; **jdm frech ~** to get cheeky with sb; **auf jeden vierten kommt ein Platz** there's one place for every fourth person; **wer kommt zuerst?** who's first?; **unter ein Auto ~** to be run over by a car; **wie hoch kommt das?** what does that cost?; **komm gut nach Hause!** safe journey (home); **~den Sonntag** next Sunday; **K~** (-s) nt coming

Kommentar [kɔmɛn'taːr] m commentary; **kein ~** no comment; **k~los** adj without comment

Kommentator [kɔmɛn'taːtɔr] m *(TV)* commentator

kommentieren [kɔmɛn'tiːrən] vt to comment on

kommerziell [kɔmɛrtsi'ɛl] adj commercial

Kommilitone [kɔmili'toːnə] (-n, -n) m fellow student

Kommissar [kɔmi'saːr] m police inspector

Kommission [kɔmɪsi'oːn] f *(COMM)* commission; *(Ausschuß)* committee

Kommode [kɔ'moːdə] f (chest of) drawers

kommunal [kɔmu'naːl] adj local; *(von Stadt auch)* municipal

Kommune [kɔ'muːnə] f commune

Kommunikation [kɔmunikatsi'oːn] f communication

Kommunion [kɔmuni'oːn] f communion

Kommuniqué [kɔmyni'keː] (-s, -s) nt communiqué

Kommunismus [kɔmu'nɪsmʊs] m communism

Kommunist(in) m(f) communist

k~isch adj communist
kommunizieren [kɔmuni'tsi:rən] vi to communicate; (REL) to receive Communion
Komödie [ko'mø:diə] f comedy
Kompagnon [kɔmpan'jõ:] (-s, -s) m (COMM) partner
kompakt [kɔm'pakt] adj compact
Kompanie [kɔmpa'ni:] f company
Kompaß ['kɔmpas] (-sses, -sse) m compass
kompatibel [kɔmpa'ti:bəl] adj compatible
kompetent [kɔmpe'tɛnt] adj competent
Kompetenz f competence, authority
komplett [kɔm'plɛt] adj complete
Komplex [kɔm'plɛks] (-es, -e) m (Gebäude~) complex
Komplikation [kɔmplikatsi'o:n] f complication
Kompliment [kɔmpli'mɛnt] nt compliment
Komplize [kɔm'pli:tsə] (-n, -n) m accomplice
kompliziert [kɔmpli'tsi:rt] adj complicated
komponieren [kɔmpo'ni:rən] vt to compose
Komponist [kɔmpo'nɪst] m composer
Komposition [kɔmpozitsi'o:n] f composition
Kompost [kɔm'pɔst] (-(e)s, -e) m compost
Kompott [kɔm'pɔt] (-(e)s, -e) nt stewed fruit
Kompromiß [kɔmpro'mɪs] (-sses, -sse) m compromise; **k~bereit** adj willing to compromise; **~lösung** f compromise solution
Kondens- [kɔn'dɛns] zW: **~ation** [kɔndɛnzatsi'o:n] f condensation; **k~ieren** [kɔndɛn'zi:rən] vt to condense; **~milch** f condensed milk
Kondition [kɔnditsi'o:n] f (WIRTS, FINANZ) condition; (Durchhaltevermögen) stamina; (körperliche Verfassung) physical condition, state of health

Konditionstraining [kɔndit-si'o:nstrɛ:nɪŋ] nt fitness training
Konditor [kɔn'di:tɔr] m pastrycook; **~ei** f café; cake shop
Kondom [kɔn'do:m] (-s, -e) nt condom
Konferenz [kɔnfe'rɛnts] f conference, meeting
Konfession [kɔnfesi'o:n] f (religious) denomination; **k~ell** [-'ɛl] adj denominational; **k~slos** adj non-denominational
Konfetti [kɔn'feti] (-(s)) nt confetti
Konfirmand [kɔnfɪr'mant] m candidate for confirmation
Konfirmation [kɔnfɪrmatsi'o:n] f (REL) confirmation
konfirmieren [kɔnfɪr'mi:rən] vt to confirm
konfiszieren [kɔnfɪs'tsi:rən] vt to confiscate
Konfitüre [kɔnfi'ty:rə] f jam
Konflikt [kɔn'flɪkt] (-(e)s, -e) m conflict
konfrontieren [kɔnfrɔn'ti:rən] vt to confront
konfus [kɔn'fu:s] adj confused
Kongreß [kɔn'grɛs] (-sses, -sse) m congress
Kongruenz [kɔngru'ɛnts] f agreement, congruence
König ['kø:nɪç] (-(e)s, -e) m king; **~in** ['kø:nɪgɪn] f queen; **k~lich** adj royal; **~reich** nt kingdom; **~tum** (-(e)s) nt kingship
Konjugation [kɔnjugatsi'o:n] f conjugation
konjugieren [kɔnju'gi:rən] vt to conjugate
Konjunktion [kɔnjuŋktsi'o:n] f conjunction
Konjunktiv ['kɔnjuŋkti:f] (-s, -e) m subjunctive
Konjunktur [kɔnjuŋk'tu:r] f economic situation; (Hoch~) boom
konkav [kɔn'ka:f] adj concave
konkret [kɔn'kre:t] adj concrete
Konkurrent(in) [kɔnku'rɛnt(ɪn)] m(f) competitor

of; **k~** *vt* to cost; (*versuchen*) to taste ♦ *vi* to taste; **was kostet ...?** what does ... cost?, how much is ...?; **~anschlag** *m* estimate; **~los** *adj* free (of charge)

köstlich ['kœstlıç] *adj* precious; (*Einfall*) delightful; (*Essen*) delicious; **sich ~ amüsieren** to have a marvellous time

Kostprobe *f* taste; (*fig*) sample

kostspielig *adj* expensive

Kostüm [kɔs'ty:m] (**-s, -e**) *nt* costume; (*Damen~*) suit; **~fest** *nt* fancy-dress party; **~ieren** [kɔsty-'mi:rən] *vt, vr* to dress up; **~verleih** *m* costume agency

Kot [ko:t] (**-(e)s**) *m* excrement

Kotelett [kɔtə'lɛt] (**-(e)s, -e** *od* **-s**) *nt* cutlet, chop; **~en** *pl* (*Bart*) sideboards

Köter ['kø:tər] (**-s, -**) *m* cur

Kotflügel *m* (*AUT* umg) mudguard

kotzen ['kɔtsən] (*umg!*) *vi* to puke (*inf*), to throw up (*inf*)

Krabbe ['krabə] *f* shrimp; **k~ln** *vi* to crawl

Krach [krax] (**-(e)s, -s** *od* **-e**) *m* crash; (*andauernd*) noise; (*umg: Streit*) quarrel, argument; **k~en** *vi* to crash; (*beim Brechen*) to crack ♦ *vr* (*umg*) to argue, to quarrel

krächzen ['krɛçtsən] *vi* to croak

Kraft [kraft] (**-, -ë**) *f* strength; power; force; (*Arbeits~*) worker; **in ~ treten** to come into force; **k~** *präp* +*gen* by virtue of; **~fahrer** *m* (motor) driver; **~fahrzeug** *nt* motor vehicle; **~fahrzeugbrief** *m* logbook; **~fahrzeugsteuer** *f* road tax; **~fahrzeugversicherung** *f* car insurance

kräftig ['krɛftıç] *adj* strong; **~en** *vt* to strengthen

Kraft- *zW:* **k~los** *adj* weak, powerless; (*JUR*) invalid; **~probe** *f* trial of strength; **k~voll** *adj* vigorous; **~werk** *nt* power station

Kragen ['kra:gən] (**-s, -**) *m* collar; **~weite** *f* collar size

Krähe ['krɛ:ə] *f* crow; **k~n** *vi* to crow

Kralle ['kralə] *f* claw; (*Vogel~*) talon; **k~n** *vt* to clutch; (*krampfhaft*) to claw

Kram [kra:m] (**-(e)s**) *m* stuff, rubbish; **k~en** *vi* to rummage; (*pej*) *m* small shop

Krampf [krampf] (**-(e)s, -ë**) *m* cramp; (*zuckend*) spasm; **~ader** *f* varicose vein; **k~haft** *adj* convulsive; (*fig: Versuche*) desperate

Kran [kra:n] (**-(e)s, -ë**) *m* crane; (*Wasser~*) tap, faucet (*US*)

Kranich ['kra:nıç] (**-s, -e**) *m* (ZOOL) crane

krank [krank] *adj* ill, sick; **K~e(r)** *mf* sick person, invalid; patient

kranken ['krankən] *vi:* **an etw** *dat* **~** (*fig*) to suffer from sth

kränken ['krɛnkən] *vt* to hurt

Kranken- *zW:* **~geld** *nt* sick pay; **~gymnastik** *f* physiotherapy; **~haus** *nt* hospital; **~kasse** *f* health insurance; **~pfleger** *m* nursing orderly; **~schein** *m* health insurance card; **~schwester** *f* nurse; **~versicherung** *f* health insurance; **~wagen** *m* ambulance

Krank- *zW:* **k~haft** *adj* diseased; (*Angst etc*) morbid; **~heit** *f* illness; disease; **~heitserreger** *m* disease-causing agent

kränklich *adj* sickly

Kränkung *f* insult, offence

Kranz [krants] (**-es, -ë**) *m* wreath, garland

kraß [kras] *adj* crass

Krater ['kra:tər] (**-s, -**) *m* crater

Kratz- ['krats] *zW:* **~bürste** *f* (*fig*) crosspatch; **k~en** *vt, vi* to scratch; **~er** (**-s, -**) *m* scratch; (*Werkzeug*) scraper

Kraul [kraul] (**-s**) *nt* crawl; **~schwimmen** to do the crawl; **k~en** *vi* (*schwimmen*) to do the crawl ♦ *vt* (*streicheln*) to fondle

kraus [kraus] *adj* crinkly; (*Haar*) frizzy; (*Stirn*) wrinkled; **K~e** ['krauzə] *f* frill, ruffle

Kraut [kraut] (**-(e)s, Kräuter**) *nt*

plant; *(Gewürz)* herb; *(Gemüse)* cabbage

Krawall [kra'val] (-s, -e) *m* row, uproar

Krawatte [kra'vatə] *f* tie

kreativ [krea'ti:f] *adj* creative

Krebs [kre:ps] (-es, -e) *m* crab; *(MED, ASTROL)* cancer

krebskrank *adj* suffering from cancer

Kredit [kre'di:t] (-(e)s, -e) *m* credit

Kreditinstitut *nt* bank

Kreditkarte *f* credit card

Kreide ['kraɪdə] *f* chalk; **k~bleich** *adj* as white as a sheet

Kreis [kraɪs] (-es, -e) *m* circle; *(Stadt~ etc)* district; **im ~ gehen** *(auch fig)* to go round in circles

kreischen ['kraɪʃən] *vi* to shriek, to screech

Kreis- ['kraɪzəl] *zW:* **~el** (-s, -) *m* top; *(Verkehrs~)* roundabout *(BRIT)*, traffic circle *(US)*; **k~en** ['kraɪzən] *vi* to spin; **~lauf** *m (MED)* circulation; *(fig: der Natur etc)* cycle; **~säge** *f* circular saw

Kreisstadt *f* county town

Kreisverkehr *m* roundabout traffic

Krematorium [krema'to:riʊm] *nt* crematorium

Kreml ['krɛm(ə)l] (-s) *m* Kremlin

krepieren [kre'pi:rən] *(umg) vi (sterben)* to die, to kick the bucket

Krepp [krɛp] (-s, -s *od* -e) *m* crepe; **~(p)apier** *nt* crepe paper; **~sohle** *f* crepe sole

Kresse ['krɛsə] *f* cress

Kreta ['kre:ta] (-s) *nt* Crete

Kreuz [krɔʏts] (-es, -e) *nt* cross; *(ANAT)* small of the back; *(KARTEN)* clubs; **k~en** *vt, vi* to cross ♦ *vi (NAUT)* to cruise; **~er** (-s, -) *m (Schiff)* cruiser; **~fahrt** *f* cruise; **~feuer** *nt:* **ins ~feuer geraten** to be under fire from all sides; **~gang** *m* cloisters *pl;* **~igen** *vt* to crucify; **~igung** *f* crucifixion; **~ung** *f (Verkehrskreuzung)* crossing, junction; *(Züchten)* cross; **~verhör** *nt* cross-examination; **~weg** *m* cross-

roads; *(REL)* Way of the Cross; **~worträtsel** *nt* crossword puzzle; **~zug** *m* crusade

Kriech- ['kri:ç] *zW:* **k~en** *(unreg) vi* to crawl, to creep; *(pej)* to grovel, to crawl; **~er** (-s, -) *m* crawler; **~spur** *f* crawler lane; **~tier** *nt* reptile

Krieg [kri:k] (-(e)s, -e) *m* war

kriegen ['kri:gən] *(umg) vt* to get

Kriegs- *zW:* **~erklärung** *f* declaration of war; **~fuß** *m:* **mit jdm/etw auf ~fuß stehen** to be at loggerheads with sb/to have difficulties with sth; **~gefangene(r)** *m* prisoner of war; **~gefangenschaft** *f* captivity; **~gericht** *nt* court-martial; **~schiff** *nt* warship; **~verbrecher** *m* war criminal; **~versehrte(r)** *m* person disabled in the war; **~zustand** *m* state of war

Krim [krɪm] (-) *f* Crimea

Krimi ['kri:mi] (-s, -s; *umg) m* thriller

Kriminal- [krimi'na:l] *zW:* **~beamte(r)** *m* detective; **~i'tät** *f* criminality; **~polizei** *f* ≈ Criminal Investigation Department *(BRIT)*, Federal Bureau of Investigation *(US)*; **~roman** *m* detective story

kriminell [krimi'nɛl] *adj* criminal; **K~e(r)** *m* criminal

Krippe ['krɪpə] *f* manger, crib; *(Kinder~)* crèche

Krise ['kri:zə] *f* crisis; **k~ln** *vi:* **es k~lt** there's a crisis

Kristall [krɪs'tal] (-s, -e) *m* crystal ♦ *nt (Glas)* crystal

Kriterium [kri'te:riʊm] *nt* criterion

Kritik [kri'ti:k] *f* criticism; *(Zeitungs~)* review, write-up; **~er** ['kri:tikər] (-s, -) *m* critic; **k~los** *adj* uncritical

kritisch ['kri:tiʃ] *adj* critical

kritisieren [kriti'zi:rən] *vt, vi* to criticize

kritzeln ['krɪtsəln] *vt, vi* to scribble, to scrawl

Kroatien [kro'a:tiən] *nt* Croatia

Krokodil [kroko'di:l] (-s, -e) *nt* crocodile

Krokus ['kro:kʊs] (-, -*od* -se) *m* crocus

Krone ['kro:nə] f crown; (Baum~)
top

krönen ['krø:nən] vt to crown

Kron- zW: ~**korken** m bottle top;
~**leuchter** m chandelier; ~**prinz** m
crown prince

Krönung ['krø:nʊŋ] f coronation

Kropf [krɔpf] (-(e)s, ⁻e) m (MED)
goitre; (von Vogel) crop

Kröte ['krø:tə] f toad

Krücke ['krʏkə] f crutch

Krug [kru:k] (-(e)s, ⁻e) m jug;
(Bier~) mug

Krümel ['kry:məl] (-s, -) m crumb;
k~n vt, vi to crumble

krumm [krʊm] adj (auch fig)
crooked; (kurvig) curved; ~**beinig**
adj bandy-legged; ~**lachen** (umg) vr
to laugh o.s. silly; ~**nehmen** (unreg)
umg) vt: jdm etw ~**nehmen** to take
sth amiss

Krümmung ['krʏmʊŋ] f bend, curve

Krüppel ['krʏpəl] (-s, -) m cripple

Kruste ['krʊstə] f crust

Kruzifix [krutsi'fɪks] (-es, -e) nt crucifix

Kübel ['ky:bəl] (-s, -) m tub; (Eimer) pail

Kubikmeter [ku'bi:kme:tər] m cubic
metre

Küche ['kʏçə] f kitchen; (Kochen)
cooking, cuisine

Kuchen ['ku:xən] (-s, -) m cake;
~**form** f baking tin; ~**gabel** f pastry
fork

Küchen- zW: ~**herd** m cooker,
stove; ~**schabe** f cockroach;
~**schrank** m kitchen cabinet

Kuckuck ['kʊkʊk] (-s, -e) m cuckoo;
~**suhr** f cuckoo clock

Kufe ['ku:fə] f (Faß) vat; (Schlit-
ten~) runner; (AVIAT) skid

Kugel ['ku:gəl] (-, -n) f ball;
(MATH) sphere; (MIL) bullet;
(Erd~) globe; (SPORT) shot;
k~förmig adj spherical; ~**kopf** m
golf ball; ~**lager** nt ball bearing;
k~rund adj (Gegenstand) round;
(umg: Person) tubby; ~**schreiber** m

ball-point (pen), biro (®); **k~sicher**
adj bulletproof; ~**stoßen** (-s) nt
shot-put

Kuh [ku:] (-, ⁻e) f cow

kühl [ky:l] adj (auch fig) cool;
K~anlage f refrigeration plant; **K~e**
(-) f coolness; ~**en** vt to cool; **K~er**
(-s, -) m (AUT) radiator;
K~erhaube f (AUT) bonnet (BRIT),
hood (US); **K~raum** m cold-storage
chamber; **K~schrank** m refrigerator; **K~truhe** f freezer; **K~ung** f
cooling; **K~wasser** nt radiator water

kühn [ky:n] adj bold, daring; **K~heit**
f boldness

Kuhstall m byre, cattle shed

Küken ['ky:kən] (-s, -) nt chicken

kulant [ku'lant] adj obliging

Kuli ['ku:li] (-s, -s) m coolie; (umg:
Kugelschreiber) biro (®)

Kulisse [ku'lisə] f scenery

kullern ['kʊlərn] vi to roll

Kult [kʊlt] (-(e)s, -e) m worship,
cult; mit etw einen ~ **treiben** to
make a cult out of sth

kultivieren [-i'vi:rən] vt to cultivate

kultiviert adj cultivated, refined

Kultur [kʊl'tu:r] f culture; civilization; (des Bodens) cultivation; ~**ba-
nause** m (umg) philistine, low-brow;
~**beutel** m toilet bag; **k~ell** [-u'rɛl]
adj cultural; ~**ministerium** nt ministry of education and the arts

Kümmel ['kʏməl] (-s, -) m caraway
seed; (Branntwein) kümmel

Kummer ['kʊmər] (-s) m grief, sorrow

kümmerlich adj miserable, wretched

kümmern ['kʏmərn] vt to concern ♦
vr: sich um jdn ~ to look after sb;
das kümmert mich nicht that
doesn't worry me; sich um etw ~
to see o sth

Kumpel ['kʊmpəl] (-s, -; umg) m
mate

kündbar ['kʏntba:r] adj redeemable,
recallable; (Vertrag) terminable

Kunde[1] ['kʊndə] (-n, -n) m customer

Kunde[2] f (Botschaft) news

Kundendienst m after-sales service

Kundenkonto nt charge account

Kund- zW: **k~geben** (unreg) vt to announce; **~gebung** f announcement; (Versammlung) rally; **k~igen** vi to give in one's notice ♦ vt to cancel; **jdm k~igen** to give sb his notice; **die Stellung/Wohnung k~igen** to give notice that one is leaving one's job/house; **jdm die Stellung/Wohnung k~igen** to give sb notice to leave his/her job/house; **~igung** f notice; **~igungsfrist** f period of notice

Kundin f customer

Kundschaft f customers pl, clientele

künftig ['kʏnftɪç] adj future ♦ adv in future

Kunst [kʊnst] (-, ∞e) f art; (Können) skill; **das ist doch keine** ~ it's easy; **~dünger** m artificial manure; **~faser** f synthetic fibre; **~fertigkeit** f skilfulness; **~gegenstand** m art object; **~gerecht** adj skilful; **~geschichte** f history of art; **~gewerbe** nt arts and crafts pl; **~griff** m trick, knack; **~händler** m art dealer

Künstler(in) ['kʏnstlər(ɪn)] (-s, -) m(f) artist; **k~isch** adj artistic; **~name** m pseudonym

künstlich ['kʏnstlɪç] adj artificial

Kunst- zW: **~sammler** (-s, -) m art collector; **~seide** f artificial silk; **~stoff** m synthetic material; **~stück** nt trick; **~turnen** nt gymnastics sg; **k~voll** adj artistic; **~werk** nt work of art

kunterbunt ['kʊntərbʊnt] adj higgledy-piggledy

Kupfer ['kʊpfər] (-s) nt copper; **k~n** adj copper

Kuppe ['kʊpə] f (Berg~) top; (Finger~) tip

Kuppelei [kʊpə'laɪ] f (JUR) procuring

Kuppel (-, -n) f dome; **k~n** vi (JUR) to procure; (AUT) to declutch ♦ vt to join

Kupplung f coupling; (AUT) clutch

Kur [kuːr] (-, -en) f cure, treatment

Kür [kyːr] (-, -en) f (SPORT) free ex-

---

ercises pl

Kurbel ['kʊrbəl] (-, -n) f crank, winder; (AUT) starting handle; **~welle** f crankshaft

Kürbis ['kʏrbɪs] (-ses, -se) m pumpkin; (exotisch) gourd

Kurgast m visitor (to a health resort)

kurieren [ku'riːrən] vt to cure

kurios [kur'ioːs] adj curious, odd; **K~i'tät** f curiosity

Kurort m health resort

Kurpfuscher m quack

Kurs [kʊrs] (-es, -e) m course; (FIN) rate; **~buch** nt timetable; **k~ieren** [kʊr'ziːrən] vi to circulate; **k~iv** adv in italics; **~us** ['kʊrzʊs] (-, Kurse) m course; **~wagen** m (EISENB) through carriage

Kurve ['kʊrvə] f curve; (Straßen~) curve, bend; **kurvig** adj (Straße) bendy

kurz [kʊrts] adj short; ~ **gesagt** in short; **zu ~ kommen** to come off badly; **den kürzeren ziehen** to get the worst of it; **K~arbeit** f short-time work; **~ärm(e)lig** adj short-sleeved

Kürze ['kʏrtsə] f shortness, brevity; **k~n** vt to cut short; (in der Länge) to shorten; (Gehalt) to reduce

kurz- zW: **~erhand** adv on the spot; **~fristig** adj short-term; **K~geschichte** f short story; **~halten** (unreg) vt to keep short; **~lebig** adj short-lived

kürzlich ['kʏrtslɪç] adv lately, recently

Kurz- zW: **~schluß** m (ELEK) short circuit; **~schrift** f shorthand; **k~sichtig** adj short-sighted

Kürzung f (eines Textes) abridgement; (eines Theaterstück, des Gehalts) cut

Kurzwelle f shortwave

kuscheln ['kʊʃəln] vr to snuggle up

Kusine [ku'ziːnə] f cousin

Kuß [kʊs] (-sses, ⸚sse) m kiss

küssen ['kʏsən] vt, vr to kiss

Küste ['kʏstə] f coast, shore

Küster ['kʏstər] (-s, -) m sexton, verger

Kutsche ['kʊtʃə] f coach, carriage; ~r (-s, -) m coachman

Kutte ['kʊtə] f habit

Kuvert [ku'veːr] (-s, -e od -s) nt envelope; cover

Kybernetik [kybɛr'neːtɪk] f cybernetics sg

Kz nt abk von **Konzentrationslager**

L

l. abk = **Liter**

labil [la'biːl] adj (MED: Konstitution) delicate

Labor [la'boːr] (-s, -e od -s) nt lab; ~ant(in) [labo'rant(ɪn)] m(f) lab(oratory) assistant

Labyrinth [laby'rɪnt] (-s, -e) nt labyrinth

Lache ['laxə] f (Flüssigkeit) puddle; (von Blut, Benzin etc) pool

lächeln ['lɛçəln] vi to smile; **L~** (-s) nt smile

lachen ['laxən] vi to laugh

lächerlich ['lɛçərlɪç] adj ridiculous

Lachgas nt laughing gas

lachhaft adj laughable

Lachs [laks] (-es, -e) m salmon

Lack [lak] (-(e)s, -e) m lacquer, varnish; (von Auto) paint; l~ieren [la'kiːrən] vt to varnish; (Auto) to spray; ~ierer [la'kiːrər] (-s, -) m varnisher

Lackmus ['lakmus] (-) m od nt litmus

Laden ['laːdən] (-s, ⸚) m shop; (Fenster~) shutter

laden ['laːdən] (unreg) vt (Lasten) to load; (JUR) to summon; (einladen) to invite

Laden- zW: ~**dieb** m shoplifter; ~**diebstahl** m shoplifting; ~**schluß** m closing time; ~**tisch** m counter

Laderaum m freight space; (FLUG, NAUT) hold

Ladung ['laːdʊŋ] f (Last) cargo, load; (Beladen) loading; (JUR) summons; (Einladung) invitation;

(Spreng~) charge

Lage ['laːgə] f position, situation; (Schicht) layer; **in der ~ sein** to be in a position

Lageplan m ground plan

Lager ['laːgər] (-s, -) nt camp; (COMM) warehouse; (Schlaf~) bed; (von Tier) lair; (TECH) bearing; ~**bestand** m stocks pl; ~**feuer** nt campfire; ~**haus** nt warehouse, store

lagern ['laːgərn] vi (Dinge) to be stored; (Menschen) to camp ♦ vt to store; (betten) to lay down; (Maschine) to bed

Lagune [la'guːnə] f lagoon

lahm [laːm] adj lame; ~**en** vi to be lame

lähmen ['lɛːmən] vt to paralyse

lahmlegen vt to paralyse

Lähmung f paralysis

Laib [laɪp] (-s, -e) m loaf

Laie ['laɪə] (-n, -n) m layman; l~**nhaft** adj amateurish

Laken ['laːkən] (-s, -) nt sheet

Lakritz m od nt = **Lakritze**

Lakritze [la'krɪtsə] f liquorice

lallen ['lalən] vt, vi to slur; (Baby) to babble

Lama (-s, -s) nt (ZOOL) llama

Lamelle [la'mɛlə] f lamella; (ELEK) lamina; (TECH) plate

Lametta [la'mɛta] (-s) nt tinsel

Lamm [lam] (-(e)s, ⸚er) nt lamb

Lampe ['lampə] f lamp; ~**nfieber** nt stage fright; ~**nschirm** m lampshade

Lampion [lampi'ɔ̃] (-s, -s) m Chinese lantern

Land [lant] (-(e)s, ⸚er) nt land; (Nation, nicht Stadt) country; (Bundes~) state; **auf dem ~** in the country; ~**besitz** m landed property; ~**ebahn** f runway; l~**en** ['landən] vt, vi to land

Landes- ['landəs] zW: ~**farben** pl national colours; ~**innere(s)** nt inland region; ~**sprache** f national language; l~**üblich** adj customary; ~**verrat** m high treason; ~**währung** f national currency

landesweit adj nationwide

Land- zW: **~haus** nt country house; **~karte** f map; **~kreis** m administrative region; **l~läufig** adj customary

ländlich ['lɛntlɪç] adj rural

Land- zW: **~schaft** f countryside; (KUNST) landscape; **~sitz** m country seat; **~straße** f country road; **~streicher** (-s, -) m tramp; **~strich** m region

Landung ['landʊŋ] f landing; **~sbrücke** f jetty, pier

Land- zW: **~wirt** m farmer; **~weg** m: etw auf dem ~weg befördern to transport sth by land; **~wirtschaft** f agriculture; **~zunge** f spit

lang [laŋ] adj long; (Mensch) tall; **~atmig** adj long-winded; **~e** adv for a long time; (dauern, brauchen) a long time

Länge ['lɛŋə] f length; (GEOG) longitude

langen ['laŋən] vi (ausreichen) to do, to suffice; (fassen): **~ (nach)** to reach (for) ♦ vt: **jdm etw ~** to hand od pass sb sth; **es langt mir** I've had enough

Längengrad m longitude

Längenmaß nt linear measure

lang- zW: **~fristig** adj long-term; **~jährig** adj (Freundschaft, Gewohnheit) long-standing; **L~lauf** m (SKI) cross-country skiing

länglich adj longish

längs [lɛŋs] präp (+gen od dat) along ♦ adv lengthwise

lang- zW: **~sam** adj slow; **L~samkeit** f slowness; **L~schläfer(in)** m(f) late riser; **L~spielplatte** f long-playing record

längst [lɛŋst] adv: das ist ~ fertig that was finished a long time ago, that has been finished for a long time; **~e(r, s)** adj longest

lang- zW: **~weilen** vt to bore ♦ vr to be bored; **~weilig** adj boring, tedious; **L~welle** f long wave; **~wierig** adj lengthy, long-drawn-out

Lanze ['lantsə] f lance

Lappalie [la'pa:liə] f trifle

Lappen ['lapən] (-s, -) m cloth, rag; (ANAT) lobe

läppisch ['lɛpɪʃ] adj foolish

Lapsus ['lapsʊs] (-, -) m slip

Lärche ['lɛrçə] f larch

Lärm [lɛrm] (-(e)s) m noise; **l~en** vi to be noisy, to make a noise

Larve ['larfə] f (BIOL) larva

lasch [laʃ] adj slack

Lasche ['laʃə] f (Schuh~) tongue

Laser ['le:zər] (-s, -) m laser

SCHLÜSSELWORT

lassen ['lasən] (pt ließ, pp gelassen od (als Hilfsverb) lassen) vt 1 (unterlassen) to stop; (momentan) to leave; laß das (sein)! don't do it(!); (hör auf) stop it(!); laß mich! leave me alone; lassen wir das! let's leave it; er kann das Trinken nicht lassen he can't stop drinking

2 (zurücklassen) to leave; etw lassen, wie es ist to leave sth (just) as it is

3 (überlassen): jdn ins Haus lassen to let sb into the house

♦ vi: laß mal, ich mache das schon leave it, I'll do it

♦ Hilfsverb **1** (veranlassen): etw machen lassen to have od get sth done; sich dat etw schicken lassen to have sth sent (to one)

2 (zulassen): jdn etw wissen lassen to let sb know sth; das Licht brennen lassen to leave the light on; jdn warten lassen to keep sb waiting; das läßt sich machen that can be done

3: laß uns gehen let's go

---

lässig ['lɛsɪç] adj casual; **L~keit** f casualness

Last [last] (-, -en) f load, burden; (NAUT, AVIAT) cargo; (meist pl: Gebühr) charge; **jdm zur ~ fallen** to be a burden to sb; **~auto** nt lorry, truck; **l~en** vi: **l~en auf +dat** to weigh on

Laster ['lastər] (-s, -) nt vice

lästern ['lɛstərn] vt, vi (Gott) to blaspheme; (schlecht sprechen) to mock

Lästerung f jibe; (Gottes~) blasphemy

lästig ['lɛstɪç] adj troublesome, tiresome

Last- zW: **~kahn** m barge; **~kraftwagen** m heavy goods vehicle; **~schrift** f debit; **~wagen** m lorry, truck; **~zug** m articulated lorry

Latein [la'taɪn] (-s) nt Latin; **~amerika** nt Latin America

latent [la'tɛnt] adj latent

Laterne [la'tɛrnə] f lantern; (Straßen~) lamp, light; **~npfahl** m lamppost

latschen ['la:tʃən] (umg) vi (gehen) to wander, to go; (lässig) to slouch

Latte ['latə] f lath; (SPORT) goalpost; (quer) crossbar

Latzhose ['latsho:zə] f dungarees pl

lau [lau] adj (Nacht) balmy; (Wasser) lukewarm

Laub [laup] (-(e)s) nt foliage; **~baum** m deciduous tree; **~frosch** m tree frog; **~säge** f fretsaw

Lauch [laux] (-(e)s, -e) m leek

Lauer ['lauər] f: auf der ~ sein od liegen to lie in wait; **l~n** vi to lie in wait; (Gefahr) to lurk

Lauf [lauf] (-(e)s, Läufe) m run; (Wett~) race; (Entwicklung, ASTRON) course; (Gewehr~) barrel; einer Sache ihren ~ lassen to let sth take its course; **~bahn** f career

laufen ['laufən] (unreg) vt, vi to run; (umg: gehen) to walk; **~d** adj running; (Monat, Ausgaben) current; auf dem ~en sein/halten to be/keep up to date; am ~den Band (fig) continuously

Läufer ['lɔyfər] (-s, -) m (Teppich, SPORT) runner; (Fußball) half-back; (Schach) bishop

Lauf- zW: **~masche** f run, ladder (BRIT); **~paß** m: jdm den ~paß geben (umg) to send sb packing (inf); **~stall** m playpen; **~steg** m catwalk; **~werk** nt (COMPUT) disk drive

Lauge ['laugə] f soapy water; (CHEM) alkaline solution

Laune ['launə] f mood, humour; (Einfall) caprice; (schlechte) temper; **l~nhaft** adj capricious, changeable

launisch adj moody; bad-tempered

Laus [laus] (-, Läuse) f louse; **~bub** m rascal, imp

lauschen ['lauʃən] vi to eavesdrop, to listen in

lauschig ['lauʃɪç] adj snug

lausig ['lauzɪç] (umg: pej) adj measly; (Kälte) perishing

laut [laut] adj loud ♦ adv loudly; (lesen) aloud ♦ präp (+gen od dat) according to; **L~** (-(e)s, -e) m sound

Laute ['lautə] f lute

lauten ['lautən] vi to say; (Urteil) to be

läuten ['lɔytən] vt, vi to ring, to sound

lauter ['lautər] adj (Wasser) clear, pure; (Wahrheit, Charakter) honest ♦ adj inv (Freude, Dummheit etc) sheer ♦ adv nothing but, only

laut- zW: **~hals** adv at the top of one's voice; **~los** adj noiseless, silent; **L~schrift** f phonetics pl; **L~sprecher** m loudspeaker; **~stark** adj vociferous; **L~stärke** f (RADIO) volume

lauwarm ['lauvarm] adj (auch fig) lukewarm

Lava ['la:va] (-, Laven) f lava

Lavendel [la'vɛndəl] (-s, -) m lavender

Lawine [la'vi:nə] f avalanche; **~ngefahr** f danger of avalanches

lax [laks] adj lax

Lazarett [latsa'rɛt] (-(e)s, -e) nt (MIL) hospital, infirmary

leasen ['li:zən] vt to lease

Leben (-s, -) nt life

leben ['le:bən] vt, vi to live; **~d** adj living; **~dig** [le'bɛndɪç] adj living, alive; (lebhaft) lively; **L~digkeit** f liveliness

Lebens- zW: **~art** f way of life:

~erwartung f life expectancy; **l~fähig** adj able to live; **~freude** f zest for life; **~gefahr** f: **~gefahr!** danger!; **in ~gefahr** dangerously ill; **l~gefährlich** adj dangerous; (*Verletzung*) critical; **~haltungskosten** pl cost of living sg; **~jahr** nt year of life; **~länglich** adj (*Strafe*) for life; **~lauf** m curriculum vitae; **~mittel** nt food sg; **~mittelgeschäft** nt grocer's (shop); **~mittelvergiftung** f (*MED*) food poisoning; **l~müde** adj tired of life; **~retter** m lifesaver; **~standard** m standard of living; **~unterhalt** m livelihood; **~versicherung** f life insurance; **~wandel** m way of life; **~weise** f lifestyle, way of life; **l~wichtig** adj vital, essential; **~zeichen** nt sign of life

Leber ['le:bər] f (-, -n) f liver; **~fleck** m mole; **~tran** m cod-liver oil; **~wurst** f liver sausage

Lebewesen nt creature

leb- ['le:p] zW: **~haft** adj lively, vivacious; **L~kuchen** m gingerbread; **~los** adj lifeless

Leck [lɛk] (-(e)s, -e) nt leak; **l~** adj leaky, leaking; **l~en** vi (*Loch haben*) to leak; (*schlecken*) to lick ♦ vt to lick

lecker ['lɛkər] adj delicious, tasty; **L~bissen** m dainty morsel

Leder ['le:dər] (-s, -) nt leather; **~hose** f lederhosen; **l~n** adj leather; **~waren** pl leather goods

ledig ['le:diç] adj single; **einer Sache** gen **~ sein** to be free of sth; **~lich** adv merely, solely

leer [le:r] adj empty, vacant; **~machen** to empty; **L~e** (-) f emptiness; **~en** vt, vr to empty; **L~gewicht** nt weight when empty; **L~lauf** m neutral; **~stehend** adj empty; **L~ung** f emptying; (*Post*) collection

legal [le'ga:l] adj legal, lawful; **~isieren** vt to legalize

legen ['le:gən] vt to lay, to put, to place; (*Ei*) to lay ♦ vr to lie down; (*fig*) to subside

Legende [le'gɛndə] f legend

leger [le'ʒe:r] adj casual

Legierung f alloy

Legislative [legisla'ti:və] f legislature

legitim [legi'ti:m] adj legitimate

legitimieren [legiti'mi:rən] vt to legitimate ♦ vr to prove one's identity

Lehm [le:m] (-(e)s, -e) m loam; **l~ig** adj loamy

Lehne ['le:nə] f arm; back; **l~n** vt, vr to lean

Lehnstuhl m armchair

Lehr- zW: **~amt** nt teaching profession; **~buch** nt textbook

Lehre ['le:rə] f teaching, doctrine; (*beruflich*) apprenticeship; (*moralisch*) lesson; (*TECH*) gauge; **l~n** vt to teach; **~r(in)** (-s, -) m(f) teacher; **~zimmer** nt staff room

Lehr- zW: **~gang** m course; **~jahre** pl apprenticeship sg; **~kraft** f (*förmlich*) teacher; **~ling** m apprentice; **~plan** m syllabus; **l~reich** adj instructive; **~stelle** f apprenticeship; **~zeit** f apprenticeship

Leib [laip] (-(e)s, -er) m body; **halt ihn mir vom ~!** keep him away from me!; **l~haftig** adj personified; (*Teufel*) incarnate; **l~lich** adj bodily; (*Vater etc*) own

Leibschmerzen pl stomach pains

Leibwache f bodyguard

Leiche ['laiçə] f corpse; **~nhalle** f mortuary; **~nwagen** m hearse

Leichnam ['laiçna:m] (-(e)s, -e) m corpse

leicht [laiçt] adj light; (*einfach*) easy; **L~athletik** f athletics sg; **~fallen** (*unreg*) vi: **jdm ~fallen** to be easy for sb; **~fertig** adj frivolous; **~gläubig** adj gullible, credulous; **~hin** adv lightly; **L~igkeit** f easiness; **mit L~igkeit** with ease; **~machen** vt: **es sich** dat **~machen** to make things easy for o.s.; **L~sinn** m carelessness; **~sinnig** adj careless

Leid [lait] (-(e)s) nt grief, sorrow; **l~** adj: **etw l~ haben** od **sein** to be tired of sth; **es tut mir/ihm l~** I'm/

am/he is sorry; **er/das tut mir l~** I am sorry for him/it; **l~en** (unreg) vt to suffer; (erlauben) to permit ♦ vi to suffer; **jdn/etw nicht l~en können** not to be able to stand sb/sth; **~en** (-s, -) nt suffering; (Krankheit) complaint; **~enschaft** f passion; **l~enschaftlich** adj passionate

leider ['laɪdər] adv unfortunately; **ja, ~** yes, I'm afraid so; **~ nicht** I'm afraid not

leidig adj worrying, troublesome

leidlich adj tolerable ♦ adv tolerably

Leidtragende(r) mf bereaved; (Benachteiligter) one who suffers

Leidwesen nt: **zu jds ~** to sb's disappointment

Leier ['laɪər] (-, -n) f lyre; (fig) old story; **~kasten** m barrel organ

Leihbibliothek f lending library

Leihbücherei f lending library

leihen ['laɪən] (unreg) vt to lend; **sich dat etw ~** to borrow sth

Leih- zW: **~gebühr** f hire charge; **~haus** nt pawnshop; **~schein** m pawn ticket; (Buchleihschein etc) borrowing slip; **~wagen** m hired car

Leim [laɪm] (-(e)s, -e) m glue; **l~en** vt to glue

Leine ['laɪnə] f line, cord; (Hunde~) leash, lead

Leinen nt linen; **l~** adj linen

Leintuch nt (Bett~) sheet; linen cloth

Leinwand f (KUNST) canvas; (CINE) screen

leise ['laɪzə] adj quiet; (sanft) soft, gentle

Leiste ['laɪstə] f ledge; (Zier~) strip; (ANAT) groin

leisten ['laɪstən] vt (Arbeit) to do; (Gesellschaft) to keep; (Ersatz) to supply; (vollbringen) to achieve; **sich dat etw ~ können** to be able to afford sth

Leistung f performance; (gute) achievement; **~sdruck** m pressure; **l~sfähig** adj efficient

Leitartikel m leading article

Leitbild nt model

leiten ['laɪtən] vt to lead; (Firma) to manage; (in eine Richtung) to direct; (ELEK) to conduct

Leiter¹ ['laɪtər] (-s, -) m leader, head; (ELEK) conductor

Leiter² (-, -n) f ladder

Leitfaden m guide

Leitplanke f crash barrier

Leitung f (Führung) direction; (CINE, THEAT etc) production; (von Firma) management; directors pl; (Wasser~) pipe; (Kabel) cable; **eine lange ~ haben** to be slow on the uptake

Leitungs- zW: **~draht** m wire; **~rohr** nt pipe; **~wasser** nt tap water

Lektion [lɛktsɪˈoːn] f lesson

Lektüre [lɛkˈtyːrə] f (Lesen) reading; (Lesestoff) reading matter

Lende ['lɛndə] f loin; (Stück) fillet

lenk- [lɛŋk] zW: **~bar** adj (Fahrzeug) steerable; (Kind) manageable; **~en** vt to steer; (Kind) to guide; (Blick, Aufmerksamkeit) to direct; **~en** (auf +akk) to direct (at); **L~rad** nt steering wheel; **L~stange** f handlebars pl

Leopard [leoˈpart] (-en, -en) m leopard

Lepra ['leːpra] f leprosy

Lerche ['lɛrçə] f lark

lernbegierig adj eager to learn

lernen ['lɛrnən] vt to learn

lesbar ['leːsbaːr] adj legible

Lesbierin ['lɛsbiərɪn] f lesbian

lesbisch ['lɛsbɪʃ] adj lesbian

Lese ['leːzə] f (Wein) harvest

Lesebrille f reading glasses

Lesebuch nt reading book, reader

lesen (unreg) vt, vi to read; (ernten) to gather, to pick

Leser(in) (-s, -) m(f) reader; **~brief** m reader's letter; **l~lich** adj legible

Lesezeichen nt bookmark

Lesung [ˈleːzʊŋ] f (PARL) reading

letzte(r, s) [ˈlɛtstə(r, s)] adj last; (neueste) latest; **zum ~nmal** for the last time; **~ns** adv lately; **~re(r, s)**

adj latter

Leuchte ['lɔʏçtə] *f* lamp, light; **l~n** *vi* to shine, to gleam; **~r (-s, -)** *m* candlestick

Leucht- *zW:* **~farbe** *f* fluorescent colour; **~rakete** *f* flare; **~reklame** *f* neon sign; **~röhre** *f* strip light; **~turm** *m* lighthouse; **~zifferblatt** *nt* luminous dial

leugnen ['lɔʏgnən] *vt* to deny

Leukämie [lɔʏkɛ'miː] *f* leukaemia

Leukoplast [lɔʏko'plast] *nt* (-(e)s, -e) *nt* elastoplast (®)

Leumund ['lɔʏmʊnt] *m* (-(e)s, -e *m* reputation

Leumundszeugnis *nt* character reference

Leute ['lɔʏtə] *pl* people *pl*

Leutnant ['lɔʏtnant] (-s, -s *od* -e) *m* lieutenant

leutselig ['lɔʏtzeːlɪç] *adj* amiable

Lexikon ['lɛksikɔn] (-s, Lexiken *od* Lexika) *nt* encyclop(a)edia

Libelle [li'bɛlə] *f* dragonfly; (TECH) spirit level

liberal [libe'raːl] *adj* liberal; **L~e(r)** *mf* liberal

Libero ['liːbero] (-s, -s) *m* (Fußball) sweeper

Licht [lɪçt] (-(e)s, -er) *nt* light; **~bild** *nt* photograph; (Dia) slide; **~blick** *m* cheering prospect; **l~empfindlich** *adj* sensitive to light; **l~en** *vt* to clear; (Anker) to weigh ♦ *vr* to clear up; (Haar) to thin; **l~erloh** *adv*: **l~erloh brennen** to be ablaze; **~hupe** *f* flashing of headlights; **~jahr** *nt* light year; **~maschine** *f* dynamo; **~schalter** *m* light switch

Lichtung *f* clearing, glade

Lid [liːt] (-(e)s, -er) *nt* eyelid; **~schatten** *m* eyeshadow

lieb [liːp] *adj* dear; **das ist ~ von dir** that's kind of you; **~äugeln** ['liːbɔʏgəln] *vi insep*: **mit etw ~äugeln** to have one's eye on sth; **mit dem Gedanken ~äugeln, etw zu tun** to toy with the idea of doing sth

Liebe ['liːbə] *f* love; **l~bedürftig** *adj*: **l~bedürftig sein** to need love; **l~n** *vt* to love; to like

liebens- *zW:* **~wert** *adj* loveable; **~würdig** *adj* kind; **~würdigerweise** *adv* kindly; **L~würdigkeit** *f* kindness

lieber ['liːbər] *adv* rather, preferably; **ich gehe ~ nicht** I'd rather not go; *siehe auch* **gern lieb**

Liebes- *zW:* **~brief** *m* love letter; **~kummer** *m*: **~kummer haben** to be lovesick; **~paar** *nt* courting couple, lovers *pl*

liebevoll *adj* loving

lieb- *zW:* **~gewinnen** (unreg) *vt* to get fond of; **~haben** (unreg) *vt* to be fond of; **L~haber (-s, -)** *m* lover; **L~habe'rei** *f* hobby; **~kosen** [liːpko:zən] *vt insep* to caress; **~lich** *adj* lovely, charming; **L~ling** *m* darling; **L~lings-** *in zW* favourite; **L~losigkeit** *f* ⟨unklar⟩

Lied [liːt] (-(e)s, -er) *nt* song; (REL) hymn; **~erbuch** ['liːdər-] *nt* songbook; hymn book

liederlich ['liːdərlɪç] *adj* slovenly; (Lebenswandel) loose, immoral; **L~keit** *f* slovenliness; immorality

lief *etc* [liːf] *vb siehe* **laufen**

Lieferant [liːfə'rant] *m* supplier

Lieferbedingungen *pl* terms of delivery

liefern ['liːfərn] *vt* to deliver; (versorgen mit) to supply; (Beweis) to produce

Liefer- *zW:* **~schein** *m* delivery note; **~termin** *m* delivery date; **~ung** *f* delivery; supply; **~wagen** *m* van; **~zeit** *f* delivery period

Liege ['liːgə] *f* bed

liegen ['liːgən] (unreg) *vi* to lie; (sich befinden) to be; **mir liegt nichts/viel daran** it doesn't matter to me/it matters a lot to me; **es liegt bei Ihnen, ob ...** it's up to you whether ...; **Sprachen ~ mir nicht** languages are not my line; **woran liegt es?** what's the cause?; **~bleiben** (unreg) *vi* (im Bett) to stay in bed; (nicht aufstehen) to stay lying down; (vergessen werden) to be left (behind); ~**lassen** (unreg) vt (vergessen) to leave behind

Liege- zW: ~**sitz** m (AUT) reclining seat; ~**stuhl** m deck chair; ~**wagen** m (EISENB) couchette

Lift [lɪft] (-(e)s e od -s) m lift

Likör [li'kø:r] (-s, -e) m liqueur

lila ['li:la] adj inv purple, lilac; **L~** (-s, -s) nt (Farbe) purple, lilac

Lilie ['li:liə] f lily

Limonade [limo'na:də] f lemonade

Limone [li'mo:nə] f lime

Linde ['lɪndə] f lime tree, linden

lindern ['lɪndərn] vt to alleviate, to soothe

Linderung f alleviation

Lineal [line'a:l] (-s, -e) nt ruler

Linie ['li:niə] f line

Linien- zW: ~**blatt** nt ruled sheet; ~**flug** m scheduled flight; ~**richter** m linesman

linieren [lin'i:rən] vt to line

Linke ['lɪŋkə] f left side; left hand; (POL) left

linkisch adj awkward, gauche

links [lɪŋks] adv left; to od on the left; ~ **von mir** on od to my left; **L~außen** [lɪŋks'ausən] (-s, -) m (SPORT) outside left; **L~händer(in)** (-s, -) m(f) left-handed person; **L~kurve** f left-hand bend; **L~verkehr** m driving on the left

Linoleum [li'no:leom] (-s) nt lino(leum)

Linse ['lɪnzə] f lentil; (optisch) lens sg

Lippe ['lɪpə] f lip; ~**nstift** m lipstick

lispeln ['lɪspəln] vi to lisp

Lissabon ['lɪsabɔn] (-s) nt Lisbon

List [lɪst] (-, -en) f cunning; trick, ruse

Liste ['lɪstə] f list

listig ['lɪstɪç] adj cunning, sly

Litanei [lita'naɪ] f litany

Liter ['li:tər] (-s, -) nt od m litre

literarisch [lɪtə'ra:rɪʃ] adj literary

Literatur [lɪtəra'tu:r] f literature

Litfaßsäule ['lɪtfaszɔylə] f advertising pillar

Lithographie [litogra'fi:] f lithography

Liturgie [litur'gi:] f liturgy

liturgisch [li'torgɪʃ] adj liturgical

Litze ['lɪtsə] f braid; (ELEK) flex

live [laɪf] adj/adv (RADIO, TV) live

Livree [li'vre:] (-, -n) f livery

Lizenz [li'tsɛnts] f licence

Lkw [ɛlka:'ve:] (-(s), -(s)) m abk = Lastkraftwagen

Lob [lo:p] (-(e)s) nt praise

Lobby ['lɔbi] f lobby

loben ['lo:bən] vt to praise; ~**swert** adj praiseworthy

löblich ['lø:plɪç] adj praiseworthy, laudable

Loch [lɔx] (-(e)s, er) nt hole; **l~en** vt to punch holes in; ~**er** (-s, -) m punch

löcherig ['lœçərɪç] adj full of holes

Lochkarte f punch card

Lochstreifen m punch tape

Locke ['lɔkə] f lock, curl; **l~n** vt to entice; (Haare) to curl; ~**nwickler** (-s, -) m curler

locker ['lɔkər] adj loose; ~**lassen** (unreg) vi: **nicht** ~**lassen** not to let up; ~**n** vt to loosen

lockig ['lɔkɪç] adj curly

Lodenmantel ['lo:dənmantəl] m thick woollen coat

lodern ['lo:dərn] vi to blaze

Löffel ['lœfəl] (-s, -) m spoon

löffeln vt to spoon

Logarithmus [loga'rɪtmos] m logarithm

Loge ['lo:ʒə] f (THEAT) box; (Freimaurer) (masonic) lodge; (Pförtner~) office

Logik ['lo:gɪk] f logic

logisch ['lo:gɪʃ] adj logical

Logopäde [logo'pɛ:də] (-n, -n) m speech therapist

Lohn [lo:n] (-(e)s, e) m reward; (Arbeits~) pay, wages pl; ~**büro** nt wages office; ~**empfänger** m wage earner

lohnen ['lo:nən] vr unpers to be worth it ♦ vt (liter): **(jdm etw)** ~ to reward (sb for sth); ~**d** adj worthwhile

Lohnerhöhung f pay rise

Lohn- zW: **~steuer** f income tax; **~streifen** m pay slip; **~tüte** f pay packet

Lokal [lo'ka:l] (-(e)s, -e) nt pub(lic house)

lokal adj local; **~i'sieren** vt to localize

Lokomotive [lokomo'ti:və] f locomotive

Lokomotivführer m engine driver

Lorbeer ['lɔrbeːr] (-s, -en) m (auch fig) laurel; **~blatt** nt (KOCH) bay leaf

Lore ['lo:rə] f (MIN) truck

Los [lo:s] (-es, -e) nt (Schicksal) lot, fate; (Lotterie~) lottery ticket

los [lo:s] adj (locker) loose; **~!** go on!; etw ~ **sein** to be rid of sth; was ist ~? what's the matter?; dort ist nichts/viel ~ there's nothing/a lot going on there; etw ~ **haben** (umg) to be clever; **~binden** (unreg) vt to untie

Löschblatt nt sheet of blotting paper

löschen ['lœʃən] vt (Feuer, Licht) to put out, to extinguish; (Durst) to quench; (COMM) to cancel; (COMPUT) to delete; (Tonband) to erase; (Fracht) to unload ♦ vi (Feuerwehr) to put out a fire; (Tinte) to blot

Lösch- zW: **~fahrzeug** nt fire engine; fire boat; **~gerät** nt fire extinguisher; **~papier** nt blotting paper; **~taste** f delete key

lose ['lo:zə] adj loose

Lösegeld nt ransom

losen ['lo:zən] vi to draw lots

lösen ['lø:zən] vt to loosen; (Rätsel etc) to solve; (Verlobung) to call off; (CHEM) to dissolve; (Partnerschaft) to break up; (Fahrkarte) to buy ♦ vr (aufgehen) to come loose; (Zucker etc) to dissolve; (Problem, Schwierigkeit) to (re)solve itself

los- zW: **~fahren** (unreg) vi to leave; **~gehen** (unreg) vi to set out; (anfangen) to start; (Bombe) to go

off; auf jdn **~gehen** to go for sb; **~kaufen** vt (Gefangene, Geiseln) to pay ransom for; **~kommen** (unreg) vi: von etw **~kommen** to get away from sth; **~lassen** (unreg) vt (Seil) to let go of; (Schimpfe) to let loose; **~laufen** (unreg) vi to run off

löslich ['lø:slɪç] adj soluble; **L~keit** f solubility

los- zW: **~lösen** vt (sich) **~lösen** to free (o.s.); **~machen** vt to loosen; (Boot) to unmoor ♦ vr to get away; **~schrauben** vt to unscrew

Losung ['lo:zuŋ] f watchword, slogan

Lösung ['lø:zuŋ] f (Lockermachen) loosening; (eines Rätsels, CHEM) solution; **~smittel** nt solvent

loswerden (unreg) vt to get rid of

losziehen (unreg; umg) vi (sich aufmachen) to set off

Lot [lo:t] (-(e)s, -e) nt plumbline; **im ~** vertical; (fig) on an even keel

löten ['lø:tən] vt to solder

Lothringen ['lo:trɪŋən] (-s) nt Lorraine

Lötkolben m soldering iron

Lotse ['lo:tsə] (-n, -n) m pilot; (AVIAT) air traffic controller; **l~n** vt to pilot; (umg) to lure

Lotterie [lɔtə'ri:] f lottery

Lotto ['lɔto] (-s, -s) nt national lottery; **~zahlen** pl winning lottery numbers

Löwe ['lø:və] (-n, -n) m lion; (ASTROL) Leo; **~nanteil** m lion's share; **~nzahn** m dandelion

loyal [loa'ja:l] adj loyal

Loyalität [loajali'tɛ:t] f loyalty

Luchs [luks] (-es, -e) m lynx

Lücke ['lykə] f gap; **~nbüßer** (-s, -) m stopgap; **l~nhaft** adj full of gaps; (care, supplies etc) inadequate; **l~nlos** adj complete

Luft [luft] (-, -e) f air; (Atem) breath; in der **~ liegen** to be in the air; jdn wie **~ behandeln** to ignore sb; **~angriff** m air raid; **~ballon** m balloon; **~blase** f air bubble; **l~dicht** adj airtight; **~druck** m atmospheric pressure

lüften ['lʏftən] vt to air; (Hut) to lift, to raise ♦ vi to let some in air

Luft- zW: **~fahrt** f aviation; **l~gekühlt** adj air-cooled; **~gewehr** nt air-rifle, airgun; **l~ig** adj (Ort) breezy; (Raum) airy; (Kleider) summery; **~kissenfahrzeug** nt hovercraft; **~kurort** m health resort; **l~leer** adj: **luftleerer Raum** vacuum; **l~linie** f: **in der Luftlinie** as the crow flies; **~loch** nt air-hole; (AVIAT) air-pocket; **~matratze** f lilo ®; BRIT) air mattress; **~pirat** m hijacker; **~post** f airmail; **~röhre** f (ANAT) windpipe; **~schlange** f streamer; **Luftschutzkeller** m air-raid shelter; **~verkehr** m air traffic; **~verschmutzung** f air pollution; **~waffe** f air force; **~zug** m draught

Lüge ['ly:gə] f lie; **jdn/etw ~n strafen** to give the lie to sb/sth; **l~n** (unreg) vi to lie

Lügner(in) (-s, -) m(f) liar

Luke ['lu:kə] f dormer window; hatch

Lump [lʊmp] (-en, -en) m scamp, rascal

Lumpen ['lʊmpən] (-s, -) m rag

lumpen ['lʊmpən] vi: **sich nicht ~ lassen** to be generous

lumpig ['lʊmpɪç] adj shabby

Lupe ['lu:pə] f magnifying glass; **unter die ~ nehmen** (fig) to scrutinize

Lupine [lu'pi:nə] f lupin

Lust [lʊst] (-, -e) f joy, delight; (Neigung) desire; **~ haben zu od auf etw** akk/**etw zu tun** to feel like sth/doing sth

lüstern ['lʏstərn] adj lustful, lecherous

lustig ['lʊstɪç] adj (komisch) amusing, funny; (fröhlich) cheerful

Lüstling m lecher

Lust- zW: **l~los** adj unenthusiastic; **~mord** m sex(ual) murder; **~spiel** nt comedy

lutschen ['lʊtʃən] vt, vi to suck; **am Daumen ~** to suck one's thumb

Lutscher (-s, -) m lollipop

luxuriös [lʊksuri'ø:s] adj luxurious

Luxus ['lʊksʊs] (-) (-) m luxury; **~artikel** pl luxury goods; **~hotel** nt luxury hotel

Lymphe ['lʏmfə] f lymph

lynchen ['lʏnçən] vt to lynch

Lyrik ['ly:rɪk] f lyric poetry; **~er** (-s, -) m lyric poet

lyrisch ['ly:rɪʃ] adj lyrical

M

m abk = Meter

Machart f make

machbar adj feasible

machen ['maxən] vt **1** to do; (herstellen, zubereiten) to make; **was machst du da?** what are you doing (there)?; **das ist nicht zu machen** that can't be done; **das Radio leiser machen** to turn the radio down; **aus Holz gemacht** made of wood

2 (verursachen, bewirken) to make; **jdm Angst machen** to make sb afraid; **das macht die Kälte** it's the cold that does that

3 (ausmachen) to matter; **das macht nichts** that doesn't matter; **die Kälte macht mir nichts** I don't mind the cold

4 (kosten, ergeben) to be; **3 und 5 macht 8** 3 and 5 is od are 8; **was od wieviel macht das?** how much does that make?

5: **was macht die Arbeit?** how's the work going?; **was macht dein Bruder?** how is your brother doing?; **das Auto machen lassen** to have the car done; **mach's gut!** take care!; (viel Glück) good luck!

♦ vi: **mach schnell!** hurry up!; **Schluß machen** to finish (off); **mach schon!** come on!; **das macht müde** it makes you tired; **in etw** dat **machen** to be od deal in sth

♦ vr to come along (nicely); **sich an**

etw *akk* **machen** to set about sth;
sich verständlich machen to make
o.s. understood; **sich** *dat* **viel aus
jdm/etw machen** to like sb/sth

Macht [maxt] (-, -e) *f* power; **~ha-
ber** (-s, -) *m* ruler

mächtig ['mɛçtɪç] *adj* powerful,
mighty; (*umg: ungeheuer*) enormous

Macht- *zW:* **~los** *adj* powerless;
~probe *f* trial of strength; **~wort**
nt: **ein ~wort sprechen** to exercise
one's authority

Mädchen ['mɛːtçən] *nt* girl; **m~haft**
adj girlish; **~name** *m* maiden name

Made ['maːdə] *f* maggot

madig ['maːdɪç] *adj* maggoty; **jdm
etw ~ machen** to spoil sth for sb

mag *etc* [maːk] *vb siehe* **mögen**

Magazin [maga'tsiːn] (-s, -e) *nt* magazine

Magen ['maːgən] (-s, - *od* -) *m*
stomach; **~geschwür** *nt* (*MED*)
stomach ulcer; **~schmerzen** *pl*
stomachache *sg*

mager ['maːgər] *adj* lean; (*dünn*)
thin; **M~keit** *f* leanness; thinness

Magie [ma'giː] *f* magic

magisch ['maːgɪʃ] *adj* magical

Magnet [ma'gneːt] (-s *od* -en, -en)
m magnet; **m~isch** *adj* magnetic;
~nadel *f* magnetic needle

Mahagoni [maha'goːni] (-s) *nt* mahogany

mähen ['mɛːən] *vt, vi* to mow

Mahl [maːl] (-(e)s, -e) *nt* meal;
m~en (*unreg*) *vt* to grind; **~zeit** *f*
meal ♦ *excl* enjoy your meal

Mahnbrief *m* reminder

Mähne ['mɛːnə] *f* mane

mahnen ['maːnən] *vt* to remind;
(*warnend*) to warn; (*wegen Schuld*)
to demand payment from

Mahnung *f* reminder; admonition,
warning

Mai [maɪ] (-(e)s, -e) *m* May; **~-
glöckchen** *nt* lily of the valley;
~käfer *m* cockchafer

Mailand *nt* Milan

mailändisch *adj* Milanese

Mais [maɪs] (-es, -e) *m* maize, corn
(*US*); **~kolben** *m* corncob; **~mehl**
nt (*KOCH*) corn meal

Majestät [majɛs'tɛːt] *f* majesty;
m~isch *adj* majestic

Major [ma'joːr] (-s, -e) *m* (*MIL*) major; (*AVIAT*) squadron leader

Majoran [majo'raːn] (-s, -e) *m* mar-
joram

makaber [ma'kaːbər] *adj* macabre

Makel ['maːkəl] (-s, -) *m* blemish;
(*moralisch*) stain; **m~los** *adj* immaculate, spotless

mäkeln ['mɛːkəln] *vi* to find fault

Makkaroni [maka'roːni] *pl* macaroni
sg

Makler(in) ['maːklər(ɪn)] (-s, -) *m(f)*
broker

Makrele [ma'kreːlə] *f* mackerel

Makrone [ma'kroːnə] *f* macaroon

Mal [maːl] (-(e)s, -e) *nt* mark, sign;
(*Zeitpunkt*) time; **m~** *adv* times;
(*umg*) *siehe* **einmal** ♦ *suffix*: **-m~**
times

Malaria (-) *f* (*MED*) malaria

malen ['maːlən] *vt, vi* to paint

Maler (-s, -) *m* painter

Male'rei *f* painting

malerisch *adj* picturesque

Malkasten *m* paintbox

Mallorca [ma'lorka] (-s) *nt* Majorca

malnehmen (*unreg*) *vt, vi* to multiply

Malz [malts] (-es) *nt* malt; **~bier** *nt*
(*KOCH*) malt beer; **~bonbon** *nt*
cough drop; **~kaffee** *m* malt coffee

Mama ['mama] (-, -s; *umg*) *f*
mum(my) (*BRIT*), mom(my) (*US*)

Mami ['mami] (-, -s; *umg*) *f*
mum(my) (*BRIT*), mom(my) (*US*)

Mammut ['mamʊt] (-s, -e *od* -s) *nt*
mammoth

man [man] *pron* one, you; **~ sagt, ...**
they *od* people say ...; **wie schreibt
~ das?** how do you write it?, how is
it written?

manch [manç] (*unver*) *pron* many a

manche(r, s) ['mançə(r, s)] *adj*
many a; (*pl: einige*) a number of ♦
pron some

mancherlei adj inv various ♦ pron inv a variety of things

manchmal adv sometimes

Mandant(in) [man'dant(ɪn)] m(f) (JUR) client

Mandarine [manda'riːnə] f mandarin, tangerine

Mandat [man'daːt] (-(e)s, -e) nt mandate

Mandel ['mandəl] (-, -n) f almond; (ANAT) tonsil

Mandelentzündung f (MED) tonsillitis

Manege [ma'neːʒə] f ring, arena

Mangel¹ ['maŋəl] (-, -n) f mangle

Mangel² (-s, ¨) m lack; (Knappheit) shortage; (Fehler) defect, fault; **Mangel an** +dat shortage of; **~erscheinung** f deficiency symptom; **m~haft** adj poor; (fehlerhaft) defective, faulty; **m~n** vi unpers: **es m~t jdm an etw** dat sb lacks sth ♦ vt (Wäsche) to mangle

mangels präp +gen for lack of

Mango (-, -s) f (BOT, KOCH) mango

Manie [ma'niː] f mania

Manier [ma'niːr] (-) f manner; style; (pej) mannerism; **~en** pl (Umgangsformen) manners

manierlich adj well-mannered

Manifest [mani'fɛst] (-es, -e) nt manifesto

Maniküre [mani'kyːrə] f manicure; **m~n** vt to manicure

manipulieren [manipu'liːrən] vt to manipulate

Manko ['maŋko] (-s, -s) nt deficiency; (COMM) deficit

Mann [man] (-(e)s, ¨er) m man; (Ehe~) husband; (NAUT) hand; **seinen ~ stehen** to hold one's own

Männchen ['mɛnçən] nt little man; (Tier) male

Mannequin [manə'kɛ̃ː] (-s, -s) nt fashion model

männlich adj (BIOL) male; (fig, GRAM) masculine

Mannschaft f (SPORT, fig) team; (AVIAT, NAUT) crew; (MIL) other ranks pl

Manöver [ma'nøːvər] (-s, -) nt manoeuvre

manövrieren [manø'vriːrən] vt, vi to manoeuvre

Mansarde [man'zardə] f attic

Manschette [man'ʃɛtə] f cuff; (TECH) collar; sleeve; **~nknopf** m cufflink

Mantel ['mantəl] (-s, ¨) m coat; (TECH) casing, jacket

Manuskript [manu'skrɪpt] (-(e)s, -e) nt manuscript

Mappe ['mapə] f briefcase; (Akten~) folder

Märchen ['mɛːrçən] nt fairy tale; **m~haft** adj fabulous; **~prinz** m Prince Charming

Marder ['mardər] (-s, -) m marten

Margarine [marga'riːnə] f margarine

Margerite [marga'riːtə] f (BOT) marguerite

Maria [ma'riːa] (-) f (REL) Mary

Marienkäfer [ma'riːənkɛːfər] m ladybird

Marine [ma'riːnə] f navy; **m~blau** adj navy-blue

marinieren [mari'niːrən] vt to marinate

Marionette [mario'nɛtə] f puppet

Mark¹ [mark] (-, -) f (Münze) mark

Mark² (-(e)s) nt (Knochen~) marrow; **jdm durch Mark und Bein gehen** to go right through sb

markant [mar'kant] adj striking

Marke ['markə] f mark; (Warensorte) brand; (Fabrikat) make; (Rabatt~, Brief~) stamp; (Essens~) ticket; (aus Metall etc) token, disc

markieren [mar'kiːrən] vt to mark; (umg) to act ♦ vi to act it

Markierung f marking

Markise [mar'kiːzə] f awning

Markstück nt one-mark piece

Markt [markt] (-(e)s, ¨e) m market; **~lücke** f (WIRTS) opening, gap in the market; **~platz** m market place; **m~üblich** adj (Preise, Mieten) standard, usual; **~wert** m (WIRTS) market value; **~wirtschaft** f market economy

Marmelade [marmə'la:də] f jam

Marmor ['marmɔr] (-s, -e) m marble; **m~ieren** [-'ri:rən] vt to marble; **m~n** adj marble

Marokko [ma'rɔko] (-s) nt Morocco

Marone [ma'ro:nə] (-, -n od **Maroni**) f chestnut

Marotte [ma'rɔtə] f fad, quirk

Marsch¹ [marʃ] (-(e)s, ⁺e) m march ♦ excl march!

Marsch² (-, -en) f marsh

Marsch- [marʃ] zW: **~befehl** m marching orders pl; **m~bereit** adj ready to move; **m~ieren** [mar'ʃi:rən] vi to march

Märtyrer(in) ['mɛrtyrər(ɪn)] (-s, -) m(f) martyr

Maria (-) f (REL) Mary

März [mɛrts] (-(e)s, -e) m March

Marzipan [martsi'pa:n] (-s, -e) nt marzipan

Masche ['maʃə] f mesh; (Strick~) stitch; **das ist die neueste ~** that's the latest thing; **~ndraht** m wire mesh; **m~nfest** adj runproof

Maschine [ma'ʃi:nə] f machine; (Motor) engine; (Schreib~) typewriter; **m~ll** [maʃi'nɛl] adj machine(-); mechanical

Maschinen- zW: **~bauer** m mechanical engineer; **~gewehr** nt machine gun; **~pistole** f submachine gun; **~schaden** m mechanical fault; **~schlosser** m fitter; **~schrift** f typescript

maschineschreiben (unreg) vi to type

Maschinist [maʃi'nɪst] m engineer

Maser ['ma:zər] (-, -n) f (von Holz) grain; **~n** pl (MED) measles sg; **~ung** f grain(ing)

Maske ['maskə] f mask; **~nball** m fancy-dress ball; **~rade** [maskə'ra:də] f masquerade

maskieren [mas'ki:rən] vt to mask; (verkleiden) to dress up ♦ vr to disguise o.s.; to dress up

Maskottchen [mas'kɔtçən] nt (lucky) mascot

Maß¹ [ma:s] (-es, -e) nt measure; (Mäßigung) moderation; (Grad) degree, extent

Maß² (-, -e) f litre of beer

Massage [ma'sa:ʒə] f massage

Maßanzug m made-to-measure suit

Maßarbeit f (fig) neat piece of work

Masse ['masə] f mass

Massen- zW: **~artikel** m mass-produced article; **~grab** nt mass grave; **m~haft** adj loads of; **~medien** pl mass media pl; **~veranstaltung** f mass meeting

massenweise adv on a large scale

Masseur [ma'sø:r] m masseur

Masseurin f masseuse

maßgebend adj authoritative

maßhalten (unreg) vi to exercise moderation

massieren [ma'si:rən] vt to massage; (MIL) to mass

massig ['masıç] adj massive; (umg) massive amount of

mäßig ['mɛ:sɪç] adj moderate; **~en** ['mɛ:sɪgən] vt to restrain, to moderate; **M~keit** f moderation

Massiv (-s, -e) nt massif

massiv [ma'si:f] adj solid; (fig) heavy, rough

Maß- zW: **~krug** m tankard; **m~los** adj extreme; **~nahme** f measure, step; **~stab** m rule, measure; (fig) standard; (GEOG) scale; **m~voll** adj moderate

Mast [mast] (-(e)s, -e(n)) m mast; (ELEK) pylon

mästen ['mɛstən] vt to fatten

Material [materi'a:l] (-s, -ien) nt material(s); **~fehler** m material defect; **~ismus** [-'lɪsmus] m materialism; **m~istisch** [-'ɪstɪʃ] adj materialistic

Materie [ma'te:riə] f matter, substance

materiell [materi'ɛl] adj material

Mathematik [matema'ti:k] f mathematics sg; **~er(in)** [mate'ma:tikər(ɪn)] (-s, -) m(f) mathematician

mathematisch [mate'ma:tɪʃ] adj mathematical

Matjeshering ['matjəshɛrɪŋ] m (KOCH) young herring

Matratze [ma'tratsə] f mattress

Matrixdrucker m dot-matrix printer

Matrize [ma'tri:tsə] f matrix; (zum Abziehen) stencil

Matrose [ma'tro:zə] (-n, -n) m sailor

Matsch [matʃ] (-(e)s) m mud; (Schnee~) slush; m~ig adj muddy; slushy

matt [mat] adj weak; (glanzlos) dull; (PHOT) matt; (SCHACH) mate

Matte ['matə] f mat

Mattscheibe f (TV) screen; ~ haben (umg) not to be quite with it

Mauer ['mauər] (-, -n) f wall; m~n vi to build; to lay bricks ♦ vt to build

Maul [maul] (-(e)s, Mäuler) nt mouth; m~en (umg) vi to grumble; ~esel m mule; ~korb m muzzle; ~sperre f lockjaw; ~tasche f (KOCH) pasta envelopes stuffed and used in soup; ~tier nt mule; ~wurf m mole

Maurer ['maurər] (-s, -) m bricklayer

Maus [maus] (-, Mäuse) f (auch COMPUT) mouse

Mause- [mauzə] zW: ~falle f mousetrap; m~n vi to catch mice ♦ vt (umg) to pinch; m~tot adj stone dead

maximal [maksi'ma:l] adj maximum ♦ adv at most

Mayonnaise [majɔ'nɛ:zə] f mayonnaise

Mechan- [me'ça:n] zW: ~ik f mechanics sg; (Getriebe) mechanics pl; ~iker (-s, -) m mechanic, engineer; m~isch adj mechanical; ~ismus [meça'nɪsmus] m mechanism

meckern ['mɛkərn] vi to bleat; (umg) to moan

Medaille [me'daljə] f medal

Medaillon [medal'jõ:] (-s, -s) nt (Schmuck) locket

Medikament [medika'mɛnt] nt medicine

Meditation f meditation

meditieren [medi'ti:rən] vi to meditate

Medizin [medi'tsi:n] (-, -en) f medicine; m~isch adj medical

Meer [me:r] (-(e)s, -e) nt sea; ~enge f straits pl; ~esspiegel m sea level; ~rettich m horseradish; ~schweinchen nt guinea-pig; ~wasser nt sea water

Megaphon [mega'fo:n] (-s, -e) nt megaphone

Mehl [me:l] (-(e)s, -e) nt flour; m~ig adj floury; ~schwitze f (KOCH) roux; ~speise f (KOCH) flummery

mehr [me:r] adj, adv more; ~deutig adj ambiguous; ~ere adj several; ~eres pron several things; ~fach adj multiple; (wiederholt) repeated; M~heit f majority; ~malig adj repeated; ~mals adv repeatedly; ~stimmig adj for several voices; ~stimmig singen to harmonize; M~wertsteuer f value added tax; M~zahl f majority; (GRAM) plural

Mehrzweck- in zW multipurpose

meiden ['maɪdən] (unreg) vt to avoid

Meile ['maɪlə] f mile; ~nstein m milestone; ~nweit adj for miles

mein(e) [main] adj my; ~e(r, s) pron mine

Meineid ['maɪnʔaɪt] m perjury

meinen ['maɪnən] vi to think ♦ vt to think; (sagen) to say; (sagen wollen) to mean; das will ich ~ I should think so

mein- zW: ~erseits adv for my part; ~etwegen adv (für mich) for my sake; (von mir) so on my account; (von mir aus) as far as I'm concerned; I don't care od mind; ~etwillen adv: um ~etwillen for my sake, on my account

Meinung ['maɪnuŋ] f opinion; ganz meine ~ I quite agree; jdm die ~ sagen to give sb a piece of one's mind

Meinungs- zW: ~austausch m exchange of views; ~umfrage f opinion poll; ~**verschiedenheit** f difference of opinion

Meise ['maızə] f tit(mouse)

Meißel ['maısəl] (-s, -) m chisel; **m~n** vt to chisel

meist [maıst] adj most ♦ adv mostly; **am ~en** the most; ~**ens** adv generally, usually

Meister ['maıstər] (-s, -) m master; (SPORT) champion; **m~haft** adj masterly; **m~n** vt (Schwierigkeiten etc) to overcome, conquer; ~**schaft** f mastery; (SPORT) championship; ~**stück** nt masterpiece; ~**werk** nt masterpiece

Melancholie [melaŋko'li:] f melancholy

melancholisch [melaŋ'ko:lıʃ] adj melancholy

Melde- ['meldə] zW: ~**frist** f registration period; **m~n** vt to report ♦ vr to report; (SCH) to put one's hand up; (freiwillig) to volunteer; (auf etw, am Telefon) to answer; **sich m~n bei** to report to; to register with; **sich zu Wort m~n** to ask to speak; ~**pflicht** f obligation to register with the police; ~**stelle** f registration office

Meldung ['meldʊŋ] f announcement; (Bericht) report

meliert [me'li:rt] adj (Haar) greying; (Wolle) flecked

melken ['mɛlkən] (unreg) vt to milk

Melodie [melo'di:] f melody, tune

melodisch [me'lo:dıʃ] adj melodious, tuneful

Melone [me'lo:nə] f melon; (Hut) bowler (hat)

Membran [mem'bra:n] (-, -en) f (TECH) diaphragm

Membrane f (TECH) diaphragm

Memoiren [memo'a:rən] pl memoirs

Menge ['mɛŋə] f quantity; (Menschen~) crowd; (große Anzahl) lot (of); **m~n** vt to mix ♦ vr: **sich m~n in** +akk to meddle with; ~**lehre** f (MATH) set theory; ~**nrabatt** m bulk discount

Mensch [mɛnʃ] (-en, -en) m human

being, man; person ♦ excl hey!; **kein ~** nobody

Menschen- zW: ~**affe** m (ZOOL) ape; ~**feind** m misanthrope; **m~freundlich** adj philanthropical; ~**kenner** m judge of human nature; **m~leer** adj deserted; **m~möglich** adj humanly possible; **m~rechte** pl human rights; **m~unwürdig** adj beneath human dignity; **M~verstand** m: **gesunder M~verstand** common sense

Mensch- zW: ~**heit** f humanity, mankind; **m~lich** adj human; (human) humane; ~**lichkeit** f humanity

Menstruation [menstruatsi'o:n] f menstruation

Mentalität [mentali'te:t] f mentality

Menü [me'ny:] (-s, -s) nt (auch COMPUT) menu

Merk- ['mɛrk] zW: ~**blatt** nt instruction sheet od leaflet; **m~en** vt to notice; **sich dat etw m~en** to remember sth; **m~lich** adj noticeable; ~**mal** nt sign, characteristic; **m~würdig** adj odd

meßbar ['mɛsba:r] adj measurable

Meßbecher m measuring jug

Messe ['mɛsə] f fair; (ECCL) mass; ~**halle** f pavilion at a fair

messen (unreg) vt to measure ♦ vr to compete

Messer ['mɛsər] (-s, -) nt knife; ~**spitze** f knife point; (in Rezept) pinch

Meßstand m stall at a fair

Meßgerät nt measuring device, gauge

Messing ['mɛsıŋ] (-s) nt brass

Metall [me'tal] (-s, -e) nt metal; **m~isch** adj metallic

Meteor [mete'o:r] (-s, -e) nt meteor

Meter ['me:tər] (-s, -) nt od m metre; ~**maß** nt tape measure

Methode [me'to:də] f method

methodisch [me'to:dıʃ] adj methodical

Metropole [metro'po:lə] f metropolis

Metzger ['mɛtsgər] (-s, -) m

butcher; **~ei** [-'raɪ] f butcher's (shop)

Meute ['mɔʏtə] f pack; **~rei** f mutiny; **m~rn** vi to mutiny

miauen [mi'auən] vi to miaow

mich [mɪç] (akk von ich) pron me; myself

Miene ['miːnə] f look, expression

mies [miːs] (umg) adj lousy

Miet- ['miːt] zW: **~auto** nt hired car; **~e** f rent; **zur ~e wohnen** to live in rented accommodation; **m~en** vt to rent; (Auto) to hire; **~er(in)** (-s, -) m(f) tenant; **~shaus** nt tenement, block of (rented) flats; **~vertrag** m lease

Migräne [mi'grɛːnə] f migraine

Mikro- ['mikro] zW: **~fon** [-'foːn] (-s, -e) nt microphone; **~phon** (-s, -e) [-'foːn] nt microphone; **~skop** (-s, -e) [-'skoːp] (-s, -e) nt microscope; **m~skopisch** adj microscopic; **~wellenherd** m microwave (oven)

Milch [mɪlç] f milk; **~glas** nt frosted glass; **m~ig** adj milky; **~kaffee** m white coffee; **~mann** (pl **-männer**) m milkman; **~mixgetränk** nt (KOCH) milkshake; **~pulver** nt powdered milk; **~straße** f Milky Way; **~zahn** m milk tooth

mild [mɪlt] adj mild; (Richter) lenient; (freundlich) kind, charitable; **M~e** [-də] f mildness; leniency; **~ern** vt to mitigate, to soften; (Schmerz) to alleviate; **~ernde Umstände** extenuating circumstances

Milieu [mili'øː] (-s, -s) nt background, environment; **m~geschädigt** adj maladjusted

Mili- [mili] zW: **m~tant** [-'tant] adj militant; **~tär** [-'tɛːr] (-s) nt military, army; **~tärgericht** nt military court; **m~tärisch** [-'tɛːrɪʃ] adj military

Milli- ['mili] zW: **~ardär** [-ar'dɛːr] m multimillionaire; **~arde** [-'ardə] f milliard; billion (bes US); **~meter** m millimetre; **~meterpapier** nt graph paper

Million [mili'oːn] (-, -en) f million; **~är** [-o'nɛːr] m millionaire

Milz [mɪlts] (-, -en) f spleen

Mimik ['miːmɪk] f mime

Mimose [mi'moːzə] f mimosa; (fig) sensitive person

minder ['mɪndər] adj inferior ♦ adv less; **M~heit** f minority; **~jährig** adj minor; **M~jährige(r)** f(m) minor; **~n** vt, vr to decrease, to diminish; **M~ung** f decrease; **~wertig** adj inferior; **M~wertigkeitskomplex** m inferiority complex

Mindest- ['mɪndəst] zW: **~alter** nt minimum age; **~betrag** m minimum amount; **m~e(r, s)** adj least; **zum m~en** at least; **m~ens** adv at least; **~lohn** m minimum wage; **~maß** nt minimum

Mine ['miːnə] f mine; (Bleistift~) lead; (Kugelschreiber~) refill; **~nfeld** nt minefield

Mineral [minɛ'raːl] (-s, -e od -ien) nt mineral; **m~isch** adj mineral; **~wasser** nt mineral water

Miniatur [minia'tuːr] f miniature

Minigolf ['miːnɪɡɔlf] nt miniature golf, crazy golf

minimal [mini'maːl] adj minimal

Minimum ['miːnimʊm] nt minimum

Minirock ['miːnirɔk] m miniskirt

Minister [mi'nɪstər] (-s, -) m minister; **m~iell** [ministeri'ɛl] adj ministerial; **~ium** [minis'teːriʊm] nt ministry; **~präsident** m prime minister

Minus ['miːnʊs] (-, -) nt deficit; **minus** adv minus; **M~zeichen** nt minus sign

Minute [mi'nuːtə] f minute; **~nzeiger** m minute hand

Minze ['mɪntsə] f mint

mir [miːr] (dat von ich) pron (to) me; **~ nichts, dir nichts** just like that

Misch- ['mɪʃ] zW: **~ehe** f mixed marriage; **m~en** vt to mix; **~ling** m half-caste; **~ung** f mixture

miserabel [mizə'raːbəl] (umg) adj (Essen, Film) dreadful

Miß- ['mɪs] zW: **~behagen** nt discomfort, uneasiness; **~bildung** f deformity; **m~'billigen** *vt insep* to disapprove of; **~brauch** *m* abuse; (*falscher Gebrauch*) misuse; **m~'brauchen** *vt insep* to abuse; **jdn zu** *od* **für etw m~brauchen** to use sb for *od* to do sth; **~erfolg** *m* failure; **~fallen** (-s) *nt* displeasure; **m~'fallen** (*unreg*) *vi insep*: **jdm m~fallen** to displease sb; **~geburt** *f* freak; (*fig*) abortion; **~geschick** *nt* misfortune; **m~glücken** [mɪs'glʏkən] *vi insep* to fail; **jdm m~glückt etw** sb does not succeed with sth; **~griff** *m* mistake; **~gunst** *f* envy; **m~günstig** *adj* envious; **m~'handeln** *vt insep* to ill-treat; **~'handlung** *f* ill-treatment

Mission [mɪsi'o:n] *f* mission; **~ar(in)** [mɪsio'na:r(ɪn)] *m(f)* missionary

Miß- *zW*: **~klang** *m* discord; **~kredit** *m* discredit; **m~lingen** [mɪs'lɪŋən] (*unreg*) *vi insep* to fail; **~mut** *m* sullenness; **m~mutig** *adj* sullen; **m~'raten** (*unreg*) *vi insep* to turn out badly ♦ *adj* ill-bred; **~stand** *m* bad state of affairs; abuse; **~stimmung** *f* ill-humour, discord; **m~'trauen** *vi insep* to mistrust; **~trauen** (-s) *nt* distrust, suspicion; **~trauensantrag** *m* (*POL*) motion of no confidence; **m~trauisch** *adj* distrustful, suspicious; **~verhältnis** *nt* disproportion; **~verständnis** *nt* misunderstanding; **m~verstehen** (*unreg*) *vt insep* to misunderstand; **~wirtschaft** *f* mismanagement

Mist [mɪst] (-(e)s) *m* dung; dirt; (*umg*) rubbish

Mistel (-, -n) *f* mistletoe

Misthaufen *m* dungheap

mit [mɪt] *präp +dat* with; (*mittels*) by ♦ *adv* along, too; **~ der Bahn** by train; **~ 10 Jahren** at the age of 10; **wollen Sie ~?** do you want to come along?

Mitarbeit ['mɪt'arbaɪt] *f* cooperation; **m~en** *vi* to cooperate, to collaborate; **~er(in)** *m(f)* collaborator; coworker ♦ *pl* (*Personal*) staff

Mit- *zW*: **~bestimmung** *f* participation in decision-making; **m~bringen** (*unreg*) *vt* to bring along

miteinander [mɪt'aɪ'nandər] *adv* together, with one another

miterleben *vt* to see, to witness

Mitesser ['mɪt'ɛsər] (-s, -) *m* blackhead

mitfahren *vi* to accompany (*auf Reise auch*) to travel with

mitfühlend *adj* sympathetic, compassionate

Mit- *zW*: **m~geben** (*unreg*) *vt* to give; **~gefühl** *nt* sympathy; **m~gehen** (*unreg*) *vi* to go/come along; **m~genommen** *adj* done in, in a bad way; **~gift** *f* dowry

Mitglied ['mɪtgli:t] *nt* member; **~sbeitrag** *m* membership fee; **~schaft** *f* membership

Mit- *zW*: **m~halten** (*unreg*) *vi* to keep up; **m~helfen** (*unreg*) *vi* to help; **~hilfe** *f* help, assistance; **m~hören** *vt* to listen in to; **m~kommen** (*unreg*) *vi* to come along; (*verstehen*) to keep up, to follow; **~läufer** *m* hanger-on; (*POL*) fellow-traveller

Mitleid *nt* sympathy; (*Erbarmen*) compassion; **m~ig** *adj* sympathetic; **m~slos** *adj* pitiless, merciless

Mit- *zW*: **m~machen** *vt* to join in, to take part in; **~mensch** *m* fellow man; **m~nehmen** (*unreg*) *vt* to take along/away; (*anstrengen*) to wear out, to exhaust; **zum ~nehmen** to take away; **m~reden** *vi*: **bei etw m~reden** to have a say in sth; **m~reißen** (*unreg*) *vt* to carry away/along; (*fig*) to thrill, captivate

mitsamt *präp +dat* together with

Mitschuld *f* complicity; **m~ig** *adj*: **m~ig (an** *+dat*) implicated (in); (*an Unfall*) partly responsible (for)

Mit- *zW*: **~schüler(in)** *m(f)* schoolmate; **m~spielen** *vi* to join in, to take part; **~spieler(in)** *m(f)* partner; **~spracherecht** ['mɪtʃpra:xərɛçt] *nt* voice, say

Mittag ['mɪta:k] (-(e)s, -e) *m* midday, lunchtime; **(zu)** ~ **essen** to have lunch; **m~** adv at lunchtime od noon; **~essen** nt lunch, dinner

mittags adv at lunchtime od noon; **M~pause** f lunch break; **M~schlaf** m early afternoon nap, siesta

Mäter(in) ['mɪtɛ:tər(ɪn)] m(f) accomplice

Mitte ['mɪtə] f middle; (POL) centre; **aus unserer ~** from our midst

mitteilen ['mɪttaɪlən] vt: **jdm etw ~** to inform sb of sth, to communicate sth to sb

Mitteilung f communication

Mittel ['mɪtəl] (-s, -) nt means; method; (MATH) average; (MED) medicine; **ein ~ zum Zweck** a means to an end; **~alter** nt Middle Ages; **m~alterlich** adj mediaeval; **~ding** nt cross; **~europa** nt Central Europe; **m~mäßig** adj mediocre, middling; **~mäßigkeit** f mediocrity; **~meer** nt Mediterranean; **~punkt** m centre; **m~stand** m middle class; **~streifen** m central reservation; **~stürmer** m centre-forward; **~weg** m middle course; **~welle** f (RADIO) medium wave

mitten ['mɪtən] adv in the middle; ~ **auf der Straße/in der Nacht** in the middle of the street/night

Mitternacht ['mɪtərnaxt] f midnight

mittlere(r, s) ['mɪtlərə(r, s)] adj middle; (durchschnittlich) medium, average

mittlerweile ['mɪtlər'vaɪlə] adv meanwhile

Mittwoch ['mɪtvɔx] (-(e)s, -e) m Wednesday; **m~s** adv on Wednesdays

mitunter [mɪt'ʊntər] adv occasionally, sometimes

Mit- zW: **m~verantwortlich** adj jointly responsible; **m~wirken** vi: **m~wirken** (bei) to contribute (to); (THEAT) to take part (in); **~wirkung** f contribution; participation

Möbel ['mø:bəl] pl furniture sg; **~wagen** m furniture od removal van

mobil [mo'bi:l] adj mobile; (MIL)

mobilized; **M~iar** [mobili'a:r] (-s, -e) nt furnishings pl; **M~machung** f mobilization; **M~telefon** nt mobile phone

möblieren [mø'bli:rən] vt to furnish; **möbliert wohnen** to live in furnished accommodation

möchte etc vb siehe **mögen**

Mode ['mo:də] f fashion

Modell [mo'dɛl] (-s, -e) nt model; **m~ieren** [-'li:rən] vt to model

Modenschau f fashion show

moderig ['mo:dərɪç] adj (Keller) musty; (Luft) stale

modern [mo'dɛrn] adj modern; (modisch) fashionable; **~isieren** vt to modernize

Mode- zW: **~schau** f fashion show; **~schmuck** m fashion jewellery; **~schöpfer(in)** m(f) fashion designer; **~wort** nt fashionable word, buzz word

modisch ['mo:dɪʃ] adj fashionable

Mofa ['mo:fa] (-s, -s) nt small moped

mogeln ['mo:gəln] (umg) vi to cheat

SCHLÜSSELWORT

mögen ['mø:gən] (pt mochte, pp gemocht od (als Hilfsverb) mögen) vt, vi to like; **magst du/mögen Sie ihn?** do you like him?; **ich möchte ... I would like ..., I'd like ...; er möchte in die Stadt** he'd like to go into town; **ich möchte nicht, daß du ... I wouldn't like you to ...; ich mag nicht mehr** I've had enough

♦ Hilfsverb to want (to); (wollen) to want; **möchtest du etwas essen?** would you like something to eat?; **sie mag nicht bleiben** she doesn't want to stay; **das mag wohl sein** that may well be; **was mag das heißen?** what might that mean?; **Sie möchten zu Hause anrufen** could you please call home?

---

möglich ['mø:klɪç] adj possible; **~erweise** adv possibly; **M~keit** f possibility; **nach M~keit** if possible;

Mohn [moːn] (-(e)s, -e) m (~blume) poppy; (~samen) poppy seed

Möhre [ˈmøːrə] f carrot

Mohrrübe f carrot

mokieren [moˈkiːrən] vr: sich ~ über +akk to make fun of

Mole [ˈmoːlə] f (harbour) mole

Molekül [moleˈkyːl] (-s, -e) nt molecule

Molkerei [mɔlkəˈraɪ] f dairy

Moll [mɔl] (-, -) nt (MUS) minor (key)

mollig adj cosy; (dicklich) plump

Moment [moˈment] (-(e)s, -e) m moment ♦ nt factor; im ~ at the moment; ~ (mal)! just a moment; m~an [-ˈtaːn] adj momentary ♦ adv at the moment

Monarch [moˈnarç] (-en, -en) m monarch; ~ie [monarˈçiː] f monarchy

Monat [ˈmoːnat] (-(e)s, -e) m month; m~elang adv for months; m~lich adj monthly; ~sgehalt nt: das dreizehnte ~sgehalt Christmas bonus (of one month's salary); ~skarte f monthly ticket

Mönch [mœnç] (-(e)s, -e) m monk

Mond [moːnt] (-(e)s, -e) m moon; ~finsternis f eclipse of the moon; m~hell adj moonlit; ~landung f moon landing; ~schein m moonlight; ~sonde f moon probe

Mono- [mono] in zW mono; ~log [-ˈloːk] (-s, -e) m monologue; ~pol [-ˈpoːl] (-s, -e) nt monopoly; m~polisieren [-poliˈziːrən] vt to monopolize; m~ton [-ˈtoːn] adj monotonous; ~tonie [-toˈniː] f monotony

Montag [ˈmoːntaːk] (-(e)s, -e) m Monday

Montage [mɔnˈtaːʒə] f (PHOT etc) montage; (TECH) assembly; (Einbauen) fitting

Monteur [mɔnˈtøːr] m fitter

montieren [mɔnˈtiːrən] vt to assemble

Monument [monuˈment] nt monument; m~al adj monumental

Moor [moːr] (-(e)s, -e) nt moor

Moos [moːs] (-es, -e) nt moss

Moped [ˈmoːpet] (-s, -s) nt moped

Mops [mɔps] (-es, -e) m pug

Moral [moˈraːl] (-, -en) f morality; (einer Geschichte) moral; m~isch adj moral

Moräne [moˈrɛːnə] f moraine

Morast [moˈrast] (-(e)s, -e) m morass, mire; m~ig adj boggy

Mord [mɔrt] (-(e)s, -e) m murder; ~anschlag m murder attempt

Mörder(in) [ˈmœrdər(ɪn)] (-s, -) m(f) murderer/murderess

mörderisch adj (fig: schrecklich) terrible, dreadful ♦ adv (umg: entsetzlich) terribly, dreadfully

Mord- zW: ~kommission f murder squad; ~sglück (umg) nt amazing luck; m~smäßig (umg) adj terrific, enormous; ~verdacht m suspicion of murder; ~waffe f murder weapon

morgen [ˈmɔrgən] adv tomorrow; M~ (-s, -) m morning; ~ früh tomorrow morning; M~mantel m dressing gown; M~rock m dressing gown; M~röte f dawn; ~s adv in the morning

morgig [ˈmɔrgɪç] adj tomorrow's; der ~e Tag tomorrow

Morphium [ˈmɔrfiʊm] nt morphine

morsch [mɔrʃ] adj rotten

Morsealphabet [ˈmɔrzə-] nt Morse code

morsen vi to send a message by morse code

Mörtel [ˈmœrtəl] (-s, -) m mortar

Mosaik [mozaˈiːk] (-s, -en od -e) nt mosaic

Moschee [mɔˈʃeː] (-, -n) f mosque

Moskito [mɔsˈkiːto] (-s, -s) m mosquito

Most [mɔst] (-(e)s, -e) m (unfermented) fruit juice; (Apfelwein) cider

Motel [moˈtel] (-s, -s) nt motel

Motiv [moˈtiːf] (-s, -e) nt motive; (MUS) theme; ~ation f motivation; m~ieren [motiˈviːrən] vt to motivate

Motor [ˈmoːtɔr, pl moˈtoːrən] (-s,

-en) m engine; (bes ELEK) motor;
~boot nt motorboat; **~haube** f
(von Auto) bonnet (BRIT), hood
(US); **m~isieren** [motori'zi:rən] vt to
motorize; **~öl** nt engine oil; **~rad** nt
motorcycle; **~schaden** m engine
trouble od failure
Motte ['mɔtə] f moth; **~nkugel** f
mothball(s)
Motto ['mɔto] (-s, -s) nt motto
Möwe ['mø:və] f seagull
Mücke ['mʏkə] f midge, gnat;
~nstich m midge od gnat bite
müde ['my:də] adj tired
Müdigkeit ['my:dɪçkaɪt] f tiredness
Muff [mʊf] (-(e)s, -e) m (Hand-
wärmer) muff
Muffel (-s, -; umg) m killjoy, sour-
puss
muffig adj (Luft) musty
Mühe ['my:ə] f trouble, pains pl; **mit
Müh und Not** with great difficulty;
sich dat **~ geben** to go to a lot of
trouble; **m~los** adj without trouble,
easy; **m~voll** adj laborious, arduous
Mühle ['my:lə] f mill; (Kaffee~)
grinder
Müh- zW: **~sal** (-, -e) f, tribulation;
m~sam adj arduous, troublesome;
m~selig adj arduous, laborious
Mulde ['mʊldə] f hollow, depression
Mull [mʊl] (-(e)s, -e) m thin muslin;
~binde f gauze bandage
Müll [mʏl] (-(e)s) m refuse; **~ab-
fuhr** f rubbish disposal; (Leute) dust-
men pl; **~abladeplatz** m rubbish
dump; **~eimer** m dustbin, garbage
can (US); **~haufen** m rubbish heap;
~schlucker (-s, -) m garbage disposal unit; **~tonne** f dustbin; **~verbren-
nungsanlage** f incinerator
mulmig ['mʊlmɪç] adj rotten; (umg)
dodgy; **jdm ist ~ sb** feels funny
multiplizieren [mʊltipli'tsi:rən] vt to
multiply
Mumie ['mu:miə] f mummy
Mumm [mʊm] (-s; umg) m gumption,
nerve
Mumps [mʊmps] (-) m od f (MED)
mumps

München ['mʏnçən] (-s) nt Munich
Mund [mʊnt, pl 'mʏndər] (-(e)s,
-er) m mouth; **~art** f dialect
Mündel ['mʏndəl] (-s, -) nt ward
münden ['mʏndən] vi: **~ in** +akk to
flow into
Mund- zW: **m~faul** adj taciturn;
~geruch m bad breath; **~harmoni-
ka** f mouth organ
mündig ['mʏndɪç] adj of age;
M~keit f majority
mündlich ['mʏntlɪç] adj oral
Mundstück nt mouthpiece; (Zigar-
etten~) tip
Mündung ['mʏndʊŋ] f (von Fluß)
mouth; (Gewehr) muzzle
Mund- zW: **~wasser** nt mouthwash;
~werk nt: **ein großes ~werk haben** to have a big mouth; **~winkel**
m corner of the mouth
Munition [munitsi'o:n] f ammunition; **~slager** nt ammunition dump
munkeln ['mʊŋkəln] vi to whisper,
to mutter
Münster ['mʏnstər] (-s, -) nt minster
munter ['mʊntər] adj lively
Münze ['mʏntsə] f coin; **m~n** vt to
coin, to mint; **auf jdn gemünzt sein**
to be aimed at sb
Münzfernsehen nt pay television
Münzfernsprecher ['mʏntsfern-
ʃprɛçər] m callbox (BRIT), pay
phone
mürb(e) ['mʏrb(ə)] adj (Gestein)
crumbly; (Holz) rotten; (Gebäck)
crisp; **jdn ~ machen** to wear sb
down; **M~teig** ['mʏrbtaɪç] m short-
crust pastry
murmeln ['mʊrməln] vt, vi to murmur, to mutter
Murmeltier ['mʊrməlti:r] nt marmot
murren ['mʊrən] vi to grumble, to
grouse
mürrisch ['mʏrɪʃ] adj sullen
Mus [mu:s] (-es, -e) nt purée
Muschel ['mʊʃəl] (-, -n) f mussel;
(~schale) shell; (Telefon~) receiver
Muse ['mu:zə] f muse
Museum [mu'ze:ʊm] (-s, Museen)
nt museum

Musik [mu'zi:k] f music; (Kapelle) band; **m~alisch** adj musical; **~ant(in)** (-en, -en) m(f) musician; **~box** f jukebox; **~er** (-s, -) m musician; **~hochschule** f college of music; **~instrument** nt musical instrument

musisch adj (Mensch) artistic

musizieren [muzi'tsi:rən] vi to make music

Muskat [mos'ka:t] (-(e)s, -e) m nutmeg

Muskel ['moskəl] (-s, -n) m muscle

Muskulatur [moskula'tu:r] f muscular system

muskulös [mosku'lø:s] adj muscular

Müsli ['my:sli] (-s, -) nt (KOCH) muesli

Muß [mos] (-) nt necessity, must

Muße ['mu:sə] (-) f leisure

SCHLÜSSELWORT

müssen ['mysən] (pt mußte, pp gemußt od (als Hilfsverb) müssen) vi **1** (Zwang) must (nur im Präsens); to have to; **ich muß es tun** I must do it, I have to do it; **ich mußte es tun** I had to do it; **er muß es nicht tun** he doesn't have to do it; **muß ich?** must I?; **wann müßt ihr zur Schule?** when do you have to go to school?; **er hat gehen müssen** he (has) had to go; **muß das sein?** is that really necessary?; **ich muß mal** (umg) I need the toilet **2** (sollen): **das mußt du nicht tun!** you oughtn't to od shouldn't do that!; **Sie hätten ihn fragen müssen** you should have asked him

3: **es muß geregnet haben** it must have rained; **es muß nicht wahr sein** it needn't be true

---

müßig ['my:sɪç] adj idle

Muster ['mostər] (-s, -) nt model; (Dessin) pattern; (Probe) sample; **m~gültig** adj exemplary; **m~n** vt (Tapete) to pattern; (fig, MIL) to examine; (Truppen) to inspect; **~ung** f (von Stoff) pattern; (MIL) inspection

Mut [mu:t] m courage; **nur ~!** cheer up!; **jdm ~ machen** to encourage sb; **m~ig** adj courageous; **m~los** adj discouraged, despondent

mutmaßlich ['mu:tma:slɪç] adj presumed ♦ adv probably

Mutprobe f test or trial of courage

Mutter¹ ['motər] (-, ¨) f mother

Mutter² (-, Muttern) f (Schrauben~) nut

mütterlich ['mytərlɪç] adj motherly; **~erseits** adv on the mother's side

Mutter- zW: **~liebe** f motherly love; **~mal** nt birthmark; **~milch** f mother's milk; **~schaft** f motherhood, maternity; **~schutz** m maternity regulations; **'m~'seelena'llein** adj all alone; **~sprache** f native language; **~tag** m Mother's Day

Mutti ['moti] (-, -s) f mum(my) (BRIT), mom(my) (US)

mutwillig ['mu:tvɪlɪç] adj malicious, deliberate

Mütze ['mytsə] f cap

MwSt abk (= Mehrwertsteuer) VAT

mysteriös [mysteri'ø:s] adj mysterious

Mythos ['my:tɔs] (-, Mythen) m myth

N

na [na] excl well!; **~ gut** okay then

Nabel ['na:bəl] (-s, -) m navel; **~schnur** f umbilical cord

---

SCHLÜSSELWORT

nach [na:x] präp +dat **1** (örtlich) to; **nach Berlin** to Berlin; **nach links/rechts** to the left/right; **nach oben/hinten** up/back

2 (zeitlich) after; **einer nach dem anderen** one after the other; **nach Ihnen!** after you!; **zehn (Minuten) nach drei** ten (minutes) past three

3 (gemäß) according to; **nach dem Gesetz** according to the law; **dem Namen nach** judging by his/her name; **nach allem, was ich weiß**

as far as I know
♦ adv: **ihm nach!** after him!; **nach und nach** gradually, little by little; **nach wie vor** still

nachahmen ['naːxˌʔaːmən] vt to imitate

Nachbar(in) ['naxbaːr(ɪn)] (-s, -e) m(f) neighbour; ~**haus** nt: **im** ~**haus** next door; **n~lich** adj neighbourly; ~**schaft** f neighbourhood; ~**staat** m neighbouring state

nach- zW: ~**bestellen** vt: **50 Stück** ~**bestellen** to order another 50; **N~bestellung** f (COMM) repeat order; **N~bildung** f imitation, copy; ~**blicken** vi to gaze after; ~**datieren** vt to postdate

nachdem [naːx'deːm] konj after; (weil) since; **je ~ (ob)** it depends (whether)

nach- zW: ~**denken** (unreg) vi to think about; **N~denken** (-s) nt reflection, meditation; ~**denklich** adj thoughtful, pensive

Nachdruck ['naːxdrʊk] m emphasis; (TYP) reprint, reproduction

nachdrücklich ['naːxdrʏklɪç] adj emphatic

nacheinander [naːx'ʔaɪˈnandər] adv one after the other

nachempfinden ['naːx'ʔɛmpfɪndən] (unreg) vt: **jdm etw ~** to feel sth with sb

Nacherzählung ['naːx'ɛrtsɛːluŋ] f reproduction (of a story)

Nachfahr ['naːxfaːr] (-s, -en) m descendant

Nachfolge ['naːxfɔlgə] f succession; **n~n** vi +dat to follow; ~**r(in)** (-s, -) m(f) successor

nachforschen vt, vi to investigate

Nachforschung f investigation

Nachfrage ['naːxfraːgə] f inquiry; (COMM) demand; **n~n** vi to inquire

nach- zW: ~**fühlen** vt; ~**füllen** vt to refill; ~**geben** (unreg) vi to give way, to yield; **N~gebühr** f (POST) excess postage

nachgehen ['naːxgeːən] (unreg) vi

(+dat) to follow; (erforschen) to inquire (into); (Uhr) to be slow

Nachgeschmack ['naːxgəʃmak] m aftertaste

nachgiebig ['naːxgiːbɪç] adj soft, accommodating; **N~keit** f softness

nachhaltig ['naːxhaltɪç] adj lasting; (Widerstand) persistent

nachhelfen ['naːxhɛlfən] (unreg) vi +dat to assist (jdm sb), to help

nachher [naːx'heːr] adv afterwards

Nachhilfeunterricht ['naːxhɪlfəʊntərɪçt] m extra tuition

nachholen ['naːxhoːlən] vt to catch up with; (Versäumtes) to make up for

Nachkomme ['naːxkɔmə] (-, -n) m descendant

nachkommen (unreg) vi to follow; (einer Verpflichtung) to fulfil; **N~schaft** f descendants pl

Nachkriegszeit ['naːxkriːkstsaɪt] f postwar period

Nach- zW: ~**laß** (-lasses, -lässe) m (COMM) discount, rebate; (Erbe) estate; ~**lassen** (unreg) vt (Strafe) to remit; (Summe) to take off; (Schulden) to cancel ♦ vi to decrease, to ease off; (Sturm) to die down, to ease off; (schlechter werden) to deteriorate; **er hat n~gelassen** he has got worse; **n~lässig** adj negligent, careless

nachlaufen ['naːxlaʊfən] (unreg) vi +dat to run after, to chase

nachlösen ['naːxløːzən] vi (Zuschlag) to pay on the train, pay at the other end; (zur Weiterfahrt) to pay the supplement

nachmachen ['naːxmaxən] vt to imitate (jdm etw sth from sb), to copy; (fälschen) to counterfeit

Nachmittag ['naːxmɪtaːk] m afternoon; **am ~** in the afternoon; **n~s** adv in the afternoon

Nach- zW: ~**nahme** f cash on delivery; **per ~nahme** C.O.D.; ~**name** m surname; ~**porto** nt excess postage

nachprüfen ['naːxpryːfən] vt to

check, to verify

nachrechnen ['naːxrɛçnən] *vt* to check

nachreichen ['naːxraɪçən] *vt* (*Unterlagen*) to hand in later

Nachricht ['naːxrɪçt] (-, -en) *f* (piece of) news; (*Mitteilung*) message; ~**en** *pl* (*Neuigkeiten*) news; ~**enagentur** *f* news agency; ~**endienst** *m* (MIL) intelligence service; ~**ensprecher(in)** *m(f)* newsreader; ~**entechnik** *f* telecommunications *sg*

Nachruf ['naːxruːf] *m* obituary

nachsagen ['naːxzaːgən] *vt* to repeat; **jdm etw** ~ to say sth of sb

nachschicken ['naːxʃɪkən] *vt* to forward

nachschlagen ['naːxʃlaːgən] (*unreg*) *vt* to look up

Nachschlagewerk *nt* reference book

Nachschlüssel *m* duplicat key

Nachschub *m* supplies *pl*; (*Truppen*) reinforcements *pl*

nachsehen ['naːxzeːən] (*unreg*) *vt* (*prüfen*) to check ♦ *vi* (*erforschen*) to look and see; **jdm etw** ~ to forgive sb sth; **das N**~ **haben** to come off worst

nachsenden ['naːxzɛndən] (*unreg*) *vt* to send on, to forward

nachsichtig *adj* indulgent, lenient

nachsitzen ['naːxzɪtsən] (*unreg*) *vi*: ~ (**müssen**) (SCH) to be kept in

Nachspeise ['naːxʃpaɪzə] *f* dessert, sweet, pudding

Nachspiel ['naːxʃpiːl] *nt* epilogue; (*fig*) sequel

nachsprechen ['naːxʃprɛçən] (*unreg*) *vt*: (**jdm**) ~ to repeat (after sb)

nächst [nɛːçst] *präp +dat* (*räumlich*) next to; (*außer*) apart from; ~**beste (r, s)** *adj* first that comes along; (*zweitbeste*) next best; **N**~**e(r)** *mf* neighbour; ~**e(r, s)** *adj* next; (*nächstgelegen*) nearest

nachstellen *vt* (TECH: *neu einstellen*) to adjust

nächst- *zW*: **N**~**enliebe** *f* love for

one's fellow men; ~**ens** *adv* shortly, soon; ~**liegend** *adj* nearest; (*fig*) obvious; ~**möglich** *adj* next possible

nachsuchen ['naːxzuːxən] *vi*: **um etw** ~ to ask *od* apply for sth

Nacht [naxt] (-, -e) *f* night; ~**dienst** *m* nightduty

Nachteil ['naːxtaɪl] *m* disadvantage; ~**ig** *adj* disadvantageous

Nachthemd *nt* (*Herren*~) nightshirt; (*Damen*~) nightdress

Nachtigall ['naxtɪgal] (-, -en) *f* nightingale

Nachtisch ['naːxtɪʃ] *m* = **Nachspeise**

Nachtleben *nt* nightlife

nächtlich ['nɛçtlɪç] *adj* nightly

Nachtlokal *nt* night club

Nach- *zW*: ~**trag** (-(e)s, -träge) *m* supplement; ~**tragen** (*unreg*) *vt* to carry; (*zufügen*) to add; **jdm etw** ~**tragen** to hold sth against sb; **n**~**träglich** *adj* later, subsequent; additional ♦ *adv* later, subsequently; additionally; **n**~**trauern** *vi*: **jdm/etw n**~**trauern** to mourn the loss of sth/sth

Nacht- *zW*: **n**~**s** *adv* at *od* by night; ~**schicht** *f* nightshift; ~**schwester** *f* night nurse; **n**~**süber** *adv* during the night; ~**tarif** *m* off-peak tariff; ~**tisch** *m* bedside table; ~**wächter** *m* night watchman

Nach- *zW*: ~**untersuchung** *f* checkup; **n**~**wachsen** (*unreg*) *vi* to grow again; ~**wahl** *f* (POL) by-election

Nachweis ['naːxvaɪs] (-es, -e) *m* proof; **n**~**bar** *adj* provable, demonstrable; ~**en** (*unreg*) *vt* to prove; **jdm etw n**~**en** to point sth out to sb; **n**~**lich** *adj* evident, demonstrable

nach- *zW*: ~**wirken** *vi* to have aftereffects; **N**~**wirkung** *f* after-effect; **N**~**wort** *nt* epilogue; **N**~**wuchs** *m* offspring; (*beruflich etc*) new recruits *pl*; **n**~**zahlen** *vt*, *vi* to pay extra; **N**~**zahlung** *f* additional payment; (*zurückdatiert*) back pay; ~**ziehen** (*unreg*) *vt* (*hinter sich her-*

ziehen: Bein) to drag; **N~zügler** (-s, -) *m* straggler
Nacken ['nakən] (-s, -) *m* nape of the neck
nackt [nakt] *adj* naked; (*Tatsachen*) plain, bare; **N~heit** *f* nakedness
Nadel ['na:dəl] (-, -n) *f* needle; (*Steck~*) pin; **~öhr** *nt* eye of a needle; **~wald** *m* coniferous forest
Nagel ['na:gəl] (-s, ⸚) *m* nail; **~bürste** *f* nailbrush; **~feile** *f* nailfile; **~lack** *m* nail varnish *od* polish (*BRIT*); **n~n** *vt, vi* to nail; **n~neu** *adj* brand-new; **~schere** *f* nail scissors *pl*
nagen ['na:gən] *vt, vi* to gnaw
Nagetier ['na:gəti:r] *nt* rodent
nah(e) ['na:(ə)] *adj* (*räumlich*) near(by); (*Verwandte*) near; (*Freunde*) close; (*zeitlich*) near, close ♦ *adv* near(by); near, close; (*verwandt*) closely ♦ *präp +dat* near (to), close to; **der Nahe Osten** the Near East; **Nahaufnahme** *f* close-up
Nähe ['nɛ:ə] (-) *f* nearness, proximity; (*Umgebung*) vicinity; **in der ~** close by; at hand; **aus der ~** from close to
nahe- *zW*: **~bei** *adv* nearby; **~gehen** (*unreg*) *vi +dat* to grieve; **~kommen** (*unreg*) *vi (+dat)* to get close (to); **~legen** *vt*: **jdm etw ~legen** to suggest sth to sb; **~liegen** (*unreg*) *vi* to be obvious; **~liegend** *adj* obvious; **~n** *vi, vr* to approach, to draw near
nähen ['nɛ:ən] *vt, vi* to sew
näher *adj, adv* nearer; (*Erklärung, Erkundigung*) more detailed; **N~e(s)** *nt* details *pl*, particulars *pl*
Näherei *f* sewing, needlework
näherkommen (*unreg*) *vi, vr* to get closer
nähern *vr* to approach
nahe- *zW*: **~stehen** (*unreg*) *vi (+dat)* to be close (to); **einer Sache ~stehen** to sympathize with sth; **~stehend** *adj* close; **~treten** (*unreg*) *vi*: **jdm (zu) ~treten** to offend sb; **~zu** *adv* nearly
Nähgarn *nt* thread
Nahkampf *m* hand-to-hand fighting
Nähkasten *m* sewing basket, workbox
nahm *etc* [na:m] *vb siehe* **nehmen**
Nähmaschine *f* sewing machine
Nähnadel *f* needle
nähren ['nɛ:rən] *vt* to feed ♦ *vr* (*Person*) to feed o.s.; (*Tier*) to feed
nahrhaft ['na:rhaft] *adj* nourishing, nutritious
Nahrung ['na:rʊŋ] *f* food; (*fig auch*) sustenance
Nahrungs- *zW*: **~mittel** *nt* foodstuffs *pl*; **~mittelindustrie** *f* food industry; **~suche** *f* search for food
Nährwert *m* nutritional value
Naht [na:t] (-, ⸚e) *f* seam; (*MED*) suture; (*TECH*) join; **n~los** *adj* seamless; **n~los ineinander übergehen** to follow without a gap
Nah- *zW*: **~verkehr** *m* local traffic; **~verkehrszug** *m* local train; **~ziel** *nt* immediate objective
Name ['na:mə] (-ns, -n) *m* name; **im ~n von** on behalf of; **n~ns** *adv* by the name of; **~nstag** *m* name day, saint's day; **n~ntlich** *adj* by name ♦ *adv* particularly, especially
namhaft ['na:mhaft] *adj* (*berühmt*) famed, renowned; (*beträchtlich*) considerable; **~ machen** to name
nämlich ['nɛ:mlɪç] *adv* that is to say, namely; (*denn*) since
nannte *etc* ['nantə] *vb siehe* **nennen**
nanu [na'nu:] *excl* well, well!
Napf [napf] (-(e)s, ⸚e) *m* bowl, dish
Narbe ['narbə] *f* scar
narbig ['narbɪç] *adj* scarred
Narkose [nar'ko:ze] *f* anaesthetic
Narr [nar] (-en, -en) *m* fool; **n~en** *vt* to fool
Närrin ['nɛrɪn] *f* fool
närrisch *adj* foolish, crazy
Narzisse [nar'tsɪsə] *f* narcissus; daffodil
naschen ['naʃən] *vt, vi* to nibble; (*heimlich kosten*) to pinch a bit
naschhaft *adj* sweet-toothed
Nase ['na:zə] *f* nose

Nasen- zW: **~bluten** (-s) nt nosebleed; **~loch** nt nostril; **~tropfen** pl nose drops

naseweis adj pert, cheeky; (neugierig) nosey

Nashorn ['nasˌhɔrn] nt rhinoceros

naß [nas] adj wet

Nässe ['nɛsə] (-) f wetness; **n~n** vt to wet

naßkalt adj wet and cold

Naßrasur f wet shave

Nation [natsiˈoːn] f nation

national [natsioˈnaːl] adj national; **N~feiertag** m national holiday; **N~hymne** f national anthem; **~isieren** [-ziːrən] vt to nationalize; **N~i'sierung** f nationalization; **N~ismus** [-'lɪsmʊs] m nationalism; **~istisch** [-'lɪstɪʃ] adj nationalistic; **N~i'tät** f nationality; **N~mannschaft** f national team; **N~sozialismus** m national socialism

Natron ['naːtrɔn] (-s) nt soda

Natter ['natər] (-, -n) f adder

Natur [naˈtuːr] f nature; (körperlich) constitution; **~ell** [natuˈrɛl] (-s, -e) nt disposition; **~erscheinung** f natural phenomenon od event; **n~farben** adj natural coloured; **n~gemäß** adj natural; **~gesetz** nt law of nature; **n~getreu** adj true to life; **~katastrophe** f natural disaster

natürlich [naˈtyːrlɪç] adj natural ♦ adv naturally; ja, ~! yes, of course; **N~keit** f naturalness

Natur- zW: **~park** m = national park; **~produkt** nt natural product; **n~rein** adj natural, pure; **~schutzgebiet** nt nature reserve; **~wissenschaft** f natural science; **~wissenschaftler(in)** m(f) scientist; **~zustand** m natural state

nautisch ['nautɪʃ] adj nautical

Nazi ['naːtsi] (-s, -s) m Nazi

NB abk (= nota bene) nb

n.Chr. abk (= nach Christus) A.D.

Nebel ['neːbəl] (-s, -) m fog, mist; **n~ig** adj foggy, misty; **~scheinwerfer** m foglamp

neben ['neːbən] präp (+akk od dat) next to; (+dat: ausgenommen) besides; **~an** [neːbənˈʔan] adv next door; **N~anschluß** m (TEL) extension; **N~ausgang** m side exit; **~bei** [neːbənˈbai] adv at the same time; (außerdem) additionally; (beiläufig) incidentally; **N~beruf** m second job; **N~beschäftigung** f second job; **N~buhler(in)** m(f) rival; **~einander** [neːbənˈʔaiˈnandər] adv side by side; **~einanderlegen** vt to put next to each other; **N~eingang** m side entrance; **N~erscheinung** f side effect; **N~fach** nt subsidiary subject; **N~fluß** m tributary; **N~gebäude** nt annexe; **N~geräusch** nt (RADIO) atmospherics pl, interference; **~her** [neːbənˈheːr] adv (zusätzlich) besides; (gleichzeitig) at the same time; (daneben) alongside; **~herfahren** (unreg) vi to drive alongside; **N~kosten** pl extra charges, extras; **N~produkt** nt by-product; **N~sache** f trifle, side issue; **~sächlich** adj minor, peripheral; **N~saison** f low season; **N~straße** f side street; **N~verdienst** m secondary income; **N~zimmer** nt adjoining room

neblig ['neːblɪç] adj foggy, misty

Necessaire [nesɛˈsɛːr] (-s, -s) nt (Näh-) needlework box; (Nagel-) manicure case

necken ['nɛkən] vt to tease

Neckerei [nɛkəˈrai] f teasing

Neffe ['nɛfə] (-n, -n) m nephew

negativ [negaˈtiːf] adj negative; **N~** (-s, -e) nt (PHOT) negative

Neger ['neːgər] (-s, -) m negro; **~in** f negress

nehmen ['neːmən] (unreg) vt to take; jdn zu sich ~ to take sb in; sich ernst ~ to take o.s. seriously; nimm dir doch bitte please help yourself

Neid [nait] (-(e)s) m envy; **~er** (-s, -) m envier; **n~isch** ['naidɪʃ] adj envious, jealous

neigen ['naigən] vt to incline, to

upper jaw; ~**körper** m upper part of body; ~**leitung** f direction; (ELEK) overhead cable; ~**licht** nt skylight; ~**lippe** f upper lip; ~**schenkel** m thigh; ~**schicht** f upper classes pl; ~**schule** f grammar school (BRIT), high school (US); ~**schwester** f (MED) matron

Oberst ['o:bərst] (-en od -s, -en od -e) m colonel; **o~e(r, s)** adj very top, topmost

Ober- zW: ~**stufe** f upper school; ~**teil** nt upper part; ~**weite** f bust/chest measurement

obgleich [ɔp'glaiç] konj although

Obhut ['ɔphu:t] (-) f care, protection; **in jds ~ sein** to be in sb's care

obig ['o:biç] adj above

Objekt [ɔp'jɛkt] (-(e)s, -e) nt object; ~**iv** [-'ti:f] (-s, -e) nt lens; **o~iv** adj objective; ~**ivität** f objectivity

Oblate [o'bla:tə] f (Gebäck) wafer; (ECCL) host

obligatorisch [ɔbliga'to:rɪʃ] adj compulsory, obligatory

Oboe [o'bo:ə] f oboe

Obrigkeit ['o:brɪçkait] f (Behörden) authorities pl, administration; (Regierung) government

obschon [ɔp'ʃo:n] konj although

Observatorium [ɔpzɛrva'to:rium] nt observatory

obskur [ɔps'ku:r] adj obscure; (verdächtig) dubious

Obst [o:pst] (-(e)s) nt fruit; ~**baum** m fruit tree; ~**garten** m orchard; ~**händler** m fruiterer, fruit merchant; ~**kuchen** m fruit flan, fruit tart; ~**salat** m (KOCH) fruit salad

obszön [ɔps'tsø:n] adj obscene; **O~ität** f obscenity

obwohl [ɔp'vo:l] konj although

Ochse ['ɔksə] (-n, -n) m ox; **o~n** (umg) vt, vi to cram, to swot (BRIT); ~**nschwanzsuppe** f oxtail soup; ~**nzunge** f oxtongue

öd(e) ['ø:d(ə)] adj (Land) waste, barren; (fig) dull; **Öde** f desert, waste(land); (fig) tedium

oder ['o:dər] konj or; **das stimmt**

~**?** that's right, isn't it?

Ofen ['o:fən] (-s, ^) m oven; (Heiz~) fire, heater; (Kohlen~) stove; (Hoch~) furnace; (Herd) cooker, stove; ~**rohr** nt stovepipe

offen ['ɔfən] adj open; (aufrichtig) frank; (Stelle) vacant; ~ **gesagt** to be honest; ~**bar** adj obvious; ~**baren** [ɔfən'ba:rən] vt to reveal, to manifest; **O~barung** f (REL) revelation; ~**bleiben** (unreg) vi (Fenster) to stay open; (Frage, Entscheidung) to remain open; ~**halten** (unreg) vt to keep open; **O~heit** f candour, frankness; ~**herzig** adj candid, frank; (Kleid) revealing; ~**kundig** adj well-known; (klar) evident; ~**lassen** (unreg) vt to leave open; ~**sichtlich** adj evident, obvious

offensiv [ɔfɛn'zi:f] adj offensive; **O~e** [-'zi:və] f offensive

offenstehen (unreg) vi to be open; (Rechnung) to be unpaid; **es steht Ihnen offen, es zu tun** you are at liberty to do it

öffentlich ['œfəntlɪç] adj public; **Ö~keit** f (Leute) public; (einer Versammlung etc) public nature; **in aller Ö~keit** in public; **an die Ö~keit treten** to reach the public ear

offiziell [ɔfitsi'ɛl] adj official

Offizier [ɔfi'tsi:r] (-s, -e) m officer; ~**skasino** nt officers' mess

öffnen ['œfnən] vt, vr to open; **jdm die Tür ~** to open the door for sb

Öffner ['œfnər] (-s, -) m opener

Öffnung ['œfnuŋ] f opening; ~**szeiten** pl opening times

oft [ɔft] adv often

öfter ['œftər] adv more often od frequently; ~**s** adv often, frequently

oh [o:] excl oh; ~ **je!** oh dear

OHG [o:ha:'ge:] abk (= Offene Handelsgesellschaft) general partnership

ohne ['o:nə] präp +akk without ♦ konj without; **das ist nicht ~** (umg) it's not bad; ~ **weiteres** without a second thought; (sofort) immediately; ~ **zu fragen** without asking;

~ daß er es wußte without him knowing it; ~**dies** [oːnə'diːs] *adv* anyway; ~**einander** [oːnə'ar'nandər] *adv* without each other; ~**gleichen** [oːnə'glaiçən] *adj* unsurpassed, without equal; ~**hin** [oːnə'hɪn] *adv* anyway, in any case

Ohnmacht ['oːnmaxt] *f* faint; (*fig*) impotence; **in** ~ **fallen** to faint

ohnmächtig ['oːnmɛçtɪç] *adj* in a faint, unconscious; (*fig*) weak, impotent; **sie ist** ~ she has fainted

Ohr [oːr] (-(e)s, -en) *nt* ear; (*Gehör*) hearing

Öhr [øːr] (-(e)s, -e) *nt* eye

Ohren- *zW*: ~**arzt** *m* ear specialist; o~**betäubend** *adj* deafening; ~**schmalz** *nt* earwax; ~**schmerzen** *pl* earache *sg*; ~**schützer** (-s, -) *m* earmuff

Ohr- *zW*: ~**feige** *f* slap on the face; box on the ears; o~**feigen** *vt*: **jdn** o~**feigen** to slap sb's face; **to box sb's ears;** ~**läppchen** *nt* ear lobe; ~**ring** *m* earring; ~**wurm** *m* earwig; (*MUS*) catchy tune

ökologisch [øko'loːgɪʃ] *adj* ecological

ökonomisch [øko'noːmɪʃ] *adj* economical

Oktan [ɔk'taːn] (-s, -e) *nt* (*bei Benzin*) octane

Oktave [ɔk'taːvə] *f* octave

Oktober [ɔk'toːbər] (-s, -) *m* October

ökumenisch [øku'meːnɪʃ] *adj* ecumenical

Öl [øːl] (-(e)s, -e) *nt* oil; ~**baum** *m* olive tree; ö~**en** *vt* to oil; (*TECH*) to lubricate; ~**farbe** *f* oil paint; ~**feld** *nt* oilfield; ~**film** *m* film of oil; ~**heizung** *f* oil-fired central heating; ö~**ig** *adj* oily; ~**industrie** *f* oil industry

oliv [o'liːf] *adj* olive-green; **O~e** *f* olive

Öl- *zW*: ~**meßstab** *m* dipstick; ~**sardine** *f* sardine; ~**standanzeiger** *m* (*AUT*) oil gauge; ~**tanker** *m* oil tanker; ~**ung** *f* lubrication; oiling;

(*ECCL*) anointment; **die Letzte** ~**ung** Extreme Unction; ~**wechsel** *m* oil change; ~**zeug** *nt* oilskins *pl*

Olymp- [o'lymp] *zW*: ~**iade** [olympi'aːdə] *f* Olympic Games *pl*; ~**iasieger(in)** [-iaziː'gər(ɪn)] *m(f)* Olympic champion; ~**iateilnehmer(in)** *m(f)* Olympic competitor; o~**isch** *adj* Olympic

Oma ['oːma] (-, -s; *umg*) *f* granny

Omelett [ɔm(ə)'lɛt] (-(e)s, -s) *nt* omelet(te)

Omen ['oːmɛn] (-s, -) *nt* omen

ominös [omi'nøːs] *adj* (*unheilvoll*) ominous

Omnibus ['ɔmnibʊs] *m* (omni)bus

Onanie [ona'niː] *f* masturbation; o~**ren** *vi* to masturbate

Onkel ['ɔŋkəl] (-s, -) *m* uncle

Opa ['oːpa] (-s, -s; *umg*) *m* grandpa

Opal [o'paːl] (-s, -e) *m* opal

Oper ['oːpər] (-, -n) *f* opera; opera house

Operation [operatsi'oːn] *f* operation; ~**ssaal** *m* operating theatre

Operette [ope'rɛtə] *f* operetta

operieren [ope'riːrən] *vt* to operate on ♦ *vi* to operate

Opern- *zW*: ~**glas** *nt* opera glasses *pl*; ~**haus** *nt* opera house; ~**sänger(in)** *m(f)* opera singer

Opfer ['ɔpfər] (-s, -) *nt* sacrifice; (*Mensch*) victim; o~**n** *vt* to sacrifice; ~**ung** *f* sacrifice

Opium ['oːpiʊm] (-s) *nt* opium

opponieren [ɔpo'niːrən] *vi*: **gegen jdn/etw** ~ to oppose sb/sth

Opportunist [ɔportu'nɪst] *m* opportunist

Opposition [ɔpozitsi'oːn] *f* opposition; o~**ell** *adj* opposing

Optik ['ɔptɪk] *f* optics *sg*; ~**er** (-s, -) *m* optician

optimal [ɔpti'maːl] *adj* optimal, optimum

Optimismus [ɔpti'mɪsmʊs] *m* optimism

Optimist [ɔpti'mɪst] *m* optimist; o~**isch** *adj* optimistic

optisch ['ɔptɪʃ] *adj* optical

Orakel [o'raːkəl] (-s, -) nt oracle

oral [o'raːl] adj (MED) oral

Orange [o'rãːʒə] f orange; **o~** adj orange; **~ade** [orã'ʒaːdə] f orangeade; **~at** [orã'ʒaːt] (-s, -e) nt candied peel

Orchester [ɔr'kɛstər] (-s, -) nt orchestra

Orchidee [ɔrçi'deːə] f orchid

Orden ['ɔrdən] (-s, -) m (ECCL) order; (MIL) decoration; **~sschwester** f nun

ordentlich ['ɔrdəntlɪç] adj (anständig) decent, respectable; (geordnet) tidy, neat; (umg: annehmbar) not bad; (: tüchtig) real, proper ♦ adv properly; **~er Professor** (full) professor; **O~keit** f respectability, tidiness, neatness

ordinär [ɔrdi'nɛːr] adj common, vulgar

ordnen ['ɔrdnən] vt to order, to put in order

Ordner (-s, -) m steward; (COMM) file

Ordnung f order; (Ordnen) ordering; (Geordnetsein) tidiness; ~ machen to tidy up; in ~! okay!

Ordnungs- zW: **o~gemäß** adj proper, according to the rules; **o~liebend** adj orderly, methodical; **o~strafe** f fine; **o~widrig** adj contrary to the rules, irregular; **~zahl** f ordinal number

Organ [ɔr'gaːn] (-s, -e) nt organ; (Stimme) voice; **~isation** [-izatsi'oːn] f organisation; **~isator** [-i'zaːtɔr] m organizer; **o~isch** adj organic; **o~isieren** [-i'ziːrən] vt to organize, to arrange; (umg: beschaffen) to acquire ♦ vr to organize; **~ismus** [-'ɪsmʊs] m organism; **~ist** [-'nɪst] m organist

Orgasmus [ɔr'gasmʊs] m orgasm

Orgel ['ɔrgəl] (-, -n) f organ

Orgie ['ɔrgiə] f orgy

Orient ['oːriɛnt] (-s) m Orient, east; **~ale** [-'taːlə] (-n, -n) m Oriental; **o~alisch** [-'taːlɪʃ] adj oriental

orientier- zW: **~en** [-'tiːrən] vt

(örtlich) to locate; (fig) to inform ♦ vr to find one's way about, to get one's bearings; to inform o.s.; **O~ung** [-'tiːrʊŋ] f orientation; (fig) information; **O~ungssinn** m sense of direction

Origano [ori'gaːno] (-) m (KOCH) oregano

original [origi'naːl] adj original; **O~** (-s, -e) nt original; **O~fassung** f original version; **O~ität** f originality

originell [origi'nɛl] adj original

Orkan [ɔr'kaːn] (-(e)s, -e) m hurricane

orkanartig adj (Wind) gale-force; (Beifall) thunderous

Ornament [ɔrna'mɛnt] nt decoration, ornament; **o~al** [-'taːl] adj decorative, ornamental

Ort [ɔrt] (-(e)s, -e od ¨er) m place; an ~ und Stelle on the spot; **o~en** vt to locate

ortho- [ɔrto] zW: **~dox** [-'dɔks] adj orthodox; **O~graphie** [-gra'fiː] f spelling, orthography; **~graphisch** [-'graːfɪʃ] adj orthographic; **~päde** [-'pɛːdə] (-n, -n) m orthopaedic specialist, orthopaedist; **O~pädie** [-pɛ'diː] f orthopaedics sg; **~pädisch** [-'pɛːdɪʃ] adj orthopaedic

örtlich ['œrtlɪç] adj local; **O~keit** f locality

ortsansässig adj local

Ortschaft f village, small town

Orts- zW: **o~fremd** adj non-local; **~gespräch** nt local (phone)call; **~name** m place-name; **~netz** nt (TEL) local telephone exchange area; **~tarif** m (TEL) tariff for local calls; **~zeit** f local time

Ortung f locating

Öse ['øːzə] f loop, eye

Ost [ɔst] asien [ɔsta'ziːən] nt Eastern Asia

Osten (-s) m east

Oster- ['oːstər] zW: **~ei** nt Easter egg; **~fest** nt Easter; **~glocke** f daffodil; **~hase** m Easter bunny; **~montag** m Easter Monday; **O~n** (-s, -) nt Easter

Österreich ['øːstəraiç] (-s) nt Aus-

tria; **~er(in)** (-s, -) m(f) Austrian;
ö~isch adj Austrian

Ostküste f east coast

östlich ['œstlɪç] adj eastern, easterly

Otter¹ ['ɔtər] (-s, -) m otter

Otter² (-s, -) f (Schlange) adder

Ouvertüre [uver'tyːrə] f overture

oval [o'vaːl] adj oval

Ovation [ovatsi'oːn] f ovation

Ovulation [ovulatsi'oːn] f ovulation

Oxyd [ɔ'ksyːt] (-(e)s, -e) nt oxide;
o~ieren vt, vi to oxidize; **~ierung** f
oxidization

Ozean ['oːtseaːn] (-s, -e) m ocean;
~dampfer m (ocean-going) liner

Ozon [o'tsoːn] (-s) nt ozone; **~loch**
nt ozone hole; **~schicht** f ozone layer

P

Paar [paːr] (-(e)s, -e) nt pair;
(Ehe~) couple; **ein p~ a** few; **p~en**
vt, vr to couple; (Tiere) to mate;
~lauf m pair skating; **p~mal** adv:
ein p~mal a few times; **(e)mal** f
combination; mating; **p~weise** adv
in pairs; in couples

Pacht [paxt] (-, -en) f lease; **p~en**
vt to lease

Pächter ['pɛçtər] (-s, -) m lease-
holder, tenant

Pack¹ [pak] (-(e)s, -e od ⁺e) m bundle, pack

Pack² (-(e)s, -e od ⁺e) nt (pej) mob,
rabble

Päckchen ['pɛkçən] nt small package; (Zigaretten) packet; (Post~)
small parcel

Pack- zW: **p~en** vt to pack; (fassen)
to grasp, to seize; (umg: schaffen) to
manage; (fig: fesseln) to grip; **p~en**
(-s, -) m bundle; (fig: Menge) heaps
of; **~esel** m (auch fig) packhorse;
~papier nt brown paper, wrapping
paper; **~ung** f packet; (Pralinen-
packung) box; (MED) compress

Pädagog· [pɛda'goːg] zW: **~e** (-n,
-n) m teacher; **~ik** f education;
p~isch adj educational, pedagogical

Paddel ['padəl] (-s, -) nt paddle;
~boot nt canoe; **p~n** vi to paddle

Page ['paːʒə] (-n, -n) m page;
~nkopf m pageboy (cut)

Paket [pa'keːt] (-(e)s, -e) nt packet;
(Post~) parcel; **~karte** f dispatch
note; **~post** f parcel post; **~schalter**
m parcels counter

Pakt [pakt] (-(e)s, -e) m pact

Palast [pa'last] (-es, Paläste) m palace

Palästina [palɛs'tiːna] (-s) nt Palestine

Palme ['palmə] f palm (tree)

Palmsonntag m Palm Sunday

Pampelmuse ['pampəlmuːzə] f
grapefruit

pampig ['pampɪç] (umg) adj (frech)
fresh

panieren [pa'niːrən] vt (KOCH) to
bread

Paniermehl [pa'niːrmeːl] nt bread-
crumbs pl

Panik ['paːnɪk] f panic

panisch ['paːnɪʃ] adj panic-stricken

Panne ['panə] f (AUT etc) breakdown; (Mißgeschick) slip; **~nhilfe** f
breakdown service

panschen ['panʃən] vi to splash
about ♦ vt to water down

Panther ['pantər] (-s, -) m panther

Pantoffel ['pantɔfəl] (-s, -n) m slipper

Pantomime [panto'miːmə] f mime

Panzer ['pantsər] (-s, -) m armour;
(Platte) armour plate; (Fahrzeug)
tank; **~glas** nt bulletproof glass;
p~n vt to armour ♦ vr (fig) to arm
o.s.

Papa [pa'pa:] (-s, -s; umg) m dad,
daddy

Papagei [papa'gai] (-s, -en) m parrot

Papier [pa'piːr] (-s, -e) nt paper;
(Wert~) security; **~fabrik** f paper
mill; **~geld** nt paper money; **~korb**
m wastepaper basket; **~tüte** f paper
bag

Papp· ['pap] zW: **~deckel** m cardboard; **~e** f cardboard; **~el** (-, -n) f

poplar; **p~en** (*umg*) *vt, vi* to stick; **p~ig** sticky; **~maché** [-ma'ʃeː] (-s, -s) *nt* papier-mâché

Paprika ['paprika] (-s, -s) *m* (*Gewürz*) paprika; (*~schote*) pepper

Papst [paːpst] (-(e)s, ⸚e) *m* pope

päpstlich ['pɛːpstlɪç] *adj* papal

Parabel [pa'raːbəl] (-, -n) *f* parable; (*MATH*) parabola

Parabolantenne [para'boːl-] *f* satellite dish

Parade [pa'raːdə] *f* (*MIL*) parade, review; (*SPORT*) save

Paradies [para'diːs] (-es, -e) *nt* paradise; **p~isch** *adj* heavenly

Paradox [para'dɔks] (-es, -e) *nt* paradox; **p~** *adj* paradoxical

Paragraph [para'graːf] (-en, -en) *m* paragraph; (*JUR*) section

parallel [para'leːl] *adj* parallel; **P~e** *f* parallel

Paranuß ['paːranʊs] *f* Brazil nut

Parasit [para'ziːt] (-en, -en) *m* (*auch fig*) parasite

parat [pa'raːt] *adj* ready

Pärchen ['pɛːrçən] *nt* couple

Parfüm [par'fyːm] (-s, -s od -e) *nt* perfume; **~erie** [-ə'riː] *f* perfumery; **p~ieren** *vt* to scent, to perfume

parieren [pa'riːrən] *vt* to parry ♦ *vi* (*umg*) to obey

Paris [pa'riːs] (-) *nt* Paris; **~er** *adj* Parisian ♦ *m* Parisian; **~erin** *f* Parisian

Park [park] (-s, -s) *m* park; **~anlage** *f* park; (*um Gebäude*) grounds *pl*; **p~en** *vt, vi* to park; **~ett** [par'kɛt] (-(e)s, -e) *nt* parquet (floor); (*THEAT*) stalls *pl*; **~haus** *nt* multistorey car park; **~lücke** *f* parking space; **~platz** *m* parking place; car park, parking lot (*US*); **~scheibe** *f* parking disc; **~uhr** *f* parking meter; **~verbot** *nt* parking ban

Parlament [parla'mɛnt] *nt* parliament; **~arier** [-'taːriər] (-s, -) *m* parliamentarian; **p~arisch** [-'taːriʃ] *adj* parliamentary

Parlaments- *zW:* **~beschluß** *m* vote of parliament; **~mitglied** *nt*

member of parliament; **~sitzung** *f* sitting (of parliament)

Parodie [paro'diː] *f* parody; **p~ren** *vt* to parody

Parole [pa'roːlə] *f* password; (*Wahlspruch*) motto

Partei [par'tai] *f* party; **~ ergreifen für jdn** to take sb's side; **p~isch** *adj* partial, bias(s)ed; **p~los** *adj* neutral, impartial; **~mitglied** *nt* party member; **programm** *nt* (party) manifesto; **~tag** *m* party conference

Parterre [par'tɛr(ə)] (-s, -s) *nt* ground floor; (*THEAT*) stalls *pl*

Partie [par'tiː] *f* part; (*Spiel*) game; (*Ausflug*) outing; (*Mann, Frau*) catch; (*COMM*) lot; **mit von der ~ sein** to join in

Partisan [parti'zaːn] (-s *od* -en, -en) *m* partisan

Partitur [parti'tuːr] *f* (*MUS*) score

Partizip [parti'tsiːp] (-s, -ien) *nt* participle

Partner(in) ['partnər(ɪn)] (-s, -) *m(f)* partner; **p~schaftlich** *adj* as partners; **~stadt** *f* twin town

Party ['paːrti] (-, -s *od* **Parties**) *f* party

Paß [pas] (-sses, -sse) *m* pass; (*Ausweis*) passport

passabel [pa'saːbəl] *adj* passable, reasonable

Passage [pa'saːʒə] *f* passage

Passagier [pasa'ʒiːr] (-s, -e) *m* passenger; **~flugzeug** *nt* airliner

Passant [pa'sant] *m* passer-by

Paßamt *nt* passport office

Paßbild *nt* passport photograph

passen ['pasən] *vi* to fit; (*Farbe*) to go; (*auf Frage, KARTEN, SPORT*) to pass; **das paßt mir nicht** that doesn't suit me; **~ zu** (*Farbe, Kleider*) to go with; **er paßt nicht zu dir** he's not right for you; **~d** *adj* suitable; (*zusammenpassend*) matching; (*angebracht*) fitting; (*Zeit*) convenient

passier- [pa'siːr] *zW:* **~bar** *adj* passable; **~en** *vt* to pass; (*durch Sieb*) to strain ♦ *vi* to happen; **P~schein** *m* pass, permit

Passion [pasi'o:n] f passion; **p~iert** [-'ni:rt] adj enthusiastic, passionate; **~sspiel** nt Passion Play

passiv ['pasi:f] adj passive; **P~** (-s, -e) nt passive; **P~a** pl (COMM) liabilities; **P~ität** f passiveness

Paß~ zW: **~kontrolle** f passport control; **~stelle** f passport office; **~straße** f (mountain) pass

Paste ['pastə] f paste

Pastell [pas'tɛl] (-(e)s, -e) nt pastel

Pastete [pas'te:tə] f pie

pasteurisieren [pastøri'zi:rən] vt to pasteurize

Pastor ['pastor] m vicar; pastor, minister

Pate ['pa:tə] (-n, -n) m godfather; **~nkind** nt godchild

Patent [pa'tɛnt] (-(e)s, -e) nt patent; (MIL) commission; **p~** adj clever; ingenious; **~amt** nt patent office

Patentante f godmother

patentieren vt to patent

Patentinhaber m patentee

Pater ['pa:tər] (-s, - od Patres) m (ECCL) Father

pathetisch [pa'te:tiʃ] adj emotional; bombastic

Pathologe [pato'lo:gə] (-n, -n) m pathologist

pathologisch adj pathological

Pathos ['pa:tɔs] (-) nt emotiveness, emotionalism

Patient(in) [patsi'ɛnt(in)] m(f) patient

Patin ['pa:tin] f godmother

Patina ['pa:tina] (-) f patina

Patriot [patri'o:t] (-en, -en) m patriot; **p~isch** adj patriotic; **~ismus** [-'tɪsmʊs] m patriotism

Patrone [pa'tro:nə] f cartridge

Patrouille [pa'trʊljə] f patrol

patrouillieren [patrʊl'ji:rən] vi to patrol

patsch [patʃ] excl splash; **P~e** (umg) f (Bedrängnis) mess, jam; **p~en** vi to smack, to slap; (im Wasser) to splash; **~naß** adj soaking wet

patzig ['patsɪç] (umg) adj cheeky,

saucy

Pauke ['paukə] f kettledrum; **auf die ~ hauen** to live it up

pauken vt (intensiv lernen) to swot up (inf) ♦ vi to swot (inf), cram (inf)

pausbäckig ['pausbɛkɪç] adj chubby-cheeked

pauschal [pau'ʃa:l] adj (Kosten) inclusive; (Urteil) sweeping; **P~e** f flat rate; **P~gebühr** f flat rate; **P~preis** m all-in price; **P~reise** f package tour; **P~summe** f lump sum

Pause ['pauzə] f break; (THEAT) interval; (Innehalten) pause; (Kopie) tracing

pausen vt to trace; **~los** adj nonstop; **P~zeichen** nt call sign; (MUS) rest

Pauspapier ['pauspapi:r] nt tracing paper

Pavian ['pa:via:n] (-s, -e) m baboon

Pavillon (-s, -s) m pavilion

Pazif~ [pa'tsi:f] zW: **~ik** (-s) m Pacific; **p~istisch** adj pacifist

Pech [pɛç] (-s, -e) nt pitch; (fig) bad luck; **~ haben** to be unlucky; **p~schwarz** adj pitch-black; **~strähne** (umg) m unlucky patch; **~vogel** (umg) m unlucky person

Pedal [pe'da:l] (-s, -e) nt pedal

Pedant [pe'dant] m pedant; **~erie** f pedantry; **p~isch** adj pedantic

Pediküre [pedi'ky:rə] f (Fußpflege) pedicure

Pegel ['pe:gəl] (-s, -) m water gauge; **~stand** m water level

peilen ['pailən] vt to get a fix on

Pein [pain] f agony, pain; **p~igen** vt to torture; (plagen) to torment; **p~lich** adj (unangenehm) embarrassing, awkward, painful; (genau) painstaking; **~lichkeit** f painfulness, awkwardness; scrupulousness

Peitsche ['paitʃə] f whip; **p~n** vt to whip; (Regen) to lash

Pelikan ['pe:lika:n] (-s, -e) m pelican

Pelle ['pɛlə] f skin; **p~n** vt to skin, to peel

Pellkartoffeln pl jacket potatoes

Pelz [pɛlts] (-es, -e) m fur

Pendel ['pɛndəl] (-s, -) nt pendulum

pendeln vi (Zug, Fähre etc) to operate a shuttle service; (Mensch) to commute; **Pendelverkehr** m shuttle traffic; (für Pendler) commuter traffic

Pendler ['pɛndlər] (-s, -) m commuter

penetrant [pene'trant] adj sharp; (Person) pushing

Penis ['peːnɪs] (-, -se) m penis

pennen ['pɛnən] (umg) vi to kip

Penner (umg: pej) m (Landstreicher) tramp

Pension [penzi'oːn] f (Geld) pension; (Ruhestand) retirement; (für Gäste) boarding od guest-house; ~är(in) [-'nɛːr(ɪn)] (-s, -e) m(f) pensioner; ~ieren vt to pension off; ~iert adj retired; ~ierung f retirement; ~sgast m boarder, paying guest

Pensum ['pɛnzʊm] (-s, Pensen) nt quota; (SCH) curriculum

per [pɛr] präp +akk by, per; (pro) per; (bis) by

Perfekt ['pɛrfɛkt] (-s, -e) nt perfect; p~ [pɛr'fɛkt] adj perfect

perforieren [pɛrfo'riːrən] vt to perforate

Pergament [pɛrga'mɛnt] nt parchment; ~papier nt greaseproof paper

Periode [peri'oːdə] f period

periodisch [peri'oːdɪʃ] adj periodic; (dezimal) recurring

Perle ['pɛrlə] f (auch fig) pearl; p~n vi to sparkle; (Tropfen) to trickle

Perlmutt ['pɛrlmʊt] (-s) nt mother-of-pearl

Perlwein m sparkling wine

perplex [pɛr'plɛks] adj dumbfounded

Person [pɛr'zoːn] (-, -en) f person; ich für meine ~ ... personally I ...

Personal [pɛrzo'naːl] (-s) nt personnel; (Bedienung) servants pl; ~ausweis m identity card; ~computer m personal computer; ~ien [-'ɪən] pl particulars; ~mangel m undermanning; ~pronomen nt personal pronoun

Personen- zW: ~aufzug m lift, elevator (US); ~kraftwagen m private motorcar; ~schaden m injury to persons; ~zug m stopping train; passenger train

personifizieren [pɛrzonifi'tsiːrən] vt to personify

persönlich [pɛr'zøːnlɪç] adj personal ♦ adv in person; personally; **P~keit** f personality

personell adj (Veränderungen) personnel

Perspektive [pɛrspɛk'tiːvə] f perspective

Perücke [pe'rʏkə] f wig

pervers [pɛr'vɛrs] adj perverse

Pessimismus [pɛsi'mɪsmʊs] m pessimism

Pessimist [pɛsi'mɪst] m pessimist; p~isch adj pessimistic

Pest [pɛst] (-) f plague

Petersilie [petər'ziːliə] f parsley

Petroleum [pe'troːleʊm] (-s) nt paraffin, kerosene (US)

Petunie f (BOT) petunia

Pfad [pfaːt] (-(e)s, -e) m path; ~finder (-s, -) m boy scout; ~finderin f girl guide

Pfahl [pfaːl] (-(e)s, -e) m post, stake

Pfand [pfant] (-(e)s, -er) nt pledge, security; (Flaschen~) deposit; (im Spiel) forfeit; ~brief m bond

pfänden ['pfɛndən] vt to seize, to distrain

Pfänderspiel nt game of forfeits

Pfandschein m pawn ticket

Pfändung ['pfɛndʊŋ] f seizure, distraint

Pfanne ['pfanə] f (frying) pan

Pfannkuchen m pancake; (Berliner) doughnut

Pfarr- ['pfar] zW: ~ei f parish; ~er (-s, -) m priest; (evangelisch) minister; ~haus nt vicarage; manse

Pfau [pfaʊ] (-(e)s) m peacock; ~enauge nt peacock butterfly

Pfeffer ['pfɛfər] (-s, -) m pepper; ~korn nt peppercorn; ~kuchen m gingerbread; ~minz nt (-es, -e) peppermint; ~**mühle** f pepper-mill; **p~n** vt to pepper; (umg: werfen) to fling; gep~te Preise/Witze steep prices/spicy jokes

Pfeife ['pfaɪfə] f whistle; (Tabak~, Orgel~) pipe; **p~n** (unreg) vt, vi to whistle; ~**r** (-s, -) m piper

Pfeil [pfaɪl] (-(e)s, -e) m arrow

Pfeiler ['pfaɪlər] (-s, -) m pillar, prop; (Brücken~) pier

Pfennig ['pfɛnɪç] (-(e)s, -e) m pfennig (hundredth part of a mark)

Pferd [pfe:rt] (-(e)s, -e) nt horse

Pferde- ['pfe:rdə] zW: ~**rennen** nt horse-race; horse-racing; ~**schwanz** m (Frisur) ponytail; ~**stall** m stable

Pfiff [pfɪf] (-(e)s, -e) m whistle

Pfifferling ['pfɪfərlɪŋ] m yellow chanterelle (mushroom); **keinen** ~ **wert** not worth a thing

pfiffig adj sly, sharp

Pfingsten ['pfɪŋstən] (-, -) nt Whitsun (BRIT), Pentecost

Pfingstrose ['pfɪŋstro:zə] f peony

Pfirsich ['pfɪrzɪç] (-s, -e) m peach

Pflanz- ['pflants] zW: ~**e** f plant; **p~en** vt to plant; ~**enfett** nt vegetable fat; **p~lich** adj vegetable; ~**ung** f plantation

Pflaster ['pflastər] (-s, -) nt plaster; (Straße) pavement; **p~n** vt to pave; ~**stein** m paving stone

Pflaume ['pflaʊmə] f plum

Pflege ['pfle:gə] f care; (von Idee) cultivation; (Kranken~) nursing; **in** ~ **sein** (Kind) to be fostered out; **p~bedürftig** adj needing care; ~**eltern** pl foster parents; ~**heim** nt nursing home; ~**kind** nt foster child; **p~leicht** adj easy-care; ~**mutter** f foster mother; **p~n** vt to look after; (Kranke) to nurse; (Beziehungen) to foster; ~**r** (-s, -) m orderly; male nurse; ~**rin** f nurse, attendant; ~**vater** m foster father

Pflicht [pflɪçt] (-, -en) f duty; (SPORT) compulsory section; **p~bewußt** adj conscientious; ~**fach** nt (SCH) compulsory subject; ~**gefühl** nt sense of duty; **p~gemäß** adj

dutiful ♦ adv as in duty bound; ~**versicherung** f compulsory insurance

pflücken ['pflʏkən] vt to pick; (Blumen) to pick, to pluck

Pflug [pflu:k] (-(e)s, -e) m plough

pflügen ['pfly:gən] vt to plough

Pforte ['pfɔrtə] f gate; door

Pförtner ['pfœrtnər] (-s, -) m porter, doorkeeper, doorman

Pfosten ['pfɔstən] (-s, -) m post

Pfote ['pfo:tə] f paw; (umg: Schrift) scrawl

Pfropfen ['pfrɔpfən] (-s, -) m (Flaschen~) stopper; (Blut~) clot; **p~** vt (stopfen) to cram; (Baum) to graft

pfui [pfʊɪ] excl ugh!

Pfund [pfʊnt] (-(e)s, -e) nt pound; **p~ig** (umg) adj great

pfuschen ['pfʊʃən] (umg) vi to be sloppy; **jdm ins Handwerk** ~ to interfere in sb's business

Pfuscher ['pfʊʃər] (-s, -; umg) m sloppy worker; (Kur~) quack; ~**ei** (umg) f sloppy work; quackery

Pfütze ['pfʏtsə] f puddle

Phänomen [fɛno'me:n] (-s, -e) nt phenomenon; **p~al** [-'na:l] adj phenomenal

Phantasie [fanta'zi:] f imagination; **p~los** adj unimaginative; **p~ren** vi to fantasize; **p~voll** adj imaginative

phantastisch [fan'tastɪʃ] adj fantastic

Phase ['fa:zə] f phase

Philologe [filo'lo:gə] (-n, -n) m philologist

Philologie [filolo'gi:] f philology

Philosoph [filo'zo:f] (-en, -en) m philosopher; ~**ie** [-'fi:] f philosophy; **p~isch** adj philosophical

phlegmatisch [flɛ'gma:tɪʃ] adj lethargic

Phonetik [fo'ne:tɪk] f phonetics sg

phonetisch adj phonetic

Phosphor ['fɔsfɔr] (-s) m phosphorus

Photo etc ['fo:to] (-s, -s) nt = Foto etc

Phrase ['fraːzə] f phrase; (pej) hollow phrase

pH-Wert m pH-value

Physik [fy'ziːk] f physics sg; **p~alisch** [-'kaːlɪʃ] adj of physics; **~er(in)** ['fyːzɪkər(ɪn)] m (f) physicist

Physiologie [fyzɪolo'giː] f physiology

physisch ['fyːzɪʃ] adj physical

Pianist(in) [pia'nɪst(ɪn)] m (f) pianist

Pickel ['pɪkəl] (-s, -) m pimple; (Werkzeug) pickaxe; **p~ig** adj pimply, spotty

picken ['pɪkən] vi to pick, to peck

Picknick ['pɪknɪk] (-s, -e od -s) nt picnic; **~ machen** to have a picnic

piepen ['piːpən] vi to chirp

piepsen ['piːpsən] vi to chirp

Piepser (umg) m pager, paging device

Pier [piːr] (-s, -s od -e) m od f pier

Pietät [pie'tɛːt] f piety, reverence; **p~los** adj impious, irreverent

Pigment [pɪ'gmɛnt] nt pigment

Pik [piːk] (-s, -s) nt (KARTEN) spades

pikant [pi'kant] adj spicy, piquant; (anzüglich) suggestive

Pilger ['pɪlgər] (-s, -) m pilgrim; **~fahrt** f pilgrimage

Pille ['pɪlə] f pill

Pilot [pi'loːt] (-en, -en) m pilot

Pilz [pɪlts] (-es, -e) m fungus; (eßbar) mushroom; (giftig) toadstool; **~krankheit** f fungal disease

Pinguin ['pɪnguiːn] (-s, -e) m penguin

Pinie ['piːniə] f pine

pinkeln ['pɪŋkəln] (umg) vi to pee

Pinnwand f noticeboard

Pinsel ['pɪnzəl] (-s, -) m paintbrush

Pinzette [pɪn'tsɛtə] f tweezers pl

Pionier [pio'niːr] (-s, -e) m pioneer; (MIL) sapper, engineer

Pirat [pi'raːt] (-en, -en) m pirate; **~ensender** m pirate radio station

Piste ['pɪstə] f (SKI) run, piste; (AVIAT) runway

Pistole [pɪs'toːlə] f pistol

Pizza ['pɪtsa] (-, -s) f pizza

Pkw [peːkaː'veː] (-(s), -(s)) m abk = Personenkraftwagen

pl. abk = pluralisch; Plural

plädieren [plɛ'diːrən] vi to plead

Plädoyer [plɛdoa'jeː] (-s, -s) nt speech for the defence; (fig) plea

Plage ['plaːgə] f plague; (Mühe) nuisance; **~geist** m pest, nuisance; **p~n** vt to torment ♦ vr to toil, to slave

Plakat [pla'kaːt] (-(e)s, -e) nt placard; poster

Plan [plaːn] (-(e)s, ⁻e) m plan; (Karte) map

Plane f tarpaulin

planen vt to plan; (Mord etc) to plot

Planer (-s, -) m planner

Planet [pla'neːt] (-en, -en) m planet

planieren [pla'niːrən] vt to plane, to level

Planke ['plaŋkə] f plank

Plankton [-s] nt plankton

planlos adj (Vorgehen) unsystematic; (Umherlaufen) aimless

planmäßig adj according to plan; systematic; (EISENB) scheduled

Planschbecken nt paddling pool

planschen ['planʃən] vi to splash

Plansoll (-s) nt output target

Plantage [plan'taːʒə] f plantation

Planung f planning

Planwirtschaft f planned economy

plappern ['plapərn] vi to chatter

plärren ['plɛrən] vi (Mensch) to cry, to whine; (Radio) to blare

Plasma ['plasma] (-s, Plasmen) nt plasma

Plastik¹ ['plastɪk] f sculpture

Plastik² [-(-s)] nt (Kunststoff) plastic; **~beutel** m plastic bag, carrier bag; **~folie** f plastic film; **~tüte** f plastic bag

plastisch ['plastɪʃ] adj plastic; stell dir das ~ vor! just picture it!

Platane [pla'taːnə] f plane (tree)

Platin ['plaːtiːn] (-s) nt platinum

platonisch [pla'toːnɪʃ] adj platonic

platsch [platʃ] excl splash; **~en** vi to splash

plätschern ['plɛtʃərn] vi to babble

platschnaß adj drenched

platt [plat] adj flat; (umg: überrascht) flabbergasted; (fig: geistlos) flat, boring; **~deutsch** adj low German; **P~e** f (Speisen~, PHOT, TECH) plate; (Steinplatte) flag; (Kachel) tile; (Schallplatte) record; **P~enspieler** m record player; **P~enteller** m turntable; **P~fuß** m flat foot

Platz [plats] (-es, ⸚e) m place; (Sitz~) seat; (Raum) space, room; (in Stadt) square; (Sport~) playing field; **~ nehmen** to take a seat; **jdm ~ machen** to make room for sb; **~angst** f (MED) agoraphobia; (umg) claustrophobia; **~anweiser(in)** (-s, -) m(f) usher(ette)

Plätzchen ['pletsçən] nt spot; (Gebäck) biscuit

Platz- zW: **p~en** vi to burst; (Bombe) to explode; **vor Wut p~en** (umg) to be bursting with anger; **~karte** f seat reservation; **~mangel** m lack of space; **~patrone** f blank cartridge; **~regen** m downpour; **~wunde** f cut

Plauderei [plaudə'raɪ] f chat, conversation; (RADIO) talk

plaudern ['plaudərn] vi to chat, to talk

plausibel [plau'ziːbəl] adj plausible

plazieren [pla'tsiːrən] vt to place ♦ vr (SPORT) to be placed; (TENNIS) to be seeded

Pleite ['plaɪtə] f bankruptcy; (umg: Reinfall) flop; **~ machen** to go bust; **p~** (umg) adj broke

Plenum ['pleːnum] (-s) nt plenum

Plombe ['plɔmbə] f lead seal; (Zahn~) filling

plombieren [plɔm'biːrən] vt to seal; (Zahn~) to fill

plötzlich ['plœtslɪç] adj sudden ♦ adv suddenly

plump [plʊmp] adj clumsy; (Hände) coarse; (Körper) shapeless; **~sen** vi to plump down, to fall

Plunder ['plʊndər] (-s) m rubbish

plündern ['plʏndərn] vt to plunder;

(Stadt) to sack ♦ vi to plunder

Plünderung ['plʏndəruŋ] f plundering, sack, pillage

Plural ['pluːral] (-s, -e) m plural; **p~istisch** adj pluralistic

Plus [plʊs] (-, -) nt plus; (FIN) profit; (Vorteil) advantage; **p~** adv plus

Plüsch [plyːʃ] (-(e)s, -e) m plush

Pluspol m (ELEK) positive pole

Pluspunkt m point; (fig) point in sb's favour

Plutonium (-s) nt plutonium

PLZ abk = Postleitzahl

Po [poː] (-s, -s) (umg) m bottom, bum

Pöbel ['pøːbəl] (-s) m mob, rabble; **~ei** f vulgarity; **p~haft** adj low, vulgar

pochen ['pɔxən] vi to knock; (Herz) to pound; **auf etw akk ~** (fig) to insist on sth

Pocken ['pɔkən] pl smallpox sing

Podium ['poːdium] nt podium; **~sdiskussion** f panel discussion

Poesie [poe'ziː] f poetry

Poet [po'eːt] (-en, -en) m poet; **p~isch** adj poetic

Pointe [po'ɛ̃tə] f point

Pokal [po'kaːl] (-s, -e) m goblet; (SPORT) cup; **~spiel** nt cup-tie

Pökelfleisch nt salt meat

pökeln ['pøːkəln] vt to pickle, to salt

Poker (-s) nt od m poker

Pol [poːl] (-s, -e) m pole; **p~ar** adj polar; **~arkreis** m Arctic circle

Pole (-n, -n) m Pole

polemisch [po'leːmɪʃ] adj polemical

Polen (-s) nt Poland

Police [po'liːs(ə)] f insurance policy

Polier [po'liːr] (-s, -e) m foreman

polieren vt to polish

Poliklinik [po'liːkliːnɪk] f outpatients (department) sg

Polin f Pole

Politik [poli'tiːk] f politics sg; (eine bestimmte) policy; **~er(in)** [po'liːtɪkər(ɪn)] m(f) politician

politisch [po'liːtɪʃ] adj political

Politur [poli'tuːr] f polish

Polizei [poli'tsaɪ] f police; **~beam-**

te(r) *m* police officer; **p~lich** *adj* police; **sich p~lich melden** to register with the police; **~revier** *nt* police station; **~staat** *m* police state; **~streife** *f* police patrol; **~stunde** *f* closing time; **~wache** *f* police station

Polizist(in) [poli'tsɪst(ɪn)] (**-en, -en**) *m(f)* policeman(woman)

Pollen ['pɔlən] (**-s, -**) *m* pollen

polnisch ['pɔlnɪʃ] *adj* Polish

Polohemd *nt* polo shirt

Polster ['pɔlstər] (**-s, -**) *nt* cushion; (**~ung**) upholstery; (*in Kleidung*) padding; (*fig: Geld*) reserves; **~er** (**-s, -**) *m* upholsterer; **~möbel** *pl* upholstered furniture *sg*; **p~n** *vt* to upholster; to pad

Polterabend *m* party on eve of wedding

poltern ['pɔltərn] *vi* (*Krach machen*) to crash; (*schimpfen*) to rant

Polyp [po'ly:p] (**-en, -en**) *m* polyp; (*umg*) cop; **~en** *pl* (*MED*) adenoids

Pomade [po'ma:də] *f* pomade

Pommes frites ['pɔm'frɪt] *pl* chips, French fried potatoes

Pomp [pɔmp] (**-(e)s**) *m* pomp

pompös [pɔm'pøːs] *adj* (*Auftritt, Fest, Haus*) ostentatious, showy

Pony ['pɔni] (**-s, -s**) *nt* (*Pferd*) pony ♦ *m* (*Frisur*) fringe

Popmusik ['pɔpmuziːk] *f* pop music

Popo [po'po:] (**-s, -s**; *umg*) *m* bottom, bum

poppig ['pɔpɪç] *adj* (*Farbe etc*) gaudy

populär [popu'lɛːr] *adj* popular

Popularität [populari'tɛːt] *f* popularity

Pore ['po:rə] *f* pore

Pornographie [pɔrnogra'fi:] *f* pornography

pornographisch [pɔrno'gra:fɪʃ] *adj* pornographic

porös [po'røːs] *adj* porous

Porree ['pɔre] (**-s, -s**) *m* leek

Portal [pɔr'ta:l] (**-s, -e**) *nt* portal

Portefeuille [pɔrt'føːj] *nt* (*POL, FIN*) portfolio

Portemonnaie [pɔrtmɔ'ne:] (**-s, -s**) *nt* purse

Portier [pɔrti'e:] (**-s, -s**) *m* porter

Portion [pɔrtsi'o:n] *f* portion, helping; (*umg: Anteil*) amount

Porto ['pɔrto] (**-s, -s**) *nt* postage; **p~frei** *adj* post-free, (postage) prepaid

Porträt (**-s, -s**) *nt* = Porträt; **p~ieren** *vt* = porträtieren

Porträt [pɔr'tre:] (**-s, -s**) *nt* portrait; **p~ieren** *vt* to paint, to portray

Portugal ['pɔrtugal] (**-s**) *nt* Portugal

Portugiese [pɔrtu'gi:zə] (**-n, -n**) *m* Portuguese

Portu'giesin *f* Portuguese

portu'giesisch *adj* Portuguese

Porzellan [pɔrtse'la:n] (**-s, -e**) *nt* china, porcelain; (*Geschirr*) china

Posaune [po'zaunə] *f* trombone

Pose ['po:zə] *f* pose

Position [pozitsi'o:n] *f* position

positiv ['po:ziti:f] *adj* positive; **P~** (**-s, -e**) *nt* (*PHOT*) positive

possessiv ['pɔsesi:f] *adj* possessive; **P~pronomen** (**-s, -**) *nt* possessive pronoun

possierlich [po'si:rlɪç] *adj* funny

Post [pɔst] (**-, -en**) *f* post (office); (*Briefe*) mail; **~amt** *nt* post office; **~anweisung** *f* postal order, money order; **~bote** *m* postman; **~en** (**-s, -**) *m* post, position; (*COMM*) item; (*auf Liste*) entry; (*MIL*) sentry; (*Streik~*) picket; **~er** (**-s, -(s)**) *nt* poster; **~fach** *nt* post-office box; **~karte** *f* postcard; **p~lagernd** *adv* poste restante (*BRIT*), general delivery (*US*); **~leitzahl** *f* postal code; **~scheckkonto** *nt* postal giro account; **~sparbuch** *nt* Post Office savings book; **~sparkasse** *f* post office savings bank; **~stempel** *m* postmark; **p~wendend** *adv* by return of post; **~wertzeichen** *nt* postage stamp

potent [po'tɛnt] *adj* potent

Potential [potɛntsi'a:l] (**-s, -e**) *nt* potential

potentiell [potɛntsi'ɛl] *adj* potential

Potenz [po'tɛnts] f power; (*eines Mannes*) potency

Pracht [praxt] (-) f splendour, magnificence

prächtig ['prɛçtɪç] adj splendid

Prachtstück nt showpiece

prachtvoll adj splendid, magnificent

Prädikat [prɛdi'kaːt] (-(e)s, -e) nt title; (*GRAM*) predicate; (*Zensur*) distinction

prägen ['prɛːgən] vt to stamp; (*Münze*) to mint; (*Ausdruck*) to coin; (*Charakter*) to form

prägnant [prɛ'gnant] adj precise, terse

Prägung ['prɛːgʊŋ] f minting, forming; (*Eigenart*) character, stamp

prahlen ['praːlən] vi to boast, to brag

Prahlerei [praːlə'raɪ] f boasting

Praktik ['praktɪk] f practice; **p~abel** [-'kaːbəl] adj practicable; **~ant(in)** [-'kant(ɪn)] m(f) trainee; **~um** (-s, **Praktika** *od* **Praktiken**) nt practical training

praktisch ['praktɪʃ] adj practical, handy; **~er Arzt** general practitioner

praktizieren [praktɪ'tsiːrən] vt, vi to practise

Praline [pra'liːnə] f chocolate

prall [pral] adj firmly rounded; (*Segel*) taut; (*Arme*) plump; (*Sonne*) blazing; **~en** vi to bounce, to rebound; (*Sonne*) to blaze

Prämie ['prɛːmiə] f premium; (*Belohnung*) award, prize; **p~ren** vt to give an award to

Präparat [prɛpa'raːt] (-(e)s, -e) nt (*BIOL*) preparation; (*MED*) medicine

Präposition [prɛpozitsi'oːn] f preposition

Prärie [prɛ'riː] f prairie

Präsens ['prɛːzɛns] (-) nt present tense

präsentieren [prɛzɛn'tiːrən] vt to present

Präservativ [prɛzɛrva'tiːf] (-s, -e) nt contraceptive

Präsident(in) [prɛzi'dɛnt(ɪn)] m(f)

president; **~schaft** f presidency

Präsidium [prɛ'ziːdiʊm] nt presidency, chair(manship); (*Polizei~*) police headquarters pl

prasseln ['prasəln] vi (*Feuer*) to crackle; (*Hagel*) to drum; (*Wörter*) to rain down

Praxis ['praksɪs] (-, **Praxen**) f practice; (*Behandlungsraum*) surgery; (*von Anwalt*) office

präzis [prɛ'tsiːs] adj precise; **P~ion** [prɛtsiːo'n] f precision

predigen ['preːdɪgən] vt, vi to preach

Prediger (-s, -) m preacher

Predigt ['preːdɪçt] (-, -en) f sermon

Preis [praɪs] (-es, -e) m price; (*Sieges~*) prize; um keinen ~ at any price

preisbewußt adj price-conscious

Preiselbeere f cranberry

preis- ['praɪzən] zW: **~en** (*unreg*) vt to praise; **~geben** (*unreg*) vt to abandon; (*opfern*) to sacrifice; (*zeigen*) to expose; **~gekrönt** adj prizewinning; **P~gericht** nt jury; **~günstig** adj inexpensive; **P~lage** f price range; **~lich** adj (*Lage, Unterschied*) price, in price; **P~liste** f price list; **P~richter** m judge (*in a competition*); **P~schild** nt price tag; **P~träger(in)** m(f) prizewinner; **~wert** adj inexpensive

prekär [pre'kɛːr] adj precarious

Prell- [prɛl] zW: **~bock** m buffers pl; **p~en** vt to bump; (*fig*) to cheat, to swindle; **~ung** f bruise

Premiere [prəmi'eːrə] f premiere

Premierminister [prəmi'eːmɪnɪstər] m prime minister, premier

Presse ['prɛsə] f press; **~agentur** f press agency; **~freiheit** f freedom of the press; **p~n** vt to press

pressieren [prɛ'siːrən] vi to be in a hurry

Preßluft ['prɛsluft] f compressed air; **~bohrer** m pneumatic drill

Prestige [prɛs'tiːʒə] (-s) nt prestige

prickeln ['prɪkəln] vt, vi to tingle; to tickle

Priester ['priːstər] (-s, -) m priest

Prima ['priːma] (-, **Primen**) f sixth form, top class

prima adj inv first-class, excellent

primär [pri'mεːr] adj primary

Primel ['priːməl] (-, -l) f primrose

primitiv [primi'tiːf] adj primitive

Prinz [prɪnts] (-en, -en) m prince; **~essin** f princess

Prinzip [prɪn'tsiːp] (-s, -ien) nt principle; **p~iell** [-i'εl] adj, adv on principle; **p~ienlos** adj unprincipled

Priorität [priori'tεːt] f priority

Prise ['priːzə] f pinch

Prisma ['prɪsma] (-s, **Prismen**) nt prism

privat [pri'vaːt] adj private; **P~patient(in)** m(f) private patient; **P~schule** f public school

Privileg [privi'leːk] (-(e)s, -ien) nt privilege

Pro (-) nt pro

pro [proː] präp +akk per

Probe ['proːbə] f test; (*Teststück*) sample; (*THEAT*) rehearsal; **jdn auf die ~ stellen** to put sb to the test; **~exemplar** nt specimen copy; **~fahrt** f test drive; **p~n** vt to try; (*THEAT*) to rehearse; **~weise** adv on approval; **~zeit** f probation period

probieren [pro'biːrən] vt to try; (*Wein, Speise*) to taste, to sample ♦ vi to try; to taste

Problem [pro'bleːm] (-s, -e) nt problem; **~atik** [-'maːtɪk] f problem; **p~atisch** [-'maːtɪʃ] adj problematic; **p~los** adj problem-free

Produkt [pro'dʊkt] (-(e)s, -e) nt product; (*AGR*) produce no pl; **~ion** [prodʊktsi'oːn] f production; output; **p~iv** [-'tiːf] adj productive; **~ivi'tät** f productivity

Produzent [produ'tsεnt] m manufacturer; (*Film*) producer

produzieren [produ'tsiːrən] vt to produce

Professor [pro'fεsɔr] m professor

Profi ['proːfi] (-s, -s) m (umg, *SPORT*) pro

Profil [pro'fiːl] (-s, -e) nt profile; (*fig*)

image

Profit [pro'fiːt] (-(e)s, -e) m profit; **p~ieren** [profi'tiːrən] vi: **p~ieren (von)** to profit (from)

Prognose [pro'gnoːzə] f prediction, prognosis

Programm [pro'gram] (-s, -e) nt programme; (*COMPUT*) program; **p~ieren** [-'miːrən] vt to programme; (*COMPUT*) to program; **~ierer(in)** (-s, -) m(f) programmer

progressiv [progrε'siːf] adj progressive

Projekt [pro'jεkt] (-(e)s, -e) nt project; **~or** [pro'jεktɔr] m projector

proklamieren [prokla'miːrən] vt to proclaim

Prokurist(in) [proku'rɪst(ɪn)] m(f) = company secretary

Prolet [pro'leːt] (-en, -en) m prole, pleb; **~arier** [-'taːriər] (-s, -) m proletarian

Prolog [pro'loːk] (-(e)s, -e) m prologue

Promenade [promə'naːdə] f promenade

Promille [pro'mɪlə] (-(s), -) nt alcohol level

prominent [promi'nεnt] adj prominent

Prominenz [promi'nεnts] f VIPs pl

Promotion [promotsi'oːn] f doctorate, Ph.D.

promovieren [promo'viːrən] vi to do a doctorate oder Ph.D.

prompt [prɔmpt] adj prompt

Pronomen [pro'noːmεn] (-s, -) nt pronoun

Propaganda [propa'ganda] (-) f propaganda

Propeller [pro'pεlər] (-s, -) m propeller

Prophet [pro'feːt] (-en, -en) m prophet

prophezeien [profe'tsaiən] vt to prophesy

Prophezeiung f prophecy

Proportion [proportsi'oːn] f proportion; **p~al** [-'naːl] adj proportional

proportioniert adj: **gut/schlecht**

~ well-/badly-proportioned

Prosa ['pro:za] (-) f prose; **p~isch** [pro'za:ɪʃ] adj prosaic

prosit ['pro:zɪt] excl cheers

Prospekt [pro'spɛkt] (-(e)s, -e) m leaflet, brochure

prost [pro:st] excl cheers

Prostituierte [prostitu'i:rtə] f prostitute

Prostitution [prostitutsi'o:n] f prostitution

Protein (-s, -e) nt protein

Protest [pro'tɛst] (-(e)s, -e) m protest; ~**ant(in)** [protɛs'tant] m(f) Protestant; **p~antisch** [protɛs'tantɪʃ] adj Protestant; ~**ieren** [protɛs'ti:rən] vi to protest

Prothese [pro'te:zə] f artificial limb; (Zahn~) dentures pl

Protokoll [proto'kɔl] (-s, -e) nt register; (von Sitzung) minutes pl; (diplomatisch) protocol; (Polizei~) statement; **p~ieren** [-'li:rən] vt to take down in the minutes

protzen ['prɔtsən] vi to show off

protzig adj ostentatious

Proviant [provi'ant] (-s, -e) m provisions pl, supplies pl

Provinz [pro'vɪnts] (-, -en) f province; **p~iell** [-i'ɛl] adj provincial

Provision [provizi'o:n] f (COMM) commission

provisorisch [provi'zo:rɪʃ] adj provisional

Provokation [provokatsi'o:n] f provocation

provozieren [provo'tsi:rən] vt to provoke

Prozedur [protse'du:r] f procedure; (pej) carry-on

Prozent [pro'tsɛnt] (-(e)s, -e) nt per cent, percentage; ~**satz** m percentage; **p~ual** [-u'a:l] adj percentage cpd; as a percentage

Prozeß [pro'tsɛs] (-sses, -sse) m trial, case

Prozession [protsesi'o:n] f procession

prüde ['pry:də] adj prudish; **P~rie** [-'ri:] f prudery

Prüf- ['pry:f] zW: **p~en** vt to examine, to test; (nach~) to check; ~**er** (-s, -) m examiner; ~**ling** m examinee; ~**ung** f examination; checking; ~**ungsausschuß** m examining board

Prügel ['pry:gəl] (-s, -) m cudgel ♦ pl (Schläge) beating; ~**ei** [-'laɪ] f fight; **p~n** vt to beat ♦ vr to fight; ~**strafe** f corporal punishment

Prunk [prʊŋk] (-(e)s, -e) m pomp, show; **p~voll** adj splendid, magnificent

PS [pe:'ɛs] abk (= Pferdestärke) H.P.

Psalm [psalm] (-s, -en) m psalm

pseudo- ['psɔʏdo] in zW pseudo

pst [pst] excl psst!

Psych- ['psyç] zW: ~**iater** [-'ia:tər] (-s, -) m psychiatrist; **p~iatrisch** adj (MED) psychiatric; **p~isch** adj psychological; ~**oanalyse** [-o'ana'ly:zə] f psychoanalysis; ~**ologe** [-o'lo:gə] (-n, -n) m psychologist; ~**ologie** f psychology; **p~ologisch** adj psychological; ~**otherapeut(in)** (-en, -en) m(f) psychotherapist

Pubertät [puber'tɛ:t] f puberty

Publikum ['pu:blikʊm] (-s) nt audience; (SPORT) crowd

publizieren [publi'tsi:rən] vt to publish, to publicize

Pudding ['pʊdɪŋ] (-s) m blancmange

Pudel ['pu:dəl] (-s) m poodle

Puder ['pu:dər] (-s, -) m powder; ~**dose** f powder compact; **p~n** vt to powder; ~**zucker** m icing sugar

Puff¹ [pʊf] (-(e)s, -e) m (Wäsche~) linen basket; (Sitz~) pouf

Puff² (-s, -e) m (Stoß) push

Puff³ (-s, -;) m od nt (Bordell) brothel

Puffer (-s, -) m buffer; ~**speicher** m (COMPUT) buffer

Pullover [pʊ'lo:vər] (-s, -) m pullover, jumper

Puls [pʊls] (-es, -e) m pulse; ~**ader** f artery; **p~ieren** vi to throb, to pulsate

Pult [pʊlt] (-(e)s, -e) nt desk

Pulver ['pʊlfər] (-s, -) nt powder; **p~ig** adj powdery; **~schnee** m powdery snow

pummelig ['pʊməlɪç] adj chubby

Pumpe ['pʊmpə] f pump; **p~n** vt to pump; (umg) to lend; to borrow

Punkt [pʊŋkt] (-(e)s, -e) m point; (bei Muster) dot; (Satzzeichen) full stop; **p~ieren** [-'tiːrən] vt to dot; (MED) to aspirate

pünktlich ['pʏŋktlɪç] adj punctual; **P~keit** f punctuality

Punktsieg m victory on points

Punktzahl f score

Punsch [pʊnʃ] (-(e)s, -e) m punch

Pupille [pu'pɪlə] f pupil

Puppe ['pʊpə] f doll; (Marionette) puppet; (Insekten~) pupa, chrysalis; **~nspieler** m puppeteer; **~nstube** f doll's house; **~ntheater** nt puppet theatre

pur [puːr] adj pure; (völlig) sheer; (Whisky) neat

Püree [py're:] (-s, -s) nt mashed potatoes pl

Purzelbaum m somersault

purzeln ['pʊrtsəln] vi to tumble

Puste ['pu:stə] (-; umg) f puff; (fig) steam; **p~n** vi to puff, to blow

Pute ['pu:tə] f turkey-hen; **~r** (-s, -) m turkey-cock

Putsch [pʊtʃ] (-(e)s, -e) m revolt, putsch

Putz [pʊts] (-es) m (Mörtel) plaster, roughcast

putzen vt to clean; (Nase) to wipe, to blow ♦ vr to clean o.s.; to dress o.s. up

Putz- zW: **~frau** f charwoman; **p~ig** adj quaint, funny; **~lappen** m cloth

Puzzle ['pasəl] (-s, -s) nt jigsaw

PVC nt abk PVC

Pyjama [py'dʒa:ma] (-s, -s) m pyjamas pl

Pyramide [pyra'mi:də] f pyramid

Pyrenäen [pyre'nɛːən] pl Pyrenees

Q

Quacksalber ['kvakzalbər] (-s, -) m quack (doctor)

Quader ['kva:dər] (-s, -) m square stone; (MATH) cuboid

Quadrat [kva'dra:t] (-(e)s, -e) nt square; **q~isch** adj square; **~meter** m square metre

quaken ['kva:kən] vi to croak; (Ente) to quack

quäken ['kvɛ:kən] vi to screech

Qual [kva:l] (-, -en) f pain, agony; (seelisch) anguish

quälen ['kvɛ:lən] vt to torment ♦ vr to struggle; (geistig) to torment o.s.; **~erei** [-ə'raɪ] f torture, torment

Qualifikation [kvalifikatsi'o:n] f qualification

qualifizieren [kvalifi'tsi:rən] vt to qualify; (einstufen) to label ♦ vr to qualify

Qualität [kvali'tɛ:t] f quality; **~sware** f article of high quality

Qualle ['kvalə] f jellyfish

Qualm [kvalm] (-(e)s) m thick smoke; **q~en** vt, vi to smoke

qualvoll ['kva:lfɔl] adj excruciating, painful, agonizing

Quant- ['kvant] zW: **~entheorie** f quantum theory; **~ität** [-i'tɛ:t] f quantity; **q~itativ** [-ita'ti:f] adj quantitative; **~um** nt quantity, amount

Quarantäne [karan'tɛ:nə] f quarantine

Quark [kvark] (-s) m curd cheese; (umg) rubbish

Quartal [kvar'ta:l] (-s, -e) nt quarter (year)

Quartier [kvar'ti:r] (-s, -e) nt accommodation; (MIL) quarters pl; (Stadt~) district

Quarz [kva:rts] (-es, -e) m quartz

quasseln ['kvasəln] (umg) vi to natter

Quatsch [kvatʃ] (-es) m rubbish

q~en vi to chat, to natter

Quecksilber ['kvɛksɪlbər] nt mercury

Quelle ['kvɛlə] f spring; (eines Flusses) source; **q~n** (unreg) vi (hervor~) to pour od gush forth; (schwellen) to swell

quer [kveːr] adv crossways, diagonally; (rechtwinklig) at right angles; ~ **auf dem Bett** across the bed; **Q~balken** m crossbeam; ~**feldein** adv across country; **Q~flöte** f flute; **Q~format** nt (PHOT) oblong format; **Q~schnitt** m cross-section; ~**schnittsgelähmt** adj paralysed below the waist; ~**straße** f intersecting road

quetschen ['kvɛtʃən] vt to squash, to crush; (MED) to bruise

Quetschung f bruise, contusion

quieken ['kviːkən] vi to squeak

quietschen ['kviːtʃən] vi to squeak

Quint- ['kvɪnt] zW: ~**a** (-, **Quinten**) f second year of secondary school; ~**essenz** [-ʔɛsɛnts] f quintessence; ~**ett** (-(e)s, -e) nt quintet

Quirl [kvɪrl] (-(e)s, -e) m whisk

quitt [kvɪt] adj quits, even

Quitte f quince

quittieren [kvɪˈtiːrən] vt to give a receipt for; (Dienst) to leave

Quittung f receipt

Quiz [kvɪs] (-, -) nt quiz

quoll etc [kvɔl] vb siehe **quellen**

Quote ['kvoːtə] f number, rate

R

Rabatt [raˈbat] (-(e)s, -e) m discount

Rabatte f flowerbed, border

Rabattmarke f trading stamp

Rabe [ˈraːbə] (-n, -n) m raven

rabiat [rabiˈaːt] adj furious

Rache [ˈraxə] (-) f revenge, vengeance

Rachen (-s, -) m throat

rächen [ˈrɛçən] vt to avenge, to revenge ♦ vr to take (one's) revenge

das wird sich ~ you'll pay for that

Rachitis [raˈxiːtɪs] f rickets sg

Rad [raːt] (-(e)s, ⁼er) nt wheel; (Fahr~) bike

Radar [ˈraːdar] (-s) m od nt radar; ~**falle** f speed trap; ~**kontrolle** f radar-controlled speed trap

Radau [raˈdau] (-s) m row

radebrechen vi insep: **deutsch** etc ~ to speak broken German etc

radeln (umg) vi to cycle

radfahr- zW: ~**en** (unreg) vi to cycle; **R~er(in)** m(f) cyclist; **R~weg** m cycle track od path

Radier- [raˈdiːr] zW: **r~en** vt to rub out, to erase; (ART) to etch; ~**gummi** m rubber, eraser; ~**ung** f etching

Radieschen [raˈdiːsçən] nt radish

radikal [radiˈkaːl] adj radical; **R~e(r)** mf radical

Radio [ˈraːdio] (-s, -s) nt radio, wireless; **r~ak'tiv** adj radioactive; ~**akti·vi'tät** f radioactivity; ~**apparat** m radio, wireless set

Radius [ˈraːdius] (-, **Radien**) m radius

Rad- zW: ~**kappe** f (AUT) hub cap; ~**ler(in)** (umg) m(f) cyclist; ~**rennen** nt cycle race; cycle racing; ~**sport** m cycling

raffen [ˈrafən] vt to snatch, to pick up; (Stoff) to gather (up); (Geld) to pile up, to rake in

Raffinade [rafiˈnaːdə] f refined sugar

raffi'niert adj crafty, cunning

ragen [ˈraːgən] vi to tower, to rise

Rahm [raːm] (-s) m cream

Rahmen [ˈraːmən] (-s, -) m frame(work); **im ~ des Möglichen** within the bounds of possibility; **r~** vt to frame

Rakete [raˈkeːtə] f rocket; ~**nstützpunkt** m missile base

rammen [ˈramən] vt to ram

Rampe [ˈrampə] f ramp; ~**nlicht** nt (THEAT) footlights pl

ramponieren [rampoˈniːrən] (umg) vt to damage

Ramsch [ramʃ] (-(e)s, -e) m junk

ran [ran] (umg) adv = **heran**

Rand [rant] (-(e)s, ⁼er) m edge,

~on Brille, Tasse etc) rim; _(Hut~)_ ... m; _(auf Papier)_ margin; _~ Schmutz, unter Augen)_ ring; _(fig)_ ... ze, brink; **außer ~ und Band** ... wild; **am ~e bemerkt** mentioned in passing

randalieren [randaˈliːrən] _vi_ to (go on the) rampage

Rang [raŋ] _(-(e)s, ⁻e) m_ rank; _(Stand)_ standing; _(Wert)_ quality; _(THEAT)_ circle

Rangier- [rãˈʒiːr] _zW:_ **~bahnhof** _m_ marshalling yard; **r~en** _vt (EISENB)_ to shunt, to switch _(US)_ **+** _vi_ to rank, to be classed; **~gleis** _nt_ siding

Ranke [ˈraŋkə] _f_ tendril, shoot

ranzig [ˈrantsiç] _adj_ rancid

Rappe [ˈrapə] _(-n, -n) m_ black horse

Rappen [ˈrapən] _m (FIN)_ rappen, centime

rar [raːr] _adj_ rare; **sich ~ machen** _(umg)_ to keep o.s. to o.s.; **R~ität** _f_ rarity; _(Sammelobjekt)_ curio

rasant [raˈzant] _adj_ quick, rapid

rasch [raʃ] _adj_ quick

rascheln _vi_ to rustle

Rasen [ˈraːzən] _(-s, -) m_ lawn; grass

rasen _vi_ to rave; _(schnell)_ to race; **~d** _adj_ furious; **~de Kopfschmerzen** a splitting headache

Rasenmäher _(-s, -) m_ lawnmower

Rasier- [raˈziːr] _zW:_ **~apparat** _m_ shaver; **~creme** _f_ shaving cream; **r~en** _vt, vr_ to shave; **~klinge** _f_ razor blade; **~messer** _nt_ razor; **~pinsel** _m_ shaving brush; **~seife** _f_ shaving soap od stick; **~wasser** _nt_ shaving lotion

Rasse [ˈrasə] _f_ race; _(Tier~)_ breed; **~hund** _m_ thoroughbred dog

rasseln [ˈrasəln] _vi_ to rattle

Rassenhaß _m_ race od racial hatred; **~trennung** _f_ racial segregation

Rassismus [raˈsɪsmus] _m_ racism

Rast [rast] _(-, -en) f_ rest; **r~en** _vi_ to rest; **~hof** _m (AUT)_ service station; **r~los** _adj_ tireless; _(unruhig)_ restless; **~platz** _m (AUT)_ layby; **~stätte** _f (AUT)_ service station

Rasur [raˈzuːr] _f_ shaving

Rat [raːt] _(-(e)s, ⁻schläge) m_ advice _no pl;_ **ein ~** a piece of advice; **jdn zu ~e ziehen** to consult sb; **keinen ~ wissen** not to know what to do

Rate _f_ instalment

raten _(unreg) vt, vi_ to guess; _(empfehlen):_ **jdm ~** to advise sb

Ratenzahlung _f_ hire purchase

Ratgeber _(-s, -) m_ adviser

Rathaus _nt_ town hall

ratifizieren [ratifiˈtsiːrən] _vt_ to ratify

Ration [ratsiˈoːn] _f_ ration; **r~al** [-ˈnaːl] _adj_ rational; **r~ali'sieren** _vt_ to rationalize; **r~ell** [-ˈnɛl] _adj_ efficient; **r~ieren** [-ˈniːrən] _vt_ to ration

Rat- _zW:_ **r~los** _adj_ at a loss, helpless; **r~sam** _adj_ advisable; **~schlag** _m_ (piece of) advice

Rätsel [ˈrɛːtsəl] _(-s, -) nt_ puzzle; _(Wort~)_ riddle; **r~haft** _adj_ mysterious; **es ist mir r~haft** it's a mystery to me

Ratte [ˈratə] _f_ rat; **~nfänger** _(-s, -) m_ ratcatcher

rattern [ˈratərn] _vi_ to rattle, to clatter

Raub [raup] _(-(e)s) m_ robbery; _(Beute)_ loot, booty; **~bau** _m_ ruthless exploitation; **r~en** [ˈraubən] _vt_ to rob; _(Mensch)_ to kidnap, to abduct

Räuber [ˈrɔybər] _(-s, -) m_ robber

Raub- _zW:_ **~mord** _m_ robbery with murder; **~tier** _nt_ predator; **~überfall** _m_ robbery with violence; **~vogel** _m_ bird of prey

Rauch [raux] _(-(e)s) m_ smoke; **r~en** _vt, vi_ to smoke; **~er(in)** _(-s, -) m(f)_ smoker; **~erabteil** _nt (EISENB)_ smoker

räuchern [ˈrɔyçərn] _vt_ to smoke, to cure

Rauchfleisch _nt_ smoked meat

rauchig _adj_ smoky

rauf [rauf] _(umg) adv =_ **herauf; hinauf**

raufen _vt (Haare)_ to pull out **+** _vi, vr_ to fight; **Raufe'rei** _f_ brawl, fight

rauh [rau] _adj_ rough, coarse; _(Wet-_

ter) harsh; **R~reif** m hoarfrost

Raum [raʊm] (-(e)s, Räume) m space; (Zimmer, Platz) room; (Gebiet) area

räumen ['rɔymən] vt to clear; (Wohnung, Platz) to vacate; (wegräumen) to shift, to move; (in Schrank etc) to put away

Raum- zW: **~fähre** f space shuttle; **~fahrt** f space travel; **~inhalt** m cubic capacity, volume

räumlich ['rɔymlɪç] adj spatial; **R~keiten** pl premises

Raum- zW: **~mangel** m lack of space; **~pflegerin** f cleaner; **~schiff** nt spaceship; **~schiffahrt** f space travel

Räumung ['rɔymʊŋ] f vacating, evacuation; clearing (away); **~sverkauf** m clearance sale; (bei Geschäftsaufgabe) closing down sale

raunen ['raʊnən] vt, vi to whisper

Raupe ['raʊpə] f caterpillar; (~nkette) (caterpillar) track; **~nschlepper** m caterpillar tractor

raus [raʊs] (umg) adv = heraus; hinaus

Rausch [raʊʃ] (-(e)s, Räusche) m intoxication

rauschen vi (Wasser) to rush; (Baum) to rustle; (Radio etc) to hiss; (Mensch) to sweep, to sail; **~d** adj (Beifall) thunderous; (Fest) sumptuous

Rauschgift nt drug; **~süchtige(r)** mf drug addict

räuspern ['rɔyspərn] vr to clear one's throat

Razzia ['ratsia] (-, Razzien) f raid

Reagenzglas [rea'gɛnts-] nt test tube

reagieren [rea'giːrən] vi: ~ (auf +akk) to react (to)

Reakt- zW: **~ion** [reaktsi'oːn] f reaction; **r~io'när** adj reactionary; **~or** [re'aktɔr] m reactor

real [re'aːl] adj real, material

realisieren vt (verwirklichen) Pläne) to carry out

Realismus [rea'lɪsmʊs] m realism

realistisch adj realistic;

Realschule f secondary school

Rebe ['reːbə] f vine

rebellieren [rebɛ'liːrən] vi to rebel; **Rebellion** f rebellion; **rebellisch** adj rebellious

Rebhuhn ['rɛphuːn] nt (KOCH, ZOOL) partridge

Rechen ['rɛçən] (-s, -) m rake; **r~** vt, vi to rake

Rechen- zW: **~fehler** m miscalculation; **~maschine** f calculating machine; **~schaft** f account; für etw **~schaft ablegen** to account for sth; **~schieber** m slide rule

Rech- [rɛç] zW: **r~nen** vt, vi to calculate; **jdn/etw r~nen zu** to count sb/sth among; **r~nen mit** to reckon with; **r~nen auf** +akk to count on; **~nen** nt arithmetic; **~ner** (-s, -) m calculator; (COMPUT) computer; **~nung** f calculation(s); (COMM) bill, check (US); **jdm/etw ~nung tragen** to take sb/sth into account; **~nungsjahr** nt financial year; **~nungsprüfer** m auditor

Recht [rɛçt] (-(e)s, -e) nt right; (JUR) law; **mit ~** rightly, justly; **von ~s wegen** by rights

recht adj right ♦ adv (vor Adjektiv) really, quite; **das ist mir ~** suits me; **jetzt erst ~** now more than ever; **~ haben** to be right; **jdm ~ geben** to agree with sb

Rechte f right (hand); (POL) Right; **r~(r, s)** adj right; (POL) right-wing; **ein ~r** a right-winger; **~(s)** nt right thing; **etwas/nichts ~s** something /nothing proper

recht- zW: **~eckig** adj rectangular; **~fertigen** vt insep to justify ♦ vr insep to justify o.s.; **R~fertigung** f justification

rechthaberisch (pej) adj (Mensch) opinionated

rechtlich adj (gesetzlich: Gleichstellung, Anspruch) legal

rechtlos adj with no rights

rechtmäßig adj legal, lawful

rechts [rɛçts] adv on/to the right; **R~anwalt** m lawyer, barrister;

rung) setback; **~schluß** *m* conclusion; **~schritt** *m* retrogression; **r~schrittlich** *adj* reactionary; retrograde; **~seite** *f* back; (*von Münze etc*) reverse; **~sicht** *f* consideration; **~sicht nehmen auf** *+akk* to show consideration for; **r~sichtslos** *adj* inconsiderate; (*Fahren*) reckless; (*unbarmherzig*) ruthless; **r~sichtsvoll** *adj* considerate; **~sitz** *m* back seat; **~spiegel** *m* (*AUT*) rear-view mirror; **~spiel** *nt* return match; **~sprache** *f* further discussion or talk; **~stand** *m* arrears *pl*; **r~ständig** *adj* backward, out-of-date; (*Zahlungen*) in arrears; **~strahler** *m* (*-s, -*) *m* rear reflector; **~tritt** *m* resignation; **~trittbremse** *f* pedal brake; **~vergütung** *f* repayment; (*COMM*) refund; **~versicherung** *f* reinsurance; **r~wärtig** *adj* rear; **r~wärts** *adv* backward(s), back; **~wärtsgang** *m* (*AUT*) reverse gear; **~weg** *m* return journey, way back; **r~wirkend** *adj* retroactive; **~wirkung** *f* reaction; retrospective effect; **~zahlung** *f* repayment; **~zug** *m* retreat

Rudel ['ruːdəl] (*-s, -*) *nt* pack; herd
Ruder ['ruːdər] (*-s, -*) *nt* oar; (*Steuer*) rudder; **~boot** *nt* rowing boat; **r~n** *vt, vi* to row
Ruf [ruːf] (*-(e)s, -e*) *m* call, cry; (*Ansehen*) reputation; **r~en** (*unreg*) *vt, vi* to call; to cry; **~name** *m* usual (first) name; **~nummer** *f* (*tele*)phone number; **~säule** *f* (*an Autobahn*) emergency telephone; **~zeichen** *nt* (*RADIO*) call sign; (*TEL*) ringing tone
rügen *vt* to rebuke
Ruhe ['ruːə] (*-*) *f* rest; (*Ungestörtheit*) peace, quiet; (*Gelassenheit, Stille*) calm; (*Schweigen*) silence; **jdn in ~ lassen** to leave sb alone; **sich zur ~ setzen** to retire; **~!** be quiet!, silence!; **r~n** *vi* to rest; **~pause** *f* break; **~stand** *m* retirement; **letzte ~stätte** final resting place; **~störung** *f* breach of the peace; **~tag** *m* (*von Geschäft*) clos-

ing day
ruhig ['ruːɪç] *adj* quiet; (*bewegungslos*) still; (*Hand*) steady; (*gelassen, friedlich*) calm; (*Gewissen*) clear; **kommen Sie ~ herein** just come on in; **tu das** ~ feel free to do that
Ruhm [ruːm] (*-(e)s*) *m* fame, glory
rühmen ['ryːmən] *vt* to praise ♦ *vr* to boast
Ruhr [ruːr] (*-*) *f* dysentery
Rühr- ['ryːr] *zW*: **~ei** *nt* scrambled egg; **r~en** *vt, vr* (*auch fig*) to move, to stir ♦ *vi*: **r~en von** to come *or* stem from; **r~en an** *+akk* to touch; (*fig*) to touch on; **r~end** *adj* touching, moving; **r~ig** *adj* active, lively; **r~selig** *adj* sentimental, emotional; **~ung** *f* emotion
Ruin [ru'iːn] (*-s, -e*) *m* ruin; **~e** *f* ruin; **r~ieren** *vt* to ruin
rülpsen ['rʏlpsən] *vi* to burp, to belch
Rum [rum] (*-s, -s*) *m* rum
Rumän- [ru'mɛːn] *zW*: **~e** (*-n, -n*) *m* Ro(u)manian; **~ien** (*-s*) *nt* Ro(u)mania; **~in** *f* Ro(u)manian; **r~isch** *adj* Ro(u)manian
Rummel ['rʊməl] (*-s; umg*) *m* hubbub; (*Jahrmarkt*) fair; **~platz** *m* fairground, fair
Rumpf [rʊmpf] (*-(e)s, æ*) *m* trunk, torso; (*AVIAT*) fuselage; (*NAUT*) hull
rümpfen ['rʏmpfən] *vt* (*Nase*) to turn up
rund [rʊnt] *adj* round ♦ *adv* (*etwa*) around; **~ um etw** round sth; **R~brief** *m* circular; **R~e** *f* round; (*in Rennen*) lap; (*Gesellschaft*) circle; **R~fahrt** *f* (round) trip
Rundfunk ['rʊntfʊŋk] (*-(e)s*) *m* broadcasting; **im ~** on the radio; **~gerät** *nt* wireless set; **~sendung** *f* broadcast, radio programme
Rund- *zW*: **r~heraus** *adv* straight out, bluntly; **r~herum** *adv* round about; all round; **r~lich** *adj* plump, rounded; **~reise** *f* round trip; **r~schreiben** *nt* (*COMM*) circular; **~(wander)weg** *m* circular path *or* route

runter ['rʊntər] (umg) adv = herunter; hinunter

Runzel ['rʊntsəl] (-, -n) f wrinkle; r~ig adj wrinkled; r~n vt to wrinkle; **die Stirn r~n** to frown

Rupfen ['rʊpfən] (-s, -) m sackcloth

rupfen vt to pluck

ruppig ['rʊpɪç] adj rough, gruff

Rüsche ['ry:ʃə] f frill

Ruß [ru:s] (-es) m soot

Russe ['rosə] (-n, -n) m Russian

Rüssel ['rysəl] (-s, -) m snout; (Elefanten~) trunk

rußig ['ru:sɪç] adj sooty

Russin ['rosɪn] f Russian

russisch adj Russian

Rußland ['roslant] (-s) nt Russia

rüsten ['rʏstən] vt to prepare ♦ vi to prepare; (MIL) to arm ♦ vr to prepare (o.s.); to arm o.s.

rüstig ['rʏstɪç] adj sprightly, vigorous

Rüstung ['rʏstʊŋ] f preparation; arming; (Ritter~) armour; (Waffen etc) armaments pl; ~skontrolle f arms control

Rute ['ru:tə] f rod

Rutsch [rotʃ] (-(e)s, -e) m slide; (Erd~) landslide; ~bahn f slide; r~en vi to slide; (ausrutschen) to slip; r~ig adj slippery

rütteln ['rʏtəln] vt, vi to shake, to jolt

S

S. abk (= Seite) p.; = Schilling

s. abk (= siehe) see

Saal [za:l] (-(e)s, Säle) m hall; room

Saarland ['za:rlant] nt: das ~ the Saar(land)

Saat [za:t] (-, -en) f seed; (Pflanzen) crop; (Säen) sowing

Säbel ['zɛ:bəl] (-s, -) m sabre, sword

Sabotage [zabo'ta:ʒə] f sabotage

Sach- ['zax] zW: ~**bearbeiter** m specialist; s~**dienlich** adj relevant, helpful; ~**e** f thing; (Angelegenheit) affair, business; (Frage) matter;

(Pflicht) task; **zur ~e** to the point; s~**kundig** adj expert; s~**lich** adj matter-of-fact; objective; (Irrtum, Angabe) factual

sächlich ['zɛxlɪç] adj neuter

Sachschaden m material damage

Sachsen ['zaksən] (-s) nt Saxony

sächsisch ['zɛksɪʃ] adj Saxon

sacht(e) ['zaxt(ə)] adv softly, gently

Sachverständige(r) mf expert

Sack [zak] (-(e)s, ϟe) m sack; ~**gasse** f cul-de-sac, dead-end street (US)

Sadismus [za'dɪsmʊs] m sadism

Sadist [za'dɪst] m sadist

säen ['zɛ:ən] vt, vi to sow

Saft [zaft] (-(e)s, ϟe) m juice; (BOT) sap; s~**ig** adj juicy; s~**los** adj dry

Sage ['za:gə] f saga

Säge ['zɛ:gə] f saw; ~**mehl** nt sawdust

sagen ['za:gən] vt, vi to say; (mitteilen): **jdm ~** to tell sb; ~ **Sie ihm, daß ...** tell him ...

sägen vt, vi to saw

sagenhaft adj legendary; (umg) great, smashing

sah [za:] vb siehe **sehen**

Sahne ['za:nə] f cream

Saison [zɛ'zõ:] (-, -s) f season

Saite ['zaitə] f string; ~**ninstrument** nt string instrument

Sakko ['zako] (-s, -s) m od nt jacket

Sakrament [zakra'mɛnt] nt sacrament

Sakristei [zakrɪs'tai] f sacristy

Salat [za'la:t] (-(e)s, -e) m salad; (Kopf~) lettuce; ~**soße** f salad dressing

Salbe ['zalbə] f ointment

Salbei [zal'bai] (-s, -) m od f sage

Saldo ['zaldo] (-s, Salden) m balance

Salmiak [zalmi'ak] (-s) m sal ammoniac; ~**geist** m liquid ammonia

salopp [za'lɔp] adj casual

Salpeter [zal'pe:tər] (-s) m saltpetre; ~**säure** f nitric acid

Salz [zalts] (-es, -e) nt salt; s~**en** (unreg) vt to salt; s~**ig** adj salty; ~**kartoffeln** pl boiled potatoes;

~säure f hydrochloric acid; **~streuer** m salt cellar; **~wasser** nt (Meerwasser) salt water

Samen ['zaːmən] (-s, -) m seed; (ANAT) sperm

Sammelband m anthology

sammeln ['zaməln] vt to collect ♦ vr to assemble, to gather; (konzentrieren) to concentrate

Sammlung ['zamlʊŋ] f collection; assembly, gathering; concentration

Samstag ['zamstaːk] m Saturday; **s~s** adv (on) Saturdays

Samt [zamt] (-(e)s, -e) m velvet

samt präp +dat (along) with, together with; **~ und sonders** each and every one (of them)

sämtlich ['zɛmtlɪç] adj all (the), entire

Sand [zant] (-(e)s, -e) m sand

Sandale [zan'daːlə] f sandal

Sand- zW: **~bank** f sandbank; **s~ig** ['zandɪç] adj sandy; **~kasten** m sandpit; **~kuchen** m Madeira cake; **~papier** nt sandpaper; **~stein** m sandstone; **s~strahlen** vt insep to sandblast ♦ vi insep to sandblast; **~strand** m sandy beach

sandte etc ['zantə] vb siehe **senden**

Sanduhr f hourglass

sanft [zanft] adj soft, gentle; **~mütig** adj gentle, meek

sang etc [zaŋ] vb siehe **singen**

Sänger(in) ['zɛŋər(ɪn)] (-s, -) m(f) singer

Sani- zW: **s~eren** [za'niːrən] vt to redevelop; (Betrieb) to make financially sound ♦ vr to line one's pockets; to become financially sound; **s~tär** [zani'tɛːr] adj sanitary; **s~täre Anlagen** sanitation sg; **~täter** [zani'tɛːtər] (-s, -) m first-aid attendant; (MIL) (medical) orderly

sanktionieren [zaŋktsio'niːrən] vt to sanction

Saphir ['zaːfiːr] (-s, -e) m sapphire

Sardelle [zar'dɛlə] f anchovy

Sardine [zar'diːnə] f sardine

Sardinien [zar'diːnjən] (-s) nt Sardinia

Sarg [zark] (-(e)s, ːe) m coffin

Sarkasmus [zar'kasmʊs] m sarcasm

saß etc [zaːs] vb siehe **sitzen**

Satan ['zaːtan] (-s, -e) m Satan; devil

Satellit [zatɛ'liːt] (-en, -en) m satellite; **~enfernsehen** nt satellite television

Satire [za'tiːrə] f satire

satirisch [za'tiːrɪʃ] adj satirical

satt [zat] adj full; (Farbe) rich, deep; **jdn/etw ~ sein** od **haben** to be fed up with sb/sth; **sich ~ hören/sehen an** +dat to hear/see enough of; **sich ~ essen** to eat one's fill; **~ machen** to be filling

Sattel ['zatəl] (-s, ːe) m saddle; (Berg) ridge; **s~n** vt to saddle; **~schlepper** m articulated lorry

sättigen ['zɛtɪɡən] vt to satisfy; (CHEM) to saturate

Satz [zats] (-es, ːe) m (GRAM) sentence; (Neben~, Adverbial~) clause; (Theorem) theorem; (MUS) movement; (TENNIS, Briefmarken etc) set; (Kaffee) grounds pl; (COMM) rate; (Sprung) jump; **~teil** m part of a sentence; **~ung** f (Statut) statute, rule; **~zeichen** nt punctuation mark

Sau [zau] (-, Säue) f sow; (umg) dirty pig

sauber ['zaubər] adj clean; (ironisch) fine; **~halten** (unreg) vt to keep clean; **S~keit** f cleanness; (einer Person) cleanliness

säuberlich ['zɔybərlɪç] adv neatly

säubern vt to clean; (POL etc) to purge

Säuberung f cleaning; purge

Sauce ['zoːsə] f sauce, gravy

sauer ['zauər] adj sour; (CHEM) acid; (umg) cross; **Saurer Regen** acid rain

Sauerei [zauə'rai] (umg) f rotten state of affairs, scandal; (Schmutz etc) mess; (Unanständigkeit) obscenity

säuerlich adj (Geschmack) sour; (mißvergnügt: Gesicht) dour

Sauer- zW: **~milch** f sour milk.

~**rahm** m (KOCH) sour cream; ~**stoff** m oxygen; ~**teig** m leaven

saufen ['zaʊfən] (unreg; ung) vt, vi to drink, to booze

Säufer ['zɔʏfər] (-s, -; ung) m boozer

saugen ['zaʊgən] (unreg) vt, vi to suck

säugen ['zɔʏgən] vt to suckle

Sauger ['zaʊgər] (-s, -) m dummy, comforter (US); (auf Flasche) teat; (Staub~) vacuum cleaner, hoover (®)

Säugetier ['zɔʏgə-] nt mammal

Säugling m infant, baby

Säule ['zɔʏlə] f column, pillar

Saum [zaʊm] (-(e)s, Säume) m hem; (Naht) seam

säumen ['zɔʏmən] vt to hem; to seam ♦ vi to delay, to hesitate

Sauna ['zaʊna] (-, -s) f sauna

Säure ['zɔʏrə] f acid; (Geschmack) sourness, acidity

sausen ['zaʊzən] vi to blow; (umg: eilen) to rush; (Ohren) to buzz; etw ~ lassen (umg) not to bother with sth

Saxophon [zakso'foːn] (-s, -e) nt saxophone

SB abk = Selbstbedienung

S-Bahn f abk (= Schnellbahn) high speed railway; (= Stadtbahn) suburban railway

schaben ['ʃaːbən] vt to scrape

schäbig ['ʃɛːbɪç] adj shabby

Schablone [ʃa'bloːnə] f stencil; (Muster) pattern; (fig) convention

Schach [ʃax] (-s, -s) nt chess; (Stellung) check; ~**brett** nt chessboard; ~**figur** f chessman; **s~matt** adj checkmate; ~**spiel** nt game of chess

Schacht [ʃaxt] (-(e)s, -e) m shaft

Schachtel (-, -n) f box; (pej: Frau) bag, cow

schade ['ʃaːdə] adj a pity od shame ♦ excl: (wie) ~! what a pity od shame; sich dat zu ~ sein für etw to consider o.s. too good for sth

Schädel ['ʃɛːdəl] (-s, -) m skull; ~**bruch** m fractured skull

Schaden ['ʃaːdən] (-s, -) m damage; (Verletzung) injury; (Nachteil) disadvantage; **s~** vi +dat to hurt; einer Sache s~ to damage sth; ~**ersatz** m compensation, damages pl; ~**freude** f malicious glee; **s~froh** adj (Mensch, Lachen) gloating

schadhaft ['ʃaːthaft] adj faulty, damaged

schäd- ['ʃɛːt] zW: ~**igen** ['ʃɛdɪgən] vt to damage; (Person) to do harm to, to harm; ~**lich** adj ~**lich (für)** harmful (to); **S~lichkeit** f harmfulness; **S~ling** m pest

Schadstoff ['ʃaːtʃtɔf] m harmful substance

Schaf [ʃaːf] (-(e)s, -e) nt sheep; ~**bock** m ram

Schäfer ['ʃɛːfər] (-s, -e) m shepherd; ~**hund** m Alsatian (dog) (BRIT), German shepherd (dog) (US)

schaffen ['ʃafən] (-s) nt (creative) activity

schaffen¹ (unreg) vt to create; (Platz) to make

schaffen² vt (erreichen) to manage, to do; (erledigen) to finish; (Prüfung) to pass; (transportieren) to take ♦ vi (umg: arbeiten) to work; sich dat etw ~ to get o.s. sth; sich an etw dat zu ~ **machen** to busy o.s. with sth

Schaffner(in) ['ʃafnər(ɪn)] (-s, -) m(f) (Bus~) conductor(tress); (EISENB) guard

Schaft [ʃaft] (-(e)s, -e) m shaft; (von Gewehr) stock; (von Stiefel) leg; (BOT) stalk; tree trunk; ~**stiefel** m high boot

Schakal [ʃa'kaːl] (-s, -e) m jackal

Schal [ʃaːl] (-s, -e) m scarf

schal adj flat; (fig) insipid

Schälchen ['ʃɛːlçən] nt cup, bowl

Schale ['ʃaːlə] f skin; (abgeschält) peel; (Nuß~, Muschel~, Ei~) shell; (Geschirr) dish, bowl

schälen ['ʃɛːlən] vt to shell; to peel ♦ vr to peel

Schall [ʃal] (-(e)s, -e) m sound;

Schrank [ʃraŋk] (-(e)s, -̈e) m cupboard; (Kleider~) wardrobe; (~/barrier; ~enwärter m (EISENB) level crossing attendant; ~koffer m trunk

Schraube ['ʃraubə] f screw; ~n vt to screw; ~nschlüssel m spanner; ~nzieher (-s, -) m screwdriver

Schraubstock ['ʃraupʃtɔk] m (TECH) vice

Schreck [ʃrɛk] (-(e)s, -e) m terror; fright; ~en (-s, -) m terror; fright; s~en vt to frighten, to scare; ~gespenst nt nightmare, nemesis; ~haft adj jumpy, easily frightened; s~lich adj terrible, dreadful

Schrei [ʃrai] (-(e)s, -e) m scream; (Ruf) shout

Schreib- ['ʃraib] zW: ~block m writing pad; s~en (unreg) vt, vi to write; (buchstabieren) to spell; ~en (-s, -) nt letter, communication; s~faul adj bad about writing letters; ~kraft f typist; ~maschine f typewriter; ~papier nt notepaper; ~tisch m desk; ~ung f spelling; ~waren pl stationery sg; ~weise f spelling; way of writing; ~zentrale f typing pool; ~zeug nt writing materials pl

schreien ['ʃraiən] (unreg) vt, vi to scream; (rufen) to shout; ~d adj (fig) glaring; (Farbe) loud

Schrein (-(e)s, -e) m shrine

Schreiner ['ʃrainər] (-s, -) m joiner; (Zimmermann) carpenter; (Möbel~) cabinetmaker; ~ei [-'rai] f joiner's workshop

schreiten ['ʃraitən] (unreg) vi to stride

schrieb etc [ʃriːp] vb siehe schreiben

Schrift [ʃrift] (-, -en) f writing; handwriting; (~art) script; (Gedrucktes) pamphlet, work; ~deutsch nt written German; ~führer m secretary; s~lich adj written ◆ adv in writing; ~sprache f written language; ~steller(in) (-s, -) m(f) writer; ~stück nt document; ~wechsel

m correspondence

schrill [ʃril] adj shrill

Schritt [ʃrit] (-(e)s, -e) m step; (Gangart) walk; (Tempo) pace; (von Hose) crutch; ~ fahren to drive at walking pace; ~macher m pacemaker; ~(t)empo nt: im ~(t)empo at a walking pace

schroff [ʃrɔf] adj steep; (zackig) jagged; (fig) brusque; (ungeduldig) abrupt

schröpfen ['ʃrœpfən] vt (fig) to fleece

Schrot [ʃroːt] (-(e)s, -e) m od nt (Blei) (small) shot; (Getreide) coarsely ground grain, groats pl; ~flinte f shotgun

Schrott [ʃrɔt] (-(e)s, -e) m scrap metal; ~haufen m scrap heap; s~reif adj ready for the scrap heap

schrubben ['ʃrubən] vt to scrub

Schrubber (-s, -) m scrubbing brush

schrumpfen ['ʃrumpfən] vi to shrink; (Apfel) to shrivel

Schub- ['ʃuːb] zW: ~fach nt drawer; ~karren m wheelbarrow; ~lade f drawer

Schubs (-es, -e) (umg) m shove (inf), push

schüchtern ['ʃyçtərn] adj shy; S~heit f shyness

Schuft [ʃuft] (-(e)s, -e) m scoundrel

schuften (umg) vi to graft, to slave away

Schuh [ʃuː] (-(e)s, -e) m shoe; ~band nt shoelace; ~creme f shoe polish; ~größe f shoe size; ~löffel m shoehorn; ~macher m shoemaker

Schul- zW: ~arbeit f homework (no pl); ~aufgaben pl homework sg; ~besuch m school attendance; ~buch nt school book

Schuld [ʃult] (-, -en) f guilt; (FIN) debt; (Verschulden) fault; s~ adj: s~ sein od haben (an +dat) to be to blame (for); er ist od hat ~ it's his fault; jdm s~ geben to blame sb; **s~en** [ˈʃʊldən] vt to owe; **s~enfrei** adj free from debt; **~gefühl** nt feeling of guilt; **s~ig** adj guilty; (*gebührend*) due; **s~ig an etw** *dat* **sein** to be guilty of sth; **jdm etw s~ig sein** to owe sb sth; **jdm etw s~ig bleiben** not to provide sb with sth; **s~los** adj innocent, without guilt; **~ner** (-s, -) m debtor; **~schein** m promissory note, IOU

Schule [ˈʃuːlə] f school; **s~n** vt to train, to school

Schüler(in) [ˈʃyːlər(ɪn)] (-s, -) m(f) pupil

Schul- zW: **~ferien** pl school holidays; **s~frei** adj: **s~freier Tag** holiday; **s~frei sein** to be a holiday; **~hof** m playground; **~jahr** nt school year; **~junge** m schoolboy; **~kind** nt schoolchild; **~mädchen** nt schoolgirl; **s~pflichtig** adj of school age; **~schiff** nt (*NAUT*) training ship; **~stunde** f period, lesson; **~tasche** f school bag

Schulter [ˈʃʊltər] (-, -n) f shoulder; **~blatt** nt shoulder blade; **s~n** vt to shoulder

Schulung f education, schooling

Schulzeugnis nt school report

Schund [ʃʊnt] (-(e)s) m trash, garbage

Schuppe [ˈʃʊpə] f scale; ~n pl (*Haarschuppen*) dandruff sg

Schuppen (-s, -) m shed

schuppen vt to scale ♦ vr to peel

schuppig [ˈʃʊpɪç] adj scaly

Schur [ʃuːr] (-, -en) f shearing

schüren [ˈʃyːrən] vt to rake; (*fig*) to stir up

schürfen [ˈʃʏrfən] vt, vi to scrape, to scratch; (*MIN*) to prospect

Schurke [ˈʃʊrkə] (-n, -n) m rogue

Schurwolle f: „reine ~" "pure new wool"

Schürze [ˈʃʏrtsə] f apron

Schuss [ʃʊs] (-sses, -sse) m shot; (*WEBEN*) woof; **~bereich** m effective range

Schüssel [ˈʃʏsəl] (-, -n) f bowl

Schuß- zW: **~linie** f line of fire;

~verletzung f bullet wound; **~waffe** f firearm

Schuster [ˈʃuːstər] (-s, -) m cobbler, shoemaker

Schutt [ʃʊt] (-(e)s) m rubbish; (*Bau-*) rubble; **~abladeplatz** m refuse dump

Schüttelfrost m shivering

schütteln [ˈʃʏtəln] vt, vr to shake

schütten [ˈʃʏtən] vt to pour; (*Zucker, Kies etc*) to tip; (*ver~*) to spill ♦ vi unpers to pour (down)

Schutthalde f dump

Schutthaufen m heap of rubble

Schutz [ʃʊts] (-es) m protection; (*Unterschlupf*) shelter; **jdn in ~ nehmen** to stand up for sb; **~anzug** m overalls pl; **~blech** nt mudguard

Schütze [ˈʃʏtsə] (-n, -n) m gunman; (*Gewehr~*) rifleman; (*Scharf~, Sport~*) marksman; (*ASTROL*) Sagittarius

schützen vt to protect; **~ vor** +*dat* **od gegen** to protect from

Schützenfest nt fair featuring shooting matches

Schutz- zW: **~engel** m guardian angel; **~gebiet** nt protectorate; (*Naturschutzgebiet*) reserve; **~impfung** f immunisation; **Schützling** m protégé(e); (*bes Kind*) charge; **s~los** adj defenceless; **~mann** m policeman; **~patron** m patron saint

Schwabe [ˈʃvaːbə] (-n, -n) m (*GEOG*) Swabian (*male*)

Schwaben [ˈʃvaːbən] nt Swabia; **Schwäbin** f (*GEOG*) Swabian (*female*); **schwäbisch** [ˈʃvɛːbɪʃ] adj Swabian

schwach [ʃvax] adj weak, feeble

Schwäche [ˈʃvɛçə] f weakness; **s~n** vt to weaken

Schwachheit f weakness

schwächlich adj weakly, delicate

Schwächling m weakling

Schwach- zW: **~sinn** m imbecility; **s~sinnig** adj mentally deficient; (*Idee*) idiotic; **~strom** m weak current

Schwächung [ˈʃvɛçʊŋ] f weakening

Schwager ['ʃvaːgər] (-s, ⸚) m brother-in-law

Schwägerin ['ʃvɛːgərɪn] f sister-in-law

Schwalbe ['ʃvalbə] f swallow

Schwall [ʃval] (-(e)s, -e) m surge; (Worte) flood, torrent

Schwamm [ʃvam] (-(e)s, ⸚e) m sponge; (Pilz) fungus

schwamm etc vb siehe schwimmen

schwammig adj spongy; (Gesicht) puffy

Schwan [ʃvaːn] (-(e)s, ⸚e) m swan

schwanger ['ʃvaŋər] adj pregnant

Schwangerschaft f pregnancy

Schwank [ʃvaŋk] (-(e)s, ⸚e) m funny story

schwanken vi to sway; (taumeln) to stagger, to reel; (Preise, Zahlen) to fluctuate; (zögern) to hesitate, to vacillate

Schwankung f fluctuation

Schwanz [ʃvants] (-es, ⸚e) m tail

schwänzen ['ʃvɛntsən] (umg) vt to skip, to cut ♦ vi to play truant

Schwarm [ʃvarm] (-(e)s, ⸚e) m swarm; (umg) heart-throb, idol

schwärm- ['ʃvɛrm] zW: **~en** vi to swarm; **~en für** to be mad or wild about; **S~erei** [-ə'raɪ] f enthusiasm; **~erisch** adj impassioned, effusive

Schwarte ['ʃvartə] f hard skin; (Speck~) rind

schwarz [ʃvarts] adj black; **~es Brett** notice board; **ins S~e treffen** (auch fig) to hit the bull's eye; **in den ~en Zahlen** in the black; **S~arbeit** f illicit work, moonlighting; **S~brot** nt black bread; **S~e(r)** f(m) black (man/woman)

Schwärze ['ʃvɛrtsə] f blackness; (Farbe) blacking; (Drucker~) printer's ink; **s~n** vt to blacken

Schwarz- zW: **s~fahren** (unreg) vi to travel without paying; to drive without a licence; **~handel** m blackmarket (trade); **~hören** vi to listen to the radio without a licence; **~markt** m black market; **s~sehen** (unreg; umg) vi to see the gloomy side of things; (TV) to watch TV without a licence; **~seher** m pessimist; (TV) viewer without a licence; **~wald** m Black Forest; **s~weiß** adj black and white

schwatzen [ʃvatsən] vi to chatter

schwätzen ['ʃvɛtsən] vi to chatter

Schwätzer ['ʃvɛtsər] (-s, -) m gasbag

schwatzhaft adj talkative, gossipy

Schwebe ['ʃveːbə] f: **in der ~** (fig) in abeyance; **~bahn** f overhead railway; **~balken** m (SPORT) beam; **s~n** vi to drift, to float; (hoch) to soar

Schwed- ['ʃveːd] zW: **~e** m Swede; **~en** nt Sweden; **~in** f Swede; **s~isch** adj Swedish

Schwefel ['ʃveːfəl] (-s) m sulphur; **s~ig** adj sulphurous; **~säure** f sulphuric acid

Schweig- ['ʃvaɪg] zW: **~egeld** nt hush money; **~en** (-s) nt silence; **s~en** (unreg) vi to be silent; to stop talking; **s~sam** ['ʃvaɪkzaːm] adj silent, taciturn; **~samkeit** f taciturnity, quietness

Schwein [ʃvaɪn] (-(e)s, -e) nt pig; (umg) (good) luck

Schweine- zW: **~fleisch** nt pork; **~rei** f mess; (Gemeinheit) dirty trick; **~stall** m pigsty

schweinisch adj filthy

Schweinsleder nt pigskin

Schweiß [ʃvaɪs] (-es) m sweat, perspiration; **s~en** vt, vi to weld; **~er** (-s, -) m welder; **~füße** pl sweaty feet; **~naht** f weld

Schweiz [ʃvaɪts] f Switzerland; **~er(in)** m(f) Swiss; **s~erisch** adj Swiss

schwelgen ['ʃvɛlgən] vi to indulge

Schwelle ['ʃvɛlə] f (auch fig) threshold; doorstep; (EISENB) sleeper (BRIT), tie (US)

schwellen (unreg) vi to swell

Schwellung f swelling

Schwemme ['ʃvɛmə] f (WIRTS: Überangebot) surplus

Schwenk- ['ʃvɛŋk] zW: **s~bar** adj swivel-mounted; **s~en** vt to swing; (Fahne) to wave; (abspülen) to rinse ♦ vi to turn, to swivel; (MIL) to wheel; **~ung** f turn; wheel

schwer [ʃveːr] adj heavy; (schwierig) difficult, hard; (schlimm) serious, bad ♦ adv (sehr) very (much) (verletzt etc) seriously, badly; **S~arbeiter** m manual worker, labourer; **S~behinderte(r)** f(m) seriously handicapped person; **S~e** f weight, heaviness; (PHYS) gravity; **~elos** adj weightless; (Kammer) zero-G; **~erziehbar** adj difficult to bring up); **~fallen** (unreg) vi: jdm **~fallen** to be difficult for sb; **~fällig** adj ponderous; **S~gewicht** nt heavyweight; (fig) emphasis; **~hörig** adj hard of hearing; **S~industrie** f heavy industry; **S~kraft** f gravity; **S~kranke(r)** mf person who is seriously ill; **~lich** adv hardly; **~machen** vt: jdm/sich etw **~machen** to make sth difficult for sb/o.s.; **~mütig** adj melancholy; **~nehmen** (unreg) vt to take to heart; **S~punkt** m centre of gravity; (fig) emphasis, crucial point

Schwert [ʃveːrt] (-(e)s, -er) nt sword; **~lilie** f iris

schwer- zW: **~tun** (unreg) vi to have difficulties; **S~verbrecher(in)** m(f) criminal, serious offender; **~verdaulich** adj indigestible, heavy; **~verletzt** adj badly injured; **S~verletzte(r)** f(m) serious casualty (bei Unfall usw auch) seriously injured person; **~wiegend** adj weighty, important

Schwester ['ʃvɛstɐ] (-, -n) f sister; (MED) nurse; **~lich** adj sisterly

Schwieger- ['ʃviːɡɐ] zW: **~eltern** pl parents-in-law; **~mutter** f mother-in-law; **~sohn** m son-in-law; **~tochter** f daughter-in-law; **~vater** m father-in-law

Schwiele ['ʃviːlə] f callus

schwierig ['ʃviːrɪç] adj difficult, hard; **S~keit** f difficulty

Schwimm- ['ʃvɪm] zW: **s~bad** nt swimming baths pl; **~becken** nt swimming pool; **s~en** (unreg) vi to swim; (treiben, nicht sinken) to float; (fig: unsicher sein) to be all at sea; **~er** (-s, -) m swimmer; (Angeln) float; **~erin** f (female) swimmer; **~lehrer** m swimming instructor; **~weste** f life jacket

Schwindel ['ʃvɪndl] (-s) m giddiness; dizzy spell; (Betrug) swindle, fraud; (Zeug) stuff; **s~frei** adj: s~frei sein to have a good head for heights; **s~n** vi (umg) to fib; (lügen) to fib; jdm **s~t** es sb feels dizzy

schwinden ['ʃvɪndən] (unreg) vi to disappear; (sich verringern) to decrease; (Kräfte) to decline

Schwindler ['ʃvɪndlɐ] m swindler; (Lügner) liar

schwindlig adj dizzy; **mir ist ~ I** feel dizzy

Schwing- ['ʃvɪŋ] zW: **s~en** (unreg) vt to swing; (Waffe etc) to brandish ♦ vi to swing; (vibrieren) to vibrate; (klingen) to sound; **~tür** f swing door(s); **~ung** f vibration; (PHYS) oscillation

Schwips [ʃvɪps] (-es, -e) m: einen ~ haben to be tipsy

schwirren ['ʃvɪrən] vi to buzz

schwitzen ['ʃvɪtsən] vi to sweat, to perspire

schwören ['ʃvøːrən] (unreg) vt, vi to swear

schwul [ʃvuːl] (umg) adj gay, queer

schwül [ʃvyːl] adj sultry, close; **S~e** (-) f sultriness

Schwule(r) (umg) f(m) gay (man/woman)

schwülstig ['ʃvʏlstɪç] adj pompous

Schwung [ʃvʊŋ] (-(e)s, ⁻e) m swing; (Triebkraft) momentum; (fig: Energie) verve, energy; (umg: Menge) batch; **s~haft** adj brisk, lively; **s~voll** adj vigorous

Schwur [ʃvuːr] (-(e)s, ⁻e) m oath; **~gericht** nt court with a jury

sechs [zɛks] num six; **~hundert** num six hundred; **~te(r, s)** adj sixth;

S~tel (-s, -) nt sixth

sechzehn ['zɛçtse:n] num sixteen

sechzig ['zɛçtsɪç] num sixty

See[1] [ze:] f -, -n f sea

See[2] (-s, -n) m lake

See [ze:] zW: **~bad** m seaside resort; **~hund** m seal; **~igel** ['ze:?i:gəl] m sea urchin; **~krank** adj seasick; **~krankheit** f seasickness; **~lachs** m rock salmon

Seele ['ze:lə] f soul; **s~nruhig** adv calmly

Seeleute ['ze:lɔytə] pl seamen

Seel- zW: **s~isch** adj mental; **~sorge** f pastoral duties pl; **~sorger** (-s, -) m clergyman

See- zW: **~macht** f naval power; **~mann** (pl -leute) m seaman, sailor; **~meile** f nautical mile; **~möwe** f (ZOOL) seagull; **~not** f distress; **~räuber** m pirate; **~rose** f water lily; **~stern** m starfish; **~tang** m (BOT) seaweed; **s~tüchtig** adj seaworthy; **~weg** m sea route; **auf dem ~weg** by sea; **~zunge** f sole

Segel ['ze:gəl] (-s, -) nt sail; **~boot** nt yacht; **~fliegen** (-s) nt gliding; **~flieger** m glider pilot; **~flugzeug** nt glider; **s~n**, vi to sail; **~schiff** nt sailing vessel; **~sport** m sailing; **~tuch** nt canvas

Segen ['ze:gən] (-s, -) m blessing; **s~sreich** adj beneficial

Segler ['ze:glɐ] (-s, -) m sailor, yachtsman

segnen ['ze:gnən] vt to bless

Seh- ['ze:] zW: **s~en** (unreg) vt, vi to see; (in bestimmte Richtung) to look; **mal s~en(, ob ...)** let's see (if ...); **siehe Seite 5** see page 5; **s~enswert** adj worth seeing; **~enswürdigkeiten** pl sights (of a town); **~er** (-s, -) m seer; **~fehler** m sight defect

Sehne ['ze:nə] f sinew; (an Bogen) string

sehnen vr: **sich ~ nach** to long od yearn for

sehnig adj sinewy

Sehn- ['ze:n] zW: **s~lich** adj ardent;

~sucht f longing; **s~süchtig** adj longing

sehr [ze:r] adv very; (mit Verben) a lot, (very) much; **zu ~** too much; **~geehrte(r)** ... dear ...

seicht [zaɪçt] adj (auch fig) shallow

Seide ['zaɪdə] f silk; **s~n** adj silk; **~npapier** nt tissue paper

seidig ['zaɪdɪç] adj silky

Seife ['zaɪfə] f soap

Seifen- zW: **~lauge** f soapsuds pl; **~schale** f soap dish; **~schaum** m lather

seihen ['zaɪən] vt to strain, to filter

Seil [zaɪl] (-(e)s, -e) nt rope; cable; **~bahn** f cable railway; **~hüpfen** (-s) nt skipping; **~springen** (-s) nt skipping; **~tänzer(in)** m(f) tightrope walker

---

SCHLÜSSELWORT

sein (pt war, pp gewesen) vi 1 to be; **ich bin I am**; **du bist you are**; **er/sie/es ist he/she/it is**; **wir sind/ihr seid/sie sind** we/you/they are; **wir waren we were**; **wir sind gewesen we have been**

2: seien Sie nicht böse don't be angry; **sei so gut und ...** be so kind as to ...; **das wäre gut** that would od that'd be a good thing; **wenn ich Sie wäre** if I were od was you; **das wär's** that's that's all, that's it; **morgen bin ich in Rom** tomorrow I'll od I will od I shall be in Rome; **waren Sie mal in Rom?** have you ever been to Rome?

3: wie ist das zu verstehen? how is that to be understood?; **er ist nicht zu ersetzen** he cannot be replaced; **mit ihr ist nicht zu reden** you can't talk to her

4: mir ist kalt I'm cold; **was ist?** what's the matter, what is it?; **ist was?** is something the matter?; **es sei denn, daß ...** unless ...; **wie dem auch sei** be that as it may; **wie wäre es mit ...?** how od what about ...?; **laß das sein!** stop that!

sein(e) ['zaɪn(ə)] *adj* his; its; ~**e(r,**
s) *pron* his; its; ~**er** (*gen von* er)
pron of him; ~**erseits** *adv* for his
part; ~**erzeit** *adv* in those days, formerly; ~**esgleichen** *pron* people like
him; ~**etwegen** (*für ihn*) for his
sake; (*wegen ihm*) on his account;
(*von ihm aus*) as far as he is concerned; ~**etwillen** *adv*: **um** ~**etwil-**
len = ~**etwegen**; ~**ige** *pron*: **der/**
die/das ~**ige** his

Seismograph [zaɪsmo'graːf] *m* (-en,
-en) *m* seismograph

seit [zaɪt] *präp* +*dat* since ♦ *konj*
since; **er ist** ~ **einer Woche hier**
he has been here for a week; ~
langem for a long time; ~**dem**
[zaɪt'deːm] *adv, konj* since

Seite ['zaɪtə] *f* side; (*Buch*~) page;
(*MIL*) flank

Seiten- *zW*: ~**ansicht** *f* side view;
~**hieb** *m* (*fig*) passing shot, dig; ~**s**
präp +*gen* on the part of; ~**schiff** *nt*
aisle; ~**sprung** *m* extramarital esca-
pade; ~**stechen** *nt* a stitch; ~**stra-**
ße *f* side road; ~**streifen** *m* verge;
(*der Autobahn*) hard shoulder

seither [zaɪt'heːr] *adv, konj* since
(then)

seitlich *adj* on one ad the side; side
cpd

seitwärts *adv* sidewards

Sekretär [zekre'tɛːr] *m* secretary;
(*Möbel*) bureau; ~**in** *f* secretary

Sekretariat [zekretari'aːt] *nt* (-(e)s, -e)
nt secretary's office, secretariat

Sekt [zɛkt] (-(e)s, -e) *m* champagne

Sekte ['zɛktə] *f* sect

Sekunde [ze'kʊndə] *f* second

selber ['zɛlbər] *pron* = **selbst**

Selbst [zɛlpst] (-) *nt* self

SCHLÜSSELWORT

selbst *pron* 1: **ich/er/wir selbst** I
myself/he himself/we ourselves; **sie**
ist die Tugend selbst she's virtue
itself; **er braut sein Bier selbst** he
brews his own beer; **wie geht's?** ~
gut, und selbst? how are things? –
fine, and yourself?

2 (*ohne Hilfe*) alone, on my/his/one's
etc own; **von selbst** by itself; **er**
kam von selbst he came of his own
accord

♦ *adv* even; **selbst wenn** even if;
selbst Gott even God (himself)

---

selbständig ['zɛlpʃtɛndɪç] *adj* independent; **S**~**keit** *f* independence

Selbst- *zW*: ~**auslöser** *m* (*PHOT*)
delayed-action shutter release; ~**be-**
dienung *f* self-service; ~**befriedi-**
gung *f* masturbation; ~**beherr-**
schung *f* self-control; ~**bestim-**
mung *f* (*POL*) self-determination; ~**beteili-**
gung *f* (*VERSICHERUNG*: *bei*
Kosten) (voluntary) excess; ~**be-**
wußt *adj* self-confident; ~**bewußt-**
sein *nt* self-confidence; ~**erhaltung** *f*
self-preservation; ~**erkenntnis** *f*
self-knowledge; **s**~**gefällig** *adj* smug,
self-satisfied; **s**~**gemacht** *adj* home-
made; ~**gespräch** *nt* conversation
with o.s.; ~**kostenpreis** *m* cost
price; **s**~**los** *adj* unselfish, selfless;
~**mord** *m* suicide; ~**mörder(in)** *m(f)*
suicide; **s**~**mörderisch** *adj* suicidal;
s~**sicher** *adj* self-assured; **s**~**süchtig**
adj (*Mensch*) selfish; **s**~**verständlich**
['zɛlpstfɛrʃtɛntlɪç] *adj* obvious ♦ *adv*
naturally; **ich halte das für**
s~**verständlich** I take that for
granted; ~**verteidigung** *f* self-
defence; ~**vertrauen** *nt* self-
confidence; ~**verwaltung** *f* autono-
my, self-government

selig ['zeːlɪç] *adj* happy, blissful;
(*REL*) blessed; (*tot*) late; **S**~**keit** *f*
bliss

Sellerie ['zɛləriː] (-s, -(s) *od* -, -) *m*
od celery

selten ['zɛltən] *adj* rare ♦ *adv* seldom, rarely; **S**~**heit** *f* rarity

Selterswasser ['zɛltɐsvasɐr] *nt*
soda water

seltsam ['zɛltzaːm] *adj* strange, curious; **S**~**keit** *f* strangeness

Semester [ze'mɛstər] (-s, -) *nt* semester

Semi- [zemi] *in zW* semi-; ~**kolon**

eous

Sinfonie [zɪnfo'niː] *f* symphony

singen ['zɪŋən] (*unreg*) *vt, vi* to sing

Singular ['zɪŋgulaːr] *m* singular

Singvogel ['zɪŋfoːgəl] *m* songbird

sinken ['zɪŋkən] (*unreg*) *vi* to sink; (*Preise etc*) to fall, to go down

Sinn [zɪn] (-(e)s, -e) *m* mind; (*Wahrnehmungs~*) sense; (*Bedeutung*) sense, meaning; ~ **für etw** sense of sth; **von ~en sein** to be out of one's mind; **es hat keinen ~** there's no point; ~**bild** *nt* symbol; **s~en** (*unreg*) *vi* to ponder; **auf etw** *akk* **s~en** to contemplate sth; ~**estäuschung** *f* illusion; **s~gemäß** *adj* faithful; (*Wiedergabe*) in one's own words; **s~ig** *adj* clever; **s~lich** *adj* sensual, sensuous; (*Wahrnehmung*) sensory; ~**lichkeit** *f* sensuality; **s~los** *adj* senseless; meaningless; ~**losigkeit** *f* senselessness; meaninglessness; **s~voll** *adj* meaningful; (*vernünftig*) sensible

Sintflut ['zɪntfluːt] *f* Flood

Sippe ['zɪpə] *f* clan, kin

Sippschaft ['zɪpʃaft] (*pej*) *f* relations *pl*, tribe; (*Bande*) gang

Sirene [zi'reːnə] *f* siren

Sirup ['ziːrʊp] (-s, -e) *m* syrup

Sitt- ['zɪt] *zW*: ~**e** *f* custom; ~**en** *pl* (*Sittlichkeit*) morals; ~**enpolizei** *f* vice squad; **s~sam** *adj* modest, demure

Situation [zituatsi'oːn] *f* situation

Sitz [zɪts] (-es, -e) *m* seat; **der Anzug hat einen guten ~** the suit is a good fit; **s~en** (*unreg*) *vi* to sit; (*Bemerkung, Schlag*) to strike home, to tell; (*Gelerntes*) to have sunk in; **s~en bleiben** to remain seated; **s~enbleiben** (*unreg*) *vi* (*SCH*) to have to repeat a year; **auf etw** *dat* **s~enbleiben** to be lumbered with sth; **s~end** *adj* (*Tätigkeit*) sedentary; **s~enlassen** (*unreg*) *vt* (*SCH*) to make (sb) repeat a year; (*Mädchen*) to jilt; (*Wartenden*) to stand up; **etw auf sich** *dat* **s~enlassen** to take sth lying down;

~**gelegenheit** *f* place to sit down; ~**platz** *m* seat; ~**streik** *m* sit-down strike; ~**ung** *f* meeting

Sizilien [zi'tsiːliən] *nt* Sicily

Skala ['skaːla] (-, Skalen) *f* scale

Skalpell [skal'pɛl] (-s, -e) *nt* scalpel

Skandal [skan'daːl] (-s, -e) *m* scandal; **s~ös** *adj* scandalous

Skandinav- [skandi'naːv] *zW*: ~**ien** *nt* Scandinavia; ~**ier(in)** *m(f)* Scandinavian; **s~isch** *adj* Scandinavian

Skelett [ske'lɛt] (-(e)s, -e) *nt* skeleton

Skepsis ['skɛpsɪs] (-) *f* scepticism

skeptisch ['skɛptɪʃ] *adj* sceptical

Ski [ʃiː] (-s, -er) *m* ski; ~ **laufen** *od* **fahren** to ski; ~**fahrer** *m* skier; ~**läufer** *m* skier; ~**lehrer** *m* ski instructor; ~**lift** *m* ski-lift; ~**springen** *nt* ski-jumping; ~**stock** *m* ski-pole

Skizze ['skɪtsə] *f* sketch

skizzieren [skɪ'tsiːrən] *vt, vi* to sketch

Sklave ['sklaːvə] (-n, -n) *m* slave; ~**rei** *f* slavery; **Sklavin** *f* slave

Skonto ['skɔnto] (-s, -s) *m od nt* discount

Skorpion [skɔrpi'oːn] (-s, -e) *m* scorpion; (*ASTROL*) Scorpio

Skrupel ['skruːpəl] (-s, -) *m* scruple; ~**los** *adj* unscrupulous

Skulptur [skʊlp'tuːr] *f* (*Gegenstand*) sculpture

Slalom ['slaːlɔm] (-s, -s) *m* slalom

Slip [slɪp] (-s, -s) *m* (under)pants

Slowenien *nt* Slovenia

Smaragd [sma'rakt] (-(e)s, -e) *m* emerald

Smoking ['smoːkɪŋ] (-s, -s) *m* dinner jacket

SCHLÜSSELWORT

so *adv* **1** (*sosehr*) so; **so groß/schön etc** so big/nice etc; **so groß/schön wie ...** as big/nice as ...; **das hat ihn so geärgert, daß ...** that annoyed him so much that ...; **so einer wie ich** somebody like me; **na so was!** well, well!

2 (*auf diese Weise*) like this; **mach**

es nicht so don't do it like that; so oder so in one way or the other; und so weiter and so on; ... oder so was ... or something like that; das ist gut so that's fine

3 (*umg: umsonst*): **ich habe es so bekommen** I got it for nothing ♦ *konj*

♦ *konj*: **so daß** so that; **so wie es jetzt ist** as things are at the moment ♦ *excl*: **so?** really?; **so, das wär's** so, that's it then

s.o. *abk* = **siehe oben**

Söckchen ['zœkçən] *nt* ankle socks

Socke ['zɔkə] *f* sock

Sockel ['zɔkəl] (**-s, -**) *m* pedestal, base

Sodawasser ['zo:davasər] *nt* soda water

Sodbrennen ['zo:tbrɛnən] (**-s, -**) *nt* heartburn

soeben [zo'e:bən] *adv* just (now)

Sofa ['zo:fa] (**-s, -s**) *nt* sofa

sofern [zo'fɛrn] *konj* if, provided (that)

sofort [zo'fɔrt] *adv* immediately, at once; **~ig** *adj* immediate

Sog [zo:k] (**-(e)s, -e**) *m* (*Strömung*) undertow

sogar [zo'ga:r] *adv* even

sogenannt [zo'gənant] *adj* so-called

sogleich [zo'glaiç] *adv* straight away, at once

Sohle ['zo:lə] *f* sole; (*Tal~ etc*) bottom; (*MIN*) level

Sohn [zo:n] (**-(e)s, ⸚e**) *m* son

Solar- *in zW* solar; **~zelle** *f* solar cell

solch [zɔlç] *pron* such; **ein ~e(r, s)** ... such a ...

Soldat [zɔl'da:t] (**-en, -en**) *m* soldier

Söldner ['zœldnər] (**-s, -**) *m* mercenary

solidarisch [zoli'da:rɪʃ] *adj* in od with solidarity; **sich ~ erklären** to declare one's solidarity

Solidarität *f* solidarity

solid(e) [zo'li:d(ə)] *adj* solid; (*Leben, Person*) respectable

Solist(in) [zo'lıst(ın)] *m(f)* soloist

Soll [zɔl] (**-(s), -(s)**) *nt* (*FIN*) debit (side); (*Arbeitsmenge*) quota, target

sollen (*pt* sollte, *pp* **gesollt** *od* (*als Hilfsverb*) **sollen**) *Hilfsverb* **1** (*Pflicht, Befehl*) to be supposed to; **du hättest nicht gehen sollen** you shouldn't have gone, you oughtn't to have gone; **soll ich?** shall I?; **soll ich dir helfen?** shall I help you?; **sag ihm, er soll warten** tell him he's to wait; **was soll ich machen?** what should I do?

2 (*Vermutung*): **sie soll verheiratet sein** she's said to be married; **was soll das heißen?** what's that supposed to mean?; **man sollte glauben, daß** ... you would think that ...; **sollte das passieren,** ... if that should happen ...

♦ *vt, vi*: **was soll das?** what's all this?; **das sollst du nicht** you shouldn't do that; **was soll's?** what the hell!

Solo [zo:lo] (**-s, -s** *od* **Soli**) *nt* solo

somit [zo'mıt] *konj* and so, therefore

Sommer ['zɔmər] (**-s, -**) *m* summer; **s~lich** *adj* summery; summer; **~schlußverkauf** *m* summer sale; **~sprossen** *pl* freckles

Sonate [zo'na:tə] *f* sonata

Sonde ['zɔndə] *f* probe

Sonder- ['zɔndər] *in zW* special; **~angebot** *nt* special offer; **s~bar** *adj* strange, odd; **~fahrt** *f* special trip; **~fall** *m* special case; **s~lich** *adj* particular; (*außergewöhnlich*) remarkable; (*eigenartig*) peculiar; **~marke** *f* special issue stamp; **s~n** *konj* but ♦ *vt* to separate; **nicht nur** ..., **s~n auch** not only ..., but also; **~zug** *m* special train

Sonnabend ['zɔn'a:bənt] *m* Saturday

Sonne ['zɔnə] *f* sun; **s~n** *vr* to sun o.s.

Sonnen- *zW*: **~aufgang** *m* sunrise;

s~baden vi to sunbathe; **~brand** m sunburn; **~brille** f sunglasses pl; **~creme** f suntan lotion; **~energie** f solar energy, solar power; **~finsternis** f solar eclipse; **~kollektor** m solar panel; **~schein** m sunshine; **~schirm** m parasol, sunshade; **~stich** m sunstroke; **~uhr** f sundial; **~untergang** m sunset; **~wende** f solstice

sonnig ['zɔnɪç] adj sunny

Sonntag ['zɔntaːk] m Sunday

sonst [zɔnst] adv otherwise; (mit pron, in Fragen) else; (zu anderer Zeit) at other times, normally ♦ konj otherwise; **~ noch etwas?** anything else?; **~ nichts** nothing else; **~ig** adj other; **~jemand** pron anybody (at all); **~wo** somewhere else; **~woher** adv from somewhere else; **~wohin** adv somewhere else

sooft [zo'ɔft] konj whenever

Sopran [zo'praːn] (-s, -e) m soprano

Sopranistin f soprano

Sorge ['zɔrgə] f care, worry

sorgen ['zɔrgən] vi: **für jdn ~** to look after sb ♦ vr: **sich ~ (um)** to worry (about); **für etw ~** to take care of od see to sth; **~frei** adj carefree; **~voll** adj troubled, worried

Sorgerecht nt custody (of a child)

Sorg- [zɔrk] zW: **~falt** (-) f care(fulness); **s~fältig** adj careful; **s~los** adj careless; (ohne Sorgen) carefree; **s~sam** adj careful

Sorte ['zɔrtə] f sort; (Waren~) brand; **~n** pl (FIN) foreign currency sg

sortieren [zɔr'tiːrən] vt to sort (out)

Sortiment [zɔrti'mɛnt] nt assortment

sosehr [zo'zeːr] konj as much as

Soße ['zoːsə] f sauce; (Braten~) gravy

Souffleur [zu'fløːr] m prompter

Souffleuse [zu'fløːzə] f prompter

soufflieren [zu'fliːrən] vt, vi to prompt

Souterrain [zutɛ'rɛː] (-s, -s) nt basement

souverän [zuvɛ'rɛːn] adj sovereign;

(überlegen) superior

so- zW: **~viel** [zo'fiːl] konj as far as I know; **~viel (wie)** as much as; **rede nicht ~viel** don't talk so much; **~weit** [zo'vaɪt] konj as far as ♦ adj: **~weit sein** to be ready; **~weit wie od als möglich** as far as possible; **ich bin ~weit zufrieden** by and large I'm quite satisfied; **~wenig** [zo'veːnɪç] konj little as ♦ pron: **~wenig (wie)** as little (as); **~wie** [zo'viː] konj (sobald) as soon as; (ebenso) as well as; **~wieso** [zovi'zoː] adv anyway

sowjetisch [zɔ'vjetɪʃ] adj Soviet

Sowjetunion f Soviet Union

sowohl [zo'voːl] konj: **~ ... als** od **wie auch both ... and**

sozial [zotsi'aːl] adj social; **S~abgaben** pl national insurance contributions; **S~arbeiter(in)** m(f) social worker; **S~demokrat** m social democrat; **S~demokratisch** adj social democratic; **~isieren** vt to socialize; **S~ismus** [-'lɪsmʊs] m socialism; **S~ist** [-'lɪst] m socialist; **s~istisch** adj socialist; **S~politik** f social welfare policy; **S~produkt** nt (net) national product; **S~staat** m welfare state; **S~wohnung** f council flat

soziologisch [zotsio'loːgɪʃ] adj sociological

sozusagen [zotsu'zaːgən] adv so to speak

Spachtel ['ʃpaxtəl] (-s, -) m spatula

spähen ['ʃpɛːən] vi to peep, to peek

Spalier [ʃpa'liːr] (-s, -e) nt (Gerüst) trellis; (Leute) guard of honour

Spalt [ʃpalt] (-(e)s, -e) m crack; (Tür~) chink; (fig: Kluft) split; **~e** f crack, fissure; (Gletscherspalte) crevasse; (in Text) column; **s~en** vt, vr (auch fig) to split; **~ung** f splitting

Span [ʃpaːn] (-(e)s, -e) m shaving

Spanferkel nt sucking-pig

Spange ['ʃpaŋə] f clasp; (Haar~) hair slide; (Schnalle) buckle; (Arm~reif) bangle

Spanien ['ʃpaːniən] nt Spain

Spanier(in) m(f) Spaniard

spanisch adj Spanish
Spann- ['ʃpan] zW: **~beton** m prestressed concrete; **~bettuch** nt fitted sheet; **~e** f (Zeitspanne) space; (Differenz) gap; **s~en** vt (straffen) to tighten, to tauten; (befestigen) to brace ♦ vi to be tight; **s~end** adj exciting, gripping; **~ung** f tension; (ELEK) voltage; (fig) suspense; (unangenehm) tension

Spar- ['ʃpaːr] zW: **~buch** nt savings book; **~büchse** f moneybox; **s~en** vt, vi to save; **sich** dat etw **s~en** to save o.s. sth; (Bemerkung) to keep sth to o.s.; **mit etw s~en** to be sparing with sth; **an etw** dat **s~en** to economize on sth; **~er** (-s, -) m saver

Spargel ['ʃpargəl] (-s, -) m asparagus
Sparkasse f savings bank
Sparkonto nt savings account
spärlich ['ʃpɛːrlɪç] adj meagre; (Bekleidung) scanty
Spar- zW: **s~sam** adj economical, thrifty; **~samkeit** f thrift, economizing; **~schwein** nt piggy bank
Sparte ['ʃpartə] f field; line of business; (PRESSE) column
Spaß [ʃpaːs] (-es, **-e**) m joke; (Freude) fun; **jdm ~ machen** to be fun (for sb); **viel ~!** have fun!; **s~en** vi to joke; **mit ihm ist nicht zu s~en** you can't take liberties with him; **s~haft** adj funny, droll; **s~ig** adj funny, droll; **~verderber** (-s, -) m spoilsport
spät [ʃpɛːt] adj, adv late; **wie ~ ist es?** what's the time?
Spaten ['ʃpaːtən] (-s, -) m spade
später adj, adv later
spätestens adv at the latest
Spatz [ʃpats] (-en, **-en**) m sparrow
spazier- [ʃpaˈtsiːr] zW: **~engehen** (unreg) vi to go for a drive; **~engehen** (unreg) vi to go for a walk; **S~gang** m walk; **S~stock** m walking stick; **S~weg** m path, walk
Specht [ʃpɛçt] (-(e)s, **-e**) m wood-

pecker
Speck [ʃpɛk] (-(e)s, -e) m bacon
Spediteur [ʃpediˈtøːr] m carrier; (Möbel~) furniture remover
Spedition [ʃpediˈtsiˑɔːn] f carriage; (Speditionsfirma) road haulage contractor; removal firm
Speer [ʃpeːr] (-(e)s, -e) m spear; (SPORT) javelin
Speiche ['ʃpaɪçə] f spoke
Speichel ['ʃpaɪçəl] (-s) m saliva, spit(tle)
Speicher ['ʃpaɪçər] (-s, -) m storehouse; (Dach~) attic, loft; (Korn~) granary; (Wasser~) tank; (TECH) store; (COMPUT) memory; **s~n** vt to store; (COMPUT) to save
speien ['ʃpaɪən] (unreg) vt, vi to spit; (erbrechen) to vomit; (Vulkan) to spew
Speise ['ʃpaɪzə] f food; **~eis** [-ˈaɪs] nt ice-cream; **~kammer** f larder, pantry; **~karte** f menu; **s~n** vt to feed; to eat ♦ vi to dine; **~röhre** f gullet, oesophagus; **~saal** m dining room; **~wagen** m dining car
Speku- [ʃpeku] zW: **~lant** m speculator; **~lation** [-latsiˈoːn] f speculation; **s~lieren** [-ˈliːrən] vi (fig) to speculate; **auf etw** akk **s~lieren** to have hopes of sth
Spelunke [ʃpeˈlʊŋkə] f dive
Spende ['ʃpɛndə] f donation; **s~n** vt to donate, to give; **~r** (-s, -) m donor, donator
spendieren [ʃpɛnˈdiːrən] vt to pay for, to buy; **jdm etw ~** to treat sb to sth, to stand sb sth
Sperling ['ʃpɛrlɪŋ] m sparrow
Sperma ['ʃpɛrma] (-s, **Spermen**) nt sperm
Sperr- [ʃpɛr] zW: **~e** f barrier; (Verbot) ban; **s~en** vt to block; (SPORT) to suspend, to bar; (vom Ball) to obstruct; (einschließen) to lock; (verbieten) to ban ♦ vr to baulk, to jib(e); **~gebiet** nt prohibited area; **~holz** nt plywood; **s~ig** adj bulky; **~müll** m bulky refuse; **~sitz** m (THEAT) stalls pl; **~stunde**

f closing time

Spesen ['ʃpeːzən] *pl* expenses

Spezial- [ʃpetsiˈaːl] *in zW* special; **~gebiet** *nt* specialist field; **s~i'sieren** *vr* to specialize; **~i'sierung** *f* specialization; **~ist** ['-lɪst] *m* specialist; **~i'tät** *f* speciality

speziell [ʃpetsiˈɛl] *adj* special

spezifisch [ʃpeˈtsiːfiʃ] *adj* specific

Sphäre ['sfɛːrə] *f* sphere

Spiegel ['ʃpiːɡəl] **(-s, -)** *m* mirror; **(Wasser~)** level; **(MIL)** tab; **~bild** *nt* reflection; **s~bildlich** *adj* reversed; **~ei** *nt* fried egg; **s~n** *vt* to mirror, to reflect ♦ *vr* to be reflected ♦ *vi* to gleam; *(widerspiegeln)* to be reflective; **~ung** *f* reflection

Spiel [ʃpiːl] **(-(e)s, -e)** *nt* game; **(Schau~)** play; **(Tätigkeit)** play(ing); **(KARTEN)** deck; **(freie) Spiel** (free) play; **s~en** *vt, vi* to play; **(um Geld)** to gamble; **(THEAT)** to perform, to act; **s~end** *adv* easily; **~er (-s, -)** *m* player; **(um Geld)** gambler; **~e'rei** *f* trifling pastime; **~feld** *nt* pitch, field; **~film** *m* feature film; **~kasino** *nt* casino; **~plan** *m* **(THEAT)** programme; **~platz** *m* playground; **~raum** *m* room to manoeuvre, scope; **~regel** *f* rule; **~sachen** *pl* toys; **~uhr** *f* musical box; **~verderber (-s, -)** *m* spoilsport; **~waren** *pl* toys; **~zeug** *nt* toy(s)

Spieß [ʃpiːs] **(-es, -e)** *m* spear; **(Brat~)** spit; **~bürger** *m* bourgeois; **~er (-s, -; ung)** *m* bourgeois

spießig *(pej) adj* (petit) bourgeois

Spikes [spaɪks] *pl* spikes; **(AUT)** studs

Spinat [ʃpiˈnaːt] **(-(e)s, -e)** *m* spinach

Spind [ʃpɪnt] **(-(e)s, -e)** *m od nt* locker

Spinn- ['ʃpɪn] *zW*: **~e** *f* spider; **s~en (unreg)** *vt, vi* to spin; *(umg)* to talk rubbish; *(verrückt sein)* to be crazy *od* mad; **~e'rei** *f* spinning mill; **~rad** *nt* spinning-wheel; **~webe** *f* cobweb

Spion [ʃpiˈoːn] **(-s, -e)** *m* spy; *(in*

Tür) spyhole; **~age** [ʃpioˈnaːʒə] *f* espionage; **s~ieren** [ʃpioˈniːrən] *vi* to spy; **~in** *f* (female) spy

Spirale [ʃpiˈraːlə] *f* spiral

Spirituosen [ʃpirituˈoːzən] *pl* spirits

Spiritus ['ʃpiːritus] **(-, -se)** *m* (methylated) spirit

Spital [ʃpiˈtaːl] **(-s, ·er)** *nt* hospital

spitz [ʃpɪts] *adj* pointed; *(Winkel)* acute; *(fig: Zunge)* sharp; *(: Bemerkung)* caustic

Spitze [ʃpɪtsə] *f* point, tip; *(Berg~)* peak; *(Bemerkung)* taunt, dig; *(erster Platz)* lead, top; *(meist pl: Gewebe)* lace

Spitzel **(-s, -)** *m* police informer

spitzen *vt* to sharpen

Spitzenmarke *f* brand leader

spitzfindig *adj* (over)subtle

Spitzname *m* nickname

Splitter ['ʃplɪtər] **(-s, -)** *m* splinter

sponsern ['sponzərn, 'ʃponzərn] *vt* to sponsor

spontan [ʃpɔnˈtaːn] *adj* spontaneous

Sport [ʃpɔrt] **(-(e)s, -e)** *m* sport; *(fig)* hobby; **~lehrer(in)** *m(f)* games *od* P.E. teacher; **~ler(in) (-s, -)** *m(f)* sportsman(woman); **s~lich** *adj* sporting; *(Mensch)* sporty; **~platz** *m* playing *od* sports field; **~schuh** *m* *(Turnschuh)* training shoe, trainer; **~stadion** *nt* sports stadium; **~verein** *m* sports club; **~wagen** *m* sports car

Spott [ʃpɔt] **(-(e)s)** *m* mockery, ridicule; **s~billig** *adj* dirt-cheap; **s~en** *vi* to mock; **s~en (über +akk)** to mock (at), to ridicule

spöttisch ['ʃpœtiʃ] *adj* mocking

sprach *etc* [ʃpraːx] *vb siehe* sprechen

Sprach- *zW*: **s~begabt** *adj* good at languages; **~e** *f* language; **~enschule** *f* language school; **~fehler** *m* speech defect; **~führer** *m* phrasebook; **~gefühl** *nt* feeling for language; **~kurs** *m* language course; **~labor** *nt* language laboratory; **s~lich** *adj* linguistic; **s~los** *adj* speechless

sprang *etc* [ʃpraŋ] *vb siehe* springen

Spray [sprei] (-s, -s) *m od nt* spray

Sprech- [ʃprɛç] *zW:* ~**anlage** *f* intercom; **s~en** (*unreg*) *vi* to speak, to talk ♦ *vt* to say; (*Sprache*) to speak; (*Person*) to speak to; **mit jdm s~en** to speak to sb; **das spricht für ihn** that's a point in his favour; ~**er(in)** (-s, -) *m(f)* speaker; (*für Gruppe*) spokesman(woman); (*RADIO, TV*) announcer; ~**stunde** *f* consultation (hour); (*doctor's*) surgery; ~**stundenhilfe** *f* (*doctor's*) receptionist; ~**zimmer** *nt* consulting room, surgery, office (*US*)

spreizen [ʃpraɪtsən] *vt* (*Beine*) to open, to spread; (*Finger, Flügel*) to spread

Spreng- [ʃprɛŋ] *zW:* **s~en** *vt* to sprinkle; (*mit Sprengstoff*) to blow up; (*Gestein*) to blast; (*Versammlung*) to break up; ~**stoff** *m* explosive(s)

sprichst *etc* [ʃpriçst] *vb siehe* **sprechen**

Sprichwort *nt* proverb

sprichwörtlich *adj* proverbial

Spring- [ʃprɪŋ] *zW:* ~**brunnen** *m* fountain; **s~en** (*unreg*) *vi* to jump; (*Glas*) to crack; (*mit Kopfsprung*) to dive; ~**er** (-s, -) *m* jumper; (*Schach*) knight

Sprit [ʃprɪt] (-(e)s, -e) (*umg*) *m* juice, gas

Spritz- [ʃprɪts] *zW:* ~**e** *f* syringe; injection; (*an Schlauch*) nozzle; **s~en** *vt* to spray; (*MED*) to inject ♦ *vi* to splash; (*heraus~*) to spurt; (*MED*) to give injections; ~**pistole** *f* spray gun

spröde [ʃprøːdə] *adj* brittle; (*Person*) reserved, coy

Sprosse [ʃprɔsə] *f* rung

Sprößling [ʃprœslɪŋ] (*umg*) *m* (*Kind*) offspring (*pl inv*)

Spruch [ʃprux] (-(e)s, ⁓e) *m* saying, maxim; (*JUR*) judgement

Sprudel [ʃpruːdəl] (-s, -) *m* mineral water; lemonade; **s~n** *vi* to bubble; ~**wasser** *nt* (*KOCH*) sparkling *od* fizzy mineral water

Sprüh- [ʃpryː] *zW:* ~**dose** *f* aerosol (can); **s~en** *vi* to spray, (*fig*) to sparkle ♦ *vt* to spray; ~**regen** *m* drizzle

Sprung [ʃpruŋ] (-(e)s, ⁓e) *m* jump; (*Riß*) crack; ~**brett** *nt* springboard; **s~haft** *adj* erratic; (*Aufstieg*) rapid; ~**schanze** *f* skijump

Spucke [ʃpukə] (-) *f* spit; **s~n** *vt, vi* to spit

Spuk [ʃpuːk] (-(e)s, -e) *m* haunting; (*fig*) nightmare; **s~en** *vi* (*Geist*) to walk; **hier s~t** es this place is haunted

Spülbecken *nt* (*in Küche*) sink

Spule [ʃpuːlə] *f* spool; (*ELEK*) coil

Spül- [ʃpyːl] *zW:* ~**e** *f* (kitchen) sink; **s~en** *vt, vi* to rinse; (*Geschirr*) to wash up; (*Toilette*) to flush; ~**maschine** *f* dishwasher; ~**mittel** *nt* washing-up liquid; ~**stein** *m* sink; ~**ung** *f* rinsing; flush; (*MED*) irrigation

Spur [ʃpuːr] (-, -en) *f* trace; (*Fuß~, Rad~, Tonband~*) track; (*Fährte*) trail; (*Fahr~*) lane

spürbar *adj* noticeable, perceptible

spüren [ʃpyːrən] *vt* to feel

spurlos *adv* without (a) trace

Spurt [ʃpurt] (-(e)s, -s *od* -e) *m* spurt

spurten *vi* to spurt

sputen [ʃpuːtən] *vr* to make haste

St. *abk* = **Stück**; (= *Sankt*) St.

Staat [ʃtaːt] (-(e)s, -en) *m* state; (*Prunk*) show; (*Kleidung*) finery; **mit etw ~ machen** to show off *od* parade with sth; **s~enlos** *adj* stateless; **s~lich** *adj* state(-); state-run

Staats- *zW:* ~**angehörige(r)** *f(m)* national; ~**angehörigkeit** *f* nationality; ~**anwalt** *m* public prosecutor; ~**bürger** *m* citizen; ~**dienst** *m* civil service; ~**examen** *nt* (*UNIV*) state exam(ination); ~**feindlich** *adj* subversive; ~**mann** (*pl* -männer) *m* statesman; ~**oberhaupt** *nt* head of state

Stab [ʃtaːp] (-(e)s, ⁓e) *m* rod; (*Git-*

ter~) bar; (Menschen) staff;
~**hochsprung** m pole vault

stabil [ʃta'biːl] adj stable; (Möbel)
sturdy; ~**isieren** v/ to stabilize

Stachel ['ʃtaxəl] (-s, -n) m spike;
(von Tier) spine; (von Insekten)
sting; ~**beere** f gooseberry; ~**draht**
m barbed wire; ~**ig** adj prickly;
~**schwein** nt porcupine

Stadion ['ʃtaːdiɔn] (-s, Stadien) nt
stadium

Stadium ['ʃtaːdiʊm] nt stage, phase

Stadt [ʃtat] (-, ⸚e) f town; ~**bücherei**
f municipal library

Städt- ['ʃtɛːt] zW: ~**ebau** m town
planning; ~**er(in)** (-s, -) m(f) town
dweller; s~**isch** adj municipal;
(nicht ländlich) urban

Stadt- zW: ~**kern** m town centre,
city centre; ~**mauer** f city wall (s);
~**mitte** f town centre; ~**plan** m
street map; ~**rand** m outskirts pl;
~**rat** m (Behörde) town council, city
council; ~**rundfahrt** f tour of a/the
city; ~**teil** m district, part of town;
~**zentrum** nt town centre

Staffel ['ʃtafəl] (-, -n) f rung;
(SPORT) relay (team); (AVIAT)
squadron; ~**lauf** m (SPORT) relay
(race); s~**n** v/ to graduate

Stahl [ʃtaːl] (-(e)s, ⸚e) m steel

stahl etc vb siehe **stehlen**

stak etc [ʃtaːk] vb siehe **stecken**

Stall [ʃtal] (-(e)s, ⸚e) m stable; (Ka-
ninchen~) hutch; (Schweine~) sty;
(Hühner~) henhouse

Stamm [ʃtam] (-(e)s, ⸚e) m
(Baum~) trunk; (Menschen~) tribe;
(GRAM) stem; ~**baum** m family
tree; (von Tier) pedigree; s~**eln** v/,
v/ to stammer; s~**en** v/: ~**en von**
od aus to come from; ~**gast** m regular (customer)

stämmig ['ʃtɛmɪç] adj sturdy;
(Mensch) stocky

Stammtisch ['ʃtamtɪʃ] m table for
the regulars

stampfen ['ʃtampfən] v/, v/ to
stamp; (stapfen) to tramp; (mit
Werkzeug) to pound

Stand [ʃtant] (-(e)s, ⸚e) m position;
(Wasser~, Benzin~ etc) level; (Ste-
hen) standing position; (Zu~) state;
(Spiel~) score; (Messe~ etc) stand;
(Klasse) class; (Beruf) profession

stand etc vb siehe **stehen**

Standard ['ʃtandart] (-s, -s) m standard

Ständer ['ʃtɛndər] (-s, -) m stand

Standes- ['ʃtandəs] zW: ~**amt** nt
registry office; ~**beamte(r)** m registrar; s~**gemäß** adj, adv according
to one's social position; ~**unterschied** m social difference

Stand- zW: s~**haft** adj steadfast;
s~**halten** (unreg) v/: (jdm/etw)
s~**halten** to stand firm (against sb/
sth), to resist (sb/sth)

ständig ['ʃtɛndɪç] adj permanent;
(ununterbrochen) constant, continual

Stand- zW: ~**licht** nt sidelights pl,
parking lights pl (US); ~**ort** m location; (MIL) garrison; ~**punkt** m
standpoint

Stange ['ʃtaŋə] f stick; (Stab) pole,
bar; rod; (Zigaretten) carton; von
der ~ (COMM) off the peg; eine ~
Geld (umg) quite a packet

Stanniol [ʃtani'oːl] (-s, -e) nt tinfoil

Stapel ['ʃtaːpəl] (-s, -) m pile;
(NAUT) stocks pl; ~**lauf** m launch;
s~**n** v/ to pile (up)

Star[1] [ʃtaːr] (-(e)s, -e) m starling;
(MED) cataract

Star[2] (-s, -s) m (Film~ etc) star

starb etc [ʃtarp] vb siehe **sterben**

stark [ʃtark] adj strong; (heftig,
groß) heavy; (Maßangabe) thick

Stärke ['ʃtɛrkə] f strength; heaviness; thickness; (KOCH, Wäsche~)
starch; s~**n** v/ to strengthen;
(Wäsche) to starch

Starkstrom m heavy current

Stärkung ['ʃtɛrkʊŋ] f strengthening;
(Essen) refreshment

starr [ʃtar] adj stiff; (unnachgiebig)
rigid; (Blick) staring; ~**en** v/ to
stare; ~**en vor** od **von** to be covered
in; (Waffen) to be bristling with;

S~heit f rigidity; **~köpfig** adj stubborn; **S~sinn** m obstinacy

Start [ʃtart] (-(e)s, -e) m start; (AVIAT) takeoff; **~automatik** f automatic choke; **~bahn** f runway; **s~en** vt to start ♦ vi to start; to take off; **~er** (-s, -) m starter; **~erlaubnis** f takeoff clearance

Station [ʃtatsiˈoːn] f station; hospital ward; **s~är** [ʃtatsioˈnɛːr] adj (MED) in-patient attr; **s~ieren** [-ˈniːrən] vt to station

Statist [ʃtaˈtɪst] m extra, supernumerary

Statistik f statistics sg; **~er** (-s, -) m statistician

statistisch adj statistical

Stativ [ʃtaˈtiːf] (-s, -e) nt tripod

statt [ʃtat] konj instead of ♦ präp (+gen od dat) instead of

Stätte [ˈʃtɛtə] f place

statt- zW: **~finden** (unreg) vi to take place; **~haft** adj admissible; **~lich** adj imposing, handsome

Statue [ˈʃtaːtuə] f statue

Status [ˈʃtaːtus] (-, -) m status; **~symbol** nt status symbol

Stau [ʃtau] (-(e)s, -e) m blockage; (Verkehrs~) (traffic) jam

Staub [ʃtaup] (-(e)s) m dust; **s~en** [ˈʃtaubən] vi to be dusty; **~ig** adj dusty; **s~saugen** vi to vacuum, to hoover (®); **~sauger** m vacuum cleaner; **~tuch** nt duster

Staudamm m dam

Staude [ˈʃtaudə] f shrub

stauen [ˈʃtauən] vt (Wasser) to dam up; (Blut) to stop the flow of ♦ vr (Wasser) to become dammed up; (MED, Verkehr) to become congested; (Menschen) to collect; (Gefühle) to build up

staunen [ˈʃtaunən] vi to be astonished; **S~** (-s) nt amazement

Stausee (-s, -n) m reservoir, manmade lake

Stauung [ˈʃtauʊŋ] f (von Wasser) damming-up; (von Blut, Verkehr) congestion

Std. abk (= Stunde) hr.

Steak [steːk] nt steak

Stech- [ˈʃtɛç] zW: **~en** (unreg) vt (mit Nadel etc) to prick; (mit Messer) to stab; (mit Finger) to poke; (Biene etc) to sting; (Mücke) to bite; (Sonne) to burn; (KARTEN) to take; (ART) to engrave; (Torf, Spargel) to cut; in See **~en** to put to sea; **~en** (-s, -) nt (SPORT) play-off; jump-off; **s~end** adj piercing, stabbing; (Geruch) pungent; **~palme** f holly; **~uhr** f time clock

Steck- [ˈʃtɛk] zW: **~brief** m "wanted" poster; **~dose** f (wall) socket; **s~en** vt to put, to insert; (Nadel) to stick; (Pflanzen) to plant; (beim Nähen) to pin ♦ vi (auch unreg) to be; (festsitzen) to be stuck; (Nadeln) to stick; **~enbleiben** (unreg) vi to get stuck; **s~enlassen** (unreg) vt to leave in; **~enpferd** nt hobby-horse; **~er** (-s, -) m plug; **~nadel** f pin

Steg [ʃteːk] (-(e)s, -e) m small bridge; (Anlege~) landing stage; **~reif** m: aus dem **~reif** just like that

stehen [ˈʃteːən] (unreg) vi to stand; (sich befinden) to be; (in Zeitung) to say; (still~) to have stopped ♦ vi unpers: es steht schlecht um jdn/etw things are bad for sb/sth; zu jdm/etw **~** to stand by sb/sth; jdm **~** to suit sb; wie steht's? how are things?; (SPORT) what's the score? **~ bleiben** to remain standing; **~bleiben** (unreg) vi (Uhr) to stop; (Fehler) to stay as it is; **~lassen** (unreg) vt to leave; (Bart) to grow

Stehlampe [ˈʃteːlampə] f standard lamp

stehlen [ˈʃteːlən] (unreg) vt to steal

Stehplatz [ˈʃteːplats] m standing place

steif [ʃtaif] adj stiff; **S~heit** f stiffness

Steig- [ʃtaik] zW: **~bügel** m stirrup; **~eisen** nt crampon; **s~en** (unreg) vi to rise; (klettern) to climb; **s~en** in +akk/auf +akk to get in/on

s~ern vt to raise; (GRAM) to compare ♦ vi (Auktion) to bid ♦ vr to increase; **~erung** f raising; (GRAM) comparison; rise; **~ung** f incline, gradient, rise

steil [ʃtail] adj steep

Stein [ʃtain] m (-(e)s, -e) m stone; (in Uhr) jewel; **~bock** m (ASTROL) Capricorn; **~bruch** m quarry; **s~ern** adj (made of) stone; (fig) stony; **~gut** nt stoneware; **s~ig** [ʃtainɪç] adj stony; **s~igen** vt to stone; **~kohle** f mineral coal; **~zeit** f Stone Age

Stelle [ʃtɛlə] f place; (Arbeit) post, job; (Amt) office; **an Ihrer/meiner ~** in your/my place

stellen [ʃtɛlən] vt to put; (Uhr etc) to set; (zur Verfügung) to supply; (fassen: Dieb) to apprehend ♦ vr (sich aufstellen) to stand; (sich einfinden) to present o.s.; (bei Polizei) to give o.s. up; (vorgeben) to pretend; **sich zu etw ~** to have an opinion of sth

Stellen- zW: **~angebot** nt offer of a post; (in Zeitung) "vacancies"; **~gesuch** nt application for a post; **~vermittlung** f employment agency

Stell- zW: **~ung** f position; (MIL) line; **~ung nehmen zu** to comment on; **~ungnahme** f comment; **s~vertretend** adj deputy, acting; **~vertreter** m deputy

Stelze [ʃtɛltsə] f stilt

Stemmbogen m (SKI) stem turn

stemmen [ʃtɛmən] vt to lift (up); (drücken) to press; **sich ~ gegen** (fig) to resist, to oppose

Stempel [ʃtɛmpəl] m (-s, -) m stamp; (BOT) pistil; **~kissen** nt inkpad; **s~n** vt to stamp; (Briefmarke) to cancel; **s~n gehen** (umg) to be od go on the dole

Stengel [ʃtɛŋəl] m (-s, -) m stalk

Steno- [ʃteno] zW: **~gramm** [-'gram] nt shorthand report; **~graphie** [-gra'fiː] f shorthand; **s~graphieren** [-gra'fiːrən] vt, vi to write (in) shorthand; **~typist(in)** [-ty'pɪst(ɪn)] m(f)

shorthand typist

Stepp- [ʃtɛp] zW: **~decke** f quilt; **~e** f prairie; steppe; **s~en** vt to stitch ♦ vi to tap-dance

Sterb- [ʃtɛrp] zW: **~efall** m death; **~ehilfe** f euthanasia; **s~en** (unreg) vi to die; **s~lich** [ʃtɛrplɪç] adj mortal; **~lichkeit** f mortality; **~lichkeitsziffer** f death rate

stereo- [ʃtereo] in zW stereo(-); **~anlage** f stereo (system); **~typ** [-'tyːp] adj stereotype

steril [ʃteˈriːl] adj sterile; **~i'sieren** vt to sterilize; **S~i'sierung** f sterilization

Stern [ʃtɛrn] m (-(e)s, -e) m star; **~bild** nt constellation; **~schnuppe** f meteor, falling star; **~stunde** f historic moment

stet [ʃteːt] adj steady; **~ig** adj constant, continual; **~s** adv continually, always

Steuer¹ [ʃtɔyər] nt (-s, -) nt (NAUT) helm; (~ruder) rudder; (AUT) steering wheel

Steuer² f (-, -n) f tax; **~berater(in)** m(f) tax consultant

Steuerbord nt (NAUT, FLUG) starboard

Steuer- [ʃtɔyər] zW: **~erklärung** f tax return; **~freibetrag** m tax allowance; **~klasse** f tax group; **~knüppel** m control column; (AVIAT, COMPUT) joystick; **~mann** (pl **~männer** od **~leute**) m helmsman; **s~n** vt, vi to steer; (Flugzeug) to pilot; (Entwicklung, Tonstärke) to control; **~rad** nt steering wheel; **~ung** f (auch AUT) steering; piloting; control; (Vorrichtung) controls pl; **~zahler** m(-s, -) taxpayer

Steward [ʃtjuːart] m (-s, -s) m steward; **~eß** [ʃtjuˈardɛs] f(-, -essen) f stewardess; air hostess

Stich [ʃtɪç] m (-(e)s, -e) m (Insekten~) sting; (Messer~) stab; (beim Nähen) stitch; (Färbung) tinge; (KARTEN) trick; (ART) engraving; **jdn im ~ lassen** to leave sb in the lurch; **s~eln** vi (fig) to jibe; **s~haltig** adj sound, tenable; **~probe** f spot check; **~straße** f cul-de-sac; **~wahl** f final ballot; **~wort** nt cue; (in Wörterbuch) headword; (für Vortrag) note

sticken ['ʃtɪkən] vt, vi to embroider

Sticke'rei f embroidery

stickig adj stuffy, close

Stickstoff m nitrogen

Stief- ['ʃtiːf] in zW step

Stiefel ['ʃtiːfəl] (-s, -) m boot

Stief- zW: **~kind** nt stepchild; (fig) Cinderella; **~mutter** f stepmother; **~mütterchen** nt pansy; **s~mütterlich** adj (fig): jdn/etw s~mütterlich behandeln to pay little attention to sb/sth; **~vater** m stepfather

Stiege ['ʃtiːgə] f staircase

stiehlst etc ['ʃtiːlst] vb siehe stehlen

Stiel [ʃtiːl] (-(e)s, -e) m handle; (BOT) stalk

Stier (-(e)s, -e) m bull; (ASTROL) Taurus

stier [ʃtiːr] adj staring, fixed; **~en** vi to stare

Stierkampf m bullfight

Stierkämpfer m bullfighter

Stift [ʃtɪft] (-(e)s, -e) m peg; (Nagel) tack; (Farb~) crayon; (Blei~) pencil ♦ nt (charitable) foundation; (ECCL) religious institution; **s~en** vt to found; (Unruhe) to cause; (spenden) to contribute; **~er(in)** (-s, -) m(f) founder; **~ung** f donation; (Organisation) foundation; **~zahn** m post crown

Stil [ʃtiːl] (-(e)s, -e) m style

still [ʃtɪl] adj quiet; (unbewegt) still; (heimlich) secret; **S~er Ozean** Pacific; **S~e** f stillness, quietness; in aller **S~e** quietly; **~en** vt to stop; (befriedigen) to satisfy; (Säugling) to breast-feed; **~halten** (unreg) vi to keep still; **~(l)egen** vt to close down; **~schweigen** (unreg) vi to be silent; **S~schweigen** nt silence; **~schweigend** adj silent; (Einverständnis) tacit ♦ adv silently; tacitly; **S~stand** m standstill; **~stehen** (unreg) vi to stand still

Stimm- ['ʃtɪm] zW: **~bänder** pl vocal chords; **s~berechtigt** adj entitled to vote; **~e** f voice; (Wahlstimme) vote; **s~en** vi (MUS) to tune ♦ vi to be right; das s~te ihn traurig that made him feel sad; **s~en für/gegen** to vote for/against; **s~t so!** that's right; **~enmehrheit** f majority (of votes); **~enthaltung** f abstention; **~gabel** f tuning fork; **~recht** nt right to vote; **~ung** f mood; atmosphere; **s~ungsvoll** adj enjoyable; full of atmosphere; **~zettel** m ballot paper

stinken ['ʃtɪŋkən] (unreg) vi to stink

Stipendium [ʃti'pɛndiʊm] nt grant

stirbst etc [ʃtɪrpst] vb siehe sterben

Stirn [ʃtɪrn] (-, -en) f forehead, brow; (Frechheit) impudence; **~band** nt headband; **~höhle** f sinus

stöbern ['ʃtøːbərn] vi to rummage

stochern ['ʃtɔxərn] vi to poke (about)

Stock¹ [ʃtɔk] (-(e)s, ⸚e) m stick; (BOT) stock

Stock² (-(e)s, - od -werke) m storey

stocken vi to stop, to pause; **~d** adj halting

Stockung f stoppage

Stockwerk nt storey, floor

Stoff [ʃtɔf] (-(e)s, -e) m (Gewebe) material, cloth; (Materie) matter; (von Buch etc) subject (matter); **s~lich** adj material; **~tier** nt soft toy; **~wechsel** m metabolism

stöhnen ['ʃtøːnən] vi to groan

stoisch ['ʃtoːɪʃ] adj stoical

Stollen ['ʃtɔlən] (-s, -) m (MIN) gallery; (KOCH) cake eaten at Christmas; (von Schuhen) stud

stolpern ['ʃtɔlpərn] vi to stumble, to trip

Stolz [ʃtɔlts] (-es) m pride; **s~** adj proud; **s~ieren** [ʃtɔl'tsiːrən] vi to strut

stopfen ['ʃtɔpfən] vt (hinein-) to stuff; (voll~) to fill (up); (nähen) to darn ♦ vi (MED) to cause constipation

Stopfgarn nt darning thread

Stoppel ['ʃtɔpəl] (-, -n) f stubble

Stopp- ['ʃtɔp] zW: **s~en** vt to stop; (mit Uhr) to time ♦ vi to stop; **~schild** nt stop sign; **~uhr** f stopwatch

Stöpsel ['ʃtœpsəl] (-s, -) m plug; (für Flaschen) stopper

Storch [ʃtɔrç] (-(e)s, ⁓e) m stork

Stör- ['ʃtøːr] zW: **s~en** vt to disturb; (behindern, RADIO) to interfere with ♦ vr: sich an etw dat **s~en** to let sth bother one; **s~end** adj disturbing, annoying; **~enfried** (-(e)s, -e) m troublemaker

störrisch ['ʃtœrɪʃ] adj stubborn, perverse

Störung f disturbance; interference

Stoß [ʃtoːs] (-es, ⁓e) m (Schub) push; (Schlag) blow; knock; (mit Schwert) thrust; (mit Fuß) kick; (Erd~) shock; (Haufen) pile; **~dämpfer** (-s, -) m shock absorber; **s~en** (unreg) vt (mit Druck) to shove, to push; (mit Schlag) to knock, to bump; (mit Fuß) to kick; (Schwert etc) to thrust; (anstoßen: Kopf etc) to bump ♦ vr to get a knock ♦ vi: **s~en an** od **auf** +akk to bump into; (finden) to come across; (angrenzen) to be next to; **sich s~en an** +dat (fig) to take exception to; **~stange** f (AUT) bumper

stottern ['ʃtɔtərn] vt, vi to stutter

Str. abk (= Straße) St.

Straf- ['ʃtraːf] zW: **~anstalt** f penal institution; **~arbeit** f (SCH) punishment; lines pl; **s~bar** adj punishable; **~e** f punishment; (JUR) penalty; (Geldstrafe) fine; **s~en** vt to punish

straff [ʃtraf] adj tight; (streng) strict; (Stil etc) concise; (Haltung) erect; **~en** vt to tighten, to tauten

Strafgefangene(r) mf prisoner, convict

Strafgesetzbuch nt penal code

sträflich ['ʃtrɛːflɪç] adj criminal

Sträfling m convict

Straf- zW: **~porto** nt excess postage

(charge); **~predigt** f telling-off; **~raum** m (SPORT) penalty area; **~recht** nt criminal law; **~stoß** m (SPORT) penalty (kick); **~tat** f punishable act; **~zettel** m ticket

Strahl [ʃtraːl] (-s, -en) m ray, beam; (Wasser~) jet; **s~en** vi to radiate; (fig) to beam; **~ung** f radiation

Strähne ['ʃtrɛːnə] f strand

stramm [ʃtram] adj tight; (Haltung) erect; (Mensch) robust

strampeln ['ʃtrampəln] vi to kick (about), to fidget

Strand [ʃtrant] (-(e)s, ⁓e) m shore; (mit Sand) beach; **~bad** nt open-air swimming pool, lido; **s~en** ['ʃtrandən] vi to run aground; (fig: Mensch) to fail; **~gut** nt flotsam; **~korb** m beach chair

Strang [ʃtraŋ] (-(e)s, ⁓e) m cord, rope; (Bündel) skein

Strapaz- zW: **~e** f [ʃtra'paːtsə] f strain, exertion; **s~ieren** [ʃtrapa'tsiːrən] vt (Material) to treat roughly, to punish; (Mensch, Kräfte) to wear out, to exhaust; **s~ierfähig** adj hard-wearing; **s~iös** [ʃtrapatsi'øːs] adj exhausting, tough

Straße ['ʃtraːsə] f street, road

Straßen- zW: **~bahn** f tram, streetcar (US); **~beleuchtung** f street lighting; **~karte** f road map; **~kehrer** (-s, -) m roadsweeper; **~sperre** f roadblock; **~verkehr** m (road) traffic; **~verkehrsordnung** f highway code

Strateg- [ʃtra'teːg] zW: **~e** (-n, -n) m strategist; **~ie** [ʃtrate'giː] f strategy; **s~isch** adj strategic

sträuben ['ʃtrɔybən] vt to ruffle ♦ vr to bristle; (Mensch): **sich (gegen etw) ~** to resist (sth)

Strauch [ʃtraux] (-(e)s, Sträucher) m bush, shrub

Strauß¹ [ʃtraus] (-es, Sträuße) m bunch; bouquet

Strauß² (-es, -e) m ostrich

Streb- [ʃtreːb] zW: **s~en** vi to strive, to endeavour; **s~en nach** to strive for; **~er** (-s, -; pej) m pusher,

climber; (SCH) swot (BRIT);
s~sam adj industrious
Strecke ['ʃtrɛkə] f stretch; (Entfernung) distance; (EISENB, MATH) line; **s~n** vt to stretch; (Waffen) to lay down; (KOCH) to eke out ♦ vr to stretch (o.s.)
Streich [ʃtraɪç] (-(e)s, -e) m trick, prank; (Hieb) blow; **s~eln** vt to stroke; **s~en** (unreg) vt (berühren) to stroke; (auftragen) to spread; (anmalen) to paint; (durchstreichen) to delete; (nicht genehmigen) to cancel ♦ vi (berühren) to brush; (schleichen) to prowl; **~holz** nt match; **~instrument** nt string instrument
Streif- ['ʃtraɪf] zW: **~e** f patrol; **s~en** vt (leicht berühren) to brush against, to graze; (Blick) to skim over; (Thema, Problem) to touch on; (abstreifen) to take off ♦ vi (gehen) to roam; **~en** (-s, -) m (Linie) stripe; (Stück) strip; (Film) film; **~schuß** m graze, grazing shot; **~zug** m scouting trip
Streik [ʃtraɪk] (-(e)s, -s) m strike; **~brecher** (-s, -) m blackleg, strikebreaker; **s~en** vi to strike; **~posten** m (strike) picket
Streit [ʃtraɪt] (-(e)s, -e) m argument; dispute; **s~en** (unreg) vi, vr to argue; to dispute; **~frage** f point at issue; **s~ig** adj: jdm etw s~ig machen to dispute sb's right to sth; **~igkeiten** pl quarrel pl, dispute sg; **~kräfte** pl (MIL) armed forces
streng [ʃtrɛŋ] adj severe; (Lehrer, Maßnahme) strict; (Geruch etc) sharp; **S~e** (-) f severity, strictness, sharpness; **s~genommen** adv strictly speaking; **s~gläubig** adj orthodox, strict; **~stens** adv strictly
Streß [ʃtrɛs] (-sses, -sse) m stress
stressen vt to put under stress
streuen ['ʃtrɔyən] vt to strew, to scatter, to spread; **Streuung** f dispersion
Strich [ʃtrɪç] (-(e)s, -e) m (Linie) line; (Feder~, Pinsel~) stroke; (von Geweben) nap; (von Fell) pile; (auf den ~ gehen (umg)) to walk the

streets; jdm gegen den ~ gehen to rub sb up the wrong way; **einen ~ machen durch** to cross out; (fig) to foil; **~kode** m (auf Waren) barcode; **~mädchen** nt streetwalker; **~punkt** m semicolon; **s~weise** adv here and there
Strick [ʃtrɪk] (-(e)s, -e) m rope; **s~en** vt, vi to knit; **~jacke** f cardigan; **~leiter** f rope ladder; **~nadel** f knitting needle; **~waren** pl knitwear sg
striegeln vt (Tiere, Fell) to groom
strikt ['strɪkt] adj strict
strittig ['ʃtrɪtɪç] adj disputed, in dispute
Stroh [ʃtro:] (-(e)s) nt straw; **~blume** f everlasting flower; **~dach** nt thatched roof; **~halm** m (drinking) straw
Strom [ʃtro:m] (-(e)s, -e) m river; (fig) stream; (ELEK) current; **s~abwärts** adv downstream; **s~aufwärts** adv upstream
strömen ['ʃtrø:mən] vi to stream, to pour
Strom- zW: **~kreis** m circuit; **s~linienförmig** adj streamlined; **~sperre** f power cut
Strömung ['ʃtrø:mʊŋ] f current
Strophe ['ʃtro:fə] f verse
strotzen ['ʃtrɔtsən] vi: ~ vor or von to abound in, to be full of
Strudel ['ʃtru:dəl] (-s, -) m whirlpool, vortex; (KOCH) strudel
Struktur [ʃtrʊk'tu:r] f structure
Strumpf [ʃtrʊmpf] (-(e)s, -e) m stocking; **~band** nt garter; **~hose** f (pair of) tights
Stube ['ʃtu:bə] f room
Stuben- zW: **~arrest** m confinement to one's room; (MIL) confinement to quarters; **~hocker** (umg) m stay-at-home; **s~rein** adj house-trained
Stuck [ʃtʊk] (-(e)s) m stucco
Stück [ʃtʏk] (-(e)s, -e) nt piece; (etwas) bit; (THEAT) play; **~chen** nt little piece; **~lohn** m piecework wages pl; **s~weise** adv bit by bit, piecemeal; (COMM) individually

Student(in) [ʃtu'dənt(ın)] *m(f)* student; **s~isch** *adj* student, academic

Studie ['ʃtu:diə] *f* study

studieren [ʃtu'di:rən] *vt, vi* to study

Studio ['ʃtu:dio] **(-s, -s)** *nt* studio

Studium ['ʃtu:diom] *nt* studies *pl*

Stufe ['ʃtu:fə] *f* step; *(Entwicklungs~)* stage; **s~nweise** *adv* gradually

Stuhl [ʃtu:l] **(-(e)s, ⁓e)** *m* chair; **~gang** *m* bowel movement

stülpen ['ʃtʏlpən] *vt (umdrehen)* to turn upside down; *(bedecken)* to put

stumm [ʃtʊm] *adj* silent; *(MED)* dumb

Stummel ['ʃtʊməl] **(-s, -)** *m* stump; *(Zigaretten~)* stub

Stummfilm *m* silent film

Stümper ['ʃtʏmpər] **(-s, -)** *m* incompetent, duffer; **s~haft** *adj* bungling, incompetent; **s~n** *vi* to bungle

Stumpf [ʃtʊmpf] **(-(e)s, ⁓e)** *m* stump; **s~** *adj* blunt; *(teilnahmslos, glanzlos)* dull; *(Winkel)* obtuse; **~sinn** *m* tediousness; **s~sinnig** *adj* dull

Stunde ['ʃtʊndə] *f* hour; *(SCH)* lesson

stunden *vt*: **jdm etw ~** to give sb time to pay sth; **S~geschwindigkeit** *f* average speed per hour; **S~kilometer** *pl* kilometres per hour; **~lang** *adj* for hours; **S~lohn** *m* hourly wage; **S~plan** *m* timetable; **~weise** *adj* by the hour; every hour

stündlich ['ʃtʏntlıç] *adj* hourly

Stups [ʃtʊps] **(-es, -e)** *m; (umg)* push; **~nase** *f* snub nose

stur [ʃtu:r] *adj* obstinate, pigheaded

Sturm [ʃtʊrm] **(-(e)s, ⁓e)** *m* storm, gale; *(MIL etc)* attack, assault

stürm~ ['ʃtʏrm] *zW*: **~en** *vi (Wind)* to blow hard, to rage; *(rennen)* to storm ♦ *vt (MIL, fig)* to storm ♦ *vb unpers*: **es ~t** there's a gale blowing; **S~er** **(-s, -)** *m (SPORT)* forward, striker; **~isch** *adj* stormy

Sturmwarnung *f* gale warning

Sturz [ʃtʊrts] **(-es, ⁓e)** *m* fall; *(POL)* overthrow

stürzen ['ʃtʏrtsən] *vt (werfen)* to hurl; *(POL)* to overthrow; *(umkehren)* to overturn ♦ *vr* to rush; *(hinein~)* to plunge ♦ *vi* to fall; *(AVIAT)* to dive; *(rennen)* to dash

Sturzflug *m* nose-dive

Sturzhelm *m* crash helmet

Stute ['ʃtu:tə] *f* mare

Stützbalken *m* brace, joist

Stütze ['ʃtʏtsə] *f* support; help

stutzen ['ʃtʊtsən] *vt* to trim; *(Ohr, Schwanz)* to dock; *(Flügel)* to clip ♦ *vi* to hesitate; to become suspicious

stützen *vt (auch fig)* to support; *(Ellbogen etc)* to prop up

stutzig *adj* perplexed, puzzled; *(mißtrauisch)* suspicious

Stützpunkt *m* point of support; *(von Hebel)* fulcrum; *(MIL, fig)* base

Styropor [ʃtyro'po:r] *(®; -s)* *nt* polystyrene

s.u. *abk* = **siehe unten**

Subjekt [zʊp'jɛkt] **(-(e)s, -e)** *nt* subject; **s~iv** [-'ti:f] *adj* subjective; **~ivität** *f* subjectivity

Substantiv ['zʊpstanti:f] **(-s, -e)** *nt* noun

Substanz [zʊp'stants] *f* substance

subtil [zʊp'ti:l] *adj* subtle

subtrahieren [zʊptra'hi:rən] *vt* to subtract

subtropisch ['zʊptro:pɪʃ] *adj* subtropical

Subvention [zʊpvɛntsi'o:n] *f* subsidy; **s~ieren** [-'ni:rən] *vt* to subsidize

Such- ['zu:x] *zW*: **~aktion** *f* search; **~e** *f* search; **s~en** *vt* to look (for), to seek; *(versuchen)* to try ♦ *vi* to seek, to search; **~er** **(-s, -)** *m* seeker, searcher; *(PHOT)* viewfinder

Sucht [zʊxt] **(-, ⁓e)** *f* mania; *(MED)* addiction, craving

süchtig ['zʏçtıç] *adj* addicted; **S~e(r)** *mf* addict

Süd- ['zy:t] *zW*: **~en** **(-s)** *m* south; **~früchte** *pl* Mediterranean fruit *sg*; **s~lich** *adj* southern; **~lich von** to the south of; **~pol** *m* South Pole; **s~wärts** *adv* southwards

süffig ['zʏfıç] *adj (Wein)* pleasant to

the taste

süffisant [zyfi'zant] *adj* smug

suggerieren [zuge'ri:rən] *vt* to suggest

Sühne ['zy:nə] *f* atonement, expiation; **~n** *vt* to atone for, to expiate

Sultan [zoltan] (-s, -e) *m* sultan; **~ine** *f* sultana

Sülze ['zʏltsə] *f* brawn

Summe ['zʊmə] *f* sum, total

summen *vt*, *vi* to buzz; (*Lied*) to hum

Sumpf [zʊmpf] (-(e)s, -e) *m* swamp, marsh; **s~ig** *adj* marshy

Sünde ['zʏndə] *f* sin; **~nbock** (*umg*) *m* scapegoat; **~nfall** *m* Fall (of man); **~r(in)** (-s, -) *m(f)* sinner; **sündigen** *vi* to sin

Super ['zu:pər] (-s) *nt* (*Benzin*) four star (petrol) (*BRIT*), premium (*US*); **~lativ** [-lati:f] (-s, -e) *m* superlative; **~macht** *f* superpower; **~markt** *m* supermarket

Suppe ['zʊpə] *f* soup; **~nteller** *m* soup plate

süß [zy:s] *adj* sweet; **S~e** (-) *f* sweetness; **~en** *vt* to sweeten; **S~igkeit** *f* sweetness; (*Bonbon etc*) sweet (*BRIT*), candy (*US*); **~lich** *adj* sweetish; (*fig*) sugary; **~sauer** *adj* (*Gurke*) pickled; (*Sauce etc*) sweet-and-sour; **S~speise** *f* pudding, sweet; **S~stoff** *m* sweetener; **S~waren** *pl* confectionery (*sing*); **S~wasser** *nt* fresh water

Sylvester [zʏl'vɛstər] (-s, -) *nt* = Silvester

Symbol [zʏm'bo:l] (-s, -e) *nt* symbol; **s~isch** *adj* symbolic(al)

Symmetrie [zʏme'tri:] *f* symmetry; **symmetrisch** [zʏ'me:trɪʃ] *adj* symmetrical

Sympathie [zʏmpa'ti:] *f* liking, sympathy; **sympathisch** [zʏm'pa:tɪʃ] *adj* likeable; **er ist mir sympathisch** I like him; **sympathi'sieren** *vi* to sympathize

Symphonie [zʏmfo'ni:] *f* (*MUS*) symphony

Symptom [zʏmp'to:m] (-s, -e) *nt*

symptom; **s~atisch** [zʏmpto'ma:tɪʃ] *adj* symptomatic

Synagoge [zyna'go:gə] *f* synagogue

synchron [zyn'kro:n] *adj* synchronous; **S~getriebe** *nt* synchromesh (gears *pl*); **~i'sieren** *vt* to synchronize; (*Film*) to dub

Synonym [zyno'ny:m] (-s, -e) *nt* synonym; **s~** *adj* synonymous

Synthese [zyn'te:zə] *f* synthesis

synthetisch [zyn'te:tɪʃ] *adj* synthetic

Syphilis ['zy:filɪs] (-) *f* syphilis

System [zʏs'te:m] (-s, -e) *nt* system; **s~atisch** [zʏste'ma:tɪʃ] *adj* systematic; **s~ati'sieren** *vt* to systematize

Szene ['stse:nə] *f* scene; **~rie** [stsenə'ri:] *f* scenery

T

t *abk* (= *Tonne*) t

Tabak ['ta:bak] (-s, -e) *m* tobacco

Tabelle [ta'bɛl] *zW:* **t~arisch** [tabe'la:rɪʃ] *adj* tabular; **~e** *f* table

Tablett [ta'blet] *nt* tray; **~e** *f* tablet, pill

Tabu [ta'bu:] *nt* taboo; **t~** *adj* taboo

Tachometer [taxo'me:tər] (-s, -) *m* (*AUT*) speedometer

Tadel ['ta:dəl] (-s, -) *m* censure; scolding; (*Fehler*) fault, blemish; **t~los** *adj* faultless, irreproachable; **t~n** *vt* to scold

Tafel ['ta:fəl] (-, -n) *f* (*auch MATH*) table; (*Anschlag~*) board; (*Wand~*) blackboard; (*Schiefer~*) slate; (*Gedenk~*) plaque; (*Illustration*) plate; (*Schalt~*) panel; (*Schokolade etc*) bar

Taft [taft] (-(e)s, -e) *m* taffeta

Tag [ta:k] (-(e)s, -e) *m* day; daylight; **unter/über ~** (*MIN*) underground/on the surface; **an den ~ kommen** to come to light; **guten ~!** good morning/afternoon!; **t~aus** *adv*: **t~aus, t~ein** day in, day out; **~dienst** *m* day duty

Tage- ['ta:gə] *zW:* **~buch** *nt*

nt diary, journal; **~geld** *nt* daily allowance; **t~lang** *adv* for days; **t~n** *vi* to sit, to meet ♦ *vb unpers:* **es tagt** dawn is breaking

Tages- *zW:* **~ablauf** *m* course of the day; **~anbruch** *m* dawn; **~fahrt** *f* day trip; **~karte** *f* menu of the day; (*Fahrkarte*) day ticket; **~licht** *nt* daylight; **~ordnung** *f* agenda; **~zeit** *f* time of day; **~zeitung** *f* daily (paper)

täglich ['tɛːklɪç] *adj, adv* daily

tagsüber ['taːksyːbər] *adv* during the day

Tagung *f* conference

Taille ['taljə] *f* waist

Takt [takt] (*-(e)s, -e*) *m* tact; (*MUS*) time; **~gefühl** *nt* tact

Taktik *f* tactics *pl*

taktisch *adj* tactical

Takt- *zW:* **~los** *adj* tactless; **~losigkeit** *f* tactlessness; **~stock** *m* (conductor's) baton; **~voll** *adj* tactful

Tal [taːl] (*-(e)s, ¨er*) *nt* valley

Talent [ta'lɛnt] (*-(e)s, -e*) *nt* talent; **t~iert** [talɛnˈtiːrt] *adj* talented, gifted

Talisman ['taːlɪsman] (*-s, -e*) *m* talisman

Talsohle *f* bottom of a valley

Talsperre *f* dam

Tamburin [tambuˈriːn] (*-s, -e*) *nt* tambourine

Tampon ['tampɔn] (*-s, -e*) *m* tampon

Tandem (*-s, -e*) *nt* tandem

Tang [taŋ] (*-(e)s, -e*) *m* seaweed

Tangente [taŋˈɡɛntə] *f* tangent

Tango (*-s, -s*) *m* tango

Tank [taŋk] (*-s, -s*) *m* tank; **t~en** *vi* to fill up with petrol (*BRIT*) *od* gas (*US*); (*AVIAT*) to refuel; **~er** (*-s, -*) *m* tanker; **~schiff** *nt* tanker; **~stelle** *f* petrol (*BRIT*) *od* gas (*US*) station; **~wart** *m* petrol pump (*BRIT*) *od* gas station (*US*) attendant

Tanne ['tanə] *f* fir; **~nbaum** *m* fir tree; **~nzapfen** *m* fir cone

Tante ['tantə] *f* aunt

Tanz [tants] (*-es, -e*) *m* dance; **t~en**

vt, vi to dance

Tänzer(in) ['tɛntsər(ɪn)] (*-s, -*) *m(f)* dancer

Tanzfläche *f* (dance) floor

Tanzschule *f* dancing school

Tapete [taˈpeːtə] *f* wallpaper; **~nwechsel** *m* (*fig*) change of scenery

tapezieren [tapeˈtsiːrən] *vt* to (wall)paper

Tapezierer [tapeˈtsiːrər] (*-s, -*) *m* (interior) decorator

tapfer ['tapfər] *adj* brave; **T~keit** *f* courage, bravery

Tarif [taˈriːf] (*-s, -e*) *m* tariff, (scale of) fares *od* charges; **~lohn** *m* standard wage rate; **~verhandlungen** *pl* wage negotiations

Tarn- ['tarn] *zW:* **t~en** *vt* to camouflage; (*Person, Absicht*) to disguise; **~farbe** *f* camouflage paint; **~ung** *f* camouflaging; disguising

Tasche ['taʃə] *f* pocket; handbag

Taschen- *in zW* pocket; **~buch** *nt* paperback; **~dieb** *m* pickpocket; **~geld** *nt* pocket money; **~lampe** *f* (electric) torch, flashlight (*US*); **~messer** *nt* penknife; **~tuch** *nt* handkerchief

Tasse ['tasə] *f* cup

Tastatur [tastaˈtuːr] *f* keyboard

Taste ['tastə] *f* push-button control; (*an Schreibmaschine*) key; **t~n** *vt* to feel, to touch ♦ *vi* to feel, to grope ♦ *vr* to feel one's way

Tat [taːt] (*-, -en*) *f* act, deed, action; **in der** ~ indeed, as a matter of fact; **t~** *etc vb siehe* **tun**; **~bestand** *m* facts *pl* of the case; **t~enlos** *adj* inactive

Tät- ['tɛːt] *zW:* **~er(in)** (*-s, -*) *m(f)* perpetrator, culprit; **t~ig** *adj* active; **in einer Firma t~ig sein** to work for a firm; **~igkeit** *f* activity; (*Beruf*) occupation; **t~lich** *adj* violent; **~lichkeit** *f* violence; **~lichkeiten** *pl* (*Schläge*) blows

tätowieren [tɛtoˈviːrən] *vt* to tattoo

Tatsache *f* fact

tatsächlich *adj* actual ♦ *adv* really

Tau¹ [tao] (-(e)s, -e) nt rope

Tau² (-(e)s) m dew

taub [taop] adj deaf; (Nuß) hollow; **T~heit** f deafness; ~**stumm** adj deaf-and-dumb

Taube ['taobə] f dove; pigeon; ~**nschlag** m dovecote; **hier geht es zu wie in einem ~nschlag** it's a hive of activity here

Tauch- ['taox] zW: **t~en** vt to dip ♦ vi to dive; (NAUT) to submerge; ~**er** (-s, -) m diver; ~**eranzug** m diving suit; ~**erbrille** f diving goggles; ~**sieder** (-s, -) m immersion coil (for boiling water)

tauen ['taoən] vt, vi to thaw ♦ vb unpers: **es taut** it's thawing

Tauf- ['taof] zW: ~**becken** nt font; ~**e** f baptism; **t~en** vt to christen, to baptize; ~**name** m Christian name; ~**pate** m godfather; ~**patin** f godmother; ~**schein** m certificate of baptism

taug- [taog] zW: ~**en** vi to be of use; ~**en für** to do for, to be good for; **nicht ~en** to be no good od useless; **T~enichts** (-es, -e) m good-for-nothing; ~**lich** ['taoklɪç] adj suitable; (MIL) fit (for service)

Taumel ['taoməl] (-s) m dizziness; (fig) frenzy; **t~n** vi to reel, to stagger

Tausch [taoʃ] (-(e)s, -e) m exchange; **t~en** vt to exchange, to swap

täuschen ['tɔyʃən] vt to deceive ♦ vi to be deceptive ♦ vr to be wrong; ~**d** adj deceptive

Tauschhandel m barter

Täuschung f deception; (optisch) illusion

tausend ['taozənt] num (a) thousand; **T~füßler** (-s, -) m centipede; millipede

Tauwetter nt thaw

Taxi ['taksi] (-(s), -(s)) nt taxi; ~**fahrer** m taxi driver; ~**stand** m taxi rank

Tech- ['tɛç] zW: ~**nik** f technology; (Methode, Kunstfertigkeit) technique;

~**niker** (-s, -) m technician; **t~nisch** adj technical; ~**nologie** f technology; **t~no'logisch** adj technological

TEE [te:'e:'e:] (-, -(s)) m abk (= Trans-Europ-Express) Trans-European Express

Tee [te:] (-s, -s) m tea; ~**beutel** m tea bag; ~**kanne** f teapot; ~**löffel** m teaspoon

Teer [te:r] (-(e)s, -e) m tar; **t~en** vt to tar

Teesieb nt tea strainer

Teich [taɪç] (-(e)s, -e) m pond

Teig [taɪk] (-(e)s, -e) m dough; **t~ig** ['taɪgɪç] adj doughy; ~**waren** pl pasta sg

Teil [taɪl] (-(e)s, -e) m od nt part; (An~) share; (Bestand~) component; **zum ~** partly; **t~bar** adj divisible; ~**betrag** m instalment; ~**chen** nt (atomic) particle; **t~en** vt, vr to divide; (mit jdm) to share; **t~haben** (unreg) vi: **t~haben an** +dat to share in; ~**haber** (-s, -) m partner; ~**kaskoversicherung** f third party, fire and theft insurance; ~**nahme** f participation; (Mitleid) sympathy; **t~nahmslos** adj disinterested, apathetic; **t~nehmen** (unreg) vi: **t~nehmen an** +dat to take part in; ~**nehmer** (-s, -) m participant; **t~s** adv partly; ~**ung** f division; **t~weise** adv partially, in part; ~**zahlung** f payment by instalments; ~**zeitarbeit** f part-time work

Teint [tɛ̃:] (-s, -s) m complexion

Telefax nt fax

Telefon [tele'fo:n] (-s, -e) nt telephone; ~**anruf** m (tele)phone call; ~**at** [telefo'na:t] (-(e)s, -e) nt (tele)phone call; ~**buch** nt telephone directory; ~**hörer** m (telephone) receiver; **t~ieren** [telefo'ni:rən] vi to telephone; ~**isch** [-ɪʃ] adj telephone; (Benachrichtigung) by telephone; ~**ist(in)** [telefo'nɪst(ɪn)] m(f) telephonist; ~**karte** f phonecard; ~**nummer** f (tele)phone number; ~**zelle** f telephone kiosk, callbox; ~**zentrale** f telephone exchange

Telegraf [tele'gra:f] (-en, -en) *m* telegraph; **~enmast** *m* telegraph pole; **~ie** [-'fi:] *f* telegraphy; **t~ieren** [-'fi:rən] *vt, vi* to telegraph, to wire; **t~isch** *adj* telegraphic

Telegramm [tele'gram] (-s, -e) *nt* telegram, cable; **~adresse** *f* telegraphic address

Tele- *zW:* **~objektiv** [te:le'ɔpjɛkti:f] *nt* telephoto lens; **t~pathisch** [tele'pa:tɪʃ] *adj* telepathic; **~skop** [tele'sko:p] (-s, -e) *nt* telescope

Telex ['te:lɛks] (-es, -e) *nt* telex

Teller ['tɛlər] (-s, -) *m* plate

Tellergericht *nt* (KOCH) one-course meal

Tempel ['tɛmpəl] (-s, -) *m* temple

Temperament [tɛmpera'mɛnt] *nt* temperament; (Schwung) vivacity, liveliness; **t~voll** *adj* high-spirited, lively

Temperatur [tɛmpera'tu:r] *f* temperature

Tempo¹ ['tɛmpo] (-s, -s) *nt* speed, pace; **Tempo!** get a move on!

Tempo² (-s, Tempi) *nt* (MUS) tempo

Tendenz [tɛn'dɛnts] *f* tendency; (Absicht) intention; **t~iös** [-iˈøːs] *adj* biased, tendentious

tendieren [tɛn'di:rən] *vi:* **~ zu** to show a tendency to, to incline towards

Tennis ['tɛnɪs] (-) *nt* tennis; **~ball** *m* tennis ball; **~platz** *m* tennis court; **~schläger** *m* tennis racket; **~schuh** *m* tennis shoe; **~spieler(in)** *m(f)* tennis player

Tenor [te'no:r] (-s, -e) *m* tenor

Teppich ['tɛpɪç] (-s, -e) *m* carpet; **~boden** *m* wall-to-wall carpeting

Termin [tɛr'mi:n] (-s, -e) *m* (Zeitpunkt) date; (Frist) time limit, deadline; (Arzt~ etc) appointment; **~kalender** *m* diary, appointments book; **~planer** *m* personal organizer

Termite [tɛr'mi:tə] *f* termite

Terpentin [tɛrpɛn'ti:n] (-s, -e) *nt* turpentine, turps *sg*

Terrasse [tɛ'rasə] *f* terrace

Terrine [tɛ'ri:nə] *f* tureen

territorial [tɛritoriˈa:l] *adj* territorial

Territorium [tɛriˈto:rium] *nt* territory

Terror ['tɛrɔr] (-s) *m* terror; reign of terror; **t~isieren** [tɛrori'zi:rən] *vt* to terrorize; **~ismus** [-'rɪsmʊs] *m* terrorism; **~ist** [-'rɪst] *m* terrorist

Terz [tɛrts] (-, -en) *f* (MUS) third; **~ett** [tɛr'sɛt] (-(e)s, -e) *nt* trio

Tesafilm ['te:zafilm] ® *m* sellotape ® (BRIT), Scotch tape ® (US)

Test [tɛst] (-s, -s) *m* test

Testament [tɛsta'mɛnt] *nt* will, testament; (REL) Testament; **t~arisch** [-'ta:rɪʃ] *adj* testamentary; **~svollstrecker** *m* executor (of a will)

testen *vt* to test

Tetanus ['te:tanʊs] (-) *m* tetanus; **~impfung** *f* (anti-)tetanus injection

teuer ['tɔyər] *adj* dear, expensive; **T~ung** *f* increase in prices; **T~ungszulage** *f* cost of living bonus

Teufel ['tɔyfəl] (-s, -) *m* devil

teuflisch ['tɔyflɪʃ] *adj* fiendish, diabolical

Text [tɛkst] (-(e)s, -e) *m* text; (Lieder~) words *pl*; **t~en** *vi* to write the words

textil [tɛks'ti:l] *adj* textile; **T~ien** *pl* textiles; **T~industrie** *f* textile industry; **T~waren** *pl* textiles

Textverarbeitung *f* word processing

Theater [te'a:tər] (-s, -) *nt* theatre; (umg) fuss; **~ spielen** (auch fig) to playact; **~besucher** *m* playgoer; **~kasse** *f* box office; **~stück** *nt* (stage)play

Theke ['te:kə] *f* (Schanktisch) bar; (Ladentisch) counter

Thema ['te:ma] (-s, Themen od -ta) *nt* theme, topic, subject

Themse ['tɛmzə] *f* Thames

Theo- [teo] *zW:* **~loge** [-'lo:gə] (-n, -n) *m* theologian; **~logie** [-lo'gi:] *f* theology; **t~logisch** [-'lo:gɪʃ] *adj* theological; **~retiker** [-'re:tikər] *m*

-) *m* theorist; **t~retisch** [-'re:tɪʃ] *adj* theoretical; **~rie** [-'ri:] *f* theory

Thera- [tera] *zW:* **~peut** [-'pɔyt] (**-en, -en**) *m* therapist; **t~peutisch** [-'pɔytɪʃ] *adj* therapeutic; **~pie** [-'pi:] *f* therapy

Therm- *zW:* **~albad** [ter'ma:lba:t] *nt* thermal bath; thermal spa; **~odrucker** ['tɛrmo-] *m* thermal printer; **~ometer** [tɛrmo'me:tər] (**-s, -**) *nt* thermometer; **~oflasche** ['tɛrmɔsflaʃə] *f* Thermos ® flask; **~ostat** [tɛrmo'staːt] (**-(e)s** *od* **-en, -e(n)**) *m* thermostat

These ['te:zə] *f* thesis

Thrombose [trɔm'bo:zə] *f* thrombosis

Thron [tro:n] (**-(e)s, -e**) *m* throne; **t~en** *vi* to sit enthroned (*fig*) to sit in state; **~folge** *f* succession (to the throne)

Thunfisch ['tu:nfɪʃ] *m* tuna

Thymian ['ty:mia:n] (**-s, -e**) *m* thyme

Tick [tɪk] (**-(e)s, -s**) *m* tic; (*Eigenart*) quirk; (*Fimmel*) craze

ticken *vi* to tick

tief [ti:f] *adj* deep; (*~sinnig*) profound; (*Ausschnitt, Preis, Ton*) low; **T~** (**-s, -s**) *nt* (*MET*) depression; **T~druck** *m* low pressure; **T~e** *f* depth; **T~ebene** *f* plain; **T~enpsychologie** *f* depth psychology; **T~enschärfe** *f* (*PHOT*) depth of focus; **T~garage** *f* underground garage; **~gekühlt** *adj* frozen; **~greifend** *adj* far-reaching; **~kühlfach** *nt* deep-freeze compartment; **Teifkühlkost** *f* (deep) frozen food; **T~kühltruhe** *f* deep-freeze, freezer; **T~punkt** *m* low point; (*fig*) low ebb; **T~schlag** *m* (*BOXEN, fig*) blow below the belt; **~schürfend** *adj* profound; **T~see** *f* deep sea; **~sinnig** *adj* profound; melancholy; **T~stand** *m* low level; **T~stwert** *m* minimum *od* lowest value

Tier [ti:r] (**-(e)s, -e**) *nt* animal; **~arzt** *m* vet(erinary surgeon); **~garten** *m* zoo(logical gardens *pl*);

~heim *nt* cat/dog home; **t~isch** *adj* animal; (*auch fig*) brutish; (*fig: Ernst etc*) deadly; **~kreis** *m* zodiac; **~kunde** *f* zoology; **t~liebend** *adj* fond of animals; **~park** *m* zoo; **~quälerei** [-kvɛːləˈraɪ] *f* cruelty to animals; **~schutzverein** *m* society for the prevention of cruelty to animals

Tiger(in) ['ti:gər(ɪn)] (**-s, -**) *m* tiger(gress)

tilgen ['tɪlgən] *vt* to erase; (*Sünden*) to expiate; (*Schulden*) to pay off

Tinte ['tɪntə] *f* ink; **~nfisch** *m* cuttlefish; **~nstift** *m* copying *od* indelible pencil

Tip [tɪp] *m* tip; **t~pen** *vt, vi* to tap, to touch; (*umg: schreiben*) to type; (*im Lotto etc*) to bet (on); **auf jdn t~pen** (*umg: raten*) to tip sb, to put one's money on sb (*fig*)

Tipp- ['tɪp] *zW:* **T~fehler** (*umg*) *m* typing error; **t~topp** (*umg*) *adj* tip-top; **~zettel** *m* (pools) coupon

Tirol [ti'ro:l] *nt* the Tyrol; **~er(in)** *m(f)* Tyrolean; **t~isch** *adj* Tyrolean

Tisch [tɪʃ] (**-(e)s, -e**) *m* table; **bei ~** at table; **vor/nach ~** before/after eating; **unter den ~ fallen** (*fig*) to be dropped; **~decke** *f* tablecloth; **~ler** (**-s, -**) *m* carpenter, joiner; **~le'rei** *f* joiner's workshop; (*Arbeit*) carpentry, joinery; **t~lern** *vi* to do carpentry *etc*; **~rede** *f* after-dinner speech; **~tennis** *nt* table tennis; **~tuch** *nt* tablecloth

Titel ['ti:təl] (**-s, -**) *m* title; **~bild** *nt* cover (picture); (*von Buch*) cover; frontispiece; **~rolle** *f* title role; **~seite** *f* cover; (*Buch~*) title page; **~verteidiger** *m* defending champion, title holder

Toast [to:st] (**-(e)s, -s** *od* **-e**) *m* toast; **~brot** *nt* bread for toasting; **~er** (**-s, -**) *m* toaster

tob- [to:b] *zW:* **~en** *vi* to rage; (*Kinder*) to romp about; **~süchtig** *adj* maniacal

Tochter ['tɔxtər] (**-, -**) *f* daughter; **~gesellschaft** *f* subsidiary (company)

Tod [toːt] (-(e)s, -e) m death; **t~ernst** adj deadly serious ♦ adv in dead earnest

Todes- ['toːdəs] zW: **~angst** [-aŋst] f mortal fear; **~anzeige** f obituary (notice); **~fall** m death; **~strafe** f death penalty; **~ursache** f cause of death; **~urteil** nt death sentence; **~verachtung** f utter disgust

todkrank adj dangerously ill

tödlich ['tøːtlɪç] adj deadly, fatal

tod- zW: **~müde** adj dead tired; **~schick** (umg) adj smart, classy; **~sicher** (umg) adj absolutely od dead certain; **T~sünde** f deadly sin

Toilette [toa'lɛtə] f toilet, lavatory; (Frisiertisch) dressing table; (Kleidung) outfit

Toiletten- zW: **~artikel** pl toiletries, toilet articles; **~papier** nt toilet paper; **~tisch** m dressing table

toi, toi, toi ['tɔy 'tɔy 'tɔy] excl touch wood

tolerant [tole'rant] adj tolerant

Toleranz [tole'rants] f tolerance

tolerieren [tole'riːrən] vt to tolerate

toll [tɔl] adj mad; (Treiben) wild; (umg) terrific; **~en** vi to romp; **T~kirsche** f deadly nightshade; **~kühn** adj daring; **T~wut** f rabies

Tomate [to'maːtə] f tomato; **~nmark** nt tomato puree

Tombola f tombola

Ton¹ [toːn] (-(e)s, -e) m (Erde) clay

Ton² (-(e)s, -e) m (Laut) sound; (MUS) note; (Redeweise) tone; (Farb~, Nuance) shade; (Betonung) stress; **~abnehmer** m pick-up; **~angebend** adj leading; **~art** f (musical) key; **~band** nt tape; **~bandgerät** nt tape recorder

tönen ['tøːnən] vi to sound ♦ vt to shade; (Haare) to tint

tönern ['tøːnərn] adj clay

Ton- zW: **~fall** m intonation; **~film** m sound film; **~leiter** f (MUS) scale; **t~los** adj soundless

Tonne ['tɔnə] f barrel; (Maß) ton

Tontaube f clay pigeon

Tonwaren pl pottery sg, earthenware sg

Topf [tɔpf] (-(e)s, -e) m pot; **~blume** f pot plant

Töpfer ['tœpfər] (-s, -) m potter; **~ei** [-'raɪ] f piece of pottery; potter's workshop; **~scheibe** f potter's wheel

topographisch [topo'graːfɪʃ] adj topographic

Tor¹ [toːr] (-en, -en) m fool

Tor² (-(e)s, -e) nt gate; (SPORT) goal; **Torbogen** m archway

Torf [tɔrf] (-(e)s) m peat

Torheit f foolishness; foolish deed

töricht ['tøːrɪçt] adj foolish

torkeln ['tɔrkəln] vi to stagger, to reel

Torpedo [tɔr'peːdo] (-s, -s) m torpedo

Torte ['tɔrtə] f cake; (Obst~) flan, tart

Tortur [tɔr'tuːr] f ordeal

Torwart (-(e)s, -e) m goalkeeper

tosen ['toːzən] vi to roar

tot [toːt] adj dead

total [to'taːl] adj total; **~itär** [totali'tɛːr] adj totalitarian; **T~schaden** m (AUT) complete write-off

Tote(r) [toːr] mf dead person

töten ['tøːtən] vt, vi to kill

Toten- ['toːtən] zW: **~bett** nt death bed; **t~blaß** adj deathly pale, white as a sheet; **~kopf** m skull; **~schein** m death certificate; **~stille** f deathly silence

tot- zW: **T~schlag** m manslaughter; **~schlagen** (unreg) vt (auch fig) to kill; **~schweigen** (unreg) vt to hush up; **~stellen** vr to pretend to be dead

Tötung ['tøːtʊŋ] f killing

Toupet [tu'peː] (-s, -s) nt toupee

toupieren [tu'piːrən] vt to backcomb

tot- zW: **~fahren** (unreg) vt to run over; **~geboren** adj stillborn; **~lachen** (umg) vr to laugh one's head off

Toto ['toːto] (-s, -s) m od nt pools pl; **~schein** m pools coupon

Tour [tuːr] (-, -en) f tour, trip; (*Umdrehung*) revolution; (*Verhaltensart*) way; **in einer ~** incessantly; **~enzähler** m rev counter; **~ismus** [tu'rɪsmʊs] m tourism; **~ist** [tu'rɪst] m tourist; **~istenklasse** f tourist class; **~nee** [tʊr'neː] (-, -n) f (THEAT etc) tour; **auf ~nee gehen** to go on tour

Trab [traːp] (-(e)s) m trot; **~antenstadt** f satellite town

traben vi to trot

Tracht [traxt] (-, -en) f (*Kleidung*) costume, dress; **eine ~ Prügel** a sound thrashing; **t~en** vi: **t~en (nach)** to strive (for); **jdm nach dem Leben t~en** to seek to kill sb; **danach t~en, etw zu tun** to strive od endeavour to do sth

trächtig ['trɛçtɪç] adj (*Tier*) pregnant

Tradition [traditsi'oːn] f tradition; **t~ell** [-'nɛl] adj traditional

traf etc [traːf] vb siehe **treffen**

Tragbahre f stretcher

tragbar adj (*Gerät*) portable; (*Kleidung*) wearable; (*erträglich*) bearable

träge ['trɛːgə] adj sluggish, slow; (PHYS) inert

tragen ['traːgən] (unreg) vt to carry; (*Kleidung, Brille*) to wear; (*Namen, Früchte*) to bear; (*erdulden*) to endure ♦ vi (*schwanger sein*) to be pregnant; (*Eis*) to hold; **sich mit einem Gedanken ~** to have an idea in mind; **zum T~ kommen** to have an effect

Träger ['trɛːgər] (-s, -) m carrier; wearer; bearer; (*Ordens~*) holder; (*an Kleidung*) shoulder strap; (*Körperschaft etc*) sponsor; **~rakete** f launch vehicle

Tragetasche f carrier bag

Tragfläche f (AVIAT) wing

Tragflügelboot nt hydrofoil

Trägheit ['trɛːkhait] f laziness; (PHYS) inertia

Tragik ['traːgɪk] f tragedy

tragisch ['traːgɪʃ] adj tragic

Tragödie [tra'gøːdiə] f tragedy

Tragweite f range; (*fig*) scope

Train- ['trɛːn] zW: **~er** (-s, -) m (SPORT) trainer, coach; (*Fußball*) manager; **t~ieren** [trɛ'niːrən] vt, vi to train; (*Mensch*) to train, to coach; (*Übung*) to practise; **~ing** (-s, -s) nt training; **~ingsanzug** m track suit

Traktor ['traktɔr] m tractor; (*von Drucker*) tractor feed

trällern ['trɛlərn] vt, vi to trill, to sing

Tram (-, -s) f tram

trampeln ['trampəln] vt, vi to trample, to stamp

trampen ['trɛmpən] vi to hitch-hike

Tramper(in) (-s, -) m(f) hitch-hiker

Tran [traːn] (-(e)s, -e) m train oil, blubber

tranchieren [trã'ʃiːrən] vt to carve

Träne ['trɛːnə] f tear; **t~n** vi to water; **~ngas** nt teargas

trank etc [traŋk] vb siehe **trinken**

tränken ['trɛŋkən] vt (*Tiere*) to water

Trans- zW: **~formator** [transfɔr'maːtɔr] m transformer; **~istor** [tran'zɪstɔr] m transistor; **~itverkehr** [tran'ziːtfɛrkeːr] m transit traffic; **~itvisum** nt transit visa; **t~parent** [transpa'rɛnt] adj transparent; **~parent** (-(e)s, -e) nt (*Bild*) transparency; (*Spruchband*) banner; **~plantation** [transplantatsi'oːn] f transplantation; (*Hauttransplantation*) graft(ing)

Transport [trans'pɔrt] (-(e)s, -e) m transport; **t~ieren** [transpɔr'tiːrən] vt to transport; **~kosten** pl transport charges, carriage sg; **~mittel** nt means sg of transportation; **~unternehmen** nt carrier

Trapez [tra'peːts] (-es, -e) nt trapeze; (MATH) trapezium

Traube ['traubə] f grape; bunch (of grapes); **~nzucker** m glucose

trauen ['trauən] vi: **jdm/etw ~** to trust sb/sth ♦ vr to dare ♦ vt to marry

Trauer ['trauər] (-) f sorrow; (*für Verstorbenen*) mourning; **~ll** m death, bereavement; **~feier** f funeral service; **~kleidung** f mourning; **~** vi to mourn; **um jdn t~n** to mourn (for) sb; **~rand** m black border; **~spiel** nt tragedy

traulich ['traulɪç] adj cosy, intimate

Traum [traum] (-(e)s, Träume) m dream

Trauma (-s, -men) nt trauma

träum- ['trɔym] zW: **~en** vt, vi to dream; **T~er** (-s, -) m dreamer; **T~e'rei** f dreaming; **~erisch** adj dreamy

traumhaft adj dreamlike; (fig) wonderful

traurig ['traurɪç] adj sad; **T~keit** f sadness

Trau- ['trau] zW: **~ring** m wedding ring; **~schein** m marriage certificate; **~ung** f wedding ceremony; **~zeuge** m witness (to a marriage); **~zeugin** f witness (at a marriage ceremony)

treffen ['trɛfən] (unreg) vt to strike, to hit; (Bemerkung) to hurt; (begegnen) to meet; (Entscheidung etc) to make; (Maßnahmen) to take ♦ vi to hit ♦ vr to meet; **er hat es gut getroffen** he did well; **~ auf** +akk to come across, to meet with; **es traf sich, daß ...** it so happened that ...; **es trifft sich gut** it's convenient; **wie es so trifft** as these things happen; **T~** (-s, -) nt meeting; **~d** adj pertinent, apposite

Treffer (-s, -) m hit; (Tor) goal; (Los) winner

Treffpunkt m meeting place

Treib- ['traib] zW: **~eis** nt drift ice; **t~en** (unreg) vt to drive; (Studien etc) to pursue; (Sport) to do, to go in for ♦ vi (Schiff etc) to drift; (Pflanzen) to sprout; (KOCH: aufgehen) to rise; (Tee, Kaffee) to be diuretic; **Unsinn t~en** to fool around; **~haus** nt greenhouse; **~hauseffekt** m greenhouse effect; **~hausgas** nt greenhouse gas; **~stoff** m fuel

trenn- ['trɛn] zW: **~bar** adj separable; **~en** vt to separate; (teilen) to

divide ♦ vr to separate; **sich ~en von** to part with; **T~ung** f separation; **T~wand** f partition (wall)

Trepp- ['trɛp] zW: **t~ab** adv downstairs; **t~auf** adv upstairs; **~e** f stair(case); **~engeländer** nt banister; **~enhaus** nt staircase

Tresor [tre'zo:r] (-s, -e) m safe

Tretboot nt pedalo, pedal boat

treten ['tre:tən] (unreg) vi to step; (Tränen, Schweiß) to appear ♦ vt (mit Fußtritt) to kick; (niedertr~) to tread, to trample; **~ nach** to kick at; **~ in** +akk to step in(to); **in Verbindung ~** to get in contact; **in Erscheinung ~** to appear

treu [trɔy] adj faithful, true; **T~e** (-) f loyalty, faithfulness; **T~hand** (-s, -) m trustee; **T~handgesellschaft** f trust company; **~herzig** adj innocent; **~los** adj faithless

Tribüne [tri'by:nə] f grandstand; (Redner~) platform

Trichter ['trɪçtər] (-s, -) m funnel; (in Boden) crater

Trick [trɪk] (-s, -e od -s) m trick; **~film** m cartoon

Trieb [tri:p] (-(e)s, -e) m urge, drive; (Neigung) inclination; (an Baum etc) shoot; **t~ etc** vb siehe treiben; **~feder** f (fig) motivating force; **~kraft** f (fig) drive; **~täter** m sex offender; **~werk** nt engine

triefen ['tri:fən] vi to drip

trifft etc [trɪft] vb siehe treffen

triftig ['trɪftɪç] adj good, convincing

Trikot [tri'ko:] (-s, -s) nt vest; (SPORT) shirt

Trimester [tri'mɛstər] (-s, -) nt term

trimmen ['trɪmən] vr to keep fit exercises

trink- ['trɪŋk] zW: **~bar** adj drinkable; **~en** (unreg) vt, vi to drink; **T~er** (-s, -) m drinker; **T~geld** nt tip; **T~halle** f refreshment kiosk; **T~wasser** nt drinking water

Tripper ['trɪpər] (-s, -) m gonorrhoea

Tritt [trɪt] (-(e)s, -e) m step; (Fuß~) kick; **~brett** nt (EISENB) step;

(AUT) running-board

Triumph [tri'ʊmf] (-(e)s, -e) m triumph; ~**bogen** m triumphal arch; ~**ieren** [triʊm'fiːrən] vi to triumph; (jubeln) to exult

trocken ['trɔkən] adj dry; T~**element** nt dry cell; T~**haube** f hair-dryer; T~**heit** f dryness; ~**legen** vt (Sumpf) to drain; (Kind) to put a clean nappy on; T~**milch** f dried milk; T~**rasur** f dry shave, electric shave

trocknen ['trɔknən] vt, vi to dry

Trödel ['trøːdəl] (-s; umg) m junk; ~**markt** m flea market; t~**n** (umg) vi to dawdle

Trog [troːk] (-(e)s, ⁻e) m trough

Trommel ['trɔməl] (-, -n) f drum; ~**fell** nt eardrum; t~**n** vt, vi to drum

Trompete [trɔm'peːtə] f trumpet; ~**r** (-s, -) m trumpeter

Tropen ['troːpən] pl tropics; ~**helm** m sun helmet

tröpfeln ['trœpfəln] vi to drop, to trickle

Tropfen ['trɔpfən] (-s, -) m drop; t~ vt, vi to drip ♦ vb unpers: es tropft a few raindrops are falling; t~**weise** adv in drops

Tropfsteinhöhle f stalactite cave

tropisch ['troːpɪʃ] adj tropical

Trost [troːst] (-es) m consolation, comfort

trösten ['trøːstən] vt to console, to comfort

trost- zW: ~**los** adj bleak; (Verhältnisse) wretched; T~**preis** m consolation prize; ~**reich** adj comforting

Trott [trɔt] (-(e)s, -e) m trot; (Routine) routine; ~**el** (-s, -; umg) m fool, dope; t~**en** vi to trot; ~**oir** [trɔto'aːr] (-s, -e od -s) nt pavement, sidewalk (US)

Trotz [trɔts] (-es) m pigheadedness; etw aus ~ **tun** to do sth just to show them; **jdm zum** ~ in defiance of sb; t~ präp (+gen od dat) in spite of; t~**dem** adv nevertheless, all the same ♦ konj although; t~**en** vi (+dat) to defy; (der Kälte, Klima

etc) to withstand; (der Gefahr) to brave; (trotzig sein) to be awkward; t~**ig** adj defiant, pig-headed; ~**kopf** m obstinate child

trüb [tryːp] adj dull; (Flüssigkeit, Glas) cloudy; (fig) gloomy

Trubel ['truːbəl] (-s) m hurly-burly

trüb- zW: ~**en** [ˈtryːbən] vt to cloud ♦ vr to become clouded; T~**heit** f dullness; cloudiness; gloom; T~**sal** (-, -e) f distress; ~**selig** adj sad, melancholy; T~**sinn** m depression; ~**sinnig** adj depressed, gloomy

Trüffel ['tryfəl] (-, -n) f truffle

trug etc [truːk] vb siehe **tragen**

trügen ['tryːgən] (unreg) vt to deceive ♦ vi to be deceptive

trügerisch adj deceptive

Trugschluß ['truːkʃlʊs] m false conclusion

Truhe ['truːə] f chest

Trümmer ['trʏmər] pl wreckage sg; (Bau~) ruins; ~**haufen** m heap of rubble

Trumpf [trʊmpf] (-(e)s, ⁻e) m (auch fig) trump; t~**en** vt, vi to trump

Trunk [trʊŋk] (-(e)s, ⁻e) m drink; t~**en** adj intoxicated; ~**enheit** f intoxication; ~**enheit am Steuer** drunken driving; ~**sucht** f alcoholism

Trupp [trʊp] (-s, -s) m troop; ~**e** f troop; (Waffengattung) force; (Schauspiel~) troupe; ~**en** pl (MIL) troops; ~**enübungsplatz** m training area

Truthahn ['truːthaːn] m turkey

Tschech- ['tʃɛç] zW: ~**e** m Czech, Czechoslovak(ian); ~**in** f Czech, Czechoslovak(ian); t~**isch** adj Czech, Czechoslovak(ian); ~**oslowake** [-ɔslo'vaːkə] m Czech, Czechoslovak(ian); ~**oslowakei** [-ɔslova'kaɪ] f: **die** ~**oslowakei** Czechoslovakia; t~**oslowakisch** [-ɔslo'vaːkɪʃ] adj Czechoslovak(ian)

tschüs [tʃys] excl cheerio

T-Shirt ['tiːʃœrt] nt T-shirt

Tube ['tuːbə] f tube

Tuberkulose [tubɛrku'loːzə] f tuberculosis

Tuch [tuːx] (-(e)s, ⁻er) nt cloth; (Hals~) scarf; (Kopf~) headscarf; (Hand~) towel

tüchtig ['tʏçtɪç] adj efficient, (cap)able; (umg: kräftig) good, sound; **T~keit** f efficiency, ability

Tücke ['tʏkə] f (Arglist) malice; (Trick) trick; (Schwierigkeit) difficulty, problem; **seine ~n haben** to be temperamental

tückisch ['tʏkɪʃ] adj treacherous; (böswillig) malicious

Tugend ['tuːgənt] (-, -en) f virtue; **t~haft** adj virtuous

Tüll [tʏl] (-s, -e) m tulle

Tülle ['tʏlə] f spout

Tulpe ['tʊlpə] f tulip

Tumor ['tuːmɔr] (-s, -e) m tumour

Tümpel ['tʏmpəl] (-s, -) m pool, pond

Tumult [tu'mʊlt] (-(e)s, -e) m tumult

tun [tuːn] (unreg) vt (machen) to do; (legen) to put ♦ vi to act ♦ vr: **es tut sich etwas/viel** something/a lot is happening; **jdm etw ~** (antun) to do sth to sb; **etw tut es auch sth will do; das tut nichts** that doesn't matter; **das tut nichts zur Sache** that's neither here nor there; **so ~, als ob** to act as if

tünchen ['tʏnçən] vt to whitewash

Tunke ['tʊŋkə] f sauce; **t~n** vt to dip, to dunk

tunlichst ['tuːnlɪçst] adv if at all possible; **~ bald** as soon as possible

Tunnel ['tʊnəl] (-s, -s od -) m tunnel

Tupfen ['tʊpfən] (-s, -) m dot, spot; **t~** vt, vi to dab; (mit Farbe) to dot

Tür [tyːr] (-, -en) f door

Turban(-s, -e) [tʊr'baːn] m turban

Turbine [tʊr'biːnə] f turbine

Türk- zW: **~e** m Turk; **~ei** [tʏr'kaɪ] f: **die ~ei** Turkey; **~in** f Turk

Türkis [tʏr'kiːs] (-es, -e) m turquoise; **t~** adj turquoise

türkisch ['tʏrkɪʃ] adj Turkish

Türklinke f doorknob, door handle

Turm [tʊrm] (-(e)s, ⁻e) m tower; (Kirch~) steeple; (Sprung~) diving platform; (SCHACH) castle, rook

türmen ['tʏrmən] vr to tower up ♦ vi (umg) to scarper, to bolt ♦ vt to heap up

Turn- ['tʊrn] zW: **t~en** vi to do gymnastic exercises ♦ vt to perform; **~en** (-s) nt gymnastics; (SCH) physical education, P.E.; **~er(in)** (-s, -) m(f) gymnast; **~halle** f gym (-nasium); **~hose** f gym shorts pl

Turnier [tʊr'niːr] (-s, -e) nt tournament

Turn- zW: **~schuh** m gym shoe; **~verein** m gymnastics club; **~zeug** nt gym things pl

Tusche ['tʊʃə] f Indian ink

tuscheln ['tʊʃəln] vt, vi to whisper

Tuschkasten m paintbox

Tüte ['tyːtə] f bag

tuten ['tuːtən] vi (AUT) to hoot (BRIT), to honk (US)

TÜV [tʏf] (-s, -s) m abk (= Technischer Überwachungsverein) MOT

Typ [tyːp] (-s, -en) m type; (TYP) type

Typhus ['tyːfus] (-) m typhoid (fever)

typisch ['tyːpɪʃ] adj: **~ (für)** typical (of)

Tyrann [ty'ran] (-en, -en) m tyrant; **~ei** [-'naɪ] f tyranny; **t~isch** adj tyrannical; **t~i'sieren** vt to tyrannize

U

u.a. abk = unter anderem

U-Bahn ['uːbaːn] f underground, tube

übel ['yːbəl] adj bad; (moralisch) bad, wicked; **jdm ist ~** sb feels sick; **Ü~** (-s, -) nt evil; (Krankheit) disease; **~gelaunt** adj bad-tempered; **Ü~keit** f nausea; **~nehmen** (unreg) vt: **jdm eine Bemerkung ~nehmen** to be offended at sb's remark etc

üben ['yːbən] vt, vi to exercise, to

practise

SCHLÜSSELWORT

über ['y:bər] *präp +dat* **1** (*räumlich*) over, above; **zwei Grad über Null** two degrees above zero

2 (*zeitlich*) over; **über der Arbeit einschlafen** to fall asleep over one's work

♦ *präp +akk* **1** (*räumlich*) over; (*hoch über auch*) above; (*quer über auch*) across

2 (*zeitlich*) over; **über Weihnachten** over Christmas; **über kurz oder lang** sooner or later

3 (*mit Zahlen*): **Kinder über 12 Jahren** children over *od* above 12 years of age; **ein Scheck über 200 Mark** a cheque for 200 marks

4 (*auf dem Wege*) via; **nach Köln über Aachen** to Cologne via Aachen; **ich habe es über die Auskunft erfahren** I found out from information

5 (*betreffend*) about; **ein Buch über ... a** book about *od* on ...; **über jdn/ etw lachen** to laugh about *od* at sb/ sth

6: Macht über jdn haben to have power over sb; **sie liebt ihn über alles** she loves him more than everything

♦ *adv* over; **über und über** over and over; **den ganzen Tag über** all day long; **jdm in etw** *dat* **über sein** to be superior to sb in sth

überall [y:bər'al] *adv* everywhere; **~hin** *adv* everywhere

überanstrengen [y:bər'anʃtrɛŋən] *vt insep* to overexert ♦ *vr insep* to overexert o.s.

überarbeiten [y:bər'arbaitən] *vt insep* to revise, to rework ♦ *vr insep* to overwork (o.s.)

überaus [y:bər'aus] *adv* exceedingly

überbelichten ['y:bərbəlɪçtən] *vt* (PHOT) to overexpose

über'bieten (*unreg*) *vt* to outbid; (*übertreffen*) to surpass; (*Re-*

kord) to break

Überbleibsel ['y:bərblaipsəl] (-s, -) *nt* residue, remainder

Überblick ['y:bərblɪk] *m* view; (*fig: Darstellung*) survey, overview; (*Fähigkeit*): **~** (*über +akk*) grasp (of), overall view (of); **ü~en** [-'blɪkən] *vt insep* to overlook

überbring [y:bər'brɪŋ] *zW:* **~en** (*unreg*) *vt insep* to deliver, to hand (over); **Ü~er** (-s, -) *m* bearer

überbrücken [y:bər'brykən] *vt insep* to bridge (over)

über'dauern *vt insep* to outlast

über'denken (*unreg*) *vt insep* to think over

überdies [y:bər'di:s] *adv* besides

überdimensional ['y:bərdimenzio'na:l] *adj* oversize

Überdruß ['y:bərdrus] (-sses) *m* weariness; **bis zum ~** *ad* nauseam

übereifrig ['y:bər'aifrɪç] *adj* overkeen

übereilt [y:bər'ailt] *adj* (over)hasty, premature

überein- [y:bər'ain] *zW:* **~ander** [-ai'nandər] *adv* one upon the other; (*sprechen*) about each other; **~kommen** (*unreg*) *vi* to agree; **Ü~kunft** (-, **-künfte**) *f* agreement; **~stimmen** *vi* to agree; **Ü~stimmung** *f* agreement

überempfindlich ['y:bər'ɛmpfɪntlɪç] *adj* hypersensitive

überfahren [y:bər'fa:rən] (*unreg*) *vt insep* (AUT) to run over; (*fig*) to walk all over

Überfahrt ['y:bərfa:rt] *f* crossing

Überfall ['y:bərfal] *m* (*Bank~, MIL*) raid; (*auf jdn*) assault; **ü~en** [-'falən] (*unreg*) *vt insep* to attack; (*Bank*) to raid; (*besuchen*) to drop in on, to descend on

überfällig ['y:bərfɛlɪç] *adj* overdue

über'fliegen (*unreg*) *vt insep* to fly over, to overfly; (*Buch*) to skim through

Überfluß ['y:bərflus] *m:* **~** (*an +dat*) (super)abundance (of), excess (of)

überflüssig ['y:bɐflʏsɪç] adj superfluous

über'fordern vt insep to demand too much of; (Kräfte etc) to overtax

über'führen vt insep (Leiche etc) to transport; (Täter) to have convicted

Über'führung f transport; conviction; (Brücke) bridge, overpass

überfüllt adj (Schulen, Straßen) overcrowded; (Kurs) oversubscribed

Übergabe ['y:bɐga:bə] f handing over; (MIL) surrender

Übergang ['y:bɐgaŋ] m crossing; (Wandel, Überleitung) transition

Übergangs- zW: ~lösung f provisional solution, stopgap; ~stadium nt transitional stage; ~zeit f transitional period

über'geben (unreg) vt insep to hand over; (MIL) to surrender ♦ vr insep to be sick; **dem Verkehr ~** to open to traffic

übergehen ['y:bɐge:ən] (unreg) vi (Besitz) to pass; (zum Feind etc) to go over, to defect; ~ **in** +akk to turn into to pass over, to omit

Übergewicht ['y:bɐgəvɪçt] nt excess weight; (fig) preponderance

überglücklich ['y:bɐglʏklɪç] adj overjoyed

überhaupt [y:bɐ'haupt] adv at all; (im allgemeinen) in general; (besonders) especially; ~ **nicht/keine** not/none at all

überheblich [y:bɐ'he:plɪç] adj arrogant; **Ü~keit** f arrogance

über'holen vt insep to overtake; (TECH) to overhaul

überholt adj out-of-date, obsolete

Überholverbot nt restriction on overtaking

über'hören vt insep not to hear; (absichtlich) to ignore

überirdisch ['y:bɐʔɪrdɪʃ] adj supernatural, unearthly

über'laden (unreg) vt insep to overload ♦ adj (fig) cluttered

über'lassen (unreg) vt insep: **jdm etw** ~ to leave sth to sb ♦ vr insep: **sich einer Sache** dat ~ to give o.s.

über'lasten vt insep to overload; (Mensch) to overtax

überlaufen ['y:bɐlaufən] (unreg) vi (Flüssigkeit) to flow over; (zum Feind etc) to go over, to defect; ~ **sein** to be inundated od besieged (Schauer etc) to run

Überläufer ['y:bɐlɔyfɐ] (-s, -) m deserter

über'leben vt insep to survive; **Ü~de(r)** mf survivor

über'legen vt insep to consider ♦ adj superior; **ich muß es mir** ~ I'll have to think about it; **Ü~heit** f superiority

Über'legung f consideration, deliberation

über'liefern vt insep to hand down, to transmit

Überlieferung f tradition

überlisten [y:bɐ'lɪstən] vt insep to outwit

überm ['y:bɐm] = über dem

Übermacht ['y:bɐmaxt] f superior force, superiority

übermächtig ['y:bɐmɛçtɪç] adj superior (in strength); (Gefühl etc) overwhelming

übermannen [y:bɐ'manən] vt insep to overcome

übermäßig ['y:bɐmɛ:sɪç] adj excessive

Übermensch ['y:bɐmɛnʃ] m superman; **ü~lich** adj superhuman

übermitteln [y:bɐ'mɪtəln] vt insep to convey

übermorgen ['y:bɐmɔrgən] adv the day after tomorrow

Übermüdung ['y:bɐmy:duŋ] f fatigue, overtiredness

Übermut ['y:bɐmu:t] m exuberance

übermütig ['y:bɐmy:tɪç] adj exuberant, high-spirited; ~ **werden** to get overconfident

übernächste(r, s) adj (Jahr) next but one

übernachten [y:bɐ'naxtən] vi insep: (bei jdm) ~ to spend the night (at sb's place)

Übernahme ['y:bərnaːmə] f taking over od on, acceptance

über'nehmen (unreg) vt insep to take on, to accept; (Amt, Geschäft) to take over ♦ vr insep to take on too much

über'prüfen vt insep to examine, to check

überqueren [y:bər'kveːrən] vt insep to cross

überragen [y:bər'raːgən] vt insep to tower above; (fig) to surpass

überraschen [y:bər'rafən] vt insep to surprise

Überraschung f surprise

überreden [y:bər'reːdən] vt insep to persuade

überreichen [y:bər'raiçən] vt insep to present, to hand over

Überrest m remains, remnants

überrumpeln [y:bər'rompəln] vt insep to take by surprise

überrunden [y:bər'rundən] vt insep to lap

übers ['y:bərs] = über das

Überschallflugzeug ['y:bərfal-] nt supersonic jet

Überschallgeschwindigkeit f supersonic speed

über'schätzen vt insep to overestimate

überschäumen vi (Bier) to foam over, bubble over; (Temperament) to boil over

Überschlag ['y:bərflaːk] m (FIN) estimate; (SPORT) somersault; **ü~en** [-'flaːgən] (unreg) vt insep (berechnen) to estimate; (auslassen: Seite) to omit ♦ vr insep to somersault; (Stimme) to crack; (AVIAT) to loop the loop (Beine) to cross ♦ vi (Wellen) to break; (Funken) to flash

über'schnappen vi (Stimme) to crack; (umg: Mensch) to flip one's lid

über'schneiden (unreg) vr insep (auch fig) to overlap; (Linien) to intersect

über'schreiben (unreg) vt insep to provide with a heading; jdm etw ~

to transfer od make over sth to sb

über'schreiten (unreg) vt insep to cross over; (fig) to exceed; (verletzen) to transgress

Überschrift ['y:bərfrift] f heading, title

Überschuß ['y:bərfus] m: ~ (an +dat) surplus (of)

überschüssig ['y:bərfysıç] adj surplus, excess

über'schütten vt insep: jdn/etw mit etw ~ to pour sth over sb/sth; jdn mit etw ~ (fig) to shower sb with sth

überschwemmen [y:bər'fvɛmən] vt insep to flood

Überschwemmung f flood

überschwenglich ['y:bərfvɛŋlıç] adj effusive

Übersee ['y:bərzeː] f: nach/in ~ overseas; **ü~isch** adj overseas

über'sehen (unreg) vt insep to look (out) over; (fig: Folgen) to see, to get an overall view of; (: nicht beachten) to overlook

über'senden (unreg) vt insep to send, to forward

übersetz- zW: ~en [-bər'zɛtsən] vt insep to translate ♦ vi to cross; **Ü~er(in)** [-'zɛtsər(ın)] (-s, -) m(f) translator; **Ü~ung** [-zɛtsoŋ] f translation; (TECH) gear ratio

Übersicht ['y:bərzıçt] f overall view; (Darstellung) survey; **ü~lich** adj clear; (Gelände) open; ~**lichkeit** f clarity, lucidity

übersiedeln ['y:bərziːdəln] vi sep to move to move

über'spannen vt insep (zu sehr spannen) to overstretch; (überdecken) to cover

über'spannt adj eccentric; (Idee) wild, crazy

überspitzt [y:bər'fpıtst] adj exaggerated

über'springen (unreg) vt insep to jump over; (fig) to skip

überstehen [y:bər'fteːən] (unreg) vt insep to overcome, to get over (Winter etc) to survive, to get through to project

über'steigen (unreg) vt insep to climb over; (fig) to exceed

über'stimmen vt insep to outvote

Überstunden ['y:bər∫tʊndən] pl overtime sg

über'stürzen vt insep to rush ♦ vr insep to follow (one another) in rapid succession

überstürzt adj (over)hasty

über'tönen vt insep to drown (out)

Übertrag ['y:bərtra:k] (-(e)s, -träge) m (COMM) amount brought forward; **ü~bar** ['-'tra:kba:r] adj transferable; (MED) infectious; **ü~en** ['-tra:gən] (unreg) vt insep to transfer; (RADIO) to broadcast; (übersetzen) to render; (Krankheit) to transmit ♦ vr insep to spread ♦ adj figurative; **ü~en** auf +akk to transfer to; **jdm etw ü~en** to assign sth to sb; **sich ü~en** auf +akk to spread to; **~ung** ['-tra:gʊŋ] f transfer(ence); (RADIO) broadcast; rendering; transmission

über'treffen (unreg) vt insep to surpass

über'treiben (unreg) vt insep to exaggerate

Übertreibung f exaggeration

übertreten [y:bər'tre:tən] (unreg) vt insep to cross; (Gebot etc) to break (über Linie, Gebiet) to step (over); (SPORT) to overstep; (zu anderem Glauben) to be converted; **'übertreten** (in +akk) (POL) to go over (to)

Über'tretung f violation, transgression

übertrieben [y:bər'tri:bən] adj exaggerated, excessive

übervölkert [y:bər'fœlkərt] adj overpopulated

übervoll ['y:bərfɔl] adj overfull

übervorteilen [y:bər'fɔrtailən] vt insep to dupe, to cheat

über'wachen vt insep to supervise; (Verdächtigen) to keep under surveillance

Überwachung f supervision; surveillance

überwältigen [y:bər'vɛltigən] vt insep to overpower; **~d** adj overwhelming

überweisen [y:bər'vaizən] (unreg) vt insep to transfer

Überweisung f transfer

über'wiegen (unreg) vi insep to predominate; **~d** adj predominant

über'winden (unreg) vt insep to overcome ♦ vr insep to make an effort, to bring o.s. (to do sth)

Überwindung f effort, strength of mind

Überzahl ['y:bərtsa:l] f superiority, superior numbers pl; **in der ~ sein** to be numerically superior

überzählig ['y:bərtsɛ:liç] adj surplus

über'zeugen vt insep to convince; **~d** adj convincing

Überzeugung f conviction

überziehen ['y:bərtsi:ən] (unreg) vt insep to put on to cover; (Konto) to overdraw

Überzug ['y:bərtsu:k] m cover; (Belag) coating

üblich ['y:pliç] adj usual

U-Boot ['u:bo:t] nt submarine

übrig ['y:briç] adj remaining; **für jdn etwas ~ haben** (umg) to be fond of sb; **die ~en** the others; **das ~e** the rest; **im ~en** besides; **~bleiben** (unreg) vi to remain, to be left (over); **~ens** ['y:brigəns] adv besides; (nebenbei bemerkt) by the way; **~lassen** (unreg) vt to leave (over)

Übung ['y:bʊŋ] f practice; (Turn-, Aufgabe etc) exercise; **~ macht den Meister** practice makes perfect

Ufer ['u:fər] (-s, -) nt bank; (Meeres-) shore

Uhr [u:r] (-, -en) f clock; (Armband-) watch; **wieviel ~ ist es?** what time is it?; **1 ~** 1 o'clock; **20 ~** 8 o'clock, 20.00 (twenty hundred) hours; **~(arm)band** nt watch strap; **~band** nt watch strap; **~kette** f watch chain; **~macher** (-s, -) m watchmaker; **~werk** nt clockwork;

works of a watch; **~zeiger** m hand; **~zeigersinn** m: **im ~zeigersinn** clockwise; **entgegen dem ~zeigersinn** anticlockwise; **~zeit** f time (of day)

Uhu ['u:hu] (-s, -s) m eagle owl
UKW [u:ka've:] abk (= Ultrakurzwelle) VHF
ulkig adj funny
Ulme ['ʊlmə] f elm
Ultimatum [ʊlti'ma:tʊm] (-s, Ultimaten) nt ultimatum
Ultraschall ['ʊltraʃal] m (PHYS) ultrasound
ultraviolett ['ʊltravio'let] adj ultraviolet

SCHLÜSSELWORT

um [ʊm] präp +akk **1** (um herum) (a)round; **um Weihnachten** around Christmas; **er schlug um sich** he hit about him
2 (mit Zeitangabe) at; **um acht (Uhr)** at eight (o'clock)
3 (mit Größenangabe) by; **etw um 4 cm kürzen** to shorten sth by 4 cm; **um 10% teurer** 10% more expensive; **um vieles besser** better by far; **um nichts besser** in the least bit better; **um so besser** so much the better
4: **der Kampf um den Titel** the battle for the title; **um Geld spielen** to play for money; **Stunde um Stunde** hour after hour; **Auge um Auge** an eye for an eye
♦ präp +gen: **um ... willen** for the sake of ...; **um Gottes willen** for goodness od (stärker) God's sake
♦ konj: **um ... zu** (in order) to ...; **zu klug, um zu ...** too clever to ...; **um so besser/schlimmer** so much the better/worse
♦ adv **1** (ungefähr) about; **um (die) 30 Leute** about od around 30 people
2 (vorbei): **die 2 Stunden sind um** the two hours are up

umändern ['ʊm'ɛndɐn] vt to alter
Umänderung f alteration

umarbeiten ['ʊm'arbaitən] vt to remodel; (Buch etc) to revise, to rework
umarmen [ʊm'arman] vt insep to embrace
Umbau ['ʊmbau] (-(e)s, -e od -ten) m reconstruction, alteration(s); **u~en** vt to rebuild, to reconstruct
umbilden ['ʊmbɪldən] vt to reorganize; (POL: Kabinett) to reshuffle
umbinden ['ʊmbɪndən] (unreg) vt (Krawatte etc) to put on
umblättern ['ʊmblɛtɐn] vt to turn over
umblicken ['ʊmblɪkən] vr to look around
umbringen ['ʊmbrɪŋən] (unreg) vt to kill
umbuchen ['ʊmbu:xən] vi to change one's reservation/flight etc ♦ vt to change
umdenken ['ʊmdɛŋkən] (unreg) vi to adjust one's views
umdrehen ['ʊmdre:ən] vt to turn (round); (Hals) to wring ♦ vr to turn (round)
Um'drehung f revolution; rotation
umeinander [ʊm'ai'nandɐr] adv round one another; (füreinander) for one another
umfahren ['ʊmfa:rən] (unreg) vt to run over; to drive round; to sail round
umfallen ['ʊmfalən] (unreg) vi to fall down od over
Umfang ['ʊmfaŋ] m extent; (von Buch) size; (Reichweite) range; (Fläche) area; (MATH) circumference; **u~reich** adj extensive; (Buch etc) voluminous
um'fassen vt insep to embrace; (umgeben) to surround; (enthalten) to include; **~d** adj comprehensive, extensive
umformen ['ʊmfɔrmən] vt to transform
Umformer (-s, -) m (ELEK) transformer, converter
Umfrage ['ʊmfra:gə] f poll
umfüllen ['ʊmfylən] vt to transfer;

(Wein) to decant

umfunktionieren ['umfuŋk-tsioni:rən] *vt* to convert, to transform

Umgang ['umgaŋ] *m* company; *(mit jdm)* dealings *pl*; *(Behandlung)* way of behaving

umgänglich ['umgεŋliç] *adj* sociable

Umgangsformen *pl* manners

Umgangssprache *f* colloquial language

umgeben [um'ge:bən] *(unreg) vt* insep to surround

Umgebung *f* surroundings *pl*; *(Milieu)* environment; *(Personen)* people in one's circle

umgehen ['umge:ən] *(unreg) vi* to go (a)round to bypass; *(MIL)* to outflank; *(Gesetz etc)* to circumvent; *(vermeiden)* to avoid; **im Schlosse** ~ to haunt the castle; **mit jdm grob etc** ~ to treat sb roughly etc; **mit Geld sparsam** ~ to be careful with one's money; **umgehend** *adj* immediate

Um'gehung *f* bypassing; outflanking; circumvention; avoidance; **Umgehungsstraße** *f* bypass

umgekehrt ['umgəke:rt] *adj* reverse(d); *(gegenteilig)* opposite ♦ *adv* the other way around; **und** ~ and vice versa

umgraben ['umgra:bən] *(unreg) vt* to dig up

Umhang ['umhaŋ] *m* wrap, cape

umhauen ['umhaoən] *vt* to fell; *(fig)* to bowl over

umher [om'he:r] *adv* about, around; **~gehen** *(unreg) vi* to walk about; **~ziehen** *(unreg) vi* to wander from place to place

umhinkönnen [om'hınkœnən] *(unreg) vi*: **ich kann nicht umhin, das zu tun** I can't help doing it

umhören ['omhø:rən] *vr* to ask around

Umkehr ['omke:r] *f* turning back; *(Änderung)* change; **u~en** *vi* to turn back ♦ *vt* to turn round, to reverse; *(Tasche etc)* to turn inside out; *(Gefäß etc)* to turn upside down

umkippen ['omkıpən] *vt* to tip over ♦ *vi* to overturn; *(ung: Mensch)* to keel over; *(fig: Meinung ändern)* to change one's mind

Umkleidekabine *f* *(im Schwimmbad)* (changing) cubicle

Umkleideraum ['umklaɪdəraʊm] *m* changing od dressing room

umkommen ['omkomən] *(unreg) vi* to die, to perish; *(Lebensmittel)* to go bad

Umkreis ['omkraɪs] *m* neighbourhood; **im** ~ **von** within a radius of

Umlage *f* share of the costs

Umlauf ['omlaʊf] *m* *(Geld-)* circulation; *(von Gestirn)* revolution; **~bahn** *f* orbit

Umlaut ['omlaʊt] *m* umlaut

umlegen ['omle:gən] *vt* to put on; *(verlegen)* to move, to shift; *(Kosten)* to share out; *(umkippen)* to tip over; *(ung: töten)* to bump off

umleiten ['omlaɪtən] *vt* to divert

Umleitung *f* diversion

umliegend ['omli:gənt] *adj* surrounding

um'rahmen *vt insep* to frame

um'randen *vt insep* to border, to edge

umrechnen ['omreçnən] *vt* to convert

Umrechnung *f* conversion; **~skurs** *m* rate of exchange

um'reißen *(unreg) vt insep* to outline, to sketch

Umriß ['omrıs] *m* outline

umrühren ['omry:rən] *vt, vi* to stir

ums [oms] = **um das**

Umsatz ['omzats] *m* turnover

Umsatzsteuer *f* sales tax

umschalten ['omʃaltən] *vt* to switch

Umschau ['omʃaʊ] *f* look(ing) round; **halten nach** to look around for; **u~en** *vr* to look round

Umschlag ['omʃlaːk] *m* cover; *(Buch- auch)* jacket; *(MED)* compress; *(Brief-)* envelope; *(Wechsel)* change; *(von Hose)* turn-up; **u~en** *(unreg) vi* to change; *(NAUT)*

capsize ♦ vt to knock over; (Ärmel) to turn up; (Seite) to turn over; (Waren) to transfer; ~platz m (COMM) distribution centre

umschreiben ['ʊmʃraɪbən] (unreg) vt (neu~) to rewrite; (übertragen) to transfer; ~ auf +akk to transfer to to paraphrase; (abgrenzen) to define

umschulen ['ʊmʃuːlən] vt to re-train; (Kind) to send to another school

Umschweife ['ʊmʃvaɪfə] pl: ohne ~ without beating about the bush, straight out

Umschwung ['ʊmʃvʊŋ] m change (around), revolution

umsehen ['ʊmzeːən] (unreg) vr to look around od about; (suchen): sich ~ (nach) to look out (for)

umseitig ['ʊmzaɪtɪç] adv overleaf

umsichtig ['ʊmzɪçtɪç] adj cautious, prudent

umsonst [ʊm'zɔnst] adv in vain; (gratis) for nothing

umspringen ['ʊmʃprɪŋən] (unreg) vi to change; (Wind auch) to veer; mit jdm ~ to treat sb badly

Umstand ['ʊmʃtant] m circumstance; Umstände pl (fig: Schwierigkeiten) fuss; in anderen Umständen sein to be pregnant; Umstände machen to go to a lot of trouble; unter Umständen possibly

umständlich ['ʊmʃtɛntlɪç] adj (Methode) cumbersome, complicated; (Ausdrucksweise, Erklärung) long-winded; (Mensch) ponderous

Umstandskleid nt maternity dress

Umstehende(n) ['ʊmʃteːəndə(n)] pl bystanders

umsteigen ['ʊmʃtaɪgən] (unreg) vi (EISENB) to change

umstellen ['ʊmʃtɛlən] vt (an anderen Ort) to change round, to rearrange; (TECH) to convert ♦ vr to adapt (o.s.); sich auf etw akk ~ to adapt to sth to surround

Umstellung ['ʊmʃtɛlʊŋ] f change; (Umgewöhnung) adjustment; (TECH) conversion

umstimmen ['ʊmʃtɪmən] vt (MUS) to retune; jdn ~ to make sb change his mind

umstoßen ['ʊmʃtoːsən] (unreg) vt to overturn; (Plan etc) to change, to upset

umstritten [ʊm'ʃtrɪtn] adj disputed

Umsturz ['ʊmʃtʊrts] m overthrow

umstürzen ['ʊmʃtʏrtsən] vt (umwerfen) to overturn ♦ vi to collapse, to fall down; (Wagen) to overturn

Umtausch ['ʊmtaʊʃ] m exchange; ~en vt to exchange

umtun ['ʊmtuːn] (unreg; umg) vr (suchen): sich nach jdm/etw ~ to look around for sb/sth

umwandeln ['ʊmvandəln] vt to change, to convert; (ELEK) to transform

umwechseln ['ʊmvɛksəln] vt to change

Umweg ['ʊmveːk] m detour, roundabout way

Umwelt ['ʊmvɛlt] f environment; u~feindlich adj ecologically harmful; u~freundlich adj not harmful to the environment, environment-friendly; ~schützer m environmentalist; ~verschmutzung f environmental pollution

umwenden ['ʊmvɛndən] (unreg) vt, vr to turn (round)

umwerfen ['ʊmvɛrfən] (unreg) vt to upset, to overturn; (Mantel) to throw on; (fig: erschüttern) to upset, to throw

umwerfend (umg) adj fantastic

umziehen ['ʊmtsiːən] (unreg) vt, vr to change ♦ vi to move

Umzug ['ʊmtsuːk] m procession; (Wohnungs-) move, removal

unab- ['ʊn'ap] zW: ~änderlich adj irreversible, unalterable; ~hängig adj independent; ~hängigkeit f independence; ~kömmlich adj indispensable; zur Zeit ~kömmlich not free at the moment; ~lässig adj incessant, constant; ~sehbar adj immeasurable; (Folgen) unforeseeable; (Kosten) incalculable; ~sichtlich adj unintentional; ~'**wendbar** adj inevitable

unachtsam ['ɔn'axtza:m] adj careless; **U~keit** f carelessness

unan- ['ɔn'an] zW: ~'**fechtbar** adj indisputable; ~'**gebracht** adj uncalled-for; ~**gemessen** adj inadequate; ~**genehm** adj unpleasant; **U~nehmlichkeit** f inconvenience; **U~nehmlichkeiten** pl (Ärger) trouble sg; ~**sehnlich** adj unsightly; ~**ständig** adj indecent, improper

unappetitlich ['ɔn'apetɪtlɪç] adj unsavoury

Unart ['ɔn'aːrt] f bad manners pl; (Angewohnheit) bad habit; **u~ig** adj naughty, badly behaved

unauf- ['ɔn'auf] zW: ~**fällig** adj unobtrusive; (Kleidung) inconspicuous; ~'**findbar** adj not to be found; ~**gefordert** adj unasked ♦ adv spontaneously; ~**haltsam** adj irresistible; ~**hörlich** adj incessant, continuous; ~**merksam** adj inattentive; ~'**richtig** adj insincere

unaus- ['ɔn'aus] zW: ~**geglichen** adj unbalanced; ~'**sprechlich** adj inexpressible; ~'**stehlich** adj intolerable

unbarmherzig ['ɔnbarmhɛrtsɪç] adj pitiless, merciless

unbeabsichtigt ['ɔnbə'apzɪçtɪçt] adj unintentional

unbeachtet ['ɔnbə'axtət] adj unnoticed, ignored

unbedenklich ['ɔnbədɛŋklɪç] adj (Plan) unobjectionable ♦ adv without hesitation

unbedeutend ['ɔnbədɔʏtənt] adj insignificant, unimportant; (Fehler) slight

unbedingt ['ɔnbədɪŋt] adj unconditional ♦ adv absolutely; **mußt du ~ gehen?** do you really have to go?

unbefangen ['ɔnbəfaŋən] adj impartial, unprejudiced; (ohne Hemmungen) uninhibited; **U~heit** f impartiality; uninhibitedness

unbefriedigend ['ɔnbəfriːdɪgənt] adj unsatisfactory

unbefriedigt [-dɪçt] adj unsatisfied, dissatisfied

unbefugt ['ɔnbəfuːkt] adj unauthorized

unbegreiflich [ɔnbə'graɪflɪç] adj inconceivable

unbegrenzt ['ɔnbəgrɛntst] adj unlimited

unbegründet ['ɔnbəgrʏndət] adj unfounded

Unbehagen ['ɔnbəhaːgən] nt discomfort

unbehaglich [-klɪç] adj uncomfortable; (Gefühl) uneasy

unbeholfen ['ɔnbəhɔlfən] adj awkward, clumsy

unbeirrt ['ɔnbə'ɪrt] adj imperturbable

unbekannt ['ɔnbəkant] adj unknown

unbekümmert ['ɔnbəkʏmərt] adj unconcerned

unbeliebt ['ɔnbəliːpt] adj unpopular

unbequem ['ɔnbəkveːm] adj (Stuhl) uncomfortable; (Mensch) bothersome; (Regelung) inconvenient

unberechenbar [ɔnbə'rɛçənbaːr] adj incalculable; (Mensch, Verhalten) unpredictable

unberechtigt ['ɔnbərɛçtɪçt] adj unjustified; (nicht erlaubt) unauthorized

unberührt ['ɔnbərʏrt] adj untouched, intact; **sie ist noch ~** she is still a virgin

unbescheiden ['ɔnbəʃaɪdən] adj presumptuous

unbeschreiblich [ɔnbə'ʃraɪplɪç] adj indescribable

unbesonnen ['ɔnbəzɔnən] adj unwise, rash, imprudent

unbeständig ['ɔnbəʃtɛndɪç] adj (Mensch) inconstant; (Wetter) unsettled; (Lage) unstable

unbestechlich [ɔnbə'ʃtɛçlɪç] adj incorruptible

unbestimmt ['ɔnbəʃtɪmt] adj indefinite; (Zukunft auch) uncertain

unbeteiligt ['ɔnbətaɪlɪçt] adj unconcerned, indifferent

unbewacht ['ɔnbəvaxt] adj unguarded, unwatched

unbeweglich ['ɔnbəveːklɪç] adj immovable

unbewußt ['ʊnbəvʊst] adj unconscious

unbezahlt ['ʊnbətsaːlt] adj (Rechnung) outstanding, unsettled; (Urlaub) unpaid

unbrauchbar ['ʊnbrauxbaːr] adj (Arbeit) useless; (Gerät auch) unusable

und [ʊnt] konj and; ~ so weiter and so on

Undank ['ʊndaŋk] m ingratitude; **u~bar** adj ungrateful

undefinierbar [ʊndefiˈniːrbaːr] adj indefinable

undenkbar [ʊnˈdɛŋkbaːr] adj inconceivable

undeutlich ['ʊndɔytlıç] adj indistinct

undicht ['ʊndıçt] adj leaky

Unding ['ʊndıŋ] nt absurdity

undurch- ['ʊndʊrç] zW: **~führbar** [-ˈfyːrbaːr] adj impracticable; **~lässig** [-lɛsıç] adj waterproof, impermeable; **~sichtig** [-zıçtıç] adj opaque; (fig) obscure

uneben ['ʊnʔeːbən] adj uneven

unecht adj (Schmuck) fake (vorgetäuscht: Freundlichkeit) false

unehelich ['ʊnʔeːəlıç] adj illegitimate

uneinig ['ʊnʔaınıç] adj divided; **~ sein** to disagree; **U~keit** f discord, dissension

uneins ['ʊnʔaıns] adj at variance, at odds

unempfindlich ['ʊnʔɛmpfıntlıç] adj insensitive; (Stoff) practical

unendlich [ʊnˈʔɛntlıç] adj infinite

unent- ['ʊnʔɛnt] zW: **~behrlich** [-ˈbeːrlıç] adj indispensable; **~geltlich** [-gɛltlıç] adj free (of charge); **~schieden** [-ʃiːdən] adj undecided; **~schieden enden** (SPORT) to end in a draw; **~schlossen** [-ʃlɔsən] adj undecided; irresolute; **~wegt** [-ˈveːkt] adj unswerving; (unaufhörlich) incessant

uner- ['ʊnʔɛr] zW: **~bittlich** [-ˈbıtlıç] adj unyielding, inexorable; **~fahren**

[-faːrən] adj inexperienced; **~freulich** [-frɔylıç] adj unpleasant; **~gründlich** adj unfathomable; **~hört** [-høːrt] adj unheard-of; (Bitte) outrageous; **~läßlich** [-lɛslıç] adj indispensable; **~laubt** adj unauthorized; **~meßlich** adj immeasurable, immense; **~müdlich** [-ˈmyːtlıç] adj indefatigable; **~reichbar** adj (Ziel) unattainable; (Ort) inaccessible; (telefonisch) unobtainable; **~schöpflich** [-ˈʃœpflıç] adj inexhaustible; **~schütterlich** [-ˈʃʏtərlıç] adj unshakeable; **~schwinglich** [-ˈʃvıŋlıç] adj (Preis) exorbitant; too expensive; **~träglich** [-ˈtrɛːklıç] adj unbearable; (Frechheit) insufferable; **~wartet** adj unexpected; **~wünscht** adj undesirable, unwelcome

unfähig ['ʊnfɛːıç] adj incapable, incompetent; **zu etw ~ sein** to be incapable of sth; **U~keit** f incapacity; incompetence

unfair ['ʊnfɛːr] adj unfair

Unfall ['ʊnfal] m accident; **~flucht** f hit-and-run (driving); **~stelle** f scene of the accident; **~versicherung** f accident insurance

unfaßbar [ʊnˈfasbaːr] adj inconceivable

unfehlbar [ʊnˈfeːlbaːr] adj infallible ♦ adv inevitably; **U~keit** f infallibility

unförmig ['ʊnfœrmıç] adj (formlos) shapeless

unfrei ['ʊnfraı] adj not free, unfree; (Paket) unfranked; **~willig** adj involuntary, against one's will

unfreundlich ['ʊnfrɔyntlıç] adj unfriendly; **U~keit** f unfriendliness

Unfriede(n) ['ʊnfriːdə(n)] m dissension, strife

unfruchtbar ['ʊnfruxtbaːr] adj infertile; (Gespräche) unfruitful; **U~keit** f infertility; unfruitfulness

Unfug ['ʊnfuːk] (-s) m (Benehmen) mischief; (Unsinn) nonsense; **grober ~** (JUR) gross misconduct; malicious damage

Ungar(in) ['ʊŋgar(ın)] m(f) Hungarian; **u~isch** adj Hungarian; **~n** nt Hungary

ungeachtet ['ongə'axtət] präp +gen notwithstanding

ungeahnt ['ongə'a:nt] adj unsuspected, undreamt-of

ungebeten ['ongəbe:tən] adj uninvited

ungebildet ['ongəbɪldət] adj uneducated; uncultured

ungedeckt ['ongədɛkt] adj (Scheck) uncovered

Ungeduld ['ongədʊlt] f impatience; **u~ig** (-ig) adj impatient

ungeeignet ['ongə'aɪgnət] adj unsuitable

ungefähr ['ongəfɛ:r] adj rough, approximate; **das kommt nicht von ~** that's hardly surprising

ungefährlich adj not dangerous, harmless

ungehalten ['ongəhaltən] adj indignant

ungeheuer ['ongəhɔʏər] adj huge ♦ adv (umg) enormously; **U~ (-s, -)** nt monster; **~lich** [-'hɔʏrlɪç] adj monstrous

ungehobelt ['ongəho:bəlt] adj (fig) uncouth

ungehörig ['ongəhø:rɪç] adj impertinent, improper

ungehorsam ['ongəho:rza:m] adj disobedient; **U~** m disobedience

ungeklärt ['ongəklɛ:rt] adj not cleared up; (Rätsel) unsolved

ungeladen ['ongəla:dən] adj not loaded; (Gast) uninvited

ungelegen ['ongəle:gən] adj inconvenient

ungelernt ['ongəlɛrnt] adj unskilled

ungelogen ['ongəlo:gən] adv really, honestly

ungemein ['ongəmaɪn] adj uncommon

ungemütlich ['ongəmy:tlɪç] adj uncomfortable; (Person) disagreeable

ungenau ['ongənaʊ] adj inaccurate; **U~igkeit** f inaccuracy

ungeniert ['onʒeni:rt] adj free and easy, unceremonious ♦ adv without embarrassment, freely

ungenießbar ['ongəni:sba:r] adj inedible; undrinkable; (umg) unbearable

ungenügend ['ongəny:gənt] adj insufficient, inadequate

ungepflegt ['ongəpfle:kt] adj (Garten etc) untended; (Person) unkempt; (Hände) neglected

ungerade ['ongəra:də] adj uneven, odd

ungerecht ['ongərɛçt] adj unjust; **~fertigt** adj unjustified; **U~igkeit** f injustice, unfairness

ungern ['ongɛrn] adv unwillingly, reluctantly

ungerührt ['ongəry:rt] adj unmoved

ungeschehen ['ongəʃe:ən] adj: **~ machen** to undo

Ungeschicklichkeit ['ongəʃɪk-lɪçkaɪt] f clumsiness

ungeschickt adj awkward, clumsy

ungeschminkt ['ongəʃmɪŋkt] adj without make-up; (fig) unvarnished

ungesetzlich ['ongəzɛtslɪç] adj illegal

ungestört ['ongəʃtø:rt] adj undisturbed

ungestraft ['ongəʃtra:ft] adv with impunity

ungestüm ['ongəʃty:m] adj impetuous; tempestuous; **U~ (-(e)s)** nt impetuosity; passion

ungesund ['ongəzʊnt] adj unhealthy

ungetrübt ['ongətry:pt] adj clear; (fig) untroubled; (Freude) unalloyed

Ungetüm ['ongəty:m] (-(e)s, -e) nt monster

ungewiß ['ongəvɪs] adj uncertain; **U~heit** f uncertainty

ungewöhnlich ['ongəvø:nlɪç] adj unusual

ungewohnt ['ongəvo:nt] adj unaccustomed

Ungeziefer ['ongətsi:fər] (-s) nt vermin

ungezogen ['ongətso:gən] adj rude, impertinent; **U~heit** f rudeness, impertinence

ungezwungen ['ongətsvoŋən]

natural, unconstrained

ungläubig ['ɔnglɔybɪç] *adj* unbelieving; **die U~en** the infidel(s)

unglaublich [ʊn'glaʊplɪç] *adj* incredible

ungleich ['ʊnglaɪç] *adj* dissimilar, unequal ♦ *adv* incomparably; **~artig** *adj* different; **U~heit** *f* dissimilarity; inequality; **~mäßig** *adj* irregular, uneven

Unglück ['ʊnglʏk] (-(e)s, -e) *nt* misfortune; (*Pech*) bad luck; (*~sfall*) calamity, disaster; (*Verkehrs~*) accident; **u~lich** *adj* unhappy; (*erfolglos*) unlucky; (*unerfreulich*) unfortunate; **u~licherweise** [-'varzə] *adv* unfortunately; **u~selig** *adj* calamitous; (*Person*) unfortunate; **~sfall** *m* accident, calamity

ungültig ['ʊngʏltɪç] *adj* invalid; **U~keit** *f* invalidity

ungünstig ['ʊngʏnstɪç] *adj* unfavourable

ungut ['ʊngu:t] *adj* (*Gefühl*) uneasy; **nichts für ~** no offence

unhaltbar ['ʊnhaltbaːr] *adj* untenable

Unheil ['ʊnhaɪl] *nt* evil; (*Unglück*) misfortune; **~ anrichten** to cause mischief; **u~bar** *adj* incurable

unheimlich ['ʊnhaɪmlɪç] *adj* weird, uncanny ♦ *adv* (*umg*) tremendously

unhöflich ['ʊnhøːflɪç] *adj* impolite; **U~keit** *f* impoliteness

unhygienisch ['ʊnhygi'eːnɪʃ] *adj* unhygienic

Uni ['ʊni] (-, -s; *umg*) *f* university

uni [y'niː] *adj* self-coloured

Uniform [uni'fɔrm] *f* uniform; **u~iert** [-'miːrt] *adj* uniformed

uninteressant ['ʊn'ɪntɛrɛsant] *adj* uninteresting

Universität [univɛrzi'tɛːt] *f* university

Universum [uni'vɛrzʊm] (-s) *nt* universe

unkenntlich ['ʊnkɛntlɪç] *adj* unrecognizable

Unkenntnis ['ʊnkɛntnɪs] *f* ignorance

unklar ['ʊnklaːr] *adj* unclear; **im**

~en sein über +*akk* to be in the dark about; (*Un~heit* *f* unclarity; (*Unentschiedenheit*) uncertainty

unklug ['ʊnkluːk] *adj* unwise

Unkosten ['ʊnkɔstən] *pl* expense(s)

Unkostenbeitrag *m* contribution to costs *or* expenses

Unkraut ['ʊnkraʊt] *nt* weed; weeds *pl*

unkündbar (*Stelle*) permanent; (*Vertrag*) binding

unlängst ['ʊnlɛŋst] *adv* not long ago

unlauter ['ʊnlaʊtər] *adj* unfair

unleserlich ['ʊnleːzərlɪç] *adj* illegible

unlogisch ['ʊnloːgɪʃ] *adj* illogical

unlösbar [ʊn'løːsbaːr] *adj* insoluble

unlöslich [ʊn'løːslɪç] *adj* insoluble

Unlust ['ʊnlʊst] *f* lack of enthusiasm

unmäßig ['ʊnmɛːsɪç] *adj* immoderate

Unmenge ['ʊnmɛŋə] *f* tremendous number, hundreds *pl*

Unmensch ['ʊnmɛnʃ] *m* ogre, brute; **u~lich** *adj* inhuman, brutal; (*ungeheuer*) awful

unmerklich [ʊn'mɛrklɪç] *adj* imperceptible

unmißverständlich ['ʊnmɪsfɛrˌʃtɛntlɪç] *adj* unmistakable

unmittelbar ['ʊnmɪtəlbaːr] *adj* immediate

unmöbliert ['ʊnmøbliːrt] *adj* unfurnished

unmodern *adj* old-fashioned

unmöglich ['ʊnmøːklɪç] *adj* impossible; **U~keit** *f* impossibility

unmoralisch ['ʊnmoraːlɪʃ] *adj* immoral

Unmut ['ʊnmuːt] *m* ill humour

unnachgiebig ['ʊnnaːxgiːbɪç] *adj* unyielding

unnahbar [ʊn'naːbaːr] *adj* unapproachable

unnötig ['ʊnnøːtɪç] *adj* unnecessary

unnütz ['ʊnnʏts] *adj* useless

unordentlich ['ʊn'ɔrdəntlɪç] *adj* untidy

Unordnung ['ʊn'ɔrdnʊŋ] *f* disorder

unparteiisch ['ʊnpartaɪʃ] *adj* impartial; **U~e(r)** *m* umpire; (*FUSS-*

BALL) referee

unpassend ['unpasənt] *adj* inappropriate; (*Zeit*) inopportune

unpäßlich ['unpɛslɪç] *adj* unwell

unpersönlich ['unpɛrzøːnlɪç] *adj* impersonal

unpolitisch ['unpoliːtɪʃ] *adj* apolitical

unpraktisch ['unpraktɪʃ] *adj* unpractical

unpünktlich ['unpʏŋktlɪç] *adj* unpunctual

unrationell ['unratsionɛl] *adj* inefficient

unrealistisch ['unrealɪstɪʃ] *adj* unrealistic

unrecht ['unrɛçt] *adj* wrong; **U~** *nt* wrong; **zu U~** wrongly; **U~ haben** to be wrong; **~mäßig** *adj* unlawful, illegal

unregelmäßig ['unreːgəlmɛsɪç] *adj* irregular; **U~keit** *f* irregularity

unreif ['unraɪf] *adj* (*Obst*) unripe; (*fig*) immature

unrentabel ['unrɛntaːbəl] *adj* unprofitable

unrichtig ['unrɪçtɪç] *adj* incorrect, wrong

Unruhe ['unruːə] *f* unrest; **~stifter** *m* troublemaker

unruhig ['unruːɪç] *adj* restless

uns [uns] (*akk, dat von* **wir**) *pron* us; ourselves

unsachlich ['unzaxlɪç] *adj* not to the point, irrelevant

unsagbar [un'zaːkbaːr] *adj* indescribable

unsanft ['unzanft] *adj* rough

unsauber ['unzaubər] *adj* unclean, dirty; (*fig*) crooked; (*MUS*) fuzzy

unschädlich ['unʃɛːtlɪç] *adj* harmless; **jdn/etw ~ machen** to render sb/sth harmless

unscharf ['unʃarf] *adj* indistinct; (*Bild etc*) out of focus, blurred

unscheinbar ['unʃaɪnbaːr] *adj* insignificant; (*Aussehen, Haus etc*) unprepossessing

unschlagbar [un'ʃlaːkbaːr] *adj* invincible

unschlüssig [un'ʃlʏsɪç] *adj* undecided

unschön *adj* (*häßlich: Anblick*) ugly, unattractive; (*unfreundlich: Benehmen*) unpleasant, ugly

Unschuld ['unʃult] *f* innocence; **u~ig** [-dɪç] *adj* innocent

unselbständig ['unzɛlpʃtɛndɪç] *adj* dependent, over-reliant on others

unser(e) ['unzər(ə)] *adj* our; **~e(r, s)** *pron* ours; **~einer** *pron* people like us; **~eins** *pron* = **unsereiner**; **~erseits** *adv* on our part; **~twegen** *adv* (*für uns*) for our sake; (*wegen uns*) on our account; **~twillen** *adv*: **um ~twillen** = **um unsertwegen**

unsicher ['unzɪçər] *adj* uncertain; (*Mensch*) insecure; **U~heit** *f* uncertainty; insecurity

unsichtbar ['unzɪçtbaːr] *adj* invisible

Unsinn ['unzɪn] *m* nonsense; **u~ig** *adj* nonsensical

Unsitte ['unzɪtə] *f* deplorable habit

unsittlich ['unzɪtlɪç] *adj* indecent

unsozial ['unzotsiaːl] *adj* (*Verhalten*) antisocial

unsportlich ['unʃpɔrtlɪç] *adj* not sporty; unfit; (*Verhalten*) unsporting

unsre ['unzrə] = **unsere**

unsterblich [un'ʃtɛrplɪç] *adj* immortal

Unstimmigkeit ['unʃtɪmɪçkaɪt] *f* inconsistency; (*Streit*) disagreement

unsympathisch ['unzʏmpaːtɪʃ] *adj* unpleasant; **er ist mir ~** I don't like him

untätig ['unteːtɪç] *adj* idle

untauglich ['untauklɪç] *adj* unsuitable; (*MIL*) unfit

unteilbar [un'taɪlbaːr] *adj* indivisible

unten ['untən] *adv* below; (*im Haus*) downstairs; (*an der Treppe etc*) at the bottom; **nach ~** down; **~ am Berg** *etc* at the bottom of the mountain *etc*; **ich bin bei ihm ~ durch** (*umg*) he's through with me

unter ['untər] *präp* +*dat* 1 (*räumlich, mit Zahlen*) under; (*drunter*) underneath, below; **unter 18 Jahren** under 18 years

2 (zwischen) among(st); **sie waren unter sich** they were by themselves; **einer unter ihnen** one of them; **unter anderem** among other things
♦ *präp +akk* under, below

Unterarm [ˈʊntərʔarm] *m* forearm

unter- *zW:* **~belichten** *vt* (*PHOT*) to underexpose; **U~bewußtsein** *nt* subconscious; **~bezahlt** *adj* underpaid

unterbieten [ʊntərˈbiːtən] (*unreg*) *vt insep* (*COMM*) to undercut; (*Rekord*) to lower

unterbrechen [ʊntərˈbrɛçən] (*unreg*) *vt insep* to interrupt

Unterbrechung *f* interruption

unterbringen [ˈʊntərbrɪŋən] (*unreg*) *vt* (*in Koffer*) to stow; (*in Zeitung*) to place; (*Person: in Hotel etc*) to accommodate, to put up; (: *beruflich*): **jdn in einer Stellung** *od* **auf einem Posten ~** to fix sb up with a job

unterdessen [ʊntərˈdɛsən] *adv* meanwhile

Unterdruck [ˈʊntərdrʊk] *m* low pressure

unterdrücken [ʊntərˈdrʏkən] *vt insep* to suppress; (*Leute*) to oppress

untere(r, s) [ˈʊntərə(r, s)] *adj* lower

untereinander [ʊntərʔaɪˈnandər] *adv* with each other; among themselves etc

unterentwickelt [ˈʊntərʔɛntvɪkəlt] *adj* underdeveloped

unterernährt [ˈʊntərʔɛrnɛːrt] *adj* undernourished, underfed

Unterernährung *f* malnutrition

Unterführung *f* subway, underpass

Untergang [ˈʊntərgaŋ] *m* (down)fall, decline; (*NAUT*) sinking; (*von Gestirn*) setting

unter'geben *adj* subordinate

untergehen [ˈʊntərgeːən] (*unreg*) *vi* to go down; (*Sonne auch*) to set; (*Staat*) to fall; (*Volk*) to perish; (*Welt*) to come to an end; (*im Lärm*) to be drowned

Untergeschoß [ˈʊntərgəʃɔs] *nt* basement

Untergewicht *nt* underweight

unter'gliedern *vt insep* to subdivide

Untergrund [ˈʊntərgrʊnt] *m* foundation; (*POL*) underground; **~bahn** *f* underground, tube, subway (*US*); **~bewegung** *f* underground (movement)

unterhalb [ˈʊntərhalp] *präp +gen* below ♦ *adv* below; **~ von** below

Unterhalt [ˈʊntərhalt] *m* maintenance; **u~en** [ʊntərˈhaltən] (*unreg*) *vt insep* to maintain; (*belustigen*) to entertain ♦ *vr insep* to talk; (*sich belustigen*) to enjoy o.s.; **u~sam** *adj* (*Abend, Person*) entertaining, amusing; **~ung** *f* maintenance; (*Belustigung*) entertainment, amusement; (*Gespräch*) talk

Unterhändler [ˈʊntərhɛntlər] *m* negotiator

Unterhemd [ˈʊntərhɛmt] *nt* vest, undershirt (*US*)

Unterhose [ˈʊntərhoːzə] *f* underpants *pl*

Unterkiefer [ˈʊntərkiːfər] *m* lower jaw

unterkommen [ˈʊntərkɔmən] (*unreg*) *vi* to find shelter; to find work; **das ist mir noch nie untergekommen** I've never met with that

unterkühlt [ʊntərˈkyːlt] *adj* (*Körper*) affected by hypothermia

Unterkunft [ˈʊntərkʊnft] (*-, -künfte*) *f* accommodation

Unterlage [ˈʊntərlaːgə] *f* foundation; (*Beleg*) document; (*Schreib~ etc*) pad

unter'lassen (*unreg*) *vt insep* (*versäumen*) to fail to do; (*sich enthalten*) to refrain from

unterlaufen [ʊntərˈlaʊfən] (*unreg*) *vi insep* to happen ♦ *adj:* **mit Blut ~** suffused with blood; (*Augen*) bloodshot

unterlegen [ʊntərˈleːgən] *vt* to lay *od* put under inferior; (*besiegt*) defeated

Unterleib [ˈʊntərlaɪp] *m* abdomen

unter'liegen (*unreg*) *vi*

(+dat) to be defeated od overcome (by); (unterworfen sein) to be subject (to)

Untermiete ['ʊntərmiːtə] f: zur ~ wohnen to be a subtenant od lodger; ~r(in) m(f) subtenant, lodger

unter'nehmen (unreg) vt insep to undertake; **U~** (-s, -) nt undertaking, enterprise (auch COMM)

Unternehmer [ʊntər'neːmər] (-s, -) m entrepreneur, businessman

unterordnen vr +dat to submit o.s. (to) ♦ vr to give o.s. second place to

Unterredung [ʊntər'reːduŋ] f discussion, talk

Unterricht ['ʊntərriçt] (-(e)s, -e) m instruction, lessons pl; **u~en** [ʊntər'rɪçtən] vt insep to instruct; (SCH) to teach ♦ vr insep: **sich u~en** (über +akk) to inform o.s. (about), to obtain information (about); **~sfach** nt subject (on school etc curriculum)

Unterrock ['ʊntərrɔk] m petticoat, slip

unter'sagen vt insep to forbid; **jdm etw untersagen** to forbid sb to do sth

Untersatz ['ʊntərzats] m coaster, saucer

unter'schätzen vt insep to underestimate

unter'scheiden (unreg) vt insep to distinguish ♦ vr insep to differ

Unter'scheidung f (Unterschied) distinction; (Unterscheiden) differentiation

Unterschied ['ʊntərʃiːt] (-(e)s, -e) m difference, distinction; **im ~ zu** as distinct from; **u~lich** adj varying, differing; (diskriminierend) discriminatory; **u~slos** adv indiscriminately

unter'schlagen (unreg) vt insep to embezzle; (verheimlichen) to suppress

Unter'schlagung f embezzlement

Unterschlupf ['ʊntərʃlʊpf] (-(e)s, -schlüpfe) m refuge

unter'schreiben (unreg) vt insep to sign

Unterschrift ['ʊntərʃrɪft] f signature

Unterseeboot ['ʊntərzeːboːt] nt submarine

Untersetzer ['ʊntərzetsər] m tablemat; (für Gläser) coaster

untersetzt [ʊntər'zetst] adj stocky

unterste(r, s) ['ʊntərstə(r, s)] adj lowest, bottom

unterstehen [ʊntər'ʃteːən] (unreg) vi insep +dat to be under ♦ vr insep to dare to shelter

unterstellen [ʊntər'ʃtelən] vt insep to subordinate; (fig) to impute ♦ vt (Auto) to garage, to park ♦ vr to take shelter

unter'streichen (unreg) vt insep (auch fig) to underline

Unterstufe ['ʊntərʃtuːfə] f lower grade

unter'stützen vt insep to support

Unter'stützung f support, assistance

unter'suchen vt insep (MED) to examine; (Polizei) to investigate

Unter'suchung f examination; investigation, inquiry; **Untersuchungsausschuß** m committee of inquiry; **Untersuchungshaft** f imprisonment on remand

Untertan ['ʊntərtaːn] (-s, -en) m subject

Untertasse ['ʊntərtasə] f saucer

untertauchen ['ʊntərtaoxən] vi to dive; (fig) to disappear, to go underground

Unterteil ['ʊntərtaɪl] nt od m lower part, bottom; **u~en** [ʊntər'taɪlən] vt insep to divide up

Untertitel ['ʊntərtiːtəl] m subtitle

Unterwäsche ['ʊntərvɛʃə] f underwear

unterwegs [ʊntər'veːks] adv on the way

unter'werfen (unreg) vt insep to subject; (Volk) to subjugate ♦ vr insep (+dat) to submit (to)

unterwürfig ['ʊntərvrrfɪç] adj obsequious, servile

unter'zeichnen vt insep to sign

unter'ziehen (unreg) vt insep to

subject ♦ *vr insep* (+*dat*) to undergo; (*einer Prüfung*) to take

untragbar [ʊn'traːkbaːr] *adj* unbearable, intolerable

untreu ['ʊntrɔʏ] *adj* unfaithful; **U~e** *f* unfaithfulness

untröstlich [ʊn'trøːstlɪç] *adj* inconsolable

unüberlegt ['ʊn'yːbərleːkt] *adj* ill-considered ♦ *adv* without thinking

unübersichtlich *adj* (*Gelände*) broken; (*Kurve*) blind

unumgänglich [ʊn'ʊmgɛŋlɪç] *adj* indispensable, vital; absolutely necessary

unumwunden [ʊn'ʊmvʊndən] *adj* candid ♦ *adv* straight out

ununterbrochen ['ʊn'ʊntərbrɔxən] *adj* uninterrupted

unver- [ʊnfɛr] *zW:* **~änderlich** [-'ɛndərlɪç] *adj* unchangeable; **~antwortlich** [-'antvɔrtlɪç] *adj* irresponsible; (*unentschuldbar*) inexcusable; **~besserlich** *adj* incorrigible; **~bindlich** *adj* not binding; (*Antwort*) curt ♦ *adv* (*COMM*) without obligation; **~bleit** *adj* (*Benzin usw*) unleaded; **ich fahre ~bleit** I use unleaded; **~blümt** [-'blyːmt] *adj* plain, blunt ♦ *adv* plainly, bluntly; **~daulich** *adj* indigestible; **~einbar** *adj* incompatible; **~fänglich** [-'fɛŋlɪç] *adj* harmless; **~froren** *adj* impudent; **~geßlich** *adj* (*Tag, Erlebnis*) unforgettable; **~hofft** [-'hɔft] *adj* unexpected; **~meidlich** [-'maɪtlɪç] *adj* unavoidable; **~mutet** *adj* unexpected; **~nünftig** [-'nʏnftɪç] *adj* foolish; **~schämt** *adj* impudent; **U~schämtheit** *f* impudence, insolence; **~sehens** [-'zeːəns] *adv* all of a sudden; **~sehrt** *adj* uninjured; **~söhnlich** [-'zøːnlɪç] *adj* irreconcilable; **~ständlich** [-'ʃtɛntlɪç] *adj* unintelligible; **~träglich** *adj* quarrelsome; (*Meinungen, MED*) incompatible; **~wüstlich** [-'vyːstlɪç] *adj* indestructible; (*Mensch*) irrepressible; **~zeihlich** *adj* unpardonable; **~züglich** [-'tsyːklɪç] *adj* immediate

unvollkommen ['ʊnfɔlkɔmən] *adj* imperfect

unvollständig *adj* incomplete

unvor- ['ʊnfoːr] *zW:* **~bereitet** *adj* unprepared; **~eingenommen** *adj* unbiased; **~hergesehen** [-heːrgəzeːən] *adj* unforeseen; **~sichtig** [-zɪçtɪç] *adj* careless, imprudent; **~stellbar** [-'ʃtɛlbaːr] *adj* inconceivable; **~teilhaft** *adj* disadvantageous

unwahr ['ʊnvaːr] *adj* untrue; **~scheinlich** *adj* improbable, unlikely ♦ *adv* (*umg*) incredibly

unweigerlich [ʊn'vaɪgərlɪç] *adj* unquestioning ♦ *adv* without fail

Unwesen ['ʊnveːzən] *nt* nuisance; (*Unfug*) mischief; **sein ~ treiben** to wreak havoc; **u~tlich** *adj* inessential, unimportant; **u~tlich besser** marginally better

Unwetter ['ʊnvɛtər] *nt* thunderstorm

unwichtig ['ʊnvɪçtɪç] *adj* unimportant

unwider- [ʊnviːdər] *zW:* **~legbar** *adj* irrefutable; **~ruflich** *adj* irrevocable; **~stehlich** *adj* irresistible

unwill- ['ʊnvɪl] *zW:* **U~e(n)** *m* indignation; **~ig** *adj* indignant; (*widerwillig*) reluctant; **~kürlich** [-kyːrlɪç] *adj* involuntary ♦ *adv* instinctively; (*lachen*) involuntarily

unwirklich ['ʊnvɪrklɪç] *adj* unreal

unwirksam *adj* (*Mittel, Methode*) ineffective

unwirsch ['ʊnvɪrʃ] *adj* cross, surly

unwirtschaftlich ['ʊnvɪrtʃaftlɪç] *adj* uneconomical

unwissen- ['ʊnvɪsən] *zW:* **~d** *adj* ignorant; **U~heit** *f* ignorance; **~tlich** *adv* unknowingly, unwittingly

unwohl ['ʊnvoːl] *adj* unwell, ill; **U~sein** (-s) *nt* indisposition

unwürdig ['ʊnvʏrdɪç] *adj* unworthy

unzählig [ʊn'tsɛːlɪç] *adj* innumerable, countless

unzer- [ʊntser] *zW:* **~brechlich** *adj* unbreakable; **~störbar** *adj* indestructible; **~trennlich** *adj* inseparable

Unzucht ['ʊntsʊxt] *f* sexual offence

unzüchtig ['ʊntsʏçtɪç] *adj* immoral; lewd

unzu- ['ʊntsu] *zW:* **~frieden** *adj* dissatisfied; **U~friedenheit** *f* discontent; **~länglich** *adj* inadequate; **~lässig** *adj* inadmissible; **~rechnungsfähig** *adj* irresponsible; **~treffend** *adj* incorrect; **~verlässig** *adj* unreliable

unzweideutig ['ʊntsvaɪdɔʏtɪç] *adj* unambiguous

üppig ['ʏpɪç] *adj* (*Frau*) curvaceous; (*Busen*) full, ample; (*Essen*) sumptuous; (*Vegetation*) luxuriant, lush

Ur- ['uːr] *in zW* original

uralt ['uːr'alt] *adj* ancient, very old

Uran [u'raːn] (**-s**) *nt* uranium

Ur- *zW:* **~aufführung** *f* first performance; **~einwohner** *m* original inhabitant; **~eltern** *pl* ancestors; **~enkel(in)** *m(f)* great-grandchild, great-grandson (daughter); **~großeltern** *pl* great-grandparents; **~großmutter** *f* great-grandmother; **~großvater** *m* great-grandfather; **~heber** (**-s**, **-**) *m* originator; (*Autor*) author

Urin [u'riːn] (**-s**, **-e**) *m* urine

Urkunde ['uːrkʊndə] *f* document, deed

Urlaub ['uːrlaʊp] (**-(e)s**, **-e**) *m* holiday(s *pl*) (*BRIT*), vacation (*US*); (*MIL etc*) leave; **~er** [-laʊbər] (**-s**, **-**) *m* holiday-maker (*BRIT*), vacationer (*US*); **~sort** *m* holiday resort

Urne ['ʊrnə] *f* urn

Urologe [uro'loːgə] *m* (*MED*) urologist

Ursache ['uːrzaxə] *f* cause; **keine ~** that's all right

Ursprung ['uːrʃprʊŋ] *m* origin, source; (*von Fluß*) source

ursprünglich ['uːrʃprʏŋlɪç] *adj* original ♦ *adv* originally

Urteil ['ʊrtaɪl] (**-s**, **-e**) *nt* opinion; (*JUR*) sentence, judgement; **u~en** *vi* to judge; **~sspruch** *m* sentence, verdict

Urwald *m* jungle

Urzeit *f* prehistoric times *pl*

USA [uːˈɛsˈʔaː] *pl abk* (= *Vereinigte Staaten von Amerika*) USA

usw. *abk* (= *und so weiter*): **~** (= *und so weiter*) etc

Utensilien [uten'ziːliən] *pl* utensils

Utopie [uto'piː] *f* pipedream

utopisch [u'toːpɪʃ] *adj* utopian

V

vag(e) [vaːk, 'vaːgə] *adj* vague

Vagina [va'giːna] (**-**, **Vaginen**) *f* vagina

Vakuum ['vaːkuʊm] (**-s**, **Vakua** *od* **Vakuen**) *nt* vacuum

Vampir [vam'piːr] *m* vampire

Vanille [va'nɪljə] (**-**) *f* vanilla

Variation [variatsi'oːn] *f* variation

variieren [vari'iːrən] *vt*, *vi* to vary

Vase ['vaːzə] *f* vase

Vater [ˈfaːtər] (**-s**, **¨**) *m* father; **~land** *nt* native country; Fatherland

väterlich [ˈfɛːtərlɪç] *adj* fatherly

Vaterschaft *f* paternity

Vaterunser (**-s**, **-**) *nt* Lord's Prayer

Vati [ˈfaːti] *m* daddy

v.Chr. *abk* (= *vor Christus*) B.C.

Vegetarier(in) [vege'taːriər(ɪn)] (**-s**, **-**) *m(f)* vegetarian

Veilchen [ˈfaɪlçən] *nt* violet

Vene [ˈveːnə] *f* vein

Ventil [vɛn'tiːl] (**-s**, **-e**) *nt* valve

Ventilator [vɛnti'laːtɔr] *m* ventilator

verab- [fɛr'ap] *zW:* **~reden** *vt* to agree, to arrange ♦ *vr*: **sich mit jdm ~reden** to arrange to meet sb; **mit jdm ~redet sein** to have arranged to meet sb; **V~redung** *f* arrangement; (*Treffen*) appointment; **~scheuen** *vt* to detest, to abhor; **~schieden** *vt* (*Gäste*) to say goodbye to; (*entlassen*) to discharge; (*Gesetz*) to pass ♦ *vr* to take one's leave; **V~schiedung** *f* leave-taking; discharge; passing

ver- [fɛr] *zW:* **~achten** *vt* to despise; **~ächtlich** [-ˈɛçtlɪç] *adj* contemptuous; (*verachtenswert*) contemptible; **jdn ~ächtlich machen** to run sb down; **V~achtung** *f* contempt

verallgemeinern [fer'algəˈmainərn] *vt* to ger.ralize

Verallgemeinerung *f* generalization

veralten [fer''altən] *vi* to become obsolete *od* out-of-date

Veranda [veˈranda] (-, **Veranden**) *f* veranda

veränder- [fer'ɛndər] *zW:* **~lich** *adj* changeable; **~n** *vt, vr* to change, to alter; **V~ung** *f* change, alteration

veran- [fer'an] *zW:* **~lagt** *adj* with a ... nature; **V~lagung** *f* disposition; **~lassen** *vt* to cause; **Maßnahmen ~lassen** to take measures; **sich ~laßt sehen** to feel prompted; **~schaulichen** *vt* to illustrate; **~schlagen** *vt* to estimate; **~stalten** *vt* to organize, to arrange; **V~stalter** (-s, -) *m* organizer; **V~staltung** *f* (*Veranstalten*) organizing; (*Konzert etc*) event, function

verantwort- [fer''antvort] *zW:* **~en** *vt* to answer for ♦ *vr* to justify o.s.; **~lich** *adj* responsible; **V~ung** *f* responsibility; **~ungsbewußt** *adj* responsible; **~ungslos** *adj* irresponsible

verarbeiten [fer''arbaitən] *vt* to process; (*geistig*) to assimilate; **etw zu etw ~** to make sth into sth

Verarbeitung *f* processing; assimilation

verärgern [fer''ɛrgərn] *vt* to annoy

verausgaben [fer''ausga:bən] *vr* to run out of money; (*fig*) to exhaust o.s.

Verb [vɛrp] (-s, -en) *nt* verb

Verband [ferˈbant] (-(e)s, ᵂe) *m* (*MED*) bandage, dressing; (*Bund*) association, society; (*MIL*) unit; **~kasten** *m* medicine chest, first-aid box; **~zeug** *nt* bandage

verbannen [ferˈbanən] *vt* to banish

Verbannung *f* exile

verbergen [ferˈbɛrgən] (*unreg*) *vt, vr:* (**sich**) **~** (**vor** +*dat*) to hide sth

verbessern [ferˈbɛsərn] *vt, vr* to improve; (*berichtigen*) to correct (o.s.)

Verbesserung *f* improvement; correction

verbeugen [ferˈbɔygən] *vr* to bow

Verbeugung *f* bow

ver'biegen (*unreg*) *vi* to bend

ver'bieten (*unreg*) *vt* to forbid; **jdm etw verbieten** to forbid sb to do sth

ver'binden (*unreg*) *vt* to connect; (*kombinieren*) to combine; (*MED*) to bandage ♦ *vr* (*auch CHEM*) to combine, to join; **jdm die Augen ~** to blindfold sb

verbindlich [ferˈbɪntlɪç] *adj* binding; (*freundlich*) friendly

Verbindung *f* connection; (*Zusammensetzung*) combination; (*CHEM*) compound; (*UNIV*) club

verbissen [ferˈbɪsən] *adj* (*Kampf*) bitter; (*Gesichtsausdruck*) grim

ver'bitten *vt:* **sich** *dat* **etw ~** not to tolerate sth, not to stand for sth

verblassen [ferˈblasən] *vi* to fade

Verbleib [ferˈblaip] (-(e)s) *m* whereabouts; **v~en** (*unreg*) *vi* to remain

verbleit [ferˈblait] *adj* (*Benzin*) leaded

verblüffen [ferˈblyfən] *vt* to stagger, to amaze

Verblüffung *f* stupefaction

ver'blühen *vi* to wither, to fade

ver'bluten *vi* to bleed to death

verborgen [ferˈbɔrgən] *adj* hidden

Verbot [ferˈboːt] (-(e)s, -e) *nt* prohibition, ban; **v~en** *adj* forbidden; **Rauchen v~en!** no smoking; **~sschild** *nt* prohibitory sign

Verbrauch [ferˈbraux] (-(e)s) *m* consumption; **v~en** *vt* to use up; **~er** (-s, -) *m* consumer; **v~t** *adj* used up, finished; (*Luft*) stale; (*Mensch*) worn-out

Verbrechen [ferˈbrɛçən] (-s, -) *nt* crime

Verbrecher [ferˈbrɛçər] (-s, -) *m* criminal; **v~isch** *adj* criminal

ver'breiten *vt, vr* to spread; **sich über etw** *akk* **~** to expound on sth

verbreitern [ferˈbraitərn] *vt* to broaden

Verbreitung f spread(ing), propagation

verbrenn- [fɛr'brɛn] zW: ~**bar** adj combustible; ~**en** (unreg) vt to burn; (Leiche) to cremate; **V~ung** f burning; (in Motor) combustion; (von Leiche) cremation; **V~ungsmotor** m internal combustion engine

ver'bringen (unreg) vt to spend

verbrühen [fɛr'bry:ən] vt to scald

verbuchen [fɛr'bu:xən] vt (FIN) to register; (Erfolg) to enjoy; (Mißerfolg) to suffer

verbunden [fɛr'bʊndən] adj connected; **jdm ~ sein** to be obliged or indebted to sb; „**falsch ~**" (TEL) "wrong number"

verbünden [fɛr'bʏndən] vr to ally o.s.

Verbündete(r) [fɛr'bʏndətə(r)] mf ally

ver'bürgen vr: **sich ~ für** to vouch for

verbüßen vt: **eine Strafe ~** to serve a sentence

Verdacht [fɛr'daxt] (-(e)s) m suspicion

verdächtig [fɛr'dɛçtɪç] adj suspicious, suspect; ~**en** [fɛr'dɛçtɪgən] vt to suspect

verdammen [fɛr'damən] vt to damn, to condemn; **verdammt!** damn!

verdammt (umg) adj, adv damned; ~ **noch mal!** damn!; dammit!

ver'dampfen vi to vaporize, to evaporate

ver'danken vt: **jdm etw ~** to owe sb sth

verdauen [fɛr'dauən] vt (auch fig) to digest

verdaulich [fɛr'daulɪç] adj digestible; **das ist schwer ~** that is hard to digest

Verdauung f digestion

Verdeck [fɛr'dɛk] (-(e)s, -e) m (AUT) hood; (NAUT) deck; **v~en** vt to cover (up); (verbergen) to hide

Verderb- [fɛr'dɛrp] zW: ~**en**

[-'dɛrbən] (-s) nt ruin; **v~en** (unreg) vt to spoil; (schädigen) to corrupt ♦ vi (Essen) to spoil, to rot; (Mensch) to go to the bad; **es mit jdm v~en** to get into sb's bad books; **v~lich** adj (Einfluß) pernicious; (Lebensmittel) perishable

verdeutlichen [fɛr'dɔytlɪçən] vt to make clear

ver'dichten vt, vr to condense

ver'dienen vt to earn; (moralisch) to deserve

Ver'dienst (-(e)s, -e) m earnings pl ♦ nt merit; (Leistung): **Verdienst (um)** service (to)

verdient [fɛr'di:nt] adj well-earned; (Person) deserving of esteem; **sich um etw ~ machen** to do a lot of work for sth

verdoppeln [fɛr'dɔpəln] vt to double

verdorben [fɛr'dɔrbən] adj spoilt; (geschädigt) ruined; (moralisch) corrupt

ver'drängen vt to oust, to displace (auch PHYS); (PSYCH) to repress

ver'drehen vt (auch fig) to twist; (Augen) to roll; **jdm den Kopf ~** (fig) to turn sb's head

verdreifachen [fɛr'draɪfaxən] vt to treble

verdrießlich [fɛr'dri:slɪç] adj peevish, annoyed

Verdruß [fɛr'drʊs] (-sses, -sse) m annoyance, worry

verdummen [fɛr'dʊmən] vt to make stupid ♦ vi to grow stupid

verdunkeln [fɛr'dʊŋkəln] vt to darken; (fig) to obscure ♦ vr to darken

Verdunk(e)lung f blackout; (fig) obscuring

ver'dünnen vt to dilute

verdunsten [fɛr'dʊnstən] vi to evaporate

verdursten [fɛr'dʊrstən] vi to die of thirst

verdutzt [fɛr'dʊtst] adj nonplussed, taken aback

verehr- [fɛr'e:r] zW: ~**en** vt to venerate, to worship (auch REL); **jdm**

etw ~en to present sb with sth; **V~er(in)** *(-s, -) m(f)* admirer, worshipper *(auch REL)*; **~t** *adj* esteemed; **V~ung** *f* respect; *(REL)* worship

Verein [fɛr'ain] *(-(e)s, -e) m* club, association; **v~bar** *adj* compatible; **v~baren** *vt* to agree upon; **~barung** *f* agreement; **v~en** *vt (Menschen, Länder)* to reconcile; **mit v~ten Kräften** having pooled resources, having joined forces; **~te Nationen** United Nations; **v~fachen** *vt* to simplify; **v~igen** *vt, vr* to unite; **~igung** *f* union; *(Verein)* association; **v~t** *adj* united; **v~zelt** *adj* isolated

vereiteln [fɛr'aitəln] *vt* to frustrate

ver'eitern *vi* to suppurate, to fester

verengen [fɛr'ɛŋən] *vr* to narrow

vererb- [fɛr'ɛrb] *zW:* **~en** *vt* to bequeath; *(BIOL)* to transmit ♦ *vr* to be hereditary; **~lich** [fɛr'ɛrpliç] *adj* hereditary; **V~ung** *f* bequeathing; *(BIOL)* transmission; *(Lehre)* heredity

verewigen [fɛr'e:vigən] *vt* to immortalize ♦ *vr (umg)* to immortalize o.s.

ver'fahren *(unreg) vi* to act ♦ *vr* to get lost ♦ *adj* tangled; **~ mit** to deal with; **V~** *(-s, -) nt* procedure; *(TECH)* process; *(JUR)* proceedings *pl*

Verfall [fɛr'fal] *(-(e)s) m* decline; *(von Haus)* dilapidation; *(FIN)* expiry; **v~en** *(unreg) vi* to decline; *(Haus)* to be falling down; *(FIN)* to lapse; **v~en in** *+akk* to lapse into; **v~en auf** *+akk* to hit upon; **einem Laster v~en sein** to be addicted to a vice; **~sdatum** *nt* expiry date; *(der Haltbarkeit)* sell-by date

verfänglich [fɛr'fɛŋliç] *adj (Frage, Situation)* awkward, tricky

ver'färben *vr* to change colour

verfassen [fɛr'fasən] *vt (Rede)* to prepare, work out

Verfasser(in) [fɛr'fasər(in)] *(-s, -) m(f)* author, writer

Verfassung *f (auch POL)* constitution

Verfassungs- *zW:* **~gericht** *nt* constitutional court; **v~widrig** *adj* unconstitutional

ver'faulen *vi* to rot

ver'fehlen *vt* to miss; **etw für verfehlt halten** to regard sth as mistaken

verfeinern [fɛr'fainərn] *vt* to refine

ver'filmen *vt* to film

verflixt [fɛr'flikst] *(umg) adj* damned, darn

ver'fluchen *vt* to curse

verfolg- [fɛr'fɔlg] *zW:* **~en** *vt* to pursue; *(gerichtlich)* to prosecute; *(grausam, bes POL)* to persecute; **V~er** *(-s, -) m* pursuer; **V~ung** *f* pursuit; prosecution; persecution

verfrüht [fɛr'fry:t] *adj* premature

verfüg- [fɛr'fy:g] *zW:* **~bar** *adj* available; **~en** *vt* to direct, to order ♦ *vi:* **~en über** *+akk* to have at one's disposal; **V~ung** *f* direction, order; **zur V~ung** at one's disposal; **jdm zur V~ung stehen** to be available to sb

verführ- [fɛr'fy:r] *zW:* **~en** *vt* to tempt; *(sexuell)* to seduce; **V~er** *m* tempter; seducer; **v~erisch** *adj* seductive; **V~ung** *f* seduction; *(Versuchung)* temptation

ver'gammeln *(umg) vi* to go to seed; *(Nahrung)* to go off

vergangen [fɛr'gaŋən] *adj* past; **V~heit** *f* past

vergänglich [fɛr'gɛŋliç] *adj* transitory; **V~keit** *f* transitoriness, impermanence

vergasen [fɛr'ga:zən] *vt (töten)* to gas

Vergaser *(-s, -) m (AUT)* carburettor

vergaß *etc* [fɛr'ga:s] *vb siehe* **vergessen**

vergeb- [fɛr'ge:b] *zW:* **~en** *(unreg) vt (verzeihen)* to forgive; *(weggeben)* to give away; **jdm etw ~en** to forgive sb *for* sth; **~ens** *adv* in vain; **~lich** [fɛr'ge:pliç] *adv* in vain ♦ *adj* vain, futile; **V~ung** f forgiveness

ver'gehen (unreg) vi to pass by or pass away ♦ vr to commit an offence; jdm vergeht etw sb loses sth; sich an jdm ~ to (sexually) assault sb; **V~** (-s, -) nt offence

ver'gelten (unreg) vt: jdm etw vergelten to pay sb back for sth, to repay sb for sth

Ver'geltung f retaliation, reprisal; **Vergeltungsschlag** m (MIL) reprisal

vergessen (unreg) vt to forget; **V~heit** f oblivion

vergeßlich [fɛr'gɛslɪç] adj forgetful; **V~keit** f forgetfulness

vergeuden [fɛr'gɔʏdən] vt to squander, to waste

vergewaltigen [fɛrgə'valtɪgən] vt to rape; (fig) to violate

Vergewaltigung f rape

vergewissern [fɛrgə'vɪsɛrn] vr to make sure

ver'gießen (unreg) vt to shed

vergiften [fɛr'gɪftən] vt to poison

Vergiftung f poisoning

Vergißmeinnicht [fɛr'gɪsmaɪnnɪçt] (-(e)s, -e) nt forget-me-not

vergißt etc [fɛr'gɪst] vb siehe **vergessen**

Vergleich [fɛr'glaɪç] (-(e)s, -e) m comparison; (JUR) settlement; im ~ mit od zu compared with od to; **v~bar** adj comparable; **v~en** (unreg) vt to compare ♦ vr to reach a settlement

vergnügen [fɛr'gnyːgən] vr to enjoy od amuse o.s.; **V~** (-s, -) nt pleasure; viel V~! enjoy yourself!

vergnügt [fɛr'gnyːkt] adj cheerful

Vergnügung f pleasure, amusement; **~spark** m amusement park

vergolden [fɛr'gɔldən] vt to gild

vergöttern [fɛr'gœtɛrn] vt to idolize

ver'graben vt to bury

ver'greifen (unreg) vr: sich an jdm ~ to lay hands on sb; sich an etw ~ to misappropriate sth; sich im Ton ~ to say the wrong thing

vergriffen [fɛr'grɪfən] adj (Buch) out of print; (Ware) out of stock

vergrößern [fɛr'grøːsɛrn] vt to enlarge; (mengenmäßig) to increase; (Lupe) to magnify

Vergrößerung f enlargement; increase; magnification; **~sglas** nt magnifying glass

Vergünstigung [fɛr'gʏnstɪgʊŋ] f concession, privilege

Vergütung f compensation

verhaften [fɛr'haftən] vt to arrest

Verhaftung f arrest

ver'hallen vi to die away

ver'halten (unreg) vr to be, to stand; (sich benehmen) to behave ♦ vt to hold or keep back; (Schritt) to check; **sich ~ (zu)** (MATH) to be in proportion (to); **V~** (-s) nt behaviour

Verhältnis [fɛr'hɛltnɪs] (-ses, -se) nt relationship; (MATH) proportion, ratio; **~se** pl (Umstände) conditions; über seine ~se leben to live beyond one's means; **v~mäßig** adj relative, comparative ♦ adv relatively, comparatively

verhandeln [fɛr'handəln] vi to negotiate; (JUR) to hold proceedings ♦ vt to discuss; (JUR) to hear; über etw akk ~ to negotiate sth od about sth

Verhandlung f negotiation; (JUR) proceedings pl; **~sbasis** f (FINANZ) basis for negotiations

ver'hängen vt (fig) to impose, to inflict

Verhängnis [fɛr'hɛŋnɪs] (-ses, -se) nt fate, doom; jdm zum ~ werden to be sb's undoing; **v~voll** adj fatal, disastrous

verharmlosen [fɛr'harmloːzən] vt to make light of, to play down

verhärten [fɛr'hɛrtən] vr to harden

verhaßt [fɛr'hast] adj odious, hateful

verhauen (unreg; umg) vt (verprügeln) to beat up

verheerend [fɛr'heːrənt] adj disastrous, devastating

verheimlichen [fɛr'haɪmlɪçən] vt: jdm etw ~ to keep sth secret from sb

verheiratet [fɛr'haɪraːtət] adj married

ver'helfen (unreg) vi: **jdm ~ zu** to help sb to get

ver'hexen vt to bewitch; **es ist wie verhext** it's jinxed

ver'hindern vt to prevent; **verhindert sein** to be unable to make it

verhöhnen [fɛr'høːnən] vt to mock, to sneer at

Verhör [fɛr'høːr] (-(e)s, -e) nt interrogation; (gerichtlich) (cross-)examination; **v~en** vt to interrogate; to (cross-)examine ♦ vr to misunderstand, to mishear

ver'hungern vi to starve, to die of hunger

ver'hüten vt to prevent, to avert

Ver'hütung f prevention; **Verhütungsmittel** nt contraceptive

verirren [fɛr'ɪrən] vr to go astray

ver'jagen vt to drive away od out

verkalken [fɛr'kalkən] vi to calcify; (umg) to become senile

verkannt [fɛr'kant] adj unappreciated

Verkauf [fɛr'kauf] m sale; **v~en** vt to sell

Verkäufer(in) [fɛr'kɔyfər(ɪn)] (-s, -) m(f) seller; salesman(woman); (in Laden) shop assistant

verkaufsoffen adj: **~er Samstag** Saturday when the shops stay open all day

Verkehr [fɛr'keːr] (-s, -e) m traffic; (Umgang, bes sexuell) intercourse; (Umlauf) circulation; **v~en** vi (Fahrzeug) to ply, to run ♦ vt, vr to turn, to transform; **v~en mit** to associate with; **bei jdm ~en** (besuchen) to visit sb regularly

Verkehrs- zW: **~ampel** f traffic lights pl; **~amt** nt tourist office; **~delikt** nt traffic offence; **v~günstig** adj convenient; **~mittel** nt means of transport; **~schild** nt road sign; **~stauung** f traffic jam, stoppage; **~stockung** f traffic jam, stoppage; **~unfall** m traffic accident; **~verein** m tourist information office; **~zeichen** nt traffic sign

verkehrt adj wrong; (umgekehrt) the wrong way round

ver'kennen (unreg) vt to misjudge, not to appreciate

ver'klagen vt to take to court

verkleiden [fɛr'klaidən] vr to disguise (o.s.); (sich kostümieren) to get dressed up ♦ vt (Wand) to cover

Verkleidung f disguise; (ARCHIT) wainscoting

verkleinern [fɛr'klainərn] vt to make smaller, to reduce in size

verklemmt [fɛr'klɛmt] adj (fig) inhibited

ver'kneifen (umg) vt: **sich dat etw ~** (Lachen) to stifle sth; (Schmerz) to hide sth; (sich versagen) to do without sth

verknüpfen [fɛr'knʏpfən] vt to tie (up), to knot; (fig) to connect

ver'kommen (unreg) vi to deteriorate, to decay; (Mensch) to go downhill, to come down in the world ♦ adj (moralisch) dissolute, depraved

verkörpern [fɛr'kœrpərn] vt to embody, to personify

verkraften [fɛr'kraftən] vt to cope with

ver'kriechen (unreg) vr to creep away, to creep into a corner

Verkrümmung f bend, warp; (ANAT) curvature

verkrüppelt [fɛr'krʏpəlt] adj crippled

ver'kühlen vr to get a chill

ver'kümmern vi to waste away

verkünden [fɛr'kʏndən] vt to proclaim; (Urteil) to pronounce

verkürzen [fɛr'kʏrtsən] vt to shorten; (Wort) to abbreviate; **sich dat die Zeit ~** to while away the time

Verkürzung f shortening; abbreviation

verladen [fɛr'laːdən] (unreg) vt (Waren, Vieh) to load; (Truppen) to embark, entrain, enplane

Verlag [fɛr'laːk] (-(e)s, -e) m publishing firm

verlangen [fɛr'laŋən] vt to demand; to desire ♦ vi: **~ nach** to ask for, to desire; **~ Sie Herrn X** ask for Mr X; **V~** (-s, -) *nt*: **V~** (**nach**) desire (for); **auf jds V~** (**hin**) at sb's request

verlängern [fɛrˈlɛŋərn] *vt* to extend; (*länger machen*) to lengthen

Verlängerung [fɛrˈlɛŋərʊŋ] *f* extension; (*SPORT*) extra time; **~sschnur** *f* extension cable

verlangsamen [fɛrˈlaŋzaːmən] *vt*, *vr* to decelerate, to slow down

Verlaß [fɛrˈlas] *m*: **auf ihn/das ist kein ~** he/it cannot be relied upon

verlassen (*unreg*) *vt* to leave ♦ *vr*: **sich verlassen auf** +*akk* to depend on ♦ *adj* desolate; (*Mensch*) abandoned

verläßlich [fɛrˈlɛslɪç] *adj* reliable

Verlauf [fɛrˈlauf] *m* course; **v~en** (*unreg*) *vi* (*zeitlich*) to pass; (*Farben*) to run ♦ *vr* to get lost; (*Menschenmenge*) to disperse

verlauten *vi*: **etw ~ lassen** to disclose sth; **wie verlautet** as reported

verlegen [fɛrˈleːgən] *vt* to move; (*verlieren*) to mislay; (*Buch*) to publish ♦ *vr*: **sich auf etw** *akk* **~** to take up *od* to sth ♦ *adj* embarrassed; **nicht ~ um** never at a loss for; **V~heit** *f* embarrassment; (*Situation*) difficulty, scrape

Verleger [fɛrˈleːgər] (-s, -) *m* publisher

Verleih [fɛrˈlai] (-(e)s, -e) *m* hire service; **v~en** (*unreg*) *vt* to lend; (*Kraft, Anschein*) to confer, to bestow; (*Preis, Medaille*) to award; **~ung** *f* lending; bestowal; award

verleiten *vt* to lead astray; **~ zu** to talk into, to tempt into

verlernen *vt* to forget, to unlearn

verlesen (*unreg*) *vt* to read out; (*aussondern*) to sort out ♦ *vr* to make a mistake in reading

verletz- [fɛrˈlɛts] *zW*: **~en** *vt* (*auch fig*) to injure, to hurt; (*Gesetz etc*) to violate; **~end** *adj* (*fig: Worte*) hurtful; **~lich** *adj* vulnerable, sensitive; **V~te(r)** *mf* injured person; **V~ung** *f* injury; (*Verstoß*) violation, infringement

verleugnen [fɛrˈlɔygnən] *vt* (*Herkunft, Glauben*) to belie; (*Menschen*) to disown

verleumden [fɛrˈlɔymdən] *vt* to slander

Verleumdung *f* slander, libel

ver'lieben *vr*: **sich verlieben (in** +*akk*) to fall in love (with)

verliebt [fɛrˈliːpt] *adj* in love

verlieren [fɛrˈliːrən] (*unreg*) *vt*, *vi* to lose ♦ *vr* to get lost

Verlierer *m* loser

verlob- [fɛrˈloːp] *zW*: **~en** *vr* to get engaged (to); **V~te(r)** [fɛrˈloːptə(r)] *mf* fiancé(e); **V~ung** *f* engagement

ver'locken *vt* to entice, to lure

Ver'lockung *f* temptation, attraction

verlogen [fɛrˈloːgən] *adj* untruthful

verlor *etc v siehe* **verlieren**

verloren [fɛrˈloːrən] *adj*; lost; (*Eier*) poached ♦ *vb siehe* **verlieren**; **~ geben** to give sth up for lost; **~gehen** (*unreg*) *vi* to get lost

verlosen [fɛrˈloːzən] *vt* to raffle, to draw lots for

Verlosung *f* raffle, lottery

verlottern [fɛrˈlɔtərn] (*umg*) *vi* to go to the dogs

verludern [fɛrˈluːdərn] (*umg*) *vi* to go to the dogs

Verlust [fɛrˈlʊst] (-(e)s, -e) *m* loss; (*MIL*) casualty

ver'machen *vt* to bequeath, to leave

Vermächtnis [fɛrˈmɛçtnɪs] (-ses, -se) *nt* legacy

Vermählung [fɛrˈmɛːlʊŋ] *f* wedding, marriage

vermarkten [fɛrˈmarktən] *vt* (*WIRTS: Artikel*) to market

vermehren [fɛrˈmeːrən] *vt*, *vr* to multiply; (*Menge*) to increase

Vermehrung *f* multiplying; increase

ver'meiden (*unreg*) *vt* to avoid

vermeintlich [fɛrˈmaintlɪç] *adj* supposed

Vermerk [fɛrˈmɛrk] (-(e)s, -e) *m* note; (*in Ausweis*) endorsement;

v~en vt to note

ver'messen (unreg) vt to survey ♦ adj presumptuous, bold; **V~heit** f presumptuousness; recklessness

Ver'messung f survey(ing)

ver'mieten vt to let, to rent (out); (Auto) to hire out, to rent

Ver'mieter(in) (-s, -) m(f) landlord(lady)

Ver'mietung f letting, renting (out); (von Autos) hiring (out)

vermindern [fɛr'mɪndərn] vt, vr to lessen, to decrease; (Preise) to reduce

Verminderung f reduction

ver'mischen vt, vr to mix, to blend

vermissen [fɛr'mɪsən] vt to miss

vermitteln [fɛr'mɪtəln] vi to mediate ♦ vt (Gespräch) to connect; jdm etw ~ to help sb to obtain sth

Vermittler [fɛr'mɪtlər] (-s, -) m (Schlichter) agent, mediator

Vermittlung f procurement; (Stellen~) agency; (TEL) exchange; (Schlichtung) mediation

ver'mögen (unreg) vt to be capable of; ~ **zu** to be able to; **V~** (-s, -) nt wealth; (Fähigkeit) ability; **ein V~ kosten** to cost a fortune; **~d** adj wealthy

vermuten [fɛr'muːtən] vt to suppose, to guess; (argwöhnen) to suspect

vermutlich adj supposed, presumed ♦ adv probably

Vermutung f supposition; suspicion

vernachlässigen [fɛr'naːxlɛsɪgən] vt to neglect

ver'nehmen (unreg) vt to perceive, to hear; (erfahren) to learn; (JUR) to (cross-)examine; **dem V~ nach** from what I/we etc hear

Vernehmung f (cross-)examination

verneigen [fɛr'naɪgən] vr to bow

verneinen [fɛr'naɪnən] vt to answer in the negative; (ablehnen) to deny; (GRAM) to negate; **~d** adj negative

Verneinung f negation

vernichten [fɛr'nɪçtən] vt to annihilate, to destroy; **~d** adj (fig) crush-

ing; (Blick) withering; (Kritik) scathing

Vernunft [fɛr'nʊnft] (-) f reason, understanding

vernünftig [fɛr'nʏnftɪç] adj sensible, reasonable

veröffentlichen [fɛr'œfəntlɪçən] vt to publish

Veröffentlichung f publication

verordnen [fɛr'ɔrdnən] vt (MED) to prescribe

Verordnung f order, decree; (MED) prescription

ver'pachten vt to lease (out)

ver'packen vt to pack

Ver'packung f packing, wrapping; **Verpackungsmaterial** nt packing, wrapping

ver'passen vt to miss; **jdm eine Ohrfeige ~** (umg) to give sb a clip round the ear

verpfänden [fɛr'pfɛndən] vt (Besitz) to mortgage

ver'pflanzen vt to transplant

Ver'pflanzung f transplant(ing)

ver'pflegen vt to feed, to cater for

Ver'pflegung f feeding, catering; (Kost) food; (in Hotel) board

verpflichten [fɛr'pflɪçtən] vt to oblige, to bind; (anstellen) to engage ♦ vr to undertake; (MIL) to sign on ♦ vi to carry obligations; **jdm zu Dank verpflichtet sein** to be obliged to sb

Verpflichtung f obligation, duty

verpönt [fɛr'pøːnt] adj disapproved (of), taboo

ver'prügeln (umg) vt to beat up, to do over

Verputz [fɛr'pʊts] m plaster, roughcast; **v~en** vt to plaster; (umg: Essen) to put away

Verrat [fɛr'raːt] (-(e)s) m treachery; (POL) treason; **v~en** (unreg) vt to betray; (Geheimnis) to divulge ♦ vr to give o.s. away

Verräter [fɛr'rɛːtər] (-s, -) m traitor(tress); **v~isch** adj treacherous

ver'rechnen vt: ~ **mit** to set off

against ♦ vr to miscalculate

Verrechnungsscheck [fer-ˈrɛçnʊŋsʃɛk] m crossed cheque

ver'regnet adj spoilt by rain, rainy

ver'reisen vi to go away (on a journey)

ver'renken [fɛrˈrɛŋkən] vt to contort; (MED) to dislocate; **sich** dat **den Knöchel ~** to sprain one's ankle

ver'richten [fɛrˈrɪçtən] vt to do, to perform

ver'riegeln [fɛrˈriːɡəln] vt to bolt up, to lock

ver'ringern [fɛrˈrɪŋərn] vt to reduce ♦ vr to diminish

Ver'ringerung f reduction; lessening

ver'rinnen (unreg) vi to run out or away; (Zeit) to elapse

ver'rosten vi to rust

ver'rotten [fɛrˈrɔtən] vi to rot

ver'rücken vt to move, to shift

verrückt [fɛrˈrʏkt] adj crazy, mad; **V~e(r)** mf lunatic; **V~heit** f madness, lunacy

Verruf [fɛrˈruːf] m: **in ~ geraten/bringen** to fall/bring into disrepute; **v~en** adj notorious, disreputable

Vers [fɛrs] (-es, -e) m verse

ver'sagen vt: **jdm/sich etw ~** to deny sb/o.s. sth ♦ vi to fail; **V~** (-s) nt failure

Versager [fɛrˈzaːɡər] (-s, -) m failure

ver'salzen (unreg) vt to put too much salt in; (fig) to spoil

ver'sammeln vt, vr to assemble, to gather

Ver'sammlung f meeting, gathering

Versand [fɛrˈzant] (-(e)s) m forwarding; dispatch; (~abteilung) dispatch department; **~haus** nt mail-order firm

ver'säumen [fɛrˈzɔymən] vt to miss; (unterlassen) to neglect, to fail

ver'schaffen vt: **jdm/sich etw ~** to get or procure sth for sb/o.s.

ver'schämt [fɛrˈʃɛːmt] adj bashful

ver'schandeln [fɛrˈʃandəln] (umg) vt to spoil

ver'schärfen [fɛrˈʃɛrfən] vt to intensify; (Lage) to aggravate ♦ vr to intensify; to become aggravated

ver'schätzen vr to be out in one's reckoning

ver'schenken vt to give away

ver'scheuchen [fɛrˈʃɔyçən] vt (Tiere) to chase off or away

ver'schicken vt to send off

ver'schieben (unreg) vt to shift; (EISENB) to shunt; (Termin) to postpone

ver'schieden [fɛrˈʃiːdən] adj different; (pl: mehrere) various; **sie sind ~ groß** they are of different sizes; **~tlich** adv several times

ver'schimmeln vi (Nahrungsmittel) to go mouldy

ver'schlafen [fɛrˈʃlaːfən] (unreg) vt to sleep through; (fig: versäumen) to miss ♦ vi to oversleep ♦ adj sleepy

Verschlag [fɛrˈʃlaːk] m shed; **v~en** (unreg) vt to board up ♦ adj cunning; **jdm den Atem v~en** to take sb's breath away; **an einen Ort v~en werden** to wind up in a place

verschlechtern [fɛrˈʃlɛçtərn] vt to make worse ♦ vr to deteriorate, to get worse

Verschlechterung f deterioration

Verschleiß [fɛrˈʃlais] (-es, -e) m wear and tear; **v~en** (unreg) vt to wear out

ver'schleppen vt to carry off, to abduct; (Krankheit) to protract; (zeitlich) to drag out

ver'schleudern vt to squander; (COMM) to sell dirt-cheap

verschließbar adj lockable

ver'schließen [fɛrˈʃliːsən] (unreg) vt to close; to lock ♦ vr: **sich einer Sache** dat **~** to close one's mind to sth

ver'schlimmern [fɛrˈʃlɪmərn] vt to make worse, to aggravate ♦ vr to get worse, to deteriorate

ver'schlingen (unreg) vt to devour, to swallow up; (Fäden) to twist

verschlossen [fɛrˈʃlɔsən] adj locked; (fig) reserved; **V~heit** f reserve

ver'schlucken vt to swallow ♦ vr to choke

Verschluß [fɛrˈʃlʊs] m lock; (von Kleid etc) fastener; (PHOT) shutter; (Stöpsel) plug; **unter ~ halten** to keep under lock and key

verschlüsseln [fɛrˈʃlʏsəln] vt to encode

verschmähen [fɛrˈʃmɛːən] vt to disdain, to scorn

verschmerzen [fɛrˈʃmɛrtsən] vt to get over

verschmieren [fɛrˈʃmiːrən] vt (verstreichen: Gips, Mörtel) to apply, spread on; (schmutzig machen: Wand etc) to smear

verschmutzen [fɛrˈʃmʊtsən] vt to soil; (Umwelt) to pollute

verschneit [fɛrˈʃnaɪt] adj snowed up, covered in snow

verschollen [fɛrˈʃɔlən] adj lost, missing

ver'schonen vt: **jdn mit etw verschonen** to spare sb sth

verschönern [fɛrˈʃøːnərn] vt to decorate; (verbessern) to improve

verschreiben [fɛrˈʃraɪbən] (unreg) vt (MED) to prescribe ♦ vr to make a mistake (in writing); **sich einer Sache** dat ~ to devote o.s. to sth

verschreibungspflichtig adj (Medikament) available on prescription only

verschroben [fɛrˈʃroːbən] adj eccentric, odd

verschrotten [fɛrˈʃrɔtən] vt to scrap

verschuld- [fɛrˈʃʊld] zW: **~et** adj to be guilty of; **V~en** (-s) nt fault, guilt; **~et** adj in debt; **V~ung** f fault; (Geld) debts pl

ver'schütten vt to spill; (zuschütten) to fill; (unter Trümmer) to bury

verschweigen (unreg) vt to keep secret; **jdm etw ~** to keep sth from sb

verschwend- [fɛrˈʃvɛnd] zW: **~en** vt to squander; **V~er** (-s, -) m

spendthrift; **~erisch** adj wasteful, extravagant; **V~ung** f waste; extravagance

verschwiegen [fɛrˈʃviːgən] adj discreet; (Ort) secluded; **V~heit** f discretion; seclusion

verschwimmen (unreg) vi to grow hazy, to become blurred

verschwinden (unreg) vi to disappear, to vanish; **V~** (-s) nt disappearance

verschwitzt [fɛrˈʃvɪtst] adj (Mensch) sweaty

verschwommen [fɛrˈʃvɔmən] adj hazy, vague

verschwör- [fɛrˈʃvøːr] zW: **~en** (unreg) vr to plot, to conspire; **V~er** (-s, -) m conspirator; **V~ung** f conspiracy, plot

ver'sehen (unreg) vt to supply, to provide; (Pflicht) to carry out; (Amt) to fill; (Haushalt) to keep ♦ vr (fig) to make a mistake; **ehe er (es) sich ~ hatte** ... before he knew it ...; **V~** (-s, -) nt oversight; **aus V~** by mistake; **versehentlich** adv by mistake

Versehrte(r) [fɛrˈzeːrtə(r)] mf disabled person

ver'senden (unreg) vt to forward, to dispatch

ver'senken vt to sink ♦ vr: **sich versenken in** +akk to become engrossed in

versessen [fɛrˈzɛsən] adj: ~ **auf** +akk mad about

ver'setzen vt to transfer; (verpfänden) to pawn; (umg) to stand up ♦ vr: **sich in jdn** od **in jds Lage ~** to put o.s. in sb's place; **jdm einen Tritt/Schlag ~** to kick/hit sb; **etw mit etw ~** to mix sth with sth; **jdn in gute Laune ~** to put sb in a good mood

Ver'setzung f transfer

verseuchen [fɛrˈzɔʏçən] vt to contaminate

versichern [fɛrˈzɪçərn] vt to assure; (mit Geld) to insure

Versicherung f assurance; insurance; **~sgesellschaft** f insurance company; **~spolice** f insurance policy

ver'siegen vi to dry up

ver'sinken (unreg) vi to sink

ver'söhnen [fɛr'zøːnən] vt to reconcile ♦ vr to become reconciled

Ver'söhnung f reconciliation

ver'sorgen vt to provide, to supply; (Familie etc) to look after

Ver'sorgung f provision; (Unterhalt) maintenance; (Alters- etc) benefit, assistance

ver'späten [fɛr'ʃpɛːtən] vr to be late

verspätet adj (Zug, Abflug, Ankunft) late; (Glückwünsche) belated

Ver'spätung f delay; ~ **haben** to be late

ver'sperren vt to bar, to obstruct

ver'spielt [fɛr'ʃpiːlt] adj (Kind, Tier) playful

ver'spotten vt to ridicule, to scoff at

ver'sprechen (unreg) vt to promise; **sich** dat **etw von etw** ~ to expect sth from sth; **V~** (-s, -) nt promise

ver'staatlichen [fɛr'ʃtaːtlɪçən] vt to nationalize

Ver'stand [fɛr'ʃtant] m intelligence; mind; **den** ~ **verlieren** to go out of one's mind; **über jds** ~ **gehen** to go beyond sb

ver'ständ- [fɛr'ʃtɛnt] zW: **~lich** adj understandable, comprehensible; **V~lichkeit** f clarity, intelligibility; **V~nis** (-ses, -se) nt understanding; **~nislos** adj uncomprehending; **~nisvoll** adj understanding, sympathetic

ver'stärk- [fɛr'ʃtɛrk] zW: **~en** vt to strengthen; (Ton) to amplify; (erhöhen) to intensify ♦ vr to intensify; **V~er** (-s, -) m amplifier; **V~ung** f strengthening; (Hilfe) reinforcements

pl; (von Ton) amplification

ver'stauchen [fɛr'ʃtaʊxən] vt to sprain

ver'stauen [fɛr'ʃtaʊən] vt to stow away

Ver'steck [fɛr'ʃtɛk] (-(e)s, -e) nt hiding (place); **v~en** vt, vr to hide; **v~t** adj hidden

ver'stehen (unreg) vt to understand ♦ vr to get on; **das versteht sich (von selbst)** that goes without saying

ver'steigern [fɛr'ʃtaɪgərn] vt to auction

Ver'steigerung f auction

ver'stell- [fɛr'ʃtɛl] zW: **~bar** adj adjustable, variable; **~en** vt to move, to shift; (Uhr) to adjust; (versperren) to block; (fig) to disguise ♦ vr to pretend, to put on an act; **V~ung** f pretence

ver'steuern [fɛr'ʃtɔʏərn] vt to pay tax on

ver'stiegen [fɛr'ʃtiːgən] adj exaggerated

ver'stimmt [fɛr'ʃtɪmt] adj out of tune; (fig) cross, put out; (Magen) upset

ver'stohlen [fɛr'ʃtoːlən] adj stealthy

ver'stopfen vt to block, to stop up; (MED) to constipate

Ver'stopfung f obstruction; (MED) constipation

ver'storben [fɛr'ʃtɔrbən] adj deceased, late

ver'stört [fɛr'ʃtøːrt] adj (Mensch) distraught

Ver'stoß [fɛr'ʃtoːs] m: ~ **(gegen)** infringement (of), violation (of); **v~en** (unreg) vt to disown, to reject ♦ vi: **v~en gegen** to offend against

ver'streichen (unreg) vt to spread ♦ vi to elapse

ver'streuen vt to scatter (about)

ver'stümmeln [fɛr'ʃtʏməln] vt to maim, to mutilate (auch fig)

ver'stummen [fɛr'ʃtʊmən] vi to go silent; (Lärm) to die out

Ver'such [fɛr'zuːx] m: **~(e)s, -e)** m attempt; (SCI) experiment; **v~en** vt to try; (*verlocken*) to tempt ♦ *vr*: **sich an etw** *dat* **~en** to try one's hand at sth; **~skaninchen** *nt* (*fig*) guinea-pig; **~ung** *f* temptation

versunken [fɛr'zʊŋkən] *adj* sunken; **~ sein in** +*akk* to be absorbed *od* engrossed in

vertagen [fɛr'taːgən] *vt, vi* to adjourn

ver'tauschen *vt* to exchange; (*versehentlich*) to mix up

verteidig- [fɛr'taɪdɪç] *zW*: **~en** *vt* to defend; **V~er** (-s, -) *m* defender; (*JUR*) defence counsel; **V~ung** *f* defence

ver'teilen *vt* to distribute; (*Rollen*) to assign; (*Salbe*) to spread

Verteilung *f* distribution, allotment

vertiefen [fɛr'tiːfən] *vt* to deepen ♦ *vr*: **sich in etw** *akk* **~** to become engrossed *od* absorbed in sth

Vertiefung *f* depression

vertikal [vɛrti'kaːl] *adj* vertical

vertilgen [fɛr'tɪlgən] *vt* to exterminate; (*umg*) to eat up, to consume

vertonen [fɛr'toːnən] *vt* to set to music

Vertrag [fɛr'traːk] (-(e)s, ⁓e) *m* contract, agreement; (*POL*) treaty; **v~en** (*unreg*) *vt* to tolerate, to stand ♦ *vr* to get along; (*sich aussöhnen*) to become reconciled; **v~lich** *adj* contractual

verträglich [fɛr'trɛːklɪç] *adj* good-natured, sociable; (*Speisen*) easily digested; (*MED*) easily tolerated; **V~keit** *f* sociability; good nature; digestibility

Vertrags- *zW*: **~bruch** *m* breach of contract; **~partner** *m* party to a contract; **v~widrig** *adj* contrary to contract

vertrauen [fɛr'traʊən] *vi*: **jdm ~** to trust sb; **~ auf** +*akk* to rely on; **V~** (-s) *nt* confidence; **~erweckend** [fɛr'traʊənʔɛrvɛkənt] *adj* inspiring trust; **~svoll** *adj* trustful; **~swürdig** *adj* trustworthy

vertraulich [fɛr'traʊlɪç] *adj* familiar; (*geheim*) confidential

vertraut [fɛr'traʊt] *adj* familiar; **V~heit** *f* familiarity

ver'treiben (*unreg*) *vt* to drive away; (*aus Land*) to expel; (*COMM*) to sell; (*Zeit*) to pass

vertret- [fɛr'treːt] *zW*: **~en** (*unreg*) *vt* to represent; (*Ansicht*) to hold, to advocate; **sich** *dat* **die Beine ~en** to stretch one's legs; **V~er** (-s, -) *m* representative; (*Verfechter*) advocate; **V~ung** *f* representation; advocacy

Vertrieb [fɛr'triːp] (-(e)s, -e) *m* marketing (department)

ver'trocknen *vi* to dry up

ver'trösten *vt* to put off

vertun [fɛr'tuːn] (*unreg*) *vt* to waste ♦ *vr* (*umg*) to make a mistake

ver'tuschen [fɛr'tʊʃən] *vt* to hush *od* cover up

verübeln [fɛr'yːbəln] *vt*: **jdm etw ~** to be cross *od* offended with sb on account of sth

verüben [fɛr'yːbən] *vt* to commit

verun- [fɛr'ʊn] *zW*: **~glimpfen** *vt* to disparage; **~glücken** *vi* to have an accident; **tödlich ~glücken** to be killed in an accident; **~reinigen** *vt* to soil; (*Umwelt*) to pollute; **~sichern** *vt* to rattle; **~treuen** [-trɔʏən] *vt* to embezzle

verur- [fɛr'uːr] *zW*: **~sachen** *vt* to cause; **~teilen** [-taɪlən] *vt* to condemn; **V~teilung** *f* condemnation; (*JUR*) sentence

verviel- [fɛr'fiːl] *zW*: **~fachen** *vt* to multiply; **~fältigen** [-fɛltɪgən] *vt* to duplicate, to copy; **V~fältigung** *f* duplication, copying

vervollkommnen [fɛr'fɔlkɔmnən] *vt* to perfect

vervollständigen *vt* to complete

ver'wackeln *vt* (*Foto*) to blur

ver'wählen *vr* (*TEL*) to dial the wrong number

verwahren *vt* to keep, to lock away ♦ *vr* to protest

verwalt- [fɛr'valt] *zW*: **~en** *vt* to manage; to administer; **V~er** (-s, -) *m* manager; (*Vermögensverwalter*) trustee; **V~ung** f administration; management

ver'wandeln vt to change, to transform ♦ vr to change; to be transformed

Ver'wandlung f change, transformation

verwandt [fɛr'vant] adj: ~ (mit) related (to); **V~e(r)** mf relative, relation; **V~schaft** f relationship; (Menschen) relations pl

ver'warnen vt to caution

Ver'warnung f caution

ver'wechseln vt: verwechseln mit to confuse with; to mistake for; **zum V~ ähnlich** as like as two peas

Ver'wechslung f confusion, mixing up

verwegen [fɛr'veːɡən] adj daring, bold

Verwehung [fɛr'veːʊŋ] f snowdrift; sanddrift

verweichlicht [fɛr'vaɪçlɪçt] adj effeminate, soft

ver'weigern vt: **jdm etw verweigern** to refuse sb sth; **den Gehorsam/die Aussage ~** to refuse to obey/testify

Ver'weigerung f refusal

Verweis [fɛr'vaɪs] (-es, -e) m reprimand, rebuke; (Hinweis) reference; **v~en** [fɛr'vaɪzən] (unreg) vt to refer; **jdn von der Schule v~en** to expel sb (from school); **jdn des Landes v~en** to deport od expel sb

ver'welken vi to fade

verwendbar [fɛr'vɛntbaːr] adj usable

ver'wenden (unreg) vt to use; (Mühe, Zeit, Arbeit) to spend ♦ vr to intercede

Ver'wendung f use

ver'werfen (unreg) vt to reject

verwerflich [fɛr'vɛrflɪç] adj reprehensible

ver'werten vt to utilize

Ver'wertung f utilization

verwesen [fɛr'veːzən] vi to decay

ver'wickeln vt to tangle (up); (fig) to involve ♦ vr to get tangled (up); **jdn in etw** akk **verwickeln** to in-

volve sb in sth; **sich in etw** akk **verwickeln** to get involved in sth

verwickelt [fɛr'vɪkəlt] adj (Situation, Fall) tricky, complicated

ver'wildern vi to run wild

ver'winden (unreg) vt to get over

verwirklichen [fɛr'vɪrklɪçən] vt to realize, to put into effect

Verwirklichung f realization

ver'wirren [fɛr'vɪrən] vt to tangle (up); (fig) to confuse

Verwirrung f confusion

ver'wittern [fɛr'vɪtərn] vi to weather

verwitwet [fɛr'vɪtvət] adj widowed

verwöhnen [fɛr'vøːnən] vt to spoil

verworfen [fɛr'vɔrfən] adj depraved

verworren [fɛr'vɔrən] adj confused

verwundbar [fɛr'vʊntbaːr] adj vulnerable

ver'wunden [fɛr'vʊndən] vt to wound

verwunderlich [fɛr'vʊndərlɪç] adj surprising

Verwunderung [fɛr'vʊndərʊŋ] f astonishment

Verwundete(r) mf injured person

Ver'wundung f wound, injury

ver'wünschen vt to curse

verwüsten [fɛr'vyːstən] vt to devastate

ver'zagen [fɛr'tsaːɡən] vi to despair

ver'zählen vr to miscount

verzehren [fɛr'tseːrən] vt to consume

ver'zeichnen vt to list; (Niederlage, Verlust) to register

Verzeichnis [fɛr'tsaɪçnɪs] (-ses, -se) nt list, catalogue; (in Buch) index

verzeih- [fɛr'tsaɪ] zW: **~en** (unreg) vt, vi to forgive; **jdm etw ~en** to forgive sb for sth; **~lich** adj pardonable; **V~ung** f forgiveness, pardon; **V~ung!** sorry!, excuse me!

verzichten [fɛr'tsɪçtən] vi: ~ **auf** +akk to forgo, to give up

ver'ziehen (unreg) vt to move ♦ vt to put out of shape; (Kind) to spoil; (Pflanzen) to thin out ♦ vr to go out of shape; (Gesicht) to contort;

(*verschwinden*) to disappear; **das Gesicht ~** to pull a face

verzieren [fɛr'tsiːrən] *vt* to decorate, to ornament

Verzierung *f* decoration

verzinsen [fɛr'tsɪnzən] *vt* to pay interest on

ver'zögern *vt* to delay

ver'zögern *vt* to delay

Ver'zögerung *f* delay, time-lag; **Verzögerungstaktik** *f* delaying tactics *pl*

verzollen [fɛr'tsɔlən] *vt* to pay duty on

verzückt [fɛr'tsʏkt] *adj* enraptured

Verzug [fɛr'tsuːk] *m* delay

verzwei-: *zW:* **~eln** *vi* to despair; **~elt** *adj* desperate; **V~lung** *f* despair

verzwickt [fɛr'tsvɪkt] (*umg*) *adj* awkward, complicated

Vesuv [ve'zuːf] (**-(s)**) *m* Vesuvius

Veto ['veːto] (**-s, -s**) *nt* veto

Vetter ['fɛtər] (**-s, -n**) *m* cousin

vgl. *abk* (= *vergleiche*) cf.

v.H. *abk* (= *vom Hundert*) p.c.

vibrieren [vi'briːrən] *vi* to vibrate

Video ['viːdeo] *nt* video; **~gerät** *nt* video recorder; **~recorder** *m* video recorder

Vieh [fiː] (**-(e)s**) *nt* cattle *pl*; **~isch** *adj* bestial

viel [fiːl] *adj* a lot of, much ♦ *adv* a lot, much; **~e** *pron pl* a lot of, many; **~ zuwenig** much too little; **~erlei** *adj* a great variety of; **~es** *pron* a lot; **~fach** *adj, adv* many times; **auf ~fachen Wunsch** at the request of many people; **V~falt** *f* variety; **~fältig** *adj* varied, many-sided

vielleicht [fi'laɪçt] *adv* perhaps

viel-: *zW:* **~mal(s)** *adv* many times; **danke ~mals** many thanks; **~mehr** *adv* rather, on the contrary; **~sagend** *adj* significant; **~seitig** *adj* many-sided; **~versprechend** *adj* promising

vier [fiːr] *num* four; **V~eck** (**-(e)s**) *nt* four-sided figure; (*gleichseitig*) square; **~eckig** *adj* square; **V~taktmotor** *m* four-stroke

---

engine; **~te(r, s)** ['fiːrtə(r, s)] *adj* fourth; **V~tel** (**-s, -**) ['fɪrtl] *nt* quarter; **V~teljahr** *nt* quarter; **~teljährlich** *adj* quarterly; **~teln** *vt* to divide into four; (*Kuchen usw*) to divide into quarters; **V~telnote** *f* crotchet; **V~tel'stunde** *f* quarter of an hour; **~zehn** ['fɪrtseːn] *num* fourteen; **in ~zehn Tagen** in a fortnight; **~zehntägig** *adj* fortnightly; **~zig** ['fɪrtsɪç] *num* forty

Villa ['vɪla] (**-, Villen**) *f* villa

violett [vio'lɛt] *adj* violet

Violin-: ['viːros] *zW:* **~e** *f* violin; **~schlüssel** *m* treble clef

Virus ['viːros] (**-, Viren**) *m od nt* (*auch: COMPUT*) virus

Visa ['viːza] *pl von* **Visum**

vis-à-vis [viza'viː] *adv* opposite

Visen ['viːzən] *pl von* **Visum**

Visier [vi'ziːr] (**-s, -e**) *nt* gunsight; (*am Helm*) visor

Visite [vi'ziːtə] *f* (*MED*) visit; **~nkarte** *f* visiting card

Visum ['viːzom] (**-s, Visa** *od* **Visen**) *nt* visa

vital [vi'taːl] *adj* lively, full of life, vital

Vitamin [vita'miːn] (**-s, -e**) *nt* vitamin

Vogel ['foːgəl] (**-s, ¨**) *m* bird; **einen ~ haben** (*umg*) to have bats in the belfry; **jdm den ~ zeigen** to tap one's forehead (*meaning that one thinks sb stupid*); **~bauer** *nt* birdcage; **~häuschen** *nt* bird house; **~perspektive** *f* bird's-eye view; **~scheuche** *f* scarecrow

Vokabel [vo'kaːbəl] (**-, -n**) *f* word

Vokabular [vokabu'laːr] (**-s, -e**) *nt* vocabulary

Vokal [vo'kaːl] (**-s, -e**) *m* vowel

Volk [fɔlk] (**-(e)s, ¨er**) *nt* people; nation

Völker- ['fœlkər] *zW:* **~recht** *nt* international law; **v~rechtlich** *adj* according to international law; **~verständigung** *f* international understanding

Volks- *zW:* **~entscheid** *m* referen-

dum; ~**fest** nt fair; ~**hochschule** f
adult education classes pl; ~**lied** nt
folksong; ~**republik** f people's republic; die ~**republik China** the
People's Republic of China; ~**schule**
f elementary school; ~**tanz** m folk
dance; ~**vertreter(in)** m(f) people's
representative; ~**wirtschaft** f economics sg; ~**zählung** f (national)
census

voll [fɔl] adj full; **etw** ~ **machen** to
fill sth up; ~ **und ganz** completely;
jdn für ~ **nehmen** (umg) to take sb
seriously; **~auf** [fɔl'ʔauf] adv amply;
V~bart m full beard; ~**bringen** (unreg) vt insep to accomplish; ~**enden**
vt insep to finish, to complete; ~**en-
det** adj (vollkommen) completed;
~**ends** ['fɔlɛnts] adv completely;
V~endung f completion; ~**er** adj
fuller; ~**er einer Sache** gen full of
sth

Volleyball ['vɔlibal] m volleyball

Vollgas nt: **mit** ~ at full throttle; ~
geben to step on it

völlig ['fœlɪç] adj complete ♦ adv
completely

voll- zW: ~**jährig** adj of age;
V~kaskoversicherung f [fɔlkasko-
fɛrzɪçəruŋ] f fully comprehensive insurance; ~**kommen** adj perfect;
V~kommenheit f perfection;
V~kornbrot nt wholemeal bread;
V~macht (-, -en) f authority, full
powers pl; **V~milch** f (KOCH) full-
cream milk; **V~mond** m full moon;
V~pension f full board; ~**ständig**
['fɔlʃtɛndɪç] adj complete; ~**strecken** vt insep to execute; ~**tanken** vt,
vi to fill up; **V~wertkost** f whole-
food; ~**zählig** ['fɔltsɛːlɪç] adj complete, in full number; ~**ziehen**
(unreg) vt insep to carry out ♦ vr
insep to happen; **V~zug** m execution

Volt [vɔlt] (- od -(e)s, -) nt volt

Volumen [vo'luːmən] (-s, - od Volu-
mina) nt volume

vom [fɔm] = **von dem**

von [fɔn] präp +dat **1** (Ausgangspunkt) from; **von ... bis from ...** to;
von morgens bis abends from
morning till night; **von ... nach ...**
from ... to ...; **von ... an** from ...;
von ... aus from ...; **von dort aus**
from there; **etw von sich aus tun** to
do sth of one's own accord; **von mir
aus** (umg) if you like, I don't mind;
von wo/wann ...? where/when ...
from?

2 (Ursache, im Passiv) by; **ein Gedicht von Schiller** a poem by Schiller; **von etw müde** tired from sth

3 (als Genitiv) of; **ein Freund von
mir** a friend of mine; **nett von dir**
nice of you; **jeweils zwei von zehn**
two out of every ten

4 (über) about; **er erzählte vom
Urlaub** he talked about his holiday

5: von wegen! (umg) no way!

voneinander adv from each other

vor [foːr] präp +dat **1** (räumlich) in
front of; **vor der Kirche links abbiegen** turn left before the church

2 (zeitlich) before; **ich war vor ihm
da** I was there before him; **vor 2
Tagen** 2 days ago; **5 (Minuten) vor
4** 5 (minutes) to 4; before a little while ago

3 (Ursache) with; **vor Wut/Liebe**
with rage/love; **vor Hunger sterben**
to die of hunger; **vor lauter Arbeit**
because of work

4: vor allem, vor allen Dingen
most of all

♦ präp +akk (räumlich) in front of

♦ adv: **vor und zurück** backwards
and forwards

Vorabend ['foːrʔaːbənt] m evening
before, eve

voran [fo'ran] adv before, ahead;
mach ~! get on with it!; ~**gehen**
(unreg) vi to go ahead; **einer Sache**

dat ~**gehen** to precede sth; ~**kom-men** (*unreg*) *vi* to come along, to make progress

Voranschlag *m* estimate

Vorarbeiter *m* foreman

voraus [foˈraus] *adv* ahead; (*zeitlich*) in advance; **jdm** ~ **sein** to be ahead of sb; **im** ~ in advance; ~**gehen** (*unreg*) *vi* to go (on) ahead; (*fig*) to precede; ~**haben** (*unreg*) *vt*: **jdm etw** ~**haben** to have the edge on sb in sth; **V**~**sage** *f* prediction; ~**sagen** *vt* to predict; ~**sehen** (*unreg*) *vt* to foresee; ~**setzen** *vt* to assume; **ge-setzt, daß** ... provided that ...; **V**~**setzung** *f* requirement, prerequisite; **V**~**sicht** *f* foresight; **aller V**~**sicht nach** in all probability; ~**sichtlich** *adv* probably

Vorbehalt [ˈfoːrbəhalt] (-(e)s, -e) *m* reservation, proviso; **v**~**en** (*unreg*) *vt*: **sich/jdm etw** ~ to reserve sth (for o.s.)/for sb; **v**~**los** *adj* unconditional ♦ *adv* unconditionally

vorbei [foˈrbai] *adv* by, past; **das ist** ~ **that's** over; ~**gehen** (*unreg*) *vi* to pass by, to go past; ~**kommen** (*unreg*) *vi*: **bei jdm** ~**kommen** to drop in *od* call in on sb

vor- *zW*: ~**belastet** [ˈfoːrbəlastət] *adj* (*fig*) handicapped; ~**bereiten** *vt* to prepare; **V**~**bereitung** *f* preparation; ~**bestraft** [ˈfoːrbəʃtraːft] *adj* previously convicted, with a record

vorbeugen [ˈfoːrbɔʏɡən] *vt, vr* to lean forward ♦ *vi* +*dat* to prevent; ~**d** *adj* preventive

Vorbeugung *f* prevention; **zur** ~ **gegen** for the prevention of

Vorbild [ˈfoːrbɪlt] *nt* model; **sich dat jdn zum** ~ **nehmen** to model o.s. on sb; **v**~**lich** *adj* model, ideal

vorbringen [ˈfoːrbrɪŋən] (*unreg*) *vt* to advance, to state

Vorder- [ˈfɔrdər] *zW*: ~**achse** *f* front axle; ~**e(r, s)** *adj* front; ~**grund** *m* foreground; ~**mann** (*pl* -**männer**) *m* man in front; **jdn auf** ~**mann brin-gen** (*umg*) to get sb to shape up; ~**seite** *f* front (side); **v**~**ste(r, s)** *adj*

front

vordrängen [ˈfoːrdrɛŋən] *vr* to push to the front

voreilig [ˈfoːrailɪç] *adj* hasty, rash

voreinander [foːraiˈnandər] *adv* (*räumlich*) in front of each other

voreingenommen [ˈfoːraɪn-ɡənɔmən] *adj* biased; **V**~**heit** *f* bias

vorenthalten [ˈfoːrɛnthaltən] (*un-reg*) *vt*: **jdm etw** ~ to withhold sth from sb

vorerst [ˈfoːrˈeːrst] *adv* for the moment *od* present

Vorfahr [ˈfoːrfaːr] (-**en**, -**en**) *m* ancestor

vorfahren (*unreg*) *vi* to drive (on) ahead; (*vors Haus etc*) to drive up

Vorfahrt *f* (*AUT*) right of way; ~ **achten!** give way!

Vorfahrts- *zW*: ~**regel** *f* right of way; ~**schild** *nt* give way sign

Vorfall [ˈfoːrfal] *m* incident; **v**~**en** (*unreg*) *vi* to occur

vorfinden [ˈfoːrfɪndən] (*unreg*) *vt* to find

Vorfreude [ˈfoːrfrɔʏdə] *f* (joyful) anticipation

vorführen [ˈfoːrfyːrən] *vt* to show, to display; **dem Gericht** ~ to bring before the court

Vorgabe [ˈfoːrɡaːbə] *f* (*SPORT*) start, handicap ♦ *in zW* (*COMPUT*) default

Vorgang [ˈfoːrɡaŋ] *m* course of events; (*bes SCI*) process

Vorgänger(in) [ˈfoːrɡɛŋər(ɪn)] (-**s**, -) *m(f)* predecessor

vorgeben [ˈfoːrɡeːbən] (*unreg*) *vt* to pretend; to use as a pretext; (*SPORT*) to give an advantage *od* a start of

vorgefaßt [ˈfoːrɡəfast] *adj* preconceived

vorgefertigt [ˈfoːrɡəfɛrtɪçt] *adj* prefabricated

vorgehen [ˈfoːrɡeːən] (*unreg*) *vi* (*voraus*) to go (on) ahead; (*nach vorn*) to go up front; (*handeln*) to act, to proceed; (*Uhr*) to be fast;

(*Vorrang haben*) to take precedence; (*passieren*) to go on; **V~** (**-s**) *nt* action

Vorgeschichte ['foːrgəʃɪçtə] *f* past history

Vorgeschmack ['foːrgəʃmak] *m* foretaste

Vorgesetzte(r) ['foːrgəzɛtstə(r)] *m(f)* superior

vorgestern ['foːrgɛstərn] *adv* the day before yesterday

vorhaben ['foːrhaːbən] (*unreg*) *vt* to intend; **hast du schon was vor?** have you got anything on?; **V~** (**-s, -**) *nt* intention

vorhalten ['foːrhaltən] (*unreg*) *vt* to hold *od* put up ♦ *vi* to last; **jdm etw ~** (*fig*) to reproach sb for sth

vorhanden [foːr'handən] *adj* existing; (*erhältlich*) available

Vorhang ['foːrhaŋ] *m* curtain

Vorhängeschloß ['foːrhɛŋəʃlɔs] *nt* padlock

vorher [foːr'heːr] *adv* before(hand); **~bestimmen** *vt* (*Schicksal*) to preordain; **~gehen** (*unreg*) *vi* to precede; **~ig** [-ɪç] *adj* previous

Vorherrschaft ['foːrhɛrʃaft] *f* predominance, supremacy

vorherrschen ['foːrhɛrʃən] *vi* to predominate

vorher- [foːr'heːr] *zW*: **V~sage** *f* forecast; **~sagen** *vt* to forecast, to predict; **~sehbar** *adj* predictable; **~sehen** (*unreg*) *vt* to foresee

vorhin [foːr'hɪn] *adv* not long ago, just now; **~ein** *adv*: **im ~ein** beforehand

vorig ['foːrɪç] *adj* previous, last

Vorkämpfer(in) ['foːrkɛmpfər(ɪn)] *m(f)* pioneer

Vorkaufsrecht ['foːrkaufsrɛçt] *nt* option to buy

Vorkehrung ['foːrkeːruŋ] *f* precaution

vorkommen ['foːrkɔmən] (*unreg*) *vi* to come forward; (*geschehen, sich zeigen*) to occur; (*scheinen*) to seem (to be); **sich** *dat* **dumm** *etc* **~** to feel stupid *etc*; **V~** (**-s, -**) *nt* occurrence

Vorkriegs- ['foːrkriːks] *in zW* prewar

Vorladung ['foːrlaːduŋ] *f* summons *sg*

Vorlage ['foːrlaːgə] *f* model, pattern; (*Gesetzes~*) bill; (*SPORT*) pass

vorlassen ['foːrlasən] (*unreg*) *vt* to admit; (*vorgehen lassen*) to allow to go in front

vorläufig ['foːrlɔyfɪç] *adj* temporary, provisional

vorlaut ['foːrlaut] *adj* impertinent, cheeky

vorlesen ['foːrleːzən] (*unreg*) *vt* to read (out)

Vorlesung *f* (*UNIV*) lecture

Vorletzte(r, s) ['foːrlɛtstə(r, s)] *adj* last but one

Vorliebe ['foːrliːbə] *f* preference, partiality

vorliebnehmen [foːr'liːpneːmən] (*unreg*) *vi*: **~ mit** to make do with

vorliegen ['foːrliːgən] (*unreg*) *vi* to be there; **etw liegt jdm vor** sb has sth; **~d** *adj* present, at issue

vormachen ['foːrmaxən] *vt*: **jdm etw ~** to show sb how to do sth; (*fig*) to fool sb; to have sb on

Vormachtstellung ['foːrmaxtʃtɛluŋ] *f* supremacy, hegemony

Vormarsch ['foːrmarʃ] *m* advance

vormerken ['foːrmɛrkən] *vt* to book

Vormittag ['foːrmɪtaːk] *m* morning; **v~s** *adv* in the morning, before noon

Vormund ['foːrmʊnt] (**-(e)s, -e** *od* **-münder**) *m* guardian

vorn ['fɔrn] *adv* in front; **von ~ anfangen** to start at the beginning; **nach ~** to the front

Vorname ['foːrnaːmə] *m* first name, Christian name

vorne *adv* = **vorn**

vornehm ['foːrneːm] *adj* distinguished; refined; elegant

vornehmen (*unreg*) *vt* (*fig*) to carry out; **sich** *dat* **etw ~** to start on sth; (*beschließen*) to decide to do sth; **sich** *dat* **jdn ~** to tell sb off

vornherein ['fɔrnhɛraɪn] *adv*: **von**

~ from the start

Vorort ['fo:rʔɔrt] m suburb

Vorrang ['fo:rraŋ] m precedence, priority; **v~ig** adj of prime importance, primary

Vorrat ['fo:rra:t] m stock, supply

vorrätig ['fo:rre:tɪç] adj in stock

Vorratskammer f pantry

Vorrecht ['fo:rreçt] nt privilege

Vorrichtung ['fo:rrɪçtʊŋ] f device, contrivance

vorrücken ['fo:rrykən] vi to advance ♦ vt to move forward

Vorsatz ['fo:rzats] m intention; (JUR) intent; **einen ~ fassen** to make a resolution

vorsätzlich ['fo:rzetslɪç] adj intentional; (JUR) premeditated ♦ adv intentionally

Vorschau ['fo:rʃau] f (RADIO, TV) (programme) preview; (Film) trailer

Vorschlag ['fo:rʃla:k] m suggestion, proposal; **v~en** (unreg) vt to suggest, to propose

vorschreiben ['fo:rʃraibən] (unreg) vt to prescribe, to specify

Vorschrift ['fo:rʃrɪft] f regulation(s); rule(s); (Anweisungen) instruction(s); **Dienst nach ~** work-to-rule; **v~smäßig** adj as per regulations/instructions

Vorschuß ['fo:rʃʊs] m advance

vorsehen ['fo:rze:ən] (unreg) vt to provide for, to plan ♦ vr to take care, to be careful ♦ vi to be visible

Vorsehung f providence

vorsetzen ['fo:rzetsən] vt to move forward; (anbieten) to offer; **~ vor +akk** to put in front of

Vorsicht ['fo:rzɪçt] f caution, care; **~!** look out!, take care!; (auf Schildern) caution!, danger!; **~, Stufe!** mind the step!; **v~ig** adj cautious, careful; **v~shalber** adv just in case

Vorsilbe ['fo:rzɪlbə] f prefix

vorsingen vt (vor Zuhörern) to sing (to); (in Prüfung, für Theater etc) to audition (for) ♦ vi to sing

Vorsitz ['fo:rzɪts] m chair(manship); **~ende(r)** mf chairman(woman)

Vorsorge ['fo:rzɔrgə] f precaution(s), provision(s); **v~n** vi: ~ **für** to make provision for; **~untersuchung** f check-up

vorsorglich ['fo:rzɔrklɪç] adv as a precaution

Vorspeise ['fo:rʃpaizə] f hors d'oeuvre, appetizer

Vorspiel ['fo:rʃpi:l] nt prelude

vorspielen ['fo:rʃpi:lən] vt: **jdm etw ~** (MUS) to play sth for or to sb ♦ vi (zur Prüfung etc) to play for or to sb

vorsprechen ['fo:rʃpreçən] (unreg) vt to say out loud, to recite ♦ vi: **bei jdm ~** to call on sb

Vorsprung ['fo:rʃprʊŋ] m projection, ledge; (fig) advantage, start

Vorstadt ['fo:rʃtat] f suburbs pl

Vorstand ['fo:rʃtant] m executive committee; (COMM) board (of directors); (Person) director, head

vorstehen ['fo:rʃte:ən] (unreg) vi to project; **etw** dat ~ (fig) to be the head of sth

vorstell- ['fo:rʃtel] zW: **~bar** adj conceivable; **~en** vt to put forward (bekannt machen) to introduce; (darstellen) to represent; **~en vor +akk** to put in front of; **sich** dat **etw ~en** to imagine sth; **V~ung** f (Bekanntmachen) introduction; (THEAT etc) performance; (Gedanke) idea, thought

vorstoßen ['fo:rʃto:sən] (unreg) vi (ins Unbekannte) to venture (forth)

Vorstrafe ['fo:rʃtra:fə] f previous conviction

Vortag ['fo:rta:k] m: **am ~ einer Sache** gen on the day before sth

vortäuschen ['fo:rtɔyʃən] vt to feign, to pretend

Vorteil ['fo:rtail] m (-s, -e) m: ~ (gegenüber) advantage (over); **im ~ sein** to have the advantage; **v~haft** adj advantageous

Vortrag ['fo:rtra:k] m (-(e)s, **Vorträge**) m talk, lecture; **v~en** (unreg) vt to carry forward; (fig) to recite; (Rede) to deliver; (Lied) to perform; (Meinung etc) to express

vortrefflich ['fo:rtrefliç] adj excellent

vortreten ['fo:rtre:tən] (unreg) vi to step forward; (Augen etc) to protrude

vorüber [fo'ry:bər] adv past, over; **~gehen** (unreg) vi to pass (by); **~gehen an** +dat (fig) to pass over; **~gehend** adj temporary, passing

Vorurteil ['fo:r|ortail] nt prejudice

Vorverkauf ['fo:rferkauf] m advance booking

Vorwahl ['fo:rva:l] f preliminary election; (TEL) dialling code

Vorwand ['fo:rvant] (-(e)s, Vorwände) m pretext

vorwärts ['fo:rverts] adv forward; **V~gang** m (AUT etc) forward gear; **~gehen** (unreg) vi to progress; **~kommen** (unreg) vi to get on, to make progress

Vorwäsche f prewash

vorweg [fo:r'vek] adv in advance; **~nehmen** (unreg) vt to anticipate

vorweisen ['fo:rvaizən] (unreg) vt to show, to produce

vorwerfen ['fo:rverfən] (unreg) vt: **jdm etw ~** to reproach sb for sth, to accuse sb of sth; **sich** dat **nichts vorzuwerfen haben** to have nothing to reproach o.s. with

vorwiegend [fo:r'vi:gənt] adj predominant ♦ adv predominantly

vorwitzig ['fo:rvitsiç] adj (Mensch, Bemerkung) cheeky

Vorwort ['fo:rvort] (-(e)s, -e) nt preface

Vorwurf ['fo:rvorf] m reproach; **jdm/sich Vorwürfe machen** to reproach sb/o.s.; **v~svoll** adj reproachful

vorzeigen ['fo:rtsaigən] vt to show, to produce

vorzeitig ['fo:rtsaitiç] adj premature

vorziehen ['fo:rtsi:ən] (unreg) vt to pull forward; (Gardinen) to draw; (lieber haben) to prefer

Vorzimmer ['fo:rtsimər] nt (Büro) outer office

Vorzug ['fo:rtsu:k] m preference

(gute Eigenschaft) merit, good quality; (Vorteil) preference

vorzüglich [fo:r'tsy:kliç] adj excellent

vulgär [vol'ge:r] adj vulgar

Vulkan [vol'ka:n] (-s, -e) m volcano

W

Waage ['va:gə] f scales pl; (ASTROL) Libra; **w~recht** adj horizontal

Wabe ['va:bə] f honeycomb

wach [vax] adj awake; (fig) alert; **W~e** f guard, watch; **W~e halten** to keep watch; **W~e stehen** to stand guard; **~en** vi to be awake; (Wache halten) to guard

Wacholder [va'xɔldər] (-s, -) m juniper

Wachs [vaks] (-es, -e) nt wax

wachsam ['vaxza:m] adj watchful, vigilant, alert

wachsen (unreg) vi to grow

Wachstuch nt oilcloth

Wachstum (-s) nt growth

Wächter ['veçtər] (-s, -) m guard, warden, keeper; (Parkplatz~) attendant

wackel- ['vakəl] zW: **~ig** adj shaky, wobbly; **W~kontakt** m loose connection; **~n** vi to shake; (fig: Position) to be shaky

wacker ['vakər] adj valiant, stout ♦ adv well, bravely

Wade ['va:də] f (ANAT) calf

Waffe ['vafə] f weapon

Waffel (-, -n) f waffle; wafer

Waffen- zW: **~schein** m gun licence; **~stillstand** m armistice, truce

Wagemut ['va:gəmu:t] m daring

wagen ['va:gən] vt to venture, to dare

Wagen ['va:gən] (-s, -) m vehicle; (Auto) car; (EISENB) carriage; (Pferde~) cart; **~heber** (-s, -) m jack

Waggon [va'gō:] (-s, -s) m carriage; (Güter~) goods van, freight truck (US)

waghalsig ['va:khalzɪç] adj foolhardy

Wagnis ['va:knɪs] (-ses, -se) nt risk

Wahl ['va:l] (-, -en) f choice; (POL) election; **zweite** ~ (COMM) seconds pl

wähl- ['ve:l] zW: **~bar** adj eligible; **~en** vt, vi to choose; (POL) to elect, to vote (for); (TEL) to dial; **W~er(in)** (-s, -) m(f) voter; **~erisch** adj fastidious, particular

Wahl- zW: **~fach** nt optional subject; **~gang** m ballot; **~kabine** f polling booth; **~kampf** m election campaign; **~kreis** m constituency; **~lokal** nt polling station; **w~los** adv at random; **~recht** nt franchise; **~spruch** m motto; **~urne** f ballot box

Wahn [va:n] (-(e)s m delusion; folly; **~sinn** m madness; **w~sinnig** adj insane, mad ♦ adv (umg) incredibly

wahr [va:r] adj true

wahren vt to maintain, to keep

während ['vɛ:rənt] präp +gen during ♦ konj while; **~dessen** adv meanwhile

wahr- zW: **~haben** (unreg) vt to refuse to admit sth; **~haft** adv (tatsächlich) truly; **~haftig** [va:r'haftɪç] adj true, real ♦ adv really; **W~heit** f truth; **~nehmen** (unreg) vt to perceive, to observe; **W~nehmung** f perception; **~sagen** vi to prophesy, to tell fortunes; **W~sager(in)** (-s, -) m(f) fortune teller; **~scheinlich** [va:r'faɪnlɪç] adj probable ♦ adv probably; **W~'scheinlichkeit** f probability; **aller W~scheinlichkeit nach** in all probability

Währung ['vɛ:rʊŋ] f currency

Waise ['vaɪzə] f orphan; **~nhaus** nt orphanage

Wald [valt] (-(e)s, -er) m wood(s); (groß) forest; **~brand** m forest fire; **~sterben** nt trees dying due to pollution

Wal(fisch) ['va:l(fɪʃ)] (-(e)s, -e) m whale

Wall [val] (-(e)s, -e) m embankment; (Bollwerk) rampart

Wallfahr- zW: **~er(in)** m(f) pilgrim; **~t** f pilgrimage

Walnuß ['valnʊs] f walnut

Walroß ['valrɔs] nt walrus

Walze ['valtsə] f (Gerät) cylinder; (Fahrzeug) roller; **w~n** vt to roll (out)

wälzen ['vɛltsən] vt to roll (over); (Bücher) to hunt through; (Probleme) to deliberate on ♦ vr to roll about; (vor Schmerzen) to roll about; (im Bett) to toss and turn

Walzer ['valtsər] (-s, -) m waltz

Wand [vant] (-, -e) f wall; (Trenn~) partition; (Berg~) precipice

Wandel ['vandəl] (-s) m change; **w~bar** adj changeable, variable; **w~n** vt, vr to change ♦ vi (gehen) to walk

Wander- ['vandər] zW: **~er** (-s,) m hiker, rambler; **~karte** f map of country walks; **w~n** vi to hike; (Blick) to wander; (Gedanken) to stray; **~schaft** f travelling; **~ung** f walk, hike; **~weg** m trail, walk

Wandlung f change, transformation

Wange ['vaŋə] f cheek

wankelmütig [vaŋkəlmy:tɪç] adj vacillating, inconstant

wanken ['vaŋkən] vi to stagger; (fig) to waver

wann [van] adv when

Wanne ['vanə] f tub

Wanze ['vantsə] f bug

Wappen ['vapən] (-s, -) nt coat of arms, crest; **~kunde** f heraldry

war etc (var) vb siehe **sein**

Ware ['va:rə] f ware

Waren- zW: **~haus** nt department store; **~lager** nt stock, store; **~probe** f sample; **~zeichen** nt: (eingetragenes) **~zeichen** (registered) trademark

warf [va:rf] vb siehe **werfen**

warm [varm] adj warm; (Essen) hot

Wärm- ['vɛrm] zW: **~e** f warmth; **w~en** vt, vr to warm (up), to heat (up); **~flasche** f hot-water bottle

warnen ['varnən] vt to warn

Warnung f warning

warten ['vartən] vi: **~ (auf** +akk) to wait (for); **auf sich ~ lassen** to take a long time

Wärter(in) ['vɛrtər(ɪn)] (-s, -) m(f) attendant

Warte- ['vartə] zW: **~raum** m (EISENB) waiting room; **~saal** m (EISENB) waiting room; **~zimmer** nt waiting room

Wartung f servicing; service; **~ und Instandhaltung** maintenance

warum [va'rʊm] adv why

Warze ['vartsə] f wart

was [vas] pron what; (umg: etwas) something; **~ für (ein)** ... what sort of ...

waschbar adj washable

Waschbecken nt washbasin

Wäsche ['vɛʃə] f wash(ing); (Bett~) linen; (Unter~) underclothing

waschecht adj colourfast; (fig) genuine

Wäscheklammer f clothes peg (BRIT), clothespin (US)

Wäscheleine f washing line (BRIT)

waschen ['vaʃən] (unreg) vt, vi to wash ♦ vr to (have a) wash; **sich** dat **die Hände ~** to wash one's hands

Wäsche'rei f laundry

Waschgelegenheit f washing facilities

Wasch- zW: **~küche** f laundry room; **~lappen** m face flannel, washcloth (US); (umg) sissy; **~maschine** f washing machine; **~mittel** nt detergent, washing powder; **~pulver** nt detergent, washing powder; **~raum** m washroom; **~salon** m Launderette (®)

Wasser ['vasər] (-s, -) nt water; **~ball** m water polo; **w~dicht** adj waterproof; **~fall** m waterfall; **~farbe** f watercolour; **~hahn** m tap, faucet (US); **~kraftwerk** nt hydro-

electric power station; **~leitung** f water pipe; **~mann** m (ASTROL) Aquarius; **~melone** f (BOT) water melon

wässern ['vɛsərn] vt, vi to water

Wasser- zW: **w~scheu** adj afraid of (the) water; **~ski** ['vasərʃi:] nt water-skiing; **~stoff** m hydrogen; **~waage** f spirit level; **~zeichen** nt watermark

wäßrig ['vɛsrɪç] adj watery

waten ['va:tən] vi to wade

watscheln ['va:tʃəln] vi to waddle

Watt¹ [vat] (-(e)s, -en) nt mud flats pl

Watt² (-s, -) nt (ELEK) watt

Watte f cotton wool, absorbent cotton (US)

WC ['ve:'tse:] (-s, -s) nt abk (= water closet) W.C.

Web- ['ve:b] zW: **w~en** (unreg) vt to weave; **~er** (-s, -) m weaver; **~e'rei** f (Betrieb) weaving mill; **~stuhl** m loom

Wechsel ['vɛksəl] (-s, -) m change; (COMM) bill of exchange; **~geld** nt change; **w~haft** adj (Wetter) variable; **~jahre** pl change of life sg; **~kurs** m rate of exchange; **w~n** vt to change; (Blicke) to exchange ♦ vi to change; to vary; (Geldwechseln) to have change; **~strom** m alternating current; **~stube** f bureau de change; **~wirkung** f interaction

wecken ['vɛkən] vt to wake (up); to call

Wecker ['vɛkər] (-s, -) m alarm clock

wedeln ['ve:dəln] vi vt (mit Schwanz) to wag; (mit Fächer etc) to wave

weder ['ve:dər] konj neither; **~** ... **noch** ... neither ... nor ...

Weg [ve:k] (-(e)s, -e) m way; (Pfad) path; (Route) route; **sich auf den ~ machen** to be on one's way; **jdm aus dem ~ gehen** to keep out of sb's way

weg [vɛk] adv away, off; **über etw** akk **~ sein** to be over sth; **er war schon ~** he had already left; **Finger**

~! hands off!
wegbleiben (*unreg*) *vi* to stay away

wegen ['ve:gən] *präp* +*gen* (*umg*: +*dat*) because of

weg- ['vɛk] *zW:* **~fallen** (*unreg*) *vi* to be left out; (*Ferien, Bezahlung*) to be cancelled; (*aufhören*) to cease; **~gehen** (*unreg*) *vi* to go away; to leave; **~lassen** (*unreg*) *vt* to leave out; **~laufen** (*unreg*) *vi* to run away *od* off; **~legen** *vt* to put aside; **~machen** (*umg*) *vt* to get rid of; **~müssen** (*unreg; umg*) *vi* to have to go; **~nehmen** (*unreg*) *vt* to take away; **~tun** (*unreg*) *vt* to put away; **W~weiser** ['ve:gvaɪzər] (*-s, -*) *m* road sign, signpost; **~werfen** (*unreg*) *vt* to throw away; **~werfend** *adj* disparaging

weh [ve:] *adj* sore; ~ **tun** to be sore; **jdm/sich** ~ **tun** to hurt sb/o.s.; **~(e)** *excl:* ~ **(e), wenn du** ... woe betide you if ...; o ~! oh dear!; ~**e!** just you dare!

wehen *vt, vi* to blow; (*Fahnen*) to flutter

weh- *zW:* **~leidig** *adj* whiny, whining; **~mütig** *adj* melancholy

Wehr¹ [ve:r] (*-(e)s, -e*) *nt* weir

Wehr² (*-, -en*) *f:* **sich zur** ~ **setzen** to defend o.s.; **~dienst** *m* military service; **~dienstverweigerer** *m* ≈ conscientious objector; **w~en** *vr* to defend o.s.; **~los** *adj* defenceless; **~pflicht** *f* compulsory military service; **w~pflichtig** *adj* liable for military service

Weib [vaɪp] (*-(e)s, -er*) *nt* woman, female; wife; **~chen** *nt* female; **w~lich** *adj* feminine

weich [vaɪç] *adj* soft; **W~e** *f* (*EISENB*) points *pl*; **~en** (*unreg*) *vi* to yield, to give way; **W~heit** *f* softness; **~lich** *adj* soft, namby-pamby; **W~ling** *m* weakling

Weide ['vaɪdə] *f* (*Baum*) willow; (*Gras*) pasture; **w~n** *vi* to graze ⬩ *vr:* **sich an etw** *dat* **w~n** to delight in sth

weidlich ['vaɪtlɪç] *adv* thoroughly

weigern ['vaɪgərn] *vt* to refuse

Weigerung ['vaɪgəruŋ] *f* refusal

Weihe ['vaɪə] *f* consecration; (*Priester~*) ordination; **w~n** *vt* to consecrate; to ordain

Weiher (*-s, -*) *m* pond

Weihnacht- *zW:* **~en** (*-*) *nt* Christmas; **w~lich** *adj* Christmas *cpd*; **~sabend** *m* Christmas Eve; **~slied** *nt* Christmas carol; **~smann** *m* Father Christmas, Santa Claus; **~smarkt** *m* Christmas fair; **~stag** *m* Christmas Day; **zweiter ~stag** *m* Boxing Day

Weihrauch *m* incense

Weihwasser *nt* holy water

weil [vaɪl] *konj* because

Weile ['vaɪlə] (*-*) *f* while, short time

Wein [vaɪn] (*-(e)s, -e*) *m* wine; (*Pflanze*) vine; **~bau** *m* cultivation of vines; **~berg** *m* vineyard; **~bergschnecke** *f* snail; **~brand** *m* brandy

weinen *vt, vi* to cry; **das ist zum W~** it's enough to make you cry *od* weep

Wein- *zW:* **~glas** *nt* wine glass; **~karte** *f* wine list; **~lese** *f* vintage; **~probe** *f* wine-tasting; **~rebe** *f* vine; **w~rot** *adj* burgundy, claret, wine-red; **~stock** *m* vine; **~stube** *f* wine bar; **~traube** *f* grape

weise ['vaɪzə] *adj* wise

Weise *f* manner, way; (*Lied*) tune; **auf diese Weise** in this way

weisen (*unreg*) *vt* to show

Weisheit ['vaɪshaɪt] *f* wisdom; **~szahn** *m* wisdom tooth

weiß [vaɪs] *adj* white ⬩ *vb siehe* **wissen**; **W~brot** *nt* white bread; **~en** *vt* to whitewash; **W~glut** *f* (*TECH*) incandescence; **jdn bis zur W~glut bringen** (*fig*) to make sb see red; **W~kohl** *m* (white) cabbage; **W~wein** *m* white wine

weit [vaɪt] *adj* wide; (*Begriff*) broad; (*Reise, Wurf*) long ⬩ *adv* far; **wie ~ ist es** ...? how far is it ...?; **in ~er Ferne** in the far distance; **das geht**

zu ~ that's going too far; **~aus** adv
by far; **~blickend** adj far-seeing;
W~e f width; (Raum) space; (von
Entfernung) distance; **~n** vt, vr to
widen

weiter ['vaɪtər] adj wider; broader;
farther (away); (zusätzlich) further
♦ adv further; ohne ~s without
further ado; just like that; **~**
nichts/niemand nothing/nobody else;
~arbeiten vi to go on working; **~bil-**
den vr to continue one's education;
~empfehlen (unreg) vt to recommend (to others); **W~fahrt** f continuation of the journey; **~führen** vi
(Straße) to lead on (to) ♦ vt (fortsetzen) to continue, carry on; **~gehen**
(unreg) vi to go on; **~hin** adv: etw
~hin tun to go on doing sth; **~kom-**
men (unreg) vi (fig: mit Arbeit) to
make progress; **~leiten** vt to pass
on; **~machen** vt, vi to continue

weit–zW: **~gehend** adj considerable
♦ adv largely; **~läufig** adj (Gebäude) spacious; (Erklärung)
lengthy; (Verwandter) distant; **~rei-**
chend adj long-range; (fig) far-
reaching; **~schweifig** adj long-
winded; **~sichtig** adj (MED) long-
sighted; (fig) far-sighted; **W~sprung**
m long jump; **~verbreitet** adj widespread; (fig) widespread;
W~winkelobjektiv nt
(PHOT) wide-angle lens

Weizen ['vaɪtsən] (-s, -) m wheat

welche(r, s) ['vɛlçə(r, s)] interrogativ pron which; **welcher von bei-**
den? which (one) of the two?; **wel-**
chen hast du genommen? which
(one) did you take?; **welche eine**
...! what a ...!; **welche Freude!**
what joy!

♦ unbestimmt pron some ♦ indef
pron; (in Fragen) any; **ich habe**
welche I have some; **haben Sie**
welche? do you have any?

♦ relativ pron (bei Menschen) who;
(bei Sachen) which, that; **welche(r,**
s) auch immer whoever/whichever

whatever

welk [vɛlk] adj withered; **~en** vi to
wither

Wellblech nt corrugated iron

Welle ['vɛlə] f wave; (TECH) shaft;
~nbereich m waveband; **~nlänge** f
(auch fig) wavelength; **~nlinie** f
wavy line; **~nsittich** m budgerigar

Welt [vɛlt] (-, -en) f world; **~all** nt
universe; **~anschauung** f philosophy
of life; **w~berühmt** adj world-
famous; **~krieg** m world war; **w~-**
lich adj worldly; (nicht kirchlich)
secular; **~macht** f world power;
~meister m world champion;
~raum m space; **~reise** f trip round
the world; **~stadt** f metropolis;
w~weit adj world-wide

wem [veːm] (dat von wer) pron to
whom

wen [veːn] (akk von wer) pron
whom

Wende ['vɛndə] f turn; (Veränderung) change; **~kreis** m
(GEOG) tropic; (AUT) turning circle; **~ltreppe** f spiral staircase;
w~n (unreg) vt, vi, vr to turn; **sich**
an jdn w~n to go/come to sb;
~punkt m turning point

wendig ['vɛndɪç] adj (Auto etc)
manœuvrable; (fig) agile

Wendung f turn; (Rede–) idiom

wenig ['veːnɪç] adj little; **~** pron pl
few pl; **~er** adj less; (mit pl)
fewer ♦ adv less; **~ste(r, s)** adj
least; **am ~sten** least; **~stens** adv
at least

wenn [vɛn] konj **1** (falls, bei
Wünschen) if; **wenn auch ...,** selbst
wenn ... even if ...; **wenn ich doch**
... if only I ...

2 (zeitlich) when; **immer wenn**
whenever

wennschon ['vɛnʃoːn] adv: na ~
so what?; ~, **dennschon!** in for a
penny, in for a pound

wer [veːr] *pron* who

Werbe- ['vɛrbə] *zW:* **~fernsehen** *nt* commercial television; **w~n** (*unreg*) *vt* to win; (*Mitglied*) to recruit ♦ *vi* to advertise; **um jdn/etw w~n** to try to win sb/sth; **für jdn/etw w~n** to promote sb/sth

Werbung *f* advertising; (*von Mitgliedern*) recruitment; **~ um** *'jdn/ etw* promotion of sb/sth

Werdegang ['veːrdəgaŋ] *m* (*Laufbahn*) development; (*beruflich*) career

werden ['veːrdən] (*pt* **wurde,** *pp* **geworden** *od* (*bei Passiv*) **worden**) *vi* to become; **was ist aus ihm/aus der Sache geworden?** what became of him/it?; **es ist nichts/gut geworden** it came to nothing/turned out well; **es wird Nacht/Tag** it's getting dark/light; **mir wird kalt** I'm getting cold; **mir wird schlecht** I fell ill; **Erster werden** to come *od* be first; **das muß anders werden** that'll have to change; **rot/zu Eis werden** to turn red/to ice; **was willst du (mal) werden?** what do you want to be?; **die Fotos sind gut geworden** the photos have come out nicely

♦ *als Hilfsverb* **1** (*bei Futur*): **er wird es tun he will** *od* **he'll do it; er wird das nicht tun** he will not *od* he won't do it; **es wird gleich regnen** it's going to rain

2 (*bei Konjunktiv*): **ich würde ... I would ...; er würde gern ... he** would *od* he'd like to ...; **ich würde lieber ... I would** *od* **I'd rather ...**

3 (*bei Vermutung*): **sie wird in der Küche sein** she will be in the kitchen

4 (*bei Passiv*): **gebraucht werden** to be used; **er ist erschossen worden** he has *od* he's been shot; **mir wurde gesagt, daß ... I was told** that ...

werfen ['vɛrfən] (*unreg*) *vt* to throw

Werft [vɛrft] (**-, -en**) *f* shipyard, dockyard

Werk [vɛrk] (**-(e)s, -e**) *nt* work; (*Tätigkeit*) job; (*Fabrik, Mechanismus*) works *pl*; **ans ~ gehen** to set to work; **~statt** (**-, -stätten**) *f* workshop; (*AUT*) garage; **~tag** *m* working day; **w~tags** *adv* on working days; **w~tätig** *adj* working; **~zeug** *nt* tool

Wermut ['veːrmuːt] (**-(e)s**) *m* wormwood; (*Wein*) vermouth

Wert [veːrt] (**-(e)s, -e**) *m* worth; (*FIN*) value; **~ legen auf** +*akk* to attach importance to; **es hat doch keinen ~** it's useless; **w~** *adj* worth; (*geschätzt*) dear; worthy; **das ist nichts/viel w~** it's not worth anything/it's worth a lot; **das ist es/ er mir w~** it's/he's worth that to me; **w~en** *vt* to rate; **~gegenstände** *mpl* valuables; **w~los** *adj* worthless; **~papier** *nt* security; **w~voll** *adj* valuable

Wesen ['veːzən] (**-s, -**) *nt* (*Geschöpf*) being; (*Natur, Character*) nature; **w~tlich** *adj* significant; (*beträchtlich*) considerable

weshalb [vɛs'halp] *adv* why

Wespe ['vɛspə] *f* wasp

wessen ['vɛsən] (*gen von* **wer**) *pron* whose

Weste ['vɛstə] *f* waistcoat, vest (*US*); (*Woll~*) cardigan

West- *zW:* **~en** (**-s**) *m* west; **~europa** *nt* Western Europe; **~indien** *nt* the West Indies; **w~lich** *adj* western ♦ *adv* to the west

weswegen [vɛs'veːgən] *adv* why

wett [vɛt] *adj* even; **W~bewerb** *m* competition; **W~e** *f* bet, wager; **~en** *vt, vi* to bet

Wetter ['vɛtər] (**-s, -**) *nt* weather; **~bericht** *m* weather report; **~dienst** *m* meteorological service; **~lage** *f* (weather) situation; **~vorhersage** *f* weather forecast; **~warte** *f* weather station

Wett- *zW:* **~kampf** *m* contest; **~lauf**

m race; **w~machen** *vt* to make good

wichtig ['vɪçtɪç] *adj* important; **W~keit** *f* importance

wickeln ['vɪkəln] *vt* to wind; (*Haare*) to set; (*Kind*) to change; **jdn/etw in etw** *akk* ~ to wrap sth/sb in sth

Widder ['vɪdər] (**-s, -**) *m* ram; (*ASTROL*) Aries

wider ['vi:dər] *präp* +*akk* against; **~fahren** (*unreg*) *vi* to happen; **~legen** *vt* to refute

widerlich ['vi:dərlɪç] *adj* disgusting, repulsive

wider- ['vi:dər] *zW*: **~rechtlich** *adj* unlawful; **W~rede** *f* contradiction; **W~ruf** *m* retraction, countermanding; **~rufen** (*unreg*) *vt insep* to retract; (*Anordnung*) to revoke; (*Befehl*) to countermand; **~setzen** *vr insep*: **sich jdm/etw ~setzen** to oppose sb/sth

widerspenstig ['vi:dərʃpɛnstɪç] *adj* wilful

widerspiegeln *vt* (*Entwicklung, Erscheinung*) to mirror, reflect ♦ *vr* to be reflected

wider'sprechen (*unreg*) *vi insep*: **jdm widersprechen** to contradict sb

Widerspruch ['vi:dərʃprʊx] *m* contradiction; **w~slos** *adv* without arguing

Widerstand ['vi:dərʃtant] *m* resistance

Widerstands- *zW*: **~bewegung** *f* resistance (movement); **w~fähig** *adj* resistant, tough; **w~los** *adj* unresisting

wider'stehen (*unreg*) *vi insep*: **jdm/etw widerstehen** to withstand sb/sth

wider- ['vi:dər] *zW*: **~wärtig** *adj* nasty, horrid; **W~wille** *m*: **W~wille (gegen)** aversion (to); **~willig** *adj* unwilling, reluctant

widmen ['vɪtmən] *vt* to dedicate; to devote ♦ *vr* to devote o.s.

widrig ['vi:drɪç] *adj* (*Umstände*) adverse

SCHLÜSSELWORT

wie [vi:] *adv* how; **wie groß/schnell?** how big/fast?; **wie wär's?** how about it?; **wie ist er?** what's he like?; **wie gut du das kannst!** you're very good at it; **wie bitte?** pardon?; (*entrüstet*) I beg your pardon!; **und wie!** and how!

♦ *konj* **1** (*bei Vergleichen*): **so schön wie ...** as beautiful as ...; **wie ich schon sagte** as I said; **wie du wie du like you; **singen wie ein ...** to sing like a ...; **wie** (*zum Beispiel*) such as (for example)

2 (*zeitlich*): **wie er das hörte, ging er** when he heard that he left; **er hörte, wie der Regen fiel** he heard the rain falling

wieder ['vi:dər] *adv* again; **~ da sein** to be back (again); **gehst du schon ~?** are you off again?; **~ ein(e) ...** another ...; **W~aufbau** [-'aufbau] *m* rebuilding; **~aufbereiten** *vt sep* to recycle; **~aufnehmen** (*unreg*) *vt* to resume; **~bekommen** (*unreg*) *vt* to get back; **~bringen** (*unreg*) *vt* to bring back; **~erkennen** (*unreg*) *vt* to recognize; **W~gabe** *f* reproduction; **~geben** (*unreg*) *vt* (*zurückgeben*) to return; (*Erzählung etc*) to repeat; (*Gefühle etc*) to convey; **~gutmachen** *vt* to make up for; (*Fehler*) to put right; **W~gutmachung** *f* reparation; **~herstellen** *vt* to restore; **~holen** *vt insep* to repeat; **W~holung** *f* repetition; **W~hören** *nt*: **W~hören** (*TEL*) goodbye; **W~kehr** (**-**) *f* return; (*von Vorfall*) repetition, recurrence; **~sehen** (*unreg*) *vt* to see again; **auf W~sehen** goodbye; **~um** *adv* again; (*andererseits*) on the other hand; **~vereinigen** *vt* to reunite; (*POL*) to reunify; **~verwerten** *vt sep* to recycle; **W~wahl** *f* reelection

Wiege ['vi:gə] *f* cradle; **w~n**[1] *vt* (*schaukeln*) to rock

wiegen[2] (unreg) vt, vi (Gewicht) to weigh

wiehern ['viːɐrn] vi to neigh, to whinny

Wien [viːn] nt Vienna

Wiese ['viːzə] f meadow

Wiesel ['viːzəl] (-s, -) nt weasel

wieso [viːˈzoː] adv why

wieviel [viˈfiːl] adj how much; ~ **Menschen** how many people; ~**mal** adv how often; ~**te(r, s)** adj: **zum ~ten Mal?** how many times?; **den W~ten haben wir?** what's the date?; **an ~ter Stelle?** in what place?; **der ~te Besucher war er?** how many visitors were there before him?

wieweit [viˈvaɪt] adv to what extent

wild [vɪlt] adj wild; **W~** (-(e)s) nt game; **W~e(r)** f(m) savage; **w~rn** vi to poach; ~**fremd** (umg) adj quite strange od unknown; **W~heit** f wildness; **W~leder** nt suede; **W~nis** (-, -se) f wilderness; **W~schwein** nt (wild) boar

will etc [vɪl] vb siehe **wollen**

Wille ['vɪlə] (-ns, -n) m will; **w~n** präp +gen: **um** ... **w~n** for the sake of ...; **w~nsstark** adj strong-willed

will- zW: **~ig** adj willing; **W~kommen** [vɪlˈkɔmən] (-s, -) nt welcome; **~kommen** adj welcome; **jdn ~kommen heißen** to welcome sb; **~kürlich** adj arbitrary; (Bewegung) voluntary

wimmeln ['vɪməln] vi: ~ (**von**) to swarm (with)

wimmern ['vɪmərn] vi to whimper

Wimper ['vɪmpər] (-, -n) f eyelash

Wimperntusche f mascara

Wind [vɪnt] (-(e)s, -e) m wind; ~**beutel** m cream puff; (fig) rake; ~**e** f (TECH) winch, windlass; (BOT) bindweed; ~**el** f nappy, diaper (US); **w~en** vi unpers to be windy ♦ vt (unreg) to wind; (Kranz) to weave; (entwinden) to twist ♦ vr (unreg) to wind; (Person) to writhe; ~**energie** f wind energy; ~**hund** m greyhound;

(Mensch) fly-by-night; **w~ig** ['vɪndɪç] adj windy; (fig) dubious; ~**mühle** f windmill; ~**pocken** pl chickenpox sg; ~**schutzscheibe** f (AUT) windscreen (BRIT), windshield (US); ~**stärke** f wind-force; **w~still** adj (Tag) still, windless; (Platz) sheltered; ~**stille** f calm; ~**stoß** m gust of wind

Wink [vɪŋk] (-(e)s, -e) m (mit Hand) wave; (mit Kopf) nod; (Hinweis) hint

Winkel ['vɪŋkəl] (-s, -) m (MATH) angle; (Gerät) set square; (in Raum) corner

winken ['vɪŋkən] vt, vi to wave

winseln ['vɪnzəln] vi to whine

Winter ['vɪntər] (-s, -) m winter; **w~fest** adj (Pflanze) hardy; ~**garten** m conservatory; **w~lich** adj wintry; ~**reifen** m winter tyre; ~**sport** m winter sports pl

Winzer ['vɪntsər] (-s, -) m vine grower

winzig ['vɪntsɪç] adj tiny

Wipfel ['vɪpfəl] (-s, -) m treetop

wir [viːr] pron we; ~ **alle** all of us, we all

Wirbel ['vɪrbəl] (-s, -) m whirl, swirl; (Trubel) hurly-burly; (Aufsehen) fuss; (ANAT) vertebra; **w~n** vi to whirl, to swirl; ~**säule** f spine

wird [vɪrt] vb siehe **werden**

wirfst etc [vɪrfst] vb siehe **werfen**

wirken ['vɪrkən] vi to have an effect; (erfolgreich sein) to work; (scheinen) to seem ♦ vt (Wunder) to work

wirklich ['vɪrklɪç] adj real ♦ adv really; **W~keit** f reality

wirksam ['vɪrkzaːm] adj effective

Wirkstoff m (biologisch, chemisch, pflanzlich) active substance

Wirkung ['vɪrkʊŋ] f effect; **w~slos** adj ineffective; **w~slos bleiben** to have no effect; **w~svoll** adj effective

wirr [vɪr] adj confused, wild; **W~warr** (-s) m disorder, chaos

Wirsing ['vɪrzɪŋ] (-s) m savoy cabbage

wirst [vɪrst] vb siehe **werden**

Wirt(in) ['vɪrt(ɪn)] (-(e)s, -e) *m* landlord; ~**schaft** *f* (Gaststätte) pub; (Haushalt) housekeeping; (eines Landes) economy; (umg: Durcheinander) mess; **w~schaftlich** *adj* economical; (POL) economic

Wirtschafts- *zW:* ~**krise** *f* economic crisis; ~**politik** *f* economic policy; ~**prüfer** *m* chartered accountant; ~**wunder** *nt* economic miracle

Wirtshaus *nt* inn

wischen *vt* to wipe

Wischer (-s, -) *m* (AUT) wiper

wispern ['vɪspərn] *vt, vi* to whisper

Wißbegier(de) ['vɪsbəgiːr(də)] *f* thirst for knowledge; **wißbegierig** *adj* inquisitive, eager for knowledge

wissen ['vɪsən] (unreg) *vt* to know; was weiß ich! I don't know!; **W~** (-s) *nt* knowledge; **W~schaft** *f* science; **W~schaftler(in)** (-s, -) *m(f)* scientist; **~schaftlich** *adj* scientific; **~swert** *adj* worth knowing; **~tlich** *adj* knowing

wittern ['vɪtərn] *vt* to scent; (fig) to suspect

Witterung *f* weather; (Geruch) scent

Witwe ['vɪtvə] *f* widow; **~r** (-s, -) *m* widower

Witz [vɪts] (-es, -e) *m* joke; ~**bold** (-es, -e) *m* joker, wit; **w~ig** *adj* funny

wo [voː] *adv* where; (umg: irgendwo) somewhere; im Augenblick, ~ ... the moment (that) ...; die Zeit, ~ ... the time when ...; **~anders** [voːʔandərs] *adv* elsewhere; **~bei** [-ˈbaɪ] *adv* (relativ) by/with which; (interrogativ) what ... in/by/with

Woche ['vɔxə] *f* week

Wochen- *zW:* ~**ende** *nt* weekend; **w~lang** *adj, adv* for weeks; ~**schau** *f* newsreel

wöchentlich ['vœçəntlɪç] *adj, adv* weekly

wodurch [voːˈdʊrç] *adv* (relativ) through which; (interrogativ) what ... through

wofür [voːˈfyːr] *adv* (relativ) for

which; (interrogativ) what ... for

wog *etc* [voːk] *vb siehe* wiegen

wo- [voː'geːgən] *zW:* ~**gegen** *adv* (relativ) against which; (interrogativ) what ... against; **~her** [-ˈheːr] *adv* where ... from; **~hin** [-ˈhɪn] *adv* where ... to

---

wohl [voːl] *adv* **1:** sich wohl fühlen (zufrieden) to feel happy; (gesundheitlich) to feel well; wohl oder übel whether one likes it or not **2** (wahrscheinlich) probably; (gewiß) certainly; (vielleicht) perhaps; sie ist wohl zu Hause she's probably at home; das ist doch wohl nicht dein Ernst! surely you're not serious!; das mag wohl sein that may well be; ob das wohl stimmt? I wonder if that's true; er weiß das sehr wohl he knows that perfectly well

---

Wohl [voːl] (-(e)s) *nt* welfare; zum ~! cheers!; **w~auf** *adv* well; ~**behagen** *nt* comfort; ~**fahrt** *f* welfare; ~**fahrtsstaat** *m* welfare state; **w~habend** *adj* wealthy; **w~ig** *adj* contented, comfortable; **w~schmeckend** *adj* delicious; ~**stand** *m* prosperity; ~**standsgesellschaft** *f* affluent society; ~**tat** *f* relief; act of charity; ~**täter(in)** *m(f)* benefactor; **w~tätig** *adj* charitable; ~**tätigkeits-** *zW:* charity, charitable; **w~tun** (unreg) *vi:* jdm ~tun to do sb good; **w~verdient** *adj* well-earned, well-deserved; **w~weislich** *adv* prudently; **~wollen** (-s) *nt* good will; **w~wollend** *adj* benevolent

wohn- ['voːn] *zW:* ~**en** *vi* to live; **W~gemeinschaft** *f* (Menschen) people sharing a flat; **~haft** *adj* resident; **W~heim** *nt* (für Studenten) hall of residence; (für Senioren) home; (bes für Arbeiter) hostel; **~lich** *adj* comfortable; **W~ort** *m* domicile; **W~sitz** *m* place of residence; **W~ung** *f* house; (Etagenwoh-

nung) flat, apartment *(US)*; **W~wagen** *m* caravan; **W~zimmer** *nt* living room

wölben ['vœlbən] *vt, vr* to curve

Wölbung *f* curve

Wolf [vɔlf] (-(e)s, **e**) *m* wolf

Wolke ['vɔlkə] *f* cloud; **~nkratzer** *m* skyscraper

wolkig ['vɔlkɪç] *adj* cloudy

Wolle ['vɔlə] *f* wool; **w~n1** *adj* woollen

SCHLÜSSELWORT

wollen2 *(pt* **wollte**, *pp* **gewollt** *od (als Hilfsverb)* **wollen)** *vt, vi* to want; **ich will nach Hause** I want to go home; **er will nicht** he doesn't want to; **er wollte das nicht** he didn't want it; **wenn du willst** if you like; **ich will, daß du mir zuhörst** I want you to listen to me

♦ *Hilfsverb:* **er will ein Haus kaufen** he wants to buy a house; **ich wollte, ich wäre ...** I wish I were ...; **etw gerade tun wollen** to be going to do sth

wollüstig ['vɔlʏstɪç] *adj* lusty, sensual

wo- *zW:* **~mit** [voː'mɪt] *adv (relativ)* with which; *(interrogativ)* what ... with; **~'möglich** *adv* probably, I suppose; **~'nach** *adv (relativ)* after/for which; *(interrogativ)* what ... for/ after; **~'ran** *adv (relativ)* what ... on/at which; *(interrogativ)* what ... on/at; **~'rauf** *adv (relativ)* on which; *(interrogativ)* what ... on; **~'raus** *adv (relativ)* from/out of which; *(interrogativ)* what ... from/out of; **~'rin** *adv (relativ)* in which; *(interrogativ)* what ... in

Wort [vɔrt] (-(e)s, **er** *od* **-e)** *nt* word; **jdn beim ~ nehmen** to take sb at his word; **mit anderen ~en** in other words; **w~brüchig** *adj* not true to one's word

Wörterbuch ['vœrtərbuːx] *nt* dictionary

Wort- *zW:* **~führer** *m* spokesman; **w~karg** *adj* taciturn; **~laut** *m* wording

wörtlich ['vœrtlɪç] *adj* literal

Wort- *zW:* **~los** *adj* mute; **w~reich** *adj* wordy, verbose; **~schatz** *m* vocabulary; **~spiel** *nt* play on words, pun

wo- *zW:* **~rüber** [voː'ryːbər] *adv (relativ)* over/about which; *(interrogativ)* what ... over/about; **~rum** *adv (relativ)* about/round which; *(interrogativ)* what ... about/round; **~'runter** *adv (relativ)* under which; *(interrogativ)* what ... under; **~'von** *adv (relativ)* from which; *(interrogativ)* what ... from; **~'vor** *adv (relativ)* in front of/before which; *(interrogativ)* in front of/before what; of what; **~'zu** *adv (relativ)* to/for which; *(interrogativ)* what ... for/to; *(warum)* why

Wrack [vrak] (-(e)s, **-s)** *nt* wreck

wringen ['vrɪŋən] *(unreg) vt* to wring

Wucher ['vuːxər] (-s) *m* profiteering; **~er** (-s, -) *m* profiteer; **w~isch** *adj* profiteering; **w~n** *vi (Pflanzen)* to grow wild; **~ung** *f (MED)* growth, tumour

Wuchs [vuːks] (-es) *m (Wachstum)* growth; *(Statur)* build

Wucht [vʊxt] (-) *f* force

wühlen ['vyːlən] *vi* to scrabble; *(Tier)* to root; *(Maulwurf)* to burrow; *(umg: arbeiten)* to slave away ♦ *vt* to dig

Wulst [vʊlst] (-es, **e**) *m* bulge; *(an Wunde)* swelling

wund [vʊnt] *adj* sore, raw; **W~e** *f* wound

Wunder ['vʊndər] (-s, -) *nt* miracle; **es ist kein ~** it's no wonder; **w~bar** *adj* wonderful, marvellous; **~kerze** *f* sparkler; **~kind** *nt* infant prodigy; **w~lich** *adj* odd, peculiar; **w~n** *vr* to be surprised ♦ *vt* to surprise; **sich w~n über** +*akk* to be surprised at; **w~schön** *adj* beautiful; **w~voll** *adj* wonderful

Wundstarrkrampf ['vʊntʃtar-
krampf] m tetanus, lockjaw
Wunsch [vʊnʃ] (-(e)s, ⁼e) m wish
wünschen ['vʏnʃən] vt to wish; **sich**
dat **etw ~** to want sth, to wish for
sth; **~swert** adj desirable
wurde etc ['vʊrdə] vb siehe **werden**
Würde ['vʏrdə] f dignity; (Stellung)
honour; **w~voll** adj dignified
würdig ['vʏrdɪç] adj worthy;
(würdevoll) dignified; **~en** ['vʏr-
dɪgən] vt to appreciate; **jdn keines
Blickes ~en** not to so much as look
at sb
Wurf [vʊrf] (-(e)s, ⁼e) m throw; (Junge)
litter
Würfel ['vʏrfəl] (-s, -) m dice;
(MATH) cube; **~becher** m (dice)
cup; **w~n** vi to play dice ♦ vt to
dice; **~zucker** m lump sugar
würgen ['vʏrgən] vti to choke
Wurm [vʊrm] (-(e)s, ⁼er) m worm
wurmstichig adj worm-ridden
Wurst [vʊrst] (-, ⁼e) f sausage; **das
ist mir ~** (umg) I don't care, I don't
give a damn
Würstchen ['vʏrstçən] nt sausage
Würze ['vʏrtsə] f seasoning, spice
Wurzel ['vʊrtsəl] (-, -n) f root
würzen ['vʏrtsən] vt to season, to
spice
würzig adj spicy
wusch etc [vʊʃ] vb siehe **waschen**
wußte etc ['vʊstə] vb siehe **wissen**
wüst [vyːst] adj untidy, messy;
(ausschweifend) wild; (öde) waste;
(umg: heftig) terrible; **W~e** f desert
Wut [vuːt] (-) f rage, fury; **~anfall** m
fit of rage
wüten ['vyːtən] vi to rage; **~d** adj
furious, mad

X

X-Beine ['ɪksbaɪnə] pl knock-knees
x-beliebig [ɪksbə'liːbɪç] adj any
(whatever)
xerokopieren [kseroko'piːrən] vt to
xerox, to photocopy

x-mal ['ɪksmaːl] adv any number of
times, n times
Xylophon [ksylo'foːn] (-s, -e) nt xylophone

Y

Ypsilon ['ypsilɔn] (-(s), -s) nt the
letter Y

Z

Zacke ['tsakə] f point; (Berg~)
jagged peak; (Gabel~) prong;
(Kamm~) tooth
zackig ['tsakɪç] adj jagged; (umg)
smart; (Tempo) brisk
zaghaft ['tsaːkhaft] adj timid
zäh [tsɛː] adj tough; (Mensch) tenacious; (Flüssigkeit) thick; (schleppend) sluggish; **Z~igkeit** f tough-
ness; tenacity
Zahl [tsaːl] (-, -en) f number; **z~bar**
adj payable; **z~en** vti to pay;
z~en bitte! the bill please!
zählen ['tsɛːlən] vti, vi to count; **~
auf** +akk to count on; **~ zu** to be
numbered among
Zahlenschloß nt combination lock
Zähler ['tsɛːlər] (-s, -) m (TECH)
meter; (MATH) numerator
Zahl- ~reich adj countless;
z~reich adj numerous; **~tag** m pay-
day; **~ung** f payment; **z~ungsfähig**
adj solvent; **~wort** nt numeral
zahm [tsaːm] adj tame
zähmen ['tsɛːmən] vt to tame; (fig)
to curb
Zahn [tsaːn] (-(e)s, ⁼e) m tooth;
~arzt m dentist; **~ärztin** f (female)
dentist; **~bürste** f toothbrush;
~fleisch nt gums pl; **~pasta** f toothpaste; **~rad** nt cog(wheel);
~schmerzen pl toothache sg; **~stein**
m tartar; **~stocher** (-s, -) m tooth-
pick
Zange [tsaŋə] f pliers pl; (Zucker~
etc) tongs pl; (Beiß~, ZOOL) pincers

pl; (MED) forceps *pl*

zanken ['tsaŋkən] *vi, vr* to quarrel

zänkisch ['tsɛŋkiʃ] *adj* quarrelsome

Zäpfchen ['tsɛpfçən] *nt* (ANAT) uvula; (MED) suppository

Zapfen ['tsapfən] (**-s**, **-**) *m* plug; (BOT) cone; (Eis~) icicle

zappeln ['tsapəln] *vi* to wriggle; to fidget

zart [tsart] *adj* (weich, leise) soft; (Fleisch) tender; (fein, schwächlich) delicate; **Z~heit** *f* softness; tenderness; delicacy

zärtlich ['tsɛːrtliç] *adj* tender, affectionate

Zauber ['tsaubər] (**-s**, **-**) *m* magic; (~bann) spell; **~ei** [-'rai] *f* magic; **~er** (**-s**, **-**) *m* magician; conjuror; **z~haft** *adj* magical, enchanting; **~künstler** *m* conjuror; **~kunststück** *nt* conjuring trick; **z~n** *vi* to conjure, to practise magic

zaudern ['tsaudərn] *vi* to hesitate

Zaum [tsaum] (**-(e)s**, **Zäume**) *m* bridle; etw im ~ halten to keep sth in check

Zaun [tsaun] (**-(e)s**, **Zäune**) *m* fence; **~könig** *m* wren

z.B. *abk* (= zum Beispiel) e.g.

Zebra ['tseːbra] *nt* zebra; **~streifen** *m* zebra crossing

Zeche ['tsɛçə] *f* (Rechnung) bill; (Bergbau) mine

Zeh [tseː] (**-s**, **-en**) *m* toe

Zehe ['tseːə] *f* toe; (Knoblauch~) clove

zehn [tseːn] *num* ten; **~te(r, s)** *adj* tenth; **Z~tel** (**-s**, **-**) *nt* tenth (part)

Zeich- ['tsaiç] *zW:* **~en** (**-s**, **-**) *nt* sign; **~nen** *vt* to draw; (kennzeichnen) to mark; (unterzeichnen) to sign ♦ *vi* to draw; to sign; **~ner** (**-s**, **-**) *m* artist; technischer **~ner** draughtsman; **~nung** *f* drawing; (Markierung) markings *pl*

Zeige- ['tsaigə] *zW:* **~finger** *m* index finger; **z~n** *vt* to show ♦ *vi* to point ♦ *vr:* **z~n** auf +akk to point to; to point at; es wird sich **z~n** time will tell; es zeigte sich,

daß it turned out that ...; **~r** (**-s**, **-**) *m* pointer; (Uhrzeiger) hand

Zeile ['tsailə] *f* line; (Häuser~) row

Zeit [tsait] (**-**, **-en**) *f* time; (GRAM) tense; zur ~ at the moment; sich *dat* ~ lassen to take one's time; von ~ zu ~ from time to time; **~alter** *nt* age; **~arbeit** *f* (WIRTS) temporary job; **z~gemäß** *adj* in keeping with the times; **~genosse** *m* contemporary; **~ig** *adj* early; **~lich** *adj* temporal; **~lupe** *f* slow motion; **~raubend** *adj* time-consuming; **~raum** *m* period; **~rechnung** *f* time, era; nach/vor unserer **~rechnung** A.D./B.C.; **~schrift** *f* periodical; **~ung** *f* newspaper; **~verschwendung** *f* waste of time; **~vertreib** *m* pastime, diversion; **z~weilig** *adj* temporary; **z~weise** *adv* for a time; **~wort** *nt* verb; **~zünder** *m* time fuse

Zelle ['tsɛlə] *f* cell; (Telefon~) call-box

Zellstoff *m* cellulose

Zelt [tsɛlt] (**-(e)s**, **-e**) *nt* tent; **z~en** *vi* to camp; **~platz** *m* camp site

Zement [tse'mɛnt] (**-(e)s**, **-e**) *m* cement; **z~ieren** *vt* to cement

zensieren [tsɛn'ziːrən] *vt* to censor; (SCH) to mark

Zensur [tsɛn'zuːr] *f* censorship; (SCH) mark

Zentimeter [tsɛnti'meːtər] *m* od *nt* centimetre

Zentner ['tsɛntnər] (**-s**, **-**) *m* hundredweight

zentral [tsɛn'traːl] *adj* central; **Z~e** *f* central office; (TEL) exchange; **Z~heizung** *f* central heating

Zentrum ['tsɛntrum] (**-s**, **Zentren**) *nt* centre

zerbrechen [tsɛr'brɛçən] (unreg) *vt*, *vi* to break

zerbrechlich *adj* fragile

zer'drücken *vt* to squash, to crush; (Kartoffeln) to mash

Zeremonie [tseremo'niː] *f* ceremony

Zerfall [tsɛr'fal] *m* decay; **z~en** (unreg) *vi* to disintegrate, to decay;

(*sich gliedern*): **z~en** (**in** +*akk*) to fall (into)

zer'gehen (*unreg*) *vi* to melt, to dissolve

zerkleinern [tsɛr'klaɪnərn] *vt* to reduce to small pieces

zerlegbar *adj* able to be dismantled

zerlegen [tsɛr'leːgən] *vt* to take to pieces; (*Fleisch*) to carve; (*Satz*) to analyse

zermürben [tsɛr'mʏrbən] *vt* to wear down

zerquetschen [tsɛr'kvɛtʃən] *vt* to squash

Zerrbild ['tsɛrbɪlt] *nt* caricature, distorted picture

zer'reißen (*unreg*) *vt* to tear to pieces ♦ *vi* to tear, to rip

zerren ['tsɛrən] *vt* to drag ♦ *vi*: ~ (**an** +*dat*) to tug (at)

zer'rinnen (*unreg*) *vi* to melt away

zerrissen [tsɛr'rɪsən] *adj* torn, tattered; **Z~heit** *f* tattered state; (*POL*) disunion, discord; (*innere Zerrissenheit*) disintegration

Zerrung *f* (*MED*): **eine** ~ **pulled muscle**

zer'rütten *vt* to wreck, to destroy

zerrüttet *adj* wrecked, shattered

zer'schlagen (*unreg*) *vt* to shatter, to smash ♦ *vr* to fall through

zer'schneiden (*unreg*) *vt* to cut up

zer'setzen *vt, vr* to decompose, to dissolve

zer'springen (*unreg*) *vi* to shatter, to burst

Zerstäuber [tsɛr'ʃtɔybər] (**-s**, **-**) *m* atomizer

zer'stören [tsɛr'ʃtøːrən] *vt* to destroy

Zerstörung *f* destruction

zerstreu~ [tsɛr'ʃtrɔy] *zW*: **~en** *vt* to disperse, to scatter; (*unterhalten*) to divert; (*Zweifel etc*) to dispel ♦ *vr* to disperse, to scatter; to be dispelled; **~t** *adj* scattered; (*Mensch*) absentminded; **Z~theit** *f* absent-mindedness; **Z~ung** *f* dispersion; (*Ablenkung*) diversion

zerstückeln [tsɛr'ʃtʏkəln] *vt* to cut

into pieces

zer'teilen *vt* to divide into parts

Zertifikat [tsɛrtifi'kaːt] (**-(e)s**, **-e**) *nt* certificate

zer'treten (*unreg*) *vt* to crush underfoot

zertrümmern [tsɛr'trʏmərn] *vt* to shatter; (*Gebäude etc*) to demolish

zetern ['tseːtərn] *vi* to shout, to shriek

Zettel ['tsɛtəl] (**-s**, **-**) *m* piece of paper, slip; (*Notiz~*) note; (*Formular*) form

Zeug [tsɔyk] (**-(e)s**, **-e**; *umg*) *nt* stuff; (*Ausrüstung*) gear; **dummes** ~ (stupid) nonsense; **das** ~ **haben zu** to have the makings of; **sich ins** ~ **legen** to put one's shoulder to the wheel

Zeuge ['tsɔygə] (**-n**, **-n**) *m* witness; **z~n** *vi* to bear witness, to testify ♦ *vt* (*Kind*) to father; **es zeugt von** ... it testifies to ...; **~naussage** *f* evidence; **Zeugin** ['tsɔygɪn] *f* witness

Zeugnis ['tsɔyknɪs] (**-ses**, **-se**) *nt* certificate; (*SCH*) report; (*Referenz*) reference; (*Aussage*) evidence, testimony; ~ **geben von** to be evidence of, to testify to

z.H(d). *abk* (= *zu Händen*) attn.

Zickzack ['tsɪktsak] (**-(e)s**, **-e**) *m* zigzag

Ziege ['tsiːgə] *f* goat

Ziegel ['tsiːgəl] (**-s**, **-**) *m* brick; (*Dach~*) tile

ziehen ['tsiːən] (*unreg*) *vt* to draw; (*zerren*) to pull; (*SCHACH etc*) to move; (*züchten*) to rear ♦ *vi* to draw; (*um~*, *wandern*) to move; (*Rauch, Wolke etc*) to drift; (*reißen*) to pull ♦ *vb unpers*: **es zieht** there is a draught, it's draughty ♦ (*Gummi*) to stretch; (*Grenze etc*) to run out; **etw nach sich** ~ to lead to sth, to entail sth

Ziehharmonika ['tsiːharmoːnika] *f* concertina; accordion

Ziehung ['tsiːʊŋ] *f* (*Los~*) drawing

Ziel [tsiːl] (**-(e)s**, **-e**) *nt* (*einer Reise*) destination; (*SPORT*) finish; (*MIL*)

target; (*Absicht*) goal; **z~bewußt** *adj* decisive; **z~en** *vi*: **z~en auf** (*+akk*) to aim (at); **z~los** *adj* aimless; **~scheibe** *f* target; **z~strebig** *adj* purposeful

ziemlich ['tsiːmlɪç] *adj* quite a; fair ♦ *adv* rather; quite a bit

zieren ['tsiːrən] *vr* to act coy

zierlich ['tsiːrlɪç] *adj* dainty

Ziffer ['tsɪfər] (**-, -n**) *f* figure, digit; **~blatt** *nt* dial, clock-face

zig [tsɪç] (*umg*) *adj* umpteen

Zigarette [tsiga'rɛtə] *f* cigarette

Zigaretten– *zW*: **~automat** *m* cigarette machine; **~schachtel** *f* cigarette packet; **~spitze** *f* cigarette holder

Zigarillo [tsiga'rɪlo] (**-s, -s**) *nt od m* cigarillo

Zigarre [tsi'garə] *f* cigar

Zigeuner(in) [tsi'gɔynər(ɪn)] (**-s, -**) *m(f)* gipsy

Zimmer ['tsɪmər] (**-s, -**) *nt* room; **~lautstärke** *f* reasonable volume; **~mädchen** *nt* chambermaid; **~mann** *m* carpenter; **z~n** *vt* to make (from wood); **~nachweis** *m* accommodation office; **~pflanze** *f* indoor plant

zimperlich ['tsɪmpərlɪç] *adj* squeamish; (*pingelig*) fussy, finicky

Zimt [tsɪmt] (**-(e)s, -e**) *m* cinnamon

Zink [tsɪŋk] (**-(e)s**) *nt* zinc

Zinn [tsɪn] (**-(e)s**) *nt* (*Element*) tin; (*in ~waren*) pewter; **~soldat** *m* tin soldier

Zins [tsɪns] (**-es, -en**) *m* interest; **~esz~** *m* compound interest; **~fuß** *m* rate of interest; **z~los** *adj* interest-free; **~satz** *m* rate of interest

Zipfel ['tsɪpfəl] (**-s, -**) *m* corner; (*spitz*) tip; (*Hemd~*) tail; (*Wurst~*) end; **~mütze** *f* stocking cap; nightcap

zirka ['tsɪrka] *adv* (round) about

Zirkel ['tsɪrkəl] (**-s, -**) *m* circle; (*MATH*) pair of compasses

Zirkus ['tsɪrkus] (**-, -se**) *m* circus

zischen ['tsɪʃən] *vi* to hiss

Zitat [tsi'taːt] (**-(e)s, -e**) *nt* quotation, quote

zitieren [tsi'tiːrən] *vt* to quote

Zitronat [tsitro'naːt] (**-(e)s, -e**) *nt* candied lemon peel

Zitrone [tsi'troːnə] *f* lemon; **~nlimonade** *f* lemonade; **~nsaft** *m* lemon juice

zittern ['tsɪtərn] *vi* to tremble

zivil [tsi'viːl] *adj* civil; (*Preis*) moderate; **Z~** (**-s**) *nt* plain clothes *pl*; (*MIL*) civilian clothing; **Z~bevölkerung** *f* civilian population; **Z~courage** *f* courage of one's convictions; **Z~dienst** *m* community service; **Z~isation** [tsivilizatsi'oːn] *f* civilization; **Z~isationskrankheit** *f* disease peculiar to civilization; **~i'sieren** *vt* to civilize; **Z~ist** [tsivi'lɪst] *m* civilian

zögern ['tsøːgərn] *vi* to hesitate

Zoll [tsɔl] (**-(e)s, ¨e**) *m* customs *pl*; (*Abgabe*) duty; **~abfertigung** *f* customs clearance; **~amt** *nt* customs office; **~beamte(r)** *m* customs official; **~erklärung** *f* customs declaration; **z~frei** *adj* duty-free; **~kontrolle** *f* customs check; **z~pflichtig** *adj* liable to duty, dutiable

Zone ['tsoːnə] *f* zone

Zoo [tsoː] (**-s, -s**) *m* zoo; **~loge** [tsoo'loːgə] (**-n, -n**) *m* zoologist; **~lo'gie** *f* zoology; **z~logisch** *adj* zoological

Zopf [tsɔpf] (**-(e)s, ¨e**) *m* plait; pigtail; **alter ~** antiquated custom

Zorn [tsɔrn] (**-(e)s**) *m* anger; **z~ig** *adj* angry

zottig ['tsɔtɪç] *adj* shaggy

z.T. *abk* = **zum Teil**

SCHLÜSSELWORT

zu [tsuː] *präp +dat* **1** (*örtlich*) to; **zum Bahnhof/Arzt gehen** to go to the station/doctor; **zur Schule/Kirche gehen** to go to school/church; **sollen wir zu euch gehen?** shall we go to your place?; **sie sah zu ihm hin** she looked towards him; **zum Fenster herein** through the window; **zu meiner Linken** to od on my left

2 (zeitlich) at; **zu Ostern** at Easter; **bis zum 1. Mai** until May 1st; (nicht später als) by May 1st; **zu meiner Zeit** in my time

3 (Zusatz) with; **Wein zum Essen trinken** to drink wine with one's meal; **sich zu jdm setzen** to sit down beside sb; **setz dich doch zu uns** (come and) sit with us; **Anmerkungen zu etw** notes on sth

4 (Zweck) for; **Wasser zum Waschen** water for washing; **Papier zum Schreiben** paper to write on; **etw zum Geburtstag bekommen** to get sth for one's birthday

5 (Veränderung) into; **zu etw werden** to turn into sth; **jdn zu etw machen** to make sb (into) sth; **zu Asche verbrennen** to burn to ashes

6 (mit Zahlen): **3 zu 2** (SPORT) 3-2; **das Stück zu 2 Mark** at 2 marks each; **zum ersten Mal** for the first time

7: **zu meiner Freude** etc to my joy etc; **zum Glück** luckily; **zu Fuß** on foot; **es ist zum Weinen** it's enough to make you cry

♦ konj to; **etw zu essen** sth to eat; **um besser sehen zu können** in order to see better; **ohne es zu wissen** without knowing it; **noch zu bezahlende Rechnungen** bills that are still to be paid

♦ adv **1** (allzu) too; **zu sehr** too much

2 (örtlich) toward(s); **er kam auf mich zu** he came up to me

3 (geschlossen) shut; closed; **die Geschäfte haben zu** the shops are closed; **auf/zu** (Wasserhahn etc) on/off

4 (umg: los): **nur zu!** just keep on!; **mach zu!** hurry up!

zuallererst [tsu''alər'|e:rst] adv first of all

zuallerletzt [tsu''alər'letst] adv last of all

Zubehör ['tsu:bəhør] (-(e)s, -e) nt accessories pl

zubereiten ['tsu:bəraɪtən] vt to prepare

zubilligen ['tsu:bɪlɪgən] vt to grant

zubinden ['tsu:bɪndən] (unreg) vt to tie up

zubringen ['tsu:brɪŋən] (unreg) vt (Zeit) to spend

Zubringer (-s, -) m (Straße) approach od slip road

Zucchini [tsu'ki:ni] pl (BOT, KOCH) courgette (BRIT), zucchini (US)

Zucht [tsʊxt] (-, -en) f (von Tieren) breeding; (von Pflanzen) cultivation; (Rasse) breed; (Erziehung) raising; (Disziplin) discipline

züchten ['tsʏçtən] vt (Tiere) to breed; (Pflanzen) to cultivate, to grow

Züchter (-s, -) m breeder; grower

Zuchthaus nt prison, penitentiary (US)

züchtigen ['tsʏçtɪgən] vt to chastise

Züchtung f (Zuchtart, Sorte: von Tier) breed(; von Pflanze) variety

zucken ['tsʊkən] vi to jerk, to twitch; (Strahl etc) to flicker ♦ vt (Schultern) to shrug

Zucker ['tsʊkər] (-s, -) m sugar; (MED) diabetes; **~guß** m icing; **z~krank** adj diabetic; **~krankheit** f (MED) diabetes; **z~n** vt to sugar; **~rohr** nt sugar cane; **~rübe** f sugar beet

Zuckung ['tsʊkʊŋ] f convulsion, spasm; (leicht) twitch

zudecken ['tsu:dɛkən] vt to cover (up)

zudem [tsu'de:m] adv in addition (to this)

zudringlich ['tsu:drɪŋlɪç] adj forward, pushing, obtrusive

zudrücken ['tsu:drʏkən] vt to close; **ein Auge ~** to turn a blind eye

zueinander [tsu'aɪ'nandər] adv to one other; (in Verbindung) together

zuerkennen ['tsu:'ɛrkɛnən] (unreg) vt to award; **jdm etw ~** to award sth to sb, to award sb sth

zuerst [tsu'ʔeːrst] *adv* first; (*zu Anfang*) at first; ~ **einmal** first of all

Zufahrt ['tsuːfaːrt] *f* approach; ~**sstraße** *f* approach road; (*von Autobahn etc*) slip road

Zufall ['tsuːfal] *m* chance; (*Ereignis*) coincidence; **durch** ~ by accident; **so ein** ~ what a coincidence; **z~en** (*unreg*) *vi* to close, to shut; (*Anteil, Aufgabe*) to fall

zufällig ['tsuːfɛlɪç] *adj* chance ♦ *adv* by chance; (*in Frage*) by any chance

Zuflucht ['tsuːfluxt] *f* recourse; (*Ort*) refuge

zufolge ['tsuːfɔlgə] *präp* (+*dat od gen*) judging by; (*laut*) according to

zufrieden [tsu'friːdən] *adj* contented, satisfied; ~**geben** (*unreg*) *vr* to be content *od* satisfied (with); ~**stellen** *vt* to satisfy

zufrieren [tsu'friːrən] (*unreg*) *vi* to freeze up *od* over

zufügen ['tsuːfyːgən] *vt* to add; (*Leid etc*): (*jdm*) **etw** ~ to cause (sb) sth

Zufuhr ['tsuːfuːr] (-, **-en**) *f* (*Herbeibringen*) supplying; (*MET*) influx

Zug [tsuːk] (-(*e*)s, ¤e) *m* (*EISENB*) train; (*Luft*~) draught; (*Ziehen*) pull(ing); (*Gesichts*~) feature; (*SCHACH etc*) move; (*Klingel*~) pull; (*Schrift*~) stroke; (*Charakter*~) trait; (*an Zigarette*) puff, pull, drag; (*Schluck*) gulp; (*Menschengruppe*) procession; (*von Vögeln*) flight; (*MIL*) platoon; **etw in vollen Zügen genießen** to enjoy sth to the full

Zu- ['tsuː] *zW*: ~**gabe** *f* extra; (*in Konzert etc*) encore; ~**gang** *m* access, approach; **z~gänglich** *adj* accessible; (*Mensch*) approachable

zugeben ['tsuːgeːbən] (*unreg*) *vt* (*beifügen*) to add, to throw in; (*gestehen*) to admit; (*erlauben*) to permit

zugehen ['tsuːgeːən] (*unreg*) *vi* (*schließen*) to shut; **es geht dort seltsam zu** there are strange goings-on there; **auf jdn/etw** ~ to walk towards sb/sth; **dem Ende** ~ to be finishing

Zugehörigkeit ['tsuːgəhøːrɪçkaɪt] *f*: ~ (**zu**) membership (of), belonging (to)

Zügel ['tsyːgəl] (-s, -) *m* rein(s); (*fig*) curb

zuge- ['tsuːgə] *zW*: **Z~ständnis** (-ses, -se) *nt* concession; ~**stehen** (*unreg*) *vt* to admit; (*Rechte*) to concede

Zugführer *m* (*EISENB*) guard

zugig ['tsuːgɪç] *adj* draughty

zügig ['tsyːgɪç] *adj* speedy, swift

zugreifen ['tsuːgraɪfən] (*unreg*) *vi* to seize *od* grab at; (*helfen*) to help; (*beim Essen*) to help o.s.

zugrunde [tsu'grʊndə] *adv*: ~ **gehen** to collapse; (*Mensch*) to perish; **einer Sache** *dat* **etw** ~ **legen** to base sth on sth; **einer Sache** *dat* ~ **liegen** to be based on sth; ~ **richten** to ruin, to destroy

zugunsten [tsu'gʊnstən] *präp* (+*gen od dat*) in favour of

zugute [tsu'guːtə] *adv*: **jdm etw** ~ **halten** to concede sth to sb; **jdm** ~ **kommen** to be of assistance to sb

Zugvogel *m* migratory bird

zuhalten ['tsuːhaltən] (*unreg*) *vt* to keep closed ♦ *vi*: **auf jdn/etw** ~ to make a beeline for sb/sth

Zuhälter ['tsuːhɛltər] (-s, -) *m* pimp

Zuhause [tsu'hausə] (-) *nt* home

zuhören ['tsuːhøːrən] *vi* to listen

Zuhörer (-s, -) *m* listener

zukleben ['tsuːkleːbən] *vt* to paste up

zukommen ['tsuːkɔmən] (*unreg*) *vi* to come up; **auf jdn** ~ to come up to sb; **jdm etw** ~ **lassen** to give sb sth; **etw auf sich** ~ **lassen** to wait and see; **jdm** ~ (*sich gehören*) to be fitting for sb

Zukunft ['tsuːkʊnft] (-, **Zukünfte**) *f* future; **zukünftig** ['tsuːkynftɪç] *adj* future ♦ *adv* in future; **mein** ~**er Mann** my husband to be

Zulage ['tsuːlaːgə] *f* bonus

zulassen ['tsuːlasən] (unreg) vt (hereinlassen) to admit; (erlauben) to permit; (Auto) to license; (umg: nicht öffnen) to (keep) shut

zulässig ['tsuːlɛsɪç] adj permissible, permitted

Zulassung f (amtlich) authorisation; (von Kfz) licensing

zulaufen ['tsuːlaofən] (unreg) vi (subj: Mensch): ~ auf jdn/etw to run up to sb/sth; (: Straße): ~ auf to lead towards

zuleide [tsuːˈlaidə] adv: jdm etw ~ tun to hurt od harm sb

zuletzt [tsuˈlɛtst] adv finally, at last

zuliebe [tsuːˈliːbə] adv: jdm ~ to please sb

zum [tsum] = zu dem; ~ dritten Mal for the third time; ~ Scherz a joke; ~ Trinken for drinking

zumachen ['tsuːmaxən] vt to shut; (Kleidung) to do up, to fasten ♦ vi (umg) to hurry up

zumal [tsuˈmaːl] konj especially (as)

zumeist [tsuˈmaist] adv mostly

zumindest [tsuˈmɪndəst] adv at least

zumut- zW: **~bar** ['tsuːmuːtbaːr] adj reasonable; **~e** adv: wie ist ihm ~e? how does he feel?; **~en** vt: (jdm) etw ~en to expect od ask sth (of sb); **Z~ung** f unreasonable expectation od demand, impertinence

zunächst [tsuˈnɛːçst] adv first of all; ~ einmal to start with

Zunahme ['tsuːnaːmə] f increase

Zuname ['tsuːnaːmə] m surname

Zünd- [tsynd] zW: **z~en** vi (Feuer) to light, to ignite; (Motor) to fire; (begeistern): bei jdm z~en to fire sb (with enthusiasm); **z~end** adj fiery; **~er** (-s, -) m fuse; (MIL) detonator; **~holz** ['tsynt-] nt match; **~kerze** f (AUT) spark(ing) plug; **~schlüssel** m ignition key; **~schnur** f fuse wire; **~stoff** m (fig) inflammatory stuff; **~ung** f ignition

zunehmen ['tsuːneːmən] (unreg) vi to increase, to grow; (Mensch) to put on weight

Zuneigung f affection

Zunft [tsunft] (-, ¨e) f guild

zünftig ['tsynftɪç] adj proper, real; (Handwerk) decent

Zunge ['tsuŋə] f tongue

zunichte [tsuˈnɪçtə] adv: ~ machen to ruin, to destroy; ~ werden to come to nothing

zunutze [tsuˈnutsə] adv: sich dat etw ~ machen to make use of sth

zuoberst [tsuˈʔoːbərst] adv at the top

zupfen ['tsupfən] vt to pull, to pick, to pluck; (Gitarre) to pluck

zur [tsuːr] = zu der

zurechnungsfähig ['tsuːrɛçnuŋs-fɛːɪç] adj responsible, accountable

zurecht- [tsuˈrɛçt] zW: **~finden** (unreg) vr to find one's way (about); **~kommen** (unreg) vi to (be able to) cope, to manage; **~legen** vt to have ready; (Ausrede etc) to have ready; **~machen** vt to prepare ♦ vr to get ready; **~weisen** (unreg) vt to reprimand; **Z~weisung** f reprimand, rebuff

zureden ['tsuːreːdən] vi: jdm ~ to persuade od urge sb

zurück [tsuˈrʏk] adv back; **~behalten** (unreg) vt to keep back; **~bekommen** (unreg) vt to get back; **~bleiben** (unreg) vi (Mensch) to remain behind; (nicht nachkommen) to fall behind, to lag; (Schaden) to remain; **~bringen** (unreg) vt to bring back; **~fahren** (unreg) vi to travel back ♦ (vor Schreck) to recoil, to start ♦ vt to drive back; **~finden** vi to find one's way back; **~fordern** vt to demand back; **~führen** vt to lead back; etw auf etw akk ~führen to trace sth back to sth; **~geben** (unreg) vt to give back; (antworten) to retort with; **~geblieben** adj retarded; **~gehen** (unreg) vi to go back; (fallen) to go down, to fall; (zeitlich) to date back (to); **~gezogen** adj retired, withdrawn; **~halten** (unreg) vt to hold back; (Mensch) to restrain; (hindern) to prevent ♦ vr (reserviert) *sein)* to be reserved; *(im Essen)* to hold back; **Z~haltung** f reserve; **~kehren** vi to return; **~kommen** *(unreg)* vi to come back; **auf etw** *akk* **~kommen** to return to sth; **~lassen** *(unreg)* vt to leave behind; **~legen** vt to put back; *(Geld)* to put by; *(reservieren)* to keep back; *(Strecke)* to cover; **~nehmen** *(unreg)* vt to take back; **~schrecken** vi: **~schrecken (vor** +dat*)* to shrink (from); **~stellen** vt to put back, to replace; *(aufschieben)* to put off, to postpone; *(MIL)* to keep; *(Interessen)* to defer; *(Ware)* to keep; **~treten** *(unreg)* vi to step back; *(vom Amt)* to retire; **gegenüber etw** od **hinter etw** dat **~treten** to diminish in importance in view of sth; **~weisen** *(unreg)* vt to turn down; *(Mensch)* to reject; **~zahlen** vt to repay, to pay back; **~ziehen** *(unreg)* vt to pull back; *(Angebot)* to withdraw ♦ vr to retire

Zuruf ['tsu:ruf] m shout, cry

Zusage ['tsu:za:gə] f promise; *(Annahme)* consent; **~n** vt to promise ♦ vi to accept; **jdm ~n** *(gefallen)* to agree with od please sb

zusammen [tsu'zamən] adv together; **Z~arbeit** f cooperation; **~arbeiten** vi to cooperate; **~beißen** *(unreg)* vt *(Zähne)* to clench; **~bleiben** *(unreg)* vi to stay together; **~brechen** *(unreg)* vi to collapse; *(Mensch auch)* to b̤eak down; **~bringen** *(unreg)* vt to bring od get together; *(Geld)* to get; *(Sätze)* to put together; **Z~bruch** m collapse; **~fassen** vt to summarize; *(vereinigen)* to unite; **Z~fassung** f summary, résumé; **~fügen** vt to join (together), to unite; **~halten** *(unreg)* vi to stick together; **Z~hang** m connection; **im/aus dem Z~hang** in/out of context; **~hängen** *(unreg)* vi to be connected od linked; **~kommen** *(unreg)* vi to meet, to assemble; *(sich ereignen)* to occur at once od together; **~legen** vt to put together; *(stapeln)*

to pile up; *(falten)* to fold; *(verbinden)* to combine, to unite; *(Termine, Fest)* to amalgamate; *(Geld)* to collect; **~nehmen** *(unreg)* vt to summon up ♦ vr to pull o.s. together; **alles ~genommen** all in all; **~passen** vi to go well together; to match; **~schließen** *(unreg)* vt, vr to join (together); **Z~schluß** m amalgamation; **~schreiben** *(unreg)* vt to write as one word; *(Bericht)* to put together; **Z~sein** *(-s)* nt get-together; **~setzen** vt to put together ♦ vr *(Stoff)* to be composed of; *(Menschen)* to get together; **Z~setzung** f composition; **~stellen** vt to put together; to compile; **Z~stoß** m collision; **~stoßen** *(unreg)* vi to collide; **~treffen** *(unreg)* vi to coincide; *(Menschen)* to meet; **~zählen** vt to add up; **~ziehen** *(unreg)* vt *(verengern)* to draw together; *(vereinigen)* to bring together; *(addieren)* to add up ♦ vr to shrink; *(sich bilden)* to form, to develop

zusätzlich ['tsu:zɛtslɪç] adj additional ♦ adv in addition

zuschauen ['tsu:ʃauən] vi to watch, to look on

Zuschauer(in) (-s, -) m(f) spectator ♦ pl *(THEAT)* audience sg

zuschicken ['tsu:ʃɪkən] vt: **jdm etw ~** to send od to forward (sth to sb)

Zuschlag ['tsu:ʃla:k] m extra charge, surcharge; **z~en** *(unreg)* vt *(Tür)* to slam; *(Ball)* to hit; *(bei Auktion)* to knock down; *(Steine etc)* to knock into shape ♦ vi *(Fenster, Tür)* to shut; *(Mensch)* to hit, to punch; **~karte** f *(EISENB)* surcharge ticket; **z~pflichtig** adj subject to surcharge

zuschneiden ['tsu:ʃnaɪdən] *(unreg)* vt to cut out; to cut to size

zuschrauben ['tsu:ʃraubən] vt to screw down od up

zuschreiben ['tsu:ʃraɪbən] *(unreg)* vt *(fig)* to ascribe, to attribute; *(COMM)* to credit

Zuschrift ['tsu:ʃrɪft] *f* letter, reply

zuschulden ['tsu:ʃʊldən] *adv*: **sich dat etw ~ kommen lassen** to make o.s. guilty of sth

Zuschuß ['tsu:ʃʊs] *m* subsidy, allowance

zusehen ['tsu:ze:ən] (*unreg*) *vi* to watch; (*dafür sorgen*) to take care; **jdm/etw ~** to watch sb/sth; **~ds** *adv* visibly

zusenden ['tsu:zɛndən] (*unreg*) *vt* to forward, to send on

zusichern ['tsu:zɪçərn] *vt*: **jdm etw ~** to assure sb of sth

zuspielen ['tsu:ʃpi:lən] *vt, vi* to pass

zuspitzen ['tsu:ʃpɪtsən] *vt* to sharpen ♦ *vr* (*Lage*) to become critical

zusprechen ['tsu:ʃprɛçən] (*unreg*) *vt* (*zuerkennen*) to award ♦ *vi* to speak; **jdm etw ~** to award sb sth *od* sth to sb; **jdm Trost ~** to comfort sb; **dem Essen/Alkohol ~** to eat/drink a lot

Zustand ['tsu:ʃtant] *m* state, condition; **z~e** ['tsu:ʃtɛndə] *adv*: **z~e bringen** to bring about; **z~e kommen** to come about

zuständig ['tsu:ʃtɛndɪç] *adj* responsible; **Z~keit** *f* competence, responsibility

zustehen ['tsu:ʃte:ən] (*unreg*) *vi*: **jdm ~** to be sb's right

zustellen ['tsu:ʃtɛlən] *vt* (*verstellen*) to block; (*Post etc*) to send

zustimmen ['tsu:ʃtɪmən] *vi* to agree

Zustimmung *f* agreement, consent

zustoßen ['tsu:ʃto:sən] (*unreg*) *vi* (*fig*) to happen

zutage [tsu:'ta:gə] *adv*: **~ bringen** to bring to light; **~ treten** to come to light

Zutaten ['tsu:ta:tən] *pl* ingredients

zuteilen ['tsu:taɪlən] *vt* (*Arbeit, Rolle*) to designate, assign; (*Aktien, Wohnung*) to allocate

zutiefst [tsu:'ti:fst] *adv* deeply

zutragen ['tsu:tra:gən] (*unreg*) *vt* to bring; (*Klatsch*) to tell ♦ *vr* to happen

zutrau- ['tsu:trao] *zW*: **Z~en** (-s) *nt*

trust (in); **~en** *vt*: **jdm etw ~en** to credit sb with sth; **~lich** *adj* trusting, friendly

zutreffen ['tsu:trɛfən] (*unreg*) *vi* to be correct; to apply

zutreffend *adj* (*richtig*) accurate; **Z~es bitte unterstreichen** please underline where applicable

Zutritt ['tsu:trɪt] *m* access, admittance

Zutun ['tsu:tu:n] (-s) *nt* assistance

zuverlässig ['tsu:fɛrlɛsɪç] *adj* reliable; **Z~keit** *f* reliability

zuversichtlich *adj* confident

zuviel [tsu:'fi:l] *adv* too much

zuvor [tsu:'fo:r] *adv* before, previously; **~kommen** (*unreg*) *vi* +*dat* to anticipate; **jdm ~kommen** to beat sb to it; **~kommend** *adj* obliging, courteous

Zuwachs ['tsu:vaks] (-es) *m* increase, growth; (*umg*) addition; **z~en** (*unreg*) *vi* to become overgrown; (*Wunde*) to heal (up)

zuwege [tsu:'ve:gə] *adv*: **etw ~ bringen** to accomplish sth

zuweilen [tsu:'vaɪlən] *adv* at times, now and then

zuweisen ['tsu:vaɪzən] (*unreg*) *vt* to assign, to allocate

zuwenden ['tsu:vɛndən] (*unreg*) *vt* (+*dat*) to turn (towards) ♦ *vr*: **sich jdm/etw ~** to devote o.s. to sb/sth; to turn to sb/sth; **jdm seine Aufmerksamkeit ~** to give sb one's attention

zuwenig [tsu:'ve:nɪç] *adv* too little

zuwider [tsu:'vi:dər] *adv*: **etw ist jdm ~** sb loathes sth, sb finds sth repugnant; **~handeln** *vi*: **einer Sache dat ~handeln** to act contrary to sth; **einem Gesetz ~handeln** to contravene a law

zuziehen ['tsu:tsi:ən] (*unreg*) *vt* (*schließen: Vorhang*) to draw, to close; (*herbeirufen: Experten*) to call in ♦ *vi* to move in, to come; **sich etw ~** (*Krankheit*) to catch sth; (*Zorn*) to incur sth

zuzüglich ['tsu:tsy:klɪç] *präp* +*gen*

plus, with the addition of

Zwang ['tsvaŋ] (-(e)s, -e) *m* compulsion, coercion

zwängen ['tsvɛŋən] *vt, vr* to squeeze

zwanglos *adj* informal

Zwangs- *zW:* **~arbeit** *f* forced labour; (*Strafe*) hard labour; **~lage** *f* predicament, tight corner; **z~läufig** *adj* necessary, inevitable

zwanzig ['tsvantsɪç] *num* twenty

zwar [tsva:r] *adv* to be sure, indeed; das ist ~ ..., aber ... that may be ... but ...; und ~ am Sonntag on Sunday to be precise; und ~ so schnell, daß ... in fact so quickly that ...

Zweck ['tsvɛk] (-(e)s, -e) *m* purpose, aim; es hat keinen ~ there's no point; **z~dienlich** *adj* practical; expedient

Zwecke *f* hobnail; (*Heft~*) drawing pin, thumbtack (*US*)

Zweck- *zW:* **z~los** *adj* pointless; **z~mäßig** *adj* suitable, appropriate; **z~s** *präp +gen* for the purpose of

zwei [tsvaɪ] *num* two; **~deutig** *adj* ambiguous; (*unanständig*) suggestive; **~erlei** *adj:* **~erlei** Stoff two different kinds of material; **~erlei** Meinung of differing opinions; **~fach** *adj* double

Zweifel ['tsvaɪfəl] (-s, -) *m* doubt; **z~haft** *adj* doubtful, dubious; **z~los** *adj* doubtless; **z~n** *vi:* (an etw *dat*) **z~n** to doubt (sth)

Zweig [tsvaɪk] (-(e)s, -e) *m* branch; **~stelle** *f* branch (office)

zwei- *zW:* **~hundert** *num* two hundred; **Z~kampf** *m* duel; **~mal** *adv* twice; **~sprachig** *adj* bilingual; **~spurig** *adj* (*AUT*) two-lane; **~stimmig** *adj* for two voices; **Z~taktmotor** *m* two-stroke engine

zweit [tsvaɪt] *adv:* **zu ~** together; (*bei mehreren Paaren*) in twos; **~beste(r, s)** *adj* second best; **~e(r, s)** *adj* second

zweiteilig *adj* (*Gruppe*) two-piece; (*Fernsehfilm*) two-part; (*Kleidung*) two-piece; **zweitens** *adv* secondly

zweitgrößte(r, s) *adj* second largest; **zweitklassig** *adj* second-class; **zweitletzte(r, s)** *adj* last but one, penultimate; **zweitrangig** *adj* second-rate

Zwerchfell ['tsvɛrçfɛl] *nt* diaphragm

Zwerg [tsvɛrk] (-(e)s, -e) *m* dwarf

Zwetsch(g)e ['tsvɛt∫(g)ə] *f* plum

Zwieback ['tsvi:bak] (-(e)s, -e) *m* rusk

Zwiebel ['tsvi:bəl] (-, -n) *f* onion; (*Blumen~*) bulb

Zwie- ['tsvi:] *zW:* **z~lichtig** *adj* shady, dubious; **z~spältig** *adj* (*Gefühle*) conflicting; (*Charakter*) contradictory; **~tracht** *f* discord, dissension

Zwilling ['tsvɪlɪŋ] (-s, -e) *m* twin; **~e** *pl* (*ASTROL*) Gemini

zwingen ['tsvɪŋən] (*unreg*) *vt* to force; **~d** *adj* (*Grund etc*) compelling

zwinkern ['tsvɪŋkərn] *vi* to blink; (*absichtlich*) to wink

Zwirn [tsvɪrn] (-(e)s, -e) *m* thread

zwischen ['tsvɪʃən] *präp* (+*akk* od *dat*) between; **Z~bemerkung** *f* (*incidental*) remark; **Z~ding** *nt* cross; **~durch** *adv* in between; (*räumlich*) here and there; **Z~ergebnis** *nt* intermediate result; **Z~fall** *m* incident; **Z~frage** *f* question; **Z~handel** *m* middlemen *pl*; middleman's trade; **Z~landung** *f* (*AVIAT*) stopover; **~menschlich** *adj* interpersonal; **Z~raum** *m* space; **Z~ruf** *m* interjection; **Z~zeit** *f* interval; in der **Z~zeit** in the interim, meanwhile

zwitschern ['tsvɪtʃərn] *vt, vi* to twitter, to chirp

zwo [tsvo:] *num* two

zwölf [tsvœlf] *num* twelve

Zyklus ['tsy:klos] (-, Zyklen) *m* cycle

Zylinder [tsi'lɪndər] (-s, -) *m* cylinder; (*Hut*) top hat

Zyniker ['tsy:nikər] (-s, -) *m* cynic

zynisch ['tsy:nɪʃ] *adj* cynical

Zypern ['tsy:pərn] *nt* Cyprus

Zyste ['tsystə] *f* cyst

z.Z(t). *abk* = **zur Zeit**

ENGLISH - GERMAN
ENGLISCH - DEUTSCH

A

A [eɪ] n (MUS) A nt; ~ **road** Hauptverkehrsstraße f

KEYWORD

a [eɪ, ə] (before vowel or silent h: an) indef art **1** (before noun) eine; ein; a **woman** eine Frau; a **book** ein Buch; an **eagle** ein Adler; **she's a doctor** sie ist Ärztin

2 (instead of the number one) ein; eine; a **year ago** vor einem Jahr; a **hundred/thousand** etc pounds (ein) hundert/(ein) tausend etc Pfund

3 (in expressing ratios, prices etc) pro; **3 a day/week** 3 pro Tag/Woche, 3 am Tag/in der Woche; **10 km an hour** 10 km pro Stunde/in der Stunde

A.A. n abbr = **Alcoholics Anonymous**; (BRIT) **Automobile Association**

A.A.A. (US) n abbr = **American Automobile Association**

aback [ə'bæk] adv: **to be taken ~** verblüfft sein

abandon [ə'bændən] vt (give up) aufgeben; (desert) verlassen ♦ n Hingabe f

abate [ə'beɪt] vi nachlassen, sich legen

abattoir ['æbətwɑ:*] (BRIT) n Schlachthaus nt

abbey ['æbɪ] n Abtei f

abbot ['æbət] n Abt m

abbreviate [ə'bri:vɪeɪt] vt abkürzen

abbreviation [əbri:vɪ'eɪʃən] n Abkürzung f

abdicate ['æbdɪkeɪt] vt aufgeben ♦ vi abdanken

abdomen ['æbdəmən] n Unterleib m

abduct [æb'dʌkt] vt entführen

aberration [æbə'reɪʃən] n (geistige) Verwirrung f

abet [ə'bet] vt see **aid**

abeyance [ə'beɪəns] n: **in ~** in der Schwebe; (disuse) außer Kraft

abhor [əb'hɔ:*] vt verabscheuen

abide [ə'baɪd] vt vertragen; leiden; ~ **by** vi sich halten an +acc

ability [ə'bɪlɪtɪ] n (power) Fähigkeit f; (skill) Geschicklichkeit f

abject ['æbdʒekt] adj (liar) übel; (poverty) größte(r, s); (apology) zerknirscht

ablaze [ə'bleɪz] adj in Flammen

able ['eɪbl] adj geschickt, fähig; **to be ~ to do sth** etw tun können; ~-**bodied** adj kräftig; (seaman) Vollmatrose m

ably ['eɪblɪ] adv geschickt

abnormal [æb'nɔ:məl] adj regelwidrig, abnorm

aboard [ə'bɔ:d] adv, prep an Bord +gen

abode [ə'bəʊd] n: **of no fixed ~** ohne festen Wohnsitz

abolish [ə'bɒlɪʃ] vt abschaffen

abolition [æbə'lɪʃən] n Abschaffung f

abominable [ə'bɒmɪnəbl] adj scheußlich

aborigine [æbə'rɪdʒɪnɪ] n Ureinwohner m

abort [ə'bɔ:t] vt abtreiben; fehlgebären; ~**ion** [ə'bɔ:ʃən] n Abtreibung f; (miscarriage) Fehlgeburt f; ~**ive** adj mißlungen

abound [ə'baʊnd] vi im Überfluß vorhanden sein; **to~ in** im Überfluß haben an +dat

KEYWORD

about [ə'baʊt] adv **1** (approximately) etwa, ungefähr; **about a hundred/thousand** etc etwa hundert/tausend etc; **at about 2 o'clock** etwa um 2 Uhr; **I've just about finished** ich bin gerade fertig

2 (referring to place) herum, umher; **to leave things lying about** Sachen herumliegen lassen; **to run/walk** etc about herumrennen/gehen etc

3: to be about to do sth im Begriff sein, etw zu tun; **he was about to go to bed** er wollte gerade ins Bett gehen

♦ prep **1** (relating to) über +acc; **a book about London** ein Buch über London; **what is it about?** worum geht es?; (book etc) wovon handelt es?; **we talked about it** wir haben darüber geredet; **what** or **how about doing this?** wollen wir das machen?

2 (referring to place) um (... herum); **to walk about the town** in der Stadt herumgehen; **her clothes were scattered about the room** ihre Kleider waren über das ganze Zimmer verstreut

about-face [ə'baut'feɪs] n Kehrtwendung f
about-turn [ə'baut'tɜːn] n Kehrtwendung f
above [ə'bʌv] adv oben ♦ prep über; ~ **all** vor allem; ~ **board** adj offen, ehrlich
abrasive [ə'breɪzɪv] adj Abschleif-; (personality) zermürbend, aufreibend
abreast [ə'brest] adv nebeneinander; **to keep** ~ **of** Schritt halten mit
abridge [ə'brɪdʒ] vt (ab)kürzen
abroad [ə'brɔːd] adv (be) im Ausland; (go) ins Ausland
abrupt [ə'brʌpt] adj (sudden) abrupt, jäh; (curt) schroff
abscess ['æbsɪs] n Geschwür nt
abscond [əb'skɒnd] vi flüchten, sich davonmachen
abseil ['æbsaɪl] vi (also: ~ down) sich abseilen
absence ['æbsəns] n Abwesenheit f
absent ['æbsənt] adj abwesend, nicht da; (lost in thought) geistesabwesend; ~**ee** [æbsən'tiː] n Abwesende(r) m; ~**eeism** [æbsən'tiːɪzəm] n Fehlen nt (am Arbeitsplatz in der Schule); ~**-minded** adj zerstreut
absolute ['æbsəluːt] adj absolut,

(pow- er) unumschränkt; (rubbish) vollkommen, rein; ~**ly** [-'luːtlɪ] adv absolut, vollkommen; ~**ly!** ganz bestimmt!
absolve [əb'zɒlv] vt entbinden; freisprechen
absorb [əb'zɔːb] vt aufsaugen, absorbieren; (fig) ganz in Anspruch nehmen, fesseln; **to be** ~**ed in a book** in ein Buch vertieft sein; ~**ent cotton** (US) n Verbandwatte f; ~**ing** adj aufsaugend; (fig) packend
absorption [əb'zɔːpʃən] n Aufsaugung f, Absorption f; (fig) Versunkenheit f
abstain [əb'steɪn] vi (in vote) sich enthalten; **to** ~ **from** (keep from) sich enthalten +gen
abstemious [əb'stiːmɪəs] adj enthaltsam
abstention [əb'stenʃən] n (in vote) (Stimm)enthaltung f
abstinence ['æbstɪnəns] n Enthaltsamkeit f
abstract ['æbstrækt] adj abstrakt
absurd [əb'sɜːd] adj absurd
abundance [ə'bʌndəns] n: ~ (**of**) Überfluß m (an +dat)
abundant [ə'bʌndənt] adj reichlich
abuse [n ə'bjuːs, vb ə'bjuːz] n (rude language) Beschimpfung f; (ill usage) Mißbrauch m; (bad practice) (Amts)mißbrauch m ♦ vt (misuse) mißbrauchen
abusive [ə'bjuːsɪv] adj beleidigend, Schimpf-
abysmal [ə'bɪzməl] adj scheußlich; (ignorance) bodenlos
abyss [ə'bɪs] n Abgrund m
AC abbr (= alternating current) Wechselstrom m
academic [ækə'demɪk] adj akademisch; (theoretical) theoretisch ♦ n Akademiker(in) m(f)
academy [ə'kædəmɪ] n (school) Hochschule f; (society) Akademie f
accelerate [æk'seləreɪt] vi schneller werden; (AUT) Gas geben ♦ vt beschleunigen
acceleration [ækselə'reɪʃən] Be-

schleunigung f

accelerator [ək'seləreitə*] n Gas(pedal) nt

accent ['æksənt] n Akzent m, Tonfall m; (mark) Akzent m; (stress) Betonung f

accept [ək'sept] vt (take) annehmen; (agree to) akzeptieren; ~**able** adj annehmbar; ~**ance** n Annahme f

access ['ækses] n Zugang m; ~**ible** [æk'sesɪbl] adj (easy to approach) zugänglich; (within reach) (leicht) erreichbar

accessory [æk'sesərɪ] n Zubehörteil nt; **toilet accessories** Toilettenartikel pl

accident ['æksɪdənt] n Unfall m; (coincidence) Zufall m; by ~ zufällig; ~**al** [æksɪ'dentl] adj unbeabsichtigt; ~**ally** [æksɪ'dentəlɪ] adv zufällig; ~**-prone** adj: to be ~-**prone** zu Unfällen neigen

acclaim [ə'kleɪm] vt zujubeln +dat ♦ n Beifall m

acclimate [ə'klaɪmət] (US) vt = ac**climatize**

acclimatize [ə'klaɪmətaɪz] vt: to be**come** ~**d** (to) sich gewöhnen (an +acc), sich akklimatisieren (in +dat)

accolade [ə'kɒleɪd] n Auszeichnung f

accommodate [ə'kɒmədeɪt] vt unterbringen; (hold) Platz haben für; (oblige) (aus)helfen +dat

accommodating [ə'kɒmədeɪtɪŋ] adj entgegenkommend

accommodation [ə'kɒmə'deɪʃən] (US ~s) n Unterkunft f

accompany [ə'kʌmpənɪ] vt begleiten

accomplice [ə'kʌmplɪs] n Helfershelfer m, Komplize m

accomplish [ə'kʌmplɪʃ] vt (fulfil) durchführen; (finish) vollenden; (aim) erreichen; ~**ed** adj vollendet, ausgezeichnet; ~**ment** n (skill) Fähigkeit f; (completion) Vollendung f; (feat) Leistung f

accord [ə'kɔːd] n Übereinstimmung f ♦ vt gewähren; **of one's own** ~ freiwillig; ~**ing** to nach, laut +gen;

~**ance** n: in ~**ance with** in Übereinstimmung mit; ~**ingly** adv danach, dementsprechend

accordion [ə'kɔːdɪən] n Akkordeon nt

accost [ə'kɒst] vt ansprechen

account [ə'kaʊnt] n (bill) Rechnung f; (narrative) Bericht m; (report) Rechenschaftsbericht m; (in bank) Konto nt; (importance) Geltung f; ~s npl (FIN) Bücher pl; on ~ auf Rechnung; of no ~ ohne Bedeutung; on no ~ keinesfalls; on ~ of wegen; to take into ~ berücksichtigen; ~ for vt fus (expenditure) Rechenschaft ablegen für; how do you ~ for that? wie erklären Sie (sich) das?; ~**able** adj verantwortlich; ~**ancy** [ə'kaʊntənsɪ] n Buchhaltung f; ~**ant** [ə'kaʊntənt] n Wirtschaftsprüfer m(f); ~ **number** n Kontonummer f

accredited [ə'kredɪtd] adj (offiziell) zugelassen

accrue [ə'kruː] vi sich ansammeln

accumulate [ə'kjuːmjʊleɪt] vt ansammeln ♦ vi sich ansammeln

accuracy [ə'kjʊərəsɪ] n Genauigkeit f

accurate ['ækjʊrət] adj genau; ~**ly** adv genau, richtig

accusation [ækjʊ'zeɪʃən] n Anklage f, Beschuldigung f

accuse [ə'kjuːz] vt anklagen, beschuldigen; ~**d** n Angeklagte(r) mf

accustom [ə'kʌstəm] vt: to ~ **sb** (to **sth**) jdn (an etw acc) gewöhnen; ~**ed** adj gewohnt

ace [eɪs] n As nt; (inf) As nt, Kanone f

ache [eɪk] n Schmerz m ♦ vi (be sore) schmerzen, weh tun

achieve [ə'tʃiːv] vt zustande bringen; (aim) erreichen; ~**ment** n Leistung f; (act) Erreichen nt

acid ['æsɪd] n Säure f ♦ adj sauer, scharf; ~ **rain** n Saure(r) Regen m

acknowledge [ək'nɒlɪdʒ] vt (receipt) bestätigen; (admit) zugeben; ~**ment** n Anerkennung f; (letter) Empfangsbestätigung f

acne ['æknɪ] n Akne f

acorn ['eɪkɔːn] n Eichel f

acoustic [ə'kuːstɪk] adj akustisch; ~s npl Akustik f

acquaint [ə'kweɪnt] vt vertraut machen; to be ~ed with sb mit jdm bekannt sein; ~ance n (person) Bekannte(r) mf; (knowledge) Kenntnis f

acquiesce [ækwɪ'es] vi: to ~ (in) sich abfinden (mit)

acquire [ə'kwaɪə*] vt erwerben

acquisition [ækwɪ'zɪʃən] n Errungenschaft f; (act) Erwerb m

acquisitive [ə'kwɪzɪtɪv] adj gewinnsüchtig

acquit [ə'kwɪt] vt (free) freisprechen; to ~ o.s. well sich bewähren; ~tal n Freispruch m

acre ['eɪkə*] n Morgen m

acrid ['ækrɪd] adj (smell, taste) bitter; (smoke) beißend

acrimonious [ækrɪ'məunɪəs] adj bitter

acrobat ['ækrəbæt] n Akrobat m

across [ə'krɒs] prep über +acc ♦ adv hinüber, herüber; he lives ~ the river er wohnt auf der anderen Seite des Flusses; ten metres ~ zehn Meter breit; he lives ~ from us er wohnt uns gegenüber; to run/swim ~ hinüberlaufen/schwimmen

acrylic [ə'krɪlɪk] adj Acryl-

act [ækt] n (deed) Tat f; (JUR) Gesetz nt; (THEAT) Akt m; (: turn) Nummer f ♦ vi (take action) handeln; (behave) sich verhalten; (pretend) vorgeben; (THEAT) spielen ♦ vt (in play) spielen; to ~ as fungieren als; ~ing adj stellvertretend ♦ n Schauspielkunst f; (performance) Aufführung f

action ['ækʃən] n (deed) Tat f, Handlung f; (motion) Bewegung f; (way of working) Funktionieren nt; (battle) Einsatz m, Gefecht nt; (lawsuit) Klage f, Prozeß m; out of ~ (person) nicht einsatzfähig; (thing) außer Betrieb; to take ~ etwas unternehmen; ~ replay n (TV) Wiederholung f

activate ['æktɪveɪt] vt (mechanism) betätigen; (CHEM, PHYS) aktivieren

active ['æktɪv] adj (brisk) rege, tatkräftig; (working) aktiv; (GRAM) aktiv, Tätigkeits-; ~ly adv aktiv; (dislike) offen

activity [æk'tɪvɪtɪ] n Aktivität f; (doings) Unternehmungen pl; (occupation) Tätigkeit f

actor ['æktə*] n Schauspieler m

actress ['æktrɪs] n Schauspielerin f

actual ['æktjuəl] adj wirklich; ~ly adv tatsächlich; ~ly no eigentlich nicht

acumen ['ækjumən] n Scharfsinn m

acute [ə'kjuːt] adj (severe) heftig, akut; (keen) scharfsinnig

ad [æd] n abbr = advertisement

A.D. adv abbr (= Anno Domini) n.Chr.

Adam ['ædəm] n Adam m

adamant ['ædəmənt] adj eisern; hartnäckig

adapt [ə'dæpt] vt anpassen ♦ vi: to ~ (to) sich anpassen (an +acc); ~able adj anpassungsfähig; ~ation [ædæp'teɪʃən] n (THEAT etc) Bearbeitung f; (adjustment) Anpassung f; ~er n (ELEC) Zwischenstecker m; ~or n (ELEC) Zwischenstecker m

add [æd] vt (join) hinzufügen; (numbers: also: ~ up) addieren; ~ up vi (make sense) stimmen; ~ up to vt fus ausmachen

adder ['ædə*] n Kreuzotter f, Natter f

addict ['ædɪkt] n Süchtige(r) mf; ~ed [ə'dɪktɪd] adj: ~ed to -süchtig; ~ion [ə'dɪkʃən] n Sucht f; ~ive adj: to be ~ive süchtig machen

addition [ə'dɪʃən] n Anhang m, Addition f; (MATH) Addition f, Zusammenzählen nt; in ~ zusätzlich, außerdem; ~al adj zusätzlich, weiter

additive ['ædɪtɪv] n Zusatz m

address [ə'dres] n Adresse f; (speech) Ansprache f ♦ vt (letter) adressieren; (speak to) ansprechen; (make speech to) eine Ansprache halten an +acc

adept ['ædept] adj geschickt; to be

~ at gut sein in +dat

adequate [ˈædɪkwɪt] *adj* angemessen

adhere [ədˈhɪə*] *vi:* to ~ to haften an +*dat;* *(fig)* festhalten an +*dat*

adhesive [ədˈhiːzɪv] *adj* klebend; Kleb(e)- ♦ *n* Klebstoff *m;* ~ **tape** *n* (*BRIT*) Klebestreifen *m;* (*US*) Heftpflaster *nt*

ad hoc [ædˈhɒk] *adj* (*decision, committee*) Ad-hoc- ♦ *adv* (*decide, appoint*) ad hoc

adjacent [əˈdʒeɪsənt] *adj* benachbart; ~ **to** angrenzend an +*acc*

adjective [ˈædʒektɪv] *n* Adjektiv *nt,* Eigenschaftswort *nt*

adjoining [əˈdʒɔɪnɪŋ] *adj* benachbart, Neben-

adjourn [əˈdʒɜːn] *vt* vertagen ♦ *vi* abbrechen

adjudicate [əˈdʒuːdɪkeɪt] *vi* entscheiden, ein Urteil fällen

adjust [əˈdʒʌst] *vt* (*alter*) anpassen; (*put right*) regulieren, richtig stellen ♦ *vi* sich anpassen; ~**able** *adj* verstellbar

ad-lib [ædˈlɪb] *vt, vi* improvisieren ♦ *adv:* **ad lib** aus dem Stegreif

administer [ədˈmɪnɪstə*] *vt* (*manage*) verwalten; (*dispense*) ausüben; (*justice*) sprechen; (*medicine*) geben

administration [ədmɪnɪsˈtreɪʃən] *n* Verwaltung *f;* (*POL*) Regierung *f*

administrative [ədˈmɪnɪstrətɪv] *adj* Verwaltungs-

administrator [ədˈmɪnɪstreɪtə*] *n* Verwaltungsbeamte(r) *m*

admiral [ˈædmərəl] *n* Admiral *m*

Admiralty [ˈædmərəltɪ] (*BRIT*) *n* Admiralität *f*

admiration [ædmɪˈreɪʃən] *n* Bewunderung *f*

admire [ədˈmaɪə*] *vt* (*respect*) bewundern; (*love*) verehren; ~**r** *n* Bewunderer *m*

admission [ədˈmɪʃən] *n* (*entrance*) Einlaß *m;* (*fee*) Eintritt(spreis *m*) *m;* (*confession*) Geständnis *nt*

admit [ədˈmɪt] *vt* (*let in*) einlassen; (*confess*) gestehen; (*accept*) anerkennen; ~**tance** *n* Zulassung *f;*

~**tedly** *adv* zugegebenermaßen

admonish [ədˈmɒnɪʃ] *vt* ermahnen

ad nauseam [ædˈnɔːsɪæm] *adv* (*repeat, talk*) endlos

ado [əˈduː] *n:* **without more** ~ ohne weitere Umstände

adolescence [ædəˈlesns] *n* Jugendalter *nt*

adolescent [ædəˈlesnt] *adj* jugendlich ♦ *n* Jugendliche(r) *mf*

adopt [əˈdɒpt] *vt* (*child*) adoptieren; (*idea*) übernehmen; ~**ion** [əˈdɒpʃən] *n* Adoption *f;* Übernahme *f*

adore [əˈdɔː*] *vt* anbeten; verehren

adorn [əˈdɔːn] *vt* schmücken

Adriatic [eɪdrɪˈætɪk] *n:* **the** ~ (**Sea**) die Adria

adrift [əˈdrɪft] *adv* Wind und Wellen preisgegeben

adult [ˈædʌlt] *n* Erwachsene(r) *mf*

adultery [əˈdʌltərɪ] *n* Ehebruch *m*

advance [ədˈvɑːns] *n* (*progress*) Vorrücken *nt;* (*money*) Vorschuß *m* ♦ *vt* (*move forward*) vorrücken; (*money*) vorschießen; (*argument*) vorbringen ♦ *vi* vorwärtsgehen; **in** ~ im voraus; ~**d** *adj* (*ahead*) vorgerückt; (*modern*) fortgeschritten; (*study*) für Fortgeschrittene; ~**ment** *n* Förderung *f;* (*promotion*) Beförderung *f*

advantage [ədˈvɑːntɪdʒ] *n* Vorteil *m;* **to have an** ~ **over sb** jdm gegenüber im Vorteil sein; **to take** ~ **of** (*misuse*) ausnutzen; (*profit from*) Nutzen ziehen aus; ~**ous** [ædvənˈteɪdʒəs] *adj* vorteilhaft

advent [ˈædvent] *n* Ankunft *f;* **A**~ Advent *m*

adventure [ədˈventʃə*] *n* Abenteuer *nt*

adventurous [ədˈventʃərəs] *adj* abenteuerlich, waghalsig

adverb [ˈædvɜːb] *n* Adverb *nt,* Umstandswort *nt*

adversary [ˈædvəsərɪ] *n* Gegner *m*

adverse [ˈædvɜːs] *adj* widrig

adversity [ədˈvɜːsɪtɪ] *n* Widrigkeit *f,* Mißgeschick *nt*

advert [ˈædvɜːt] *n* Anzeige *f*

advertise ['ædvətaɪz] vt werben für ♦ vi annoncieren; **to ~ for sth** etw (per Anzeige) suchen

advertisement [əd'vəːtɪsmənt] n Anzeige f, Inserat nt

advertiser ['ædvətaɪzə*] n (in newspaper etc) Inserent m

advertising ['ædvətaɪzɪŋ] n Werbung f

advice [əd'vaɪs] n Rat(schlag) m; (notification) Benachrichtigung f

advisable [əd'vaɪzəbl] adj ratsam

advise [əd'vaɪz] vt: **to ~ (sb)** (jdm) raten

advisedly [əd'vaɪzɪdlɪ] adv (deliberately) bewußt

adviser n Berater m

advisory [əd'vaɪzərɪ] adj beratend, Beratungs-

advocate [vb 'ædvəkeɪt, n 'ædvəkɪt] vt vertreten ♦ n Befürworter(in) m(f)

Aegean [iː'dʒiːən] n: **the ~ (Sea)** die Ägäis

aerial ['ɛərɪəl] n Antenne f ♦ adj Luft-

aerobics [ɛər'əʊbɪks] n Aerobic nt

aerodynamic ['ɛərəʊdaɪ'næmɪk] adj aerodynamisch

aeroplane ['ɛərəpleɪn] n Flugzeug nt

aerosol ['ɛərəsɒl] n Aerosol nt; Sprühdose f

aesthetic [ɪs'θetɪk] adj ästhetisch

afar [ə'faː*] adv: **from ~** aus der Ferne

affable ['æfəbl] adj umgänglich

affair [ə'fɛə*] n (concern) Angelegenheit f; (event) Ereignis nt; (love ~) Verhältnis n; **~s** npl (business) Geschäfte pl

affect [ə'fekt] vt (influence) (ein)wirken auf +acc; (move deeply) bewegen; **this change doesn't ~ us** diese Änderung betrifft uns nicht; **~ed** adj affektiert, gekünstelt

affection [ə'fekʃən] n Zuneigung f; **~ate** [ə'fekʃənɪt] adj liebevoll

affiliated [ə'fɪlɪeɪtɪd] adj angeschlossen

affinity [ə'fɪnɪtɪ] n (attraction) gegenseitige Anziehung f; (relationship) Verwandtschaft f

affirmation [æfə'meɪʃən] n Behauptung f

affirmative [ə'fəːmətɪv] adj bestätigend

affix [ə'fɪks] vt aufkleben, anheften

afflict [ə'flɪkt] vt quälen; heimsuchen

affluence ['æfluəns] n (wealth) Wohlstand m

affluent ['æfluənt] adj wohlhabend, Wohlstands-

afford [ə'fɔːd] vt sich dat leisten; (yield) bieten, einbringen

affront [ə'frʌnt] n Beleidigung f

Afghanistan [æf'gænɪstɑːn] n Afghanistan n

afield [ə'fiːld] adv: **far ~** weit fort

afloat [ə'fləʊt] adj: **to be ~** schwimmen

afoot [ə'fʊt] adv im Gang

afraid [ə'freɪd] adj ängstlich; **to be ~ of** Angst haben vor +dat; **to be ~ to do sth** sich scheuen, etw zu tun; **I am ~ I have ...** ich habe leider ...; **I'm ~ so/not** leider/leider nicht; **I am ~ that ...** ich fürchte(, daß) ...

afresh [ə'freʃ] adv von neuem

Africa ['æfrɪkə] n Afrika nt; **~n** adj afrikanisch ♦ n Afrikaner(in) m(f)

aft [ɑːft] adv achtern

after ['ɑːftə*] prep nach; (following, seeking) hinter ... dat ... her; (in imitation) nach, im Stil von ♦ adv: **soon ~** bald danach ♦ conj nachdem; **what are you ~?** was wollen Sie?; ~ **he left** nachdem er gegangen war; ~ **you!** nach Ihnen!; ~ **all** letzten Endes; ~ **having shaved** als er sich rasiert hatte; **~effects** npl Nachwirkungen pl; **~math** n Auswirkungen pl; **~noon** n Nachmittag m; **~s** (inf) n (dessert) Nachtisch m; **~-sales service** (BRIT) n Kundendienst m; **~-shave (lotion)** n Rasierwasser nt; **~thought** n nachträgliche(r) Einfall m; **~wards** adv danach, nachher

again [ə'gen] adv wieder, noch einmal; (besides) außerdem, ferner; ~

and ~ immer wieder

against [ə'genst] *prep* gegen

age [eɪdʒ] *n* (*of person*) Alter *nt*; (*in history*) Zeitalter *nt* ♦ *vi* altern, alt werden ♦ *vt* älter machen; **to come of** ~ mündig werden; **20 years of** ~ 20 Jahre alt; **it's been** ~**s since** ... es ist ewig her, seit ...; **~d** adj ... Jahre alt, -jährig; ['eɪdʒɪd] (*elderly*) betagt ♦ *npl*: **the** ~ *die Alten pl*; ~ **group** *n* Altersgruppe *f*; ~ **limit** *n* Altersgrenze *f*

agency ['eɪdʒənsɪ] *n* Agentur *f*; Vermittlung *f*; (*CHEM*) Wirkung *f*; **through** *or* **by the** ~ **of** ... mit Hilfe von ...

agenda [ə'dʒendə] *n* Tagesordnung *f*

agent ['eɪdʒənt] *n* (*COMM*) Vertreter *m*; (*spy*) Agent *m*

aggravate ['ægrəveɪt] *vt* (*make worse*) verschlimmern; (*irritate*) reizen

aggregate ['ægrɪgɪt] *n* Summe *f*

aggression [ə'greʃən] *n* Aggression *f*

aggressive [ə'gresɪv] *adj* aggressiv

aggrieved [ə'griːvd] *adj* bedrückt, verletzt

aghast [ə'gɑːst] *adj* entsetzt

agile ['ædʒaɪl] *adj* flink, agil; (*mind*) rege

agitate ['ædʒɪteɪt] *vt* rütteln; **to** ~ **for sth** sich stark machen für

ago [ə'gəʊ] *adv*: **two days** ~ vor zwei Tagen; **not long** ~ vor kurzem; **it's so long** ~ es ist schon so lange her

agog [ə'gɒg] *adj* gespannt

agonizing ['ægənaɪzɪŋ] *adj* quälend

agony ['ægənɪ] *n* Qual *f*; **to be in** ~ Qualen leiden

agree [ə'griː] *vt* (*date*) vereinbaren ♦ *vi* (*have same opinion, correspond*) übereinstimmen; (*consent*) zustimmen; (*be in harmony*) sich vertragen; **to** ~ **to sth** einer Sache *dat* zustimmen; **to** ~ **that** ... (*admit*) zugeben, daß ...; **to** ~ **to do sth** sich bereit erklären, etw zu tun; **garlic doesn't** ~ **with me** Knoblauch vertrage ich nicht; **I** ~ einverstanden,

ich stimme zu; **to** ~ **on sth** sich auf etw *acc* einigen; **~able** *adj* (*pleasing*) liebenswürdig; (*willing to consent*) einverstanden; **~d** *adj* vereinbart; **~ment** *n* (*agreeing*) Übereinstimmung *f*, (*contract*) Vereinbarung *f*, Vertrag *m*; **to be in** ~**ment** übereinstimmen

agricultural [ægrɪ'kʌltʃərəl] *adj* landwirtschaftlich, Landwirtschafts-

agriculture ['ægrɪkʌltʃə*] *n* Landwirtschaft *f*

aground [ə'graʊnd] *adv*: **to run** ~ auf Grund laufen

ahead [ə'hed] *adv* vorwärts; **to be** ~ voraus sein; **~ of time** der Zeit voraus; **go right** *or* **straight** ~ gehen Sie geradeaus; fahren Sie geradeaus

aid [eɪd] *n* (*assistance*) Hilfe *f*, (*person*) Hilfe *f*; (*thing*) Hilfsmittel *nt* ♦ *vt* unterstützen, helfen +*dat*; **to** ~ **sb to do sth** jdm dabei helfen, etw zu tun; **to** ~ **and abet sb** jdm Beihilfe leisten

aide [eɪd] *n* (*person*) Gehilfe *m*; (*MIL*) Adjutant *m*

AIDS [eɪdz] *n abbr* (= *acquired immune deficiency syndrome*) Aids *nt*

ailing ['eɪlɪŋ] *adj* kränkelnd

ailment ['eɪlmənt] *n* Leiden *nt*

aim [eɪm] *vt* (*gun, camera*) richten ♦ *vi* (*with gun; also: take* ~) zielen; (*intend*) beabsichtigen ♦ *n* (*intention*) Absicht *f*, Ziel *nt*; (*pointing*) Zielen *nt*, Richten *nt*; **to** ~ **at sth** auf etw *acc* richten; (*fig*) etw anstreben; **to** ~ **to do sth** vorhaben, etw zu tun; **~less** *adj* ziellos; **~lessly** *adv* ziellos

ain't [eɪnt] (*inf*) = **am not; are not; is not; has not; have not**

air [eə*] *n* Luft *f*; (*manner*) Miene *f*, Anschein *m*; (*MUS*) Melodie *f* ♦ *vt* lüften; (*fig*) an die Öffentlichkeit bringen ♦ *cpd* Luft-; **by** ~ (*travel*) auf dem Luftweg; **to be on the** ~ (*RADIO, TV*): *programme*) gesendet werden; **~bed** (*BRIT*) *n* Luftmatratze *f*; **~borne** *adj* in der Luft; **~-conditioned** *adj* mit Klimaanlage-

~-conditioning n Klimaanlage f; **~craft** n Flugzeug nt, Maschine f; **~craft carrier** n Flugzeugträger m; **~field** n Flugplatz m; **~ force** n Luftwaffe f; **~ freshener** n Raumspray nt; **~gun** n Maschinengewehr nt; **~hostess** (BRIT) n Stewardeß f; **~letter** (BRIT) n Luftpostbrief m; **~lift** n Luftbrücke f; **~line** n Luftverkehrsgesellschaft f; **~liner** n Verkehrsflugzeug nt; **~lock** n Luftblase f; **~mail** n: **by ~mail** mit Luftpost; **~plane** (US) n Flugzeug nt; **~port** n Flughafen m, Flugplatz m; **~ raid** n Luftangriff m; **~sick** adj luftkrank; **~space** n Luftraum m; **~strip** n Landestreifen m; **~ terminal** n Terminal m; **~tight** adj luftdicht; **~ traffic controller** n Fluglotse m; **~y** adj luftig; (manner) leichtfertig

aisle [aıl] n Gang m

ajar [ə'dʒɑː*] adv angelehnt; einen Spalt offen

akin [ə'kın] adj: **~ to** ähnlich +dat

alacrity [ə'lækrıtı] n Bereitwilligkeit f

alarm [ə'lɑːm] n (warning) Alarm m; (bell etc) Alarmanlage f; (anxiety) Sorge f ♦ vt erschrecken; **~ call** n (in hotel etc) Weckruf m; **~ clock** n Wecker m

alas [ə'læs] excl ach

Albania [æl'beınıə] n Albanien nt

albeit [ɔːl'biːıt] conj obgleich

album [ælbəm] n Album nt

alcohol [ælkəhɒl] n Alkohol m; **~ic** [ælkə'hɒlık] adj (drink) alkoholisch ♦ n Alkoholiker(in) m(f); **~ism** n Alkoholismus m

ale [eıl] n Ale nt

alert [ə'lɜːt] adj wachsam ♦ n Alarm m ♦ vt alarmieren; **to be on the ~** wachsam sein

algebra [ældʒıbrə] n Algebra f

Algeria [æl'dʒıərıə] n Algerien nt

alias [eılıəs] adv alias ♦ n Deckname m

alibi [ælıbaı] n Alibi nt

alien [eılıən] n Ausländer m ♦ adj (foreign) ausländisch; (strange) fremd; **~ to** fremd +dat; **~ate** vt

entfremden

alight [ə'laıt] adj brennend; (of building) in Flammen ♦ vi (descend) aussteigen; (bird) sich setzen

align [ə'laın] vt ausrichten

alike [ə'laık] adj gleich, ähnlich ♦ adv gleich, ebenso; **to look ~** sich dat ähnlich sehen

alimony [ælımənı] n Unterhalt m, Alimente pl

alive [ə'laıv] adj (living) lebend; (lively) lebendig, aufgeweckt; **~ (with)** (full of) voll (von), wimmelnd (von)

---

all [ɔːl] adj alle(r, s); **all day/night** den ganzen Tag/die ganze Nacht; **all men are equal** alle Menschen sind gleich; **all five came** alle fünf kamen; **all the books/food** die ganzen Bücher/das ganze Essen; **all the time** die ganze Zeit (über); **all his life** sein ganzes Leben (lang)

♦ pron 1 alles; **I ate it all, I ate all of it** ich habe alles gegessen; **all of us/the boys went** wir gingen alle/alle Jungen gingen; **we all sat down** wir setzten uns alle

2 (in phrases): **above all** vor allem; **after all** schließlich; **at all: not at all** (in answer to question) überhaupt nicht; (in answer to thanks) gern geschehen; **I'm not at all tired** ich bin überhaupt nicht müde; **anything at all will do** es ist egal, welche(r, s); **all in all** alles in allem

♦ adv ganz; **all alone** ganz allein; **it's not as hard as all that** so schwer ist es nun auch wieder nicht; **all the more/the better** um so mehr/besser; **all but** fast; **the score is 2 all** es steht 2 zu 2

allay [ə'leı] vt (fears) beschwichtigen

all clear n Entwarnung f

allegation [ælı'geıʃən] n Behauptung f

allege [ə'ledʒ] vt (declare) behaupten; (falsely) vorgeben; **~dly**

[ə'ledʒɪdlɪ] *adv* angeblich

allegiance [ə'liːdʒəns] *n* Treue *f*

allergic [ə'lɜːdʒɪk] *adj*: ~ (to) allergisch (gegen)

allergy ['ælədʒɪ] *n* Allergie *f*

alleviate [ə'liːvɪeɪt] *vt* lindern

alley ['ælɪ] *n* Gasse *f*, Durchgang *m*

alliance [ə'laɪəns] *n* Bund *m*, Allianz *f*

allied ['ælaɪd] *adj* vereinigt; (*powers*) alliiert; ~ (to) verwandt (mit)

alligator ['ælɪgeɪtə*] *n* Alligator *m*

all-in ['ɔːlɪn] (*BRIT*) *adj*, *adv* (*charge*) alles inbegriffen, Gesamt-; ~ **wrestling** *n* Freistilringen *nt*

all-night ['ɔːl'naɪt] *adj* (*café*, *cinema*) die ganze Nacht geöffnet, Nacht-

allocate ['æləkeɪt] *vt* zuteilen

allot [ə'lɒt] *vt* zuteilen; ~**ment** *n* (*share*) Anteil *m*; (*plot*) Schrebergarten *m*

all-out ['ɔːl'aʊt] *adj*, *adv* total; **all out** mit voller Kraft

allow [ə'laʊ] *vt* (*permit*) erlauben (*sb jdm*), gestatten; (*grant*) bewilligen; (*deduct*) abziehen; (*concede*): to ~ that ... annehmen, daß ...; to ~ **sb** **sth** jdm etw erlauben, jdm etw gestatten; to ~ **sb to do sth** jdm erlauben *or* gestatten, etw zu tun; ~ **for** *vt fus* berücksichtigen, einplanen; ~**ance** *n* Beihilfe *f*; to **make** ~**ances for** berücksichtigen

alloy ['ælɔɪ] *n* Metallegierung *f*

all right *adv* (*well*) gut; (*correct*) richtig; (*as answer*) okay

all-round ['ɔːl'raʊnd] *adj* (*sportsman*) allseitig, Allround-; (*view*) Rundum-

all-time ['ɔːl'taɪm] *adj* (*record*, *high*) ... aller Zeiten, Höchst-

allude [ə'luːd] *vi*: to ~ **to** hinweisen auf +*acc*, anspielen auf +*acc*

alluring [ə'ljʊərɪŋ] *adj* verlockend

allusion [ə'luːʒən] *n* Anspielung *f*

ally ['ælaɪ, *vb* ə'laɪ] *n* Verbündete(r) *mf*; (*POL*) Alliierte(r) *f(m)* ♦ *vr*: to ~ **o.s.** with sich verbünden mit

almighty [ɔːl'maɪtɪ] *adj* allmächtig

almond ['ɑːmənd] *n* Mandel *f*

almost ['ɔːlməʊst] *adv* fast, beinahe

alms [ɑːmz] *npl* Almosen *nt*

aloft [ə'lɒft] *adv* (*be*) in der Luft; (*throw*) in die Luft

alone [ə'ləʊn] *adj*, *adv* allein; to **leave sth** ~ etw sein lassen; **let** ~ ... geschweige denn ...

along [ə'lɒŋ] *prep* entlang, längs ♦ *adv* (*onward*) vorwärts, weiter; ~ **with** zusammen mit; **he was limping** ~ er humpelte einher; **all** ~ (*all the time*) die ganze Zeit; ~**side** *adv* (*walk*) nebenher; (*come*) nebendran; (*be*) daneben ♦ *prep* (*walk*, *compared*) neben +*dat*; (*come*) neben +*acc*; (*be*) entlang, neben +*dat*; (*of ship*) längsseits +*gen*

aloof [ə'luːf] *adj* zurückhaltend ♦ *adv* fern; to **stand** ~ abseits stehen

aloud [ə'laʊd] *adv* laut

alphabet ['ælfəbet] *n* Alphabet *nt*; ~**ical** [ælfə'betɪkl] *adj* alphabetisch

alpine ['ælpaɪn] *adj* alpin, Alpen-

Alps [ælps] *npl*: **the** ~ **die** Alpen *pl*

already [ɔːl'redɪ] *adv* schon, bereits

alright ['ɔːl'raɪt] (*BRIT*) *adv* = **all right**

Alsatian [æl'seɪʃən] *n* (*dog*) Schäferhund *m*

also ['ɔːlsəʊ] *adv* auch, außerdem

altar ['ɔːltə*] *n* Altar *m*

alter ['ɔːltə*] *vt* ändern; (*dress*) umändern; ~**ation** [ɔltə'reɪʃən] *n* Änderung *f*; Umänderung *f*; (*to build-ing*) Umbau *m*

alternate [*adj* ɒl'tɜːnɪt, *vb* 'ɒltɜːneɪt] *adj* abwechselnd ♦ *vi* abwechseln; **on** ~ **days** jeden zweiten Tag

alternating ['ɒltɜːneɪtɪŋ] *adj*: ~ **current** Wechselstrom *m*

alternative [ɒl'tɜːnətɪv] *adj* andere(r, s) ♦ *n* Alternative *f*; ~**ly** *adv* im anderen Falle; ~**ly one could ...** oder man könnte ...

alternator ['ɒltɜːneɪtə*] *n* (*AUT*) Lichtmaschine *f*

although [ɔːl'ðəʊ] *conj* obwohl

altitude ['æltɪtjuːd] *n* Höhe *f*

alto ['æltəʊ] *n* Alt *m*

altogether [ɔːltə'geðə*] *adv* (*on the*

whole) im ganzen genommen; (*entirely*) ganz und gar

aluminium [ælju'mɪnɪəm] (*BRIT*) n Aluminium nt

aluminum [ə'luːmɪnəm] (*US*) n Aluminium nt

always ['ɔːlweɪz] adv immer

Alzheimer's (disease) ['æltsɪarmaz-] n (*MED*) Alzheimer-Krankheit f

am [æm] *see* be

a.m. adv abbr (= *ante meridiem*) vormittags

amalgamate [ə'mælgəmeɪt] vi (*combine*) sich vereinigen ♦ vt (*mix*) amalgamieren

amass [ə'mæs] vt anhäufen

amateur ['æmətə:*] n Amateur m; (*pej*) Amateur m, Stümper m; **~ish** (*pej*) dilettantisch, stümperhaft

amaze [ə'meɪz] vt erstaunen; **to be ~d (at)** erstaunt sein (über); **~ment** n höchste(s) Erstaunen nt

amazing [ə'meɪzɪŋ] adj höchst erstaunlich

Amazon ['æməzən] n (*GEOG*) Amazonas m

ambassador [æm'bæsədə:*] n Botschafter m

amber ['æmbə:*] n Bernstein m; **at ~** (*BRIT: AUT*) (auf) gelb

ambiguous [æm'bɪgjuəs] adj zweideutig; (*not clear*) unklar

ambition [æm'bɪʃən] n Ehrgeiz m

ambitious [æm'bɪʃəs] adj ehrgeizig

ambivalent [æm'bɪvələnt] adj (*attitude*) zwiespältig

amble ['æmbl] vi (*usu: ~ along*) schlendern

ambulance ['æmbjuləns] n Krankenwagen m; **~man** (*irreg*) n Sanitäter m

ambush ['æmbuʃ] n Hinterhalt m ♦ vt (aus dem Hinterhalt) überfallen

amenable [ə'miːnəbl] adj gefügig; **~ (to)** (*reason*) zugänglich (+dat); (*flattery*) empfänglich für; (*law*) unterworfen (+dat)

amend [ə'mend] vt (*law etc*) abändern, ergänzen; **to make ~s**

etw wiedergutmachen; **~ment** n Abänderung f

amenities [ə'miːnɪtɪz] npl Einrichtungen pl

America [ə'merɪkə] n Amerika nt; **~n** adj amerikanisch ♦ n Amerikaner(in) m(f)

amiable ['eɪmɪəbl] adj liebenswürdig

amicable ['æmɪkəbl] adj freundschaftlich; (*settlement*) gütlich

amid(st) [ə'mɪd(st)] prep mitten in or unter +dat

amiss [ə'mɪs] adv: **to take sth ~** etw übelnehmen; **there's something ~** da stimmt irgend etwas nicht

ammonia [ə'məunɪə] n Ammoniak nt

ammunition [æmju'nɪʃən] n Munition f

amnesia [æm'niːzɪə] n Gedächtnisverlust m

amnesty ['æmnɪstɪ] n Amnestie f

amok [ə'mɔk] adv: **to run ~** Amok laufen

among(st) [ə'mʌŋ(st)] prep unter

amoral [eɪ'mɔrəl] adj unmoralisch

amorous ['æmərəs] adj verliebt

amount [ə'maunt] n (*of money*) Betrag m; (*of water, sand*) Menge f ♦ vi: **to ~ to** (*total*) sich belaufen auf +acc; **a great ~ of time/energy** ein großer Aufwand an Zeit/Energie (dat); **this ~s to treachery** das kommt Verrat gleich; **it ~s to the same** es läuft aufs gleiche hinaus; **he won't ~ to much** aus ihm wird nie was

amp(ère) ['æmp(εə*)] n Ampere nt

amphibian [æm'fɪbɪən] n Amphibie f

amphibious [æm'fɪbɪəs] adj amphibisch, Amphibien-

ample ['æmpl] adj (*portion*) reichlich; (*dress*) weit, groß; **~ time** genügend Zeit

amplifier ['æmplɪfaɪə*] n Verstärker m

amuse [ə'mjuːz] vt (*entertain*) unterhalten; (*make smile*) belustigen; **~ment** n (*feeling*) Unterhaltung f; (*recreation*) Zeitvertreib m; (*at*

arcade n Spielhalle f

an [æn] see a

anaemia [ə'niːmɪə] n Anämie f

anaemic [ə'niːmɪk] n blutarm

anaesthetic [ænɪs'θetɪk] n Betäubungsmittel nt; under ~ unter Narkose

anaesthetist [æ'niːsθɪtɪst] n Anästhesist m(f)

analgesic [ænæl'dʒiːsɪk] n schmerzlindernde(s) Mittel nt

analog(ue) [ˈænəlɒg] adj Analog

analogy [ə'nælədʒɪ] n Analogie f

analyse [ˈænəlaɪz] (BRIT) vt analysieren

analyses [ə'næləsɪz] npl of analysis

analysis [ə'næləsɪs] (pl analyses) n Analyse f

analyst [ˈænəlɪst] n Analytiker m(f)

analytic(al) [ænə'lɪtɪk(əl)] adj analytisch

analyze [ˈænəlaɪz] (US) vt = analyse

anarchy [ˈænəkɪ] n Anarchie f

anathema [ə'næθɪmə] n (fig) Greuel nt

anatomy [ə'nætəmɪ] n (structure) anatomische(r) Aufbau m; (study) Anatomie f

ancestor [ˈænsestə*] n Vorfahr m

anchor [ˈæŋkə*] n Anker m ♦ vi (also: to drop ~) ankern, vor Anker gehen ♦ vt verankern; to weigh ~ den Anker lichten

anchovy [ˈæntʃəvɪ] n Sardelle f

ancient [ˈeɪnʃənt] adj alt; (car etc) uralt

ancillary [æn'sɪlərɪ] adj Hilfs-

and [ænd] conj und; ~ so on und so weiter; try ~ come versuche zu kommen; better ~ better immer besser

Andes [ˈændiːz] npl: the ~ die Anden pl

anemia [ə'niːmɪə] (US) n = anaemia

anesthetic [ænɪs'θetɪk] (US) n = anaesthetic

anew [ə'njuː] adv von neuem

angel [ˈeɪndʒəl] n Engel m

anger [ˈæŋgə*] n Zorn m ♦ vt ärgern

angina [æn'dʒaɪnə] n Angina f

angle [ˈæŋgl] n Winkel m; (point of view) Standpunkt m

angler [ˈæŋglə*] n Angler m

Anglican [ˈæŋglɪkən] adj anglikanisch ♦ n Anglikaner(in) m(f)

angling [ˈæŋglɪŋ] n Angeln nt

Anglo- [ˈæŋgləʊ] prefix Anglo-

angrily [ˈæŋgrɪlɪ] adv ärgerlich, böse

angry [ˈæŋgrɪ] adj ärgerlich, ungehalten, böse; (wound) entzündet; to be ~ with sb auf jdn böse sein; to be ~ at sth über etw acc verärgert sein

anguish [ˈæŋgwɪʃ] n Qual f

angular [ˈæŋgjʊlə*] adj eckig, winkelförmig; (face) kantig

animal [ˈænɪməl] n Tier nt; (living creature) Lebewesen nt ♦ adj tierisch

animate [vb ˈænɪmeɪt, adj ˈænɪmət] vt beleben ♦ adj lebhaft; ~d adj lebendig; (film) Zeichentrick-

animosity [ænɪ'mɒsɪtɪ] n Feindseligkeit f, Abneigung f

aniseed [ˈænɪsiːd] n Anis m

ankle [ˈæŋkl] n (Fuß)knöchel m; ~ sock n Söckchen nt

annex [n ˈæneks, vb ə'neks] n (also: BRIT: annexe) Anbau m ♦ vt anfügen; (POL) annektieren, angliedern

annihilate [ə'naɪəleɪt] vt vernichten

anniversary [ænɪ'vɜːsərɪ] n Jahrestag m

annotate [ˈænəteɪt] vt kommentieren

announce [ə'naʊns] vt ankündigen, anzeigen; ~ment n Ankündigung f; (official) Bekanntmachung f; ~r n Ansager(in) m(f)

annoy [ə'nɔɪ] vt ärgern; don't get ~ed! reg dich nicht auf!; ~ance n Ärgernis nt, Störung f; ~ing adj ärgerlich; (person) lästig

annual [ˈænjʊəl] adj jährlich; (salary) Jahres- ♦ n (plant) einjährige Pflanze f; (book) Jahrbuch nt; ~ly adv jährlich

annul [ə'nʌl] vt aufheben, annullieren

annum ['ænəm] n see per

anomaly [ə'nɒməlɪ] n Abweichung f von der Regel

anonymous [ə'nɒnɪməs] adj anonym

anorak ['ænəræk] n Anorak m, Windjacke f

anorexia [ænə'reksɪə] n (MED) Magersucht f

another [ə'nʌðə*] adj, pron (different) ein(e) andere(r, s); (additional) noch eine(r, s); see also one

answer ['ɑ:nsə*] n Antwort f ♦ vi antworten; (on phone) sich melden ♦ vt (person) antworten +dat; (letter, question) beantworten; (telephone) gehen an +acc, abnehmen; (door) öffnen; **in ~ to your letter** in Beantwortung Ihres Schreibens; **to ~ the phone** ans Telefon gehen; **to ~ the bell** or **the door** aufmachen; **~ back** vi frech sein; **~ for** vt: **to ~ for sth** für etw verantwortlich sein; **~able** adj: **to be ~able to sb** for **sth** jdm gegenüber für etw verantwortlich sein; **~ing machine** n Anrufbeantworter m

ant [ænt] n Ameise f

antagonism [æn'tægənɪzəm] n Antagonismus m

antagonize [æn'tægənaɪz] vt reizen

Antarctic [ænt'ɑ:ktɪk] adj antarktisch ♦ n: **the ~** die Antarktis

antelope ['æntɪləʊp] n Antilope f

antenatal [æntɪ'neɪtl] adj vor der Geburt; **~ clinic** n Sprechstunde f für werdende Mütter

antenna [æn'tenə] n (BIOL) Fühler m; (RADIO) Antenne f

antennae [æn'teni:] npl of antenna

anthem ['ænθəm] n Hymne f; **national ~** Nationalhymne f

anthology [æn'θɒlədʒɪ] n Gedichtsammlung f, Anthologie f

anti- ['æntɪ] pref Gegen-, Anti-

anti-aircraft [æntɪ'ɛəkrɑ:ft] adj Flugabwehr-

antibiotic ['æntɪbaɪ'ɒtɪk] n Antibiotikum n

antibody ['æntɪbɒdɪ] n Antikörper m

anticipate [æn'tɪsɪpeɪt] vt (expect: trouble, question) erwarten, rechnen mit; (look forward to) sich freuen auf +acc; (do first) vorwegnehmen; (foresee) ahnen, vorhersehen

anticipation [æntɪsɪ'peɪʃən] n Erwartung f; (foreshadowing) Vorwegnahme f

anticlimax ['æntɪ'klaɪmæks] n Ernüchterung f

anticlockwise ['æntɪ'klɒkwaɪz] adv entgegen dem Uhrzeigersinn

antics ['æntɪks] npl Possen pl

anticyclone ['æntɪ'saɪkləʊn] n Hoch nt, Hochdruckgebiet nt

antidote ['æntɪdəʊt] n Gegenmittel nt

antifreeze ['æntɪfri:z] n Frostschutzmittel nt

antihistamine [æntɪ'hɪstəmi:n] n Antihistamin n

antiquated ['æntɪkweɪtɪd] adj antiquiert

antique [æn'ti:k] n Antiquität f ♦ adj antik; (old-fashioned) altmodisch; **~ shop** n Antiquitätenladen m

antiquity [æn'tɪkwɪtɪ] n Altertum nt

antiseptic [æntɪ'septɪk] n Antiseptikum nt ♦ adj antiseptisch

antisocial ['æntɪ'səʊʃl] adj (person) ungesellig; (law) unsozial

antlers ['æntləz] npl Geweih nt

anus ['eɪnəs] n After m

anvil ['ænvɪl] n Amboß m

anxiety [æŋ'zaɪətɪ] n Angst f; (worry) Sorge f

anxious ['æŋkʃəs] adj ängstlich; (worried) besorgt; **to be ~ to do sth** etw unbedingt tun wollen

---

KEYWORD

any ['enɪ] adj **1** (in questions etc): **have you any butter?** haben Sie (etwas) Butter?; **have you any children?** haben Sie Kinder?; **if there are any tickets left** falls noch Karten da sind

2 (with negative): **I haven't any money/books** ich habe kein Geld/

keine Bücher

3 (*no matter which*) jede(r, s) (beliebige); *any colour* jede (all) jede beliebige Farbe; *choose any book you like* nehmen Sie ein beliebiges Buch
4 (*in phrases*): *in any case* in jedem Fall; *any day now* jeden Tag; *at any moment* jeden Moment; *at any rate* auf jeden Fall
♦ *pron* **1** (*in questions etc*) have you got any? haben Sie welche?; *can any of you sing?* kann ich irgend(ein)er von euch singen?
2 (*with negative*): *I haven't any (of them)* ich habe keinen/keines (davon)
3 (*no matter which one(s)*): take any of those books (you like) nehmen Sie irgendeines dieser Bücher
♦ *adv* **1** (*in questions etc*): do you want any more soup/sandwiches? möchten Sie noch Suppe/Brote?; *are you feeling any better?* fühlen Sie sich etwas besser?
2 (*with negative*): *I can't hear him any more* ich kann ihn nicht mehr hören

anybody ['enɪbɔdɪ] *pron* (*no matter who*) jede(r, s); (*in questions etc*) (irgend) eine(r); (*with negative*): *I can't see* ~ ich kann niemanden sehen

anyhow ['enɪhaʊ] *adv* (*at any rate*): *I shall go* ~ ich gehe sowieso; (*haphazardly*): *do it* ~ machen Sie es, wie Sie wollen

anyone ['enɪwʌn] *pron* = **anybody**

KEYWORD

anything ['enɪθɪŋ] *pron* **1** (*in questions etc*) (irgend) etwas; *can you see anything?* können Sie etwas sehen?
2 (*with negative*): *I can't see anything* ich kann nichts sehen
3 (*no matter what*): *you can say anything you like* Sie können sagen, was Sie wollen; *anything will do* ir-

gend etwas(, wird genügen); *anything(, will genügen); he'll eat anything* er ißt alles

anyway ['enɪweɪ] *adv* (*at any rate*) auf jeden Fall; (*besides*): ~, I couldn't come even if I wanted to jedenfalls könnte ich nicht kommen, selbst wenn ich wollte; *why are you phoning,* ~? warum rufst du überhaupt an?

anywhere ['enɪwɛə*] *adv* (*in questions etc*) irgendwo; (: *with direction*) irgendwohin; (*no matter where*) überall; (: *with direction*) überallhin; (*with negative*): *I can't see him* ~ ich kann ihn nirgendwo or nirgends sehen; *can you see him* ~? siehst du ihn irgendwo?; *put the books down* ~ leg die Bücher irgendwohin

apart [ə'pɑːt] *adv* (*parted*) auseinander; (*away*) beiseite, abseits; *10 miles* ~ 10 Meilen auseinander; *to take* ~ auseinandernehmen; ~ *from prep* außer

apartheid [ə'pɑːteɪt] *n* Apartheid *f*

apartment [ə'pɑːtmənt] *n* (*US*) Wohnung *f*; ~ *building* (*US*) *n* Wohnhaus *nt*

apathy ['æpəθɪ] *n* Teilnahmslosigkeit *f*, Apathie *f*

ape [eɪp] *n* (Menschen)affe *m* ♦ *vt* nachahmen

aperitif *n* Aperitif *m*

aperture ['æpətjʊə*] *n* Öffnung *f*; (*PHOT*) Blende *f*

apex ['eɪpɛks] *n* Spitze *f*

apiece [ə'piːs] *adv* pro Stück; (*per person*) pro Kopf

apologetic [əpɔlə'dʒetɪk] *adj* entschuldigend; *to be* ~ sich sehr entschuldigen

apologize [ə'pɔlədʒaɪz] *vi*: *to* ~ (*for sth to sb*) sich (für etw bei jdm) entschuldigen

apology [ə'pɔlədʒɪ] *n* Entschuldigung *f*

apostle [ə'pɔsl] *n* Apostel *m*

apostrophe [ə'pɔstrəfɪ] *n* Apostroph *m*

appal [ə'pɔːl] vt erschrecken; ~**ling**
[ə'pɔːlɪŋ] adj schrecklich

apparatus [æpə'reɪtəs] n Gerät nt

apparel [ə'pærəl] (US) n Kleidung f

apparent [ə'pærənt] adj offenbar;
~**ly** adv anscheinend

apparition n (ghost) Erscheinung f, Geist m; (appearance)
Erscheinen nt

appeal [ə'piːl] vi dringend ersuchen;
(JUR) Berufung einlegen ♦ n Aufruf
m; (JUR) Berufung f; to ~ for dringend bitten um; to ~ to sich wenden
an +acc; (to public) appellieren an
+acc; (to please) ~ to me es gefällt
mir nicht; ~**ing** adj ansprechend

appear [ə'pɪə*] vi (come into sight)
erscheinen; (be seen) auftauchen;
(seem) scheinen; it would ~ that ...
anscheinend; ~**ance** n (coming
into sight) Erscheinen nt; (outward
show) Äußere(s) nt

appease [ə'piːz] vt beschwichtigen

appendices [ə'pendɪsiːz] npl of appendix Anhang

appendicitis [əpendɪ'saɪtɪs] n Blind-
darmentzündung f

appendix [ə'pendɪks] (pl appendices) n (in book) Anhang m; (MED)
Blinddarm m

appetite ['æpɪtaɪt] n Appetit m; (fig)
Lust f

appetizer ['æpətaɪzə*] n Appetitanre-
ger m

appetizing ['æpɪtaɪzɪŋ] adj appetit-
anregend

applaud [ə'plɔːd] vi Beifall klatschen, applaudieren ♦ vt Beifall klatschen +dat

applause [ə'plɔːz] n Beifall m, Applaus m

apple ['æpl] n Apfel m; ~ **tree** n Ap-
felbaum m

appliance [ə'plaɪəns] n Gerät nt

applicable [ə'plɪkəbl] adj anwend-
bar; (in forms) zutreffend

applicant ['æplɪkənt] n Bewerber(in)
m(f)

application [æplɪ'keɪʃən] n (request)
Antrag m; (for job) Bewerbung f;

(putting into practice) Anwendung f;
(hard work) Fleiß m; ~ **form** n Be-
werbungsformular nt

applied [ə'plaɪd] adj angewandt

apply [ə'plaɪ] vi (be suitable) zutreffen; (ask): to ~ (to) sich wenden
(an +acc); (request): to ~ for sich
melden für ♦ vt (place on) auflegen;
(cream) auftragen; (put into practice) anwenden; to ~ for sth sich
um etw bewerben; to ~ o.s. to sth
sich bei etw anstrengen

appoint [ə'pɔɪnt] vt (to office) ernennen, berufen; (settle) festsetzen;
~**ment** n (meeting) Verabredung f;
(at hairdresser etc) Bestellung f; (in
business) Termin m; (choice for a
position) Ernennung f; (UNIV) Berufung f

appraisal [ə'preɪzl] n Beurteilung f

appreciable [ə'priːʃəbl] adj (perceptible) merklich; (able to be estimated) abschätzbar

appreciate [ə'priːʃɪeɪt] vt (value) zu
schätzen wissen; (understand) einsehen ♦ vi (increase in value) im Wert
steigen

appreciation [əpriːʃɪ'eɪʃən] n Wertschätzung f; (COMM) Wertzuwachs
m

appreciative [ə'priːʃɪətɪv] adj (showing thanks) dankbar; (showing liking) anerkennend

apprehend [æprɪ'hend] vt (arrest)
festnehmen; (understand) erfassen

apprehension [æprɪ'henʃən] n
Angst f

apprehensive [æprɪ'hensɪv] adj
furchtsam

apprentice [ə'prentɪs] n Lehrling m;
~**ship** n Lehrzeit f

approach [ə'prəʊtʃ] vi sich nähern ♦
vt herantreten an +acc; (problem)
herangehen an +acc ♦ n Annäherung
f; (to problem) Ansatz m; (path) Zugang m, Zufahrt f; ~**able** adj zugänglich

appropriate [adj ə'prəʊprɪət, vb
ə'prəʊprɪeɪt] adj angemessen; (remark) angebracht ♦ vt (take for

o.s.) sich aneignen; (set apart) bereitstellen

approval [ə'pru:vəl] n (show of satisfaction) Beifall m; (permission) Billigung f; **on ~** (COMM) bei Gefallen

approve [ə'pru:v] vt, vi billigen; **I don't ~ of it/him** ich halte nichts davon/von ihm; **~d school** (BRIT) n Erziehungsheim nt

approximate [adj ə'prɒksɪmɪt, vb ə'prɒksɪmeɪt] adj annähernd, ungefähr ♦ vt nahekommen +dat; **~ly** [-lɪ] adv rund, ungefähr

apricot ['eɪprɪkɒt] n Aprikose f

April ['eɪprəl] n April m; **~ Fools' Day** n der erste April

apron ['eɪprən] n Schürze f

apt [æpt] adj (suitable) passend; (able) begabt; (likely): **to be ~ to do sth** dazu neigen, etw zu tun

aptitude ['æptɪtju:d] n Begabung f

aqualung ['ækwəlʌŋ] n Unterwasseratmungsgerät nt

aquarium [ə'kwɛərɪəm] n Aquarium nt

Aquarius [ə'kwɛərɪəs] n Wassermann m

aquatic [ə'kwætɪk] adj Wasser-

Arab ['ærəb] n Araber(in) m(f)

Arabia [ə'reɪbɪə] n Arabien nt

Arabian [ə'reɪbɪən] adj arabisch

Arabic ['ærəbɪk] adj arabisch ♦ n Arabisch nt

arable ['ærəbl] adj bebaubar, Kulturland

arbitrary ['ɑ:bɪtrərɪ] adj willkürlich

arbitration [ɑ:bɪ'treɪʃən] n Schlichtung f

arc [ɑ:k] n Bogen m

arcade [ɑ:'keɪd] n Säulengang m

arch [ɑ:tʃ] n Bogen m ♦ vt überwölben; (back) krumm machen

archaeologist [ɑ:kɪ'ɒlədʒɪst] n Archäologe m

archaeology [ɑ:kɪ'ɒlədʒɪ] n Archäologie f

archaic [ɑ:'keɪɪk] adj altertümlich

archbishop [ɑ:tʃ'bɪʃəp] n Erzbischof m

archenemy [ɑ:tʃ'enəmɪ] n Erzfeind m

archeology etc (US) = **archaeology** etc

archer [ɑ:tʃə*] n Bogenschütze m; **~y** n Bogenschießen nt

archipelago [ɑ:kɪ'pelɪgəʊ] n Archipel m; (sea) Inselmeer nt

architect ['ɑ:kɪtekt] n Architekt(in) m(f); **~ural** [ɑ:kɪ'tektʃərəl] adj architektonisch; **~ure** ['ɑ:kɪtektʃə*] n Architektur f

archives ['ɑ:kaɪvz] npl Archiv nt

archway ['ɑ:tʃweɪ] n Bogen m

Arctic ['ɑ:ktɪk] adj arktisch ♦ n: **the ~** die Arktis

ardent ['ɑ:dənt] adj glühend

arduous ['ɑ:djʊəs] adj mühsam

are [ɑ:*] see **be**

area ['ɛərɪə] n Fläche f; (of land) Gebiet nt; (part of sth) Teil m, Abschnitt m

arena [ə'ri:nə] n Arena f

aren't [ɑːnt] = **are not**

Argentina [ɑ:dʒən'ti:nə] n Argentinien nt

Argentinian [ɑ:dʒən'tɪnɪən] adj argentinisch ♦ n Argentinier(in) m(f)

arguably ['ɑ:gjʊəblɪ] adv wohl

argue ['ɑ:gju:] vi diskutieren; (angrily) streiten

argument ['ɑ:gjʊmənt] n (theory) Argument nt; (reasoning) Argumentation f; (row) Auseinandersetzung f, Streit m; **to have an ~** sich streiten; **~ative** [ɑ:gjʊ'mentətɪv] adj streitlustig

aria ['ɑ:rɪə] n Arie f

arid ['ærɪd] adj trocken

Aries ['ɛəriːz] n Widder m

arise [ə'raɪz] (pt **arose**, pp **arisen**) vi aufsteigen; (get up) aufstehen; (difficulties etc) entstehen; (case) vorkommen; **to ~ from sth** herrühren von etw; **arisen** [ə'rɪzn] pp of **arise**

aristocracy [ærɪs'tɒkrəsɪ] n Adel m, Aristokratie f

aristocrat ['ærɪstəkræt] n Adlige(r) mf, Aristokrat(in) m(f)

arithmetic [ə'rɪθmətɪk] n Rechnen nt, Arithmetik f

ark [ɑ:k] n: **Noah's A~** die Arche

Noah

arm [ɑːm] n Arm m; (branch of military service) Zweig m ♦ vt bewaffnen; ~s npl (weapons) Waffen pl

armaments ['ɑːməmənts] npl Ausrüstung f

armchair n Lehnstuhl m

armed adj (forces) Streit-, bewaffnet; ~ **robbery** n bewaffnete(r) Raubüberfall m

armistice ['ɑːmɪstɪs] n Waffenstillstand m

armour ['ɑːmə] (US **armor**) n (knight's) Rüstung f; (MIL) Panzerplatte f; ~**ed car** n Panzerwagen m; ~**y** n Waffenlager nt; (factory) Waffenfabrik f

armpit ['ɑːmpɪt] n Achselhöhle f

armrest ['ɑːmrest] n Armlehne f

army ['ɑːmɪ] n Armee f, Heer nt; (host) Heer nt

aroma [ə'rəʊmə] n Duft m, Aroma nt; ~**tic** [ærə'mætɪk] adj aromatisch, würzig

arose [ə'rəʊz] pt of arise

around [ə'raʊnd] adv ringsherum; (almost) ungefähr ♦ prep um ... herum; is he ~? ist er hier?

arouse [ə'raʊz] vt wecken

arrange [ə'reɪndʒ] vt (time, meeting) festsetzen; (holidays) festlegen; (flowers, hair, objects) anordnen; I ~d to meet him ich habe mit ihm ausgemacht, ihn zu treffen; it's all ~d es ist alles arrangiert; ~**ment** n (order) Reihenfolge f; (agreement) Vereinbarung f; ~**ments** npl (plans) Pläne pl

array [ə'reɪ] n (collection) Ansammlung f

arrears [ə'rɪəz] npl (of debts) Rückstand m; (of work) Unerledigte(s) nt; in ~ in Rückstand

arrest [ə'rest] vt (person) verhaften; (stop) aufhalten ♦ n Verhaftung f; under ~ in Haft

arrival [ə'raɪvl] n Ankunft f

arrive [ə'raɪv] vi ankommen; to ~ at ankommen in +dat, ankommen bei

arrogance ['ærəgəns] n Überhebigkeit f, Arroganz f

arrogant ['ærəgənt] adj überheblich, arrogant

arrow ['ærəʊ] n Pfeil m

arse [ɑːs] (inf!) n Arsch m (!)

arsenal ['ɑːsɪnl] n Waffenlager nt, Zeughaus nt

arsenic ['ɑːsnɪk] n Arsen nt

arson ['ɑːsn] n Brandstiftung f

art [ɑːt] n Kunst f; **A~s** npl (UNIV) Geisteswissenschaften pl

artery ['ɑːtərɪ] n Schlagader f, Arterie f

artful ['ɑːtfʊl] adj verschlagen

art gallery n Kunstgalerie f

arthritis [ɑː'θraɪtɪs] n Arthritis f

artichoke ['ɑːtɪtʃəʊk] n Artischocke f; **Jerusalem** ~ Erdartischocke f

article ['ɑːtɪkl] n (PRESS, GRAM) Artikel m; (thing) Gegenstand m, Artikel m; (clause) Abschnitt m, Paragraph m; ~ **of clothing** Kleidungsstück nt

articulate [adj ɑː'tɪkjʊlɪt, vb ɑː'tɪkjʊleɪt] adj (able to express o.s.) redegewandt; (speaking clearly) deutlich, verständlich ♦ vt (connect) zusammenfügen, gliedern; to be ~ sich gut ausdrücken können; ~**d vehicle** n Sattelschlepper m

artificial [ɑːtɪ'fɪʃəl] adj künstlich, Kunst-; ~ **respiration** n künstliche Atmung f

artisan ['ɑːtɪzæn] n gelernte(r) Handwerker m

artist ['ɑːtɪst] n Künstler(in) m(f); ~**ic** [ɑː'tɪstɪk] adj künstlerisch; ~**ry** n künstlerische(s) Können nt

artless ['ɑːtlɪs] adj ungekünstelt; (character) arglos

art school n Kunsthochschule f

KEYWORD

as [æz] conj 1 (referring to time) als; as the years went by mit den Jahren; he came in as I was leaving als er hereinkam, ging ich gerade; as from tomorrow ab morgen 2 (in comparisons): as big as so groß wie; twice as big as zweimal

so groß wie; **as much/many** soviel/
so viele wie; **as soon as** sobald
3 (since, because) da; **he left early
as he had to be home by 10** er
ging früher, da er um 10 zu Hause
sein mußte
4 (referring to manner, way) wie; **do
as you wish** mach was du willst; **as
she said** wie sie sagte
5 (concerning): **as for** or **to that**
was das betrifft or angeht
6: as if or **though** als ob

♦ prep als; see also **long**; **he works
as a driver** er arbeitet als Fahrer;
see also **such**; **he gave it to me as
a present** er gab es mir als Geschenk gegeben; see also **well**

a.s.a.p. abbr = **as soon as possible**
ascend [ə'sɛnd] vi aufsteigen ♦ vt
besteigen; **~ancy** n Oberhand f
ascent [ə'sɛnt] n Aufstieg m; Be-
steigung f
ascertain [æsə'teɪn] vt feststellen
ascribe [əs'kraɪb] vt: **to ~ sth to
sth/sb** etw einer Sache/jdm
etw zuschreiben
ash [æʃ] n Asche f; (tree) Esche f
ashamed [ə'ʃeɪmd] adj beschämt; **to
be ~ of sth** sich für etw schämen
ashen ['æʃən] adj (pale) aschfahl
ashore [ə'ʃɔː] adv an Land
ashtray ['æʃtreɪ] n Aschenbecher m
Ash Wednesday n Aschermitt-
woch m
Asia ['eɪʃə] n Asien nt; **~n** adj asia-
tisch ♦ n Asiat(in) m(f)
aside [ə'saɪd] adv beiseite ♦ n beiseite gesprochene Worte pl
ask [ɑːsk] vt fragen; (permission) bitten um; **~ him his name** frage ihn
nach seinem Namen; **to ~ed to see
you** er wollte dich sehen; **to ~ sb to
do sth** jdn bitten, etw zu tun; **to ~
sb about sth** jdn nach etw fragen;
to ~ (sb) a question jdn etwas fragen; **to ~ sb out to dinner** jdn zum
Essen einladen ♦ fragen nach bitten um
askance [əs'kɑːns] adv: **to look ~
at sb** jdn schief ansehen

askew [əs'kjuː] adv schief
asking price ['ɑːskɪŋ-] n Verkaufspreis m
asleep [ə'sliːp] adj: **to be ~** schlafen; **to fall ~** einschlafen
asparagus [əs'pærəgəs] n Spargel m
aspect ['æspɛkt] n Aspekt m
aspersions [əs'pɜːʃənz] npl: **to cast
~ on sb/sth** sich abfällig über jdn/
etw äußern
asphyxiation [əsfɪksɪ'eɪʃən] n Ersti-
ckung f
aspirations [æspə'reɪʃənz] npl: **to
have ~ towards sth** etw anstreben
aspire [əs'paɪə] vi: **to ~ to** streben
nach
aspirin ['æsprɪn] n Aspirin nt
ass [æs] n (also fig) Esel m; (US:
inf!) Arsch m (!)
assailant [ə'seɪlənt] n Angreifer m
assassin [ə'sæsɪn] n Attentäter(in)
m(f); **~ate** [ə'sæsɪneɪt] vt ermorden
assassination [əsæsɪ'neɪʃən] n (ge-
glückte(s)) Attentat nt
assault [ə'sɔːlt] n Angriff m ♦ vt
überfallen; (woman) herfallen über
+acc
assemble [ə'sɛmbl] vt versammeln;
(parts) zusammensetzen ♦ vi sich
versammeln
assembly [ə'sɛmblɪ] n (meeting)
Versammlung f; (construction) Zusammensetzung f, Montage f; **~ line**
n Fließband nt
assent [ə'sɛnt] n Zustimmung f
assert [ə'sɜːt] vt erklären; **~ion**
[ə'sɜːʃən] n Behauptung f
assess [ə'sɛs] vt schätzen; **~ment** n
Bewertung f, Einschätzung f; **~or** n
Steuerberater m
asset ['æsɛt] n Vorteil m, Wert m;
~s npl (FIN) Vermögen nt; (estate)
Nachlaß m
assiduous [ə'sɪdjʊəs] adj fleißig, aufmerksam
assign [ə'saɪn] vt zuweisen
assignment [ə'saɪnmənt] n Aufgabe f,
Auftrag m
assimilate [ə'sɪmɪleɪt] vt sich einver-
nen, aufnehmen

assist [ə'sɪst] vt beistehen +dat; **~ance** n Unterstützung f, Hilfe f; **~ant** n Assistent(in) m(f), Mitarbeiter(in) m(f); (BRIT: also: shop **~ant**) Verkäufer(in) m(f)

assizes [ə'saɪzɪz] npl Landgericht nt

associate [ə'səʊfɪt, vb ə'səʊfɪeɪt] n (partner) Kollege m, Teilhaber m; (member) außerordentliche(s) Mitglied nt ♦ vt verbinden ♦ vi (keep company) verkehren

association [əsəʊsɪ'eɪʃən] n Verband m, Verein m; (PSYCH) Assoziation f; (link) Verbindung f

assorted [ə'sɔːtɪd] adj gemischt

assortment [ə'sɔːtmənt] n Sammlung f; (COMM): ~ (of) Sortiment nt (von), Auswahl f (an +dat)

assume [ə'sjuːm] vt (take for granted) annehmen; (put on) annehmen, sich geben; **~d name** n Deckname m

assumption [ə'sʌmpʃən] n Annahme f

assurance [ə'ʃʊərəns] n (firm statement) Versicherung f; (confidence) Selbstsicherheit f; (insurance) (Lebens)versicherung f

assure [ə'ʃʊə*] vt (make sure) sicherstellen; (convince) versichern +dat; (life) versichern

asterisk ['æstərɪsk] n Sternchen nt

astern [ə'stɜːn] adv achtern

asthma ['æsmə] n Asthma nt

astonish [ə'stɒnɪʃ] vt erstaunen; **~ment** n Erstaunen nt

astound [ə'staʊnd] vt verblüffen

astray [ə'streɪ] adv in die Irre; auf Abwege; to go ~ (go wrong) sich vertun; to lead ~ irreführen

astride [ə'straɪd] adv rittlings ♦ prep rittlings auf

astrologer [ə'strɒlədʒə*] n Astrologe m, Astrologin f

astrology [ə'strɒlədʒɪ] n Astrologie f

astronaut ['æstrənɔːt] n Astronaut(in) m(f)

astronomer [ə'strɒnəmə*] n Astronom m

astronomical [æstrə'nɒmɪkəl] adj astronomisch; (success) riesig

astronomy [ə'strɒnəmɪ] n Astronomie f

astute [ə'stjuːt] adj scharfsinnig; schlau, gerissen

asylum [ə'saɪləm] n (home) Heim nt; (refuge) Asyl nt

at [æt] prep **1** (referring to position, direction) an +dat, bei +dat; (with place) in +dat; **at the top** an der Spitze; **at home/school** zu Hause/in der Schule; **at the baker's** beim Bäcker; **to look at sth** auf etw acc blicken; **to throw sth at sb** etw nach jdm werfen

2 (referring to time): **at 4 o'clock** um 4 Uhr; **at night** bei Nacht; **at Christmas** zu Weihnachten; **at times** manchmal

3 (referring to rates, speed etc): **at £1 a kilo** zu £1 pro Kilo; **two at a time** zwei auf einmal; **at 50 km/h** mit 50 km/h

4 (referring to manner): **at a stroke** mit einem Schlag; **at peace** in Frieden

5 (referring to activity): **to be at work** bei der Arbeit sein; **to play at cowboys** Cowboy spielen; **to be good at sth** gut in etw dat sein

6 (referring to cause): **shocked/surprised/annoyed at sth** schockiert/überrascht/verärgert über etw acc; **I went at his suggestion** ich ging auf seinen Vorschlag hin

ate [et, eɪt] pt of **eat**

atheist ['eɪθɪɪst] n Atheist(in) m(f)

Athens ['æθɪnz] n Athen nt

athlete ['æθliːt] n Athlet m, Sportler m

athletic [æθ'letɪk] adj sportlich, athletisch; **~s** n Leichtathletik f

Atlantic [ət'læntɪk] adj atlantisch ♦ n: **the ~** (Ocean) der Atlantik

atlas ['ætləs] n Atlas m

atmosphere ['ætməsfɪə*] n Atmosphäre f

atom ['ætəm] n Atom nt; (fig) bißchen nt; **~ic** ['ætomik] adj atomar, Atom-; **~(ic) bomb** n Atombombe f; **~izer** ['ætəmaizə*] n Zerstäuber m

atone [ə'təun] vi sühnen; **to ~ for** sth auf etw acc sühnen

atrocious [ə'trəʊʃəs] adj gräßlich

atrocity [ə'trɒsiti] n Scheußlichkeit f; (deed) Greueltat f

attach [ə'tætʃ] vt (fasten) befestigen; **to be ~ed to** sb/sth an jdm/etw hängen; **to ~ importance etc to** sth Wichtigkeit etc auf etw acc legen, einer Sache dat Wichtigkeit etc beimessen

attaché case [ə'tæʃei-] n Aktenkoffer m

attachment [ə'tætʃmənt] n (tool) Zubehörteil nt; (love): **~ (to sb)** Zuneigung f (zu jdm)

attack [ə'tæk] vt angreifen ♦ n Angriff m; (MED) Anfall m; **~er** n Angreifer(in) m(f)

attain [ə'tein] vt erreichen; **~ments** npl Kenntnisse pl

attempt [ə'tempt] n Versuch m ♦ vt versuchen; **~ed murder** Mordversuch m

attend [ə'tend] vt (go to) teilnehmen (an +dat); (lectures) besuchen; **~ to** (needs) nachkommen +dat; (person) sich kümmern um; **~ance** n (presence) Anwesenheit f; (people present) Besucherzahl f; **good ~ance** gute Teilnahme; **~ant** n (companion) Gesellschafter(in) m(f); (in car park etc) Wächter(in) m(f); (servant) Bedienstete(r) mf ♦ adj begleitend; (fig) damit verbunden

attention [ə'tenʃən] n Aufmerksamkeit f; (care) Fürsorge f; (for machine etc) Pflege f ♦ excl (MIL) Achtung!; **for the ~ of ...** zu Händen (von) ...

attentive [ə'tentiv] adj aufmerksam

attest [ə'test] vi: **to ~ to** sich verbürgen für

attic ['ætik] n Dachstube f, Mansarde f

attitude ['ætitju:d] n (mental) Einstellung f

attorney [ə'tɜ:ni] n (solicitor) Rechtsanwalt m; **A~ General** n Justizminister m

attract [ə'trækt] vt anziehen; (attention) erregen; **~ion** [ə'trækʃən] n Anziehungskraft f; (thing) Attraktion f; **~ive** adj attraktiv

attribute [n 'ætribju:t, vb ə'tribju:t] n Eigenschaft f, Attribut nt ♦ vt zuschreiben

attrition [ə'trɪʃən] n: **war of ~** Zermürbungskrieg m

aubergine ['əʊbəʒi:n] n Aubergine f

auburn ['ɔ:bən] adj kastanienbraun

auction ['ɔ:kʃən] n (also: sale by ~) Versteigerung f, Auktion f ♦ vt versteigern; **~eer** [ɔ:kʃə'niə*] n Versteigerer m

audacity [ɔ:'dæsiti] n (boldness) Wagemut m; (impudence) Unverfrorenheit f

audible ['ɔ:dibl] adj hörbar

audience ['ɔ:diəns] n Zuhörer pl, Zuschauer pl; (with king etc) Audienz f

audiotypist ['ɔ:diəʊ'taipist] n Phonotypistin f

audiovisual ['ɔ:diəʊ'vizjuəl] adj audiovisuell

audit ['ɔ:dit] vt prüfen

audition [ɔ:'dɪʃən] n Probe f

auditor ['ɔ:ditə*] n (accountant) Rechnungsprüfer(in) m(f), Buchprüfer m

auditorium [ɔ:di'tɔ:riəm] n Zuschauerraum m

augment [ɔ:g'ment] vt vermehren

augur ['ɔ:gə*] vi bedeuten, voraussagen; **this ~s well** das ist ein gutes Omen

August ['ɔ:gəst] n August m

aunt [ɑ:nt] n Tante f; **~ie** n Tantchen nt; **~y** n = auntie

au pair ['əʊ'pɛə*] n (also: ~ girl) Au-pair-Mädchen nt

aura ['ɔ:rə] n Nimbus m

auspices ['ɔ:spisiz] npl: **under the ~ of** unter der Schirmherrschaft von

auspicious [ɔ:s'pɪʃəs] adj günstig,

verheißungsvoll

austere [ɒsˈtɪə*] adj streng; (room) nüchtern

austerity [ɒsˈterɪtɪ] n Strenge f; (POL) wirtschaftliche Einschränkung f

Australia [ɒsˈtreɪlɪə] n Australien nt; ~n adj australisch ♦ n Australier(in) m(f)

Austria [ˈɒstrɪə] n Österreich nt; ~n adj österreichisch ♦ n Österreicher(in) m(f)

authentic [ɔːˈθentɪk] adj echt, authentisch

author [ˈɔːθə*] n Autor m, Schriftsteller m; (beginner) Urheber m, Schöpfer m

authoritarian [ɔːθɒrɪˈtɛərɪən] adj autoritär

authoritative [ɔːˈθɒrɪtətɪv] adj (account) maßgeblich; (manner) herrisch

authority [ɔːˈθɒrɪtɪ] n (power) Autorität f; (expert) Autorität f, Fachmann m; **the authorities** npl (ruling body) die Behörden pl

authorize [ˈɔːθəraɪz] vt bevollmächtigen; (permit) genehmigen

auto [ˈɔːtəʊ] (US) n Auto nt, Wagen m

autobiography [ɔːtəʊbaɪˈɒgrəfɪ] n Autobiographie f

autograph [ˈɔːtəgrɑːf] n (of celebrity) Autogramm nt ♦ vt mit Autogramm versehen

automatic [ɔːtəˈmætɪk] adj automatisch ♦ n (gun) Selbstladepistole f; (car) Automatik m; ~ally adv automatisch

automation [ɔːtəˈmeɪʃən] n Automatisierung f

automobile [ˈɔːtəməbiːl] (US) n Auto(mobil) nt

autonomous [ɔːˈtɒnəməs] adj autonom

autumn [ˈɔːtəm] n Herbst m

auxiliary [ɔːgˈzɪlɪərɪ] adj Hilfs-

Av. abbr = avenue

avail [əˈveɪl] vt: to ~ o.s. of sth sich einer Sache gen bedienen ♦ n: to no

~ nutzlos

availability [əˌveɪləˈbɪlɪtɪ] n Erhältlichkeit f, Vorhandensein nt

available [əˈveɪləbl] adj erhältlich; zur Verfügung stehend; (person) erreichbar, abkömmlich

avalanche [ˈævəlɑːnʃ] n Lawine f

avarice [ˈævərɪs] n Habsucht f, Geiz m

Ave. abbr = avenue

avenge [əˈvendʒ] vt rächen, sühnen

avenue [ˈævənjuː] n Allee f

average [ˈævərɪdʒ] n Durchschnitt m ♦ adj durchschnittlich, Durchschnitts- ♦ vt (figures) den Durchschnitt nehmen von; (perform) durchschnittlich leisten; (in car etc) im Schnitt fahren; on ~ durchschnittlich, im Durchschnitt; ~ out vi: to ~ out at im Durchschnitt betragen

averse [əˈvɜːs] adj: to be ~ to doing sth eine Abneigung dagegen haben, etw zu tun

avert [əˈvɜːt] vt (turn away) abkehren; (prevent) abwehren

aviary [ˈeɪvɪərɪ] n Vogelhaus nt

aviation [eɪvɪˈeɪʃən] n Luftfahrt f, Flugwesen nt

avid [ˈævɪd] adj: ~ (for) gierig (auf +acc)

avocado [ævəˈkɑːdəʊ] n (also: BRIT: ~ pear) Avocado(birne) f

avoid [əˈvɔɪd] vt vermeiden

await [əˈweɪt] vt erwarten, entgegensehen +dat

awake [əˈweɪk] (pt awoke, pp awoken or awaked) adj wach ♦ vt (auf)wecken ♦ vi aufwachen; to be ~ wach sein; ~ning n Erwachen nt

award [əˈwɔːd] n (prize) Preis m ♦ vt: to ~ (sb sth) (jdm etw) zuerkennen

aware [əˈwɛə*] adj bewußt; to be ~ sich bewußt sein; ~ness n Bewußtsein nt

awash [əˈwɒʃ] adj überflutet

away [əˈweɪ] adv weg, fort; two hours ~ by car zwei Autostunden entfernt; the holiday was two weeks ~ es war noch zwei Wochen bis zum Urlaub; **two kilometres ~** zwei Kilometer entfernt; ~ **match** n (SPORT) Auswärtsspiel nt

awe [ɔː] n Ehrfurcht f; ~**-inspiring** adj ehrfurchtgebietend; ~**some** adj ehrfurchtgebietend

awful [ˈɔːfʊl] adj (very bad) furchtbar; ~**ly** adv furchtbar, sehr

awhile [əˈwaɪl] adv eine Weile

awkward [ˈɔːkwəd] adj (clumsy) ungeschickt, linkisch; (embarrassing) peinlich

awning [ˈɔːnɪŋ] n Markise f

awoke [əˈwəʊk] pt of **awake**; **awoken** [əˈwəʊkən] pp of **awake**

awry [əˈraɪ] adv schief; **to go ~** (person) fehlgehen; (plans) schiefgehen

axe [æks] (US **ax**) n Axt f, Beil nt ♦ vt (end suddenly) streichen

axes¹ [ˈæksɪz] npl of **axe**

axes² [ˈæksiːz] npl of **axis**

axis [ˈæksɪs] (pl **axes**) n Achse f

axle [ˈæksl] n Achse f

ay(e) [aɪ] excl (yes) ja

azalea [əˈzeɪlɪə] n Azalee f

B

B [biː] n (MUS) H nt

B.A. n abbr = **Bachelor of Arts**

babble [ˈbæbl] vi schwätzen; (stream) murmeln

baby [ˈbeɪbɪ] n Baby nt; ~ **carriage** (US) n Kinderwagen m; ~**-sit** vi Kinder hüten, babysitten; ~**-sitter** n Babysitter m

bachelor [ˈbætʃələ*] n Junggeselle m; B~ of Arts Bakkalaureus m der philosophischen Fakultät; B~ of Science Bakkalaureus m der Naturwissenschaften

back [bæk] n (of person, horse) Rücken m; (of house) Rückseite f; (of train) Ende nt; (FOOTBALL) Verteidiger m ♦ vt (support) unterstützen; (wager) wetten auf +acc; (car) rückwärts fahren ♦ vi (go

backwards) rückwärts gehen or fahren ♦ adj hintere(r, s) ♦ adv zurück; (to the rear) nach hinten; ~ **down** vi zurückweichen; ~ **out** vi sich zurückziehen; (inf) kneifen; ~ **up** vt (support) unterstützen; (car) zurücksetzen; (COMPUT) eine Sicherungskopie machen von; ~**bencher** (BRIT) n Parlamentarier(in) m(f); ~**bone** n Rückgrat nt; (support) Rückhalt m; ~**cloth** n Hintergrund m; ~**date** vt rückdatieren; ~**drop** n (THEAT) = backcloth; (background) Hintergrund m; ~**fire** vi (plan) fehlschlagen; (TECH) fehlzünden; ~**ground** n Hintergrund m; (person's education) Vorbildung f; **family ~ground** Familienverhältnisse pl; ~**hand** n (TENNIS: also: ~hand stroke) Rückhand f; ~**hander** (BRIT) n (bribe) Schmiergeld nt; ~**ing** n (support) Unterstützung f; ~**lash** n (fig) Gegenschlag m; ~**log** n (of work) Rückstand m; ~**number** n (PRESS) alte Nummer f; ~**pack** n Rucksack m; ~ **pay** n (Gehalts- or Lohn)nachzahlung f; ~ **payments** npl Zahlungsrückstände pl; ~ **seat** n (AUT) Rücksitz m; ~**side** n (inf) Hintern m; ~**stage** adv hinter den Kulissen; ~**stroke** n Rückenschwimmen nt; ~**up** adj (train) Zusatz-; (plane) Sonder-; (COMPUT) Sicherungs- ♦ n (see adj) Zusatzzug m; Sondermaschine f; Sicherungskopie f; ~**ward** adj (less developed) (primitive) rückständig; ~**wards** adv rückwärts; ~**water** n (fig) Kaff nt; ~**yard** n Hinterhof m

bacon [ˈbeɪkən] n Schinkenspeck m

bacteria [bækˈtɪərɪə] npl Bakterien pl

bad [bæd] adj schlecht, schlimm; **to go ~** schlecht werden

bade [bæd] pt of **bid**

badge [bædʒ] n Abzeichen nt

badger [ˈbædʒə*] n Dachs m

badly [ˈbædlɪ] adv schlecht, schlimm; ~ **wounded** schwerverwundet; **he**

needs it ~ er braucht es dringend; **to be ~ off (for money)** dringend Geld nötig haben

badminton ['bædmɪntən] n Federball m, Badminton nt

bad-tempered ['bæd'tempəd] adj schlecht gelaunt

baffle ['bæfl] vt (puzzle) verblüffen

bag [bæg] n (sack) Beutel m; (paper) Tüte f; (hand~) Tasche f; (suitcase) Koffer m; (booty) Jagdbeute f; (inf: old woman) alte Schachtel f ♦ vt (put in sack) in einen Sack stecken; (hunting) erlegen; ~s npl (inf: lots of) eine Menge +acc; **~gage** ['bægɪdʒ] n Gepäck nt; **~gy** ['bægɪ] adj bauschig, sackartig; **~pipes** ['bægpaɪps] npl Dudelsack m

Bahamas [bə'hɑːməz] npl: **the ~** die Bahamas pl

bail [beɪl] n (money) Kaution f ♦ vt (prisoner: usu: grant ~ to) gegen Kaution freilassen; (boat: also: ~ out) ausschöpfen; **on ~** (prisoner) gegen Kaution freigelassen; **to ~ sb out** die Kaution für jdn stellen; see also **bale**

bailiff ['beɪlɪf] n Gerichtsvollzieher(in) m(f)

bait [beɪt] n Köder m ♦ vt mit einem Köder versehen; (fig) ködern

bake [beɪk] vt, vi backen; **~d beans** gebackene Bohnen pl; **~r** n Bäcker m; **~ry** n Bäckerei f

baking ['beɪkɪŋ] n Backen nt; **~ powder** n Backpulver nt

balance ['bæləns] n (scales) Waage f; (equilibrium) Gleichgewicht nt; (FIN: state of account) Saldo m; (difference) Bilanz f; (amount remain- ing) Restbetrag m ♦ vt (weigh) wägen; (make equal) ausgleichen; **~ of trade/payments** Handels-/Zahlungsbilanz f; **~d** adj ausgeglichen; **~ sheet** n Bilanz f, Rechnungsabschluß m

balcony ['bælkənɪ] n Balkon m

bald [bɔːld] adj kahl; (statement) knapp

bale [beɪl] n Ballen m (from a plane)

abspringen

ball [bɔːl] n Ball m; **~ bearing** n Kugellager nt

ballet ['bæleɪ] n Ballett nt; **~ dancer** n Ballettänzer(in) m(f)

balloon [bə'luːn] n (Luft)ballon m

ballot ['bælət] n (geheime) Abstimmung f

ballpoint (pen) ['bɔːlpɔɪnt] n Kugelschreiber m

ballroom ['bɔːlrʊm] n Tanzsaal m

Baltic ['bɔːltɪk] n: **the ~ (Sea)** die Ostsee

bamboo [bæm'buː] n Bambus m

ban [bæn] n Verbot nt ♦ vt verbieten

banana [bə'nɑːnə] n Banane f

band [bænd] n Band nt; (group) Gruppe f; (of criminals) Bande f; (MUS) Kapelle f, Band f; **~ to- gether** vi sich zusammentun

bandage ['bændɪdʒ] n Verband m; (elastic) Bandage f ♦ vt (cut) verbinden; (broken limb) bandagieren

bandaid ['bændeɪd] ® (US) n Heftpflaster nt

bandwagon ['bændwægən] n: **to jump on the ~** (fig) auf den fahrenden Zug aufspringen

bandy ['bændɪ] vt wechseln; **~- legged** ['bændɪ'legɪd] adj o-beinig

bang [bæŋ] n (explosion) Knall m; (blow) Hieb m ♦ vt, vi knallen

Bangladesh [bæŋglə'deʃ] n Bangladesch nt

bangle ['bæŋgl] n Armspange f

bangs [bæŋz] (US) npl (fringe) Pony m

banish ['bænɪʃ] vt verbannen

banister(s) ['bænɪstə(z)] n(pl) (Treppen)geländer nt

bank [bæŋk] n (raised ground) Erdwall m; (of lake etc) Ufer nt; (FIN) Bank f ♦ vt (tilt: AVIAT) in die Kurve bringen; (money) einzahlen; **~ on** vt fus: **to ~ on sth** mit etw rechnen; **~ account** n Bankkonto nt; **~ card** n Scheckkarte f; **~er** n Bankier m; **~er's card** (BRIT) n = **bank card**; **B~ holiday** (BRIT) n gesetzliche(r) Feiertag m; **~ing** n Bankwesen n

~note n Banknote f; ~ rate n Banksatz m

bankrupt ['bæŋkrʌpt] adj: to be ~ bankrott sein; to go ~ Bankrott machen; ~cy n Bankrott m

bank statement n Kontoauszug m

banner ['bænə*] n Banner nt

banns [bænz] npl Aufgebot nt

baptism ['bæptizəm] n Taufe f

baptize [bæp'taiz] vt taufen

bar [bɑː*] n (rod) Stange f; (obstacle) Hindernis nt; (of chocolate) Tafel f; (of soap) Stück nt; (for food, drink) Buffet nt, Bar f; (pub) Wirtschaft f; (MUS) Taktstrich m ♦ vt (fasten) verriegeln; (hinder) versperren; (exclude) ausschließen; behind ~s hinter Gittern; the B~: to be called to the B~ als Anwalt zugelassen werden; ~ none ohne Ausnahme

barbaric [bɑː'bærɪk] adj primitiv, unkultiviert

barbecue ['bɑːbɪkjuː] n Barbecue nt

barbed wire ['bɑːbd-] n Stacheldraht m

barber ['bɑːbə*] n Herrenfriseur m

bar code n (on goods) Registrierkode f

bare [bɛə*] adj nackt; (trees, country) kahl; (mere) bloß ♦ vt entblößen; ~back adv ungesattelt; ~faced adj unverfroren; ~foot adj, adv barfuß; ~ly adv kaum, knapp

bargain ['bɑːgɪn] n (sth cheap) günstiger Kauf; (agreement: written) Kaufvertrag m; (: oral) Geschäft n; into the ~ obendrein; ~ for vt: he got more than he ~ed for er erlebte sein blaues Wunder

barge [bɑːdʒ] n Lastkahn m; ~ in vi hereinplatzen; ~ into vt rennen

bark [bɑːk] n (of tree) Rinde f; (of dog) Bellen nt ♦ vi (dog) bellen

barley ['bɑːlɪ] n Gerste f; ~ sugar n Malzbonbon nt

barmaid ['bɑːmeɪd] n Bardame f

barman ['bɑːmən] (irreg) n Barkellner m

barn [bɑːn] n Scheune f

barometer [bə'rɒmɪtə*] n Barometer nt

baron ['bærən] n Baron m; ~ess n Baronin f

barracks ['bærəks] npl Kaserne f

barrage [bæ'rɑːʒ] n (gunfire) Sperrfeuer nt; (dam) Staudamm m; Talsperre f

barrel ['bærəl] n Faß nt; (of gun) Lauf m

barren ['bærən] adj unfruchtbar

barricade [bærɪ'keɪd] n Barrikade f ♦ vt verbarrikadieren

barrier ['bærɪə*] n (obstruction) Hindernis nt; (fence) Schranke f

barring ['bɑːrɪŋ] prep außer im Falle +gen

barrister ['bærɪstə*] (BRIT) n Rechtsanwalt m

barrow ['bærəu] n (cart) Schubkarren m

bartender ['bɑːtendə*] (US) n Barmann or -kellner m

barter ['bɑːtə*] vt handeln

base [beɪs] n (bottom) Boden m, Basis f; (MIL) Stützpunkt m ♦ vt gründen; (opinion, theory): to be ~d on basieren auf +dat ♦ adj (low) gemein; ~ball n Baseball m; ~ment ['beɪsmənt] n Kellergeschoß nt

bases¹ ['beɪsiːz] npl of base

bases² ['beɪsiːz] npl of basis

bash [bæʃ] (inf) vt (heftig) schlagen

bashful ['bæʃful] adj schüchtern

basic ['beɪsɪk] adj grundlegend; ~s npl: the ~s das Wesentliche (sg); ~ally adv im Grunde

basil ['bæzl] n Basilikum n

basin ['beɪsn] n (dish) Schüssel f; (for washing, also valley) Becken nt; (dock) (Trocken)becken nt

basis ['beɪsɪs] (pl bases) n Basis f, Grundlage f

bask [bɑːsk] vi: to ~ in the sun sich sonnen

basket ['bɑːskɪt] n Korb m; ~ball n Basketball m

bass [beɪs] n (MUS, also instrument) Baß m

Baß m; (voice) Baßstimme f

bassoon [bə'su:n] n Fagott nt

bastard ['bɑ:stəd] n Bastard m; (inf!) Arschloch nt (!)

bastion ['bæstɪən] n (also fig) Bollwerk nt

bat [bæt] n (SPORT) Schlagholz nt; Schläger m; (ZOOL) Fledermaus ♦ vt: he didn't ~ an eyelid er hat nicht mit der Wimper gezuckt

batch [bætʃ] n (of letters) Stoß m; (of samples) Satz m

bated ['beɪtɪd] adj: with ~ breath mit angehaltenem Atem

bath [bɑ:θ, pl bɑ:ðz] n (~ tub) Badewanne f ♦ vt baden; to have a ~ baden; see also baths

bathe [beɪð] vt, vi baden; ~r n Badende(r) mf

bathing ['beɪðɪŋ] n Baden nt; ~ cap n Badekappe f; ~ costume n Badeanzug m; ~ suit n (US) n Badeanzug m; ~ trunks (BRIT) npl Badehose f

bathrobe ['bɑ:θrəʊb] n Bademantel m

bathroom ['bɑ:θrʊm] n Bad(ezimmer nt) nt

baths [bɑ:ðz] npl (Schwimm)bad nt

bath towel n Badetuch nt

baton ['bætən] n (of police) Gummiknüppel m; (MUS) Taktstock m

batter ['bætə*] vt verprügeln ♦ n Schlagteig m; (for cake) Biskuitteig m; ~ed adj (hat, pan) verbeult

battery ['bætərɪ] n (ELEC) Batterie f; (MIL) Geschützbatterie f

battle ['bætl] n Schlacht f; (small) Gefecht nt ♦ vi kämpfen; ~field n Schlachtfeld nt; ~ship n Schlachtschiff nt

Bavaria n Bayern nt; ~n adj bay(e)risch ♦ n (person) Bayer(in) m(f); (LING) Bay(e)risch nt

bawdy ['bɔ:dɪ] adj unflätig

bawl [bɔ:l] vi brüllen

bay [beɪ] n (of sea) Bucht f ♦ vi bellen; to keep at ~ unter Kontrolle halten

bay window n Erkerfenster nt

bazaar [bə'zɑ:*] n Basar m

B. & B. abbr = bed and breakfast

BBC n abbr (= British Broadcasting Corporation) BBC f or m

B.C. adv abbr (= before Christ) v.Chr.

be [bi:] (pt was, were, pp been) aux vb **1** (with present participle: forming continuous tenses): what are you doing? was machst du (gerade)?; it is raining es regnet; I've been waiting for you for hours ich warte schon seit Stunden auf dich

2 (with pp: forming passives): to be killed getötet werden; the thief was nowhere to be seen der Dieb war nirgendwo zu sehen

3 (in tag questions): it was fun, wasn't it? es hat Spaß gemacht, nicht wahr?

4 (+to +infin): the house is to be sold das Haus soll verkauft werden; he's not to open it er darf es nicht öffnen

♦ vb +complement **1** (usu with adj, n): I'm tired ich bin müde; I'm hot/cold mir ist heiß/kalt; he's a doctor er ist Arzt; **2 and 2 are 4** 2 und 2 ist or sind 4; she's tall/pretty sie ist groß/hübsch; be careful/quiet sei vorsichtig/ruhig

2 (of health): how are you? wie geht es dir?; he's very ill er ist sehr krank; I'm fine now mir geht es mir gut

3 (of age): how old are you? wie alt bist du?; I'm sixteen (years) old ich bin sechzehn (Jahre alt)

4 (cost): how much was the meal? was or wieviel hat das Essen gekostet?; that'll be £5.75, please das macht 5,75, bitte

♦ vi **1** (exist, occur etc) sein; is there a God? gibt es einen Gott?; be that as it may wie dem auch sei; so be it also gut

2 (referring to place) sein; I won't be here tomorrow ich werde mor-

gen nicht hier sein
3 (referring to movement): **where have you been?** wo bist du gewesen?; **I've been in the garden** ich war im Garten
♦ impers vb **1** (referring to time, distance, weather) sein; **it's 5 o'clock** es ist 5 Uhr; **it's 10 km to the village** es sind 10 km bis zum Dorf; **it's too hot/cold** es ist zu heiß/kalt
2 (emphatic): **it's me** ich bin's; **it's the postman** es ist der Briefträger

beach [biːtʃ] n Strand m ♦ vt (ship) auf den Strand setzen
beacon ['biːkən] n (signal) Leuchtfeuer nt; (traffic ~) Bake f
bead [biːd] n Perle f; (drop) Tropfen m
beak [biːk] n Schnabel m
beaker ['biːkə*] n Becher m
beam [biːm] n (of wood) Balken m; (of light) Strahl m; (smile) strahlende(s) Lächeln nt ♦ vi strahlen
bean [biːn] n Bohne f; **~ sprouts** npl Sojasprossen pl
bear [bɛə*] (pt bore, pp borne) n Bär m; (of weight, crops) tragen; (tolerate) ertragen; (young) gebären ♦ vi: **to ~ right/left** sich rechts/links halten; **~ out** vt (suspicions etc) bestätigen; **~ up** vi sich halten
beard [bɪəd] n Bart m; **~ed** adj bärtig
bearer ['bɛərə*] n Träger m
bearing ['bɛərɪŋ] n (posture) Haltung f; (relevance) Relevanz f; (relation) Bedeutung f; (TECH) Kugellager nt; **~s** npl (direction) Orientierung f; (also: **ball ~s**) (Kugel)lager nt
beast [biːst] n Tier nt, Vieh nt; (person) Biest nt; **~ly** adj viehisch; (inf) scheußlich
beat [biːt] (pt beat, pp beaten) n (stroke) Schlag m; (pulsation) Herz)schlag m; (police round) Runde f; Revier nt; (MUS) Takt m; Beat m ♦ vt, vi schlagen; **to ~ it** abhauen; **off the ~en track** abge-

gen; **~ off** vt abschlagen; zusammenschlagen; **beaten** pp of beat; **~ing** n Prügel pl
beautiful ['bjuːtɪful] adj schön; **~ly** adv ausgezeichnet
beauty ['bjuːtɪ] n Schönheit f; **~ salon** n Schönheitssalon m; **~ spot** n Schönheitsfleck m; (BRIT: TOURISM) (besonders) schöne(r) Ort m
beaver ['biːvə*] n Biber m
became [bɪ'keɪm] pt of become
because [bɪ'kɒz] conj weil ♦ prep: **~ of** wegen +gen, wegen +dat (inf)
beck [bɛk] n: **to be at the ~ and call of sb** nach jds Pfeife tanzen
beckon ['bɛkən] vt, vi: **(to ~ to sb)** jdm ein Zeichen geben
become [bɪ'kʌm] (irreg: like come) vi werden ♦ vt werden; (clothes) stehen +dat
becoming [bɪ'kʌmɪŋ] adj (suitable) schicklich; (clothes) kleidsam
bed [bɛd] n Bett nt; (of river) Flußbett nt; (foundation) Schicht f; (in garden) Beet nt; **to go to ~** zu Bett gehen; **~ and breakfast** n Übernachtung f mit Frühstück; **~clothes** npl Bettwäsche f; **~ding** n Bettzeug nt
bedlam ['bɛdləm] n (uproar) tolle(s) Durcheinander nt
bedraggled [bɪ'dræɡld] adj ramponiert
bed: **~ridden** adj bettlägerig; **~room** n Schlafzimmer nt; **~side** n: **at the ~side** am Bett; **~sit(ter)** (BRIT) n Einzimmerwohnung f, möblierte(s) Zimmer nt; **~spread** n Tagesdecke f; **~time** n Schlafenszeit f
bee [biː] n Biene f
beech [biːtʃ] n Buche f
beef [biːf] n Rindfleisch nt; **roast ~** n Roastbeef nt; **~burger** n Hamburger m
beehive ['biːhaɪv] n Bienenstock m
beeline ['biːlaɪn] n: **to make a ~ for** schnurstracks zugehen auf +acc
been [biːn] pp of be
beer [bɪə*] n Bier nt

beet [biːt] n (vegetable) Rübe f; (US: also: red ~) rote Bete f or Rübe f

beetle ['biːtl] n Käfer m

beetroot ['biːtruːt] (BRIT) n rote Bete f

before [bɪ'fɔː*] prep vor ♦ conj bevor ♦ adv (of time) zuvor; früher; **the week ~** die Woche zuvor or vorher; **I've done it ~** das hab' ich schon mal getan; **~ going** bevor er sie geht/ging; **~ she goes** bevor sie geht; **~hand** adv im voraus

beg [beg] vt, vi (implore) dringend bitten; (alms) betteln

began [bɪ'gæn] pt of begin

beggar ['begə*] n Bettler(in) m(f)

begin [bɪ'gɪn] (pt began, pp begun) vt, vi anfangen, beginnen; (found) gründen; **to ~ doing** or **to do sth** anfangen or beginnen, etw zu tun; **to ~ with** zunächst (einmal); **~ner** n Anfänger m; **~ning** n Anfang m

begun [bɪ'gʌn] pp of begin

behalf [bɪ'hɑːf] n: **on ~ of** im Namen +gen; **on my ~** für mich

behave [bɪ'heɪv] vi sich benehmen

behaviour [bɪ'heɪvjə*] (US behavior) n Benehmen nt

behead [bɪ'hed] vt enthaupten

beheld [bɪ'held] pt, pp of behold

behind [bɪ'haɪnd] prep hinter ♦ adv (late) im Rückstand; (in the rear) hinten ♦ n (inf) Hinterteil nt; **~ the scenes** (fig) hinter den Kulissen

behold [bɪ'həʊld] (irreg: like hold) vt erblicken

beige [beɪʒ] adj beige

Beijing ['beɪ'dʒɪŋ] n Peking nt

being ['biːɪŋ] n (existence) (Da)sein nt; (person) Wesen nt; **to come into ~** entstehen

belated [bɪ'leɪtɪd] adj verspätet

belch [beltʃ] vi rülpsen ♦ vt (smoke) ausspeien

belfry ['belfrɪ] n Glockenturm m

Belgian ['beldʒən] adj belgisch ♦ n Belgier(in) m(f)

Belgium ['beldʒəm] n Belgien nt

belie [bɪ'laɪ] vt Lügen strafen +acc

belief [bɪ'liːf] n Glaube m; (conviction) Überzeugung f; **in sb/sth** Glaube an jdn/etw

believe [bɪ'liːv] vt glauben +dat; (think) glauben, meinen, denken ♦ vi (have faith) glauben; **to ~ in sth** an etw acc glauben; **~r** n Gläubige(r) mf

belittle [bɪ'lɪtl] vt herabsetzen

bell [bel] n Glocke f

belligerent [bɪ'lɪdʒərənt] adj (person) streitsüchtig; (country) kriegsführend

bellow ['beləʊ] vt, vi brüllen

bellows ['beləʊz] npl (TECH) Gebläse nt; (for fire) Blasebalg m

belly ['belɪ] n Bauch m

belong [bɪ'lɒŋ] vi gehören; **to ~ to sb** jdm gehören; **to ~ to a club** etc einem Club etc angehören; **it does not ~ here** es gehört nicht hierher; **~ings** npl Habe f

beloved [bɪ'lʌvɪd] adj innig geliebt ♦ n Geliebte(r) mf

below [bɪ'ləʊ] prep unter ♦ adv unten

belt [belt] n (band) Riemen m; (round waist) Gürtel m ♦ vt (inf: beat) schlagen; **~way** (US) n (AUT: ring road) Umgehungsstraße f

bemused [bɪ'mjuːzd] adj verwirrt

bench [bentʃ] n (seat) Bank f; (workshop) Werkbank f; (judge's seat) Richterbank f; (judges) Richter pl

bend [bend] (pt, pp bent) vt (curve) biegen; (stoop) beugen ♦ vi sich biegen; sich beugen ♦ n Biegung f; (BRIT: in road) Kurve f; **~ down** or **over** vi sich bücken

beneath [bɪ'niːθ] prep unter ♦ adv darunter

benefactor ['benɪfæktə*] n Wohltäter(in) m(f)

beneficial [benɪ'fɪʃl] adj vorteilhaft; (to health) heilsam

benefit ['benɪfɪt] n (advantage) Nutzen m ♦ vt fördern ♦ vi: **to ~ (from)** Nutzen ziehen (aus)

Benelux [ˈbenɪlʌks] n Beneluxstaaten pl

benevolent [bɪˈnevələnt] adj wohlwollend

benign [bɪˈnaɪn] adj (person) gütig; (climate) mild

bent [bent] pt, pp of bend ♦ n (inclination) Neigung f ♦ adj (inf: dishonest) unehrlich; **to be ~ on** versessen sein auf +acc

bequest [bɪˈkwest] n Vermächtnis nt

bereaved [bɪˈriːvd] npl: **the ~** die Hinterbliebenen pl

bereft [bɪˈreft] adj: **~ of** bar +gen

beret [ˈbereɪ] n Baskenmütze f

Berlin [bɜːˈlɪn] n Berlin nt

berm [bɜːm] n (US) n (AUT) Seitenstreifen m

Bermuda [bɜːˈmjuːdə] n Bermuda nt

berry [ˈberɪ] n Beere f

berserk [bəˈsɜːk] adj: **to go ~** wild werden

berth [bɜːθ] n (for ship) Ankerplatz m; (in ship) Koje f; (in train) Bett nt ♦ vt am Kai festmachen ♦ vi anlegen

beseech [bɪˈsiːtʃ] (pt, pp besought) vt anflehen

beset [bɪˈset] (pt, pp beset) vt bedrängen

beside [bɪˈsaɪd] prep neben, bei; (except) außer; **to be ~ o.s. (with)** außer sich sein (vor +dat); **that's ~ the point** das tut nichts zur Sache

besides [bɪˈsaɪdz] prep außer, neben ♦ adv außerdem

besiege [bɪˈsiːdʒ] vt (MIL) belagern; (surround) umlagern, bedrängen

besought [bɪˈsɔːt] pt, pp of beseech

best [best] adj (+r, s) ♦ adv am besten; **the ~ part of** (quantity) das meiste +gen; **at ~** höchstens; **to make the ~ of it** das Beste daraus machen; **to do one's ~** sein Bestes tun; **to the ~ of my knowledge** meines Wissens; **to the ~ of my ability** so gut ich kann; **for the ~** zum Besten; **~ man** n Trauzeuge m

bestow [bɪˈstəʊ] vt verleihen

bet [bet] (pt, pp bet or betted) n

Wette f ♦ vt, vi wetten

betray [bɪˈtreɪ] vt verraten

better [ˈbetə*] adj, adv besser ♦ vt verbessern ♦ n: **to get the ~ of sb** jdn überwinden; **he thought ~ of it** er hat sich eines Besseren besonnen; **you had ~ leave** Sie gehen jetzt wohl besser; **to get ~** (MED) gesund werden; **~ off** adj (richer) wohlhabender

betting [ˈbetɪŋ] n Wetten nt; **~ shop** (BRIT) n Wettbüro nt

between [bɪˈtwiːn] prep zwischen; (among) unter ♦ adv dazwischen

beverage [ˈbevərɪdʒ] n Getränk nt

bevy [ˈbevɪ] n Schar f

beware [bɪˈweə*] vt, vi sich hüten vor +dat; **"~ of the dog"** „Vorsicht, bissiger Hund!"

bewildered [bɪˈwɪldəd] adj verwirrt

bewitching [bɪˈwɪtʃɪŋ] adj bestrickend

beyond [bɪˈjɒnd] prep (place) jenseits +gen; (time) über ... hinaus; (out of reach) außerhalb +gen ♦ adv darüber hinaus; **~ doubt** ohne Zweifel; **~ repair** nicht mehr zu reparieren

bias [ˈbaɪəs] n (slant) Neigung f; (prejudice) Vorurteil nt; **~(s)ed** adj voreingenommen

bib [bɪb] n Latz m

Bible [ˈbaɪbl] n Bibel f

bicarbonate of soda [baɪˈkɑːbənɪt-] n Natron nt

bicker [ˈbɪkə*] vi zanken

bicycle [ˈbaɪsɪkl] n Fahrrad nt

bid [bɪd] (pt bade or bid, pp bid(den)) n (offer) Gebot nt; (attempt) Versuch m ♦ vt, vi (offer) bieten; **to ~ farewell** Lebewohl sagen; **bidden** [ˈbɪdn] pp of bid; **~der** n (person) Steigerer m; **the highest ~der** der Meistbietende; **~ding** n (command) Geheiß nt

bide [baɪd] vt: **to ~ one's time** abwarten

bifocals [baɪˈfəʊkəlz] npl Bifokalbrille f

big [bɪg] adj groß

big dipper [-'dɪpə*] n Achterbahn f
bigheaded ['bɪg'hedɪd] adj eingebildet

bigot ['bɪgət] n Frömmler m; **~ed**
adj bigott; **~ry** n Bigotterie f
big top n Zirkuszelt nt
bike [baɪk] n Rad nt
bikini [bɪ'ki:nɪ] n Bikini m
bile [baɪl] n (BIOL) Galle f
bilingual [baɪ'lɪŋgwəl] adj zweisprachig

bill [bɪl] n (account) Rechnung f;
(POL) Gesetzentwurf m; (US: FIN)
Geldschein m; **to fit** or **fill the ~**
(fig) der/die/das richtige sein; "**post
no ~s**" "Plakate ankleben verboten"; **~board** ['bɪlbɔːd] n Reklameschild nt

billet ['bɪlɪt] n Quartier nt
billfold ['bɪlfəʊld] (US) n Geldscheintasche f
billiards ['bɪljədz] n Billard nt
billion ['bɪljən] n (BRIT) Billion f;
(US) Milliarde f
bin [bɪn] n Kasten m; (dust~) (Abfall)eimer m
bind [baɪnd] (pt, pp **bound**) vt (tie)
binden; (tie together) zusammenbinden; (oblige) verpflichten; **~ing** n
(Buch)einband m ♦ adj verbindlich
binge [bɪndʒ] (inf) n Sauferei f
bingo ['bɪngəʊ] n Bingo nt
binoculars [bɪ'nɒkjʊləz] npl Fernglas nt

bio... [baɪəʊ] prefix: **~chemistry** n
Biochemie f; **~graphy** n Biographie
f; **~logical** [baɪə'lɒdʒɪkəl] adj biologisch; **~logy** [baɪ'ɒlədʒɪ] n Biologie f
birch [bɜːtʃ] n Birke f

bird [bɜːd] n Vogel m; (BRIT: inf:
girl) Mädchen nt; **~'s-eye view** n
Vogelschau f; **~ watcher** n Vogelbeobachter(in) m(f)

Biro [baɪərəʊ] ® n Kugelschreiber
m

birth [bɜːθ] n Geburt f; **to give ~ to**
zur Welt bringen; **~ certificate** n Geburtsurkunde f; **~ control** n Geburtenkontrolle f; **~day** n Geburtstag
m; **~day card** n Geburtstagskarte f;

~place n Geburtsort m; **~ rate** n
Geburtenrate f

biscuit ['bɪskɪt] n Keks m
bisect [baɪ'sekt] vt halbieren
bishop ['bɪʃəp] n Bischof m

bit [bɪt] pt of **bite** ♦ n bißchen,
Stückchen nt; (horse's) Gebiß nt;
(COMPUT) Bit nt; **a ~ tired** etwas
müde

bitch [bɪtʃ] n (dog) Hündin f; (unpleasant woman) Weibsstück nt
bite [baɪt] (pt **bit**, pp **bitten**) vt, vi
beißen ♦ n Biß m; (mouthful) Bissen
m; **to ~ one's nails** Nägel kauen;
let's have a ~ to eat laß uns etwas
essen

biting ['baɪtɪŋ] adj beißend
bitten ['bɪtn] pp of **bite**
bitter ['bɪtə*] adj bitter; (memory
etc) schmerzlich; (person) verbittert
♦ n (BRIT: beer) dunkle(s) Bier nt;
~ness n Bitterkeit f
blab [blæb] vi klatschen ♦ vt (also: ~
out) ausplaudern

black [blæk] adj schwarz; (night)
finster ♦ vt schwärzen; (shoes) wichsen; (eye) blau schlagen; (BRIT: INDUSTRY) boykottieren; **to give sb a
~ eye** jdm ein blaues Auge schlagen; **in the ~** (bank account) in den
schwarzen Zahlen; **~ and blue** adj
grün und blau; **~berry** n Brombeere
f; **~bird** n Amsel f; **~board** n
(Wand)tafel f; **~ coffee** n schwarze(r) Kaffee m; **~currant** n schwarze Johannisbeere f; **~en** vt
schwärzen; (fig) verunglimpfen; **B-
Forestblack** n Schwarzwald m; **~ ice**
n Glatteis m; **~** (US) n Siebzehn und
Vier; **~leg** (BRIT) n Streikbrecher(in) m(f); **~list** n schwarze Liste f; **~mail** n Erpressung f ♦ vt erpressen; **~ market** n Schwarzmarkt
m; **~out** n Verdunklung f; (MED):
to have a ~out bewußtlos werden;
~ Sea n: the ~ Sea das Schwarze
Meer; **~ sheep** n schwarze(s) Schaf
nt; **~smith** n Schmied m; **~ spot** n
(AUT) Gefahrenstelle f; (for unemployment etc) schwer betroffene(s)

Gebiet *nt*

bladder ['blædə*] *n* Blase *f*

blade [bleɪd] *n* (*of weapon*) Klinge *f*; (*of grass*) Halm *m*; (*of oar*) Ruderblatt *nt*

blame [bleɪm] *n* Tadel *m*, Schuld *f* ♦ *vt* Vorwürfe machen +*dat*; **to ~ sb for sth** jdm die Schuld an etw *dat* geben; **he is to ~** er ist daran schuld

bland [blænd] *adj* mild

blank [blæŋk] *adj* leer, unbeschrieben; (*look*) verdutzt; (*verse*) Blank- ♦ *n* (*space*) Lücke *f*; Zwischenraum *m*; (*cartridge*) Platzpatrone *f*; **~ cheque** *n* Blankoscheck *m*; Freibrief *m*

blanket ['blæŋkɪt] *n* (Woll)decke *f*

blare [blɛə*] *vi* (*radio*) plärren; (*horn*) tuten; (*MUS*) schmettern

blasé ['blɑːzeɪ] *adj* blasiert

blast [blɑːst] *n* Explosion *f*; (*of wind*) Windstoß *m* ♦ *vt* (*blow up*) sprengen; **~!** (*inf*) verflixt!; **~-off** *n* (*SPACE*) (Raketen)abschuß *m*

blatant ['bleɪtənt] *adj* offenkundig

blaze [bleɪz] *n* (*fire*) lodernde(s) Feuer *nt* ♦ *vi* lodern ♦ *vt*: **to ~ a trail** Bahn brechen

blazer ['bleɪzə*] *n* Blazer *m*

bleach [bliːtʃ] *n* (*also: household ~*) Bleichmittel *nt* ♦ *vt* bleichen

bleachers ['bliːtʃəz] (*US*) *npl* (*SPORT*) unüberdachte Tribüne *f*

bleak [bliːk] *adj* kahl, rauh; (*future*) trostlos

bleary-eyed ['blɪərɪaɪd] *adj* triefäugig; (*on waking up*) mit verschlafenen Augen

bleat [bliːt] *vi* blöken; (*fig: complain*) meckern

bled [bled] *pt*, *pp* *of* **bleed**

bleed [bliːd] (*pt*, *pp* **bled**) *vi* bluten ♦ *vt* (*draw blood*) zur Ader lassen; **to ~ to death** verbluten

bleeper ['bliːpə*] *n* (*of doctor etc*) Funkrufempfänger *m*

blemish ['blemɪʃ] *n* Makel *m* ♦ *vt* verunstalten

blend [blend] *n* Mischung *f* ♦ *vt* mi-

schen ♦ *vi* sich mischen

bless [bles] (*pt*, *pp* **blessed** *or* **blest**) *vt* segnen; (*give thanks*) preisen; (*make happy*) glücklich machen; **~ you!** Gesundheit!; **~ing** *n* Segen *m*; (*at table*) Tischgebet *nt*; (*happiness*) Wohltat *f*; Segen *m*; (*good wish*) Glück *nt*

blest [blest] *pt*, *pp* *of* **bless**

blew [bluː] *pt* *of* **blow**

blight [blaɪt] *vt* zunichte machen

blimey ['blaɪmɪ] (*BRIT: inf*) *excl* verflucht

blind [blaɪnd] *adj* blind; (*corner*) unübersichtlich ♦ *n* (*for window*) Rouleau *nt* ♦ *vt* blenden; **~ alley** *n* Sackgasse *f*; **~fold** *n* Augenbinde *f* ♦ *adj*, *adv* mit verbundenen Augen ♦ *vt*: **to ~fold sb** jdm die Augen verbinden; **~ly** *adv* blind; (*fig*) blindlings; **~ness** *n* Blindheit *f*; **~ spot** *n* (*AUT*) tote(r) Winkel *m*; (*fig*) schwache(r) Punkt *m*

blink [blɪŋk] *vi* blinzeln; **~ers** *npl* Scheuklappen *pl*

bliss [blɪs] *n* (Glück)seligkeit *f*

blister ['blɪstə*] *n* Blase *f* ♦ *vi* Blasen werfen

blithe [blaɪð] *adj* munter

blitz [blɪts] *n* Luftkrieg *m*

blizzard ['blɪzəd] *n* Schneesturm *m*

bloated ['bləʊtɪd] *adj* aufgedunsen; (*inf: full*) nudelsatt

blob [blɒb] *n* Klümpchen *nt*

bloc [blɒk] *n* (*POL*) Block *m*

block [blɒk] *n* (*of wood*) Block *m*, Klotz *m*; (*of houses*) Häuserblock *m* ♦ *vt* hemmen; **~ade** [blɒ'keɪd] *n* Blockade *f* ♦ *vt* blockieren; **~age** *n* Verstopfung *f*; **~buster** *n* Knüller *m*; **~ of flats** (*BRIT*) *n* Häuserblock *m*; **~ letters** *npl* Blockbuchstaben *pl*

bloke [bləʊk] (*BRIT: inf*) *n* Kerl *m*, Typ *m*

blond(e) [blɒnd] *adj* blond ♦ *n* Blondine *f*

blood [blʌd] *n* Blut *nt*; **~ donor** *n* Blutspender *m*; **~ group** *n* Blutgruppe *f*; **~ pressure** *n* Blutdruck *m*; **~shed** *n* Blutvergießen *nt*; **~shot**

adj blutunterlaufen; **~stained** *adj* blutbefleckt; **~stream** *n* Blut *nt*, Blutkreislauf *m*; **~ test** *n* Blutprobe *f*; **~thirsty** *adj* blutrünstig; **~y** *adj* blutig; (*BRIT: inf*) verdammt; **~y-minded** (*BRIT: inf*) *adj* stur

bloom [blu:m] *n* Blüte *f*; (*freshness*) Glanz *m* ♦ *vi* blühen

blossom ['blɒsəm] *n* Blüte *f* ♦ *vi* blühen

blot [blɒt] *n* Klecks *m* ♦ *vt* beklecksen; (*ink*) (ab)löschen; **~ out** *vt* auslöschen

blotchy ['blɒtʃɪ] *adj* fleckig

blotting paper ['blɒtɪŋ-] *n* Löschpapier *nt*

blouse [blauz] *n* Bluse *f*

blow [bləʊ] (*pt* **blew**, *pp* **blown**) *n* Schlag *m* ♦ *vt* blasen ♦ *vi* (*wind*) wehen; **to ~ one's nose** sich *dat* die Nase putzen; **~ away** *vt* wegblasen; **~ down** *vt* umwehen; **~ out** *vi* ausgehen; **~ over** *vi* vorübergehen; **~ up** *vi* explodieren ♦ *vt* sprengen; **dry** *vi*: **to have a ~dry** sich fönen lassen ♦ *vt* fönen; **~lamp** (*BRIT*) *n* Lötlampe *f*; **~n** [bləʊn] *pp of* **blow**; **~out** *n* (*AUT*) geplatzte(r) Reifen *m*; **~torch** *n* = **blowlamp**

blue [blu:] *adj* blau; (*unhappy*) niedergeschlagen; (*obscene*) pornographisch; (*joke*) anzüglich; **out of the ~** (*fig*) aus heiterem Himmel; **to have the ~s** traurig sein; **~bell** *n* Glockenblume *f*; **~bottle** *n* Schmeißfliege *f*; **~ film** *n* Pornofilm *m*; **~print** *n* (*fig*) Entwurf *m*

bluff [blʌf] *vi* bluffen, täuschen ♦ *n* (*deception*) Bluff *m*; **to call sb's ~** es darauf ankommen lassen

blunder ['blʌndə*] *n* grobe(r) Fehler *m*, Schnitzer *m* ♦ *vi* einen groben Fehler machen

blunt [blʌnt] *adj* (*knife*) stumpf; (*talk*) unverblümt ♦ *vt* abstumpfen

blur [blɜ:*] *n* Fleck *m* ♦ *vt* verschwommen machen

blurb [blɜ:b] *n* Waschzettel *m*

blurt [blɜ:t] *vt*: **~ out** herausplatzen mit

blush [blʌʃ] *vi* erröten ♦ *n* (Scham)röte *f*

blustery ['blʌstərɪ] *adj* stürmisch

boar [bɔ:*] *n* Keiler *m*, Eber *m*

board [bɔ:d] *n* (*of wood*) Brett *nt*; (*of card*) Pappe *f*; (*committee*) Ausschuß *m*; (*of firm*) Aufsichtsrat *m*; (*SCH*) Direktorium *nt* ♦ *vt* (*train*) einsteigen in +*acc*; (*ship*) an Bord gehen +*gen*; **on ~** (*AVIAT, NAUT*) an Bord; **~ and lodging** Unterkunft *f* und Verpflegung; **full/half ~** (*BRIT*) Voll-/Halbpension *f*; **to go by the ~** flachfallen, über Bord gehen; **~ up** *vt* mit Brettern vernageln; **~er** *n* Kostgänger *m*; (*SCH*) Internatsschüler(in) *m(f)*; **~ing card** *n* (*AVIAT, NAUT*) Bordkarte *f*; **~ing house** *n* Pension *f*; **~ing school** *n* Internat *nt*; **~ room** *n* Sitzungszimmer *nt*

boast [bəʊst] *vi* prahlen ♦ *vt* sich rühmen +*gen* ♦ *n* Großtuerei *f*; Prahlerei *f*; **to ~ about** *or* **of sth** mit etw prahlen

boat [bəʊt] *n* Boot *nt*; (*ship*) Schiff *nt*; **~er** *n* (*hat*) Kreissäge *f*; **~swain** *n* = **bosun**

bob [bɒb] *vi* sich auf und nieder bewegen ♦ *n* (*BRIT: inf*) = **shilling**; **~ up** *vi* auftauchen

bobbin ['bɒbɪn] *n* Spule *f*

bobby ['bɒbɪ] (*BRIT: inf*) *n* Bobby *m*

bobsleigh ['bɒbsleɪ] *n* Bob *m*

bode [bəʊd] *vi*: **to ~ well/ill** ein gutes/schlechtes Zeichen sein

bodily ['bɒdɪlɪ] *adj, adv* körperlich

body ['bɒdɪ] *n* Körper *m*; (*dead*) Leiche *f*; (*group*) Mannschaft *f*; (*AUT*) Karosserie *f*; (*trunk*) Rumpf *m*; **~guard** *n* Leibwache *f*; **~work** *n* Karosserie *f*

bog [bɒg] *n* Sumpf *m* ♦ *vt*: **to get ~ged down** sich festfahren

boggle ['bɒgl] *vi* stutzen; **the mind ~s** es ist kaum auszumalen

bogus ['bəʊgəs] *adj* unecht, Schein-

boil [bɔɪl] *vt, vi* kochen ♦ *n* (*MED*) Geschwür *nt*; **to come to the**

(BRIT) or a *(US)* ~ zu kochen anfangen; **to ~ down to** *(fig)* hinauslaufen auf +*acc*; ~ **over** vi überkochen; ~**ed egg** n gekochte(s) Ei *nt*; ~**ed potatoes** *npl* Salzkartoffeln *pl*; ~**er** n Boiler m; ~**er suit** *(BRIT)* n Arbeitsanzug m; ~**ing point** n Siedepunkt m

boisterous ['bɔɪstərəs] *adj* ungestüm

bold [bəʊld] *adj (fearless)* unerschrocken; *(handwriting)* fest und klar

bollard ['bɒləd] n *(NAUT)* Poller m; *(BRIT: AUT)* Pfosten m

bolster ['bəʊlstə*] : ~ **up** vt unterstützen

bolt [bəʊlt] n Bolzen m; *(lock)* Riegel m ♦ *adv*: ~ **upright** kerzengerade ♦ vt verriegeln; *(swallow)* verschlingen ♦ vi *(horse)* durchgehen

bomb [bɒm] n Bombe f ♦ vt bombardieren; ~**ard** [bɒm'bɑːd] vt bombardieren; ~**ardment** n Beschießung f; ~ **disposal** n Bombenräumkommando *nt*; ~**shell** n *(fig)* Bombe f

bona fide ['bəʊnə'faɪdɪ] *adj* echt

bond [bɒnd] n *(link)* Band *nt*; *(FIN)* Schuldverschreibung f

bondage ['bɒndɪdʒ] n Sklaverei f

bone [bəʊn] n Knochen m; *(of fish)* Gräte f; *(piece of)* ~ Knochensplitter m ♦ vt die Knochen herausnehmen +*dat*; *(fish)* entgräten; ~ **idle** *adj* stinkfaul

bonfire ['bɒnfaɪə*] n Feuer *nt* im Freien

bonnet ['bɒnɪt] n Haube f; *(for baby)* Häubchen *nt*; *(BRIT: AUT)* Motorhaube f

bonus ['bəʊnəs] n Bonus m; *(annual ~)* Prämie f

bony ['bəʊnɪ] *adj* knochig, knochendürr

boo [buː] vt auspfeifen

booby trap ['buːbɪ-] n Falle f

book [bʊk] n Buch *nt* ♦ vt *(ticket etc)* vorbestellen; *(person)* verwarnen; ~**s** *npl (COMM)* Bücher *pl*; ~**case** n Bücherregal *nt*, Bücher-

schrank m; ~**ing office** *(BRIT)* n *(RAIL)* Fahrkartenschalter m; *(THEAT)* Vorverkaufsstelle f; ~**keeping** n Buchhaltung f; ~**let** n Broschüre f; ~**maker** n Buchmacher m; ~**seller** n Buchhändler m; ~**shop, ~store** n Buchhandlung f

boom [buːm] n *(noise)* Dröhnen *nt*; *(busy period)* Hochkonjunktur f ♦ vi dröhnen

boon [buːn] n Wohltat f, Segen m

boost [buːst] n Auftrieb m; *(fig)* Reklame f ♦ vt Auftrieb geben; ~**er** n *(MED)* Wiederholungsimpfung f

boot [buːt] n Stiefel m; *(BRIT: AUT)* Kofferraum m ♦ vt *(kick)* einen Fußtritt geben; *(COMPUT)* laden; **to ~** *(in addition)* obendrein

booth [buːð] n *(at fair)* Bude f; *(telephone)* Zelle f; *(voting)* Kabine f

booze [buːz] *(inf)* n Alkohol m, Schnaps m ♦ vi saufen

border ['bɔːdə*] n Grenze f; *(edge)* Kante f; *(in garden)* *(Blumen)*rabatte f ♦ *adj* Grenz-; **the B~s** *Grenzregion f zwischen England und Schottland*; ~ **on** vt grenzen an +*acc*; ~**line** n Grenze f; ~**line case** n Grenzfall m

bore [bɔː*] pt of **bear** ♦ vt bohren; *(weary)* langweilen ♦ n *(person)* Langweiler m; *(thing)* langweilige Sache f; *(of gun)* Kaliber *nt*; **I am ~d** ich langweile mich; ~**dom** n Langeweile f

boring ['bɔːrɪŋ] *adj* langweilig

born [bɔːn] *adj*: **to be ~** geboren werden

borne [bɔːn] pp of **bear**

borough ['bʌrə] n Stadt(gemeinde) f, Stadtbezirk m

borrow ['bɒrəʊ] vt borgen

Bosnia (and) Herzegovina ['bɒznɪə (ənd) hɜːtsəgəʊ'viːnə] Bosnien und Herzegowina *nt*

bosom ['bʊzəm] n Busen m

boss [bɒs] n Chef m, Boß m ♦ vt: **to ~ around** herumkommandieren; ~**y** *adj* herrisch

bosun ['bəʊsn] n Bootsmann m

botany ['bɒtənɪ] n Botanik f

botch [bɒtʃ] vt (also: ~ up) verpfuschen

both [bəʊθ] adj beide(s) ♦ pron beide(s) ♦ adv: ~ X and Y sowohl X wie or als auch Y; ~ (of) the books beide Bücher; ~ of us went, we ~ went wir gingen beide

bother ['bɒðə*] vt (pester) quälen; vi (fuss) sich aufregen ♦ n Mühe f, Umstand m; to ~ doing sth sich die Mühe machen, etw zu tun; what a ~! wie ärgerlich!

bottle ['bɒtl] n Flasche f ♦ vt (in Flaschen) abfüllen; ~ up vt aufstauen; ~ **bank** n Altglascontainer m; ~**neck** n (also fig) Engpaß m; ~**opener** n Flaschenöffner m

bottom ['bɒtəm] n Boden m; (of person) Hintern m; (riverbed) Flußbett nt ♦ adj unterste(r, s)

bough [baʊ] n Zweig m, Ast m

bought [bɔːt] pt, pp of buy

boulder ['bəʊldə*] n Felsbrocken m

bounce [baʊns] vi (ball) hochspringen; (person) herumhüpfen; (cheque) platzen ♦ vt (auf)springen lassen ♦ n (rebound) Aufprall m; ~r n Rausschmeißer m

bound [baʊnd] pt, pp of bind ♦ n Grenze f; (leap) Sprung m ♦ vi (spring, leap) (auf)springen ♦ adj (obliged) gebunden, verpflichtet; out of ~s Zutritt verboten; to be ~ to do sth verpflichtet sein, etw zu tun; it's ~ to happen es muß so kommen; to be ~ for ... nach ... fahren

boundary ['baʊndərɪ] n Grenze f

bouquet [bʊ'keɪ] n Strauß m; (of wine) Blume f

bourgeois ['bʊəʒwɑː] adj kleinbürgerlich, bourgeois ♦ n Spießbürger(in) m(f)

bout [baʊt] n (of illness) Anfall m; (of contest) Kampf m

bow¹ [bəʊ] n (ribbon) Schleife f; (weapon, MUS) Bogen m

bow² [baʊ] n (with head, body) Verbeugung f; (of ship) Bug m ♦ vi sich

verbeugen; (submit): to bow to sich beugen +dat

bowels ['baʊəlz] npl Darm m; (centre) Innere nt

bowl [bəʊl] n (basin) Schüssel f; (of pipe) (Pfeifen)kopf m; (wooden ball) (Holz)kugel f ♦ vt, vi (die Kugel) rollen; ~s n (game) Bowls-Spiel m

bow-legged ['bəʊ'legɪd] adj o-beinig

bowler ['bəʊlə*] n Werfer m; (BRIT: also: ~ hat) Melone f

bowling ['bəʊlɪŋ] n Kegeln nt; ~ alley n Kegelbahn f; ~ green n Rasen m zum Bowling-Spiel

bow tie ['bəʊ'taɪ] n Fliege f

box [bɒks] n (also: cardboard ~) Schachtel f; (bigger) Kasten m; (THEAT) Loge f ♦ vt einpacken ♦ vi boxen; ~**er** n Boxer m; ~**ing** n (SPORT) Boxen nt; **B~ing Day** (BRIT) n zweite(r) Weihnachtsfeiertag m; ~**ing gloves** npl Boxhandschuhe pl; ~**ing ring** n Boxring m; ~ **office** n (Theater)kasse f; ~**room** n Rumpelkammer f

boy [bɔɪ] n Junge m

boycott ['bɔɪkɒt] n Boykott m ♦ vt boykottieren

boyfriend ['bɔɪfrend] n Freund m

boyish ['bɔɪɪʃ] adj jungenhaft

B.R. n abbr = British Rail

bra [brɑː] n BH m

brace [breɪs] n (TECH) Stütze f; (MED) Klammer f ♦ vt stützen; ~s npl (BRIT) Hosenträger pl; to ~ o.s. for sth (fig) sich auf etw acc gefaßt machen

bracelet ['breɪslɪt] n Armband nt

bracing ['breɪsɪŋ] adj kräftigend

bracken ['brækən] n Farnkraut nt

bracket ['brækɪt] n Halter m, Klammer f; (in punctuation) Klammer f; (group) Gruppe f ♦ vt einklammern; (fig) in dieselbe Gruppe einordnen

brag [bræg] vi sich rühmen

braid [breɪd] n (hair) Flechte f; (trim) Borte f

Braille [breɪl] n Blindenschrift f

brain [breɪn] n (ANAT) Gehirn nt; (intellect) Intelligenz f, Verstand m

braise — (*person*) kluge(r) Kopf *m*; **~s** *npl* (*intelligence*) Verstand *m*; **~child** *n* Erfindung *f*; **~wash** *vt* eine Gehirnwäsche vornehmen bei; **~wave** *n* Geistesblitz *m*; **~y** *adj* gescheit

braise [breɪz] *vt* schmoren

brake [breɪk] *n* Bremse *f* ♦ *vt, vi* bremsen; **~ fluid** *n* Bremsflüssigkeit *f*; **~ light** *n* Bremslicht *nt*

bramble ['bræmbl] *n* Brombeere *f*

bran [bræn] *n* Kleie *f*; (*food*) Frühstücksflocken *pl*

branch [brɑːntʃ] *n* Ast *m*; (*division*) Zweig *m* ♦ *vi* (*also:* **~ out:** *road*) sich verzweigen

brand [brænd] *n* (*COMM*) Marke *f*, Sorte *f*; (*on cattle*) Brandmal *nt* ♦ *vt* brandmarken; (*COMM*) ein Warenzeichen geben ♦ *dat*

brandish ['brændɪʃ] *vt* (*drohend*) schwingen

brand-new ['brænd'njuː] *adj* funkelnagelneu

brandy ['brændɪ] *n* Weinbrand *m*, Kognak *m*

brash [bræʃ] *adj* unverschämt

brass [brɑːs] *n* Messing *nt*; **the ~** (*MUS*) das Blech; **~ band** *n* Blaskapelle *f*

brassière ['bræsɪə*] *n* Büstenhalter *m*

brat [bræt] *n* Gör *nt*

bravado [brə'vɑːdəʊ] *n* Tollkühnheit *f*

brave [breɪv] *adj* tapfer ♦ *n* indianische(r) Krieger *m* ♦ *vt* die Stirn bieten ♦ *dat*

bravery ['breɪvərɪ] *n* Tapferkeit *f*

brawl [brɔːl] *n* Rauferei *f*

brawn [brɔːn] *n* (*ANAT*) Muskeln *pl*; (*strength*) Muskelkraft *f*

bray [breɪ] *vi* schreien

brazen ['breɪzn] *adj* (*shameless*) unverschämt ♦ *vt*: **to ~ it out** sich mit Lügen und Betrügen durchsetzen

brazier ['breɪzɪə*] *n* (*of workmen*) offene(r) Kohlenofen *m*

Brazil [brə'zɪl] *n* Brasilien *nt*; **~ian** *adj* brasilianisch ♦ *n* Brasilianer(in) *m(f)*

breach [briːtʃ] *n* (*gap*) Lücke *f*; (*MIL*) Durchbruch *m*; (*of discipline*) Verstoß *m* (gegen die Disziplin); (*of faith*) Vertrauensbruch *m* ♦ *vt* durchbrechen; **~ of contract** Vertragsbruch *m*; **~ of the peace** öffentliche Ruhestörung *f*

bread [bred] *n* Brot *nt*; **~ and butter** Butterbrot *nt*; **~bin** *n* Brotkasten *m*; **~box** (*US*) *n* Brotkasten *m*; **~crumbs** *npl* Brotkrumen *pl*; (*COOK*) Paniermehl *nt*; **~line** *n*: **to be on the ~line** sich gerade so durchschlagen

breadth [bretθ] *n* Breite *f*

breadwinner ['bredwɪnə*] *n* Ernährer *m*

break [breɪk] (*pt* **broke**, *pp* **broken**) *vt* (*destroy*) (ab- *or* zer)brechen; (*promise*) brechen, nicht einhalten ♦ *vi* (*fall apart*) auseinanderbrechen; (*collapse*) zusammenbrechen; (*dawn*) anbrechen ♦ *n* (*gap*) Lücke *f*; (*chance*) Chance *f*, Gelegenheit *f*; (*fracture*) Bruch *m*; (*rest*) Pause *f*. **~ down** *vt* (*figures, data*) aufschlüsseln; (*undermine*) überwinden ♦ *vi* (*car*) eine Panne haben; (*person*) zusammenbrechen; **~ even** *vi* die Kosten decken; **~ free** *vi* sich losreißen; **~ in** *vt* (*animal*) einreißen ♦ *vi* (*burglar*) einbrechen; **~ into** *vt fus* (*house*) einbrechen in +*acc*; **~ loose** *vi* sich losreißen; **~ off** *vi* abbrechen; **~ open** *vt* (*door etc*) aufbrechen; **~ out** *vi* ausbrechen; **to ~ out in spots** Pickel bekommen; **~ up** *vi* zerbrechen; (*fig*) sich zerstreuen; (*BRIT: SCH*) in die Ferien gehen ♦ *vt* brechen; **~age** *n* Bruch *m*, Beschädigung *f*; **~down** *n* (*TECH*) Panne *f*; (*MED*: also: **nervous ~down**) Zusammenbruch *m*; **~down van** (*BRIT*) *n* Abschleppwagen *m*; **~er** *n* Brecher *m*

breakfast ['brekfəst] *n* Frühstück *n*

break- **~in** *n* Einbruch *m*; **~ing** *n*: **~ing and entering** (*JUR*) Einbruch *m*; **~through** *n* Durchbruch *m*;

~**water** n Wellenbrecher m
breast [brest] n Brust f; ~**-feed** (ir-reg: like feed) vt, vi stillen; ~**-stroke** n Brustschwimmen nt

breath [breθ] n Atem m; **out of** ~ außer Atem; **under one's** ~ flüsternd

Breathalyzer ['breθəlaızə*] (®) n Röhrchen nt

breathe [bri:ð] vt, vi atmen; ~ **in** vt, vi einatmen; ~ **out** vt, vi ausatmen; ~**r** n Verschnaufpause f

breathing ['bri:ðiŋ] n Atmung f
breathless ['breθlis] adj atemlos
breathtaking ['breθteikiŋ] adj atemberaubend

bred [bred] pt, pp of breed
breed [bri:d] (pt, pp bred) vi sich vermehren ♦ vt züchten ♦ n (race) Rasse f, Zucht f; ~**er** n (person) Züchter m; ~**ing** n Züchtung f; (up-bringing) Erziehung f; (education) Bildung f

breeze [bri:z] n Brise f
breezy ['bri:zi] adj windig; (manner) munter

brevity ['breviti] n Kürze f
brew [bru:] vt brauen; (plot) anzetteln ♦ vi (storm) sich zusammenziehen; ~**ery** n Brauerei f

bribe [braib] n Bestechungsgeld nt, Bestechungsgeschenk nt ♦ vt bestechen; ~**ry** ['braibəri] n Bestechung f

bric-a-brac ['brikəbræk] n Nippes pl
brick [brik] n Backstein m; ~**layer** n Maurer m; ~**works** n Ziegelei f

bridal ['braidl] adj Braut-
bride [braid] n Braut f; ~**groom** n Bräutigam m; ~**smaid** n Brautjungfer f

bridge [bridʒ] n Brücke f; (NAUT) Kommandobrücke f; (CARDS) Bridge nt; (ANAT) Nasenrücken m ♦ vt (fig) überbrücken

bridle ['braidl] n Zaum m ♦ vt (fig) zügeln; (horse) aufzäumen; ~ **path** n Reitweg m

brief [bri:f] adj kurz ♦ n (JUR) Akten pl ♦ vt instruieren; ~**s** npl (un-derwear) Schlüpfer m, Slip m; ~**case** n Aktentasche f; ~**ing** n (ge-naue) Anweisung f; ~**ly** adv kurz

brigadier [brigə'diə*] n Brigadegeneral m

bright [brait] adj hell; (cheerful) heiter; (idea) klug; ~**en** (**up**) ['braitn-] vt aufhellen; (person) aufheitern ♦ vi sich aufheitern

brilliance ['briljəns] n Glanz m; (of person) Scha fsinn m

brilliant ['briljənt] adj glänzend
brim [brim] n Rand m
brine [brain] n Salzwasser nt
bring [briŋ] (pt, pp brought) vt bringen; ~ **about** vt zustande bringen; ~ **back** vt zurückbringen; ~ **down** vt (price) senken; ~ **forward** vt (meeting) vorverlegen; (COMM) übertragen; ~ **in** vt hereinbringen; (harvest) einbringen; ~ **off** vt davontragen; (success) erzielen; ~ **out** vt (object) herausbringen; ~ **round** or **to** vt wieder zu sich bringen; ~ **up** vt aufziehen; (question) zur Sprache bringen

brink [briŋk] n Rand m
brisk [brisk] adj lebhaft
brisket ['briskit] n Bruststück nt
bristle ['brisl] n Borste f ♦ vi sich sträuben; **bristling with** strotzend vor +dat

Britain ['britən] n (also: Great ~) Großbritannien nt

British ['britiʃ] adj britisch ♦ npl: **the** ~ die Briten pl; **the** ~ **Isles** npl die Britischen Inseln pl; ~ **Rail** n die Britischen Eisenbahnen pl

Briton ['britən] n Brite m, Britin f
brittle ['britl] adj spröde
broach [brəʊtʃ] vt (subject) anschneiden

broad [brɔːd] adj breit; (hint) deutlich; (daylight) helllicht; (general) allgemein; (accent) stark; **in** ~ **daylight** am helllichten Tag; ~**cast** (pt, pp broadcast) n Rundfunkübertragung f ♦ vt, vi übertragen, senden; ~**en** vt erweitern ♦ vi sich erweitern; ~**ly** adv allgemein gesagt; ~-**minded** adj tolerant

broccoli ['brɒkəlɪ] n Brokkoli pl

brochure ['brəʊʃʊə*] n Broschüre f

broil [brɔɪl] vt (grill) grillen

broke [brəʊk] pt of **break** ♦ adj (inf) pleite

broken ['brəʊkən] pp of **break** ♦ adj: ~ **leg** gebrochenes Bein; **in** ~ **English** in gebrochenem Englisch; ~-**hearted** adj untröstlich

broker ['brəʊkə*] n Makler m

brolly ['brɒlɪ] n (BRIT: inf) Schirm m

bronchitis [brɒŋ'kaɪtɪs] n Bronchitis f

bronze [brɒnz] n Bronze f

brooch [brəʊtʃ] n Brosche f

brood [bruːd] n Brut f ♦ vi brüten

brook [brʊk] n Bach m

broom [bruːm] n Besen m; ~**stick** n Besenstiel m

Bros. abbr = **Brothers**

broth [brɒθ] n Suppe f, Fleischbrühe f

brothel ['brɒθl] n Bordell nt

brother ['brʌðə*] n Bruder m; ~-**in-law** n Schwager m

brought [brɔːt] pt, pp of **bring**

brow [braʊ] n (eyebrow) (Augen)braue f; (forehead) Stirn f; (of hill) Bergkuppe f

brown [braʊn] adj braun ♦ n Braun nt ♦ vt bräunen; ~ **bread** n Mischbrot nt; **B~ie** n Wichtel m; ~ **paper** n Packpapier nt; ~ **sugar** n brauner(r) Zucker m

browse [braʊz] vi (in books) blättern; (in shop) schmökern, herumschauen

bruise [bruːz] n Bluterguß m, blaue(r) Fleck m ♦ vi einen blauen Fleck geben ♦ vi einen blauen Fleck bekommen

brunt [brʌnt] n volle Wucht f

brush [brʌʃ] n Bürste f; (for sweeping) Handbesen m; (for painting) Pinsel m; (fight) kurze(r) Kampf m; (MIL) Scharmützel nt; (fig) Auseinandersetzung f ♦ vt (clean) bürsten; (sweep) fegen; (usu: ~ past, ~

against) streifen; ~ **aside** vt abtun; ~ **up** vt (knowledge) auffrischen; ~**wood** n Gestrüpp nt

brusque [bruːsk] adj schroff

Brussels ['brʌslz] n Brüssel nt; ~ **sprout** n Rosenkohl m

brutal ['bruːtl] adj brutal

brute [bruːt] n (person) Scheusal nt ♦ adj: **by** ~ **force** mit roher Kraft

B.Sc. n abbr = **Bachelor of Science**

bubble ['bʌbl] n (Luft)blase f ♦ vi sprudeln; (with joy) übersprudeln; ~ **bath** n Schaumbad nt; ~**gum** n Kaugummi m or nt

buck [bʌk] n Bock m; (US: inf) Dollar m ♦ vi bocken; **to pass the** ~ (**to sb**) die Verantwortung (auf jdn) abschieben; ~ **up** (inf) vi sich zusammenreißen

bucket ['bʌkɪt] n Eimer m

buckle ['bʌkl] n Schnalle f ♦ vt (an or zusammen)schnallen ♦ vi (bend) sich verziehen

bud [bʌd] n Knospe f ♦ vi knospen, keimen

Buddhism ['bʊdɪzəm] n Buddhismus m

budding ['bʌdɪŋ] adj angehend

buddy ['bʌdɪ] (inf) n Kumpel m

budge [bʌdʒ] vt, vi (sich) von der Stelle rühren

budgerigar ['bʌdʒərɪgɑː*] n Wellensittich m

budget ['bʌdʒɪt] n Budget nt; (POL) Haushalt m ♦ vi: **to** ~ **for sth** etw einplanen

budgie ['bʌdʒɪ] n = **budgerigar**

buff [bʌf] adj (colour) lederfarben ♦ n (enthusiast) Fan m

buffalo ['bʌfələʊ] (pl ~ or ~**es**) n (BRIT) Büffel m; (US: bison) Bison m

buffer ['bʌfə*] n Puffer m; (COMPUT) Pufferspeicher m

buffet[1] ['bʌfɪt] n (blow) Schlag m ♦ vt (herum)stoßen

buffet[2] ['bʊfeɪ] (BRIT) n (bar) Imbißraum m, Erfrischungsraum m; (food) (kaltes) Büffet nt; ~ **car** n (BRIT) n Speisewagen m

bug [bʌg] n (also fig) Wanze f ♦ vt verwanzen

bugle ['bju:gl] n Jagdhorn nt; (MIL; MUS) Bügelhorn nt

build [bɪld] (pt, pp built) vt bauen ♦ n Körperbau m; ~ **up** vt aufbauen; ~**er** n Bauunternehmer m; ~**ing** n Gebäude nt; ~**ing society** (BRIT) n Bausparkasse f

built [bɪlt] pt, pp of build

built-in adj (cupboard) eingebaut

built-up area n Wohngebiet nt

bulb [bʌlb] n (BOT) (Blumen)zwiebel f; (ELEC) Glühlampe f, Birne f

Bulgaria [bʌl'gɛərɪə] n Bulgarien nt; ~**n** adj bulgarisch ♦ n Bulgare m, Bulgarin f; (LING) Bulgarisch nt

bulge [bʌldʒ] n (Aus)bauchung f ♦ vi sich (aus)bauchen

bulk [bʌlk] n Größe f, Masse f; (greater part) Großteil m; **in** ~ (COMM) en gros; **the** ~ **of** der größte Teil +gen; ~**head** n Schott nt; ~**y** adj (sehr) umfangreich; (goods) sperrig

bull [bʊl] n (animal) Bulle m; (cattle) Stier m; (papal) Bulle f; ~**dog** n Bulldogge f

bulldozer ['bʊldəʊzə*] n Planierraupe f

bullet ['bʊlɪt] n Kugel f

bulletin ['bʊlɪtɪn] n Bulletin nt, Bekanntmachung f

bulletproof ['bʊlɪtpru:f] adj kugelsicher

bullfight ['bʊlfaɪt] n Stierkampf m; ~**er** n Stierkämpfer m

bullion ['bʊljən] n Barren m

bullock ['bʊlək] n Ochse m

bullring ['bʊlrɪŋ] n Stierkampfarena f

bull's-eye ['bʊlzaɪ] n Zentrum nt

bully ['bʊlɪ] n Raufbold m ♦ vt einschüchtern

bum [bʌm] n (inf: backside) Hintern m; (tramp) Landstreicher m

bumblebee ['bʌmblbi:] n Hummel f

bump [bʌmp] n (blow) Stoß m; (swelling) Beule f ♦ vt, vi stoßen, prallen; ~ **into** vt fus stoßen gegen

♦ vt (person) treffen; ~ **cars** (US) npl (dodgems) Autoskooter pl; ~**er** n (AUT) Stoßstange f ♦ adj (edition) dick; (harvest) Rekord-

bumptious ['bʌmpʃəs] adj aufgeblasen

bumpy ['bʌmpɪ] adj holprig

bun [bʌn] n Korinthenbrötchen nt

bunch [bʌntʃ] n (of flowers) Strauß m; (of keys) Bund m; (of people) Haufen m

bundle ['bʌndl] n Bündel nt ♦ vt (also: ~ **up**) bündeln

bungalow ['bʌŋgələu] n einstöckige(s) Haus nt, Bungalow m

bungle ['bʌŋgl] vt verpfuschen

bunion ['bʌnjən] n entzündete(r) Fußballen m

bunk [bʌŋk] n Schlafkoje f; ~ **beds** npl Etagenbett nt

bunker ['bʌŋkə*] n (coal store) Kohlenbunker m; (GOLF) Sandloch nt

bunny ['bʌnɪ] n (also: ~ **rabbit**) Häschen nt

bunting ['bʌntɪŋ] n Fahnentuch nt

buoy [bɔɪ] n Boje f; (life~) Rettungsboje f; ~ **up** vt Auftrieb geben +dat; ~**ant** adj (floating) schwimmend; (fig) heiter

burden ['bɜ:dn] n (weight) Ladung f, Last f; (fig) Bürde f ♦ vt belasten

bureau ['bjuərəu] (pl ~**x**) n (BRIT: writing desk) Sekretär m; (US: chest of drawers) Kommode f; (for information etc) Büro nt

bureaucracy [bjuə'rɔkrəsɪ] n Bürokratie f

bureaucrat ['bjuərəkræt] n Bürokrat(in) m(f)

bureaux ['bjuərəuz] npl of bureau

burglar ['bɜ:glə*] n Einbrecher m; ~ **alarm** n Einbruchssicherung f; ~**y** n Einbruch m

burial ['bɛrɪəl] n Beerdigung f

burly ['bɜ:lɪ] adj stämmig

Burma ['bɜ:mə] n Birma nt

burn [bɜ:n] (pt, pp **burned** or **burnt**) vt verbrennen ♦ vi brennen ♦ n Brandwunde f; ~ **down** vi, vi abbrennen; ~**er** n Brenner m; (also:

adj brennend; **~t** [bɜːnt] *pt, pp of* **burn**

burrow [ˈbʌrəʊ] *n (of fox)* Bau *m*; *(of rabbit)* Höhle *f* ♦ *vt* eingraben

bursar [ˈbɜːsə*] *n* Kassenverwalter *m*, Quästor *m*; **~y** (BRIT) *n* Stipendium *nt*

burst [bɜːst] *(pt, pp* burst) *vt* zerbrechen ♦ *vi* platzen ♦ *n* Explosion *f*; *(outbreak)* Ausbruch *m*; *(in pipe)* Bruch(stelle *f*) *m*; **to ~ into flames** in Flammen aufgehen; **~ into tears** in Tränen ausbrechen; **to ~ out laughing** in Gelächter ausbrechen; **~ into** *vt fus (room etc)* platzen in *+acc*; **~ open** *vi* aufbrechen

bury [ˈberɪ] *vt* vergraben; *(in grave)* beerdigen

bus [bʌs] *n* (Auto)bus *m*, Omnibus *m*

bush [bʊʃ] *n* Busch *m*; **to beat about the ~** wie die Katze um den heißen Brei herumgehen

bushy [ˈbʊʃɪ] *adj* buschig

busily [ˈbɪzɪlɪ] *adv* geschäftig

business [ˈbɪznɪs] *n* Geschäft *nt*; *(concern)* Angelegenheit *f*; **it's none of your ~** es geht dich nichts an; **to mean ~** es ernst meinen; **to be away on ~** geschäftlich verreist sein; **it's my ~ to ...** es ist meine Sache, zu ...; **~-like** *adj* geschäftsmäßig; **~man** *(irreg) n* Geschäftsmann *m*; **~ trip** *n* Geschäftsreise *f*; **~woman** *(irreg) n* Geschäftsfrau *f*

busker [ˈbʌskə*] *n* (BRIT) *n* Straßenmusikant *m*

bus stop *n* Bushaltestelle *f*

bust [bʌst] *n* Büste *f* ♦ *adj (broken)* kaputt(gegangen); *(business)* pleite; **to go ~** pleite machen

bustle [ˈbʌsl] *n* Getriebe *nt* ♦ *vi* hasten

bustling [ˈbʌslɪŋ] *adj* geschäftig

busy [ˈbɪzɪ] *adj* beschäftigt; *(road)* belebt ♦ *vt*: **to ~ o.s.** sich beschäftigen; **~body** *n* Übereifrige(r) *mf*; **~ signal** *(US) n* (TEL) Besetztzeichen *nt*

but [bʌt] *conj* **1** *(yet)* aber; **not X but Y** nicht X sondern Y

2 *(however)*: **I'd love to come, but I'm busy** ich würde gern kommen, bin aber beschäftigt

3 *(showing disagreement, surprise etc)*: **but that's fantastic!** (aber) das ist ja fantastisch! ♦ *prep (apart from, except)*: **nothing but trouble** nichts als Ärger; **no-one but him can do it** niemand außer ihn kann es machen; **but for you/your help** ohne dich/deine Hilfe; **anything but that** alles, nur das nicht

♦ *adv (just, only)*: **she's but a child** sie ist noch ein Kind; **had I but known** wenn ich es nur gewußt hätte; **I can but try** ich kann es immerhin versuchen; **all but finished** so gut wie fertig

butcher [ˈbʊtʃə*] *n* Metzger *m*; *(murderer)* Schlächter *m* ♦ *vt* schlachten; *(kill)* abschlachten; **~'s** *(shop) n* Metzgerei *f*

butler [ˈbʌtlə*] *n* Butler *m*

butt [bʌt] *n (cask)* große(s) Faß *nt*; *(BRIT: fig: target)* Zielscheibe *f*; *(thick end)* dicke(s) Ende *nt*; *(of gun)* Kolben *m*; *(of cigarette)* Stummel *m* ♦ *vt* (mit dem Kopf) stoßen; **~ in** *vi (interrupt)* sich einmischen

butter [ˈbʌtə*] *n* Butter *f* ♦ *vt* buttern; **~ bean** *n* Wachsbohne *f*; **~cup** *n* Butterblume *f*

butterfly [ˈbʌtəflaɪ] *n* Schmetterling *m*; *(SWIMMING: also ~ stroke)* Butterflystil *m*

buttocks [ˈbʌtəks] *npl* Gesäß *nt*

button [ˈbʌtn] *n* Knopf *m* ♦ *vt, vi (also: ~ up)* zuknöpfen

buttress [ˈbʌtrɪs] *n* Strebepfeiler *m*; Stützbogen *m*

buxom [ˈbʌksəm] *adj* drall

buy [baɪ] *(pt, pp* bought) *vt* kaufen ♦ *n* Kauf *m*; **to ~ sb a drink** jdm einen Drink spendieren; **~er** *n*

Käufer(in) m(f)

buzz [bʌz] n Summen nt ♦ vi summen

buzzer ['bʌzə*] n Summer m

buzz word n Modewort nt

KEYWORD

by [baɪ] prep 1 (referring to cause, agent) von, durch; **killed by lightning** vom Blitz getötet; **a painting by Picasso** ein Gemälde von Picasso 2 (referring to method, means): **by bus/car/train** mit dem Bus/Auto/Zug; **to pay by cheque** per Scheck bezahlen; **by moonlight** bei Mondschein; **by saving hard, he ...** indem er eisern sparte, ... er ...

3 (via, through) über +acc; **he came in by the back door** er kam durch die Hintertür herein

4 (close to, past) bei, an +dat; **a holiday by the sea** ein Urlaub am Meer; **she rushed by me** sie eilte an mir vorbei

5 (not later than): **by 4 o'clock** bis 4 Uhr; **by this time tomorrow** morgen um diese Zeit; **by the time I got here** it was too late als ich hier ankam, war es zu spät

6 (during): **by day** bei Tag

7 (amount): **by the kilo/metre** kiloweise/meterweise; **paid by the hour** stundenweise bezahlt

8 (MATH, measure): **to divide by 3** durch 3 teilen; **to multiply by 3** mit 3 malnehmen; **a room 3 metres by 4** ein Zimmer 3 mal 4 Meter; **it's broader by a metre** es ist um einen Meter breiter

9 (according to) nach; **it's all right by me** von mir aus gern

10: **(all) by oneself** etc ganz allein

11: **by the way** übrigens

♦ adv 1 see go; pass etc

2: **by and by** irgendwann; (with past tenses) nach einiger Zeit; **by and large** (on the whole) im großen und ganzen

bye(-bye) ['baɪ('baɪ)] excl (auf) Wiedersehen

by(e)-law ['baɪlɔ:] n Verordnung f

by-election ['baɪɪlekʃən] (BRIT) n Nachwahl f

bygone ['baɪɡɒn] adj vergangen ♦ n: **let ~s be ~s** laß(t) das Vergangene vergangen sein

bypass ['baɪpɑ:s] n Umgehungsstraße f ♦ vt umgehen

by-product ['baɪprɒdʌkt] n Nebenprodukt nt

bystander ['baɪstændə*] n Zuschauer m

byte [baɪt] n (COMPUT) Byte nt

byword ['baɪwɜ:d] n Inbegriff m

C

C [si:] n (MUS) C nt

C. abbr (= centigrade) C

C.A. abbr = chartered accountant

cab [kæb] n Taxi nt; (of train) Führerstand m; (of truck) Führersitz m

cabaret ['kæbəreɪ] n Kabarett nt

cabbage ['kæbɪdʒ] n Kohl(kopf) m

cabin ['kæbɪn] n Hütte f; (NAUT) Kajüte f; (AVIAT) Kabine f; **~ cruiser** n Motorjacht f

cabinet ['kæbɪnɪt] n Schrank m; (for china) Vitrine f; (POL) Kabinett nt; **~-maker** n Kunsttischler m

cable ['keɪbl] n Drahtseil nt, Tau nt; (TEL) (Leitungs)kabel nt; (telegram) Kabel nt ♦ vt kabeln, telegraphieren; **~-car** n Seilbahn f; **~ television** n Kabelfernsehen nt

cache [kæʃ] n geheime(s) (Waffen)lager nt, geheime(s) (Proviant)lager nt

cackle ['kækl] vi gackern

cacti ['kæktaɪ] npl of **cactus**

cactus ['kæktəs] (pl **cacti**) n Kaktus m, Kaktee f

caddie ['kædɪ] n (GOLF) Golfjunge m

caddy n = **caddie**

cadet [kə'det] n Kadett m

cadge [kædʒ] vt schmarotzen

Caesarean [siːˈzɛəriən] adj: ~ (section) Kaiserschnitt m

café [ˈkæfɪ] n Café nt, Restaurant nt

cafeteria [kæfɪˈtɪəriə] n Selbstbedienungsrestaurant nt

caffein(e) [ˈkæfiːn] n Koffein nt

cage [keɪdʒ] n Käfig m ♦ vt einsperren

cagey [ˈkeɪdʒɪ] adj geheimnistuerisch, zurückhaltend

cagoule [kəˈguːl] n Windhemd nt

Cairo [ˈkaɪərəʊ] n Kairo nt

cajole [kəˈdʒəʊl] vt überreden

cake [keɪk] n Kuchen m; (of soap) Stück nt; ~d adj verkrustet

calamity [kəˈlæmɪtɪ] n Unglück nt, (Schicksals)schlag m

calcium [ˈkælsɪəm] n Kalzium nt

calculate [ˈkælkjuleɪt] vt berechnen, kalkulieren; **calculating** adj berechnend; **calculation** [kælkjuˈleɪʃən] n Berechnung f; **calculator** n Rechner m

calculus [ˈkælkjʊləs] n Infinitesimalrechnung f

calendar [ˈkælɪndə*] n Kalender m; ~ **month** n Kalendermonat m

calf [kɑːf] (pl **calves**) n Kalb nt; (also: ~skin) Kalbsleder nt; (ANAT) Wade f

calibre [ˈkælɪbə*] (US **caliber**) n Kaliber nt

call [kɔːl] vt rufen; (name) nennen; (meeting) einberufen; (awaken) wecken; (TEL) anrufen ♦ vi (shout) rufen; (visit: also: ~ in, ~ round) vorbeikommen ♦ n (shout) Ruf m; (TEL) Anruf m; to be ~ed heißen; on ~ in Bereitschaft; ~ **back** vi (return) wiederkommen; (TEL) zurückrufen; ~ **for** vt fus (demand) erfordern, verlangen; (fetch) abholen; ~ **off** vt (cancel) absagen; ~ **on** vt fus (visit) besuchen; (turn to) bitten; ~ **out** vi rufen; ~ **up** vt (MIL) einberufen; ~**box** (BRIT) n Telefonzelle f; ~**er** n Besucher(in) m(f); (TEL) Anrufer m; ~ **girl** n Call-Girl nt; ~**in** (US) n (phone-in) Phone-in nt; ~**ing** n (vocation) Berufung f; ~**ing**

card (US) n Visitenkarte f

callous [ˈkæləs] adj herzlos

calm [kɑːm] n Ruhe f; (NAUT) Flaute f ♦ vt beruhigen ♦ adj ruhig; (person) gelassen; ~ **down** vi sich beruhigen ♦ vt beruhigen

Calor gas [ˈkælə-] ® n Propangas nt

calorie [ˈkælərɪ] n Kalorie f

calves [kɑːvz] npl of **calf**

camber [ˈkæmbə*] n Wölbung f

Cambodia [kæmˈbəʊdʒə] n Kambodscha nt

camcorder [ˈkæmkɔːdə*] n Camcorder m

came [keɪm] pt of **come**

cameo [ˈkæmɪəʊ] n Kamee f

camera [ˈkæmərə] n Fotoapparat m; (CINE, TV) Kamera f; **in** ~ unter Ausschluß der Öffentlichkeit; ~**man** (irreg) n Kameramann m

camouflage [ˈkæməflɑːʒ] n Tarnung f ♦ vt tarnen

camp [kæmp] n Lager nt ♦ vi zelten, campen ♦ adj affektiert

campaign [kæmˈpeɪn] n Kampagne f; (MIL) Feldzug m ♦ vi Krieg führen; (fig) werben, Propaganda machen; (POL) den Wahlkampf führen

campbed [ˈkæmpˈbed] (BRIT) n Campingbett nt

camper [ˈkæmpə*] n Camper(in) m(f); (vehicle) Camping-wagen m

camping [ˈkæmpɪŋ] n: to go ~ zelten, Camping machen

campsite [ˈkæmpsaɪt] n Campingplatz m

campus [ˈkæmpəs] n Universitätsgelände nt, Campus m

can[1] [kæn] n Büchse f, Dose f; (for water) Kanne f ♦ vt konservieren, in Büchsen einmachen

---

KEYWORD

can[2] [kæn] (negative **cannot**, **can't**; conditional **could**) aux vb 1 (be able to, know how to) können; **I can see you tomorrow, if you like** ich könnte Sie morgen sehen, wenn Sie wollen; **I can swim** ich kann schwimmen; **can you speak German?** sprechen Sie Deutsch? **2** (*may*) können, dürfen; **could I have a word with you?** könnte ich Sie kurz sprechen?

Canada ['kænədə] *n* Kanada *nt*
Canadian [kə'neidiən] *adj* kanadisch ♦ *n* Kanadier(in) *m(f)*
canal [kə'næl] *n* Kanal *m*
canary [kə'neəri] *n* Kanarienvogel *m*
cancel ['kænsəl] *vt* absagen; (*delete*) durchstreichen; (*train*) streichen; **~lation** [kænsə'leiʃən] *n* Absage *f*; Streichung *f*
cancer ['kænsə*] *n* (*also: ASTROL: C~*) Krebs *m*
candid ['kændid] *adj* offen, ehrlich
candidate ['kændideit] *n* Kandidat(in) *m(f)*
candle ['kændl] *n* Kerze *f*; **~light** *n* Kerzenlicht *nt*; **~stick** *n* (*also: ~ holder*) Kerzenhalter *m*
candour ['kændə*] (*US* **candor**) *n* Offenheit *f*
candy ['kændi] *n* Kandis(zucker) *m*; (*US*) Bonbons *pl*; **~floss** (*BRIT*) *n* Zuckerwatte *f*
cane [kein] *n* (*BOT*) Rohr *nt*; (*stick*) Stock *m* ♦ *vt* (*BRIT: SCH*) schlagen
canine ['keinain] *adj* Hunde-
canister ['kænistə*] *n* Blechdose *f*
cannabis ['kænəbis] *n* Hanf *m*, Haschisch *nt*
canned [kænd] *adj* Büchsen-, eingemacht
cannibal ['kænibəl] *n* Menschenfresser *m*
cannon ['kænən] (*pl* ~ *or* **~s**) *n* Kanone *f*
cannot ['kænɔt] = can not
canny ['kæni] *adj* schlau
canoe [kə'nu:] *n* Kanu *nt*
canon ['kænən] *n* (*clergyman*) Domherr *m*; (*standard*) Grundsatz *m*
canonize ['kænənaiz] *vt* heiligsprechen
can-opener [-'əupnə*] *n* Büchsenöffner *m*

canopy ['kænəpi] *n* Baldachin *m*
can't [kɑːnt] = can not
cantankerous [kæn'tæŋkərəs] *adj* zänkisch, mürrisch
canteen [kæn'ti:n] *n* Kantine *f*; (*BRIT: of cutlery*) Besteckkasten *m*; (*bottle*) Feldflasche *f*
canter ['kæntə*] *n* Kanter *m* ♦ *vi* in kurzem Galopp reiten
canvas ['kænvəs] *n* Segeltuch *nt*; (*sail*) Segel *nt*; (*for painting*) Leinwand *f*; **under ~** (*camping*) in Zelten
canvass ['kænvəs] *vi* um Stimmen werben; **~ing** *n* Wahlwerbung *f*
canyon ['kænjən] *n* Felsenschlucht *f*
cap [kæp] *n* Mütze *f*; (*of pen*) Kappe *f*; (*of bottle*) Deckel *m* ♦ *vt* (*surpass*) übertreffen; (*SPORT*) aufstellen; (*put limit on*) einen Höchstsatz festlegen für
capability [keipə'biliti] *n* Fähigkeit *f*
capable ['keipəbl] *adj* fähig
capacity [kə'pæsiti] *n* Fassungsvermögen *nt*; (*ability*) Fähigkeit *f*; (*position*) Eigenschaft *f*
cape [keip] *n* (*garment*) Cape *nt*, Umhang *m*; (*GEOG*) Kap *nt*
caper ['keipə*] *n* (*COOK: usu: ~s*) Kaper *f*; (*prank*) Kapriole *f*
capital ['kæpitl] *n* (*~ city*) Hauptstadt *f*; (*FIN*) Kapital *nt*; (*~ letter*) Großbuchstabe *m*; **~ gains tax** *n* Kapitalertragssteuer *f*; **~ism** *n* Kapitalismus *m*; **~ist** *adj* kapitalistisch ♦ *n* Kapitalist(in) *m(f)*; **~ize**: **~ize on** *vi* Kapital schlagen aus; **~ punishment** *n* Todesstrafe *f*
capitulate [kə'pitjuleit] *vi* kapitulieren
capricious [kə'priʃəs] *adj* launisch
Capricorn ['kæprikɔ:n] *n* Steinbock *m*
capsize [kæp'saiz] *vt, vi* kentern
capsule ['kæpsju:l] *n* Kapsel *f*
captain ['kæptin] *n* Kapitän *m*; (*MIL*) Hauptmann *m* ♦ *vt* anführen
caption ['kæpʃən] *n* (*heading*) Überschrift *f*; (*to picture*) Unterschrift *f*

captivate ['kæptɪveɪt] vt fesseln

captive ['kæptɪv] n Gefangene(r) mf ♦ adj gefangen(gehalten)

captivity [kæp'tɪvɪtɪ] n Gefangenschaft f

capture ['kæptʃə*] vt gefangennehmen; (place) erobern; (attention) erregen ♦ n Gefangennahme f; (data ~) Erfassung f

car [kɑ:*] n Auto nt, Wagen m; (RAIL) Wagen m

carat ['kærət] n Karat nt

caravan ['kærəvæn] n (BRIT) Wohnwagen m; (in desert) Karawane f; ~ site (BRIT) n Campingplatz m für Wohnwagen

carbohydrate [kɑ:bəʊ'haɪdreɪt] n Kohlenhydrat nt

carbon ['kɑ:bən] n Kohlenstoff m; ~ copy n Durchschlag m; ~ paper n Kohlepapier nt

carburettor ['kɑ:bjʊretə*] (US **carburetor**) n Vergaser m

carcass ['kɑ:kəs] n Kadaver m

card [kɑ:d] n Karte f; ~board n Pappe f; ~ game n Kartenspiel nt

cardiac ['kɑ:dɪæk] adj Herz-

cardigan ['kɑ:dɪgən] n Strickjacke f

cardinal ['kɑ:dɪnl] adj: ~ number Kardinalzahl f ♦ n (REL) Kardinal m

card index n Kartei f; (in library) Katalog m

care [kɛə*] n (of teeth, car etc) Pflege f; (of children) Fürsorge f; (carefulness) Sorgfalt f; (worry) Sorge f ♦ vi: to ~ about sich kümmern um; ~ of bei; in sb's ~ in jds Obhut; I don't ~ das ist mir egal; I couldn't ~ less es ist mir doch völlig egal; to take ~ auffassen; to take ~ of sorgen für; to take ~ to do sth sich bemühen, etw zu tun; ~ for vt sorgen für; (like) mögen

career [kə'rɪə*] n Karriere f, Laufbahn f ♦ vi (also: ~ along) rasen

carefree ['kɛəfri:] adj sorgenfrei

careful ['kɛəfʊl] adj sorgfältig; (be) ~! paß auf!

careless ['kɛəlɪs] adj nachlässig;

~ness n Nachlässigkeit f

carer ['kɛərə*] n (MED) Betreuer(in) m(f)

caress [kə'res] n Liebkosung f ♦ vt liebkosen

caretaker ['kɛəteɪkə*] n Hausmeister m

car-ferry ['kɑ:ferɪ] n Autofähre f

cargo ['kɑ:gəʊ] (pl ~es) n Schiffsladung f

car hire n Autovermietung f

Caribbean [kærɪ'bɪən] n: the ~ (Sea) die Karibik

caricature ['kærɪkətjʊə*] n Karikatur f

caring ['kɛərɪŋ] adj (society, organization) sozial eingestellt; (person) liebevoll

carnage ['kɑ:nɪdʒ] n Blutbad nt

carnal ['kɑ:nl] adj fleischlich

carnation [kɑ:'neɪʃən] n Nelke f

carnival ['kɑ:nɪvəl] n Karneval m, Fasching m; (US: fun fair) Kirmes f

carnivorous [kɑ:'nɪvərəs] adj fleischfressend

carol ['kærəl] n (Christmas ~) (Weihnachts)lied nt

carp [kɑ:p] n (fish) Karpfen m; ~ at vt herummorgeln an +dat

car park (BRIT) n Parkplatz m; (covered) Parkhaus m

carpenter ['kɑ:pɪntə*] n Zimmermann m

carpentry ['kɑ:pɪntrɪ] n Zimmerei f

carpet ['kɑ:pɪt] n Teppich m ♦ vt mit einem Teppich auslegen; ~ slippers n Pantoffeln pl; ~ sweeper n Teppichkehrer m

car phone n (TEL) Autotelefon nt

carriage ['kærɪdʒ] n Kutsche f, (RAIL, of typewriter) Wagen m; (of goods) Beförderung f; (bearing) Haltung f; ~ return n (on typewriter) Rücklauftaste f; ~way (BRIT) n Fahrbahn f

carrier ['kærɪə*] n Träger(in) m(f); (COMM) Spediteur m; ~ bag (BRIT) n Tragetasche f

carrot ['kærət] n Möhre f, Karotte f

carry ['kærɪ] vt, vi tragen; to get

carried away (fig) sich nicht mehr bremsen können; ~ **on** vi (continue) weitermachen; (inf: complain) Theater machen; ~ **out** vt (orders) ausführen; (investigation) durchführen; ~**cot** (BRIT) n Babytragetasche f; ~**on** (inf) n (fuss) Theater nt

cart [kɑːt] n Wagen m, Karren m ♦ vt schleppen

cartilage ['kɑːtɪlɪdʒ] n Knorpel m

carton ['kɑːtən] n Karton m; (of milk) Tüte f

cartoon [kɑːtuːn] n (PRESS) Karikatur f; (comic strip) Comics pl; (CINE) (Zeichen)trickfilm m

cartridge ['kɑːtrɪdʒ] n Patrone f

carve [kɑːv] vt (wood) schnitzen; (stone) meißeln; (meat) (vor)schneiden; ~ **up** vt aufschneiden

carving ['kɑːvɪŋ] n Schnitzerei f; ~ **knife** n Tranchiermesser nt

car wash n Autowäsche f

cascade [kæskeɪd] n Wasserfall m ♦ vi kaskadenartig herabfallen

case [keɪs] n (box) Kasten m; (BRIT: also: suit~) Koffer m; (JUR, matter) Fall m; **in** ~ falls, im Falle; **in any** ~ jedenfalls, auf jeden Fall

cash [kæʃ] n (Bar)geld nt ♦ vt einlösen; ~ **on delivery** per Nachnahme; ~ **book** n Kassenbuch nt; ~ **card** n Scheckkarte f; ~ **desk** (BRIT) n Kasse f; ~ **dispenser** n Geldautomat m

cashew [kæ'ʃuː] n (also: ~ **nut**) Cashewnuß f

cash flow n Cash-flow m

cashier [kæ'ʃɪə*] n Kassierer(in) m(f)

cashmere ['kæʃmɪə*] n Kaschmirwolle f

cash register n Registrierkasse f

casing ['keɪsɪŋ] n Gehäuse nt

casino [kə'siːnəʊ] n Kasino nt

cask [kɑːsk] n Faß nt

casket ['kɑːskɪt] n Kästchen nt; (US: coffin) Sarg m

casserole ['kæsərəʊl] n Kasserolle f; (food) Auflauf m

cassette [kæ'set] n Kassette f; ~

player n Kassettengerät nt

cast [kɑːst] (pt, pp cast) vt werfen; (horns) verlieren; (metal) gießen; (THEAT) besetzen; (vote) abgeben ♦ n (THEAT) Besetzung f; (also: plaster ~) Gipsverband m; ~ **off** vi (NAUT) losmachen

castaway ['kɑːstəweɪ] n Schiffbrüchige(r) mf

caste [kɑːst] n Kaste f

caster sugar ['kɑːstə-] (BRIT) n Raffinade f

casting vote ['kɑːstɪŋ-] (BRIT) n entscheidende Stimme f

cast iron n Gußeisen nt

castle ['kɑːsl] n Burg f; Schloß nt; (CHESS) Turm m

castor ['kɑːstə*] n (wheel) Laufrolle f

castor oil n Rizinusöl nt

castrate [kæs'treɪt] vt kastrieren

casual ['kæʒjʊl] adj (attitude) nachlässig; (dress) leger; (meeting) zufällig; (work) Gelegenheits-; ~**ly** adv (dress) zwanglos, leger; (remark) beiläufig

casualty ['kæʒjʊltɪ] n Verletzte(r) mf; (dead) Tote(r) mf; ~ **department** n Unfallstation f

cat [kæt] n Katze f

catalogue ['kætəlɒg] (US catalog) n Katalog m ♦ vt katalogisieren

catalyst ['kætəlɪst] n Katalysator m

catalytic convertor [kætə'lɪtɪk kən'vɜːtə*] n Katalysator m

catapult ['kætəpʌlt] n Schleuder f

cataract ['kætərækt] n (MED) graue(r) Star m

catarrh [kə'tɑː*] n Katarrh m

catastrophe [kə'tæstrəfɪ] n Katastrophe f

catch [kætʃ] (pt, pp caught) vt fangen; (arrest) fassen; (train) erreichen; (person: by surprise) ertappen; (also: ~ **up**) einholen ♦ vi (fire) in Gang kommen; (in branches etc) hängenbleiben ♦ n (fish etc) Fang m; (trick) Haken m; (of lock) Sperrhaken m; **to** ~ **an illness** sich dat eine Krankheit holen; **to** ~ **fire**

Feuer fangen; ~ **on** vi (understand) begreifen; (grow popular) ankommen; ~ **up** vi (fig) aufholen

catching ['kætʃɪŋ] adj ansteckend

catchment area n ['kætʃmənt-] (BRIT) n Einzugsgebiet nt

catch phrase n Slogan m

catchy ['kætʃɪ] adj (tune) eingängig

catechism ['kætɪkɪzəm] n Katechismus m

categoric(al) [kætə'gɒrɪk(l)] adj kategorisch

category ['kætɪgərɪ] n Kategorie f

cater ['keɪtə*] vi versorgen; ~ **for** (BRIT) vt fus (party) ausrichten; (needs) eingestellt sein auf +acc; ~**er** n Lieferant(in) m(f) von Speisen und Getränken; ~**ing** n Gastronomie f

caterpillar ['kætəpɪlə*] n Raupe f; ~ **track** ® n Gleiskette f

cathedral [kə'θiːdrəl] n Kathedrale f, Dom m

catholic ['kæθəlɪk] adj (tastes etc) vielseitig; **C~** adj (REL) katholisch ♦ n Katholik(in) m(f)

cat's-eye ['kætsaɪ] (BRIT) n (AUT) Katzenauge nt

cattle ['kætl] npl Vieh nt

catty ['kætɪ] adj gehässig

caucus ['kɔːkəs] n (POL) Gremium nt; (US: meeting) Sitzung f

caught [kɔːt] pt, pp of **catch**

cauliflower ['kɒlɪflauə*] n Blumenkohl m

cause [kɔːz] n Ursache f; (purpose) Sache f ♦ vt verursachen

causeway ['kɔːzweɪ] n Damm m

caustic ['kɔːstɪk] adj ätzend; (fig) bissig

caution ['kɔːʃən] n Vorsicht f; (warning) Verwarnung f ♦ vt verwarnen

cautious ['kɔːʃəs] adj vorsichtig

cavalier [kævə'lɪə*] adj blasiert

cavalry ['kævəlrɪ] n Kavallerie f

cave [keɪv] n Höhle f; ~ **in** vi einstürzen; ~**man** (irreg) n Höhlenmensch m

cavern ['kævən] n Höhle f

caviar(e) ['kævɪɑː*] n Kaviar m

cavity ['kævɪtɪ] n Loch nt

cavort [kə'vɔːt] vi umherspringen

C.B. n abbr = Citizens' Band (Radio)) CB

C.B.I. n abbr = Confederation of British Industry) ≈ BDI m

cc n abbr = carbon copy; cubic centimetres

CD n abbr (= compact disc) CD f; (: player) CD-Spieler m

CD-ROM n abbr (= compact disk read-only memory) CD-Rom f

cease [siːs] vi aufhören ♦ vt beenden; ~**fire** n Feuereinstellung f; ~**less** adj unaufhörlich

cedar ['siːdə*] n Zeder f

cede [siːd] vt abtreten

ceiling ['siːlɪŋ] n Decke f; (fig) Höchstgrenze f

celebrate ['selɪbreɪt] vt, vi feiern; ~**d** adj gefeiert

celebration [selɪ'breɪʃən] n Feier f

celebrity [sɪ'lebrɪtɪ] n gefeierte Persönlichkeit f

celery ['selərɪ] n Sellerie m or f

celestial [sɪ'lestɪəl] adj himmlisch

celibacy ['selɪbəsɪ] n Zölibat nt or m

cell [sel] n Zelle f; (ELEC) Element nt

cellar ['selə*] n Keller m

'cello ['tʃeləʊ] n Cello nt

cellophane ['seləfeɪn] (®) n Cellophan nt ®

cellphone n Funktelefon nt

cellular ['seljulə*] adj zellular

cellulose ['seljuləʊs] n Zellulose f

Celt [kelt, selt] n Kelte m, Keltin f; ~**ic** ['keltɪk, 'seltɪk] adj keltisch

cement [sɪ'ment] n Zement m ♦ vt zementieren; ~ **mixer** n Betonmischmaschine f

cemetery ['semɪtrɪ] n Friedhof m

cenotaph ['senəʊtɑːf] n Ehrenmal nt

censor ['sensə*] n Zensor m ♦ vt zensieren; ~**ship** n Zensur f

censure ['senʃə*] vt rügen

census ['sensəs] n Volkszählung f

cent [sent] n (US: coin) Cent m; see also **per cent**

centenary [sen'ti:nərɪ] n Jahrhundertfeier f

center ['sentə*] (US) n = centre

centigrade ['sentɪgreɪd] adj Celsius

centimetre ['sentɪmi:tə*] (US **centimeter**) n Zentimeter nt

centipede ['sentɪpi:d] n Tausendfüßler m

central ['sentrəl] adj zentral; C~ **America** n Mittelamerika nt; ~ **heating** n Zentralheizung f; ~**ize** vt zentralisieren; ~ **reservation** (BRIT) (AUT) Mittelstreifen m

centre ['sentə*] (US **center**) n Zentrum nt ♦ vt zentrieren; ~**forward** n (SPORT) Mittelstürmer m; ~**half** n (SPORT) Stopper m

century ['sentjʊrɪ] n Jahrhundert nt

ceramic [sɪ'ræmɪk] adj keramisch; ~**s** npl Keramiken pl

cereal ['sɪərɪəl] n (grain) Getreide nt; (at breakfast) Getreideflocken pl

cerebral ['serɪbrəl] adj zerebral; (intellectual) geistig

ceremony ['serɪmənɪ] n Zeremonie f; **to stand on** ~ förmlich sein

certain ['sɜːtən] adj sicher; (particular) gewiß; **for** ~ ganz bestimmt; ~**ly** adv sicher, bestimmt; ~**ty** n Gewißheit f

certificate [sə'tɪfɪkɪt] n Bescheinigung f; (SCH etc) Zeugnis nt

certified mail ['sɜːtɪfaɪd-] (US) n Einschreiben nt

certified public accountant ['sɜːtɪfaɪd-] (US) n geprüfte(r) Buchhalter m

certify ['sɜːtɪfaɪ] vt bescheinigen

cervical ['sɜːvɪkl] adj (smear, cancer) Gebärmutterhals-

cervix ['sɜːvɪks] n Gebärmutterhals m

cessation [se'seɪʃən] n Einstellung f, Ende nt

cf. abbr (= compare) vgl.

CFC n abbr (= chlorofluorocarbon) FCKW m

ch. abbr (= chapter) Kap.

chafe [tʃeɪf] vt scheuern

chaffinch ['tʃæfɪntʃ] n Buchfink m

chagrin ['ʃægrɪn] n Verdruß m

chain [tʃeɪn] n Kette f ♦ vt (also: ~ up) anketten; ~ **reaction** n Kettenreaktion f; ~**smoke** vi kettenrauchen; ~ **store** n Kettenladen m

chair [tʃeə*] n Stuhl m; (arm~) Sessel m; (UNIV) Lehrstuhl m ♦ vt (meeting) den Vorsitz führen bei; ~**lift** n Sessellift m; ~**man** (irreg) n Vorsitzende(r) m

chalet ['ʃæleɪ] n Chalet nt

chalice ['tʃælɪs] n Kelch m

chalk [tʃɔːk] n Kreide f

challenge ['tʃælɪndʒ] n Herausforderung f ♦ vt herausfordern; (contest) bestreiten

challenging ['tʃælɪndʒɪŋ] adj (tone) herausfordernd; (work) anspruchsvoll

chamber ['tʃeɪmbə*] n Kammer f; ~ **of commerce** Handelskammer f; ~**maid** n Zimmermädchen nt; ~ **music** n Kammermusik f

chamois ['ʃæmwɑː] n Gemse f

champagne [ʃæm'peɪn] n Champagner m, Sekt m

champion ['tʃæmpɪən] n (SPORT) Meister(in) m(f); (of cause) Verfechter(in) m(f); ~**ship** n Meisterschaft f

chance [tʃɑːns] n (luck) Zufall m; (possibility) Möglichkeit f; (opportunity) Gelegenheit f, Chance f; (risk) Risiko nt ♦ adj zufällig ♦ vt: **to** ~ **it** es darauf ankommen lassen; **by** ~ zufällig; **to take a** ~ ein Risiko eingehen

chancellor ['tʃɑːnsələ*] n Kanzler m; **C~ of the Exchequer** (BRIT) n Schatzkanzler m

chandelier [ʃændɪ'lɪə*] n Kronleuchter m

change [tʃeɪndʒ] vt ändern; (replace, COMM: money) wechseln; (exchange) umtauschen; (transform) verwandeln ♦ vi sich ändern; (~ trains) umsteigen; (~ clothes) sich umziehen ♦ n Veränderung f; (money returned) Wechselgeld nt; (coins) Kleingeld nt; **to** ~ **one's mind** es sich dat anders überlegen; **to** ~ **into**

sth (*be transformed*) sich in etw acc verwandeln; **for a** ~ zur Abwechslung; **~able** adj (*weather*) wechselhaft; ~ **machine** n Geldwechselautomat m; **~over** n Umstellung f

changing ['tʃeɪndʒɪŋ] adj veränderlich; ~ **room** (BRIT) n Umkleideraum m

channel ['tʃænl] n (*stream*) Bachbett nt; (NAUT) Straße f; (TV) Kanal m; (*fig*) Weg m ♦ vt (*efforts*) lenken; **the (English) C~** der Ärmelkanal; **C~ Islands** npl: **the C~ Islands** die Kanalinseln pl

chant [tʃɑ:nt] n Gesang m; (*of football fans etc*) Sprechchor m ♦ vt intonieren

chaos ['keɪɔs] n Chaos nt

chap [tʃæp] (*inf*) n Kerl m

chapel ['tʃæpəl] n Kapelle f

chaperon ['ʃæpərəʊn] n Anstandsdame f

chaplain ['tʃæplɪn] n Kaplan m

chapped [tʃæpt] adj (*skin, lips*) spröde

chapter ['tʃæptə*] n Kapitel nt

char [tʃɑ:*] vt (*burn*) verkohlen ♦ n (BRIT) = **charlady**

character ['kærɪktə*] n Charakter m, Wesen nt; (*in novel, film*) Figur f; **~istic** [kærɪktə'rɪstɪk] adj: **~istic (of sb/sth)** (für jdn/etw) charakteristisch ♦ n Kennzeichen nt; **~ize** vt charakterisieren, kennzeichnen

charade [ʃə'rɑ:d] n Scharade f

charcoal ['tʃɑ:kəʊl] n Holzkohle f

charge [tʃɑ:dʒ] n (*cost*) Preis m; (JUR) Anklage f; (*explosive*) Ladung f; (*attack*) Angriff m ♦ vt (*gun, battery*) laden; (*price*) verlangen; (JUR) anklagen; (MIL) angreifen ♦ vi (*rush*) (an)stürmen; **bank ~s** Bankgebühren pl; **free of ~** kostenlos; **to reverse the ~s** (TEL) ein R-Gespräch führen; **to be in ~ of** verantwortlich sein für; **to take ~** (die Verantwortung) übernehmen; **to ~ sth (up) to sb's account** jdm etw in Rechnung stellen; ~ **card** n Kundenkarte f

charitable ['tʃærɪtəbl] adj wohltätig; (*lenient*) nachsichtig

charity ['tʃærɪtɪ] n (*institution*) Hilfswerk nt; (*attitude*) Nächstenliebe f

charlady ['tʃɑ:leɪdɪ] (BRIT) n Putzfrau f

charlatan ['ʃɑ:lətən] n Scharlatan m

charm [tʃɑ:m] n Charme m; (*spell*) Bann m; (*object*) Talisman m ♦ vt bezaubern; **~ing** adj reizend

chart [tʃɑ:t] n Tabelle f; (NAUT) Seekarte f ♦ vt (*course*) abstecken

charter ['tʃɑ:tə*] vt chartern ♦ n Schutzbrief m; **~ed accountant** n Wirtschaftsprüfer(in) m(f); ~ **flight** n Charterflug m

charwoman ['tʃɑ:wʊmən] n = **charlady**

chase [tʃeɪs] vt jagen, verfolgen ♦ n Jagd f

chasm ['kæzəm] n Kluft f

chassis ['ʃæsɪ] n Fahrgestell nt

chastity ['tʃæstɪtɪ] n Keuschheit f

chat [tʃæt] vi (*also: have a* ~) plaudern ♦ n Plauderei f; ~ **show** (BRIT) n Talkshow f

chatter ['tʃætə*] vi schwatzen; (*teeth*) klappern ♦ n Geschwätz nt; **~box** n Quasselstrippe f

chatty ['tʃætɪ] adj geschwätzig

chauffeur ['ʃəʊfə*] n Chauffeur m

chauvinist ['ʃəʊvɪnɪst] n (*male* ~) Chauvi m (*inf*); (*nationalist*) Chauvinist(in) m(f)

cheap [tʃi:p] adj, adv billig; **~ly** adv billig

cheat [tʃi:t] vi, vt betrügen; (SCH) mogeln ♦ n Betrüger(in) m(f)

check [tʃek] vt (*examine*) prüfen; (*make sure*) nachsehen; (*control*) kontrollieren; (*restrain*) zügeln; (*stop*) anhalten ♦ n (*examination, restraint*) Kontrolle f; (*bill*) Rechnung f; (*pattern*) Karo(muster) nt; (US) = **cheque** ♦ adj (*pattern, cloth*) kariert; ~ **in** vi (*in hotel, airport*) einchecken ♦ vt (*luggage*) abfertigen lassen; ~ **out** vi (*of hotel*) abreisen; ~ **up** vi nachschauen; ~ **up on** vt kontrollieren; **~ered** (US) adj

chequered; **~ers** (US) n (draughts) Damespiel nt; **~in** (desk) n Abfertigung f; **~ing account** (US) = current account) Girokonto nt; **~mate** n Schachmatt nt; **~out** n Kasse f; **~point** n Kontrollpunkt m; **~ room** (US) = left-luggage office) Gepäckaufbewahrung f; **~up** n (Nach)prüfung f; (MED) (ärztliche) Untersuchung f

cheek [tʃiːk] n Backe f; (fig) Frechheit f; **~bone** n Backenknochen m; **~y** adj frech

cheep [tʃiːp] vi piepsen

cheer [tʃɪə*] n (usu pl) Hurra- or Beifallsruf ♦ vt zujubeln; (encourage) aufmuntern ♦ vi jauchzen; **~!** Prost!; **~ up** vi bessere Laune bekommen ♦ vt aufmuntern; **~ up!** nun lach doch mal!; **~ful** adj fröhlich

cheerio ['tʃɪərɪ'əʊ] (BRIT) excl tschüs!

cheese [tʃiːz] n Käse m; **~board** n (gemischte) Käseplatte f

cheetah ['tʃiːtə] n Gepard m

chef [ʃef] n Küchenchef m

chemical ['kemɪkəl] adj chemisch ♦ n Chemikalie f

chemist ['kemɪst] n (BRIT: pharmacist) Apotheker m, Drogist m; (scientist) Chemiker m; **~ry** n Chemie f; **~'s (shop)** (BRIT) n Apotheke f, Drogerie f

cheque [tʃek] (BRIT) n Scheck m; **~book** n Scheckbuch nt; **~ card** n Scheckkarte f

chequered ['tʃekəd] adj (fig) bewegt

cherish ['tʃerɪʃ] vt (person) lieben; (hope) hegen

cherry ['tʃerɪ] n Kirsche f

chess [tʃes] n Schach nt; **~board** n Schachbrett nt; **~man** (irreg) n Schachfigur f

chest [tʃest] n (ANAT) Brust f; (box) Kiste f; **~ of drawers** n Kommode f

chestnut ['tʃesnʌt] n Kastanie f; **~ tree** n Kastanienbaum m

chew [tʃuː] vt, vi kauen; **~ing gum** n Kaugummi m

chic [ʃiːk] adj schick, elegant

chick [tʃɪk] n Küken nt; (US: inf: girl) Biene f

chicken ['tʃɪkɪn] n Huhn nt; (food) Hähnchen nt; **~ out** (inf) vi kneifen (inf)

chickenpox ['tʃɪkɪnpɒks] n Windpocken pl

chicory ['tʃɪkərɪ] n (in coffee) Zichorie f; (plant) Chicorée f

chief [tʃiːf] n (of tribe) Häuptling m; (COMM) Chef m ♦ adj Haupt-; **~ executive** n Geschäftsführer(in) m(f); **~ly** adv hauptsächlich

chiffon ['ʃɪfɒn] n Chiffon m

chilblain ['tʃɪlbleɪn] n Frostbeule f

child [tʃaɪld] (pl **children**) n Kind nt; **~birth** n Entbindung f; **~hood** n Kindheit f; **~ish** adj kindisch; **~like** adj kindlich; **~ minder** (BRIT) n Tagesmutter f

children ['tʃɪldrən] npl of child

Chile ['tʃɪlɪ] n Chile nt; **~an** adj chilenisch

chill [tʃɪl] n Kühle f; (MED) Erkältung f ♦ vt (CULIN) kühlen

chilli ['tʃɪlɪ] n Peperoni pl; (meal, spice) Chili m

chilly ['tʃɪlɪ] adj kühl, frostig

chime [tʃaɪm] n Geläut nt ♦ vi ertönen

chimney ['tʃɪmnɪ] n Schornstein m; **~ sweep** n Schornsteinfeger(in) m(f)

chimpanzee [tʃɪmpæn'ziː] n Schimpanse m

chin [tʃɪn] n Kinn nt

China ['tʃaɪnə] n China nt

china ['tʃaɪnə] n Porzellan nt

Chinese [tʃaɪ'niːz] adj chinesisch ♦ n (inv) Chinese m, Chinesin f; (LING) Chinesisch

chink [tʃɪŋk] n (opening) Ritze f; (noise) Klirren nt

chip [tʃɪp] n (of wood etc) Splitter m; (in poker etc) Chip m; (US: crisp) Chip m ♦ vt absplittern; **~s** npl (BRIT: COOK) Pommes frites pl; **~ in** (inf) vi Zwischenbemerkungen machen

chiropodist [kɪˈrɔpədɪst] (*BRIT*) *n* Fußpfleger(in) *m(f)*

chirp [tʃəːp] *vi* zwitschern

chisel [ˈtʃɪzl] *n* Meißel *m*

chit [tʃɪt] *n* Notiz *f*

chitchat [ˈtʃɪttʃæt] *n* Plauderei *f*

chivalrous [ˈʃɪvəlrəs] *adj* ritterlich

chivalry [ˈʃɪvəlrɪ] *n* Ritterlichkeit *f*

chives [tʃaɪvz] *npl* Schnittlauch *m*

chlorine [ˈklɔːriːn] *n* Chlor *nt*

chock [tʃɔk] *n* Bremsklotz *m*; **~-a-block** *adj* vollgepfropft; **~-full** *adj* vollgepfropft

chocolate [ˈtʃɔklɪt] *n* Schokolade *f*

choice [tʃɔɪs] *n* Wahl *f*; (*of goods*) Auswahl *f* ♦ *adj* Qualitäts-

choir [ˈkwaɪə*] *n* Chor *m*; **~boy** *n* Chorknabe *m*

choke [tʃəuk] *vi* ersticken ♦ *vt* erdrosseln; (*block*) (ab)drosseln ♦ *n* (*AUT*) Starterklappe *f*

cholera [ˈkɔlərə] *n* Cholera *f*

cholesterol [kəˈlestərɔl] *n* Cholesterin *nt*

choose [tʃuːz] (*pt* chose, *pp* chosen) *vt* wählen

choosy [ˈtʃuːzi] *adj* wählerisch

chop [tʃɔp] *vt* (*wood*) spalten; (*COOK: also: ~ up*) (zer)hacken ♦ *n* Hieb *m*; (*COOK*) Kotelett *nt*; **~s** *npl* (*jaws*) Lefzen *pl*

chopper [ˈtʃɔpə*] *n* (*helicopter*) Hubschrauber *m*

choppy [ˈtʃɔpi] *adj* (*sea*) bewegt

chopsticks [ˈtʃɔpstiks] *npl* (Eß)stäbchen *pl*

choral [ˈkɔːrəl] *adj* Chor-

chord [kɔːd] *n* Akkord *m*

chore [tʃɔː*] *n* Pflicht *f*; **~s** *npl* (*housework*) Hausarbeit *f*

choreographer [kɔrɪˈɔgrəfə*] *n* Choreograph(in) *m(f)*

chorister [ˈkɔrɪstə*] *n* Chorsänger(in) *m(f)*

chortle [ˈtʃɔːtl] *vi* glucksen

chorus [ˈkɔːrəs] *n* Chor *m*; (*in song*) Refrain *m*

chose [tʃəuz] *pt of* choose

chosen [ˈtʃəuzn] *pp of* choose

Christ [kraɪst] *n* Christus *m*

christen [ˈkrɪsn] *vt* taufen

Christian [ˈkrɪstɪən] *adj* christlich ♦ *n* Christ(in) *m(f)*; **~ity** [krɪstɪˈænɪtɪ] *n* Christentum *nt*; **~ name** *n* Vorname *m*

Christmas [ˈkrɪsməs] *n* Weihnachten *pl*; Happy or Merry ~! Frohe or fröhliche Weihnachten!; **~ card** *n* Weihnachtskarte *f*; **~ Day** *n* erster Weihnachtstag; **~ Eve** *n* Heiligabend *m*; **~ tree** *n* Weihnachtsbaum *m*

chrome [krəum] *n* = **chromium plating**

chromium [ˈkrəumɪəm] *n* Chrom *nt*; **~ plating** [krəmɪəˈpleɪtɪŋ] *n* Verchromung *f*

chronic [ˈkrɔnɪk] *adj* chronisch

chronicle [ˈkrɔnɪkl] *n* Chronik *f*

chronological [krɔnəˈlɔdʒɪkəl] *adj* chronologisch

chubby [ˈtʃʌbi] *adj* rundlich

chuck [tʃʌk] *n* werfen; (*BRIT*: *also*: **~ up**) hinwerfen; **~ out** *vt* (*person*) rauswerfen; (*old clothes etc*) wegwerfen

chuckle [ˈtʃʌkl] *vi* in sich hineinlachen

chug [tʃʌg] *vi* tuckern

chum [tʃʌm] *n* Kumpel *m*

chunk [tʃʌŋk] *n* Klumpen *m*; (*of food*) Brocken *m*

church [tʃəːtʃ] *n* Kirche *f*; **~yard** *n* Kirchhof *m*

churlish [ˈtʃəːlɪʃ] *adj* grob

churn [tʃəːn] *n* (*for butter*) Butterfaß *nt*; (*for milk*) Milchkanne *f*; **~ out** *vt* produzieren

chute [ʃuːt] *n* Rutsche *f*; (*rubbish* ~) Müllschlucker *m*

CIA (*US*) *n abbr* (= Central Intelligence Agency) CIA *m*

CID (*BRIT*) *n abbr* (= Criminal Investigation Department) ≈ Kripo *f*

cider [ˈsaɪdə*] *n* Apfelwein *m*

cigar [sɪˈgɑː*] *n* Zigarre *f*

cigarette [sɪgəˈret] *n* Zigarette *f*; **~ case** *n* Zigarettenetui *nt*; **~ end** *n* Zigarettenstummel *m*

Cinderella [sɪndəˈrelə] *n* Aschenbrödel *nt*

cinders ['sɪndəz] *npl* Asche *f*

cine-camera ['sɪnɪ'kæmərə] (*BRIT*) *n* Filmkamera *f*

cine-film ['sɪnɪfɪlm] (*BRIT*) *n* Schmalfilm *m*

cinema ['sɪnəmə] *n* Kino *nt*

cinnamon ['sɪnəmən] *n* Zimt *m*

cipher ['saɪfə*] *n* (*code*) Chiffre *f*

circle ['sɜːkl] *n* Kreis *m*; (*in cinema etc*) Rang *m* ♦ *vi* kreisen ♦ *vt* (*surround*) umgeben; (*move round*) kreisen um

circuit ['sɜːkɪt] *n* (*track*) Rennbahn *f*; (*lap*) Runde *f*; (*ELEC*) Stromkreis *m*; **~ous** [sɜː'kjuːɪtəs] *adj* weitschweifig

circular ['sɜːkjələ*] *adj* rund ♦ *n* Rundschreiben *nt*

circulate ['sɜːkjʊleɪt] *vi* zirkulieren ♦ *vt* in Umlauf setzen; **circulation** [sɜːkjʊ'leɪʃən] *n* (*of blood*) Kreislauf *m*; (*of newspaper*) Auflage *f*; (*of money*) Umlauf *m*

circumcise ['sɜːkəmsaɪz] *vt* beschneiden

circumference [sə'kʌmfərəns] *n* (*Kreis*)umfang *m*

circumspect ['sɜːkəmspekt] *adj* umsichtig

circumstances ['sɜːkəmstənsɪz] *npl* Umstände *pl*; (*financial condition*) Verhältnisse *pl*

circumvent [sɜːkəm'vent] *vt* umgehen

circus ['sɜːkəs] *n* Zirkus *m*

CIS *n abbr* (= *Commonwealth of Independent States*) GUS *f*

cistern ['sɪstən] *n* Zisterne *f*; (*of W.C.*) Spülkasten *m*

cite [saɪt] *vt* zitieren, anführen

citizen ['sɪtɪzn] *n* Bürger(in) *m(f)*; **~ship** *n* Staatsbürgerschaft *f*

citrus fruit ['sɪtrəs fruːt] *n* Zitrusfrucht *f*

city ['sɪtɪ] *n* Großstadt *f*; **the C~** die City, das Finanzzentrum Londons

civic ['sɪvɪk] *adj* (*of town*) städtisch; (*of citizen*) Bürger-; **~ centre** *n* Stadtverwaltung *f*

civil ['sɪvl] *adj* bürgerlich; (*not mili-*

tary) zivil; (*polite*) höflich; **~ engineer** *n* Bauingenieur *m*; **~ian** [sɪ'vɪlɪən] *n* Zivilperson *f* ♦ *adj* zivil, Zivil-

civilization [sɪvɪlaɪ'zeɪʃən] *n* Zivilisation *f*

civilized ['sɪvɪlaɪzd] *adj* zivilisiert

civil : **~ law** *n* Zivilrecht *nt*; **~ servant** *n* Staatsbeamte(r) *m*; **C~ Service** *n* Staatsdienst *m*; **~ war** *n* Bürgerkrieg *m*

clad [klæd] *adj*: **~ in** gehüllt in +*acc*

claim [kleɪm] *vt* beanspruchen; (*have opinion*) behaupten ♦ *vi* (*for insurance*) Ansprüche geltend machen ♦ *n* (*demand*) Forderung *f*; (*right*) Anspruch *m*; (*pretension*) Behauptung *f*; **~ant** *n* Antragsteller(in) *m(f)*

clairvoyant [klɛə'vɔɪənt] *n* Hellseher(in) *m(f)*

clam [klæm] *n* Venusmuschel *f*

clamber ['klæmbə*] *vi* kraxeln

clammy ['klæmɪ] *adj* klamm

clamour ['klæmə*] *vi*: **~ to ~ for sth** nach etw verlangen

clamp [klæmp] *n* Schraubzwinge *f* ♦ *vt* einspannen; **~ down on** *vt fus* Maßnahmen ergreifen gegen

clan [klæn] *n* Clan *m*

clandestine [klæn'destɪn] *adj* geheim

clang [klæŋ] *vi* scheppern

clap [klæp] *vi* klatschen ♦ *vt* Beifall klatschen +*dat* ♦ *n* (*of hands*) Klatschen *nt*; (*of thunder*) Donnerschlag *m*; **~ping** *n* Klatschen *nt*

claret ['klærət] *n* rote(r) Bordeaux(wein) *m*

clarify ['klærɪfaɪ] *vt* klären, erklären

clarinet [klærɪ'net] *n* Klarinette *f*

clarity ['klærɪtɪ] *n* Klarheit *f*

clash [klæʃ] *n* (*fig*) Konflikt *m* ♦ *vi* zusammenprallen; (*colours*) sich beißen; (*argue*) sich streiten

clasp [klɑːsp] *n* Griff *m*; (*on jewels, bag*) Verschluß *m* ♦ *vt* umklammern

class [klɑːs] *n* Klasse *f* ♦ *vt* einordnen; **~-conscious** *adj* klassenbewußt

classic ['klæsɪk] *n* Klassiker *m* ♦ *adj* klassisch; **~al** *adj* klassisch

classified ['klæsıfaıd] adj (information) Geheim-; ~ **advertisement** n Kleinanzeige f

classify ['klæsıfaı] vt klassifizieren

classmate ['klɑːsmeıt] n Klassenkamerad(in) m(f)

classroom ['klɑːsrʊm] n Klassenzimmer nt

clatter ['klætə*] vi klappern; (feet) trappeln

clause [klɔːz] n (JUR) Klausel f; (GRAM) Satz m

claustrophobia [klɔːstrə'fəʊbıə] n Platzangst f

claw [klɔː] n Kralle f ♦ vt (zer)kratzen

clay [kleı] n Lehm m; (for pots) Ton m

clean [kliːn] adj sauber ♦ vt putzen; (clothes) reinigen; ~ **out** vt gründlich putzen; ~ **up** vt aufräumen; ~**-cut** adj (person) adrett; (clear) klar; ~**er** n (person) Putzfrau f; ~**ing** n Putzen nt; (clothes) Reinigung f; ~**liness** ['klenlınıs] n Reinlichkeit f

cleanse [klenz] vt reinigen; ~**r** n (for face) Reinigungsmilch f

clean-shaven ['kliːn'feıvn] adj glattrasiert

cleansing department ['klenzıŋ-] (BRIT) n Stadtreinigung f

clear [klıə*] adj klar; (road) frei ♦ vt (road etc) freimachen; (obstacle) beseitigen; (JUR: suspect) freisprechen ♦ vi klarwerden; (fog) sich lichten ♦ adv: ~ of von ... entfernt; to ~ **the table** den Tisch abräumen; ~ **up** vt aufräumen; (solve) aufklären; ~**ance** ['klıərəns] n (removal) Räumung f; (free space) Lichtung f; (permission) Freigabe f; ~**-cut** adj (case) eindeutig; ~**ing** n Lichtung f; ~**ing bank** (BRIT) n Clearingbank f; ~**ly** adv klar; (obviously) eindeutig; ~**way** (BRIT) n (Straße f mit) Halteverbot nt

cleaver ['kliːvə*] n Hackbeil f

clef [klef] n Notenschlüssel m

cleft [kleft] n (in rock) Spalte f

clemency ['klemənsı] n Milde f

clench [klentʃ] vt (teeth) zusammenbeißen; (fist) ballen

clergy ['klɜːdʒı] n Geistliche(n) pl; ~**man** (irreg) n Geistliche(r) m

clerical ['klerıkəl] adj (office) Schreib-, Büro-; (REL) geistlich

clerk [klɑːk, (US) klɜːk] n (in office) Büroangestellte(r) mf; (US: sales person) Verkäufer(in) m(f)

clever ['klevə*] adj klug; (crafty) schlau

cliché [kliːʃ] n Klischee nt

click [klık] vt (heels) zusammenklappen; (tongue) schnalzen mit

client ['klaıənt] n Klient(in) m(f); ~**ele** [kliːɑːn'tel] n Kundschaft f

cliff [klıf] n Klippe f

climate ['klaımıt] n Klima nt

climax ['klaımæks] n Höhepunkt m

climb [klaım] vt besteigen ♦ vi steigen, klettern ♦ n Aufstieg m; ~**-down** n Abstieg m; ~**er** n Bergsteiger(in) m(f); ~**ing** n Bergsteigen nt

clinch [klıntʃ] vt (decide) entscheiden; (deal) festmachen

cling [klıŋ] (pt, pp **clung**) vi (clothes) eng anliegen; to ~ **to** sich festklammern an +dat

clinic ['klınık] n Klinik f; ~**al** adj klinisch

clink [klıŋk] vi klimpern

clip [klıp] n Spange f; (also: paper ~) Klammer f ♦ vt (papers) heften; (hair, hedge) stutzen; ~**pers** npl (for hedge) Heckenschere f; (for hair) Haarschneidemaschine f; ~**ping** n Ausschnitt m

cloak [kləʊk] n Umhang m ♦ vt hüllen; ~**room** n (for coats) Garderobe f; (BRIT: W.C.) Toilette f

clock [klɒk] n Uhr f; ~ **in** or **on** vt stempeln; ~ **off** or **out** vi stempeln; ~**wise** adv im Uhrzeigersinn; ~**work** n Uhrwerk nt ♦ adj zum Aufziehen

clog [klɒg] n Holzschuh m ♦ vt verstopfen

cloister ['klɔıstə*] n Kreuzgang m

clone [kləʊn] n Klon m

close¹ [kləʊs] *adj* (*near*) in der Nähe; (*friend, connection, print*) eng; (*relative*) nahe; (*result*) knapp; (*examination*) scharf; (*weather*) schwül; (*room*) stickig ♦ *adv* nahe, dicht; ~ **by** in der Nähe; ~ **at hand** in der Nähe; **to have a ~ shave** (*fig*) mit knapper Not davorkommen

close² [kləʊz] *vt* (*shut*) schließen; (*end*) beenden ♦ *vi* (*shop etc*) schließen; (*door etc*) sich schließen ♦ *n* Ende *nt* ♦ *vt* (*shut*) schließen; ~ **down** *vi* schließen; ~**d** (*shop etc*) geschlossen; ~**d shop** *n* Gewerkschaftszwang *m*

close-knit [kləʊs'nɪt] *adj* eng zusammengewachsen

closely ['kləʊslɪ] *adv* eng; (*carefully*) genau

closet ['klɒzɪt] *n* Schrank *m*

close-up ['kləʊsʌp] *n* Nahaufnahme *f*

closure ['kləʊʒə*] *n* Schließung *f*

clot [klɒt] *n* (*of blood*) Blutgerinnsel *nt*; (*fool*) Blödmann *m* ♦ *vi* gerinnen

cloth [klɒθ] *n* (*material*) Tuch *nt*; (*rag*) Lappen *m*

clothe [kləʊð] *vt* kleiden; ~**s** *npl* Kleider *pl*; ~**s brush** *n* Kleiderbürste *f*; ~**s line** *n* Wäscheleine *f*; ~**s peg** (*US → pin*) *n* Wäscheklammer *f*

clothing [kləʊðɪŋ] *n* Kleidung *f*

cloud [klaʊd] *n* Wolke *f*; ~**burst** *n* Wolkenbruch *m*; ~**y** *adj* bewölkt; (*liquid*) trüb

clout [klaʊt] *vt* hauen

clove [kləʊv] *n* Gewürznelke *f*; ~ **of garlic** Knoblauchzehe *f*

clover ['kləʊvə*] *n* Klee *m*

clown [klaʊn] *n* Clown *m* ♦ *vi* (*also*: ~ **about,** ~ **around**) kaspern

cloying ['klɔɪɪŋ] *adj* (*taste, smell*) übersüß

club [klʌb] *n* (*weapon*) Knüppel *m*; (*society*) Klub *m*; (*also*: *golf* ~) Golfschläger *m* ♦ *vt* prügeln ♦ *vi*: **to ~ together** zusammentun; ~**s** (*CARDS*) Kreuz *nt*; ~ **car** (*US*) *n* (*RAIL*) Speisewagen *m*; ~**house** *n*

Klubhaus *nt*

cluck [klʌk] *vi* glucken

clue [kluː] *n* Anhaltspunkt *m*; (*in crosswords*) Frage *f*; **I haven't a ~** (ich hab') keine Ahnung

clump [klʌmp] *n* Gruppe *f*

clumsy ['klʌmzɪ] *adj* (*person*) unbeholfen; (*shape*) unförmig

clung [klʌŋ] *pt, pp of* **cling**

cluster ['klʌstə*] *n* (*of trees etc*) Gruppe *f* ♦ *vi* sich drängen, sich scharen

clutch [klʌtʃ] *n* Griff *m*; (*AUT*) Kupplung *f* ♦ *vt* sich festklammern an +*dat*

clutter ['klʌtə*] *vt* vollpfropfen; (*desk*) übersäen

CND *n abbr* = Campaign for Nuclear Disarmament

Co. *abbr* = county; company

c/o *abbr* = (*care of*) c/o

coach [kəʊtʃ] *n* (*bus*) Reisebus *m*; (*horse-drawn*) Kutsche *f*; (*RAIL*) (Personen)wagen *m*; (*trainer*) Trainer *m* ♦ *vt* (*SCH*) Nachhilfeunterricht geben +*dat*; (*SPORT*) trainieren; ~ **trip** *n* Busfahrt *f*

coagulate [kəʊˈægjʊleɪt] *vi* gerinnen

coal [kəʊl] *n* Kohle *f*; ~ **face** *n* Streb *m*; ~ **field** *n* Kohlengebiet *nt*

coalition [kəʊəˈlɪʃən] *n* Koalition *f*

coalman ['kəʊlmən] *n* Kohlenhändler *m*

coal merchant *n* = coalman

coal mine *n* Kohlenbergwerk *nt*

coarse [kɔːs] *adj* grob; (*fig*) ordinär

coast [kəʊst] *n* Küste *f* ♦ *vi* dahinrollen; (*AUT*) im Leerlauf fahren; ~**al** *adj* Küsten-; ~**guard** *n* Küstenwache *f*; ~**line** *n* Küste(nlinie) *f*

coat [kəʊt] *n* Mantel *m*; (*on animals*) Fell *nt*; (*of paint*) Schicht *f* ♦ *vt* überstreichen; ~ **of arms** *n* Wappen *nt*; ~**hanger** *n* Kleiderbügel *m*; ~**ing** *n* Überzug *m*; (*of paint*) Schicht *f*

coax [kəʊks] *vt* beschwatzen

cob [kɒb] *n see* **corn**

cobbler ['kɒblə*] *n* Schuster *m*

cobbles ['kɒblz] *npl* Pflastersteine *pl*

cobblestones ['kɒblstəʊnz] npl Pflastersteine pl

cobweb ['kɒbweb] n Spinnennetz nt

cocaine [kə'keɪn] n Kokain nt

cock [kɒk] n Hahn m ♦ vt (gun) entsichern; ~**erel** n junge(r) Hahn m; ~-**eyed** adj (fig) verrückt

cockle ['kɒkl] n Herzmuschel f

cockney ['kɒknɪ] n echte(r) Londoner m

cockpit ['kɒkpɪt] n (AVIAT) Pilotenkanzel f

cockroach ['kɒkrəʊtʃ] n Küchenschabe f

cocktail ['kɒkteɪl] n Cocktail m; ~ **cabinet** n Hausbar f; ~ **party** n Cocktailparty f

cocoa ['kəʊkəʊ] n Kakao m

coconut ['kəʊkənʌt] n Kokosnuß f

cocoon [kə'kuːn] n Kokon m

cod [kɒd] n Kabeljau m

C.O.D. abbr = **cash on delivery**

code [kəʊd] n Kode m; (JUR) Kodex m

cod-liver oil ['kɒdlɪvər-] n Lebertran m

coercion [kəʊ'ɜːʃən] n Zwang m

coffee ['kɒfɪ] n Kaffee m; ~ **bar** (BRIT) n Café nt; ~ **bean** n Kaffeebohne f; ~ **break** n Kaffeepause f; ~**pot** n Kaffeekanne f; ~ **table** n Couchtisch m

coffin ['kɒfɪn] n Sarg m

cog [kɒg] n (Rad)zahn m

cogent ['kəʊdʒənt] adj triftig, überzeugend, zwingend

cognac ['kɒnjæk] n Kognak m

coherent [kəʊ'hɪərənt] adj zusammenhängend; (person) verständlich

cohesion [kəʊ'hiːʒən] n Zusammenhang m

coil [kɔɪl] n Rolle f; (ELEC) Spule f; (contraceptive) Spirale f ♦ vt aufwickeln

coin [kɔɪn] n Münze f ♦ vt prägen; ~**age** n (word) Prägung f; ~-**box** (BRIT) n Münzfernsprecher m

coincide [kəʊɪn'saɪd] vi (happen together) zusammenfallen; (agree) übereinstimmen; ~**nce** [kəʊ'ɪnsɪdns] n Zufall m

Coke [kəʊk] ® n (drink) Coca-Cola f (®)

coke [kəʊk] n Koks m

colander ['kɒləndə*] n Durchschlag m

cold [kəʊld] adj kalt ♦ n Kälte f; (MED) Erkältung f; **I'm** ~ mir ist kalt; **to catch** ~ sich erkälten; **in** ~ **blood** kaltblütig; **to give sb the** ~ **shoulder** jdm die kalte Schulter zeigen; ~**ly** adv kalt; ~-**shoulder** vt die kalte Schulter zeigen +dat; ~ **sore** n Erkältungsbläschen nt

coleslaw ['kəʊlslɔː] n Krautsalat m

colic ['kɒlɪk] n Kolik f

collaborate [kə'læbəreɪt] vi zusammenarbeiten

collaboration [kəlæbə'reɪʃən] n Zusammenarbeit f; (POL) Kollaboration f

collapse [kə'læps] vi (people) zusammenbrechen; (things) einstürzen ♦ n Zusammenbruch m; Einsturz m

collapsible [kə'læpsəbl] adj zusammenklappbar, Klapp-

collar ['kɒlə*] n Kragen m; ~**bone** n Schlüsselbein nt

collateral [kɒ'lætərəl] n (zusätzliche) Sicherheit f

colleague ['kɒliːg] n Kollege m, Kollegin f

collect [kə'lekt] vt sammeln; (BRIT: call and pick up) abholen ♦ vi sich sammeln ♦ adv: **to call** ~ (US: TEL) ein R-Gespräch führen; ~**ion** [kə'lekʃən] n Sammlung f; (REL) Kollekte f; (of post) Leerung f

collective [kə'lektɪv] adj gemeinsam; (POL) kollektiv

collector [kə'lektə*] n Sammler m; (tax ~) (Steuer)einnehmer m

college ['kɒlɪdʒ] n (UNIV) College nt; (TECH) Fach-, Berufsschule f

collide [kə'laɪd] vi zusammenstoßen

colliery ['kɒlɪərɪ] (BRIT) n Zeche f

collision [kə'lɪʒən] n Zusammenstoß m

colloquial [kə'ləʊkwɪəl] adj umgangssprachlich

collusion [kə'luːʒən] n geheime(s) Einverständnis nt

colon ['kəʊlən] n Doppelpunkt m; (MED) Dickdarm m

colonel ['kɜːnl] n Oberst m

colonial [kə'ləʊnɪəl] adj Kolonial-

colonize ['kɒlənaɪz] vt kolonisieren

colony ['kɒlənɪ] n Kolonie f

colour ['kʌlə*] (US **color**) n Farbe f ♦ vt (also fig) färben ♦ vi sich verfärben; ~s npl (of club) Fahne f; ~ bar n Rassenschranke f; ~-blind adj farbenblind; ~ed adj farbig; ~ film n Farbfilm m; ~ful adj bunt; (personality) schillernd; ~ing n (complexion) Gesichtsfarbe f; (substance) Farbstoff m; ~ scheme n Farbgebung f; ~ television n Farbfernsehen nt

colt [kəʊlt] n Fohlen nt

column ['kɒləm] n Säule f; (MIL) Kolonne f; (of print) Spalte f; ~ist ['kɒləmnɪst] n Kolumnist m

coma ['kəʊmə] n Koma nt

comb [kəʊm] n Kamm m ♦ vt kämmen; (search) durchkämmen

combat ['kɒmbæt] n Kampf m ♦ vt bekämpfen

combination [kɒmbɪ'neɪʃən] n Kombination f

combine [vb kəm'baɪn, n 'kɒmbaɪn] vt verbinden ♦ vi sich vereinigen ♦ n (COMM) Konzern m; ~ (harvester) n Mähdrescher m

combustion [kəm'bʌstʃən] n Verbrennung f

come [kʌm] (pt **came**, pp **come**) vi kommen; **to** ~ **undone** aufgehen; ~ **about** vi geschehen; ~ **across** vt fus (find) stoßen auf +acc; ~ **away** vi (person) weggehen; (handle etc) abgehen; ~ **back** vi zurückkommen; ~ **by** vt fus (find): **to** ~ **by sth** zu etw kommen; ~ **down** vi (price) fallen; ~ **forward** vi (volunteer) sich melden; ~ **from** vi (result) kommen von; **where do you** ~ **from?** wo kommen Sie her?; **I** ~ **from London** ich komme aus London; ~ **in** vi hereinkommen; (train) einfahren; ~ **in**

for vt fus abkriegen; ~ **into** vt fus (inherit) erben; ~ **off** vi (handle) abgehen; (succeed) klappen; ~ **on** vi (progress) vorankommen; ~ **on!** komm!; (hurry) beeil dich!; ~ **out** vi herauskommen; ~ **round** vi (MED) wieder zu sich kommen; ~ **to** vi (MED) wieder zu sich kommen ♦ vt (bill) sich belaufen auf +acc; ~ **up** vi hochkommen; (sun) aufgehen; (problem) auftauchen; ~ **up against** vt fus (resistance, difficulties) stoßen auf +acc; ~ **upon** vt fus stoßen auf +acc; ~ **up with** vt fus sich einfallen lassen

comedian [kə'miːdɪən] n Komiker m

comedienne [kəmiːdɪ'en] n Komikerin f

comedown ['kʌmdaʊn] n Abstieg m

comedy ['kɒmədɪ] n Komödie f

comet ['kɒmɪt] n Komet m

comeuppance [kʌm'ʌpəns] n: **to get one's** ~ seine Quittung bekommen

comfort ['kʌmfət] n Komfort m; (consolation) Trost m ♦ vt trösten; ~**able** adj bequem; ~**ably** adv (sit etc) bequem; (live) angenehm; ~ **station** (US) n öffentliche Toilette f

comic ['kɒmɪk] n Comic(heft) nt; (comedian) Komiker m ♦ adj (also: ~**al**) komisch

coming ['kʌmɪŋ] n Kommen nt; ~(**s**) **and going(s)** n(pl) Kommen und Gehen nt

comma ['kɒmə] n Komma nt

command [kə'mɑːnd] n Befehl m; (control) Führung f; (MIL) Kommando nt; (mastery) Beherrschung f ♦ vt befehlen +dat; (MIL) kommandieren; (be able to get) verfügen über +acc; ~**eer** [kəmən'dɪə*] vt requirieren; ~**er** n Kommandant m

commandment [kə'mɑːndmənt] n (REL) Gebot nt

commando [kə'mɑːndəʊ] n Kommandotruppe nt; (person) Mitglied nt einer Kommandotruppe

commemorate [kə'meməreɪt] vt gedenken +gen

commence [kə'mɛns] vt, vi beginnen

commend [kə'mɛnd] vt (recommend) empfehlen; (praise) loben

commensurate [kə'mɛnsjʊrɪt] adj: ~ with sth einer Sache adj entsprechend

comment ['kɒmɛnt] n Bemerkung f ♦ vi: to ~ (on) sich äußern (zu); ~**ary** ['kɒmɛntrɪ] n Kommentar m; ~**ator** ['kɒmɛnteɪtə*] n Kommentator m; (TV) Reporter(in) m(f)

commerce ['kɒmɜːs] n Handel m

commercial [kə'mɜːʃəl] adj kommerziell, geschäftlich; (training) kaufmännisch ♦ n (TV) Fernsehwerbung f; ~ **break** n Werbespot m; ~**ize** vt kommerzialisieren

commiserate [kə'mɪzəreɪt] vi: to ~ with Mitleid haben mit

commission [kə'mɪʃən] n (act) Auftrag m; (fee) Provision f; (body) Kommission f ♦ vt beauftragen; (MIL) zum Offizier ernennen; (work of art) in Auftrag geben; **out of ~** außer Betrieb; ~**aire** [kəmɪʃə'nɛə*] (BRIT) n Portier m; ~**er** n (POLICE) Polizeipräsident m

commit [kə'mɪt] vt (crime) begehen; (entrust) anvertrauen; to ~ o.s. sich festlegen; ~**ment** n Verpflichtung f

committee [kə'mɪtɪ] n Ausschuß m

commodity [kə'mɒdɪtɪ] n Ware f

common ['kɒmən] adj (cause) gemeinsam; (pej) gewöhnlich; (widespread) üblich, häufig ♦ n Gemeindeland nt; ~**s** npl (BRIT): **the C~s** das Unterhaus; ~ **er** n Bürgerliche(r) m/f; ~ **law** n Gewohnheitsrecht nt; **C~ Market** n Gemeinsame(r) Markt m; ~**ly** adv alltäglich; ~**place** adj alltäglich; ~**room** n Gemeinschaftsraum m; ~ **sense** n gesunde(r) Menschenverstand m; **C~wealth** n: **the C~wealth** das Commonwealth

commotion [kə'məʊʃən] n Aufsehen nt

communal ['kɒmjuːnl] adj Gemeinde-; Gemeinschafts-

commune [n 'kɒmjuːn, vb kə'mjuːn] n Kommune f ♦ vi: to ~ with sich mitteilen +dat

communicate [kə'mjuːnɪkeɪt] vt (transmit) übertragen ♦ vi (be in touch) in Verbindung stehen; (make self understood) sich verständigen

communication [kəmjuːnɪ'keɪʃən] n (message) Mitteilung f; (making understood) Kommunikation f; ~ **cord** (BRIT) n Notbremse f

communion [kə'mjuːnɪən] n (also: Holy C~) Abendmahl nt, Kommunion f

communism ['kɒmjʊnɪzəm] n Kommunismus m

communist ['kɒmjʊnɪst] n Kommunist(in) m(f) ♦ adj kommunistisch

community [kə'mjuːnɪtɪ] n Gemeinschaft f; ~ **centre** n Gemeinschaftszentrum nt; ~ **chest** (US) n Wohltätigkeitsfonds m; ~ **home** (BRIT) n Erziehungsheim nt

commutation ticket [kɒmjʊ'teɪʃən-] (US) n Zeitkarte f

commute [kə'mjuːt] vi pendeln ♦ vt umwandeln; ~**r** n Pendler m

compact [adj kəm'pækt] adj kompakt ♦ n (for make-up) Puderdose f; ~ **disc** n Compact-disc f; ~ **disc player** n CD-Spieler m

companion [kəm'pænjən] n Begleiter(in) m(f); ~**ship** n Gesellschaft f

company ['kʌmpənɪ] n Gesellschaft f; (COMM) Firma f, Gesellschaft f; **to keep sb** ~ jdm Gesellschaft leisten; ~ **secretary** (BRIT) n ≈ Prokurist(in) m(f)

comparable ['kɒmpərəbl] adj vergleichbar

comparative [kəm'pærətɪv] adj (relative) relativ; ~**ly** adv verhältnismäßig

compare [kəm'pɛə*] vt vergleichen ♦ vi sich vergleichen lassen

comparison [kəm'pærɪsn] n Vergleich m; **in** ~ **(with)** im Vergleich (mit or zu)

compartment [kəm'pɑːtmənt] n (RAIL) Abteil nt; (in drawer etc)

Fach nt

compass ['kʌmpəs] n Kompaß m; ~es npl (MATH etc: also: pair of ~es) Zirkel m.

compassion [kəm'pæʃən] n Mitleid nt; ~ate adj mitfühlend

compatible [kəm'pætɪbl] adj vereinbar; (COMPUT) kompatibel

compel [kəm'pel] vt zwingen

compensate ['kɒmpenseɪt] vt entschädigen ♦ vi: to ~ for Ersatz leisten für

compensation [kɒmpen'seɪʃən] n Entschädigung f

compère ['kɒmpeə*] n Conférencier m

compete [kəm'piːt] vi (take part) teilnehmen; (vie with) konkurrieren

competent ['kɒmpɪtənt] adj kompetent

competition [kɒmpɪ'tɪʃən] n (contest) Wettbewerb m; (COMM, rivalry) Konkurrenz f

competitive [kəm'petɪtɪv] adj Konkurrenz-; (COMM) konkurrenzfähig

competitor [kəm'petɪtə*] n (COMM) Konkurrent(in) m(f); (participant) Teilnehmer(in) m(f)

compile [kəm'paɪl] vt zusammenstellen

complacency [kəm'pleɪsnsɪ] n Selbstzufriedenheit f

complacent [kəm'pleɪsnt] adj selbstzufrieden

complain [kəm'pleɪn] vi sich beklagen; (formally) sich beschweren; ~t n Klage f; (formal ~t) Beschwerde f; (MED) Leiden nt

complement [n 'kɒmplɪmənt, vb 'kɒmplɪment] n Ergänzung f; (ship's crew etc) Bemannung f ♦ vt ergänzen; ~ary [kɒmplɪ'mentərɪ] adj (sich) ergänzend

complete [kəm'pliːt] adj (full) völlig; (finished) fertig ♦ vt vervollständigen; (finish) beenden; (fill in: form) ausfüllen; ~ly adv ganz

completion [kəm'pliːʃən] n Fertig-

stellung f; (of contract etc) Abschluß m

complex ['kɒmpleks] adj kompliziert

complexion [kəm'plekʃən] n Gesichtsfarbe f; (fig) Aspekt m

complexity [kəm'pleksɪtɪ] n Kompliziertheit f

compliance [kəm'plaɪəns] n Fügsamkeit f, Einwilligung f; in ~ with sth einer Sache dat gemäß

complicate ['kɒmplɪkeɪt] vt komplizieren; ~d adj kompliziert

complication [kɒmplɪ'keɪʃən] n Komplikation f

complicity [kəm'plɪsɪtɪ] n: ~ (in) Mittäterschaft f (bei)

compliment [n 'kɒmplɪmənt, vb 'kɒmplɪment] n Kompliment nt ♦ vt ein Kompliment machen +dat; ~s npl (greetings) Grüße pl; to pay sb a ~ jdm ein Kompliment machen; ~ary [kɒmplɪ'mentərɪ] adj schmeichelhaft; (free) Frei-, Gratis-

comply [kəm'plaɪ] vi: to ~ with erfüllen +acc; entsprechen +dat

component [kəm'pəʊnənt] adj Teil- ♦ n Bestandteil m

compose [kəm'pəʊz] vt (music) komponieren; (poetry) verfassen; to ~ o.s. sich sammeln; ~d adj gefaßt; ~r n Komponist(in) m(f)

composite ['kɒmpəzɪt] adj zusammengesetzt

composition [kɒmpə'zɪʃən] n (MUS) Komposition f; (SCH) Aufsatz m; (structure) Zusammensetzung f; Aufbau m

compost ['kɒmpɒst] n Kompost m

composure [kəm'pəʊʒə*] n Fassung f

compound [n (CHEM) Verbindung f; (enclosure) Lager m; (LING) Kompositum f ♦ adj zusammengesetzt; (fracture) kompliziert; ~ interest n Zinseszins m

comprehend [kɒmprɪ'hend] vt begreifen

comprehension [kɒmprɪ'henʃən] n Verständnis nt

comprehensive [kɒmprɪ'hensɪv] adj

umfassend ♦ n = **comprehensive school**; ~ **insurance** n Volkasko nt; ~ **school** (BRIT) n Gesamtschule f

compress [vb kəm'pres, n 'kɒmpres] vt komprimieren ♦ n (MED) Kompresse f

comprise [kəm'praɪz] vt (also: be ~d of) umfassen, bestehen aus

compromise ['kɒmprəmaɪz] n Kompromiß m ♦ vt kompromittieren ♦ vi einen Kompromiß schließen

compulsion [kəm'pʌlʃən] n Zwang m

compulsive [kəm'pʌlsɪv] adj zwanghaft

compulsory [kəm'pʌlsərɪ] adj obligatorisch

computer [kəm'pjuːtə*] n Computer m, Rechner m; ~ **game** n Computerspiel nt; ~**ize** vt (information) computerisieren; (company, accounts) auf Computer umstellen; ~ **programmer** n Programmierer(in) m(f); ~ **programming** n Programmieren nt; ~ **science** n Informatik f

computing [kəm'pjuːtɪŋ] n (science) Informatik f; (work) Computerei f

comrade ['kɒmrɪd] n Kamerad m; (POL) Genosse m

con [kɒn] vt hereinlegen ♦ n Schwindel nt

concave [kɒn'keɪv] adj konkav

conceal [kən'siːl] vt (secret) verschweigen; (hide) verbergen

concede [kən'siːd] vt (grant) gewähren; (point) zugeben ♦ vi (admit defeat) nachgeben

conceit [kən'siːt] n Einbildung f; ~**ed** adj eingebildet

conceivable [kən'siːvəbl] adj vorstellbar

conceive [kən'siːv] vt (idea) ausdenken; (imagine) sich vorstellen; (baby) empfangen ♦ vi empfangen

concentrate ['kɒnsəntreɪt] vi konzentrieren ♦ vt konzentrieren; to ~ **on sth** sich auf etw acc konzentrieren

concentration [kɒnsən'treɪʃən] n Konzentration f; ~ **camp** n Konzentrationslager nt, KZ nt

concept ['kɒnsept] n Begriff m

conception [kən'sepʃən] n (idea) Vorstellung f; (BIOL) Empfängnis f

concern [kən'sɜːn] n (affair) Angelegenheit f; (COMM) Unternehmen nt; (worry) Sorge f ♦ vt (interest) angehen; (be about) handeln von; (have connection with) betreffen; to be ~**ed** (about) sich Sorgen machen (um); ~**ing** prep hinsichtlich +gen

concert ['kɒnsət] n Konzert nt

concerted [kən'sɜːtɪd] adj gemeinsam

concert hall n Konzerthalle f

concertina [kɒnsə'tiːnə] n Handharmonika f

concerto [kən'tʃɜːtəʊ] n Konzert nt

concession [kən'seʃən] n (yielding) Zugeständnis nt; **tax** ~ Steuer-Konzession f

conciliation [kənsɪlɪ'eɪʃən] n Versöhnung f; (official) Schlichtung f

concise [kən'saɪs] adj präzis

conclude [kən'kluːd] vt (end) beenden; (treaty) (ab)schließen; (decide) schließen, folgern

conclusion [kən'kluːʒən] n (Ab)schluß m; (deduction) Schluß m

conclusive [kən'kluːsɪv] adj schlüssig

concoct [kən'kɒkt] vt zusammenbrauen; ~**ion** [kən'kɒkʃən] n Gebräu nt

concourse ['kɒŋkɔːs] n (Bahnhofs)halle f, Vorplatz m

concrete ['kɒŋkriːt] n Beton m ♦ adj konkret

concur [kən'kɜː*] vi übereinstimmen

concurrently [kən'kʌrəntlɪ] adv gleichzeitig

concussion [kən'kʌʃən] n (Gehirn)erschütterung f

condemn [kən'dem] vt (JUR) verurteilen; (building) abbruchreif erklären

condensation [kɒnden'seɪʃən] n Kondensation f

condense [kən'dens] vi (CHEM) kondensieren ♦ vt (fig) zusammen-

drängen; ~d milk n Kondensmilch f
condescending [kɔndɪˈsendɪŋ] adj
herablassend
condition [kənˈdɪʃən] n (state) Zustand m; (presupposition) Bedingung f ♦ vt (hair etc) behandeln; (accustom) gewöhnen; ~s npl (circumstances) Verhältnisse pl; on ~ that ... unter der Bedingung, daß ...; ~al adj bedingt; (LING) Bedingungs-; ~er n (for hair) Spülung f; (for fabrics) Weichspüler m
condolences [kənˈdəʊlənsɪz] npl Beileid nt
condom [ˈkɔndəm] n Kondom nt or m
condominium [kɔndəˈmɪnɪəm] (US) n Eigentumswohnung f; (block) Eigentumsblock m
condone [kənˈdəʊn] vt gutheißen
conducive [kənˈdjuːsɪv] adj: ~ to dienlich +dat
conduct [n ˈkɔndʌkt, vb kənˈdʌkt] n (behaviour) Verhalten nt; (management) Führung f ♦ vt führen; (MUS) dirigieren; ~ed tour n Führung f; ~or [kənˈdʌktə*] n (of orchestra) Dirigent m; (in bus, US: on train) Schaffner m; (ELEC) Leiter m; ~ress [kənˈdʌktrɪs] n (in bus) Schaffnerin f
cone [kəʊn] n (MATH) Kegel m; (for ice cream) (Waffel)tüte f; (BOT) Tannenzapfen m
confectioner [kənˈfekʃənə*] n Konditor m; ~'s (shop) n Konditorei f; ~y n Süßigkeiten pl
confederation [kənfedəˈreɪʃən] n Bund m
confer [kənˈfɜː*] vt (degree) verleihen ♦ vi (discuss) konferieren, verhandeln; ~ence [ˈkɔnfərəns] n Konferenz f
confess [kənˈfes] vt, vi gestehen; (ECCL) beichten; ~ion [kənˈfeʃən] n Geständnis nt; (ECCL) Beichte f; ~ional n Beichtstuhl m
confetti [kənˈfetɪ] n Konfetti nt
confide [kənˈfaɪd] vi: to ~ in (sich) anvertrauen +dat

confidence [ˈkɔnfɪdəns] n Vertrauen nt; (assurance) Selbstvertrauen nt; (secret) Geheimnis nt; in ~ (speak, write) vertraulich; ~ trick n Schwindel m
confident [ˈkɔnfɪdənt] adj (sure) überzeugt; (self-assured) selbstsicher
confidential [kɔnfɪˈdenʃəl] adj vertraulich
confine [kənˈfaɪn] vt (limit) beschränken; (lock up) einsperren; ~d adj (space) eng; ~ment n (in prison) Haft f; (MED) Wochenbett nt; ~s [ˈkɔnfaɪnz] npl Grenzen pl
confirm [kənˈfɜːm] vt bestätigen; ~ation [kɔnfəˈmeɪʃən] n Bestätigung f; (REL) Konfirmation f; ~ed adj unverbesserlich; (bachelor) eingefleischt
confiscate [ˈkɔnfɪskeɪt] vt beschlagnahmen
conflict [n ˈkɔnflɪkt, vb kənˈflɪkt] n Konflikt m ♦ vi im Widerspruch stehen; ~ing [kənˈflɪktɪŋ] adj widersprüchlich
conform [kənˈfɔːm] vi: to ~ (to) (things) entsprechen +dat; (people) sich anpassen +dat; (to rules) sich richten (nach)
confound [kənˈfaʊnd] vt verblüffen; (throw into confusion) durcheinanderbringen
confront [kənˈfrʌnt] vt (enemy) entgegentreten +dat; (problems) sich stellen +dat; to ~ sb with sth jdn mit etw konfrontieren; ~ation [kɔnfrənˈteɪʃən] n Konfrontation f
confuse [kənˈfjuːz] vt verwirren; (sth with sth) verwechseln; ~d adj verwirrt; confusing adj verwirrend; confusion [kənˈfjuːʒən] n (perplexity) Verwirrung f; (mixing up) Verwechslung f; (tumult) Aufruhr m
congeal [kənˈdʒiːl] vi (freeze) gefrieren; (clot) gerinnen
congenial [kənˈdʒiːnɪəl] adj angenehm
congenital [kənˈdʒenɪtəl] adj angeboren
congested [kənˈdʒestɪd] adj über-

füllt

congestion [kənˈdʒɛstʃən] n Stau m

conglomerate [kənˈglɒmərət] n (COMM, GEOL) Konglomerat nt

conglomeration [kənglɒməˈreɪʃən] n Anhäufung f

congratulate [kənˈgrætjʊleɪt] vt: to ~ sb (on sth) jdn (zu etw) beglückwünschen

congratulations [kəngrætjʊˈleɪʃənz] npl Glückwünsche pl; ~! gratuliere!, herzlichen Glückwunsch!

congregate [ˈkɒŋgrɪgeɪt] vi sich versammeln

congregation [kɒŋgrɪˈgeɪʃən] n Gemeinde f

congress [ˈkɒŋgrɛs] n Kongreß m; **~man** (US: irreg) n Mitglied nt des amerikanischen Repräsentantenhauses

conical [ˈkɒnɪkəl] adj kegelförmig

conifer [ˈkɒnɪfə*] n Nadelbaum m

conjecture [kənˈdʒɛktʃə*] n Vermutung f

conjugal [ˈkɒndʒʊgəl] adj ehelich

conjugate [ˈkɒndʒʊgeɪt] vt konjugieren

conjunction [kənˈdʒʌŋkʃən] n Verbindung f; (GRAM) Konjunktion f

conjunctivitis [kəndʒʌŋktɪˈvaɪtɪs] n Bindehautentzündung f

conjure [ˈkʌndʒə*] vi zaubern; **~ up** vt heraufbeschwören; **~r** n Zauberkünstler(in) m(f)

conk out [kɒŋk-] (inf) vi den Geist aufgeben

con man (irreg) n Schwindler m

connect [kəˈnɛkt] vt verbinden; (ELEC) anschließen; to be ~ed with in Beziehung haben zu; (be related to) verwandt sein mit; **~ion** [kəˈnɛkʃən] n Verbindung f; (relation) Zusammenhang m; (ELEC, TEL, RAIL) Anschluß m

connive [kəˈnaɪv] vi: to ~ at stillschweigend dulden

connoisseur [kɒnɪˈsɜː*] n Kenner m

conquer [ˈkɒŋkə*] vt (feelings) überwinden; (enemy) besiegen; (country) erobern; **~or** n Eroberer

m

conquest [ˈkɒŋkwɛst] n Eroberung f

cons [kɒnz] npl see **convenience**; **pro**

conscience [ˈkɒnʃəns] n Gewissen nt

conscientious [kɒnʃɪˈɛnʃəs] adj gewissenhaft

conscious [ˈkɒnʃəs] adj bewußt; (MED) bei Bewußtsein; **~ness** n Bewußtsein nt

conscript [ˈkɒnskrɪpt] n Wehrpflichtige(r) m; **~ion** [kənˈskrɪpʃən] n Wehrpflicht f

consecrate [ˈkɒnsɪkreɪt] vt weihen

consecutive [kənˈsɛkjʊtɪv] adj aufeinanderfolgend

consensus [kənˈsɛnsəs] n allgemeine Übereinstimmung f

consent [kənˈsɛnt] n Zustimmung f
♦ vi zustimmen

consequence [ˈkɒnsɪkwəns] n (importance) Bedeutung f; (effect) Folge f

consequently [ˈkɒnsɪkwəntlɪ] adv folglich

conservation [kɒnsəˈveɪʃən] n Erhaltung f; (nature ~) Umweltschutz m

conservative [kənˈsɜːvətɪv] adj konservativ; **C~** (BRIT) adj konservativ ♦ n Konservative(r) mf

conservatory [kənˈsɜːvətrɪ] n (room) Wintergarten m

conserve [kənˈsɜːv] vt erhalten

consider [kənˈsɪdə*] vt überlegen; (take into account) in Betracht ziehen; (regard as) halten für; to ~ doing sth daran denken, etw zu tun

considerable [kənˈsɪdərəbl] adj beträchtlich

considerably adv beträchtlich

considerate [kənˈsɪdərɪt] adj rücksichtsvoll

consideration [kənsɪdəˈreɪʃən] n Rücksicht(nahme) f; (thought) Erwägung f; (reward) Entgelt nt

considering [kənˈsɪdərɪŋ] prep in Anbetracht +gen

consign [kənˈsaɪn] vt übergeben; **~ment** n Sendung f

consist [kənˈsɪst] vi: to ~ of bestehen aus
consistency [kənˈsɪstənsɪ] n (of material) Konsistenz f; (of argument,
person) Konsequenz f
consistent [kənˈsɪstənt] adj (person)
konsequent; (argument) folgerich-
tig
consolation [kɔnsəˈleɪʃən] n Trost
m
console[1] [kənˈsəʊl] vt trösten
console[2] [ˈkɔnsəʊl] n Kontroll(pult)
nt
consolidate [kənˈsɔlɪdeɪt] vt festigen
consommé [kənˈsɔmeɪ] n Fleischbrühe f
consortium [kənˈsɔːtɪəm] n
(COMM) Konsortium nt
conspicuous [kənˈspɪkjʊəs] adj
(prominent) auffällig; (visible) deutlich sichtbar
conspiracy [kənˈspɪrəsɪ] n Ver-
schwörung f
conspire [kənˈspaɪə*] vi sich verschwören
constable [ˈkʌnstəbl] (BRIT) n Poliz-
ist(in) m(f); **chief ~** Polizeipräsident m
constabulary [kənˈstæbjʊlərɪ] n Polizei f
constant [ˈkɔnstənt] adj (continuous) ständig; (unchanging) kon-
stant; ~ly adv ständig
constellation [kɔnstəˈleɪʃən] n
Sternbild nt
consternation [kɔnstəˈneɪʃən] n Bestürzung f
constipated [ˈkɔnstɪpeɪtəd] adj ver-
stopft
constipation [kɔnstɪˈpeɪʃən] n Verstopfung f
constituency [kənˈstɪtjʊənsɪ] n
Wahlkreis m
constituent [kənˈstɪtjʊənt] n (person) Wähler m; (part) Bestandteil m
constitute [ˈkɔnstɪtjuːt] vt (make
up) bilden; (amount to) darstellen
constitution [kɔnstɪˈtjuːʃən] n Verfassung f; ~al adj Verfassungs-

constraint [kənˈstreɪnt] n Zwang m;
(shyness) Befangenheit f
construct [kənˈstrʌkt] vt bauen;
~ion [kənˈstrʌkʃən] n Konstruktion f;
(building) Bau m; ~ive adj konstruk-
tiv
construe [kənˈstruː] vt deuten
consul [ˈkɔnsl] n Konsul m; ~ate
[ˈkɔnsjʊlət] n Konsulat nt
consult [kənˈsʌlt] vt um Rat fragen;
(doctor) konsultieren; (book) nachschlagen in +dat; ~ant n (MED)
Facharzt m; (other specialist) Gu-
tachter m; ~ation [kɔnslˈteɪʃən] n
Beratung f; (MED) Konsultation f;
~ing room n Sprechzimmer nt
consume [kənˈsjuːm] vt verbrauchen; (food) konsumieren; ~r n Ver-
braucher m; ~r goods npl Konsum-
güter pl; ~rism n Konsum m; ~r
society n Konsumgesellschaft f
consummate [ˈkɔnsəmeɪt] vt (marriage) vollziehen
consumption [kənˈsʌmpʃən] n Verbrauch m; (of food) Konsum m
cont. abbr (= continued) Forts.
contact [ˈkɔntækt] n (touch) Berührung f; (connection) Verbindung
f; (person) Kontakt m ♦ vt sich in
Verbindung setzen mit; ~ lenses npl
Kontaktlinsen pl
contagious [kənˈteɪdʒəs] adj ansteckend
contain [kənˈteɪn] vt enthalten; to ~
o.s. sich zügeln; ~er n Behälter m;
(transport) Container m
contaminate [kənˈtæmɪneɪt] vt verunreinigen
contamination [kəntæmɪˈneɪʃən] n
Verunreinigung f
cont'd abbr (= continued) Forts.
contemplate [ˈkɔntəmpleɪt] vt (look
at) (nachdenklich) betrachten; (think
about) überdenken; (plan) vorhaben
contemporary [kənˈtempərərɪ] adj
zeitgenössisch ♦ n Zeitgenosse m
contempt [kənˈtempt] n Verachtung
f; ~ of court (JUR) Mißachtung f
des Gerichts; ~ible adj verachtenswert; ~uous adj verächtlich

contend [kən'tend] *vt* (*argue*) behaupten ♦ *vi* kämpfen; **~er** *n* (*for post*) Bewerber(in) *m(f)*; (*SPORT*) Wettkämpfer(in) *m(f)*

content [*adj, vb* kən'tent, *n* 'kɒntent] *adj* zufrieden ♦ *vt* befriedigen ♦ *n* (*also: ~s*) Inhalt *m*; **~ed** zufrieden

contention [kən'tenʃən] *n* (*dispute*) Streit *m*; (*argument*) Behauptung *f*

contentment [kən'tentmənt] *n* Zufriedenheit *f*

contest [*n* 'kɒntest, *vb* kən'test] *n* (Wett)kampf *m* ♦ *vt* (*dispute*) bestreiten; (*JUR*) anfechten; (*POL*) kandidieren in +*dat*; **~ant** [kən'testənt] *n* Bewerber(in) *m(f)*

context ['kɒntekst] *n* Zusammenhang *m*

continent ['kɒntinənt] *n* Kontinent *m*; **the C~** (*BRIT*) das europäische Festland; **~al** [kɒnti'nentl] *adj* kontinental; **~al quilt** (*BRIT*) *n* Federbett *nt*

contingency [kən'tindʒənsɪ] *n* Möglichkeit *f*

contingent [kən'tindʒənt] *n* Kontingent *nt*

continual [kən'tinjuəl] *adj* (*endless*) fortwährend; (*repeated*) immer wiederkehrend; **~ly** *adv* immer wieder

continuation [kəntɪnju'eɪʃən] *n* Fortsetzung *f*

continue [kən'tinju:] *vi* (*person*) weitermachen; (*thing*) weitergehen ♦ *vt* fortsetzen

continuity [kɒntɪ'njuːɪtɪ] *n* Kontinuität *f*

continuous [kən'tinjuəs] *adj* ununterbrochen; **~ stationery** *n* Endlospapier *nt*

contort [kən'tɔːt] *vt* verdrehen; **~ion** [kən'tɔːʃən] *n* Verzerrung *f*

contour ['kɒntuə*] *n* Umriß *m*; (*also: ~ line*) Höhenlinie *f*

contraband ['kɒntrəbænd] *n* Schmuggelware *f*

contraception [kɒntrə'sepʃən] *n* Empfängnisverhütung *f*

contraceptive [kɒntrə'septɪv] *n* empfängnisverhütende(s) Mittel *nt* ♦ *adj* empfängnisverhütend

contract [*n* 'kɒntrækt, *vb* kən'trækt] *n* Vertrag *m* ♦ *vi* (*muscle, metal*) sich zusammenziehen ♦ *vt* zusammenziehen; to **~ to do sth** (*COMM*) sich vertraglich verpflichten, etw zu tun; **~ion** [kən'trækʃən] *n* (*shortening*) Verkürzung *f*; **~or** [kən'træktə*] *n* Unternehmer *m*

contradict [kɒntrə'dikt] *vt* widersprechen +*dat*; **~ion** [kɒntrə'dikʃən] *n* Widerspruch *m*; **~ory** *adj* widersprüchlich

contraption [kən'træpʃən] (*inf*) *n* Apparat *m*

contrary[1] ['kɒntrərɪ] *adj* (*opposite*) entgegengesetzt ♦ *n* Gegenteil *nt*; **on the contrary** im Gegenteil

contrary[2] [kən'treərɪ] *adj* (*obstinate*) widerspenstig

contrast [*n* 'kɒntrɑːst, *vb* kən'trɑːst] *n* Kontrast *m* ♦ *vt* entgegensetzen; **~ing** [kən'trɑːstɪŋ] *adj* Kontrast-

contravene [kɒntrə'viːn] *vt* verstoßen gegen

contribute [kən'trɪbjuːt] *vt, vi*: to **~ to** beitragen zu

contribution [kɒntrɪ'bjuːʃən] *n* Beitrag *m*

contributor [kən'trɪbjutə*] *n* Beitragende(r) *mf*

contrive [kən'traɪv] *vt* ersinnen ♦ *vi*: to **~ to do sth** es schaffen, etw zu tun

control [kən'trəul] *vt* (*direct, test*) kontrollieren ♦ *n* Kontrolle *f*; **~s** *npl* (*of vehicle*) Steuerung *f*; (*of business, office*) Schalttafel *f*; **to be in ~ of** (*business, office*) leiten; (*group of children*) beaufsichtigen; **out of ~** außer Kontrolle; **under ~** unter Kontrolle; **~ panel** *n* Schalttafel *f*; **~ room** *n* Kontrollraum *m*; **~ tower** *n* (*AVIAT*) Kontrollturm *m*

controversial [kɒntrə'vəːʃəl] *adj* umstritten

controversy ['kɒntrəvəːsɪ] *n* Kontroverse *f*

conurbation [kɒnəː'beɪʃən] *n* Ballungsgebiet nt

convalesce [kɔnvə'les] vi genesen; **~nce** n Genesung f

convector [kən'vektə*] n Heizlüfter m

convene [kən'viːn] vt zusammenrufen ♦ vi sich versammeln

convenience [kən'viːnɪəns] n Annehmlichkeit f; **all modern ~s** mit allem Komfort; **all mod cons** (BRIT) mit allem Komfort; **at your ~** wann es Ihnen paßt

convenient [kən'viːnɪənt] adj günstig

convent ['kɔnvənt] n Kloster nt

convention [kən'venʃən] n Versammlung f; (custom) Konvention f; **~al** adj konventionell

converge [kən'vɜːdʒ] vi zusammenlaufen

conversant [kən'vɜːsənt] adj: **to be ~ with** bewandert sein in +dat

conversation [kɔnvə'seɪʃən] n Gespräch nt; **~al** adj Unterhaltungs-

converse [n 'kɔnvɜːs, vb kən'vɜːs] n Gegenteil nt ♦ vi sich unterhalten

conversion [kən'vɜːʃən] n Umwandlung f; (esp REL) Bekehrung f

convert [vb kən'vɜːt, n 'kɔnvɜːt] vt (change) umwandeln; (REL) bekehren ♦ n Bekehrte(r) mf; Konvertit(in) m(f); **~ible** n (AUT) Kabriolett nt ♦ adj umwandelbar; (FIN) konvertierbar

convex [kɔn'veks] adj konvex

convey [kən'veɪ] vt (carry) befördern; (feelings) vermitteln; **~or belt** n Fließband nt

convict [vb kən'vɪkt, n 'kɔnvɪkt] vt verurteilen ♦ n Häftling m; **~ion** [kən'vɪkʃən] n (verdict) Verurteilung f; (belief) Überzeugung f

convince [kən'vɪns] vt überzeugen; **~d** adj: **~d that** überzeugt davon, daß; **convincing** adj überzeugend

convoluted [kɔnvə'luːtɪd] adj verwickelt; (style) gewunden

convoy ['kɔnvɔɪ] n (of vehicles) Kolonne f; (protected) Konvoi m

convulse [kən'vʌls] vt zusammenzucken lassen; **to be ~d with laughter** sich vor Lachen krümmen

convulsion [kən'vʌlʃən] n (esp MED) Zuckung f, Krampf m

coo [kuː] vi gurren

cook [kuk] vt, vi kochen ♦ n Koch m, Köchin f; **~ book** n Kochbuch nt; **~er** n Herd m; **~ery** n Kochkunst f; **~ery book** (BRIT) n = cook book; **~ie** (US) n Plätzchen nt; **~ing** n Kochen nt

cool [kuːl] adj kühl ♦ vt, vi (ab)kühlen; **~ down** vt, vi (fig) (sich) beruhigen; **~ness** n Kühle f; (of temperament) kühle(r) Kopf m

coop [kuːp] n Hühnerstall m ♦ vt: **~ up** (fig) einpferchen

cooperate [kəʊ'ɔpəreɪt] vi zusammenarbeiten; **cooperation** [kəʊpə'reɪʃən] n Zusammenarbeit f

cooperative [kəʊ'ɔpərətɪv] adj hilfsbereit; (COMM) genossenschaftlich ♦ n (of farmers) Genossenschaft f; (~ store) Konsumladen m

coordinate [vb kəʊ'ɔːdɪneɪt, n kəʊ'ɔːdɪnət] vt koordinieren ♦ n (MATH) Koordinate f; **~s** npl (clothes) Kombinationen pl

coordination [kəʊɔːdɪ'neɪʃən] n Koordination f

cop [kɔp] (inf) n Polyp m, Bulle m

cope [kəʊp] vi: **to ~ with** fertig werden mit

copious ['kəʊpɪəs] adj reichhaltig

copper ['kɔpə*] n (metal) Kupfer nt; (inf: policeman) Polyp m, Bulle m; **~s** npl (money) Kleingeld nt

coppice ['kɔpɪs] n Unterholz nt

copse [kɔps] n Unterholz nt

copulate ['kɔpjʊleɪt] vi sich paaren

copy ['kɔpɪ] n (imitation) Kopie f; (of book etc) Exemplar nt; (of newspaper) Nummer f ♦ vt kopieren, abschreiben; **~right** n Copyright nt

coral ['kɔrəl] n Koralle f; **~ reef** n Korallenriff nt

cord [kɔːd] n Schnur f; (ELEC) Kabel nt

cordial ['kɔːdɪəl] adj herzlich ♦ n Fruchtsaft m

cordon ['kɔːdn] n Absperrkette f; ~ **off** vt abriegeln

corduroy ['kɔːdərɔɪ] n Kord(samt) m

core [kɔː*] n Kern m ♦ vt entkernen

cork [kɔːk] n (bark) Korkrinde f; (stopper) Korken m; ~**screw** n Korkenzieher m

corn [kɔːn] n (BRIT: wheat) Getreide nt, Korn nt; (US: maize) Mais m; (on foot) Hühnerauge nt; ~ **on the cob** Maiskolben m

cornea ['kɔːnɪə] n Hornhaut f

corned beef ['kɔːnd-] n Corned Beef nt

corner ['kɔːnə*] n Ecke f; (on road) Kurve f ♦ vt in die Enge treiben; (market) monopolisieren ♦ vi (AUT) in die Kurve gehen; ~**stone** n Eckstein m

cornet ['kɔːnɪt] n (MUS) Kornett nt; (BRIT: of ice cream) Eistüte f

cornflakes ['kɔːnfleɪks] npl Cornflakes pl ®

cornflour ['kɔːnflaʊə*] (BRIT) n Maizena f ®

cornstarch ['kɔːnstɑːtʃ] (US) n Maizena f ®

Cornwall ['kɔːnwəl] n Cornwall nt

corny ['kɔːnɪ] adj (joke) blöd(e)

corollary [kə'rɒlərɪ] n Folgesatz m

coronary ['kɒrənərɪ] n (also: ~ thrombosis) Herzinfarkt m

coronation [kɒrə'neɪʃən] n Krönung f

coroner ['kɒrənə*] n Untersuchungsrichter m

coronet ['kɒrənɪt] n Adelskrone f

corporal ['kɔːpərəl] n Obergefreite(r) m ♦ adj: ~ **punishment** Prügelstrafe f

corporate ['kɔːpərɪt] adj gemeinschaftlich, korporativ

corporation [kɔːpə'reɪʃən] n (of town) Gemeinde f; (COMM) Körperschaft f, Aktiengesellschaft f

corps [kɔː*, pl kɔːz] (pl corps) n (Armee)korps nt

corpse [kɔːps] n Leiche f

corpuscle ['kɔːpʌsl] n Blutkör-

perchen nt

corral [kə'rɑːl] n Pferch m, Korral m

correct [kə'rekt] adj (accurate) richtig; (proper) korrekt ♦ vt korrigieren; ~**ion** [kə'rekʃən] n Berichtigung f

correlation [kɒrɪ'leɪʃən] n Wechselbeziehung f

correspond [kɒrɪs'pɒnd] vi (agree) übereinstimmen; (exchange letters) korrespondieren; ~**ence** n (similarity) Entsprechung f; (letters) Briefwechsel m, Korrespondenz f; ~**ence course** n Fernkurs m; ~**ent** n (PRESS) Berichterstatter m

corridor ['kɒrɪdɔː*] n Gang m

corroborate [kə'rɒbəreɪt] vt bestätigen

corrode [kə'rəʊd] vt zerfressen ♦ vi rosten

corrosion [kə'rəʊʒən] n Korrosion f

corrugated ['kɒrəgeɪtɪd] adj gewellt; ~ **iron** n Wellblech nt

corrupt [kə'rʌpt] adj korrupt ♦ vt verderben; (bribe) bestechen; ~**ion** [kə'rʌpʃən] n (of society) Verdorbenheit f; (bribery) Bestechung f

corset ['kɔːsɪt] n Korsett nt

Corsica ['kɔːsɪkə] n Korsika f

cortège [kɔː'teɪʒ] n Zug m; (of funeral) Leichenzug m

cosh [kɒʃ] (BRIT) n Totschläger m

cosmetics npl Kosmetika pl

cosmic ['kɒzmɪk] adj kosmisch

cosmonaut ['kɒzmənɔːt] n Kosmonaut(in) m(f)

cosmopolitan [kɒzmə'pɒlɪtən] adj international; (city) Welt-

cosmos ['kɒzmɒs] n Kosmos m

cosset ['kɒsɪt] vt verwöhnen

cost [kɒst] (pt, pp cost) n Kosten pl, Preis m ♦ vt, vi kosten; ~**s** npl (JUR) Kosten pl; **how much does it** ~? wieviel kostet das?; **at all** ~**s** um jeden Preis

co-star ['kəʊstɑː*] n zweite(r) or weitere(r) Hauptdarsteller(in) m(f)

cost-effective ['kɒstɪ'fektɪv] adj rentabel

costly ['kɒstlɪ] adj kostspielig

cost-of-living ['kɒstəv'lɪvɪŋ] adj (allowance, index) Lebenshaltungskosten-

cost price n Selbstkostenpreis m

costume ['kɒstjuːm] n Kostüm nt; (fancy dress) Maskenkostüm nt; (BRIT: also: swimming ~) Badeanzug m; ~ **jewellery** n Modeschmuck m

cosy ['kəʊzɪ] (BRIT) adj behaglich; (atmosphere) gemütlich

cot [kɒt] n (BRIT: child's) Kinderbett(chen) nt; (US: campbed) Feldbett nt

cottage ['kɒtɪdʒ] n kleines Haus nt; ~ **cheese** n Hüttenkäse m; ~ **industry** n Heimindustrie f; ~ **pie** n Auflauf m mit Hackfleisch und Kartoffelbrei m

cotton ['kɒtn] n Baumwolle f; (thread) Garn nt; ~ **on to** (inf) vt kapieren; ~ **candy** (US) n Zuckerwatte f; ~ **wool** (BRIT) n Watte f

couch [kaʊtʃ] n Couch f

couchette [kuː'ʃet] n (on train, boat) Liegewagenplatz m

cough [kɒf] vi husten ♦ n Husten m; ~ **drop** n Hustenbonbon nt

could [kʊd] pt of **can²**; ~**n't** = could not

council ['kaʊnsl] n (of town) Stadtrat m; ~ **estate** (BRIT) n Siedlung f des sozialen Wohnungsbaus; ~ **house** (BRIT) n Haus nt des sozialen Wohnungsbaus; ~**lor** ['kaʊnsɪlə²] n Stadtrat m/-rätin f

counsel ['kaʊnsl] n (barrister) Anwalt m; (advice) Rat(schlag) m ♦ vt beraten; ~**lor** n Berater m

count [kaʊnt] vt, vi zählen ♦ n (reckoning) Abrechnung f; (nobleman) Graf m; ~ **on** vt zählen auf +acc; ~**down** n Countdown m

countenance ['kaʊntɪnəns] n (old) Antlitz nt ♦ vt (tolerate) gutheißen

counter ['kaʊntə²] n (in shop) Ladentisch m; (in café) Theke f; (in bank, post office) Schalter m ♦ vt entgegnen; ~**act** [kaʊntə'rækt] vt ent-

gegenwirken +dat; ~**espionage** n Spionageabwehr f

counterfeit ['kaʊntəfiːt] n Fälschung f ♦ vt fälschen ♦ adj gefälscht

counterfoil ['kaʊntəfɔɪl] n (Kontroll)abschnitt m

countermand ['kaʊntəmɑːnd] vt rückgängig machen

counterpart ['kaʊntəpɑːt] n (object) Gegenstück nt; (person) Gegenüber nt

counterproductive ['kaʊntəprə'dʌktɪv] adj destruktiv

countersign ['kaʊntəsaɪn] vt gegenzeichnen

countess ['kaʊntɪs] n Gräfin f

countless ['kaʊntlɪs] adj zahllos, unzählig

country ['kʌntrɪ] n Land nt; ~ **dancing** (BRIT) n Volkstanz m; ~**man** (irreg) n Landmann m; (national) Landsmann m; (rural) Bauer m; ~**side** n Landschaft f

county ['kaʊntɪ] n Landkreis m; (BRIT) Grafschaft f

coup [kuː] (pl ~s) n Coup m; (also: ~ d'état) Staatsstreich m, Putsch m

coupé [kuː'peɪ] n (AUT) Coupé nt

couple ['kʌpl] n Paar nt ♦ vt koppeln; a ~ of ein paar

coupon ['kuːpɒn] n Gutschein m

coups [kuːz] npl of **coup**

courage ['kʌrɪdʒ] n Mut m; ~**ous** [kə'reɪdʒəs] adj mutig

courgette [kʊə'ʒet] (BRIT) n Zucchini f

courier ['kʊrɪə²] n (for holiday) Reiseleiter m; (messenger) Kurier m

course [kɔːs] n (race) Bahn f; (of stream) Lauf m; (golf ~) Platz m; (NAUT, SCH) Kurs m; (in meal) Gang m; of ~ natürlich

court [kɔːt] n (royal) Hof m; (JUR) Gericht nt ♦ vt (woman) gehen mit; (danger) herausfordern; to take to ~ vor Gericht bringen

courteous ['kɜːtɪəs] adj höflich

courtesan [kɔːtɪ'zæn] n Kurtisane f

courtesy ['kɜːtəsɪ] n Höflichkeit f

court-house ['kɔːthaʊs] (US) n Gerichtsgebäude nt

courtier ['kɔːtɪə*] n Höfling m

court-martial ['kɔːt'mɑːʃəl] (pl **courts-martial**) n Kriegsgericht nt ♦ vt vor ein Kriegsgericht stellen

courtroom ['kɔːtrum] n Gerichtssaal m

courts-martial ['kɔːts'mɑːʃəl] npl of **court-martial**

courtyard ['kɔːtjɑːd] n Hof m

cousin ['kʌzn] n Cousin m, Vetter m; Kusine f

cove [kəuv] n kleine Bucht f

covenant ['kʌvənənt] n (ECCL) Bund m; (JUR) Verpflichtung f

cover ['kʌvə*] vt (spread over) bedecken; (shield) abschirmen; (include) sich erstrecken über +acc; (protect) decken; (distance) zurücklegen; (report on) berichten über +acc ♦ n (lid) Deckel m; (for bed) Decke f; (MIL) Bedeckung f; (of book) Einband m; (of magazine) Umschlag m; (insurance) Versicherung f; **to take** ~ (from rain) sich unterstellen; (MIL) in Deckung gehen; **under** ~ (indoors) drinnen; **under** ~ **of** im Schutze +gen; **under separate** ~ (COMM) mit getrennter Post; **to** ~ **up for sb** jdn decken; **~age** n (PRESS: reports) Berichterstattung f; (distribution) Verbreitung f; ~ **charge** n Bedienungsgeld nt; **~ing** n Bedeckung f; **~ing letter** (US **cover letter**) n Begleitbrief m; ~ **note** n (INSURANCE) vorläufige(r) Versicherungsschein m

covert ['kʌvət] adj geheim

cover-up ['kʌvərʌp] n Vertuschung f

covet ['kʌvɪt] vt begehren

cow [kau] n Kuh f ♦ vt einschüchtern

coward ['kauəd] n Feigling m; **~ice** ['kauədɪs] n Feigheit f; **~ly** adj feige

cowboy ['kaubɔɪ] n Cowboy m

cower ['kauə*] vi kauern

coxswain ['kɒksn] n (abbr: cox) Steuermann m

coy [kɔɪ] adj schüchtern

coyote [kɔɪ'əutɪ] n Präriewolf m

cozy ['kəuzɪ] (US) adj = cosy

CPA (US) n abbr = **certified public accountant**

crab [kræb] n Krebs m; ~ **apple** n Holzapfel m

crack [kræk] n Riß m, Sprung m; (noise) Knall m; (drug) Crack nt ♦ vt (break) springen lassen; (joke) reißen; (nut, safe) knacken; (whip) knallen lassen ♦ vi springen ♦ adj erstklassig; (troops) Elite-; ~ **down on** hart durchgreifen (bei); ~ **up** vi (fig) zusammenbrechen; **~er** n (firework) Knallkörper m, Kracher m; (Christmas ~) Knallbonbon nt

crackle ['krækl] vi knistern; (fire) prasseln

cradle ['kreɪdl] n Wiege f

craft [krɑːft] n (skill) (Hand- or Kunst)fertigkeit f; (trade) Handwerk nt; (NAUT) Schiff nt; **~sman** (irreg) n Handwerker m; **~smanship** n (quality) handwerkliche Ausführung f; (ability) handwerkliche(s) Können nt; ~**y** adj schlau

crag [kræg] n Klippe f

cram [kræm] vt vollstopfen ♦ vi (learn) pauken; **to** ~ **sth into sth** etw in etw acc stopfen

cramp [kræmp] n Krampf m ♦ vt (limit) einengen; (hinder) hemmen; **~ed** adj (position) verkrampft; (space) eng

crampon ['kræmpən] n Steigeisen nt

cranberry ['krænbərɪ] n Preiselbeere f

crane [kreɪn] n (machine) Kran m; (bird) Kranich m

crank [kræŋk] n (lever) Kurbel f; (person) Spinner m; **~shaft** n Kurbelwelle f

cranny ['krænɪ] n see **nook**

crash [kræʃ] n (noise) Krachen nt; (with cars) Zusammenstoß m; (with plane) Absturz m; (COMM) Zusammenbruch m ♦ vt (plane) abstürzen mit ♦ vi (cars) zusammenstoßen; (plane) abstürzen; (economy) zusammenbrechen; (noise) knallen; ~ **course** n Schnellkurs m; ~ **helmet** n

Sturzhelm *m*; ~ **landing** *n* Bruchlandung *f*

crass [kræs] *adj* kraß

crate [kreɪt] *n (also fig)* Kiste *f*

crater ['kreɪtə*] *n* Krater *m*

cravat(e) [krə'væt] *n* Halstuch *nt*

crave [kreɪv] *vt* verlangen nach

crawl [krɔ:l] *vi* krabbeln ♦ *n* Kriechen *nt; (swim)* Kraul *nt*

crayfish ['kreɪfɪʃ] *n inv (freshwater)* Krebs *m; (saltwater)* Languste *f*

crayon ['kreɪən] *n* Buntstift *m*

craze [kreɪz] *n* Fimmel *m*

crazy ['kreɪzɪ] *adj* verrückt; ~ **paving** *n* Mosaikpflaster *nt*

creak [kri:k] *vi* knarren

cream [kri:m] *n (from milk)* Rahm *m*, Sahne *f; (polish, cosmetic)* Creme *f; (fig: people)* Elite *f* ♦ *adj* cremfarbig; ~ **cake** *n* Sahnetorte *f;* ~ **cheese** *n* Rahmquark *m;* ~**y** *adj* sahnig

crease [kri:s] *n* Falte *f* ♦ *vt* falten; *(untidy)* zerknittern ♦ *vi (wrinkle up)* knittern

create [krɪ'eɪt] *vt* erschaffen; *(cause)* verursachen

creation [krɪ'eɪʃən] *n* Schöpfung *f*

creative [krɪ'eɪtɪv] *adj* kreativ

creator [krɪ'eɪtə*] *n* Schöpfer *m*

creature ['kri:tʃə*] *n* Geschöpf *nt*

crèche [kreʃ] *n* Krippe *f*

credence ['kri:dəns] *n*: **to lend** or **give** ~ **to sth** etw *dat* Glauben schenken

credentials [krɪ'denʃəlz] *npl* Beglaubigungsschreiben *nt*

credibility [kredɪ'bɪlɪtɪ] *n* Glaubwürdigkeit *f*

credible ['kredɪbl] *adj (person)* glaubwürdig; *(story)* glaubhaft

credit ['kredɪt] *n (also COMM)* Kredit *m* ♦ *vt* Glauben schenken +*dat;* (COMM) gutschreiben; ~**s** *npl (of film)* Mitwirkenden *pl;* ~**able** *adj* rühmlich; ~ **card** *n* Kreditkarte *f;* ~**or** *n* Gläubiger *m*

creed [kri:d] *n* Glaubensbekenntnis *nt*

creek [kri:k] *n (inlet)* kleine Bucht *f;*

(US: river) kleine(r) Wasserlauf *m*

creep [kri:p] *(pt, pp* **crept)** *vi* kriechen; ~ **er** *n* Kletterpflanze *f;* ~**y** *adj (frightening)* gruselig

cremate [krɪ'meɪt] *vt* einäschern

cremation [krɪ'meɪʃən] *n* Einäscherung *f*

crêpe [kreɪp] *n* Krepp *m;* ~ **bandage** *(BRIT) n* Elastikbinde *f*

crept [krept] *pt, pp of* **creep**

crescent ['kresnt] *n (of moon)* Halbmond *m*

cress [kres] *n* Kresse *f*

crest [krest] *n (of cock)* Kamm *m; (of wave)* Wellenkamm *m; (coat of arms)* Wappen *nt;* ~**fallen** *adj* niedergeschlagen

Crete [kri:t] *n* Kreta *nt*

crevice ['krevɪs] *n* Riß *m*

crew [kru:] *n* Besatzung *f,* Mannschaft *f;* ~**cut** *n* Bürstenschnitt *m;* ~**neck** *n* runde(r) Ausschnitt *m*

crib [krɪb] *n (bed)* Krippe *f* ♦ *vt (inf)* spicken

crick [krɪk] *n* Muskelkrampf *m*

cricket ['krɪkɪt] *n (insect)* Grille *f; (game)* Kricket *nt*

crime [kraɪm] *n* Verbrechen *nt*

criminal ['krɪmɪnl] *n* Verbrecher *m* ♦ *adj* kriminell; *(act)* strafbar

crimson ['krɪmzn] *adj* leuchtend rot

cringe [krɪndʒ] *vi* sich ducken

crinkle ['krɪŋkl] *vt* zerknittern

cripple ['krɪpl] *n* Krüppel *m* ♦ *vt* lahmlegen; *(MED)* verkrüppeln

crises ['kraɪsi:z] *npl of* **crisis**

crisis ['kraɪsɪs] *(pl* **crises)** *n* Krise *f*

crisp [krɪsp] *adj* knusprig; ~**s** *(BRIT) npl* Chips *pl*

crisscross ['krɪskros] *adj* gekreuzt, Kreuz-

criteria [kraɪ'tɪərɪə] *npl of* **criterion**

criterion [kraɪ'tɪərɪən] *(pl* **criteria)** *n* Kriterium *nt*

critic ['krɪtɪk] *n* Kritiker(in) *m(f);* ~**al** *adj* kritisch; ~**ally** *adv* kritisch; *(ill)* gefährlich; ~**ism** ['krɪtɪsɪzəm] *n* Kritik *f;* ~**ize** ['krɪtɪsaɪz] *vt* kritisieren

croak [krəʊk] *vi* krächzen; *(frog)*

quaken

Croatia [krəʊˈeːʃə] n Kroatien nt

crochet [ˈkrəʊʃeɪ] n Häkelei f

crockery [ˈkrɒkərɪ] n Geschirr nt

crocodile [ˈkrɒkədaɪl] n Krokodil nt

crocus [ˈkrəʊkəs] n Krokus m

croft [krɒft] (BRIT) n kleine(s) Pachtgut nt

crony [ˈkrəʊnɪ] (inf) n Kumpel m

crook [krʊk] n (criminal) Gauner m; (stick) Hirtenstab m; **~ed** [ˈkrʊkɪd] adj krumm

crop [krɒp] n (harvest) Ernte f; (riding ~) Reitpeitsche f ♦ vt ernten; **~ up** vi passieren

croquet [ˈkrəʊkeɪ] n Krocket nt

croquette [krəʊˈket] n Krokette f

cross [krɒs] n Kreuz nt ♦ vt (road) überqueren; (legs) übereinander legen; kreuzen ♦ adj (annoyed) böse; **~ out** vt streichen; **~ over** vi hinübergehen; **~bar** n Querstange f; **~country** (race) n Geländelauf m; **~-examine** vt im Kreuzverhör vernehmen; **~-eyed** adj: to be **~-eyed** schielen; **~fire** n Kreuzfeuer nt; **~ing** n (crossroads) (Straßen)kreuzung f; (of ship) Überfahrt f; (for pedestrians) Fußgängerüberweg m; **~ing guard** (US) n Schülerlotse m; **~ purposes** npl: to be at **~ purposes** aneinander vorbeireden; **~reference** n Querverweis m; **~roads** n Straßenkreuzung f; (fig) Scheideweg m; **~ section** n Querschnitt m; **~walk** (US) n Fußgängerüberweg m; **~wind** n Seitenwind m; **~word** (puzzle) n Kreuzworträtsel nt

crotch [krɒtʃ] n Zwickel m; (ANAT) Unterleib m

crotchet [ˈkrɒtʃɪt] n Viertelnote f

crotchety [ˈkrɒtʃɪtɪ] adj launenhaft

crouch [kraʊtʃ] vi hocken

croupier [ˈkruːpɪeɪ] n Croupier m

crow [krəʊ] n (bird) Krähe f; (of cock) Krähen nt ♦ vi krähen

crowbar [ˈkrəʊbɑːʳ] n Stemmeisen nt

crowd [kraʊd] n Menge f ♦ vt (fill)

überfüllen ♦ vi drängen; **~ed** adj überfüllt

crown [kraʊn] n Krone f; (of head, hat) Kopf m ♦ vt krönen; **~ jewels** npl Kronjuwelen pl; **~ prince** n Kronprinz m

crow's-feet [ˈkrəʊzfiːt] npl Krähenfüße pl

crucial [ˈkruːʃəl] adj entscheidend

crucifix [ˈkruːsɪfɪks] n Kruzifix nt; **~ion** [kruːsɪˈfɪkʃən] n Kreuzigung f

crude [kruːd] adj (raw) roh; (humour, behaviour) grob; (basic) primitiv; **~ (oil)** n Rohöl nt

cruel [ˈkrʊəl] adj grausam; **~ty** n Grausamkeit f

cruet [ˈkruːɪt] n Gewürzständer m

cruise [kruːz] n Kreuzfahrt f ♦ vi kreuzen; **~r** n (MIL) Kreuzer m

crumb [krʌm] n Krume f

crumble [ˈkrʌmbl] vt, vi zerbröckeln

crumbly [ˈkrʌmblɪ] adj krümelig

crumpet [ˈkrʌmpɪt] n Tee(pfann)kuchen m

crumple [ˈkrʌmpl] vt zerknittern

crunch [krʌntʃ] n: the **~** (fig) der Knackpunkt ♦ vt knirschen; **~y** adj knusprig

crusade [kruːˈseɪd] n Kreuzzug m

crush [krʌʃ] n Gedränge nt ♦ vt zerdrücken; (rebellion) unterdrücken

crust [krʌst] n Kruste f

crutch [krʌtʃ] n Krücke f

crux [krʌks] n springende(r) Punkt m

cry [kraɪ] vi (shout) schreien; (weep) weinen ♦ n (call) Schrei m; **~ off** vi (plötzlich) absagen

crypt [krɪpt] n Krypta f

cryptic [ˈkrɪptɪk] adj hintergründig

crystal [ˈkrɪstl] n Kristall m; (glass) Kristallglas nt; (mineral) Bergkristall m; **~-clear** adj kristallklar

crystallize vt, vi kristallisieren; (fig) klären

cub [kʌb] n Junge(s) nt; (also: C~ scout) Wölfling m

Cuba [ˈkjuːbə] n Kuba nt; **~n** adj kubanisch ♦ n Kubaner(in) m(f)

cubbyhole [ˈkʌbɪhəʊl] n Eckchen nt

cube [kjuːb] n Würfel m ♦ vt

cubic (MATH) hoch drei nehmen; **~ root** n Kubikwurzel f

cubic ['kju:bik] adj würfelförmig; (centimetre etc) Kubik-; **~ capacity** n Fassungsvermögen nt

cubicle ['kju:bikl] n Kabine f

cuckoo ['kuku:] n Kuckuck m; **~ clock** n Kuckucksuhr f

cucumber ['kju:kʌmbə*] n Gurke f

cuddle ['kʌdl] vt, vi herzen, drücken (inf)

cue [kju:] n (THEAT) Stichwort nt; (snooker ~) Billardstock m

cuff [kʌf] n (BRIT: of shirt, coat etc) Manschette f; Aufschlag m; (US) = **turn-up; off the ~** aus dem Handgelenk; **~link** n Manschettenknopf m

cuisine [kwi'zi:n] n Kochkunst f, Küche f

cul-de-sac ['kʌldəsæk] n Sackgasse f

culinary ['kʌlinəri] adj Koch-

cull [kʌl] vt (flowers) pflücken; (select) auswählen

culminate ['kʌlmineit] vi gipfeln

culmination [kʌlmi'neiʃən] n Höhepunkt m

culottes [kju'lɒts] npl Hosenrock m

culpable ['kʌlpəbl] adj schuldig

culprit ['kʌlprit] n Täter m

cult [kʌlt] n Kult m

cultivate ['kʌltiveit] vt (AGR) bebauen; (mind) bilden

cultivation [kʌlti'veiʃən] n (AGR) Bebauung f; (of person) Bildung f

cultural ['kʌltʃərəl] adj kulturell, Kultur-

culture ['kʌltʃə*] n Kultur f; **~d** adj gebildet

cumbersome ['kʌmbəsəm] adj (object) sperrig

cumulative ['kju:mjulətiv] adj gehäuft

cunning ['kʌniŋ] n Verschlagenheit f ♦ adj schlau

cup [kʌp] n Tasse f; (prize) Pokal m

cupboard ['kʌbəd] n Schrank m

Cupid ['kju:pid] n Amor m

cup tie (BRIT) n Pokalspiel nt

curate ['kjuərit] n (Catholic) Kurat m; (Protestant) Vikar m

curator [kjuə'reitə*] n Kustos m

curb [kɜ:b] vt zügeln ♦ n (on spending etc) Einschränkung f; (US) Bordstein m

curdle ['kɜ:dl] vi gerinnen

cure [kjuə*] n Heilmittel nt; (process) Heilverfahren nt ♦ vt heilen

curfew ['kɜ:fju:] n Ausgangssperre f; Sperrstunde f

curio ['kjuəriəu] n Kuriosität f

curiosity [kjuəri'ɒsiti] n Neugier f

curious ['kjuəriəs] adj neugierig; (strange) seltsam

curl [kɜ:l] n Locke f ♦ vi sich locken; **~ up** vi sich zusammenrollen; (person) sich ankuscheln; **~er** n Lockenwickler m; **~y** ['kɜ:li] adj lockig

currant ['kʌrənt] n Korinthe f

currency ['kʌrənsi] n Währung f; **to gain ~** an Popularität gewinnen

current ['kʌrənt] n Strömung f ♦ adj (expression) gängig, üblich; (issue) neueste; **~ account** (BRIT) n Girokonto nt; **~ affairs** npl Zeitgeschehen nt; **~ly** adv zur Zeit

curricula [kə'rikjulə] npl of **curriculum**

curriculum [kə'rikjuləm] (pl **~s** or **curricula**) n Lehrplan m; **~ vitae** n Lebenslauf m

curry ['kʌri] n Currygericht nt ♦ vt: **to ~ favour with** sich einschmeicheln bei; **~ powder** n Currypulver nt

curse [kɜ:s] vi (swear): **to ~ (at)** fluchen (auf or über) +acc ♦ vt (insult) verwünschen ♦ n Fluch m

cursor ['kɜ:sə*] n (COMPUT) Cursor m

cursory ['kɜ:səri] adj flüchtig

curt [kɜ:t] adj schroff

curtail [kɜ:'teil] vt abkürzen; (rights) einschränken

curtain ['kɜ:tn] n Vorhang m

curts(e)y ['kɜ:tsi] n Knicks m ♦ vi knicksen

curve [kɜ:v] n Kurve f ♦ vi (of body, vase etc) Rundung f ♦ vi sich biegen; (hips, breasts) sich runden; (road) einen Bogen machen

cushion ['kuʃən] n Kissen nt ♦ vt dämpfen

custard ['kʌstəd] n Vanillesoße f

custodian [kʌs'təudiən] n Kustos m, Verwalter(in) m(f)

custody ['kʌstədɪ] n Aufsicht f; (po-lice ~) Haft f; **to take into ~** verhaften

custom ['kʌstəm] n (tradition) Brauch m; (COMM) Kundschaft f; **~ary** adj üblich

customer ['kʌstəmə*] n Kunde m, Kundin f

customized ['kʌstəmaɪzd] adj. (car etc) mit Spezialausrüstung

custom-made ['kʌstəm'meɪd] adj speziell angefertigt

customs ['kʌstəmz] npl Zoll m; **~ duty** n Zollabgabe f; **~ officer** n Zollbeamte(r) m, Zollbeamtin f

cut [kʌt] (pt, pp cut) vt schneiden; (wages) kürzen; (prices) herabsetzen ♦ vi schneiden; (intersect) sich schneiden ♦ n (in skin) Schnitt m; (wound) Schnittwunde f; (in book, income etc) Kürzung f; (share) Anteil m; **to ~ a tooth** zahnen; **~ down** vt (tree) fällen; (reduce) einschränken; **~ off** vt (also fig) abschneiden; (allowance) sperren; **~ out** vt (shape) ausschneiden; (delete) streichen; **~ up** vt (meat) aufschneiden; **~back** n Kürzung f; (CINE) Rückblende f

cute [kjuːt] adj niedlich

cuticle ['kjuːtɪkl] n Nagelhaut f

cutlery ['kʌtlərɪ] n Besteck nt

cutlet ['kʌtlɪt] n (pork) Kotelett nt; (veal) Schnitzel nt

cut: **~out** n (cardboard ~out) Ausschneidemodell nt; **~price** (US cut-rate) adj verbilligt; **~throat** n Verbrecher(typ) m ♦ adj mörderisch

cutting ['kʌtɪŋ] adj schneidend ♦ n (BRIT: PRESS) Ausschnitt m; (: RAIL) Durchstich m

CV n abbr = **curriculum vitae**

cwt abbr = **hundredweight(s)**

cyanide ['saɪənaɪd] n Zyankali m

cycle ['saɪkl] n Fahrrad nt; (series) Reihe f ♦ vi radfahren; **cycling**

['saɪklɪŋ] n Radfahren nt; **cyclist** ['saɪklɪst] n Radfahrer(in) m(f)

cyclone ['saɪkləun] n Zyklon m

cygnet ['sɪgnɪt] n junge(r) Schwan m

cylinder ['sɪlɪndə*] n Zylinder m; (TECH) Walze f; **~head gasket** n Zylinderkopfdichtung f

cymbals ['sɪmbəlz] npl Becken nt

cynic ['sɪnɪk] n Zyniker(in) m(f); **~al** adj zynisch; **~ism** ['sɪnɪsɪzəm] n Zynismus m

cypress ['saɪprəs] n Zypresse f

Cyprus ['saɪprəs] n Zypern nt

cyst [sɪst] n Zyste f

cystitis [sɪs'taɪtɪs] n Blasentzündung f

czar [zɑː*] n Zar m

Czech [tʃɛk] adj tschechisch ♦ n Tscheche m, Tschechin f

Czechoslovakia [tʃɛkəslə'vækɪə] n die Tschechoslowakei; **~n** adj tschechoslowakisch ♦ n Tschechoslowake m, Tschechoslowakin f

D

D [diː] n (MUS) D nt

dab [dæb] vt (wound, paint) betupfen ♦ n (little bit) bißchen nt; (of paint) Tupfer m

dabble ['dæbl] vi: **to ~ in sth** in etw dat machen

dad [dæd] n Papa m, Vati m; **~dy** ['dædɪ] n Papa m, Vati m; **~dy-long-legs** n Weberknecht m

daffodil ['dæfədɪl] n Osterglocke f

daft [dɑːft] (inf) adj blöd(e), doof

dagger ['dægə*] n Dolch m

daily ['deɪlɪ] adj täglich ♦ n (PRESS) Tageszeitung f; (BRIT: cleaning woman) Haushaltshilfe f ♦ adv täglich

dainty ['deɪntɪ] adj zierlich

dairy ['dɛərɪ] n (shop) Milchgeschäft nt; (on farm) Molkerei f ♦ adj Milch-; **~ farm** n Hof m mit Milchwirtschaft; **~ produce** n Molkereiprodukte pl; **~ store** (US) n Milchgeschäft nt

dais ['deɪɪs] n Podium nt

daisy ['deɪzɪ] n Gänseblümchen nt; ~ **wheel** n (on printer) Typenrad nt

dale [deɪl] n Tal nt

dam [dæm] n (Stau)damm m ♦ vt stauen

damage ['dæmɪdʒ] n Schaden m ♦ vt beschädigen; ~**s** npl (JUR) Schaden(s)ersatz m

damn [dæm] vt verdammen ♦ n (inf): **I don't give a** ~ **das ist mir total egal** ♦ adj (: also: ~ed) verdammt; ~ **it!** verflixt!; ~**ing** adj vernichtend

damp [dæmp] adj feucht ♦ n Feuchtigkeit f ♦ vt (also: ~en) befeuchten; (discourage) dämpfen

damson ['dæmzən] n Damaszenerpflaume f

dance [dɑːns] n Tanz m ♦ vi tanzen; ~ **hall** n Tanzlokal nt; ~**r** n Tänzer m

dancing ['dɑːnsɪŋ] n Tanzen nt

dandelion ['dændɪlaɪən] n Löwenzahn m

dandruff ['dændrəf] n (Kopf)schuppen pl

Dane [deɪn] n Däne m, Dänin f

danger ['deɪndʒə*] n Gefahr f; ~**!** (sign) Achtung!; **to be in** ~ **of doing sth Gefahr laufen, etw zu tun;** ~**ous** adj gefährlich

dangle ['dæŋgl] vi baumeln ♦ vt herabhängen lassen

Danish ['deɪnɪʃ] adj dänisch ♦ n Dänisch nt

dapper ['dæpə*] adj elegant

dare [deə*] vt herausfordern ♦ vi: **to** ~ **(to) do sth es wagen, etw zu tun;** **I** ~ **say ich würde sagen;** ~**devil** n Draufgänger(in) m(f)

daring ['deərɪŋ] adj (audacious) verwegen; (bold) wagemutig; (dress) gewagt ♦ n Mut m

dark [dɑːk] adj dunkel; (fig) düster, trübe; (deep colour) dunkel- ♦ n Dunkelheit f; **to be left in the** ~ **about sth im dunkeln sein über** +acc; **after** ~ **nach Anbruch der Dunkelheit;** ~**en** vt, vi verdunkeln; ~ **glasses** npl Sonnenbrille f; ~**ness** n Finsternis nt; ~**room** n Dunkelkammer f

darling ['dɑːlɪŋ] n Liebling m ♦ adj lieb

darn [dɑːn] vt stopfen

dart [dɑːt] n (weapon) Pfeil m; (in sewing) Abnäher m ♦ vi sausen; ~**s** n (game) Pfeilwerfen nt; ~**board** n Zielscheibe f

dash [dæʃ] n Sprung m; (mark) (Gedanken)strich m; (small amount) bißchen nt ♦ vt (hopes) zunichte machen ♦ vi stürzen; ~ **away** vi davonstürzen; ~ **off** vi davonstürzen

dashboard ['dæʃbɔːd] n Armaturenbrett nt

dashing ['dæʃɪŋ] adj schneidig

data ['deɪtə] npl Einzelheiten pl, Daten pl; ~**base** n Datenbank f; ~ **processing** n Datenverarbeitung f

date [deɪt] n Datum nt; (for meeting etc) Termin m; (with person) Verabredung f; (fruit) Dattel f ♦ vt (letter etc) datieren; (person) gehen mit; ~ **of birth Geburtsdatum** nt; **to** ~ **bis heute; out of** ~ **überholt; up to** ~ **(clothes) modisch; (report) up-to-date; (with news) auf dem laufenden;** ~**d** adj altmodisch

daub [dɔːb] vt beschmieren; (paint) schmieren

daughter ['dɔːtə*] n Tochter f; ~-**in-law** n Schwiegertochter f

daunting ['dɔːntɪŋ] adj entmutigend

dawdle ['dɔːdl] vi trödeln

dawn [dɔːn] n Morgendämmerung f ♦ vi dämmern; (fig): **it ~ed on him that ... es dämmerte ihm, daß ...**

day [deɪ] n Tag m; **the** ~ **before/after am Tag zuvor/danach; the** ~ **after tomorrow übermorgen; the** ~ **before yesterday vorgestern; by** ~ **am Tage;** ~**break** n Tagesanbruch m; ~**dream** n vi mit offenen Augen träumen; ~**light** n Tageslicht nt; ~ **return** (BRIT) n Tagesrückfahrkarte f; ~**time** n Tageszeit f; ~-**to-day** adj alltäglich

daze [deɪz] vt betäuben ♦ n Betäubung f; **in a** ~ **benommen**

dazzle ['dæzl] *vt* blenden

DC *abbr* (= *direct current*) Gleichstrom *m*

D-day ['di:deɪ] *n* (HIST) Tag der Invasion durch die Alliierten (6.6.44); (*fig*) der Tag X

deacon ['di:kən] *n* Diakon *m*

dead [ded] *adj* tot; (*without feeling*) gefühllos ♦ *adv* ganz; (*exactly*) genau ♦ *npl*: die ~ die Toten *pl*; to shoot sb ~ jdn erschießen; ~ **tired** todmüde; to **stop** ~ abrupt stehenbleiben; ~**en** *vt* (*pain*) abtöten; (*sound*) ersticken; ~**end** *n* Sackgasse *f*; ~ **heat** *n* tote(s) Rennen *nt*; ~**line** *n* Stichtag *m*; ~**lock** *n* Stillstand *m*; ~ **loss** (*inf*) *n* to be a ~ loss ein hoffnungsloser Fall sein; ~**ly** *adj* tödlich; ~**pan** *adj* undurchdringlich; **D~ Sea** *n* the **D~ Sea** das Tote Meer

deaf [def] *adj* taub; ~**en** *vt* taub machen; ~**mute** *n* Taubstumme(r) *mf*; ~**ness** *n* Taubheit *f*

deal [di:l] (*pt, pp* **dealt**) *n* Geschäft *nt* ♦ *vt* austeilen; (CARDS) geben; a **great** ~ of sehr viel; ~ **in** *vt fus* handeln mit; ~ **with** *vt fus* (*person*) behandeln; (*subject*) sich befassen mit; (*problem*) in Angriff nehmen; ~**er** *n* (COMM) Händler *m*; (CARDS) Kartengeber *m*; ~**ings** *npl* (FIN) Geschäfte *pl*; (*relations*) Beziehungen *pl*; ~**t** [delt] *pt, pp* of **deal**

dean [di:n] *n* (*Protestant*) Superintendent *m*; (*Catholic*) Dechant *m*; (UNIV) Dekan *m*

dear [dɪə*] *adj* lieb; (*expensive*) teuer ♦ *n* Liebling *m* ♦ *excl*: ~ **me!** du liebe Zeit!; **D~ Sir** Sehr geehrter Herr!; **D~ John** Lieber John!; ~**ly** *adv* (*love*) herzlich; (*pay*) teuer

death [deθ] *n* Tod *m*; (*statistic*) Todesfall *m*; ~ **certificate** *n* Totenschein *m*; ~ **duties** (BRIT) *npl* Erbschaftssteuer *f*; ~**ly** *adj* totenähnlich, Toten-; ~ **penalty** *n* Todesstrafe *f*; ~ **rate** *n* Sterblichkeitsziffer *f*

debar [dɪ'bɑ:*] *vt* ausschließen

debase [dɪ'beɪs] *vt* entwerten

debatable [dɪ'beɪtəbl] *adj* anfechtbar

debate [dɪ'beɪt] *n* Debatte *f* ♦ *vt* debattieren, diskutieren; (*consider*) überlegen

debauchery [dɪ'bɔ:tʃərɪ] *n* Ausschweifungen *pl*

debilitating [dɪ'bɪlɪteɪtɪŋ] *adj* schwächend

debit ['debɪt] *n* Schuldposten *m* ♦ *vt* belasten

debris ['debri:] *n* Trümmer *pl*

debt [det] *n* Schuld *f*; to **be in** ~ verschuldet sein; ~**or** *n* Schuldner *m*

debunk [dɪ'bʌŋk] *vt* entlarven

decade ['dekeɪd] *n* Jahrzehnt *nt*

decadence ['dekədəns] *n* Dekadenz *f*

decaffeinated [dɪ'kæfɪneɪtɪd] *adj* koffeinfrei

decanter [dɪ'kæntə*] *n* Karaffe *f*

decay [dɪ'keɪ] *n* Verfall *m*; (*tooth* ~) Karies *m* ♦ *vi* verfallen; (*teeth, meat etc*) faulen; (*leaves etc*) verrotten

deceased [dɪ'si:st] *adj* verstorben

deceit [dɪ'si:t] *n* Betrug *m*; ~**ful** *adj* falsch

deceive [dɪ'si:v] *vt* täuschen

December [dɪ'sembə*] *n* Dezember *m*

decency ['di:sənsɪ] *n* Anstand *m*

decent [dɪsənt] *adj* (*respectable*) anständig; (*pleasant*) annehmbar

deception [dɪ'sepʃən] *n* Betrug *m*

deceptive [dɪ'septɪv] *adj* irreführend

decibel ['desɪbel] *n* Dezibel *nt*

decide [dɪ'saɪd] *vt* entscheiden ♦ *vi* sich entscheiden; to ~ **on sth** etw beschließen; ~**d** *adj* entschieden; ~**dly** [dɪ'saɪdɪdlɪ] *adv* entschieden

deciduous [dɪ'sɪdjʊəs] *adj* Laub-

decimal ['desɪməl] *adj* dezimal ♦ *n* Dezimalzahl *f*; ~ **point** *n* Komma *nt*

decimate ['desɪmeɪt] *vt* dezimieren

decipher [dɪ'saɪfə*] *vt* entziffern

decision [dɪ'sɪʒən] *n* Entscheidung *f*, Entschluß *m*

decisive [dɪ'saɪsɪv] *adj* entscheidend; (*person*) entschlossen

deck [dek] *n* (NAUT) Deck *nt*; (*of*

cards) Pack m; ~**chair** n Liegestuhl m

declaration [dekləˈreɪʃən] n Erklärung f

declare [dɪˈklɛə*] vt erklären; (CUSTOMS) verzollen

decline [dɪˈklaɪn] n (decay) Verfall m; (lessening) Rückgang m ♦ vt (invitation) ablehnen ♦ vi (of strength) nachlassen; (say no) ablehnen

declutch [ˈdiːˈklʌtʃ] vi auskuppeln

decode [ˈdiːˈkəud] vt entschlüsseln

decoder n (TV) decoder m

decompose [diːkəmˈpəuz] vi (sich) zersetzen

décor [ˈdeɪkɔː*] n Ausstattung f

decorate [ˈdekəreɪt] vt (room: paper) tapezieren; (: paint) streichen; (adorn) (aus)schmücken; (cake) verzieren; (honour) auszeichnen

decoration [dekəˈreɪʃən] n (of house) (Wand)dekoration f; (medal) Orden m

decorator [ˈdekəreɪtə*] n Maler m, Anstreicher m

decorum [dɪˈkɔːrəm] n Anstand m

decoy [ˈdiːkɔɪ] n Lockvogel m

decrease [n ˈdiːkriːs, vb diːˈkriːs] n Abnahme f ♦ vt vermindern ♦ vi abnehmen

decree [dɪˈkriː] n Erlaß m; ~ **nisi** n vorläufige(s) Scheidungsurteil nt

decrepit [dɪˈkrepɪt] adj hinfällig

dedicate [ˈdedɪkeɪt] vt widmen

dedication [dedɪˈkeɪʃən] n (devotion) Ergebenheit; (in book) Widmung f

deduce [dɪˈdjuːs] vt: to ~ **sth** (from sth) etw (aus etw) ableiten, etw (aus etw) schließen

deduct [dɪˈdʌkt] vt abziehen; ~**ion** [dɪˈdʌkʃən] n (of money) Abzug m; (conclusion) Schluß folgerung f

deed n Tat f; (document) Urkunde f

deem [diːm] vt: to ~ **sb/sth** (to be) sth jdn/etw für etw halten

deep [diːp] adj tief ♦ adv: the spectators stood 20 ~ die Zuschauer standen in 20 Reihen hintereinander; to be 4m ~ 4 Meter tief sein; ~**en**

vt vertiefen ♦ vi (darkness) tiefer werden; ~**freeze** n Tiefkühlung f; ~**fry** vt fritieren; ~**ly** adv tief; ~ **sea diving** n Tiefseetauchen nt; ~**seated** adj tiefsitzend

deer [dɪə*] n Reh nt; ~**skin** n Hirsch-/Rehleder f

deface [dɪˈfeɪs] vt entstellen

defamation [defəˈmeɪʃən] n Verleumdung f

default [dɪˈfɔːlt] n Versäumnis nt; (COMPUT) Standardwert m ♦ vi versäumen; by ~ durch Nichterscheinen

defeat [dɪˈfiːt] n Niederlage f ♦ vt schlagen; ~**ist** adj defätistisch ♦ n Defätist m

defect [n ˈdiːfekt, vb dɪˈfekt] n Fehler m ♦ vi überlaufen; ~**ive** [dɪˈfektɪv] adj fehlerhaft

defence [dɪˈfens] n Verteidigung f; ~**less** adj wehrlos

defend [dɪˈfend] vt verteidigen; ~**ant** n Angeklagte(r) m; ~**er** n Verteidiger m

defense [dɪˈfens] (US) n = **defence**

defensive [dɪˈfensɪv] adj defensiv ♦ n: on the ~ in der Defensive

defer [dɪˈfɜː*] vt verschieben

deference [ˈdefərəns] n Rücksichtnahme f

defiance [dɪˈfaɪəns] n Trotz m, Unnachgiebigkeit f; in ~ of sth einer Sache dat zum Trotz

defiant [dɪˈfaɪənt] adj trotzig, unnachgiebig

deficiency [dɪˈfɪʃənsɪ] n (lack) Mangel m; (weakness) Schwäche f

deficient [dɪˈfɪʃənt] adj mangelhaft

deficit [ˈdefɪsɪt] n Defizit nt

defile [vb dɪˈfaɪl, n ˈdiːfaɪl] vt beschmutzen ♦ n Hohlweg m

define [dɪˈfaɪn] vt bestimmen; (explain) definieren

definite [ˈdefɪnɪt] adj (fixed) definitiv; (clear) eindeutig; ~**ly** adv bestimmt

definition [defɪˈnɪʃən] n Definition f; (PHOT) Schärfe f

deflate [diːˈfleɪt] vt die Luft ablassen

aus

deflect [dɪ'flɛkt] vt ablenken

deform [dɪ'fɔːm] vt deformieren; ~ity n Mißbildung f

defraud [dɪ'frɔːd] vt betrügen

defray [dɪ'freɪ] vt (costs) übernehmen

defrost [diː'frɒst] vt (fridge) abtauen; (food) auftauen; ~er (US) n (demister) Gebläse nt

deft [dɛft] adj geschickt

defunct [dɪ'fʌŋkt] adj verstorben

defuse [diː'fjuːz] vt entschärfen

defy [dɪ'faɪ] vt (disobey) sich widersetzen +dat; (orders, death) trotzen +dat; (challenge) herausfordern

degenerate [vb dɪ'dʒɛnəreɪt, adj dɪ'dʒɛnərɪt] vi degenerieren ♦ adj degeneriert

degrading [dɪ'greɪdɪŋ] adj erniedrigend

degree [dɪ'griː] n Grad m; (UNIV) Universitätsabschluß m; by ~s allmählich; to some ~ zu einem gewissen Grad

dehydrated [diːhaɪ'dreɪtɪd] adj (person) ausgetrocknet; (food) Trockende-ice [diː'aɪs] vt enteisen

deign [deɪn] vi sich herablassen

deity [diːɪtɪ] n Gottheit f

dejected [dɪ'dʒɛktɪd] adj niedergeschlagen

delay [dɪ'leɪ] vt (hold back) aufschieben ♦ vi (train) sich aufhalten ♦ n Aufschub m, Verzögerung f; (of train etc) Verspätung f; to be ~ed (train) Verspätung haben; without ~ unverzüglich

delectable [dɪ'lɛktəbl] adj köstlich; (fig) reizend

delegate [n 'dɛlɪgɪt, vb 'dɛlɪgeɪt] n Delegierte(r) mf ♦ vt delegieren

delete [dɪ'liːt] vt (aus)streichen

deliberate [adj dɪ'lɪbərɪt, vb dɪ'lɪbəreɪt] adj (intentional) absichtlich; (slow) bedächtig ♦ vi (consider) überlegen; (debate) sich beraten; ~ly adv absichtlich

delicacy ['dɛlɪkəsɪ] n Zartheit f; (weakness) Anfälligkeit f; (food) Delikatesse f

delicate ['dɛlɪkɪt] adj (fine) fein; (fragile) zart; (situation) heikel; (MED) empfindlich

delicatessen [dɛlɪkə'tɛsn] n Feinkostgeschäft nt

delicious [dɪ'lɪʃəs] adj lecker

delight [dɪ'laɪt] n Wonne f ♦ vt entzücken; to take ~ in sth Freude an etw dat haben; ~ed: ~ed (at or with sth) entzückt (über +acc etw); ~ed to do sth etw sehr gern tun; ~ful adj entzückend, herrlich

delinquency [dɪ'lɪŋkwənsɪ] n Kriminalität f

delinquent [dɪ'lɪŋkwənt] n Straffällige(r) mf ♦ adj straffällig

delirious [dɪ'lɪrɪəs] adj im Fieberwahn

deliver [dɪ'lɪvə*] vt (goods) (ab)liefern; (letter) zustellen; (speech) halten; ~y n (Ab)lieferung f; (of letter) Zustellung f; (of speech) Vortragsweise f; (MED) Entbindung f; to take ~y of in Empfang nehmen

delude [dɪ'luːd] vt täuschen

deluge ['dɛljuːdʒ] n Überschwemmung f; (fig) Flut f ♦ vt überfluten

delusion [dɪ'luːʒən] n (Selbst)täuschung f

de luxe [dɪ'lʌks] adj Luxus-

delve [dɛlv] vi: to ~ into sich vertiefen in +acc

demand [dɪ'mɑːnd] vt verlangen ♦ n (request) Verlangen nt; (COMM) Nachfrage f; in ~ gefragt; on ~ auf Verlangen; ~ing adj anspruchsvoll

demarcation [diːmɑː'keɪʃən] n Abgrenzung f

demean [dɪ'miːn] vt: to ~ o.s. sich erniedrigen

demeanour [dɪ'miːnə*] (US demeanor) n Benehmen nt

demented [dɪ'mɛntɪd] adj wahnsinnig

demise [dɪ'maɪz] n Ableben nt

demister [diː'mɪstə*] n (AUT) Gebläse nt

demo ['deməʊ] (inf) n abbr (= demonstration) Demo f

democracy [dɪ'mɒkrəsɪ] n Demokratie f

democrat ['deməkræt] n Demokrat m; **~ic** [demə'krætɪk] adj demokratisch

demolish [dɪ'mɒlɪʃ] vt abreißen; (fig) vernichten

demolition [demə'lɪʃən] n Abbruch m

demon ['di:mən] n Dämon m

demonstrate ['demənstreɪt] vt, vi demonstrieren

demonstration [demən'streɪʃən] n Demonstration f

demonstrator ['demənstreɪtə*] n (POL) Demonstrant(in) m(f)

demote [dɪ'məʊt] vt degradieren

demure [dɪ'mjʊə*] adj ernst

den [den] n (of animal) Höhle f; (study) Bude f

denatured alcohol [di:'neɪtʃəd-] (US) n ungenießbar gemachte(r) Alkohol m

denial [dɪ'naɪəl] n Leugnung f; official ~ Dementi nt

denim ['denɪm] adj Denim-; **~s** pl Denim-Jeans pl

Denmark ['denma:k] n Dänemark nt

denomination [dɪnɒmɪ'neɪʃən] n (ECCL) Bekenntnis nt; (type) Klasse f; (FIN) Wert m

denominator [dɪ'nɒmɪneɪtə*] n Nenner m

denote [dɪ'nəʊt] vt bedeuten

denounce [dɪ'naʊns] vt brandmarken

dense [dens] adj dicht; (stupid) schwer von Begriff; **~ly** adv dicht

density ['densɪtɪ] n Dichte f; single-/double-density disk Diskette f mit einfacher/doppelter Dichte

dent [dent] n Delle f ♦ vt (also: make a ~ in) einbeulen

dental ['dentl] adj Zahn-; **~ surgeon** n = dentist

dentist ['dentɪst] n Zahnarzt(ärztin) m(f); **~ry** n Zahnmedizin f

dentures ['dentʃəz] npl Gebiß nt

deny [dɪ'naɪ] vt leugnen; (officially) dementieren; (help) abschlagen

deodorant [di:'əʊdərənt] n Deodorant nt

depart [dɪ'pɑ:t] vi abfahren; to ~ from (fig: differ from) abweichen von

department [dɪ'pɑ:tmənt] n (COMM) Abteilung f; (UNIV) Seminar nt; (POL) Ministerium nt; ~ store n Warenhaus nt

departure [dɪ'pɑ:tʃə*] n (of person) Abreise f; (of train) Abfahrt f; (of plane) Abflug m; new ~ Neuerung f; ~ lounge n (at airport) Abflughalle f

depend [dɪ'pend] vi: to ~ on abhängen von; (rely on) angewiesen sein auf +acc; it ~s es kommt darauf an; **~ing on the result ...** abhängend vom Resultat ...; **~able** adj zuverlässig; **~ant** n Angehörige(r) mf; **~ence** n Abhängigkeit f; **~ent** adj abhängig ♦ n = dependant; **~ent on** abhängig von

depict [dɪ'pɪkt] vt schildern

depleted [dɪ'pli:tɪd] adj aufgebraucht

deplorable [dɪ'plɔ:rəbl] adj bedauerlich

deplore [dɪ'plɔ:*] vt mißbilligen

deploy [dɪ'plɔɪ] vt einsetzen

depopulation ['di:pɒpjʊ'leɪʃən] n Entvölkerung f

deport [dɪ'pɔ:t] vt deportieren; **~ation** [di:pɔ:'teɪʃən] n Abschiebung f

deportment [dɪ'pɔ:tmənt] n Betragen nt

depose [dɪ'pəʊz] vt absetzen

deposit [dɪ'pɒzɪt] n (in bank) Guthaben nt; (down payment) Anzahlung f; (security) Kaution f; (CHEM) Niederschlag m ♦ vt (in bank) deponieren; (put down) niederlegen; ~ account n Sparkonto nt

depot ['depəʊ] n Depot nt

depraved [dɪ'preɪvd] adj verkommen

depreciate [dɪ'pri:ʃɪeɪt] vi im Wert sinken; **depreciation** [dɪpri:ʃɪ'eɪʃən] n Wertminderung f

depress [dɪ'pres] vt (press down) niederdrücken; (in mood) deprimieren; ~ed adj deprimiert; ~ing adj deprimierend; ~ion [dɪ'preʃən] n (in mood) Depression f; (in trade) Wirtschaftskrise f; (hollow) Vertiefung f; (MET) Tief(druckgebiet) nt

deprivation [deprɪ'veɪʃən] n Not f

deprive [dɪ'praɪv] vt: to ~ sb of sth jdn einer Sache gen berauben; ~d adj (child) sozial benachteiligt; (area) unterentwickelt

depth [depθ] n Tiefe f; in the ~s of despair in tiefster Verzweiflung

deputation [depju'teɪʃən] n Abordnung f

deputize ['depjʊtaɪz] vi: to ~ (for sb) (jdn) vertreten

deputy ['depjʊtɪ] adj stellvertretend ♦ n (Stell)vertreter m

derail [dɪ'reɪl] vt: to be ~ed entgleisen; ~ment n Entgleisung f

deranged [dɪ'reɪndʒd] adj verrückt

derby ['dɜːbɪ] (US) n (bowler hat) Melone f

derelict ['derɪlɪkt] adj verlassen

deride [dɪ'raɪd] vt auslachen

derisory [dɪ'raɪsərɪ] adj spöttisch

derivative [dɪ'rɪvətɪv] n Derivat nt ♦ adj abgeleitet

derive [dɪ'raɪv] vt (get) gewinnen; (deduce) ableiten ♦ vi (come from) abstammen

dermatitis [dɜːmə'taɪtɪs] n Hautentzündung f

derogatory [dɪ'rɒgətərɪ] adj geringschätzig

derrick ['derɪk] n Drehkran m

descend [dɪ'send] vt, vi hinuntersteigen; to ~ from abstammen von; ~ant n Nachkomme m

descent [dɪ'sent] n (coming down) Abstieg m; (origin) Abstammung f

describe [dɪs'kraɪb] vt beschreiben

description [dɪs'krɪpʃən] n Beschreibung f; (sort) Art f

descriptive [dɪs'krɪptɪv] adj beschreibend; (word) anschaulich

desecrate ['desɪkreɪt] vt schänden

desert [n 'dezət, vb dɪ'zɜːt] n Wüste f

♦ vt verlassen; (temporarily) im Stich lassen ♦ vi (MIL) desertieren; ~s npl (what one deserves): to get one's just ~s seinen gerechten Lohn bekommen; ~er n Deserteur m; ~ion [dɪ'zɜːʃən] n (of wife) Verlassen nt; (MIL) Fahnenflucht f; ~ island n einsame Insel f

deserve [dɪ'zɜːv] vt verdienen

deserving [dɪ'zɜːvɪŋ] adj verdienstvoll

design [dɪ'zaɪn] n (plan) Entwurf m; (planning) Design nt ♦ vt entwerfen

designate [vb 'dezɪgneɪt, adj 'dezɪgnɪt] vt bestimmen ♦ adj designiert

designer [dɪ'zaɪnə*] n (TECH) Konstrukteur(in) m(f); (fashion ~) Modeschöpfer(in) m(f)

desirable [dɪ'zaɪərəbl] adj wünschenswert

desire [dɪ'zaɪə*] n Wunsch m, Verlangen nt ♦ vt (lust) begehren; (ask for) wollen

desk [desk] n Schreibtisch m; (BRIT: in shop, restaurant) Kasse f

desolate ['desəlɪt] adj öde; (sad) trostlos

desolation [desə'leɪʃən] n Trostlosigkeit f

despair [dɪs'pεə*] n Verzweiflung f ♦ vi: to ~ (of) verzweifeln (an +dat)

despatch [dɪs'pætʃ] n, vt = dispatch

desperate ['despərɪt] adj verzweifelt; ~ly ['despərɪtlɪ] adv verzweifelt

desperation [despə'reɪʃən] n Verzweiflung f

despicable [dɪs'pɪkəbl] adj abscheulich

despise [dɪs'paɪz] vt verachten

despite [dɪs'paɪt] prep trotz +gen

despondent [dɪs'pɒndənt] adj mutlos

dessert [dɪ'zɜːt] n Nachtisch m; ~spoon n Dessertlöffel m

destination [destɪ'neɪʃən] n (of person) (Reise)ziel nt; (of goods) Bestimmungsort m

destiny ['destɪnɪ] n Schicksal nt

destitute ['destɪtjuːt] adj notleidend

destroy [dɪs'trɔɪ] vt zerstören; **~er** n (NAUT) Zerstörer m

destruction [dɪs'trʌkʃən] n Zerstörung f

destructive [dɪs'trʌktɪv] adj zerstörend

detach [dɪ'tætʃ] vt loslösen; **~able** adj abtrennbar; **~ed** adj (attitude) distanziert; (house) Einzel-; **~ment** n (MIL) Sonderkommando nt; (fig) Abstand m

detail [ˈdiːteɪl] n Einzelheit f, Detail nt ♦ vt (relate) ausführlich berichten; (appoint) abkommandieren; **in ~** im Detail; **~ed** adj detailliert

detain [dɪ'teɪn] vt aufhalten; (imprison) in Haft halten

detect [dɪ'tekt] vt entdecken; **~ion** [dɪ'tekʃən] n Aufdeckung f; **~ive** n Detektiv m; **~ive story** n Kriminalgeschichte f, Krimi m; **~or** n Detektor m

détente [ˈdeɪtɑ̃ːnt] n Entspannung f

detention [dɪ'tenʃən] n Haft f; (SCH) Nachsitzen nt

deter [dɪ'tɜː*] vt abschrecken

detergent [dɪ'tɜːdʒənt] n Waschmittel nt

deteriorate [dɪ'tɪərɪəreɪt] vi sich verschlechtern; **deterioration** [dɪtɪərɪə'reɪʃən] n Verschlechterung f

determination [dɪtɜːmɪ'neɪʃən] n Entschlossenheit f

determine [dɪ'tɜːmɪn] vt bestimmen; **~d** adj entschlossen

deterrent [dɪ'terənt] n Abschreckungsmittel nt

detest [dɪ'test] vt verabscheuen

detonate [ˈdetəneɪt] vt explodieren lassen ♦ vi detonieren

detour [ˈdiːtuə*] n Umweg m; (US: AUT: diversion) Umleitung f ♦ vt (: traffic) umleiten

detract [dɪ'trækt] vi: **to ~ from** schmälern

detriment [ˈdetrɪmənt] n: **to the ~ of** zum Schaden +gen; **~al** [detrɪ'mentl] adj schädlich

devaluation [diːvæljʊˈeɪʃən] n Abwertung f

devastate [ˈdevəsteɪt] vt verwüsten

devastating [ˈdevəsteɪtɪɡ] adj verheerend

develop [dɪ'veləp] vt entwickeln; (resources) erschließen ♦ vi sich entwickeln; **~ing country** n Entwicklungsland nt; **~ment** n Entwicklung f

deviate [ˈdiːvɪeɪt] vi abweichen; **deviation** [diːvɪ'eɪʃən] n Abweichung f

device [dɪ'vaɪs] n Gerät nt

devil [ˈdevl] n Teufel m; **~ish** adj teuflisch

devious [ˈdiːvɪəs] adj (means) krumm; (person) verschlagen

devise [dɪ'vaɪz] vt entwickeln

devoid [dɪ'vɔɪd] adj: **~ of** ohne

devolution [diːvə'luːʃən] n (POL) Dezentralisierung f

devote [dɪ'vəʊt] vt: **to ~ sth (to sth)** etw (einer Sache dat) widmen; **~d** adj ergeben; **~e** [devəʊ'tiː] n Anhänger(in) m(f), Verehrer(in) m(f)

devotion [dɪ'vəʊʃən] n (piety) Andacht f; (loyalty) Ergebenheit f, Hingabe f

devour [dɪ'vaʊə*] vt verschlingen

devout [dɪ'vaʊt] adj andächtig

dew [djuː] n Tau m

dexterity [deks'terɪtɪ] n Geschicklichkeit f

DHSS (BRIT) n abbr = Department of Health and Social Security

diabetes [daɪə'biːtiːz] n Zuckerkrankheit f

diabetic [daɪə'betɪk] adj zuckerkrank; (food) Diabetiker- ♦ n Diabetiker m

diabolical [daɪə'bɒlɪkl] (inf) adj (weather, behaviour) saumäßig

diagnose [ˈdaɪəɡnəʊz] vt diagnostizieren

diagnoses [daɪəɡ'nəʊsiːz] npl of diagnosis

diagnosis [daɪəɡ'nəʊsɪs] n Diagnose f

diagonal [daɪ'æɡənl] adj diagonal ♦ n Diagonale f

diagram [ˈdaɪəɡræm] n Diagramm nt, Schaubild nt

dial ['daɪəl] n (TEL) Wählscheibe f; (of clock) Zifferblatt nt ♦ vt wählen; ~ **code** (US) n = **dialling code**

dialect ['daɪəlekt] n Dialekt m

dialling code ['daɪəlɪŋ-] n Vorwahl f

dialling tone ['daɪəlɪŋ-] n Amtszeichen nt

dialogue ['daɪəlɔg] n Dialog m

dial tone (US) n = **dialling tone**

diameter [daɪ'æmɪtə*] n Durchmesser m

diamond ['daɪəmənd] n Diamant m; ~**s** npl (CARDS) Karo nt

diaper ['daɪəpə*] (US) n Windel f

diaphragm ['daɪəfræm] n Zwerchfell nt

diarrhoea [daɪə'riːə] (US **diarrhea**) n Durchfall m

diary ['daɪərɪ] n Taschenkalender m; (account) Tagebuch n

dice [daɪs] n Würfel pl ♦ vt in Würfel schneiden

dichotomy [dɪ'kɔtəmɪ] n Kluft f

dictate [dɪk'teɪt] vt diktieren; ~**s** ['dɪkteɪts] npl Gebote pl

dictation [dɪk'teɪʃən] n Diktat nt

dictator [dɪk'teɪtə*] n Diktator m; ~**ship** [dɪk'teɪtəʃɪp] n Diktatur f

diction ['dɪkʃən] n Ausdrucksweise f

dictionary ['dɪkʃənrɪ] n Wörterbuch nt

did [dɪd] pt of **do**

didn't ['dɪdənt] = **did not**

die [daɪ] vi sterben; **to be dying for sth** etw unbedingt haben wollen; **to be dying to do sth**, darauf brennen, etw zu tun; ~ **away** vi schwächer werden; ~ **down** vi nachlassen; ~ **out** vi aussterben

diehard ['daɪhɑːd] n Dickkopf m; (POL) Reaktionär m

diesel ['diːzl] n (car) Diesel m; ~ **engine** n Dieselmotor m; ~ **oil** n Dieselkraftstoff m

diet ['daɪət] n Nahrung f; (special food) Diät f; (slimming) Abmagerungskur f ♦ vi (also: **be on a** ~) eine Abmagerungskur machen

differ ['dɪfə*] vi sich unterscheiden; (disagree) anderer Meinung sein;

~**ence** n Unterschied m; ~**ent** adj anders; (two things) verschieden; ~**ential** [dɪfə'renʃəl] n (in wages) Lohnstufe f; ~**entiate** [dɪfə'renʃɪeɪt] vt, vi unterscheiden; ~**ently** adv anders; (from one another) unterschiedlich

difficult ['dɪfɪkəlt] adj schwierig; ~**y** n Schwierigkeit f

diffident ['dɪfɪdənt] adj schüchtern

diffuse [adj dɪ'fjuːs, vb dɪ'fjuːz] adj langatmig ♦ vt verbreiten

dig [dɪg] (pt, pp **dug**) vt graben ♦ n (prod) Stoß m; (remark) Spitze f; (archaeological) Ausgrabung f; ~ **in** vi (MIL) sich eingraben; ~ **into** vt fus (sb's past) wühlen in +dat; (savings) angreifen; ~ **up** vt ausgraben; (fig) aufgabeln

digest [vb daɪ'dʒest, n 'daɪdʒest] vt verdauen ♦ n Auslese f; ~**ion** [dɪ'dʒestʃən] n Verdauung f

digit ['dɪdʒɪt] n Ziffer f; (ANAT) Finger m; ~**al** adj digital, Digital-

dignified ['dɪgnɪfaɪd] adj würdevoll

dignity ['dɪgnɪtɪ] n Würde f

digress [daɪ'gres] vi abschweifen

digs [dɪgz] (BRIT: inf) npl Bude f

dilapidated [dɪ'læpɪdeɪtɪd] adj baufällig

dilate [daɪ'leɪt] vt weiten ♦ vi sich weiten

dilemma [daɪ'lemə] n Dilemma nt

diligent ['dɪlɪdʒənt] adj fleißig

dilute [daɪ'luːt] vt verdünnen

dim [dɪm] adj trübe; (stupid) schwer von Begriff ♦ vt verdunkeln; **to** ~ **one's headlights** (esp US) abblenden

dime [daɪm] (US) n Zehncentstück nt

dimension [dɪ'menʃən] n Dimension f

diminish [dɪ'mɪnɪʃ] vt, vi verringern

diminutive [dɪ'mɪnjʊtɪv] adj winzig ♦ n Verkleinerungsform f

dimmer ['dɪmə*] (US) n (AUT) Abblendschalter m; ~**s** npl Abblendlicht nt; (sidelights) Begrenzungsleuchten pl

dimple ['dɪmpl] n Grübchen nt

din [dɪn] n Getöse nt

dine [daɪn] vi speisen; **~r** n Tischgast m; (RAIL) Speisewagen m

dinghy ['dɪŋgɪ] n Dinghy nt; **rubber ~** Schlauchboot nt

dingy ['dɪndʒɪ] adj armselig

dining car ['daɪnɪŋ-] (BRIT) n Speisewagen m

dining room ['daɪnɪŋ-] n Eßzimmer nt; (in hotel) Speisezimmer nt

dinner ['dɪnə*] n (lunch) Mittagessen nt; (evening) Abendessen nt; (public) Festessen nt; **~ jacket** n Smoking m; **~ party** n Tischgesellschaft f; **~ time** n Tischzeit f

dinosaur ['daɪnəsɔ:*] n Dinosaurier m

dint [dɪnt] n: **by ~ of** durch

diocese ['daɪəsɪs] n Diözese f

dip [dɪp] n (hollow) Senkung f; (bathe) kurze(s) Baden nt ♦ vt eintauchen; (BRIT: AUT: lights) abblenden ♦ vi (slope) sich senken, abfallen

diploma [dɪ'pləʊmə] n Diplom nt

diplomacy [dɪ'pləʊməsɪ] n Diplomatie f

diplomat ['dɪpləmæt] n Diplomat(in) m(f); **~ic** [dɪplə'mætɪk] adj diplomatisch

dip stick n Ölmeßstab m

dipswitch (BRIT) n (AUT) Abblendschalter m

dire [daɪə*] adj schrecklich

direct [daɪ'rekt] adj direkt ♦ vt leiten; (film) die Regie führen +gen; (aim) richten; (order) anweisen; **can you ~ me to ...?** können Sie mir sagen, wo ich zu ... komme?

direction [dɪ'rekʃən] n Richtung f; (CINE) Regie f; Leitung f; **~s** npl (for use) Gebrauchsanleitung f; (orders) Anweisungen pl; **sense of ~** Orientierungssinn m

directly [dɪ'rektlɪ] adv direkt; (at once) sofort

director [dɪ'rektə*] n Direktor m; (of film) Regisseur m

directory [dɪ'rektərɪ] n (TEL) Telefonbuch nt

dirt [dɜ:t] n Schmutz m, Dreck m; **~-cheap** adj spottbillig; **~y** schmutzig ♦ vt beschmutzen; **~y trick** n gemeine(r) Trick m

disability [dɪsə'bɪlɪtɪ] n Körperbehinderung f

disabled [dɪs'eɪbld] adj körperbehindert

disadvantage [dɪsəd'vɑ:ntɪdʒ] n Nachteil m

disaffection [dɪsə'fekʃən] n Entfremdung f

disagree [dɪsə'gri:] vi nicht übereinstimmen; (quarrel) (sich) streiten; (food): **to ~ with sb** jdm nicht bekommen; **~able** adj unangenehm; **~ment** (between persons) Streit m; (between things) Widerspruch m

disallow [dɪsə'laʊ] vt nicht zulassen

disappear [dɪsə'pɪə*] vi verschwinden; **~ance** n Verschwinden nt

disappoint [dɪsə'pɔɪnt] vt enttäuschen; **~ed** adj enttäuscht; **~ing** adj enttäuschend; **~ment** n Enttäuschung f

disapproval [dɪsə'pru:vəl] n Mißbilligung f

disapprove [dɪsə'pru:v] vi: **to ~ of** mißbilligen

disarm [dɪs'ɑ:m] vt entwaffnen; (POL) abrüsten; **~ament** n Abrüstung f

disarray ['dɪsə'reɪ] n: **to be in ~** (army) in Auflösung (begriffen) sein; (clothes) in unordentlichem Zustand sein

disaster [dɪ'zɑ:stə*] n Katastrophe f

disastrous [dɪ'zɑ:strəs] adj verhängnisvoll

disband [dɪs'bænd] vt auflösen ♦ vi auseinandergehen

disbelief ['dɪsbə'li:f] n Ungläubigkeit f

disc [dɪsk] n Scheibe f; (record) (Schall)platte f; (COMPUT) = disk

discard [dɪs'kɑ:d] vt ablegen

discern [dɪ'sɜ:n] vt erkennen; **~ing** adj scharfsinnig

discharge [vb dɪs'tʃɑ:dʒ, n

'dɪstʃɑːdʒ] vt (ship) entladen; (duties) nachkommen +dat; (dismiss)
entlassen; (gun) abschießen; (JUR)
freisprechen ♦ n (of ship, ELEC)
Entladung f; (dismissal) Entlassung
f; (MED) Ausfluß m

disciple [dɪ'saɪpl] n Jünger m

discipline ['dɪsɪplɪn] n Disziplin f ♦
vt (train) schulen; (punish) bestrafen

disc jockey n Diskjockey m

disclaim [dɪs'kleɪm] vt nicht anerkennen

disclose [dɪs'kləuz] vt enthüllen

disclosure [dɪs'kləuʒə*] n Ent-
hüllung f

disco ['dɪskəu] n abbr = discotheque

discoloured [dɪs'kʌləd] (US discol-
ored) adj verfärbt

discomfort [dɪs'kʌmfət] n Unbehagen nt

disconcert [dɪskən'sɜːt] vt aus der
Fassung bringen

disconnect [dɪskə'nekt] vt abtrennen

discontent [dɪskən'tent] n Unzufriedenheit f; ~ed adj unzufrieden

discontinue ['dɪskən'tɪnjuː] vt einstellen

discord ['dɪskɔːd] n Zwietracht f;
(noise) Dissonanz f; ~ant
[dɪs'kɔːdənt] adj uneinig

discotheque ['dɪskəutek] n Disko-
thek f

discount [n 'dɪskaunt, vb dɪs'kaunt]
n Rabatt m ♦ vt außer acht lassen

discourage [dɪs'kʌrɪdʒ] vt entmutigen; (prevent) abraten

discouraging [dɪs'kʌrɪdʒɪŋ] adj entmutigend

discourteous [dɪs'kɜːtɪəs] adj unhöflich

discover [dɪs'kʌvə*] vt entdecken;
~y n Entdeckung f

discredit [dɪs'kredɪt] vt in Verruf
bringen

discreet [dɪs'kriːt] adj diskret

discrepancy [dɪs'krepənsɪ] n Diskre-
panz f

discriminate [dɪs'krɪmɪneɪt] vi
unterscheiden; to ~ against diskri-

minieren

discriminating [dɪs'krɪmɪneɪtɪŋ] adj
anspruchsvoll

discrimination [dɪskrɪmɪ'neɪʃən] n
Urteilsvermögen nt; (pej) Diskrimi-
nierung f

discuss [dɪs'kʌs] vt diskutieren, besprechen; ~ion [dɪs'kʌʃən] n Diskus-
sion f, Besprechung f

disdain [dɪs'deɪn] n Verachtung f ♦ n
Verachtung f

disease [dɪ'ziːz] n Krankheit f

disembark [dɪsɪm'bɑːk] vi aussteigen lassen ♦ vi von Bord gehen

disenchanted ['dɪsɪn'tʃɑːntɪd] adj
desillusioniert

disengage [dɪsɪn'geɪdʒ] vt (AUT)
auskuppeln

disentangle ['dɪsɪn'tæŋgl] vt entwirren

disfigure [dɪs'fɪgə*] vt entstellen

disgrace [dɪs'greɪs] n Schande f ♦
Schande bringen über +acc; ~ful adj
unerhört

disgruntled [dɪs'grʌntld] adj verärgert

disguise [dɪs'gaɪz] vt verkleiden;
(feelings) verhehlen ♦ n Verkleidung
f; in ~ verkleidet, maskiert

disgust [dɪs'gʌst] n Abscheu f ♦ vt
anwidern; ~ing adj widerlich

dish [dɪʃ] n Schüssel f; (food) Gericht
nt; to do or wash the ~es abwaschen; ~ up vt auftischen; ~cloth n
Spüllappen m

dishearten [dɪs'hɑːtn] vt entmutigen

dishevelled [dɪ'ʃevəld] adj (hair)
zerzaust; (clothing) ungepflegt

dishonest [dɪs'ɒnɪst] adj unehrlich;
~y n Unehrlichkeit f

dishonour [dɪs'ɒnə*] (US dishonor)
n Unehre f; ~able adj unehrenhaft

dishtowel ['dɪʃtauəl] n Geschirrtuch
nt

dishwasher ['dɪʃwɒʃə*] n Geschirrs-
pülmaschine f

disillusion [dɪsɪ'luːʒən] vt enttäuschen, desillusionieren

disincentive ['dɪsɪn'sentɪv] n Entmu-
tigung f

disinfect [dɪsɪn'fɛkt] vt desinfizieren; **~ant** n Desinfektionsmittel nt

disintegrate [dɪs'ɪntɪgreɪt] vi sich auflösen

disinterested [dɪs'ɪntrɪstɪd] adj uneigennützig; (inf) uninteressiert

disjointed [dɪs'dʒɔɪntɪd] adj unzusammenhängend

disk [dɪsk] n (COMPUT) Diskette f; single-/double-sided ~ einseitige/ beidseitige Diskette; ~ drive n Diskettenlaufwerk nt; ~ette (US) n = disk

dislike [dɪs'laɪk] n Abneigung f ♦ vt nicht leiden können

dislocate ['dɪsləkeɪt] vt auskugeln

dislodge [dɪs'lɒdʒ] vt verschieben, (MIL) aus der Stellung werfen

disloyal ['dɪs'lɔɪəl] adj treulos

dismal ['dɪzməl] adj trostlos, trübe

dismantle [dɪs'mæntl] vt demontieren

dismay [dɪs'meɪ] n Bestürzung f ♦ vt bestürzen

dismiss [dɪs'mɪs] vt (employee) entlassen; (idea) von sich weisen; (send away) wegschicken; (JUR) abweisen; **~al** n Entlassung f

dismount [dɪs'maʊnt] vi absteigen

disobedience [dɪsə'biːdɪəns] n Ungehorsam m

disobedient [dɪsə'biːdɪənt] adj ungehorsam

disobey ['dɪsə'beɪ] vt nicht gehorchen +dat

disorder [dɪs'ɔːdə*] n (confusion) Verwirrung f; (commotion) Aufruhr m; (MED) Erkrankung f

disorderly [dɪs'ɔːdəlɪ] adj (untidy) unordentlich; (unruly) ordnungswidrig

disorganized [dɪs'ɔːgənaɪzd] adj unordentlich

disorientated [dɪs'ɔːrɪenteɪtɪd] adj (person: after journey, deep sleep) verwirrt

disown [dɪs'əʊn] vt (child) verstoßen

disparaging [dɪs'pærɪdʒɪŋ] adj geringschätzig

disparity [dɪs'pærɪtɪ] n Verschiedenheit f

dispassionate [dɪs'pæʃnɪt] adj objektiv

dispatch [dɪs'pætʃ] vt (goods) abschicken, abfertigen ♦ n Absendung f; (esp MIL) Meldung f

dispel [dɪs'pel] vt zerstreuen

dispensary [dɪs'pensərɪ] n Apotheke f

dispense [dɪs'pens] vt verteilen, austeilen; ~ **with** vt fus verzichten auf +acc; **~r** n (container) Spender m

dispensing [dɪs'pensɪŋ] adj: ~ **chemist** (BRIT) Apotheker m

dispersal [dɪs'pɜːsəl] n Zerstreuung f

disperse [dɪs'pɜːs] vt zerstreuen ♦ vi sich verteilen

dispirited [dɪs'pɪrɪtɪd] adj niedergeschlagen

displace [dɪs'pleɪs] vt verschieben; **~d person** n Verschleppte(r) mf

display [dɪs'pleɪ] n (of goods) Auslage f; (of feeling) Zurschaustellung f ♦ vt zeigen; (ostentatiously) vorführen; (goods) ausstellen

displease [dɪs'pliːz] vt mißfallen +dat

displeasure [dɪs'pleʒə*] n Mißfallen nt

disposable [dɪs'pəʊzəbl] adj Wegwerf-; ~ **nappy** n Papierwindel f

disposal [dɪs'pəʊzəl] n (of property) Verkauf m; (throwing away) Beseitigung f; to be at one's ~ einem zur Verfügung stehen

dispose [dɪs'pəʊz] vi: to ~ of loswerden

disposed [dɪs'pəʊzd] adj geneigt

disposition [dɪspə'zɪʃən] n Wesen nt

disproportionate [dɪsprə'pɔːʃnɪt] adj unverhältnismäßig

disprove [dɪs'pruːv] vt widerlegen

dispute [dɪs'pjuːt] n Streit m; (also: industrial ~) Arbeitskampf m ♦ vt bestreiten

disqualify [dɪs'kwɒlɪfaɪ] vt disqualifizieren

disquiet [dɪs'kwaɪət] n Unruhe f

disregard [dɪsrɪ'gɑːd] vt nicht (be)achten

disrepair [ˈdɪsrɪˈpɛə*] n: to fall into ~ verfallen

disreputable [dɪsˈrɛpjʊtəbl] adj verrufen

disrespectful [dɪsrɪsˈpɛktfʊl] adj respektlos

disrupt [dɪsˈrʌpt] vt stören; (service) unterbrechen; ~ion [dɪsˈrʌpʃən] n Störung f; Unterbrechung f

dissatisfaction [ˈdɪssætɪsˈfækʃən] n Unzufriedenheit f

dissatisfied [ˈdɪssætɪsfaɪd] adj unzufrieden

dissect [dɪˈsɛkt] vt zerlegen, sezieren

disseminate [dɪˈsɛmɪneɪt] vt verbreiten

dissent [dɪˈsɛnt] n abweichende Meinung f

dissertation [dɪsəˈteɪʃən] n wissenschaftliche Arbeit f; (Ph.D.) Doktorarbeit f

disservice [dɪsˈsɜːvɪs] n: to do sb a ~ jdm einen schlechten Dienst erweisen

dissident [ˈdɪsɪdənt] adj andersdenkend ♦ n Dissident m

dissimilar [ˈdɪˈsɪmɪlə*] adj: ~ (to sb/sth) (jdm/etw) unähnlich

dissipate [ˈdɪsɪpeɪt] vt (waste) verschwenden; (scatter) zerstreuen

dissociate [dɪˈsəʊʃɪeɪt] vt trennen

dissolute [ˈdɪsəluːt] adj liederlich

dissolution [dɪsəˈluːʃən] n Auflösung f

dissolve [dɪˈzɒlv] vt auflösen ♦ vi sich auflösen

dissuade [dɪˈsweɪd] vt: to ~ sb from doing sth jdn davon abbringen, etw zu tun

distance [ˈdɪstəns] n Entfernung f; in the ~ in der Ferne

distant [ˈdɪstənt] adj entfernt, fern; (with time) fern; (formal) distanziert

distaste [dɪsˈteɪst] n Abneigung f; ~ful adj widerlich

distended [dɪsˈtɛndɪd] adj (stomach) aufgebläht

distil [dɪsˈtɪl] vt destillieren; ~lery n Brennerei f

distinct [dɪsˈtɪŋkt] adj (separate) getrennt; (clear) klar, deutlich; as ~ from im Unterschied zu; ~ion [dɪsˈtɪŋkʃən] n Unterscheidung f; (eminence) Auszeichnung f; ~ive adj bezeichnend

distinguish [dɪsˈtɪŋgwɪʃ] vt unterscheiden; ~ed adj (eminent) berühmt; ~ing adj bezeichnend

distort [dɪsˈtɔːt] vt verdrehen; (misrepresent) entstellen; ~ion [dɪsˈtɔːʃən] n Verzerrung f

distract [dɪsˈtrækt] vt ablenken; ~ing adj verwirrend; ~ion [dɪsˈtrækʃən] n (distress) Raserei f; (diversion) Zerstreuung f

distraught [dɪsˈtrɔːt] adj bestürzt

distress [dɪsˈtrɛs] n Not f; (suffering) Qual f ♦ vt quälen; ~ing adj erschütternd; ~ signal n Notsignal nt

distribute [dɪsˈtrɪbjuːt] vt verteilen; ~ion [dɪstrɪˈbjuːʃən] n Verteilung f

distributor [dɪsˈtrɪbjʊtə*] n Verteiler m

district [ˈdɪstrɪkt] n (of country) Kreis m; (of town) Bezirk m; ~ attorney (US) n Oberstaatsanwalt m; ~ nurse n Kreiskrankenschwester f

distrust [dɪsˈtrʌst] n Mißtrauen nt ♦ vt mißtrauen +dat

disturb [dɪsˈtɜːb] vt stören; (agitate) erregen; ~ance n Störung f; ~ed adj beunruhigt; emotionally ~ed emotional gestört; ~ing adj beunruhigend

disuse [ˈdɪsˈjuːs] n: to fall into ~ außer Gebrauch kommen

disused [dɪsˈjuːzd] adj außer Gebrauch; (mine, railway line) stillgelegt

ditch [dɪtʃ] n Graben m ♦ vt (person) loswerden; (plan) fallenlassen

dither [ˈdɪðə*] vi verdattert sein

ditto [ˈdɪtəʊ] adv dito, ebenfalls

divan [dɪˈvæn] n Liegesofa nt

dive [daɪv] n (into water) Kopfsprung m; (AVIAT) Sturzflug m ♦ vi tauchen; ~r n Taucher m

diverge [daɪˈvɜːdʒ] vi auseinandergehen

diverse [daɪˈvɜːs] adj verschieden

diversion [daɪˈvɜːʃən] n Ablenkung f; (BRIT: AUT) Umleitung f

diversity [daɪˈvɜːsɪtɪ] n Vielfalt f

divert [daɪˈvɜːt] vt ablenken; (traffic) umleiten

divide [dɪˈvaɪd] vt teilen ♦ vi sich teilen; ~d highway (US) n Schnellstraße f

divine [dɪˈvaɪn] adj göttlich

diving [ˈdaɪvɪŋ] n (SPORT) Turmspringen nt; (underwater ~) Tauchen nt; ~ board n Sprungbrett nt

divinity [dɪˈvɪnɪtɪ] n Gottheit f; (subject) Religion f

division [dɪˈvɪʒən] n Teilung f; (MIL) Division f; (part) Abteilung f; (in opinion) Uneinigkeit f; (BRIT: POL) (Abstimmung f durch) Hammelsprung f

divorce [dɪˈvɔːs] n (Ehe)scheidung f ♦ vt scheiden; ~d adj geschieden; ~e [dɪvɔːˈsiː] n Geschiedene(r) mf

divulge [daɪˈvʌldʒ] vt preisgeben

D.I.Y. (BRIT) n abbr = do-it-yourself

dizzy [ˈdɪzɪ] adj schwindlig

DJ n abbr = disc jockey

KEYWORD

do [duː] (pt **did**, pp **done**) n (inf: party etc) Fete f
♦ aux vb 1 (in negative constructions and questions): **I don't understand** ich verstehe nicht; **didn't you know?** wußtest du das nicht?; **what do you think?** was meinen Sie?
2 (for emphasis, in polite expressions): **she does seem rather tired** sie scheint wirklich sehr müde zu sein; **do sit down/help yourself** setzen Sie sich doch hin/greifen Sie doch zu
3 (used to avoid repeating vb): **she swims better than I do** sie schwimmt besser als ich; **she lives in Glasgow - so do I** sie wohnt in Glasgow - ich auch
4 (in question tags): **you like him,**

don't you? du magst ihn doch, oder?
♦ vt 1 (carry out, perform etc) tun, machen; **what are you doing tonight?** was machst du heute abend?; **I've got nothing to do** ich habe nichts zu tun; **to do one's hair/nails** sich die Haare/Nägel machen
2 (AUT etc) fahren
♦ vi 1 (act, behave): **do as I do** mach es wie ich
2 (get on, fare): **he's doing well/badly at school** er ist gut/schlecht in der Schule; **how do you do?** guten Tag
3 (be suitable) gehen; (be sufficient) reichen; **to make do (with)** auskommen mit

do away with vt (kill) umbringen; (abolish: law etc) abschaffen

do up vt (laces, dress, buttons) zumachen; (renovate: room, house) renovieren

do with vt (need) brauchen; (be connected) zu tun haben mit

do without vt, vi auskommen ohne

docile [ˈdəʊsaɪl] adj gefügig

dock [dɔk] n Dock nt; (JUR) Anklagebank f ♦ vi ins Dock gehen; ~er n Hafenarbeiter m; ~yard n Werft f

doctor [ˈdɔktə*] n Arzt m, Ärztin f; (UNIV) Doktor m ♦ vt (fig) fälschen; (drink etc) etw beimischen +dat; **D~ of Philosophy** n Doktor m der Philosophie

document [ˈdɔkjʊmənt] n Dokument nt; ~ary [dɔkjʊˈmɛntərɪ] n Dokumentarbericht m; (film) Dokumentarfilm m ♦ adj dokumentarisch; ~ation [dɔkjʊmɛnˈteɪʃən] n dokumentarische(r) Nachweis m

dodge [dɔdʒ] n Kniff m ♦ vt ausweichen +dat; ~ms (BRIT) npl Autoskooter m

doe [dəʊ] n (roe deer) Ricke f; (red deer) Hirschkuh f; (rabbit) Weibchen nt

does [dʌz] vb see **do**; ~n't = **does not**

dog [dɔg] n Hund m; ~ **collar** n Hundehalsband nt; (ECCL) Kragen m des Geistlichen; **~eared** adj mit Eselsohren

dogged ['dɔgɪd] adj hartnäckig

dogsbody ['dɔgzbɔdɪ] n Mädchen nt für alles

doings ['duːɪŋz] npl (activities) Treiben nt

do-it-yourself ['duːɪtjə'self] n Do-it-yourself nt

doldrums ['dɔldrəmz] npl: to be in the ~ (business) Flaute haben; (person) deprimiert sein

dole [dəul] (BRIT) n Stempelgeld nt; to be on the ~ stempeln gehen; ~ out vt ausgeben, austeilen

doleful ['dəulful] adj traurig

doll [dɔl] n Puppe f ♦ vt: to ~ o.s. up sich aufdonnern

dollar ['dɔlə*] n Dollar m

dolphin ['dɔlfɪn] n Delphin m

dome [dəum] n Kuppel f

domestic [də'mestɪk] adj häuslich; (within country) Innen-, Binnen-; (animal) Haus-; **~ated** adj (person) häuslich; (animal) zahm

dominant ['dɔmɪnənt] adj vorherrschend

dominate ['dɔmɪneɪt] vt beherrschen

domineering [dɔmɪ'nɪərɪŋ] adj herrisch

dominion [də'mɪnɪən] n (rule) Regierungsgewalt f; (land) Staatsgebiet nt mit Selbstverwaltung

domino ['dɔmɪnəu] (pl dominoes) n Dominostein m; **~es** pl (game) Domino(spiel) nt

don [dɔn] (BRIT) n akademische(r) Lehrer m

donate [dəu'neɪt] vt (blood, little money) spenden; (lot of money) stiften

donation [dəu'neɪʃən] n Spende f

done [dʌn] pp of do

donkey ['dɔŋkɪ] n Esel m

donor ['dəunə*] n Spender m

don't [dəunt] = do not

doodle ['duːdl] vi kritzeln

doom [duːm] n böse(s) Geschick nt;

(downfall) Verderben nt ♦ vt: to be ~ed zum Untergang verurteilt sein; **~sday** n der Jüngste Tag

door [dɔː*] n Tür f; **~bell** n Türklingel f; **~handle** n Türklinke f; **~man** (irreg) n Türsteher m; **~mat** n Fußmatte f; **~step** n Türstufe f; **~way** n Türöffnung f

dope [dəup] n (drug) Aufputschmittel nt ♦ vt (horse etc) dopen

dopey ['dəupɪ] (inf) adj bekloppt

dormant ['dɔːmənt] adj latent

dormitory ['dɔːmɪtrɪ] n Schlafsaal m

dormouse ['dɔːmaus] (pl -mice) n Haselmaus f

DOS [dɔs] n abbr (= disk operating system) DOS nt

dosage ['dəusɪdʒ] n Dosierung f

dose [dəus] n Dosis f

doss house ['dɔs-] (BRIT) n Bleibe f

dot [dɔt] n Punkt m; **~ted** with übersät mit; on the ~ pünktlich

dote [dəut] : to ~ on vt fus vernarrt sein in +acc

dot matrix printer n Matrixdrucker m

dotted line n punktierte Linie f

double ['dʌbl] adj, adv doppelt ♦ n Doppelgänger m ♦ vt verdoppeln ♦ vi sich verdoppeln; **~s** npl (TENNIS) Doppel nt; on or at the ~ im Laufschritt; **~ bass** n Kontrabaß m; **~ bed** n Doppelbett nt; **~ bend** (BRIT) n S-Kurve f; **~breasted** adj zweireihig; **~cross** vt hintergehen; **~decker** n Doppeldecker m; **~ glazing** (BRIT) n Doppelverglasung f; **~ room** n Doppelzimmer nt

doubly ['dʌblɪ] adv doppelt

doubt [daut] n Zweifel m ♦ vt bezweifeln; **~ful** adj zweifelhaft; **~less** adv ohne Zweifel

dough [dəu] n Teig m; **~nut** n Berliner m

douse [dauz] vt (drench) mit Wasser begießen, durchtränken; (extinguish) ausmachen

dove [dʌv] n Taube f

Dover n (GEO) Dover nt

dovetail ['dʌvteɪl] vi (plans) übereinstimmen

dowdy ['daʊdɪ] adj unmodern

down [daʊn] n (fluff) Flaum m; (hill) Hügel m ♦ adv unten; (motion) herunter; hinunter ♦ prep: to go ~ the street die Straße hinuntergehen ♦ vt niederschlagen; ~ with X!: nieder mit X!; **~-and-out** n Tramp m; **~at-heel** adj schäbig; **~cast** adj niedergeschlagen; **~fall** n Sturz m; **~hearted** adj niedergeschlagen; **~hill** adv bergab; **~ payment** n Anzahlung f; **~pour** n Platzregen m; **~right** adj ausgesprochen

Down's syndrome ['daʊnzdrəʊm] n (MED) Down-Syndrom n

down: **~stairs** adv unten; (motion) nach unten; **~stream** adv flußabwärts; **~-to-earth** adj praktisch; **~town** adv in der Innenstadt; (motion) in die Innenstadt; **~ under** (BRIT: inf) adv in/nach Australien/Neuseeland; **~ward** adv abwärts, nach unten ♦ adj abwärts, nach unten; **~wards** adv abwärts, nach unten

doz. abbr (= dozen) Dtzd.

doze [dəʊz] vi dösen; **~ off** vi einnicken

dozen ['dʌzn] n Dutzend nt; **a ~ books** ein Dutzend Bücher; **~s of** Dutzende von

Dr. abbr = doctor; driver

drab [dræb] adj düster, eintönig

draft [drɑːft] n Entwurf m; (FIN) Wechsel m; (US: MIL) Einberufung f ♦ vt skizzieren; see also **draught**

draftsman ['drɑːftsmən] (US: irreg) n = **draughtsman**

drag [dræg] vt schleppen; (river) mit einem Schleppnetz absuchen ♦ vi sich (dahin)schleppen ♦ n (bore) etwas Blödes; **in ~** als Tunte; **a man in ~** eine Tunte; **~ on** vi sich in die Länge ziehen

dragon ['drægən] n Drache m; **~fly** ['drægənflaɪ] n Libelle f

drain [dreɪn] n Abfluß m; (fig: burden) Belastung f ♦ vt ableiten; (ex-

haust) erschöpfen ♦ vi (of water) abfließen; **~age** n Kanalisation f; **~ing board** (US drainboard) n Ablaufbrett nt; **~pipe** n Abflußrohr nt

dram [dræm] n Schluck m

drama ['drɑːmə] n Drama nt; **~tic** [drə'mætɪk] adj dramatisch; **~tist** ['dræmətɪst] n Dramatiker m; **~tize** vt (events) dramatisieren; (adapt: for TV, cinema) bearbeiten

drank [dræŋk] pt of **drink**

drape [dreɪp] vt drapieren; **~r** (BRIT) n Tuchhändler m; **~s** (US) npl Vorhänge pl

drastic ['dræstɪk] adj drastisch

draught [drɑːft] (US **draft**) n Zugluft f; (NAUT) Tiefgang m; **~s** n Damespiel nt; **on ~** (beer) vom Faß; **~board** (BRIT) n Zeichenbrett n

draughtsman ['drɑːftsmən] (irreg) n technische(r) Zeichner m

draw [drɔː] (pt **drew**, pp **drawn**) vt ziehen; (crowd) anlocken; (picture) zeichnen; (money) abheben; (water) schöpfen ♦ vi (SPORT) unentschieden spielen ♦ n Unentschieden nt; (lottery) Ziehung f; **~ near** vi näherrücken; **~ out** vi (train) ausfahren; (lengthen) sich hinziehen; **~ up** vi (stop) halten ♦ vt (document) aufsetzen; **~back** n Nachteil m; **~bridge** n Zugbrücke f

drawer [drɔː*] n Schublade f

drawing ['drɔːɪŋ] n Zeichnung f; Zeichnen nt; **~ board** n Reißbrett nt; **~ pin** (BRIT) n Reißzwecke f; **~ room** n Salon m

drawl [drɔːl] n schleppende Sprechweise f

drawn [drɔːn] pp of **draw**

dread [dred] n Furcht f ♦ vt fürchten; **~ful** adj furchtbar

dream [driːm] (pt, pp **dreamed** or **dreamt**) n Traum m ♦ vt träumen ♦ vi: **to ~ (about)** träumen (von); **~er** n Träumer m; **dreamt** [dremt] pt, pp of **dream**; **~y** adj verträumt

dreary ['drɪərɪ] adj trostlos, öde

dredge [dredʒ] vt ausbaggern

dregs [dregz] npl Bodensatz m; (fig)

Abschaum m

drench [drentʃ] vt durchnässen

dress [dres] n Kleidung f; (garment) Kleid nt ♦ vt anziehen; (MED) verbinden; **to get ~ed** sich anziehen; **~ up** vi sich fein machen; **~ circle** (BRIT) n erste(r) Rang m; **~er** n (furniture) Anrichte f; (MED) Verband m; (COOK) Soße f; **~ing gown** (BRIT) n Morgenrock m; **~ing room** n (THEAT) Garderobe f; (SPORT) Umkleideraum m; **~ing table** n Toilettentisch m; **~maker** n Schneiderin f; **~ rehearsal** n Generalprobe f

drew [dru:] pt of draw

dribble ['drɪbl] vi sabbern ♦ vt (ball) dribbeln

dried [draɪd] adj getrocknet; (fruit) Dörr-, gedörrt; (~ milk) n Milchpulver nt

drier ['draɪə*] n = dryer

drift [drɪft] n Strömung f; (snow~) Schneewehe f; (fig) Richtung f ♦ vi sich treiben lassen; **~wood** n Treibholz nt

drill [drɪl] n Bohrer m; (MIL) Drill m ♦ vt bohren; (MIL) ausbilden ♦ vi: **to ~ (for)** bohren (nach)

drink [drɪŋk] (pt drank, pp drunk) n Getränk nt; (spirits) Drink m ♦ vt, vi trinken; **to have a ~** etwas trinken; **~er** n Trinker m; **~ing water** n Trinkwasser nt

drip [drɪp] n Tropfen m ♦ vi tropfen; **~-dry** adj bügelfrei; **~ping** n Bratenfett nt

drive [draɪv] (pt drove, pp driven) n Fahrt f; (road) Einfahrt f; (campaign) Aktion f; (energy) Schwung m; (SPORT) Schlag m; (also: disk ~) Diskettenlaufwerk nt ♦ vt (car) fahren; (animals, people, objects) treiben; (power) antreiben ♦ vi fahren; **left-hand/right-hand ~** Links-/Rechtssteuerung f; **to ~ sb mad** jdn verrückt machen

drivel ['drɪvl] n Faselei f

driven ['drɪvn] pp of drive

driver ['draɪvə*] n Fahrer m; **~'s li-**

cense (US) n Führerschein m

driveway ['draɪvweɪ] n Auffahrt f; (longer) Zufahrtsstraße f

driving ['draɪvɪŋ] adj (rain) stürmisch; **~ instructor** n Fahrlehrer m; **~ lesson** n Fahrstunde f; **~ licence** (BRIT) n Führerschein m; **~ school** n Fahrschule f; **~ test** n Fahrprüfung f

drizzle ['drɪzl] n Nieselregen m ♦ vi nieseln

droll [drəʊl] adj drollig

drone [drəʊn] n (sound) Brummen nt; (bee) Drohne f

drool [dru:l] vi sabbern

droop [dru:p] vi (schlaff) herabhängen

drop [drɒp] n (of liquid) Tropfen m; (fall) Fall m ♦ vt fallen lassen; (lower) senken; (abandon) fallenlassen ♦ vi (fall) herunterfallen; **~s** npl (MED) Tropfen pl; **~ off** vi (sleep) einschlafen ♦ vt (passenger) absetzen; **~ out** vi (withdraw) ausscheiden; **~out** n Aussteiger m; **~per** n Pipette f; **~pings** npl Kot m

drought [draʊt] n Dürre f

drove [drəʊv] pt of drive

drown [draʊn] vt ertränken; (sound) übertönen ♦ vi ertrinken

drowsy ['draʊzɪ] adj schläfrig

drudgery ['drʌdʒərɪ] n Plackerei f

drug [drʌg] n (MED) Arznei f; (narcotic) Rauschgift nt ♦ vt betäuben; **~ addict** n Rauschgiftsüchtige(r) m(f); **~gist** (US) n Drogist(in) m(f); **~store** (US) n Drogerie f

drum [drʌm] n Trommel f ♦ vi trommeln; **~s** npl (MUS) Schlagzeug nt; **~mer** n Trommler m

drunk [drʌŋk] pp of drink ♦ adj betrunken ♦ n (also: **~ard**) Trinker(in) m(f); **~en** adj betrunken

dry [draɪ] adj trocken ♦ vt (ab)trocknen ♦ vi trocknen; **~ up** vt austrocknen ♦ vt (dishes) abtrocknen; **~ cleaning** n chemische Reinigung f; **~er** n Trockner m; (US: spindryer) (Wäsche)schleuder f; **~ goods store** (US) n Kurzwarengeschäft nt; **~ness** n Trockenheit f; **~rot** n Hausschwamm m

DSS n abbr (= Department of Social Security) ≈ Sozialministerium nt

dual ['djʊəl] adj doppelt; **~ carriageway** (BRIT) n zweispurige Fahrbahn f; **~ nationality** n doppelte Staatsangehörigkeit f; **~-purpose** adj Mehrzweck-

dubbed [dʌbd] adj (film) synchronisiert

dubious ['djuːbɪəs] adj zweifelhaft

duchess ['dʌtʃɪs] n Herzogin f

duck [dʌk] n Ente f ♦ vi sich ducken; **~ling** n Entchen nt

duct [dʌkt] n Röhre f

dud [dʌd] n Niete f ♦ adj (cheque) ungedeckt

due [djuː] adj fällig; (fitting) angemessen ♦ n Gebühr f; (right) Recht nt ♦ adv (south etc) genau; **~s** pl (for club, union) Beitrag m; (in harbour) Gebühren pl; **~ to** wegen +gen

duel ['djʊəl] n Duell nt

duet [dju:'et] n Duett nt

duffel ['dʌfl] adj: **~ bag** Matchbeutel m, Matchsack m; **~ coat** n Dufflecoat m

dug [dʌg] pt, pp of **dig**

duke [djuːk] n Herzog m

dull [dʌl] adj (colour, weather) trübe; (stupid) schwer von Begriff; (boring) langweilig ♦ vt abstumpfen

duly ['djuːlɪ] adv ordnungsgemäß

dumb [dʌm] adj stumm; (inf: stupid) doof, blöde; **~founded** [dʌm'faʊndəd] adj verblüfft

dummy ['dʌmɪ] n Schneiderpuppe f; (substitute) Attrappe f; (BRIT: for baby) Schnuller m ♦ adj Schein-

dump [dʌmp] n Abfallhaufen m; (MIL) Stapelplatz m; (inf: place) Nest nt ♦ vt abladen, auskippen; **~ing** n (COMM) Schleuderexport m; (of rubbish) Schuttabladen nt

dumpling ['dʌmplɪŋ] n Kloß m, Knödel m

dumpy ['dʌmpɪ] adj pummelig

dunce [dʌns] n Dummkopf m

dune [djuːn] n Düne f

dung [dʌŋ] n Dünger m

dungarees [dʌŋgə'riːz] npl Latzhose f

dungeon ['dʌndʒən] n Kerker m

dupe [djuːp] n Gefoppte(r) m ♦ vt hintergehen, anführen

duplex ['djuːpleks] (US) n zweistöckige Wohnung f

duplicate [n 'djuːplɪkɪt, vb 'djuːplɪkeɪt] n Duplikat nt ♦ vt verdoppeln; (make copies) kopieren; **in ~** in doppelter Ausführung

duplicity [djuː'plɪsɪtɪ] n Doppelspiel nt

durable ['djʊərəbl] adj haltbar

duration [djʊə'reɪʃən] n Dauer f

duress [djʊə'res] n: **under ~** unter Zwang

during ['djʊərɪŋ] prep während +gen

dusk [dʌsk] n Abenddämmerung f

dust [dʌst] n Staub m ♦ vt abstauben; (sprinkle) bestäuben; **~bin** (BRIT) n Mülleimer m; **~er** n Staubtuch nt; **~ jacket** n Schutzumschlag m; **~man** (BRIT: irreg) n Müllmann m; **~y** adj staubig

Dutch [dʌtʃ] adj holländisch, niederländisch ♦ n (LING) Holländisch nt, Niederländisch nt; **the ~** npl (people) die Holländer pl, die Niederländer pl; **to go ~** getrennte Kasse machen; **~man/woman** (irreg) n Holländer(in) m(f), Niederländer(in) m(f)

dutiful ['djuːtɪfʊl] adj pflichtbewußt

duty ['djuːtɪ] n Pflicht f; (job) Aufgabe f; (tax) Einfuhrzoll m; **on ~** im Dienst; **~-free** adj zollfrei

duvet ['duːveɪ] (BRIT) n Daunendecke f

dwarf [dwɔːf] (pl dwarves) n Zwerg m ♦ vt überragen

dwell [dwel] (pt, pp dwelt) vi wohnen; **~ on** vt fus verweilen bei; **~ing** n Wohnung f

dwelt [dwelt] pt, pp of **dwell**

dwindle ['dwɪndl] vi schwinden

dye [daɪ] n Farbstoff m ♦ vt färben

dying ['daɪɪŋ] adj (person) sterbend; (moments) letzt

dyke [daɪk] (BRIT) n (channel) Kanal m; (barrier) Deich m, Damm m

dynamic [daɪ'næmɪk] adj dynamisch

dynamite ['daɪnəmaɪt] n Dynamit nt

dynamo ['daɪnəməʊ] n Dynamo m

dyslexia [dɪs'leksɪə] n Legasthenie f

E

E [i:] n (MUS) E nt

each [i:tʃ] adj jeder/jede/jedes ♦ pron (ein) jeder/(eine) jede/(ein) jedes; ~ other einander; they have two books – sie haben je 2 Bücher; ~ other, sich

eager ['i:gə*] adj eifrig

eagle ['i:gl] n Adler m

ear [ɪə*] n Ohr nt; (of corn) Ähre f; ~ache n Ohrenschmerzen pl; ~drum n Trommelfell nt

earl [ɜːl] n Graf m

early ['ɜːlɪ] adj, adv früh; ~ retirement n vorzeitige Pensionierung

earmark ['ɪəmɑːk] vt vorsehen

earn [ɜːn] vt verdienen

earnest ['ɜːnɪst] adj ernst; in ~ im Ernst

earnings ['ɜːnɪŋz] npl Verdienst m

earphones ['ɪəfəʊnz] npl Kopfhörer pl

earring ['ɪərɪŋ] n Ohrring m

earshot ['ɪəʃɒt] n Hörweite f

earth [ɜːθ] n Erde f; (BRIT: ELEC) Erdung f ♦ vt erden; ~enware n Steingut nt

earthquake [-kweɪk] n Erdbeben nt

earthy ['ɜːθɪ] adj roh; (sensual) sinnlich

earwig ['ɪəwɪg] n Ohrwurm m

ease [i:z] n (simplicity) Leichtigkeit f; (social) Ungezwungenheit f ♦ vt (soothe) lindern; (burden) erleichtern; at ~ ungezwungen; (MIL) rührt euch!; ~ off or up vi nachlassen

easel ['i:zl] n Staffelei f

easily ['i:zɪlɪ] adv leicht

east [i:st] n Osten m ♦ adj östlich ♦ adv nach Osten

Easter ['i:stə*] n Ostern nt; ~ egg n

Osterei nt

easterly ['i:stəlɪ] adj östlich, Ost-

eastern ['i:stən] adj östlich

eastward(s) ['i:stwəd(z)] adv ostwärts

easy ['i:zɪ] adj (task) einfach; (life) bequem; (manner) ungezwungen, natürlich ♦ adv leicht; ~ chair n Sessel m; ~-going adj gelassen; (lax) lässig

eat [i:t] (pt ate, pp eaten) vt essen; (animals) fressen; (destroy) (zer)fressen ♦ vi essen; fressen; ~ away vt zerfressen; ~ into vt fus zerfressen

eaten pp of eat

eau de Cologne [əʊdəkə'ləʊn] n Kölnisch Wasser nt

eaves [i:vz] npl Dachrand m

eavesdrop ['i:vzdrɒp] vi lauschen; to ~ on sb jdn belauschen

ebb [eb] n Ebbe f ♦ vi (fig: also: ~ away) (ab)ebben

ebony ['ebənɪ] n Ebenholz nt

ebullient [ɪ'bʌlɪənt] adj sprudelnd, temperamentvoll

EC n abbr (= European Community) EG f

eccentric [ɪk'sentrɪk] adj exzentrisch ♦ n Exzentriker(in) m(f)

ecclesiastical [ɪkliːzɪ'æstɪkəl] adj kirchlich

echo ['ekəʊ] (pl ~es) n Echo nt ♦ vt zurückwerfen; (fig) nachbeten ♦ vi widerhallen

eclipse [ɪ'klɪps] n Finsternis f ♦ vt verfinstern

ecology [ɪ'kɒlədʒɪ] n Ökologie f

economic [i:kə'nɒmɪk] adj wirtschaftlich; ~al adj wirtschaftlich; (person) sparsam; ~s n Volkswirtschaft f

economist [ɪ'kɒnəmɪst] n Volkswirt(schaftler) m

economize [ɪ'kɒnəmaɪz] vi sparen

economy [ɪ'kɒnəmɪ] n (thrift) Sparsamkeit f; (of country) Wirtschaft f

ecstasy ['ekstəsɪ] n Ekstase f; (drug) Ecstasy nt

ecstatic [eks'tætɪk] adj hingerissen

ECU ['eɪkjuː] n abbr (= European Currency Unit) ECU m

ecumenical [iːkjʊˈmenɪkəl] adj ökumenisch

eczema ['eksɪmə] n Ekzem nt

edge [edʒ] n Rand m; (of knife) Schneide f ♦ vt (SEWING) einfassen; **on** ~ (fig) = **edgy**; **to** ~ **away from** langsam abrücken von; ~**ways** adv: **he couldn't get a word in** ~**ways** er kam überhaupt nicht zu Wort

edgy ['edʒɪ] adj nervös

edible ['edɪbl] adj eßbar

edict ['iːdɪkt] n Erlaß m

edifice ['edɪfɪs] n Gebäude nt

Edinburgh [edɪnbərə] n (GEO) Edinburgh nt

edit ['edɪt] vt redigieren; ~**ion** [ɪˈdɪʃən] n Ausgabe f; ~**or** n (of newspaper) Redakteur m; (of book) Lektor m

editorial [edɪˈtɔːrɪəl] adj Redaktions- ♦ n Leitartikel m

educate ['edjʊkeɪt] vt erziehen, (aus)bilden

education [edjʊˈkeɪʃən] n (teaching) Unterricht m; (system) Schulwesen nt; (schooling) Erziehung f; Bildung f; ~**al** adj pädagogisch

eel [iːl] n Aal m

eerie ['ɪərɪ] adj unheimlich

effect [ɪˈfekt] n Wirkung f ♦ vt bewirken; ~**s** npl (sound, visual) Effekte pl; **in** ~ in der Tat; **to take** ~ (law) in Kraft treten; (drug) wirken; ~**ive** adj wirksam, effektiv; ~**ively** adv wirksam, effektiv

effeminate [ɪˈfemɪnɪt] adj weibisch

effervescent [efəˈvesnt] adj (also fig) sprudelnd

efficacy ['efɪkəsɪ] n Wirksamkeit f

efficiency [ɪˈfɪʃənsɪ] n Leistungsfähigkeit f

efficient [ɪˈfɪʃənt] adj tüchtig; (TECH) leistungsfähig; (method) wirksam

effigy ['efɪdʒɪ] n Abbild nt

effort ['efət] n Anstrengung f; ~**less** adj mühelos

effrontery [ɪˈfrʌntərɪ] n Unverfroren-

heit f

effusive [ɪˈfjuːsɪv] adj überschwenglich

e.g. adv abbr (= exempli gratia) z.B.

egalitarian [ɪgælɪˈtɛərɪən] adj Gleichheits-, egalitär

egg [eg] n Ei nt; ~ **on** vt anstacheln; ~**cup** n Eierbecher m; ~**plant** (esp US) n Aubergine f; ~**shell** n Eierschale f

ego ['iːgəʊ] n Ich nt, Selbst nt

egotism ['egəʊtɪzəm] n Ichbezogenheit f

egotist ['egəʊtɪst] n Egozentriker m

Egypt ['iːdʒɪpt] n Ägypten nt; ~**ian** [ɪˈdʒɪpʃən] adj ägyptisch ♦ n Ägypter(in) m(f)

eiderdown ['aɪdədaʊn] n Daunendecke f

eight [eɪt] num acht; ~**een** num achtzehn; ~**h** [eɪtθ] adj achte(r, s) ♦ n Achtel nt; ~**y** num achtzig

Eire ['ɛərə] n Irland nt

either ['aɪðə*] conj: ~ ... **or** entweder ... oder ♦ pron: ~ **of the two** eine(r, s) von beiden ♦ adj: **on** ~ **side** auf beiden Seiten ♦ adv: **I don't** ~ ich auch nicht; **I don't want** ~ ich will keins von beiden

eject [ɪˈdʒekt] vt ausstoßen, vertreiben

eke [iːk] vt: **to** ~ **out** strecken

elaborate [adj ɪˈlæbərɪt, vb ɪˈlæbəreɪt] adj sorgfältig ausgearbeitet, ausführlich ♦ vt sorgfältig ausarbeiten ♦ vi ausführlich darstellen

elapse [ɪˈlæps] vi vergehen

elastic [ɪˈlæstɪk] n Gummiband nt ♦ adj elastisch; ~ **band** (BRIT) n Gummiband nt

elated [ɪˈleɪtɪd] adj froh

elation [ɪˈleɪʃən] n gehobene Stimmung f

elbow ['elbəʊ] n Ellbogen m

elder ['eldə*] adj älter ♦ n Ältere(r) mf; ~**ly** adj ältere(r, s) ♦ npl: **the** ~**ly** die Älteren pl

eldest ['eldɪst] adj älteste(r, s) ♦ n Älteste mf

elect [ɪ'lekt] vt wählen ♦ adj zukünftig; **~ion** [ɪ'lekʃən] n Wahl f; **~ioneering** [ɪlekʃə'nɪərɪŋ] n Wahlpropaganda f; **~or** n Wähler m; **~oral** adj Wahl-; **~orate** n Wähler pl, Wählerschaft f

electric [ɪ'lektrɪk] adj elektrisch, Elektro-; **~al** adj elektrisch; **~ blanket** n Heizdecke f; **~ chair** n elektrische(r) Stuhl m; **~ fire** n elektrische(r) Heizofen m

electrician [ɪlek'trɪʃən] n Elektriker m

electricity [ɪlek'trɪsɪtɪ] n Elektrizität f

electrify [ɪ'lektrɪfaɪ] vt elektrifizieren; (fig) elektrisieren

electrocute [ɪ'lektrəkjuːt] vt durch elektrischen Strom töten

electronic [ɪlek'trɒnɪk] adj elektronisch, Elektronen-; **~ mail** n elektronische(r) Briefkasten m; **~s** n Elektronik f

elegance ['elɪɡəns] n Eleganz f

elegant ['elɪɡənt] adj elegant

element ['elɪmənt] n Element nt; **~ary** [elɪ'mentərɪ] adj einfach; (primary) Grund-

elephant ['elɪfənt] n Elefant m

elevate ['elɪveɪt] vt emporheben

elevation [elɪ'veɪʃən] n (height) Erhebung f; (ARCHIT) (Quer)schnitt m

elevator ['elɪveɪtə*] n (US) n Fahrstuhl m, Aufzug m

eleven [ɪ'levn] num elf; **~ses** (BRIT) npl ≈ zweite(s) Frühstück nt; **~th** adj elfte(r, s)

elf [elf] (pl **elves**) n Elfe f

elicit [ɪ'lɪsɪt] vt herausbekommen

eligible ['elɪdʒəbl] adj wählbar; to be **~ for** a pension pensionsberechtigt sein

eliminate [ɪ'lɪmɪneɪt] vt ausschalten

elimination [ɪlɪmɪ'neɪʃən] n Ausschaltung f

elite [eɪ'liːt] n Elite f

elm [elm] n Ulme f

elocution [elə'kjuːʃən] n Sprecherziehung f

elongated ['iːlɒŋɡeɪtɪd] adj verlängert

elope [ɪ'ləup] vi entlaufen

eloquence ['eləkwəns] n Beredsamkeit f

eloquent ['eləkwənt] adj redegewandt

else [els] adv sonst; who **~**? wer sonst?; somebody **~** jemand anders; or **~** sonst; **~where** adv anderswo, woanders

elucidate [ɪ'luːsɪdeɪt] vt erläutern

elude [ɪ'luːd] vt entgehen +dat

elusive [ɪ'luːsɪv] adj schwer faßbar

elves [elvz] npl of **elf**

emaciated [ɪ'meɪsɪeɪtɪd] adj abgezehrt

emanate ['eməneɪt] vi: to **~ from** ausströmen aus

emancipate [ɪ'mænsɪpeɪt] vt emanzipieren; (slave) freilassen

emancipation [ɪmænsɪ'peɪʃən] n Emanzipation f; Freilassung f

embankment [ɪm'bæŋkmənt] n (of river) Uferböschung f; (of road) Straßendamm m

embargo [ɪm'bɑːɡəu] (pl **~es**) n Embargo nt

embark [ɪm'bɑːk] vi sich einschiffen; **~ on** vt fus unternehmen; **~ation** [embɑː'keɪʃən] n Einschiffung f

embarrass [ɪm'bærəs] vt in Verlegenheit bringen; **~ed** adj verlegen; **~ing** adj peinlich; **~ment** n Verlegenheit f

embassy ['embəsɪ] n Botschaft f

embed [ɪm'bed] vt einbetten

embellish [ɪm'belɪʃ] vt verschönern

embers ['embəz] npl Glut(asche) f

embezzle [ɪm'bezl] vt unterschlagen; **~ment** n Unterschlagung f

embitter [ɪm'bɪtə*] vt verbittern

embody [ɪm'bɒdɪ] vt (ideas) verkörpern; (new features) (in sich) vereinigen

embossed [ɪm'bɒst] adj geprägt

embrace [ɪm'breɪs] vt umarmen (include) einschließen ♦ vi sich umarmen ♦ n Umarmung f

embroider [ɪm'brɔɪdə*] vt (be-)sticken; (story) ausschmücken; **~y** n

Stickerei f
emerald ['ɛmərəld] n Smaragd m
emerge [ɪ'mɜːdʒ] vi auftauchen; (truth) herauskommen
emergence [ɪ'mɜːdʒəns] n Erscheinen nt
emergency [ɪ'mɜːdʒənsɪ] n Notfall m; ~ **cord** (US) n Notbremse f; ~ **exit** n Notausgang m; ~ **landing** n Notlandung f; ~ **services** npl Notdienste pl
emery board ['ɛmərɪ-] n Papiernagelfeile f
emetic [ɪ'mɛtɪk] n Brechmittel nt
emigrant ['ɛmɪgrənt] n Auswanderer m
emigrate ['ɛmɪgreɪt] vi auswandern
emigration [ɛmɪ'greɪʃən] n Auswanderung f
eminence ['ɛmɪnəns] n hohe(r) Rang m
eminent ['ɛmɪnənt] adj bedeutend
emission [ɪ'mɪʃən] n Ausströmen nt; ~s npl Emissionen fpl
emit [ɪ'mɪt] vt von sich dat geben
emotion [ɪ'məʊʃən] n Emotion f, Gefühl nt; ~**al** adj (person) emotional; (scene) ergreifend
emotive [ɪ'məʊtɪv] adj gefühlsbetont
emperor ['ɛmpərə*] n Kaiser m
emphases ['ɛmfəsiːz] npl of emphasis
emphasis ['ɛmfəsɪs] n (LING) Betonung f; (fig) Nachdruck m
emphasize ['ɛmfəsaɪz] vt betonen
emphatic [ɪm'fætɪk] adj nachdrücklich; ~**ally** [ɪm'fætɪkəlɪ] adv nachdrücklich
empire ['ɛmpaɪə*] n Reich nt
empirical [ɛm'pɪrɪkəl] adj empirisch
employ [ɪm'plɔɪ] vt (hire) anstellen; (use) verwenden; ~**ee** [ɛmplɔɪ'iː] n Angestellte(r) mf; ~**er** n Arbeitgeber(in) m(f); ~**ment** n Beschäftigung f; ~**ment agency** n Stellenvermittlung f
empower [ɪm'paʊə*] vt: to ~ sb to do sth jdn ermächtigen, etw zu tun
empress ['ɛmprɪs] n Kaiserin f
emptiness ['ɛmptɪnɪs] n Leere f

empty ['ɛmptɪ] adj leer ♦ n (bottle) Leergut nt ♦ vt (contents) leeren; (container) ausleeren ♦ vi (water) abfließen; (river) münden; (house) sich leeren; ~**-handed** adj mit leeren Händen
emulate ['ɛmjʊleɪt] vt nacheifern +dat
emulsion [ɪ'mʌlʃən] n Emulsion f
enable [ɪ'neɪbl] vt: to ~ sb to do sth jdm ermöglichen, etw zu tun
enact [ɪn'ækt] vt (law) erlassen; (play) aufführen; (role) spielen
enamel [ɪ'næməl] n Email nt; (of teeth) (Zahn)schmelz m
encased [ɪn'keɪst] adj: ~ in (enclosed) eingeschlossen in +dat; (covered) verkleidet mit
enchant [ɪn'tʃɑːnt] vt bezaubern; ~**ing** adj entzückend
encircle [ɪn'sɜːkl] vt umringen
encl. abbr (= enclosed) Anl.
enclose [ɪn'kləʊz] vt einschließen; to ~ sth (in or with a letter) etw (einem Brief) beilegen; ~**d** (in letter) beiliegend, anbei
enclosure [ɪn'kləʊʒə*] n Einfriedung f; (in letter) Anlage f
encompass [ɪn'kʌmpəs] vt (include) umfassen
encore ['ɒŋkɔː*] n Zugabe f
encounter [ɪn'kaʊntə*] n Begegnung f; (MIL) Zusammenstoß m ♦ vt treffen; (resistance) stoßen auf +acc
encourage [ɪn'kʌrɪdʒ] vt ermutigen; ~**ment** n Ermutigung f, Förderung f
encouraging [ɪn'kʌrɪdʒɪŋ] adj ermutigend, vielversprechend
encroach [ɪn'krəʊtʃ] vi: to ~ (up)on eindringen in +acc; (time) in Anspruch nehmen
encrusted [ɪn'krʌstəd] adj: ~ with besetzt mit
encumber [ɪn'kʌmbə*] vt: to be ~ed with (parcels) beladen sein mit; (debts) belastet sein mit
encyclop(a)edia [ɛnsaɪkləʊ'piːdɪə] n Konversationslexikon nt
end [ɛnd] n Ende nt, Schluß m; (purpose) Zweck m ♦ vt (also: bring to

an ~, put an ~ to) beenden ♦ vi zu Ende gehen; **in the** ~ zum Schluß; **on** ~ (object) hochkant; **to stand on** ~ (hair) zu Berge stehen; **for hours on** ~ stundenlang; ~ **up** vi landen

endanger [ɪn'deɪndʒə*] vt gefährden

endearing [ɪn'dɪərɪŋ] adj gewinnend

endeavour [ɪn'devə*] (US **endeavor**) n Bestrebung f ♦ vi sich bemühen

ending ['endɪŋ] n Ende nt

endive ['endaɪv] n Endivie f

endless ['endlɪs] adj endlos

endorse [ɪn'dɔːs] vt unterzeichnen; (approve) unterstützen; ~**ment** n (on licence) Eintrag m

endow [ɪn'dau] vt: **to** ~ **sb with sth** jdm etw verleihen; (with money) jdm etw stiften

endurance [ɪn'djuərəns] n Ausdauer f

endure [ɪn'djuə*] vt ertragen ♦ vi (last) (fort)dauern

enemy ['enɪmɪ] n Feind m ♦ adj feindlich

energetic [enə'dʒetɪk] adj tatkräftig

energy ['enədʒɪ] n Energie f

enforce [ɪn'fɔːs] vt durchsetzen

engage [ɪn'geɪdʒ] vt (employ) einstellen; (in conversation) verwickeln; (TECH) einschalten ♦ vi ineinandergreifen; (clutch) fassen; **to** ~ **in** sich beteiligen an +dat; ~**d** adj verlobt; (BRIT: TEL, toilet) besetzt; (: busy) beschäftigt; **to get** ~**d** sich verloben; ~**d tone** (BRIT) n (TEL) Besetztzeichen nt; ~**ment** n (appointment) Verabredung f; (to marry) Verlobung f; (MIL) Gefecht nt; ~**ment ring** n Verlobungsring m

engaging [ɪn'geɪdʒɪŋ] adj gewinnend

engender [ɪn'dʒendə*] vt hervorrufen

engine ['endʒɪn] n (AUT) Motor m; (RAIL) Lokomotive f; ~ **driver** n (RAIL) Lok(omotiv)führer(in) m(f)

engineer [endʒɪ'nɪə*] n Ingenieur m; (US: RAIL) Lok(omotiv)führer(in) m(f); ~**ing** [endʒɪ'nɪərɪŋ] n Technik f

England ['ɪŋglənd] n England nt

English ['ɪŋglɪʃ] adj (LING) Englisch nt; **the** ~ npl (people) die Engländer pl; **the** ~ **Channel** n der Ärmelkanal m; ~**man/woman** (irreg) n Engländer(in) m(f)

engraving [ɪn'greɪvɪŋ] n Stich m

engrossed [ɪn'grəust] adj vertieft

engulf [ɪn'gʌlf] vt verschlingen

enhance [ɪn'hɑːns] vt steigern, heben

enigma [ɪ'nɪgmə] n Rätsel nt; ~**tic** [enɪg'mætɪk] adj rätselhaft

enjoy [ɪn'dʒɔɪ] vt genießen; (privilege) besitzen; **to** ~ **o.s.** sich amüsieren; ~**able** adj erfreulich; ~**ment** n Genuß m, Freude f

enlarge [ɪn'lɑːdʒ] vt erweitern; (PHOT) vergrößern ♦ vi: **to** ~ **on sth** etw weiter ausführen; ~**ment** n Vergrößerung f

enlighten [ɪn'laɪtn] vt aufklären; ~**ment** n: **the E~ment** (HIST) die Aufklärung

enlist [ɪn'lɪst] vt gewinnen ♦ vi (MIL) sich melden

enmity ['enmɪtɪ] n Feindschaft f

enormity [ɪ'nɔːmɪtɪ] n Ungeheuerlichkeit f

enormous [ɪ'nɔːməs] adj ungeheuer

enough [ɪ'nʌf] adj, adv genug; **funnily** ~ komischerweise

enquire [ɪn'kwaɪə*] vt, vi = **inquire**

enrage [ɪn'reɪdʒ] vt wütend machen

enrich [ɪn'rɪtʃ] vt bereichern

enrol [ɪn'rəul] vt einschreiben ♦ vi (register) sich anmelden; ~**ment** n (for course) Anmeldung f

en route [ɑ̃'ruːt] adv unterwegs

ensign ['ensaɪn, 'ensən] n (NAUT) Flagge f; (MIL) Fähnrich m

enslave [ɪn'sleɪv] vt versklaven

ensue [ɪn'sjuː] vi folgen, sich ergeben

ensure [ɪn'ʃuə*] vt garantieren

entail [ɪn'teɪl] vt mit sich bringen

entangle [ɪn'tæŋgl] vt verwirren, verstricken; ~**d** adj: **to become** ~**d** (**in**) (in net, rope etc) sich verfangen (in +dat)

enter ['entə*] vt eintreten in +dat,

betreten; (club) beitreten +dat; (in book) eintragen ♦ vi hereinkommen, hineingehen; ~ **for** vt fus sich beteiligen an +dat; ~ **into** vt fus (agreement) eingehen; (plans) eine Rolle spielen bei; ~ **(up)on** vt fus betreten
enterprise ['entəpraɪz] n (in person) Initiative f; (COMM) Unternehmen nt
enterprising ['entəpraɪzɪŋ] adj unternehmungslustig
entertain [entə'teɪn] vt (guest) bewirten; (amuse) unterhalten; ~**er** n Unterhaltungskünstler(in) f(m); ~**ing** adj unterhaltsam; ~**ment** n Unterhaltung f
enthralled [ɪn'θrɔːld] adj gefesselt
enthusiasm [ɪn'θuːzɪæzm] n Begeisterung f
enthusiast [ɪn'θuːzɪæst] n Enthusiast m; ~**ic** [ɪnθuːzɪ'æstɪk] adj begeistert
entice [ɪn'taɪs] vt verleiten, locken
entire [ɪn'taɪə*] adj ganz; ~**ly** adv ganz, völlig; ~**ty** [ɪn'taɪərətɪ] n: in its ~ty in seiner Gesamtheit
entitle [ɪn'taɪtl] vt (allow) berechtigen; (name) betiteln; ~**d** adj (book) mit dem Titel; to be ~d to sth dazu berechtigt sein, etw zu tun; to be ~d to do sth das Recht haben, etw zu tun
entity ['entɪtɪ] n Ding nt, Wesen nt
entourage [ɒntu'rɑːʒ] n Gefolge nt
entrails ['entreɪlz] npl Eingeweide pl
entrance [n 'entrəns, vb ɪn'trɑːns] n Eingang m; (entering) Eintritt m ♦ vt hinreißen; ~ **examination** n Aufnahmeprüfung f; ~ **fee** n Eintrittsgeld nt; ~ **ramp** (US) n (AUT) Einfahrt f
entrant ['entrənt] n (for exam) Kandidat m; (in race) Teilnehmer m
entreat [ɪn'triːt] vt anflehen
entrenched [ɪn'trentʃt] adj (fig) verwurzelt
entrepreneur [ɒntrəprə'nɜː*] n Unternehmer(in) f(m)
entrust [ɪn'trʌst] vt: to ~ sb with sth or sth to sb jdm etw anvertrauen

entry ['entrɪ] n Eingang m; (THEAT) Auftritt m; (in account) Eintragung f; (in dictionary) Eintrag m; "no ~" "Eintritt verboten"; (for cars) "Einfahrt verboten"; ~ **form** n Anmeldeformular nt; ~ **phone** n Sprechanlage f
enumerate [ɪ'njuːməreɪt] vt aufzählen
enunciate [ɪ'nʌnsɪeɪt] vt aussprechen
envelop [ɪn'veləp] vt einhüllen
envelope ['envələup] n Umschlag m
enviable ['envɪəbl] adj beneidenswert
envious ['envɪəs] adj neidisch
environment [ɪn'vaɪərənmənt] n Umgebung f; (ECOLOGY) Umwelt f; ~**al** [ɪnvaɪrən'mentl] adj Umwelt-; ~**friendly** adj umweltfreundlich
envisage [ɪn'vɪzɪdʒ] vt sich dat vorstellen
envoy ['envɔɪ] n Gesandte(r) mf
envy ['envɪ] n Neid m ♦ vt: to ~ sb sth jdn um etw beneiden
enzyme ['enzaɪm] n Enzym nt
ephemeral [ɪ'femərəl] adj flüchtig
epic ['epɪk] n Epos nt ♦ adj episch
epidemic [epɪ'demɪk] n Epidemie f
epilepsy ['epɪlepsɪ] n Epilepsie f
epileptic [epɪ'leptɪk] adj epileptisch ♦ n Epileptiker(in) f(m)
episode ['epɪsəud] n (incident) Vorfall m; (story) Episode f
epitaph ['epɪtɑːf] n Grabinschrift f
epithet ['epɪθet] n Beiname m
epitome [ɪ'pɪtəmɪ] n Inbegriff m
epitomize [ɪ'pɪtəmaɪz] vt verkörpern
equable ['ekwəbl] adj ausgeglichen
equal ['iːkwəl] adj gleich ♦ n Gleichgestellte(r) mf ♦ vt gleichkommen +dat; to ~ **the task** der Aufgabe gewachsen; ~**ity** [ɪ'kwɒlɪtɪ] n Gleichheit f; (~ **rights**) Gleichberechtigung f; ~**ize** vt gleichmachen ♦ vi (SPORT) ausgleichen; ~**izer** n (SPORT) Ausgleich(streffer) m; ~**ly** adv gleich
equanimity [ekwə'nɪmɪtɪ] n Gleichmut m
equate [ɪ'kweɪt] vt gleichsetzen

equation 91 **ethical**

equation [ɪ'kweɪʒən] n Gleichung f

equator [ɪ'kweɪtə*] n Äquator m

equestrian [ɪ'kwestrɪən] adj Reit-

equilibrium [i:kwɪ'lɪbrɪəm] n Gleichgewicht nt

equinox ['i:kwɪnɒks] n Tag- und
Nachtgleiche f

equip [ɪ'kwɪp] vt ausrüsten; **~ment**
n Ausrüstung f; (TECH) Gerät nt

equitable ['ekwɪtəbl] adj gerecht,
billig

equities ['ekwɪtɪz] (BRIT) npl (FIN)
Stammaktien pl

equivalent [ɪ'kwɪvələnt] adj gleichwertig, entsprechend ♦ n Äquivalent
nt; (in money) Gegenwert m; **~ to**
gleichwertig +dat, entsprechend +dat

equivocal [ɪ'kwɪvəkəl] adj zweideutig

era ['ɪərə] n Epoche f, Ära f

eradicate [ɪ'rædɪkeɪt] vt ausrotten

erase [ɪ'reɪz] vt auslöschen; (tape)
löschen; **~r** n Radiergummi m

erect [ɪ'rekt] adj aufrecht ♦ vt errichten

erection [ɪ'rekʃən] n Errichtung f;
(ANAT) Erektion f

ergonomics [ɜ:gə'nɒmɪks] n Ergonomie f, Ergonomik f

ERM n abbr (= Exchange Rate
Mechanism) Wechselkursmechanis-
mus m

erode [ɪ'rəʊd] vt zerfressen; (land)
auswaschen

erotic [ɪ'rɒtɪk] adj erotisch; **~ism**
[ɪ'rɒtɪsɪzəm] n Erotik f

err [ɜ:*] vi sich irren

errand ['erənd] n Besorgung f

erratic [ɪ'rætɪk] adj unberechenbar

erroneous [ɪ'rəʊnɪəs] adj irrig

error ['erə*] n Fehler m

erudite ['erʊdaɪt] adj gelehrt

erupt [ɪ'rʌpt] vi ausbrechen; **~ion**
[ɪ'rʌpʃən] n Ausbruch m

escalate ['eskəleɪt] vi sich steigern

escalator ['eskəleɪtə*] n Rolltreppe f

escape [ɪs'keɪp] n Flucht f; (of gas)
Entweichen nt ♦ vi entkommen; (pri-
soners) fliehen; (leak) entweichen ♦
vt entkommen +dat

escapism [ɪs'keɪpɪzəm] n Flucht f
(vor der Wirklichkeit)

escort [n 'eskɔ:t, vb ɪs'kɔ:t] n (person accompanying) Begleiter m;
(guard) Eskorte f ♦ vt (lady) begleiten; (MIL) eskortieren

especially [ɪs'peʃəlɪ] adv besonders

espionage ['espɪənɑ:ʒ] n Spionage f

esplanade ['espləneɪd] n Promenade
f

espouse [ɪ'spaʊz] vt Partei ergreifen
für

Esquire [ɪs'kwaɪə*] n: J. Brown **~**
Herrn J. Brown

essay ['eseɪ] n Aufsatz m; (LITER)
Essay m

essence ['esəns] n (quality) Wesen
nt; (extract) Essenz f

essential [ɪ'senʃl] adj (necessary)
unentbehrlich; (basic) wesentlich ♦ n
Allernötigste(s) nt; **~ly** adv eigentlich

establish [ɪs'tæblɪʃ] vt (set up)
gründen; (prove) nachweisen; **~ed**
adj anerkannt; (belief, laws etc) herrschend; **~ment** n (setting up) Einrichtung f; the E**~ment** das Establish-
ment

estate [ɪs'teɪt] n Gut nt; (BRIT: housing **~**) Siedlung f; (will) Nachlaß
m; **~ agent** (BRIT) n Grund-
stücksmakler m; **~ car** (BRIT) n
Kombiwagen m

esteem [ɪs'ti:m] n Wertschätzung f

esthetic [ɪs'θetɪk] (US) adj =
aesthetic

estimate [n 'estɪmət, vb 'estɪmeɪt] n
Schätzung f; (of price) (Ko-
sten)voranschlag m ♦ vt schätzen

estimation [estɪ'meɪʃən] n Einschätzung f; (esteem) Achtung f

estranged [ɪ'streɪndʒd] adj entfrem-
det

estuary ['estjʊərɪ] n Mündung f

etc abbr (= et cetera) usw

etching ['etʃɪŋ] n Kupferstich m

eternal [ɪ'tɜ:nl] adj ewig

eternity [ɪ'tɜ:nɪtɪ] n Ewigkeit f

ether ['i:θə*] n Äther m

ethical ['eθɪkəl] adj ethisch

ethics ['eθɪks] n Ethik f ♦ npl Moral f

Ethiopia [i:θɪ'əʊpɪə] n Äthiopien nt

ethnic ['eθnɪk] adj Volks-, ethnisch

ethos ['i:θɒs] n Gesinnung f

etiquette ['etɪket] n Etikette f

euphemism ['ju:fɪmɪzəm] n Euphemismus m

Eurocheque ['jʊərəʊ'tʃek] n Euroscheck m

Europe ['jʊərəp] n Europa nt; **~an** [jʊərə'pi:ən] adj europäisch ♦ n Europäer(in) m(f)

euro-sceptic n Kritiker(in) f(m) der Europäischen Gemeinschaft

evacuate [ɪ'vækjʊeɪt] vt (place) räumen; (people) evakuieren

evacuation [ɪvækjʊ'eɪʃən] n Räumung f; Evakuierung f

evade [ɪ'veɪd] vt (escape) entkommen +dat; (avoid) meiden; (duty) sich entziehen +dat

evaluate [ɪ'væljʊeɪt] vt bewerten; (information) auswerten

evaporate [ɪ'væpəreɪt] vi verdampfen ♦ vt verdampfen lassen; **~d milk** n Kondensmilch f

evasion [ɪ'veɪʒən] n Umgehung f

evasive [ɪ'veɪzɪv] adj ausweichend

eve [i:v] n: **on the ~ of** am Vorabend +gen

even ['i:vən] adj eben; gleichmäßig; (score etc) unentschieden; (number) gerade ♦ adv sogar; you ~ du; to get ~ with sb jdm heimzahlen; ~ if selbst wenn; ~ so dennoch; ~ though obwohl; ~ more sogar noch mehr; ~ out vi sich ausgleichen

evening ['i:vnɪŋ] n Abend m; in the ~ abends, am Abend; ~ class n Abendschule f; ~ dress n (man's) Gesellschaftsanzug m; (woman's) Abendkleid nt

event [ɪ'vent] n (happening) Ereignis nt; (SPORT) Disziplin f; in the ~ of im Falle +gen; ~ful adj ereignisreich

eventual [ɪ'ventʃʊəl] adj (final) schließlich; **~ity** [ɪventʃʊ'ælɪtɪ] n Möglichkeit f; **~ly** adv (at last) am

Ende; (given time) schließlich

ever ['evə] adv (always) immer; (at any time) je(mals); ~ since seitdem ♦ conj seit; have you ~ seen it? haben Sie es je gesehen?; **~green** n Immergrün nt; **~lasting** adj immerwährend

every ['evrɪ] adj jede(r, s); ~ other/third day jeden zweiten/dritten Tag; ~ one of them alle; I have ~ confidence in him ich habe uneingeschränktes Vertrauen in ihn; we wish you ~ success wir wünschen Ihnen viel Erfolg; he's ~ bit as clever as his brother er ist genauso klug wie sein Bruder; ~ now and then ab und zu; **~body** pron = everyone; **~day** adj (daily) täglich; (commonplace) alltäglich, Alltags-; **~one** pron jeder, alle pl; **~thing** pron alles; **~where** adv überall(hin); (wherever) wohin; ~where you go wohin du auch gehst

evict [ɪ'vɪkt] vt ausweisen; **~ion** n Ausweisung f

evidence ['evɪdəns] n (sign) Spur f; (proof) Beweis m; (testimony) Aussage f

evident ['evɪdənt] adj augenscheinlich; **~ly** adv offensichtlich

evil ['i:vl] adj böse ♦ n Böse nt

evocative [ɪ'vɒkətɪv] adj: to be ~ of sth an etw acc erinnern

evoke [ɪ'vəʊk] vt hervorrufen

evolution [i:və'lu:ʃən] n Entwicklung f; (of life) Evolution f

evolve [ɪ'vɒlv] vt entwickeln ♦ vi sich entwickeln

ewe [ju:] n Mutterschaf nt

ex- [eks] prefix Ex-, Alt-, ehemalig

exacerbate [ek'sæsəbeɪt] vt verschlimmern

exact [ɪg'zækt] adj genau ♦ vt (demand) verlangen; **~ing** adj anspruchsvoll; **~ly** adv genau

exaggerate [ɪg'zædʒəreɪt] vt, vi übertreiben

exaggeration [ɪgzædʒə'reɪʃən] n Übertreibung f

exalted [ɪg'zɔ:ltɪd] adj (position, style) hoch; (person) exaltiert

exam [ɪg'zæm] n abbr = **examination**

examination [ɪgzæmɪ'neɪʃən] n Untersuchung f; (SCH) Prüfung f, Examen nt; (customs) Kontrolle f

examine [ɪg'zæmɪn] vt untersuchen; (SCH) prüfen; (consider) erwägen; **~r** n Prüfer m

example [ɪg'zɑːspərɪt] vt zum Beispiel m; for ~ zum Beispiel

exasperate [ɪg'zɑːspəreɪt] vt zum Verzweifeln bringen

exasperating [ɪg'zɑːspəreɪtɪŋ] adj ärgerlich, zum Verzweifeln bringend

exasperation [ɪgzɑːspə'reɪʃən] n Verzweiflung f

excavate ['ekskəveɪt] vt ausgraben

excavation [ekskə'veɪʃən] n Ausgrabung f

exceed [ɪk'siːd] vt überschreiten; (hopes) übertreffen

exceedingly adv (enormously: stupid, rich, pleasant) äußerst

excel [ɪk'sel] vi sich auszeichnen

excellence ['eksələns] n Vortrefflichkeit f

excellency ['eksələnsɪ] n: His E~ Seine Exzellenz f

excellent [ɪk'sept] adj ausgezeichnet

except [ɪk'sept] prep (also: ~ for, ~ing) außer +dat ♦ vt ausnehmen; **~ion** [ɪk'sepʃən] n Ausnahme f; to take ~ion to Anstoß nehmen an +dat; **~ional** [ɪk'sepʃənl] adj außergewöhnlich

excerpt ['eksɜːpt] n Auszug m

excess [ɪk'ses] n Übermaß nt; an ~ of ein Übermaß an +dat; ~ **baggage** n Mehrgepäck nt; ~ **fare** n Nachlösegebühr f; **~ive** adj übermäßig

exchange [ɪks'tʃeɪndʒ] n Austausch m; (also: telephone ~) Zentrale f ♦ vt (goods) tauschen; (greetings) austauschen; (money, blows) wechseln; ~ **rate** n Wechselkurs m

Exchequer [ɪks'tʃekə*] (BRIT) n: the ~ das Schatzamt

excise [n 'eksaɪz, vb ek'saɪz] n Verbrauchssteuer f ♦ vt (MED) herausschneiden

excite [ɪk'saɪt] vt erregen; to get ~d sich aufregen; **~ment** n Aufregung f

exciting [ɪk'saɪtɪŋ] adj spannend

exclaim [ɪks'kleɪm] vi ausrufen

exclamation [eksklə'meɪʃən] n Ausruf m; ~ **mark** n Ausrufezeichen nt

exclude [ɪks'kluːd] vt ausschließen

exclusion [ɪks'kluːʒən] n Ausschluß m

exclusive [ɪks'kluːsɪv] adj (select) exklusiv; (sole) ausschließlich, Allein-; ~ of exclusive +gen; **~ly** adv nur, ausschließlich

excommunicate [ekskə'mjuːnɪkeɪt] vt exkommunizieren

excrement ['ekskrɪmənt] n Kot m

excruciating [ɪks'kruːʃɪeɪtɪŋ] adj qualvoll

excursion [ɪks'kɜːʃən] n Ausflug m

excusable [ɪks'kjuːzəbl] adj entschuldbar

excuse [n ɪks'kjuːs, vb ɪks'kjuːz] n Entschuldigung f ♦ vt entschuldigen; ~ me! entschuldigen Sie!

ex-directory ['eksdaɪ'rektərɪ] (BRIT) adj: to be ~ nicht im Telefonbuch stehen

execute ['eksɪkjuːt] vt (carry out) ausführen; (kill) hinrichten

execution [eksɪ'kjuːʃən] n Ausführung f; (killing) Hinrichtung f; **~er** n Scharfrichter m

executive [ɪg'zekjʊtɪv] n (COMM) Geschäftsführer m; (POL) Exekutive f ♦ adj Exekutiv-, ausführend

executor [ɪg'zekjʊtə*] n Testamentsvollstrecker m

exemplary [ɪg'zemplərɪ] adj musterhaft

exemplify [ɪg'zemplɪfaɪ] vt veranschaulichen

exempt [ɪg'zempt] adj befreit ♦ vt befreien; **~ion** [ɪg'zempʃən] n Befreiung f

exercise ['eksəsaɪz] n Übung f; (power) ausüben; (muscle, patience) üben; (dog) ausführen ♦ vi üben treiben; ~ **bike** n Heimtrainer m; ~ **book** n (Schul)heft nt

exert [ɪg'zɜːt] vt (influence) ausüben; to ~ o.s. sich anstrengen; ~**ion** [ɪg'zɜːʃən] n Anstrengung f

exhale [eks'heɪl] vt, vi ausatmen

exhaust [ɪg'zɔːst] n (fumes) Abgase pl; (pipe) Auspuffrohr nt ♦ vt erschöpfen; ~**ed** adj erschöpft; ~**ion** [ɪg'zɔːstʃən] n Erschöpfung f; ~**ive** adj erschöpfend

exhibit [ɪg'zɪbɪt] n (ART) Ausstellungsstück nt; (JUR) Beweisstück nt ♦ vt ausstellen; ~**ion** [eksɪ'bɪʃən] n (ART) Ausstellung f; (of temper etc) Zurschaustellung f; ~**ionist** [eksɪ'bɪʃənɪst] n Exhibitionist m

exhilarating [ɪg'zɪləreɪtɪŋ] adj erhebend

exhort [ɪg'zɔːt] vt ermahnen

exile ['eksaɪl] n Exil nt; (person) Verbannte(r) mf ♦ vt verbannen

exist [ɪg'zɪst] vi existieren; ~**ence** n Existenz f; ~**ing** adj bestehend

exit ['eksɪt] n Ausgang m; (THEAT) Abgang m ♦ vi abtreten; (COMPUT) aus einem Programm herausgehen; ~ **ramp** (US) n (AUT) Ausfahrt f

exodus ['eksədəs] n Auszug m

exonerate [ɪg'zɔnəreɪt] vt entlasten

exorbitant [ɪg'zɔːbɪtənt] adj übermäßig; (price) Phantasie-

exotic [ɪg'zɔtɪk] adj exotisch

expand [ɪks'pænd] vt, vi erweitern; sich ausdehnen

expanse [ɪks'pæns] n Fläche f

expansion [ɪks'pænʃən] n Erweiterung f

expatriate [eks'pætrɪt] n Ausländer(in) m(f)

expect [ɪks'pekt] vt erwarten; (suppose) annehmen ♦ vi: to be ~ing ein Kind erwarten; ~**ancy** n Erwartung f; ~**ant mother** n werdende Mutter f; ~**ation** [ekspek'teɪʃən] n Hoffnung f

expedience [ɪks'piːdɪəns] n Zweckdienlichkeit f

expediency [ɪks'piːdɪənsɪ] n Zweckdienlichkeit f

expedient [ɪks'piːdɪənt] adj zweckdienlich ♦ n (Hilfs)mittel nt

expedition [ekspɪ'dɪʃən] n Expedition f

expel [ɪks'pel] vt ausweisen; (student) verweisen

expend [ɪks'pend] vt (effort) aufwenden; ~**iture** [ɪk'spendɪtʃə*] n Ausgaben pl

expense [ɪks'pens] n Kosten pl; ~**s** npl (COMM) Spesen pl; at the ~ of auf Kosten von; ~ **account** n Spesenkonto nt

expensive [ɪks'pensɪv] adj teuer

experience [ɪks'pɪərɪəns] n (incident) Erlebnis nt; (practice) Erfahrung f ♦ vt erleben; ~**d** adj erfahren

experiment [n ɪks'perɪmənt, vb ɪks'perɪment] n Versuch m, Experiment nt ♦ vi experimentieren; ~**al** [ɪkspserɪ'mentl] adj experimentell

expert ['eksp3ːt] n Fachmann m; (official) Sachverständige(r) m ♦ adj erfahren; ~**ise** [eksp3ː'tiːz] n Sachkenntnis f

expire [ɪks'paɪə*] vi (end) ablaufen; (ticket) verfallen; (die) sterben

expiry [ɪks'paɪərɪ] n Ablauf m

explain [ɪks'pleɪn] vt erklären

explanation [eksplə'neɪʃən] n Erklärung f

explanatory [ɪks'plænətərɪ] adj erklärend

explicit [ɪks'plɪsɪt] adj ausdrücklich

explode [ɪks'pləud] vi explodieren ♦ vt (bomb) sprengen; (theory) platzen lassen

exploit [n 'eksplɔɪt, vb ɪks'plɔɪt] n (Helden)tat f ♦ vt ausbeuten; ~**ation** [eksplɔɪ'teɪʃən] n Ausbeutung f

exploration [eksplɔː'reɪʃən] n Erforschung f

exploratory [eks'plɔrətərɪ] adj Probe-

explore [ɪks'plɔː*] vt (travel) erforschen; (search) untersuchen; ~**r** n Erforscher(in) m(f)

explosion [ɪks'pləuʒən] n Explosion f; (fig) Ausbruch m

explosive [ɪks'pləuzɪv] adj explosiv,

Spreng-♦ *n* Sprengstoff *m*

exponent [eks'pəʊnənt] *n* Exponent *m*

export [*vb* eks'pɔːt, *n* 'ekspɔːt] *vt* exportieren ♦ *n* Export *m* ♦ *cpd* (*trade*) Export-; ~**er** *n* Exporteur *m*

expose [iks'pəʊz] *vt* (*to danger etc*) aussetzen; (*impostor*) entlarven; to ~ **sb** to **sth** jdn einer Sache *dat* aussetzen; ~**d** [iks'pəʊzd] *adj* (*position*) exponiert

exposure [iks'pəʊʒə*] *n* (*MED*) Unterkühlung *f*; (*PHOT*) Belichtung *f*; ~ **meter** *n* Belichtungsmesser *m*

expound [iks'paʊnd] *vt* entwickeln

express [iks'pres] *adj* ausdrücklich; (*speedy*) Expreß-, Eil- ♦ *n* (*RAIL*) Schnellzug *m* ♦ *adv* (*send*) per Expreß ♦ *vt* ausdrücken; to ~ **o.s.** sich ausdrücken; ~**ion** [iks'preʃən] *n* Ausdruck *m*; ~**ive** *adj* ausdrucksvoll; ~**ly** *adv* ausdrücklich; ~**way** (*US*) *n* (*urban motorway*) Schnellstraße *f*

expulsion [iks'pʌlʃən] *n* Ausweisung *f*

expurgate ['ekspə:geit] *vt* zensieren

exquisite [eks'kwizit] *adj* erlesen

extend [iks'tend] *vt* (*visit etc*) verlängern; (*building*) ausbauen; (*hand*) ausstrecken; (*welcome*) bieten ♦ *vi* (*land*) sich erstrecken

extension [iks'tenʃən] *n* Erweiterung *f*; (*of building*) Anbau *m*; (*TEL*) Apparat *m*

extensive [iks'tensiv] *adj* (*knowledge*) umfassend; (*use*) weitgehend

extent [iks'tent] *n* Ausdehnung *f*; (*fig*) Ausmaß *nt*; **to a certain** ~ bis zu einem gewissen Grade; **to such an** ~ **that** ... dermaßen, daß ...; **to what** ~? inwieweit?

extenuating [eks'tenjueitiŋ] *adj* mildernd

exterior [eks'tiəriə*] *adj* äußere(r, s), Außen- ♦ *n* Äußere(s) *nt*

exterminate [eks'tə:mineit] *vt* ausrotten

external [eks'tə:nl] *adj* äußere(r, s), Außen-

extinct [iks'tiŋkt] *adj* ausgestorben;

~**ion** [iks'tiŋkʃən] *n* Aussterben *nt*

extinguish [iks'tiŋgwiʃ] *vt* (aus-)löschen; ~**er** *n* Löschgerät *nt*

extort [iks'tɔːt] *vt* erpressen; ~**ion** [iks'tɔːʃən] *n* Erpressung *f*; ~**ionate** [iks'tɔːʃənit] *adj* überhöht, erpresserisch

extra ['ekstrə] *adj* zusätzlich ♦ *adv* besonders ♦ *n* (*for car etc*) Extra *nt*; (*charge*) Zuschlag *m*; (*THEAT*) Statist *m* ♦ *prefix* außer...

extract [*vb* iks'trækt, *n* 'ekstrækt] *vt* (*heraus*)ziehen ♦ *n* (*from book etc*) Auszug *m*; (*COOK*) Extrakt *m*

extracurricular ['ekstrəkə'rikjulə*] *adj* außerhalb des Stundenplans

extradite ['ekstrədait] *vt* ausliefern

extramarital ['ekstrə'mæritl] *adj* außerehelich

extramural ['ekstrə'mjuərl] *adj* (*course*) Volkshochschul-

extraordinary [iks'trɔːdnri] *adj* außerordentlich; (*amazing*) erstaunlich

extravagance [iks'trævəgəns] *n* Verschwendung *f*; (*lack of restraint*) Zügellosigkeit *f*; (*an* ~) Extravaganz *f*

extravagant [iks'trævəgənt] *adj* extravagant

extreme [iks'triːm] *adj* (*edge*) äußerste(r, s), hinterste(r, s); (*cold*) äußerste(r, s); (*behaviour*) außergewöhnlich, übertrieben ♦ *n* Extrem *nt*; ~**ly** *adv* äußerst, höchst

extremity [iks'tremiti] *n* (*end*) Spitze *f*, äußerste(s) Ende *nt*; (*hardship*) bitterste Not *f*; (*ANAT*) Hand *f*; Fuß *m*

extricate ['ekstrikeit] *vt* losmachen, befreien

extrovert ['ekstrəvə:t] *n* extrovertierte(r) Mensch *m*

exuberant [ig'zu:bərənt] *adj* ausgelassen

exude [ig'zju:d] *vt* absondern

exult [ig'zʌlt] *vi* frohlocken

eye [ai] *n* Auge *nt*; (*of needle*) Öhr *nt* ♦ *vt* betrachten; (*up and down*) mustern; **to keep an** ~ **on** aufpassen auf +*acc*; **~ball** *n* Augapfel *m*; **~bath** *n* Augenbad *nt*; **~brow** *n* Augenbraue *f*; **~brow pencil** *n* Augenbrauenstift *m*; **~drops** *npl* Augentropfen *pl*; **~lash** *n* Augenwimper *f*; **~lid** *n* Augenlid *nt*; **~liner** *n* Eyeliner *nt*; **~opener** *n*: that was an **~opener** das hat mir/ihm *etc* die Augen geöffnet; **~shadow** *n* Lidschatten *m*; **~sight** *n* Sehkraft *f*; **~sore** *n* Schandfleck *m*; **~ witness** *n* Augenzeuge *m*

F

F [ɛf] *n* (*MUS*) F *nt*
F. *abbr* (= *Fahrenheit*) F
fable ['feɪbl] *n* Fabel *f*
fabric ['fæbrɪk] *n* Stoff *m*; (*fig*) Gefüge *nt*
fabrication [fæbrɪ'keɪʃən] *n* Erfindung *f*
fabulous ['fæbjʊləs] *adj* sagenhaft
face [feɪs] *n* Gesicht *nt*; (*surface*) Oberfläche *f*; (*of clock*) Zifferblatt *nt* ♦ *vt* (*point towards*) liegen nach; (*situation, difficulty*) sich stellen +*dat*; **~ down** (*person*) mit dem Gesicht nach unten; (*card*) mit der Vorderseite nach unten; **to make** *or* **pull a ~** das Gesicht verziehen; **in the ~ of** angesichts +*gen*; **on the ~ of it** so, wie es aussieht; **~ to ~** Auge in Auge; **to ~ up to sth** einer Sache *dat* ins Auge sehen; **~ cloth** (*BRIT*) *n* Waschlappen *m*; **~ cream** *n* Gesichtscreme *f*; **~ lift** *n* Face-lifting *nt*; **~ powder** *n* (Gesichts)puder *m*
facet ['fæsɪt] *n* Aspekt *m*; (*of gem*) Facette *f*
facetious [fə'siːʃəs] *adj* witzig
face value *n* Nennwert *m*; **to take sth at** (**its**) **~** (*fig*) etw für bare Münze nehmen
facial ['feɪʃəl] *adj* Gesichts-
facile ['fæsaɪl] *adj* oberflächlich; (*US: easy*) leicht
facilitate [fə'sɪlɪteɪt] *vt* erleichtern
facilities [fə'sɪlɪtɪz] *npl* Einrichtungen

pl; **credit ~** Kreditmöglichkeiten *pl*
facing ['feɪsɪŋ] *adj* zugekehrt ♦ *prep* gegenüber
facsimile [fæk'sɪmɪlɪ] *n* Faksimile *nt*; (*machine*) Telekopierer *m*
fact [fækt] *n* Tatsache *f*; **in ~** in der Tat
faction ['fækʃən] *n* Splittergruppe *f*
factor ['fæktə*] *n* Faktor *m*
factory ['fæktərɪ] *n* Fabrik *f*
factual ['fæktjʊəl] *adj* sachlich
faculty ['fækəltɪ] *n* Fähigkeit *f*; (*UNIV*) Fakultät *f*; (*US: teaching staff*) Lehrpersonal *nt*
fad [fæd] *n* Tick *m*; (*fashion*) Masche *f*
fade [feɪd] *vi* (*lose colour*) verblassen; (*grow dim*) nachlassen; (*sound, memory*) schwächer werden; (*wither*) verwelken
fag [fæg] (*inf*) *n* (*cigarette*) Kippe *f*
fail [feɪl] *vt* (*exam*) nicht bestehen; (*student*) durchfallen lassen; (*courage*) verlassen; (*memory*) im Stich lassen ♦ *vi* (*supplies*) zu Ende gehen; (*student*) durchfallen; (*eyesight*) nachlassen; (*light*) schwächer werden; (*crop*) fehlschlagen; (*remedy*) nicht wirken; **to ~ to do sth** (*neglect*) es unterlassen, etw zu tun; (*be unable*) es nicht schaffen, etw zu tun; **without ~** unbedingt; **~ing** *n* Schwäche *f* ♦ *prep* mangels +*gen*; **~ure** *n* (*person*) Versager *m*; (*act*) Versagen *nt*; (*TECH*) Defekt *m*
faint [feɪnt] *adj* schwach ♦ *n* Ohnmacht *f* ♦ *vi* ohnmächtig werden
fair [fɛə*] *adj* (*just*) gerecht, fair; (*hair*) blond; (*skin*) hell; (*weather*) schön; (*not very good*) mittelmäßig; (*sizeable*) ansehnlich ♦ *adv* (*play*) fair ♦ *n* (*COMM*) Messe *f*; (*BRIT: fun*~) Jahrmarkt *m*; **~ly** *adv* (*honestly*) gerecht, fair; (*rather*) ziemlich; **~ness** *n* Fairneß *f*
fairy ['fɛərɪ] *n* Fee *f*; **~ tale** *n* Märchen *n*
faith [feɪθ] *n* Glaube *m*; (*trust*) Vertrauen *nt*; (*sect*) Bekenntnis *nt*; **~ful** *adj* treu; **~fully** *adv* treu; **yours**

fake [feɪk] *n* (*thing*) Fälschung *f*; (*person*) Schwindler *m* ♦ *adj* vorgetäuscht ♦ *vt* fälschen

falcon ['fɔːlkən] *n* Falke *m*

fall [fɔːl] (*pt* **fell**, *pp* **fallen**) *n* Fall *m*, Sturz *m*; (*decrease*) Fallen *nt*; (*of snow*) (Schnee)fall *m*; (*US: autumn*) Herbst *m* ♦ *vi* (*also fig*) fallen; (*night*) hereinbrechen; ~s *npl* (*waterfall*) Fälle *pl*; **to** ~ **flat** platt hinfallen; (*joke*) nicht ankommen; ~ **back** *vi* zurückweichen; ~ **back on** *vt fus* zurückgreifen auf +*acc*; ~ **behind** *vi* zurückbleiben; ~ **down** *vi* (*person*) hinfallen; (*building*) einstürzen; ~ **for** *vt fus* (*trick*) hereinfallen auf +*acc*; (*person*) sich verknallen in +*acc*; ~ **in** *vi* (*roof*) einstürzen; ~ **off** *vi* herunterfallen; (*diminish*) sich vermindern; ~ **out** *vi* sich streiten; (*MIL*) wegtreten; ~ **through** *vi* (*plan*) ins Wasser fallen

fallacy ['fæləsɪ] *n* Trugschluß *m*

fallen ['fɔːlən] *pp* of **fall**

fallible ['fæləbl] *adj* fehlbar

fallout ['fɔːlaʊt] *n* radioaktive(r) Niederschlag *m*; ~ **shelter** *n* Atombunker *m*

fallow ['fæləʊ] *adj* brach(liegend)

false [fɔːls] *adj* falsch; (*artificial*) künstlich; **under** ~ **pretences** unter Vorspiegelung falscher Tatsachen; ~ **alarm** *n* Fehlalarm *m*; ~ **teeth** (*BRIT*) *npl* Gebiß *nt*

falter ['fɔːltə*] *vi* schwanken; (*in speech*) stocken

fame [feɪm] *n* Ruhm *m*

familiar [fə'mɪlɪə*] *adj* bekannt; (*intimate*) familiär; **to be** ~ **with** vertraut sein mit; ~**ize** *vt* vertraut machen

family ['fæmɪlɪ] *n* Familie *f*; (*relations*) Verwandtschaft *f*; ~ **business** *n* Familienunternehmen *nt*; ~ **doctor** *n* Hausarzt *m*

famine ['fæmɪn] *n* Hungersnot *f*

famished ['fæmɪʃt] *adj* ausgehungert

famous ['feɪməs] *adj* berühmt; ~**ly** *adv* (*get on*) prächtig

fan [fæn] *n* (*folding*) Fächer *m*; (*ELEC*) Ventilator *m*; (*admirer*) Fan *m* ♦ *vt* fächeln; ~ **out** *vi* sich (fächerförmig) ausbreiten

fanatic [fə'nætɪk] *n* Fanatiker(in) *m(f)*

fan belt *n* Keilriemen *m*

fanciful ['fænsɪfʊl] *adj* (*odd*) seltsam; (*imaginative*) phantasievoll

fancy ['fænsɪ] *n* (*liking*) Neigung *f*; (*imagination*) Einbildung *f* ♦ *adj* schick ♦ *vt* (*like*) gern haben; wollen; (*imagine*) sich einbilden; **he fancies her** er mag sie; ~ **dress** *n* Maskenkostüm *nt*; ~-**dress ball** *n* Maskenball *m*

fang [fæŋ] *n* Fangzahn *m*; (*of snake*) Giftzahn *m*

fantastic [fæn'tæstɪk] *adj* phantastisch

fantasy ['fæntəzɪ] *n* Phantasie *f*

far [fɑː*] *adj* weit ♦ *adv* weit entfernt; (*very much*) weitaus, ~ **by** ~ bei weitem; **so** ~ soweit; bis jetzt; **go as** ~ **as the** ~**m** gehen Sie bis zum Bauernhof; **as** ~ **as I know** soweit or soviel ich weiß; ~-**away** *adj* weit entfernt

farce [fɑːs] *n* Farce *f*

farcical ['fɑːsɪkəl] *adj* lächerlich

fare [fɛə*] *n* Fahrpreis *m*; Fahrgeld *nt*; (*food*) Kost *f*; **half/full** ~ halber/voller Fahrpreis *m*

Far East *n* **the** ~ der Ferne Osten

farewell [fɛə'wel] *n* Abschied(sgruß) *m* ♦ *excl* lebe wohl!

farm [fɑːm] *n* Bauernhof *m*, Farm *f* ♦ *vt* bewirtschaften; ~**er** *n* Bauer *m*, Landwirt *m*; ~**hand** *n* Landarbeiter *m*; ~**house** *n* Bauernhaus *nt*; ~**ing** *n* Landwirtschaft *f*; ~**land** *n* Ackerland *nt*; ~**yard** *n* Hof *m*

far-reaching [fɑː'riːtʃɪŋ] *adj* (*reform, effect*) weitreichend

fart [fɑːt] (*inf!*) *n* Furz *m* ♦ *vi* furzen

farther ['fɑːðə*] *adv* weiter

farthest ['fɑːðɪst] *adj* fernste(r, s) ♦ *adv* am weitesten

fascinate ['fæsɪneɪt] *vt* faszinieren

fascination [fæsɪ'neɪʃən] *n* Faszina

tion f

fascism ['fæʃızəm] n Faschismus m

fashion ['fæʃən] n (of clothes) Mode f; (manner) Art f (und Weise) ♦ vt machen; **in ~** in Mode; **out of ~** unmodisch; **~able** adj (clothes) modisch; (place) elegant; **~ show** n Mode(n)schau f

fast [fɑːst] adj schnell; (firm) fest ♦ adv schnell; fest ♦ n Fasten nt ♦ vi fasten; **to be ~** (clock) vorgehen

fasten ['fɑːsn] vt (attach) befestigen; (with rope) zuschnüren; (seat belt) festmachen; (coat) zumachen ♦ vi sich schließen lassen; **~er** n Verschluß m; **~ing** n Verschluß m

fast food n Fast food nt

fastidious [fæs'tɪdɪəs] adj wählerisch

fat [fæt] adj dick ♦ n Fett nt

fatal ['feɪtl] adj tödlich; (disastrous) verhängnisvoll; **~ity** [fə'tælɪtɪ] n (road death etc) Todesopfer nt; **~ly** adv tödlich

fate [feɪt] n Schicksal nt; **~ful** adj (prophetic) schicksalsschwer; (important) schicksalhaft

father ['fɑːðə*] n Vater m; (REL) Pater m; **~-in-law** n Schwiegervater m; **~ly** adj väterlich

fathom ['fæðəm] n Klafter m ♦ vt ausloten; (fig) ergründen

fatigue [fə'tiːɡ] n Ermüdung f

fatten ['fætn] vt dick machen; (animals) mästen ♦ vi dick werden

fatty ['fætɪ] adj fettig ♦ n (inf) Dickerchen nt

fatuous ['fætjuəs] adj albern, affig

faucet ['fɔːsɪt] (US) n Wasserhahn m

fault [fɔːlt] n (defect) Defekt m; (ELEC) Störung f; (blame) Schuld f; (GEOG) Verwerfung f ♦ vt: **it's your ~** du bist daran schuld; **to find ~ with (sth/sb)** etwas auszusetzen haben an (etw/jdm); **at ~** im Unrecht; **~less** adj tadellos; **~y** adj fehlerhaft, defekt

favour ['feɪvə*] (US favor) n (approval) Wohlwollen nt; (kindness) Gefallen m ♦ vt (prefer) vorziehen; **in ~ of** für; zugunsten +gen; **to find ~**

with sb bei jdm Anklang finden; **~able** adj günstig; **~ite** ['feɪvərɪt] adj Lieblings- ♦ n (child) Liebling m; (SPORT) Favorit m

fawn [fɔːn] adj rehbraun ♦ n (colour) Rehbraun nt; (animal) (Reh)kitz nt ♦ vi: **to ~ (up)on** (fig) katzbuckeln vor +dat

fax [fæks] n (document) Fax nt; (machine) Telefax nt ♦ vt: **to ~ sth to sb** jdm etw faxen

FBI ['efbi:'aɪ] (US) n abbr (= Federal Bureau of Investigation) FBI nt

fear [fɪə*] n Furcht f ♦ vt fürchten; **~ful** adj (timid) furchtsam; (terrible) fürchterlich; **~less** adj furchtlos

feasible ['fiːzəbl] adj durchführbar

feast [fiːst] n Festmahl nt; (REL: also: **~ day**) Feiertag m ♦ vi: **to ~ (on)** sich gütlich tun (an +dat)

feat [fiːt] n Leistung f

feather ['feðə*] n Feder f

feature ['fiːtʃə*] n (Gesichts)zug m; (important part) Grundzug m; (CINE, PRESS) Feature nt ♦ vt darstellen; (advertising etc) groß herausbringen ♦ vi vorkommen; **featuring X** mit X; **~ film** n Spielfilm m

February ['februərɪ] n Februar m

fed [fed] pt, pp of **feed**

federal ['fedərəl] adj Bundes-

federation [fedə'reɪʃən] n (society) Verband m; (of states) Staatenbund m

fed up adj: **to be ~ with sth** etw satt haben; **I'm ~** ich habe die Nase voll

fee [fiː] n Gebühr f

feeble ['fiːbl] adj (person) schwach; (excuse) lahm

feed [fiːd] (pt, pp **fed**) n (for baby) Essen nt; (for animals) Futter nt ♦ vt füttern; (support) ernähren; (data) eingeben; **to ~ on** fressen; **~back** n (information) Feedback nt; **~ing bottle** (BRIT) n Flasche f

feel [fiːl] (pt, pp **felt**) n: **it has a soft ~** es fühlt sich weich an ♦ vt (sense) fühlen; (touch) anfassen; (think) meinen ♦ vi (person) sich fühlen; (thing) sich anfühlen; to get the ~ of sth sich an etw acc gewöhnen; I ~ cold mir ist kalt; I ~ like a cup of tea ich habe Lust auf eine Tasse Tee; ~ **about** or **around** vi herumsuchen; ~er n Fühler m; ~ing n Gefühl nt; (opinion) Meinung f

feet [fiːt] npl of foot

feign [feɪn] vt vortäuschen

feline ['fiːlaɪn] adj katzenartig

fell [fɛl] pt of fall ♦ vt (tree) fällen

fellow ['fɛləʊ] n (man) Kerl m; ~ **citizen** n Mitbürger(in) m(f); ~ **countryman** (irreg) n Landsmann m; ~ **men** npl Mitmenschen pl; ~**ship** n (group) Körperschaft f; (friendliness) Kameradschaft f; (scholarship) Forschungsstipendium nt; ~ **student** n Kommilitone m, Kommilitonin f

felony ['fɛlənɪ] n schwere(s) Verbrechen nt

felt [fɛlt] pt, pp of feel ♦ n Filz m; ~**tip pen** n Filzstift m

female ['fiːmeɪl] n (of animals) Weibchen nt ♦ adj weiblich

feminine ['fɛmɪnɪn] adj (LING) weiblich; (qualities) fraulich

feminist ['fɛmɪnɪst] n Feminist(in) m(f)

fence [fɛns] n Zaun m ♦ vt (also: ~ in) einzäunen ♦ vi fechten

fencing ['fɛnsɪŋ] n Zaun m; (SPORT) Fechten nt

fend [fɛnd] vi: to ~ for o.s. sich (allein) durchschlagen; ~ **off** vt abwehren

fender ['fɛndə*] n Kaminvorsetzer m; (US: AUT) Kotflügel m

ferment [vb fə'mɛnt, n 'fɜːmɛnt] vi (CHEM) gären ♦ n (excitement) Unruhe f

fern [fɜːn] n Farn m

ferocious [fə'rəʊʃəs] adj wild, grausam

ferret ['fɛrɪt] n Frettchen nt ♦ vt: to ~ **out** aufspüren

ferry ['fɛrɪ] n Fähre f ♦ vt übersetzen

fertile ['fɜːtaɪl] adj fruchtbar

fertilize ['fɜːtɪlaɪz] vt (AGR) düngen;

(BIOL) befruchten; ~**r** ['fɜːtɪlaɪzə*] n (Kunst)dünger m

fervent ['fɜːvənt] adj (admirer) glühend; (hope) innig

fervour ['fɜːvə*] (US fervor) n Leidenschaft f

fester ['fɛstə*] vi eitern

festival ['fɛstɪvəl] n (REL etc) Fest nt; (ART, MUS) Festspiele pl

festive ['fɛstɪv] adj festlich; the ~ **season** (Christmas) die Festzeit

festivities [fɛs'tɪvɪtɪz] npl Feierlichkeiten pl

festoon [fɛs'tuːn] vt: to ~ **with** schmücken mit

fetch [fɛtʃ] vt holen; (in sale) einbringen

fetching ['fɛtʃɪŋ] adj reizend

fête [feɪt] n Fest nt

fetus ['fiːtəs] (US) n = foetus

feud [fjuːd] n Fehde f

feudal ['fjuːdl] adj feudal

fever ['fiːvə*] n Fieber nt; ~**ish** adj (MED) fiebrig; (fig) fieberhaft

few [fjuː] adj wenig; a ~ einige; ~**er** adj weniger; ~**est** adj wenigste(r, s)

fiancé [fɪ'ɑːnseɪ] n Verlobte(r) m; ~**e** n Verlobte f

fib [fɪb] n Flunkerei f ♦ vi flunkern

fibre ['faɪbə*] (US fiber) n Faser f; ~**glass** n Glaswolle f

fickle ['fɪkl] adj unbeständig

fiction ['fɪkʃən] n (novels) Romanliteratur f; (story) Erdichtung f; ~**al** adj erfunden

fictitious [fɪk'tɪʃəs] adj erfunden, fingiert

fiddle ['fɪdl] n Geige f; (trick) Schwindelei f ♦ vt (BRIT: accounts) frisieren; ~ **with** vt fus herummeln an +dat

fidelity [fɪ'dɛlɪtɪ] n Treue f

fidget ['fɪdʒɪt] vi zappeln

field [fiːld] n Feld nt; (range) Gebiet nt; ~ **marshal** n Feldmarschall m; ~**work** n Feldforschung f

fiend [fiːnd] n Teufel m

fierce [fɪəs] adj wild

fiery ['faɪərɪ] adj (hot-tempered) hitzig

fifteen [fɪf'tiːn] num fünfzehn

fifth [fɪfθ] adj fünfte(r, s) ♦ n Fünftel nt

fifty [fɪftɪ] num fünfzig; **~-fifty** adj, adv halbe halbe, fifty fifty (inf)

fig [fɪg] n Feige f

fight [faɪt] (pt, pp fought) n Kampf m; (brawl) Schlägerei f; (argument) Streit m ♦ vt kämpfen gegen; sich schlagen mit; (fig) bekämpfen ♦ vi kämpfen; sich schlagen; streiten; **~er** n Kämpfer(in) m(f); (plane) Jagdflugzeug nt; **~ing** n Kämpfen nt; (war) Kampfhandlungen pl

figment [ˈfɪgmənt] n: **~ of the imagination** reine Einbildung f

figurative [ˈfɪgərətɪv] adj bildlich

figure [ˈfɪgə*] n (of person) Figur f; (person) Gestalt f; (number) Ziffer f ♦ vt (US: imagine) glauben ♦ vi (appear) erscheinen; **~ out** vt herausbekommen; **~head** n (NAUT, fig) Galionsfigur f; **~ of speech** n Redensart f

filament [ˈfɪləmənt] n Faden m; (ELEC) Glühfaden m

filch [fɪltʃ] (inf) vt filzen

file [faɪl] n (tool) Feile f; (dossier) Akte f; (folder) Aktenordner m; (COMPUT) Datei f; (row) Reihe f ♦ vt (metal, nails) feilen; (papers) abheften; (claim) einreichen ♦ vi: to **in/out** hintereinander hereinkommen/hinausgehen; to **~ past** vorbeimarschieren

filing [ˈfaɪlɪŋ] n Ablage f; **~ cabinet** n Aktenschrank m

fill [fɪl] vt füllen; (occupy) ausfüllen; (satisfy) sättigen ♦ n: to eat one's **~** sich richtig satt essen; **~ in** vt (hole) (auf)füllen; (form) ausfüllen; **~ up** vt (container) auffüllen ♦ vi (AUT) tanken

fillet [ˈfɪlɪt] n Filet nt; **~ steak** n Filetsteak nt

filling [ˈfɪlɪŋ] n (COOK) Füllung f; (for tooth) (Zahn)plombe f; **~ station** n Tankstelle f

film [fɪlm] n Film m ♦ vt (scene) filmen; **~ star** n Filmstar m; **~ strip** n Filmstreifen m

filter [ˈfɪltə*] n Filter m ♦ vt filtern; **~ lane** (BRIT) n Abbiegespur f; **~-tipped** adj Filter-

filth [fɪlθ] n Dreck m; **~y** adj dreckig; (weather) scheußlich

fin [fɪn] n Flosse f

final [ˈfaɪnl] adj letzte(r, s); End-; (conclusive) endgültig ♦ n (FOOTBALL etc) Endspiel nt; **~s** npl (UNIV) Schlußrunde f; **~e** [fɪˈnɑːlɪ] n (MUS) Finale nt; **~ist** n (SPORT) Schlußrundenteilnehmer m; **~ize** vt endgültige Form geben +dat; abschließen; **~ly** adv (lastly) zuletzt; (eventually) endlich; (irrevocably) endgültig

finance [faɪˈnæns] n Finanzwesen nt ♦ vt finanzieren; **~s** npl (funds) Finanzen pl

financial [faɪˈnænʃəl] adj Finanz-; finanziell

find [faɪnd] (pt, pp found) vt finden ♦ n Fund m; to **~ sb guilty** jdn für schuldig erklären; **~ out** vt herausfinden; **~ings** npl (JUR) Ermittlungsergebnis nt; (of report) Befund m

fine [faɪn] adj fein; (good) gut; (weather) schön ♦ adv (well) gut; (small) klein ♦ n (JUR) Geldstrafe f ♦ vt mit einer Geldstrafe belegen; **~ arts** npl schöne(n) Künste pl

finery [ˈfaɪnərɪ] n Putz m

finger [ˈfɪŋgə*] n Finger m ♦ vt befühlen; **~nail** n Fingernagel m; **~print** n Fingerabdruck m; **~tip** n Fingerspitze f

finicky [ˈfɪnɪkɪ] adj pingelig

finish [ˈfɪnɪʃ] n Ende nt; (SPORT) Ziel nt; (of object) Verarbeitung f; (of paint) Oberflächenwirkung f ♦ vt beenden; (book) zu Ende lesen ♦ vi aufhören; (SPORT) ans Ziel kommen; to be **~ed with** sth fertig sein mit etw; to **~ doing** sth mit etw fertig werden; **~ off** vt (complete) fertigmachen; (kill) den Gnadenstoß geben +dat; (knock out) erledigen (*umg*); ~ **up** vt (*food*) aufessen; (*drink*) austrinken ♦ vi (*end up*) enden; ~**ing line** n Ziellinie f; ~**ing school** n Mädchenpensionat nt

finite ['faɪnaɪt] adj endlich, begrenzt

Finland ['fɪnlənd] n Finnland nt

Finn [fɪn] n Finne m, Finnin f; ~**ish** adj finnisch ♦ n (LING) Finnisch nt

fir [fɜ:*] n Tanne f

fire [faɪə*] n Feuer nt; (*in house etc*) Brand m ♦ vt (*gun*) abfeuern; (*imagination*) entzünden; (*dismiss*) hinauswerfen ♦ vi (AUT) zünden; to be on ~ brennen; ~ **alarm** n Feueralarm m; ~**arm** n Schußwaffe f; ~ **brigade** (BRIT) n Feuerwehr f; ~ **department** (US) n Feuerwehr f; ~ **engine** n Feuerwehrauto nt; ~ **escape** n Feuerleiter f; ~ **extinguisher** n Löschgerät nt; ~**man** (*irreg*) n Feuerwehrmann m; ~**place** n Kamin m; ~**side** n Kamin m; ~ **station** n Feuerwache f; ~**works** npl Feuerwerk nt

firing ['faɪərɪŋ] n Schießen nt; ~ **squad** n Exekutionskommando nt

firm [fɜ:m] adj fest ♦ n Firma f

firmly adv (*grasp, speak*) fest; (*push, tug*) energisch; (*decide*) endgültig

first [fɜ:st] adj erste(r, s) ♦ adv zuerst; (*arrive*) als erste(r); (*happen*) zum erstenmal ♦ n (*person: in race*) Erste(r) m/f; (UNIV) Eins f; (AUT) erste(r) Gang m; at ~ zuerst; ~ **of all** zu allererst; ~ **aid** n Erste Hilfe f; ~**aid kit** n Verbandskasten m; ~**class** adj erstklassig; (*travel*) erster Klasse; ~**hand** adj aus erster Hand; ~ **lady** (US) n First Lady f; ~**ly** adv erstens; ~ **name** n Vorname m; ~**rate** adj erstklassig

fiscal ['fɪskəl] adj Finanz-

fish [fɪʃ] n inv Fisch m ♦ vi fischen; angeln; to **go** ~**ing** angeln gehen; (*in sea*) fischen gehen; ~**erman** (*irreg*) n Fischer m; ~ **farm** n Fischzucht f; ~ **fingers** (BRIT) npl Fischstäbchen pl; ~**ing boat** n Fischer-

boot nt; ~**ing line** n Angelschnur f; ~**ing rod** n Angel(rute) f; ~**monger's (shop)** n Fischhändler m; ~ **slice** n Fischvorleger m; ~ **sticks** (US) npl = **fish fingers**; ~**y** (*inf*) adj (*suspicious*) faul

fission ['fɪʃən] n Spaltung f

fissure ['fɪʃə*] n Riß m

fist [fɪst] n Faust f

fit [fɪt] adj (MED) gesund; (SPORT) in Form, fit; (*suitable*) geeignet ♦ vt passen +dat; (*insert, attach*) einsetzen ♦ vi passen; (*in space, gap*) hineinpassen ♦ n (*of clothes*) Sitz m; (MED, *of anger*) Anfall m; (*of laughter*) Krampf m; **by** ~**s and starts** (*move*) ruckweise; (*work*) unregelmäßig; ~ **in** vi hineinpassen; (*fig: person*) passen; ~ **out** vt (*also: fit up*) ausstatten; ~**ful** adj (*sleep*) unruhig; ~**ment** n Einrichtungsgegenstand m; ~**ness** n (*suitability*) Eignung f; (MED) Gesundheit f; (SPORT) Fitneß f; ~**ted carpet** n Teppichboden m; ~**ted kitchen** n Einbauküche f; ~**ter** n (TECH) Monteur m; ~**ting** adj passend ♦ n (*of dress*) Anprobe f; (*piece of equipment*) (Ersatz)teil nt; ~**tings** npl (*equipment*) Zubehör nt; ~**ting room** n Anproberaum m

five [faɪv] num fünf; ~**r** (*inf*) n (BRIT) Fünf-Pfund-Note f; (US) Fünf-Dollar-Note f

fix [fɪks] vt befestigen; (*settle*) festsetzen; (*repair*) reparieren ♦ n: **in a** ~ in der Klemme; ~ **up** vt (*meeting*) arrangieren; to ~ **sb up with sth** jdm etw acc verschaffen; ~**ation** [fɪks'eɪʃən] n Fixierung f; ~**ed** [fɪkst] adj fest; ~**ture** ['fɪkstʃə*] n Installationsteil nt; (SPORT) Spiel nt

fizzle ['fɪzl] vi: to ~ **out** verpuffen

fizzy ['fɪzɪ] adj Sprudel-, sprudelnd

flabbergasted ['flæbəgɑ:stɪd] (*inf*) adj platt

flabby ['flæbɪ] adj wabbelig

flag [flæg] n Fahne f ♦ vi (*strength*) nachlassen; (*spirit*) erlahmen; ~ **down** vt anhalten

flagpole ['flægpəʊl] n Fahnenstange f

flagrant ['fleɪgrənt] adj kraß

flair [fleə*] n Talent n

flak [flæk] n Flakfeuer nt

flake [fleɪk] n (of snow) Flocke f; (of rust) Schuppe f ♦ vi (also: ~ off) abblättern

flamboyant [flæm'bɔɪənt] adj extravagant

flame [fleɪm] n Flamme f

flamingo [flə'mɪŋgəʊ] n Flamingo m

flammable ['flæməbl] adj brennbar

flan [flæn] n (BRIT) Obsttorte f

flank [flæŋk] n Flanke f ♦ vt flankieren

flannel ['flænl] n Flanell m; (BRIT: also: face ~) Waschlappen m; (: inf) Geschwafel nt; ~s npl (trousers) Flanellhose f

flap [flæp] n Klappe f; (inf: crisis) (helle) Aufregung f ♦ vt (wings) schlagen mit ♦ vi flattern

flare [fleə*] n (signal) Leuchtsignal nt; (in skirt etc) Weite f; ~ up vi aufflammen; (fig) aufbrausen; (revolt) (plötzlich) ausbrechen

flash [flæʃ] n Blitz m; (also: news ~) Kurzmeldung f; (PHOT) Blitzlicht nt ♦ vt aufleuchten lassen ♦ vi aufleuchten; in a ~ im Nu; ~ by or past vi vorbeirasen; ~back n Rückblende f; ~bulb n Blitzlichtbirne f; ~ cube n Blitzwürfel m; ~light n Blitzlicht nt

flashy ['flæʃɪ] (pej) adj knallig

flask [flɑːsk] n (CHEM) Kolben m; (also: vacuum ~) Thermosflasche f (®)

flat [flæt] adj flach; (dull) matt; (MUS) erniedrigt; (beer) schal; (tyre) platt ♦ n (BRIT: rooms) Wohnung f; (MUS) b nt; (AUT) Platte(r) m; to work ~ out auf Hochtouren arbeiten; ~ly adv glatt; ~ten vt (also: ~ten out) ebnen

flatter ['flætə*] vt schmeicheln +dat; ~ing adj schmeichelhaft; ~y n Schmeichelei f

flatulence ['flætjʊləns] n Blähungen pl

flaunt [flɔːnt] vt prunken mit

flavour ['fleɪvə*] (US **flavor**) n Geschmack m ♦ vt würzen; ~ed adj: strawberry-flavoured mit Erdbeergeschmack; ~ing n Würze f

flaw [flɔː] n Fehler m; ~less adj einwandfrei

flax [flæks] n Flachs m; ~en adj flachsfarben

flea [fliː] n Floh m

fleck [flek] n (mark) Fleck m; (pattern) Tupfen m

fled [fled] pt, pp of flee

flee [pt, pp fled] vi fliehen ♦ vt fliehen vor +dat; (country) fliehen aus

fleece [fliːs] n Vlies nt; (inf) schröpfen

fleet [fliːt] n Flotte f

fleeting ['fliːtɪŋ] adj flüchtig

Flemish ['flemɪʃ] adj flämisch

flesh [fleʃ] n Fleisch nt; ~ wound n Fleischwunde f

flew [fluː] pt of fly

flex [fleks] n Kabel nt ♦ vt beugen; ~ibility [fleksɪ'bɪlɪtɪ] n Biegsamkeit f; (fig) Flexibilität f; ~ible adj biegsam; (plans) flexibel

flick [flɪk] n leichte(r) Schlag m ♦ vt leicht schlagen; ~ through vt fus durchblättern

flicker ['flɪkə*] n Flackern nt ♦ vi flackern

flier ['flaɪə*] n Flieger m

flight [flaɪt] n Flug m; (fleeing) Flucht f; (also: ~ of steps) Treppe f; to take ~ die Flucht ergreifen; ~ attendant (US) n Steward(eß) m(f); ~ deck n Flugdeck nt

flimsy ['flɪmzɪ] adj (thin) hauchdünn; (excuse) fadenscheinig

flinch [flɪntʃ] vi: to ~ (away from) zurückschrecken (vor +dat)

fling [flɪŋ] (pt, pp flung) vt schleudern

flint [flɪnt] n Feuerstein m

flip [flɪp] vt werfen

flippant ['flɪpənt] adj schnippisch

flipper ['flɪpə*] n Flosse f

flirt [flɜːt] vi flirten ♦ n: he/she is a ~ er/sie flirtet gern; ~ation [flɜː'teɪʃən] n Flirt m

flit [flɪt] vi flitzen

float [fləʊt] n (FISHING) Schwimmer m; (esp in procession) Plattformwagen m ♦ vi (also: ~ about) schweben ♦ vt (COMM) gründen; (currency) floaten

flock [flɒk] n (of sheep, REL) Herde f; (of birds) Schwarm m; (of people) Schar f

flog [flɒg] vt prügeln; (inf: sell) verkaufen

flood [flʌd] n Überschwemmung f; (fig) Flut f ♦ vt überschwemmen; ~ing n Überschwemmung f; ~light n Flutlicht nt

floor [flɔː*] n (Fuß)boden m; (storey) Stock m ♦ vt (person) zu Boden schlagen; **ground ~** (BRIT) Erdgeschoß nt; **first ~** erste(r) Stock m; (US) Erdgeschoß nt; **~board** n Diele f; **~ show** n Kabarettvorstellung f

flop [flɒp] n Plumps m; (failure) Reinfall m ♦ vi (fail) durchfallen

floppy ['flɒpɪ] adj hängend; **~ (disk)** n (COMPUT) Diskette f

flora ['flɔːrə] n Flora f; **~l** adj Blumen-

florid ['flɒrɪd] adj (style) blumig

florist ['flɒrɪst] n Blumenhändler(in) m(f); **~'s (shop)** n Blumengeschäft nt

flotation n (FINANCE) Auflegung f

flounce [flaʊns] n Volant m

flounder ['flaʊndə*] vi (fig) ins Schleudern kommen ♦ n (ZOOL) Flunder f

flour ['flaʊə*] n Mehl nt

flourish ['flʌrɪʃ] vi blühen; gedeihen ♦ n (waving) Schwingen nt; (of trumpets) Tusch m, Fanfare f; **~ing** adj blühend

flout [flaʊt] vt mißachten

flow [fləʊ] n Fließen nt; (of sea) Flut f ♦ vi fließen; **~ chart** n Flußdiagramm nt

flower ['flaʊə*] n Blume f ♦ vi blühen; **~ bed** n Blumenbeet nt; **~pot** n Blumentopf m; **~y** adj (style) blumenreich

flown [fləʊn] pp of fly

flu [fluː] n Grippe f

fluctuate ['flʌktjʊeɪt] vi schwanken

fluctuation [flʌktjʊ'eɪʃən] n Schwankung f

fluency ['fluːənsɪ] n Flüssigkeit f

fluent ['fluːənt] adj fließend; **~ly** adv fließend

fluff [flʌf] n Fussel f; **~y** adj flaumig

fluid ['fluːɪd] n Flüssigkeit f ♦ adj flüssig; (fig: plans) veränderbar

fluke [fluːk] (inf) n Dusel m

flung [flʌŋ] pt, pp of fling

fluoride ['flʊəraɪd] n Fluorid nt; **~ toothpaste** n Fluorzahnpasta f

flurry ['flʌrɪ] n (of snow) Gestöber nt; (of activity) Aufregung f

flush [flʌʃ] n Erröten nt; (of excitement) Glühen nt ♦ vt (aus)spülen ♦ vi erröten ♦ adj glatt; **~ out** vt ausstöbern; **~ed** adj rot

flustered ['flʌstəd] adj verwirrt

flute [fluːt] n Querflöte f

flutter ['flʌtə*] n Flattern nt ♦ vi flattern

flux [flʌks] n: **in a state of ~** im Fluß

fly [flaɪ] (pt flew, pp flown) n (insect) Fliege f; (on trousers: also: **flies**) (Hosen)schlitz m ♦ vt fliegen ♦ vi fliegen; (flee) fliehen; (flag) wehen; **~ away** or **off** (bird, insect) wegfliegen; **~ing** n Fliegen nt ♦ adj: **with ~ing colours** mit fliegenden Fahnen; **~ing start** gute(r) Start m; **~ing visit** Stippvisite f; **~ing saucer** n fliegende Untertasse f; **~over** (BRIT) n Überführung f; **~past** n Luftparade f; **~sheet** n (for tent) Regendach nt

foal [fəʊl] n Fohlen nt

foam [fəʊm] n Schaum m ♦ vi schäumen; **~ rubber** n Schaumgummi m

fob [fɒb] vt: **to ~ sb off with sth** jdm etw andrehen; (with promise) jdm etw abspeisen

focal ['fəʊkəl] adj Brenn-; **~ point** n (of room, activity) Mittelpunkt m

focus ['fəʊkəs] (pl **~es**) n Brennpunkt m ♦ vt (attention) konzentrieren; (camera) scharf einstellen ♦ vi: to ~ (on) sich konzentrieren (auf +acc); in ~ scharf eingestellt; out of ~ unscharf

fodder ['fɒdə*] n Futter nt

foe [fəu] n Feind m

foetus ['fi:təs] (US fetus) n Fötus m

fog [fɒg] n Nebel m; ~gy adj neblig; ~ lamp n (AUT) Nebellampe f

foil [fɔil] vt vereiteln ♦ n (metal, also fig) Folie f; (FENCING) Florett nt

fold [fəuld] n (bend, crease) Falte f; (AGR) Pferch m ♦ vt (map etc) zusammenfalten ♦ vi (business) eingehen; ~er n Schnellhefter m; (ing adj (chair etc) Klapp-

foliage ['fəulIidʒ] n Laubwerk nt

folk [fəuk] npl Leute pl ♦ adj Volks-; ~s npl (family) Leute pl; ~lore ['fəuklɔ:*] n (study) Volkskunde f; (tradition) Folklore f; ~ song n Volkslied nt; (modern) Folksong m

follow ['fɒləu] vt folgen +dat; (fashion) mitmachen ♦ vi folgen; ~ up vt verfolgen; ~er n Anhänger(in) m(f); ~ing adj folgend ♦ n (people) Gefolgschaft f

folly ['fɒlI] n Torheit f

fond [fɒnd] adj: to be ~ of gern haben

fondle ['fɒndl] vt streicheln

font [fɒnt] n Taufbecken nt

food [fu:d] n Essen nt, (for animals) Futter nt; ~ mixer n Küchenmixer m; ~ poisoning n Lebensmittelvergiftung f; ~ processor n Küchenmaschine f; ~stuffs npl Lebensmittel pl

fool [fu:l] n Narr m, Närrin f ♦ vt (deceive) hereinlegen ♦ vi (also: ~ around) (herum)albern; ~hardy adj tollkühn; ~ish adj albern; ~proof adj idiotensicher

foot [fut] (pl feet) n Fuß m ♦ vt (bill) bezahlen; on ~ zu Fuß; ~age n (CINE) Filmmaterial nt; ~ball n Fußball m; (game: BRIT) Fußball m; (: US) Football m; ~ball player

n (BRIT: also: ~baller) Fußballspieler m, Fußballer m; (US) Footballer m; ~brake n Fußbremse f; ~bridge n Fußgängerbrücke f; ~hills npl Ausläufer pl; ~hold n Halt m; ~ing n Halt m; (fig) Verhältnis nt; ~lights npl Rampenlicht nt; ~man (irreg) n Bediensteter m; ~note n Fußnote f; ~path n Fußweg m; ~print n Fußabdruck m; ~sore adj fußkrank; ~step n Schritt m; ~wear n Schuhzeug nt

for [fɔ:*] prep 1 für; is this for me? ist das für mich?; the train for London der Zug nach London; he went for the paper er ging die Zeitung holen; give it to me - what for? gib es mir - warum?

2 (because of) wegen; for this reason aus diesem Grunde

3 (referring to distance): there are roadworks for 5 km die Baustelle ist 5 km lang; we walked for miles wir sind meilenweit gegangen

4 (referring to time) seit; (: with future sense) für; he was away for 2 years er war zwei Jahre lang weg

5 (with infin clauses): it is not for me to decide das kann ich nicht entscheiden; for this to be possible ... damit dies möglich wird/wurde ...

6 (in spite of) trotz +gen (inf); for all his complaints obwohl er sich ständig beschwert

♦ conj denn

forage ['fɒrIidʒ] n (Vieh)futter nt

foray ['fɒreI] n Raubzug m

forbad(e) [fə'bæd] pt of forbid

forbid [fə'bId] (pt forbad(e), pp forbidden) vt verbieten; ~den [fə'bIdn] pp of forbid; ~ding adj einschüchternd

force [fɔ:s] n Kraft f; (compulsion) Zwang m ♦ vt zwingen; (lock) aufbrechen; the F~s npl (BRIT) die Streitkräfte; in ~ (rule) gültig; (group) in großer Stärke; ~d

adj (smile) gezwungen; (landing)
Not-; **~feed** vt zwangsernähren;
~ful *adj* (speech) kraftvoll; (personality) resolut

forceps ['fɔːseps] *npl* Zange f

forcibly ['fɔːsəblɪ] *adv* zwangsweise

ford [fɔːd] *n* Furt f ♦ vt durchwaten

fore [fɔː*] *n*: to the ~ in den Vorder-
grund

forearm ['fɔːrɑːm] *n* Unterarm m

foreboding [fɔː'bəudɪŋ] *n* Vorahnung f

forecast ['fɔːkɑːst] (irreg: like cast)
n Vorhersage f ♦ vt voraussagen

forecourt ['fɔːkɔːt] *n* (of garage)
Vorplatz m

forefathers ['fɔːfɑːðəz] *npl* Vorfahren pl

forefinger ['fɔːfɪŋgə*] *n* Zeigefinger
m

forefront ['fɔːfrʌnt] *n* Spitze f

forego [fɔː'gəu] (irreg: like go) vt
verzichten auf +acc

foregone ['fɔːgɒn] *adj*: it's a ~
conclusion es steht von vornherein
fest

foreground ['fɔːgraund] *n* Vorder-
grund m

forehead ['fɔrɪd] *n* Stirn f

foreign ['fɔrɪn] *adj* Auslands-; (accent) ausländisch; (trade) Außen-;
(body) Fremd-; **~er** *n* Ausländer(in)
m(f); ~ **exchange** *n* Devisen pl; F~
Office (BRIT) *n* Außenministerium
nt; F~ **Secretary** (BRIT) *n* Außen-
minister m

foreleg ['fɔːleg] *n* Vorderbein nt

foreman ['fɔːmən] (irreg) *n* Vorarbeiter m

foremost ['fɔːməust] *adj* erste(r, s)
♦ *adv*: first and ~ vor allem

forensic [fə'rensɪk] *adj* gerichtsmedi-
zinisch

forerunner ['fɔːrʌnə*] *n* Vorläufer m

foresee [fɔː'siː] (irreg: like see) vt
vorhersehen; **~able** *adj* absehbar

foreshadow [fɔː'ʃædəu] vt andeuten

foresight ['fɔːsaɪt] *n* Voraussicht f

forest ['fɔrɪst] *n* Wald m

forestall [fɔː'stɔːl] vt zuvorkommen

+dat

forestry ['fɔrɪstrɪ] *n* Forstwirtschaft f

foretaste ['fɔːteɪst] *n* Vorgeschmack
m

foretell [fɔː'tel] (irreg: like tell) vt
vorhersagen

forever [fə'revə*] *adv* für immer

foreword ['fɔːwəːd] *n* Vorwort nt

forfeit ['fɔːfɪt] *n* Einbuße f ♦ vt ver-
wirken

forgave [fə'geɪv] *pt of* forgive

forge [fɔːdʒ] *n* Schmiede f ♦ vt
fälschen; (iron) schmieden; ~ **ahead**
vi Fortschritte machen; **~r** *n*
Fälscher m; **~ry** *n* Fälschung f

forget [fə'get] (pt forgot, pp forgotten) vt, vi vergessen; **~ful** *adj* vergeßlich; **~-me-not** *n* Vergißmeinnicht nt

forgive [fə'gɪv] (pt forgave, pp of
forgiven) vt verzeihen; to ~ sb (for
sth) jdm (etw) verzeihen; **~n** pp of
forgive; **~ness** *n* Verzeihung f

forgo [fɔː'gəu] (irreg: like go) vt
verzichten auf +acc

forgot [fə'gɒt] *pt of* forget

forgotten [fə'gɒtn] *pp of* forget

fork [fɔːk] *n* Gabel f; (in road) Gabe-
lung f ♦ vi (road) sich gabeln; ~ **out**
(inf) vt (pay) blechen; **~-lift truck** *n*
Gabelstapler m

forlorn [fə'lɔːn] *adj* (person) verlassen; (hope) vergeblich

form [fɔːm] *n* Form f; (figure) Gestalt f; (SCH) Klasse f;
(bench) (Schul)bank f; (document)
Formular nt ♦ vt formen; (be part
of) bilden

formal ['fɔːməl] *adj* formell; (occasion) offiziell; **~ly** *adv* (ceremonious-
ly) formell; (officially) offiziell

format ['fɔːmæt] *n* Format nt ♦ vt
(COMPUT) formatieren

formation [fɔː'meɪʃən] *n* Bildung f;
(AVIAT) Formation f

formative ['fɔːmətɪv] *adj* (years)
formend

former ['fɔːmə*] *adj* früher; (opposite of latter) erstere(r, s); **~ly** *adv*
früher

formidable ['fɔːmɪdəbl] *adj* furcht-bar

formula ['fɔːmjʊlə] (*pl* ~e *or* ~s) *n* Formel *f*; **formulae** ['fɔːmjʊliː] *npl of* **formula**; **~te** ['fɔːmjʊleɪt] *vt* formulieren

forsake [fə'seɪk] (*pt* **forsook**, *pp* **forsaken**) *vt* verlassen; **forsaken** *pp of* **forsake**

forsook [fə'sʊk] *pt of* **forsake**

fort [fɔːt] *n* Feste *f*, Fort *nt*

forte ['fɔːtɪ] *n* Stärke *f*, starke Seite *f*

forth [fɔːθ] *adv*: **and so ~** und so weiter; **~coming** *adj* kommend; (*character*) entgegenkommend; **~right** *adj* offen; **~with** *adv* umgehend

fortify ['fɔːtɪfaɪ] *vt* (ver)stärken; (*protect*) befestigen

fortitude ['fɔːtɪtjuːd] *n* Seelenstärke *f*

fortnight ['fɔːtnaɪt] *n* (*BRIT*) vierzehn Tage *pl*; **~ly** (*BRIT*) *adj* wöchentlich ♦ *adv* alle vierzehn Tage

fortress ['fɔːtrɪs] *n* Festung *f*

fortuitous [fɔː'tjuːɪtəs] *adj* zufällig

fortunate ['fɔːtʃənɪt] *adj* glücklich; **~ly** *adv* glücklicherweise, zum Glück

fortune ['fɔːtʃən] *n* Glück *nt*; (*money*) Vermögen *nt*; **~-teller** *n* Wahrsager(in) *m(f)*

forty ['fɔːtɪ] *num* vierzig

forum ['fɔːrəm] *n* Forum *nt*

forward ['fɔːwəd] *adj* vordere(r, s); (*movement*) Vorwärts-; (*person*) vorlaut; (*planning*) Voraus- ♦ *adv* vorwärts ♦ *n* (*SPORT*) Stürmer *m* ♦ *vt* (*send*) schicken; (*help*) fördern; **~s** *adv* vorwärts

forwent [fɔː'went] *pt of* **forgo**

fossil ['fɒsl] *n* Fossil *n*, Versteinerung *f*

foster ['fɒstə*] *vt* (*talent*) fördern; **~ child** *n* Pflegekind *nt*; **~ mother** *n* Pflegemutter *f*

fought [fɔːt] *pt*, *pp of* **fight**

foul [faʊl] *adj* schmutzig; (*language*) gemein; (*weather*) schlecht ♦ *n* (*SPORT*) Foul *nt* ♦ *vt* (*mechanism*) blockieren; (*SPORT*) foulen; **~ play** *n* (*SPORT*) Foulspiel *nt*; (*LAW*) Ver-

brechen *nt*

found [faʊnd] *pt*, *pp of* **find** ♦ *vt* gründen; **~ation** [faʊn'deɪʃən] *n* (*act*) Gründung *f*; (*fig*) Fundament *nt*; (*also*: **~ cream**) Grundierungscreme *f*; **~ations** *npl* (*of house*) Fundament *nt*

founder ['faʊndə*] *n* Gründer *m(f)* ♦ *vi* sinken

foundry ['faʊndrɪ] *n* Gießerei *f*

fount [faʊnt] *n* Quelle *f*; **~ain** ['faʊntɪn] *n* (*Spring*)brunnen *m*; **~ain pen** *n* Füllfederhalter *m*

four [fɔː*] *num* vier; **on all ~s** auf allen vieren; **~-poster** *n* Himmelbett *nt*; **~some** *n* Quartett *nt*; **~teen** *num* vierzehn; **~teenth** *adj* vierzehnte(r, s); **~th** *adj* vierte(r, s)

fowl [faʊl] *n* Huhn *nt*; (*food*) Geflügel *nt*

fox [fɒks] *n* Fuchs *m* ♦ *vt* täuschen

foyer ['fɔɪeɪ] *n* Foyer *n*, Vorhalle *f*

fraction ['frækʃən] *n* (*MATH*) Bruch *m*; (*part*) Bruchteil *m*

fracture ['fræktʃə*] *n* (*MED*) Bruch *m* ♦ *vt* brechen

fragile ['frædʒaɪl] *adj* zerbrechlich

fragment ['frægmənt] *n* Bruchstück *n*; (*small part*) Splitter *m*

fragrance ['freɪgrəns] *n* Duft *m*

fragrant ['freɪgrənt] *adj* duftend

frail [freɪl] *adj* schwach, gebrechlich

frame [freɪm] *n* Rahmen *m*; (*of spectacles*: *also*: **~s**) Gestell *nt*; (*body*) Gestalt *f* ♦ *vt* einrahmen; **to ~ sb** (*inf*: *incriminate*) jdm etwas anhängen; **~ of mind** Verfassung *f*; **~work** *n* Rahmen *m*; (*of society*) Gefüge *nt*

France [frɑːns] *n* Frankreich *nt*

franchise ['fræntʃaɪz] *n* (*POL*) (aktives) Wahlrecht *nt*; (*COMM*) Lizenz *f*

frank [fræŋk] *adj* offen ♦ *vt* (*letter*) frankieren; **~ly** *adv* offen gesagt; **~ness** *n* Offenheit *f*

frantic ['fræntɪk] *adj* verzweifelt

fraternal [frə'tɜːnl] *adj* brüderlich

fraternity [frə'tɜːnɪtɪ] *n* (*club*) Vereinigung *f*; (*spirit*) Brüderlichkeit *f*; (*US: SCH*) Studentenverbindung *f*

fraternize ['frætənaɪz] vi fraternisieren

fraud [frɔːd] n (trickery) Betrug m; (person) Schwindler(in) m(f)

fraudulent ['frɔːdjʊlənt] adj betrügerisch

fraught [frɔːt] adj: ~ with voller +gen

fray [freɪ] n Rauferei f ♦ vt, vi ausfransen; tempers were ~ed die Gemüter waren erhitzt

freak [friːk] n Monstrosität f ♦ cpd (storm etc) anormal

freckle ['frekl] n Sommersprosse f

free [friː] adj frei; (loose) lose; (liberal) freigebig ♦ vt (set free) befreien; (unblock) freimachen; ~ (of charge) gratis, umsonst; for ~ (inf) gratis, umsonst; ~dom ['friːdəm] n Freiheit f; ~for-all n (fight) allgemeine(s) Handgemenge nt; ~ gift n Geschenk nt; ~hold property n (free(r)) Grundbesitz m; ~ kick n Freistoß m; ~lance adj frei; (artist) freischaffend; ~ly adv frei; (admit) offen; ~mason n Freimaurer m; ~post n Gebühr zahlt Empfänger; ~range adj (hen) Farmhof-; (eggs) Land-; ~ trade n Freihandel m; ~way (US) n Autobahn f; ~wheel vi im Freilauf fahren; ~ will n: of one's own ~ will aus freien Stücken

freeze [friːz] (pt froze, pp frozen) vi gefrieren; (feel cold) frieren ♦ vt (also fig) einfrieren ♦ n (fig, FIN) Stopp m; ~r n Tiefkühltruhe f; (in fridge) Gefrierfach nt

freezing ['friːzɪŋ] adj eisig; (~ cold) eiskalt; ~ point n Gefrierpunkt m

freight [freɪt] n Fracht f; ~ train n Güterzug m

French [frentʃ] adj französisch ♦ n (LING) Französisch nt; the ~ npl (people) die Franzosen pl; ~ bean n grüne Bohne f; ~ fried potatoes (BRIT) npl Pommes frites pl; ~ fries (US) npl Pommes frites pl; ~man/woman (irreg) n Franzose

m/Französin f; ~ window n Verandatür f

frenzy ['frenzɪ] n Raserei f

frequency ['friːkwənsɪ] n Häufigkeit f; (PHYS) Frequenz f

frequent [adj 'friːkwənt, vb frɪ'kwent] adj häufig ♦ vt (regelmäßig) besuchen; ~ly adv (oft(en)) häufig, oft

fresco ['freskəʊ] n Fresko nt

fresh [freʃ] adj frisch; ~en vi (also: ~en up) (sich) auffrischen; (person) sich frisch machen; ~er (BRIT: inf) n (UNIV) Erstsemester nt; ~ly adv gerade; ~man (US; irreg) n = fresher; ~ness n Frische f; ~water adj (fish) Süßwasser-

fret [fret] vi sich dat Sorgen machen

friar ['fraɪə*] n Klosterbruder m

friction ['frɪkʃən] n (also fig) Reibung f

Friday ['fraɪdeɪ] n Freitag m

fridge [frɪdʒ] (BRIT) n Kühlschrank m

fried [fraɪd] adj gebraten

friend [frend] n Freund(in) m(f); ~ly adj freundlich; (relations) freundschaftlich; ~ship n Freundschaft f

frieze [friːz] n Fries m

frigate ['frɪgɪt] n Fregatte f

fright [fraɪt] n Schrecken m; to take ~ es mit der Angst zu tun bekommen; ~en vt erschrecken; to be ~ened Angst haben; ~ening adj schrecklich; ~ful (inf) adj furchtbar; ~fully (inf) adv furchtbar

frigid ['frɪdʒɪd] adj (woman) frigide

frill [frɪl] n Rüsche f

fringe [frɪndʒ] n Besatz m; (BRIT: of hair) Pony m; (fig) Peripherie f; ~ benefits npl zusätzliche Leistungen pl

frisk [frɪsk] vt durchsuchen

frisky ['frɪskɪ] adj lebendig, ausgelassen

fritter ['frɪtə*] vt: to ~ away vergeuden

frivolous ['frɪvələs] adj frivol

frizzy ['frɪzɪ] adj kraus

fro [frəu] *see* to

frock [frɔk] *n* Kleid *nt*

frog [frɔg] *n* Frosch *m*; ~**man** (*irreg*) *n* Froschmann *m*

frolic [ˈfrɔlɪk] *vi* ausgelassen sein

KEYWORD

from [frɔm] *prep* **1** (*indicating starting place*) von; (*indicating origin etc*) aus +*dat*; **a letter/telephone call from my sister** ein Brief/Anruf von meiner Schwester; **where do you come from?** woher kommen Sie?; **to drink from the bottle** aus der Flasche trinken

2 (*indicating time*) von ... an; (: *past*) seit; **from one o'clock to** *or* **until** *or* **till two** von ein Uhr bis zwei; **from January (on)** ab Januar

3 (*indicating distance*) von ... (entfernt)

4 (*indicating price, number etc*) ab +*dat*; **from £10** ab £10; **there were from 20 to 30 people** there es waren zwischen 20 und 30 Leute da

5 (*indicating difference*): **he can't tell red from green** er kann nicht zwischen rot und grün unterscheiden; **to be different from sb/sth** anders sein als jd/etw

6 (*because of, on the basis of*): **from what he says** aus dem, was er sagt; **weak from hunger** schwach vor Hunger

front [frʌnt] *n* Vorderseite *f*; (*of house*) Fassade *f*; (*promenade: also*: **sea** ~) Strandpromenade *f*; (*MIL, POL, MET*) Front *f*; (*fig: appearances*) Fassade *f* ♦ *adj* (*forward*) vordere(r, s), Vorder-; (*first*) vorderste(r, s) ♦ *n*: **in** ~ vorne; **in** ~ **of** vor; ~**age** *n* Vorderfront *f*; ~**al** *adj* frontal, Vorder-; ~ **door** *n* Haustür *f*; ~**ier** [ˈfrʌntɪə*] *n* Grenze *f*; ~ **page** *n* Titelseite *f*; ~ **room** (*BRIT*) *n* Wohnzimmer *nt*; ~**wheel drive** *n* Vorderradantrieb *m*

frost [frɔst] *n* Frost *m*; ~**bite** *n* Erfrierung *f*; ~**ed** *adj* (*glass*) Milch-;

~**y** *adj* frostig

froth [frɔθ] *n* Schaum *m*

frown [fraun] *n* Stirnrunzeln *nt* ♦ *vi* die Stirn runzeln

froze [frəuz] *pt of* **freeze**

frozen [ˈfrəuzn] *pp of* **freeze**

frugal [ˈfruːgəl] *adj* sparsam, bescheiden

fruit [fruːt] *n inv* (*as collective*) Obst *nt*; (*particular*) Frucht *f*; ~**erer** *n* Obsthändler *m*; ~**ful** *adj* fruchtbar; ~**ion** [fruːˈɪʃən] *n*: **to come to** ~**ion** in Erfüllung gehen; ~ **juice** *n* Fruchtsaft *m*; ~ **machine** (*BRIT*) *n* Spielautomat *m*; ~ **salad** *n* Obstsalat *m*

frustrate [frʌsˈtreɪt] *vt* vereiteln; ~**d** *adj* gehemmt; (*PSYCH*) frustriert

fry [fraɪ] (*pt, pp* **fried**) *vt* braten ♦ *npl*: **small** ~ kleine Fische *pl*; ~**ing pan** *n* Bratpfanne *f*

ft. *abbr* = **foot**; **feet**

fuddy-duddy [ˈfʌdɪdʌdɪ] *n* altmodische(r) Kauz *m*

fudge [fʌdʒ] *n* Fondant *m*

fuel [fjuəl] *n* Treibstoff *m*; (*for heating*) Brennstoff *m*; (*for lighter*) Benzin *nt*; ~ **oil** *n* (*diesel fuel*) Heizöl *nt*; ~ **tank** *n* Tank *m*

fugitive [ˈfjuːdʒɪtɪv] *n* Flüchtling *m*

fulfil [fulˈfɪl] *vt* (*duty*) erfüllen; (*promise*) einhalten; ~**ment** *n* Erfüllung *f*

full [ful] *adj* (*box, bottle, price*) voll; (*person: satisfied*) satt; (*member, power, employment, moon*) Voll-; (*complete*) vollständig, Voll-; (*speed*) höchste(r, s); (*skirt*) weit ♦ *adv*: **well** *or* **well** sehr wohl; **in** ~ vollständig; **a** ~ **two hours** volle zwei Stunden; ~**length** *adj* (*lifesize*) lebensgroß; **a** ~**length photograph** eine Ganzaufnahme; ~ **moon** *n* Vollmond *m*; ~**scale** *adj* (*attack*) General-; (*drawing*) in Originalgröße; ~ **stop** *n* Punkt *m*; ~**time** *adj* (*job*) Ganztags- ♦ *adv* (*work*) ganztags ♦ *n* (*SPORT*) Spielschluß *nt*; ~**y** *adv* völlig; ~**y-fledged** *adj* (*also fig*) flügge

fulsome ['fulsəm] adj übertrieben

fumble ['fʌmbl] vi: to ~ (with) herumfummeln (an +dat)

fume [fju:m] vi qualmen; (fig) kochen (inf); ~s npl (of fuel, car) Abgase pl

fumigate ['fju:mɪgeɪt] vt ausräuchern

fun [fʌn] n Spaß m; to make ~ of sich lustig machen über +acc

function ['fʌŋkʃən] n Funktion f; (occasion) Veranstaltung f ♦ vi funktionieren; ~al adj funktionell

fund [fʌnd] n (money) Geldmittel pl, Fonds m; (store) Vorrat m; ~s npl (resources) Mittel pl

fundamental [fʌndə'mentl] adj fundamental, grundlegend

funeral ['fju:nərəl] n Beerdigung f; ~ parlour n Leichenhalle f; ~ service n Trauergottesdienst m

funfair ['fʌnfeə*] (BRIT) n Jahrmarkt m

fungi ['fʌŋgaɪ] npl of fungus

fungus ['fʌŋgəs] n Pilz m

funnel ['fʌnl] n Trichter m; (NAUT) Schornstein m

funny ['fʌnɪ] adj komisch

fur [fɜ:*] n Pelz m; ~ coat n Pelzmantel m

furious ['fjʊərɪəs] adj wütend; (attempt) heftig

furlong ['fɜ:lɒŋ] n = 201.17 m

furlough ['fɜ:ləʊ] n Urlaub m

furnace ['fɜ:nɪs] n (Brenn)ofen m

furnish ['fɜ:nɪʃ] vt einrichten; (supply) versehen; ~ings npl Einrichtung f

furniture ['fɜ:nɪtʃə*] n Möbel pl; piece of ~ Möbelstück n

furrow ['fʌrəʊ] n Furche f

furry ['fɜ:rɪ] adj (tongue) pelzig; (animal) Pelz-

further ['fɜ:ðə*] adj weitere(r, s) ♦ adv weiter ♦ vt fördern; ~ education n Weiterbildung f, Erwachsenenbildung f; ~more adv ferner

furthest ['fɜ:ðɪst] superl of far

furtive ['fɜ:tɪv] adj verstohlen

fury ['fjʊərɪ] n Wut f, Zorn m

fuse [fju:z] n (ELEC) Sicherung f; (of bomb) Zünder m ♦ vt verschmelzen ♦ vi (BRIT: ELEC) durchbrennen; ~ box n Sicherungskasten m

fuselage ['fju:zəlɑ:ʒ] n Flugzeugrumpf m

fusion ['fju:ʒən] n Verschmelzung f

fuss [fʌs] n Theater nt; ~y adj kleinlich

futile ['fju:taɪl] adj zwecklos, sinnlos

futility [fju:'tɪlɪtɪ] n Zwecklosigkeit f

future ['fju:tʃə*] adj zukünftig ♦ n Zukunft f; in (the) ~ in Zukunft

fuze [fju:z] (US) = fuse

fuzzy ['fʌzɪ] adj (indistinct) verschwommen; (hair) kraus

G

G [dʒi:] n (MUS) G nt

G7 n abbr (= Group of Seven) G7 f

gabble ['gæbl] vi plappern

gable ['geɪbl] n Giebel m

gadget ['gædʒɪt] n Vorrichtung f

Gaelic ['geɪlɪk] adj gälisch ♦ n (LING) Gälisch nt

gaffe [gæf] n Fauxpas m

gag [gæg] n Knebel m; (THEAT) Gag m ♦ vt knebeln

gaiety ['geɪətɪ] n Fröhlichkeit f

gaily ['geɪlɪ] adv lustig, fröhlich

gain [geɪn] vt (obtain) erhalten; gewinnen ♦ vi (clock) vorgehen ♦ n Gewinn m; to ~ in sth an etw dat gewinnen; ~ on sth fus einholen

gait [geɪt] n Gang m

gal. abbr = gallon

gala ['gɑ:lə] n Fest nt

galaxy ['gæləksɪ] n Sternsystem nt

gale [geɪl] n Sturm m

gallant ['gælənt] adj tapfer; (polite) galant; ~ry n Tapferkeit f; Galanterie f

gallbladder ['gɔ:l] n Gallenblase f

gallery ['gælərɪ] n (also: art ~) Galerie f

galley ['gælɪ] n (ship's kitchen) Kombüse f; (ship) Galeere f

gallon ['gælən] *n* Gallone *f*

gallop ['gæləʊ] *n* Galopp *m* ♦ *vi* galoppieren

gallows ['gæləʊz] *n* Galgen *m*

gallstone ['gɔːlstəʊn] *n* Gallenstein *m*

galore [gə'lɔː*] *adv* in Hülle und Fülle

galvanize ['gælvənaɪz] *vt* (*metal*) galvanisieren; (*fig*) elektrisieren

gambit ['gæmbɪt] *n* (*fig*): **opening ~** (einleitende*r*) Schachzug *m*

gamble ['gæmbl] *vi* (um Geld) spielen ♦ *vt* (*risk*) aufs Spiel setzen ♦ *n* Risiko *nt*; **~r** *n* Spieler(in) *m(f)*

gambling ['gæmblɪŋ] *n* Glücksspiel *nt*

game [geɪm] *n* Spiel *nt*; (*hunting*) Wild *nt* ♦ *adj*: **~ (for)** bereit (zu); **~keeper** *n* Wildhüter *m*; **~s console** *n* (*COMPUT*) Gameboy *m* (®), Konsole *f*

gammon ['gæmən] *n* geräucherte*r* Schinken *m*

gamut ['gæmət] *n* Tonskala *f*

gang [gæŋ] *n* (*of criminals, youths*) Bande *f*; (*of workmen*) Kolonne *f* ♦ *vi*: **to ~ up on sb** sich gegen jdn verschwören

gangrene ['gæŋgriːn] *n* Brand *m*

gangster ['gæŋstə*] *n* Gangster *m*

gangway ['gæŋweɪ] *n* (*NAUT*) Laufplanke *f*; (*aisle*) Gang *m*

gaol [dʒeɪl] (*BRIT*) *n*, *vt* = **jail**

gap [gæp] *n* Lücke *f*

gape [geɪp] *vi* glotzen

gaping ['geɪpɪŋ] *adj* (*wound*) klaffend; (*hole*) gähnend

garage ['gærɑːʒ] *n* Garage *f*; (*for repair*) (Auto)reparaturwerkstatt *f*; (*for petrol*) Tankstelle *f*

garbage ['gɑːbɪdʒ] *n* Abfall *m*; **~ can** (*US*) *n* Mülltonne *f*

garbled ['gɑːbld] *adj* (*story*) verdreht

garden ['gɑːdn] *n* Garten *m*; **~er** *n* Gärtner(in) *m(f)*; **~ing** *n* Gärtnern *nt*

gargle ['gɑːgl] *vi* gurgeln

gargoyle ['gɑːgɔɪl] *n* Wasserspeier *m*

garish ['gɛərɪʃ] *adj* grell

garland ['gɑːlənd] *n* Girlande *f*

garlic ['gɑːlɪk] *n* Knoblauch *m*

garment ['gɑːmənt] *n* Kleidungsstück *nt*

garnish ['gɑːnɪʃ] *vt* (*food*) garnieren

garrison ['gærɪsən] *n* Garnison *f*

garrulous ['gærʊləs] *adj* geschwätzig

garter ['gɑːtə*] *n* Strumpfband *nt*; (*US*) Strumpfhalter *m*

gas [gæs] *n* Gas *nt*; (*esp US: petrol*) Benzin *nt* ♦ *vt* vergasen; **~ cooker** (*BRIT*) *n* Gasherd *m*; **~ cylinder** (*BRIT*) *n* Gasflasche *f*; **~ fire** *n* Gasofen *m*

gash [gæʃ] *n* klaffende Wunde *f* ♦ *vt* tief verwunden

gasket ['gæskɪt] *n* Dichtungsring *m*

gas mask *n* Gasmaske *f*

gas meter *n* Gaszähler *m*

gasoline ['gæsəliːn] (*US*) *n* Benzin *nt*

gasp [gɑːsp] *vi* keuchen; (*in astonishment*) tief Luft holen ♦ *n* Keuchen *nt*

gas ring *n* Gasring *m*

gas tap *n* Gashahn *m*

gastric ['gæstrɪk] *adj* Magen-

gate [geɪt] *n* Tor *nt*; (*barrier*) Schranke *f*; **~crash** (*BRIT*) *vt* (*party*) platzen in +*acc*; **~way** *n* Toreingang *m*

gather ['gæðə*] *vt* (*people*) versammeln; (*things*) sammeln; (*understand*) annehmen ♦ *vi* (*assemble*) sich versammeln; **to ~ speed** schneller werden; **to ~ (from)** schließen (aus); **~ing** *n* Versammlung *f*

gauche [gəʊʃ] *adj* linkisch

gaudy ['gɔːdɪ] *adj* schreiend

gauge [geɪdʒ] *n* (*instrument*) Meßgerät *nt*; (*RAIL*) Spurweite *f*; (*dial*) Anzeiger *m*; (*measure*) Maß *nt* ♦ *vt* (ab)messen; (*fig*) abschätzen

gaunt [gɔːnt] *adj* hager

gauntlet ['gɔːntlɪt] *n* (*knight's*) (Fehde)handschuh *m*

gauze [gɔːz] *n* Gaze *f*

gave [geɪv] *pt of* **give**

gay [geɪ] *adj* (*homosexual*) schwul; (*lively*) lustig

gaze [geɪz] *n* Blick *m* ♦ *vi* starren;

to ~ at sth etw *dat* anstarren

gazelle [gə'zɛl] *n* Gazelle *f*

gazetteer [gæzɪ'tɪə*] *n* geographische(s) Lexikon *nt*

gazumping [gə'zʌmpɪŋ] (BRIT) *n* Hausverkauf zu höherbietenden trotz Zusage an anderen

GB *n abbr* = Great Britain

GCE (BRIT) *n abbr* = General Certificate of Education

GCSE (BRIT) *n abbr* = General Certificate of Secondary Education

gear [gɪə*] *n* Getriebe *nt*; (equipment) Ausrüstung *f*; (AUT) Gang *m* ♦ *vt* (fig: adapt): **to be ~ed to** ausgerichtet sein auf +acc; **top ~** höchste(r) Gang *m*; **high ~** (US) höchste(r) Gang *m*; **low ~** niedrige(r) Gang *m*; **in ~** eingekuppelt; ~**box** *n* Getriebe(gehäuse) *nt*; ~**lever** *n* Schalthebel *m*; ~**shift** (US) *n* Schalthebel *m*

geese [giːs] *npl of* **goose**

gel [dʒɛl] *n* Gel *nt*

gelatin(e) ['dʒɛlətiːn] *n* Gelatine *f*

gelignite ['dʒɛlɪgnaɪt] *n* Plastiksprengstoff *m*

gem [dʒɛm] *n* Edelstein *m*; (fig) Juwel *nt*

Gemini ['dʒɛmɪniː] *n* Zwillinge *pl*

gender ['dʒɛndə*] *n* (GRAM) Geschlecht *nt*

gene [dʒiːn] *n* Gen *nt*

general ['dʒɛnərəl] *n* General *m* ♦ *adj* allgemein; ~ **delivery** (US) *n* Ausgabe(schalter *m*) *f* postlagernder Sendungen; ~ **election** *n* allgemeine Wahlen *pl*; ~**ization** [dʒɛnərəlaɪ'zeɪʃən] *n* Verallgemeinerung *f*; ~**ize** *vi* verallgemeinern; ~**ly** *adv* allgemein, im allgemeinen; ~ **practitioner** *n* praktische(r) Arzt *m*, praktische Ärztin *f*

generate ['dʒɛnəreɪt] *vt* erzeugen

generation [dʒɛnə'reɪʃən] *n* Generation *f*; (act) Erzeugung *f*

generator ['dʒɛnəreɪtə*] *n* Generator *m*

generosity [dʒɛnə'rɒsɪtɪ] *n* Groß-

zügigkeit *f*

generous ['dʒɛnərəs] *adj* großzügig

genetic engineering [dʒɪ'nɛtɪk] *n* Gentechnologie *f*; ~ **fingerprinting** *n* genetische Fingerabdrücke *pl*

genetics [dʒɪ'nɛtɪks] *n* Genetik *f*

Geneva [dʒɪ'niːvə] *n* Genf *nt*

genial ['dʒiːnɪəl] *adj* freundlich, jovial

genitals ['dʒɛnɪtlz] *npl* Genitalien *pl*

genius ['dʒiːnɪəs] *n* Genie *nt*

genocide ['dʒɛnəusaɪd] *n* Völkermord *m*

gent [dʒɛnt] *n abbr* = **gentleman**

genteel [dʒɛn'tiːl] *adj* (polite) wohlanständig; (affected) affektiert

gentle ['dʒɛntl] *adj* sanft, zart

gentleman ['dʒɛntlmən] (irreg) *n* Herr *m*; (polite) Gentleman *m*

gentleness ['dʒɛntlnɪs] *n* Zartheit *f*, Milde *f*

gently ['dʒɛntlɪ] *adv* zart, sanft

gentry ['dʒɛntrɪ] *n* Landadel *m*

gents [dʒɛnts] *n*: G~ (lavatory) Herren *pl*

genuine ['dʒɛnjuɪn] *adj* echt

geographic(al) [dʒɪə'græfɪk(əl)] *adj* geographisch

geography [dʒɪ'ɒgrəfɪ] *n* Geographie *f*

geological [dʒɪəu'lɒdʒɪkəl] *adj* geologisch

geologist [dʒɪ'ɒlədʒɪst] *n* Geologe *m*, Geologin *f*

geology [dʒɪ'ɒlədʒɪ] *n* Geologie *f*

geometric(al) [dʒɪə'mɛtrɪk(l)] *adj* geometrisch

geometry [dʒɪ'ɒmɪtrɪ] *n* Geometrie *f*

geranium [dʒɪ'reɪnɪəm] *n* Geranie *f*

geriatric [dʒɛrɪ'ætrɪk] *adj* Alten-, Greis(in) *m(f)*

germ [dʒɜːm] *n* Keim *m*; (MED) Bacillus *m*

German ['dʒɜːmən] *adj* deutsch ♦ *n* Deutsche(r) *mf*; (LING) Deutsch *nt*; ~ **measles** *n* Röteln *pl*

Germany ['dʒɜːmənɪ] *n* Deutschland *nt*

germination [dʒɜːmɪ'neɪʃən] *n* Keimen *nt*

gesticulate [dʒes'tɪkjʊleɪt] vi gestikulieren

gesture ['dʒestʃə*] n Geste f

KEYWORD
---

get [get] (pt, pp **got**, pp **gotten** (US)) vi **1** (become, be) werden; to get old/tired alt/müde werden; to get married heiraten

2 (go) (an)kommen, gehen

3 (begin): to get to know sb jdn kennenlernen; let's get going or started fangen wir an!

♦ (modal aux vb): you've got to do it du mußt es tun

♦ vt **1**: to get sth done (do) etw machen; (have done) etw machen lassen; to get sth going or to go etw in Gang bringen or bekommen; to get sb to do sth jdn dazu kriegen, etw zu tun

2 (obtain: money, permission, results) erhalten; (find: job, flat) finden; (fetch: person, doctor, object) holen; to get sth for sb jdm etw besorgen; get me Mr Jones, please (TEL) verbinden Sie mich bitte mit Mr Jones

3 (receive: present, letter) bekommen, kriegen; (acquire: reputation etc) erwerben

4 (catch) bekommen, kriegen; (hit: target etc) treffen, erwischen; get him! (to dog) faß!

5 (take, move) bringen; to get sth to sb jdm etw bringen

6 (understand) verstehen; (hear) mitbekommen; I've got it! ich hab's!

7 (have, possess): to have got sth etw haben

get about vi herumkommen; (news) sich verbreiten

get along vi (people) (gut) zurechtkommen; (depart) sich acc auf den Weg machen

get at vt (facts) herausbekommen; to get at sb (nag) an jdm herumnörgeln

get away vi (leave) sich acc davon

machen; (escape): to get away from sth von etw dat loskommen; to get away with sth mit etw davon kommen

get back vi (return) zurückkommen

♦ vt zurückbekommen

get by vi (pass) vorbeikommen; (manage) zurechtkommen

get down vi (her)untergehen ♦ vt (depress) fertigmachen; to get down to in Angriff nehmen; (find time to do) kommen zu

get in vi (train) ankommen; (arrive home) heimkommen

get into vt (enter) hinein-/ hereinkommen in +acc; (: car, train etc) einsteigen in +acc; (clothes) anziehen

get off vi (from train etc) aussteigen; (from horse) absteigen ♦ vt aussteigen aus; absteigen von

get on vi (progress) vorankommen; (be friends) auskommen; (age) alt werden; (onto train etc) einsteigen; (onto horse) aufsteigen ♦ vt einsteigen in +acc ♦ vi aufsteigen auf +acc

get out vi (of house) herauskommen; (of vehicle) aussteigen ♦ vt (take out) herausholen

get out of vt (duty etc) herumkommen um

get over vt (illness) sich acc erholen von; (surprise) verkraften; (news) fassen; (loss) sich abfinden mit

get round vt herumkommen; (fig: person) herumkriegen

get through to vt (TEL) durchkommen zu

get together vi zusammenkommen

get up vi aufstehen ♦ vt hinaufbringen; (go up) hinaufgehen; (organize) auf die Beine stellen

get up to vt (reach) erreichen; (prank etc) anstellen

getaway ['getəweɪ] n Flucht f

get-up ['getʌp] (inf) n Aufzug m

geyser ['giːzə*] n Geiser m; (heater) Durchlauferhitzer m

ghastly ['gɑːstlɪ] adj gräßlich

gherkin ['gɜːkɪn] n Gewürzgurke f

ghetto ['getəʊ] n G(h)etto nt; ~ **blaster** n (groß(er)) Radiorekorder m

ghost [gəʊst] n Gespenst nt

giant ['dʒaɪənt] n Riese m ♦ adj riesig, Riesen-

gibberish ['dʒɪbərɪʃ] n dumme(s) Geschwätz nt

gibe [dʒaɪb] n spöttische Bemerkung f

giblets ['dʒɪblɪts] npl Geflügelinnereien pl

Gibraltar [dʒɪ'brɔːltə*] n Gibraltar nt

giddiness ['gɪdɪnəs] n Schwindelgefühl nt

giddy ['gɪdɪ] adj schwindlig

gift [gɪft] n Geschenk nt; (ability) Begabung f; ~ed adj begabt; ~ token, ~ voucher n Geschenkgutschein m

gigantic [dʒaɪ'gæntɪk] adj riesenhaft

giggle ['gɪgl] vi kichern ♦ n Gekicher nt

gild [gɪld] vt vergolden

gill [dʒɪl] n (1/4 pint) Viertelpinte f

gills [gɪlz] npl (of fish) Kiemen pl

gilt [gɪlt] n Vergoldung f ♦ adj vergoldet; ~-edged adj mündelsicher

gimmick ['gɪmɪk] n Gag m

ginger ['dʒɪndʒə*] n Ingwer m; ~ **ale** n Ingwerbier nt; ~ **beer** n Ingwerbier nt; ~**bread** n Pfefferkuchen m; ~**haired** adj rothaarig

gingerly ['dʒɪndʒəlɪ] adv behutsam

gipsy ['dʒɪpsɪ] n Zigeuner(in) m(f)

giraffe ['dʒɪrɑːf] n Giraffe f

girder ['gɜːdə*] n Eisenträger m

girdle ['gɜːdl] n Hüftgürtel m

girl [gɜːl] n Mädchen nt; **an English ~** eine (junge) Engländerin f; ~**friend** n Freundin f; ~**ish** adj mädchenhaft

giro ['dʒaɪrəʊ] n (bank ~) Giro nt; (post office ~) Postscheckverkehr m

girth [gɜːθ] n (measure) Umfang m; (strap) Sattelgurt m

gist [dʒɪst] n Wesentliche(s) nt

give [gɪv] (pt gave, pp given) vt geben ♦ vi (break) nachgeben; ~ **away** vt verschenken; (betray) verraten; ~ **back** vt zurückgeben; ~ **in**

vi nachgeben ♦ vt (hand in) abgeben; ~ **off** vt abgeben; ~ **out** vt verteilen; (announce) bekanntgeben; ~ **up** vt, vi aufgeben; **to ~ o.s. up** sich stellen; (after siege) sich ergeben; ~ **way** vi (BRIT: traffic) Vorfahrt lassen; (to feelings): **to ~ way to** nachgeben +dat; ~**n** pp of **give**

glacier ['glæsɪə*] n Gletscher m

glad [glæd] adj froh

gladly ['glædlɪ] adv gern(e)

glamorous ['glæmərəs] adj reizvoll

glamour ['glæmə*] n Glanz m

glance [glɑːns] n Blick m ♦ vi: **to ~ (at)** (hin)blicken (auf +acc); ~ **off** vt fus (fly off) abprallen von

glancing ['glɑːnsɪŋ] adj (blow) Streif-

gland [glænd] n Drüse f

glare [glɛə*] n (light) grelle(s) Licht nt; (stare) wilde(r) Blick m ♦ vi grell scheinen; (angrily): **to ~ at** böse ansehen

glaring ['glɛərɪŋ] adj (injustice) schreiend; (mistake) kraß

glass [glɑːs] n Glas nt; (mirror: also: looking ~) Spiegel m; ~**es** npl (spectacles) Brille f; ~**house** n Gewächshaus nt; ~**ware** n Glaswaren pl; ~**y** adj glasig

glaze [gleɪz] vt verglasen; (finish with a ~) glasieren ♦ n Glasur f; ~**d** adj (eye) glasig; (pottery) glasiert

glazier ['gleɪzɪə*] n Glaser m

gleam [gliːm] n Schimmer m ♦ vi schimmern; ~**ing** adj schimmernd

glean [gliːn] vt (fig) ausfindig machen

glen [glen] n Bergtal nt

glib [glɪb] adj oberflächlich

glide [glaɪd] vi gleiten; ~**r** n (AVIAT) Segelflugzeug nt

gliding ['glaɪdɪŋ] n Segelfliegen nt

glimmer ['glɪmə*] n Schimmer m

glimpse [glɪmps] n flüchtige(r) Blick m ♦ vt flüchtig erblicken

glint [glɪnt] n Glitzern nt ♦ vi glitzern

glisten ['glɪsn] vi glänzen

glitter ['glɪtə*] vi funkeln ♦ n Funkeln nt

gloat ['gləʊt] vi: to ~ **over** sich weiden an +dat

globe [gləʊb] n Erdball m; (sphere) Globus m

gloom [glu:m] n (darkness) Dunkel nt; (depression) düstere Stimmung f; ~**y** adj düster

glorify ['glɔ:rɪfaɪ] vt verherrlichen

glorious ['glɔ:rɪəs] adj glorreich

glory ['glɔ:rɪ] n Ruhm m

gloss [glɒs] n (shine) Glanz m; ~ **over** vt fus übertünchen

glossary ['glɒsərɪ] n Glossar nt

glossy ['glɒsɪ] adj (surface) glänzend

glove [glʌv] n Handschuh m; ~ **compartment** n (AUT) Handschuhfach nt

glow [gləʊ] vi glühen ♦ n Glühen nt

glower ['glaʊə*] vi: to ~ **at** finster anblicken

glucose ['glu:kəʊs] n Traubenzucker m

glue [glu:] n Klebstoff m ♦ vt kleben

glum [glʌm] adj bedrückt

glut [glʌt] n Überfluß m

glutton ['glʌtn] n Vielfraß m; a ~ **for work** ein Arbeitstier nt; ~**y** n Völlerei f

glycerin(e) ['glɪsəri:n] n Glyzerin nt

gnarled [nɑ:ld] adj knorrig

gnat [næt] n Stechmücke f

gnaw [nɔ:] vt nagen an +dat

gnome [nəʊm] n Gnom m

go [gəʊ] (pt went, pp gone; pl ~es) vi gehen; (travel) reisen, fahren; (depart: train) (ab)fahren; (be sold) verkauft werden; (work) gehen, funktionieren; (fit, suit) passen; (become) werden; (break etc) nachgeben ♦ n (energy) Schwung m; (attempt) Versuch m; he's ~**ing** to do it er wird es tun; to ~ **for a walk** spazieren gehen; to ~ **dancing** tanzen gehen; how did it ~? wie war's?; to ~ **with** (be suitable) passen zu; to have a ~ **at sth** etw versuchen; to be on the ~ auf Trab sein; whose ~ **is it?** wer ist dran?; ~ **about** vi (rumour) umgehen ♦ vt fus: how do I ~ **about this?** wie packe ich das an?; ~ **ahead** vi (proceed) weiterge-

hen; ~ **along** vi dahingehen, dahinfahren ♦ vt entlanggehen, entlangfahren; to ~ **along with** (agree to support) zustimmen +dat; ~ **away** vi (depart) weggehen; ~ **back** vi (return) zurückgehen; ~ **back on** vt fus (promise) nicht halten; ~ **by** (years, time) vergehen ♦ vt fus sich richten nach; ~ **down** vi (sun) untergehen ♦ vt fus hinuntergehen, hinunterfahren; ~ **for** vt fus (fetch) holen (gehen); (like) mögen; (attack) sich stürzen auf +acc; ~ **in** vi hineingehen; ~ **in for** vt fus (competition) teilnehmen an; ~ **into** vt fus (enter) hineingehen in +acc; (study) sich befassen mit; ~ **off** vi (depart) weggehen; (lights) ausgehen; (milk etc) sauer werden; (explode) losgehen ♦ vt fus (dislike) nicht mehr mögen; ~ **on** vi (continue) weitergehen; (inf: complain) meckern; (lights) angehen; to ~ **on with sth** mit etw weitermachen; ~ **out** vi (fire, light) ausgehen; (of house) hinausgehen; ~ **over** vi (ship) kentern ♦ vt fus (examine, check) durchgehen; ~ **through** vt fus (town etc) durchgehen, durchfahren; ~ **up** vi (price) steigen; ~ **without** vt fus sich behelfen ohne; (food) entbehren

goad [gəʊd] vt anstacheln

go-ahead ['gəʊəhɛd] adj zielstrebig; (progressive) fortschrittlich ♦ n grüne(s) Licht nt

goal [gəʊl] n Ziel nt; (SPORT) Tor nt; ~**keeper** n Torwart m; ~**post** n Torpfosten m

goat [gəʊt] n Ziege f

gobble ['gɒbl] vt (also: ~ **down, ~ up**) hinunterschlingen

go-between ['gəʊbɪtwi:n] n Mittelsmann m

goblet ['gɒblɪt] n Kelch(glas nt) m

god [gɒd] n Gott m; G~ n Gott m; ~**child** n Patenkind nt; ~**daughter** n Patentochter f; ~**dess** n Göttin f; ~**father** n Pate m; ~**forsaken** adj gottverlassen; ~**mother** n Patin f; ~**send** n Geschenk nt des Himmels;

~son n Patensohn m

goggles ['gɒglz] npl Schutzbrille f

going ['gəʊɪŋ] n (HORSE-RACING) Bahn f ♦ adj (rate) gängig; (concern) gutgehend; it's hard ~ es ist schwierig

gold [gəʊld] n Gold nt ♦ adj golden; ~en adj golden, Gold-; ~fish n Goldfisch m; ~ mine n Goldgrube f; ~-plated adj vergoldet; ~smith n Goldschmied (in) m(f)

golf [gɒlf] n Golf nt; ~ball n Golfball m; (on typewriter) Kugelkopf m; ~club n (society) Golfklub m; (stick) Golfschläger m; ~ course n Golfplatz m; ~er n Golfspieler(in) m(f)

gondola ['gɒndələ] n Gondel f

gone [gɒn] pp of go

gong [gɒŋ] n Gong m

good [gʊd] n (benefit) Wohl nt; (moral excellence) Güte f ♦ adj gut; ~s npl (merchandise etc) Waren pl, Güter pl; a ~ deal (of) ziemlich viel; a ~ many ziemlich viele; ~ morning! guten Morgen!; ~ afternoon! guten Tag!; ~ evening! guten Abend!; ~ night! gute Nacht!; would you be ~ enough to ...? könnten Sie bitte ...?; ~bye excl auf Wiedersehen!; G~ Friday n Karfreitag m; ~-looking adj gutaussehend; ~-natured adj gutmütig; (joke) harmlos; ~ness n Güte f; (virtue) Tugend f; ~s train (BRIT) n Güterzug m; ~will n (favour) Wohlwollen nt; (COMM) Firmenansehen nt

goose [guːs] (pl geese) n Gans f

gooseberry ['gʊzbərɪ] n Stachelbeere f

gooseflesh ['guːsfleʃ] n Gänsehaut f

goose pimples npl Gänsehaut f

gore [gɔː*] vt aufspießen ♦ n Blut nt

gorge [gɔːdʒ] n Schlucht f ♦ vt: to ~ o.s. (sich voll) fressen

gorgeous ['gɔːdʒəs] adj prächtig

gorilla [gə'rɪlə] n Gorilla m

gorse [gɔːs] n Stechginster m

gory ['gɔːrɪ] adj blutig

go-slow ['gəʊ'sləʊ] (BRIT) n Bum-

melstreik m

gospel ['gɒspəl] n Evangelium nt

gossip ['gɒsɪp] n Klatsch m; (person) Klatschbase f ♦ vi klatschen

got [gɒt] pt, pp of get

gotten ['gɒtən] (US) pp of get

gout [gaʊt] n Gicht f

govern ['gʌvən] vt regieren; verwalten

governess ['gʌvənɪs] n Gouvernante f

government ['gʌvnmənt] n Regierung f

governor ['gʌvənə*] n Gouverneur m

gown [gaʊn] n Gewand nt; (UNIV) Robe f

G.P. n abbr = general practitioner

grab [græb] vt packen

grace [greɪs] n Anmut f; (blessing) Gnade f; (prayer) Tischgebet nt ♦ vt (adorn) zieren; (honour) auszeichnen; 5 days' ~ 5 Tage Aufschub; ~ful adj anmutig

gracious ['greɪʃəs] adj gnädig; (kind) freundlich

grade [greɪd] n Grad m; (slope) Gefälle f ♦ vt (classify) einstufen; ~ crossing (US) n Bahnübergang m; ~ school (US) n Grundschule f

gradient ['greɪdɪənt] n Steigung f; Gefälle nt

gradual ['grædjʊəl] adj allmählich; ~ly adv allmählich

graduate [n 'grædjʊɪt, vb 'grædjʊeɪt] n: to be a ~ das Staatsexamen haben ♦ vi das Staatsexamen machen

graduation [grædjʊ'eɪʃən] n Abschlussfeier f

graffiti [grə'fiːtɪ] npl Graffiti pl

graft [grɑːft] n (hard work) Schufterei f; (MED) Verpflanzung f ♦ vt propfen; (fig) aufpropfen; (MED) verpflanzen

grain [greɪn] n Korn nt; (in wood) Maserung f

gram [græm] n Gramm nt

grammar ['græmə*] n Grammatik f; ~ school (BRIT) n Gymnasium nt

grammatical [grə'mætɪkl] adj grammat(ikal)isch

gramme [græm] n = gram

granary [ˈgrænəri] n Kornspeicher m

grand [grænd] adj großartig; ~**child** (pl **grandchildren**) n Enkelkind nt, Enkel(in) m(f); ~**dad** n Opa m; ~**daughter** n Enkelin f; ~**eur** [ˈgrændjə*] n Erhabenheit f; ~**father** n Großvater m; ~**iose** [ˈgrændiəus] adj (imposing) großartig; (pompous) schwülstig; ~**ma** n Oma f; ~**mother** n Großmutter f; ~**pa** n granddad; ~**parents** npl Großeltern pl; ~**piano** n Flügel m; ~**son** n Enkel m; ~**stand** n Haupttribüne f

granite [ˈgrænɪt] n Granit m

granny [ˈgrænɪ] n Oma f

grant [grɑːnt] vt gewähren ♦ n Unterstützung f; (UNIV) Stipendium nt; **to take sth for ~ed** etw als selbstverständlich (an)nehmen

granulated sugar [ˈgrænjuleɪtɪd-] n Zuckerraffinade f

granule [ˈgrænjuːl] n Körnchen n

grape [greɪp] n (Wein)traube f

grapefruit [ˈgreɪpfruːt] n Pampelmuse f, Grapefruit f

graph [grɑːf] n Schaubild nt; ~**ic** [ˈgræfɪk] adj (descriptive) anschaulich; (drawing) graphisch; ~**ics** npl Grafik f

grapple [ˈgræpl] vi: **to ~ with** kämpfen mit

grasp [grɑːsp] vt ergreifen; (understand) begreifen ♦ n Griff m; (of subject) Beherrschung f; ~**ing** adj habgierig

grass [grɑːs] n Gras nt; ~**hopper** n Heuschrecke f; ~**land** n Weideland nt; ~**roots** adj an der Basis; ~**snake** n Ringelnatter f

grate [greɪt] n Kamin m ♦ vi (sound) knirschen ♦ vt (cheese etc) reiben; **to ~ on the nerves** auf die Nerven gehen

grateful [ˈgreɪtful] adj dankbar

grater [ˈgreɪtə*] n Reibe f

gratify [ˈgrætɪfaɪ] vt befriedigen; ~**ing** [ˈgrætɪfaɪɪŋ] adj erfreulich

grating [ˈgreɪtɪŋ] n (iron bars) Gitter

nt ♦ adj (noise) knirschend

gratitude [ˈgrætɪtjuːd] n Dankbarkeit f

gratuity [grəˈtjuːɪtɪ] n Gratifikation f

grave [greɪv] n Grab nt ♦ adj (serious) ernst

gravel [ˈgrævəl] n Kies m

gravestone [ˈgreɪvstəun] n Grabstein m

graveyard [ˈgreɪvjɑːd] n Friedhof m

gravity [ˈgrævɪtɪ] n Schwerkraft f; (seriousness) Schwere f

gravy [ˈgreɪvɪ] n (Braten)soße f

gray [greɪ] adj = grey

graze [greɪz] vi grasen ♦ vt (touch) streifen; (MED) abschürfen ♦ n Abschürfung f

grease [griːs] n (fat) Fett nt; (lubricant) Schmiere f ♦ vt (lub)schmieren; ~**proof** (BRIT) adj (paper) Butterbrot-

greasy [ˈgriːsɪ] adj fettig

great [greɪt] adj groß; (inf: good) prima; **G~ Britain** n Großbritannien nt; ~**grandfather** n Urgroßvater m; ~**grandmother** n Urgroßmutter f; ~**ly** adv sehr; ~**ness** n Größe f

Greece [griːs] n Griechenland nt

greed [griːd] n (also: ~**iness**) Gier f; (meanness) Geiz m; ~**iness** for Gier nach; ~**y** adj gierig

Greek [griːk] adj griechisch ♦ n Grieche m, Griechin f; (LING) Griechisch nt

green [griːn] adj grün; (village ~) Dorfwiese f; ~ **belt** n Grüngürtel m; ~ **card** n (AUT) grüne Versicherungskarte f; ~**ery** n Grün nt; ~**gage** n Reineclaude f; ~**grocer** (BRIT) n Obst- und Gemüsehändler m; ~**house** n Gewächshaus nt; ~**house effect** n Treibhauseffekt m; ~**house gas** n Treibhausgas nt; ~**ish** adj grünlich

Greenland [ˈgriːnlənd] n Grönland nt

greet [griːt] vt grüßen; ~**ing** n Gruß m; ~**ing(s) card** n Glückwunschkarte f

gregarious [grɪ'gɛərɪəs] adj gesellig
grenade [grɪ'neɪd] n Granate f
grew [gru:] pt of grow
grey [greɪ] adj grau; **~-haired** adj
grauhaarig; **~hound** n Windhund m;
~ish adj gräulich
grid [grɪd] n Gitter nt; (ELEC) Lei-
tungsnetz nt; (on map) Gitternetz nt
grief [gri:f] n Gram m, Kummer m
grievance ['gri:vəns] n Beschwerde f
grieve [gri:v] vi sich grämen ♦ vt betrüben
grievous ['gri:vəs] adj: **~ bodily
harm** (JUR) schwere Körperverletzung f
grill [grɪl] n Grill m ♦ vt (BRIT) grillen; (question) in die Mangel nehmen
grille [grɪl] n (on car etc)
(Kühler)gitter nt
grim [grɪm] adj grimmig; (situation)
düster
grimace [grɪ'meɪs] n Grimasse f ♦ vi
Grimassen schneiden
grime [graɪm] n Schmutz m
grimy ['graɪmɪ] adj schmutzig
grin [grɪn] n Grinsen nt ♦ vi grinsen
grind [graɪnd] (pt, pp ground) vt
mahlen; (US: meat) durch den
Fleischwolf drehen; (sharpen) schleifen; (teeth) knirschen mit ♦ n (bore)
Plackerei f
grip [grɪp] n Griff m; (suitcase)
Handkoffer m ♦ vt packen; **~ping**
adj (exciting) spannend
grisly ['grɪzlɪ] adj gräßlich
gristle ['grɪsl] n Knorpel m
grit [grɪt] n Splitt m; (courage) Mut
m ♦ vt (teeth) zusammenbeißen;
(road) (mit Splitt be)streuen
groan [grəʊn] n Stöhnen nt ♦ vi
stöhnen
grocer ['grəʊsə*] n Lebensmittel-
händler m; **~ies** npl Lebensmittel pl;
~'s (shop) n Lebensmittelgeschäft nt
groggy ['grɒgɪ] adj benommen
groin [grɔɪn] n Leistengegend f
groom [gru:m] n (also: bride**~**)
Bräutigam m; (for horses) Pferde-
knecht m ♦ vt (horse) striegeln;
(well-)groomed gepflegt

groove [gru:v] n Rille f, Furche f
grope [grəʊp] vi tasten; **~ for** vt fus
suchen nach
gross [grəʊs] adj (coarse) dick,
plump; (bad) grob, schwer; (COMM)
brutto; **~ly** adv höchst
grotesque [grəʊ'tesk] adj grotesk
grotto ['grɒtəʊ] n Grotte f
ground [graʊnd] pt, pp of grind ♦ n
Boden m; (land) Grundbesitz m;
(reason) Grund m; (US: also: **~**
wire) Endleitung f; **~s** npl (of coffee)
Bodensatz m; (around house) (Garten)anlagen pl; **on the ~** am Boden;
to the ~ zu Boden; **to gain/lose ~**
Boden gewinnen/verlieren; **~ cloth**
(US) n = ground sheet; **~ing** n (instruction) Anfangsunterricht m;
~less adj grundlos; **~sheet** (BRIT)
n Zeltboden m; **~ staff** n Bodenper-
sonal nt; **~ swell** n (of sea) Dünung
f; (fig) Zunahme f; **~work** n Grundlage f
group [gru:p] n Gruppe f ♦ vt (also:
~ together) gruppieren ♦ vi sich
gruppieren
grouse [graʊs] n inv (bird) schotti-
sche(s) Moorhuhn nt ♦ vi (complain)
meckern
grove [grəʊv] n Gehölz m, Hain m
grovel ['grɒvl] vi (fig) kriechen
grow [grəʊ] (pt grew, pp grown) vi
wachsen; (become) werden ♦ vt
(raise) anbauen; **~ up** vi aufwachsen; **~er** n Züchter m; **~ing**
adj zunehmend
growl [graʊl] vi knurren
grown [grəʊn] pp of grow; **~-up** n
Erwachsene(r) mf
growth [grəʊθ] n Wachstum nt; (increase) Zunahme f; (of beard etc)
Wuchs m
grub [grʌb] n Made f, Larve f; (inf:
food) Futter nt; **~by** ['grʌbɪ] adj
schmutzig
grudge [grʌdʒ] n Groll m ♦ vt: **to**
sb sth jdm etw mißgönnen; **to bear**
sb a ~ einen Groll gegen jdn hegen
gruelling ['grʊəlɪŋ] adj (climb, race)

mörderisch

gruesome ['gru:səm] *adj* grauenhaft

gruff [grʌf] *adj* barsch

grumble ['grʌmbl] *vi* murren

grumpy ['grʌmpɪ] *adj* verdrießlich

grunt [grʌnt] *vi* grunzen ♦ *n* Grunzen *nt*

G-string ['dʒi:-] *n* Minislip *m*

guarantee [gærən'ti:] *n* Garantie *f* ♦ *vt* garantieren

guard [gɑːd] *n* (*sentry*) Wache *f*; (*BRIT: RAIL*) Zugbegleiter *m* ♦ *vt* bewachen; **~ed** *adj* vorsichtig; **~ian** *n* Vormund *m*; (*keeper*) Hüter *m*; **~'s van** (*BRIT*) *n* (*RAIL*) Dienstwagen *m*

guerrilla [gə'rɪlə] *n* Guerilla(kämpfer) *m*; **~ warfare** *n* Guerillakrieg *m*

guess [ges] *vt, vi* (*er*)raten, schätzen ♦ *n* Vermutung *f*; **~work** *n* Raterei *f*

guest [gest] *n* Gast *m*; **~house** *n* Pension *f*; **~ room** *n* Gastzimmer *nt*

guffaw [gʌ'fɔ:] *vi* schallend lachen

guidance ['gaɪdəns] *n* (*control*) Leitung *f*; (*advice*) Beratung *f*

guide [gaɪd] *n* Führer *m*; (*also: girl ~*) Pfadfinderin *f* ♦ *vt* führen; **~book** *n* Reiseführer *m*; **~ dog** *n* Blindenhund *m*; **~lines** *npl* Richtlinien *pl*

guild [gɪld] *n* (*HIST*) Gilde *f*; **~hall** (*BRIT*) *n* Stadthalle *f*

guile [gaɪl] *n* Arglist *f*

guillotine [gɪlə'tiːn] *n* Guillotine *f*

guilt [gɪlt] *n* Schuld *f*; **~y** *adj* schuldig

guinea pig ['gɪnɪ-] *n* Meerschweinchen *nt*; (*fig*) Versuchskaninchen *nt*

guise [gaɪz] *n*: **in the ~ of** in der Form +*gen*

guitar [gɪ'tɑ:*] *n* Gitarre *f*

gulf [gʌlf] *n* Golf *m*; (*fig*) Abgrund *m*

gull [gʌl] *n* Möwe *f*

gullet ['gʌlɪt] *n* Schlund *m*

gullible ['gʌlɪbl] *adj* leichtgläubig

gully ['gʌlɪ] *n* (*Wasser*)rinne *f*

gulp [gʌlp] *vt* (*also: ~ down*) hinunterschlucken ♦ *vi* (*gasp*) schlucken

gum [gʌm] *n* (*around teeth*) Zahn-

fleisch *nt*; (*glue*) Klebstoff *m*; (*also: chewing~*) Kaugummi *m* ♦ *vt* gummieren; **~boots** (*BRIT*) *npl* Gummistiefel *pl*

gumption ['gʌmpʃən] (*inf*) *n* Mumm *m*

gun [gʌn] *n* Schußwaffe *f*; **~boat** *n* Kanonenboot *nt*; **~fire** *n* Geschützfeuer *nt*; **~man** (*irreg*) *n* bewaffneter Verbrecher *m*; **~point** *n*: **at ~point** mit Waffengewalt; **~powder** *n* Schießpulver *nt*; **~shot** *n* Schuß *m*

gurgle ['gɜːgl] *vi* gluckern

guru ['guru:] *n* Guru *m*

gush [gʌʃ] *vi* (*rush out*) hervorströmen; (*fig*) schwärmen

gust [gʌst] *n* Windstoß *m*, Bö *f*

gusto ['gʌstəu] *n* Genuß *m*, Lust *f*

gut [gʌt] *n* (*ANAT*) Gedärm *pl*; (*string*) Darm *m*; **~s** *npl* (*fig*) Schneid *m*

gutter ['gʌtə*] *n* Dachrinne *f*; (*in street*) Gosse *f*

guttural ['gʌtərəl] *adj* guttural, Kehl-

guy [gaɪ] *n* (*also: ~rope*) Halteseil *nt*; (*man*) Typ *m*, Kerl *m*

guzzle ['gʌzl] *vt, vi* (*drink*) saufen; (*eat*) fressen

gym [dʒɪm] *n* (*also: gymnasium*) Turnhalle *f*; (*: gymnastics*) Turnen *nt*; **~nast** [dʒɪmˈnæst] *n* Turner(in) *m(f)*; **~nastics** [dʒɪmˈnæstɪks] *n* Turnen *nt*, Gymnastik *f*; **~ shoes** *npl* Turnschuhe *pl*; **~ slip** (*BRIT*) *n* Schultragerrock *m*

gynaecologist [gaɪnɪˈkɒlədʒɪst] (*US* **gynecologist**) *n* Frauenarzt(ärztin) *m(f)*

gypsy ['dʒɪpsɪ] *n* = **gipsy**

gyrate [dʒaɪˈreɪt] *vi* kreisen

H

haberdashery [hæbəˈdæʃərɪ] (*BRIT*) *n* Kurzwaren *pl*

habit ['hæbɪt] *n* (*An*)gewohnheit *f*; (*monk's*) Habit *m* or *nt*

habitable ['hæbɪtəbl] *adj* bewohnbar

habitat ['hæbɪtæt] n Lebensraum m
habitual [hə'bɪtjʊəl] adj gewohnheitsmäßig; **~ly** adv gewöhnlich
hack [hæk] vt haken ♦ n Hieb m; (writer) Schreiberling m
hacker ['hækə*] n (COMPUT) Hacker m
hackneyed ['hæknɪd] adj abgedroschen
had [hæd] pt, pp of have
haddock ['hædək] (pl ~ or ~s) n Schellfisch m
hadn't ['hædnt] = had not
haemorrhage ['hemərɪdʒ] (US hemorrhage) n Blutung f
haemorrhoids ['hemərɔɪdz] (US hemorrhoids) npl Hämorrhoiden pl
haggard ['hægəd] adj abgekämpft
haggle ['hægl] vi feilschen
Hague [heɪg] n: The ~ Den Haag nt
hail [heɪl] n Hagel m ♦ vt umjubeln ♦ vi hageln; **~stone** n Hagelkorn nt
hair [heə*] n Haar nt, Haare pl; (one ~) Haar nt; **~brush** n Haarbürste f; **~cut** n Haarschnitt m; **to get a ~cut** sich dat die Haare schneiden lassen; **~do** n Frisur f; **~dresser** n Friseur m, Friseuse f; **~dresser's** n Friseursalon m; **~ dryer** n Trockenhaube f; (hand-held) Fön m; **~grip** n Klemme f; **~net** n Haarnetz nt; **~pin** n Haarnadel f; **~pin bend** (US **hairpin curve**) n Haarnadelkurve f; **~raising** adj haarsträubend; **~removing cream** n Enthaarungscreme nt; **~spray** n Haarspray nt; **~style** n Frisur f; **~y** adj haarig
hake [heɪk] n Seehecht m
half [hɑːf] (pl **halves**) n Hälfte f ♦ adj halb ♦ adv halb, zur Hälfte; **~-an-hour** eine halbe Stunde; **two and a ~** zweieinhalb; **to cut sth in ~** etw halbieren; **~ a dozen** ein halbes Dutzend, sechs; **~back** n Läufer m; **~ board** n Halbpension f; **~caste** n Mischling m; **~-hearted** adj lustlos; **~hour** n halbe Stunde f; **~penny** ['heɪpnɪ] (BRIT) n halber Penny m; (at) **~-price** zum halben Preis; **~ term** (BRIT) n (SCH) Ferien pl in

der Mitte des Trimesters; **~-time** n Halbzeit f; **~way** adv halbwegs, auf halbem Wege
halibut ['hælɪbət] n inv Heilbutt m
hall [hɔːl] n Saal m; (entrance ~) Hausflur m; (building) Halle f; **~ of residence** (BRIT) n Studentenwohnheim nt
hallmark ['hɔːlmɑːk] n Stempel m
hallo [hə'ləʊ] excl = hello
Hallowe'en ['hæləʊ'iːn] n Tag m vor Allerheiligen
hallucination [həluːsɪ'neɪʃən] n Halluzination f
hallway ['hɔːlweɪ] n Korridor m
halo ['heɪləʊ] n Heiligenschein m
halt [hɔːlt] n Halt m ♦ vt, vi anhalten
halve [hɑːv] vt halbieren
halves [hɑːvz] pl of half
ham [hæm] n Schinken m
hamburger ['hæmbɜːgə*] n Hamburger m
hamlet ['hæmlɪt] n Weiler m
hammer ['hæmə*] n Hammer m ♦ vt, vi hämmern
hammock ['hæmək] n Hängematte f
hamper ['hæmpə*] vt (be)hindern ♦ n Picknickkorb m
hand [hænd] n Hand f; (of clock) (Uhr)zeiger m; (worker) Arbeiter m ♦ vt (pass) geben; **to give sb a ~** jdm helfen; **at ~** nahe; **to ~** zur Hand; **in ~** (under control) unter Kontrolle; (being done) im Gange; (extra) übrig; **on ~** zur Verfügung; **on the one ~ ..., on the other ~ ...** einerseits ..., andererseits ...; **~ in** vt abgeben; (forms) einreichen; **~ out** vt austeilen; **~ over** vt (deliver) übergeben; (surrender) ausliefern; **~bag** n Handtasche f; **~book** n Handbuch nt; **~brake** n Handbremse f; **~cuffs** npl Handschellen pl; **~ful** n Handvoll f; (inf: person) Plage f
handicap ['hændɪkæp] n Handikap nt ♦ vt benachteiligen; **mentally/physically ~ped** geistig/körperlich behindert
handicraft ['hændɪkrɑːft] n Kunst-

handwerk nt
handiwork ['hændɪwɜːk] n Arbeit f; (fig) Werk nt

handkerchief ['hæŋkətʃɪf] n Taschentuch nt

handle ['hændl] n (of door etc) Klinke f; (of cup etc) Henkel m; (for winding) Kurbel f ♦ vt (touch) anfassen; (deal with: things) sich befassen mit; ⊢ (: people) umgehen mit; ~**bar(s)** n(pl) Lenkstange f

hand: ~ **luggage** n Handgepäck nt; ~**made** adj handgefertigt; ~**out** n (distribution) Verteilung f; (charity) Geldzuwendung f; (leaflet) Flugblatt nt; ~**rail** n Geländer nt; (on ship) Reling f; ~**shake** n Händedruck f

handsome ['hænsəm] adj gutaussehend

handwriting ['hændraɪtɪŋ] n Handschrift f

handy ['hændɪ] adj praktisch; (shops) leicht erreichbar; ~**man** ['hændɪmən] (irreg) n Bastler m

hang [hæŋ] (pt, pp **hung**) vt aufhängen; (criminal: pt, pp **hanged**) hängen ♦ vi hängen ♦ to: **to get the ~ of sth** (inf) den richtigen Dreh bei etw herauskriegen; ~ **about** vi sich herumtreiben; ~ **on** vi (wait) warten; ~ **up** vi (TEL) auflegen

hangar ['hæŋə*] n Hangar m

hanger ['hæŋə*] n Kleiderbügel m

hanger-on ['hæŋər'ɒn] n Anhänger(in) m(f)

hang-gliding ['hæŋglaɪdɪŋ] n Drachenfliegen nt

hangover ['hæŋəuvə*] n Kater m

hang-up ['hæŋʌp] n Komplex m

hanker ['hæŋkə*] vi: **to ~ for** or **after** sich sehnen nach

hankie ['hæŋkɪ] n abbr = **handkerchief**

hanky ['hæŋkɪ] n abbr = **handkerchief**

haphazard ['hæp'hæzəd] adj zufällig

happen ['hæpən] vi sich ereignen, passieren; **as it ~s** I'm going there today zufällig(erweise) gehe ich heute (dort)hin; ~**ing** n Ereignis nt

happily ['hæpɪlɪ] adv glücklich; (fortunately) glücklicherweise

happiness ['hæpɪnɪs] n Glück nt

happy ['hæpɪ] adj glücklich; ~ **birthday!** alles Gute zum Geburtstag!; ~**go-lucky** adj sorglos

harass ['hærəs] vt plagen; ~**ment** n Belästigung f

harbour ['hɑːbə*] (US **harbor**) n Hafen m ♦ vt (hope etc) hegen; (criminal etc) Unterschlupf gewähren

hard [hɑːd] adj (firm) hart; (difficult) schwer; (harsh) hart(herzig) ♦ adv (work) hart; (try) sehr; (push, hit) fest; **no ~ feelings!** ich nehme es dir nicht übel; ~ **of hearing** schwerhörig; **to be ~ done by** übel dran sein; ~**back** n kartonierte Ausgabe f; ~ **cash** n Bargeld nt; ~ **disk** n (COMPUT) Festplatte f; ~**en** vt erhärten; (fig) verhärten ♦ vi hart werden; (fig) sich verhärten; ~**headed** adj nüchtern; ~ **labour** n Zwangsarbeit f

hardly ['hɑːdlɪ] adv kaum

hard: ~**ness** n Härte f; (difficulty) Schwierigkeit f; ~**ship** n Not f; ~**up** adj knapp bei Kasse; ~**ware** n Eisenwaren pl; (COMPUT) Hardware f; ~**ware shop** n Eisenwarenhandlung f; ~**wearing** adj strapazierfähig; ~**working** adj fleißig

hardy ['hɑːdɪ] adj widerstandsfähig

hare [hɛə*] n Hase m; ~**brained** adj schwachsinnig

harm [hɑːm] n Schaden m ♦ vt schaden +dat; **out of ~'s way** in Sicherheit; ~**ful** adj schädlich; ~**less** adj harmlos

harmonica [hɑː'mɒnɪkə] n Mundharmonika f

harmonious [hɑː'məunɪəs] adj harmonisch

harmonize ['hɑːmənaɪz] vt abstimmen ♦ vi harmonieren

harmony ['hɑːmənɪ] n Harmonie f

harness ['hɑːnɪs] n Geschirr nt ♦ vt (horse) anschirren; (fig) nutzbar machen

harp [hɑːp] n Harfe f ♦ vi: **to ~**

about sth auf etw *dat* herumreiten

harpoon [hɑːˈpuːn] *n* Harpune *f*

harrowing [ˈhærəʊɪŋ] *adj* nervenaufreibend

harsh [hɑːʃ] *adj* (*rough*) rauh; (*severe*) streng; **~ness** *n* Härte *f*

harvest [ˈhɑːvɪst] *n* Ernte *f* ♦ *vt, vi* ernten; **~er** [ˈhɑːvɪstə*] *n* Mähdrescher *m*

has [hæz] *vb see* have

hash [hæʃ] *vt* kleinhacken ♦ *n* (*mess*) Kuddelmuddel *m*; (*meat*) Haschee *nt*

hashish [ˈhæʃɪʃ] *n* Haschisch *nt*

hasn't [ˈhæznt] = has not

hassle [ˈhæsl] (*inf*) *n* Theater *nt*

haste [heɪst] *n* Eile *f*; **~n** [ˈheɪsn] *vt* beschleunigen ♦ *vi* eilen

hasty [ˈheɪstɪ] *adj* hastig; (*rash*) vorschnell

hat [hæt] *n* Hut *m*

hatch [hætʃ] *n* (NAUT: *also*: **~way**) Luke *f*; (*in house*) Durchreiche *f* ♦ *vi* (*young*) ausschlüpfen ♦ *vt* (*brood*) ausbrüten; (*plot*) aushecken

hatchback [ˈhætʃbæk] *n* (AUT) (Auto *nt* mit) Heckklappe *f*

hatchet [ˈhætʃɪt] *n* Beil *nt*

hate [heɪt] *vt* hassen ♦ *n* Haß *m*; **~ful** *adj* verhaßt

hatred [ˈheɪtrɪd] *n* Haß *m*

haughty [ˈhɔːtɪ] *adj* hochnäsig, überheblich

haul [hɔːl] *vt* ziehen ♦ *n* (*catch*) Fang *m*; **~age** *n* Spedition *f*; **~ier** (US **hauler**) *n* Spediteur *m*

haunch [hɔːntʃ] *n* Lende *f*

haunt [hɔːnt] *vt* (*ghost*) spuken in +*dat*; (*memory*) verfolgen; (*pub*) häufig besuchen ♦ *n* Lieblingsplatz *m*; **the castle is ~ed** in dem Schloß spukt es

---

KEYWORD

have [hæv] (*pt, pp* **had**) *aux vb* **1** haben; (*esp with vbs of motion*) sein; **to have arrived/slept** angekommen sein/geschlafen haben; **to have been** gewesen sein; **having eaten** *or* **when he had eaten**, **he left** nachdem er gegessen hatte, ging er

2 (*in tag questions*): **you've done it, haven't you?** du hast es doch gemacht, oder nicht?

3 (*in short answers and questions*): **you've made a mistake - so I have/no I haven't** du hast einen Fehler gemacht - ja, stimmt/nein; **we haven't paid - yes we have!** wir haben nicht bezahlt - doch; **I've been there before, have you?** ich war schon einmal da, du auch?

♦ *modal aux vb* (*be obliged*): **to have (got) to do sth** etw tun müssen; **you haven't to tell her** du darfst es ihr nicht erzählen

♦ *vt* **1** (*possess*) haben; **he has (got) blue eyes** er hat blaue Augen; **I have (got) an idea** ich habe eine Idee

2 (*referring to meals etc*): **to have breakfast/a cigarette** frühstücken/ eine Zigarette rauchen

3 (*receive, obtain etc*) haben; **may I have your address?** kann ich Ihre Adresse haben?; **to have a baby** ein Kind bekommen

4 (*maintain, allow*): **he will have it that he is right** er besteht darauf, daß er recht hat; **I won't have it** das lasse ich mir nicht bieten

5: **to have sth done** etw machen lassen; **to have sb do sth** jdn etw machen lassen; **he soon had them all laughing** er brachte sie alle zum Lachen

6 (*experience, suffer*): **she had her bag stolen** man hat ihr die Tasche gestohlen; **he had his arm broken** er hat sich den Arm gebrochen

7 (+*noun: take, hold etc*): **to have a walk/rest** spazierengehen/sich ausruhen; **to have a meeting/party** eine Besprechung/Party haben

have out *vt*: **to have it out with sb** (*settle a problem etc*) etw mit jdm bereden

haven [ˈheɪvn] *n* Zufluchtsort *m*

haven't [ˈhævnt] = have not

haversack [ˈhævəsæk] *n* Rucksack *m*

havoc ['hævək] n Verwüstung f
Hawaii [hə'waiiː] n Hawaii nt
hawk [hɔːk] n Habicht m
hay [heɪ] n Heu nt; ~ **fever** n Heuschnupfen m; ~**stack** n Heuschober m
haywire ['heɪwaɪə*] (inf) adj durcheinander
hazard ['hæzəd] n Risiko nt ♦ vt aufs Spiel setzen; ~**ous** adj gefährlich; ~ **(warning) lights** npl (AUT) Warnblinklicht nt
haze [heɪz] n Dunst m
hazelnut ['heɪzlnʌt] n Haselnuß f
hazy ['heɪzɪ] adj (misty) dunstig; (vague) verschwommen
he [hiː] pron er
head [hed] n Kopf m; (leader) Leiter m ♦ vt (an)führen, leiten; (ball) köpfen; ~**s** (or **tails**) Kopf (oder Zahl); ~ **first** mit dem Kopf nach unten; ~ **over heels** kopfüber; ~ **for** vt fus zugehen auf +acc; ~**ache** n Kopfschmerzen pl; ~**dress** n Kopfschmuck m; ~**ing** n Überschrift f; ~**lamp** (BRIT) n Scheinwerfer m; ~**land** n Landspitze f; ~**light** n Scheinwerfer m; ~**line** n Schlagzeile f; ~**long** adv kopfüber; ~**master** n (of primary school) Rektor m; (of secondary school) Direktor m; ~**mistress** n Rektorin f; Direktorin f; ~**office** n Zentrale f; ~-**on** adj Frontal-; ~**phones** npl Kopfhörer pl; ~**quarters** npl Zentrale f; (MIL) Hauptquartier nt; ~**rest** n Kopfstütze f; ~**room** n (of bridges etc) lichte Höhe f; ~**scarf** n Kopftuch nt; ~**strong** adj eigenwillig; ~**waiter** n Oberkellner m; ~**way** n Fortschritte pl; ~**wind** n Gegenwind m; ~**y** adj berauschend
heal [hiːl] vt heilen ♦ vi verheilen
health [helθ] n Gesundheit f; ~ **food** n Reformkost f; **the H**~ **Service** (BRIT) n das Gesundheitswesen; ~**y** adj gesund
heap [hiːp] n Haufen m ♦ vt häufen
hear [hɪə*] (pt, pp **heard**) vt hören; (listen to) anhören ♦ vi hören; ~**d** [hɜːd] pt, pp of **hear**; ~**ing** n Gehör

nt; (JUR) Verhandlung f; ~**ing aid** n Hörapparat m; ~**say** n Hörensagen nt
hearse [hɜːs] n Leichenwagen m
heart [hɑːt] n Herz nt; ~**s** npl (CARDS) Herz nt; **by** ~ auswendig; ~ **attack** n Herzanfall m; ~**beat** n Herzschlag m; ~**breaking** adj herzzerbrechend; ~**broken** adj untröstlich; ~**burn** n Sodbrennen nt; ~ **failure** n Herzschlag m; ~**felt** adj aufrichtig
hearth [hɑːθ] n Herd m
heartily ['hɑːtɪlɪ] adv herzlich; (eat) herzhaft
heartless ['hɑːtlɪs] adj herzlos
hearty ['hɑːtɪ] er kräftig; (friendly) freundlich
heat [hiːt] n Hitze f; (of food, water etc) Wärme f; (SPORT: also: qualifying ~) Ausscheidungsrunde f ♦ vt (house) heizen; (substance) heiß machen, erhitzen; ~ **up** vi warm werden ♦ vt aufwärmen; ~**ed** adj erhitzt; (fig) hitzig; ~**er** n (Heiz)ofen m
heath [hiːθ] (BRIT) n Heide f
heathen ['hiːðən] n Heide m/Heidin f ♦ adj heidnisch, Heiden-
heather ['heðə*] n Heidekraut nt
heating ['hiːtɪŋ] n Heizung f
heatstroke ['hiːtstrəʊk] n Hitzschlag m
heat wave n Hitzewelle f
heave [hiːv] vt hochheben; (sigh) ausstoßen ♦ vi wogen; (breast) sich heben ♦ n Heben nt
heaven ['hevn] n Himmel m; ~**ly** adj himmlisch
heavy ['hevɪ] adj schwer; ~ **goods vehicle** n Lastkraftwagen m; ~**weight** n (SPORT) Schwergewicht nt
Hebrew ['hiːbruː] adj hebräisch ♦ n (LING) Hebräisch nt
Hebrides ['hebrɪdiːz] npl Hebriden pl
heckle ['hekl] vt unterbrechen
hectic ['hektɪk] adj hektisch
he'd [hiːd] = **he had; he would**

hedge [hedʒ] n Hecke f ♦ vt einzäunen ♦ vi (fig) ausweichen; **to ~ one's bets** sich absichern

hedgehog ['hedʒhɔg] n Igel m

heed [hi:d] vt (also: **take ~ of**) beachten ♦ n Beachtung f; **~less** adj achtlos

heel [hi:l] n Ferse f; (of shoe) Absatz m ♦ vt (shoes) mit Absätzen versehen

hefty ['heftɪ] adj (person) stämmig; (portion) reichlich

heifer ['hefə*] n Färse f

height [haɪt] n (of person) Größe f; (of object) Höhe f; **~en** vt erhöhen

heir [ɛə*] n Erbe m; **~ess** ['ɛərɪs] n Erbin f; **~loom** n Erbstück nt

held [held] pt, pp of **hold**

helicopter ['helɪkɔptə*] n Hubschrauber m

heliport ['helɪpɔ:t] n Hubschrauberlandeplatz m

hell [hel] n Hölle f ♦ excl verdammt!

he'll [hi:l] = **he will**; **he shall**

hellish ['helɪʃ] adj höllisch, verteufelt

hello [hʌ'ləʊ] excl hallo

helm [helm] n Ruder nt, Steuer nt

helmet ['helmɪt] n Helm m

help [help] n Hilfe f ♦ vt helfen +dat; **I can't ~** it ich kann nichts dafür; **~ yourself** bedienen Sie sich; **~er** n Helfer m; **~ful** adj hilfreich; **~ing** n Portion f; **~less** adj hilflos

hem [hem] n Saum m ♦ vt säumen; **~ in** vt einengen

hemorrhage ['hemərɪdʒ] (US) n = **haemorrhage**

hemorrhoids ['hemərɔɪdz] (US) npl = **haemorrhoids**

hen [hen] n Henne f

hence [hens] adv von jetzt an; (therefore) daher; **~forth** adv von nun an; (from then on) von da an

henchman ['hentʃmən] (irreg) n Gefolgsmann m

her [hɜ:*] pron (acc) sie; (dat) ihr ♦ adj ihr; see also **my**

herald ['herəld] n (Vor)bote m ♦ vt verkünden

heraldry ['herəldrɪ] n Wappenkunde f

herb [hɜ:b] n Kraut nt

herd [hɜ:d] n Herde f

here [hɪə*] adv hier; (to this place) hierher; **~after** adv hernach, künftig ♦ n Jenseits nt; **~by** adv hiermit

hereditary [hɪ'redɪtərɪ] adj erblich

heredity [hɪ'redɪtɪ] n Vererbung f

heresy ['herəsɪ] n Ketzerei f

heretic ['herətɪk] n Ketzer m

heritage ['herɪtɪdʒ] n Erbe nt

hermetically [hɜ:'metɪkəlɪ] adv: **~ sealed** hermetisch verschlossen

hermit ['hɜ:mɪt] n Einsiedler m

hernia ['hɜ:nɪə] n Bruch m

hero ['hɪərəʊ] (pl **~es**) n Held m; **~ic** [hɪ'rəʊɪk] adj heroisch

heroin ['herəʊɪn] n Heroin f

heroine ['herəʊɪn] n Heldin f

heroism ['herəʊɪzəm] n Heldentum nt

heron ['herən] n Reiher m

herring ['herɪŋ] n Hering m

hers [hɜ:z] pron ihre(r, s); see also **mine**

herself [hɜ:'self] pron sich (selbst); (emphatic) selbst; see also **oneself**

he's [hi:z] = **he is**; **he has**

hesitant ['hezɪtənt] adj zögernd

hesitate ['hezɪteɪt] vi zögern

hesitation [hezɪ'teɪʃən] n Zögern nt

hew [hju:] (pt **hewed**, pp **hewn**) vt hauen, hacken

hexagon ['heksəgən] n Sechseck nt; **~al** [hek'sægənəl] adj sechseckig

heyday ['heɪdeɪ] n Blüte f, Höhepunkt m

HGV n abbr = **heavy goods vehicle**

hi [haɪ] excl he, hallo

hiatus [haɪ'eɪtəs] n (gap) Lücke f

hibernate ['haɪbəneɪt] vi Winterschlaf m halten

hibernation [haɪbə'neɪʃən] n Winterschlaf m

hiccough ['hɪkʌp] vi den Schluckauf haben; **~s** npl Schluckauf m

hiccup ['hɪkʌp] n = **hiccough**

hid [hɪd] pt of **hide**; **~den** ['hɪdn] pp of **hide**

hide [haɪd] (pt **hid**, pp **hidden**) n (skin) Haut f, Fell nt ♦ vt verstecken

hideous ♦ *vi* sich verstecken; **~-and-seek** *n* Versteckspiel *nt*; **~away** *n* Versteck *nt*

hideous ['hɪdɪəs] *adj* abscheulich

hiding ['haɪdɪŋ] *n* (*beating*) Tracht *f* Prügel; **to be in** ~ (*concealed*) sich versteckt halten; ~ **place** *n* Versteck *nt*

hi-fi ['haɪfaɪ] *n* Hi-Fi *nt* ♦ *adj* Hi-Fi-

high [haɪ] *adj*, *adv* hoch; (*wind*) stark ♦ *adv* hoch; **it is 20m** = es ist 20 Meter hoch; **~brow** *adj* (betont) intellektuell; **~chair** *n* Hochstuhl *m*; **~er education** *n* Hochschulbildung *f*; **~-handed** *adj* eigenmächtig; **~-heeled** *adj* hochhackig; ~ **jump** *n* (SPORT) Hochsprung *m*; **the H~lands** *npl* das schottische Hochland; ~ **light** *n* (*fig*) Höhepunkt *m* ♦ *vt* hervorheben; **~ly** *adv* höchst; **~ly strung** *adj* überempfindlich; **~ness** *n* Höhe *f*; **Her H~ness** *ihre* Hoheit *f*; **~-pitched** *adj* hoch; **~-rise block** *n* Hochhaus *nt*; **~ school** (US) *n* Oberschule *f*; ~ **season** (BRIT) *n* Hochsaison *f*; **~ street** (BRIT) *n* Hauptstraße *f*

highway ['haɪweɪ] *n* Landstraße *f*, **H~ Code** (BRIT) *n* Straßenverkehrsordnung *f*

hijack ['haɪdʒæk] *vt* entführen; **~er** *n* Entführer(in) *m(f)*

hike [haɪk] *vi* wandern ♦ *n* Wanderung *f*; **~r** *n* Wanderer *m*

hilarious [hɪ'lɛərɪəs] *adj* lustig

hill [hɪl] *n* Berg *m*; **~side** *n* (Berg)hang *m*; **~y** *adj* hügelig

hilt [hɪlt] *n* Heft *nt*; (**up**) **to the** ~ ganz und gar

him [hɪm] *pron* (*acc*) ihn; (*dat*) ihm; *see also* me

himself [hɪm'self] *pron* sich (selbst); (*emphatic*) selbst; *see also* oneself

hind [haɪnd] *adj* hinter, Hinter-

hinder ['hɪndə*] *vt* (*stop*) hindern; (*delay*) behindern

hindrance ['hɪndrəns] *n* (*delay*) Behinderung *f*; (*obstacle*) Hindernis *nt*

hindsight ['haɪndsaɪt] *n*: **with** ~ im nachhinein

Hindu ['hɪnduː] *n* Hindu *m*

hinge [hɪndʒ] *n* Scharnier *nt*; (*on door*) Türangel *f* ♦ *vi* (*fig*): **to** ~ **on** abhängen von

hint [hɪnt] *n* Tip *m*; (*trace*) Anflug *m* ♦ *vt*: **to** ~ **that** andeuten, daß ♦ *vi*: **to** ~ **at** andeuten

hip [hɪp] *n* Hüfte *f*

hippopotami [hɪpə'pɒtəmaɪ] *npl of* hippopotamus

hippopotamus [hɪpə'pɒtəməs] (*pl* ~**es** *or* hippopotami) *n* Nilpferd *nt*

hire ['haɪə*] *vt* (*worker*) anstellen; (BRIT: *car*) mieten ♦ *n* Miete *f*; **for** ~ (*taxi*) frei; ~ **purchase** (BRIT) *n* Teilzahlungskauf *m*

his [hɪz] *adj* sein ♦ *pron* seine(r, s); *see also* my mine

hiss [hɪs] *vi* zischen ♦ *n* Zischen *nt*

historian [hɪs'tɔːrɪən] *n* Historiker *m*

historic [hɪs'tɒrɪk] *adj* historisch

historical [hɪs'tɒrɪkəl] *adj* historisch, geschichtlich

history ['hɪstərɪ] *n* Geschichte *f*

hit [hɪt] (*pt*, *pp* hit) *vt* schlagen; (*injure*) treffen ♦ *n* (*blow*) Schlag *m*; (*success*) Erfolg *m*; (MUS) Hit *m*; **to** ~ **it off with sb** prima mit jdm auskommen; **~-and-run driver** *n* jemand, der Fahrerflucht begeht

hitch [hɪtʃ] *vt* festbinden; (*also*: ~ **up**) hochziehen ♦ *n* (*difficulty*) Haken *m*; **to** ~ **a lift** trampen

hitchhike ['hɪtʃhaɪk] *vi* trampen; **~r** *n* Tramper *m*

hi-tech ['haɪtek] *adj* Hi-tech- ♦ *n* Spitzentechnologie *f*

hitherto ['hɪðə'tuː] *adv* bislang

HIV *n abbr*: **HIV-negative/-positive** HIV-negativ/-positiv

hive [haɪv] *n* Bienenkorb *m*; ~ **off** *vt* ausgliedern

HMS *abbr* = His (Her) Majesty's Ship

hoard [hɔːd] *n* Schatz *m* ♦ *vt* horten, hamstern

hoarding ['hɔːdɪŋ] *n* Bretterzaun *m*; (BRIT: *for advertising*) Reklamewand *f*

hoarse [hɔːs] *adj* heiser, rauh

hoax [həʊks] n Streich m
hob [hɒb] n Kochmulde f
hobble [ˈhɒbl] vi humpeln
hobby [ˈhɒbɪ] n Hobby nt; **~-horse** n (fig) Steckenpferd nt
hobo [ˈhəʊbəʊ] (US) n Tippelbruder m
hock [hɒk] n (wine) weiße(r) Rheinwein m
hockey [ˈhɒkɪ] n Hockey nt
hoe [həʊ] n Hacke f ♦ vt hacken
hog [hɒg] n Schlachtschwein nt ♦ vt mit Beschlag belegen; **to go the whole ~** aufs Ganze gehen
hoist [hɔɪst] n Winde f ♦ vt hochziehen
hold [həʊld] (pt, pp **held**) vt halten; (contain) enthalten; (be able to contain) fassen; (breath) anhalten; (meeting) abhalten ♦ vi (withstand pressure) aushalten ♦ n (grasp) Halt m; (NAUT) Schiffsraum m; **~ the line!** (TEL) bleiben Sie am Apparat!; **to ~ one's own** sich behaupten; **~ back** vt zurückhalten; **~ down** vt niederhalten; (job) behalten; **~ off** vt (enemy) abwehren; **~ on** vi sich festhalten; (resist) standhalten; (wait) warten; **~ on to** vt fus festhalten an +dat; (keep) behalten; **~ out** vt hinhalten ♦ vi aushalten; **~ up** vt (delay) aufhalten; (rob) überfallen; **~all** (BRIT) n Reisetasche f; **~er** n Behälter m; (of share) (Aktien)anteil m; **~up** n (BRIT: in traffic) Stockung f; (robbery) Überfall m; (delay) Verzögerung f
hole [həʊl] n Loch nt ♦ vt durchlöchern
holiday [ˈhɒlədɪ] n (day) Feiertag m; (time off) Tag m, (vacation) Urlaub m; (SCH) Ferien pl; **~ camp** n Ferienlager nt; **~-maker** (BRIT) n Urlauber(in) m(f); **~ resort** n Ferienort m
holiness [ˈhəʊlɪnɪs] n Heiligkeit f
Holland [ˈhɒlənd] n Holland nt
hollow [ˈhɒləʊ] adj hohl; (fig) leer ♦ n Vertiefung f; **~ out** vt aushöhlen

holly [ˈhɒlɪ] n Stechpalme f
holocaust [ˈhɒləkɔːst] n Inferno nt
holster [ˈhəʊlstə*] n Pistolenhalfter m
holy [ˈhəʊlɪ] adj heilig; **the H~ Ghost** or **Spirit** nt der Heilige Geist
homage [ˈhɒmɪdʒ] n Huldigung f; **to pay ~** to huldigen +dat
home [həʊm] n Zuhause nt; (institution) Heim nt, Anstalt f ♦ adj einheimisch; (POL) inner ♦ adv heim, nach Hause; **at ~** zu Hause; **~ address** n Heimatadresse f; **~coming** n Heimkehr f; **~land** n Heimat(land nt) f; **~less** adj obdachlos; **~ly** (US: ugly) unscheinbar; **~-made** adj selbstgemacht; **H~ Office** (BRIT) n Innenministerium nt; **~ rule** n Selbstverwaltung f; **H~ Secretary** (BRIT) n Innenminister(in) m(f); **~sick** adj: **to be ~sick** Heimweh haben; **~ town** n Heimatstadt f; **~ward** adj (journey) Heim-; **~work** n Hausaufgaben pl
homicide [ˈhɒmɪsaɪd] (US) n Totschlag m
homoeopathy [həʊmɪˈɒpəθɪ] n Homöopathie f
homogeneous [hɒməˈdʒiːnɪəs] adj homogen
homosexual [hɒməˈsɛksjʊəl] adj homosexuell ♦ n Homosexuelle(r) m f
honest [ˈɒnɪst] adj ehrlich; **~ly** adv ehrlich; **~y** n Ehrlichkeit f
honey [ˈhʌnɪ] n Honig m; **~comb** n Honigwabe f; **~moon** n Flitterwochen pl, Hochzeitsreise f; **~suckle** n Geißblatt nt
honk [hɒŋk] vi hupen
honor [ˈɒnə*] (US) vt, n = **honour**
honorary [ˈɒnərərɪ] adj Ehren-
honour [ˈɒnə*] (US **honor**) vt ehren; (cheque) einlösen ♦ n Ehre f; **~able** adj ehrenwert; (intention) ehrenhaft; **~s degree** n (UNIV) akademischer Grad mit Prüfung im Spezialfach
hood [hʊd] n Kapuze f; (BRIT: AUT) Verdeck nt; (US) Kühlerhaube f
hoodlum [ˈhuːdləm] n Rowdy m

(member of gang) Gangster *m*

hoodwink ['hodwiŋk] *vt* reinlegen

hoof [hu:f] *(pl* hooves) *n* Huf *m*

hook [hʊk] *n* Haken *m* ♦ *vt* einhaken

hooligan ['hu:lɪgən] *n* Rowdy *m*

hoop [hu:p] *n* Reifen *m*

hoot [hu:t] *vi (AUT)* hupen; **~er** *n (NAUT)* Dampfpfeife *f*; *(BRIT: AUT)* (Auto)hupe *f*

hoover ['hu:vəʳ] ® *(R: BRIT) n* Staubsauger *m* ♦ *vt* staubsaugen

hooves [hu:vz] *pl* of **hoof**

hop [hɒp] *vi* hüpfen, hopsen ♦ *n (jump)* Hopser *m*

hope [həʊp] *vt, vi* hoffen ♦ *n* Hoffnung *f*; **I ~** so/not hoffentlich/ hoffentlich nicht; **~ful** *adj* hoffnungsvoll; *(promising)* vielversprechend; **~fully** *adv* hoffentlich; **~less** *adj* hoffnungslos

hops [hɒps] *npl* Hopfen *m*

horizon [hə'raɪzn] *n* Horizont *m*; **~tal** [hɒrɪ'zɒntl] *adj* horizontal

hormone ['hɔ:məʊn] *n* Hormon *nt*

horn [hɔ:n] *n* Horn *nt*; *(AUT)* Hupe *f*

hornet ['hɔ:nɪt] *n* Hornisse *f*

horny ['hɔ:nɪ] *adj* schwielig; *(US: inf)* scharf

horoscope ['hɒrəskəʊp] *n* Horoskop *nt*

horrendous [hə'rendəs] *adj (crime)* abscheulich; *(error)* schrecklich

horrible ['hɒrɪbl] *adj* fürchterlich

horrid ['hɒrɪd] *adj* scheußlich

horrify ['hɒrɪfaɪ] *vt* entsetzen

horror ['hɒrəʳ] *n* Schrecken *m*; **~ film** *n* Horrorfilm *m*

hors d'oeuvre [ɔ:'də:vr] *n* Vorspeise *f*

horse [hɔ:s] *n* Pferd *nt*; **~back** *n*: **on ~back** beritten; **~chestnut** *n* Roßkastanie *f*; **~man/woman** *(irreg) n* Reiter(in) *m(f)*; **~power** *n* Pferdestärke *f*; **~racing** *n* Pferderennen *nt*; **~radish** *n* Meerrettich *m*; **~shoe** *n* Hufeisen *nt*

horticulture ['hɔ:tɪkʌltʃəʳ] *n* Gartenbau *m*

hose [həʊz] *n (also: ~pipe)* Schlauch *m*

hosiery ['həʊzɪərɪ] *n* Strumpfwaren *pl*

hospitable [hɒs'pɪtəbl] *adj* gastfreundlich

hospital ['hɒspɪtl] *n* Krankenhaus *nt*

hospitality [hɒspɪ'tælɪtɪ] *n* Gastfreundschaft *f*

host [həʊst] *n* Gastgeber *m*; *(innkeeper)* (Gast)wirt *m*; *(large number)* Heerschar *f*; *(ECCL)* Hostie *f*

hostage ['hɒstɪdʒ] *n* Geisel *f*

hostel ['hɒstl] *n* Herberge *f*; *(also: youth ~)* Jugendherberge *f*

hostess ['həʊstes] *n* Gastgeberin *f*

hostile ['hɒstaɪl] *adj* feindlich

hostility [hɒs'tɪlɪtɪ] *n* Feindschaft *f*; **hostilities** *npl (fighting)* Feindseligkeiten *pl*

hot [hɒt] *adj* heiß; *(drink, food, water)* warm; *(spiced)* scharf; **I'm ~** mir ist heiß; **~bed** *n (fig)* Nährboden *m*; **~ dog** *n* heiße(s) Würstchen *nt*

hotel [həʊ'tel] *n* Hotel *nt*; **~ier** *n* Hotelier *m*

hot: **~headed** *adj* hitzig; **~house** *n* Treibhaus *nt*; **~ line** *n (POL)* heiße(r) Draht *m*; **~ly** *adv (argue)* hitzig; **~plate** *n* Kochplatte *f*; **~water bottle** *n* Wärmflasche *f*

hound [haʊnd] *n* Jagdhund *m* ♦ *vt* hetzen

hour ['aʊəʳ] *n* Stunde *f*; *(time of day)* (Tages)zeit *f*; **~ly** *adj, adv* stündlich

house [*n* haus, *pl* 'haʊzɪz, *vb* hauz] *n* Haus *nt* ♦ *vt* unterbringen; **on the ~** auf Kosten des Hauses; **~ arrest** *n (POL, MIL)* Hausarrest *m*; **~boat** *n* Hausboot *nt*; **~breaking** *n* Einbruch *m*; **~coat** *n* Morgenmantel *m*; **~hold** *n* Haushalt *m*; **~keeper** *n* Haushälterin *f*; **~keeping** *n* Haushaltung *f*; **~warming party** *n* Einweihungsparty *f*; **~wife** *(irreg) n* Hausfrau *f*; **~work** *n* Hausarbeit *f*

housing ['haʊzɪŋ] *n (act)* Unterbringung *f*; *(houses)* Wohnungen *pl*; *(POL)* Wohnungsbau *m*; *(covering)* Gehäuse *nt*; **~ estate** *(US* housing development) n (Wohn)siedlung f

hovel ['hɔvəl] n elende Hütte f

hover ['hɔvə*] vi (bird) schweben; (person) herumstehen; ~craft n Luftkissenfahrzeug nt

how [hau] adv wie; ~ are you? wie geht es Ihnen?; ~ much milk? wieviel Milch?; ~ many people? wie viele Leute?

however [hau'evə*] adv (but) (je)doch, aber; ~ you phrase it wie Sie es auch ausdrücken

howl [haul] n Heulen nt ♦ vi heulen

H.P. abbr = hire purchase

h.p. abbr = horsepower

H.Q. abbr = headquarters

hub [hʌb] n Radnabe f

hubbub ['hʌbʌb] n Tumult m

hubcap ['hʌbkæp] n Radkappe f

huddle ['hʌdl] vi: to ~ together sich zusammendrängen

hue [hju:] n Färbung f; ~ and cry n Zetergeschrei nt

huff [hʌf] n: to go into a ~ einschnappen

hug [hʌg] vt umarmen ♦ n Umarmung f

huge [hju:dʒ] adj groß, riesig

hulk [hʌlk] n (ship) abgetakelte(s) Schiff nt; (person) Koloß m

hull [hʌl] n Schiffsrumpf m

hullo [hʌ'ləu] excl = hello

hum [hʌm] vt, vi summen

human ['hju:mən] adj menschlich ♦ n (also: ~ being) Mensch m

humane [hju:'meɪn] adj human

humanitarian [hju:mænɪ'tɛərɪən] adj humanitär

humanity [hju:'mænɪtɪ] n Menschheit f; (kindliness) Menschlichkeit f

humble ['hʌmbl] adj demütig; (modest) bescheiden ♦ vt demütigen

humbug ['hʌmbʌg] n Humbug m; (BRIT: sweet) Pfefferminzbonbon nt

humdrum ['hʌmdrʌm] adj stumpfsinnig

humid ['hju:mɪd] adj feucht; ~ity n Feuchtigkeit f

humiliate [hju:'mɪlɪeɪt] vt demütigen

humiliation [hju:mɪlɪ'eɪʃən] n Demütigung f

humility [hju:'mɪlɪtɪ] n Demut f

humor ['hju:mə*] (US) n, vt = humour

humorous ['hju:mərəs] adj humorvoll

humour ['hju:mə*] (US humor) n (fun) Humor m; (mood) Stimmung f ♦ vt bei Stimmung halten

hump [hʌmp] n Buckel m

hunch [hʌntʃ] n Buckel m; (premonition) (Vor)ahnung f; ~back n Bucklige(r) m/f; ~ed adj gekrümmt

hundred ['hʌndrɪd] num hundert; ~weight n Zentner m (BRIT = 50.8kg; US =45.3kg)

hung [hʌŋ] pt, pp of hang

Hungarian [hʌŋ'gɛərɪən] adj ungarisch ♦ n Ungar(in) m(f); (LING) Ungarisch nt

Hungary ['hʌŋgərɪ] n Ungarn nt

hunger ['hʌŋgə*] n Hunger m ♦ vi hungern

hungry ['hʌŋgrɪ] adj hungrig; to be ~ Hunger haben

hunk [hʌŋk] n (of bread) Stück m

hunt [hʌnt] vt, vi jagen ♦ n Jagd f; to ~ for suchen; ~er n Jäger m; ~ing n Jagd f

hurdle ['hɜ:dl] n (also fig) Hürde f

hurl [hɜ:l] vt schleudern

hurrah [hu'rɑ:] n Hurra nt

hurray [hu'reɪ] n Hurra nt

hurricane ['hʌrɪkən] n Orkan m

hurried ['hʌrɪd] adj eilig; (hasty) übereilt; ~ly adv übereilt, hastig

hurry ['hʌrɪ] n Eile f ♦ vi sich beeilen ♦ vt (an)treiben; (job) übereilt; to be in a ~ es eilig haben; ~ up vi sich beeilen ♦ vt (person) zur Eile antreiben; (work) vorantreiben

hurt [hɜ:t] (pt, pp hurt) vt weh tun +dat; (injure, fig) verletzen ♦ vi weh tun; ~ful adj schädlich; (remark) verletzend

hurtle ['hɜ:tl] vi sausen

husband ['hʌzbənd] n (Ehe)mann m

hush [hʌʃ] n Stille f ♦ vt zur Ruhe bringen ♦ excl pst, still

husk [hʌsk] n Spelze f

husky ['hʌskɪ] *adj (voice)* rauh ♦ *n* Eskimohund *m*

hustle ['hʌsl] *vt (push)* stoßen; *(hurry)* antreiben ♦ *n*: ~ **and bustle** Geschäftigkeit *f*

hut [hʌt] *n* Hütte *f*

hutch [hʌtʃ] *n* (Kaninchen)stall *m*

hyacinth ['haɪəsɪnθ] *n* Hyazinthe *f*

hybrid ['haɪbrɪd] *n* Kreuzung *f* ♦ *adj* Misch-

hydrant ['haɪdrənt] *n (also: fire* ~) Hydrant *m*

hydraulic [haɪ'drɔlɪk] *adj* hydraulisch

hydroelectric [haɪdrəʊ'lektrɪk] *adj (energy)* durch Wasserkraft erzeugt; ~ **power station** *n* Wasserkraftwerk *nt*

hydrofoil ['haɪdrəʊfɔɪl] *n* Tragflügelboot *nt*

hydrogen ['haɪdrɪdʒən] *n* Wasserstoff *m*

hyena [haɪ'iːnə] *n* Hyäne *f*

hygiene ['haɪdʒiːn] *n* Hygiene *f*

hygienic [haɪ'dʒiːnɪk] *adj* hygienisch

hymn [hɪm] *n* Kirchenlied *nt*

hype [haɪp] *(inf)* Publicity *f*

hypermarket ['haɪpəmɑːkɪt] *(BRIT)* Hypermarkt *m*

hyphen ['haɪfən] *n* Bindestrich *m*

hypnosis [hɪp'nəʊsɪs] *n* Hypnose *f*

hypnotic [hɪp'nɒtɪk] *adj* hypnotisierend

hypnotize ['hɪpnətaɪz] *vt* hypnotisieren

hypocrisy [hɪ'pɒkrɪsɪ] *n* Heuchelei *f*

hypocrite ['hɪpəkrɪt] *n* Heuchler *m*

hypocritical [hɪpə'krɪtɪkəl] *adj* scheinheilig, heuchlerisch

hypothermia [haɪpəʊ'θɜːmɪə] *n* Unterkühlung *f*

hypotheses [haɪ'pɒθɪsiːz] *npl of* **hypothesis**

hypothesis [haɪ'pɒθɪsɪs] *(pl* **hypotheses)** *n* Hypothese *f*

hypothetic(al) [haɪpəʊ'θetɪk(əl)] *adj* hypothetisch

hysterical [hɪs'terɪkəl] *adj* hysterisch

hysterics [hɪs'terɪks] *npl* hysterische(r) Anfall *m*

I

I [aɪ] *pron* ich

ice [aɪs] *n* Eis *nt* ♦ *vt (COOK)* mit Zuckerguß überziehen ♦ *vi (also:* ~ **up)** vereisen; ~ **axe** *n* Eispickel *m*; ~**berg** *n* Eisberg *m*; ~**box** *(US)* *n* Kühlschrank *m*; ~ **cream** *n* Eis *nt*; ~ **cube** *n* Eiswürfel *m*; ~ **hockey** *n* Eishockey *nt*

Iceland ['aɪslənd] *n* Island *nt*

ice: ~ **lolly** *(BRIT)* *n* Eis *nt* am Stiel; ~ **rink** *n* (Kunst)eisbahn *f*; ~ **skating** *n* Schlittschuhlaufen *nt*

icicle ['aɪsɪkl] *n* Eiszapfen *m*

icing ['aɪsɪŋ] *n (on cake)* Zuckerguß *m*; *(on window)* Vereisung *f*; ~ **sugar** *(BRIT)* *n* Puderzucker *m*

icon ['aɪkɒn] *n* Ikone *f*

icy ['aɪsɪ] *adj (slippery)* vereist; *(cold)* eisig

I'd [aɪd] = **I would; I had**

idea [aɪ'dɪə] *n* Idee *f*

ideal [aɪ'dɪəl] *n* Ideal *nt* ♦ *adj* ideal; ~**ist** *n* Idealist *m*

identical [aɪ'dentɪkəl] *adj* identisch; *(twins)* eineiig

identification [aɪdentɪfɪ'keɪʃən] *n* Identifizierung *f*; **means of** ~ Ausweispapiere *pl*

identify [aɪ'dentɪfaɪ] *vt* identifizieren; *(regard as the same)* gleichsetzen

Identikit picture [aɪ'dentɪkɪt-] *n* Phantombild *nt*

identity [aɪ'dentɪtɪ] *n* Identität *f*; ~ **card** *n* Personalausweis *m*

ideology [aɪdɪ'ɒlədʒɪ] *n* Ideologie *f*

idiom ['ɪdɪəm] *n (expression)* Redewendung *f*; *(dialect)* Idiom *nt*; ~**atic** [ɪdɪə'mætɪk] *adj* idiomatisch

idiosyncrasy [ɪdɪə'sɪŋkrəsɪ] *n* Eigenart *f*

idiot ['ɪdɪət] *n* Idiot(in) *m(f)*; ~**ic** [ɪdɪ'ɒtɪk] *adj* idiotisch

idle ['aɪdl] *adj (doing nothing)* untätig; *(lazy)* faul; *(useless)* nutzlos; *(machine)* still(stehend); *(threat, talk)* leer ♦ *vi (machine)* leerlaufen

♦ vt: to ~ away the time die Zeit vertrödeln; ~**ness** n Müßiggang m; Faulheit f

idol ['aɪdl] n Idol nt; ~**ize** vt vergöttern

i.e. abbr (= id est) d.h.

KEYWORD

if [ɪf] conj **1** wenn; (in case also) falls; if I were you wenn ich Sie wäre

2 (although): (even) if (selbst or auch) wenn

3 (whether) ob

4: if so/not wenn ja/nicht; if only ... wenn ... doch nur ...; see also as; if only I could wenn ich doch nur könnte

ignite [ɪg'naɪt] vt (an)zünden ♦ vi sich entzünden

ignition [ɪg'nɪʃən] n Zündung f; to switch on/off the ~ den Motor anlassen/abstellen; ~ **key** n (AUT) Zündschlüssel m

ignorance ['ɪgnərəns] n Unwissenheit f

ignorant ['ɪgnərənt] adj unwissend; to be ~ of nicht wissen

ignore [ɪg'nɔː*] vt ignorieren

I'll [aɪl] = I will; I shall

ill [ɪl] adj krank ♦ n Übel nt ♦ adv schlecht; ~**-advised** adj unklug; ~**-at-ease** adj unbehaglich

illegal [ɪ'liːgəl] adj illegal

illegible [ɪ'ledʒəbl] adj unleserlich

illegitimate [ɪlɪ'dʒɪtɪmət] adj unehelich

ill-fated [ɪl'feɪtɪd] adj unselig

ill feeling n Verstimmung f

illicit [ɪ'lɪsɪt] adj verboten

illiterate [ɪ'lɪtərət] adj ungebildet

ill-mannered ['ɪl'mænəd] adj ungehobelt

illness ['ɪlnəs] n Krankheit f

illogical [ɪ'lɒdʒɪkl] adj unlogisch

ill-treat ['ɪl'triːt] vt mißhandeln

illuminate [ɪ'luːmɪneɪt] vt beleuchten

illumination [ɪluːmɪ'neɪʃən] n Beleuchtung f; ~**s** pl (decorative lights)

festliche Beleuchtung f

illusion [ɪ'luːʒən] n Illusion f; to be under the ~ that ... sich dat einbilden, daß ...

illusory [ɪ'luːsərɪ] adj trügerisch

illustrate ['ɪləstreɪt] vt (book) illustrieren; (explain) veranschaulichen

illustration [ɪlə'streɪʃən] n Illustration f; (explanation) Veranschaulichung f

illustrious [ɪ'lʌstrɪəs] adj berühmt

ill will n Groll m

I'm [aɪm] = I am

image ['ɪmɪdʒ] n Bild nt; (public ~) Image nt; ~**ry** n Symbolik f

imaginary [ɪ'mædʒɪnərɪ] adj eingebildet; (world) Phantasie-

imagination [ɪmædʒɪ'neɪʃən] n Einbildung f; (creative) Phantasie f

imaginative [ɪ'mædʒɪnətɪv] adj phantasiereich, einfallsreich

imagine [ɪ'mædʒɪn] vt sich vorstellen; (wrongly) sich einbilden

imbalance [ɪm'bæləns] n Unausgeglichenheit f

imbecile ['ɪmbəsiːl] n Schwachsinnige(r) mf

imbue [ɪm'bjuː] vt: to ~ sth with etw erfüllen mit

imitate ['ɪmɪteɪt] vt imitieren

imitation [ɪmɪ'teɪʃən] n Imitation f

immaculate [ɪ'mækjʊlɪt] adj makellos; (dress) tadellos; (ECCL) unbefleckt

immaterial [ɪmə'tɪərɪəl] adj unwesentlich; it is ~ whether ... es ist unwichtig, ob ...

immature [ɪmə'tjʊə*] adj unreif

immediate [ɪ'miːdɪət] adj (instant) sofortig; (near) unmittelbar; (relatives) nächste(r, s); (needs) dringlich; ~**ly** adv sofort; ~**ly next to** direkt neben

immense [ɪ'mens] adj unermeßlich

immerse [ɪ'mɜːs] vt eintauchen; to be ~d in (fig) vertieft sein in +acc

immersion heater [ɪ'mɜːʃən-] (BRIT) n Boiler m

immigrant ['ɪmɪgrənt] n Einwanderer m

immigrate ['ɪmɪgreɪt] *vi* einwandern

immigration [ɪmɪ'greɪʃən] *n* Einwanderung *f*

imminent ['ɪmɪnənt] *adj* bevorstehend

immobile [ɪ'məʊbaɪl] *adj* unbeweglich

immobilize [ɪ'məʊbɪlaɪz] *vt* lähmen

immoral [ɪ'mɒrəl] *adj* unmoralisch; **~ity** [ɪmə'rælɪtɪ] *n* Unsittlichkeit *f*

immortal [ɪ'mɔːtl] *adj* unsterblich

immune [ɪ'mjuːn] *adj* (*secure*) sicher; (*MED*) immun; **~ from** sicher vor +*dat*

immunity [ɪ'mjuːnɪtɪ] *n* (*MED, JUR*) Immunität *f*; (*fig*) Freiheit *f*

immunize ['ɪmjʊnaɪz] *vt* immunisieren

imp [ɪmp] *n* Kobold *m*

impact ['ɪmpækt] *n* Aufprall *m*; (*fig*) Wirkung *f*

impair [ɪm'peə*] *vt* beeinträchtigen

impale [ɪm'peɪl] *vt* aufspießen

impart [ɪm'pɑːt] *vt* mitteilen; (*knowledge*) vermitteln; (*exude*) abgeben

impartial [ɪm'pɑːʃəl] *adj* unparteiisch

impassable [ɪm'pɑːsəbl] *adj* unpassierbar

impasse [æm'pɑːs] *n* Sackgasse *f*

impassive [ɪm'pæsɪv] *adj* gelassen

impatience [ɪm'peɪʃəns] *n* Ungeduld *f*

impatient [ɪm'peɪʃənt] *adj* ungeduldig

impeccable [ɪm'pekəbl] *adj* tadellos

impede [ɪm'piːd] *vt* (be)hindern

impediment [ɪm'pedɪmənt] *n* Hindernis *nt*; (*in speech*) Sprachfehler *m*

impending [ɪm'pendɪŋ] *adj* bevorstehend

impenetrable [ɪm'penɪtrəbl] *adj* (*also fig*) undurchdringlich

imperative [ɪm'perətɪv] *adj* (*necessary*) unbedingt erforderlich ♦ *n* (*GRAM*) Imperativ *m*, Befehlsform *f*

imperceptible [ɪmpə'septəbl] *adj* nicht wahrnehmbar

imperfect [ɪm'pɜːfɪkt] *adj* (*faulty*) fehlerhaft; **~ion** [ɪmpə'fekʃən] *n* Un-

vollkommenheit *f*; (*fault*) Fehler *m*

imperial [ɪm'pɪərɪəl] *adj* kaiserlich; **~ism** *n* Imperialismus *m*

impersonal [ɪm'pɜːsnl] *adj* unpersönlich

impersonate [ɪm'pɜːsəneɪt] *vt* sich ausgeben als; (*for amusement*) imitieren

impertinent [ɪm'pɜːtɪnənt] *adj* unverschämt, frech

impervious [ɪm'pɜːvɪəs] *adj* (*fig*): **~ (to)** unempfänglich (für)

impetuous [ɪm'petjʊəs] *adj* ungestüm

impetus ['ɪmpɪtəs] *n* Triebkraft *f*; (*fig*) Auftrieb *m*

impinge [ɪm'pɪndʒ]: **~ on** *vt* beeinträchtigen

implacable [ɪm'plækəbl] *adj* unerbittlich

implement [*n* 'ɪmplɪmənt, *vb* 'ɪmplɪment] *n* Werkzeug *nt* ♦ *vt* ausführen

implicate ['ɪmplɪkeɪt] *vt* verwickeln

implication [ɪmplɪ'keɪʃən] *n* (*effect*) Auswirkung *f*; (*in crime*) Verwicklung *f*

implicit [ɪm'plɪsɪt] *adj* (*suggested*) unausgesprochen; (*utter*) vorbehaltlos

implore [ɪm'plɔː*] *vt* anflehen

imply [ɪm'plaɪ] *vt* (*hint*) andeuten; (*be evidence for*) schließen lassen auf +*acc*

impolite [ɪmpə'laɪt] *adj* unhöflich

import [*vb* ɪm'pɔːt, *n* 'ɪmpɔːt] *vt* einführen ♦ *n* Einfuhr *f*; (*meaning*) Bedeutung *f*

importance [ɪm'pɔːtəns] *n* Bedeutung *f*

important [ɪm'pɔːtənt] *adj* wichtig; **it's not ~** es ist unwichtig

importer [ɪm'pɔːtə*] *n* Importeur *m*

impose [ɪm'pəʊz] *vt, vi*: **to ~ (on)** auferlegen (+*dat*); (*penalty, sanctions*) verhängen (gegen); **to ~ (o.s.) on sb** sich jdm aufdrängen

imposing [ɪm'pəʊzɪŋ] *adj* eindrucksvoll

imposition [ɪmpə'zɪʃən] *n* (*of bur-*

den, fine) Auferlegung f; (SCH) Strafarbeit f; **to be an ~** (on person) eine Zumutung sein

impossible [ɪmˈposəbl] adj unmöglich

impostor [ɪmˈpostə*] n Hochstapler m

impotent [ˈɪmpətənt] adj machtlos; (sexually) impotent

impound [ɪmˈpaʊnd] vt beschlagnahmen

impoverished [ɪmˈpovərɪʃt] adj verarmt

impracticable [ɪmˈpræktɪkəbl] adj undurchführbar

impractical [ɪmˈpræktɪkəl] adj unpraktisch

imprecise [ɪmprəˈsaɪs] adj ungenau

impregnable [ɪmˈpregnəbl] adj (castle) uneinnehmbar

impregnate [ˈɪmpregneɪt] vt (saturate) sättigen; (fertilize) befruchten

impress [ɪmˈpres] vt (influence) beeindrucken; (imprint) (auf)drücken; **to ~ sth on sb** jdm etw einschärfen

impression [ɪmˈpreʃən] n Eindruck m; (on wax, footprint) Abdruck m; (of book) Auflage f; (take-off) Nachahmung f; **I was under the ~** ich hatte den Eindruck; **~able** adj leicht zu beeindrucken; **~ist** n Impressionist m

impressive [ɪmˈpresɪv] adj eindrucksvoll

imprint [ˈɪmprɪnt] n Abdruck m

imprison [ɪmˈprɪzn] vt ins Gefängnis schicken; **~ment** n Inhaftierung f

improbable [ɪmˈprobəbl] adj unwahrscheinlich

impromptu [ɪmˈpromptju:] adj, adv aus dem Stegreif, improvisiert

improper [ɪmˈpropə*] adj (indecent) unanständig; (unsuitable) unpassend

improve [ɪmˈpru:v] vt verbessern ♦ vi besser werden; **~ment** n (Ver)besserung f

improvise [ˈɪmprəvaɪz] vt, vi improvisieren

imprudent [ɪmˈpru:dənt] adj unklug

impudent [ˈɪmpjʊdənt] adj unverschämt

impulse [ˈɪmpʌls] n Impuls m; **to act on ~** spontan handeln

impulsive [ɪmˈpʌlsɪv] adj impulsiv

impunity [ɪmˈpju:nɪtɪ] n Straflosigkeit f

impure [ɪmˈpjʊə*] adj (dirty) verunreinigt; (bad) unsauber

impurity [ɪmˈpjʊərɪtɪ] n Unreinheit f; (TECH) Verunreinigung f

---

KEYWORD

in [ɪn] prep 1 (indicating place, position) in +dat; (with motion) in +acc; **in here/there** hier/dort; **in London** in London; **in the United States** in den Vereinigten Staaten

2 (indicating time: during) in +dat; **in summer** im Sommer; **in 1988** (im Jahre) 1988; **in the afternoon** nachmittags, am Nachmittag

3 (indicating time: in the space of) innerhalb von; **I'll see you in 2 weeks** or **in 2 weeks' time** ich sehe Sie in zwei Wochen

4 (indicating manner, circumstances, state etc) in +dat; **in the sun/in the rain** in der Sonne/im Regen; **in English/French** auf Englisch/Französisch; **in a loud/soft voice** mit lauter/leiser Stimme

5 (with ratios, numbers): **1 in 10** jeder zehnte; **20 pence in the pound** 20 Pence pro Pfund; **they lined up in twos** sie stellten sich in Zweierreihe auf

6 referring to people, works): **the disease is common in children** die Krankheit ist bei Kindern häufig; **in Dickens** bei Dickens; **we have a loyal friend in him** er ist uns ein treuer Freund

7 (indicating profession etc): **to be in teaching/the army** Lehrer(in)/beim Militär sein; **to be in publishing** im Verlagswesen arbeiten

8 (with present participle): **in saying this, I ...** wenn ich das sage, ...; **in accepting this view, he** ...

weil er diese Meinung akzeptierte, ... er

♦ *adv*: **to be in** (*person: at home, work*) dasein; (*train, ship, plane*) eingekommen sein; (*in fashion*) in sein; **to ask sb in** jdn hereinbitten; **to run/limp** *etc* **in** hereingerannt/gehumpelt *etc* kommen

♦ *n*: **the ins and outs** (*of proposal, situation etc*) die Feinheiten

in. *abbr* = **inch**

inability [ɪnə'bɪlɪtɪ] *n* Unfähigkeit *f*

inaccessible [ɪnæk'sesəbl] *adj* unzugänglich

inaccurate [ɪn'ækjʊrət] *adj* ungenau; (*wrong*) unrichtig

inactivity [ɪnæk'tɪvɪtɪ] *n* Untätigkeit *f*

inadequate [ɪn'ædɪkwət] *adj* unzulänglich

inadvertently [ɪnəd'vɜːtəntlɪ] *adv* unabsichtlich

inadvisable [ɪnəd'vaɪzəbl] *adj* nicht ratsam

inane [ɪ'neɪn] *adj* dumm, albern

inanimate [ɪn'ænɪmət] *adj* leblos

inappropriate [ɪnə'prəʊprɪət] *adj* (*clothing*) ungeeignet; (*remark*) unangebracht

inarticulate [ɪnɑː'tɪkjʊlət] *adj* unklar

inasmuch as [ɪnəz'mʌtʃəz] *adv* da; (*in so far as*) soweit

inaudible [ɪn'ɔːdəbl] *adj* unhörbar

inaugural [ɪn'ɔːgjʊrəl] *adj* Eröffnungs-

inaugurate [ɪn'ɔːgjʊreɪt] *vt* (*open*) einweihen; (*admit to office*) (feierlich) einführen

inauguration [ɪnɔːgjʊ'reɪʃən] *n* Eröffnung *f*; (*feierliche*) Amtseinführung *f*

inborn [ɪn'bɔːn] *adj* angeboren

inbred [ɪn'bred] *adj* angeboren

Inc. *abbr* = **incorporated**

incalculable [ɪn'kælkjʊləbl] *adj* (*consequences*) unabsehbar

incapable [ɪn'keɪpəbl] *adj*: ~ (**of**) unfähig (, etw zu tun)

incapacitate [ɪnkə'pæsɪteɪt] *vt* untauglich machen

incapacity [ɪnkə'pæsɪt] *n* Unfähigkeit *f*

incarcerate [ɪn'kɑːsəreɪt] *vt* einkerkern

incarnation [ɪnkɑː'neɪʃən] *n* (*ECCL*) Menschwerdung *f*; (*fig*) Inbegriff *m*

incendiary [ɪn'sendɪərɪ] *adj* Brand-

incense [*n* 'ɪnsens, *vb* ɪn'sens] *n* Weihrauch *m* ♦ *vt* erzürnen

incentive [ɪn'sentɪv] *n* Anreiz *m*

incessant [ɪn'sesnt] *adj* unaufhörlich; ~**ly** *adv* unaufhörlich

incest ['ɪnsest] *n* Inzest *m*

inch [ɪntʃ] *n* Zoll *m* ♦ *vi*: **to ~ forward** sich Stückchen für Stückchen vorwärts bewegen; **to be within an ~ of** kurz davor sein; **he didn't give an ~** er gab keinen Zentimeter nach

incidence ['ɪnsɪdəns] *n* Auftreten *nt*; (*of crime*) Quote *f*

incident ['ɪnsɪdənt] *n* Vorfall *m*; (*disturbance*) Zwischenfall *m*

incidental [ɪnsɪ'dentl] *adj* (*music*) Begleit-; (*unimportant*) nebensächlich; (*remark*) beiläufig; ~**ly** *adv* übrigens

incinerator [ɪn'sɪnəreɪtə*] *n* Verbrennungsofen *m*

incipient [ɪn'sɪpɪənt] *adj* beginnend

incision [ɪn'sɪʒən] *n* Einschnitt *m*

incisive [ɪn'saɪsɪv] *adj* (*style*) treffend; (*person*) scharfsinnig

incite [ɪn'saɪt] *vt* anstacheln

inclination [ɪnklɪ'neɪʃən] *n* Neigung *f*

incline [*n* 'ɪnklaɪn, *vb* ɪn'klaɪn] *n* Abhang *m* ♦ *vt* neigen; (*fig*) veranlassen ♦ *vi* sich neigen; **to be ~d to do sth** dazu neigen, etw zu tun

include [ɪn'kluːd] *vt* einschließen; (*on list, in group*) aufnehmen

including [ɪn'kluːdɪŋ] *prep*: ~ X X inbegriffen

inclusion [ɪn'kluːʒən] *n* Aufnahme *f*

inclusive [ɪn'kluːsɪv] *adj* einschließlich; (*COMM*) inklusive; ~ **of** einschließlich +*gen*

incoherent [ɪnkəʊ'hɪərənt] *adj* zusammenhanglos

income ['ɪnkʌm] n Einkommen nt; (from business) Einkünfte pl; ~ **tax** n Lohnsteuer f; (of self-employed) Einkommenssteuer f

incoming ['ɪnkʌmɪŋ] adj: ~ flight eintreffende Maschine f

incomparable [ɪn'kɒmpərəbl] adj unvergleichlich

incompatible [ɪnkəm'pætəbl] adj unvereinbar; (people) unverträglich

incompetence [ɪn'kɒmpɪtəns] n Unfähigkeit f

incompetent [ɪn'kɒmpɪtənt] adj unfähig

incomplete [ɪnkəm'pliːt] adj unvollständig

incomprehensible [ɪnkɒmprɪ'hensəbl] adj unverständlich

inconceivable [ɪnkən'siːvəbl] adj unvorstellbar

incongruous [ɪn'kɒŋgruəs] adj seltsam; (remark) unangebracht

inconsiderate [ɪnkən'sɪdərət] adj rücksichtslos

inconsistency [ɪnkən'sɪstənsɪ] n Widersprüchlichkeit f; (state) Unbeständigkeit f

inconsistent [ɪnkən'sɪstənt] adj (action, speech) widersprüchlich; (person, work) unbeständig; ~ with nicht übereinstimmend mit

inconspicuous [ɪnkən'spɪkjuəs] adj unauffällig

incontinent [ɪn'kɒntɪnənt] adj (MED) nicht fähig, Stuhl und Harn zurückzuhalten

inconvenience [ɪnkən'viːnɪəns] n Unbequemlichkeit f; (trouble to others) Unannehmlichkeiten pl

inconvenient [ɪnkən'viːnɪənt] adj ungelegen; (journey) unbequem

incorporate [ɪn'kɔːpəreɪt] vt (include) aufnehmen; (contain) enthalten

incorporated [ɪn'kɔːpəreɪtɪd] adj: ~ company (US) eingetragene Aktiengesellschaft f

incorrect [ɪnkə'rekt] adj unrichtig

incorrigible [ɪn'kɒrɪdʒəbl] adj unverbesserlich

incorruptible [ɪnkə'rʌptəbl] adj unzerstörbar; (person) unbestechlich

increase [n 'ɪnkriːs, vb ɪn'kriːs] n Zunahme f; (pay ~) Gehaltserhöhung f; (in size) Vergrößerung f ♦ vt erhöhen; (wealth, rage) vermehren; (business) erweitern ♦ vi zunehmen; (prices) steigen; (in size) größer werden; (in number) sich vermehren

increasing [ɪn'kriːsɪŋ] adj steigend

increasingly [ɪn'kriːsɪŋlɪ] adv zunehmend

incredible [ɪn'kredəbl] adj unglaublich

incredulous [ɪn'kredjuləs] adj ungläubig

increment ['ɪnkrɪmənt] n Zulage f

incriminate [ɪn'krɪmɪneɪt] vt belasten

incubation [ɪnkju'beɪʃən] n Ausbrüten nt

incubator ['ɪnkjubeɪtə*] n Brutkasten m

incumbent [ɪn'kʌmbənt] n Amtsinhaber(in) m(f) ♦ adj: it is ~ on him to ... es obliegt ihm, ...

incur [ɪn'kɜː*] vt sich zuziehen; (debts) machen

incurable [ɪn'kjuərəbl] adj unheilbar; (fig) unverbesserlich

incursion [ɪn'kɜːʃən] n Einfall m

indebted [ɪn'detɪd] adj (obliged): ~ to sb) (jdm) verpflichtet

indecent [ɪn'diːsnt] adj unanständig; ~ assault (BRIT) n Notzucht f; ~ exposure n Exhibitionismus m

indecisive [ɪndɪ'saɪsɪv] adj (battle) nicht entscheidend; (person) unentschlossen

indeed [ɪn'diːd] adv tatsächlich, in der Tat; yes ~! Allerdings!; ~ definitely adv auf unbestimmte Zeit; (wait) unbegrenzt lange

indelible [ɪn'deləbl] adj unauslöschlich

independence [ɪndɪ'pendəns] n Unabhängigkeit f

independent [ɪndɪ'pendənt] adj unabhängig

indestructible [ˌɪndɪsˈtrʌktəbl] *adj* unzerstörbar

indeterminate [ˌɪndɪˈtɜːmɪnɪt] *adj* unbestimmt

index [ˈɪndeks] *n* Index *m*; ~ **card** *n* Karteikarte *f*; ~ **finger** *n* Zeigefinger *m*; ~**-linked** (*US* **indexed**) *adj* (*salaries*) der Inflationsrate *dat* angeglichen; (*pensions*) dynamisch

India [ˈɪndɪə] *n* Indien *nt*; ~**n** *adj* indisch ♦ *n* Inder(in) *m(f)*; **Red** ~**n** Indianer(in) *m(f)*; **the** ~**n Ocean** *n* der Indische Ozean

indicate [ˈɪndɪkeɪt] *vt* anzeigen; (*hint*) andeuten

indication [ɪndɪˈkeɪʃən] *n* Anzeichen *nt*; (*information*) Angabe *f*

indicative [ɪnˈdɪkətɪv] *adj*: ~ **of** bezeichnend für ♦ *n* (*GRAM*) Indikativ *m*

indicator [ˈɪndɪkeɪtə*] *n* (*sign*) (An)zeichen *nt*; (*AUT*) Richtungsanzeiger *m*

indices [ˈɪndɪsiːz] *npl of* **index**; **indictment** *n* Anklage *f*

indifference [ɪnˈdɪfrəns] *n* Gleichgültigkeit *f*; Unwichtigkeit *f*

indifferent [ɪnˈdɪfrənt] *adj* gleichgültig; (*mediocre*) mäßig

indigenous [ɪnˈdɪdʒɪnəs] *adj* einheimisch

indigestion [ɪndɪˈdʒestʃən] *n* Verdauungsstörung *f*

indignant [ɪnˈdɪgnənt] *adj*: **to be** ~ **about sth** über etw *acc* empört sein

indignation [ɪndɪgˈneɪʃən] *n* Entrüstung *f*

indignity [ɪnˈdɪgnɪtɪ] *n* Demütigung *f*

indirect [ɪndɪˈrekt] *adj* indirekt; ~**ly** *adv* indirekt

indiscreet [ɪndɪsˈkriːt] *adj* (*insensitive*) taktlos; (*telling secrets*) indiskret

indiscretion [ɪndɪsˈkreʃən] *n* Taktlosigkeit *f*; Indiskretion *f*

indiscriminate [ɪndɪsˈkrɪmɪnət] *adj* wahllos; kritiklos

indispensable [ɪndɪsˈpensəbl] *adj* unentbehrlich

indisposed [ɪndɪsˈpəʊzd] *adj* unpäßlich

indisputable [ɪndɪsˈpjuːtəbl] *adj* unbestreitbar; (*evidence*) unanfechtbar

indistinct [ɪndɪsˈtɪŋkt] *adj* undeutlich

individual [ɪndɪˈvɪdjuəl] *n* Individuum *nt* ♦ *adj* individuell; (*case*) Einzel-; (*of, for one person*) eigen, individuell; (*characteristic*) eigentümlich; ~**ly** *adv* einzeln, individuell

indivisible [ɪndɪˈvɪzəbl] *adj* unteilbar

indoctrinate [ɪnˈdɒktrɪneɪt] *vt* indoktrinieren

indolent [ˈɪndələnt] *adj* träge

Indonesia [ɪndəˈniːzɪə] *n* Indonesien *nt*

indoor [ˈɪndɔː*] *adj* Haus-; Zimmer-; Innen-; (*SPORT*) Hallen-; ~**s** [ɪnˈdɔːz] *adv* drinnen, im Haus

induce [ɪnˈdjuːs] *vt* dazu bewegen; (*reaction*) herbeiführen; ~**ment** *n* Veranlassung *f*; (*incentive*) Anreiz *m*

induction course [BRIT] *n* Einführungskurs *m*

indulge [ɪnˈdʌldʒ] *vt* (*give way*) nachgeben +*dat*; (*gratify*) frönen +*dat* ♦ *vi*: **to** ~ (**in**) frönen (+*dat*); ~**nce** *n* Nachsicht *f*; (*enjoyment*) Genuß *m*; ~**nt** *adj* nachsichtig; (*pej*) nachgiebig

industrial [ɪnˈdʌstrɪəl] *adj* Industrie-, industriell; (*dispute, injury*) Arbeits-; ~ **action** *n* Arbeitskampfmaßnahmen *pl*; ~ **estate** (*BRIT*) *n* Industriegebiet *nt*; ~**ist** *n* Industrielle(r) *mf*; ~**ize** *vt* industrialisieren; ~ **park** (*US*) *n* Industriegebiet *nt*

industrious [ɪnˈdʌstrɪəs] *adj* fleißig

industry [ˈɪndəstrɪ] *n* Industrie *f*; (*diligence*) Fleiß *m*

inebriated [ɪˈniːbrɪeɪtɪd] *adj* betrunken

inedible [ɪnˈedɪbl] *adj* ungenießbar

ineffective [ɪnɪˈfektɪv] *adj* unwirksam; (*person*) untauglich

ineffectual [ɪnɪˈfektʃuəl] *adj* = **ineffective**

inefficiency [ɪnɪˈfɪʃənsɪ] *n* Ineffizienz *f*

inefficient [ɪnɪˈfɪʃənt] *adj* ineffizient; (*ineffective*) unwirksam

inept [ɪ'nept] adj (remark) unpassend; (person) ungeeignet

inequality [ɪnɪ'kwɒlɪtɪ] n Ungleichheit f

inert [ɪ'nɜːt] adj träge; (CHEM) inaktiv; (motionless) unbeweglich

inertia [ɪ'nɜːʃə] n Trägheit f

inescapable [ɪnɪs'keɪpəbl] adj unvermeidbar

inevitable [ɪn'evɪtəbl] adj unvermeidlich

inevitably [ɪn'evɪtəblɪ] adv zwangsläufig

inexcusable [ɪnɪks'kjuːzəbl] adj unverzeihlich

inexhaustible [ɪnɪg'zɔːstəbl] adj unerschöpflich

inexorable [ɪn'eksərəbl] adj unerbittlich

inexpensive [ɪnɪks'pensɪv] adj preiswert

inexperience [ɪnɪks'pɪərɪəns] n Unerfahrenheit f; **~d** [ɪnɪks'pɪərɪənst] adj unerfahren

inexplicable [ɪnɪks'plɪkəbl] adj unerklärlich

inextricably [ɪnɪks'trɪkəblɪ] adv untrennbar

infallible [ɪn'fæləbl] adj unfehlbar

infamous [ɪn'fəməs] adj (place) verrufen; (deed) schändlich; (person) niederträchtig

infamy [ɪn'fəmɪ] n Verruftheit f; Niedertracht f; (disgrace) Schande f

infancy [ɪn'fənsɪ] n frühe Kindheit f; (fig) Anfangsstadium nt

infant [ɪn'fənt] n kleine(s) Kind nt; Säugling m; **~ile** adj kindisch, infantil; **~ school** (BRIT) n Vorschule f

infatuated [ɪn'fætjʊeɪtɪd] adj vernarrt; **to become ~ with** sich vernarren in +acc

infatuation [ɪnfætjʊ'eɪʃən] n: **~ (with)** Vernarrtheit f (in +acc)

infect [ɪn'fekt] vt anstecken (also fig); (with illness) infiziert mit; **~ed with** (illness) infiziert mit; **~ion** [ɪn'fekʃən] n Infektion f; **~ious** [ɪn'fekʃəs] adj ansteckend

infer [ɪn'fɜː*] vt schließen; **~ence** [ɪn'fərəns] n Schlußfolgerung f

inferior [ɪn'fɪərɪə*] adj (rank) untergeordnet; (quality) minderwertig ♦ n Untergebene(r) m; **~ity** [ɪnfɪərɪ'ɒrɪtɪ] n Minderwertigkeit f; (in rank) untergeordnete Stellung f; **~ity complex** n Minderwertigkeitskomplex m

infernal [ɪn'fɜːnl] adj höllisch

infertile [ɪn'fɜːtaɪl] adj unfruchtbar

infertility [ɪnfɜː'tɪlɪtɪ] n Unfruchtbarkeit f

infested [ɪn'festɪd] adj: **to be ~ with** wimmeln von

infidelity [ɪnfɪ'delɪtɪ] n Untreue f

infighting [ɪn'faɪtɪŋ] n Nahkampf m

infiltrate [ɪn'fɪltreɪt] vt infiltrieren; (spies) einschleusen ♦ vi (MIL, liquid) einsickern; (POL): **to ~ (into)** unterwandern (+acc)

infinite [ɪn'fɪnɪt] adj unendlich

infinitive [ɪn'fɪnɪtɪv] n Infinitiv m

infinity [ɪn'fɪnɪtɪ] n Unendlichkeit f

infirm [ɪn'fɜːm] adj gebrechlich

infirmary [ɪn'fɜːmərɪ] n Krankenhaus nt

infirmity [ɪn'fɜːmɪtɪ] n Schwäche f, Gebrechlichkeit f

inflamed [ɪn'fleɪmd] adj entzündet

inflammable [ɪn'flæməbl] (BRIT) adj feuergefährlich

inflammation [ɪnflə'meɪʃən] n Entzündung f

inflatable [ɪn'fleɪtəbl] adj aufblasbar

inflate [ɪn'fleɪt] vt aufblasen; (tyre) aufpumpen; (prices) hochtreiben

inflation [ɪn'fleɪʃən] n Inflation f; **~ary** [ɪn'fleɪʃənrɪ] adj (increase) inflationistisch; (situation) inflationär

inflexible [ɪn'fleksəbl] adj (person) nicht flexibel; (opinion) starr; (thing) unbiegsam

inflict [ɪn'flɪkt] vt: **to ~ sth on sb** jdm etw zufügen; (wound) jdm etw beibringen

influence [ɪn'fluːəns] n Einfluß m ♦ vt beeinflussen

influential [ɪnflʊ'enʃəl] adj einflußreich

influenza [ɪnflʊ'enzə] n Grippe f

influx [ɪn'flʌks] n (of people) Zustrom m; (of ideas) Eindringen nt

inform [ɪn'fɔːm] vt informieren ♦ vi:
to ~ on sb jdn denunzieren; to keep
sb ~ed jdn auf dem laufenden halten

informal [ɪn'fɔːməl] adj zwanglos;
~ity [ɪnfɔːˈmælɪtɪ] n Ungezwungenheit
f

informant [ɪn'fɔːmənt] n Informant(in) m(f)

information [ɪnfəˈmeɪʃən] n Auskunft f, Information f; **a piece of ~**
eine Auskunft, eine Information; **~
office** n Informationsbüro nt

informative [ɪn'fɔːmətɪv] adj informativ; (person) mitteilsam

informer [ɪn'fɔːmə*] n Denunziant(in) m(f)

infra-red [ɪnfrə'red] adj infrarot

infrequent [ɪn'friːkwənt] adj selten

infringe [ɪn'frɪndʒ] vt (law) verstoßen gegen; **~ upon** vt verletzen;
~ment n Verstoß m, Verletzung f

infuriating [ɪn'fjʊərɪeɪtɪŋ] adj ärgerlich

infusion [ɪn'fjuːʒən] n (tea etc) Aufguß m

ingenious [ɪn'dʒiːnɪəs] adj genial

ingenuity [ɪndʒɪ'njuːɪtɪ] n Genialität
f

ingenuous [ɪn'dʒenjuəs] adj aufrichtig; (naive) naiv

ingot ['ɪŋgət] n Barren m

ingrained [ɪn'greɪnd] adj tiefsitzend

ingratiate [ɪn'greɪʃɪeɪt] vt: to ~ o.s.
with sb sich bei jdm einschmeicheln

ingratitude [ɪn'grætɪtjuːd] n Undankbarkeit f

ingredient [ɪn'griːdɪənt] n Bestandteil m; (COOK) Zutat f

inhabit [ɪn'hæbɪt] vt bewohnen; **~ant**
[ɪn'hæbɪtnt] n Bewohner(in) f; (of
island, town) Einwohner(in) m(f)

inhale [ɪn'heɪl] vt einatmen; (MED,
cigarettes) inhalieren

inherent [ɪn'hɪərənt] adj: ~ (in) innewohnend (+dat)

inherit [ɪn'herɪt] vt erben; **~ance** n
Erbe nt, Erbschaft f

inhibit [ɪn'hɪbɪt] vt hemmen; to ~
sb from doing sth jdn daran hindern, etw zu tun; **~ion** [ɪnhɪ'bɪʃən] n

Hemmung f

inhospitable [ɪnhɒs'pɪtəbl] adj (person) ungastlich; (country) unwirtlich

inhuman [ɪn'hjuːmən] adj unmenschlich

inimitable [ɪ'nɪmɪtəbl] adj unnachahmlich

iniquity [ɪ'nɪkwɪtɪ] n Ungerechtigkeit f

initial [ɪ'nɪʃəl] adj anfänglich,
Anfangs- ♦ n Initiale f ♦ vt abzeichnen; (POL) paraphieren; **~ly** adv
anfangs

initiate [ɪ'nɪʃɪeɪt] vt einführen; (negotiations) einleiten; to ~ sb into a
secret jdn in ein Geheimnis einweihen; to ~ proceedings against sb
(JUR) gerichtliche Schritte gegen jdn
einleiten

initiation [ɪnɪʃɪ'eɪʃən] n Einführung
f, Einleitung f

initiative [ɪ'nɪʃətɪv] n Initiative f

inject [ɪn'dʒekt] vt einspritzen, (fig)
einflößen; **~ion** [ɪn'dʒekʃən] n Spritze
f

injunction [ɪn'dʒʌŋkʃən] n Verfügung f

injure ['ɪndʒə*] vt verletzen; **~d** adj
(person, arm) verletzt

injury ['ɪndʒərɪ] n Verletzung f; to
play ~ time (SPORT) nachspielen

injustice [ɪn'dʒʌstɪs] n Ungerechtigkeit f

ink [ɪŋk] n Tinte f

inkling ['ɪŋklɪŋ] n (dunkle) Ahnung f

inlaid ['ɪn'leɪd] adj eingelegt, Einlege-

inland [adj 'ɪnlænd, adv 'ɪn'lænd] adj
Binnen-; (domestic) Inlands- ♦ adv
landeinwärts; **I~ revenue** (BRIT) n
Fiskus m

in-laws ['ɪnlɔːz] npl (parents-in-law)
Schwiegereltern pl; (others) angeheiratete Verwandte pl

inlet ['ɪnlet] n Einlaß m; (bay) kleine
Bucht f

inmate ['ɪnmeɪt] n Insasse m

inn [ɪn] n Gasthaus nt, Wirtshaus nt

innate [ɪ'neɪt] adj angeboren

inner ['ɪnə*] adj inner, Innen-; (fig)
verborgen; ~ **city** n Innenstadt f

tube n (of tyre) Schlauch m

innings ['ɪnɪŋz] n (CRICKET) Innenrunde f

innocence ['ɪnəsns] n Unschuld f; (ignorance) Unkenntnis f

innocent ['ɪnəsnt] adj unschuldig

innocuous [ɪ'nɔkjuəs] adj harmlos

innovation [ɪnəu'veɪʃən] n Neuerung f

innuendo [ɪnju'endəu] n (versteckte) Anspielung f

innumerable [ɪ'nju:mərəbl] adj unzählig

inoculation [ɪnɔkju'leɪʃən] n Impfung f

inopportune [ɪn'ɔpətju:n] adj (remark) unangebracht; (visit) ungelegen

inordinately [ɪ'nɔ:dɪnɪtlɪ] adv unmäßig

inpatient ['ɪnpeɪʃənt] n stationäre(r) Patient m/stationäre Patientin f

input ['ɪnput] n (COMPUT) Eingabe f; (power ~) Energiezufuhr f; (of energy, work) Aufwand m

inquest ['ɪnkwest] n gerichtliche Untersuchung f

inquire [ɪn'kwaɪə*] vi sich erkundigen ♦ vt (price) sich erkundigen nach; ~ **into** vt untersuchen

inquiry [ɪn'kwaɪərɪ] n (question) Erkundigung f; (investigation) Untersuchung f; ~ **office** (BRIT) n Auskunft(sbüro nt) f

inquisitive [ɪn'kwɪzɪtɪv] adj neugierig

inroad ['ɪnrəud] n (MIL) Einfall m; (fig) Eingriff m

ins. abbr = **inches**

insane [ɪn'seɪn] adj wahnsinnig; (MED) geisteskrank

insanity [ɪn'sænɪtɪ] n Wahnsinn m

insatiable [ɪn'seɪʃəbl] adj unersättlich

inscribe [ɪn'skraɪb] vt eingravieren

inscription [ɪn'skrɪpʃən] n (on coin) Inschrift f; (in book) Widmung f

inscrutable [ɪn'skru:təbl] adj unergründlich

insect ['ɪnsekt] n Insekt nt; ~**icide**

[ɪn'sektɪsaɪd] n Insektenvertilgungsmittel nt

insecure [ɪnsɪ'kjuə*] adj (person) unsicher; (thing) nicht fest or sicher

insecurity [ɪnsɪ'kjuərɪtɪ] n Unsicherheit f

insemination [ɪnsemɪ'neɪʃən] n: **artificial ~** künstliche Befruchtung f

insensible [ɪn'sensɪbl] adj (unconscious) bewußtlos

insensitive [ɪn'sensɪtɪv] adj (to pain) unempfindlich; (without feelings) gefühllos

inseparable [ɪn'sepərəbl] adj (people) unzertrennlich; (word) untrennbar

insert [vb ɪn'sɜ:t, n 'ɪnsɜ:t] vt einfügen; (coin) einwerfen; (stick into) hineinstecken; (advertisement) aufgeben ♦ n (in book) Einlage f; (in magazine) Beilage f; ~**ion** [ɪn'sɜ:ʃən] n Einfügung f; (PRESS) Inserat nt

in-service [ɪn'sɜ:vɪs] adj (training) berufsbegleitend

inshore ['ɪn'ʃɔ:*] adj Küsten- ♦ adv an der Küste

inside ['ɪn'saɪd] n Innenseite f, Innere(s) nt ♦ adj innere(r, s), Innen- ♦ adv (place) innen; (direction) nach innen, hinein ♦ prep (place) in +dat; (direction) in +acc ... hinein; (time) innerhalb +gen; ~**s** npl (inf) Eingeweide nt; ~ **10 minutes** unter 10 Minuten; ~ **lane** n (AUT: in Britain) linke Spur; ~ **out** adv linksherum; (know) inner und auswendig

insider dealing n (STOCK EXCHANGE) Insiderhandel m

insider trading n (STOCK EXCHANGE) Insiderhandel m

insidious [ɪn'sɪdɪəs] adj heimtückisch

insight ['ɪnsaɪt] n Einsicht f; ~ **into** Einblick m in +acc

insignificant [ɪnsɪg'nɪfɪkənt] adj unbedeutend

insincere [ɪnsɪn'sɪə*] adj unaufrichtig

insinuate [ɪn'sɪnjueɪt] vt (hint) andeuten

insipid [ɪnˈsɪpɪd] *adj* fad(e)

insist [ɪnˈsɪst] *vi*: **to ~ (on)** bestehen (auf +*acc*); **~ence** *n* Bestehen *nt*; **~ent** *adj* hartnäckig; (*urgent*) dringend

insole [ˈɪnsəʊl] *n* Einlegesohle *f*

insolence [ˈɪnsələns] *n* Frechheit *f*

insolent [ˈɪnsələnt] *adj* frech

insoluble [ɪnˈsɒljʊbl] *adj* unlösbar; (CHEM) unlöslich

insolvent [ɪnˈsɒlvənt] *adj* zahlungsunfähig

insomnia [ɪnˈsɒmnɪə] *n* Schlaflosigkeit *f*

inspect [ɪnˈspekt] *vt* prüfen; (*officially*) inspizieren; **~ion** [ɪnˈspekʃən] *n* Inspektion *f*; **~or** *n* (*official*) Inspektor *m*; (*police*) Polizeikommissar *m*; (BRIT: *on buses, trains*) Kontrolleur *m*

inspiration [ɪnspɪˈreɪʃən] *n* Inspiration *f*

inspire [ɪnˈspaɪə*] *vt* (*person*) inspirieren; **to ~ sth in sb** (*respect*) jdm etw einflößen; (*hope*) etw in jdm wecken

instability [ɪnstəˈbɪlɪtɪ] *n* Unbeständigkeit *f*, Labilität *f*

install [ɪnˈstɔːl] *vt* (*put in*) installieren; (*telephone*) anschließen; (*establish*) einsetzen; **~ation** [ɪnstəˈleɪʃən] *n* (*of person*) (Amts)einsetzung *f*; (*of machinery*) Installierung *f*; (*machines etc*) Anlage *f*

instalment [ɪnˈstɔːlmənt] (US **installment**) *n* Rate *f*; (*of story*) Fortsetzung *f*; **to pay in ~s** in Raten zahlen

instance [ˈɪnstəns] *n* Fall *m*; (*example*) Beispiel *nt*; **for ~** zum Beispiel; **in the first ~** zunächst

instant [ˈɪnstənt] *n* Augenblick *m* ♦ *adj* augenblicklich, sofortig

instantaneous [ɪnstənˈteɪnɪəs] *adj* unmittelbar

instant coffee *n* Pulverkaffee *m*

instantly [ˈɪnstəntlɪ] *adv* sofort

instead [ɪnˈsted] *adv* statt dessen; **~ of** *prep* anstatt +*gen*

instep [ˈɪnstep] *n* Spann *m*; (*of shoe*)

Blatt *nt*

instil [ɪnˈstɪl] *vt* (*fig*): **to ~ sth in sb** jdm etw beibringen

instinct [ˈɪnstɪŋkt] *n* Instinkt *m*; **~ive** [ɪnˈstɪŋktɪv] *adj* instinktiv

institute [ˈɪnstɪtjuːt] *n* Institut *nt* ♦ *vt* einführen; (*search*) einleiten

institution [ɪnstɪˈtjuːʃən] *n* Institution *f*; (*home*) Anstalt *f*

instruct [ɪnˈstrʌkt] *vt* anweisen; (*officially*) instruieren; **~ion** [ɪnˈstrʌkʃən] *n* Unterricht *m*; **~ions** *npl* (*orders*) Anweisungen *pl*; (*for use*) Gebrauchsanweisung *f*; **~ive** *adj* lehrreich; **~or** *n* Lehrer *m*; (MIL) Ausbilder *m*

instrument [ˈɪnstrʊmənt] *n* Instrument *nt*; **~al** [ɪnstrʊˈmentl] *adj* (MUS) Instrumental-; (*helpful*): **~al (in)** behilflich (bei); **~ panel** *n* Armaturenbrett *nt*

insubordinate [ɪnsəˈbɔːdənət] *adj* aufsässig, widersetzlich

insubordination [ɪnsəbɔːdɪˈneɪʃən] *n* Gehorsamsverweigerung *f*

insufferable [ɪnˈsʌfərəbl] *adj* unerträglich

insufficient [ɪnsəˈfɪʃənt] *adj* ungenügend

insular [ˈɪnsjələ*] *adj* (*fig*) engstirnig

insulate [ˈɪnsjʊleɪt] *vt* (ELEC) isolieren; (*fig*): **to ~ (from)** abschirmen (vor +*dat*)

insulating tape *n* Isolierband *nt*

insulation [ɪnsjʊˈleɪʃən] *n* Isolierung *f*

insulin [ˈɪnsjʊlɪn] *n* Insulin *nt*

insult [*n* ˈɪnsʌlt, *vb* ɪnˈsʌlt] *n* Beleidigung *f* ♦ *vt* beleidigen; **~ing** [ɪnˈsʌltɪŋ] *adj* beleidigend

insuperable [ɪnˈsuːpərəbl] *adj* unüberwindlich

insurance [ɪnˈʃʊərəns] *n* Versicherung *f*; **fire/life** ~ Feuer-/Lebensversicherung, **~ agent** *n* Versicherungsvertreter *m*; **~ policy** *n* Versicherungspolice *f*

insure [ɪnˈʃʊə*] *vt* versichern

insurrection [ɪnsəˈrekʃən] *n* Aufstand *m*

intact [ɪnˈtækt] *adj* unversehrt

intake ['ınteık] n (place) Einlaß-
öffnung f; (act) Aufnahme f; (BRIT:
SCH): **an ~ of 200 a year** ein Neu-
zugang von 200 im Jahr

intangible [ın'tændʒəbl] adj nicht
greifbar

integral ['ıntıgrəl] adj (essential) wesentlich; (complete) vollständig;
(MATH) Integral-

integrate ['ıntıgreıt] vt integrieren ♦
vi sich integrieren

integrity [ın'tegrıtı] n (honesty) Red-
lichkeit f, Integrität f

intellect ['ıntəlekt] n Intellekt m;
~ual [ıntı'lektjʊəl] adj geistig, intellektuell ♦ n Intellektuelle(r) mf

intelligence [ın'telıdʒəns] n (understanding) Intelligenz f; (news) Information f; (MIL) Geheimdienst m

intelligent [ın'telıdʒənt] adj intelligent; **~ly** adv klug; (write, speak)
verständlich

intelligentsia [ıntelı'dʒentsıə] n Intelligenz f

intelligible [ın'telıdʒəbl] adj verständlich

intend [ın'tend] vt beabsichtigen;
that was ~ed for you das war für
dich gedacht

intense [ın'tens] adj stark, intensiv;
(person) ernsthaft; **~ly** adv äußerst;
(study) intensiv

intensify [ın'tensıfaı] vt verstärken,
intensivieren

intensity [ın'tensıtı] n Intensität f

intensive [ın'tensıv] adj intensiv; **~
care unit** n Intensivstation f

intent [ın'tent] n Absicht f ♦ adj: **to
be ~ on doing sth** fest entschlossen
sein, etw zu tun; **to all ~s and purposes** praktisch

intention [ın'tenʃən] n Absicht f;
~al adj absichtlich; **~ly** adv
absichtlich

intently [ın'tentlı] adv konzentriert

interact [ıntər'ækt] vi aufeinander
einwirken; **~ion** n Wechselwirkung f

interactive adj (COMPUT) interak-
tiv

intercede [ıntə'si:d] vi sich verwen-

den

intercept [ıntə'sept] vt abfangen

interchange [n 'ıntətʃeındʒ, vb
ıntə'tʃeındʒ] n (exchange) Austausch
m; (on roads) Verkehrskreuz n ♦ vt
austauschen; **~able** [ıntə'tʃeındʒəbl]
adj austauschbar

intercom ['ıntəkom] n (Gegen)-
sprechanlage f

intercourse ['ıntəkɔ:s] n (exchange)
Beziehungen pl; (sexual) Geschlechtsverkehr m

interest ['ıntrest] n Interesse nt;
(FIN) Zinsen pl; (COMM: share) Anteil m; (group) Interessengruppe f
♦ vt interessieren; **~ed** adj (having
claims) beteiligt; (attentive) interes-
siert; **to be ~ed in** sich interessieren für; **~ing** adj interessant; **~
rate** n Zinssatz m

interface ['ıntəfeıs] n (COMPUT)
Schnittstelle f, Interface nt

interfere [ıntə'fıə*] vi: **to ~ (with)**
(meddle) sich einmischen (in +acc);
(disrupt) stören +acc

interference [ıntə'fıərəns] n Ein-
mischung f; (TV) Störung f

interim ['ıntərım] n: **in the ~** inzwischen

interior [ın'tıərıə*] n Innere(s) nt ♦
adj innere(r, s), Innen-; **~ designer**
n Innenarchitekt(in) m(f)

interjection [ıntə'dʒekʃən] n Ausruf
m

interlock [ıntə'lok] vi ineinandergreifen

interlude ['ıntəlu:d] n Pause f

intermarry [ıntə'mærı] vi untereinander heiraten

intermediary [ıntə'mi:dıərı] n Vermittler m

intermediate [ıntə'mi:dıət] adj
Zwischen-, Mittel-

interminable [ın'tɜ:mınəbl] adj endlos

intermission [ıntə'mıʃən] n Pause f

intermittent [ıntə'mıtənt] adj periodisch, stoßweise

intern [vb ın'tɜ:n, n 'ıntɜ:n] vt inter-
nieren ♦ n (US) Assistenzarzt m/-

ärztin f

internal [ɪn'tɜːnl] adj (inside) inne-re(r, s); (domestic) Inlands-; **~ly** adv innen; (MED) innerlich; **"not to be taken ~ly"** „nur zur äußerlichen Anwendung"; **I~ Revenue Service** (US) n Finanzamt nt

international [ɪntə'næʃnəl] adj international ♦ n (SPORT) National-spieler(in) m(f); (: match) internationale(s) Spiel nt

interplay ['ɪntəpleɪ] n Wechselspiel nt

interpret [ɪn'tɜːprɪt] vt (explain) auslegen, interpretieren; (translate) dolmetschen; **~ation** [ɪntɜːprɪ'teɪʃən] n Interpretation f; **~er** n Dolmet-scher(in) m(f)

interrelated [ɪntərɪ'leɪtɪd] adj unter-einander zusammenhängend

interrogate [ɪn'terəgeɪt] vt verhören

interrogation [ɪntərə'geɪʃən] n Ver-hör nt

interrogative [ɪntə'rɒgətɪv] adj Frage-

interrupt [ɪntə'rʌpt] vt unterbre-chen; **~ion** [ɪntə'rʌpʃən] n Unter-brechung f

intersect [ɪntə'sekt] vt (durch)-schneiden ♦ vi sich schneiden; **~ion** [ɪntə'sekʃən] n (of roads) Kreuzung f; (of lines) Schnittpunkt m

intersperse [ɪntə'spɜːs] vt: **to ~ sth with** etw mit etw durchsetzen

intertwine [ɪntə'twaɪn] vt verflech-ten ♦ vi sich verflechten

interval ['ɪntəvl] n Abstand m; (BRIT: SCH, THEAT, SPORT) Pause f; **at ~s** in Abständen

intervene [ɪntə'viːn] vi dazwischen-liegen; (act): **to ~ (in)** einschreiten (gegen)

intervention [ɪntə'venʃən] n Ein-greifen nt, Intervention f

interview ['ɪntəvjuː] n (PRESS etc) Interview nt; (for job) Vorstellungs-gespräch nt ♦ vt interviewen; **~er** n Interviewer m

intestine [ɪn'testɪn] n: **large/small ~** Dick-/Dünndarm m

intimacy ['ɪntɪməsɪ] n Intimität f

intimate ['ɪntɪmət, vb 'ɪntɪmeɪt] adj (inmost) innerste(r, s); (know-ledge) staunlich; (familiar) vertraut; (friends) eng ♦ vt andeuten

intimidate [ɪn'tɪmɪdeɪt] vt ein-schüchtern

intimidation [ɪntɪmɪ'deɪʃən] n Ein-schüchterung f

into ['ɪntu] prep (motion) in +acc ... hinein; **5 ~ 25** 25 durch 5

intolerable [ɪn'tɒlərəbl] adj uner-träglich

intolerance [ɪn'tɒlərns] n Unduld-samkeit f

intolerant [ɪn'tɒlərnt] adj: **~ of** un-duldsam gegen(über)

intoxicate [ɪn'tɒksɪkeɪt] vt berau-schen; **~d** adj betrunken

intoxication [ɪntɒksɪ'keɪʃən] n Rausch m

intractable [ɪn'træktəbl] adj schwer zu handhaben; (problem) schwer lösbar

intransigent [ɪn'trænsɪdʒənt] adj un-nachgiebig

intransitive [ɪn'trænsɪtɪv] adj intran-sitiv

intravenous [ɪntrə'viːnəs] adj intra-venös

in-tray ['ɪntreɪ] n Eingangskorb m

intrepid [ɪn'trepɪd] adj unerschro-cken

intricate ['ɪntrɪkət] adj kompliziert

intrigue [ɪn'triːg] n Intrige f ♦ vt fas-zinieren ♦ vi intrigieren

intriguing [ɪn'triːgɪŋ] adj faszinie-rend

intrinsic [ɪn'trɪnsɪk] adj innere(r, s); (difference) wesentlich

introduce [ɪntrə'djuːs] vt (person) vorstellen; (sth new) einführen; (sub-ject) anschneiden; **to ~ sb to sth** jdm zu etw bringen; **to ~ sb to sb** jdn jdm vorstellen; jdn in etw einführen

introduction [ɪntrə'dʌkʃən] n Ein-führung f; (to book) Einleitung f

introductory [ɪntrə'dʌktərɪ] adj Einführungs-, Vor-

introspective [ɪntrəʊ'spektɪv] adj

nach innen gekehrt

introvert ['ɪntrəʊvɜːt] n Introvertierte(r) mf ♦ adj introvertiert

intrude [ɪn'truːd] vi: to ~ (on sb/sth) (jdn/etw) stören; ~r n Eindringling m

intrusion [ɪn'truːʒən] n Störung f

intrusive [ɪn'truːsɪv] adj aufdringlich

intuition [ɪntjuːˈɪʃən] n Intuition f

inundate ['ɪnʌndeɪt] vt (also fig) überschwemmen

invade [ɪn'veɪd] vt einfallen in +acc; ~r n Eindringling m

invalid [n 'ɪnvəlɪd, adj ɪn'vælɪd] n (disabled) Invalide m ♦ adj (ill) krank; (disabled) invalide; (not valid) ungültig

invaluable [ɪn'væljuəbl] adj unschätzbar

invariable [ɪn'vɛərɪəbl] adj unveränderlich

invariably [ɪn'vɛərɪəblɪ] adv ausnahmslos

invasion [ɪn'veɪʒən] n Invasion f

invent [ɪn'vent] vt erfinden; ~ion [ɪn'venʃən] n Erfindung f; ~ive adj erfinderisch; ~or n Erfinder m

inventory ['ɪnvəntrɪ] n Inventar nt

inverse ['ɪn'vɜːs] n Umkehrung f ♦ adj umgekehrt

invert [ɪn'vɜːt] vt umdrehen; ~ed commas (BRIT) npl Anführungsstriche pl

invest [ɪn'vest] vt investieren

investigate [ɪn'vestɪgeɪt] vt untersuchen

investigation [ɪnvestɪ'geɪʃən] n Untersuchung f

investigator [ɪn'vestɪgeɪtə*] n Untersuchungsbeamte(r) m

investiture [ɪn'vestɪtʃə*] n Amtseinsetzung f

investment [ɪn'vestmənt] n Investition f

investor [ɪn'vestə*] n (Geld)anleger m

inveterate [ɪn'vetərət] adj unverbesserlich

invidious [ɪn'vɪdɪəs] adj unangenehm; (distinctions, remark) unge-

recht

invigilate [ɪn'vɪdʒɪleɪt] vi (in exam) Aufsicht führen ♦ vt Aufsicht führen bei

invigorating [ɪn'vɪgəreɪtɪŋ] adj stärkend

invincible [ɪn'vɪnsəbl] adj unbesiegbar

invisible [ɪn'vɪzəbl] adj unsichtbar

invitation [ɪnvɪ'teɪʃən] n Einladung f

invite [ɪn'vaɪt] vt einladen

inviting [ɪn'vaɪtɪŋ] adj einladend

invoice ['ɪnvɔɪs] n Rechnung f ♦ vt (goods): to ~ sb for sth jdm etw acc in Rechnung stellen

invoke [ɪn'vəʊk] vt anrufen

involuntary [ɪn'vɒləntərɪ] adj unabsichtlich

involve [ɪn'vɒlv] vt (entangle) verwickeln; (entail) mit sich bringen; ~d adj verwickelt; ~ment n Verwicklung f

inward ['ɪnwəd] adj innere(r, s); (curve) Innen- ♦ adv nach innen; ~ly adv im Innern; ~s adv nach innen

I/O abbr (COMPUT: = input/output) I/O

iodine ['aɪədiːn] n Jod nt

iota [aɪ'əʊtə] n (fig) bißchen nt

IOU n abbr (= I owe you) Schuldschein m

IQ n abbr (= intelligence quotient) IQ m

IRA n abbr (= Irish Republican Army) IRA f

Iran [ɪ'rɑːn] n Iran m; ~ian adj iranisch ♦ n Iraner(in) m(f); (LING) Iranisch nt

Iraq [ɪ'rɑːk] n Irak m; ~i adj irakisch ♦ n Iraker(in) m(f); (LING) Irakisch nt

irascible [ɪ'ræsɪbl] adj reizbar

irate [aɪ'reɪt] adj zornig

Ireland ['aɪələnd] n Irland nt

iris ['aɪrɪs] (pl ~es) n Iris f

Irish ['aɪrɪʃ] adj irisch ♦ npl: the ~ die Iren pl, die Irländer pl; ~man (irreg) n Ire m, Irländer m; ~ Sea n (GEO): the ~ Sea die Irische See f;

~woman (irreg) n Irin f, Irländerin f

irksome ['ɜːksəm] adj lästig

iron ['aɪən] n Eisen nt; (for ironing) Bügeleisen nt ♦ adj eisern ♦ vt bügeln; **~ out** vt (also fig) ausbügeln; **I~ Curtain** n Eiserne(r) Vorhang m

ironic(al) [aɪ'rɒnɪk(əl)] adj ironisch; (coincidence etc) witzig

ironing ['aɪənɪŋ] n Bügeln nt; (laundry) Bügelwäsche f; **~ board** n Bügelbrett nt

irony ['aɪərənɪ] n Ironie f

irrational [ɪ'ræʃənl] adj irrational

irreconcilable [ɪrekən'saɪləbl] adj unvereinbar

irrefutable [ɪrɪ'fjuːtəbl] adj unwiderlegbar

irregular [ɪ'regjʊlə*] adj unregelmäßig; (shape) ungleich(mäßig); (fig) unüblich; (: behaviour) ungehörig; **~ity** [ɪregjʊ'lærɪtɪ] n Unregelmäßigkeit f; Ungleichmäßigkeit f; (fig) Vergehen nt

irrelevant [ɪ'reləvənt] adj belanglos, irrelevant

irreparable [ɪ'repərəbl] adj nicht wiedergutzumachen

irreplaceable [ɪrɪ'pleɪsəbl] adj unersetzlich

irresistible [ɪrɪ'zɪstəbl] adj unwiderstehlich

irrespective [ɪrɪ'spektɪv]: **~ of** prep ungeachtet +gen

irresponsible [ɪrɪ'spɒnsəbl] adj verantwortungslos

irreverent [ɪ'revərənt] adj respektlos

irrevocable [ɪ'revəkəbl] adj unwiderrufbar

irrigate ['ɪrɪgeɪt] vt bewässern

irrigation [ɪrɪ'geɪʃən] n Bewässerung f

irritable ['ɪrɪtəbl] adj reizbar

irritate ['ɪrɪteɪt] vt irritieren, reizen (also MED)

irritation [ɪrɪ'teɪʃən] n (anger) Ärger m; (MED) Reizung f

IRS n abbr = Internal Revenue Service

is [ɪz] vb see **be**

Islam ['ɪzlɑːm] n Islam m

island ['aɪlənd] n Insel f; **~er** n Inselbewohner(in) m(f)

isle [aɪl] n (kleine) Insel f

isn't ['ɪznt] = is not

isolate ['aɪsəleɪt] vt isolieren; **~d** adj isoliert; (case) Einzel-

isolation [aɪsə'leɪʃən] n Isolierung f

Israel ['ɪzreɪl] n Israel nt; **~i** [ɪz'reɪlɪ] adj israelisch ♦ n Israeli mf

issue ['ɪʃuː] n (matter) Frage f; (outcome) Ausgang m; (of newspaper, shares) Ausgabe f; (offspring) Nachkommenschaft f ♦ vt ausgeben; (warrant) erlassen; (documents) ausstellen; (orders) erteilen; (books) herausgeben; (verdict) aussprechen; **to be at ~** zur Debatte stehen; **to take ~ with sb over sth** jdm in etw dat widersprechen

isthmus ['ɪsməs] n Landenge f

KEYWORD

it [ɪt] pron **1** (specific: subject) er/sie/es; (: direct object) ihn/sie/es; (: indirect object) ihm/ihr/ihm; **about/from/in/of** it darüber/davon/darin/davon

2 (impers) es; **it's raining** es regnet; **it's Friday tomorrow** morgen ist Freitag; **who is it? - it's me** wer ist da? - ich (bin's)

Italian [ɪ'tæljən] adj italienisch ♦ n Italiener(in) m(f); (LING) Italienisch nt

italic [ɪ'tælɪk] adj kursiv; **~s** npl Kursivschrift f

Italy ['ɪtəlɪ] n Italien nt

itch [ɪtʃ] n Juckreiz m; (fig) Lust f ♦ vi jucken; **to be ~ing to do sth** darauf brennen, etw zu tun; **~y** adj juckend

it'd ['ɪtd] = it would; it had

item ['aɪtəm] n Gegenstand m; (on list) Posten m; (in programme) Nummer f; (in agenda) (Programm)punkt m; (in newspaper) (Zeitungs)notiz f; **~ize** vt verzeichnen

itinerant [ı'tınərənt] *adj* (person) umherreisend

itinerary [aı'tınərərı] *n* Reiseroute *f*

it'll ['ıtl] = it will; it shall

its [ıts] *adj* (masculine, neuter) sein; (feminine) ihr

it's [ıts] = it is; it has

itself [ıt'self] *pron* sich (selbst); (emphatic) selbst

ITV (BRIT) *n abbr* = Independent Television

I.U.D. *n abbr* (= intra-uterine device) Pessar *nt*

I've [aıv] = I have

ivory ['aıvərı] *n* Elfenbein *nt*

ivy ['aıvı] *n* Efeu *m*

J

jab [dʒæb] *vt* (hinein)stechen ♦ *n* Stich *m*, Stoß *m*; (inf) Spritze *f*

jabber ['dʒæbə*] *vi* plappern

jack [dʒæk] *n* (AUT) (Wagen)heber *m*; (CARDS) Bube *m*; ~ **up** *vt* aufbocken

jackal ['dʒækəl] *n* (ZOOL) Schakal *m*

jackdaw ['dʒækdɔ:] *n* Dohle *f*

jacket ['dʒækıt] *n* Jacke *f*; (of book) Schutzumschlag *m*; (TECH) Ummantelung *f*

jackknife ['dʒæknaıf] *vi* (truck) sich zusammenschieben

jack plug *n* (ELEC) Buchsenstecker *m*

jackpot ['dʒækpɔt] *n* Haupttreffer *m*

jaded ['dʒeıdıd] *adj* ermattet

jagged ['dʒægıd] *adj* zackig

jail [dʒeıl] *n* Gefängnis *nt* ♦ *vt* einsperren; ~**er** *n* Gefängniswärter *m*

jam [dʒæm] *n* Marmelade *f*; (also: traffic ~) (Verkehrs)stau *m*; (inf: trouble) Klemme *f* ♦ *vt* (wedge) einklemmen; (cram) hineinzwängen; (obstruct) blockieren ♦ *vi* sich verklemmen; to ~ **sth into sth** etw in etw *acc* hineinstopfen

Jamaica [dʒə'meıkə] *n* Jamaika *f*

jangle ['dʒæŋgl] *vt, vi* klimpern

janitor ['dʒænıtə*] *n* Hausmeister *m*

January ['dʒænjuərı] *n* Januar *m*

Japan [dʒə'pæn] *n* Japan *nt*; ~**ese** [dʒæpə'ni:z] *adj* japanisch ♦ *n inv* Japaner(in) *m(f)*; (LING) Japanisch *nt*

jar [dʒɑ:*] *n* Glas *nt* ♦ *vi* kreischen; (colours etc) nicht harmonieren

jargon ['dʒɑ:gən] *n* Fachsprache *f*, Jargon *m*

jaundice ['dʒɔ:ndıs] *n* Gelbsucht *f*; ~**d** *adj* (fig) mißgünstig

jaunt [dʒɔ:nt] *n* Spritztour *f*; ~**y** (lively) munter; (brisk) flott

javelin ['dʒævlın] *n* Speer *m*

jaw [dʒɔ:] *n* Kiefer *m*

jay [dʒeı] *n* (ZOOL) Eichelhäher *m*

jaywalker ['dʒeıwɔ:kə*] *n* unvorsichtige(r) Fußgänger *m*

jazz [dʒæz] *n* Jazz *m*; ~ **up** *vt* (MUS) verjazzen; (enliven) aufpolieren; ~**y** *adj* (colour) schreiend, auffallend

jealous ['dʒeləs] *adj* (envious) mißgünstig; (husband) eifersüchtig; ~**y** *n* Mißgunst *f*; Eifersucht *f*

jeans [dʒi:nz] *npl* Jeans *pl*

jeep [dʒi:p] *n* Jeep *m*

jeer [dʒıə*] *vi*: to ~ (at sb) (über jdn) höhnisch lachen, (jdn) verspotten

jelly ['dʒelı] *n* Gelee *nt*; (dessert) Grütze *f*; ~**fish** *n* Qualle *f*

jeopardize ['dʒepədaız] *vt* gefährden

jeopardy ['dʒepədı] *n*: to be in ~ in Gefahr sein

jerk [dʒɜ:k] *n* Ruck *m*; (inf: idiot) Trottel *m* ♦ *vt* ruckartig bewegen ♦ *vi* sich ruckartig bewegen

jerkin ['dʒɜ:kın] *n* Wams *nt*

jerky ['dʒɜ:kı] *adj* (movement) ruckartig; (ride) rüttelnd

jersey ['dʒɜ:zı] *n* Pullover *m*

Jesus ['dʒi:zəs] *n* Jesus *m*

jet [dʒet] *n* (stream: of water etc) Strahl *m*; (spout) Düse *f*; (AVIAT) Düsenflugzeug *nt*; ~**-black** *adj* rabenschwarz; ~ **engine** *n* Düsenmotor *m*; ~**-lag** *n* Jet-lag *m*

jettison ['dʒetısn] *vt* über Bord werfen

jetty ['dʒetɪ] n Landesteg m, Mole f
Jew [dʒuː] n Jude m
jewel ['dʒuːəl] n (also fig) Juwel nt; ~**ler** (US **jeweler**) n Juwelier m; ~**ler's (shop)** n Juwelier m; ~**lery** (US **jewelry**) n Schmuck m
Jewess ['dʒuːɪs] n Jüdin f
Jewish ['dʒuːɪʃ] adj jüdisch
jib [dʒɪb] n (NAUT) Klüver m
jibe [dʒaɪb] n spöttische Bemerkung f
jiffy ['dʒɪfɪ] (inf) n: in a ~ sofort
jigsaw ['dʒɪgsɔː] n (also: ~ puzzle) Puzzle(spiel) nt
jilt [dʒɪlt] vt den Laufpaß geben +dat
jingle ['dʒɪŋgl] n (advertisement) Werbesong m ♦ vi klimpern; (bells) bimmeln ♦ vt klimpern mit; bimmeln lassen
jinx [dʒɪŋks] n: there's a ~ on it es ist verhext
jitters ['dʒɪtəz] (inf) npl: to get the ~ einen Bammel kriegen
job [dʒɒb] n (piece of work) Arbeit f; (position) Stellung f; (duty) Aufgabe f; (difficulty) Mühe f; **it's a good ~ he** ... es ist ein Glück, daß er ...; **just the ~** genau das Richtige; **J~centre** (BRIT) n Arbeitsamt nt; ~**less** adj arbeitslos
jockey ['dʒɒkɪ] n Jockei m ♦ vi: to ~ **for position** sich in eine gute Position drängen
jocular ['dʒɒkjʊlə*] adj scherzhaft
jog [dʒɒg] vt an(stoßen ♦ vi (run) joggen; to ~ **along** vi sich vor sich hinwursteln; (work) seinen Gang gehen; ~**ging** n Jogging nt
join [dʒɔɪn] vt (club) beitreten +dat; (person) sich anschließen +dat; (put together) to ~ (sth to sth) (etw mit etw) verbinden ♦ vi (unite) sich vereinigen ♦ n Verbindungsstelle f, Naht f; ~ **in** vt, vi: to ~ **in** (sth) (bei etw) mitmachen; ~ **up** vi (MIL) zur Armee gehen
joiner ['dʒɔɪnə*] n Schreiner m; ~**y** n Schreinerei f
joint [dʒɔɪnt] n (TECH) Fuge f; (of bones) Gelenk nt; (of meat) Braten

m; (inf: place) Lokal nt ♦ adj gemeinsam; ~ **account** n (with bank etc) gemeinsame(s) Konto nt; ~**ly** adv gemeinsam
joke [dʒəʊk] n Witz m ♦ vi Witze machen; **to play a** ~ on sb jdm einen Streich spielen; ~**r** n Witzbold m; (CARDS) Joker m
jolly ['dʒɒlɪ] adj lustig ♦ adv (inf) ganz schön
jolt [dʒəʊlt] n (shock) Schock m; (jerk) Stoß m ♦ vt (push) stoßen; (shake) durchschütteln; (fig) aufrütteln ♦ vi holpern
Jordan ['dʒɔːdən] n Jordanien nt; (river) Jordan m
jostle ['dʒɒsl] vt anrempeln
jot [dʒɒt] n: not one ~ kein Jota nt; ~ **down** vt notieren; ~**ter** (BRIT) n Notizblock m
journal ['dʒɜːnl] n (diary) Tagebuch nt; (magazine) Zeitschrift f; ~**ism** n Journalismus m; ~**ist** n Journalist(in m(f))
journey ['dʒɜːnɪ] n Reise f
jovial ['dʒəʊvɪəl] adj froh
joy [dʒɔɪ] n Freude f; ~**ful** adj freudig; ~**ous** adj freudig; ~ **ride** n Schwarzfahrt f; ~**rider** n Autodieb m, der den Wagen nur für eine Spritztour stiehlt; ~**stick** n Steuerknüppel m; (COMPUT) Joystick m
J.P. n abbr = Justice of the Peace
Jr abbr = **junior**
jubilant ['dʒuːbɪlənt] adj triumphierend
jubilee ['dʒuːbɪliː] n Jubiläum nt
judge [dʒʌdʒ] n Richter m; (fig) Kenner m ♦ vt (JUR: person) die Verhandlung führen über +acc; (case) verhandeln; (assess) beurteilen; (estimate) einschätzen; ~**ment** n (JUR) Urteil nt; (ECCL) Gericht nt; (ability) Urteilsvermögen nt
judicial [dʒuː'dɪʃl] adj gerichtlich, Justiz-
judiciary [dʒuː'dɪʃɪərɪ] n Gerichtsbehörden pl; (judges) Richterstand m
judicious [dʒuː'dɪʃəs] adj weise

judo ['dʒu:dəʊ] n Judo nt

jug [dʒʌg] n Krug m

juggernaut ['dʒʌgənɔ:t] (BRIT) n (huge truck) Schwertransporter m

juggle ['dʒʌgl] vt, vi jonglieren; **~r** n Jongleur m

Jugoslav etc = Yugoslav etc

juice [dʒu:s] n Saft m

juicy ['dʒu:sɪ] adj (also fig) saftig

jukebox ['dʒu:kbɒks] n Musikautomat m

July [dʒu:'laɪ] n Juli m

jumble ['dʒʌmbl] n Durcheinander nt ♦ vt (also: ~ up) durcheinanderwerfen; (facts) durcheinanderbringen; **~ sale** (BRIT) n Basar m, Flohmarkt m

jumbo (jet) n Jumbo(-Jet) m

jump [dʒʌmp] vi springen; (nervously) zusammenzucken ♦ vt überspringen ♦ n Sprung m; **to ~ the queue** (BRIT) sich vordrängeln

jumper ['dʒʌmpə*] n (BRIT: pullover) Pullover m; (US: dress) Trägerkleid nt; **~ cables** (US) npl = jump leads

jump leads (BRIT) npl Überbrückungskabel nt

jumpy ['dʒʌmpɪ] adj nervös

Jun. abbr = junior

junction ['dʒʌŋkʃən] n (BRIT: of roads) (Straßen)kreuzung f; (RAIL) Knotenpunkt m

juncture ['dʒʌŋktʃə*] n: **at this ~** in diesem Augenblick

June [dʒu:n] n Juni m

jungle ['dʒʌŋgl] n Dschungel m

junior ['dʒu:nɪə*] adj (younger) jünger; (after name) junior; (SPORT) Junioren-; (lower position) untergeordnet; (for young people) Junioren- ♦ n (Jüngere(r) m/f; **~ school** (BRIT) n Grundschule f

junk [dʒʌŋk] n (rubbish) Plunder m; (ship) Dschunke f; **~ food** n Plastikessen nt; **~ mail** n Reklame f die unangefordert in den Briefkasten gesteckt ist; **~shop** n Ramschladen m

Junr abbr = junior

jurisdiction [dʒʊərɪs'dɪkʃən] n Gerichtsbarkeit f; (range of authority) Zuständigkeit (sbereich m) f

juror ['dʒʊərə*] n Geschworene(r) m/f; (in competition) Preisrichter m

jury ['dʒʊərɪ] n (court) Geschworene pl; (in competition) Jury f

just [dʒʌst] adj gerecht ♦ adv (recently, now) gerade, eben; (barely) gerade noch; (exactly) genau, gerade; (only) nur, bloß; (a small distance) gleich; (absolutely) einfach; **~ as I arrived** gerade als ich ankam; **~ as nice** genauso nett; **~ as well** um so besser; **~ now** soeben, gerade; **~ try** versuch es mal; **she's ~ left** sie ist gerade or (so)eben gegangen; **he's ~ done it** er hat es gerade or (so)eben getan; **~ before** gerade or kurz bevor; **~ enough** gerade genug; **he ~ missed** er hat fast or beinahe getroffen

justice ['dʒʌstɪs] n (fairness) Gerechtigkeit f; **~ of the peace** n Friedensrichter m

justifiable ['dʒʌstɪfaɪəbl] adj berechtigt

justification [dʒʌstɪfɪ'keɪʃən] n Rechtfertigung f

justify ['dʒʌstɪfaɪ] vt rechtfertigen; (text) justieren

justly ['dʒʌstlɪ] adv (say) mit Recht; (condemn) gerecht

jut [dʒʌt] vi (also: ~ out) herausragen, vorstehen

juvenile ['dʒu:vənaɪl] adj (young) jugendlich; (for the young) Jugend- ♦ n Jugendliche(r) m/f

juxtapose ['dʒʌkstəpəʊz] vt nebeneinanderstellen

K

K abbr (= one thousand) Tsd.; (= Kilobyte) K

kangaroo [kæŋgə'ru:] n Känguruh nt

karate [kə'rɑ:tɪ] n Karate nt

kebab [kə'bæb] n Kebab m

keel [ki:l] n Kiel m; **on an even ~** (fig) im Lot

keen [ki:n] *adj* begeistert; *(intelligence, wind, blade)* scharf ♦ *(sight, hearing)* gut; **to be ~ to do** or **on doing sth** etw unbedingt tun wollen; **to be ~ on sth/sb** scharf auf etw/jdn sein

keep [ki:p] *(pt, pp* **kept)** *vt (retain)* behalten; *(have)* haben; *(animals, one's word)* halten; *(support)* versorgen; *(maintain in state)* halten; *(preserve)* aufbewahren; *(restrain)* abhalten ♦ *vi (continue in direction)* sich halten; *(food)* sich halten; *(remain: quiet etc)* bleiben ♦ *n* Unterhalt *m*; *(tower)* Burgfried *m*; *(inf):* **for ~s** für immer; **to ~ sth to o.s.** etw für sich behalten; **it ~s happening** es passiert immer wieder; **~ back** *vt* fernhalten; *(secret)* verschweigen; **~ on** *vi:* **to ~ on doing sth** etw immer weiter tun; **~ out** *vt* nicht hereinlassen; **"~ out"** "Eintritt verboten!"; **~ up** *vi* Schritt halten ♦ *vt* aufrechterhalten; *(continue)* weitermachen; **to ~ up with** Schritt halten mit; **~er** *n* Wärter(in) *m(f)*; *(goalkeeper)* Torhüter(in) *m(f)*; **~fit** *n* Keep-fit *nt*; **~ing** *n (care)* Obhut *f*; **in ~ing with** in Übereinstimmung mit; **~sake** *n* Andenken *nt*

keg [keg] *n* Faß *nt*

kennel [ˈkɛnl] *n* Hundehütte *f*; **~s** *npl (for boarding):* **to put a dog in ~s** einen Hund in Pflege geben

Kenya [ˈkɛnjə] *n* Kenia *nt*; **~n** *adj* kenianisch ♦ *n* Kenianer(in) *m(f)*

kept [kɛpt] *pt, pp of* **keep**

kerb [kɜ:b] *(BRIT) n* Bordstein *m*

kernel [ˈkɜ:nl] *n* Kern *m*

kerosene [ˈkɛrəsi:n] *n* Kerosin *nt*

ketchup [ˈkɛtʃəp] *n* Ketchup *nt* or *m*

kettle [ˈkɛtl] *n* Kessel *m*; **~drum** *n* Pauke *f*

key [ki:] *n* Schlüssel *m*; *(of piano, typewriter)* Taste *f*; *(MUS)* Tonart *f* ♦ *vt (also:* **~ in)** eingeben; **~board** *n* Tastatur *f*; **~ed up** *adj (person)* überdreht; **~hole** *n* Schlüsselloch *nt*; **~note** *n* Grundton *m*; **~ ring** *n* Schlüsselring *m*

khaki [ˈkɑ:kɪ] *n* K(h)aki *nt* ♦ *adj* k(h)aki(farben)

kick [kɪk] *vt* einen Fußtritt geben +*dat*, treten ♦ *vi* treten; *(baby)* strampeln; *(horse)* ausschlagen ♦ *n* (Fuß)tritt *m*; *(thrill)* Spaß *m*; **he does it for ~s** er macht das aus Jux; **~ off** *vi (SPORT)* anstoßen; **~off** *n (SPORT)* Anstoß *m*

kid [kɪd] *n (inf: child)* Kind *nt*; *(goat)* Zicklein *nt*; *(leather)* Glacéleder *nt* ♦ *vi (inf)* Witze machen

kidnap [ˈkɪdnæp] *vt* entführen; **~per** *n* Entführer *m*; **~ping** *n* Entführung *f*

kidney [ˈkɪdnɪ] *n* Niere *f*

kill [kɪl] *vt* töten, umbringen ♦ *vi* töten ♦ *n* Tötung *f*; *(hunting)* (Jagd)beute *f*; **~er** *n* Mörder(in) *m(f)*; **~ing** *n* Mord *m*; **~joy** *n* Spaßverderber(in) *m(f)*

kiln [kɪln] *n* Brennofen *m*

kilo [ˈki:ləʊ] *n* Kilo *nt*; **~byte** *n (COMPUT)* Kilobyte *nt*; **~gram(me)** [ˈkɪləʊgræm] *n* Kilogramm *nt*; **~metre** [ˈkɪləmi:tə*] *(US* **kilometer)** *n* Kilometer *m*; **~watt** *n* Kilowatt *nt*

kilt [kɪlt] *n* Schottenrock *m*

kind [kaɪnd] *adj* freundlich ♦ *n* Art *f*; **a ~ of** eine Art von; **(two) of a ~** (zwei) von der gleichen Art; **in ~** *(in goods)* in Naturalien

kindergarten [ˈkɪndəgɑ:tn] *n* Kindergarten *m*

kind-hearted [kaɪndˈhɑ:tɪd] *adj* gutherzig

kindle [ˈkɪndl] *vt (set on fire)* anzünden; *(rouse)* reizen, (er)wecken

kindly [ˈkaɪndlɪ] *adj* freundlich ♦ *adv* liebenswürdig(erweise); **would you ...?** wären Sie so freundlich und ...?

kindness [ˈkaɪndnəs] *n* Freundlichkeit *f*

kindred [ˈkɪndrɪd] *adj:* **~ spirit** Gleichgesinnte(r) *mf*

king [kɪŋ] *n* König *m*; **~dom** *n* Königreich *nt*; **~fisher** *n* Eisvogel *m*; **~-size** *adj (cigarette)* Kingsize

kinky ['kɪŋkɪ] (*inf*) *adj* (person, ideas) verrückt (*inf*); (sexual) abartig

kiosk ['kiːɒsk] (*BRIT*) *n* (*TEL*) Telefonhäuschen *nt*

kipper ['kɪpə*] *n* Räucherhering *m*

kiss [kɪs] *n* Kuß *m* ♦ *vt* küssen ♦ *vi*: **they ~ ed** sie küßten sich

kit [kɪt] *n* Ausrüstung *f*; (tools) Werkzeug *nt*

kitchen ['kɪtʃən] *n* Küche *f*; ~ **sink** *n* Spülbecken *nt*

kite [kaɪt] *n* Drachen *m*

kith [kɪθ] *n*: ~ **and kin** Blutsverwandte *pl*

kitten ['kɪtn] *n* Kätzchen *nt*

kitty ['kɪtɪ] *n* (money) Kasse *f*

km *abbr* (= *kilometre*) *m*

knack [næk] *n* Dreh *m*, Trick *m*

knapsack ['næpsæk] *n* Rucksack *m*; (*MIL*) Tornister *m*

knead [niːd] *vt* kneten

knee [niː] *n* Knie *nt*; ~**cap** *n* Kniescheibe *f*

kneel [niːl] (*pt*, *pp* **knelt**) *vi* (*also*: ~ **down**) knien

knell [nel] *n* Grabgeläute *nt*

knelt [nelt] *pt*, *pp of* **kneel**

knew [njuː] *pt of* **know**

knickers ['nɪkəz] (*BRIT*) *npl* Schlüpfer *m*

knife [naɪf] (*pl* **knives**) *n* Messer *nt* ♦ *vt* erstechen

knight [naɪt] *n* Ritter *m*; (chess) Springer *m*; ~**hood** *n* (title): **to get a ~hood** zum Ritter geschlagen werden

knit [nɪt] *vt* stricken ♦ *vi* stricken; (bones) zusammenwachsen; ~**ting** *n* (occupation) Stricken *nt*; (work) Strickzeug *nt*; ~**ting needle** *n* Stricknadel *f*; ~**wear** *n* Strickwaren *pl*

knives [naɪvz] *pl of* **knife**

knob [nɒb] *n* Knauf *m*; (on instrument) Knopf *m*; (*BRIT*: of butter etc) kleine(s) Stück *nt*

knock [nɒk] *vt* schlagen; (criticize) heruntermachen; *vi*: **to ~ at** *or* **on the door** an die Tür klopfen ♦ *n* Schlag *m*; (on door) Klopfen *nt*; ~ **down** *vt* umwerfen; (with car) an-

fahren; ~ **off** *vt* (do quickly) hinhauen; (*inf*: steal) klauen ♦ *vi* (finish) Feierabend machen; ~ **out** *vt* ausschlagen; (*BOXING*) k.o. schlagen; ~ **over** *vt* (person, object) umwerfen; (with car) anfahren; ~**er** *n* (on door) Türklopfer *m*; ~**-kneed** *adj* x-beinig; ~**out** *n* K.o.-Schlag *m*; (fig) Sensation *f*

knot [nɒt] *n* Knoten *m* ♦ *vt* (ver)knoten

knotty ['nɒtɪ] *adj* (fig) kompliziert

know [nəʊ] (*pt* **knew**, *pp* **known**) *vt*, *vi* wissen; (be able to) können; (be acquainted with) kennen; (recognize) erkennen; **to ~ how to do sth** wissen, wie man etw macht, etw tun können; **to ~ about** *or* **of sth/sb** etw/jdn kennen; ~**-all** *n* Alleswisser *m*; ~**-how** *n* Kenntnis *f*, Know-how *nt*; ~**ing** *adj* (look, smile) wissend; ~**ingly** *adv* wissend; (intentionally) wissentlich

knowledge ['nɒlɪdʒ] *n* Wissen *nt*, Kenntnis *f*; ~**able** *adj* informiert

known [nəʊn] *pp of* **know**

knuckle ['nʌkl] *n* Fingerknöchel *m*

K.O. *n abbr* = **knockout**

Koran [kɔ'rɑːn] *n* Koran *m*

Korea [kə'rɪə] *n* Korea *nt*

kosher ['kəʊʃə*] *adj* kosher

L

l. *abbr* = **litre**

lab [læb] (*inf*) *n* Labor *nt*

label ['leɪbl] *n* Etikett *nt* ♦ *vt* etikettieren

labor *etc* (*US*) = **labour** *etc*

laboratory [lə'bɒrətərɪ] *n* Laboratorium *nt*

laborious [lə'bɔːrɪəs] *adj* mühsam

labour ['leɪbə*] (*US* **labor**) *n* Arbeit *f*; (workmen) Arbeitskräfte *pl*; (*MED*) Wehen *pl* ♦ *vi*: **to ~ (at)** sich abmühen (mit) ♦ *vt* breittreten (*inf*); **in ~** (*MED*) in den Wehen; **L~** (*BRIT*: also the Labour party) die Labour Party; ~**ed** *adj* (move-

ment) gequält; (*style*) schwerfällig; ~er *n* Arbeiter *m*; farm ~er (Land)arbeiter *m*

lace [leɪs] *n* (*fabric*) Spitze *f*; (*of shoe*) Schnürsenkel *m*; (*braid*) Litze *f* ♦ *vt* (*also:* ~ *up*) (zu)schnüren

lack [læk] *n* Mangel *m* ♦ *vt* nicht haben; sb ~s sth jdm fehlt etw *nom*; to be ~ing sb is ~ing in sth es fehlt jdm an etw *dat*; through or for ~ of aus Mangel an +*dat*

lacquer ['lækə*] *n* Lack *m*

lad [læd] *n* Junge *m*

ladder ['lædə*] *n* Leiter *f*; (*BRIT: in tights*) Laufmasche *f* ♦ *vt* (*: tights*) Laufmaschen bekommen in +*dat*

laden ['leɪdn] *adj* beladen, voll

ladle ['leɪdl] *n* Schöpfkelle *f*

lady ['leɪdɪ] *n* Dame *f*; (*title*) Lady *f*; young ~ junge Dame *f*; the ladies' (room) die Damentoilette; ~bird (*US* ladybug) *n* Marienkäfer *m*; ~like *adj* damenhaft, vornehm; ~ship *n*: your ~ship Ihre Ladyschaft

lag [læg] *vi* (*also:* ~ behind) zurückbleiben ♦ *vt* (*pipes*) verkleiden

lager ['lɑːgə*] *n* helle(s) Bier *nt*

lagging ['lægɪŋ] *n* Isolierung *f*

lagoon [lə'guːn] *n* Lagune *f*

laid [leɪd] *pt, pp of* lay; ~ back (*inf*) *adj* cool

lain [leɪn] *pp of* lie

lair [lɛə*] *n* Lager *nt*

laity ['leɪɪtɪ] *n* Laien *pl*

lake [leɪk] *n* See *m*

lamb [læm] *n* Lamm *nt*; (*meat*) Lammfleisch *nt*; ~ chop *n* Lammkotelett *nt*; ~swool *n* Lammwolle *f*

lame [leɪm] *adj* lahm; (*excuse*) faul

lament [lə'ment] *n* Klage *f* ♦ *vt* beklagen

laminated ['læmɪneɪtɪd] *adj* geschichtet

lamp [læmp] *n* Lampe *f*; (*in street*) Straßenlaterne *f*

lamppost ['læmppəʊst] *n* Laternenpfahl *m*

lampshade ['læmpʃeɪd] *n* Lampen-

schirm *m*

lance [lɑːns] *n* Lanze *f* ♦ *vt* (*MED*) aufschneiden; ~ corporal (*BRIT*) *n* Obergefreite(r) *m*

land [lænd] *n* Land *nt* ♦ *vi* (*from ship*) an Land gehen; (*AVIAT, end up*) landen ♦ *vt* (*obtain*) kriegen; (*passengers*) absetzen; (*goods*) abladen; (*troops, space probe*) landen; ~fill site *n* Mülldeponie *f*; ~ing *n* Landung *f*; (*on stairs*) (Treppen)absatz *m*; ~ing gear *n* Fahrgestell *nt*; ~ing stage (*BRIT*) *n* Landesteg *m*; ~ing strip *n* Landebahn *f*; ~lady *n* (Haus)wirtin *f*; ~locked *adj* landumschlossen, Binnen-; ~lord *n* (*of house*) Hauswirt *m*, Besitzer *m*; (*of pub*) Gastwirt *m*; (*of land*) Grundbesitzer *m*; ~mark *n* Wahrzeichen *nt*; (*fig*) Meilenstein *m*; ~owner *n* Grundbesitzer *m*

landscape ['lændskeɪp] *n* Landschaft *f*

landslide ['lændslaɪd] *n* (*GEOG*) Erdrutsch *m*; (*POL*) überwältigende(r) Sieg *m*

lane [leɪn] *n* (*in town*) Gasse *f*; (*in country*) Weg *m*; (*of motorway*) Fahrbahn *f*, Spur *f*; (*SPORT*) Bahn *f*

language ['læŋgwɪdʒ] *n* Sprache *f*; bad ~ unanständige Ausdrücke *pl*; ~ laboratory *n* Sprachlabor *nt*

languid ['læŋgwɪd] *adj* schlaff, matt

languish ['læŋgwɪʃ] *vi* schmachten

lank [læŋk] *adj* dürr

lanky ['læŋkɪ] *adj* schlaksig

lantern ['læntən] *n* Laterne *f*

lap [læp] *n* Schoß *m*; (*SPORT*) Runde *f* ♦ *vt* (*also:* ~ up) auflecken ♦ *vi* (*water*) plätschern

lapel [lə'pel] *n* Revers *nt or m*

Lapland ['læplænd] *n* Lappland *nt*

lapse [læps] *n* (*moral*) Fehltritt *m* ♦ *vi* (*decline*) nachlassen; (*expire*) ablaufen; (*claims*) erlöschen; to ~ into bad habits sich schlechte Gewohnheiten angewöhnen

laptop (computer) ['læptɒp] *n* Laptop(-Computer) *m*

larceny ['lɑːsənɪ] *n* Diebstahl *m*

lard [lɑ:d] n Schweineschmalz nt

larder ['lɑ:də*] n Speisekammer f

large [lɑ:dʒ] adj groß; **at ~** auf freiem Fuß; **~ly** adv zum größten Teil; **~scale** adj groß angelegt, Groß-

largesse [lɑ:'ʒes] n Freigebigkeit f

lark [lɑ:k] n (bird) Lerche f; (joke) Jux m; **~ about** (inf) vi herumalbern

laryngitis [lærin'dʒaitis] n Kehlkopfentzündung f

larynx ['læriŋks] n Kehlkopf m

laser ['leizə*] n Laser m; **~ printer** n Laserdrucker m

lash [læʃ] n Peitschenhieb m; (eye~) Wimper f ♦ vt (rain) schlagen gegen; (whip) peitschen; (bind fast) festbinden; **~ out** vi (with fists) um sich schlagen; (spend money) sich in Unkosten stürzen ♦ vt (money etc) springen lassen

lass [læs] n Mädchen nt

lasso [læ'su:] n Lasso nt

last [lɑ:st] adj letzte(r, s) ♦ adv zuletzt; (last time) das letztemal ♦ vi (continue) dauern; (remain good) sich halten; (money) ausreichen; **at ~** endlich; **~ night** gestern abend; **~ week** letzte Woche; **~ but one** vorletzte(r, s); **~ditch** adj (attempt) in letzter Minute; **~ing** adj dauerhaft; (shame etc) andauernd; **~ly** adv schließlich; **~-minute** adj in letzter Minute

latch [lætʃ] n Riegel m

late [leit] adj spät; (dead) verstorben ♦ adv spät; (after proper time) zu spät; **to be ~** zu spät kommen; **of ~** in letzter Zeit; **in ~ May** Ende Mai; **~comer** n Nachzügler(in) m(f); **~ly** adv in letzter Zeit

later ['leitə*] adj (date etc) später; (version etc) neuer ♦ adv später

lateral ['lætərəl] adj seitlich

latest ['leitist] adj (fashion) neueste(r, s) ♦ n (news) Neue(ste)s nt; **at the ~** spätestens

lathe [leið] n Drehbank f

lather ['lɑːðə*] n (Seifen)schaum m

♦ vt einschäumen ♦ vi schäumen

Latin ['lætin] n Latein nt ♦ adj lateinisch; (Roman) römisch; **~ America** n Lateinamerika nt; **~-American** adj lateinamerikanisch

latitude ['lætitju:d] n (GEOG) Breite f; (freedom) Spielraum m

latter ['lætə*] adj (second of two) letztere; (coming at end) letzte(r, s) späte(r, s) ♦ n: **the ~** die/der/das letztere, die, die letzteren; **~ly** adv in letzter Zeit

lattice ['lætis] n Gitter nt

laudable ['lɔːdəbl] adj löblich

laugh [lɑːf] n Lachen nt ♦ vi lachen; **~ at** vt lachen über +acc; **~ off** vt lachend abtun; **~able** adj lachhaft; **~ing stock** n Zielscheibe f des Spottes; **~ter** n Gelächter nt

launch [lɔːntʃ] n (of ship) Stapellauf m; (of rocket) Abschuß m; (boat) Barkasse f; (of product) Einführung f ♦ vt (set afloat) vom Stapel lassen; (rocket) (ab)schießen; (product) auf den Markt bringen; **~(ing) pad** n Abschußrampe f

launder ['lɔːndə*] vt waschen

launderette [lɔːn'dret] n (BRIT) Waschsalon m

Laundromat ['lɔːndrəmæt] n ® (US) n Waschsalon m

laundry ['lɔːndri] n (place) Wäscherei f; (clothes) Wäsche f; **to do the ~** waschen

laureate ['lɔːriət] adj see poet

laurel ['lɒrəl] n Lorbeer m

lava ['lɑːvə] n Lava f

lavatory ['lævətəri] n Toilette f

lavender ['lævində*] n Lavendel m

lavish ['læviʃ] adj (extravagant) verschwenderisch; (generous) großzügig ♦ vt (money): **to ~ sth on sb** etw auf etw acc verschwenden; (attention, gifts): **to ~ sth on sb** jdn mit etw überschütten

law [lɔː] n Gesetz nt; (system) Recht nt; (as studies) Jura no m; **~-abiding** adj gesetzestreu; **~ and order** n Recht nt und Ordnung f; **~ court** n Gerichtshof m; **~ful** adj gesetzlich; ~**less** adj gesetzlos

lawn [lɔːn] n Rasen m; ~**mower** n Rasenmäher m; ~ **tennis** n Rasentennis m

law school n Rechtsakademie f

lawsuit [ˈlɔːsuːt] n Prozeß m

lawyer [ˈlɔːjə*] n Rechtsanwalt m, Rechtsanwältin f

lax [læks] adj (behaviour) nachlässig; (standards) lax

laxative [ˈlæksətɪv] n Abführmittel nt

lay [leɪ] (pt, pp **laid**) pt of **lie** ♦ adj Laien- ♦ vt (place) legen; (table) decken; (egg) legen; (trap) stellen; (money) wetten; ~ **aside** vt zurücklegen; ~ **by** vt (set aside) beiseite legen; ~ **down** vt hinlegen; (rules) vorschreiben; (arms) strecken; **to** ~ **down the law** Vorschriften machen; ~ **off** vt (workers) (vorübergehend) entlassen; ~ **on** vt (water, gas) anschließen; (concert etc) veranstalten; ~ **out** vt (her)auslegen; (money) ausgeben; (corpse) aufbahren; ~ **up** vt (subj: illness) ans Bett fesseln; (supplies) anlegen; ~**about** n Faulenzer m; ~**by** n (BRIT) Parkbucht f; (bigger) Rastplatz m

layer [ˈleɪə*] n Schicht f

layette [leɪˈet] n Babyausstattung f

layman [ˈleɪmən] n Laie m

layout [ˈleɪaʊt] n Anlage f; (ART) Layout m

laze [leɪz] vi faulenzen

laziness [ˈleɪzɪnɪs] n Faulheit f

lazy [ˈleɪzɪ] adj faul; (slow-moving) träge

lb. abbr = **pound** (weight)

lead¹ [led] n (chemical) Blei nt; (of pencil) (Bleistift)mine f ♦ adj bleiern, Blei-

lead² [liːd] (pt, pp **led**) n (front position) Führung f; (distance, time ahead) Vorsprung m; (example) Vorbild nt; (clue) Tip m; (of hunting) Spur f; (THEAT) Hauptrolle f; (dog's) Leine f ♦ vt (guide) führen; (group etc) leiten ♦ vi (be first) führen; **in the** ~ (SPORT, fig) in Führung; ~ **astray** vt irreführen; ~ **away** vt wegführen; (prisoner) abführen; ~ **back** vi zurückführen; ~ **on** vt anführen; ~ **on to** vt (induce) dazu bringen; ~ **to** vt (street) (hin)führen nach; (result in) führen zu; ~ **up to** vt (drive) führen zu; (speaker etc) hinführen auf +acc

leaden [ˈledn] adj (sky, sea) bleiern; (heavy: footsteps) bleischwer

leader [ˈliːdə*] n Führer m, Leiter m; (of party) Vorsitzende/r m; (PRESS) Leitartikel m; ~**ship** n (office) Leitung f; (quality) Führerschaft f

lead-free [ˈledfriː] adj (petrol) bleifrei

leading [ˈliːdɪŋ] adj führend; ~ **lady** n (THEAT) Hauptdarstellerin f; ~ **light** n (person) führende/r Geist m

leaf [liːf] (pl **leaves**) n Blatt nt ♦ vi: **to** ~ **through** durchblättern; **to turn over a new** ~ einen neuen Anfang machen

leaflet [ˈliːflɪt] n (advertisement) Prospekt m; (pamphlet) Flugblatt nt; (for information) Merkblatt nt

league [liːg] n (union) Bund m; (SPORT) Liga f; **to be in** ~ **with** unter einer Decke stecken mit

leak [liːk] n undichte Stelle f; (in ship) Leck nt ♦ vt (liquid etc) durchlassen ♦ vi (pipe etc) undicht sein; (liquid etc) auslaufen; **the information was** ~**ed to the enemy** die Information wurde dem Feind zugespielt; ~ **out** vi (liquid etc) auslaufen; (information) durchsickern

leaky [ˈliːkɪ] adj undicht

lean [liːn] (pt, pp **leaned** or **leant**) adj mager ♦ vi sich neigen ♦ vt (an)lehnen; **to** ~ **against sth** an etw dat angelehnt sein; sich an etw acc anlehnen; ~ **back** vi sich zurücklehnen; ~ **forward** vi sich vorbeugen; ~ **on** vt fus sich stützen auf +acc; ~ **out** vi sich hinauslehnen; ~ **over** vi sich hinüberbeugen; ~**ing** n Neigung f ♦ adj schief; **leant** pt, pp of **lean**; ~**-to** n Anbau m

leap [li:p] (pt, pp **leaped** or **leapt**) n Sprung m ♦ vi springen; **~frog** n Bockspringen nt; **leapt** [lept] (pt, pp) of leap; **~ year** n Schaltjahr nt

learn [lə:n] (pt, pp **learned** or **learnt**) vt, vi lernen; (find out) erfahren; to **~ how to do sth** etw (er)lernen; **~ed** [lə:nɪd] adj gelehrt; **~er** n Anfänger(in) m(f); (AUT: BRIT: also **~ driver**) Fahrschüler(in) m(f); **~ing** n Gelehrsamkeit f; **~t** [lə:nt] pt, pp of learn

lease [li:s] n (of property) Mietvertrag m ♦ vt pachten

leash [li:ʃ] n Leine f

least [li:st] adj geringste(r, s) ♦ adv am wenigsten ♦ n Mindeste(s) nt; the **~ possible effort** möglichst geringer Aufwand; at **~** zumindest; not in the **~!** durchaus nicht!

leather ['leðə*] n Leder nt

leave [li:v] (pt, pp **left**) vt verlassen; (~ behind) zurücklassen; (forget) vergessen; (allow to remain) lassen; (after death) hinterlassen; (entrust): to **~** sth to sb jdm etw überlassen ♦ vi weggehen, wegfahren; (for journey) abreisen; (bus, train) abfahren ♦ n Erlaubnis f; (MIL) Urlaub m; to be **~** (remain) übrigbleiben; there's some milk **left** over es ist noch etwas Milch übrig; on **~** auf Urlaub; **~ behind** vt (person, object) dalassen; (~ forget) liegenlassen, stehenlassen; **~ out** vt auslassen; **~** of absence n Urlaub m

leaves [li:vz] pl of leaf

Lebanon ['lebənən] n Libanon m

lecherous ['letʃərəs] adj lüstern

lecture ['lektʃə*] n Vortrag m; (UNIV) Vorlesung f ♦ vi einen Vortrag halten; (UNIV) lesen ♦ vt (scold) abkanzeln; to give a **~** on sth einen Vortrag über etwas halten; **~r** ['lektʃərə*] n Vortragende(r) mf; (BRIT: UNIV) Dozent(in) m(f)

led [led] pt, pp of lead²

ledge [ledʒ] n Leiste f; (window ~) Sims m or nt; (of mountain) (Fels)vorsprung m

ledger ['ledʒə*] n Hauptbuch nt

leech [li:tʃ] n Blutegel m

leek [li:k] n Lauch m

leer [lɪə*] vi: to **~** (at sb) (nach jdm) schielen

leeway ['li:weɪ] n (fig): to have some **~** etwas Spielraum haben

left [left] pt, pp of leave ♦ adj linke(r, s) ♦ n (side) linke Seite f ♦ adv links; on the **~** links; to the **~** nach links; the L**~** (POL) die Linke f; **~-handed** adj linkshändig; **~-hand side** n linke Seite f; **~-luggage (office)** (BRIT) n Gepäckaufbewahrung f; **~-overs** npl Reste pl; **~-wing** adj linke(r, s)

leg [leg] n Bein nt; (of meat) Keule f; (stage) Etappe f; 1st/2nd **~** (SPORT) 1./2. Etappe

legacy ['legəsɪ] n Erbe nt, Erbschaft f

legal ['li:gəl] adj gesetzlich; (allowed) legal; **~ holiday** (US) n gesetzliche(r) Feiertag m; **~ize** vt legalisieren; **~ly** adv gesetzlich; legal; **~ tender** n gesetzliche(s) Zahlungsmittel nt

legend ['ledʒənd] n Legende f; **~ary** adj legendär

legible ['ledʒəbl] adj leserlich

legislation [ledʒɪs'leɪʃən] n Gesetzgebung f

legislative ['ledʒɪslətɪv] adj gesetzgebend

legislature ['ledʒɪslətʃə*] n Legislative f

legitimate [lɪ'dʒɪtɪmət] adj rechtmäßig, legitim; (child) ehelich

legroom ['legrum] n Platz m für die Beine

leisure ['leʒə*] n Freizeit f; to be at **~** Zeit haben; **~ centre** n Freizeitzentrum nt; **~ly** adj gemächlich

lemon ['lemən] n Zitrone f; (colour) Zitronengelb nt; **~ade** [lemə'neɪd] n Limonade f; **~ tea** n Zitronentee m

lend [lend] (pt, pp **lent**) vt leihen; to **~** sb sth jdm etw leihen; **~ing library** n Leihbibliothek f

length [leŋθ] n Länge f; (section of

road, pipe etc) Strecke *f*; (*of material*) Stück *nt*; **at ~** (*lengthily*) ausführlich; (*at last*) schließlich; **~en** *vt* verlängern ♦ *vi* länger werden; **~ways** *adv* längs; **~y** *adj* sehr lang, langatmig

lenient ['li:nɪənt] *adj* nachsichtig

lens [lenz] *n* Linse *f*; (*PHOT*) Objektiv *nt*

Lent [lent] *n* Fastenzeit *f*

lent *pt, pp of* **lend**

lentil ['lentl] *n* Linse *f*

Leo ['li:əu] *n* Löwe *m*

leotard ['li:ətɑːd] *n* Trikot *nt*, Gymnastikanzug *m*

leper ['lepə*] *n* Leprakranke(r) *f(m)*

leprosy ['leprəsɪ] *n* Lepra *f*

lesbian ['lezbɪən] *adj* lesbisch ♦ *n* Lesbierin *f*

less [les] *adj, adv* weniger ♦ *n* weniger ♦ *pron* weniger; **~ than half** weniger als die Hälfte; **~ than ever** weniger denn je; **~ and ~** immer weniger; **the ~ he works** je weniger er arbeitet

lessen ['lesn] *vi* abnehmen ♦ *vt* verringern, verkleinern

lesser ['lesə*] *adj* kleiner, geringer; **to a ~ extent** in geringerem Maße

lesson ['lesn] *n* (*SCH*) Stunde *f*; (*unit of study*) Lektion *f*; (*fig*) Lehre *f*; (*ECCL*) Lesung *f*; **a maths ~** eine Mathestunde

lest [lest] *conj*: **~ it happen** damit es nicht passiert

let [let] (*pt, pp* **let**) *vt* lassen; (*BRIT: lease*) vermieten; **to ~ sb do sth** jdn etw tun lassen; **to ~ sb know sth** jdn etw wissen lassen; **~'s go!** gehen wir!; **~ him come** soll er doch kommen; **~ down** *vt* hinunterlassen; (*disappoint*) enttäuschen; **~ go** *vi* loslassen ♦ *vt* (*things*) loslassen; (*person*) gehen lassen; **~ in** *vt* hereinlassen; (*water*) durchlassen; **~ off** *vt* (*gun*) abfeuern; (*steam*) ablassen; (*forgive*) laufen lassen; **~ on** *vi* durchblicken lassen; (*pretend*) vorgeben; **~ out** *vt* herauslassen; (*scream*) fahren lassen; **~ up** *vi*

nachlassen; (*stop*) aufhören

lethal ['li:θəl] *adj* tödlich

lethargic [le'θɑːdʒɪk] *adj* lethargisch

letter ['letə*] *n* (*of alphabet*) Buchstabe *m*; (*message*) Brief *m*; **~ bomb** *n* Briefbombe *f*; **~box** (*BRIT*) *n* Briefkasten *m*; **~ing** *n* Beschriftung *f*; **~ of credit** *n* Akkreditiv *m*

lettuce ['letɪs] *n* (Kopf)salat *m*

let-up ['letʌp] (*inf*) *n* Nachlassen *nt*

leukaemia [luː'kiːmɪə] (*US* **leukemia**) *n* Leukämie *f*

level ['levl] *adj* (*ground*) eben; (*at same height*) auf gleicher Höhe; (*equal*) gleich gut; (*head*) kühl ♦ *adv* auf gleicher Höhe ♦ *n* (*instrument*) Wasserwaage *f*; (*altitude*) Höhe *f*; (*flat place*) ebene Fläche *f*; (*position on scale*) Niveau *nt*; (*amount, degree*) Grad *m* ♦ *vt* (*ground*) einebnen; **to draw ~ with** gleichziehen mit; **to be ~ with** auf einer Höhe sein mit; **A ~s** (*BRIT*) Abitur *nt*; **O ~s** = mittlere Reife *f*; **on the ~** (*fig: honest*) ehrlich; **to sth at sb** (*blow*) jdm etw versetzen; (*remark*) etw gegen jdn richten; **~ off** *or* **out** *vi* flach *or* eben werden; (*fig*) sich ausgleichen; (*plane*) horizontal fliegen ♦ *vt* (*ground*) planieren; (*differences*) ausgleichen; **~ crossing** (*BRIT*) *n* Bahnübergang *m*; **~-headed** *adj* vernünftig

lever ['li:və*] *n* Hebel *m*; (*fig*) Druckmittel *nt* ♦ *vt* (hoch)stemmen; **~age** *n* Hebelkraft *f*; (*fig*) Einfluß *m*

levity ['levɪtɪ] *n* Leichtfertigkeit *f*

levy ['levɪ] *n* (*of taxes*) Erhebung *f*; (*tax*) Abgaben *pl*; (*MIL*) Aushebung *f* ♦ *vt* erheben; (*MIL*) ausheben

lewd [luːd] *adj* unzüchtig, unanständig

liability [laɪə'bɪlɪtɪ] *n* (*burden*) Belastung *f*; (*duty*) Pflicht *f*; (*debt*) Verpflichtung *f*; (*proneness*) Anfälligkeit *f*; (*responsibility*) Haftung *f*

liable ['laɪəbl] *adj* (*responsible*) haftbar; (*prone*) anfällig; **to be ~ for sth** für etw haftbar sein; **it's ~ to happen** es kann leicht vorkommen

liaise [lɪ:'eɪz] vi: to ~ (with sb) (mit jdm) zusammenarbeiten

liaison [lɪ:'eɪzɒn] n Verbindung f

liar ['laɪə*] n Lügner m

libel ['laɪbəl] n Verleumdung f ♦ vt verleumden

liberal ['lɪbərəl] adj (generous) großzügig; (open-minded) aufgeschlossen; (POL) liberal

liberate ['lɪbəreɪt] vt befreien

liberation [lɪbə'reɪʃən] n Befreiung f

liberty ['lɪbətɪ] n Freiheit f; (permission) Erlaubnis f; to be at ~ (to do sth) etw tun dürfen; to take the ~ of doing sth sich dat erlauben, etw zu tun

Libra ['lɪ:brə] n Waage f

librarian [laɪ'breərɪən] n Bibliothekar(in) m(f)

library ['laɪbrərɪ] n Bibliothek f; (lending ~) Bücherei f

Libya ['lɪbɪə] n Libyen nt; ~n adj libysch ♦ n Libyer(in) m(f)

lice [laɪs] npl of louse

licence ['laɪsəns] (US license) n (permit) Erlaubnis f; (also: driving ~, US driver's ~) Führerschein m; (excess) Zügellosigkeit f

license ['laɪsəns] n (US) = licence ♦ vt genehmigen, konzessionieren; ~d adj (for alcohol) konzessioniert (für den Alkoholausschank)

license plate (US) n (AUT) Nummernschild nt

licentious [laɪ'senʃəs] adj ausschweifend

lichen ['laɪkən] n Flechte f

lick [lɪk] vt lecken ♦ n Lecken nt; a ~ of paint ein bißchen Farbe

licorice ['lɪkərɪs] (US) n = liquorice

lid [lɪd] n Deckel m; (eye~) Lid nt

lie [laɪ] (pt lay, pp lain) vi (rest, be situated) liegen; (put o.s. in position) sich legen; (pt, pp lied: tell lies) lügen ♦ n Lüge f; to ~ low (fig) untertauchen; ~ **about** vi (things) herumliegen; (people) faulenzen; ~-**down** (BRIT) n: to have a ~-down ein Nickerchen machen; ~-**in** (BRIT) n: to have a ~-in sich ausschlafen

lieu [lu:] n: in ~ of anstatt +gen

lieutenant [lef'tenənt, (US) lu:'tenənt] n Leutnant m

life [laɪf] (pl lives) n Leben nt; ~ **assurance** (BRIT) n = life insurance; ~**belt** (BRIT) n Rettungsring m; ~**boat** n Rettungsboot nt; ~**guard** n Rettungsschwimmer m; ~ **insurance** n Lebensversicherung f; ~ **jacket** n Schwimmweste f; ~**less** adj (dead) leblos; (dull) langweilig; ~**like** adj lebensnah, naturgetreu; ~**line** n Rettungsleine f; (fig) Rettungsanker m; ~**long** adj lebenslang; ~ **preserver** (US) n = lifebelt; ~**saver** n Lebensretter(in) m(f); ~ **sentence** n lebenslängliche Freiheitsstrafe f; ~**sized** adj in Lebensgröße; ~ **span** n Lebensspanne f; ~**style** n Lebensstil m; ~ **support system** n (MED) Lebenserhaltungssystem nt; ~**time** n: in his ~time während er lebte; once in a ~time einmal im Leben

lift [lɪft] vt hochheben ♦ vi sich heben ♦ n (BRIT: elevator) Aufzug m, Lift m; to give sb a ~ jdn mitnehmen; ~**off** n Abheben nt (vom Boden)

ligament ['lɪgəmənt] n Band nt

light [laɪt] (pt, pp **lighted** or **lit**) n Licht nt; (for cigarette etc): have you got a ~? haben Sie Feuer? ♦ vt beleuchten (lamp); anmachen; (fire, cigarette) anzünden ♦ adj (bright) hell; (pale) hell-; (not heavy, easy) leicht; (punishment) milde; (touch) leicht; ~**s** npl (AUT) Beleuchtung f; ~ **up** vi (lamp) aufleuchten; (face) aufleuchten ♦ vt (illuminate) beleuchten; (lights) anmachen; ~ **bulb** n Glühbirne f; ~**en** vi (brighten) hell werden; (lightning) blitzen ♦ vt (give light to) erhellen; (hair) aufhellen; (gloom) aufheitern; (make less heavy) leichter machen; (fig) erleichtern; ~**er** n Feuerzeug nt; ~**headed** adj (thoughtless) leichtsinnig; (giddy) schwindlig; ~**hearted** adj leichtherzig, fröhlich; ~**house** n Leuchtturm m; ~**ing** n Beleuchtung f; ~**ly** adv leicht; (irresponsibly) leichtfertig; **to get off** ~**ly** mit einem blauen Auge davonkommen; ~**ness** n (of weight) Leichtigkeit f; (of colour) Helle f

lightning ['laɪtnɪŋ] n Blitz m; ~ **conductor** (US **lightning rod**) n Blitzableiter m

light: ~ **pen** n Lichtstift m; ~**weight** adj (suit) leicht; ~**weight boxer** n Leichtgewichtler m; ~ **year** n Lichtjahr nt

like [laɪk] vt mögen, gernhaben ♦ prep wie ♦ adj (similar) ähnlich; (equal) gleich ♦ n: **the** ~ dergleichen; **I would** ~ or **I'd** ~ ich möchte gern; **would you** ~ **a coffee?** möchten Sie einen Kaffee?; **to be** or **look** ~ sb/sth jdm/etw ähneln; **that's just** ~ **him** das ist typisch für ihn; **do it** ~ **this** mach es so; **it is nothing** ~ ... es ist nicht zu vergleichen mit ...; **what does it look** ~? wie sieht es aus?; **what does it sound** ~? wie hört es sich an?; **what does it taste** ~? wie schmeckt es?; **his** ~**s and dislikes** was er mag und was er nicht mag; ~**able** adj sympathisch

likelihood ['laɪklɪhʊd] n Wahrscheinlichkeit f

likely ['laɪklɪ] adj wahrscheinlich; **he's** ~ **to leave** er geht möglicherweise; **not** ~! wohl kaum!

likeness ['laɪknɪs] n Ähnlichkeit f; (portrait) Bild nt

likewise ['laɪkwaɪz] adv ebenso

liking ['laɪkɪŋ] n Zuneigung f; (taste) Vorliebe f

lilac ['laɪlək] n Flieder m ♦ adj (colour) fliederfarben

lily ['lɪlɪ] n Lilie f; ~ **of the valley** n Maiglöckchen nt

limb [lɪm] n Glied nt

limber ['lɪmbə*] n: ~ **up** vi sich auflockern; (fig) sich vorbereiten

limbo ['lɪmbəʊ] n: **to be in** ~ (fig) in der Schwebe sein

lime [laɪm] n (tree) Linde f; (fruit) Limone f; (substance) Kalk m

limelight ['laɪmlaɪt] n: **to be in the**

~ (fig) im Rampenlicht stehen

limestone ['laɪmstəʊn] n Kalkstein m

limit ['lɪmɪt] n Grenze f; (inf) Höhe f ♦ vt begrenzen, einschränken; ~**ation** n Einschränkung f; ~**ed** adj beschränkt; **to be** ~**ed to** sich beschränken auf +acc; ~**ed (liability) company** (BRIT) n Gesellschaft f mit beschränkter Haftung

limp [lɪmp] n Hinken nt ♦ vi hinken ♦ adj schlaff

limpet ['lɪmpɪt] n (fig) Klette f

line [laɪn] n Linie f; (rope) Leine f; (on face) Falte f; (row) Reihe f; (of hills) Kette f; (US: queue) Schlange f; (company) Linie f, Gesellschaft f; (RAIL) Strecke f; (TEL) Leitung f; (written) Zeile f; (direction) Richtung f; (fig: business) Branche f; (range of items) Kollektion f ♦ vt (coat) füttern; (border) säumen; ~**s** npl (RAIL) Gleise pl; **in** ~ **with** in Übereinstimmung mit; ~ **up** vi sich aufstellen ♦ vt aufstellen; (prepare) sorgen für; (support) mobilisieren; (surprise) planen

linear ['lɪnɪə*] adj gerade; (measure) Längen-

lined [laɪnd] adj (face) faltig; (paper) liniert

linen ['lɪnɪn] n Leinen nt; (sheets etc) Wäsche f

liner [laɪnə*] n Überseedampfer m

linesman ['laɪnzmən] (irreg) n (SPORT) Linienrichter m

line-up ['laɪnʌp] n Aufstellung f

linger ['lɪŋgə*] vi (remain long) verweilen; (taste) (zurück)bleiben; (delay) zögern, verharren

lingerie ['lænʒərɪ] n Damenunterwäsche f

lingering ['lɪŋgərɪŋ] adj (doubt) zurückbleibend; (disease) langwierig; (taste) nachhaltend; (look) lang

lingo ['lɪŋgəʊ] (pl ~**es**, inf) n Sprache f

linguist ['lɪŋgwɪst] n Sprachkundige(r) mf; (UNIV) Sprachwissenschaftler(in) m(f)

linguistic [lɪŋˈgwɪstɪk] *adj* sprachlich; sprachwissenschaftlich; **~s** [lɪŋˈgwɪstɪks] *n* Sprachwissenschaft *f*, Linguistik *f*

lining [ˈlaɪnɪŋ] *n* Futter *nt*

link [lɪŋk] *n* Glied *nt*; (*connection*) Verbindung *f* ♦ *vt* verbinden; **~s** *npl* (*GOLF*) Golfplatz *m*; **~ up** *vt* verbinden ♦ *vi* zusammenkommen; (*companies*) sich zusammenschließen; **~-up** *n* (*TEL*) Verbindung *f*; (*of spaceships*) Kopplung *f*

lino [ˈlaɪnəʊ] *n* = linoleum

linoleum [lɪˈnəʊlɪəm] *n* Linoleum *nt*

linseed oil [ˈlɪnsiːd-] *n* Leinöl *nt*

lion [ˈlaɪən] *n* Löwe *m*; **~ess** *n* Löwin *f*

lip [lɪp] *n* Lippe *f*; (*of jug*) Schnabel *m*; **to pay ~ service** (**to**) ein Lippenbekenntnis ablegen (*zu*); **~read** (*irreg*) *vi* von den Lippen ablesen; **~ salve** *n* Lippenbalsam *m*; **~stick** *n* Lippenstift *m*

liqueur [lɪˈkjʊə*] *n* Likör *m*

liquid [ˈlɪkwɪd] *n* Flüßigkeit *f* ♦ *adj* flüssig

liquidate [ˈlɪkwɪdeɪt] *vt* liquidieren

liquidation [lɪkwɪˈdeɪʃən] *n* Liquidation *f*

liquidize [ˈlɪkwɪdaɪz] *vt* (*CULIN*) (im Mixer) pürieren; **~r** [ˈlɪkwɪdaɪzə*] *n* Mixgerät *nt*

liquor [ˈlɪkə*] *n* Alkohol *m*

liquorice [ˈlɪkərɪs] (*BRIT*) *n* Lakritze *f*

liquor store (*US*) *n* Spirituosengeschäft *nt*

Lisbon [ˈlɪzbən] *n* Lissabon *nt*

lisp [lɪsp] *n* Lispeln *nt* ♦ *vt, vi* lispeln

list [lɪst] *n* Liste *f*, Verzeichnis, *nt*; (*of ship*) Schlagseite *f* ♦ *vt* (*write down*) eine Liste machen von; (*verbally*) aufzählen ♦ *vi* (*ship*) Schlagseite haben

listen [ˈlɪsn] *vi* hören; **~ to** *vt* zuhören +*dat*; **~er** *n* (Zu)hörer(in) *m(f)*

listless [ˈlɪstlɪs] *adj* lustlos

lit [lɪt] *pt, pp* of **light**

liter [ˈliːtə*] (*US*) *n* = litre

literacy [ˈlɪtərəsɪ] *n* Fähigkeit *f* zu lesen und zu schreiben

literal [ˈlɪtərəl] *adj* buchstäblich; (*translation*) wortwörtlich; **~ly** *adv* wörtlich; buchstäblich

literary [ˈlɪtərərɪ] *adj* literarisch

literate [ˈlɪtərət] *adj* des Lesens und Schreibens kundig

literature [ˈlɪtrətʃə*] *n* Literatur *f*

lithe [laɪð] *adj* geschmeidig

litigation [lɪtɪˈgeɪʃən] *n* Prozeß *m*

litre [ˈliːtə*] (*US* liter) *n* Liter *m*

litter [ˈlɪtə*] *n* (*rubbish*) Abfall *m*; (*of animals*) Wurf *m* ♦ *vt* in Unordnung bringen; **to be ~ed with** übersät sein mit; **~ bin** (*BRIT*) *n* Abfalleimer *m*

little [ˈlɪtl] *adj* klein ♦ *adv, n* wenig; **a ~** ein bißchen; **~ by ~** nach und nach

live¹ [laɪv] *adj* lebendig; (*MIL*) scharf; (*ELEC*) geladen; (*broadcast*) live

live² [lɪv] *vi* leben; (*dwell*) wohnen ♦ *vt* (*life*) führen; **~ down** *vt*: **I'll never ~ it down** das wird man mir nie vergessen; **~ on** *vi* weiterleben ♦ *vt fus*: **to live on sth** von etw leben; **~ together** *vi* zusammenleben; (*share a flat*) zusammenwohnen; **~ up to** *vt* (*standards*) gerecht werden +*dat*; (*principles*) anstreben; (*hopes*) entsprechen +*dat*

livelihood [ˈlaɪvlɪhʊd] *n* Lebensunterhalt *m*

lively [ˈlaɪvlɪ] *adj* lebhaft, lebendig

liven up [ˈlaɪvn-] *vt* beleben

liver [ˈlɪvə*] *n* (*ANAT*) Leber *f*

lives [laɪvz] *pl* of **life**

livestock [ˈlaɪvstɒk] *n* Vieh *nt*

livid [ˈlɪvɪd] *adj* bläulich; (*furious*) fuchsteufelswild

living [ˈlɪvɪŋ] *n* (Lebens)unterhalt *m* ♦ *adj* lebendig; (*language etc*) lebend; **to earn** *or* **make a ~** sich *dat* seinen Lebensunterhalt verdienen; **~ conditions** *npl* Wohnverhältnisse *pl*; **~ room** *n* Wohnzimmer *nt*; **~ standards** *npl* Lebensstandard *m*; **~ wage** *n* ausreichender Lohn *m*

lizard ['lɪzəd] n Eidechse f

load [ləʊd] n (burden) Last f; (amount) Ladung f ♦ vt (also: ~ up) (be)laden; (COMPUT) laden; (camera) Film einlegen in +acc; (gun) laden; **a ~ of, ~s of** (fig) jede Menge; **~ed** adj beladen; (dice) präpariert; (question) fangend; (inf: rich) steinreich; **~ing bay** n Ladeplatz m

loaf [ləʊf] (pl **loaves**) n Brot nt ♦ vi (also: ~ about, ~ around) herumlungern, faulenzen

loan [ləʊn] n Leihgabe f, (FIN) Darlehen nt ♦ vt leihen; **on ~** geliehen

loath [ləʊθ] adj: **to be ~ to do sth** etw ungern tun

loathe [ləʊð] vt verabscheuen

loathing ['ləʊðɪŋ] n Abscheu f

loaves [ləʊvz] pl of **loaf**

lobby ['lɒbɪ] n Vorhalle f; (POL) Lobby f ♦ vt politisch beeinflussen (wollen)

lobe [ləʊb] n Ohrläppchen nt

lobster ['lɒbstə*] n Hummer m

local ['ləʊkəl] adj ortsansässig, Orts- ♦ n (pub) Stammwirtschaft f; the **~s** npl (people) die Ortsansässigen pl; **~ anaesthetic** n (MED) örtliche Betäubung f; **~ authority** n städtische Behörden pl; **~ call** n (TEL) Ortsgespräch nt; **~ government** n Gemeinde-/Kreisverwaltung f; **~ity** [ləʊˈkælɪtɪ] n Ort m; **~ly** adv örtlich, am Ort

locate [ləʊˈkeɪt] vt ausfindig machen; (establish) errichten

location [ləʊˈkeɪʃən] n Platz m, Lage f; **on ~** (CINE) auf Außenaufnahme

loch [lɒx] (SCOTTISH) n See m

lock [lɒk] n Schloß nt; (NAUT) Schleuse f; (of hair) Locke f ♦ vt (fasten) (ver)schließen ♦ vi (door etc) sich schließen (lassen); (wheels) blockieren; **~ up** vt (criminal, mental patient) einsperren; (house) abschließen

locker ['lɒkə*] n Spind m

locket ['lɒkɪt] n Medaillon nt

lock-out ['lɒkaʊt] n Aussperrung f

locksmith ['lɒksmɪθ] n Schlosser(in) m(f)

lockup ['lɒkʌp] n (jail) Gefängnis nt; (garage) Garage f

locomotive [ləʊkəˈməʊtɪv] n Lokomotive f

locum ['ləʊkəm] n (MED) Vertreter(in) m(f)

locust ['ləʊkəst] n Heuschrecke f

lodge [lɒdʒ] n (gatehouse) Pförtnerhaus nt; (freemasons') Loge f ♦ vi (get stuck) stecken(bleiben); (in Untermiete): **to ~ (with)** wohnen (bei) ♦ vt (protest) einreichen; **~r** n (Unter)mieter m

lodgings ['lɒdʒɪŋz] n (Miet)wohnung f

loft [lɒft] n (Dach)boden m

lofty ['lɒftɪ] adj hoch(ragend); (proud) hochmütig

log [lɒg] n Klotz m; (book) = **log-book**

logbook ['lɒgbʊk] n Bordbuch nt; (for lorry) Fahrtenschreiber m; (AUT) Kraftfahrzeugbrief m

loggerheads ['lɒgəhedz] npl: **to be at ~** sich in den Haaren liegen

logic ['lɒdʒɪk] n Logik f; **~al** adj logisch

logistics [lɒˈdʒɪstɪks] npl Logistik f

logo ['ləʊgəʊ] n Firmenzeichen nt

loin [lɔɪn] n Lende f

loiter ['lɔɪtə*] vi herumstehen

loll [lɒl] vi (also: ~ about) sich rekeln

lollipop ['lɒlɪpɒp] n (Dauer)lutscher m; **~ man/lady** (BRIT) n = Schülerlotse m

London ['lʌndən] n London nt; **~er** n Londoner(in) m(f)

lone [ləʊn] adj einsam

loneliness ['ləʊnlɪnəs] n Einsamkeit f

lonely ['ləʊnlɪ] adj einsam

loner ['ləʊnə*] n Einzelgänger(in) m(f)

long [lɒŋ] adj lang; (distance) weit ♦ adv lange ♦ vi: **to ~ for** sich sehnen nach; **before ~** bald; **as ~ as** solange; **in the ~ run** auf die Dauer; **don't be ~!** beeil dich!; **how ~ is**

the street? wie lang ist die Straße?; how ~ is the lesson? wie lange dauert die Stunde?; **6 metres** ~ 6 Meter lang; **6 months** ~ 6 Monate lang; **all night** ~ die ganze Nacht; he no ~er comes er kommt nicht mehr; ~ ago vor langer Zeit; ~ before lange vorher; at ~ last endlich; ~**distance** adj Fern-

longevity [lon'dʒevɪtɪ] n Langlebigkeit f

long: ~ **-haired** adj langhaarig; ~**hand** n Langschrift f; ~**ing** n Sehnsucht f ♦ adj sehnsüchtig

longitude ['lɒŋgɪtjuːd] n Längengrad m

long: ~ **jump** n Weitsprung m; ~ **lost** adj längst verloren geglaubt; ~**playing record** n Langspielplatte f; ~**range** adj Langstrecken-, Fern-; ~**sighted** adj weitsichtig; ~**standing** adj alt, seit langer Zeit bestehend; ~**suffering** adj schwer geprüft; ~**term** adj langfristig; ~**wave** n Langwelle f; ~**winded** adj langatmig

loo [luː] (BRIT: inf) n Klo nt

look [luk] vi schauen; (seem) aussehen; (building etc): **to** ~ **on to** the sea aufs Meer gehen ♦ n Blick m; ~s npl (appearance) Aussehen nt; ~ **after** vt (care for) sorgen für; (watch) aufpassen auf +acc; ~ **at** vt ansehen; (consider) sich überlegen; ~ **back** vi sich umsehen; (fig) zurückblicken; ~ **down** on vt (fig) herabsehen auf +acc; ~ **for** vt (seek) suchen; ~ **forward to** vt sich freuen auf +acc; (in letters): **we** ~ **forward to hearing from you** wir hoffen, bald von Ihnen zu hören; ~ **into** vt untersuchen; ~ **out** vi zusehen; ~ **out** vi hinaussehen; (beware) aufpassen; ~**out** **for** vt Ausschau halten nach; (be careful) achtgeben auf +acc; ~ **round** vi sich umsehen; ~ **to** vt (take care of) achtgeben auf +acc; (rely on) sich verlassen auf +acc; ~ **up** vi aufblicken; (improve) sich bessern ♦ vt

(word) nachschlagen; (person) besuchen; ~ **up to** vt aufsehen zu; ~**out** n (watch) Ausschau f; (person) Wachposten m; (place) Ausguck m; (prospect) Aussichten pl; **to be on the** ~**out for sth** nach etw Ausschau halten

loom [luːm] n Webstuhl m ♦ vi sich abzeichnen

loony ['luːnɪ] (inf) n Verrückte(r) mf

loop [luːp] n Schlaufe f; ~**hole** n (fig) Hintertürchen nt

loose [luːs] adj lose, locker; (free) frei; (inexact) unpräzise ♦ vt lösen, losbinden; ~ **change** n Kleingeld nt; ~ **chippings** npl (on road) Rollsplitt m; ~ **end**: **to be at a** ~ **end** (BRIT) or at ~**ends** (US) nicht wissen, was man tun soll; ~**ly** adv locker, lose; ~**n** vt lockern, losmachen

loot [luːt] n Beute f ♦ vt plündern

lop off vt abhacken

lopsided ['lɒp'saɪdɪd] adj schief

lord [lɔːd] n (ruler) Herr m; (BRIT: title) Lord m; **the L~** (Gott) der Herr; **the (House of) L~s** das Oberhaus; ~**ship** n: **your L~ship** Eure Lordschaft

lore [lɔː*] n Überlieferung f

lorry ['lɒrɪ] (BRIT) n Lastwagen m; ~ **driver** (BRIT) n Lastwagenfahrer(in m) f

lose [luːz] (pt, pp **lost**) vt verlieren; (chance) verpassen ♦ vi verlieren; ~ **(time)** (clock) nachgehen; ~**r** n Verlierer m

loss [lɒs] n Verlust m; **at a** ~ (COMM) mit Verlust; (unable) außerstande

lost [lɒst] pt, pp of **lose** ♦ adj verloren; ~ **property** (US lost and found) n Fundsachen pl

lot [lɒt] n (quantity) Menge f; (fate, at auction) Los nt; (inf: people, things) Haufen m; **the** ~ alles; (people) alle; **a** ~ **of** (with sg) viel; (with pl) viele; ~**s of** massenhaft, viel(e); **I read a** ~ ich lese viel; **to draw** ~**s for sth** etw verlosen

lotion ['ləuʃən] n Lotion f

lottery ['lɒtəri] n Lotterie f

loud [laud] adj laut; (showy) schreiend ♦ adv laut; **~hailer** (BRIT) n Megaphon nt; **~ly** adv laut; **~speaker** n Lautsprecher m

lounge [laundʒ] n (in hotel) Gesellschaftsraum m; (in house) Wohnzimmer nt ♦ vi sich herumlümmeln; **~ suit** (BRIT) n Straßenanzug m

louse [laus] (pl **lice**) n Laus f

lousy ['lauzi] adj (fig) miserabel

lout [laut] n Lümmel m

louvre ['luːvə*] (US **louver**) adj (door, window) Jalousie-

lovable ['lʌvəbl] adj liebenswert

love [lʌv] n Liebe f; (person) Liebling m; (SPORT) null ♦ vt (person) lieben; (activity) gerne mögen; **to be in ~ with sb** in jdn verliebt sein; **to make ~** sich lieben; **for the ~ of** aus Liebe zu; **"15 ~"** (TENNIS) „15 null"; **to ~ to do sth** etw (sehr) gerne tun; **~ affair** n (Liebes)verhältnis nt; **~ letter** n Liebesbrief m; **~ life** n Liebesleben nt

lovely ['lʌvli] adj schön

lover ['lʌvə*] n Liebhaber(in) m(f)

loving ['lʌvɪŋ] adj liebend, liebevoll

low [ləu] adj niedrig; (rank) niedere(r, s); (level, neck, neckline) tief; (intelligence, density) gering; (vulgar) ordinär; (not loud) leise; (depressed) gedrückt ♦ adv (not high) niedrig; (not loudly) leise ♦ n (low point) Tiefstand m; (MET) Tief nt; **to feel ~** sich mies fühlen; **to turn (down) ~** leiser stellen; **~cut** adj (dress) tiefausgeschnitten

lower ['ləuə*] vt herunterlassen; (eyes, gun) senken; (reduce) herabsetzen, senken ♦ vr: **to ~ o.s. to** (fig) sich herablassen zu

low: ~fat adj fettarm, Mager-; **~lands** npl (GEOG) Flachland nt; **~ly** adj bescheiden; **~lying** adj tiefgelegen

loyal ['lɔɪəl] adj treu; **~ty** n Treue f

lozenge ['lɒzindʒ] n Pastille f

L.P. n abbr = **long-playing record**

L-plates ['elpleits] (BRIT) npl L-Schild nt (für Fahrschüler)

Ltd abbr (= limited company) GmbH.

lubricant ['luːbrikənt] n Schmiermittel nt

lubricate ['luːbrikeit] vt schmieren

lucid ['luːsid] adj klar; (sane) bei klarem Verstand; (moment) licht

luck [lʌk] n Glück nt; **bad or hard or tough ~!** (so ein) Pech!; **good ~!** viel Glück!; **~ily** adv glücklicherweise, zum Glück; **~y** adj Glücks-; **to be ~y** Glück haben

lucrative ['luːkrətiv] adj einträglich

ludicrous ['luːdikrəs] adj grotesk

lug [lʌg] vt schleppen

luggage ['lʌgidʒ] n Gepäck nt; **~ rack** n Gepäcknetz nt

lukewarm ['luːkwɔːm] adj lauwarm; (indifferent) lau

lull [lʌl] n Flaute f ♦ vt einlullen; (calm) beruhigen

lullaby ['lʌləbai] n Schlaflied nt

lumbago [lʌm'beigəu] n Hexenschuß m

lumber ['lʌmbə*] n Plunder m; (wood) Holz nt; **~jack** n Holzfäller m

luminous ['luːminəs] adj Leucht-

lump [lʌmp] n Klumpen m; (MED) Schwellung f; (in breast) Knoten m; (of sugar) Stück nt ♦ vt (also: **~ together**) zusammentun; (judge together) in einen Topf werfen; **~ sum** n Pauschalsumme f; **~y** adj klumpig

lunacy ['luːnəsi] n Irrsinn m

lunar ['luːnə*] adj Mond-

lunatic ['luːnətik] n Wahnsinnige(r) m/f ♦ adj wahnsinnig, irr

lunch [lʌntʃ] n Mittagessen nt

luncheon ['lʌntʃən] n Mittagessen nt; **~ meat** n Frühstücksfleisch nt; **~ voucher** (BRIT) n Essensmarke f

lunchtime n Mittagszeit f

lung [lʌŋ] n Lunge f

lunge [lʌndʒ] vi (also: **~ forward**) (los)stürzen; **to ~** at sich stürzen auf +acc

lurch [lɜːtʃ] vi taumeln; (NAUT) schlingern ♦ n Ruck m; (NAUT) Schlingern nt; **to leave sb in the**

jdn im Stich lassen

lure [ljuə*] n Köder m; (fig) Lockung f ♦ vt (ver)locken

lurid ['ljuərɪd] adj (shocking) grausig, widerlich; (colour) grell

lurk [lɜːk] vi lauern

luscious ['lʌʃəs] adj köstlich

lush [lʌʃ] adj satt; (vegetation) üppig

lust [lʌst] n (sensation) Wollust f; (greed) Gier f ♦ vi: to ~ after gieren nach

lustre ['lʌstə*] (US **luster**) n Glanz m

lusty ['lʌstɪ] adj gesund und munter

Luxembourg ['lʌksəmbɜːg] n Luxemburg f

luxuriant [lʌg'zjuərɪənt] adj üppig

luxurious [lʌg'zjuərɪəs] adj luxuriös, Luxus-

luxury ['lʌkʃərɪ] n Luxus m ♦ cpd Luxus-

lying ['laɪɪŋ] n Lügen nt ♦ adj verlogen

lynx [lɪŋks] n Luchs m

lyric ['lɪrɪk] n Lyrik f ♦ adj lyrisch; ~s pl (words for song) (Lied)text m; ~al adj lyrisch, gefühlvoll

M

M. abbr = metre; m; ~ abbr; mile; million

M.A. n abbr = Master of Arts

mac [mæk] (BRIT: inf) n Regenmantel m

macaroni [mækə'rəʊnɪ] n Makkaroni pl

machine [mə'ʃiːn] n Maschine f ♦ vt (dress etc) mit der Maschine nähen; ~ gun n Maschinengewehr nt; ~ language n (COMPUT) Maschinensprache f; ~ry [mə'ʃiːnərɪ] n Maschinerie f

macho ['mætʃəʊ] adj macho

mackerel ['mækrəl] n Makrele f

mackintosh ['mækɪntɒʃ] (BRIT) n Regenmantel m

mad [mæd] adj verrückt; (dog) tollwütig; (angry) wütend; ~ about

(fond of) verrückt nach, versessen auf +acc

madam ['mædəm] n gnädige Frau f

madden ['mædn] vt verrückt machen; (make angry) ärgern

made [meɪd] pt, pp of **make**

Madeira [mə'dɪərə] n (GEOG) Madeira nt; (wine) Madeira m

made-to-measure ['meɪdtə'meʒə*] (BRIT) adj Maß-

madly ['mædlɪ] adv wahnsinnig

madman ['mædmən] (irreg) n Verrückte(r) m, Irre(r) m

madness ['mædnəs] n Wahnsinn m

Madrid [mə'drɪd] n Madrid nt

magazine [mægə'ziːn] n Zeitschrift f; (in gun) Magazin n

maggot ['mægət] n Made f

magic ['mædʒɪk] n Zauberei f, Magie f; (fig) Zauber m ♦ adj magisch, Zauber-; ~al adj magisch; ~ian [mə'dʒɪʃən] n Zauberer m

magistrate ['mædʒɪstreɪt] n (Friedens)richter m

magnanimous [mæg'nænɪməs] adj großmütig

magnesium [mæg'niːzɪəm] n Magnesium nt

magnet ['mægnɪt] n Magnet m; ~ic [mæg'netɪk] adj magnetisch; ~ic tape n Magnetband nt; ~ism n Magnetismus m; (fig) Ausstrahlungskraft f

magnificent [mæg'nɪfɪsənt] adj großartig

magnify ['mægnɪfaɪ] vt vergrößern; ~ing glass n Lupe f

magnitude ['mægnɪtjuːd] n (size) Größe f; (importance) Ausmaß nt

magpie ['mægpaɪ] n Elster f

mahogany [mə'hɒgənɪ] n Mahagoni nt ♦ cpd Mahagoni-

maid [meɪd] n Dienstmädchen nt; old ~ alte Jungfer f

maiden ['meɪdn] n Maid f ♦ adj (flight, speech) Jungfern-

mail [meɪl] n Post f ♦ vt aufgeben; ~ box n (US) Briefkasten m; ~ing list n Anschreibeliste f; ~ order n Bestellung f durch die Post; ~ order

firm n Versandhaus nt

maim [meɪm] vt verstümmeln

main [meɪn] adj hauptsächlich, Haupt- ♦ n (pipe) Hauptleitung f; **the ~s** npl (ELEC) das Stromnetz; **in the ~** im großen und ganzen; **~frame** n (COMPUT) Großrechner m; **~land** n Festland nt; **~ly** adv hauptsächlich; **~ road** n Hauptstraße f; **~stay** n (fig) Hauptstütze f; **~stream** n Hauptrichtung f

maintain [meɪnˈteɪn] vt (machine, roads) instand halten; (support) unterhalten; (keep up) aufrechterhalten; (claim) behaupten; (innocence) beteuern

maintenance [ˈmeɪntənəns] n (TECH) Wartung f; (of family) Unterhalt m

maize [meɪz] n Mais m

majestic [məˈdʒestɪk] adj majestätisch

majesty [ˈmædʒɪstɪ] n Majestät f

major [ˈmeɪdʒə*] n Major m ♦ adj (MUS) Dur; (more important) Haupt-; (bigger) größer

Majorca [məˈjɔːkə] n Mallorca nt

majority [məˈdʒɒrɪtɪ] n Mehrheit f; (JUR) Volljährigkeit f

make [meɪk] (pt, pp made) vt machen; (appoint) ernennen (zu); (cause to do sth) veranlassen; (reach) erreichen; (in time) schaffen; (earn) verdienen ♦ n Marke f; **to ~ sth happen** etw geschehen lassen; **to ~ it** es schaffen; **what time do you ~ it?** wie spät hast du es?; **to ~ do with** auskommen mit; **~ for** vt gehen/fahren nach; **~ out** vt (write out) ausstellen; (understand) verstehen; (write: cheque) ausstellen; **~ up** vt machen; (face) schminken; (quarrel) beilegen; (story etc) erfinden ♦ vi sich versöhnen; **~ up for** vt wiedergutmachen; (COMM) vergüten; **~believe** n Phantasie f; **~r** n (COMM) Hersteller m; **~shift** adj behelfsmäßig, Not-; **~up** n Schminke f, Make-up nt; **~up remover** n Make-up-Entferner m

making [ˈmeɪkɪŋ] n: **in the ~** im Entstehen; **to have the ~s of** das Zeug haben zu

malaise [mæˈleɪz] n Unbehagen nt

malaria [məˈleərɪə] n Malaria f

Malaysia [məˈleɪzɪə] n Malaysia nt

male [meɪl] n Mann m; (animal) Männchen nt ♦ adj männlich

malevolent [məˈlevələnt] adj übelwollend

malfunction [mælˈfʌŋkʃən] n (MED) Funktionsstörung f; (of machine) Defekt m

malice [ˈmælɪs] n Bosheit f

malicious [məˈlɪʃəs] adj böswillig, gehässig

malign [məˈlaɪn] vt verleumden ♦ adj böse

malignant [məˈlɪgnənt] adj bösartig

mall [mɔːl] n (also: shopping ~) Einkaufszentrum nt

malleable [ˈmælɪəbl] adj formbar

mallet [ˈmælɪt] n Holzhammer m

malnutrition [ˈmælnjuˈtrɪʃən] n Unterernährung f

malpractice [ˈmælˈpræktɪs] n Amtsvergehen nt

malt [mɔːlt] n Malz nt

Malta [ˈmɔːltə] n Malta nt; **Maltese** [ˈmɔːlˈtiːz] adj inv maltesisch ♦ n inv Malteser(in) m(f)

maltreat [mælˈtriːt] vt mißhandeln

mammal [ˈmæməl] n Säugetier nt

mammoth [ˈmæməθ] n Mammut nt ♦ adj Mammut-

man [mæn] (pl men) n Mann m; (human race) der Mensch, die Menschen pl ♦ vt bemannen; **an old ~** ein alter Mann, ein Greis m; **~ and wife** Mann und Frau

manage [ˈmænɪdʒ] vi zurechtkommen ♦ vt (control) leiten, leiten; (cope with) fertigwerden mit; **~able** adj (person, animal) fügsam; (object) handlich; **~ment** n (control) Führung f, Leitung f; (directors) Management n; **~r** n Geschäftsführer m; **~ress** [mænɪdʒəˈres] n Geschäftsführerin f; **~rial** [mænəˈdʒɪərɪəl] adj (post) leitend; (problem etc) Management-

managing ['mænɪdʒɪŋ] adj: ~ director Betriebsleiter m

mandarin ['mændərɪn] n (fruit) Mandarine f

mandatory ['mændətərɪ] adj obligatorisch

mane [meɪn] n Mähne f

maneuver [mə'nuːvə*] (US) = manoeuvre

manfully ['mænfʊlɪ] adv mannhaft

mangle ['mæŋgl] vt verstümmeln ♦ n Mangel f

mango ['mæŋgəʊ] (pl ~es) n Mango(pflaume) f

mangy ['meɪndʒɪ] adj (dog) räudig

manhandle ['mænhændl] vt grob behandeln

manhole ['mænhəʊl] n (Straßen)-schacht m

manhood ['mænhʊd] n Mannesalter nt; (manliness) Männlichkeit f

man-hour ['mæn'aʊə*] n Arbeitsstunde f

manhunt ['mænhʌnt] n Fahndung f

mania ['meɪnɪə] n Manie f; ~c ['meɪnɪæk] n Wahnsinnige(r) mf

manic ['mænɪk] adj (behaviour, activity) hektisch

manicure ['mænɪkjʊə*] n Maniküre f; ~ set n Necessaire nt

manifest ['mænɪfest] vt offenbaren ♦ adj offenkundig; ~ation n (sign) Anzeichen nt

manifesto [mænɪ'festəʊ] n Manifest nt

manipulate [mə'nɪpjʊleɪt] vt handhaben; (fig) manipulieren

mankind [mæn'kaɪnd] n Menschheit f

manly ['mænlɪ] adj männlich; mannhaft

man-made ['mæn'meɪd] adj (fibre) künstlich

manner ['mænə*] n Art f, Weise f; ~s npl (behaviour) Manieren pl; in a ~ of speaking sozusagen; ~ism n (of person) Angewohnheit f; (of style) Manieriertheit f

manoeuvre [mə'nuːvə*] (US = ma-

neuver) vt, vi manövrieren ♦ n (MIL) Feldzug m; (general) Manöver nt, Schachzug m

manor ['mænə*] n Landgut nt; ~ house n Herrenhaus nt

manpower ['mænpaʊə*] n Arbeitskräfte pl

mansion ['mænʃən] n Villa f

manslaughter ['mænslɔːtə*] n Totschlag m

mantelpiece ['mæntlpiːs] n Kaminsims m

manual ['mænjʊəl] adj manuell, Hand- ♦ n Handbuch nt

manufacture [mænjʊ'fæktʃə*] vt herstellen ♦ n Herstellung f; ~r n Hersteller m

manure [mə'njʊə*] n Dünger m

manuscript ['mænjʊskrɪpt] n Manuskript nt

Manx [mæŋks] adj der Insel Man

many ['menɪ] adj, pron viele; a great ~ sehr viele; ~ a time oft

map [mæp] n (Land)karte f; (of town) Stadtplan m ♦ vt eine Karte machen von; ~ out vt (fig) ausarbeiten

maple ['meɪpl] n Ahorn m

mar [mɑː*] vt verderben

marathon ['mærəθən] n (SPORT) Marathonlauf m; (fig) Marathon m

marauder [mə'rɔːdə*] n Plünderer m

marble ['mɑːbl] n Marmor m; (for game) Murmel f

March [mɑːtʃ] n März m

march [mɑːtʃ] vi marschieren ♦ n Marsch m

mare [mɛə*] n Stute f

margarine [mɑːdʒə'riːn] n Margarine f

margin ['mɑːdʒɪn] n Rand m; (extra amount) Spielraum m; (COMM) Spanne f; ~al adj (note) Rand-; (difference etc) geringfügig; ~al (seat) n (POL) Wahlkreis, der nur mit knapper Mehrheit gehalten wird

marigold ['mærɪgəʊld] n Ringelblume f

marijuana [mærɪ'wɑːnə] n Marihuanä nt

marina [mə'ri:nə] n Yachthafen m

marinate ['mærɪneɪt] vt marinieren

marine [mə'ri:n] adj Meeres-, See- n (MIL) Marineinfanterist m

marital ['mærɪtl] adj ehelich; Ehe-; ~ **status** n Familienstand m

maritime ['mærɪtaɪm] adj See-

mark [ma:k] n (coin) Mark f; (spot) Fleck m; (scar) Kratzer m; (sign) Zeichen nt; (target) Ziel nt; (SCH) Note f ♦ vt (make ~ on) Flecken/ Kratzer machen auf +acc; (indicate) markieren; (exam) korrigieren; to ~ **time** (also fig) auf der Stelle treten; ~ **out** vt bestimmen; (area) abstecken; ~ed adj deutlich; ~er n (in book) (Lese)zeichen nt; (on road) Schild n

market ['ma:kɪt] n Markt m; (stock ~) Börse f ♦ vt (COMM: new product) auf den Markt bringen; (sell) vertreiben; ~ **garden** (BRIT) n Handelsgärtnerei f; ~ing n Marketing nt; ~ **research** n Marktforschung f; ~ **value** n Marktwert m

marksman ['ma:ksmən] (irreg) n Scharfschütze m

marmalade ['ma:məleɪd] n Orangenmarmelade f

maroon [mə'ru:n] vt aussetzen ♦ adj (colour) kastanienbraun

marquee [ma:'ki:] n große(s) Zelt nt

marriage ['mærɪdʒ] n Ehe f; (wedding) Heirat f; ~ **bureau** n Heiratsinstitut nt; ~ **certificate** n Heiratsurkunde f

married ['mærɪd] adj (person) verheiratet; (couple, life) Ehe-

marrow ['mærəʊ] n (Knochen)mark nt; (vegetable) Kürbis m

marry ['mærɪ] vt (join) trauen; (take as husband, wife) heiraten ♦ vi (also: get married) heiraten

Mars [ma:z] n (planet) Mars m

marsh [ma:ʃ] n Sumpf m

marshal ['ma:ʃəl] n (US) Bezirkspolizeichef m ♦ vt (an)ordnen, arrangieren

marshy ['ma:ʃɪ] adj sumpfig

martial ['ma:ʃəl] adj kriegerisch; ~ **law** n Kriegsrecht nt

martyr ['ma:tə*] n (also fig) Märtyrer(in) m(f) ♦ vt zum Märtyrer machen; ~dom n Martyrium nt

marvel ['ma:vəl] n Wunder nt ♦ vi: to ~ (at) sich wundern (über +acc); ~lous (US marvelous) adj wunderbar

Marxist ['ma:ksɪst] n Marxist(in) m(f)

marzipan [ma:zɪ'pæn] n Marzipan nt

mascara [mæs'ka:rə] n Wimperntusche f

mascot ['mæskət] n Maskottchen nt

masculine ['mæskjʊlɪn] adj männlich

mash [mæʃ] n Brei m; ~ed potatoes npl Kartoffelbrei m or -püree nt

mask [ma:sk] n (also fig) Maske f ♦ vt maskieren, verdecken

mason ['meɪsn] n (stone~) Steinmetz m; (free~) Freimaurer m; ~ic [mə'sɒnɪk] adj Freimaurer-; ~ry n Mauerwerk nt

masquerade [mæskə'reɪd] n Maskerade f ♦ vi: to ~ as sich ausgeben als

mass [mæs] n Masse f; (greater part) Mehrheit f; (REL) Messe f ♦ vi sich sammeln; the ~es npl (people) die Masse(n) f(pl)

massacre ['mæsəkə*] n Blutbad nt ♦ vt niedermetzeln, massakrieren

massage ['mæsɑ:ʒ] n Massage f ♦ vt massieren

massive ['mæsɪv] adj gewaltig, massiv

mass media npl Massenmedien pl

mass production n Massenproduktion f

mast [ma:st] n Mast m

master ['ma:stə*] n Herr m; (NAUT) Kapitän m; (teacher) Lehrer m; (artist) Meister m ♦ vt meistern; (language etc) beherrschen; ~ly adj meisterhaft; ~mind n Kapazität f ♦ vt geschickt lenken; M~ **of Arts** n Magister m der philosophischen; M~ **of Science** n Magister m der naturwissenschaftlichen; **~piece** n Meisterwerk nt; **~ plan** n kluge(r) Plan m; **~y** n Können nt

masturbate ['mæstəbeɪt] vi masturbieren, onanieren

mat [mæt] n Matte f; (for table) Untersetzer m ♦ adj = **mat(t)**

match [mætʃ] n Streichholz nt; (sth corresponding) Pendant nt; (SPORT) Wettkampf m; (ball games) Spiel nt ♦ vt (be like, suit) passen zu; (equal) gleichkommen +dat ♦ vi zusammenpassen; it's a good ~ (for) es paßt gut zu; **~box** n Streichholzschachtel f; **~ing** adj passend

mate [meɪt] n (companion) Kamerad m; (spouse) Lebensgefährte m; (of animal) Weibchen nt/Männchen nt; (NAUT) Schiffsoffizier m ♦ vi (animals) sich paaren ♦ vt paaren

material [mə'tɪərɪəl] n Material nt; (for book, cloth) Stoff m ♦ adj (important) wesentlich; (damage) Sach-; (comforts etc) materiell; ~s npl (for building etc) Materialien pl; **~istic** adj materialistisch; **~ize** vi sich verwirklichen, zustande kommen

maternal [mə'tɜːnl] adj mütterlich, Mutter-

maternity [mə'tɜːnɪtɪ] adj (dress) Umstands-; (benefit) Wochen-; **~ hospital** n Entbindungsheim nt

math [mæθ] (US) n = **maths**

mathematical [mæθə'mætɪkl] adj mathematisch

mathematics [mæθə'mætɪks] n Mathematik f

maths [mæθs] (US **math**) n Mathe f

matinée ['mætɪneɪ] n Matinee f

mating call ['meɪtɪŋ-] n Lockruf m

matrices ['meɪtrɪsiːz] npl of **matrix**

matriculation [mətrɪkju'leɪʃən] n Immatrikulation f

matrimonial [mætrɪ'məʊnɪəl] adj ehelich, Ehe-

matrimony ['mætrɪmənɪ] n Ehestand m

matrix ['meɪtrɪks] (pl **matrices**) n Matrize f; (GEOL etc) Matrix f

matron ['meɪtrən] n (MED) Oberin f; (SCH) Hausmutter f; **~ly** adj matronenhaft

mat(t) [mæt] adj (paint) matt

matted ['mætɪd] adj verfilzt

matter ['mætə*] n (substance) Materie f; (affair) Angelegenheit f ♦ vi darauf ankommen; no ~ how/what egal wie/was; what is the ~? was ist los?; as a ~ of course selbstverständlich; as a ~ of fact eigentlich; it doesn't ~ es macht nichts; **~-of-fact** adj sachlich, nüchtern

mattress ['mætrəs] n Matratze f

mature [mə'tjʊə*] adj reif ♦ vi reif werden

maturity [mə'tjʊərɪtɪ] n Reife f

maudlin ['mɔːdlɪn] adj gefühlsduselig

maul [mɔːl] vt übel zurichten

maxima ['mæksɪmə] npl of **maximum**

maximum ['mæksɪməm] (pl **maxima**) adj Höchst-, Maximal- ♦ n Maximum nt

May [meɪ] n Mai m

may [meɪ] (conditional **might**) vi (be possible) können; (have permission) dürfen; he ~ come er kommt vielleicht

maybe ['meɪbiː] adv vielleicht

May Day n der 1. Mai

mayhem ['meɪhem] n Chaos nt; (US) Körperverletzung f

mayonnaise [meɪə'neɪz] n Mayonnaise f

mayor [meə*] n Bürgermeister m; **~ess** (wife) (die) Frau f Bürgermeister; (lady ~) Bürgermeisterin f

maypole ['meɪpəʊl] n Maibaum m

maze [meɪz] n Irrgarten m; (fig) Wirrwarr m

M.D. abbr = Doctor of Medicine

┌─────────── KEYWORD ───────────┐

me [miː] pron **1** (direct) mich; it's me ich bin's

2 (indirect) mir; give them to me gib sie mir

3 (after prep: +acc) mich; (: +dat)

mir; **with/without me** mit mir/ohne mich

meadow ['medəʊ] n Wiese f

meagre ['miːgə*] (US **meager**) adj dürftig, spärlich

meal [miːl] n Essen nt, Mahlzeit f; (grain) Schrotmehl nt; **to have a ~** essen (gehen); **~time** n Essenszeit f

mean [miːn] (pt, pp **meant**) adj (stingy) geizig; (spiteful) gemein; (average) durchschnittlich, Durchschnitts- ♦ vt (signify) bedeuten; (intend) vorhaben, beabsichtigen ♦ n (average) Durchschnitt m; **~s** npl (wherewithal) Mittel pl; (wealth) Vermögen nt; **do you ~ me?** meinst du mich?; **do you ~ it?** meinst du das ernst?; **what do you ~?** was willst du damit sagen?; **to be ~t for sb/sth** für jdn/etw bestimmt sein; **by ~s of** durch; **by all ~s** selbstverständlich; **by no ~s** keineswegs

meander [mɪ'ændə*] vi sich schlängeln

meaning ['miːnɪŋ] n Bedeutung f; (of life) Sinn m; **~ful** adj bedeutungsvoll; (life) sinnvoll; **~less** adj sinnlos

meanness ['miːnnəs] n (stinginess) Geiz m; (spitefulness) Gemeinheit f

meant [ment] pt, pp of **mean**

meantime ['miːntaɪm] adv inzwischen

meanwhile ['miːnwaɪl] adv inzwischen

measles ['miːzlz] n Masern pl

measly ['miːzlɪ] (inf) adj popelig

measure ['meʒə*] vt, vi messen ♦ n Maß nt; (step) Maßnahme f; **~ments** npl Maße pl

meat [miːt] n Fleisch nt; **cold ~** Aufschnitt m; **~ ball** n Fleischkloß m; **~ pie** n Fleischpastete f; **~y** adj fleischig; (fig) gehaltvoll

Mecca ['mekə] n Mekka nt (also fig)

mechanic [mɪ'kænɪk] n Mechaniker m; **~al** adj mechanisch; **~s** n Mechanik f ♦ npl Technik f

mechanism ['mekənɪzəm] n Mechanismus m

mechanize ['mekənaɪz] vt mechanisieren

medal ['medl] n Medaille f; (decoration) Orden m; **~list** (US **medalist**) n Medaillengewinner(in) m(f)

meddle ['medl] vi: **to ~ (in)** sich einmischen (in +acc); **to ~ with sth** sich an etw dat zu schaffen machen

media ['miːdɪə] npl Medien pl

mediaeval [medɪ'iːvəl] adj = **medieval**

median ['miːdɪən] (US) n (also: **~ strip**) Mittelstreifen m

mediate ['miːdɪeɪt] vi vermitteln

mediator ['miːdɪeɪtə*] n Vermittler m

Medicaid ['medɪkeɪd] (®: US) n medizinisches Versorgungsprogramm für Sozialschwache

medical ['medɪkəl] adj medizinisch; Medizin-; ärztlich ♦ n (ärztliche) Untersuchung f

Medicare ['medɪkeə*] (US) n staatliche Krankenversicherung besonders für Ältere

medicated ['medɪkeɪtɪd] adj medizinisch

medication [medɪ'keɪʃən] n (drugs etc) Medikamente pl

medicinal [me'dɪsɪnl] adj medizinisch, Heil-

medicine ['medsɪn] n Medizin f; (drugs) Arznei f

medieval [medɪ'iːvəl] adj mittelalterlich

mediocre [miːdɪ'əʊkə*] adj mittelmäßig

mediocrity [miːdɪ'ɒkrɪtɪ] n Mittelmäßigkeit f

meditate ['medɪteɪt] vi meditieren; **to ~ (on sth)** (über etw acc) nachdenken

meditation [medɪ'teɪʃən] n Nachsinnen nt; Meditation f

Mediterranean [medɪtə'reɪnɪən] adj Mittelmeer-; (person) südländisch; **the ~ (Sea)** das Mittelmeer

medium ['miːdɪəm] adj mittlere(r, s) Mittel-, mittel-; ~ in Mitte f; (means) Mittel nt; (person) Medium nt; happy ~ goldener Mittelweg; ~ wave n Mittelwelle f

medley ['medlɪ] n Gemisch nt

meek [miːk] adj sanft(mütig); (pej) duckmäuserisch

meet [miːt] (pt, pp met) vt (encounter) begegnen +dat; (by arrangement) sich treffen mit; (difficulties) stoßen auf +acc; (become acquainted with) kennenlernen; (fetch) abholen; (join) zusammentreffen mit; (satisfy) entsprechen +dat ♦ vi sich treffen; (become acquainted) sich kennenlernen; ~ with vt (problems) stoßen auf +acc; (US: people) zusammentreffen mit; ~ing n Treffen nt; (business meeting) Besprechung f; (of committee) Sitzung f; (assembly) Versammlung f

megabyte ['megəbaɪt] n (COMPUT) Megabyte nt

megaphone ['megəfəʊn] n Megaphon nt

melancholy ['melənkəlɪ] adj (person) melancholisch; (sight, event) traurig

mellow ['meləʊ] adj mild, weich; (fruit) reif; (fig) gesetzt ♦ vi reif werden

melodious [mɪ'ləʊdɪəs] adj wohlklingend

melody ['melədɪ] n Melodie f

melon ['melən] n Melone f

melt [melt] vi schmelzen; (anger) verfliegen ♦ vt schmelzen; ~ away vi dahinschmelzen; ~ down vt einschmelzen; ~down n (in nuclear reactor) Kernschmelze f; ~ing point n Schmelzpunkt m; ~ing pot n (fig) Schmelztiegel m

member ['membə*] n Mitglied nt; (of tribe, species) Angehörige(r) m; (ANAT) Glied nt; M~ of Parliament (BRIT) n Parlamentsmitglied n; M~ of the European Parliament (BRIT) n Mitglied nt des Europäischen Parlaments; ~ship n Mitgliedschaft f; to seek ~ship of einen Antrag auf Mitgliedschaft stellen; ~ship card n Mitgliedskarte f

memento [mə'mentəʊ] n Andenken nt

memo ['meməʊ] n Mitteilung f

memoirs ['memwɑːz] npl Memoiren pl

memorable ['memərəbl] adj denkwürdig

memoranda [memə'rændə] npl of memorandum

memorandum [memə'rændəm] (pl memoranda) n Mitteilung f

memorial [mɪ'mɔːrɪəl] n Denkmal nt ♦ adj Gedenk-

memorize ['memraɪz] vt sich einprägen

memory ['memərɪ] n Gedächtnis nt; (of computer) Speicher m; (sth recalled) Erinnerung f

men [men] pl of man ♦ (human race) die Menschen pl

menace ['menɪs] n Drohung f; Gefahr f ♦ vt bedrohen

menacing ['menɪsɪŋ] adj drohend

menagerie [mɪ'nædʒərɪ] n Tierschau f

mend [mend] vt reparieren, flicken ♦ vi (ver)heilen ♦ n ausgebesserte Stelle f; on the ~ auf dem Wege der Besserung; ~ing n (articles) Flickarbeit f

menial ['miːnɪəl] adj niedrig

meningitis [menɪn'dʒaɪtɪs] n Hirnhautentzündung f, Meningitis f

menopause ['menəʊpɔːz] n Wechseljahre pl, Menopause f

menstruation [menstru'eɪʃən] n Menstruation f

mental ['mentl] adj geistig, Geistes-; (arithmetic) Kopf-; (hospital) Nerven-; (cruelty) seelisch; (inf: abnormal) verrückt; ~ity [men'tælɪtɪ] n Mentalität f

menthol ['menθɒl] n Menthol nt

mention ['menʃən] n Erwähnung f ♦ vt erwähnen; don't ~ it! bitte (sehr), gern geschehen

mentor ['mentɔː*] n Mentor m

menu ['menjuː] n Speisekarte f

MEP n abbr = Member of the European Parliament

mercenary ['mɜːsɪnərɪ] adj (person) geldgierig; (MIL) Söldner- ♦ n Söldner m

merchandise ['mɜːtʃəndaɪz] n (Handels)ware f

merchant ['mɜːtʃənt] n Kaufmann m; ~ **navy** (US merchant marine) n Handelsmarine f

merciful ['mɜːsɪful] adj gnädig

merciless ['mɜːsɪləs] adj erbarmungslos

mercury ['mɜːkjʊrɪ] n Quecksilber nt

mercy ['mɜːsɪ] n Erbarmen nt; Gnade f; at the ~ of ausgeliefert +dat

mere [mɪə*] adj bloß

merely adv bloß

merge [mɜːdʒ] vt verbinden; (COMM) fusionieren ♦ vi verschmelzen; (roads) zusammenlaufen; (COMM) fusionieren; ~r n (COMM) Fusion f

meringue [mə'ræŋ] n Baiser nt

merit ['merɪt] n Verdienst nt; (advantage) Vorzug m ♦ vt verdienen

mermaid ['mɜːmeɪd] n Wassernixe f

merry ['merɪ] adj fröhlich; ~-**go-round** n Karussell nt

mesh [meʃ] n Masche f ♦ vi (gears) ineinandergreifen

mesmerize ['mezməraɪz] vt hypnotisieren; (fig) faszinieren

mess [mes] n Unordnung f; (dirt) Schmutz m; (trouble) Schwierigkeiten pl; (MIL) Messe f; ~ **about** or **around** vi (play the fool) herumalbern; (do nothing in particular) herumgammeln; ~ **about** or **around with** vt fus (tinker with) herummurksen an +dat; ~ **up** vt (make untidy) in Unordnung bringen

message ['mesɪdʒ] n Mitteilung f; to get the ~ kapieren

messenger ['mesɪndʒə*] n Bote m

Messrs ['mesəz] abbr (on letters) die Herren

messy ['mesɪ] adj schmutzig; (untidy) unordentlich

met [met] pt, pp of **meet**

metabolism [me'tæbəlɪzəm] n Stoffwechsel m

metal ['metl] n Metall nt

metaphor ['metəfə*] n Metapher f

mete [miːt] : to ~ **out** vt austeilen

meteorology [miːtɪə'rɒlədʒɪ] n Meteorologie f

meter ['miːtə*] n Zähler m; (US) = **metre**

method ['meθəd] n Methode f; ~**ical** [mɪ'θɒdɪkəl] adj methodisch; **M~ist** ['meθədɪst] adj methodistisch ♦ n Methodist(in) m(f); ~**ology** [meθə'dɒlədʒɪ] n Methodik f

meths [meθs] (BRIT) n = **methylated spirit(s)**

methylated spirit(s) ['meθɪleɪtɪd 'spɪrɪts] (BRIT) n (Brenn)spiritus m

meticulous [mɪ'tɪkjʊləs] adj (über)genau

metre ['miːtə*] (US **meter**) n Meter m or nt

metric ['metrɪk] adj (also: ~al) metrisch

metropolitan [metrə'pɒlɪtən] adj der Großstadt; **the M~ Police** (BRIT) n die Londoner Polizei

mettle ['metl] n Mut m

mew [mjuː] vi (cat) miauen

mews [mjuːz] n: ~ **cottage** (BRIT) ehemaliges Kutscherhäuschen

Mexican ['meksɪkən] adj mexikanisch ♦ n Mexikaner(in) m(f)

Mexico ['meksɪkəʊ] n Mexiko nt; ~ **City** n Mexiko City f

miaow [miː'aʊ] vi miauen

mice [maɪs] pl of **mouse**

micro ['maɪkrəʊ] n (also: ~**computer**) Mikrocomputer m

microchip ['maɪkrəʊtʃɪp] n Mikrochip m

microcosm ['maɪkrəʊkɒzəm] n Mikrokosmos m

microfilm ['maɪkrəʊfɪlm] n Mikrofilm m ♦ vt auf Mikrofilm aufnehmen

microphone ['maɪkrəfəʊn] n Mikrophon nt

microprocessor ['maɪkrəʊprəʊsesə*] n Mikroprozessor m

microscope ['maɪkrəskəʊp] n Mikroskop nt

microwave ['maɪkrəʊweɪv] n (also: ~ oven) Mikrowelle(nherd nt) f

mid [mɪd] adj: **in** ~ **afternoon** am Nachmittag; **in** ~ **air** in der Luft; **in** ~ **May** Mitte Mai

midday ['mɪd'deɪ] n Mittag m

middle ['mɪdl] n Mitte f; (waist) Taille f ♦ adj mittlere(r, s), Mittel-; **in the** ~ **of** mitten in +dat; **~-aged** adj mittleren Alters; **the M~ Ages** npl das Mittelalter; **~-class** adj Mittelstands-; **the M~ East** n der Nahe Osten; **~man** (irreg) n (COMM) Zwischenhändler m; ~ **name** n zweiter Vorname m; ~ **weight** n (BOXING) Mittelgewicht nt

middling ['mɪdlɪŋ] adj mittelmäßig

midge [mɪdʒ] n Mücke f

midget ['mɪdʒɪt] n Liliputaner(in m) f

Midlands ['mɪdləndz] npl Midlands pl

midnight ['mɪdnaɪt] n Mitternacht f

midriff ['mɪdrɪf] n Taille f

midst [mɪdst] n: **in the** ~ **of** (persons) mitten unter +dat; (things) mitten in +dat

midsummer ['mɪd'sʌmə*] n Hochsommer m

midway ['mɪd'weɪ] adv auf halbem Wege ♦ adj Mittel-

midweek ['mɪd'wiːk] adv in der Mitte der Woche

midwife ['mɪdwaɪf] (irreg) n Hebamme f; **~ry** ['mɪdwɪfərɪ] n Geburtshilfe f

midwinter ['mɪd'wɪntə*] n tiefste(r) Winter m

might [maɪt] vi see **may** ♦ n Macht f, Kraft f; **I** ~ **come** ich komme vielleicht; **~y** adj, adv mächtig

migraine ['miːgreɪn] n Migräne f

migrant ['maɪgrənt] adj Wander-; (bird) Zug-

migrate [maɪ'greɪt] vi (ab)wandern; (birds) (fort)ziehen

migration [maɪ'greɪʃən] n Wanderung f, Zug m

mike [maɪk] n = **microphone**

Milan [mɪ'læn] n Mailand nt

mild [maɪld] adj mild; (medicine, interest) leicht; (person) sanft

mildew ['mɪldjuː] n (on plants) Mehltau m; (on food) Schimmel m

mildly ['maɪldlɪ] adv leicht; **to put it** ~ gelinde gesagt

mile [maɪl] n Meile f; **~age** n Meilenzahl f

mileometer n = **milometer**

milestone n (also fig) Meilenstein m

military ['mɪlɪtərɪ] adj militärisch, Militär-, Wehr-

militate ['mɪlɪteɪt] vi: **to** ~ **against** entgegenwirken +dat

militia [mɪ'lɪʃə] n Miliz f

milk [mɪlk] n Milch f ♦ vt (also fig) melken; **~ chocolate** n Milchschokolade f; **~man** (irreg) n Milchmann m; **~ shake** n Milchmixgetränk nt; **~y** adj milchig; **M~y Way** n Milchstraße f

mill [mɪl] n Mühle f; (factory) Fabrik f ♦ vt mahlen ♦ vi (move around) umherlaufen

millennia [mɪ'lenɪə] npl of **millennium**

millennium [mɪ'lenɪəm] (pl ~s or **millennia**) n Jahrtausend nt

miller ['mɪlə*] n Müller m

millet ['mɪlɪt] n Hirse f

milligram(me) ['mɪlɪgræm] n Milligramm nt

millimetre ['mɪlɪmiːtə*] (US **millimeter**) n Millimeter m

million ['mɪljən] n Million f; **a** ~ **times** tausendmal; **~aire** [mɪljə'nɛə*] n Millionär(in m) f

millstone ['mɪlstəʊn] n Mühlstein m

milometer [maɪ'lɒmɪtə*] n = Kilometerzähler m

mime [maɪm] n Pantomime f ♦ vt, vi mimen

mimic ['mɪmɪk] n Mimiker m ♦ vt, vi nachahmen; **~ry** ['mɪmɪkrɪ] n Nachahmung f; (BIOL) Mimikry f

min. abbr = **minutes**; **minimum**

minaret [mɪnə'ret] n Minarett nt

mince [mɪns] vt (zer)hacken ♦ vi (walk) trippeln ♦ n (meat) Hackfleisch nt; **~meat** n süße Pastetenfüllung f; **~ pie** n gefüllte (süße) Pastete f; **~r** n Fleischwolf m

mind [maɪnd] n Verstand m, Geist m; (opinion) Meinung f ♦ vt aufpassen auf +acc; (object to) etwas haben gegen; **on my ~** auf dem Herzen; **to my ~** meiner Meinung nach; **to be out of one's ~** wahnsinnig sein; **to bear** or **keep in ~** bedenken; **to change one's ~** es sich dat anders überlegen; **to make up one's ~** sich entschließen; **I don't ~** das macht mir nichts aus; **~ you, ...** allerdings ...; **never ~!** macht nichts!; **"~ the step"** "Vorsicht Stufe"; **~ your own business** kümmern Sie sich um Ihre eigenen Angelegenheiten; **~er** n Aufpasser(in) m(f); **~ful** adj: **~ful of** achtsam auf +acc; **~less** adj sinnlos

mine¹ [maɪn] n (coal~) Bergwerk nt; (MIL) Mine f ♦ vt ausbeuten; (MIL) verminen

mine² [maɪn] pron meine(r, s); that book is mine das Buch gehört mir; a friend of mine ein Freund von mir

minefield ['maɪnfi:ld] n Minenfeld nt

miner ['maɪnə*] n Bergarbeiter m

mineral ['mɪnərəl] adj mineralisch, Mineral- ♦ n Mineral nt; **~s** npl (BRIT: soft drinks) alkoholfreie Getränke pl; **~ water** n Mineralwasser nt

minesweeper ['maɪnswi:pə*] n Minensuchboot nt

mingle ['mɪŋgl] vi: **to ~ (with)** sich mischen (unter +acc)

miniature ['mɪnɪtʃə*] adj Miniatur- ♦ n Miniatur f

minibus ['mɪnɪbʌs] n Kleinbus m

minim ['mɪnɪm] n halbe Note f

minimal ['mɪnɪməl] adj minimal

minimize ['mɪnɪmaɪz] vt auf das Mindestmaß beschränken

minimum ['mɪnɪməm] (pl **minima**)

n Minimum n ♦ adj Mindest-

mining ['maɪnɪŋ] n Bergbau m ♦ adj Bergbau-, Berg-

miniskirt ['mɪnɪskɜ:t] n Minirock m

minister ['mɪnɪstə*] n (BRIT: POL) Minister m; (ECCL) Pfarrer m ♦ vi: **to ~ to sb/sb's needs** sich um jdn kümmern; (sb's needs) nachkommen +dat; **~ial** [mɪnɪs'tɪərɪəl] adj ministeriell, Minister-

ministry ['mɪnɪstrɪ] n (BRIT: POL) Ministerium nt; (ECCL: office) geistliche(s) Amt nt

mink [mɪŋk] n Nerz m

minnow ['mɪnəu] n Elritze f

minor ['maɪnə*] adj kleiner; (operation) leicht; (problem, poet) unbedeutend; (MUS) Moll ♦ n (BRIT: under 18) Minderjährige(r) mf

minority [maɪ'nɒrɪtɪ] n Minderheit f

mint [mɪnt] n Minze f; (sweet) Pfefferminzbonbon nt ♦ vt (coins) prägen; the (Royal (BRIT) or US (US)) M~ die Münzanstalt; **in ~ condition** in tadellosem Zustand

minus ['maɪnəs] n Minuszeichen nt; (amount) Minusbetrag m ♦ prep minus, weniger

minuscule ['mɪnəskju:l] adj winzig

minute¹ [maɪ'nju:t] adj winzig; (detailed) minuziös

minute² ['mɪnɪt] n Minute f; (moment) Augenblick m; **minutes** npl (of meeting etc) Protokoll nt

miracle ['mɪrəkl] n Wunder nt

miraculous [mɪ'rækjuləs] adj wunderbar

mirage ['mɪrɑ:ʒ] n Fata Morgana f

mire [maɪə*] n Morast m

mirror ['mɪrə*] n Spiegel m ♦ vt (wider)spiegeln

mirth [mɜ:θ] n Heiterkeit f

misadventure [mɪsəd'ventʃə*] n Mißgeschick nt, Unfall m

misanthropist [mɪ'zænθrəpɪst] n Menschenfeind m

misapprehension ['mɪsæprɪ'henʃən] n Mißverständnis nt

misbehave ['mɪsbɪ'heɪv] vi sich schlecht benehmen

miscalculate ['mɪs'kælkjuleɪt] vt

falsch berechnen
miscarriage ['miskærɪdʒ] n (MED) Fehlgeburt f; ~ **of justice** Fehlurteil nt
miscellaneous [misi'leiniəs] adj verschieden
mischance [mis'tʃɑːns] n Mißgeschick nt
mischief ['mistʃif] n Unfug m
mischievous ['mistʃivəs] adj (person) durchtrieben; (glance) verschmitzt; (rumour) bösartig
misconception ['miskən'sepʃən] n fälschliche Annahme f
misconduct [mis'kɒndʌkt] n Vergehen nt; **professional** ~ Berufsvergehen nt
misconstrue [miskən'struː] vt mißverstehen
misdeed [mis'diːd] n Untat f
misdemeanour [misdi'miːnə*] (US **misdemeanor**) n Vergehen nt
miser ['maizə*] n Geizhals m
miserable ['mizərəbl] adj (unhappy) unglücklich; (headache, weather) fürchterlich; (poor) elend; (contemptible) erbärmlich
miserly ['maizəli] adj geizig
misery ['mizəri] n Elend nt, Qual f
misfire [mis'faiə*] vi (gun) versagen; (engine) fehlzünden; (plan) fehlgehen
misfit ['misfit] n Außenseiter m
misfortune [mis'fɔːtʃən] n Unglück nt
misgiving(s) [mis'givin(z)] n(pl) Bedenken pl
misguided [mis'gaidid] adj fehlgeleitet; (opinions) irrig
mishandle [mis'hændl] vt falsch handhaben
mishap ['mishæp] n Mißgeschick nt
misinform [misin'fɔːm] vt falsch unterrichten
misinterpret [misin'tɜːprit] vt falsch auffassen
misjudge [mis'dʒʌdʒ] vt falsch beurteilen
mislay [mis'lei] (irreg: like lay) vt verlegen

mislead [mis'liːd] (irreg: like lead) vt (deceive) irreführen; ~**ing** adj irreführend
mismanage ['mis'mænidʒ] vt schlecht verwalten
misnomer ['mis'nəumə*] n falsche Bezeichnung f
misogynist [mi'sɒdʒinist] n Weiberfeind m
misplace ['mis'pleis] vt verlegen
misprint ['misprint] n Druckfehler m
Miss [mis] n Fräulein nt
miss [mis] vt (fail to hit, catch) verfehlen; (not notice) verpassen; (be too late) versäumen, verpassen; (omit) auslassen; (regret the absence of) vermissen ♦ vi fehlen ♦ n (shot) Fehlschuß m; (failure) Fehlschlag m; **I ~ you** du fehlst mir; ~ **out** vt auslassen
missal ['misəl] n Meßbuch nt
misshapen ['mis'ʃeipən] adj mißgestaltet
missile ['misail] n Rakete f
missing ['misiŋ] adj (person) vermißt; (thing) fehlend; **to be** ~ fehlen
mission ['miʃən] n (work) Auftrag m; (people) Delegation f; (REL) Mission f; ~**ary** n Missionar (in) m(f)
misspell ['mis'spel] (irreg: like spell) vt falsch schreiben
misspent ['mis'spent] adj (youth) vergeudet
mist [mist] n Dunst m, Nebel m ♦ vi (also: ~ over, ~ up) sich trüben; (BRIT: windows) sich beschlagen
mistake [mis'teik] (irreg: like take) n Fehler m ♦ vt (misunderstand) mißverstehen; (mix up): **to** ~ (for sth) (etw mit etw) verwechseln; **to make a** ~ einen Fehler machen; **by** ~ aus Versehen; **to** ~ **A for B** A mit B verwechseln; **mistaken** pp of **mistake** ♦ adj (idea) falsch; **to be** ~ sich irren
mister ['mistə*] n (inf) Herr m; see **Mr**
mistletoe ['misltəu] n Mistel f
mistook [mis'tuk] pt of **mistake**

mistress ['mɪstrɪs] n (teacher) Lehrerin f; (in house) Herrin f; (lover) Geliebte f; see Mrs

mistrust ['mɪs'trʌst] vt mißtrauen +dat

misty ['mɪstɪ] adj neblig

misunderstand ['mɪsʌndə'stænd] (irreg: like **understand**) vt, vi mißverstehen, falsch verstehen; **~ing** n Mißverständnis nt; (disagreement) Meinungsverschiedenheit f

misuse [n 'mɪs'juːs, vb 'mɪs'juːz] n falsche(r) Gebrauch m ♦ vt falsch gebrauchen

mitigate ['mɪtɪgeɪt] vt mildern

mitt(en) ['mɪt(n)] n Fausthandschuh m

mix [mɪks] vt (blend) (ver)mischen ♦ vi (liquids) sich (ver)mischen lassen; (people: get on) sich vertragen; (: associate) Kontakt haben ♦ n (mixture) Mischung f; **~ up** vt zusammenmischen; (confuse) verwechseln; **~ed** adj gemischt; **~ed-up** adj durcheinander; **~er** n (for food) Mixer m; **~ture** n Mischung f; **~up** n Durcheinander nt

mm abbr (= millimetre(s)) mm

moan [məʊn] n Stöhnen nt; (complaint) Klage f ♦ vi stöhnen; (complain) maulen

moat [məʊt] n (Burg)graben m

mob [mɒb] n Mob m; (the masses) Pöbel m ♦ vt (star) herfallen über +acc

mobile ['məʊbaɪl] adj beweglich; (library etc) fahrbar ♦ n (decoration) Mobile nt; **~ home** n Wohnwagen m; **~ phone** n (TEL) Mobiltelefon nt

mobility [məʊ'bɪlɪtɪ] n Beweglichkeit f

mobilize ['məʊbɪlaɪz] vt mobilisieren

moccasin ['mɒkəsɪn] n Mokassin m

mock [mɒk] vt verspotten; (defy) trotzen +dat ♦ adj Schein-; **~ery** n Spott m; (person) Gespött nt

mod [mɒd] adj see convenience

mode [məʊd] n (Art f und) Weise f

model ['mɒdl] n Modell nt; (example) Vorbild nt; (in fashion) Manne-

quin nt ♦ adj (railway) Modell-; (perfect) Muster-; vorbildlich ♦ vt (make) bilden; (clothes) vorführen ♦ vi als Mannequin arbeiten

modem ['məʊdem] n (COMPUT) Modem nt

moderate [adj, n 'mɒdərət, vb 'mɒdəreɪt] adj gemäßigt ♦ n (POL) Gemäßigte(r) mf ♦ vi sich mäßigen ♦ vt mäßigen

moderation [mɒdə'reɪʃən] n Mäßigung f; in ~ mit Maßen

modern ['mɒdən] adj modern; (history, languages) neuere(r, s); (Greek etc) Neu-; **~ize** vt modernisieren

modest ['mɒdɪst] adj bescheiden; **~y** n Bescheidenheit f

modicum ['mɒdɪkəm] n bißchen n

modification [mɒdɪfɪ'keɪʃən] n (Ab)änderung f

modify ['mɒdɪfaɪ] vt abändern

module ['mɒdjuːl] n (component) (Bau)element nt; (SPACE) (Raum)kapsel f

mogul ['məʊgəl] n (fig) Mogul m

mohair ['məʊheə*] n Mohair m

moist [mɔɪst] adj feucht; **~en** ['mɔɪsn] vt befeuchten; **~ure** ['mɔɪstʃə*] n Feuchtigkeit f; **~urizer** ['mɔɪstʃəraɪzə*] n Feuchtigkeitscreme f

molar ['məʊlə*] n Backenzahn m

molasses [mə'læsɪz] n Melasse f

mold [məʊld] n (US) = **mould**

mole [məʊl] n (spot) Leberfleck m; (animal) Maulwurf m; (pier) Mole f

molest [məʊ'lest] vt belästigen

mollycoddle ['mɒlɪkɒdl] vt verhätscheln

molt [məʊlt] vi (US) = **moult**

molten ['məʊltən] adj geschmolzen

mom [mɒm] (US) n = **mum**

moment ['məʊmənt] n Moment m, Augenblick m; (importance) Tragweite f; at the ~ im Augenblick; **~ary** adj kurz; **~ous** [məʊ'mentəs] adj folgenschwer

momentum [məʊ'mentəm] n Schwung m; to gather ~ in Fahrt kommen

mommy ['mɒmɪ] (US) n = **mummy**

Monaco ['mɒnəkəʊ] n Monaco nt

monarch ['mɒnək] n Herrscher(in m(f)); ~y n Monarchie f

monastery ['mɒnəstrɪ] n Kloster nt

monastic [mə'næstɪk] adj klösterlich, Kloster-

Monday ['mʌndeɪ] n Montag m

monetary ['mʌnɪtərɪ] adj Geld-; (of currency) Währungs-

money ['mʌnɪ] n Geld nt; **to make** ~ Geld verdienen; ~**lender** n Geldverleiher m; ~ **order** n Postanweisung f; ~**spinner** (inf) n Verkaufsschlager m (inf)

mongol ['mɒŋgəl] n (MED) mongoloide(s) Kind nt ♦ adj mongolisch; (MED) mongoloid

mongrel ['mʌŋgrəl] n Promenadenmischung f

monitor ['mɒnɪtə*] n (SCH) Klassenordner m; (television ~) Monitor m ♦ vt (broadcasts) abhören; (control) überwachen

monk [mʌŋk] n Mönch m

monkey ['mʌŋkɪ] n Affe m; ~ **nut** (BRIT) n Erdnuß f; ~ **wrench** n (TECH) Engländer m, Franzose m

monochrome ['mɒnəkrəʊm] adj schwarz-weiß

monopolize [mə'nɒpəlaɪz] vt beherrschen

monopoly [mə'nɒpəlɪ] n Monopol nt

monosyllable ['mɒnəsɪləbl] n einsilbige(s) Wort nt

monotone ['mɒnətəʊn] n gleichbleibende(r) Ton(fall) m; **to speak in a** ~ monoton sprechen

monotonous [mə'nɒtənəs] adj eintönig

monotony [mə'nɒtənɪ] n Eintönigkeit f, Monotonie f

monsoon [mɒn'suːn] n Monsun m

monster ['mɒnstə*] n Ungeheuer nt; (person) Scheusal nt

monstrosity [mɒn'strɒsɪtɪ] n Ungeheuerlichkeit f; (thing) Monstrosität f

monstrous ['mɒnstrəs] adj (shocking) gräßlich, ungeheuerlich; (huge) riesig

month [mʌnθ] n Monat m; ~**ly** adj monatlich, Monats- ♦ adv einmal im Monat ♦ n (magazine) Monatsschrift f

monument ['mɒnjʊmənt] n Denkmal nt; ~**al** [mɒnjʊ'mentl] adj (huge) gewaltig; (ignorance) ungeheuer

mood [muːd] n Stimmung f, Laune f; **to be in a good/bad** ~ guter/ schlechter Laune haben; ~**y** adj launisch

moon [muːn] n Mond m; ~**light** n Mondlicht nt; ~**lighting** n Schwarzarbeit f; ~**lit** adj mondhell

moor [muə*] n Heide f, Hochmoor nt ♦ vt (ship) festmachen, verankern ♦ vi anlegen; ~**ings** npl Liegeplatz m

moorland ['muələnd] n Heidemoor nt

moose [muːs] n Elch m

mop [mɒp] n Mop m ♦ vt (auf)wischen; ~ **up** vt aufwischen

mope [məʊp] vi Trübsal blasen

moped ['məʊped] n Moped nt

moral ['mɒrəl] adj moralisch; (values) sittlich; (virtuous) tugendhaft ♦ n Moral f; ~**s** npl (ethics) Moral f; ~**e** [mɒ'rɑːl] n Moral f; ~**ity** [mə'rælɪtɪ] n Sittlichkeit f

morass [mə'ræs] n Sumpf m

morbid ['mɔːbɪd] adj krankhaft; (jokes) makaber

KEYWORD

more [mɔː*] adj (greater in number etc) mehr; (additional) noch mehr; **do you want (some) more tea?** möchten Sie noch etwas Tee?; **I have no** or **I don't have any more money** ich habe kein Geld mehr ♦ pron (greater amount) mehr; (further or additional amount) noch mehr; **is there any more?** gibt es noch mehr?; (left over) ist noch etwas da?; **there's no more** es ist nichts mehr da

♦ adv mehr; **more dangerous/ easily etc (than)** gefährlicher/ einfacher etc (als); **more and more** immer mehr; **more and more excited** immer aufgeregter; **more or less** mehr oder weniger; **more than ever** mehr denn je; **more beautiful than ever** schöner denn je

moreover [mɔːˈrəʊvə*] adv überdies

morgue [mɔːg] n Leichenschauhaus nt

moribund [ˈmɔrɪbʌnd] adj aussterbend

Mormon [ˈmɔːmən] n Mormone m, Mormonin f

morning [ˈmɔːnɪŋ] n Morgen m; **in the ~** am Morgen; **7 o'clock in the ~** 7 Uhr morgens

Morocco [məˈrɒkəʊ] n Marokko nt

moron [ˈmɔːrɒn] n Schwachsinnige(r) mf

morose [məˈrəʊs] adj mürrisch

morphine [ˈmɔːfiːn] n Morphium nt

Morse [mɔːs] n (also: ~ code) Morsealphabet nt

morsel [ˈmɔːsl] n Bissen m

mortal [ˈmɔːtl] adj sterblich; (deadly) tödlich; (very great) Todes- ♦ n (human being) Sterbliche(r) mf; **~ity** [mɔːˈtælɪtɪ] n Sterblichkeit f; (death rate) Sterblichkeitsziffer f

mortar [ˈmɔːtə*] n (for building) Mörtel m; (bowl) Mörser m; (MIL) Granatwerfer m

mortgage [ˈmɔːgɪdʒ] n Hypothek f ♦ vt hypothekarisch belasten = Bausparkasse f

mortify [ˈmɔːtɪfaɪ] vt beschämen

mortuary [ˈmɔːtjʊərɪ] n Leichenhalle f

mosaic [məʊˈzeɪɪk] n Mosaik nt

Moscow [ˈmɒskəʊ] n Moskau nt

Moslem [ˈmɒzləm] = **Muslim**

mosque [mɒsk] n Moschee f

mosquito [mɒsˈkiːtəʊ] (pl ~es) n Moskito m

moss [mɒs] n Moos nt

most [məʊst] adj meiste(r, s) ♦ adv am meisten; (very) höchst ♦ n die meiste, der größte Teil; (people) die meisten; **~ men** die meisten Männer; **at the (very) ~** aller-

höchstens; **to make the ~ of** das Beste machen aus; **a ~ interesting book** ein höchst interessantes Buch; **~ly** adv größtenteils

MOT (BRIT) n abbr (= Ministry of Transport): **the ~ (test)** = der TÜV

motel [məʊˈtel] n Motel nt

moth [mɒθ] n Nachtfalter m; (wool-eating) Motte f; **~ball** n Mottenkugel f

mother [ˈmʌðə*] n Mutter f ♦ vt bemuttern; **~hood** n Mutterschaft f; **~-in-law** n Schwiegermutter f; **~ly** adj mütterlich; **~-to-be** n werdende Mutter f; **~ tongue** n Muttersprache f

motif [məʊˈtiːf] n Motiv nt

motion [ˈməʊʃən] n Bewegung f; (in meeting) Antrag m ♦ vt, vi: **to ~ (to) sb** jdm winken, jdm ein Zeichen geben; **~less** adj regungslos; **~ picture** n Film m

motivated [ˈməʊtɪveɪtɪd] adj motiviert

motivation [məʊtɪˈveɪʃən] n Motivierung f

motive [ˈməʊtɪv] n Motiv nt, Beweggrund m ♦ adj treibend

motley [ˈmɒtlɪ] adj bunt

motor [ˈməʊtə*] n Motor m; (BRIT: inf: vehicle) Auto nt ♦ adj Motor-; **~bike** n Motorrad nt; **~boat** n Motorboot nt; **~car** (BRIT) n Auto nt; **~cycle** n Motorrad nt; **~cyclist** n Motorradfahrer(in) m(f); **~ing** (BRIT) n Autofahren nt ♦ adj Auto-; **~ist** [ˈməʊtərɪst] n Autofahrer(in) m(f); **~ racing** (BRIT) n Autorennen nt; **~ vehicle** n Kraftfahrzeug nt; **~way** (BRIT) n Autobahn f

mottled [ˈmɒtld] adj gesprenkelt

motto [ˈmɒtəʊ] (pl ~es) n Motto nt

mould [məʊld] (US mold) n Form f; (mildew) Schimmel m ♦ vt (also fig) formen; **~er** vi (decay) vermodern; **~y** adj schimmelig

moult [məʊlt] (US molt) vi sich mausern

mound [maʊnd] n (Erd)hügel m

mount [maʊnt] n (liter: hill) Berg

m; (horse) Pferd nt; (for jewel etc)
Fassung f ♦ vt (horse) steigen auf
+acc; (put in setting) fassen; (exhibition) veranstalten; (attack) unternehmen ♦ vi (also: ~ up) sich
häufen; (on horse) aufsitzen

mountain ['mauntɪn] n Berg m ♦
cpd Berg-; ~ **bike** n Mountain-Bike
nt; ~**eer** [mauntɪ'nɪəⁱ] n Bergstei-
ger(in m(f)); ~**eering** n Bergsteigen
nt; ~**ous** adj bergig; ~ **rescue team**
n Bergwacht f; ~**side** n
Berg(ab)hang m

mourn [mɔːn] vt betrauern, beklagen
♦ vi: **to** ~ (**for sb**) (um jdn)
trauern; ~**er** n Trauernde(r) mf;
~**ful** adj traurig; ~**ing** n (grief)
Trauer f ♦ cpd (dress) Trauer-; **in**
~**ing** (period etc) in Trauer; (dress)
in Trauerkleidung f

mouse [maus] (pl **mice**) n Maus f;
~**trap** n Mausefalle f

mousse [muːs] n (CULIN) Creme f;
(cosmetic) Schaumfestiger m

moustache [məs'taːʃ] n Schnurrbart
m

mousy ['mausɪ] adj (colour) maus-
grau; (person) schüchtern

mouth [mauθ, pl mauðz] n Mund m;
(opening) Öffnung f; (of river)
Mündung f; ~**ful** n Mundvoll m;
~ **organ** n Mundharmonika f; ~**piece** n
Mundstück nt; (fig) Sprachrohr nt;
~**wash** n Mundwasser nt; ~**watering** adj lecker, appetitlich

movable ['muːvəbl] adj beweglich

move [muːv] n (movement) Bewegung f; (in game) Zug m; (step)
Schritt m; (of house) Umzug m ♦ vt
bewegen; (people) transportieren;
(in job) versetzen; (emotionally) bewegen ♦ vi sich bewegen; (vehicle,
ship) fahren; (go to another house)
umziehen; **to get a** ~ **on** sich beeil-
en; **to** ~ **sb to do sth** jdn veranlassen zu etw zun; ~ **about or around**
vi sich hin- und herbewegen; (travel)
unterwegs sein; ~ **along** vi weitergehen; (cars) weiterfahren; ~ **away** vi
weggehen; ~ **back** vi zurückgehen;

(to the rear) zurückweichen; ~ **forward** vi vorwärtsgehen, sich vor-
wärtsbewegen ♦ vt vorschieben; ~
(time) vorverlegen; ~ **in** vi (to
house) einziehen; (troops) einrücken;
~ **on** vi weitergehen ♦ vt weitergehen lassen; ~ **out** vi (of house) ausziehen; (troops) abziehen; ~ **over** vi
zur Seite rücken; ~ **up** vi aufsteigen;
(in job) befördert werden ♦ vt nach
oben bewegen; (in job) befördern

movement ['muːvmənt] n Bewegung f

movie ['muːvɪ] n Film m; **to go to**
the ~**s** ins Kino gehen; ~ **camera** n
Filmkamera f

moving ['muːvɪŋ] adj beweglich;
(touching) ergreifend

mow [məu] (pt **mowed**, pp **mowed**
or **mown**) vt mähen; ~ **down** vt
(fig) niedermähen; ~**er** n (machine)
Mähmaschine f; (lawn-) Rasenmäher m

mown [məun] pp of **mow**

MP n abbr = **Member of Parliament**

m.p.h. abbr = **miles per hour**

Mr ['mɪstəⁱ] (US **Mr.**) n Herr m

Mrs ['mɪsɪz] (US **Mrs.**) n Frau f

Ms [mɪz] (US **Ms.**) n (= Miss or Mrs)
Frau f

M.Sc. n abbr = **Master of Science**

much [mʌtʃ] adj viel ♦ adv sehr;
viel ♦ n viel, eine Menge; **how** ~ **is**
it? wieviel kostet das?; **too** ~ zuviel; **it's not** ~ es ist nicht viel; **as**
~ **as** sosehr, soviel; **however** ~ **he**
tries sosehr er es auch versucht

muck [mʌk] n Mist m; (fig) Schmutz
m; ~ **to about or around** (with
sth) (an etw dat) herumalbern; ~
up vt (inf: ruin) vermasseln; (dirty)
dreckig machen; ~**y** adj (dirty)
dreckig

mucus ['mjuːkəs] n Schleim m

mud [mʌd] n Schlamm m

muddle ['mʌdl] n Durcheinander nt
♦ vt (also: ~ **up**) durcheinanderbringen; ~ **through** vi sich durchwur-

muddy ['mʌdɪ] *adj* schlammig

mudguard ['mʌdgɑ:d] *n* Schutzblech *nt*

mud-slinging ['mʌdslɪŋɪŋ] (*inf*) *n* Verleumdung *f*

muff [mʌf] *n* Muff *m* ♦ *vt* (*chance*) verpassen; (*lines*) verpatzen (*inf*)

muffin ['mʌfɪn] *n* süße(s) Teilchen *nt*

muffle ['mʌfl] *vt* (*sound*) dämpfen; (*wrap up*) einhüllen; **~d** *adj* gedämpft

muffler ['mʌflə*] (*US*) *n* (*AUT*) Schalldämpfer *m*

mug [mʌg] *n* (*cup*) Becher *m*; (*inf: face*) Visage *f*; (: *fool*) Trottel *m* ♦ *vt* überfallen und ausrauben; **~ging** *n* Überfall *m*

muggy ['mʌgɪ] *adj* (*weather*) schwül

mule [mju:l] *n* Maulesel *m*

mull [mʌl]: **~ over** *vt* nachdenken über +*acc*

mulled [mʌld] *adj* (*wine*) Glüh-

multi- ['mʌltɪ] *prefix* Multi-, multi-

multicoloured ['mʌltɪ'kʌləd] (*US* **multicolored**) *adj* mehrfarbig

multi-level ['mʌltɪlevl] (*US*) *adj* = **multistorey**

multiple ['mʌltɪpl] *n* Vielfache(s) *nt* ♦ *adj* mehrfach; (*many*) mehrere; **~ sclerosis** *n* multiple Sklerose *f*

multiply ['mʌltɪplaɪ] *vt*: **to ~ (by)** multiplizieren (mit) ♦ *vi* (*BIOL*) sich vermehren

multistorey ['mʌltɪ'stɔ:rɪ] (*BRIT*) *adj* (*building, car park*) mehrstöckig

multitude ['mʌltɪtju:d] *n* Menge *f*

mum [mʌm] *n* (*BRIT: inf*) Mutti *f* ♦ *adj*: **to keep ~ (about)** den Mund halten (über +*acc*)

mumble ['mʌmbl] *vt, vi* murmeln ♦ *n* Gemurmel *nt*

mummy ['mʌmɪ] *n* (*dead body*) Mumie *f*; (*BRIT: inf*) Mami *f*

mumps [mʌmps] *n* Mumps *m*

munch [mʌntʃ] *vt, vi* mampfen

mundane [mʌn'deɪn] *adj* banal

municipal [mju:'nɪsɪpl] *adj* städtisch, Stadt-; **~ity** [mju:nɪsɪ'pælɪtɪ] *n* Stadt *f* mit Selbstverwaltung

mural ['mjʊərəl] *n* Wandgemälde *nt*

murder ['mɜ:də*] *n* Mord *m* ♦ *vt* ermorden; **~er** *n* Mörder *m*; **~ous** *adj* Mord-; (*fig*) mörderisch

murky ['mɜ:kɪ] *adj* finster

murmur ['mɜ:mə*] *n* Murmeln *nt*; (*of water, wind*) Rauschen *nt* ♦ *vt, vi* murmeln

muscle ['mʌsl] *n* Muskel *m*; **~ in** *vi* mitmischen

muscular ['mʌskjʊlə*] *adj* Muskel-; (*strong*) muskulös

muse [mju:z] *vi* (nach)sinnen

museum [mju:'zɪəm] *n* Museum *nt*

mushroom ['mʌʃrʊm] *n* Champignon *m*; Pilz *m* ♦ *vi* (*fig*) emporschießen

music ['mju:zɪk] *n* Musik *f*; (*printed*) Noten *pl*; **~al** *adj* (*sound*) melodisch; (*person*) musikalisch ♦ *n* (*show*) Musical *nt*; **~al instrument** *n* Musikinstrument *nt*; **~ hall** (*BRIT*) *n* Varieté *nt*; **~ian** [mju:'zɪʃən] *n* Musiker(in) *m(f)*

musk [mʌsk] *n* Moschus *m*

Muslim ['mʌzlɪm] *adj* moslemisch ♦ *n* Moslem *m*

muslin ['mʌzlɪn] *n* Musselin *m*

mussel ['mʌsl] *n* Miesmuschel *f*

must [mʌst] *vb aux* müssen; (*in negation*) dürfen ♦ *n* Muß *nt*; **the film is a ~** den Film muß man einfach gesehen haben

mustard ['mʌstəd] *n* Senf *m*

muster ['mʌstə*] *vt* (*MIL*) antreten lassen; (*courage*) zusammennehmen

mustn't ['mʌsnt] = **must not**

musty ['mʌstɪ] *adj* muffig

mute [mju:t] *adj* stumm ♦ *n* (*person*) Stumme(r) *mf*; (*MUS*) Dämpfer *m*

muted ['mju:tɪd] *adj* gedämpft

mutilate ['mju:tɪleɪt] *vt* verstümmeln

mutiny ['mju:tɪnɪ] *n* Meuterei *f* ♦ *vi* meutern

mutter ['mʌtə*] *vt, vi* murmeln

mutton ['mʌtn] *n* Hammelfleisch *nt*

mutual ['mju:tjʊəl] *adj* gegenseitig; beiderseitig; **~ly** *adv* gegenseitig; für beide Seiten

muzzle ['mʌzl] *n* (*of animal*) Schnau-

ze f; (for animal) Maulkorb m; (of gun) Mündung f ♦ vt einen Maulkorb anlegen +dat

my [maɪ] adj mein; **this is ~ car** das ist mein Auto; **I've washed ~ hair** ich habe mir die Haare gewaschen

myopic [maɪˈɒpɪk] adj kurzsichtig

myriad [ˈmɪrɪəd] n: **a ~ of** (people, things) unzählige

myself [maɪˈself] pron mich acc; mir dat; (emphatic) selbst; see also oneself

mysterious [mɪsˈtɪərɪəs] adj geheimnisvoll

mystery [ˈmɪstərɪ] n (secret) Geheimnis nt; (sth difficult) Rätsel nt

mystify [ˈmɪstɪfaɪ] vt ein Rätsel sein +dat; verblüffen

mystique [mɪsˈtiːk] n geheimnisvolle Natur f

myth [mɪθ] n Mythos m; (fig) Erfindung f; ~ology [mɪˈθɒlədʒɪ] n Mythologie f

N

n/a abbr (= not applicable) nicht zutreffend

nab [næb] (inf) vt schnappen

nag [næg] n (horse) Gaul m; (person) Nörgler(in) m(f) ♦ vt, vi: **to ~ (at)** sb an jdm herumnörgeln; **~ging** adj (doubt) nagend ♦ n Nörgelei f

nail [neɪl] n Nagel m ♦ vt: **to ~ sb down to doing sth** jdn darauf festnageln, etw zu tun; **~brush** n Nagelbürste f; **~file** n Nagelfeile f; **~ polish** n Nagellack m; **~ polish remover** n Nagellackentferner m; **~ scissors** npl Nagelschere f; **~ varnish** (BRIT) n = nail polish

naïve [naɪˈiːv] adj naiv

naked [ˈneɪkɪd] adj nackt

name [neɪm] n Name m; (reputation) Ruf m ♦ vt nennen; (sth new) benennen; (appoint) ernennen; **by ~** mit Namen; **I know him only by ~**

ich kenne ihn nur dem Namen nach; **what's your ~?** wie heißen Sie?; **in the ~ of** im Namen +gen; (for the sake of) um +gen ...willen; **~less** adj namenlos; **~ly** adv nämlich; **~sake** n Namensvetter m

nanny [ˈnænɪ] n Kindermädchen nt

nap [næp] n (sleep) Nickerchen nt; (on cloth) Strich m ♦ vi: **to be caught ~ping** (fig) überrumpelt werden

nape [neɪp] n Nacken m

napkin [ˈnæpkɪn] n (at table) Serviette f; (BRIT: for baby) Windel f

nappy [ˈnæpɪ] (BRIT) n (for baby) Windel f; ~ **liner** n Windeleinlage f; ~ **rash** n wunde Stellen pl

narcissi [nɑːˈsɪsaɪ] npl of narcissus

narcissus [nɑːˈsɪsəs] n (BOT) Narzisse f

narcotic [nɑːˈkɒtɪk] adj betäubend ♦ n Betäubungsmittel nt

narrative [ˈnærətɪv] n Erzählung f ♦ adj erzählend

narrator [nəˈreɪtə*] n Erzähler(in) m(f)

narrow [ˈnærəʊ] adj eng, schmal; (limited) beschränkt ♦ vi sich verengen; **to have a ~ escape** mit knapper Not davonkommen; **to ~ sth down to** sth etw auf etw acc einschränken; **~ly** adv (miss) knapp; (escape) mit knapper Not; **~minded** adj engstirnig

nasty [ˈnɑːstɪ] adj ekelhaft, fies; (business, wound) schlimm

nation [ˈneɪʃən] n Nation f, Volk nt; ~**al** [ˈnæʃnl] adj national, National-, Landes- ♦ n Staatsangehörige(r) m(f); ~**al dress** n Tracht f; **N~al Health Service** (BRIT) n Staatliche(r) Gesundheitsdienst m; **N~al Insurance** (BRIT) n Sozialversicherung f; ~**alism** [ˈnæʃnəlɪzəm] n Nationalismus m; ~**alist** [ˈnæʃnəlɪst] n Nationalist(in) m(f) ♦ adj nationalistisch; ~**ality** [næʃəˈnælɪtɪ] n Staatsangehörigkeit f; ~**alize** [ˈnæʃnəlaɪz] vt verstaatlichen; ~**ally** [ˈnæʃnəlɪ] adv national, auf Staatsebene; ~**wide**

['neɪʃənwaɪd] *adj, adv* allgemein, landesweit

native ['neɪtɪv] *n (born in)* Einheimische(r) *mf*; *(original inhabitant)* Eingeborene(r) *mf* ♦ *adj (coming from a certain place)* einheimisch; *(of the original inhabitants)* Eingeborenen-; *(belonging by birth)* heimatlich, Heimat-; *(inborn)* angeboren, natürlich; **a ~ of Germany** ein gebürtiger Deutscher; **a ~ speaker of French** ein französischer Muttersprachler; **~ American** *n* Indianer(in) *m(f)*, Ureinwohner Americas; **~ language** *n* Muttersprache *f*

Nativity [nə'tɪvɪtɪ] *n:* **the ~** Christi Geburt *no art*

NATO ['neɪtəʊ] *n abbr (= North Atlantic Treaty Organization)* NATO *f*

natter ['nætə*] *(BRIT; inf)* *vi* quatschen ♦ *n* Gequatsche *nt*

natural ['nætʃrəl] *adj* natürlich; Natur-; *(inborn)* angeboren; **~ gas** *n* Erdgas *nt*; **~ist** *n* Naturkundler(in) *m(f)*; **~ize** *vt (foreigner)* einbürgern; *(plant etc)* einführen; **~ly** *adv* natürlich

nature ['neɪtʃə*] *n* Natur *f*; **by ~** von Natur (aus)

naught [nɔːt] *n* = nought

naughty ['nɔːtɪ] *adj (child)* unartig, ungezogen; *(action)* ungehörig

nausea ['nɔːsɪə] *n (sickness)* Übelkeit *f*; *(disgust)* Ekel *m*; **~te** ['nɔːsɪeɪt] *vt* anekeln

nautical ['nɔːtɪkəl] *adj* nautisch; See-; *(expression)* seemännisch

naval ['neɪvəl] *adj* Marine-, Flotten-; **~ officer** *n* Marineoffizier *m*

nave [neɪv] *n* Kirchen(haupt)schiff *nt*

navel ['neɪvəl] *n* Nabel *m*

navigate ['nævɪgeɪt] *vi* navigieren

navigation [nævɪ'geɪʃən] *n* Navigation *f*

navigator ['nævɪgeɪtə*] *n* Steuermann *m*; *(AVIAT)* Navigator *m*; *(AUT)* Beifahrer(in) *m(f)*

navvy ['nævɪ] *(BRIT)* *n* Straßenarbeiter *m*

navy ['neɪvɪ] *n (Kriegs)marine *f* ♦

adj marineblau

Nazi ['nɑːtsɪ] *n* Nazi *m*

NB *abbr (= nota bene)* NB

near [nɪə*] *adj* nah ♦ *adv* in der Nähe ♦ *prep (also: ~ to: space)* in der Nähe +*gen*; (: *time)* um +*acc* ... herum ♦ *vt* sich nähern +*dat*; **a ~ miss** knapp daneben; **~by** *adj* nahe (gelegen) ♦ *adv* in der Nähe; **~ly** *adv* fast; **I ~ly fell** ich wäre fast gefallen; **~side** *n (AUT)* Beifahrerseite *f* ♦ *adj* auf der Beifahrerseite

near-sighted *adj* kurzsichtig

neat ['niːt] *adj (tidy)* ordentlich; *(solution)* sauber; *(pure)* pur; **~ly** *adv* *(tidily)* ordentlich

nebulous ['nebjʊləs] *adj* nebulös

necessarily ['nesɪsərɪlɪ] *adv* unbedingt

necessary ['nesɪsərɪ] *adj* notwendig, nötig; **he did all that was ~** er erledigte alles, was nötig war; **it is ~ to/that ...** man muß ...

necessitate [nɪ'sesɪteɪt] *vt* erforderlich machen

necessity [nɪ'sesɪtɪ] *n (need)* Not *f*; *(compulsion)* Notwendigkeit *f*; **necessities** *npl (things needed)* das Notwendigste

neck [nek] *n* Hals *m* ♦ *vi (inf)* knutschen; **~ and ~** Kopf an Kopf

necklace ['neklɪs] *n* Halskette *f*

neckline ['neklaɪn] *n* Ausschnitt *m*

necktie ['nektaɪ] *(US)* *n* Krawatte *f*

née [neɪ] *adj* geborene

need [niːd] *n* Bedürfnis *nt*; *(lack)* Mangel *m*; *(necessity)* Notwendigkeit *f*; *(poverty)* Not *f* ♦ *vt* brauchen; **I ~ to do it** ich muß es tun; **you don't ~ to go** du brauchst nicht zu gehen

needle ['niːdl] *n* Nadel *f* ♦ *vt (fig: inf)* ärgern

needless ['niːdlɪs] *adj* unnötig; **~ to say** natürlich

needlework ['niːdlwɜːk] *n* Handarbeit *f*

needn't ['niːdnt] = need not

needy ['niːdɪ] *adj* bedürftig

negation [nɪ'geɪʃən] *n* Verneinung *f*

negative ['negətiv] n (PHOT) Negativ nt ♦ adj negativ; (answer) abschlägig

neglect [nɪ'glekt] vt vernachlässigen ♦ n Vernachlässigung f

negligée ['neglɪʒeɪ] n Negligé nt

negligence ['neglɪdʒəns] n Nachlässigkeit f

negligible ['neglɪdʒəbl] adj unbedeutend, geringfügig

negotiable [nɪ'gəʊʃɪəbl] adj (cheque) übertragbar, einlösbar

negotiate [nɪ'gəʊʃɪeɪt] vi verhandeln ♦ vt (treaty) abschließen; (difficulty) überwinden; (corner) nehmen; **negotiation** [nɪgəʊʃɪ'eɪʃən] n Verhandlung f; **negotiator** n Unterhändler m

Negress ['niːgrɛs] n Negerin f

Negro ['niːgrəʊ] n Neger m ♦ adj Neger-

neigh [neɪ] vi wiehern

neighbour ['neɪbə*] (US neighbor) n Nachbar(in) m(f); **~hood** n Nachbarschaft f; Umgebung f; **~ing** adj benachbart, angrenzend; **~ly** adj (person, attitude) nachbarlich

neither ['naɪðə*] adj, pron keine(r, s) (von beiden) ♦ conj: **he can't do it, and ~ can I** er kann es nicht und ich auch nicht ♦ adv: **~ good nor bad** weder gut noch schlecht; **~ story is true** keine der beiden Geschichten stimmt

neon ['niːɔn] n Neon nt

nephew ['nefjuː] n Neffe m

nerve [nɜːv] n Nerv m; (courage) Mut m; (impudence) Frechheit f; **to have a fit of ~s** in Panik geraten; **~-racking** adj nervenaufreibend

nervous ['nɜːvəs] adj (of the nerves) Nerven-; (timid) nervös, ängstlich; **~ breakdown** n Nervenzusammenbruch m; **~ness** n Nervosität f

nest [nest] n Nest nt ♦ vi nisten; **~ egg** n (fig) Notgroschen m

nestle ['nesl] vi sich kuscheln

net [net] n Netz nt ♦ adj netto, Netto- ♦ vt netto einnehmen; **~ball** n Netzball m; **~ curtain** n Store m

Netherlands ['neðələndz] npl: **the**

~ die Niederlande pl

nett [net] adj = **nett**

netting ['netɪŋ] n Netz(werk) nt

nettle ['netl] n Nessel f

network ['netwɜːk] n Netz nt

neurotic [njʊə'rɔtɪk] adj neurotisch ♦ n Neurotiker(in) m(f)

neuter ['njuːtə*] adj (BIOL) geschlechtslos; (GRAM) sächlich ♦ vt kastrieren

neutral ['njuːtrəl] adj neutral ♦ n (AUT) Leerlauf m; **~ity** n Neutralität f; **~ize** vt (fig) ausgleichen

never ['nevə*] adv nie(mals); **I ~ went** ich bin gar nicht gegangen; **~ in my life** nie in meinem Leben; **~-ending** adj endlos; **~theless** [nevəðə'les] adv trotzdem, dennoch

new [njuː] adj neu; **N~ Age** n New-Age-; **~born** adj neugeboren; **~comer** ['njuːkʌmə*] n Neuankömmling m; **~-fangled** (pej) adj neumodisch; **~-found** adj neuentdeckt; **~ly** adv frisch, neu; **~lyweds** npl Frischvermählte pl; **~ moon** n Neumond m

news [njuːz] n Nachricht f; (RAD, TV) Nachrichten pl; **a piece of ~** eine Nachricht; **~ agency** n Nachrichtenagentur f; **~agent** (BRIT) n Zeitungshändler m; **~caster** n Nachrichtensprecher(in) m(f); **~ dealer** (US) n = **newsagent**; **~ flash** n Kurzmeldung f; **~letter** n Rundschreiben nt; **~paper** n Zeitung f; **~print** n Zeitungspapier nt; **~reader** n = **newscaster**; **~reel** n Wochenschau f; **~ stand** n Zeitungsstand m

newt [njuːt] n Wassermolch m

New Year n Neujahr nt; **~'s Day** n Neujahrstag m; **~'s Eve** n Silvester(abend m) nt

New York [-'jɔːk] n New York nt

New Zealand [-'ziːlənd] n Neuseeland nt; **~er** n Neuseeländer(in) m(f)

next [nekst] adj nächste(r, s) ♦ adv (after) dann, darauf; (~ time) das nächstemal; **the ~ day** am nächsten or folgenden Tag; **~ time** das nächste Mal; **~ year** nächstes Jahr; **~ door** adv nebenan ♦ adj (neighbour, flat) von nebenan; **~ of kin** n nächste(r) Verwandte(r) mf; **~ to** prep neben; **~ to nothing** so gut wie nichts

NHS n abbr = **National Health Service**

nib [nɪb] n Spitze f

nibble ['nɪbl] vt knabbern an +dat

nice [naɪs] adj (person) nett; (thing) schön; (subtle) fein; **~-looking** adj gutaussehend; **~ly** adv gut, nett; **~ties** ['naɪsɪtɪz] npl Feinheiten pl

nick [nɪk] n Einkerbung f ♦ vt (inf: steal) klauen; **in the ~ of time** gerade rechtzeitig

nickel ['nɪkl] n Nickel nt; (US) Nickel m (5 cents)

nickname ['nɪkneɪm] n Spitzname m ♦ vt taufen

niece [niːs] n Nichte f

Nigeria [naɪ'dʒɪərɪə] n Nigeria nt

niggling ['nɪglɪŋ] adj pedantisch; (doubt, worry) quälend; (detail) kleinlich

night [naɪt] n Nacht f; (evening) Abend m; **the ~ before last** vorletzte Nacht; **at** or **by ~** (after midnight) nachts; (before midnight) abends; **~cap** n (drink) Schlummertrunk m; **~club** n Nachtlokal nt; **~dress** n Nachthemd nt; **~fall** n Einbruch der Nacht; **~ gown** n = **nightdress**; **~ie** ['naɪtɪ] (inf) n Nachthemd nt

nightingale ['naɪtɪŋgeɪl] n Nachtigall f

nightlife ['naɪtlaɪf] n Nachtleben nt

nightly ['naɪtlɪ] adj, adv jeden Abend; jede Nacht

nightmare ['naɪtmeə*] n Alptraum m

night : ~ porter n Nachtportier m; **~ school** n Abendschule f; **~ shift** n Nachtschicht f; **~ time** n Nacht f

nil [nɪl] n Null f

Nile [naɪl] n: **the ~** der Nil

nimble ['nɪmbl] adj beweglich

nine [naɪn] num neun; **~teen** num

neunzehn; **~ty** num neunzig

ninth [naɪnθ] adj neunte(r, s)

nip [nɪp] vt kneifen ♦ n Kneifen nt

nipple ['nɪpl] n Brustwarze f

nippy ['nɪpɪ] (inf) adj (person) flink; (BRIT: car) flott; (: cold) frisch

nitrogen ['naɪtrədʒən] n Stickstoff m

KEYWORD

---

no [nəʊ] (pl **~es**) adv (opposite of yes) nein; **to answer no** (to question) mit Nein antworten; (to request) nein sagen; **no thank you** nein, danke

♦ adj (not any) kein(e); **I have no money/time** ich habe kein Geld/ keine Zeit; **no smoking** Rauchen verboten

♦ n Nein nt; (no vote) Neinstimme f

---

nobility [nəʊ'bɪlɪtɪ] n Adel m

noble ['nəʊbl] adj (rank) adlig; (splendid) nobel, edel

nobody ['nəʊbədɪ] pron niemand, keiner

nocturnal [nɒk'tɜːnl] adj (tour, visit) nächtlich; (animal) Nacht-

nod [nɒd] vi nicken ♦ vt nicken mit ♦ n Nicken nt; **~ off** vi einnicken

noise [nɔɪz] n (sound) Geräusch m; (unpleasant, loud) Lärm m

noisy ['nɔɪzɪ] adj laut; (crowd) lärmend

nominal ['nɒmɪnl] adj nominell

nominate ['nɒmɪneɪt] vt (suggest) vorschlagen; (in election) aufstellen; (appoint) ernennen

nomination [nɒmɪ'neɪʃən] n (election) Nominierung f; (appointment) Ernennung f

nominee [nɒmɪ'niː] n Kandidat(in) m(f)

non- [nɒn] prefix Nicht-, un-; **~alcoholic** adj alkoholfrei; **~-aligned** adj bündnisfrei

nonchalant ['nɒnʃələnt] adj lässig

non-committal ['nɒnkə'mɪtl] adj (reserved) zurückhaltend; (uncommitted) unverbindlich

nondescript ['nɒndɪskrɪpt] adj mittelmäßig

none [nʌn] adj, pron kein(e, er, es)
♦ adv: he's ~ the worse for it es
hat ihm nicht geschadet; it's too late,
isn't it? es ist zu spät, oder or nicht
wahr?; ~ of von keiner; I've ~ left ich
habe keinen mehr

nonentity [nɔ'nentiti] n Null f (inf)

nonetheless ['nʌnðə'les] adv nichts-
destoweniger

non-existent ['nɔnig'zistənt] adj
nicht vorhanden

non-fiction ['nɔn'fikʃən] n Sach-
bücher pl

nonplussed ['nɔn'plʌst] adj verdutzt

nonsense ['nɔnsəns] n Unsinn m

non : ~-smoker n Nichtraucher(in)
m(f); ~-stick adj (pan, surface)
Teflon-(®); ~-stop adj Nonstop-

noodles ['nuːdlz] npl Nudeln pl

nook [nʊk] n Winkel m; ~s and
crannies Ecken und Winkel

noon [nuːn] n (12 Uhr) Mittag m

no one ['nəʊwʌn] pron = nobody

noose [nuːs] n Schlinge f

nor [nɔː*] conj = neither ♦ adv see
neither

norm [nɔːm] n (convention) Norm f;
(rule, requirement) Vorschrift f

normal ['nɔːml] adj normal; ~ly
adv normal; (usually) normalerweise

north [nɔːθ] n Norden m ♦ adj
nördlich, Nord- ♦ adv nördlich, nach
or im Norden; N~ Africa n Nordafri-
ka nt; ~-east n Nordosten m; ~erly
['nɔːðəlɪ] adj nördlich; ~ern ['nɔːðən]
adj nördlich, Nord-; N~ern Ireland n
Nordirland nt; N~ Pole n Nordpol
m; N~ Sea n Nordsee f; ~ward(s)
['nɔːθwəd(z)] adv nach Norden; ~-
west n Nordwesten m

Norway ['nɔːweɪ] n Norwegen nt

Norwegian [nɔː'wiːdʒən] adj norwegisch ♦ n Norweger(in) m(f);
(LING) Norwegisch nt

nose [nəʊz] n Nase f ♦ vi: to ~
about herumschnüffeln; ~bleed n
Nasenbluten nt; ~-dive n Sturzflug
m; ~y adj = nosy

nostalgia [nɔs'tældʒɪə] n Nostalgie f;
nostalgic adj nostalgisch

nostril ['nɔstrɪl] n Nasenloch nt

nosy ['nəʊzɪ] (inf) adj neugierig

not [nɔt] adv nicht; he is ~ or isn't
here er ist nicht hier; it's too late,
isn't it? es ist zu spät, oder or nicht
wahr?; ~ yet/now noch nicht/nicht
jetzt; see also only

notably ['nəʊtəblɪ] adv (especially)
besonders; (noticeably) bemerkenswert

notary ['nəʊtərɪ] n Notar(in) m(f)

notch [nɔtʃ] n Kerbe f, Einschnitt m

note [nəʊt] n (MUS) Note f, Ton m;
(short letter) Nachricht f; (POL)
Note f; (comment, attention) Notiz f;
(of lecture etc) Aufzeichnung f;
(bank-) Schein m; (fame) Ruf m ♦
vt (observe) bemerken; (write down)
notieren; ~book n Notizbuch nt; ~d
['nəʊtɪd] adj bekannt; ~pad n Notizblock m; ~paper n Briefpapier nt

nothing ['nʌθɪŋ] n nichts; ~ new/
much nichts Neues/viel; for ~
umsonst

notice ['nəʊtɪs] n (announcement)
Bekanntmachung f; (warning) Ankündigung f; (dismissal) Kündigung f
♦ vt bemerken; to take ~ of beachten; at short ~ kurzfristig; until
further ~ bis auf weiteres; to hand
in one's ~ kündigen; ~able adj
merklich; ~board n Anschlagtafel f

notify ['nəʊtɪfaɪ] vt benachrichtigen

notion ['nəʊʃən] n Idee f

notorious [nəʊ'tɔːrɪəs] adj berüchtigt

notwithstanding [nɔtwɪθ'stændɪŋ]
adv trotzdem; ~ this ungeachtet dessen

nought [nɔːt] n Null f

noun [naʊn] n Substantiv nt

nourish ['nʌrɪʃ] vt nähren; ~ing adj
nahrhaft; ~ment n Nahrung f

novel ['nɔvəl] n Roman m ♦ adj
neu(artig); ~ist n Schriftsteller(in)
m(f); ~ty n Neuheit f

November [nəʊ'vembə*] n November m

novice ['nɔvɪs] n Neuling m; (ECCL)
Novize m

now [nau] *adv* jetzt; **right ~** jetzt, gerade; **by ~** inzwischen; **just ~** gerade; **~ and then, ~ and again** ab und zu, manchmal; **from ~ on** von jetzt an; **~adays** ['nauədeiz] *adv* heutzutage

nowhere ['nəuwεə*] *adv* nirgends

nozzle ['nɔzl] *n* Düse *f*

nubile ['nju:bail] *adj (woman)* gut entwickelt

nuclear ['nju:kliə*] *adj (energy etc)* Atom-, Kern-

nuclei ['nju:kliai] *npl of* nucleus

nucleus ['nju:kliəs] *n* Kern *m*

nude [nju:d] *adj nackt ♦ n (ART)* Akt *m*; **in the ~** nackt

nudge [nʌdʒ] *vt* leicht anstoßen

nudist ['nju:dist] *n* Nudist(in) *m(f)*

nudity ['nju:diti] *n* Nacktheit *f*

nuisance ['nju:sns] *n* Ärgernis *nt*; **what a ~!** wie ärgerlich!

nuke [nju:k] *(inf) n* Kernkraftwerk *nt ♦ vt* atomar vernichten

null [nʌl] *adj*: **~ and void** null und nichtig

numb [nʌm] *adj* taub, gefühllos ♦ *vt* betäuben

number ['nʌmbə*] *n* Nummer *f*; *(numeral also)* Zahl *f*; *(quantity)* (An)zahl *f ♦ vt (give a ~ to)* numerieren; *(amount to)* sein; **to be ~ed among** gezählt werden zu; **a ~ of** *(several)* einige; **they were ten in ~** sie waren zehn an der Zahl; **~ plate** *(BRIT) n (AUT)* Nummernschild *nt*

numeral ['nju:mərəl] *n* Ziffer *f*

numerate ['nju:mərit] *adj* rechenkundig

numerical [nju:'merikəl] *adj (order)* zahlenmäßig

numerous ['nju:mərəs] *adj* zahlreich

nun [nʌn] *n* Nonne *f*

nurse [nə:s] *n* Krankenschwester *f*; *(for children)* Kindermädchen *nt ♦ vt (patient)* pflegen; *(doubt etc)* hegen

nursery ['nə:səri] *n (for children)* Kinderzimmer *nt*; *(for plants)* Gärtnerei *f*; *(for trees)* Baumschule

f; **~ rhyme** *n* Kinderreim *m*; **~ school** *n* Kindergarten *m*; **~ slope** *(BRIT) n (SKI)* Idiotenhügel *m (inf)*, Anfängerhügel *m*

nursing ['nə:siŋ] *n (profession)* Krankenpflege *f*; **~ home** *n* Privatklinik *f*

nurture ['nə:tʃə*] *vt* aufziehen

nut [nʌt] *n* Nuß *f*; *(screw)* Schraubenmutter *f*; *(inf)* Verrückte(r) *m*; **he's ~s** er ist verrückt

nutcrackers ['nʌtkrækəz] *npl* Nußknacker *m*

nutmeg ['nʌtmeg] *n* Muskat(nuß *f*) *m*

nutrient ['nju:triənt] *n* Nährstoff *m*

nutrition [nju:'trifən] *n* Nahrung *f*

nutritious [nju:'trifəs] *adj* nahrhaft

nylon ['nailɔn] *n* Nylon *nt ♦ adj* Nylon-

O

oak [əuk] *n* Eiche *f ♦ adj* Eichen(holz)-

O.A.P. *abbr =* old-age pensioner

oar [ɔ:*] *n* Ruder *nt*

oases [əu'eisi:z] *npl of* oasis

oasis [əu'eisis] *n* Oase *f*

oath [əuθ] *n (statement)* Eid *m*, Schwur *m*; *(swearword)* Fluch *m*

oatmeal ['əutmi:l] *n* Haferschrot *m*

oats [əuts] *npl* Hafer *m*

obedience [ə'bi:diəns] *n* Gehorsam *m*

obedient [ə'bi:diənt] *adj* gehorsam

obesity [əu'bi:siti] *n* Fettleibigkeit *f*

obey [ə'bei] *vt, vi*: **to ~ (sb)** (jdm) gehorchen

obituary [ə'bitjuəri] *n* Nachruf *m*

object [*n* 'ɔbdʒikt, *vb* əb'dʒekt] *n (thing)* Gegenstand *m*, Objekt *nt*; *(purpose)* Ziel *nt ♦ vi* dagegen sein; **expense is no ~** Ausgaben spielen keine Rolle; **I ~!** ich protestiere!; **to ~ to sth** Einwände gegen etw haben; *(morally)* Anstoß an etw *acc* nehmen; **to ~ that** einwenden, daß; **~ion** [əb'dʒekʃən] *n (reason against)*

Einwand *m*, Einspruch *m*; (*dislike*) Abneigung *f*; **I have no ~ion to ...** ich habe nichts gegen ... einzuwenden; **~ionable** [əˈdʒekʃnəbl] *adj* nicht einwandfrei; (*language*) anstößig; **~ive** [əˈdʒektɪv] *n* Ziel *nt* ♦ *adj* objektiv

obligation [ɔblɪˈɡeɪʃən] *n* Verpflichtung *f*; **without ~** unverbindlich

obligatory [əˈblɪɡətərɪ] *adj* obligatorisch

oblige [əˈblaɪdʒ] *vt* (*compel*) zwingen; (*do a favour*) einen Gefallen tun +*dat*; **to be ~d to sb for sth** jdm für etw verbunden sein

obliging [əˈblaɪdʒɪŋ] *adj* entgegenkommend

oblique [əˈbliːk] *adj* schräg, schief ♦ *n* Schrägstrich *m*

obliterate [əˈblɪtəreɪt] *vt* auslöschen

oblivion [əˈblɪvɪən] *n* Vergessenheit *f*

oblivious [əˈblɪvɪəs] *adj* nicht bewußt

oblong [ˈɔblɔŋ] *n* Rechteck *nt* ♦ *adj* länglich

obnoxious [əbˈnɔkʃəs] *adj* widerlich

obscene [əbˈsiːn] *adj* obszön

obscenity [əbˈsenɪtɪ] *n* Obszönität *f*; **obscenities** *npl* (*swearwords*) Zoten *pl*

obscure [əbˈskjʊə*] *adj* unklar; (*indistinct*) undeutlich; (*unknown*) unbekannt, obskur; (*dark*) düster ♦ *vt* verdunkeln; (*view*) verbergen; (*confuse*) verwirren

obscurity [əbˈskjʊərɪtɪ] *n* Unklarheit *f*; (*darkness*) Dunkelheit *f*

obsequious [əbˈsiːkwɪəs] *adj* servil

observance [əbˈzɜːvəns] *n* Befolgung *f*

observant [əbˈzɜːvənt] *adj* aufmerksam

observation [ɔbzəˈveɪʃən] *n* (*noticing*) Beobachtung *f*; (*surveillance*) Überwachung *f*; (*remark*) Bemerkung *f*

observatory [əbˈzɜːvətrɪ] *n* Sternwarte *f*, Observatorium *nt*

observe [əbˈzɜːv] *vt* (*notice*) bemerken; (*watch*) beobachten; (*customs*) einhalten; **~r** *n* Beobachter(in) *m(f)*

obsess [əbˈses] *vt* verfolgen, quälen; **~ion** [əbˈseʃən] *n* Besessenheit *f*, Wahn *m*; **~ive** *adj* krankhaft

obsolescence [ɔbsəˈlesns] *n* Veraltetheit *nt*

obsolete [ˈɔbsəliːt] *adj* überholt, veraltet

obstacle [ˈɔbstəkl] *n* Hindernis *nt*; **~race** *n* Hindernisrennen *nt*

obstetrics [ɔbˈstetrɪks] *n* Geburtshilfe *f*

obstinate [ˈɔbstɪnət] *adj* hartnäckig, stur

obstruct [əbˈstrʌkt] *vt* versperren; (*pipe*) verstopfen; (*hinder*) hemmen; **~ion** [əbˈstrʌkʃən] *n* Versperrung *f*; Verstopfung *f*; (*obstacle*) Hindernis *nt*

obtain [əbˈteɪn] *vt* erhalten, bekommen; (*result*) erzielen

obtrusive [əbˈtruːsɪv] *adj* aufdringlich

obvious [ˈɔbvɪəs] *adj* offenbar, offensichtlich; **~ly** *adv* offensichtlich

occasion [əˈkeɪʒən] *n* Gelegenheit *f*; (*special event*) Ereignis *nt*; (*reason*) Anlaß *m* ♦ *vt* veranlassen; **~al** *adj* gelegentlich; **~ally** *adv* gelegentlich

occupant [ˈɔkjʊpənt] *n* Inhaber(in) *m(f)*; (*of house etc*) Bewohner(in) *m(f)*

occupation [ɔkjʊˈpeɪʃən] *n* (*employment*) Tätigkeit *f*, Beruf *m*; (*pastime*) Beschäftigung *f*; (*of country*) Besetzung *f*, Okkupation *f*; **~al hazard** *n* Berufsrisiko *nt*

occupier [ˈɔkjʊpaɪə*] *n* Bewohner(in) *m(f)*

occupy [ˈɔkjʊpaɪ] *vt* (*take possession of*) besetzen; (*seat*) belegen; (*live in*) bewohnen; (*position, office*) bekleiden; (*position in sb's life*) einnehmen; (*time*) beanspruchen; **to ~ o.s. with sth** sich mit etw beschäftigen; **to ~ o.s. by doing sth** sich damit beschäftigen, etw zu tun

occur [əˈkɜː*] *vi* vorkommen; **to ~ to sb** jdm einfallen; **~rence** *n* (*event*) Ereignis *nt*; (*appearing*) Auftreten *nt*

ocean [ˈəuʃən] n Ozean m, Meer nt;
~**-going** adj Hochsee-

o'clock [əˈklɔk] adv: it is 5 ~ es ist
5 Uhr

OCR n abbr = optical character
reader

octagonal [ɔkˈtægənl] adj achteckig

October [ɔkˈtəubə*] n Oktober m

octopus [ˈɔktəpəs] n Krake f (small) Tintenfisch m

odd [ɔd] adj (strange) sonderbar;
(not even) ungerade; (the other part
missing) einzeln; (surplus) übrig;
60-odd so um die 60; at ~ times ab
und zu; to be the ~ one out (person) das fünfte Rad am Wagen sein;
(thing) nicht dazugehören; ~**ity** n
(strangeness) Merkwürdigkeit f;
(queer person) seltsamer Kauz m;
(thing) Kuriosität f; ~-**job man** (irreg) n Mädchen nt für alles; ~ **jobs**
npl gelegentlich anfallende Arbeiten;
~**ly** adv seltsam; ~**ments** npl Reste
pl; ~**s** npl Chancen pl; (betting) Gewinnchancen pl; it makes no ~s es
spielt keine Rolle; at ~s uneinig; ~**s**
and ends npl Krimskrams m

odious [ˈəudiəs] adj verhaßt; (action) abscheulich

odometer [əuˈdɔmətə*] (esp US) n
Tacho(meter) m

odour [ˈəudə*] (US **odor**) n Geruch
m

---

men; the 5th of July der 5 Juli
3 (from, out of) aus; a bridge made
of wood eine Holzbrücke, eine
Brücke aus Holz

off [ɔf] adj, adv (absent) weg, fort;
(switch) aus(geschaltet), ab(geschaltet); (BRIT: food: bad) schlecht;
(cancelled) abgesagt ♦ prep von
+dat; to be ~ (to leave) gehen; to
be ~ **sick** krank sein; a day ~ ein
freier Tag; to have an ~ **day** einen
schlechten Tag haben; he had his
coat ~ er hatte seinen Mantel aus;
10% ~ (COMM) 10% Rabatt; 5 km
~ (the road) 5 km (von der Straße)
entfernt; ~ **the coast** vor der Küste;
I'm ~ **meat** (no longer eat it) ich esse kein Fleisch mehr;
(no longer like it) ich mag kein
Fleisch mehr; on the ~ **chance** auf
gut Glück

offal [ˈɔfəl] n Innereien pl

offbeat [ˈɔfbiːt] adj unkonventionell

off-colour [ˈɔfˈkʌlə*] adj nicht wohl

offence [əˈfɛns] (US **offense**) n
(crime) Vergehen nt, Straftat f; (insult) Beleidigung f; to take ~ at gekränkt sein wegen

offend [əˈfɛnd] vt beleidigen; ~**er** n
Gesetzesübertreter m

offense [əˈfɛns] (US) n = offence

offensive [əˈfɛnsiv] adj (unpleasant)
übel, abstoßend; (weapon) Kampf-;
(remark) verletzend ♦ n Angriff m

offer [ˈɔfə*] n Angebot f ♦ vt anbieten; (opinion) äußern; (resistance)
leisten; on ~ zum Verkauf angeboten; ~**ing** n Gabe f

offhand [ˈɔfˈhænd] adj lässig ♦ adv
ohne weiteres

office [ˈɔfis] n Büro nt; (position)
Amt nt; doctor's ~ (US) Praxis f;
to take ~ sein Amt antreten; (POL)
die Regierung übernehmen; ~ **auto-**
mation n Büroautomatisierung f; ~
block (US **office building**) n
Büro(hoch)haus nt; ~ **hours** npl
Dienstzeit f; (US: MED) Sprechstunde f

officer [ˈɒfɪsə*] n (MIL) Offizier m; (public ~) Beamte(r) m

official [əˈfɪʃl] adj offiziell, amtlich ♦ n Beamte(r) m; ~**dom** n Beamtentum nt

officiate [əˈfɪʃɪeɪt] vi amtieren

officious [əˈfɪʃəs] adj aufdringlich

offing [ˈɒfɪŋ] n: **in the** ~ in (Aus)sicht

off: ~**licence** (BRIT) n (shop) Wein- und Spirituosenhandlung f; ~**line** adj (COMPUT) Off-line ♦ adv off line; ~**peak** adj (charges) verbilligt; ~**putting** (BRIT) adj (person, remark etc) abstoßend; ~**season** adj außer Saison

offset [ˈɒfset] (irreg: like set) vt ausgleichen ♦ n (also: ~ printing) Offset(druck) m

offshoot [ˈɒfʃuːt] n (fig: of organization) Zweig m; (: of discussion etc) Randergebnis nt

offshore [ˈɒfˈʃɔː*] adv in einiger Entfernung von der Küste ♦ adj küstennah, Küsten-

offside [ˈɒfˈsaɪd] adj (SPORT) im Abseits ♦ adv abseits ♦ n (AUT) Fahrerseite f

offspring [ˈɒfsprɪŋ] n Nachkommenschaft f; (one) Sprößling m

off: ~**stage** adv hinter den Kulissen; ~**the-cuff** adj unvorbereitet, aus dem Stegreif; ~**the-peg** (US off-**the-rack**) adv von der Stange; ~**white** adj naturweiß

often [ˈɒfn] adv oft

ogle [ˈəʊgl] vt liebäugeln mit

oh [əʊ] excl oh, ach

oil [ɔɪl] n Öl nt ♦ vt ölen; ~**can** n Ölkännchen nt; ~**field** n Ölfeld nt; ~**filter** n (AUT) Ölfilter m; ~**fired** adj Öl-; ~**painting** n Ölgemälde nt; ~**rig** n Ölplattform f; ~**skins** npl Ölzeug nt; ~**tanker** n (Öl)tanker m; ~ **well** n Ölquelle f; ~**y** adj ölig; (dirty) ölbeschmiert

ointment [ˈɔɪntmənt] n Salbe f

O.K. [ˈəʊˈkeɪ] excl in Ordnung, O.K. ♦ adj in Ordnung ♦ vt genehmigen

okay [ˈəʊˈkeɪ] = **O.K.**

old [əʊld] adj alt; how ~ are you? wie alt bist du?; he's 10 years ~ er ist 10 Jahre alt; ~**er brother** ältere(r) Bruder m; ~ **age** n Alter nt; ~**age pensioner** (BRIT) n Rentner(in) m(f); ~**fashioned** adj altmodisch

olive [ˈɒlɪv] n (fruit) Olive f; (colour) Olive f ♦ adj Oliven-; (coloured) olivenfarbig; ~ **oil** n Olivenöl nt

Olympic [əʊˈlɪmpɪk] adj olympisch; **the** ~ **Games, the** ~**s** die Olympischen Spiele

omelet(te) [ˈɒmlət] n Omelett nt

omen [ˈəʊmən] n Omen nt

ominous [ˈɒmɪnəs] adj bedrohlich

omission [əʊˈmɪʃən] n Auslassung f; (neglect) Versäumnis nt

omit [əʊˈmɪt] vt auslassen; (fail to do) versäumen

KEYWORD

on [ɒn] prep **1** (indicating position) auf +dat; (with vb of motion) auf +acc; (on vertical surface, part of body) an +dat/acc; **it's on the table** es ist auf dem Tisch; **she put the book on the table** sie legte das Buch auf den Tisch; **on the left** links

2 (indicating means, method, condition) **on foot** (go) zu Fuß; **on the train/plane** (go) mit dem Zug/Flugzeug; (be) im Zug/Flugzeug; **on the telephone/television** am Telefon/im Fernsehen; **to be on drugs** Drogen nehmen; **to be on holiday/business** im Urlaub/auf Geschäftsreise sein

3 (referring to time): **on Friday** (am) Freitag; **on Fridays** freitags; **on June 20th** am 20. Juni; **a week on Friday** Freitag in einer Woche; **on arrival he** ... als er ankam, ... er

4 (about, concerning) über +acc ♦ adv **1** (referring to dress) an; **she put her boots/hat on** sie zog ihre Stiefel an/setzte ihren Hut auf

2 (further, continuously) weiter;

walk on weitergehen
♦ adj 1 (functioning, in operation: machine, TV, light) an; (: tap) aufgedreht; (: brakes) angezogen; **is the meeting still on?** findet die Versammlung noch statt?; **there's a good film on** es läuft ein guter Film 2: **that's not on!** (inf: of behaviour) das liegt nicht drin!

once [wʌns] adv einmal ♦ conj wenn ... einmal; ~ **he had left/it was done** nachdem er gegangen war/es fertig war; **at ~** sofort; (at the same time) gleichzeitig; ~ **a week** einmal in der Woche; ~ **more** noch einmal; ~ **and for all** ein für allemal; ~ **upon a time** es war einmal

oncoming ['ɒnkʌmɪŋ] adj (traffic) Gegen-, entgegenkommend

KEYWORD

---

one [wʌn] num eins; (with noun, referring back to noun) ein/eine/ein; **it is one o'clock** es ist eins, es ist ein Uhr; **one hundred and fifty** einhundertfünfzig

♦ adj 1 (sole) einzige(r, s); **the one book which** das einzige Buch, welches

2 (same) derselbe/dieselbe/dasselbe; **they came in the one car** sie kamen alle in dem einen Auto

3 (indef): **one day I discovered ...** eines Tages bemerkte ich ...

♦ pron 1 eine(r, s); **do you have a red one?** haben Sie einen roten/eine rote/ein rotes?; **this one** diese(r, s); **that one** der/die/das; **which one?** welche(r, s)?; **one by one** einzeln

2: **one another** einander; **do you two ever see one another?** seht ihr beide euch manchmal?

3 (impers) man; **one never knows** man kann nie wissen; **to cut one's finger** sich in den Finger schneiden

one: ~-**armed bandit** n einarmiger Bandit m; ~-**day excursion** (US) n (day return) Tagesrückfahrkarte f;

~-**man** adj Einmann-; ~-**man band** n Einmannkapelle f; (fig) Einmannbetrieb m; ~-**off** (BRIT: inf) n Einzelfall m

oneself [wʌn'sɛlf] pron (reflexive: after prep) sich; (~ personally) sich selbst or selber; (emphatic) (sich) selbst; **to hurt** ~ sich verletzen

one: ~-**sided** adj (argument) einseitig; ~-**to-one** adj (relationship) eins-zu-eins; ~-**upmanship** n die Kunst, anderen um eine Nasenlänge voraus zu sein; ~-**way** adj (street) Einbahn-

ongoing ['ɒngəʊɪŋ] adj momentan; (progressing) sich entwickelnd

onion ['ʌnjən] n Zwiebel f

on-line ['ɒn'laɪn] adj (COMPUT) Online-

onlooker ['ɒnlʊkə*] n Zuschauer(in) m(f)

only ['əʊnlɪ] adv nur, bloß ♦ adj einzige(r, s) ♦ conj nur, bloß; **an ~ child** ein Einzelkind; **not ~ ... but also ...** nicht nur ... sondern auch ...

onset ['ɒnsɛt] n (beginning) Beginn m

onshore ['ɒn'ʃɔ:] adj (wind) See-

onslaught ['ɒnslɔ:t] n Angriff m

onto ['ɒntʊ] prep = on to

onus ['əʊnəs] n Last f, Pflicht f

onward(s) ['ɒnwəd(z)] adv (place) voran, vorwärts; **from that day onwards** von dem Tag an; **from today onwards** ab heute

ooze [u:z] vi sickern

opaque [əʊ'peɪk] adj undurchsichtig

OPEC ['əʊpɛk] n abbr (= Organization of Petroleum-Exporting Countries) OPEC f

open ['əʊpən] adj offen; (public) öffentlich; (mind) aufgeschlossen ♦ vt öffnen, aufmachen; (trial, motorway, account) eröffnen ♦ vi (begin) anfangen; (shop) aufmachen; (door, flower) aufgehen; (play) Premiere haben; **in the ~ (air)** im Freien; **to on to** vi fus sich öffnen auf +acc; ~ **up** vt (route) erschließen; (shop, prospects) eröffnen ♦ vi öffnen,

~**ing** n (hole) Öffnung f; (beginning) Anfang m; (good chance) Gelegenheit f; ~**ly** adv offen; (publicly) öffentlich; ~**minded** adj aufgeschlossen; ~**necked** adj offen; ~**plan** adj (office) Großraum-; (flat etc) offen angelegt

opera ['ɔpərə] n Oper f; ~ **house** n Opernhaus nt

operate ['ɔpəreɪt] vt (machine) bedienen; (brakes, light) betätigen ♦ vi (machine) laufen, in Betrieb sein; (person) arbeiten; (MED): to ~ on operieren

operatic [ɔpə'rætɪk] adj Opern-

operating ['ɔpəreɪtɪŋ]: ~ **table/theatre** Operationstisch m/-saal m

operation [ɔpə'reɪʃən] n (working) Betrieb m; (MED) Operation f; (undertaking) Unternehmen nt; (MIL) Einsatz m; to be in ~ (JUR) in Kraft sein; (machine) in Betrieb sein; to have an ~ (MED) operiert werden; ~**al** adj einsatzbereit

operative ['ɔpərətɪv] adj wirksam; (MED) operativ

operator ['ɔpəreɪtə*] n (of machine) Arbeiter m; (TEL) Telefonist(in) m(f)

ophthalmic [ɔf'θælmɪk] adj Augen-

opinion [ə'pɪnjən] n Meinung f; in my ~ meiner Meinung nach; ~**ated** adj starrsinnig; ~ **poll** n Meinungsumfrage f

opponent [ə'pəʊnənt] n Gegner m

opportunity [ɔpə'tjuːnɪtɪ] n Gelegenheit f, Möglichkeit f; **to take the** ~ **of doing sth** die Gelegenheit ergreifen, etw zu tun

oppose [ə'pəʊz] vt entgegentreten +dat; (argument, idea) ablehnen; (plan) bekämpfen; **to be** ~**d to sth** gegen etw sein; **as** ~**d to** im Gegensatz zu

opposing [ə'pəʊzɪŋ] adj gegnerisch; (points of view) entgegengesetzt

opposite ['ɔpəzɪt] adj (house) gegenüberliegend; (direction) entgegengesetzt ♦ adv gegenüber ♦ prep gegenüber ♦ n Gegenteil nt

opposition [ɔpə'zɪʃən] n (resistance) Widerstand m; (POL) Opposition f; (contrast) Gegensatz m

oppress [ə'pres] vt unterdrücken; (heat etc) bedrücken; ~**ion** [ə'preʃən] n Unterdrückung f; ~**ive** adj (authority, law) repressiv; (burden, thought) bedrückend; (heat) drückend

opt [ɔpt] vi: **to** ~ **for** sich entscheiden für; **to** ~ **to do sth** sich entscheiden, etw zu tun; **to** ~ **out of** sich drücken vor +dat; (of society) ausflippen aus

optical ['ɔptɪkəl] adj optisch; ~ **character reader** n optische(s) Lesegerät nt

optician [ɔp'tɪʃən] n Optiker m

optimist ['ɔptɪmɪst] n Optimist m; ~**ic** ['ɔptɪ'mɪstɪk] adj optimistisch

optimum ['ɔptɪməm] adj optimal

option ['ɔpʃən] n Wahl f; (COMM) Option f; **to keep one's** ~**s open** sich alle Möglichkeiten offenhalten; ~**al** adj freiwillig; (subject) wahlfrei; ~**al extras** npl Extras auf Wunsch

opulent ['ɔpjʊlənt] adj sehr reich

or [ɔː*] conj oder; **he could not read** ~ **write** er konnte weder lesen noch schreiben; ~ **else** sonst

oral ['ɔːrəl] adj mündlich ♦ n (exam) mündliche Prüfung f

orange ['ɔrɪndʒ] n (fruit) Apfelsine f, Orange f; (colour) Orange nt ♦ adj orange

orator ['ɔrətə*] n Redner(in) m(f)

orbit ['ɔːbɪt] n Umlaufbahn f

orchard ['ɔːtʃəd] n Obstgarten m

orchestra ['ɔːkɪstrə] n Orchester nt; (US: seating) Parkett nt; ~**l** [ɔː'kestrəl] adj Orchester-, orchestral

orchid ['ɔːkɪd] n Orchidee f

ordain [ɔː'deɪn] vt (ECCL) weihen; (decide) verfügen

ordeal [ɔː'diːl] n Qual f

order ['ɔːdə*] n (sequence) Reihenfolge f; (good arrangement) Ordnung f; (command) Befehl m; (JUR) Anordnung f; (peace) Ordnung f; (con-

dition) Zustand *m*; (*rank*) Klasse *f*;
(*COMM*) Bestellung *f*; (*ECCL, honour*) Orden *m* ♦ *vt* (*also: put in* ~)
ordnen; (*command*) befehlen;
(*COMM*) bestellen; **in** ~ in der Reihenfolge; (*in* (*working*) ~ in gutem
Zustand; **in** ~ **to do sth** um etw zu
tun; **on** ~ (*COMM*) auf Bestellung;
to ~ **sb to do sth** jdm befehlen, etw
zu tun; **to** ~ **sth** (*command*) etw *acc*
befehlen; ~ **form** *n* Bestellschein *m*;
~**ly** *n* (*MIL*) Sanitäter *m*; (*MED*)
Pfleger *m* ♦ *adj* (*tidy*) ordentlich;
(*well-behaved*) ruhig

ordinary ['ɔːdnrɪ] *adj* gewöhnlich;
out of the ~ außergewöhnlich

ordnance ['ɔːdnəns] *n* Artillerie *f*;
O~ Survey (*BRIT*) *n* amtliche(r)
Kartographiedienst *m*

ore [ɔː*] *n* Erz *nt*

organ ['ɔːgən] *n* (*MUS*) Orgel *f*;
(*BIOL, fig*) Organ *nt*

organic [ɔː'gænɪk] *adj* (*food, farming
etc*) biodynamisch

organization [ɔːgənaɪ'zeɪʃən] *n* Organisation *f*; (*make-up*) Struktur *f*

organize ['ɔːgənaɪz] *vt* organisieren;
~**r** *n* Organisator *m*, Veranstalter *m*

orgasm ['ɔːgæzəm] *n* Orgasmus *m*

orgy ['ɔːdʒɪ] *n* Orgie *f*

Orient ['ɔːrɪənt] *n* Orient *m*

oriental [ɔːrɪ'entəl] *adj* orientalisch

origin ['ɒrɪdʒɪn] *n* Ursprung *m*; (*of
the world*) Anfang *m*, Entstehung *f*

original [ə'rɪdʒɪnl] *adj* (*first*) ursprünglich; (*painting*) original;
(*idea*) originell ♦ *n* Original *nt*; ~**ly**
adv ursprünglich; originell

originate [ə'rɪdʒɪnɛɪt] *vi* entstehen ♦
vt ins Leben rufen; **to** ~ **from** stammen aus

Orkneys ['ɔːknɪz] *npl* (*also: the Orkney Islands*) die Orkneyinseln *pl*

ornament ['ɔːnəmənt] *n* Schmuck
m; (*on mantelpiece*) Nippesfigur *f*;
~**al** [ɔː'nəmentl] *adj* Zier-

ornate [ɔː'neɪt] *adj* reich verziert

orphan ['ɔːfn] *n* Waise *f*, Waisenkind *nt* ♦ *vt*: **to be** ~**ed** Waise werden; ~**age** *n* Waisenhaus *nt*

orthodox ['ɔːθədɒks] *adj* orthodox;
~**y** *n* Orthodoxie *f*, Konventionalität *f*

orthopaedic [ɔːθəʊ'piːdɪk] (*US orthopedic*) *adj* orthopädisch

ostensibly [ɒs'tensəblɪ] *adv* vorgeblich, angeblich

ostentatious [ɒsten'teɪʃəs] *adj* großtuerisch, protzig

ostracize ['ɒstrəsaɪz] *vt* ausstoßen

ostrich ['ɒstrɪtʃ] *n* Strauß *m*

other ['ʌðə*] *adj* andere(r, s) ♦ *pron*
andere(r, s) ♦ *adv*: ~ **than** anders
als; **the** ~ (**one**) der/die/das andere;
the ~ **day** neulich; ~**s** (~ *people*)
andere; ~**wise** *adv* (*in a different
way*) anders; (*or else*) sonst

ouch [autʃ] *excl* aua

ought [ɔːt] *vb aux* sollen; **I** ~ **to do
it** ich sollte es tun; **this** ~ **to have
been corrected** das hätte korrigiert
werden sollen

ounce [auns] *n* Unze *f*

our ['auə*] *adj* unser; see also **my**;
~**s** *pron* unsere(r, s); see also **mine**;
~**selves** *pron* uns (selbst); (*emphatic*) (wir) selbst; see also **oneself**

oust [aust] *vt* verdrängen

out [aut] *adv* hinaus/heraus; (*not indoors*) draußen; (*not alight*) aus;
(*unconscious*) bewußtlos; (*results*)
bekanntgegeben; **to eat/go** ~ auswärts essen/ausgehen; ~ **there** da
draußen; **he is** ~ (*absent*) er ist
nicht da; **he was** ~ **in his calculations** seine Berechnungen waren
nicht richtig; ~ **loud** laut; ~ **of** aus;
(*away from*) außerhalb +*gen*; **to be**
~ **of milk** *etc* keine Milch *etc* mehr
haben; ~ **of order** außer Betrieb;
~**-and-out** *adj* (*liar, thief etc*) ausgemacht

outback ['autbæk] *n* Hinterland *nt*

outboard (motor) ['autbɔːd-] *n*
Außenbordmotor *m*

outbreak ['autbreɪk] *n* Ausbruch *m*

outburst ['autbɜːst] *n* Ausbruch *m*

outcast ['autkɑːst] *n* Ausgestoßene(r)
mf

outcome ['autkʌm] *n* Ergebnis *nt*

outcrop ['aʊtkrɔp] n (of rock) Felsnase f

outcry ['aʊtkraɪ] n Protest m

outdated [aʊt'deɪtɪd] adj überholt

outdo [aʊt'duː] (irreg: like do) vt übertrumpfen

outdoor ['aʊtdɔː*] adj Außen- (SPORT) im Freien; **~s** adv im Freien

outer ['aʊtə*] adj äußere(r, s); **~ space** n Weltraum m

outfit ['aʊtfɪt] n Kleidung f; **~ters** (BRIT) n (for men's clothes) Herrenausstatter m

outgoing ['aʊtgəʊɪŋ] adj (character) aufgeschlossen; **~s** (BRIT) npl Ausgaben pl

outgrow [aʊt'grəʊ] (irreg: like grow) vt (clothes) herauswachsen aus; (habit) ablegen

outhouse ['aʊthaʊs] n Nebengebäude nt

outing ['aʊtɪŋ] n Ausflug m

outlandish [aʊt'lændɪʃ] adj eigenartig

outlaw ['aʊtlɔː] n Geächtete(r) m ♦ vt ächten; (thing) verbieten

outlay ['aʊtleɪ] n Auslage f

outlet ['aʊtlɛt] n Auslaß m, Abfluß m; (also: retail ~) Absatzmarkt m; (US: ELEC) Steckdose f; (for emotions) Ventil nt

outline ['aʊtlaɪn] n Umriß m

outlive [aʊt'lɪv] vt überleben

outlook ['aʊtlʊk] n (also fig) Aussicht f; (attitude) Einstellung f

outlying ['aʊtlaɪɪŋ] adj entlegen; (district) Außen-

outmoded [aʊt'məʊdɪd] adj veraltet

outnumber [aʊt'nʌmbə*] vt zahlenmäßig überlegen sein +dat

out-of-date [aʊtəv'deɪt] adj (passport) abgelaufen; (clothes etc) altmodisch; (ideas etc) überholt

out-of-the-way [aʊtəvðə'weɪ] adj abgelegen

outpatient ['aʊtpeɪʃənt] n ambulante(r) Patient m/ambulante Patientin f

outpost ['aʊtpəʊst] n (MIL, fig) Vorposten m

output ['aʊtpʊt] n Leistung f, Produktion f; (COMPUT) Ausgabe f

outrage ['aʊtreɪdʒ] n (cruel deed) Ausschreitung f; (indecency) Skandal m ♦ vt (morals) verstoßen gegen; (person) empören; **~ous** [aʊt'reɪdʒəs] adj unerhört

outright [adv aʊt'raɪt, adj 'aʊtraɪt] adv (at once) sofort; (openly) ohne Umschweife ♦ adj (denial) völlig; (sale) Total-; (winner) unbestritten

outset ['aʊtsɛt] n Beginn m

outside ['aʊt'saɪd] n Außenseite f ♦ adj äußere(r, s), Außen-; (chance) gering ♦ adv außen ♦ prep außerhalb +gen; **at the ~** (fig) maximal; (time) spätestens; **to go ~** nach draußen gehen; **~ lane** n (AUT) äußere Spur f; **~ line** n (TEL) Amtsanschluß m; **~r** n Außenseiter(in) m(f)

outsize ['aʊtsaɪz] adj übergroß

outskirts ['aʊtskɜːts] npl Stadtrand m

outspoken [aʊt'spəʊkən] adj freimütig

outstanding [aʊt'stændɪŋ] adj hervorragend; (debts etc) ausstehend

outstay [aʊt'steɪ] vt: **to ~ one's welcome** länger bleiben als erwünscht

outstretched ['aʊtstrɛtʃt] adj ausgestreckt

outstrip [aʊt'strɪp] vt übertreffen

out-tray ['aʊttreɪ] n Ausgangskorb m

outward ['aʊtwəd] adj äußere(r, s); (journey) Hin-; (freight) ausgehend ♦ adv nach außen; **~ly** adv äußerlich

outweigh [aʊt'weɪ] vt (fig) überwiegen

outwit [aʊt'wɪt] vt überlisten

oval ['əʊvəl] adj oval ♦ n Oval nt

ovary ['əʊvərɪ] n Eierstock m

ovation [əʊ'veɪʃən] n Beifallssturm m

oven ['ʌvn] n Backofen m; **~proof** adj feuerfest

over ['əʊvə*] adv (across) hinüber/ herüber; (finished) vorbei; (left) übrig; *(again)* wieder, noch einmal ♦ *prep* über ♦ *prefix (excessively)* übermäßig; ~ **here** hier(hin); ~ **there** dort(hin); **all** ~ *(everywhere)* überall; *(finished)* vorbei; ~ **and** ~ immer wieder; ~ **and above dar-** über hinaus; **to ask sb** ~ jdn einladen; **to bend** ~ sich bücken

overall [adj. 'əʊvərɔːl, adv əʊvər'ɔːl] *adj (situation)* allgemein; *(length)* Gesamt- ♦ *n (BRIT)* Kittel *m* ♦ *adv* insgesamt; **~s** *npl (for man)* Overall *m*

overawe [əʊvər'ɔː] *vt (frighten)* einschüchtern; *(make impression)* überwältigen

overbalance [əʊvə'bæləns] *vi* Übergewicht bekommen

overbearing [əʊvə'beərɪŋ] *adj* aufdringlich

overboard ['əʊvəbɔːd] *adv* über Bord

overbook [əʊvə'bʊk] *vi* überbuchen

overcast ['əʊvəkɑːst] *adj* bedeckt

overcharge ['əʊvə'tʃɑːdʒ] *vt*: **to ~ sb** von jdm zuviel verlangen

overcoat ['əʊvəkəʊt] *n* Mantel *m*

overcome [əʊvə'kʌm] *(irreg: like come)* *vt* überwinden

overcrowded [əʊvə'kraʊdɪd] *adj* überfüllt

overcrowding [əʊvə'kraʊdɪŋ] *n* Überfüllung *f*

overdo [əʊvə'duː] *(irreg: like do)* *vt (cook too much)* verkochen; *(exaggerate)* übertreiben

overdose ['əʊvədəʊs] *n* Überdosis *f*

overdraft ['əʊvədrɑːft] *n* (Konto)überziehung *f*

overdrawn [əʊvə'drɔːn] *adj (account)* überzogen

overdue ['əʊvə'djuː] *adj* überfällig

overestimate ['əʊvər'estɪmeɪt] *vt* überschätzen

overexcited ['əʊvərɪk'saɪtɪd] *adj* überreizt; *(children)* aufgeregt

overflow [*vb* əʊvə'fləʊ, *n* 'əʊvəfləʊ] *vi* überfließen ♦ *n (excess)* Überschuß *m*; *(also:* ~ *pipe)* Überlaufrohr *nt*

overgrown [əʊvə'grəʊn] *adj (garden)* verwildert

overhaul [*vb* əʊvə'hɔːl, *n* 'əʊvəhɔːl] *vt (car)* überholen; *(plans)* überprüfen ♦ *n* Überholung *f*

overhead [*adv* əʊvə'hed, *adj, n* 'əʊvəhed] *adv* oben ♦ *adj* Hoch-; *(wire)* oberirdisch; *(lighting)* Decken- ♦ *n (US)* = **overheads**; **~s** *npl (costs)* allgemeine Unkosten *pl*

overhear [əʊvə'hɪə*] *vt (like hear)* *vt (mit an)*hören

overheat [əʊvə'hiːt] *vi (engine)* heiß laufen

overjoyed [əʊvə'dʒɔɪd] *adj* überglücklich

overkill ['əʊvəkɪl] *n (fig)* Rundumschlag *m*

overland [*adj* 'əʊvəlænd, *adv* əʊvə'lænd] *adj* Überland- ♦ *adv (trav- el)* über Land

overlap [*vb* əʊvə'læp, *n* 'əʊvəlæp] *vi* sich überschneiden; *(objects)* sich teilweise decken ♦ *n* Überschneidung *f*

overleaf [əʊvə'liːf] *adv* umseitig

overload ['əʊvə'ləʊd] *vt* überladen

overlook [əʊvə'lʊk] *vt (view from above)* überblicken; *(not notice)* übersehen; *(pardon)* hinwegsehen über +*acc*

overnight [*adv* 'əʊvə'naɪt, *adj* 'əʊvənaɪt] *adv* über Nacht ♦ *adj (journey)* Nacht-; ~ **stay** Übernachtung *f*; **to stay** ~ übernachten

overpass ['əʊvəpɑːs] *n* Überführung *f*

overpower [əʊvə'paʊə*] *vt* überwältigen; **~ing** *adj* überwältigend

overrate [əʊvə'reɪt] *vt* überschätzen

override [əʊvə'raɪd] *(irreg: like ride)* *vt (order, decision)* aufheben; *(objection)* übergehen; **overriding** [əʊvə'raɪdɪŋ] *adj* vorherrschend

overrule [əʊvə'ruːl] *vt* verwerfen

overrun [əʊvə'rʌn] *(irreg: like run)* *vt (country)* einfallen in; *(time limit)* überziehen

overseas ['əuvə'si:z] adv nach/in Übersee ♦ adj überseeisch

overseer ['əuvəsiə*] n Aufseher m

overshadow [əuvə'ʃædəu] vt überschatten

overshoot [əuvə'ʃu:t] (irreg: like shoot) vt (runway) hinausschießen über +acc

oversight ['əuvəsait] n (mistake) Versehen nt

oversleep ['əuvə'sli:p] (irreg: like sleep) vi verschlafen

overspill ['əuvəspil] n (Bevölkerungs)überschuß m

overstate ['əuvə'steit] vt übertreiben

overstep ['əuvə'step] vt: to ~ the mark zu weit gehen

overt [əu'vз:t] adj offen(kundig)

overtake [əuvə'teik] (irreg: like take) vt, vi überholen

overthrow [əuvə'θrəu] (irreg: like throw) vt (POL) stürzen

overtime ['əuvətaim] n Überstunden pl

overtone ['əuvətəun] n (fig) Note f

overture ['əuvətjuə*] n Ouvertüre f

overturn [əuvə'tз:n] vt, vi umkippen

overweight ['əuvə'weit] adj zu dick

overwhelm [əuvə'welm] vt überwältigen; **~ing** adj überwältigend

overwork ['əuvə'wз:k] n Überarbeitung f ♦ vt überlasten ♦ vi sich überarbeiten

overwrought ['əuvə'rɔ:t] adj überreizt

owe [əu] vt schulden; to ~ sth to sb (money) jdm etw schulden; (favour etc) jdm etw verdanken

owing to ['əuiŋ-] prep wegen +gen

owl [aul] n Eule f

own [əun] vt besitzen ♦ adj eigen; a room of my ~ mein eigenes Zimmer; to get one's ~ back sich rächen; on one's ~ allein; to ~ up: to ~ up (to sth) (etw) zugeben; ~er n Besitzer(in) m(f); ~ership n Besitz m

ox [ɔks] (pl oxen) n Ochse m

oxen ['ɔksn] npl of ox

oxtail ['ɔksteil] n: ~ soup Ochsen-

schwanzsuppe f

oxygen ['ɔksidʒən] n Sauerstoff m; ~ mask n Sauerstoffmaske f; ~ tent n Sauerstoffzelt nt

oyster ['ɔistə*] n Auster f

oz. abbr = **ounce(s)**

ozone ['əuzəun] n Ozon nt; ~-friendly adj (aerosol) ohne Treibgas; (fridge) FCKW-frei; ~ hole n Ozonloch nt; ~ layer n Ozonschicht f

P

p [pi:] abbr = **penny; pence**

pa [pɑ:] (inf) n Papa m

P.A. n abbr = **personal assistant; public address system**

p.a. abbr = **per annum**

pace [peis] n Schritt m; (speed) Tempo nt ♦ vi schreiten; to keep ~ with Schritt halten mit; ~-maker n Schrittmacher m

pacific [pə'sifik] adj pazifisch ♦ n: the P~ (Ocean) der Pazifik

pacifist ['pæsifist] n Pazifist m

pacify ['pæsifai] vt befrieden; (calm) beruhigen

pack [pæk] n (of goods) Packung f; (of hounds) Meute f; (of cards) Spiel nt; (gang) Bande f ♦ vt (case) packen; (clothes) einpacken ♦ vi packen; to ~ sb off to ... jdn nach ... schicken; ~ it in! laß es gut sein!

package ['pækidʒ] n Paket nt; ~ tour n Pauschalreise f

packed lunch ['pækt-] n Lunchpaket nt

packet ['pækit] n Päckchen nt

packing ['pækiŋ] n (action) Packen nt; (material) Verpackung f; ~ case n (Pack)kiste f

pact [pækt] n Pakt m, Vertrag m

pad [pæd] n (of paper) (Schreib)block m; (stuffing) Polster nt ♦ vt polstern; ~ding n Polsterung f

paddle ['pædl] n Paddel nt; (US: for table tennis) Schläger m ♦ vt (boat) paddeln ♦ vi (in sea) planschen; ~ steamer n Raddampfer m

paddling pool ['pædlɪŋ-] (BRIT) n Planschbecken nt

paddock ['pædək] n Koppel f

paddy field ['pædɪ-] n Reisfeld nt

padlock ['pædlɒk] n Vorhängeschloß nt ♦ vt verschließen

paediatrics [pi:dɪ'ætrɪks] (US **pediatrics**) n Kinderheilkunde f

pagan ['peɪgən] adj heidnisch ♦ n Heide m, Heidin f

page [peɪdʒ] n Seite f; (person) Page m ♦ vt (in hotel etc) ausrufen lassen

pageant ['pædʒənt] n Festzug m; ~ry n Gepränge nt

pager ['peɪdʒə*] n (TEL) Funkrufempfänger m, Piepser m (inf)

paging device ['peɪdʒɪŋ-] n (TEL) = pager

paid [peɪd] pt, pp of **pay** ♦ adj bezahlt; to put ~ to (BRIT) zunichte machen

pail [peɪl] n Eimer m

pain [peɪn] n Schmerz m; to be in ~ Schmerzen haben; on ~ of death bei Todesstrafe; to take ~s to do sth sich dat Mühe geben, etw zu tun; ~ed adj (expression) gequält; ~ful adj (physically) schmerzhaft; (embarrassing) peinlich; (difficult) mühsam; ~fully adv (fig: very) schrecklich; ~killer n Schmerzmittel nt; ~less adj schmerzlos; ~staking ['peɪnzteɪkɪŋ] adj gewissenhaft

paint [peɪnt] n Farbe f ♦ vt anstreichen; (picture) malen; to ~ the door blue die Tür blau streichen; ~brush n Pinsel m; ~er n Maler m; ~ing n Malerei f; (picture) Gemälde nt; ~work n Anstrich m; (of car) Lack m

pair [peə*] n Paar nt; ~ of scissors Schere f; ~ of trousers Hose f

pajamas [pə'dʒɑːməz] (US) npl Schlafanzug m

Pakistan [pɑːkɪ'stɑːn] n Pakistan nt; ~i adj pakistanisch ♦ n Pakistani m/f

pal [pæl] (inf) n Kumpel m

palace ['pæləs] n Palast m, Schloß nt

palatable ['pælətəbl] adj schmackhaft

palate ['pælɪt] n Gaumen m

palatial [pə'leɪʃəl] adj palastartig

pale [peɪl] adj blaß, bleich ♦ n: to be beyond the ~ die Grenzen überschreiten

Palestine ['pælɪstaɪn] n Palästina nt

Palestinian [pælɪs'tɪnɪən] adj palästinensisch ♦ n Palästinenser(in) m(f)

palette ['pælɪt] n Palette f

paling ['peɪlɪŋ] n (stake) Zaunpfahl m; (fence) Lattenzaun m

pall [pɔːl] n (of smoke) (Rauch)wolke f ♦ vi jeden Reiz verlieren, verblassen

pallet ['pælɪt] n (for goods) Palette f

pallid ['pælɪd] adj blaß, bleich

pallor ['pælə*] n Blässe f

palm [pɑːm] n (of hand) Handfläche f; (also: ~ tree) Palme f ♦ vt: to ~ sth off on sb jdm etw andrehen; P~ **Sunday** n Palmsonntag m

palpable ['pælpəbl] adj (also fig) greifbar

palpitation [pælpɪ'teɪʃən] n Herzklopfen nt

paltry ['pɔːltrɪ] adj armselig

pamper ['pæmpə*] vt verhätscheln

pamphlet ['pæmflət] n Broschüre f

pan [pæn] n Pfanne f ♦ vi (CINE) schwenken

panacea [pænə'sɪə] n (fig) Allheilmittel nt

panache [pə'næʃ] n Schwung m

pancake ['pænkeɪk] n Pfannkuchen m

pancreas ['pæŋkrɪəs] n Bauchspeicheldrüse f

panda ['pændə] n Panda m; ~ **car** (BRIT) n (Funk)streifenwagen m

pandemonium [pændɪ'məʊnɪəm] n Hölle f; (noise) Höllenlärm m

pander ['pændə*] vi: to ~ to sich richten nach

pane [peɪn] n (Fenster)scheibe f

panel ['pænl] n (of wood) Tafel f; (TV) Diskussionsrunde f; ~ling (US **paneling**) n Täfelung f

pang [pæŋ] n: ~s of hunger quälende(r) Hunger m; ~s of conscience Gewissensbisse pl

panic ['pænɪk] n Panik f ♦ vi in Panik geraten; **don't ~** (nur) keine Panik; **~ky** adj überängstlich; **~-stricken** adj von panischem Schrecken erfaßt; (look) panisch

pansy ['pænzɪ] n (flower) Stiefmütterchen nt; (inf) Schwule(r) m

pant [pænt] vi keuchen; (dog) hecheln

panther ['pænθə*] n Panther m

panties ['pæntɪz] npl (Damen)slip m

pantihose ['pæntɪhəuz] (US) n Strumpfhose f

pantomime ['pæntəmaɪm] (BRIT) n Märchenkomödie f um Weihnachten

pantry ['pæntrɪ] n Vorratskammer f

pants [pænts] npl (BRIT: woman's) Schlüpfer m; (: man's) Unterhose f; (US: trousers) Hose f

papal ['peɪpəl] adj päpstlich

paper ['peɪpə*] n Papier nt; (news-) Zeitung f; (essay) Referat nt ♦ adj Papier-, aus Papier ♦ vt (wall) tapezieren; **~s** npl (identity ~s) Ausweis(papiere pl) m; **~back** n Taschenbuch nt; **~ bag** n Tüte f; **~ clip** n Büroklammer f; **~ hankie** n Tempotaschentuch nt ®; **~weight** n Briefbeschwerer m; **~work** n Schreibarbeit f

par [pɑ:*] n (COMM) Nennwert m; (GOLF) Par nt; **on a ~ with** ebenbürtig +dat

parable ['pærəbl] n (REL) Gleichnis nt

parachute ['pærəʃu:t] n Fallschirm m ♦ vi (mit dem Fallschirm) abspringen

parade [pə'reɪd] n Parade f ♦ vt aufmarschieren lassen; (fig) zur Schau stellen ♦ vi paradieren, vorbeimarschieren

paradise ['pærədaɪs] n Paradies nt

paradox ['pærədɔks] n Paradox nt; **~ically** [pærə'dɔksɪkəlɪ] adv paradoxerweise

paraffin ['pærəfɪn] (BRIT) n Paraffin nt

paragon ['pærəgən] n Muster nt

paragraph ['pærəgrɑ:f] n Absatz m

parallel ['pærəlel] adj parallel ♦ n Parallele f

paralyse ['pærəlaɪz] (BRIT) vt (MED) lähmen, paralysieren; (fig: organization, production etc) lahmlegen

paralysis [pə'rælɪsɪs] n Lähmung f

paralyze ['pærəlaɪz] vt lähmen

parameter [pə'ræmɪtə*] n Parameter m; **~s** npl (framework, limits) Rahmen m

paramount ['pærəmaunt] adj höchste(r, s), oberste(r, s)

paranoid ['pærənɔɪd] adj (person) paranoid, an Verfolgungswahn leidend; (feeling) krankhaft

parapet ['pærəpɪt] n Brüstung f

paraphernalia ['pærəfə'neɪlɪə] n Zubehör nt, Utensilien pl

paraphrase ['pærəfreɪz] vt umschreiben

paraplegic [pærə'pli:dʒɪk] n Querschnittsgelähmte(r) mf

parasite ['pærəsaɪt] n (also fig) Schmarotzer m, Parasit m

parasol ['pærəsɔl] n Sonnenschirm m

paratrooper ['pærətru:pə*] n Fallschirmjäger m

parcel ['pɑ:sl] n Paket nt ♦ vt (also: ~ up) einpacken

parch [pɑ:tʃ] vt (aus)dörren; **~ed** adj ausgetrocknet; (person) am Verdursten

parchment ['pɑ:tʃmənt] n Pergament nt

pardon ['pɑ:dn] n Verzeihung f ♦ vt (JUR) begnadigen; **~ me!; I beg your ~!** verzeihen Sie bitte!; (US) **~ me?** wie bitte?; **(I beg your) ~?** wie bitte?; **(US) ~?** (I beg you) ~? wie bitte?

parent ['pɛərənt] n Elternteil m; **~s** npl (mother and father) Eltern pl; **~al** [pə'rentl] adj elterlich, Eltern-

parentheses [pə'renθɪsi:z] npl of parenthesis

parenthesis [pə'renθɪsɪs] n Klammer f; (sentence) Parenthese f

Paris ['pærɪs] n Paris nt

parish ['pærɪʃ] n Gemeinde f

parity ['pærɪtɪ] n (FIN) Umrechnungskurs m, Parität f

park [pɑːk] n Park m ♦ vt, vi parken

parking ['pɑːkɪŋ] n Parken nt; "no ~" „Parken verboten"; ~ **lot** (US) n Parkplatz m; ~ **meter** n Parkuhr f; ~ **ticket** n Strafzettel m

parlance ['pɑːləns] n Sprachgebrauch m

parliament ['pɑːləmənt] n Parlament nt; ~**ary** [pɑːlə'mentərɪ] adj parlamentarisch, Parlaments-

parlour ['pɑːlə*] (US **parlor**) n Salon m

parochial [pə'rəukɪəl] adj Gemeinde-; (narrow-minded) eng(stirnig)

parole [pə'rəul] n: **on** ~ (prisoner) auf Bewährung

paroxysm ['pærəksɪzəm] n Anfall m

parrot ['pærət] n Papagei m

parry ['pærɪ] vt parieren, abwehren

parsimonious [pɑːsɪ'məunɪəs] adj knauserig

parsley ['pɑːslɪ] n Petersilie f

parsnip ['pɑːsnɪp] n Pastinake f

parson ['pɑːsn] n Pfarrer m

part [pɑːt] n (piece) Teil m; (THEAT) Rolle f; (of machine) Teil nt ♦ adv = **partly** ♦ vt trennen; (hair) scheiteln ♦ vi (people) sich trennen; **to take** ~ **in** teilnehmen an +dat; **to take sth in good** ~ etw nicht übelnehmen; **to take sb's** ~ sich auf jds Seite acc stellen; **for my** ~ ich für meinen Teil; **for the most** ~ meistens, größtenteils; **in** ~ exchange (BRIT) in Zahlung; ~ **with** vt fus hergeben; (renounce) aufgeben; ~**ial** ['pɑːʃəl] adj (incomplete) teilweise; (biased) parteiisch; **to be** ~**ial to** eine (besondere) Vorliebe haben für

participant [pɑː'tɪsɪpənt] n Teilnehmer(in) m(f)

participate [pɑː'tɪsɪpeɪt] vi: **to** ~ (**in**) teilnehmen (an +dat)

participation [pɑːtɪsɪ'peɪʃən] n Teilnahme f; (sharing) Beteiligung f

participle ['pɑːtɪsɪpl] n Partizip nt

particle ['pɑːtɪkl] n Teilchen nt;

(GRAM) Partikel m

particular [pə'tɪkjələ*] adj bestimmt; (exact) genau; (fussy) eigen; in ~ besonders; ~**ly** adv besonders; ~**s** npl (details) Einzelheiten pl; (of person) Personalien pl

parting ['pɑːtɪŋ] n (separation) Abschied m; (BRIT: of hair) Scheitel m ♦ adj Abschieds-

partition [pɑː'tɪʃən] n (wall) Trennwand f; (division) Teilung f ♦ vt aufteilen

partly ['pɑːtlɪ] adv zum Teil, teilweise

partner ['pɑːtnə*] n Partner m ♦ vt der Partner sein von; ~**ship** n Partnerschaft f; (COMM) Teilhaberschaft f

partridge ['pɑːtrɪdʒ] n Rebhuhn n

part-time ['pɑːt'taɪm] adj Teilzeit- ♦ adv stundenweise

party ['pɑːtɪ] n (POL, JUR) Partei f; (group) Gesellschaft f; (celebration) Party f ♦ adj (dress) Party-; (politics) Partei-; ~ **line** n (TEL) Gemeinschaftsanschluß m

pass [pɑːs] vt (on foot) vorbeigehen an +dat; (driving) vorbeifahren an +dat; (surpass) übersteigen; (hand on) weitergeben; (approve) verabschieden; (time) verbringen; (exam) bestehen ♦ vi (go by) vorbeigehen, vorbeifahren; (years) vergehen; (be successful) bestehen ♦ n (in mountains, SPORT) Paß m; (permission) Passierschein m (in exam): **to get a** ~ bestehen; **to** ~ **sth through sth** etw durch etw führen; **to make a** ~ **at sb** (inf) bei jdm Annäherungsversuche machen; ~ **away** vi (euph) verscheiden; ~ **by** vi vorbeigehen; vorbeifahren; (years) vergehen; ~ **for** vt fus gehalten werden für; ~ **on** vt weitergeben; ~ **out** vi (faint) ohnmächtig werden; ~ **up** vt vorbeigehen lassen; ~**able** adj (road) passierbar; (fairly good) passabel

passage ['pæsɪdʒ] n (corridor) Gang m; (in book) (Text)stelle f; (voyage)

Überfahrt f; **~way** n Durchgang m

passbook ['pɑːsbʊk] n Sparbuch n

passenger ['pæsɪndʒə*] n Passagier m; (on bus) Fahrgast m

passer-by ['pɑːsə'baɪ] n Passant(in) m(f)

passing ['pɑːsɪŋ] adj (car) vorbeifahrend; (thought, affair) momentan ♦ n: **in ~** en passant; **~ place** n (AUT) Ausweichstelle f

passion ['pæʃən] n Leidenschaft f; **~ate** adj leidenschaftlich

passive ['pæsɪv] adj passiv; (LING) passivisch; **~ smoking** n passives Rauchen nt

Passover ['pɑːsəʊvə*] n Passahfest nt

passport ['pɑːspɔːt] n (Reise)paß m; **~ control** n Paßkontrolle f

password ['pɑːswɜːd] n Parole f, Kennwort nt, Losung f

past [pɑːst] prep (motion) an +dat ... vorbei; (position) hinter +dat; (later than) nach ♦ adj (years) vergangen; (president etc) ehemalig ♦ n Vergangenheit f; **he's ~ forty** er ist über vierzig; **for the ~ few/3 days** in den letzten paar/3 Tagen; **to run ~** vorbeilaufen; **ten/quarter ~ eight** zehn/viertel nach acht

pasta ['pæstə] n Teigwaren pl

paste [peɪst] n (fish ~ etc) Paste f; (glue) Kleister m ♦ vt kleben; (put ~ on) mit Kleister bestreichen

pasteurized ['pæstəraɪzd] adj pasteurisiert

pastime ['pɑːstaɪm] n Zeitvertreib m

pastor ['pɑːstə*] n Pfarrer m

pastry ['peɪstrɪ] n Blätterteig m; **pastries** npl (tarts etc) Stückchen pl

pasture ['pɑːstʃə*] n Weide f

pasty [n 'pæstɪ, adj 'peɪstɪ] n (Fleisch)pastete f ♦ adj bläßlich, käsig

pat [pæt] n leichte(r) Schlag m, Klaps m ♦ vt tätscheln

patch [pætʃ] n Fleck m ♦ vt flicken; (to go through) **a bad ~** eine Pechsträhne (haben); **~ up** vt flicken;

(quarrel) beilegen; **~y** adj (irregular) ungleichmäßig

pâté ['pæteɪ] n Pastete f

patent ['peɪtənt] n Patent nt ♦ vt patentieren lassen; (by authorities) patentieren ♦ adj offenkundig; **~ leather** n Lackleder nt

paternal [pə'tɜːnl] adj väterlich

paternity [pə'tɜːnɪtɪ] n Vaterschaft f

path [pɑːθ] n Pfad m; Weg m; (of the sun) Bahn f

pathetic [pə'θetɪk] adj (very bad) kläglich

pathological [pæθə'lɒdʒɪkl] adj pathologisch

pathology [pə'θɒlədʒɪ] n Pathologie f

pathos ['peɪθɒs] n Rührseligkeit f

pathway ['pɑːθweɪ] n Weg m

patience ['peɪʃəns] n Geduld f; (BRIT: CARDS) Patience f

patient ['peɪʃənt] n Patient(in) m(f), Kranke(r) mf ♦ adj geduldig

patio ['pætɪəʊ] n Terrasse f

patriotic [pætrɪ'ɒtɪk] adj patriotisch

patrol [pə'trəʊl] n Patrouille f; (police) Streife f ♦ vt patrouillieren in +dat ♦ vi (police) die Runde machen; (MIL) patrouillieren; **~ car** n Streifenwagen m; **~man** n (US; irreg) n (Streifen)polizist m

patron ['peɪtrən] n (in shop) (Stamm)kunde m; (in hotel) (Stamm)gast m; (supporter) Förderer m; **~ of the arts** Mäzen m; **~age** ['pætrənɪdʒ] n Schirmherrschaft f; **~ize** ['pætrənaɪz] vt (support) unterstützen; (shop) besuchen; (treat condescendingly) von oben herab behandeln; **~ saint** n Schutzpatron(in) m(f)

patter ['pætə*] n (sound: of feet) Trappeln nt; (: of rain) Prasseln nt; (sales talk) Gerede nt ♦ vi (feet) trappeln; (rain) prasseln

pattern ['pætən] n Muster nt; (SEWING) Schnittmuster nt; (KNITTING) Strickanleitung f

paunch [pɔːntʃ] n Wanst m

pauper ['pɔːpə*] n Arme(r) m

pause [pɔːz] n Pause f ♦ vi innehalten

pave [peɪv] vt pflastern; **to ~ the way for** den Weg bahnen für

pavement ['peɪvmənt] n (BRIT) Bürgersteig m

pavilion [pə'vɪlɪən] n Pavillon m; (SPORT) Klubhaus nt

paving ['peɪvɪŋ] n Straßenpflaster nt; **~ stone** n Pflasterstein m

paw [pɔː] n Pfote f; (of big cats) Tatze f, Pranke f ♦ vt (scrape) scharren; (handle) betatschen

pawn [pɔːn] n Pfand nt; (chess) Bauer m ♦ vt verpfänden; **~broker** n Pfandleiher m; **~shop** n Pfandhaus nt

pay [peɪ] (pt, pp **paid**) n Bezahlung f, Lohn m ♦ vt bezahlen ♦ vi zahlen; (be profitable) sich bezahlt machen; **to ~ attention (to)** achtgeben (auf +acc); **to ~ sb a visit** jdn besuchen; **~ back** vt zurückzahlen; **~ for** vt fus bezahlen; **~ in** vt einzahlen; **~ off** vt abzahlen ♦ vi (scheme, decision) sich bezahlt machen; **~ up** vi bezahlen; **~able** adj zahlbar, fällig; **~ee** [peɪ'iː] n Zahlungsempfänger m; **~ envelope** (US) n Lohntüte f; **~ment** n Bezahlung f; **advance ~ment** Vorauszahlung f; **monthly ~ment** monatliche Rate f; **~ packet** (BRIT) n Lohntüte f; **~ phone** n Münzfernsprecher m; **~roll** n Lohnliste f; **~ slip** n Lohn-/Gehaltsstreifen m; **~ television** n Münzfernsehen nt

PC n abbr = **personal computer**

p.c. abbr = **per cent**

pea [piː] n Erbse f

peace [piːs] n Friede(n) m; **~able** adj friedlich; **~ful** adj friedlich, ruhig; **~-keeping** adj Friedens-

peach [piːtʃ] n Pfirsich m

peacock ['piːkɔk] n Pfau m

peak [piːk] n Spitze f; (of mountain) Gipfel m; (fig) Höhepunkt m; **~ hours** npl (traffic) Hauptverkehrszeit f; (telephone, electricity) Hauptbelastungszeit f; **~ period** n Stoßzeit f, Hauptzeit f

peal [piːl] n (Glocken)läuten nt; **~s of laughter** schallende(s) Gelächter nt

peanut ['piːnʌt] n Erdnuß f; **~ butter** n Erdnußbutter f

pear [peə*] n Birne f

pearl [pɜːl] n Perle f

peasant ['pezənt] n Bauer m

peat [piːt] n Torf m

pebble ['pebl] n Kiesel m

peck [pek] vt, vi picken ♦ n (with beak) Schnabelhieb m; (kiss) flüchtige(r) Kuß m; **~ing order** n Hackordnung f; **~ish** (BRIT: inf) adj ein bißchen hungrig

peculiar [pɪ'kjuːlɪə*] adj (odd) seltsam; **~ to** charakteristisch für; **~ity** [pɪkjuːlɪ'ærɪt] n (singular quality) Besonderheit f; (strangeness) Eigenartigkeit f

pedal ['pedl] n Pedal nt ♦ vt, vi (cycle) fahren, radfahren

pedantic [pɪ'dæntɪk] adj pedantisch

peddle ['pedlə*] n Hausierer (in) m(f); (of drugs) Drogenhändler(in) m(f)

pedestal ['pedɪstl] n Sockel m

pedestrian [pɪ'destrɪən] n Fußgänger m ♦ adj Fußgänger-; (humdrum) langweilig; **~ crossing** (BRIT) n Fußgängerüberweg m

pediatrics [piːdɪ'ætrɪks] (US) n = **paediatrics**

pedigree ['pedɪgriː] n Stammbaum m ♦ cpd (animal) reinrassig, Zucht-

pedlar ['pedlə*] n = **peddler**

pee [piː] (inf) vi pissen, pinkeln

peek [piːk] vi gucken

peel [piːl] n Schale f ♦ vt schälen ♦ vi (paint etc) abblättern; (skin) sich schälen

peep [piːp] n (BRIT: look) kurze(r) Blick m; (sound) Piepsen nt ♦ vi (BRIT: look) gucken; **~ out** vi herausgucken; **~hole** n Guckloch nt

peer [pɪə*] vi starren; (peep) gucken ♦ n (nobleman) Peer m; (equal) Ebenbürtige(r) m; **~age** n Peerswürde f

peeved [piːvd] adj ärgerlich; (person) sauer

peevish ['pi:vɪʃ] adj verdrießlich

peg [peg] n (stake) Pflock m; (BRIT: also: clothes ~) Wäscheklammer f

Peking [pi:'kɪŋ] n Peking nt

pelican ['pelɪkən] n Pelikan m; ~ **crossing** (BRIT) n (AUT) Ampelüberweg m

pellet ['pelɪt] n Kügelchen nt

pelmet ['pelmɪt] n Blende f

pelt [pelt] vt bewerfen ♦ vi (rain) schütten ♦ n Pelz m, Fell nt

pelvis ['pelvɪs] n Becken nt

pen [pen] n (fountain ~) Federhalter m; (ball-point ~) Kuli m; (for sheep) Pferch m

penal ['pi:nl] adj Straf-; ~**ize** vt (punish) bestrafen; (disadvantage) benachteiligen; ~**ty** ['penltɪ] n Strafe f; (FOOTBALL) Elfmeter m; ~**ty (kick)** n Elfmeter m

penance ['penəns] n Buße f

pence [pens] (BRIT) npl of penny

pencil ['pensl] n Bleistift m; ~ **case** n Federmäppchen nt; ~ **sharpener** n Bleistiftspitzer m

pendant ['pendənt] n Anhänger m

pending ['pendɪŋ] prep bis (zu) ♦ adj unentschieden, noch offen

pendulum ['pendjʊləm] n Pendel nt

penetrate ['penɪtreɪt] vt durchdringen; (enter into) eindringen in +acc

penetration [penɪ'treɪʃən] n Durchdringen nt; Eindringen n

penfriend ['penfrend] (BRIT) n Brieffreund(in) m(f)

penguin ['pengwɪn] n Pinguin m

penicillin [penɪ'sɪlɪn] n Penizillin nt

peninsula [pɪ'nɪnsjʊlə] n Halbinsel f

penis ['pi:nɪs] n Penis m

penitence ['penɪtəns] n Reue f

penitent ['penɪtənt] adj reuig

penitentiary [penɪ'tenʃərɪ] (US) n Zuchthaus nt

penknife ['pennaɪf] n Federmesser nt

pen name n Pseudonym nt

penniless ['penɪlɪs] adj mittellos

penny ['penɪ] (pl **pennies** or BRIT **pence**) n Penny m; (US) Centstück

nt

penpal ['penpæl] n Brieffreund(in) m(f)

pension ['penʃən] n Rente f; ~**er** (BRIT) n Rentner(in) m(f); ~ **fund** n Rentenfonds m

pensive ['pensɪv] adj nachdenklich

Pentecost ['pentɪkɒst] n Pfingsten pl or nt

penthouse ['penthaʊs] n Dachterrassenwohnung f

pent-up ['pentʌp] adj (feelings) angestaut

penultimate [pɪ'nʌltɪmət] adj vorletzte(r, s)

people ['pi:pl] n (nation) Volk nt ♦ npl (persons) Leute pl; (inhabitants) Bevölkerung f ♦ vt besiedeln; several ~ came mehrere Leute kamen; ~ say that ... man sagt, daß ...

pep [pep] (inf) n Schwung m, Schmiß m; ~ **up** vt aufmöbeln

pepper ['pepə*] n Pfeffer m; (vegetable) Paprika m ♦ vt (pelt) bombardieren; ~**mint** n (plant) Pfefferminze f; (sweet) Pfefferminz nt

peptalk ['pepto:k] (inf) n Anstachelung f

per [pɜ:*] prep pro; ~ **day/person** pro Tag/Person; ~ **annum** adv pro Jahr; ~ **capita** adj (income) Pro-Kopf- ♦ adv pro Kopf

perceive [pə'si:v] vt (realize) wahrnehmen; (understand) verstehen

per cent [pə'sent] n Prozent nt

percentage [pə'sentɪdʒ] n Prozentsatz m

perception [pə'sepʃən] n Wahrnehmung f; (insight) Einsicht f

perceptive [pə'septɪv] adj (person) aufmerksam; (analysis) tiefgehend

perch [pɜ:tʃ] n Stange f; (fish) Flußbarsch m ♦ vi sitzen, hocken

percolator ['pɜ:kəleɪtə*] n Kaffeemaschine f

percussion [pə'kʌʃən] n (MUS) Schlagzeug nt

peremptory [pə'remptərɪ] adj schroff

perennial [pə'renɪəl] adj wiederkehrend; (*everlasting*) unvergänglich

perfect [*adj*, *n* 'pɜ:fɪkt, *vb* pə'fekt] *adj* vollkommen; (*crime, solution*) perfekt ♦ *vt* (*GRAM*) Perfekt *nt* ♦ *vt* vervollkommnen; ~**ion** [pə'fekʃən] *n* Vollkommenheit *f*; ~**ionist** [pə'fekʃənɪst] *n* Perfektionist *m*; ~**ly** *adv* vollkommen, perfekt; (*quite*) ganz, einfach

perforate ['pɜ:fəreɪt] *vt* durchlöchern

perforation [pɜ:fə'reɪʃən] *n* Perforieren *nt*; (*line of holes*) Perforation *f*

perform [pə'fɔ:m] *vt* (*carry out*) durch- or ausführen; (*task*) verrichten; (*THEAT etc*) spielen, geben ♦ *vi* auftreten; ~**ance** *n* Durchführung *f*; (*efficiency*) Leistung *f*; (*show*) Vorstellung *f*; ~**er** *n* Künstler(in) *m(f)*; ~**ing** *adj* (*animal*) dressiert

perfume ['pɜ:fju:m] *n* Duft *m*; (*lady's*) Parfüm *nt*

perfunctory [pə'fʌŋktərɪ] *adj* oberflächlich, mechanisch

perhaps [pə'hæps] *adv* vielleicht

peril ['perɪl] *n* Gefahr *f*

perimeter [pə'rɪmɪtə*] *n* Peripherie *f*; (*of circle etc*) Umfang *m*

period ['pɪərɪəd] *n* Periode *f*; (*GRAM*) Punkt *m*; (*MED*) Periode *f* ♦ *adj* (*costume*) historisch; ~**ic** [pɪərɪ'ɒdɪk] *adj* periodisch; ~**ical** [pɪərɪ'ɒdɪkl] *n* Zeitschrift *f*; ~**ically** [pɪərɪ'ɒdɪklɪ] *adv* periodisch

peripheral [pə'rɪfərəl] *adj* Rand-, peripher ♦ *n* (*COMPUT*) Peripheriegerät *nt*

perish ['perɪʃ] *vi* umkommen; (*fruit*) verderben; ~**able** *adj* leicht verderblich

perjury ['pɜ:dʒərɪ] *n* Meineid *m*

perk [pɜ:k] (*inf*) *n* (*fringe benefit*) Vergünstigung *f*; ~ **up** *vi* munter werden; ~**y** *adj* (*cheerful*) keck

perm [pɜ:m] *n* Dauerwelle *f*

permanent ['pɜ:mənənt] *adj* dauernd, ständig

permeate ['pɜ:mɪeɪt] *vt, vi* durchdringen

permissible [pə'mɪsəbl] *adj* zulässig

permission [pə'mɪʃən] *n* Erlaubnis *f*

permissive [pə'mɪsɪv] *adj* nachgiebig; the ~ **society** die permissive Gesellschaft

permit [*n* 'pɜ:mɪt, *vb* pə'mɪt] *n* Zulassung *f* ♦ *vt* erlauben, zulassen

pernicious [pɜ:'nɪʃəs] *adj* schädlich

perpendicular [pɜ:pən'dɪkjələ*] *adj* senkrecht

perpetrate ['pɜ:pɪtreɪt] *vt* begehen

perpetual [pə'petjʊəl] *adj* dauernd, ständig

perpetuate [pə'petjʊeɪt] *vt* verewigen, bewahren

perplex [pə'pleks] *vt* verblüffen

persecute ['pɜ:sɪkju:t] *vt* verfolgen

persecution [pɜ:sɪ'kju:ʃən] *n* Verfolgung *f*

perseverance [pɜ:sɪ'vɪərəns] *n* Ausdauer *f*

persevere [pɜ:sɪ'vɪə*] *vi* durchhalten

Persian ['pɜ:ʃən] *adj* persisch ♦ *n* Perser(in) *m(f)*; the (**Persian**) Gulf der Persische Golf

persist [pə'sɪst] *vi* (*in belief etc*) bleiben; (*rain, smell*) andauern; (*continue*) nicht aufhören; to ~ **in** bleiben bei; ~**ence** *n* Beharrlichkeit *f*; ~**ent** *adj* beharrlich; (*unending*) ständig

person ['pɜ:sn] *n* Person *f*; **in** ~ persönlich; ~**able** *adj* gut aussehend; ~**al** *adj* persönlich; (*private*) privat; (*of body*) körperlich, Körper-; ~**al assistant** *n* Assistent(in) *m(f)*; ~**al computer** *n* Personalcomputer *m*; ~**ality** [pɜ:sə'nælɪtɪ] *n* Persönlichkeit *f*; ~**ally** *adv* persönlich; ~**al organiser** *n* Terminplaner *m*, Zeitplaner *m*; (*electronic*) elektronisches Notizbuch *nt*; ~**al stereo** *n* Walkman *m* ®; ~**ify** [pɜ:'sɒnɪfaɪ] *vt* verkörpern

personnel [pɜ:sə'nel] *n* Personal *nt*

perspective [pə'spektɪv] *n* Perspektive *f*

Perspex ['pɜ:speks] ® *n* Acrylglas *nt*

perspiration [pɜ:spə'reɪʃən] *n* Transpiration *f*

perspire [pə'spaɪə*] *vi* transpirieren

persuade [pə'sweɪd] *vt* überreden; (*convince*) überzeugen

persuasion [pə'sweɪʒən] n Überredung f; Überzeugung f
persuasive [pə'sweɪsɪv] adj überzeugend
pert [pɜːt] adj keck
pertaining [pɜː'teɪnɪŋ]: ~ **to** prep betreffend +acc
pertinent ['pɜːtɪnənt] adj relevant
perturb [pə'tɜːb] vt beunruhigen
peruse [pə'ruːz] vt lesen
pervade [pə'veɪd] vt erfüllen
perverse [pə'vɜːs] adj pervers; (obstinate) eigensinnig
pervert ['pɜːvɜːt, vb pə'vɜːt] n perverse(r) Mensch m ♦ vt verdrehen; (morally) verderben
pessimist ['pesɪmɪst] n Pessimist m; ~**ic** [pesɪ'mɪstɪk] adj pessimistisch
pest [pest] n (insect) Schädling m; (fig: person) Nervensäge f; (: thing) Plage f
pester ['pestə*] vt plagen
pesticide ['pestɪsaɪd] n Insektenvertilgungsmittel nt
pet [pet] n (animal) Haustier nt ♦ vt liebkosen, streicheln ♦ vi (inf) Petting machen
petal ['petl] n Blütenblatt nt
peter out ['piːtə-] vi allmählich zu Ende gehen
petite [pə'tiːt] adj zierlich
petition [pə'tɪʃən] n Bittschrift f
petrified ['petrɪfaɪd] adj versteinert; (person) starr (vor Schreck)
petrify ['petrɪfaɪ] vt versteinern; (person) erstarren lassen
petrol ['petrəl] (BRIT) n Benzin nt, Kraftstoff m; **two-/four-star** ~ = Normal-/Superbenzin nt; ~ **can** n Benzinkanister m
petroleum [pɪ'trəʊlɪəm] n Petroleum nt
petrol: ~ **pump** (BRIT) n (in car) Benzinpumpe f; (at garage) Zapfsäule f; ~ **station** (BRIT) n Tankstelle f; ~ **tank** (BRIT) n Benzintank m
petticoat ['petɪkəʊt] n Unterrock m
petty ['petɪ] adj (unimportant) unbedeutend; (mean) kleinlich; ~ **cash**

Portokasse f; ~ **officer** n Maat m
petulant ['petjʊlənt] adj leicht reizbar
pew [pjuː] n Kirchenbank f
pewter ['pjuːtə*] n Zinn nt
pharmacist ['fɑːməsɪst] n Pharmazeut m; (druggist) Apotheker m
pharmacy ['fɑːməsɪ] n Pharmazie f; (shop) Apotheke f
phase [feɪz] n Phase f ♦ vt: **to** ~ **sth in/out** etw allmählich einführen; **to** ~ **out** etw auslaufen lassen
Ph.D. n abbr = Doctor of Philosophy
pheasant ['feznt] n Fasan m
phenomena [fɪ'nɒmɪnə] npl of phenomenon
phenomenon [fɪ'nɒmɪnən] n Phänomen nt
philanthropist [fɪ'lænθrəpɪst] n Philanthrop m, Menschenfreund m
Philippines ['fɪlɪpiːnz] npl: **the** ~ die Philippinen pl
philosopher [fɪ'lɒsəfə*] n Philosoph m
philosophical [fɪlə'sɒfɪkl] adj philosophisch
philosophy [fɪ'lɒsəfɪ] n Philosophie f
phlegm [flem] n (MED) Schleim m; (calmness) Gelassenheit f; ~**atic** [fleg'mætɪk] adj gelassen
phobia ['fəʊbjə] n (irrational fear: of insects, flying, water etc) Phobie f
phone [fəʊn] n Telefon nt ♦ vt, vi telefonieren, anrufen; **to be on the** ~ telephonieren; ~ **back** vt, vi zurückrufen; ~ **up** vt, vi anrufen; ~ **book** n Telefonbuch nt; ~ **booth** n Telefonzelle f; ~ **box** n Telefonzelle f; ~ **call** n Telefonanruf m; ~**card** n (TEL) Telefonkarte f; ~-**in** n (RADIO, TV) Phone-in nt
phonetics [fə'netɪks] n Phonetik f
phoney ['fəʊnɪ] (inf) adj unecht ♦ n (person) Schwindler m; (thing) Fälschung f; (banknote) Blüte f
phony ['fəʊnɪ] adj, n = phoney
photo ['fəʊtəʊ] n Foto nt
photocopier ['fəʊtəʊ'kɒpɪə*] n Kopiergerät nt

photocopy ['fəʊtəʊkɒpɪ] n Fotokopie f ♦ vt fotokopieren

photogenic [fəʊtəʊ'dʒenɪk] adj fotogen

photograph ['fəʊtəɡrɑːf] n Fotografie f, Aufnahme f ♦ vt fotografieren; **~er** [fə'tɒɡrəfə*] n Fotograf m; **~ic** ['fəʊtə'ɡræfɪk] adj fotografisch; **~y** [fə'tɒɡrəfɪ] n Fotografie f

phrase [freɪz] n Satz m; (expression) Ausdruck m ♦ vt ausdrücken, formulieren; **~ book** n Sprachführer m

physical ['fɪzɪkəl] adj physikalisch; (bodily) körperlich, physisch; **~ education** n Turnen nt; **~ly** adv physikalisch

physician [fɪ'zɪʃən] n Arzt m

physicist ['fɪzɪsɪst] n Physiker(in) m(f)

physics ['fɪzɪks] n Physik f

physiotherapy [fɪzɪə'θerəpɪ] n Heilgymnastik f, Physiotherapie f

physique [fɪ'ziːk] n Körperbau m

pianist ['pɪənɪst] n Pianist(in) m(f)

piano [pɪ'ænəʊ] n Klavier nt

pick [pɪk] n (tool) Pickel m; (choice) Auswahl f ♦ vt (fruit) pflücken; (choose) aussuchen; **take your ~** such dir etwas aus; **to ~ sb's pocket** jdn bestehlen; **~ off** vt (kill) abschießen; **~ on** vt fus (person) herumhacken auf +dat; **~ out** vt auswählen; **~ up** vi (improve) sich erholen ♦ vt (lift up) aufheben; (learn) (schnell) mitbekommen; (collect) abholen; (girl) sich dat anlachen; (AUT: passenger) mitnehmen; (speed) gewinnen an +dat; **to ~ o.s. up** aufstehen

picket ['pɪkɪt] n (striker) Streikposten m ♦ vt (factory) (Streik)posten aufstellen vor +dat ♦ vi (Streik)posten stehen

pickle ['pɪkl] n (salty mixture) Pökel m; (inf) Klemme f ♦ vt (in Essig) einlegen; einpökeln

pickpocket ['pɪkpɒkɪt] n Taschendieb m

pick-up ['pɪkʌp] n (BRIT: on record player) Tonabnehmer m; (small truck) Lieferwagen m

picnic ['pɪknɪk] n Picknick nt ♦ vi picknicken

pictorial [pɪk'tɔːrɪəl] adj in Bildern

picture ['pɪktʃə*] n Bild nt ♦ vt (visualize) sich dat vorstellen; **the ~s** npl (BRIT) das Kino; **~ book** n Bilderbuch nt

picturesque [pɪktʃə'resk] adj malerisch

pie [paɪ] n (meat) Pastete f; (fruit) Torte f

piece [piːs] n Stück nt ♦ vt: **to ~ together** zusammenstückeln; (fig) sich dat zusammenreimen; **to take to ~s** in Einzelteile zerlegen; **~meal** adv stückweise, Stück für Stück; **~work** n Akkordarbeit f

pie chart n Kreisdiagramm nt

pier [pɪə*] n Pier m, Mole f

pierce [pɪəs] vt durchstechen, durchbohren (also look); **piercing** ['pɪəsɪŋ] adj (cry) durchdringend

piety ['paɪətɪ] n Frömmigkeit f

pig [pɪɡ] n Schwein nt

pigeon ['pɪdʒən] n Taube f; **~hole** n (compartment) Ablegefach nt

piggy bank ['pɪɡɪ-] n Sparschwein nt

pigheaded ['pɪɡ'hedɪd] adj dickköpfig

piglet ['pɪɡlət] n Ferkel nt

pigskin ['pɪɡskɪn] n Schweinsleder nt

pigsty ['pɪɡstaɪ] n (also fig) Schweinestall m

pigtail ['pɪɡteɪl] n Zopf m

pike [paɪk] n Pike f; (fish) Hecht m

pilchard ['pɪltʃəd] n Sardine f

pile [paɪl] n Haufen m; (of books, wood) Stapel m; (in ground) Pfahl m; (on carpet) Flausch m ♦ vt (also: **~ up**) anhäufen ♦ vi sich anhäufen

piles [paɪlz] npl Hämorrhoiden pl

pile-up ['paɪlʌp] n (AUT) Massenzusammenstoß m

pilfering ['pɪlfərɪŋ] n Diebstahl m

pilgrim ['pɪlɡrɪm] n Pilger(in) m(f); **~age** n Wallfahrt f

pill [pɪl] n Tablette f, Pille f; **the ~**

die (Antibaby)pille

pillage ['pɪlɪdʒ] vt plündern

pillar ['pɪlə*] n Pfeiler m, Säule f (also fig); ~ **box** (BRIT) n Briefkasten m

pillion ['pɪljən] n Soziussitz m

pillory ['pɪlərɪ] vt (fig) anprangern

pillow ['pɪləu] n Kissen nt; ~**case** n Kissenbezug m

pilot ['paɪlət] n Pilot m; (NAUT) Lotse m ♦ adj (scheme etc) Versuchs-♦ vt führen; (ship) lotsen; ~ **light** n Zündflamme f

pimp [pɪmp] n Zuhälter m

pimple ['pɪmpl] n Pickel m

pimply ['pɪmplɪ] adj pick(e)lig

pin [pɪn] n Nadel f; (for sewing) Stecknadel f; (TECH) Stift m, Bolzen m ♦ vt stecken; (keep in one position) pressen, drücken; to ~ sth to sth etw an etw acc heften; to ~ sth on sb (fig) jdm etw anhängen; ~s **and needles** Kribbeln n; ~ **down** vt (fig: person): to ~ **sb down** to sth jdn auf etw acc festnageln

pinafore ['pɪnəfɔː*] n Schürze f; ~ **dress** n Kleiderrock m

pinball ['pɪnbɔːl] n Flipper m

pincers ['pɪnsəz] npl Kneif- or Beißzange f; (MED) Pinzette f

pinch [pɪntʃ] n Zwicken nt, Kneifen nt; (of salt) Prise f ♦ vt zwicken, kneifen; (inf: steal) klauen; (: arrest) schnappen ♦ vi (shoe) drücken; at a ~ notfalls, zur Not

pincushion ['pɪnkuʃən] n Nadelkissen nt

pine [paɪn] n (also: ~ **tree**) Kiefer f ♦ vi: to ~ **for** sich sehnen nach; ~ **away** vi sich zu Tode sehnen

pineapple ['paɪnæpl] n Ananas f

ping [pɪŋ] n Klingeln nt; ~**pong** ® n Pingpong nt

pink [pɪŋk] adj rosa inv ♦ n Rosa nt; (BOT) Nelke f

pinnacle ['pɪnəkl] n Spitze f

PIN (number) n Geheimnummer f

pinpoint ['pɪnpɔɪnt] vt festlegen

pinstripe ['pɪnstraɪp] n Nadelstreifen m

pint [paɪnt] n Pint nt; (BRIT: inf: of beer) große(s) Bier nt

pioneer [paɪə'nɪə*] n Pionier m; (fig also) Bahnbrecher m

pious ['paɪəs] adj fromm

pip [pɪp] n Kern m; **the** ~**s** npl (BRIT: time signal on radio) das Zeitzeichen

pipe [paɪp] n (smoking) Pfeife f; (tube) Rohr nt; (in house) (Rohr)leitung f ♦ vt (durch Rohre) leiten; (MUS) blasen; ~**s** npl (also: bagpipes) Dudelsack m; ~ **down** vi (be quiet) die Luft anhalten; ~**cleaner** n Pfeifenreiniger m; ~**dream** n Luftschloß nt; ~**line** n (for oil) Pipeline f; ~**r** n Pfeifer m; (bagpipes) Dudelsackbläser m

piping ['paɪpɪŋ] adv: ~ **hot** siedend heiß

pique [piːk] n gekränkte(r) Stolz m

pirate ['paɪərɪt] n Pirat m, Seeräuber m; ~ **radio** (BRIT) n Piratensender m

Pisces ['paɪsiːz] n Fische pl

piss [pɪs] (inf!) vi pissen; ~**ed** (inf!) adj (drunk) voll

pistol ['pɪstl] n Pistole f

piston ['pɪstən] n Kolben m

pit [pɪt] n Grube f; (THEAT) Parterre nt; (orchestra ~) Orchestergraben m ♦ vt (mark with scars) zerfressen; (compare): to ~ **sb against sb** jdn an jdm messen; **the** ~**s** npl (MOTOR RACING) die Boxen

pitch [pɪtʃ] n Wurf m; (of trader) Stand m; (SPORT) (Spiel)feld nt; (MUS) Tonlage f; (substance) Pech nt ♦ vt werfen; (set up) aufschlagen ♦ vi (NAUT) rollen; to ~ **a tent** ein Zelt aufbauen; ~**black** adj pechschwarz; ~**ed battle** n offene Schlacht f

pitcher ['pɪtʃə*] n Krug m

piteous ['pɪtɪəs] adj kläglich, erbärmlich

pitfall ['pɪtfɔːl] n (fig) Falle f

pith [pɪθ] n Mark nt

pithy ['pɪθɪ] adj prägnant

pitiful ['pɪtɪful] adj (deserving pity)

bedauernswert; (*contemptible*) jämmerlich

pitiless ['pɪtɪləs] *adj* erbarmungslos

pittance ['pɪtəns] *n* Hungerlohn *m*

pity ['pɪtɪ] *n* (*sympathy*) Mitleid *nt* ♦ *vt* Mitleid haben mit; **what a ~!** wie schade!

pivot ['pɪvət] *n* Drehpunkt *m* ♦ *vi*: to ~ (**on**) sich drehen (um)

pixie ['pɪksɪ] *n* Elf *m*, Elfe *f*

pizza ['pɪːtsə] *n* Pizza *f*

placard ['plækɑːd] *n* Plakat *nt*, Anschlag *m*

placate [plə'keɪt] *vt* beschwichtigen

place [pleɪs] *n* Platz *m*; (*spot*) Stelle *f*; (*town etc*) Ort *m* ♦ *vt* setzen, stellen, legen; (*order*) aufgeben; (*SPORT*) plazieren; (*identify*) unterbringen; **to take ~** stattfinden; **out of ~** nicht am rechten Platz; (*fig: remark*) unangebracht; **in the first ~** erstens; **to change ~s with sb** mit jdm den Platz tauschen; **to be ~d third** (*in race, exam*) auf dem dritten Platz liegen

placid ['plæsɪd] *adj* gelassen, ruhig

plagiarism ['pleɪdʒɪərɪzəm] *n* Plagiat *nt*

plague [pleɪg] *n* Pest *f*; (*fig*) Plage *f* ♦ *vt* plagen

plaice [pleɪs] *n* Scholle *f*

plain [pleɪn] *adj* (*clear*) klar, deutlich; (*simple*) einfach, schlicht; (*not beautiful*) alltäglich ♦ *n* Ebene *f*; **in ~ clothes** (*police*) in Zivil(kleidung); ~ **chocolate** *n* Bitterschokolade *f*

plaintiff ['pleɪntɪf] *n* Kläger *m*

plaintive ['pleɪntɪv] *adj* wehleidig

plait [plæt] *n* Zopf *m* ♦ *vt* flechten

plan [plæn] *n* Plan *m* ♦ *vt, vi* planen; **according to ~** planmäßig; **to ~ to do sth** vorhaben, etw zu tun

plane [pleɪn] *n* Ebene *f*; (*AVIAT*) Flugzeug *nt*; (*tool*) Hobel *m*; (*tree*) Platane *f*

planet ['plænɪt] *n* Planet *m*

plank [plæŋk] *n* Brett *nt*

planning ['plænɪŋ] *n* Planung *f*; **family ~** Familienplanung *f*; ~ **per-**

mission *n* Baugenehmigung *f*

plant [plɑːnt] *n* Pflanze *f*; (*TECH*) (Maschinen)anlage *f*; (*factory*) Fabrik *f*, Werk *nt* ♦ *vt* pflanzen; (*set firmly*) stellen

plantation [plæn'teɪʃən] *n* Plantage *f*

plaque [plæk] *n* Gedenktafel *f*; (*on teeth*) (Zahn)belag *m*

plaster ['plɑːstə*] *n* Gips *m*; (*in house*) Verputz *m*; (*BRIT: also: sticking ~*) Pflaster *nt*; (*for fracture:* ~ *of Paris*) Gipsverband *m* ♦ *vt* gipsen; (*hole*) zugipsen; (*ceiling*) verputzen; (*fig: with pictures etc*) bekleben, verkleben; ~**ed** (*inf*) *adj* besoffen; ~**er** *n* Gipser *m*

plastic ['plæstɪk] *n* Plastik *nt or f* ♦ *adj* (*made of* ~) Plastik-; (*ART*) plastisch, bildend; ~ **bag** *n* Plastiktüte *f*

plasticine ['plæstɪsiːn] ® *n* Plastilin *nt*

plastic surgery *n* plastische Chirurgie *f*

plate [pleɪt] *n* Teller *m*; (*gold/silver* ~) vergoldete(s)/versilberte(s) Tafelgeschirr *nt*; (*flat sheet*) Platte *f*; (*in book*) (Bild)tafel *f*

plateau ['plætəʊ] (*pl* ~**s** *or* ~**x**) *n* (*GEO*) Plateau *nt*, Hochebene *f*

plateaux ['plætəʊz] *npl of* plateau

plate glass *n* Tafelglas *nt*

platform ['plætfɔːm] *n* (*at meeting*) Plattform *f*, Podium *nt*; (*RAIL*) Bahnsteig *m*; (*POL*) Parteiprogramm *nt*; ~ **ticket** *n* Bahnsteigkarte *f*

platinum ['plætɪnəm] *n* Platin *nt*

platoon [plə'tuːn] *n* (*MIL*) Zug *m*

platter ['plætə*] *n* Platte *f*

plausible ['plɔːzɪbl] *adj* (*theory, excuse, statement*) plausibel; (*person*) überzeugend

play [pleɪ] *n* (*also TECH*) Spiel *nt*; (*THEAT*) (Theater)stück *nt* ♦ *vt* spielen; (*another team*) spielen gegen ♦ *vi* spielen; **to ~ safe** auf Nummer sicher gehen; ~ **down** *vt* herunterspielen; ~ **up** *vi* (*cause trouble*) frech werden; (*bad leg etc*) weh tun ♦ *vt* (*person*) plagen; **to ~ up to**

sb jdm flattieren; **~-acting** *n* Schauspielerei *f*; **~boy** *n* Playboy *m*; **~er** *n* Spieler(in) *m(f)*; **~ful** *adj* spielerisch; **~ground** *n* Spielplatz *m*; **~group** *n* Kindergarten *m*; **~ing card** *n* Spielkarte *f*; **~ing field** *n* Sportplatz *m*; **~mate** *n* Spielkamerad *m*; **~-off** *n* (SPORT) Entscheidungsspiel *nt*; **~pen** *n* Laufstall *m*; **~school** = playgroup; **~thing** *n* Spielzeug *nt*; **~wright** *n* Theaterschriftsteller *m*

plc *abbr* (= public limited company) AG

plea [pli:] *n* Bitte *f*; (general appeal) Appell *m*; (JUR) Plädoyer *nt*

plead [pli:d] *vt* (poverty) zur Entschuldigung anführen; (JUR: sb's case) vertreten ♦ *vi* (beg) dringend bitten; (JUR) plädieren; **to ~ with sb** jdn dringend bitten

pleasant ['pleznt] *adj* angenehm; **~ness** *n* Angenehme(s) *nt*; (of person) Freundlichkeit *f*; **~ries** *npl* (polite remarks) Nettigkeiten *pl*

please [pli:z] *vt, vi* (be agreeable to) gefallen +*dat*; **~!** bitte!; **~ your-self!** wie du willst!; **~d** *adj* zufrieden; (glad): **~d (about sth)** erfreut (über etw *acc*); **~d to meet you** angenehm

pleasing ['pli:zɪŋ] *adj* erfreulich

pleasure ['pleʒə*] *n* Freude *f*; (old: will) Wünsche *pl* ♦ *cpd* Vergnügungs-; **"it's a ~"** "gern geschehen"

pleat [pli:t] *n* Falte *f*

plectrum ['plektrəm] *n* Plektron *nt*

pledge [pledʒ] *n* Pfand *nt*; (promise) Versprechen *nt* ♦ *vt* verpfänden; (promise) geloben, versprechen

plentiful ['plentifʊl] *adj* reichlich

plenty ['plentɪ] *n* Fülle *f*, Überfluß *m*; **~ of** eine Menge, viel

pleurisy ['plʊərɪsɪ] *n* Rippenfellentzündung *f*

pliable ['plaɪəbl] *adj* biegsam; (person) beeinflußbar

pliers ['plaɪəz] *npl* (Kneif)zange *f*

plight [plaɪt] *n* (Not)lage *f*

plimsolls ['plɪmsəlz] (BRIT) *npl* Turnschuhe *pl*

plinth [plɪnθ] *n* Sockel *m*

plod [plɒd] *vi* (work) sich abplagen; (walk) trotten; **~der** *n* Arbeitstier *nt*

plonk [plɒŋk] *n* (BRIT: inf: wine) billige(r) Wein *m* ♦ *vt*: **to ~ sth down** etw hinknallen

plot [plɒt] *n* Komplott *nt*; (story) Handlung *f*; (of land) Grundstück *nt* ♦ *vt* markieren; (curve) zeichnen; (movements) nachzeichnen ♦ *vi* (plan secretly) sich verschwören; **~ter** *n* (instrument) Plotter *m*

plough [plaʊ] (US plow) *n* Pflug *m* ♦ *vt* pflügen; **~ back** *vt* (COMM) wieder in das Geschäft stecken; **~ through** *vt fus* (water) durchpflügen; (book) sich kämpfen durch

plow [plaʊ] = plough

ploy [plɔɪ] *n* Masche *f*

pluck [plʌk] *vt* (fruit) pflücken; (guitar) zupfen; (goose etc) rupfen ♦ *n* Mut *m*; **to ~ up courage** all seinen Mut zusammennehmen; **~y** *adj* beherzt

plug [plʌg] *n* Stöpsel *m*; (ELEC) Stecker *m*; (inf: publicity) Schleichwerbung *f*; (AUT) Zündkerze *f* ♦ *vt* (zu)stopfen; (inf: advertise) Reklame machen für; **~ in** *vt* (ELEC) anschließen

plum [plʌm] *n* Pflaume *f*, Zwetsch(g)e *f* ♦ *adj* (job etc) Bomben-

plumage ['plu:mɪdʒ] *n* Gefieder *nt*

plumb [plʌm] *adj* senkrecht ♦ *n* Lot *nt* ♦ *adv* (exactly) genau ♦ *vt* ausloten; (fig) sondieren

plumber ['plʌmə*] *n* Klempner *m*, Installateur *m*

plumbing ['plʌmɪŋ] *n* (craft) Installieren *nt*; (fittings) Leitungen *pl*

plume [plu:m] *n* Feder *f*; (of smoke etc) Fahne *f*

plummet ['plʌmɪt] *vi* (ab)stürzen

plump [plʌmp] *adj* rundlich, füllig ♦ *vt* plumpsen lassen; **to ~ for** (inf: choose) sich entscheiden für

plunder ['plʌndə*] *n* Plünderung *f*;

(*loot*) Beute *f* ♦ *vt* plündern

plunge [plʌndʒ] *n* Sturz *m* ♦ *vt* stoßen ♦ *vi* (sich) stürzen; **to take the ~** den Sprung wagen

plunging [plʌndʒɪŋ] *adj* (*neckline*) offenherzig

pluperfect [plu:ˈpɜ:fɪkt] *n* Plusquamperfekt *nt*

plural [ˈpluərəl] *n* Plural *m*, Mehrzahl *f*

plus [plʌs] *n* (*also: ~ sign*) Plus(zeichen) *nt* ♦ *prep* plus, und; **ten/twenty ~** mehr als zehn/zwanzig

plush [plʌʃ] *adj* (*also ~y: inf: luxurious*) feudal

ply [plaɪ] *vt* (*trade*) (be)treiben; (*with questions*) zusetzen +*dat*; (*ship, taxi*) befahren ♦ *vi* verkehren ♦ *n*: **to ~ sb with drink** jdn zum Trinken animieren; **~wood** *n* Sperrholz *nt*

P.M. *n abbr* = Prime Minister

p.m. *adv abbr* (= post meridiem) nachmittags

pneumatic [nju:ˈmætɪk] *adj* pneumatisch; (*TECH*) Luft-; **~ drill** *n* Preßlufthammer *m*

pneumonia [nju:ˈməunɪə] *n* Lungenentzündung *f*

poach [pəutʃ] *vt* (*COOK*) pochieren; (*game*) stehlen ♦ *vi* (*steal*) wildern; **~ed** *adj* (*egg*) verloren; **~er** *n* Wilddieb *m*

P.O. Box *n abbr* = Post Office Box

pocket [ˈpɒkɪt] *n* Tasche *f*; (*of resistance*) (Widerstands)nest *nt* ♦ *vt* einstecken ♦ *vi*; **to be out of** (*BRIT*) draufzahlen; **~book** *n* Taschenbuch *nt*; **~ knife** *n* Taschenmesser *nt*; **~ money** *n* Taschengeld *nt*

pod [pɒd] *n* Hülse *f*; (*of peas also*) Schote *f*

podgy [ˈpɒdʒɪ] *adj* pummelig

podiatrist [pɒˈdi:ətrɪst] (*US*) *n* Fußpfleger(in) *m(f)*

poem [ˈpəuɪm] *n* Gedicht *nt*

poet [ˈpəuɪt] *n* Dichter *m*, Poet *m*; **~ic** [pəuˈetɪk] *adj* poetisch, dichterisch; **~ laureate** *n* Hofdichter *m*; **~ry** *n* Poesie *f*; (*poems*) Gedichte *pl*

poignant [ˈpɔɪnjənt] *adj* (*touching*) ergreifend

point [pɔɪnt] *n* (*also in discussion, scoring*) Punkt *m*; (*spot*) Punkt *m*, Stelle *f*; (*sharpened tip*) Spitze *f*; (*moment*) (Zeit)punkt *m*; (*purpose*) Zweck *m*; (*idea*) Argument *nt*; (*decimal*) Dezimalstelle *f*; (*personal characteristic*) Seite *f* ♦ *vt* zeigen mit; (*gun*) richten ♦ *vi* zeigen; **~s** *npl* (*RAIL*) Weichen *pl*; **to be on the ~ of doing sth** drauf und dran sein, etw zu tun; **to make a ~** of Wert darauf legen; **to get the ~** verstehen, worum es geht; **to come to the ~** zur Sache kommen; **there's no ~ (in doing sth)** es hat keinen Sinn(, etw zu tun); **~ out** *vt* hinweisen auf +*acc*; **~ to** *vt fus* zeigen auf +*acc*; **~-blank** *adv* (*at close range*) aus nächster Entfernung; (*bluntly*) unverblümt; **~ed** *adj* (*also fig*) spitz, scharf; (*fig*) spitz; **~er** *n* Zeigestock *m*; (*on dial*) Zeiger *m*; **~less** *adj* sinnlos; **~ of view** *n* Stand- or Gesichtspunkt *m*

poise [pɔɪz] *n* Haltung *f*; (*fig*) Gelassenheit *f*

poison [ˈpɔɪzn] *n* (*also fig*) Gift *nt* ♦ *vt* vergiften; **~ing** *n* Vergiftung *f*; **~ous** *adj* giftig, Gift-

poke [pəuk] *vt* stoßen; (*put*) stecken; (*fire*) schüren; (*hole*) bohren; **~ about** *vi* herumstochern; (*nose around*) herumwühlen

poker [ˈpəukə*] *n* Schürhaken *m*; (*CARDS*) Poker *nt*; **~-faced** *adj* undurchdringlich

poky [ˈpəukɪ] *adj* eng

Poland [ˈpəulənd] *n* Polen *nt*

polar [ˈpəulə*] *adj* Polar-, polar; **~ bear** *n* Eisbär *m*; **~ize** *vt* polarisieren

Pole [pəul] *n* Pole *m*, Polin *f*

pole [pəul] *n* Stange *f*, Pfosten *m*; (*flag-, telegraph*) Stange *f*, Mast *m*; (*ELEC, GEOG*) Pol *m*; (*SPORT: vaulting ~*) Stab *m*; (*ski ~*) Stock *m*; **~ bean** (*US*) *n* (*runner bean*) Stangenbohne *f*; **~ vault** *n* hochsprung m

police [pəˈliːs] n Polizei ♦ vt kontrollieren; ~ **car** n Polizeiwagen m; ~ **man** (irreg) n Polizist m; ~ **state** n Polizeistaat m; ~ **station** n (Polizei)revier nt, Wache f; ~ **woman** (irreg) n Polizistin f

policy [ˈpɒlɪsɪ] n Politik f; (insurance) (Versicherungs)police f

polio [ˈpəʊlɪəʊ] n (spinale) Kinderlähmung f, Polio f

Polish [ˈpəʊlɪʃ] adj polnisch ♦ n (LING) Polnisch nt

polish [ˈpɒlɪʃ] n Politur f; (for floor) Wachs nt; (for shoes) Creme f; (for nails) Lack m; (shine) Glanz m; (of furniture) Politur f; (fig) Schliff m ♦ vt polieren; (shoes) putzen; (fig) den letzten Schliff geben +dat; ~ **off** vt (inf: work) erledigen; (: food) verputzen; (: drink) hinunterschütten; ~**ed** adj (also fig) glänzend; (manners) verfeinert

polite [pəˈlaɪt] adj höflich; ~**ness** n Höflichkeit f

politic [ˈpɒlɪtɪk] adj (prudent) diplomatisch; ~**al** [pəˈlɪtɪkl] adj politisch; ~**ally** adv politisch; ~**ian** [pɒlɪˈtɪʃən] n Politiker m; ~**s** npl Politik f

polka dot n Tupfen m

poll [pəʊl] n Abstimmung f; (in election) Wahl f; (votes cast) Wahlbeteiligung f; (opinion ~) Umfrage f ♦ vt (votes) erhalten

pollen [ˈpɒlən] n (BOT) Blütenstaub m, Pollen m

pollination [pɒlɪˈneɪʃən] n Befruchtung f

polling [ˈpəʊlɪŋ] (BRIT) : ~ **booth** (BRIT) n Wahlkabine f; ~ **day** (BRIT) n Wahltag m; ~ **station** (BRIT) n Wahllokal nt

pollute [pəˈluːt] vt verschmutzen, verunreinigen; **pollution** [pəˈluːʃən] n Verschmutzung f

polo [ˈpəʊləʊ] n Polo nt; ~**neck** n Rollkragen m; Rollkragenpullover m; ~ **shirt** n Polohemd nt

polystyrene [pɒlɪˈstaɪriːn] n Styropor nt

polytechnic [pɒlɪˈteknɪk] n technische Hochschule f

polythene [ˈpɒlɪθiːn] n Plastik nt

pomegranate [ˈpɒmɪgrænɪt] n Granatapfel m

pommel [ˈpʌml] vt mit den Fäusten bearbeiten ♦ n Sattelknopf m

pompom [ˈpɒmpɒm] n Troddel f, Pompon m

pompous [ˈpɒmpəs] adj aufgeblasen; (language) geschwollen

pond [pɒnd] n Teich m, Weiher m

ponder [ˈpɒndə*] vt nachdenken über +acc; ~**ous** adj schwerfällig

pong [pɒŋ] (BRIT) n Mief m

pontiff [ˈpɒntɪf] n Pontifex m

pontificate [pɒnˈtɪfɪkeɪt] vi (fig) geschwollen reden

pontoon [pɒnˈtuːn] n Ponton m; (CARDS) 17-und-4 nt

pony [ˈpəʊnɪ] n Pony nt; ~**tail** n Pferdeschwanz m; ~ **trekking** (BRIT) n Ponyreiten nt

poodle [ˈpuːdl] n Pudel m

pool [puːl] n (swimming ~) Schwimmbad nt; (: private) Swimmingpool m; (of spilt liquid, blood) Lache f; (fund) (gemeinsame) Kasse f; (billiards) Poolspiel nt ♦ vt (money etc) zusammenlegen; **typing** ~ n Schreibzentrale f; (football) ~**s** Toto nt

poor [pʊə*] adj arm; (not good) schlecht ♦ npl: **the** ~ die Armen pl; ~ **in** (resources etc) arm an +dat; ~**ly** adv schlecht; (dressed) ärmlich ♦ adj schlecht

pop [pɒp] n Knall m; (music) Popmusik f; (drink) Limonade f; (US: inf) Pa m ♦ vt (put) stecken; (balloon) platzen lassen ♦ vi knallen; ~ **in** vi kurz vorbeigehen or vorbeikommen; ~ **out** vi (person) kurz rausgehen; (thing) herausspringen; ~ **up** vi auftauchen; ~**corn** n Puffmais m

pope [pəʊp] n Papst m

poplar [ˈpɒplə*] n Pappel f

poppy [ˈpɒpɪ] n Mohn m (ice

Popsicle [ˈpɒpsɪkl] (®; US) n (ice

lolly) Eis *nt* am Stiel

populace ['pɒpjʊlɪs] *n* Volk *nt*

popular ['pɒpjʊlə*] *adj* beliebt, populär; *(of the people)* volkstümlich; *(widespread)* allgemein; **~ity** [pɒpjʊ'lærɪtɪ] *n* Beliebtheit *f*, Popularität *f*; **~ize** [pɒpjʊlərɪz] *vt* popularisieren; **~ly** *adv* allgemein, überall

population [pɒpjʊ'leɪʃən] *n* Bevölkerung *f*; *(of town)* Einwohner *pl*

populous ['pɒpjʊləs] *adj* dicht besiedelt

porcelain ['pɔːslɪn] *n* Porzellan *nt*

porch [pɔːtʃ] *n* Vorbau *m*, Veranda *f*

porcupine ['pɔːkjʊpaɪn] *n* Stachelschwein *nt*

pore [pɔː*] *n* Pore *f* ♦ *vi*: **to ~ over** brüten über +*dat*

pork [pɔːk] *n* Schweinefleisch *nt*

pornography [pɔː'nɒɡrəfɪ] *n* Pornographie *f*

porous ['pɔːrəs] *adj* porös; *(skin)* porig

porpoise ['pɔːpəs] *n* Tümmler *m*

porridge ['pɒrɪdʒ] *n* Haferbrei *m*

port [pɔːt] *n* Hafen *m*; *(town)* Hafenstadt *f*; *(NAUT: left side)* Backbord *nt*; *(wine)* Portwein *m*; **~ of call** Anlaufhafen *m*

portable ['pɔːtəbl] *adj* tragbar

portent ['pɔːtent] *n* schlimme(s) Vorzeichen *nt*

porter ['pɔːtə*] *n* Pförtner(in) *m(f)*; *(for luggage)* Gepäckträger *m*

portfolio [pɔːt'fəʊlɪəʊ] *n (case)* Mappe *f*; *(POL)* Geschäftsbereich *m*; *(FIN)* Portefeuille *nt*; *(of artist)* Kollektion *f*

porthole ['pɔːthəʊl] *n* Bullauge *nt*

portion ['pɔːʃən] *n* Teil *m*, Stück *nt*; *(of food)* Portion *f*

portly ['pɔːtlɪ] *adj* korpulent, beleibt

portrait ['pɔːtrɪt] *n* Porträt *nt*

portray [pɔː'treɪ] *vt* darstellen; **~al** *n* Darstellung *f*

Portugal ['pɔːtjʊɡəl] *n* Portugal *nt*

Portuguese [pɔːtjʊ'ɡiːz] *adj* portugiesisch ♦ *n inv* Portugiese *m*, Portugiesin *f*; *(LING)* Portugiesisch *nt*

pose [pəʊz] *n* Stellung *f*, Pose *f*; *(af-*

fectation) Pose *f* ♦ *vi* posieren ♦ *vt* stellen

posh [pɒʃ] *(inf) adj* (piek)fein

position [pə'zɪʃən] *n* Stellung *f*; *(place)* Lage *f*; *(job)* Stelle *f*; *(attitude)* Standpunkt *m* ♦ *vt* aufstellen

positive ['pɒzɪtɪv] *adj* positiv; *(convinced)* sicher; *(definite)* eindeutig

posse ['pɒsɪ] *(US) n* Aufgebot *nt*

possess [pə'zes] *vt* besitzen; **~ion** [pə'zeʃən] *n* Besitz *m*; **~ive** *adj* besitzergreifend, eigensüchtig

possibility [pɒsɪ'bɪlɪtɪ] *n* Möglichkeit *f*

possible ['pɒsəbl] *adj* möglich; **as big as ~** so groß wie möglich, möglichst groß

possibly ['pɒsəblɪ] *adv* möglicherweise, vielleicht; **I cannot ~ come** ich kann unmöglich kommen

post [pəʊst] *n (BRIT: letters, delivery)* Post *f*; *(pole)* Pfosten *m*, Pfahl *m*; *(place of duty)* Posten *m*; *(job)* Stelle *f* ♦ *vt (notice)* anschlagen; *(BRIT: letters)* aufgeben; *(: appoint)* versetzen; *(soldiers)* aufstellen; **~age** *n* Postgebühr *f*, Porto *nt*; **~al** *adj* Post-; *(order)* Post-; **~al order** *n* Postanweisung *f*; **~box** *(BRIT) n* Briefkasten *m*; **~card** *n* Postkarte *f*; **~code** *(BRIT) n* Postleitzahl *f*

postdate [pəʊst'deɪt] *vt (cheque)* nachdatieren

poster ['pəʊstə*] *n* Plakat *nt*, Poster *nt*

poste restante [pəʊst'restɑ̃ːnt] *n* Aufbewahrungsstelle *f* für postlagernde Sendungen

posterior [pɒs'tɪərɪə*] *(inf) n* Hintern *m*

posterity [pɒs'terɪtɪ] *n* Nachwelt *f*

postgraduate ['pəʊst'ɡrædjʊət] *n* Weiterstudierende(r) *mf*

posthumous ['pɒstjʊməs] *adj* post(h)um

postman ['pəʊstmən] *(irreg) n* Briefträger *m*

postmark ['pəʊstmɑːk] *n* Poststempel *m*

post-mortem ['pəʊst'mɔːtəm] *n* Autopsie f

post office n Postamt nt, Post f; (organization) Post f; **Post Office Box** n Postfach nt

postpone [pə'spəʊn] vt verschieben

postscript ['pəʊsskrɪpt] n Postskript nt; (to affair) Nachspiel nt

postulate ['pɒstjʊleɪt] vt voraussetzen; (maintain) behaupten

posture ['pɒstʃə*] n Haltung f ♦ vi posieren

postwar ['pəʊst'wɔː*] adj Nachkriegs-

posy ['pəʊzɪ] n Blumenstrauß m

pot [pɒt] n Topf m; (tea~) Kanne f; (inf: marijuana) Hasch m ♦ vt (plant) eintopfen; to go to ~ (inf: work, performance) auf den Hund kommen

potato [pə'teɪtəʊ] (pl ~es) n Kartoffel f; ~ peeler n Kartoffelschäler m

potent ['pəʊtənt] adj stark; (argument) zwingend

potential [pə'tenʃəl] adj potentiell ♦ n Potential nt; ~ly adv potentiell

pothole ['pɒthəʊl] n (in road) Schlagloch nt; (BRIT: underground) Höhle f

potholing ['pɒthəʊlɪŋ] (BRIT) n: to go ~ Höhlen erforschen

potion ['pəʊʃən] n Trank m

potluck ['pɒt'lʌk] n: to take ~ with sth eine auf gut Glück nehmen

potshot ['pɒtʃɒt] n: to take a ~ at sth auf etw acc ballern

potted ['pɒtɪd] adj (food) eingelegt, eingemacht; (plant) Topf-; (fig: book, version) konzentriert

potter ['pɒtə*] n Töpfer m ♦ vi herumhantieren; ~y n Töpferwaren pl; (place) Töpferei f

potty ['pɒtɪ] adj (inf: mad) verrückt ♦ n Töpfchen nt

pouch [paʊtʃ] n Beutel m

pouf(fe) [puːf] n Sitzkissen nt

poultry ['pəʊltrɪ] n Geflügel nt

pounce [paʊns] vi sich stürzen ♦ n Sprung m, Satz m; to ~ on sich stürzen auf +acc

pound [paʊnd] n (FIN, weight) Pfund nt; (for cars, animals) Auslösestelle f ♦ vt (zer)stampfen ♦ vi klopfen, hämmern; ~ sterling n Pfund Sterling nt

pour [pɔː*] vt gießen, schütten ♦ vi gießen; (crowds etc) strömen; ~ away vt abgießen; ~ in vi (people) hereinströmen; ~ off vt abgießen; ~ out vi (people) herausströmen ♦ vt (drink) einschenken; ~ing adj: ~ing rain strömende(r) Regen m

pout [paʊt] vi schmollen

poverty ['pɒvətɪ] n Armut f; ~-stricken adj verarmt, sehr arm

powder ['paʊdə*] n Pulver nt; (cosmetic) Puder m ♦ vt pulverisieren; to ~ one's nose sich dat die Nase pudern; ~ compact n Puderdose f; ~ed milk n Milchpulver nt; ~ room n Damentoilette f; ~y adj pulverig

power ['paʊə*] n (also POL) Macht f; (ability) Fähigkeit f; (strength) Stärke f; (MATH) Potenz f; (ELEC) Strom m ♦ vt betreiben, antreiben; to be in ~ (POL etc) an der Macht sein; ~ cut n Stromausfall m; ~ed adj: ~ed by betrieben mit; ~ failure (US) n Stromausfall m; ~ful adj (person) mächtig; (engine, government) stark; ~less adj machtlos; ~ point (BRIT) n elektrische(r) Anschluß m; ~ station n Elektrizitätswerk nt

p.p. abbr (= per procurationem) = J. Smith i.A. J. Smith

PR n abbr = public relations

practicable ['præktɪkəbl] adj durchführbar

practical ['præktɪkəl] adj praktisch; ~ity [præktɪ'kælɪtɪ] n (of person) praktische Veranlagung f; (of situation etc) Durchführbarkeit f; ~ joke n Streich m; ~ly adv praktisch

practice ['præktɪs] n Übung f; (reality, also of doctor, lawyer) Praxis f; (custom) Brauch m; (in business) Usus m ♦ vt, vi (US) = practise; in ~ (in reality) in der Praxis; out of ~ außer Übung

practicing (US) adj = practising

practise ['præktɪs] (*US* **practice**) *vt* üben; (*profession*) ausüben ♦ *vi* (sich) üben; (*doctor, lawyer*) praktizieren

practising ['præktɪsɪŋ] *adj* (*US* **practicing**) praktizierend; (*Christian etc*) aktiv

practitioner [præk'tɪʃənə*] *n* praktische(r) Arzt *m*

pragmatic [præg'mætɪk] *adj* pragmatisch

prairie ['prɛərɪ] *n* Prärie *f*, Steppe *f*

praise [preɪz] *n* Lob *nt* ♦ *vt* loben; **~worthy** *adj* lobenswert

pram [præm] (*BRIT*) *n* Kinderwagen *m*

prance [prɑːns] *vi* (*horse*) tänzeln; (*person*) stolzieren; (: *gaily*) herumhüpfen

prank [præŋk] *n* Streich *m*

prattle ['prætl] *vi* schwatzen, plappern

prawn [prɔːn] *n* Garnele *f*; Krabbe *f*

pray [preɪ] *vi* beten; **~er** [prɛə*] *n* Gebet *nt*

preach [priːtʃ] *vi* predigen; **~er** *n* Prediger *m*

preamble [pri'æmbl] *n* Einleitung *f*

precarious [prɪ'kɛərɪəs] *adj* prekär, unsicher

precaution [prɪ'kɔːʃən] *n* (Vorsichts)maßnahme *f*

precede [prɪ'siːd] *vi* vorausgehen ♦ *vt* vorausgehen +*dat*; **~nce** ['presɪdəns] *n* Vorrang *m*; **~nt** ['presɪdənt] *n* Präzedenzfall *m*

preceding [prɪ'siːdɪŋ] *adj* vorhergehend

precept ['priːsept] *n* Gebot *nt*, Regel *f*

precinct ['priːsɪŋkt] *n* (*US*: *district*) Bezirk *m*; **~s** *npl* (*round building*) Gelände *nt*; (*area, environs*) Umgebung *f*; **pedestrian ~** Fußgängerzone *f*; **shopping ~** Geschäftsviertel *nt*

precious ['preʃəs] *adj* kostbar, wertvoll; (*affected*) preziös, geziert

precipice ['presɪpɪs] *n* Abgrund *m*

precipitate [*adj* prɪ'sɪpɪtɪt, *vb*

**pri'sɪpɪteɪt] *adj* überstürzt, übereilt ♦ *vt* hinunterstürzen; (*events*) heraufbeschwören

precise [prɪ'saɪs] *adj* genau, präzis; **~ly** *adv* genau, präzis

precision [prɪ'sɪʒən] *n* Präzision *f*

preclude [prɪ'kluːd] *vt* ausschließen

precocious [prɪ'kəʊʃəs] *adj* frühreif

preconceived ['priːkən'siːvd] *adj* (*idea*) vorgefaßt

precondition ['priːkən'dɪʃən] *n* Vorbedingung *f*, Voraussetzung *f*

precursor [priː'kɜːsə*] *n* Vorläufer *m*

predator ['predətə*] *n* Raubtier *nt*

predecessor ['priːdɪsesə*] *n* Vorgänger *m*

predestination [priːdestɪ'neɪʃən] *n* Vorherbestimmung *f*

predicament [prɪ'dɪkəmənt] *n* mißliche Lage *f*

predict [prɪ'dɪkt] *vt* voraussagen; **~able** *adj* vorhersagbar; **~ion** [prɪ'dɪkʃən] *n* Voraussage *f*

predominantly [prɪ'dɒmɪnəntlɪ] *adv* überwiegend, hauptsächlich

predominate [prɪ'dɒmɪneɪt] *vi* vorherrschen, (*fig*) vorherrschen, überwiegen

pre-eminent [priː'emɪnənt] *adj* hervorragend, herausragend

pre-empt [priː'empt] *vt* (*action, decision*) vorwegnehmen

preen [priːn] *vt* putzen; **to ~ o.s.** (*person*) sich brüsten

prefab ['priːfæb] *n* Fertighaus *nt*

prefabricated ['priːfæbrɪkeɪtɪd] *adj* vorgefertigt, Fertig-

preface ['prefɪs] *n* Vorwort *nt*

prefect ['priːfekt] *n* Präfekt *m*; (*SCH*) Aufsichtsschüler(in) *m(f)*

prefer [prɪ'fɜː*] *vt* vorziehen, lieber mögen; **to ~ to do sth** etw lieber tun; **~ably** *adv* vorzugsweise, am liebsten; **~ence** ['prefrəns] *n* Präferenz *f*, Vorzug *m*; **~ential** [prefə'renʃəl] *adj* bevorzugt, Vorzugs-

prefix ['priːfɪks] *n* Vorsilbe *f*, Präfix *nt*

pregnancy ['pregnənsɪ] *n* Schwan

gerschaft f

pregnant ['pregnənt] adj schwanger

prehistoric ['pri:hɪs'tɒrɪk] adj prähistorisch, vorgeschichtlich

prejudice ['predʒʊdɪs] n (opinion) Vorurteil nt; (bias) Voreingenommenheit f; (harm) Schaden m ♦ vt beeinträchtigen; **~d** adj (person) voreingenommen

preliminary [prɪ'lɪmɪnərɪ] adj einleitend, Vor-

prelude ['prelju:d] n Vorspiel nt, (fig) Auftakt m

premarital ['pri:'mærɪtl] adj vorehelich

premature ['premətʃʊə*] adj vorzeitig, verfrüht; (birth) Früh-

premeditated ['pri:'medɪteɪtɪd] adj geplant; (murder) vorsätzlich

premier ['premɪə*] adj erste(r, s) ♦ n Premier m

première [premɪ'eə*] n Premiere f; Uraufführung f

premise ['premɪs] n Voraussetzung f, Prämisse f; **~s** npl (shop) Räumlichkeiten pl; (grounds) Gelände nt; **on the ~s** im Hause

premium ['pri:mɪəm] n Prämie f; **to be at a ~** über pari stehen; **~ bond** (BRIT) n Prämienanleihe f

premonition [premə'nɪʃən] n Vorahnung f

preoccupation [pri:ɒkju'peɪʃən] n Sorge f

preoccupied [pri:'ɒkjupaɪd] adj (look) geistesabwesend

prep [prep] n (SCH: study) Hausaufgabe f

prepaid ['pri:'peɪd] adj vorausbezahlt; (letter) frankiert

preparation [prepə'reɪʃən] n Vorbereitung f

preparatory [prɪ'pærətərɪ] adj Vor(bereitungs)-; **~ school** n (BRIT) private Vorbereitungsschule für die Public School; (US) private Vorbereitungsschule für die Hochschule

prepare [prɪ'peə*] vt vorbereiten ♦ vi sich vorbereiten; **to ~ for/ prepare sth for** sich/etw vorbereiten

auf +acc; **to be ~d to ...** bereit sein zu ...

preponderance [prɪ'pɒndərəns] n Übergewicht nt

preposition [prepə'zɪʃən] n Präposition f, Verhältniswort nt

preposterous [prɪ'pɒstərəs] adj absurd

prep school n = **preparatory school**

prerequisite ['pri:'rekwɪzɪt] n (unerläßliche) Voraussetzung f

prerogative [prɪ'rɒgətɪv] n Vorrecht nt

Presbyterian [prezbɪ'tɪərɪən] adj presbyterianisch ♦ n Presbyterier(in) m(f)

preschool ['pri:sku:l] adj Vorschul-

prescribe [prɪs'kraɪb] vt vorschreiben; (MED) verschreiben

prescription [prɪs'krɪpʃən] n (MED) Rezept nt

presence ['prezns] n Gegenwart f; **~ of mind** Geistesgegenwart f

present [adj, n 'preznt, vb prɪ'zent] adj (here) anwesend; (current) gegenwärtig ♦ n Gegenwart f; (gift) Geschenk nt ♦ vt vorlegen; (introduce) vorstellen; (show) zeigen; (give) **to ~ sb with sth** jdm etw überreichen; **at ~** im Augenblick; **to give sb a ~** jdm ein Geschenk machen; **~able** [prɪ'zentəbl] adj präsentabel; **~ation** [prezn'teɪʃən] n Überreichung f; **~-day** adj heutig; **~er** [prɪ'zentə*] n (RADIO, TV) Moderator(in) m(f); **~ly** adv bald; (at present) im Augenblick

preservation [prezə'veɪʃən] n Erhaltung f

preservative [prɪ'zɜ:vətɪv] n Konservierungsmittel nt

preserve [prɪ'zɜ:v] vt erhalten; (food) einmachen ♦ n (jam) Eingemachte(s) nt; (hunting) Schutzgebiet nt

preside [prɪ'zaɪd] vi den Vorsitz haben

presidency ['prezɪdənsɪ] n (POL) Präsidentschaft f

president ['prezidənt] n Präsident m; **~ial** [prezi'denʃəl] adj Präsidenten-; (election) Präsidentschafts-; (system) Präsidial-.

press [pres] n Presse f; (printing house) Druckerei f ♦ vt drücken; (iron) bügeln; (urge) (be)drängen ♦ vi (push) drücken; to be **~ed** for time unter Zeitdruck stehen; to **~** for sth drängen auf etw acc; to **~** on vi vorwärtsdrängen; **~ agency** n Presseagentur f; **~ conference** n Pressekonferenz f; **~ing** adj dringend; **~-stud** (BRIT) n Druckknopf m; **~-up** (BRIT) n Liegestütz m.

pressure ['preʃə*] n Druck m; **~cooker** n Schnellkochtopf m; **~gauge** n Druckmesser m.

pressurized ['preʃəraizd] adj Druck-.

prestige [pres'ti:ʒ] n Prestige nt.

prestigious [pres'tidʒəs] adj Prestige-.

presumably [pri'zju:məbli] adv vermutlich.

presume [pri'zju:m] vt, vi annehmen; to **~** to do sth sich erlauben, etw zu tun.

presumption [pri'zʌmpʃən] n Annahme f.

presumptuous [pri'zʌmptjʊəs] adj anmaßend.

presuppose [pri:sə'pəʊz] vt voraussetzen.

pretence [pri'tens] (US **pretense**) n Vorgabe f, Vortäuschung f; (false claim) Vorwand m.

pretend [pri'tend] vt vorgeben, so tun als ob ... ♦ vi so tun; to **~** to sth Anspruch erheben auf etw acc.

pretense [pri'tens] (US) n = **pretence**.

pretension [pri'tenʃən] n Anspruch m; (impudent claim) Anmaßung f.

pretentious [pri'tenʃəs] adj angeberisch.

pretext ['pri:tekst] n Vorwand m.

pretty ['priti] adj hübsch ♦ adv (inf) ganz schön.

prevail [pri'veil] vi siegen; (custom) vorherrschen; to **~** against or over

siegen über +acc; to **~** (up)on sb to do sth jdn dazu bewegen, etw zu tun; **~ing** adj vorherrschend.

prevalent ['prevələnt] adj vorherrschend.

prevent [pri'vent] vt (stop) verhindern, verhüten; to **~** sb from doing sth jdn (daran) hindern, etw zu tun; **~ative** n Vorbeugungsmittel nt; **~ion** [pri'venʃən] n Verhütung f; **~ive** adj vorbeugend, Schutz-.

preview ['pri:vju:] n private Voraufführung f; (trailer) Vorschau f.

previous ['pri:viəs] adj früher, vorherig; **~ly** adv früher.

prewar ['pri:'wɔ:*] adj Vorkriegs-.

prey [prei] n Beute f; **~ on** vt fus Jagd machen auf +acc; it was **~ing on his mind** es quälte sein Gewissen.

price [prais] n Preis m; (value) Wert m ♦ vt (label) auszeichnen; **~less** adj (also fig) unbezahlbar; **~ list** n Preisliste f.

prick [prik] n Stich m ♦ vt, vi stechen; to **~ up one's ears** die Ohren spitzen.

prickle ['prikl] n Stachel m, Dorn m.

prickly ['prikli] adj stachelig; (fig: person) reizbar; **~ heat** n Hitzebläschen pl.

pride [praid] n Stolz m; (arrogance) Hochmut m ♦ vt: to **~ o.s. on sth** auf etw acc stolz sein.

priest [pri:st] n Priester m; **~ess** n Priesterin f; **~hood** n Priesteramt nt.

prig [prig] n Selbstgefällige(r) mf.

prim [prim] adj prüde.

primarily ['praimərili] adv vorwiegend.

primary ['praiməri] adj (main) Haupt-; (SCH) Grund-; **~ school** (BRIT) n Grundschule f.

prime [praim] adj erste(r, s); (excellent) erstklassig ♦ vt vorbereiten; (gun) laden; in the **~ of** life in der Blüte der Jahre; **P~ Minister** n Premierminister m, Ministerpräsident m; **~r** ['praimə*] n Fibel f.

primeval [prai'mi:vəl] adj vorzeitlich; (forests) Ur-

primitive ['prɪmɪtɪv] adj primitiv

primrose ['prɪmrəʊz] n (gelbe) Primel f

primus (stove) ['praɪməs-] n (®); BRIT) n Primuskocher m

prince [prɪns] n Prinz m; (ruler) Fürst m; ~ss [prɪn'ses] n Prinzessin f; Fürstin f

principal ['prɪnsɪpəl] adj Haupt- ♦ n (SCH) (Schul)direktor m, Rektor m; (money) (Grund)kapital nt

principle ['prɪnsɪpl] n Grundsatz m, Prinzip nt; in ~ im Prinzip; on ~ aus Prinzip, prinzipiell

print [prɪnt] n Druck m; (made by feet, fingers) Abdruck m; (PHOT) Abzug m ♦ vt drucken; (name) in Druckbuchstaben schreiben; (PHOT) abziehen; out of ~ vergriffen; ~ed matter n Drucksache f; ~er n Drucker m; ~ing n Drucken nt; (of photos) Abziehen nt; ~out n (COMPUT) Ausdruck m

prior ['praɪə*] adj früher ♦ n Prior m; ~ to sth vor etw dat; ~ to going abroad, she had ... bevor sie ins Ausland ging, hatte sie ...

priority [praɪ'ɒrɪtɪ] n Vorrang m; Priorität f

prise [praɪz] vt: to ~ open aufbrechen

prison ['prɪzn] n Gefängnis nt ♦ adj Gefängnis-; (system etc) Strafvollzugs-; ~er n Gefangene(r) m/f

pristine ['prɪstiːn] adj makellos

privacy ['prɪvəsɪ] n Ungestörtheit f, Ruhe f; Privatleben nt

private ['praɪvɪt] adj privat, Privat-; (secret) vertraulich, geheim ♦ n einfache(r) Soldat m; "~" (on envelope) „persönlich"; in ~ privat, unter vier Augen; ~ enterprise n Privatunternehmen nt; ~ eye n Privatdetektiv m; ~ly adv privat; vertraulich, geheim; ~ property n Privatbesitz m; ~ school n Privatschule f; privatize vt privatisieren

privet ['prɪvɪt] n Liguster m

privilege ['prɪvɪlɪdʒ] n Privileg nt; ~d adj bevorzugt, privilegiert

privy ['prɪvɪ] adj geheim, privat; P~ Council n Geheime(r) Staatsrat m

prize [praɪz] n Preis m ♦ adj (example) erstklassig; (idiot) Voll- ♦ vt (hoch)schätzen; ~-giving n Preisverteilung f; ~winner n Preisträger(in) m(f)

pro [prəʊ] n (professional) Profi m; the ~s and cons (for and against) das Für und Wider

probability [prɒbə'bɪlɪtɪ] n Wahrscheinlichkeit f

probable ['prɒbəbl] adj wahrscheinlich

probably adv wahrscheinlich

probation [prə'beɪʃən] n Probe(zeit) f; (JUR) Bewährung f; on ~ auf Probe; auf Bewährung

probe [prəʊb] n Sonde f; (enquiry) Untersuchung f ♦ vt, vi erforschen

problem ['prɒbləm] n Problem nt; ~atic [prɒblɪ'mætɪk] adj problematisch

procedure [prə'siːdʒə*] n Verfahren nt

proceed [prə'siːd] vi (advance) vorrücken; (start) anfangen; (carry on) fortfahren; (set about) vorgehen; ~ings npl Verfahren nt; ~s ['prəʊsiːdz] npl Erlös m

process ['prəʊses] n Prozeß m; (method) Verfahren nt ♦ vt bearbeiten; (food) verarbeiten; (film) entwickeln; ~ing n (PHOT) Entwickeln nt

procession [prə'seʃən] n Prozession f, Umzug m; funeral ~ Trauerprozession f

proclaim [prə'kleɪm] vt verkünden

proclamation [prɒklə'meɪʃən] n Verkündung f

procrastinate [prəʊ'kræstɪneɪt] vi zaudern

procreation [prəʊkrɪ'eɪʃən] n (Er)zeugung f

procure [prə'kjʊə*] vt beschaffen

prod [prɒd] vt stoßen ♦ n Stoß m

prodigal ['prɒdɪgəl] adj: ~ (with or

of) verschwenderisch (mit)

prodigious [prə'dɪdʒəs] adj gewaltig; (wonderful) wunderbar

prodigy ['prodɪdʒɪ] n Wunder nt

produce [n 'prodjuːs, vb prə'djuːs] n (AGR) (Boden)produkte pl, (Natur)erzeugnis nt ♦ vt herstellen, produzieren; (cause) hervorrufen, (farmer) erzeugen; (yield) liefern, bringen; (play) inszenieren; ~r n Hersteller m, Produzent m (also CINE); Erzeuger m

product ['prodʌkt] n Produkt nt, Erzeugnis nt

production [prə'dʌkʃən] n Produktion f, Herstellung f; (thing) Erzeugnis nt, Produkt nt; (THEAT) Inszenierung f; ~ line n Fließband nt

productive [prə'dʌktɪv] adj produktiv; (fertile) ertragreich, fruchtbar

productivity [prodʌk'tɪvɪtɪ] n Produktivität f

profane [prə'feɪn] adj (secular, lay) weltlich, profan; (language etc) gotteslästerlich

profess [prə'fes] vt bekennen; (show) zeigen; (claim to be) vorgeben

profession [prə'feʃən] n Beruf m; (declaration) Bekenntnis nt; ~al n Fachmann m; (SPORT) Berufsspieler(in) m(f) ♦ adj Berufs-; (expert) fachlich; (player) professionell

professor [prə'fesə*] n Professor m

proficiency [prə'fɪʃənsɪ] n Können nt

proficient [prə'fɪʃənt] adj fähig

profile ['prəʊfaɪl] n Profil nt; (fig: report) Kurzbiographie f

profit ['profɪt] n Gewinn m ♦ vi: to ~ (by or from) profitieren (von); ~ability [profɪtə'bɪlɪtɪ] n Rentabilität f; ~able adj einträglich, rentabel

profiteering [profɪ'tɪərɪŋ] n Profitmacherei f

profound [prə'faʊnd] adj tief

profuse [prə'fjuːs] adj überreich; ~ly [prə'fjuːslɪ] adv überschwenglich; (sweat) reichlich

profusion [prə'fjuːʒən] n: ~ (of) Überfülle f (von), Überfluß m (an

+dat)

progeny ['prodʒɪnɪ] n Nachkommenschaft f

programme ['prəʊgræm] (US program) n Programm nt ♦ vt planen; (computer) programmieren

programmer (US **programer**) n Programmierer(in) m(f)

programming ['prəʊgræmɪŋ] (US **programing**) n Programmieren nt

progress [n 'prəʊgres, vb prə'gres] n Fortschritt m ♦ vi fortschreiten, weitergehen; **in ~** im Gang; ~**ion** [prə'greʃən] n Folge f; ~**ive** [prə'gresɪv] adj fortschrittlich, progressiv

prohibit [prə'hɪbɪt] vt verbieten; to ~ **sb from doing sth** jdm untersagen, etw zu tun; ~**ion** [prəʊɪ'bɪʃən] n Verbot nt; (US) Alkoholverbot nt, Prohibition f; ~**ive** adj (price etc) unerschwinglich

project [n 'prodʒekt, vb prə'dʒekt] n Projekt nt ♦ vt vorausplanen; (film etc) projizieren; (personality, voice) zum Tragen bringen ♦ vi (stick out) hervorragen, (her)vorstehen

projectile [prə'dʒektaɪl] n Geschoß nt

projection [prə'dʒekʃən] n Projektion f; (sth prominent) Vorsprung m

projector [prə'dʒektə*] n Projektor m

proletariat [prəʊlə'teərɪət] n Proletariat nt

proliferate [prə'lɪfəreɪt] vi sich vermehren

prolific [prə'lɪfɪk] adj fruchtbar; (author etc) produktiv

prologue ['prəʊlɒg] n Prolog m; (event) Vorspiel nt

prolong [prə'lɒŋ] vt verlängern

prom [prom] n abbr = promenade; **promenade concert** n (US: college ball) Studentenball m

promenade [promɪ'nɑːd] n Promenade f; ~ **concert** n Promenadenkonzert nt

prominence ['promɪnəns] n (große

Bedeutung f

prominent ['prɒmɪnənt] adj bedeutend; (politician) prominent; (easily seen) herausragend, auffallend

promiscuous [prə'mɪskjʊəs] adj lose

promise ['prɒmɪs] n Versprechen nt; (hope: promise of sth) Aussicht f auf etw acc ♦ vt, vi versprechen

promising ['prɒmɪsɪŋ] adj vielversprechend

promontory ['prɒməntrɪ] n Vorsprung m

promote [prə'məʊt] vt befördern; (help on) fördern, unterstützen; ~r n (in sport, entertainment) Veranstalter m; (for charity etc) Organisator m

promotion [prə'məʊʃən] n (in rank) Beförderung f; (furtherance) Förderung f; (COMM): ~ (of) Werbung f (für)

prompt [prɒmpt] adj prompt, schnell ♦ adv (punctually) genau ♦ n (COMPUT) Meldung f ♦ vt veranlassen; (THEAT) soufflieren +dat; to ~ sb to do sth jdn dazu veranlassen, etw zu tun; ~ly adv sofort

prone [prəʊn] adj hingestreckt; to be ~ to sth zu etw neigen

prong [prɒŋ] n Zinke f

pronoun ['prəʊnaʊn] n Fürwort nt

pronounce [prə'naʊns] vt aussprechen; (JUR) verkünden ♦ vi (give an opinion): to ~ (on) sich äußern (zu); ~d adj ausgesprochen; ~ment n Erklärung f

pronunciation [prənʌnsɪ'eɪʃən] n Aussprache f

proof [pruːf] n Beweis m; (PRINT) Korrekturfahne f; (of alcohol) Alkoholgehalt m ♦ adj sicher

prop [prɒp] n (also fig) Stütze f; (THEAT) Requisit nt ♦ vt (also: ~ up) stützen

propaganda [prɒpə'gændə] n Propaganda f

propagate ['prɒpəgeɪt] vt fortpflanzen; (news) propagieren, verbreiten

propel [prə'pel] vt (an)treiben; ~ler n Propeller m; ~ling pencil (BRIT)

n Drehbleistift m

propensity [prə'pensɪtɪ] n Tendenz f

proper ['prɒpə*] adj richtig; (seemly) schicklich; ~ly adv richtig; ~ noun n Eigenname m

property ['prɒpətɪ] n Eigentum nt; (quality) Eigenschaft f; (land) Grundbesitz m; ~ owner n Grundbesitzer m

prophecy ['prɒfɪsɪ] n Prophezeiung f

prophesy ['prɒfɪsaɪ] vt prophezeien

prophet ['prɒfɪt] n Prophet m

proportion [prə'pɔːʃən] n Verhältnis nt; (share) Teil m ♦ vt: to ~ (to) abstimmen (auf +acc); ~al adj proportional; ~ate adj verhältnismäßig

proposal [prə'pəʊzl] n Vorschlag m; (of marriage) Heiratsantrag m

propose [prə'pəʊz] vt vorschlagen; (toast) ausbringen ♦ vi (offer marriage) einen Heiratsantrag machen; to ~ to do sth beabsichtigen, etw zu tun

proposition [prɒpə'zɪʃən] n Angebot nt; (statement) Satz m

proprietor [prə'praɪətə*] n Besitzer m, Eigentümer m

propriety [prə'praɪətɪ] n Anstand m

pro rata [prəʊ'rɑːtə] adv anteilmäßig

prose [prəʊz] n Prosa f

prosecute ['prɒsɪkjuːt] vt (strafrechtlich) verfolgen

prosecution [prɒsɪ'kjuːʃən] n (JUR) strafrechtliche Verfolgung f; (party) Anklage f

prosecutor ['prɒsɪkjuːtə*] n Vertreter m der Anklage; Public P~ n Staatsanwalt m

prospect [n 'prɒspekt, vb prə'spekt] n Aussicht f ♦ vi auf Bodenschätze hin untersuchen ♦ vi: to ~ (for) suchen (nach); ~ing [prə'spektɪŋ] n (for minerals) Suche f; ~or n (Gold)sucher m; ~us n (Werbe)prospekt m

prosper ['prɒspə*] vi blühen, gedeihen; (person) erfolgreich sein; ~ity [prɒ'sperɪtɪ] n Wohlstand m; ~ous adj wohlhabend, reich

prostitute ['prɒstɪtjuːt] n Prostituierte f

prostrate ['prɒstreɪt] adj ausgestreckt (liegend); ~ **with grief/exhaustion** von Schmerz/Erschöpfung übermannt

protagonist [prəʊ'tægənɪst] n Hauptperson f, Held m

protect [prə'tekt] vt (be)schützen; ~**ion** n Schutz m; ~**ive** adj Schutz-, (be)schützend

protégé ['prɒteʒeɪ] n Schützling m

protein ['prəʊtiːn] n Protein n, Eiweiß nt

protest [n 'prəʊtest, vb prə'test] n Protest m ♦ vi protestieren ♦ vt (affirm) beteuern

Protestant ['prɒtɪstənt] adj protestantisch ♦ n Protestant(in) m(f)

protester [prə'testə*] n (demonstrator) Demonstrant(in) m(f)

protracted [prə'træktɪd] adj sich hinziehend

protrude [prə'truːd] vi (her)vorstehen

proud [praʊd] adj: ~ (**of**) stolz (auf +acc)

prove [pruːv] vt beweisen ♦ vi: to ~ (**to be**) correct sich als richtig erweisen; to ~ o.s. sich bewähren

proverb ['prɒvɜːb] n Sprichwort nt; ~**ial** [prə'vɜːbɪəl] adj sprichwörtlich

provide [prə'vaɪd] vt versehen; (supply) besorgen; to ~ **sb with sth** jdn mit etw versorgen; ~ **for** vt fus sorgen für; (emergency) Vorkehrungen treffen für; ~**d** (**that**) conj vorausgesetzt (, daß); **P~nce** ['prɒvɪdəns] n die Vorsehung

providing [prə'vaɪdɪŋ] conj vorausgesetzt (, daß)

province ['prɒvɪns] n Provinz f; (division of work) Bereich m

provincial [prə'vɪnʃəl] adj provinziell, Provinz-

provision [prə'vɪʒən] n Vorkehrung f; (condition) Bestimmung f; ~**s** npl (food) Vorräte pl, Proviant m; ~**al** adj provisorisch

proviso [prə'vaɪzəʊ] n Bedingung f

provocative [prə'vɒkətɪv] adj provo-

zierend

provoke [prə'vəʊk] vt provozieren; (cause) hervorrufen

prow [praʊ] n Bug m

prowess ['praʊes] n überragende(s) Können nt

prowl [praʊl] vi herumstreichen; (animal) schleichen ♦ n: **on the** ~ umherstreifend; ~**er** n Herumtreiber(in) m(f)

proximity [prɒk'sɪmɪtɪ] n Nähe f

proxy ['prɒksɪ] n (Stell)vertreter m; (authority, document) Vollmacht f; **by** ~ durch einen Stellvertreter

prudence ['pruːdəns] n Umsicht f

prudent ['pruːdənt] adj klug, umsichtig

prudish ['pruːdɪʃ] adj prüde

prune [pruːn] n Backpflaume f ♦ vt ausputzen; (fig) zurechtstutzen

pry [praɪ] vi: to ~ (**into**) seine Nase stecken (in +acc)

PS n abbr (= postscript) PS

pseudo- ['sjuːdəʊ] prefix Pseudo-; ~**nym** ['sjuːdənɪm] n Pseudonym nt, Deckname m

psychiatric [saɪkɪ'ætrɪk] adj psychiatrisch

psychiatrist [saɪ'kaɪətrɪst] n Psychiater m

psychic ['saɪkɪk] adj (also: ~**al**) paranormal übersinnlich; (person) übersinnlich begabt

psychoanalyse [saɪkəʊ'ænəlaɪz] (US **psychoanalyze**) vt psychoanalytisch behandeln

psychoanalyst [saɪkəʊ'ænəlɪst] n Psychoanalytiker(in) m(f)

psychological [saɪkə'lɒdʒɪkəl] adj psychologisch

psychologist [saɪ'kɒlədʒɪst] n Psychologe m, Psychologin f

psychology [saɪ'kɒlədʒɪ] n Psychologie f

PTO abbr = please turn over

pub [pʌb] n abbr (= public house) Kneipe f

pubic ['pjuːbɪk] adj Scham-

public ['pʌblɪk] adj öffentlich ♦ n (also: **general** ~) Öffentlichkeit f; **in**

~ in der Öffentlichkeit; ~ **address system** n Lautsprecheranlage f

publican ['pʌblɪkən] n Wirt m

publication [pʌblɪ'keɪʃən] n Veröffentlichung f

public: ~ **company** n Aktiengesellschaft f; ~ **convenience** (BRIT) n öffentliche Toiletten pl; ~ **holiday** n gesetzliche(r) Feiertag m; ~ **house** (BRIT) n Lokal nt, Kneipe f

publicity [pʌb'lɪsɪtɪ] n Publicity f, Werbung f

publicize ['pʌblɪsaɪz] vt bekannt machen; (advertise) Publicity machen für

publicly ['pʌblɪklɪ] adv öffentlich

public: ~ **opinion** n öffentliche Meinung f; ~ **relations** npl Public Relations pl; ~ **school** n (BRIT) Privatschule f; (US) staatliche Schule f; **~-spirited** adj mit Gemeinschaftssinn; ~ **transport** n öffentliche Verkehrsmittel pl

publish ['pʌblɪʃ] vt veröffentlichen; (event) bekanntgeben; **~er** n Verleger m; **~ing** n (business) Verlagswesen nt

pucker ['pʌkə*] vt (face) verziehen; (lips) kräuseln

pudding ['pʊdɪŋ] n (BRIT: course) Nachtisch m; Pudding m; **black ~** ≈ Blutwurst f

puddle ['pʌdl] n Pfütze f

puff [pʌf] n (of wind etc) Stoß m; (cosmetic) Puderquaste f ♦ vt blasen, pusten; (pipe) paffen ♦ vi keuchen, schnaufen; (smoke) paffen; to ~ **out smoke** Rauch ausstoßen; **~ed** (inf) adj (out of breath) außer Puste; **~ pastry** (US ~ **paste**) n Blätterteig m; **~y** adj aufgedunsen

pull [pʊl] n Ruck m; (influence) Beziehung f ♦ vt ziehen; (trigger) abdrücken ♦ vi ziehen; to ~ **sb's leg** jdn auf den Arm nehmen; to ~ to ~ **pieces** in Stücke reißen; (fig) verreißen; to ~ **one's punches** sich zurückhalten; to ~ **one's weight** sich in die Riemen legen; to ~ **o.s. together** sich zusammenreißen; ~

apart vt (break) zerreißen; (dismantle) auseinandernehmen; (fighters) trennen; ~ **down** vt (house) abreißen; ~ **in** vi hineinfahren; (stop) anhalten; (RAIL) einfahren; ~ **off** vt (deal etc) abschließen; ~ **out** vi (car) herausfahren; (fig: partner) aussteigen ♦ vt herausziehen; ~ **over** vi (AUT) an die Seite fahren; ~ **round** vi durchkommen; ~ **through** vi durchkommen; ~ **up** vi anhalten ♦ vt (uproot) herausreißen; (stop) anhalten

pulley ['pʊlɪ] n Rolle f, Flaschenzug m

pullover ['pʊləʊvə*] n Pullover m

pulp [pʌlp] n Brei m; (of fruit) Fruchtfleisch nt

pulpit ['pʊlpɪt] n Kanzel f

pulsate [pʌl'seɪt] vi pulsieren

pulse [pʌls] n Puls m

pummel ['pʌml] vt mit den Fäusten bearbeiten

pump [pʌmp] n Pumpe f; (shoe) leichter (Tanz)schuh m ♦ vt pumpen; ~ **up** vt (tyre) aufpumpen

pumpkin ['pʌmpkɪn] n Kürbis m

pun [pʌn] n Wortspiel nt

punch [pʌntʃ] n (tool) Locher m; (blow) (Faust)schlag m; (drink) Punsch m, Bowle f ♦ vt lochen; (strike) schlagen, boxen; ~ **line** n Pointe f; **~-up** (BRIT: inf) n Keilerei f

punctual ['pʌŋktjʊəl] adj pünktlich

punctuate ['pʌŋktjʊeɪt] vt mit Satzzeichen versehen; (fig) unterbrechen

punctuation [pʌŋktjʊ'eɪʃən] n Zeichensetzung f, Interpunktion f

puncture ['pʌŋktʃə*] n Loch nt; (AUT) Reifenpanne f ♦ vt durchbohren

pundit ['pʌndɪt] n Gelehrte(r) mf

pungent ['pʌndʒənt] adj scharf

punish ['pʌnɪʃ] vt bestrafen; (in boxing etc) übel zurichten; **~ment** n Strafe f; (action) Bestrafung f

punk [pʌŋk] n (also: ~ **rocker**) Punker(in) m(f); (: ~ **rock**) Punk m; (US: inf: hoodlum) Ganove m

punt [pʌnt] n Stechkahn m

punter ['pʌntə*] n (better) Wetter m

puny ['pju:nɪ] adj kümmerlich

pup [pʌp] n = **puppy**

pupil ['pju:pl] n Schüler(in) m(f); (in eye) Pupille f

puppet ['pʌpɪt] n Puppe f; Marionette f

puppy ['pʌpɪ] n junge(r) Hund m

purchase ['pɜ:tʃɪs] n Kauf m; (grip) Halt m ♦ vt kaufen, erwerben; ~r n Käufer(in) m(f)

pure [pjuə*] adj (also fig) rein; ~ly ['pjuəlɪ] adv rein

purgatory ['pɜ:gətərɪ] n Fegefeuer nt

purge [pɜ:dʒ] n (also POL) Säuberung f; (medicine) Abführmittel nt ♦ vt reinigen; (body) entschlacken

purify ['pjuərɪfaɪ] vt reinigen

purity ['pjuərɪtɪ] n Reinheit f

purl [pɜ:l] n linke Masche f

purple ['pɜ:pl] adj violett; (face) dunkelrot

purport [pə'pɔ:t] vi vorgeben

purpose ['pɜ:pəs] n Zweck m, Ziel nt; (of person) Absicht f; on ~ absichtlich; ~ful adj zielbewußt, entschlossen

purr [pɜ:*] n Schnurren f ♦ vi schnurren

purse [pɜ:s] n Portemonnaie nt, Geldbeutel m ♦ vt (lips) zusammenpressen, schürzen

purser ['pɜ:sə*] n Zahlmeister m

pursue [pə'sju:] vt verfolgen; (study) nachgehen +dat; ~r n Verfolger m

pursuit [pə'sju:t] n Verfolgung f; (occupation) Beschäftigung f

purveyor [pɜ:'veɪə*] n Lieferant m

pus [pʌs] n Eiter m

push [puʃ] n Stoß m, Schub m; (MIL) Vorstoß m ♦ vt stoßen, schieben; (button) drücken; (idea) durchsetzen ♦ vi stoßen, schieben; ~ aside vt beiseiteschieben; ~ off (inf) vi abschieben; ~ on vi weitermachen; ~ through vt durchdrücken; (policy) durchsetzen; ~ up vt (total)

erhöhen; (prices) hochtreiben; ~chair (BRIT) n (Kinder-)sportwagen m; ~over (inf) n Kinderspiel nt; ~up (US) n (press-up) Liegestütz m; ~y (inf) adj aufdringlich

puss [pus] n Mieze(katze) f; ~y(-cat) ['pusi(kæt)] n Mieze(katze) f

put [put] (pt, pp put) vt setzen, stellen, legen; (express) ausdrücken, sagen; (write) schreiben; ~ about vi (turn back) wenden ♦ vt (spread) verbreiten; ~ across vt (explain) erklären; ~ away vt weglegen; (store) beiseitelegen; ~ back vt zurückstellen or -legen; ~ by vt zurücklegen, sparen; ~ down vt hinstellen or -legen; (rebellion) niederschlagen; (animal) einschläfern; (in writing) niederschreiben; ~ forward vt (idea) vorbringen; (clock) vorstellen; ~ in vt (application, complaint) einreichen; ~ off vt verschieben; (discourage) abhalten; to ~ sb off sth jdn von etw abbringen; ~ on vt (clothes etc) anziehen; (light etc) anschalten, anmachen; (play etc) aufführen; (brake) anziehen; ~ out vt (hand etc) (her)ausstrecken; (news, rumour) verbreiten; (light etc) ausschalten, ausmachen; ~ through vt (TEL: person) verbinden; (: call) durchstellen; ~ up vt (tent) aufstellen; (building) errichten; (price) erhöhen; (person) unterbringen; ~ up with vt fus sich abfinden mit

putrid ['pju:trɪd] adj faul

putt [pʌt] n (golf) putten ♦ n Putten nt; ~ing green n kleine(r) Golfplatz m nur zum Putten

putty ['pʌtɪ] n Kitt m; (fig) Wachs nt

put-up ['putʌp] adj: ~ job abgekartete(s) Spiel nt

puzzle ['pʌzl] n Rätsel nt; (toy) Geduldspiel nt ♦ vt verwirren ♦ vi sich den Kopf zerbrechen

puzzling ['pʌzlɪŋ] adj rätselhaft, verwirrend

pyjamas [pɪ'dʒɑ:məz] (BRIT) npl Schlafanzug m, Pyjama m

pylon ['paɪlən] n Mast m

pyramid ['pɪrəmɪd] n Pyramide f

Q

quack [kwæk] n Quaken nt; (doctor) Quacksalber m ♦ vi quaken

quad [kwɒd] n abbr = quadrangle; quadruplet

quadrangle ['kwɒdræŋgl] n (court) Hof m; (MATH) Viereck nt

quadruple [kwɒ'dru:pl] adj vierfach ♦ vi sich vervierfachen ♦ vt vervierfachen

quadruplets [kwɒ'dru:pləts] npl Vierlinge pl

quagmire ['kwægmaɪə*] n Morast m

quail [kweɪl] n (bird) Wachtel f ♦ vi (vor Angst) zittern

quaint [kweɪnt] adj kurios; malerisch

quake [kweɪk] vi beben, zittern ♦ n abbr = **earthquake**

qualification [kwɒlɪfɪ'keɪʃən] n Qualifikation f; (sth which limits) Einschränkung f

qualified ['kwɒlɪfaɪd] adj (competent) qualifiziert; (limited) bedingt

qualify ['kwɒlɪfaɪ] vt (prepare) befähigen; (limit) einschränken ♦ vi sich qualifizieren; to ~ as a doctor/lawyer sein juristisches/medizinisches Staatsexamen machen

quality ['kwɒlɪtɪ] n Qualität f; (characteristic) Eigenschaft f

qualm [kwɑːm] n Bedenken nt

quandary ['kwɒndərɪ] n: to be in a ~ in Verlegenheit sein

quantity ['kwɒntɪtɪ] n Menge f; ~ surveyor n Baukostenkalkulator m

quarantine ['kwɒrəntiːn] n Quarantäne f

quarrel ['kwɒrəl] n Streit m ♦ vi sich streiten; **~some** adj streitsüchtig

quarry ['kwɒrɪ] n Steinbruch m; (animal) Wild nt; (fig) Opfer nt

quart [kwɔːt] n Quart nt

quarter ['kwɔːtə*] n Viertel nt; (of year) Quartal nt ♦ vt (divide) vierteln; (MIL) einquartieren; **~s** npl (esp MIL) Quartier nt; ~ of an hour Viertelstunde f; ~ **final** n Viertelfinale nt; **~ly** adj vierteljährlich

quartet(te) [kwɔː'tet] n Quartett nt

quartz [kwɔːts] n Quarz m

quash [kwɒʃ] vt (verdict) aufheben

quasi- ['kwɑːzɪ] prefix Quasi-

quaver ['kweɪvə*] n (BRIT: MUS) Achtelnote f ♦ vi (tremble) zittern

quay [kiː] n Kai m

queasy ['kwiːzɪ] adj übel

queen [kwiːn] n Königin f; ~ **mother** n Königinmutter f

queer [kwɪə*] adj seltsam ♦ n (inf: homosexual) Schwule(r) m

quell [kwel] vt unterdrücken

quench [kwentʃ] vt (thirst) löschen

querulous ['kwerʊləs] adj nörglerisch

query ['kwɪərɪ] n (question) (An)frage f; (question mark) Fragezeichen nt ♦ vt in Zweifel ziehen, in Frage stellen

quest [kwest] n Suche f

question ['kwestʃən] n Frage f ♦ vt (ask) (be)fragen; (suspect) verhören; (doubt) in Frage stellen, bezweifeln; **beyond** ~ ohne Frage; **out of the** ~ ausgeschlossen; **~able** adj zweifelhaft; ~ **mark** n Fragezeichen nt

questionnaire [kwestʃə'nɛə*] n Fragebogen m

queue [kjuː] (BRIT) n Schlange f ♦ vi (also: ~ up) Schlange stehen

quibble ['kwɪbl] vi kleinlich sein

quick [kwɪk] adj schnell ♦ n (of nail) Nagelhaut f; **be** ~! mach schnell!; **cut to the** ~ (fig) tief getroffen; **~en** vt (hasten) beschleunigen ♦ vi sich beschleunigen; **~ly** adj schnell; **~sand** n Treibsand m; **~witted** adj schlagfertig

quid [kwɪd] (BRIT: inf) n (£1) Pfund nt

quiet ['kwaɪət] adj (without noise) leise; (peaceful, calm) still, ruhig ♦ n Stille f, Ruhe f ♦ vt, vi (US) =

quieten; keep ~! sei still!; ~en vi (also: ~en down) ruhig werden ♦ vt beruhigen; ~ly adv leise, ruhig; ~ness n Ruhe f, Stille f

quilt [kwɪlt] n (continental ~) Steppdecke f

quin [kwɪn] n abbr = quintuplet

quinine [kwɪˈniːn] n Chinin nt

quintuplets [kwɪnˈtjuːplɪts] npl Fünflinge pl

quip [kwɪp] n witzige Bemerkung f

quirk [kwɜːk] n (oddity) Eigenart f

quit [kwɪt] (pt, pp quit or quitted) vt verlassen ♦ vi aufhören

quite [kwaɪt] adv (completely) ganz, völlig; (fairly) ziemlich; ~ a few of them ziemlich viele von ihnen; ~ (so)! richtig!

quits [kwɪts] adj quitt; let's call it ~ lassen wir's gut sein

quiver [ˈkwɪvə*] vi zittern ♦ n (for arrows) Köcher m

quiz [kwɪz] n (competition) Quiz nt ♦ vt prüfen; ~zical adj fragend

quorum [ˈkwɔːrəm] n beschlußfähige Anzahl f

quota [ˈkwəʊtə] n Anteil m; (COMM) Quote f

quotation [kwəʊˈteɪʃən] n Zitat nt; (price) Kostenvoranschlag m; ~ marks npl Anführungszeichen pl

quote [kwəʊt] n = quotation; vi (from book) zitieren ♦ vt zitieren; (price) angeben

R

rabbi [ˈræbaɪ] n Rabbiner m; (title) Rabbi m

rabbit [ˈræbɪt] n Kaninchen nt; ~hole n Kaninchenbau m; ~ hutch n Kaninchenstall m

rabble [ˈræbl] n Pöbel m

rabies [ˈreɪbiːz] n Tollwut f

RAC (BRIT) n abbr = Royal Automobile Club

raccoon [rəˈkuːn] n Waschbär m

race [reɪs] n (species) Rasse f; (competition) Rennen nt; (on foot) Rennen

nt, Wettlauf m; (rush) Hetze f ♦ vi um die Wette laufen mit; (horses) laufen lassen ♦ vi (run) rennen; (in contest) am Rennen teilnehmen; ~car (US) n = racing car; ~ car driver (US) n racing driver; ~course n (for horses) Rennbahn f; ~horse n Rennpferd nt; ~track n (for cars etc) Rennstrecke f

racial [ˈreɪʃəl] adj Rassen-; ~ist adj rassistisch ♦ n Rassist m

racing [ˈreɪsɪŋ] n Rennen nt; ~ car (BRIT) n Rennwagen m; ~ driver (BRIT) n Rennfahrer m

racism [ˈreɪsɪzəm] n Rassismus m

racist [ˈreɪsɪst] n Rassist m ♦ adj rassistisch

rack [ræk] n Ständer m, Gestell nt ♦ vt plagen; to go to ~ and ruin verfallen; to ~ one's brains sich dat den Kopf zerbrechen

racket [ˈrækɪt] n (din) Krach m; (scheme) (Schwindel)geschäft nt; (TENNIS: also racquet) (Tennis)schläger m

racoon [rəˈkuːn] n = raccoon

racquet [ˈrækɪt] n (Tennis)schläger m

racy [ˈreɪsɪ] adj gewagt; (style) spritzig

radar [ˈreɪdɑː*] n Radar nt or m

radial [ˈreɪdɪəl] adj (also: US: ~-ply) radial

radiance [ˈreɪdɪəns] n strahlende(r) Glanz m

radiant [ˈreɪdɪənt] adj strahlend; (giving out rays) Strahlungs-

radiate [ˈreɪdɪeɪt] vi ausstrahlen; (roads, lines) strahlenförmig wegführen ♦ vt ausstrahlen

radiation [reɪdɪˈeɪʃən] n (Aus)strahlung f

radiator [ˈreɪdɪeɪtə*] n (for heating) Heizkörper m; (AUT) Kühler m

radical [ˈrædɪkəl] adj radikal

radii [ˈreɪdɪaɪ] npl of radius

radio [ˈreɪdɪəʊ] n Rundfunk m, Radio nt; (set) Radio nt, Radioapparat m; on the ~ im Radio; ~active [reɪdɪəʊˈæktɪv] adj radioaktiv; ~logy [reɪdɪ'ɒledʒɪ] n Strahlenkunde f; ~ **station** n Rundfunkstation f; ~**therapy** ['reɪdɪəʊ'θerəpɪ] n Röntgentherapie f

radish ['rædɪʃ] n (big) Rettich m; (small) Radieschen nt

radius ['reɪdɪəs] n (pl **radii**) n Radius m; (circ) Umkreis m

RAF n abbr = **Royal Air Force**

raffle ['ræfl] n Verlosung f, Tombola f ♦ vt verlosen

raft [rɑːft] n Floß nt

rafter ['rɑːftə*] n Dachsparren m

rag [ræg] n (cloth) Lumpen m, Lappen m; (inf: newspaper) Käseblatt nt; (UNIV: for charity) studentische Sammelaktion f ♦ vt (BRIT) auf den Arm nehmen; ~**s** npl (clothes) Lumpen pl; ~-**and-bone man** (irreg, BRIT) n = **ragman**; ~ **doll** n Flickenpuppe f

rage [reɪdʒ] n Wut f; (fashion) große Mode f ♦ vi wüten, toben

ragged ['rægɪd] adj (edge) gezackt; (clothes) zerlumpt

ragman ['rægmæn] (irreg) n Lumpensammler m

raid [reɪd] n Überfall m; (MIL) Angriff m; (by police) Razzia f ♦ vt überfallen

rail [reɪl] n (also RAIL) Schiene f; (on stair) Geländer nt; (of ship) Reling f; ~**s** npl (RAIL) Geleise pl; by ~ per Bahn; ~**ing(s)** nt(pl) Geländer nt; ~**road** (US) n Eisenbahn f; ~**way** (BRIT) n Eisenbahn f; ~**way line** (BRIT) n (Eisen)bahnlinie f; (track) Gleis nt; ~**wayman** (irreg; BRIT) n Eisenbahner m; ~**way station** (BRIT) n Bahnhof m

rain [reɪn] n Regen m ♦ vt, vi regnen; **in the** ~ im Regen; **it's** ~**ing** es regnet; ~**bow** n Regenbogen m; ~**coat** n Regenmantel m; ~**drop** n Regentropfen m; ~**fall** n Niederschlag m; ~**forest** n Regenwald m; ~**y** adj (region, season) Regen-; (day) regnerisch, verregnet

raise [reɪz] n (esp US: increase) (Ge-halts)erhöhung f ♦ vt (lift)

(hoch)heben; (increase) erhöhen; (question) aufwerfen; (doubts) äußern; (funds) beschaffen; (family) großziehen; (livestock) züchten; **to** ~ **one's voice** die Stimme erheben

raisin ['reɪzən] n Rosine f

rake [reɪk] n Rechen m, Harke f; (person) Wüstling m ♦ vt rechen, harken; (with gun) (mit Feuer) bestreichen; (search) (durch)suchen

rakish ['reɪkɪʃ] adj verwegen

rally ['rælɪ] n (POL etc) Kundgebung f; (AUT) Rallye f ♦ vt (MIL) sammeln ♦ vi Kräfte sammeln; ~ **round** vt fus (sich) scharen um; (help) zu Hilfe kommen +dat ♦ vi zu Hilfe kommen

RAM n abbr (= random access memory) RAM m

ram [ræm] n Widder m; (instrument) Ramme f ♦ vt (strike) rammen; (stuff) hineinstopfen

ramble ['ræmbl] n Wanderung f ♦ vi (talk) schwafeln; ~**r** n Wanderer m

rambling ['ræmblɪŋ] adj (speech) weitschweifig; (town) ausgedehnt

ramp [ræmp] n Rampe f; **on/off** ~ (US: AUT) Ein-/Ausfahrt f

rampage [ræm'peɪdʒ] n: **to be on the** ~ randalieren ♦ vi randalieren

rampant ['ræmpənt] adj wild wuchernd

rampart ['ræmpɑːt] n (Schutz)wall m

ramshackle ['ræmʃækl] adj baufällig

ran [ræn] pt of **run**

ranch [rɑːntʃ] n Ranch f

rancid ['rænsɪd] adj ranzig

rancour ['ræŋkə*] (US **rancor**) n Verbitterung f, Groll m

random ['rændəm] adj ziellos, wahllos ♦ n: **at** ~ aufs Geratewohl; ~ **access** (COMPUT) wahlfreie(r) Zugriff m

randy ['rændɪ] (BRIT: inf) adj geil, scharf

rang [ræŋ] pt of **ring**

range [reɪndʒ] n (of mountains) Kette f; (COMM) Sortiment nt; (reach) (Reich)weite f; (of gun) Schußweite f; (for shooting practice)

Schießplatz m; (stove) (großer) Herd m ♦ vt (set in row) anordnen, aufstellen; (roam) durchstreifen ♦ vi: **to ~ over** (wander) umherstreifen in +dat; (extend) sich erstrecken auf +acc; **a ~ of** (selection) eine (große) Auswahl an +dat; **prices ranging from £5 to £10** Preise, die sich zwischen £5 und £10 bewegen; **~r** ['reɪŋdʒə*] n Förster m

rank [ræŋk] n (row) Reihe f; (BRIT: also: taxi ~) (Taxi)stand m; (MIL) Rang m; (social position) Stand m ♦ vi (have ~): **to ~ among** gehören zu ♦ adj (strong-smelling) stinkend; (extreme) krass; **the ~ and file** (fig) die breite Masse

rankle ['ræŋkl] vi nagen

ransack ['rænsæk] vt (plunder) plündern; (search) durchwühlen

ransom ['rænsəm] n Lösegeld nt; **to hold sb to ~** jdn gegen Lösegeld festhalten

rant [rænt] vi hochtrabend reden

rap [ræp] n Schlag m; (music) Rap m ♦ vt klopfen

rape [reɪp] n Vergewaltigung f; (BOT) Raps m ♦ vt vergewaltigen; **~(seed) oil** n Rapsöl nt

rapid ['ræpɪd] adj rasch, schnell; **~ity** [rə'pɪdɪtɪ] n Schnelligkeit f; **~ly** adv schnell; **~s** npl Stromschnellen pl

rapist ['reɪpɪst] n Vergewaltiger m

rapport [ræ'pɔ:*] n gute(s) Verhältnis nt

rapture ['ræptʃə*] n Entzücken nt

rapturous ['ræptʃərəs] adj (applause) stürmisch; (expression) verzückt

rare [reə*] adj selten, rar; (underdone) nicht durchgebraten

rarely ['reəlɪ] adv selten

raring ['reərɪŋ] adj: **to be ~ to go** (inf) es kaum erwarten können, bis es losgeht

rarity ['reərɪtɪ] n Seltenheit f

rascal ['rɑːskəl] n Schuft m

rash [ræʃ] adj übereilt; (reckless) unbesonnen ♦ n (Haut)ausschlag m

rasher ['ræʃə*] n Speckscheibe f

raspberry ['rɑːzbərɪ] n Himbeere f

rasping ['rɑːspɪŋ] adj (noise) kratzend; (voice) krächzend

rat [ræt] n (animal) Ratte f; (person) Halunke m

rate [reɪt] n (proportion) Rate f; (price) Tarif m; (speed) Tempo nt ♦ vt (ein)schätzen; **~s** npl (BRIT: tax) Grundsteuer f; **to ~ as** für etw halten; **~able value** (BRIT) n Einheitswert m (als Bemessungsgrundlage); **~payer** (BRIT) n Steuerzahler(in) m(f)

rather ['rɑːðə*] adv (in preference) lieber, eher; (to some extent) ziemlich; **I would** or **I'd ~ go** ich würde lieber gehen; **it's ~ expensive** (quite) es ist ziemlich teuer; (too) es ist etwas zu teuer; **there's ~ a lot** es ist ziemlich viel

ratify ['rætɪfaɪ] vt bestätigen; (POL) ratifizieren

rating ['reɪtɪŋ] n Klasse f; (BRIT: sailor) Matrose m

ratio ['reɪʃɪəʊ] n Verhältnis nt; **in the ~ of 100 to 1** im Verhältnis 100 zu 1

ration ['ræʃən] n (usu pl) Ration f ♦ vt rationieren

rational ['ræʃənl] adj rational; **~e** [ræʃə'nɑːl] n Grundprinzip nt; **~ize** ['ræʃnəlaɪz] vt rationalisieren; **~ly** adv rational

rat race n Konkurrenzkampf m

rattle ['rætl] n (sound) Rasseln nt; (toy) Rassel f ♦ vi rasseln, klappern ♦ vt rasseln mit; **~snake** n Klapperschlange f

raucous ['rɔːkəs] adj heiser, rauh

ravage ['rævɪdʒ] vt verheeren; **~s** npl verheerende Wirkungen pl

rave [reɪv] vi (talk wildly) phantasieren; (rage) toben

raven ['reɪvn] n Rabe m

ravenous ['rævənəs] adj heißhungrig

ravine [rə'viːn] n Schlucht f

raving ['reɪvɪŋ] adj: **~ lunatic** völlig Wahnsinnige(r) mf

ravishing ['rævɪʃɪŋ] adj atemberaubend

raw [rɔː] *adj* roh; *(tender)* wund(gerieben); *(inexperienced)* unerfahren; **to get a ~ deal** *(inf)* schlecht wegkommen; **~ material** *n* Rohmaterial *nt*

ray [reɪ] *n (of light)* Strahl *m*; **~ of hope** Hoffnungsschimmer *m*

raze [reɪz] *vt (also: raze to the ground)* dem Erdboden gleichmachen

razor ['reɪzə*] *n* Rasierapparat *m*; **~-blade** *n* Rasierklinge *f*

Rd *abbr* = **road**

re [riː] *prep (COMM)* betreffs +*gen*

reach [riːtʃ] *n* Reichweite *f*; *(of river)* Strecke *f* ♦ *vt (arrive at)* erreichen; *(give)* reichen ♦ *vi (stretch)* sich erstrecken; **within ~** *(shops etc)* in erreichbarer Weite or Entfernung; **out of ~** außer Reichweite; **to ~ for** *(try to get)* langen nach; **~ out** *vi* die Hand ausstrecken; **to ~ out for sth** nach etw greifen

react [riːˈækt] *vi* reagieren; **~ion** [riːˈækʃən] *n* Reaktion *f*

reactor [riːˈæktə*] *n* Reaktor *m*

read[1] [red] *pt, pp of* **read**

read[2] [riːd] *(pt, pp* read) *vt, vi* lesen; *(aloud)* vorlesen; **~ out** *vt* vorlesen; **~able** *adj* leserlich; *(worth reading)* lesenswert; **~er** *n (person)* Leser(in) *m(f)*; *(book)* Lesebuch *nt*; **~ership** *n* Leserschaft *f*

readily ['redɪlɪ] *adv (willingly)* bereitwillig; *(easily)* prompt

readiness ['redɪnəs] *n (willingness)* Bereitwilligkeit *f*; *(being ready)* Bereitschaft *f*; **in ~** *(prepared)* bereit

reading ['riːdɪŋ] *n* Lesen *nt*

readjust ['riːəˈdʒʌst] *vt* neu einstellen ♦ *vi (person)*: **to ~** to sich wieder anpassen an +*acc*

ready ['redɪ] *adj (prepared, willing)* bereit ♦ *adv*: **~-cooked** vorgekocht ♦ *n*: **at the ~** bereit; **~-made** *adj* gebrauchsfertig, Fertig-; *(clothes)* Konfektions-; **~ money** *n* Bargeld *nt*; **~ reckoner** *n* Rechentabelle *f*; **~-to-wear** *adj* Konfektions-

real [rɪəl] *adj* wirklich; *(actual)* eigentlich; *(not fake)* echt; **in ~**

terms effektiv; **~ estate** *n* Grundbesitz *m*; **~-istic** [rɪəˈlɪstɪk] *adj* realistisch

reality [riːˈælɪtɪ] *n* Wirklichkeit *f*, Realität *f*; **in ~** in Wirklichkeit

realization [rɪəlaɪˈzeɪʃən] *n (understanding)* Erkenntnis *f*; *(fulfilment)* Verwirklichung *f*

realize ['rɪəlaɪz] *vt (understand)* begreifen; *(make real)* verwirklichen; *(money)* einbringen; **I didn't ~** ... ich wußte nicht, ...

really ['rɪəlɪ] *adv* wirklich; **~?** *(indicating interest)* tatsächlich?; *(expressing surprise)* wirklich?

realm [relm] *n* Reich *nt*

realtor ['rɪəltɔː*] *n* (®; *US*) *n* Grundstücksmakler(in) *m(f)*

reap [riːp] *vt* ernten

reappear ['riːəˈpɪə*] *vi* wieder erscheinen

rear [rɪə*] *adj* hintere, Rück- ♦ *n* Rückseite *f*; *(last part)* Schluß *m* ♦ *vt (bring up)* aufziehen ♦ *vi (horse)* sich aufbäumen; **~guard** *n* Nachhut *f*

rearmament ['riːˈɑːməmənt] *n* Wiederaufrüstung *f*

rearrange ['riːəˈreɪndʒ] *vt* umordnen

rear-view mirror ['rɪəvjuː-] *n* Rückspiegel *m*

reason ['riːzn] *n (cause)* Grund *m*; *(ability to think)* Verstand *m*; *(sensible thoughts)* Vernunft *f* ♦ *vi (think)* denken; *(use arguments)* argumentieren; **it stands to ~ that** es ist logisch, daß; **to ~ with sb** mit jdm diskutieren; **~able** *adj* vernünftig; **~ably** *adv* vernünftig; *(fairly)* ziemlich; **~ed** *adj (argument)* durchdacht; **~ing** *n* Urteilen *nt*; *(argumentation)* Beweisführung *f*

reassurance ['riːəˈʃʊərəns] *n* Beruhigung *f*; *(confirmation)* Bestätigung *f*

reassure ['riːəˈʃʊə*] *vt* beruhigen; **to ~ sb of sth** jdm etw versichern

reassuring ['riːəˈʃʊərɪŋ] *adj* beruhigend

rebate ['riːbeɪt] *n* Rückzahlung *f*

rebel [*n* 'rebl, *vb* rɪ'bel] *n* Rebell *m*

vi rebellieren; **~lion** [rɪˈbeljən] *n* Rebellion *f*, Aufstand *m*; **~lious** *adj* (*subject, child, behaviour*) rebellisch

rebirth [ˈriːˈbɜːθ] *n* Wiedergeburt *f*

rebound [*vb* rɪˈbaʊnd, *n* ˈriːbaʊnd] *vi* zurückprallen ♦ *n* Rückprall *m*

rebuff [rɪˈbʌf] *n* Abfuhr *f* ♦ *vt* abblitzen lassen

rebuild [ˈriːˈbɪld] (*irreg*) *vt* wiederaufbauen; (*fig*) wiederherstellen

rebuke [rɪˈbjuːk] *n* Tadel *m* ♦ *vt* tadeln, rügen

rebut [rɪˈbʌt] *vt* widerlegen

recalcitrant [rɪˈkælsɪtrənt] *adj* widerspenstig

recall [rɪˈkɔːl] *vt* (*call back*) zurückrufen; (*remember*) sich erinnern an +*acc* ♦ *n* Rückruf *m*

recant [rɪˈkænt] *vi* widerrufen

recap [ˈriːkæp] *vt*, *vi* wiederholen

recapitulate [riːkəˈpɪtjuleɪt] *vt*, *vi* = recap

rec'd *abbr* (= received) Eing.

recede [rɪˈsiːd] *vi* zurückweichen

receding [rɪˈsiːdɪŋ] *adj*: ~ **hairline** Stirnglatze *f*

receipt [rɪˈsiːt] *n* (*document*) Quittung *f*; (*receiving*) Empfang *m*; **~s** *npl* (ECON) Einnahmen *pl*

receive [rɪˈsiːv] *vt* erhalten; (*visitors etc*) empfangen; **~r** [rɪˈsiːvə*] *n* (TEL) Hörer *m*

recent [ˈriːsnt] *adj* vor kurzem (geschehen), neuerlich; (*modern*) neu; **~ly** *adv* kürzlich, neulich

receptacle [rɪˈseptəkl] *n* Behälter *m*

reception [rɪˈsepʃən] *n* Empfang *m*; **~ desk** *n* Empfang *m*; (*in hotel*) Rezeption *f*; **~ist** *n* (*in hotel*) Empfangschef *m*, Empfangsdame *f*; (MED) Sprechstundenhilfe *f*

receptive [rɪˈseptɪv] *adj* aufnahmebereit

recess [rɪˈses] *n* (*break*) Ferien *pl*; (*hollow*) Nische *f*; **~ion** [rɪˈseʃən] *n* Rezession *f*

recharge [ˈriːˈtʃɑːdʒ] *vt* (*battery*) aufladen

recipe [ˈresɪpɪ] *n* Rezept *nt*

recipient [rɪˈsɪpɪənt] *n* Empfänger *m*

reciprocal [rɪˈsɪprəkəl] *adj* gegenseitig; (*mutual*) wechselseitig

recital [rɪˈsaɪtl] *n* Vortrag *m*

recite [rɪˈsaɪt] *vt* vortragen, aufsagen

reckless [ˈrekləs] *adj* leichtsinnig; (*driving*) fahrlässig

reckon [ˈrekən] *vt* (*count*) rechnen, berechnen, errechnen; (*estimate*) schätzen; (*think*): **I ~ that ...** ich nehme an, daß ...; **~ on** *vt fus* rechnen mit; **~ing** *n* (*calculation*) Rechnen *nt*

reclaim [rɪˈkleɪm] *vt* (*expenses*) zurückverlangen; (*land*): **to ~ (from sth)** (etw *dat*) gewinnen

reclamation [rekləˈmeɪʃən] *n* (*of land*) Gewinnung *f*

recline [rɪˈklaɪn] *vi* sich zurücklehnen

reclining [rɪˈklaɪnɪŋ] *adj* Liege-

recluse [rɪˈkluːs] *n* Einsiedler *m*

recognition [rekəgˈnɪʃən] *n* (*recognizing*) Erkennen *nt*; (*acknowledgement*) Anerkennung *f*; **transformed beyond ~** völlig verändert

recognizable [ˈrekəgnaɪzəbl] *adj* erkennbar

recognize [ˈrekəgnaɪz] *vt* erkennen; (POL, *approve*) anerkennen; **to ~ as** anerkennen als; **to ~ by** erkennen an +*dat*

recoil [rɪˈkɔɪl] *vi* (*in horror*) zurückschrecken; (*rebound*) zurückprallen; (*person*): **to ~ from doing sth** davor zurückschrecken, etw zu tun

recollect [rekəˈlekt] *vt* sich erinnern an +*acc*; **~ion** [rekəˈlekʃən] *n* Erinnerung *f*

recommend [rekəˈmend] *vt* empfehlen; **~ation** *n* Empfehlung *f*

recompense [ˈrekəmpens] *n* (*compensation*) Entschädigung *f*; (*reward*) Belohnung *f* ♦ *vt* entschädigen; belohnen

reconcile [ˈrekənsaɪl] *vt* (*facts*) vereinbaren; (*people*) versöhnen; **to ~ o.s. to sth** sich mit etw abfinden

reconciliation [rekənsɪlɪˈeɪʃən] *n* Versöhnung *f*

recondition [ˈriːkənˈdɪʃən] *vt* (*ma-*

chine) generalüberholen

reconnaissance [rɪˈkɒnɪsəns] n Aufklärung f

reconnoitre [rekəˈnɔɪtə*] (US **reconnoiter**) vt erkunden ♦ vi aufklären

reconsider [ˈriːkənˈsɪdə*] vt von neuem erwägen, noch einmal überdenken ♦ vi es noch einmal überdenken

reconstruct [ˈriːkənˈstrʌkt] vt wiederaufbauen; (crime) rekonstruieren; **~ion** [ˈriːkənˈstrʌkʃən] n Rekonstruktion f

record [n ˈrekɔːd, vb rɪˈkɔːd] n Aufzeichnung f; (MUS) Schallplatte f; (best performance) Rekord m ♦ vt aufzeichnen; (music etc) aufnehmen; **off the ~** vertraulich ♦ adv im Vertrauen; **in ~ time** in Rekordzeit; **~ card** n (in file) Karteikarte f; **~ed delivery** (BRIT) n (POST) Einschreiben nt; **~er** n (TECH) Registriergerät nt; (MUS) Blockflöte f; **~ holder** n (SPORT) Rekordhalter m; **~ing** n (MUS) Aufnahme f; **~ player** n Plattenspieler m

recount [rɪˈkaʊnt] vt (tell) berichten

re-count [ˈriːkaʊnt] n Nachzählung f ♦ vt nachzählen

recoup [rɪˈkuːp] vt: **to ~ one's losses** seinen Verlust wiedergutmachen

recourse [rɪˈkɔːs] n: **to have ~ to** Zuflucht nehmen zu or bei

recover [rɪˈkʌvə*] vt (get back) zurückerhalten ♦ vi sich erholen

re-cover [riːˈkʌvə*] vt (quilt etc) neu überziehen

recovery [rɪˈkʌvərɪ] n Wiedererlangung f; (of health) Erholung f

recreate [riːkrɪˈeɪt] vt wiederherstellen

recreation [rekrɪˈeɪʃən] n Erholung f; **~al** adj Erholungs-

recrimination [rɪkrɪmɪˈneɪʃən] n Gegenbeschuldigung f

recruit [rɪˈkruːt] n Rekrut m ♦ vt rekrutieren; **~ment** n Rekrutierung f

rectangle [ˈrektæŋgl] n Rechteck nt

rectangular [rekˈtæŋgjələ*] adj rech-

teckig, rechtwinklig

rectify [ˈrektɪfaɪ] vt berichtigen

rector [ˈrektə*] n (REL) Pfarrer m; (SCH) Direktor(in) m(f); **~y** [ˈrektərɪ] n Pfarrhaus nt

recuperate [rɪˈkuːpəreɪt] vi sich erholen

recur [rɪˈkɜː*] vi sich wiederholen; **~rence** n Wiederholung f; **~rent** adj wiederkehrend

recycle [riːˈsaɪkl] vt wiederverwerten, wiederaufbereiten

red [red] n Rot nt; (POL) Rote(r) m ♦ adj rot; **in the ~** in den roten Zahlen; **~ carpet treatment** n Sonderbehandlung f, große(r) Bahnhof m; **R~ Cross** n Rote(s) Kreuz nt; **~currant** n rote Johannisbeere f; **~den** vi sich röten; (blush) erröten ♦ vt röten; **~dish** adj rötlich

redeem [rɪˈdiːm] vt (COMM) einlösen; (save) retten

redeeming [rɪˈdiːmɪŋ] adj: **~ feature** versöhnende(s) Moment nt

redeploy [ˈriːdɪˈplɔɪ] vt (resources) umverteilen

red-haired [ˈredˈhɛəd] adj rothaarig

red-handed [ˈredˈhændɪd] adv: **to be caught ~** auf frischer Tat ertappt werden

redhead [ˈredhɛd] n Rothaarige(r) mf

red herring n Ablenkungsmanöver nt

red-hot [ˈredˈhɒt] adj rotglühend

redirect [ˈriːdaɪˈrekt] vt umleiten

red light n: **to go through a ~** (AUT) bei Rot über die Ampel fahren; **red-light district** n Strichviertel nt

redo [ˈriːˈduː] (irreg: like do) vt nochmals machen

redolent [ˈredəlant] adj: **~ of** riechend nach; (fig) erinnernd an +acc

redouble [riːˈdʌbl] vt: **to ~ one's efforts** seine Anstrengungen verdoppeln

redress [rɪˈdres] n Entschädigung f ♦ vt wiedergutmachen

Red Sea n: **the ~** das Rote Meer

redskin ['redskɪn] n Rothaut f
red tape n Bürokratismus m
reduce [rɪ'dʒuːs] vt (speed, temperature) vermindern; (photo) verkleinern; "~ speed now" (AUT) = „langsam"; to ~ the price (to) den Preis herabsetzen (auf +acc); at a ~d price zum ermäßigten Preis
reduction [rɪ'dʌkʃən] n Verminderung f; Verkleinerung f; Herabsetzung f; (amount of money) Nachlaß m
redundancy [rɪ'dʌndənsɪ] n Überflüssigkeit f; (of workers) Entlassung f
redundant [rɪ'dʌndənt] adj überflüssig; (workers) ohne Arbeitsplatz; to be made ~ arbeitslos werden
reed [riːd] n Schilf nt; (MUS) Rohrblatt nt
reef [riːf] n Riff nt
reek [riːk] vi: to ~ (of) stinken (nach)
reel [riːl] n Spule f, Rolle f ♦ vt (also: ~ in) wickeln, spulen ♦ vi (stagger) taumeln
ref [ref] (inf) n abbr (= referee) Schiri m
refectory [rɪ'fektərɪ] n (UNIV) Mensa f; (SCH) Speisesaal m; (ECCL) Refektorium nt
refer [rɪ'fɜː*] vt: to ~ sb to sb/sth jdn an jdn/etw verweisen ♦ vi: to ~ to (to book) nachschlagen in +dat; (mention) sich beziehen auf +acc
referee [refə'riː] n Schiedsrichter m; (BRIT: for job) Referenz f ♦ vt schiedsrichtern
reference ['refrəns] n (for job) Referenz f; (in book) Verweis m; (number, code) Aktenzeichen nt; (allusion): ~ (to) Anspielung (auf +acc); with ~ to in bezug auf +acc; ~ book n Nachschlagewerk nt; ~ number n Aktenzeichen nt
referenda [refə'rendə] npl of referendum
referendum [refə'rendəm] (pl -da) n Volksabstimmung f
refill [vb 'riː'fɪl, n 'riːfɪl] vt nachfüllen ♦ n (for pen) Ersatzmine f

refine [rɪ'faɪn] vt (purify) raffinieren; ~d adj kultiviert; ~ment n Kultiviertheit f
reflect [rɪ'flekt] vt (light) reflektieren; (fig) (wider)spiegeln ♦ vi (meditate): to ~ (on) nachdenken (über +acc); it ~s badly/well on him das stellt ihn in ein schlechtes/gutes Licht; ~ion [rɪ'flekʃən] n Reflexion f; (image) Spiegelbild nt; (thought) Überlegung f; on ~ion wenn man sich dat das recht überlegt
reflex ['riːfleks] adj Reflex- ♦ n Reflex m; ~ive [rɪ'fleksɪv] adj reflexiv
reform [rɪ'fɔːm] n Reform f ♦ vt (person) bessern; the R~ation n die Reformation; ~atory (US) n Besserungsanstalt f
refrain [rɪ'freɪn] vi: to ~ from unterlassen ♦ n Refrain m
refresh [rɪ'freʃ] vt erfrischen; ~er course (BRIT) n Wiederholungskurs m; ~ing adj erfrischend; ~ments npl Erfrischungen pl
refrigeration [rɪfrɪdʒə'reɪʃən] n Kühlung f
refrigerator [rɪ'frɪdʒəreɪtə*] n Kühlschrank m
refuel ['riː'fjʊəl] vt, vi auftanken
refuge ['refjuːdʒ] n Zuflucht f; to take ~ in sich flüchten in +acc
refugee [refjʊ'dʒiː] n Flüchtling m
refund [n 'riːfʌnd, vb rɪ'fʌnd] n Rückvergütung f ♦ vt zurückerstatten
refurbish ['riː'fɜːbɪʃ] vt aufpolieren
refusal [rɪ'fjuːzəl] n (Ver)weigerung f; first ~ Vorkaufsrecht nt
refuse[1] [rɪ'fjuːz] vt abschlagen ♦ vi sich weigern
refuse[2] ['refjuːs] n Abfall m, Müll m; ~ collection n Müllabfuhr f
refute [rɪ'fjuːt] vt widerlegen
regain [rɪ'geɪn] vt wiedergewinnen; (consciousness) wiedererlangen
regal ['riːgəl] adj königlich
regalia [rɪ'geɪlɪə] npl Insignien pl
regard [rɪ'gɑːd] n Achtung f ♦ vt ansehen; to send one's ~s to sb jdn

grüßen lassen; **"with kindest ~s"** „mit freundlichen Grüßen"; **~ing** or **as ~s** or **with ~** to bezüglich +*gen*, in bezug auf +*acc*; **~less** *adj*: **~less** of ohne Rücksicht auf +*acc* ♦ *adv* trotzdem

regenerate [rɪ'dʒenəreɪt] *vt* erneuern

régime [reɪ'ʒiːm] *n* Regime *nt*

regiment [*n* 'redʒɪmənt, *vb* 'redʒɪment] *n* Regiment *nt* ♦ *vt* (*fig*) reglementieren; **~al** [redʒɪ'mentl] *adj* Regiments-

region ['riːdʒən] *n* Region *f*; **in the ~ of** (*fig*) so um; **~al** *adj* örtlich, regional

register ['redʒɪstə*] *n* Register *nt* ♦ *vt* (*list*) registrieren; (*emotion*) zeigen; (*write down*) eintragen ♦ *vi* (*at hotel*) sich eintragen; (*with police*) sich melden; (*make impression*) wirken, ankommen; **to ~ with the police** sich bei der Polizei melden, sich polizeilich melden; **~ed** (*BRIT*) *adj* (*letter*) Einschreibe-, eingeschrieben; **~ed trademark** *n* eingetragene(s) Warenzeichen *nt*

registrar [redʒɪs'trɑː*] *n* Standesbeamte(r) *m*

registration [redʒɪs'treɪʃən] *n* (*act*) Registrierung *f*; (*AUT*: *also*: **~ number**) polizeiliche(s) Kennzeichen *nt*

registry ['redʒɪstrɪ] *n* Sekretariat *nt*; **~ office** (*BRIT*) *n* Standesamt *nt*; **to get married in a ~ office** standesamtlich heiraten

regret [rɪ'gret] *n* Bedauern *nt* ♦ *vt* bedauern; **~fully** *adv* mit Bedauern, ungern; **~table** *adj* bedauerlich

regroup [riː'gruːp] *vt* umgruppieren ♦ *vi* sich umgruppieren

regular ['regjʊlə*] *adj* regelmäßig; (*usual*) üblich; (*inf*) regelrecht ♦ *n* (*client etc*) Stammkunde *m*; **~ity** [regjʊ'lærɪtɪ] *n* Regelmäßigkeit *f*; **~ly** *adv* regelmäßig

regulate ['regjʊleɪt] *vt* regeln, regulieren

regulation [regjʊ'leɪʃən] *n* (*rule*) Vorschrift *f*; (*control*) Regulierung *f*

rehabilitation ['riːhəbɪlɪ'teɪʃən] *n* (*of criminal*) Resozialisierung *f*

rehearsal [rɪ'həːsl] *n* Probe *f*

rehearse [rɪ'həːs] *vt or* proben

reign [reɪn] *n* Herrschaft *f* ♦ *vi* herrschen

reimburse [riːɪm'bəːs] *vt*: **to ~ sb for sth** jdn für etw entschädigen, jdm etw zurückzahlen

rein [reɪn] *n* Zügel *m*

reincarnation ['riːɪnkɑː'neɪʃən] *n* Wiedergeburt *f*

reindeer ['reɪndɪə*] *n* Ren *nt*

reinforce [riːɪn'fɔːs] *vt* verstärken; **~d concrete** *n* Stahlbeton *m*; **~ment** *n* Verstärkung *f*; **~ments** *npl* (*MIL*) Verstärkungstruppen *pl*

reinstate [riːɪn'steɪt] *vt* wiedereinsetzen

reissue ['riː'ɪʃuː] *vt* neu herausgeben

reiterate [riː'ɪtəreɪt] *vt* wiederholen

reject [*n* 'riːdʒekt, *vb* rɪ'dʒekt] *n* (*COMM*) Ausschuß(artikel) *m* ♦ *vt* ablehnen; **~ion** [rɪ'dʒekʃən] *n* Zurückweisung *f*

rejoice [rɪ'dʒɔɪs] *vi*: **to ~ at** or **over** sich freuen über +*acc*

rejuvenate [rɪ'dʒuːvɪneɪt] *vt* verjüngen

rekindle ['riː'kɪndl] *vt* wieder anfachen

relapse [rɪ'læps] *n* Rückfall *m*

relate [rɪ'leɪt] *vt* (*tell*) erzählen; (*connect*) verbinden ♦ *vi*: **to ~ to** zusammenhängen mit; (*form relationship*) eine Beziehung aufbauen zu; **~d** *adj*: **~d (to)** verwandt (mit); **relating** *prep*: **relating to** bezüglich +*gen*

relation [rɪ'leɪʃən] *n* Verwandte(r) *mf*; (*connection*) Beziehung *f*; **~ship** *n* Verhältnis *n*, Beziehung *f*

relative ['relətɪv] *n* Verwandte(r) *mf* ♦ *adj* relativ; **~ly** *adv* verhältnismäßig

relax [rɪ'læks] *vi* (*slacken*) sich lockern; (*muscles*, *person*) sich entspannen ♦ *vt* (*ease*) lockern, entspannen; **~ation** [riːlæk'seɪʃən] *n* Entspannung *f*; **~ed** *adj* entspannt, locker; **~ing** adj entspannend

relay ['ri:leɪ] n (SPORT) Staffel f ♦ vt (message) weiterleiten; (RADIO, TV) übertragen

release [rɪ'li:s] n (freedom) Entlassung f; (TECH) Auslöser m ♦ vt befreien; (prisoner) entlassen; (report, news) verlautbaren, bekanntgeben

relegate ['relɪɡeɪt] vt (SPORT): to be ~d absteigen

relent [rɪ'lent] vi nachgeben; **~less** adj unnachgiebig; **~lessly** adv unnachgiebig

relevant ['relɪvənt] adj wichtig, relevant; **~ to** relevant für

reliability [rɪlaɪə'bɪlɪtɪ] n Zuverlässigkeit f

reliable [rɪ'laɪəbl] adj zuverlässig; **reliably** adv zuverlässig; **to be reliably informed that ...** aus zuverlässiger Quelle wissen, daß ...

reliance [rɪ'laɪəns] n: **~ (on)** Abhängigkeit f (von)

relic ['relɪk] n (from past) Überbleibsel nt; (REL) Reliquie f

relief [rɪ'li:f] n (from pain) Erleichterung f; (help) Hilfe f; (person) Ablösung f

relieve [rɪ'li:v] vt (ease) erleichtern; (bring help) entlasten; (person) ablösen; **to ~ sb of sth** jdm etw abnehmen; **to ~ o.s.** (euph) sich erleichtern

religion [rɪ'lɪdʒən] n Religion f

religious [rɪ'lɪdʒəs] adj religiös

relinquish [rɪ'lɪŋkwɪʃ] vt aufgeben

relish ['relɪʃ] n Würze f ♦ vt genießen; **to ~ doing** gern tun

relocate [ri:ləʊ'keɪt] vt verlegen ♦ vi umziehen

reluctance [rɪ'lʌktəns] n Widerstreben nt, Abneigung f

reluctant [rɪ'lʌktənt] adj widerwillig; **~ly** adv ungern

rely [rɪ'laɪ]: **to ~ on** vt fus sich verlassen auf +acc

remain [rɪ'meɪn] vi (be left) übrigbleiben; (stay) bleiben; **~der** n Rest m; **~ing** adj übrig(geblieben); **~s** npl Überreste pl

remand [rɪ'mɑːnd] n: **on ~** in Untersuchungshaft ♦ vt: **to ~ in custody** in Untersuchungshaft schicken; **~ home** n (BRIT) Untersuchungsgefängnis nt für Jugendliche

remark [rɪ'mɑːk] n Bemerkung f ♦ vt bemerken; **~able** adj bemerkenswert

remarry [ri:'mærɪ] vi sich wieder verheiraten

remedial [rɪ'mi:dɪəl] adj Heil-; (teaching) Hilfsschul-

remedy ['remɪdɪ] n Mittel nt ♦ vt (pain) abhelfen +dat; (trouble) in Ordnung bringen

remember [rɪ'membə*] vt sich erinnern an +acc

remembrance [rɪ'membrəns] n Erinnerung f; (official) Gedenken nt

remind [rɪ'maɪnd] vt: **to ~ sb to do sth** jdn daran erinnern, etw zu tun; **to ~ sb of sth** jdn an etw acc erinnern; **she ~s me of her mother** sie erinnert mich an ihre Mutter; **~er** n Mahnung f

reminisce [remɪ'nɪs] vi in Erinnerungen schwelgen

reminiscent [remɪ'nɪsnt] adj: **to be ~ of sth** an etw acc erinnern

remiss [rɪ'mɪs] adj nachlässig

remission [rɪ'mɪʃən] n Nachlaß m; (of debt, sentence) Erlaß m

remit [rɪ'mɪt] vt (money): **to ~ (to)** überweisen, (an +acc); **~tance** n Geldanweisung f

remnant ['remnənt] n Rest m; **~s** npl (COMM) Einzelstücke pl

remorse [rɪ'mɔːs] n Gewissensbisse pl; **~ful** adj reumütig; **~less** adj unbarmherzig; **~lessly** adv unbarmherzig

remote [rɪ'məʊt] adj abgelegen; (slight) gering; **~ control** n Fernsteuerung f; **~ly** adv entfernt

remould [ri:'məʊld] (BRIT) n runderneuerte(r) Reifen m

removable [rɪ'mu:vəbl] adj entfernbar

removal [rɪ'mu:vəl] n Beseitigung f; (of furniture) Umzug m; (from office) Entlassung f; **~ van** (BRIT)

Möbelwagen m

remove [rɪ'muːv] vt beseitigen, entfernen; **~rs** npl Möbelspedition f

remuneration [rɪmjuːnə'reɪʃən] n Vergütung f, Honorar m

render ['rendə*] vt machen; (translate) übersetzen; **~ing** n (MUS) Wiedergabe f

rendezvous ['rɒndɪvuː] n (meeting) Rendezvous nt; (place) Treffpunkt m ♦ vi sich treffen

renew [rɪ'njuː] vt erneuern; (contract, licence) verlängern; (replace) ersetzen

renewable adj regenerierbar; **renewal** n Erneuerung f; Verlängerung f

renounce [rɪ'naʊns] vt (give up) verzichten auf +acc; (disown) verstoßen

renovate ['renəveɪt] vt renovieren; (building) restaurieren

renown [rɪ'naʊn] n Ruf m; **~ed** adj namhaft

rent [rent] n Miete f; (for land) Pacht f ♦ vt (hold as tenant) mieten; pachten; (let) vermieten; verpachten; (car etc) mieten; (firm) vermieten; **~al** n Miete f

renunciation [rɪnʌnsɪ'eɪʃən] n: ~ (of) Verzicht m (auf +acc)

reorganize [riː'ɔːgənaɪz] vt umgestalten, reorganisieren

rep [rep] n abbr (COMM) = representative; (THEAT) = repertory

repair [rɪ'peə*] n Reparatur f ♦ vt reparieren; (damage) wiedergutmachen; **in good/bad** ~ in gutem/ schlechtem Zustand; ~ **kit** n Werkzeugkasten m

repartee [repɑː'tiː] n Witzeleien pl

repatriate [riː'pætrɪeɪt] vt in die Heimat zurückschicken

repay [riː'peɪ] (irreg) vt zurückzahlen; (reward) vergelten; **~ment** n Rückzahlung f; (fig) Vergeltung f

repeal [rɪ'piːl] n Aufhebung f ♦ vt aufheben

repeat [rɪ'piːt] n (RADIO, TV) Wiederholung(ssendung) f ♦ vt wiederholen; **~edly** adv wiederholt

repel [rɪ'pel] vt (drive back) zurückschlagen; (disgust) abstoßen; **~lent** adj abstoßend ♦ n: **insect** ~lent Insektenmittel nt

repent [rɪ'pent] vt, vi: to ~ (of) bereuen; **~ance** n Reue f

repercussion [riːpə'kʌʃən] n Auswirkung f; **to have** ~s ein Nachspiel haben

repertoire ['repətwɑː] n Repertoire nt

repertory ['repətəri] n Repertoire nt

repetition [repɪ'tɪʃən] n Wiederholung f

repetitive [rɪ'petɪtɪv] adj sich wiederholend

replace [rɪ'pleɪs] vt ersetzen; (put back) zurückstellen; **~ment** n Ersatz m

replay ['riːpleɪ] n (of match) Wiederholungsspiel nt; (of tape, film) Wiederholung f

replenish [rɪ'plenɪʃ] vt ergänzen

replete [rɪ'pliːt] adj (zum Platzen) voll

replica ['replɪkə] n Kopie f

reply [rɪ'plaɪ] n Antwort f ♦ vi antworten; ~ **coupon** n Antwortschein m

report [rɪ'pɔːt] n Bericht m; (BRIT: SCH) Zeugnis nt ♦ vt (tell) berichten; (give information against) melden; (to police) anzeigen ♦ vi (make report) Bericht erstatten; (present o.s.): to ~ (to sb) (present o.s.) sich (bei jdm) melden; ~ **card** (US, SCOTTISH) n Zeugnis nt; **~edly** adv wie verlautet; **~er** n Reporter m

repose [rɪ'pəʊz] n: **in** ~ (face, body) entspannt; (mind) gelassen

reprehensible [reprɪ'hensɪbl] adj tadelnswert

represent [reprɪ'zent] vt darstellen; (speak for) vertreten; **~ation** [reprɪzen'teɪʃən] n Darstellung f; (being represented) Vertretung f; **~ations** npl (protest) Vorhaltungen pl; **~ative** n (person) Vertreter m; (US: POL) Abgeordnete(r) mf ♦ adj repräsentativ

repress [rɪ'pres] vt unterdrücken; **~ion** [rɪ'preʃən] n Unterdrückung f

reprieve [rɪ'priːv] n (JUR) Begnadigung f; (fig) Gnadenfrist f ♦ vt (JUR) begnadigen

reprimand [reprɪ'mɑːnd] n Verweis m ♦ vt einen Verweis erteilen +dat

reprint [n 'riːprɪnt, vb 'riː'prɪnt] n Neudruck m ♦ vt wieder abdrucken

reprisal [rɪ'praɪzəl] n Vergeltung f

reproach [rɪ'prəʊtʃ] n Vorwurf m ♦ vt Vorwürfe machen +dat; to ~ sb with sth jdm etw vorwerfen; **~ful** adj vorwurfsvoll

reproduce [riːprə'djuːs] vt reproduzieren ♦ vi (have offspring) sich vermehren

reproduction [riːprə'dʌkʃən] n (ART, PHOT) Reproduktion f; (breeding) Fortpflanzung f

reproductive [riːprə'dʌktɪv] adj reproduktiv; (breeding) Fortpflanzungs-

reproof [rɪ'pruːf] n Tadel m

reprove [rɪ'pruːv] vt tadeln

reptile ['reptaɪl] n Reptil n

republic [rɪ'pʌblɪk] n Republik f

repudiate [rɪ'pjuːdɪeɪt] vt zurückweisen

repugnant [rɪ'pʌgnənt] adj widerlich

repulse [rɪ'pʌls] vt (drive back) zurückschlagen; (reject) abweisen

repulsive [rɪ'pʌlsɪv] adj abstoßend

reputable ['repjʊtəbl] adj angesehen

reputation [repjʊ'teɪʃən] n Ruf m

repute [rɪ'pjuːt] n hohe(s) Ansehen nt; **~d** adj angeblich; **~dly** adv angeblich

request [rɪ'kwest] n Bitte f ♦ vt (thing) erbitten; to ~ sth of or from sb jdn um etw bitten; (formally) jdn um etw ersuchen; ~ **stop** (BRIT) n Bedarfshaltestelle f

require [rɪ'kwaɪə*] vt (need) brauchen; (demand) erfordern; ~**ment** n (condition) Anforderung f; (need) Bedarf m

requisite ['rekwɪzɪt] n Erfordernis n ♦ adj erforderlich

requisition [rekwɪ'zɪʃən] n Anforderung f ♦ vt beschlagnahmen

resale ['riːseɪl] n Weiterverkauf m

rescind [rɪ'sɪnd] vt aufheben

rescue ['reskjuː] n Rettung f ♦ vt retten; ~ **party** n Rettungsmannschaft f; **~r** n Retter m

research [rɪ'sɜːtʃ] n Forschung f ♦ vi forschen ♦ vt erforschen; **~er** n Forscher m

resemblance [rɪ'zembləns] n Ähnlichkeit f

resemble [rɪ'zembl] vt ähneln +dat

resent [rɪ'zent] vt übelnehmen; **~ful** adj nachtragend, empfindlich; **~ment** n Verstimmung f, Unwille m

reservation [rezə'veɪʃən] n (booking) Reservierung f; (THEAT) Vorbestellung f; (doubt) Vorbehalt m; (land) Reservat nt

reserve [rɪ'zɜːv] n (store) Vorrat m, Reserve f; (manner) Zurückhaltung f; (game ~) Naturschutzgebiet n; (SPORT) Ersatzspieler(in) m(f) ♦ vt reservieren; (judgement) sich dat vorbehalten; **~s** npl (MIL) Reserve f; **in** ~ in Reserve f; **~d** adj reserviert

reshape ['riː'ʃeɪp] vt umformen

reshuffle ['riː'ʃʌfl] n (POL): **cabinet** ~ Kabinettsumbildung f ♦ vt (POL) umbilden

reside [rɪ'zaɪd] vi wohnen, ansässig sein

residence ['rezɪdəns] n (house) Wohnsitz m; (living) Aufenthalt m

resident ['rezɪdənt] n (in house) Bewohner m; (in area) Einwohner m ♦ adj wohnhaft, ansässig; **~ial** [rezɪ'denʃəl] adj Wohn-

residue ['rezɪdjuː] n Rest m; (CHEM) Rückstand m; (fig) Bodensatz m

resign [rɪ'zaɪn] vt (office) aufgeben, zurücktreten von ♦ vi (from office) zurücktreten; (employee) kündigen; to be ~**ed** to sth, to ~ o.s. to sth sich mit etw abfinden; ~**ation** [rezɪg'neɪʃən] n (from job) Kündigung f; (POL) Rücktritt m; (submission) Resignation f; ~**ed** adj resigniert

resilience [rɪ'zɪlɪəns] n Spannkraft f; (of person) Unverwüstlichkeit f

resilient [rɪ'zɪlɪənt] adj unverwüstlich

resin ['rezɪn] n Harz nt

resist [rɪ'zɪst] vt widerstehen +dat; **~ance** n Widerstand m

resolute ['rezəluːt] adj entschlossen, resolut

resolution [rezə'luːʃən] n (firmness) Entschlossenheit f; (intention) Vorsatz m; (decision) Beschluß m

resolve [rɪ'zɔlv] n Entschlossenheit f ♦ vt (decide) beschließen ♦ vi sich lösen; **~d** adj (fest) entschlossen

resonant ['rezənənt] adj voll

resort [rɪ'zɔːt] n (holiday place) Erholungsort m; (help) Zuflucht f ♦ vi: **to ~ to** Zuflucht nehmen zu; **as a last ~** als letzter Ausweg

resound [rɪ'zaʊnd] vi: **to ~ (with)** widerhallen (von); **~ing** [rɪ'zaʊndɪŋ] adj nachhallend; (success) groß

resource [rɪ'sɔːs] n Findigkeit f; **~s** npl (financial) Geldmittel pl; (natural) Bodenschätze pl; **~ful** adj findig

respect [rɪs'pekt] n Respekt m ♦ vt achten, respektieren; **~s** npl (regards) Grüße pl; **with ~ to** in bezug auf +acc, hinsichtlich +gen; **in this ~** in dieser Hinsicht; **~ability** [rɪspektə'bɪlɪtɪ] n Anständigkeit f; **~able** adj (decent) anständig; (fairly good) leidlich; **~ful** adj höflich

respective [rɪs'pektɪv] adj jeweilig; **~ly** adv beziehungsweise

respiration [respɪ'reɪʃən] n Atmung f

respite ['respaɪt] n Ruhepause f

resplendent [rɪs'plendənt] adj strahlend

respond [rɪs'pɔnd] vi antworten; (react): **to ~ (to)** reagieren (auf +acc)

response [rɪs'pɔns] n Antwort f, Reaktion f; (to advertisement etc) Resonanz f

responsibility [rɪspɔnsə'bɪlɪtɪ] n Verantwortung f

responsible [rɪs'pɔnsəbl] adj verantwortlich; (reliable) verantwortungsvoll

responsive [rɪs'pɔnsɪv] adj empfänglich

rest [rest] n Ruhe f; (break) Pause f; (remainder) Rest m ♦ vi sich ausruhen; (be supported) (auf)liegen ♦ vt (lean): **to ~ sth on/against sth** etw gegen etw acc lehnen; **the ~ of them** die übrigen; **it ~s with him to ...** es liegt bei ihm, zu ...

restaurant ['restərɔŋ] n Restaurant nt; **~ car** (BRIT) n Speisewagen m

restful ['restful] adj erholsam, ruhig

rest home n Erholungsheim nt

restive ['restɪv] adj unruhig

restless ['restləs] adj unruhig

restoration [restə'reɪʃən] n Rückgabe f; (of building etc) Rückerstattung f

restore [rɪs'tɔː] vt (order) wiederherstellen; (customs) wieder einführen; (person to position) wiedereinsetzen; (give back) zurückgeben; (paintings, buildings) restaurieren

restrain [rɪs'treɪn] vt zurückhalten; (curiosity etc) beherrschen; (person): **to ~ sb from doing sth** jdn davon abhalten, etw zu tun; **~ed** adj (style etc) gedämpft, verhalten; **~t** n (self-control) Zurückhaltung f

restrict [rɪs'trɪkt] vt einschränken; **~ion** [rɪs'trɪkʃən] n Einschränkung f; **~ive** adj einschränkend

rest room (US) n Toilette f

restructure ['riː'strʌktʃə] vt umstrukturieren

result [rɪ'zʌlt] n Resultat nt, Folge f; (of exam, game) Ergebnis nt ♦ vi: **to ~ in sth** etw zur Folge haben; **as a ~ of** als Folge +gen

resume [rɪ'zjuːm] vt fortsetzen; (occupy again) wieder einnehmen ♦ vi (work etc) wieder beginnen

résumé ['reɪzjuːmeɪ] n Zusammenfassung f

resumption [rɪ'zʌmpʃən] n Wiederaufnahme f

resurgence [rɪ'sɜːdʒəns] n Wiedererwachen nt

resurrection [rezə'rekʃən] n Auferstehung f

resuscitate [rɪ'sʌsɪteɪt] vt wiederleben

resuscitation [rɪsʌsɪˈteɪʃən] n Wiederbelebung f

retail [n, adj ˈriːteɪl, vb riːˈteɪl] n Einzelhandel m ♦ adj Einzelhandels- ♦ vt im kleinen verkaufen ♦ vi im Einzelhandel kosten; ~**er** [ˈriːteɪlə*] n Einzelhändler m, Kleinhändler m; ~ **price** n Ladenpreis m

retain [rɪˈteɪn] vt (keep) (zurück)behalten; ~**er** n (servant) Gefolgsmann m; (fee) (Honorar)vorschuß m

retaliate [rɪˈtælɪeɪt] vi zum Vergeltungsschlag ausholen

retaliation [rɪtælɪˈeɪʃən] n Vergeltung f

retarded [rɪˈtɑːdɪd] adj zurückgeblieben

retch [retʃ] vi würgen

retentive [rɪˈtentɪv] adj (memory) gut

reticent [ˈretɪsənt] adj schweigsam

retina [ˈretɪnə] n Netzhaut f

retinue [ˈretɪnjuː] n Gefolge nt

retire [rɪˈtaɪə*] vi (from work) in den Ruhestand treten; (withdraw) sich zurückziehen; (go to bed) schlafen gehen; ~**d** adj (person) pensioniert, im Ruhestand; ~**ment** n Ruhestand m

retiring [rɪˈtaɪərɪŋ] adj zurückhaltend

retort [rɪˈtɔːt] n (reply) Erwiderung f; (SCI) Retorte f ♦ vi (scharf) erwidern

retrace [rɪˈtreɪs] vt zurückverfolgen; to ~ one's steps denselben Weg zurückgehen

retract [rɪˈtrækt] vt (statement) zurücknehmen; (claws) einziehen ♦ vi eine Rückziehen machen; ~**able** adj (aerial) ausziehbar

retrain [riːˈtreɪn] vt umschulen; ~**ing** n Umschulung f

retread [rɪˈtred] n (tyre) Reifen m mit erneuerter Lauffläche

retreat [rɪˈtriːt] n Rückzug m; (place) Zufluchtsort m ♦ vi sich zurückziehen

retribution [retrɪˈbjuːʃən] n Strafe f

retrieval [rɪˈtriːvəl] n Wiedergewinn-

ung f

retrieve [rɪˈtriːv] vt wiederbekommen; (rescue) retten; ~**r** n Apportierhund m

retrograde [ˈretrəʊgreɪd] adj (step) Rück-; (policy) rückschrittlich

retrospect [ˈretrəʊspekt] n: in ~ im Rückblick, rückblickend; ~**ive** [retrəʊˈspektɪv] adj (action) rückwirkend; (look) rückblickend

return [rɪˈtɜːn] n Rückkehr f; (profits) Ertrag m; (BRIT: rail ticket etc) Rückfahrkarte f; (: plane ticket) Rückflugkarte f ♦ adj (journey, match) Rück- ♦ vi zurückkehren, zurückkommen ♦ vt zurückgeben, zurücksenden; (pay back) zurückzahlen; (elect) wählen; (verdict) aussprechen; ~**s** npl (COMM) Gewinn m; (receipts) Einkünfte pl; in ~ dafür; by ~ of post postwendend; many happy ~s (of the day)! herzlichen Glückwunsch zum Geburtstag!

reunion [riːˈjuːnjən] n Wiedervereinigung f; (SCH etc) Treffen nt

reunite [riːjuːˈnaɪt] vt wiedervereinigen

rev [rev] n abbr (AUT: = revolution) Drehzahl f ♦ vt (also: ~ up: engine) auf Touren bringen ♦ vi (also: ~ up) den Motor auf Touren bringen

revamp [riːˈvæmp] vt aufpolieren

reveal [rɪˈviːl] vt enthüllen; ~**ing** adj aufschlußreich

reveille [rɪˈvælɪ] n Wecken nt

revel [ˈrevl] vi: to ~ in sth/in doing sth seine Freude an etw dat haben/daran haben, etw zu tun

revelation [revəˈleɪʃən] n Offenbarung f

revelry [ˈrevlrɪ] n Rummel m

revenge [rɪˈvendʒ] n Rache f; to take ~ on sich rächen an +dat

revenue [ˈrevənjuː] n Einnahmen pl

reverberate [rɪˈvɜːbəreɪt] vi widerhallen

revere [rɪˈvɪə*] vt (ver)ehren; ~**nce** [ˈrevərəns] n Ehrfurcht f

Reverend [ˈrevərənd] adj: the ~

Robert Martin ≈ Pfarrer Robert Martin

reverent ['rɛvərənt] adj ehrfurchtsvoll

reversal [rɪ'vɜːsl] n Umkehrung f

reverse [rɪ'vɜːs] n Rückseite f; (AUT: gear) Rückwärtsgang m ♦ adj (order, direction) entgegengesetzt ♦ vt umkehren ♦ vi (BRIT: AUT) rückwärts fahren; **~-charge call** (BRIT) n R-Gespräch nt; **reversing lights** npl (AUT) Rückfahrscheinwerfer pl

revert [rɪ'vɜːt] vi: **to ~ to** zurückkehren zu; (to bad state) zurückfallen in +acc

review [rɪ'vjuː] n (MIL) Truppenschau f; (of book) Rezension f; (magazine) Zeitschrift f ♦ vt Rückschau halten auf +acc; (MIL) mustern; (book) rezensieren; (reexamine) von neuem untersuchen; **~er** n (critic) Rezensent m

revile [rɪ'vaɪl] vt verunglimpfen

revise [rɪ'vaɪz] vt (book) überarbeiten; (reconsider) ändern, revidieren

revision [rɪ'vɪʒən] n Prüfung f; (COMM) Revision f; (SCH) Wiederholung f

revitalize ['riː'vaɪtəlaɪz] vt neu beleben

revival [rɪ'vaɪvəl] n Wiederbelebung f; (REL) Erweckung f; (THEAT) Wiederaufnahme f

revive [rɪ'vaɪv] vt wiederbeleben; (fig) wieder auffrischen ♦ vi wiedererwachen; (fig) wieder aufleben

revoke [rɪ'vəʊk] vt aufheben

revolt [rɪ'vəʊlt] n Aufstand m, Revolte f ♦ vi sich auflehnen ♦ vt entsetzen; **~ing** adj widerlich

revolution [rɛvə'luːʃən] n (turn) Umdrehung f; (POL) Revolution f; **~ary** adj revolutionär ♦ n Revolutionär m; **~ize** vt revolutionieren

revolve [rɪ'vɒlv] vi kreisen; (on own axis) sich drehen

revolver [rɪ'vɒlvə*] n Revolver m

revolving door [rɪ'vɒlvɪŋ-] n Dreh-

tür f

revulsion [rɪ'vʌlʃən] n Ekel m

reward [rɪ'wɔːd] n Belohnung f ♦ vt belohnen; **~ing** adj lohnend

rewire ['riː'waɪə*] vt (house) neu verkabeln

reword ['riː'wɜːd] vt anders formulieren

rewrite ['riː'raɪt] (irreg: like write) vt umarbeiten, neu schreiben

rheumatism ['ruːmətɪzəm] n Rheumatismus m, Rheuma nt

Rhine [raɪn] n: **the ~** der Rhein

rhinoceros [raɪ'nɒsərəs] n Nashorn nt

Rhone [rəʊn] n: **the ~** die Rhone

rhubarb ['ruːbɑːb] n Rhabarber m

rhyme [raɪm] n Reim m

rhythm ['rɪðəm] n Rhythmus m

rib [rɪb] n Rippe f ♦ vt (mock) hänseln, aufziehen

ribald ['rɪbəld] adj saftig

ribbon ['rɪbən] n Band nt; **in ~s** (torn) in Fetzen

rice [raɪs] n Reis m; **~ pudding** n Milchreis m

rich [rɪtʃ] adj reich; (food) reichhaltig ♦ npl: **the ~** die Reichen pl; **~es** npl Reichtum m; **~ly** adv reich; (deserve) völlig

rickets ['rɪkɪts] n Rachitis f

rickety ['rɪkɪtɪ] adj wack(e)lig

rickshaw ['rɪkʃɔː] n Rickscha f

ricochet ['rɪkəʃeɪ] n Abprallen nt; (shot) Querschläger m ♦ vi abprallen

rid [rɪd] (pt, pp rid) vt befreien; **to get ~ of** loswerden

riddle ['rɪdl] n Rätsel nt ♦ vt: **to be ~d with** völlig durchlöchert sein von

ride [raɪd] (pt rode, pp ridden) n (in vehicle) Fahrt f; (on horse) Ritt m ♦ vt (horse) reiten; (bicycle) fahren ♦ vi fahren, reiten; **to take sb for a ~** mit jdm eine Fahrt etc machen; (fig) jdn aufs Glatteis führen; **~r** n Reiter m; (addition) Zusatz m

ridge [rɪdʒ] n Kamm m; (of roof) First m

ridicule ['rɪdɪkjuːl] n Spott m ♦ vt lächerlich machen

ridiculous [rɪˈdɪkjuləs] adj lächerlich; **~ly** adv lächerlich

riding [ˈraɪdɪŋ] n Reiten nt; **~ school**
n Reitschule f

rife [raɪf] adj weit verbreitet; **to be ~**
grassieren; **to be ~ with** voll sein
von

riffraff [ˈrɪfræf] n Pöbel m

rifle [ˈraɪfl] n Gewehr nt ♦ vt berauben; **~ range** n Schießstand m

rift [rɪft] n Spalte f, (fig) Bruch m

rig [rɪg] n (outfit) Takelung f, (fig)
Aufmachung f; (oil ~) Bohrinsel f
♦ vt (election etc) manipulieren; **~ out**
(BRIT) vt ausstatten; **~ up** vt zu-
sammenbasteln; **~ging** n Takelage f

right [raɪt] adj (correct, just) richtig,
recht; (~ side) rechte(r, s) ♦ n
Recht nt; (not left, POL) Rechte f ♦
adv (on the ~) rechts; (to the ~)
nach rechts; (look, work) richtig,
recht; (directly) gerade; (exactly)
genau ♦ vt in Ordnung bringen, korrigieren ♦ excl gut; **on the ~**
rechts; **to be in the ~** im Recht
sein; **by ~s** von Rechts wegen; **to
be ~** recht haben; **~ away** sofort;
~ now in diesem Augenblick; **~
in the middle** genau in der Mitte; **~
angle** n rechte(r) Winkel m;
~eous [ˈraɪtʃəs] adj rechtschaffen;
~ful adj rechtmäßig; **~-handed**
adj rechtshändig; **~-hand man** (irreg)
n rechte Hand f; **~-hand side** n rechte
Seite f; **~ly** adv mit Recht; **~ of
way** n Vorfahrt f; **~-wing** adj
rechtsorientiert

rigid [ˈrɪdʒɪd] adj (stiff) starr, steif;
(strict) streng; **~ity** [rɪˈdʒɪdɪtɪ] n
Starrheit f, Strenge f

rigmarole [ˈrɪgmərəʊl] n Gewäsch nt

rigor (US) n = **rigour**

rigorous [ˈrɪgərəs] adj streng

rigour [ˈrɪgə*] (US **rigor**) n Strenge
f, Härte f

rile [raɪl] vt ärgern

rim [rɪm] n (edge) Rand m; (of
wheel) Felge f

rind [raɪnd] n Rinde f

ring [rɪŋ] n (pt **rang**, pp **rung**) n Ring

m; (of people) Kreis m; (arena) Manege f; (of telephone) Klingeln nt ♦
vt, vi (bell) läuten; (BRIT) anrufen;
~ back (BRIT) vt, vi zurückrufen;
~ off (BRIT) vi aufhängen; **~ up**
(BRIT) vt anrufen; **~ing** n Klingeln
nt; (of large bell) Läuten nt; (in
ears) Klingen nt; **~ing tone** n
(TEL) Rufzeichen nt

ringleader [ˈrɪŋliːdə*] n Anführer m,
Rädelsführer m

ringlets [ˈrɪŋlɪts] npl Ringellocken pl

ring road (BRIT) n Umgehungsstraße f

rink [rɪŋk] n (ice ~) Eisbahn f

rinse [rɪns] n Spülen nt ♦ vt spülen

riot [ˈraɪət] n Aufruhr m ♦ vi randalieren; **to run ~** (people) randalieren; (vegetation) wuchern; **~er** n
Aufrührer m; **~ous** adj aufrührerisch; (noisy) lärmend; **~ously**
adv aufrührerisch

rip [rɪp] n Schlitz m, Riß m ♦ vt, vi
(zer)reißen; **~cord** [ˈrɪpkɔːd] n Reiß-
leine f

ripe [raɪp] adj reif; **~n** vi reifen ♦ vt
reifen lassen

rip-off [ˈrɪpɔf] (inf) n: **it's a ~!** das
ist Wucher!

ripple [ˈrɪpl] n kleine Welle f ♦ vt
kräuseln ♦ vi sich kräuseln

rise [raɪz] (pt **rose**, pp **risen**) n
(slope) Steigung f; (esp in wages:
BRIT) Erhöhung f; (growth) Aufstieg
m ♦ vi (sun) aufgehen; (smoke) aufsteigen; (mountain) sich erheben;
(ground) ansteigen; (prices) steigen;
(in revolt) sich erheben; **to give ~
to** Anlaß geben zu; **to ~ to the occasion** sich der Lage gewachsen zeigen; **risen** [ˈrɪzn] pp of **rise**

rising adj (increasing: tide, numbers, prices) steigend; (sun, moon)
aufgehend ♦ n (uprising) Aufstand m

risk [rɪsk] n Gefahr f, Risiko nt ♦ vt
(venture) wagen; (chance loss of)
riskieren, aufs Spiel setzen; **to take
or run the ~ of doing** das Risiko
eingehen, zu tun; **at ~** in Gefahr; **at
one's own ~** auf eigene Gefahr; **~y**

adj riskant

risqué ['riːskeɪ] *adj* gewagt

rissole ['rɪsəʊl] *n* Fleischklößchen *nt*

rite [raɪt] *n* Ritus *m*; **last ~s** Letzte Ölung *f*

ritual ['rɪtjʊəl] *n* Ritual *nt* ♦ *adj* rituell, Ritual-; (*fig*) rituell

rival ['raɪvəl] *n* Rivale *m*, Konkurrent *m* ♦ *adj* rivalisierend ♦ *vt* rivalisieren mit; (*COMM*) konkurrieren mit; **~ry** *n* Rivalität *f*; Konkurrenz *f*

river ['rɪvə*] *n* Fluß *m*, Strom *m* ♦ *cpd* (*port, traffic*) Fluß-; **up/down ~** flußaufwärts/-abwärts; **~bank** *n* Flußufer *nt*; **~bed** *n* Flußbett *nt*

rivet ['rɪvɪt] *n* Niete *f*, ♦ *vt* (*fasten*) (ver)nieten

Riviera [rɪvɪ'eərə] *n*: **the ~** die Riviera

road [rəʊd] *n* Straße *f* ♦ *cpd* Straßen-; **major/minor ~** Haupt-/Nebenstraße *f*; **~block** *n* Straßensperre *f*; **~hog** *n* Verkehrsrowdy *m*; **~map** *n* Straßenkarte *f*; **~ safety** *n* Verkehrssicherheit *f*; **~side** *n* Straßenrand *m* ♦ *adj* an der Landstraße (gelegen); **~ sign** *n* Straßenschild *nt*; **~ user** *n* Verkehrsteilnehmer *m*; **~way** *n* Fahrbahn *f*; **~ works** *npl* Straßenbauarbeiten *pl*; **~worthy** *adj* verkehrssicher

roam [rəʊm] *vi* (umher)streifen ♦ *vt* durchstreifen

roar [rɔː*] *n* Brüllen *nt*, Gebrüll *nt* ♦ *vi* brüllen; **to ~ with laughter** vor Lachen brüllen; **to do a ~ing trade** ein Riesengeschäft machen

roast [rəʊst] *n* Braten *m* ♦ *vt* braten, schmoren; **~ beef** *n* Roastbeef *nt*

rob [rɒb] *vt* bestehlen, berauben; (*bank*) ausrauben; **to ~ sb of sth** jdm etw rauben; **~ber** *n* Räuber *m*; **~bery** *n* Raub *m*

robe [rəʊb] *n* (*dress*) Gewand *nt*; (*US*) Hauskleid *nt*; (*judge's*) Robe *f*

robin ['rɒbɪn] *n* Rotkehlchen *nt*

robot ['rəʊbɒt] *n* Roboter *m*

robust [rəʊ'bʌst] *adj* (*person*) robust; (*appetite, economy*) gesund

rock [rɒk] *n* Felsen *m*; (*BRIT:*

sweet) Zuckerstange *f* ♦ *vt, vi* wiegen, schaukeln; **on the ~s** (*drink*) mit Eis(würfeln); (*marriage*) gescheitert; (*ship*) aufgelaufen; **~ and roll** *n* Rock and Roll *m*; **~bottom** *n* (*fig*) Tiefpunkt *m*; **~ery** *n* Steingarten *m*

rocket ['rɒkɪt] *n* Rakete *f*

rocking chair ['rɒkɪŋ-] *n* Schaukelstuhl *m*

rocking horse ['rɒkɪŋ-] *n* Schaukelpferd *nt*

rocky ['rɒkɪ] *adj* felsig

rod [rɒd] *n* (*bar*) Stange *f*; (*stick*) Rute *f*

rode [rəʊd] *pt of* ride

rodent ['rəʊdənt] *n* Nagetier *nt*

roe [rəʊ] *n* (*deer*) Reh *nt*; (*of fish: also:* **hard ~**) Rogen *m*; **soft ~** Milch *f*

rogue [rəʊg] *n* Schurke *m*

role [rəʊl] *n* Rolle *f*

roll [rəʊl] *n* Rolle *f*; (*bread*) Brötchen *nt*; (*list*) (Namen)liste *f*; (*of drum*) Wirbel *m* ♦ *vt* (*turn*) rollen, (herum)wälzen; (*grass etc*) walzen ♦ *vi* (*swing*) schlingern; (*sound*) rollen, grollen; **~ about** *or* **around** *vi* herumkugeln; (*ship*) schlingern; (*dog etc*) sich wälzen; **~ by** *vi* (*time*) verfließen; **~ in** *vi* (*mail*) hereinkommen; **~ over** *vi* sich (herum)drehen; **~ up** *vi* (*arrive*) kommen, auftauchen ♦ *vt* (*carpet*) aufrollen; **~ call** *n* Namensaufruf *m*; **~er** *n* Rolle *f*, Walze *f*; (*road roller*) Straßenwalze *f*; **~er coaster** *n* Achterbahn *f*; **~er skates** *npl* Rollschuhe *pl*

rolling ['rəʊlɪŋ] *adj* (*landscape*) wellig; **~ pin** *n* Nudel- *or* Wellholz *nt*; **~ stock** *n* Wagenmaterial *nt*

ROM [rɒm] *n abbr* (= *read only memory*) ROM *m*

Roman ['rəʊmən] *adj* römisch ♦ *n* Römer(in) *m(f)*; **~ Catholic** *adj* römisch-katholisch ♦ *n* Katholik(in) *m(f)*

romance [rəʊ'mæns] *n* Romanze *f*; (*story*) (Liebes)roman *m*

Romania [rəʊ'meɪnɪə] *n* = **Ruma-**

Roman numeral n römische Ziffer

romantic [rəʊˈmæntɪk] adj romantisch; **~ism** [rəʊˈmæntɪsɪzəm] n Romantik f

Rome [rəʊm] n Rom nt

romp [rɒmp] n Tollen f ♦ vi (also: ~ about) herumtollen

rompers [ˈrɒmpəz] npl Spielanzug m

roof [ruːf] (pl **roofs**) n Dach nt; (of mouth) Gaumen m ♦ vt überdachen, überdecken; **~ing** n Deckmaterial nt; **~ rack** n (AUT) Dachgepäckträger m

rook [rʊk] n (bird) Saatkrähe f; (chess) Turm m

room [ruːm] n Zimmer nt, Raum m; (space) Platz m; (fig) Spielraum m; **~s** npl (accommodation) Wohnung f; **"~s to let** (BRIT) or **for rent** (US)" "Zimmer zu vermieten"; **single/double ~** Einzel-/Doppelzimmer nt; **~ing house** (US) n Mietshaus nt (mit möblierten Wohnungen); **~mate** n Mitbewohner(in) m(f); **~ service** n Zimmerbedienung f; **~y** adj geräumig

roost [ruːst] n Hühnerstange f ♦ vi auf der Stange hocken

rooster [ˈruːstə*] n Hahn m

root [ruːt] n (also fig) Wurzel f ♦ vi wurzeln; **~ about** vi (fig) herumwühlen; **~ for** vt fus Stimmung machen für; **~ out** vt ausjäten; (fig) ausrotten

rope [rəʊp] n Seil nt ♦ vt (tie) festschnüren; **to know the ~s** sich auskennen; **to ~ sb in** jdn gewinnen; **~ off** vt absperren; **~ ladder** n Strickleiter f

rosary [ˈrəʊzərɪ] n Rosenkranz m

rose [rəʊz] pt of **rise** ♦ n Rose f ♦ adj Rosen-, rosenrot

rosé [ˈrəʊzeɪ] n Rosé m

rosebud [ˈrəʊzbʌd] n Rosenknospe f

rosebush [ˈrəʊzbʊʃ] n Rosenstock m

rosemary [ˈrəʊzmərɪ] n Rosmarin m

rosette [rəʊˈzɛt] n Rosette f

roster [ˈrɒstə*] n Dienstplan m

rostrum [ˈrɒstrəm] n Rednerbühne f

rosy [ˈrəʊzɪ] adj rosig

rot [rɒt] n Fäulnis f; (nonsense) Quatsch m ♦ vi verfaulen ♦ vt verfaulen lassen

rota [ˈrəʊtə] n Dienstliste f

rotary [ˈrəʊtərɪ] adj rotierend

rotate [rəʊˈteɪt] vi rotieren lassen; (two or more things in order) turnusmäßig wechseln ♦ vi rotieren

rotating [rəʊˈteɪtɪŋ] adj rotierend

rotation [rəʊˈteɪʃən] n Umdrehung f

rote [rəʊt] n: **by ~** auswendig

rotten [ˈrɒtn] adj faul; (fig) schlecht, gemein; **to feel ~** (ill) sich elend fühlen

rotund [rəʊˈtʌnd] adj rundlich

rouble [ˈruːbl] (US **ruble**) n Rubel m

rough [rʌf] adj (not smooth) rauh; (path) uneben; (violent) roh, grob; (crossing) stürmisch; (without comforts) hart, unbequem; (unfinished, makeshift) grob; (approximate) ungefähr ♦ n (BRIT: person) Rowdy m, Rohling m; (GOLF): **in the ~** im Rauh ♦ vt: **to ~ it** primitiv leben; **to sleep ~** im Freien schlafen; **~age** n Ballaststoffe pl; **~-and-ready** adj provisorisch; (work) zusammengehauen; **~ copy** n Entwurf m; **~ draft** n Entwurf m; **~en** vt aufrauhen; **~ly** adv grob; (about) ungefähr; **~ness** n Rauheit f; (of manner) Ungeschliffenheit f

roulette [ruːˈlɛt] n Roulett(e) nt

Roumania [ruːˈmeɪnɪə] n = **Rumania**

round [raʊnd] adj rund; (figures) aufgerundet ♦ adv (in a circle) rundherum ♦ prep um ... herum ♦ n Runde f; (of ammunition) Magazin nt ♦ vt (corner) biegen um; **all ~** überall; **the long way ~** der Umweg; **all the year ~** das ganze Jahr über; **it's just ~ the corner** (fig) es ist gerade um die Ecke; **~ the clock** rund um die Uhr; **to go ~ to sb's (house)** jdn besuchen; **to go ~ the back** hinterherum gehen; **to go ~ a house** um ein Haus herumgehen; **enough to go ~** genug für alle; **to go the ~s** (story) die Runde machen; **a**

~ of applause ein Beifall m; a ~ of
drinks eine Runde Drinks; a ~ of
sandwiches ein Sandwich nt or m,
ein belegtes Brot; ~ **off** vt abrunden;
~ **up** vt (end) abschließen; (figures)
aufrunden; (criminals) hochnehmen;
~**about** n (BRIT: traffic) Kreisverkehr m; (: merry-go-round) Karussell m ♦ adj auf Umwegen; ~**ers** npl
(game) ~ Schlagball m; ~**ly** adv
(fig) gründlich; ~**shouldered** adj
mit abfallenden Schultern; ~ **trip** n
Rundreise f; ~**up** n Zusammentrei-
ben nt, Sammeln nt

rouse [raʊz] vt (waken) (auf)-
wecken; (stir up) erregen

rousing ['raʊzɪŋ] adj (welcome)
stürmisch; (speech) zündend

route [ruːt] n Weg m, Route f; ~
map (BRIT) n (for journey) Strec-
kenkarte f

routine [ruːˈtiːn] n Routine f ♦ adj
Routine-

row[1] [raʊ] n (noise) Lärm m; (dispute) Streit m ♦ vi sich streiten

row[2] [rəʊ] n (line) Reihe f ♦ vt, vi
(boat) rudern; **in a row** (fig) hintereinander

rowboat ['rəʊbəʊt] (US) n Ruderboot nt

rowdy ['raʊdɪ] adj rüpelhaft ♦ n
(person) Rowdy m

rowing ['rəʊɪŋ] n Rudern nt;
(SPORT) Rudersport m; ~ **boat**
(BRIT) n Ruderboot nt

royal ['rɔɪəl] adj königlich, Königs-;
R~ **Air Force** n Königliche Luftwaffe
f

royalty ['rɔɪəltɪ] n (family) königliche Familie f; (for book) Tantieme
f

rpm abbr (= revs per minute) U/min

R.S.V.P. abbr (= répondez s'il vous
plaît) u.A.w.g.

Rt. Hon. (BRIT) abbr (= Right Honourable) Abgeordnete(r) mf

rub [rʌb] n (with cloth) Polieren nt;
(on person) Reiben nt ♦ vt reiben; to
~ **sb up** (BRIT) or to ~ **sb** (US)
the wrong way jdn aufreizen; ~ **off**

vi (also fig): to ~ **off** (on) abfärben
(auf +acc); ~ **out** vt herausreiben;
(with eraser) ausradieren

rubber ['rʌbə*] n Gummi m; (BRIT)
Radiergummi m; ~ **band** n Gummiband nt; ~ **plant** n Gummibaum m;
~**y** adj gummiartig

rubbish ['rʌbɪʃ] n (waste) Abfall m;
(nonsense) Blödsinn m, Quatsch m;
~ **bin** (BRIT) n Mülleimer m; ~
dump n Müllabladeplatz m

rubble ['rʌbl] n (Stein)schutt m

ruby ['ruːbɪ] n Rubin m ♦ adj rubin-
rot

rucksack ['rʌksæk] n Rucksack m

ructions ['rʌkʃənz] npl Krach m

rudder ['rʌdə*] n Steuerruder nt

ruddy ['rʌdɪ] adj (colour) rötlich;
(inf: bloody) verdammt

rude [ruːd] adj unverschämt; (shock)
hart; (awakening) unsanft; (unrefi-
ned, rough) grob; ~**ness** n Unver-
schämtheit f; Grobheit f

rudiment ['ruːdɪmənt] n Grundlage f

rueful ['ruːfʊl] adj reuevoll; (situation) beklagenswert

ruffian ['rʌfɪən] n Rohling m

ruffle ['rʌfl] vt kräuseln

rug [rʌg] n Brücke f; (in bedroom)
Bettvorleger m; (BRIT: for knees)
(Reise)decke f

rugby ['rʌgbɪ] n (also: ~ football)
Rugby nt

rugged ['rʌgɪd] adj (coastline) zer-
klüftet; (features) markig

rugger ['rʌgə*] (BRIT: inf) n Rugby
nt

ruin ['ruːɪn] n Ruine f; (downfall)
Ruin m ♦ vt ruinieren; ~**s** npl (fig)
Trümmer pl; (ruins) nt

rule [ruːl] n Regel f; (government)
Regierung f; (for measuring) Lineal
nt ♦ vt (govern) herrschen über
+acc, regieren; (decide) anordnen,
entscheiden; (make lines on) linieren
♦ vi herrschen, regieren; entscheiden; **as a** ~ in der Regel; ~ **out** vt
ausschließen; ~**d** adj (paper) liniert;
~**r** n Lineal nt; Herrscher m

ruling ['ruːlɪŋ] adj (party) Regie-

rungs-; (class) herrschend ♦ n
(JUR) Entscheid m

rum [rʌm] n Rum m

Rumania [ruːˈmeɪnɪə] n Rumänien
nt; **~n** adj rumänisch ♦ n Rumäne
m, Rumänin f; (LING) Rumänisch nt

rumble [ˈrʌmbl] n Rumpeln nt; (of
thunder) Grollen nt ♦ vi rumpeln;
grollen

rummage [ˈrʌmɪdʒ] vi durchstöbern

rumour [ˈruːmə*] (US **rumor**) n Gerücht nt ♦ vt: it is ~ed that man
sagt or man munkelt, daß

rump [rʌmp] n Hinterteil nt; **~ steak**
n Rumpsteak nt

rumpus [ˈrʌmpəs] n Spektakel m

run [rʌn] (pt **ran**, pp **run**) n Lauf m;
(in car) (Spazier)fahrt f; (series
Serie f, Reihe f; (ski ~) (Ski)abfahrt f;
(in stocking) Laufmasche f ♦ vt
(cause to ~) laufen lassen; (car,
train, bus) fahren; (race, distance)
laufen, rennen; (manage) leiten;
(COMPUT) laufen lassen; (pass:
hand, eye) gleiten lassen ♦ vi laufen;
(move quickly) laufen, rennen; (bus,
train) fahren; (flow) fließen, laufen;
(colours) (ab)färben; **there was a
~ on** (meat, tickets) es gab einen
Ansturm auf +acc; **on the** ~ auf der
Flucht; **in the long** ~ auf die
Dauer; **I'll ~ you to the station** ich
fahre dich zum Bahnhof; **to ~ a risk**
ein Risiko eingehen; **~ about** or
around vi (children) umherspringen;
~ across vt fus (find) stoßen auf
+acc; **~ away** vi weglaufen; **~
down** vi (clock) ablaufen ♦ vt (production, factory) allmählich auflösen;
(with car) überfahren; (talk against)
heruntermachen; **to be ~ down** erschöpft or abgespannt sein; **~ in**
(BRIT) vt (car) einfahren; **~ into** vt
fus (meet: person) zufällig treffen;
(: trouble) bekommen; (collide with)
rennen gegen; fahren gegen; **~ off** vi
fortlaufen; **~ out** vi (person) hinauslaufen; (liquid) auslaufen; (lease)
ablaufen; (money) ausgehen; **he ran
out of money/petrol** ihm ging das

Geld/Benzin aus; **~ over** vt (in accident) überfahren ♦ vi (instructions)
durchgehen; **~ through** vt (instructions) durchgehen; (debt, bill)
machen; **~ up** against vt fus
(difficulties) stoßen auf +acc; **~
away** adj (horse) ausgebrochen;
(person) flüchtig

rung [rʌŋ] pp of **ring** ♦ n Sprosse f

runner [ˈrʌnə*] n Läufer(in) m(f);
(for sleigh) Kufe f; (plant) (BRIT)
Stangenbohne f; **~-up** n Zweite(r)
mf

running [ˈrʌnɪŋ] n (of business) Leitung f; (of machine) Betrieb m ♦ adj
(water) fließend; (commentary) lau-
fend; **to be in/out of the ~** for sth
im/aus dem Rennen für etw sein; **3
days ~** 3 Tage lang or hintereinander

runny [ˈrʌnɪ] adj dünn; (nose) lau-
fend

run-of-the-mill [rʌnəvðəˈmɪl] adj
gewöhnlich, alltäglich

runt [rʌnt] n (animal) Kümmerer m;
(pej: person) Wicht m

run-up [ˈrʌnʌp] n: the ~ to (election
etc) die Endphase vor +dat

runway [ˈrʌnweɪ] n Startbahn f

rupee [ruːˈpiː] n Rupie f

rupture [ˈrʌptʃə*] n (MED) Bruch m

rural [ˈrʊərəl] adj ländlich, Land-

ruse [ruːz] n Kniff m, List f

rush [rʌʃ] n Eile f, Hetze f; (FIN)
starke Nachfrage f ♦ vt (carry
along) auf schnellstem Wege
schaffen or transportieren; (attack)
losstürmen auf +acc ♦ vi (hurry) eilen, stürzen; **don't ~ me** dräng
mich nicht; **~ hour** n Hauptverkehrszeit f

rusk [rʌsk] n Zwieback m

Russia [ˈrʌʃə] n Rußland nt; **~n** adj
russisch ♦ n Russe m, Russin f;
(LING) Russisch nt

rust [rʌst] n Rost m ♦ vi rosten

rustic [ˈrʌstɪk] adj bäuerlich, ländlich

rustle [ˈrʌsl] vi rauschen, rascheln ♦
vt rascheln lassen; (cattle) stehlen

rustproof [ˈrʌstpruːf] adj rostfrei

rusty [ˈrʌstɪ] adj rostig

rut [rʌt] n (in track) Radspur f; **to be in a ~** im Trott stecken
ruthless ['ruːθləs] adj rücksichtslos
rye [raɪ] n (in) Roggen m; **~ bread** n Roggenbrot nt

S

sabbath ['sæbəθ] n Sabbat m
sabotage ['sæbətɑːʒ] n Sabotage f ♦ vt sabotieren
saccharin ['sækərɪn] n Saccharin nt
sachet ['sæfeɪ] n (of shampoo etc) Briefchen nt, Kissen nt
sack [sæk] n Sack m ♦ vt (inf) hinauswerfen; (pillage) plündern; **to get the ~** rausfliegen; **~ing** n (material) Sackleinen nt; (inf) Rausschmiß m
sacrament ['sækrəmənt] n Sakrament nt
sacred ['seɪkrɪd] adj heilig
sacrifice ['sækrɪfaɪs] n Opfer nt ♦ vt (also fig) opfern
sacrilege ['sækrɪlɪdʒ] n Schändung f
sad [sæd] adj traurig; **~den** vt traurig machen, betrüben
saddle ['sædl] n Sattel m ♦ vt (burden): **to ~ sb with sth** jdm etw aufhalsen; **~bag** n Satteltasche f
sadistic [sə'dɪstɪk] adj sadistisch
sadly ['sædlɪ] adv traurig; (unfortunately) leider
sadness ['sædnəs] n Traurigkeit f
sae abbr (= stamped addressed envelope) adressierte(r) Rückumschlag m
safe [seɪf] adj (free from danger) sicher; (careful) vorsichtig ♦ n Safe m; **~ and sound** gesund und wohl; **(just) to be on the ~ side** um ganz sicher zu gehen; **~ from** (attack) sicher vor +dat; **~conduct** n freie(s) Geleit nt; **~deposit** n (vault) Tresorraum m; (box) Banksafe m; **~guard** n Sicherung f ♦ vt sichern, schützen; **~keeping** n sichere Verwahrung f; **~ly** adv sicher; (arrive) wohlbehalten; **~ sex** n (MED) geschützter Sex m

safety ['seɪftɪ] n Sicherheit f; **~ belt** n Sicherheitsgurt m; **~ pin** n Sicherheitsnadel f; **~ valve** n Sicherheitsventil nt
sag [sæg] vi (durch)sacken
sage [seɪdʒ] n (herb) Salbei f; (person) Weise(r) mf
Sagittarius [sædʒɪ'tɛərɪəs] n Schütze m
Sahara [sə'hɑːrə] n: **the ~ (Desert)** die (Wüste) Sahara
said [sed] pt, pp of **say**
sail [seɪl] n Segel nt; (trip) Fahrt f ♦ vt segeln ♦ vi segeln; (begin voyage: person) abfahren; (: ship) auslaufen; (fig: cloud etc) dahinsegeln; **to go for a ~** segeln gehen; **they ~ed into Copenhagen** sie liefen in Kopenhagen ein; **~ through** vt fus, vi (fig) (es) spielend schaffen; **~boat** (US) n Segelboot nt; **~ing** n Segeln nt; **~ing ship** n Segelschiff nt; **~or** n Matrose m, Seemann m
saint [seɪnt] n Heilige(r) mf; **~ly** adj heilig, fromm
sake [seɪk] n: **for the ~ of** um +gen willen
salad ['sæləd] n Salat m; **~ bowl** n Salatschüssel f; **~ cream** (BRIT) n gewürzte Mayonnaise f; **~ dressing** n Salatsoße f
salami [sə'lɑːmɪ] n Salami f
salary ['sælərɪ] n Gehalt nt
sale [seɪl] n Verkauf m; (reduced prices) Schlußverkauf m; **"for ~"** "zu verkaufen"; **on ~** zu verkaufen; **~room** n Verkaufsraum m; **~s assistant** n Verkäufer(in) m(f); **~s clerk** (US) n Verkäufer(in) m(f); **~sman** (irreg) n Verkäufer m; (representative) Vertreter m; **~swoman** (irreg) n Verkäuferin f
salient ['seɪlɪənt] adj bemerkenswert
saliva [sə'laɪvə] n Speichel m
sallow ['sæləʊ] adj fahl; (face) bleich
salmon ['sæmən] n Lachs m
saloon [sə'luːn] n (BRIT: AUT) Limousine f; (ship's lounge) Salon m
salt [sɔːlt] n Salz nt ♦ vt (cure)

salzen; *(flavour)* salzen; ~ **away**
(inf) vt *(money)* auf die hohe Kante
legen; ~**cellar** n Salzfaß nt; ~**water**
adj Salzwasser-; ~**y** adj salzig

salutary ['sæljʊtərɪ] adj nützlich

salute [sə'luːt] n *(MIL)* Gruß m;
(with guns) Salutschüsse pl ♦ vt
(MIL) salutieren

salvage ['sælvɪdʒ] n *(from ship)*
Bergung f; *(property)* Rettung f ♦ vt
bergen; retten

salvation [sæl'veɪʃən] n Rettung f;
S~ **Army** n Heilsarmee f

same [seɪm] adj, pron *(similar)* glei-
che(r, s); *(identical)* derselbe/
dieselbe/dasselbe; the ~ **book** as
das gleiche Buch wie; at the ~ **time**
zur gleichen Zeit, gleichzeitig; *(however)* zugleich, andererseits; all or
just the ~ trotzdem; the ~ to you!
gleichfalls!; to do the ~ (as sb)
das gleiche tun (wie jd)

sample ['sɑːmpl] n Probe f ♦ vt probieren

sanctify ['sæŋktɪfaɪ] vt weihen

sanctimonious [sæŋktɪ'məʊnɪəs]
adj scheinheilig

sanction ['sæŋkʃən] n Sanktion f

sanctity ['sæŋktɪtɪ] n Heiligkeit f;
(fig) Unverletzlichkeit f

sanctuary ['sæŋktjʊərɪ] n *(for fugitive)* Asyl nt; *(refuge)* Zufluchtsort
m; *(for animals)* Schutzgebiet nt

sand [sænd] n Sand m ♦ vt *(furniture)* schmirgeln

sandal ['sændl] n Sandale f

sand : ~**box** (US) n; ~**castle** n
Sandburg f; ~ **dune** n (Sand)düne f;
~**paper** n Sandpapier nt; ~**pit** n
Sandkasten m; ~**stone** n Sandstein
m

sandwich ['sænwɪdʒ] n Sandwich m
or nt ♦ vt *(also:* ~ *in)* einklemmen;
cheese/ham ~ Käse-/Schinkenbrot;
~**ed between** eingeklemmt zwischen; ~ **board** n Reklametafel f; ~
course (BRIT) n theorie- und praxis-
abwechselnde(r) Ausbildungsgang

sandy ['sændɪ] adj sandig; *(hair)* rot-
blond

sane [seɪn] adj geistig gesund or normal; *(sensible)* vernünftig, gescheit

sang [sæŋ] pt of **sing**

sanitary ['sænɪtərɪ] adj hygienisch;
~ **napkin** (US) n *(Monats)*binde f; ~
towel n *(Monats)*binde f

sanitation [sænɪ'teɪʃən] n sanitäre
Einrichtungen pl; ~ **department**
(US) n Stadtreinigung f

sanity ['sænɪtɪ] n geistige Gesundheit
f; *(good sense)* Vernunft f

sank [sæŋk] pt of **sink**

Santa Claus [sæntə'klɔːz] n Niko-
laus m, Weihnachtsmann m

sap [sæp] n *(of plants)* Saft m ♦ vt
(strength) schwächen

sapling ['sæplɪŋ] n junge(r) Baum m

sapphire ['sæfaɪə*] n Saphir m

sarcasm ['sɑːkæzəm] n Sarkasmus m

sarcastic [sɑː'kæstɪk] adj sarkastisch

sardine [sɑː'diːn] n Sardine f

Sardinia [sɑː'dɪnɪə] n Sardinien nt

sardonic [sɑː'dɒnɪk] adj zynisch

sash [sæʃ] n Schärpe f

sat [sæt] pt, pp of **sit**

Satan ['seɪtn] n Satan m

satchel ['sætʃəl] n *(for school)* Schul-
mappe f

sated ['seɪtɪd] adj *(appetite, person)*
gesättigt

satellite dish n *(TECH)* Parabolantenne f

satellite television n Satelliten-
fernsehen nt

satisfaction [sætɪs'fækʃən] n Befriedigung f, Genugtuung f

satisfactory [sætɪs'fæktərɪ] adj zu-
friedenstellend, befriedigend

satisfy ['sætɪsfaɪ] vt befriedigen, zu-
friedenstellen; *(convince)* überzeugen; *(conditions)* erfüllen; ~**ing**
adj befriedigend; *(meal)* sättigend

saturate ['sætʃəreɪt] vt *(durch)*-
tränken

saturation [sætʃə'reɪʃən] n Durch-
tränkung f; *(CHEM, fig)* Sättigung f

Saturday ['sætədeɪ] n Samstag m,
Sonnabend m

sauce [sɔːs] n Soße f, Sauce f; ~**pan**
n Kasserolle f

saucer ['sɔːsə*] n Untertasse f

saucy ['sɔːsɪ] adj frech, keck

Saudi ['saʊdɪ] : ~ **Arabia** n Saudi-Arabien m ♦ ~ **(Arabian)** adj saudiarabisch ♦ n Saudiaraber(in) m(f)

sauna ['sɔːnə] n Sauna f

saunter ['sɔːntə*] vi schlendern

sausage ['sɒsɪdʒ] n Wurst f; ~ **roll** n Wurst f im Schlafrock, Wurstpastete f

sauté ['səʊteɪ] adj Röst-

savage ['sævɪdʒ] adj wild ♦ n Wilde(r) mf ♦ vt (animals) zerfleischen; ~**ry** n Roheit f, Grausamkeit f

save [seɪv] vt retten; (money, electricity etc) sparen; (strength etc) aufsparen; (COMPUT) speichern ♦ vi (also: ~ up) sparen ♦ n (SPORT) (Ball)abwehr f ♦ prep, conj außer, ausgenommen

saving ['seɪvɪŋ] adj: the ~ **grace** of das Versöhnende an +dat ♦ n Sparen nt, Ersparnis f; ~s pl (money) Ersparnisse pl; ~**s account** n Sparkonto nt; ~**s bank** n Sparkasse f

saviour ['seɪvjə*] (US **savior**) n (REL) Erlöser m

savour ['seɪvə*] (US **savor**) vt (taste) schmecken; (fig) genießen; ~**y** adj pikant, würzig

saw [sɔː] (pt **sawed**, pp **sawed** or **sawn**) pt of **see** ♦ n (tool) Säge f ♦ vt, vi sägen; ~**dust** n Sägemehl nt; ~**mill** n Sägewerk nt; **sawn** [sɔːn] pp of **saw**; ~**n-off shotgun** n Gewehr nt mit abgesägtem Lauf

say [seɪ] (pt, pp **said**) n: to have a/no ~ in sth Mitspracherecht/kein Mitspracherecht bei etw haben ♦ vt, vi sagen; let him have his ~ laß ihn doch reden; to ~ yes/no ja/nein sagen; that goes without ~ing das versteht sich von selbst; that is to ~ das heißt; ~**ing** n Sprichwort nt

scab [skæb] n Schorf m; (pej) Streikbrecher m

scaffold ['skæfəʊld] n (for execution) Schafott nt; ~**ing** n (Bau)gerüst nt

scald [skɔːld] n Verbrühung f ♦ vt (burn) verbrühen; (clean) (ab)brühen

scale [skeɪl] n (of fish) Schuppe f; (MUS) Tonleiter f; (on map, size) Maßstab m; (gradation) Skala f ♦ vt (climb) erklimmen; ~s npl (balance) Waage f; **on a large** ~ (fig) im großen, in großem Umfang; ~ **of charges** Gebührenordnung f; ~ **down** vt verkleinern; ~ **model** n maßstabgetreue(s) Modell nt

scallop ['skɒləp] n Kammuschel f

scalp [skælp] n Kopfhaut f

scamper ['skæmpə*] vi: to ~ **away** or **off** sich davonmachen

scampi ['skæmpɪ] npl Scampi pl

scan [skæn] vt (examine) genau prüfen; (quickly) überfliegen; (horizon) absuchen; (poetry) skandieren

scandal ['skændl] n Skandal m; (piece of gossip) Skandalgeschichte f

Scandinavia [skændɪ'neɪvɪə] n Skandinavien nt; ~**n** adj skandinavisch ♦ n Skandinavier(in) m(f)

scant [skænt] adj knapp; ~**ily** adv knapp, dürftig; ~**y** adj knapp, unzureichend

scapegoat ['skeɪpɡəʊt] n Sündenbock m

scar [skɑː*] n Narbe f ♦ vt durch Narben entstehen

scarce ['skɛəs] adj selten, rar; (goods) knapp; ~**ly** adv kaum

scarcity ['skɛəsɪtɪ] n Mangel m

scare ['skɛə*] n Schrecken m ♦ vt erschrecken; **bomb** ~ Bombendrohung f; to ~ **sb stiff** jdn zu Tode erschrecken; **to be** ~**d** Angst haben; ~**crow** n Vogelscheuche f

scarf [skɑːf] (pl **scarves**) n Schal m; (head-) Kopftuch nt

scarlet ['skɑːlət] adj scharlachrot ♦ n Scharlachrot nt; ~ **fever** n Scharlach m

scarves [skɑːvz] npl of **scarf**

scary ['skɛərɪ] (inf) adj schaurig

scathing ['skeɪðɪŋ] adj scharf, vernichtend

scatter ['skætə*] vt (sprinkle) (ver)streuen; (disperse) zerstreuen ♦ vi sich zerstreuen; ~**brained** adj flatterhaft, schusselig

scavenger ['skævɪndʒə*] n (animal) Aasfresser m

scenario [sɪ'nɑːrɪəʊ] n (THEAT, CINE) Szenarium nt; (fig) Szenario nt

scene [siːn] n (of happening) Ort m; (of play, incident) Szene f; (view) Anblick m; (argument) Szene f, Auftritt m; **~ry** ['siːnərɪ] n (THEAT) Bühnenbild nt; (landscape) Landschaft f

scenic ['siːnɪk] adj landschaftlich

scent [sɛnt] n Parfüm nt; (smell) Duft m ♦ vt parfümieren

sceptical ['skɛptɪkəl] (US **skeptical**) adj skeptisch

schedule ['ʃɛdjuːl, (US) 'skɛdjuːl] n (list) Liste f; (plan) Programm nt; (of work) Zeitplan m ♦ vt planen; on ~ pünktlich; to be ahead of/behind ~ dem Zeitplan voraus/im Rückstand sein; ~d flight n (not charter) Linienflug m

scheme [skiːm] n Schema nt; (dishonest) Intrige f; (plan of action) Plan m ♦ vi intrigieren ♦ vt planen

scheming ['skiːmɪŋ] adj intrigierend

scholar ['skɒlə*] n Gelehrte(r) m; (holding ~ship) Stipendiat m; ~ly adj gelehrt; ~ship n Gelehrsamkeit f; (grant) Stipendium nt

school [skuːl] n Schule f; (UNIV) Fakultät f ♦ vt schulen; (dog) trainieren; ~ age n schulpflichtige(s) Alter nt; ~book n Schulbuch nt; ~boy n Schüler m; ~children npl Schulkinder pl; ~days npl (alte) Schulzeit f; ~girl n Schülerin f; ~ing n Schulung f, Ausbildung f; ~master n Lehrer m; ~mistress n Lehrerin f; ~teacher n Lehrer(in) m(f)

sciatica [saɪ'ætɪkə] n Ischias m or nt

science ['saɪəns] n Wissenschaft f; (natural ~) Naturwissenschaft f

scientific [saɪən'tɪfɪk] adj wissenschaftlich; (natural sciences) naturwissenschaftlich

scientist ['saɪəntɪst] n Wissenschaftler(in) m(f)

scintillating ['sɪntɪleɪtɪŋ] adj sprühend

scissors ['sɪzəz] npl Schere f; a pair of ~ eine Schere

scoff [skɒf] vt (BRIT: inf: eat) fressen ♦ vi (mock): to ~ (at) spotten (über +acc)

scold [skəʊld] vt schimpfen

scone [skɒn] n weiche(s) Teegebäck nt

scoop [skuːp] n Schaufel f; (news) sensationelle Erstmeldung f; ~ out vt herausschaufeln; (liquid) herausschöpfen; ~ up vt aufschaufeln; (liquid) aufschöpfen

scooter ['skuːtə*] n Motorroller m; (child's) Roller m

scope [skəʊp] n Ausmaß nt; (opportunity) (Spiel)raum m

scorch [skɔːtʃ] n Brandstelle f ♦ vt versengen; ~ing adj brennend

score [skɔː*] n (in game) Punktzahl f; (final ~) (Spiel)ergebnis nt; (MUS) Partitur f; (line) Kratzer m; (twenty) zwanzig, zwanzig Stück m ♦ vt (goal) schießen; (points) machen; (mark) einritzen ♦ vi (keep record) Punkte zählen; on that ~ in dieser Hinsicht; what's the ~? wie steht's?; to ~ 6 out of 10 6 von 10 Punkten erzielen; ~ out vt ausstreichen; ~board n Anschreibetafel f; ~r n Torschütze m; (recorder) (Auf)schreiber m

scorn [skɔːn] n Verachtung f ♦ vt verhöhnen; ~ful adj verächtlich

Scorpio ['skɔːpɪəʊ] n Skorpion m

Scot [skɒt] n Schotte m, Schottin f

Scotch [skɒtʃ] n Scotch m

scotch [skɒtʃ] vt (end) unterbinden

scot-free ['skɒt'friː] adv: to get off ~ (unpunished) ungeschoren davonkommen

Scotland ['skɒtlənd] n Schottland nt

Scots [skɒts] adj schottisch; ~man/woman (irreg) n Schotte m/Schottin f

Scottish ['skɒtɪʃ] adj schottisch

scoundrel ['skaʊndrəl] n Schuft m

scour ['skaʊə*] vt (search) absuchen; (clean) schrubben

scourge [skɔːdʒ] n (whip) Geißel f; (plague) Qual f

scout [skaut] n (MIL) Späher m; (also: boy ~) Pfadfinder m; ~ **around** vi: to ~ **around** (for) sich umsehen (nach)

scowl [skaul] n finstere(r) Blick m ♦ vi finster blicken

scrabble ['skræbl] (also: ~ around: search) (herum)tasten ♦ vi; (claw): to ~ (at) kratzen (an +dat) ♦ n: S~ ® Scrabble nt ®

scraggy ['skrægɪ] adj dürr, hager

scram [skræm] (inf) vi abhauen

scramble ['skræmbl] n (climb) Kletterei f; (struggle) Kampf m ♦ vi klettern; (fight) sich schlagen; to ~ out/through krabbeln aus/durch; to ~ **for** sth sich um etw raufen; ~**d eggs** npl Rührei nt

scrap [skræp] n (bit) Stückchen nt; (fight) Keilerei f; (also: ~ iron) Schrott m ♦ vt verwerfen ♦ vi (fight) streiten, sich prügeln; ~**s** npl (left-overs) Reste pl; (waste) Abfall m; ~**book** n Einklebealbum nt; ~ **dealer** n Schrotthändler(in) m(f)

scrape [skreɪp] n Kratzen m; (trouble) Klemme f ♦ vt kratzen; (car) zerkratzen; (clean) abkratzen ♦ vi (make harsh noise) kratzen; to ~ **through** gerade noch durchkommen; ~**r** n Kratzer m

scrap: ~ **heap** n Schrotthaufen m; **on the** ~ **heap** (fig) beim alten Eisen; ~ **iron** n Schrott m; ~ **merchant** (BRIT) n Altwarenhändler(in) m(f)

scrappy ['skræpɪ] adj zusammengestoppelt

scratch [skrætʃ] n (wound) Kratzer m, Schramme f ♦ adj: ~ **team** zusammengewürfelte Mannschaft ♦ vt kratzen; (car) zerkratzen ♦ vi (sich) kratzen; **to start from** ~ ganz von vorne anfangen; **to be up to** ~ den Anforderungen entsprechen

scrawl [skrɔːl] n Gekritzel nt ♦ vt, vi kritzeln

scrawny ['skrɔːnɪ] adj (person, neck) dürr

scream [skriːm] n Schrei m ♦ vi schreien

scree [skriː] n Geröll(halde f) nt

screech [skriːtʃ] n Schrei m ♦ vi kreischen

screen [skriːn] n (protective) Schutzschirm m; (CINE) Leinwand f; (TV) Bildschirm m ♦ vt (shelter) (be)schirmen; (film) zeigen, vorführen; ~**ing** n (MED) Untersuchung f; ~**play** n Drehbuch nt

screw [skruː] n Schraube f ♦ vt (fasten) schrauben; (vulgar) bumsen; ~ **up** vt (paper etc) zerknüllen; (inf: ruin) vermasseln (inf); ~**driver** n Schraubenzieher m

scribble ['skrɪbl] n Gekritzel nt ♦ vt kritzeln

script [skrɪpt] n (handwriting) Handschrift f; (for film) Drehbuch nt; (THEAT) Manuskript nt, Text m

Scripture ['skrɪptʃə*] n Heilige Schrift f

scroll [skrəul] n Schriftrolle f

scrounge [skraundʒ] (inf) vt: to ~ sth off or from sb etw bei jdm abstauben ♦ n: **on the** ~ beim Schnorren

scrub [skrʌb] n (clean) Schrubben nt; (in countryside) Gestrüpp nt ♦ vt (clean) schrubben; (reject) fallenlassen

scruff [skrʌf] n: **by the** ~ **of the neck** am Genick

scruffy ['skrʌfɪ] adj unordentlich, vergammelt

scrum(mage) ['skrʌm(ɪdʒ)] n Getümmel nt

scruple ['skruːpl] n Skrupel m, Bedenken nt

scrupulous ['skruːpjuləs] adj peinlich genau, gewissenhaft

scrutinize ['skruːtɪnaɪz] vt genau prüfen

scrutiny ['skruːtɪnɪ] n genaue Untersuchung f

scuff [skʌf] vt (shoes) abstoßen

scuffle ['skʌfl] n Handgemenge nt

scullery ['skʌlərɪ] n Spülküche f

sculptor ['skʌlptə*] n Bildhauer(in) m(f)

sculpture ['skʌlptʃə*] n (ART) Bildhauerei f; (statue) Skulptur f

scum [skʌm] n (also: fig) Abschaum m

scupper ['skʌpə*] vt (NAUT) versenken; (fig) zerstören

scurrilous ['skʌrɪləs] adj unflätig

scurry ['skʌrɪ] vi huschen

scuttle ['skʌtl] n (also: coal ~) Kohleneimer m ♦ vt (ship) versenken ♦ vi (scamper): **to ~ away** or **off** sich davonmachen

scythe [saɪð] n Sense f

SDP (BRIT) n abbr = **Social Democratic Party**

sea [siː] n Meer nt, See f; (fig) Meer nt ♦ adj Meeres-, See-; **by ~** (travel) auf dem Seeweg; **on the ~** (boat) auf dem Meer; (town) am Meer; **out to ~** aufs Meer hinaus; **out at ~** aufs Meer; **to be all at ~** (fig) nicht durchblicken; **~board** n Küste f; **~food** n Meeresfrüchte pl; **~ front** n Strandpromenade f; **~going** adj seetüchtig, Hochsee-; **~gull** n Möwe f

seal [siːl] n (animal) Robbe f, Seehund m; (stamp, impression) Siegel nt ♦ vt versiegeln

sea level n Meeresspiegel m

sea lion n Seelöwe m

seam [siːm] n Saum m; (edges joining) Naht f; (of coal) Flöz nt

seaman ['siːmən] (irreg) n Seemann m

seamy ['siːmɪ] adj (people, café) zwielichtig; (life) anrüchig

seaplane ['siːpleɪn] n Wasserflugzeug nt

seaport ['siːpɔːt] n Seehafen m

search [sɜːtʃ] n (for person, thing) Suche f; (of drawer, pockets, house) Durchsuchung f ♦ vi suchen ♦ vt durchsuchen; **in ~ of** auf der Suche nach; **to ~ for** suchen nach; **through** vt durchsuchen; **~ing** adj (look) forschend; **~light** n Scheinwerfer m; **~ party** n Suchmann-

schaft f; **~ warrant** n Durchsuchungsbefehl m

seashore ['siːʃɔː*] n Meeresküste f

seasick ['siːsɪk] adj seekrank; **~ness** n Seekrankheit f

seaside ['siːsaɪd] n Küste f; **~ resort** n Badeort m

season ['siːzn] n Jahreszeit f; (Christmas etc) Zeit f, Saison f ♦ vt (flavour) würzen; **~al** adj Saison-; **~ed** adj (fig) erfahren; **~ing** n Gewürz nt, Würze f; **~ ticket** n (RAIL) Zeitkarte f; (THEAT) Abonnement nt

seat [siːt] n Sitz m, Platz m; (in Parliament) Sitz m; (part of body) Gesäß nt; (of trousers) Hosenboden m ♦ vt (place) setzen; (have space for) Sitzplätze bieten für; **to be ~ed** sitzen; **~ belt** n Sicherheitsgurt m

sea water n Meerwasser nt

seaweed ['siːwiːd] n (See)tang m

seaworthy ['siːwɜːðɪ] adj seetüchtig

sec. abbr (= second(s)) Sek.

secluded [sɪ'kluːdɪd] adj abgelegen

seclusion [sɪ'kluːʒən] n Zurückgezogenheit f

second ['sekənd] adj zweite(r,s) ♦ adv (in ~ position) an zweiter Stelle ♦ n Sekunde f; (person) Zweite(r) m; (COMM: imperfect) zweite Wahl f; (SPORT) Sekundant m; (AUT: also: ~ gear) zweite(r) Gang m; (BRIT: UNIV: degree) mittlere Note bei Abschlußprüfungen ♦ vt (support) unterstützen; **~ary** adj zweitrangig; **~ary school** n höhere Schule f, Mittelschule f; **~class** adj zweiter Klasse; **~hand** adj aus zweiter Hand; (rare etc) gebraucht; **~ hand** n (on clock) Sekundenzeiger m; **~ly** adv zweitens; **~ment** n [sɪ'kɒndmənt] (BRIT) n Abordnung f; **~rate** adj mittelmäßig; **~ thoughts** npl: **to have ~ thoughts** sich dat anders überlegen; **on ~ thoughts** (BRIT) or **thought** (US) oder lieber (doch)

secrecy ['siːkrəsɪ] n Geheimhaltung f

secret ['siːkrət] n Geheimnis nt ♦ adj geheim, Geheim-; **in ~** geheim

secretarial [sekrə'teərɪəl] adj

Sekretärinnen-

secretary ['sekrətrı] n Sekretär(in) m(f)

Secretary of State (BRIT) n (POL): ~ (for) Minister(in) m(f) (für)

secretion [sɪ'kri:ʃən] n Absonderung f

secretive ['si:krətɪv] adj geheimtuerisch

secretly adv geheim

sectarian [sek'teərɪən] adj (riots etc) Konfessions-, zwischen den Konfessionen

section ['sekʃən] n Teil m; (department) Abteilung f; (of document) Abschnitt m

sector ['sektə*] n Sektor m

secular ['sekjulə*] adj weltlich, profan

secure [sɪ'kjuə*] adj (safe) sicher; (firmly fixed) fest ♦ vt (make firm) befestigen, sichern; (obtain) sichern

security [sɪ'kjuərɪtɪ] n Sicherheit f; (pledge) Pfand nt; (document) Wertpapier nt; (national ~) Staatssicherheit f

sedan [sɪ'dæn] (US) n (AUT) Limousine f

sedate [sɪ'deɪt] adj gesetzt ♦ vt (MED) ein Beruhigungsmittel geben +dat

sedation [sɪ'deɪʃən] n (MED) Einfluß m von Beruhigungsmittel

sedative ['sedətɪv] n Beruhigungsmittel nt ♦ adj beruhigend, einschläfernd

sedentary ['sedntrɪ] adj (job) sitzend

sediment ['sedɪmənt] n (Boden)satz m

sedition [sə'dɪʃən] n Aufwiegelung f

seduce [sɪ'dju:s] vt verführen

seduction [sɪ'dʌkʃən] n Verführung f

seductive [sɪ'dʌktɪv] adj verführerisch

see [si:] (pt saw, pp seen) vt sehen; (understand) (ein)sehen, erkennen; (visit) besuchen ♦ vi (be aware) sehen; (find out) nachsehen ♦ n (ECCL: R.C.) Bistum nt; (: Protestant) Kirchenkreis m; to ~ sb to the door jdn hinausbegleiten; to ~ that (ensure) dafür sorgen, daß; ~ you soon! bis bald!; ~ about vt fus sich kümmern um; ~ off vt: to ~ sb off jdn zum Zug ed begleiten; ~ through vt: to ~ sth through etw durchfechten; to ~ through sb/sth jdn/etw durchschauen; ~ to vt fus: to ~ to it dafür sorgen

seed [si:d] n Samen m ♦ vt (TENNIS) plazieren; to go to ~ (plant) schießen; (fig) herunterkommen; ~ling n Setzling m; ~y adj (café) übel; (person) zweifelhaft

seeing ['si:ɪŋ] conj: ~ (that) da

seek [si:k] (pt, pp sought) vt suchen

seem [si:m] vi scheinen; it ~s that ... es scheint, daß ...; ~ingly adv anscheinend

seen [si:n] pp of see

seep [si:p] vi sickern

seesaw ['si:sɔ:] n Wippe f

seethe [si:ð] vi: to ~ with anger vor Wut kochen

see-through ['si:θru:] adj (dress etc) durchsichtig

segment ['segmənt] n Teil m; (of circle) Ausschnitt m

segregate ['segrɪgeɪt] vt trennen

seize [si:z] vt (grasp) (er)greifen, packen; (power) ergreifen; (take legally) beschlagnahmen; ~ (up)on vt fus sich stürzen auf +acc; ~ up vt (TECH) sich festfressen

seizure ['si:ʒə*] n (illness) Anfall m

seldom ['seldəm] adv selten

select [sɪ'lekt] adj ausgewählt ♦ vt auswählen; ~ion [sɪ'lekʃən] n Auswahl f; ~ive adj (of person) wählerisch

self [self] (pl selves) pron selbst ♦ n Selbst nt, Ich nt; the ~ das Ich; ~-assured adj selbstbewußt; ~-catering (BRIT) adj für Selbstversorger; ~-centred (US self-centered) adj egozentrisch; ~-coloured (US self-colored) adj (of one colour) einfarbig, uni; ~-

confidence n Selbstvertrauen nt, Selbstbewußtsein nt; **~-conscious** adj gehemmt, befangen; **~-contained** adj (complete) (in sich) geschlossen; (person) verschlossen; (BRIT: flat) separat; **~-control** n Selbstbeherrschung f; **~-defence** (US self-defense) n Selbstverteidigung f; (JUR) Notwehr f; **~-discipline** n Selbstdisziplin f; **~-employed** adj frei(schaffend); **~-evident** adj offensichtlich; **~-governing** adj selbstverwaltet; **~-indulgent** adj zügellos; **~-interest** n Eigennutz m; **~-ish** adj egoistisch, selbstsüchtig; **~-ishness** n Egoismus m, Selbstsucht f; **~-lessly** adv selbstlos; **~-made** adj: **~ man** Selfmademan m; **~-pity** n Selbstmitleid nt; **~-portrait** n Selbstbildnis nt; **~-possessed** adj selbstbeherrscht; **~-preservation** n Selbsterhaltung f; **~-reliant** adj unabhängig; **~-respect** n Selbstachtung f; **~-righteous** adj selbstgerecht; **~-sacrifice** n Selbstaufopferung f; **~-satisfied** adj selbstzufrieden; **~-service** adj Selbstbedienungs-; **~-sufficient** adj selbstgenügsam; **~-taught** adj selbsterlernt; **~-taught person** Autodidakt m

sell [sɛl] (pt, pp **sold**) vt verkaufen ♦ vi verkaufen; (goods) sich verkaufen; **to ~ at or for £10** für £10 verkaufen; **~ off** vt verkaufen; **~ out** vi alles verkaufen; **~-by date** n Verfalldatum nt; **~er** n Verkäufer m; **~ing price** n Verkaufspreis m

Sellotape [ˈsɛləʊteɪp] (®, BRIT) n Tesafilm m (®)

sellout [ˈsɛlaʊt] n (of tickets): **it was a ~** es war ausverkauft

selves [sɛlvz] npl of **self**

semaphore [ˈsɛməfɔː*] n Winkzeichen pl

semblance [ˈsɛmbləns] n Anschein m

semen [ˈsiːmən] n Sperma nt

semester [sɪˈmɛstə*] (US) n Semester nt

semi [ˈsɛmɪ] n = **semidetached**

house; **~circle** n Halbkreis m; **~colon** n Semikolon nt; **~conductor** n Halbleiter m; **~detached house** (BRIT) n halbe(s) Doppelhaus nt; **~final** n Halbfinale nt

seminary [ˈsɛmɪnəɪ] n (REL) Priesterseminar nt

semiskilled [ˈsɛmɪˈskɪld] adj angelernt

senate [ˈsɛnɪt] n Senat m; **senator** n Senator m

send [sɛnd] (pt, pp **sent**) vt senden, schicken; (inf: inspire) hinreißen; **~away** vt wegschicken; **~away for** vt fus anfordern; **~ back** vt zurückschicken; **~ for** vt fus holen lassen; **~ off** vt (goods) abschicken; (BRIT: SPORT: player) vom Feld schicken; **~ out** vt (invitation) aussenden; **~ up** vt hinaufsenden; (BRIT: parody) verulken; **~er** n Absender m; **~-off** n: **to give sb a good ~-off** jdn (ganz) groß verabschieden

senior [ˈsiːnɪə*] adj (older) älter; (higher rank) Ober- ♦ n (older person) Ältere(r) m; (higher ranking) Rangältere(r) m; (in service) ältere(r) Mitbürger(in) m(f); **~ity** n (of age) höhere(s) Alter nt; (in rank) höhere(r) Dienstgrad m

sensation [sɛnˈseɪʃən] n Gefühl nt; (excitement) Sensation f, Aufsehen nt

sense [sɛns] n Sinn m; (understanding) Verstand m, Vernunft f; (feeling) Gefühl nt ♦ vt fühlen, spüren; **~ of humour** Humor m; **to make ~** Sinn ergeben; **~less** adj sinnlos; (unconscious) besinnungslos

sensibility [sɛnsɪˈbɪlɪtɪ] n Empfindsamkeit f; (feeling hurt) Empfindlichkeit f; **sensibilities** npl (feelings) Zartgefühl nt

sensible [ˈsɛnsəbl] adj vernünftig

sensitive [ˈsɛnsɪtɪv] adj: **~ (to)** empfindlich (gegen)

sensitivity [sɛnsɪˈtɪvɪtɪ] n Empfindlichkeit f; (artistic) Feingefühl nt; (tact) Feinfühligkeit f

sensual ['sensjuəl] *adj* sinnlich

sensuous ['sensjuəs] *adj* sinnlich

sent [sent] *pt, pp of* send

sentence ['sentəns] *n* Satz *m*; (JUR) Strafe *f*; Urteil *nt* ♦ *vt*: to ~ sb to death/to 5 years jdn zum Tode/zu 5 Jahren verurteilen

sentiment ['sentɪmənt] *n* Gefühl *nt*; (thought) Gedanke *m*; ~al [sentɪ'mentl] *adj* sentimental; (of feelings rather than reason) gefühlsmäßig

sentry ['sentrɪ] *n* (Schild)wache *f*

separate [*adj* 'seprɪt, *vb* 'sepəreɪt] *adj* getrennt, separat ♦ *vt* trennen ♦ *vi* sich trennen; ~ly *adv* getrennt; ~s *npl* (clothes) Röcke, Pullover *etc*

separation [sepə'reɪʃən] *n* Trennung *f*

September [sep'tembə*] *n* September *m*

septic ['septɪk] *adj* vereitert, septisch; ~ tank *n* Klärbehälter *m*

sequel ['si:kwəl] *n* Folge *f*

sequence ['si:kwəns] *n* (Reihen)folge *f*

sequin ['si:kwɪn] *n* Paillette *f*

Serbia ['sɜ:bɪə] *n* Serbien *nt*

serene [sə'ri:n] *adj* heiter

serenity [sɪ'renɪtɪ] *n* Heiterkeit *f*

sergeant ['sɑ:dʒənt] *n* Feldwebel *m*; (POLICE) (Polizei)wachtmeister *m*

serial ['sɪərɪəl] *n* Fortsetzungsroman *m*; (TV) Fernsehserie *f* ♦ *adj* (number) (fort)laufend; ~ize *vt* in Fortsetzungen veröffentlichen; in Fortsetzungen senden

series ['sɪərɪz] *n inv* Serie *f*, Reihe *f*

serious ['sɪərɪəs] *adj* ernst; (injury) schwer; ~ly *adv* ernst(haft); (hurt) schwer; ~ness *n* Ernst *m*, Ernsthaftigkeit *f*

sermon ['sɜ:mən] *n* Predigt *f*

serrated [se'reɪtɪd] *adj* gezackt

servant ['sɜ:vənt] *n* Diener(in) *m(f)*

serve [sɜ:v] *vt* dienen +*dat*; (guest, customer) bedienen; (food) servieren ♦ *vi* dienen, nützen; (at table) servieren; (TENNIS) geben, aufschlagen; it ~s him right das geschieht ihm recht; that'll ~ as a table das geht als Tisch; ~ *n* (on sb) (jdn) vor Gericht laden; ~ out *or* up *vt* (food) auftragen, servieren

service ['sɜ:vɪs] *n* (help) Dienst *m*; (trains etc) Verbindung *f*; (hotel) Service *m*, Bedienung *f*; (set of dishes) Service *nt*; (REL) Gottesdienst *m*; (car) Inspektion *f*; (for TVs etc) Kundendienst *m*; (TENNIS) Aufschlag *m* ♦ *vt* (AUT, TECH) warten, überholen; the S~s *npl* (armed forces) die Streitkräfte *pl*; to be of ~ to sb jdm einen großen Dienst erweisen; ~able *adj* brauchbar; ~ area *n* (on motorway) Raststätte *f*; ~ charge *n* (BRIT) Bedienung *f*; ~man (*irreg*) *n* (soldier etc) Soldat *m*; ~ station *n* (Groß)tankstelle *f*

serviette [sɜ:vɪ'et] *n* Serviette *f*

servile ['sɜ:vaɪl] *adj* unterwürfig

session ['seʃən] *n* Sitzung *f*; (POL) Sitzungsperiode *f*; to be in ~ tagen

set [set] (*pt, pp* set) *n* (collection of things) Satz *m*, Set *nt*; (RADIO, TV) Apparat *m*; (TENNIS) Satz *m*; (group of people) Kreis *m*; (CINE) Szene *f*; (THEAT) Bühnenbild *nt* ♦ *adj* festgelegt; (ready) bereit ♦ *vt* (place) setzen, stellen, legen; (arrange) ordnen; (table) decken; (time, price) festsetzen; (alarm, watch, task) stellen; (jewels) (ein)fassen; (exam) ausarbeiten ♦ *vi* (sun) untergehen; (become hard) fest werden; (bone) zusammenwachsen; to ~ on doing sth etw unbedingt tun wollen; to ~ to music vertonen; to ~ on fire anstecken; to ~ free freilassen; to ~ sth going etw in Gang bringen; to ~ sail losfahren; ~ about *vt fus* (task) anpacken; ~ aside *vt* beiseitelegen; ~ back *vt*: to ~ back (by) zurückwerfen (um); ~ off *vi* aufbrechen ♦ *vt* (explode) sprengen; (alarm) losgehen lassen; (show up well) hervorheben; ~ out *vi*: to ~ out to do sth vorhaben, etw zu tun (*arrange*) anlegen, arrangieren; (*state*) darlegen; ~ **up** *vt* aufziehen; (*record*) aufstellen; (*monument*) erstellen; ~**back** *n* Rückschlag *m*; ~ **menu** *n* Tageskarte *f*

settee [se'ti:] *n* Sofa *nt*

setting ['setıŋ] *n* Hintergrund *m*

settle ['setl] *vt* beruhigen; (*pay*) begleichen, bezahlen; (*agree*) regeln ♦ *vi* sich einleben; (*come to rest*) sich niederlassen; (*sink*) sich setzen; (*calm down*) sich beruhigen; **to ~ for sth** sich mit etw zufriedengeben; **to ~ on sth** sich für etw entscheiden; **to ~ up with sb** mit jdm abrechnen; ~ **down** *vi* (*feel at home*) sich einleben; (*calm down*) sich beruhigen; ~ **in** *vi* sich eingewöhnen; ~**ment** *n* Regelung *f*; (*payment*) Begleichung *f*; (*colony*) Siedlung *f*; ~**r** *n* Siedler *m*

setup ['setʌp] *n* (*situation*) Lage *f*

seven ['sevn] *num* sieben; ~**teen** *num* siebzehn; ~**th** *adj* siebte(r, s) ♦ *n* Siebtel *nt*; ~**ty** *num* siebzig

sever ['sevə*] *vt* abtrennen

several ['sevrəl] *adj* mehrere, verschiedene ♦ *pron* mehrere; ~ **of us** einige von uns

severance ['sevərəns] *n*: ~ **pay** Abfindung *f*

severe [sı'vıə*] *adj* (*strict*) streng; (*serious*) schwer; (*climate*) rauh

severity [sı'verıtı] *n* Strenge *f*; Schwere *f*; Rauheit *f*

sew [səu] (*pt* **sewed**, *pp* **sewn**) *vt, vi* nähen; ~ **up** *vt* zunähen

sewage ['sju:ıdʒ] *n* Abwässer *pl*

sewer ['sjuə*] *n* (*Abwasser*)kanal *m*

sewing ['səuıŋ] *n* Näharbeit *f*; ~ **machine** *n* Nähmaschine *f*

sewn [səun] *pp* of **sew**

sex [seks] *n* Sex *m*; (*gender*) Geschlecht *nt*; **to have ~ with sb** mit jdm Geschlechtsverkehr haben; ~**ist** *adj* sexistisch ♦ *n* Sexist(in) *m(f)*

sexual ['seksjuəl] *adj* sexuell, geschlechtlich, Geschlechts-

sexy ['seksı] *adj* sexy

shabby ['ʃæbı] *adj* (*also fig*) schäbig

shack [ʃæk] *n* Hütte *f*

shackles ['ʃæklz] *npl* (*also fig*) Fesseln *pl*, Ketten *pl*

shade [ʃeıd] *n* Schatten *m*; (*for lamp*) Lampenschirm *m*; (*colour*) Farbton *m* ♦ *vt* abschirmen; **in the ~** im Schatten; **a ~ smaller** ein bißchen kleiner

shadow ['ʃædəu] *n* Schatten *m* ♦ *vt* (*follow*) beschatten ♦ *adj*: ~ **cabinet** (*BRIT: POL*) Schattenkabinett *nt*; ~**y** *adj* schattig

shady ['ʃeıdı] *adj* schattig; (*fig*) zwielichtig

shaft [ʃɑ:ft] *n* (*of spear etc*) Schaft *m*; (*in mine*) Schacht *m*; (*TECH*) Welle *f*; (*of light*) Strahl *m*

shaggy ['ʃægı] *adj* struppig

shake [ʃeık] (*pt* **shook**, *pp* **shaken**) *vt* schütteln, rütteln; (*shock*) erschüttern ♦ *vi* (*move*) schwanken; (*tremble*) zittern, beben ♦ *n* (*jerk*) Schütteln *nt*, Rütteln *nt*; **to ~ hands with** die Hand geben +*dat*; **to ~ one's head** den Kopf schütteln; ~ **off** *vt* abschütteln; ~ **up** *vt* aufschütteln; (*fig*) aufrütteln; **shaken** ['ʃeıkn] *pp* of **shake**

shaky ['ʃeıkı] *adj* zittrig; (*weak*) unsicher

shall [ʃæl] *vb aux*: **I** ~ **go** ich werde gehen; ~ **I open the door?** soll ich die Tür öffnen?; ~ **I?** soll ich?; **we'll buy some cake, ~ I?** wir werden einen Kuchen kaufen, ~ I? soll ich Kuchen kaufen?, ich kaufe Kuchen, oder?

shallow ['ʃæləu] *adj* seicht

sham [ʃæm] *n* Schein *m* ♦ *adj* unecht, falsch

shambles ['ʃæmblz] *n* Durcheinander *nt*

shame [ʃeım] *n* Scham *f*; (*disgrace, pity*) Schande *f* ♦ *vt* beschämen; **it is a ~ that** es ist schade, daß; **it is a ~ to do ...** es ist eine Schande, ... zu tun; **what a ~!** wie schade!; ~**faced** *adj* beschämt; ~**ful** *adj* schändlich; ~**less** *adj* schamlos

shampoo [ʃæm'pu:] *n* Shampoo(n) *nt* ♦ *vt* (*hair*) waschen; ~ **and set**

Waschen nt und Legen

shamrock ['ʃæmrɔk] n Kleeblatt nt

shandy ['ʃændɪ] n Bier nt mit Limonade

shan't [ʃɑːnt] = shall not

shanty town ['ʃæntɪ-] n Bidonville f

shape [ʃeɪp] n Form f ♦ vt formen, gestalten ♦ vi (also: ~ up) sich entwickeln; **to take** ~ Gestalt annehmen; **-shaped** suffix: **heart-shaped** herzförmig; **~less** adj formlos; **~ly** adj wohlproportioniert

share [ʃɛə*] n (An)teil m; (FIN) Aktie f ♦ vt teilen; **to** ~ **out** (among/between) verteilen (unter/zwischen); **~holder** n Aktionär (in f) m

shark [ʃɑːk] n Hai(fisch) m; (swindler) Gauner m

sharp [ʃɑːp] adj scharf; (pin) spitz; (person) clever; (MUS) erhöht ♦ n Kreuz nt ♦ adv zu hoch; **nine o'clock** ~ Punkt neun; **~en** vt schärfen; (pencil) spitzen; **~ener** n (also: **pencil ~ener**) Anspitzer m; **~-eyed** adj scharfsichtig; **~ly** adv (turn, stop) plötzlich; (stand out, contrast) deutlich; (criticize, retort) scharf

shatter ['ʃætə*] vt zerschmettern; (fig) zerstören ♦ vi zerspringen

shave [ʃeɪv] n Rasur f ♦ vt rasieren ♦ vi sich rasieren; **to have a** ~ sich rasieren (lassen); **~r** n (also: **electric ~r**) Rasierapparat m

shaving ['ʃeɪvɪŋ] n (action) Rasieren nt; **~s** npl (of wood etc) Späne pl; **~ brush** n Rasierpinsel m; **~ cream** n Rasiercreme f; **~ foam** n Rasierschaum m

shawl [ʃɔːl] n Schal m, Umhang m

she [ʃiː] pron sie ♦ adj weiblich; **~-bear** Bärenweibchen nt

sheaf [ʃiːf] (pl **sheaves**) n Garbe f

shear [ʃɪə*] (pt **~ed**, pp **~ed** or **shorn**) vt scheren; ~ **off** vi abbrechen; **~s** npl Heckenschere f

sheath [ʃiːθ] n Scheide f; (condom) Kondom m or nt

shed [ʃed] (pt, pp **shed**) n Schuppen m;

(for animals) Stall m ♦ vt (leaves etc) verlieren; (tears) vergießen

she'd [ʃiːd] = she had; she would

sheen [ʃiːn] n Glanz m

sheep [ʃiːp] n inv Schaf nt; **~dog** n Schäferhund m; **~ish** adj verlegen; **~skin** n Schaffell nt

sheer [ʃɪə*] adj bloß, rein; (steep) steil; (transparent) (hauch)dünn ♦ adv (directly) direkt

sheet [ʃiːt] n Bettuch nt, Bettlaken nt; (of paper) Blatt nt; (of metal etc) Platte f; (of ice) Fläche f

sheik(h) [ʃeɪk] n Scheich m

shelf [ʃelf] (pl **shelves**) n Bord nt, Regal nt

shell [ʃel] n Schale f; (sea~) Muschel f; (explosive) Granate f ♦ vt (peas) schälen; (fire on) beschießen

she'll [ʃiːl] = she will; she shall

shellfish ['ʃelfɪʃ] n Schalentier (-e); (as food) Meeresfrüchte pl

shell suit n Ballonseidenanzug m

shelter ['ʃeltə*] n Schutz m; (air-raid ~) Bunker m ♦ vt schützen, bedecken; (refugees) aufnehmen ♦ vi sich unterstellen; **~ed** adj (life) behütet; (spot) geschützt

shelve [ʃelv] vt aufschieben ♦ vi abfallen

shelves [ʃelvz] npl of **shelf**

shepherd ['ʃepəd] n Schäfer m ♦ vt treiben, führen; **~'s pie** n Auflauf m aus Hackfleisch und Kartoffelbrei

sheriff ['ʃerɪf] n Sheriff m; (SCOTTISH) Friedensrichter m

sherry ['ʃerɪ] n Sherry m

she's [ʃiːz] = she is; she has

Shetland ['ʃetlənd] n (also: the ~s, the ~ Isles) die Shetlandinseln pl

shield [ʃiːld] n Schild m; (fig) Schirm m ♦ vt (be)schirmen; (TECH) abschirmen

shift [ʃɪft] n Verschiebung f; (work) Schicht f ♦ vt (ver)rücken, verschieben; (arm) wegnehmen ♦ vi sich verschieben; **~less** adj (person) träge; ~ **work** n Schichtarbeit f; **~y** adj verschlagen

shilly-shally [ˈʃɪliˌʃæli] vi zögern
shin [ʃɪn] n Schienbein nt
shine [ʃaɪn] (pt, pp **shone**) n Glanz
m, Schein m ♦ vt polieren ♦ vi scheinen; (fig) glänzen; to ~ a torch on
sb jdn mit (einer Lampe) anleuchten
shingle [ˈʃɪŋgl] n Strandkies m; ~s
npl (MED) Gürtelrose f
shiny [ˈʃaɪni] adj glänzend
ship [ʃɪp] n Schiff nt ♦ vt verschif-
fen; ~**building** n Schiffbau m;
~**ment** n Verschiffung f; ~**per** n
Verschiffer m; ~**ping** n (act) Verschiffung f; (ships) Schiffahrt f;
~**wreck** n Schiffbruch m; (destroyed
ship) Wrack nt ♦ vt: to be ~
wrecked Schiffbruch erleiden;
~**yard** n Werft f
shire [ˈʃaɪə*] (BRIT) n Grafschaft f
shirk [ʃɜːk] vt ausweichen +dat
shirt [ʃɜːt] n (Ober)hemd nt; in ~
sleeves in Hemdsärmeln; ~**y** (inf)
adj mürrisch
shit [ʃɪt] (inf!) excl Scheiße (!)
shiver [ˈʃɪvə*] n Schauer m ♦ vi
frösteln, zittern
shoal [ʃəʊl] n (Fisch)schwarm m
shock [ʃɔk] n Erschütterung f; (mental) Schock m; (ELEC) Schlag m ♦
vt erschüttern; (offend) schockieren;
~ **absorber** n Stoßdämpfer m; ~**ing**
adj unerhört
shod [ʃɔd] pt, pp of **shoe** ♦ adj be-
schuht
shoddy [ˈʃɔdi] adj schäbig
shoe [ʃuː] (pt, pp **shod**) n Schuh m;
(of horse) Hufeisen nt ♦ vt (horse)
beschlagen; ~**brush** n Schuhbürste f;
~**horn** n Schuhlöffel m; ~**lace** n
Schnürsenkel m; ~ **polish** n Schuh-
creme f; ~ **shop** n Schuhgeschäft nt;
~**string** n (fig): on a ~**string** mit
sehr wenig Geld
shone [ʃɔn] pt, pp of **shine**
shoo [ʃuː] excl sch; (to dog etc) pfui
shook [ʃʊk] pt, pp of **shake**
shoot [ʃuːt] (pt, pp **shot**) n (branch)
Schößling m ♦ vt (gun) abfeuern;
(goal, arrow) schießen; (person) an-
schießen; (kill) erschießen; (film)

drehen ♦ vi (gun, move quickly)
schießen; to ~ (at) schießen (auf
+acc); ~ **down** vt abschießen; ~ **in**
vi hineinschießen; ~ **out** vi hinausschießen; ~ **up** vi (fig) aus dem Boden schießen; ~**ing** n Schießerei f;
~**ing star** n Sternschnuppe f
shop [ʃɔp] n (esp BRIT) Geschäft nt,
Laden m; (work~) Werkstatt f ♦ vi
(also: go ~ping) einkaufen gehen; ~
assistant (BRIT) n Verkäufer(in)
m(f); ~ **floor** (BRIT) n Werkstatt f;
~**keeper** n Geschäftsinhaber m; ~**lifting** n Ladendiebstahl m; ~**per** n
Käufer(in) m(f); ~**ping** n Einkaufen
nt, Einkauf m; ~**ping bag** n Ein-
kaufstasche f; ~**ping centre** (US
~**ping center**) n Einkaufszentrum
nt; ~**soiled** adj angeschmutzt; ~
steward (BRIT) n (INDUSTRY) Be-
triebsrat m; ~ **window** n Schaufenster nt
shore [ʃɔː*] n Ufer nt; (of sea)
Strand m ♦ vt: to ~ up abstützen
shorn [ʃɔːn] pp of **shear**
short [ʃɔːt] adj kurz; (person) klein;
(curt) kurz angebunden; (measure)
zu knapp ♦ adv (suddenly) plötzlich ♦ n
(also: ~ film) Kurzfilm
m ♦ adv (suddenly) plötzlich ♦ vi
(ELEC) einen Kurzschluß haben; ~s
npl (clothes) Shorts pl; to be ~ of
sth nicht genug von etw haben; in
kurz gesagt; ~ of doing sth ohne so
weit zu gehen, etw zu tun; everything ~ of ... alles außer ...; it is ~
for das ist die Kurzform von; to cut
~ abkürzen; to fall ~ of sth etw
nicht erreichen; to stop ~ plötzlich
anhalten; to stop ~ of haltmachen
vor; ~**age** n Knappheit f, Mangel m;
~**bread** n Mürbegebäck nt; ~
change vt: to ~**change** sb jdm zu
wenig herausgeben; ~**circuit** n Kurzschluß m ♦ vi einen Kurzschluß haben ♦ vt kurzschließen; ~**coming** n
Mangel m; ~ **(crust) pastry** (BRIT) n
Mürbeteig m; ~**cut** n Abkürzung f;
~**en** vt (ab)kürzen; (clothes) kürzer
machen; ~**fall** n Defizit nt; ~**hand**
(BRIT) n Stenographie f; ~**hand**

typist (BRIT) n Stenotypistin f; **~list** (BRIT) n (for job) engere Wahl f; **~lived** adj kurzlebig; **~ly** adv bald; **~sighted** (BRIT) adj (also fig) kurzsichtig; **~staffed** adj: to be ~staffed zu wenig Personal haben; **~story** n Kurzgeschichte f; **~tempered** adj leicht aufbrausend; **~term** adj (effect) kurzfristig; **~wave** n (RADIO) Kurzwelle f

shot [ʃɒt] pt, pp of **shoot ♦** n (from gun) Schuß m; (person) Schütze m; (try) Versuch m; (injection) Spritze f; (PHOT) Aufnahme f; **like a ~** wie der Blitz **♦ ~gun** n Schrotflinte f

should [ʃʊd] vb aux: **I ~** go now ich sollte jetzt gehen; **he ~** be there now er sollte eigentlich schon da sein; **I ~** go if **I** were you ich würde gehen, wenn ich du wäre; **I ~** like to ich möchte gerne

shoulder [ˈʃəʊldə*] n Schulter f; (BRIT: of road): **hard ~** Seitenstreifen m **♦** vt (rifle) schultern; (fig) auf sich nehmen; **~ bag** n Umhängetasche f; **~ blade** n Schulterblatt nt; **~ strap** n (MIL) Schulterklappe f; (of dress etc) Träger m

shouldn't [ˈʃʊdnt] = **should not**

shout [ʃaʊt] n Schrei m **♦** vt rufen **♦** vi schreien; **~ down** vt niederbrüllen; **~ing** n Geschrei nt

shove [ʃʌv] n Schubs m, Stoß m **♦** vt schieben, stoßen, schubsen; (inf: put): **to ~ sth in(to) sth** etw in etw acc hineinschieben; **~ off** vi (NAUT) abstoßen; (fig: inf) abhauen

shovel [ˈʃʌvl] n Schaufel f **♦** vt schaufeln

show [ʃəʊ] (pt **showed**, pp **shown**) n (display) Schau f; (exhibition) Ausstellung f; (CINE, THEAT) Vorstellung f, Show f **♦** vt zeigen; (kindness) erweisen **♦** vi zu sehen sein; **to be on ~** (exhibits etc) ausgestellt sein; **to ~ sb in** jdn hereinführen; **to ~ sb out** jdn hinausbegleiten; **~ off** vi (pej) angeben **♦** vt (display) ausstellen; **~ up** vi (stand out) sich abheben; (arrive) erscheinen **♦**

vt (unmask) bloßstellen; **~ business** n Showbusineß nt; **~down** n Kraftprobe f

shower [ˈʃaʊə*] n Schauer m; (of stones) (Stein)hagel m; (~ bath) Dusche f **♦** vi duschen **♦** vt: **to ~ sb with sth** jdn mit etw überschütten; **~proof** adj wasserabstoßend

showing [ˈʃəʊɪŋ] n Vorführung f

show jumping n Turnierreiten nt

shown [ʃəʊn] pp of **show**

show: **~off** [ˈʃəʊɒf] n Angeber(in) m(f); **~piece** [ˈʃəʊpiːs] n Paradestück nt; **~room** [ˈʃəʊrʊm] n Ausstellungsraum m

shrank [ʃræŋk] pt of **shrink**

shred [ʃred] n Fetzen m **♦** vt zerfetzen; (COOK) raspeln; **~der** n (for vegetables) Gemüseschneider m; (for documents) Reißwolf m

shrewd [ʃruːd] adj clever

shriek [ʃriːk] n Schrei m **♦** vt, vi kreischen, schreien

shrimp [ʃrɪmp] n Krabbe f, Garnele f

shrink [ʃrɪŋk] (pt **shrank**, pp **shrunk**) vi schrumpfen, eingehen **♦** vt einschrumpfen lassen; **~ from doing sth** davor zurückschrecken, etw zu tun; **~age** n Schrumpfung f; **~wrap** vt einschweißen

shrivel [ˈʃrɪvl] vt, vi (also: **~ up**) schrumpfen, schrumpeln

shroud [ʃraʊd] n Leichentuch nt **♦** vt: **~ed in mystery** mit einem Geheimnis umgeben

Shrove Tuesday [ˈʃrəʊv-] n Fastnachtsdienstag m

shrub [ʃrʌb] n Busch m, Strauch m; **~bery** n Gebüsch nt

shrug [ʃrʌg] n Achselzucken nt **♦** vt, vi: **to ~ (one's shoulders)** die Achseln zucken; **~ off** vt auf die leichte Schulter nehmen

shrunk [ʃrʌŋk] pp of **shrink**

shudder [ˈʃʌdə*] n Schauder m **♦** vi schaudern

shuffle [ˈʃʌfl] n (CARDS) (Karten)mischen nt **♦** vt (cards) mischen; **to ~ one's feet** schlurfen

shun [ʃʌn] vt scheuen, (ver)meiden

shunt [ʃʌnt] vt rangieren

shut [ʃʌt] (pt, pp **shut**) vt schließen, zumachen ♦ vi sich schließen (lassen); ~ **down** vt, vi schließen; ~ **off** vt (supply) abdrehen; ~ **up** vi (keep quiet) den Mund halten ♦ vt (close) zuschließen; ~**ter** n Fensterladen m; (PHOT) Verschluß m

shuttle [ˈʃʌtl] n (plane, train etc) Pendelflugzeug nt/-zug m etc; (space ~) Raumtransporter m; (also: ~ service) Pendelverkehr m

shuttlecock [ˈʃʌtlkɔk] n Federball m

shy [ʃaɪ] adj schüchtern; ~**ness** n Schüchternheit f

Siamese [saɪəˈmiːz] adj: ~ **cat** Siamkatze f

Siberia [saɪˈbɪərɪə] n Sibirien nt

sibling [ˈsɪblɪŋ] n Geschwister nt

Sicily [ˈsɪsɪlɪ] n Sizilien nt

sick [sɪk] adj krank; (joke) makaber; **I feel ~** mir ist schlecht; **I was ~** ich habe gebrochen; **to be ~ of** sth/sth jdn/etw satt haben; ~ **bay** n (Schiffs)lazarett nt; ~**en** vt (disgust) krankmachen ♦ vi krank werden; ~**ening** adj (sight) widerlich; (annoying) zum Weinen

sickle [ˈsɪkl] n Sichel f

sick: ~ **leave** n krank geschrieben sein; ~**ly** adj kränklich, blaß; (causing nausea) widerlich; ~**ness** n Krankheit f; (vomiting) Übelkeit f, Erbrechen nt; ~ **pay** n Krankengeld nt

side [saɪd] n Seite f ♦ adj (door, entrance) Seiten-, Neben- ♦ vi: **to ~ with sb** jds Partei ergreifen; **by the ~ of** neben; **to take ~s (with)** Partei nehmen (für); **from all ~s** von allen Seiten; ~**boards** npl (BRIT) npl Koteletten pl; ~**burns** npl Koteletten pl; ~**car** n Beiwagen m; ~ **drum** n (MUS) kleine Trommel; ~ **effect** n Nebenwirkung f; ~**light** n (AUT) Parkleuchte f; ~**line** n (SPORT) Seitenlinie f; (fig: hobby) Nebenbeschäftigung f;

~**long** adj Seiten-; ~**saddle** adv im Damensattel; ~**show** n Nebenausstellung f; ~**step** vt (fig) ausweichen; ~ **street** n Seitenstraße f; ~**track** vt (fig) ablenken; ~**walk** (US) n Bürgersteig m; ~**ways** adv seitwärts

siding [ˈsaɪdɪŋ] n Nebengleis nt

sidle [ˈsaɪdl] vi: **to ~ up (to)** sich heranmachen (an +acc)

siege [siːdʒ] n Belagerung f

sieve [sɪv] n Sieb nt ♦ vt sieben

sift [sɪft] vt sieben; (fig) sichten

sigh [saɪ] n Seufzer m ♦ vi seufzen

sight [saɪt] n (power of seeing) Sehvermögen nt; (look) Blick m; (fact of seeing) Anblick m; (of gun) Visier nt ♦ vt sichten; **in ~** in Sicht; **out of ~** außer Sicht; ~**seeing** n Besuch m von Sehenswürdigkeiten; **to go ~seeing** Sehenswürdigkeiten besichtigen

sign [saɪn] n Zeichen nt; (notice, road etc) Schild nt ♦ vt unterschreiben; **to ~ sth over to sb** jdm etw überschreiben; ~ **on** vi (MIL) sich verpflichten; (as unemployed) sich (arbeitslos) melden ♦ vt (MIL) verpflichten; (employee) anstellen; ~ **up** vi (MIL) sich verpflichten ♦ vt verpflichten

signal [ˈsɪgnl] n Signal nt ♦ vi ein Zeichen geben +dat; ~**man** (irreg) n (RAIL) Stellwerkswärter m

signature [ˈsɪgnətʃə*] n Unterschrift f; ~ **tune** n Erkennungsmelodie f

signet ring [ˈsɪgnət-] n Siegelring m

significance [sɪgˈnɪfɪkəns] n Bedeutung f

significant [sɪgˈnɪfɪkənt] adj (meaning sth) bedeutsam; (important) bedeutend

signify [ˈsɪgnɪfaɪ] vt bedeuten; (show) andeuten, zu verstehen geben

sign language n Zeichensprache f, Fingersprache f

signpost [ˈsaɪnpəust] n Wegweiser m

silence [ˈsaɪləns] n Stille f; (of person) Schweigen nt ♦ vt zum Schweigen bringen; ~**r** n (on gun) Schalldämpfer m; (BRIT: AUT) Auspufftopf m

silent ['saɪlənt] adj still; (person) schweigsam; **to remain ~** schweigen; **~ partner** n (COMM) stille(r) Teilhaber m

silicon chip ['sɪlɪkən-] n Siliciumchip nt

silk [sɪlk] n Seide f ♦ adj seiden, Seiden-; **~y** adj seidig

silly ['sɪlɪ] adj dumm, albern

silt [sɪlt] n Schlamm m, Schlick m

silver ['sɪlvə*] n Silber nt ♦ adj silbern, Silber-; **~ paper** (BRIT) n Silberpapier nt; **~-plated** adj versilbert; **~smith** n Silberschmied m; **~ware** n Silber nt; **~y** adj silbern

similar ['sɪmɪlə*] adj: **~ (to)** ähnlich (+dat); **~ity** [sɪmɪ'lærɪtɪ] n Ähnlichkeit f; **~ly** adv in ähnlicher Weise

simile ['sɪmɪlɪ] n Vergleich m

simmer ['sɪmə*] vi sieden ♦ vt sieden lassen

simpering ['sɪmpərɪŋ] adj albern

simple ['sɪmpl] adj einfach; **~ (-minded)** adj einfältig; **~ton** n Einfaltspinsel m

simplicity [sɪm'plɪsɪtɪ] n Einfachheit f; (of person) Einfältigkeit f

simplify ['sɪmplɪfaɪ] vt vereinfachen

simply ['sɪmplɪ] adv einfach

simulate ['sɪmjʊleɪt] vt simulieren

simultaneous [sɪmʌl'teɪnɪəs] adj gleichzeitig

sin [sɪn] n Sünde f ♦ vi sündigen

since [sɪns] adv seither ♦ prep seit, seitdem ♦ conj (time) seit; (because) da, weil; **~ then** seitdem

sincere [sɪn'sɪə*] adj aufrichtig; **~ly** adv: **yours ~ly** mit freundlichen Grüßen

sincerity [sɪn'serɪtɪ] n Aufrichtigkeit f

sinew ['sɪnjuː] f Sehne f

sinful ['sɪnfʊl] adj sündig, sündhaft

sing [sɪŋ] (pt sang, pp sung) vt, vi singen

Singapore [sɪŋgə'pɔː*] n Singapur nt

singe [sɪndʒ] vt versengen

singer ['sɪŋə*] n Sänger(in) m(f)

single ['sɪŋgl] adj (one only) einzig; (bed, room) Einzel-, einzeln; (unmarried) ledig; (ticket) einfach; (having one part only) einzeln ♦ n (BRIT: also: ~ ticket) einfache Fahrkarte f; **in ~ file** hintereinander; **~ out** vt aussuchen, auswählen; **~ bed** n Einzelbett nt; **~-breasted** adj einreihig; **~-handed** adj allein; **~-minded** adj zielstrebig; **~ room** n Einzelzimmer nt; **~s** n (TENNIS) Einzel nt

singlet ['sɪŋglət] n Unterhemd nt

singly ['sɪŋglɪ] adv einzeln, allein

singular ['sɪŋgjʊlə*] adj (GRAM) Singular-; (odd) merkwürdig, seltsam ♦ n (GRAM) Einzahl f, Singular m

sinister ['sɪnɪstə*] adj (evil) böse; (ghostly) unheimlich

sink [sɪŋk] (pt sank, pp sunk) n Spülbecken nt ♦ vt (ship) versenken ♦ vi sinken; **to ~ sth into** (teeth, claws) etw schlagen in +acc; **~ in** vi (news etc) eingehen

sinner ['sɪnə*] n Sünder(in) m(f)

sinus ['saɪnəs] n (ANAT) Sinus m

sip [sɪp] n Schlückchen nt ♦ vi nippen an +dat

siphon ['saɪfən] n Siphon(flasche f) m; **~ off** vt absaugen; (fig) abschöpfen

sir [sɜː*] n (respect) Herr m; (knight) Sir m; **S~ John Smith** Sir John Smith; **yes ~** ja(wohl, mein Herr)

siren ['saɪərən] n Sirene f

sirloin ['sɜːlɔɪn] n Lendenstück nt

sissy ['sɪsɪ] (inf) n Waschlappen m

sister ['sɪstə*] n Schwester f; (BRIT: nurse) Oberschwester f; (nun) Ordensschwester f; **~-in-law** n Schwägerin f

sit [sɪt] (pt, pp sat) vi sitzen; (hold session) tagen ♦ vt (exam) machen; **~ down** vi sich hinsetzen; **~ in on** vt fus dabeisein bei; **~ up** vi (after lying) sich aufsetzen; (straight) sich gerade setzen; (at night) aufbleiben

sitcom ['sɪtkɒm] n abbr (= situation

comedy) Situationskomödie f

site [saɪt] n Platz m; (also: building ~) Baustelle f ♦ vt legen

sitting ['sɪtɪŋ] n (meeting) Sitzung f; ~ **room** n Wohnzimmer nt

situated ['sɪtjʊeɪtɪd] adj: to be ~ liegen

situation [sɪtjʊ'eɪʃən] n Situation f, Lage f; (place) Lage f; (employment) Stelle f; "~s vacant" (BRIT) „Stellenangebote" pl

six [sɪks] num sechs; ~**teen** num sechzehn; ~**th** adj sechste(r, s) ♦ n Sechstel nt; ~**ty** num sechzig

size [saɪz] n Größe f; (of project) Umfang m; ~ **up** vt (assess) abschätzen, einschätzen; ~**able** adj ziemlich groß, ansehnlich

sizzle ['sɪzl] vi zischen; (COOK) brutzeln

skate [skeɪt] n Schlittschuh m; (fish: pl inv) Rochen m ♦ vi Schlittschuh laufen; ~**r** n Schlittschuhläufer(in) m(f)

skating ['skeɪtɪŋ] n Eislauf m; to go ~ Eislaufen gehen; ~ **rink** n Eisbahn f

skeleton ['skelɪtn] n Skelett nt; (fig) Gerüst nt; ~ **key** n Dietrich m; ~ **staff** n Notbesetzung f

skeptical ['skeptɪkl] (US) adj = sceptical

sketch [sketʃ] n Skizze f; (THEAT) Sketch m ♦ vt skizzieren; ~**book** n Skizzenbuch nt; ~**y** adj skizzenhaft

skewer ['skjʊə*] n Fleischspieß m

ski [skiː] n Ski m, Schi m ♦ vi Ski or Schi laufen; ~ **boot** n Skistiefel m

skid [skɪd] n (AUT) Schleudern nt ♦ vi rutschen; (AUT) schleudern

skier ['skiːə*] n Skiläufer(in) m(f)

skiing ['skiːɪŋ] n: to go ~ Skilaufen gehen

ski-jump n Sprungschanze f ♦ vi Ski springen

skilful ['skɪlful] adj geschickt

ski-lift n Skilift m

skill [skɪl] n Können nt; (worker) Fach-, gelernt; ~**ed** adj geschickt; (worker) Fach-, gelernt

skim [skɪm] vt (liquid) abschöpfen;

(glide over) gleiten über +acc ♦ vi: ~ **through** (book) überfliegen; ~**med milk** n Magermilch f

skimp [skɪmp] vt (do carelessly) oberflächlich tun; ~**y** adj (work) schlecht gemacht; (dress) knapp

skin [skɪn] n Haut f; (peel) Schale f ♦ vt abhäuten; schälen; ~ **cancer** n Hautkrebs m; ~-**deep** adj oberflächlich; ~ **diving** n Schwimmtauchen nt; ~**ny** adj dünn; ~**tight** adj (dress etc) hauteng

skip [skɪp] n Sprung m ♦ vi hüpfen; (with rope) Seil springen ♦ vt (pass over) übergehen

ski pants npl Skihosen pl

ski pole n Skistock m

skipper ['skɪpə*] n Kapitän m ♦ vt führen

skipping rope ['skɪpɪŋ-] (BRIT) n Hüpfseil nt

skirmish ['skɜːmɪʃ] n Scharmützel nt

skirt [skɜːt] n Rock m ♦ vt herumgehen um; (fig) umgehen; ~**ing board** (BRIT) n Fußleiste f

ski suit n Skianzug m

skit [skɪt] n Parodie f

skittle ['skɪtl] n Kegel m; ~**s** n (game) Kegeln nt

skive [skaɪv] (BRIT: inf) vi schwänzen

skulk [skʌlk] vi sich herumdrücken

skull [skʌl] n Schädel m

skunk [skʌŋk] n Stinktier nt

sky [skaɪ] n Himmel m; ~**light** n Oberlicht nt; ~**scraper** n Wolkenkratzer m

slab [slæb] n (of stone) Platte f

slack [slæk] adj (loose) locker; (business) flau; (careless) nachlässig, lasch ♦ vi nachlässig sein ♦ n: to take up the ~ straffziehen; ~**s** npl (trousers) Hose(n pl) f; ~**en** vi (also: ~en off) locker werden; (: become slower) nachlassen, stocken ♦ vt (: loosen) lockern

slag [slæg] n Schlacke f; ~ **heap** n Halde f

slain [sleɪn] pp of slay

slam [slæm] n Knall m ♦ vt (door)

zuschlagen; *(throw down)* knallen ♦ *vi* zuschlagen

slander ['slɑːndə*] *n* Verleumdung *f* ♦ *vt* verleumden

slant [slɑːnt] *n* Schräge *f*; *(fig)* Tendenz *f* ♦ *vt* schräg legen ♦ *vi* schräg liegen; ~**ed** *adj* schräg; ~**ing** *adj* schräg

slap [slæp] *n* Klaps *m* ♦ *vt* einen Klaps geben +*dat* ♦ *adv* (*directly*) geradewegs; ~**dash** *adj* salopp; ~**stick** *n* (*comedy*) Klamauk *m*; ~**up** *adj* (*BRIT*) (*meal*) erstklassig, prima

slash [slæʃ] *n* Schnittwunde *f* ♦ *vt* (*auf*)schlitzen; (*expenditure*) radikal kürzen

slat [slæt] *n* (*of wood, plastic*) Leiste *f*

slate [sleɪt] *n* (*stone*) Schiefer *m*; (*roofing*) Dachziegel *m* ♦ *vt* (*criticize*) verreißen

slaughter ['slɔːtə*] *n* (*of animals*) Schlachten *nt*; (*of people*) Gemetzel *nt* ♦ *vt* schlachten; (*people*) niedermetzeln; ~**house** *n* Schlachthof *m*

Slav [slɑːv] *adj* slawisch

slave [sleɪv] *n* Sklave *m*, Sklavin *f* ♦ *vi* schuften, sich schinden; ~**ry** *n* Sklaverei *f*; (*work*) Schinderei *f*

slay [sleɪ] (*pt* slew, *pp* slain) *vt* ermorden

sleazy ['sliːzɪ] *adj* (*place*) schmierig

sledge [sledʒ] *n* Schlitten *m*; ~**hammer** *n* Schmiedehammer *m*

sleek [sliːk] *adj* glatt; (*shape*) rassig

sleep [sliːp] (*pt, pp* slept) *n* Schlaf *m* ♦ *vi* schlafen; **to go to** ~ einschlafen; ~ **in** *vi* ausschlafen; (*oversleep*) verschlafen; ~**er** *n* (*person*) Schläfer *m*; (*BRIT: RAIL*) Schlafwagen *m*; (: *beam*) Schwelle *f*; ~**ing bag** *n* Schlafsack *m*; ~**ing car** *n* Schlafwagen *m*; ~**ing pill** *n* Schlaftablette *f*; ~**less** *adj* (*night*) schlaflos; ~**walker** *n* Schlafwandler(in) *m(f)*; ~**y** *adj* schläfrig

sleet [sliːt] *n* Schneeregen *m*

sleeve [sliːv] *n* Ärmel *m*; (*of record*) Umschlag *m*; ~**less** *adj* ärmellos

sleigh [sleɪ] *n* Pferdeschlitten *m*

sleight [slaɪt] *n*: ~ **of hand** Fingerfertigkeit *f*

slender ['slendə*] *adj* schlank; *(fig)* gering

slept [slept] *pt, pp of* sleep

slew [sluː] *vi* (*veer*) (herum)schwenken ♦ *pt of* slay

slice [slaɪs] *n* Scheibe *f* ♦ *vt* in Scheiben schneiden

slick [slɪk] *adj* (*clever*) raffiniert, aalglatt ♦ *n* Ölteppich *m*

slid [slɪd] *pt, pp of* slide

slide [slaɪd] (*pt, pp* slid) *n* Rutschbahn *f*; (*PHOT*) Dia(positiv) *nt*; (*BRIT: for hair*) (Haar)spange *f* ♦ *vt* schieben ♦ *vi* (*slip*) gleiten, rutschen

sliding ['slaɪdɪŋ] *adj* (*door*) Schiebe-; ~ **scale** *n* gleitende Skala *f*

slight [slaɪt] *adj* zierlich; (*trivial*) geringfügig; (*small*) gering ♦ *n* Kränkung *f* ♦ *vt* (*offend*) kränken; **not in the** ~**est** nicht im geringsten; ~**ly** *adv* etwas, ein bißchen

slim [slɪm] *adj* schlank; (*book*) dünn; (*chance*) gering ♦ *vi* eine Schlankheitskur machen

slime [slaɪm] *n* Schleim *m*

slimming ['slɪmɪŋ] *n* Schlankheitskur *f*

slimy ['slaɪmɪ] *adj* glitschig; (*dirty*) schlammig; (*person*) schmierig

sling [slɪŋ] (*pt, pp* slung) *n* Schlinge *f*; (*weapon*) Schleuder *f* ♦ *vt* schleudern

slip [slɪp] *n* (*mistake*) Flüchtigkeitsfehler *m*; (*petticoat*) Unterrock *m*; (*of paper*) Zettel *m* ♦ *vt* (*put*) stecken, schieben ♦ *vi* (*lose balance*) ausrutschen; (*move*) gleiten, rutschen; (*decline*) nachlassen; (*move smoothly*): **to** ~ **in/out** (*person*) hinein-/hinausschlüpfen; **to give sb the** ~ jdm entwischen; ~ **of the tongue** Versprecher *m*; **it** ~**ped my mind** das ist mir entfallen; **to** ~ **sth on/off** etw über-/abstreifen; ~ **away** *vi* sich wegstehlen; ~ **by** *vi* (*time*) verstreichen; ~ **in** *vt* hineingleiten lassen ♦ *vi* (*errors*) sich einschleichen; **~ped disc** n Bandscheibenschaden m

slipper ['slɪpə*] n Hausschuh m

slippery ['slɪpərɪ] adj glatt

slip: **~-road** (BRIT) n Auffahrt f/ Ausfahrt f; **~shod** ['slɪpʃɒd] adj schlampig; **~-up** ['slɪpʌp] n Panne f; **~way** ['slɪpweɪ] n Auslaufbahn f

slit [slɪt] (pt, pp **slit**) n Schlitz m ♦ vt aufschlitzen

slither ['slɪðə*] vi schlittern; (snake) sich schlängeln

sliver ['slɪvə*] n (of glass, wood) Splitter m; (of cheese etc) Scheibchen nt

slob [slɒb] (inf) n Klotz m

slog [slɒg] vi (work hard) schuften ♦ n: **it was a ~** es war eine Plackerei

slogan ['sləʊgən] n Schlagwort nt; (COMM) Werbespruch m

slop [slɒp] vi (also: ~ over) überschwappen ♦ vt verschütten

slope [sləʊp] n Neigung f; (of mountains) (Ab)hang m ♦ vi: **to ~ down** sich senken; **to ~ up** ansteigen

sloping ['sləʊpɪŋ] adj schräg

sloppy ['slɒpɪ] adj schlampig

slot [slɒt] n Schlitz m ♦ vt: **to ~ sth in** etw einlegen

sloth [sləʊθ] n (laziness) Faulheit f

slot machine n (BRIT: vending machine) Automat m; (for gambling) Spielautomat m

slouch [slaʊtʃ] vi: **to ~ about** (laze) herumhängen (inf)

slovenly ['slʌvnlɪ] adj schlampig; (speech) salopp

slow [sləʊ] adj langsam ♦ adv langsam; **to be ~** (clock) nachgehen; (stupid) begriffsstutzig sein; **"~"** (road sign) „Langsam"; **in ~ motion** in Zeitlupe; **~ down** vi langsamer werden ♦ vt verlangsamen; **~ up** vi sich verlangsamen, sich verzögern ♦ vt aufhalten, langsamer machen; **~ly** adv langsam

sludge [slʌdʒ] n Schlamm m

slug [slʌg] n Nacktschnecke f; (inf: bullet) Kugel f; **~gish** adj träge; (COMM) schleppend

sluice [slu:s] n Schleuse f

slum [slʌm] n (house) Elendsquartier nt

slumber ['slʌmbə*] n Schlummer m

slump [slʌmp] n Rückgang m ♦ vi fallen, stürzen

slung [slʌŋ] pt, pp of **sling**

slur [slɜː*] n Undeutlichkeit f; (insult) Verleumdung f; **~red** [slɜːd] adj (pronunciation) undeutlich

slush [slʌʃ] n (snow) Schneematsch m; **~ fund** n Schmiergeldfonds m

slut [slʌt] n Schlampe f

sly [slaɪ] adj schlau

smack [smæk] n Klaps m ♦ vt einen Klaps geben +dat ♦ vi: **to ~ of** riechen nach; **to ~ one's lips** schmatzen, sich die Lippen lecken

small [smɔːl] adj klein; **in the ~ hours** in den frühen Morgenstunden; **~ ads** (BRIT) npl Kleinanzeigen pl; **~ change** n Kleingeld nt; **~ holder** (BRIT) n Kleinbauer m; **~pox** n Pocken pl; **~ talk** n Geplauder nt

smart [smɑːt] adj (fashionable) elegant, schick; (neat) adrett; (clever) clever; (quick) scharf ♦ vi brennen, schmerzen; **~en up** vi sich in Schale werfen ♦ vt herausputzen

smash [smæʃ] n Zusammenstoß m; (TENNIS) Schmetterball m; (break) zerschmettern; (destroy) vernichten ♦ vt (break) zerspringen; **~ing** (inf) adj toll

smattering ['smætərɪŋ] n oberflächliche Kenntnis f

smear [smɪə*] n Fleck m ♦ vt beschmieren

smell [smel] (pt, pp **smelt** or **smelled**) n Geruch m; (sense) Geruchssinn m ♦ vt riechen ♦ vi: **to ~ (of)** riechen (nach); (fragrantly) duften (nach); **~y** adj übelriechend

smile [smaɪl] n Lächeln nt ♦ vi lächeln

smirk [smɜːk] n blöde(s) Grinsen nt

smith [smɪθ] n Schmied m; **~y** ['smɪðɪ] n Schmiede f

smock [smɒk] n Kittel m

smoke [sməʊk] n Rauch m ♦ vt rauchen; (food) räuchern ♦ vi rauchen; ~**d** adj (bacon) geräuchert; (glass) Rauch-; ~**r** n Raucher(in) m(f); (RAIL) Raucherabteil nt; ~ **screen** n Rauchwand f

smoking ['sməʊkɪŋ] n: "no ~" „Rauchen verboten"

smoky ['sməʊkɪ] adj rauchig; (room) verraucht; (taste) schmalzig

smolder ['sməʊldə*] (US) vi = **smoulder**

smooth [smuːð] adj glatt ♦ vt (also: ~ out) glätten, glattstreichen

smother ['smʌðə*] vt ersticken

smoulder ['sməʊldə*] (US **smolder**) vi schwelen

smudge [smʌdʒ] n Schmutzfleck m ♦ vt beschmieren

smug [smʌg] adj selbstgefällig

smuggle ['smʌgl] vt schmuggeln; ~**r** n Schmuggler m

smuggling ['smʌglɪŋ] n Schmuggel m

smutty ['smʌtɪ] adj schmutzig

snack [snæk] n Imbiß m; ~ **bar** n Imbißstube f

snag [snæg] n Haken m

snail [sneɪl] n Schnecke f

snake [sneɪk] n Schlange f

snap [snæp] n Schnappen nt; (photograph) Schnappschuß m ♦ adj (decision) schnell ♦ vt (break) zerbrechen; (PHOT) knipsen ♦ vi (break) brechen; (speak) anfauchen; ~ **shut** zuschnappen; ~ **at** vt fus schnappen nach; ~ **off** vt (break) abbrechen; ~ **up** vt aufschnappen; ~**py** adj flott; ~**shot** n Schnappschuß m

snare [snɛə*] n Schlinge f ♦ vt mit einer Schlinge fangen

snarl [snɑːl] vi (person) Zähnefletschen n; (dog) knurren

snatch [snætʃ] n (small amount) Bruchteil m ♦ vt schnappen, packen

sneak [sniːk] vi schleichen ♦ n (inf) Petze f; ~**ers** ['sniːkəz] (US) npl Freizeitschuhe pl

sneaky ['sniːkɪ] adj raffiniert

sneer [snɪə*] n Hohnlächeln nt ♦ vi spötteln

sneeze [sniːz] n Niesen nt ♦ vi niesen

sniff [snɪf] n Schnüffeln nt ♦ vi schnieben; (smell) schnüffeln ♦ vt schnuppern

snigger ['snɪgə*] n Kichern nt ♦ vi hämisch kichern

snip [snɪp] n Schnippel m, Schnipsel m ♦ vt schnippeln

sniper ['snaɪpə*] n Heckenschütze m

snippet ['snɪpɪt] n Schnipsel m; (of conversation) Fetzen m

snivelling ['snɪvlɪŋ] adj weinerlich

snooker ['snuːkə*] n Snooker nt

snoop [snuːp] vi: to ~ **about** herumschnüffeln

snooty ['snuːtɪ] adj hochnäsig

snooze [snuːz] n Nickerchen nt ♦ vi ein Nickerchen machen, dösen

snore [snɔː*] n schnarchen ♦ vi Schnarchen nt

snorkel ['snɔːkl] n Schnorchel m

snort [snɔːt] n Schnauben nt ♦ vi schnauben

snout [snaʊt] n Schnauze f

snow [snəʊ] n Schnee m ♦ vi schneien; ~**ball** n Schneeball m ♦ vi eskalieren; ~**bound** adj eingeschneit; ~**drift** n Schneewehe f; ~**drop** n Schneeglöckchen nt; ~**fall** n Schneefall m; ~**flake** n Schneeflocke f; ~**man** (irreg) n Schneemann m; ~**plough** (US **snowplow**) n Schneepflug m; ~**shoe** n Schneeschuh m; ~**storm** n Schneesturm m

snub [snʌb] vt schroff abfertigen ♦ n Verweis m; ~**-nosed** adj stupsnasig

snuff [snʌf] n Schnupftabak m

snug [snʌg] adj gemütlich, behaglich

snuggle ['snʌgl] vi: to ~ **up** to sb sich an jdn kuscheln

KEYWORD

so [səʊ] adv 1 (thus) so; (likewise) auch; **so saying he walked away** indem er das sagte, ging er; **if so** wenn ja; **I didn't do it - you did**

so! ich hab das nicht gemacht - hast du wohl!; so ja, so ja; I *etc* ich auch; so it is! tatsächlich!; I hope/ think so hoffentlich/ich glaube schon; so far bis jetzt

2 (*in comparisons etc*): so such a degree): so quickly/big (that) so schnell/groß, daß; I'm so glad to see you ich freue mich so, dich zu sehen

3: so many so viele; so much work so viel Arbeit; I love you so much ich liebe dich so sehr

4 (*phrases*): or so etwa 10; so long! (*inf*: goodbye) tschüs!

♦ *conj* **1** (*expressing purpose*): so as to um ... zu; so (that) damit

2 (*expressing result*) also; so I was right after all ich hatte also doch recht; so you see ... wie du siehst ...

soak [səʊk] *vt* durchnässen; (*leave in liquid*) einweichen ♦ *vi* (ein)weichen; ~ **in** *vi* einsickern; ~ **up** *vt* aufsaugen

so-and-so ['səʊənsəʊ] *n* (*somebody*) Soundso *m*

soap [səʊp] *n* Seife *f*; ~ **flakes** *npl* Seifenflocken *pl*; ~ **opera** *n* Familienserie *f* (*im Fernsehen, Radio*); ~ **powder** *n* Waschpulver *nt*; ~**y** *adj* seifig, Seifen-

soar [sɔː*] *vi* aufsteigen; (*prices*) in die Höhe schnellen

sob [sɒb] *n* Schluchzen *nt* ♦ *vi* schluchzen

sober ['səʊbə*] *adj* (*also fig*) nüchtern; ~ **up** *vi* nüchtern werden

so-called ['səʊ'kɔːld] *adj* sogenannt

soccer ['sɒkə*] *n* Fußball *m*

sociable ['səʊʃəbl] *adj* gesellig

social ['səʊʃəl] *adj* sozial; (*friendly, living with others*) gesellig ♦ *n* gesellige(r) Abend *m*; ~ **club** *n* Verein *m* (*für Freizeitgestaltung*); ~**ism** *n* Sozialismus *m*; ~**ist** *n* Sozialist(in) *m(f)* ♦ *adj* sozialistisch; ~**ize** *vi*: to ~**ize** (with) gesellschaftlich verkehren (mit); ~**ly** *adv* gesellschaftlich, privat; ~ **security** *n* Sozialversiche-

rung *f*; ~ **work** *n* Sozialarbeit *f*; ~ **worker** *n* Sozialarbeiter(in) *m(f)*

society [sə'saɪətɪ] *n* Gesellschaft *f*; (*fashionable world*) die große Welt

sociology [səʊsɪ'ɒlədʒɪ] *n* Soziologie *f*

sock [sɒk] *n* Socke *f*

socket ['sɒkɪt] *n* (*ELEC*) Steckdose *f*; (*of eye*) Augenhöhle *f*; (*TECH*) Rohransatz *m*

sod [sɒd] *n* Rasenstück *nt*; (*inf!*) Saukerl *m* (*!*)

soda ['səʊdə] *n* Soda *f*; (*also*: ~ *water*) Soda(wasser) *nt*; (*US: also*: ~ *pop*) Limonade *f*

sodden ['sɒdn] *adj* durchweicht

sodium ['səʊdɪəm] *n* Natrium *nt*

sofa ['səʊfə] *n* Sofa *nt*

soft [sɒft] *adj* weich; (*not loud*) leise; (*weak*) nachgiebig; ~ **drink** *n* alkoholfreie(s) Getränk *nt*; ~ **en** ['sɒfn] *vt* weich machen; (*blow*) abschwächen, mildern ♦ *vi* weich werden; ~**ly** *adv* sanft; leise; ~**ness** *n* Weichheit *f*; (*fig*) Sanftheit *f*

software ['sɒftwɛə*] *n* (*COMPUT*) Software *f*

soggy ['sɒgɪ] *adj* (*ground*) sumpfig; (*bread*) aufgeweicht

soil [sɔɪl] *n* Erde *f* ♦ *vt* beschmutzen; ~**ed** *adj* beschmutzt

solace ['sɒləs] *n* Trost *m*

solar ['səʊlə*] *adj* Sonnen-; ~ **cell** *n* Solarzelle *f*; ~ **energy** *n* Sonnenenergie *f*; ~ **panel** *n* Sonnenkollektor *m*; ~ **power** *n* Sonnenenergie *f*

sold [səʊld] *pt, pp of* **sell**; ~ **out** (*COMM*) ausverkauft

solder ['səʊldə*] *vt* löten ♦ *n* Lötmetall *nt*

soldier ['səʊldʒə*] *n* Soldat *m*

sole [səʊl] *n* Sohle *f*; (*fish*) Seezunge *f* ♦ *adj* alleinig, Allein-; ~**ly** *adv* ausschließlich

solemn ['sɒləm] *adj* feierlich

sole trader *n* (*COMM*) Einzelunternehmen *nt*

solicit [sə'lɪsɪt] *vt* (*request*) bitten um ♦ *vi* (*prostitute*) Kunden anwerben

solicitor [sə'lɪsɪtə*] *n* Rechtsanwalt

m/-anwältin *f*

solid ['sɔlɪd] *adj* (*hard*) fest; (*of same material, not hollow*) massiv; (*without break*) voll, ganz; (*reliable, sensible*) solide ♦ *n* Festkörper *m*

solidarity [sɔlɪ'dærɪtɪ] *n* Solidarität *f*

solidify [sə'lɪdɪfaɪ] *vi* fest werden

solitary ['sɔlɪtərɪ] *adj* einsam, einzeln; ~ **confinement** *n* Einzelhaft *f*

solitude ['sɔlɪtjuːd] *n* Einsamkeit *f*

solo ['səuləu] *n* Solo *nt*

soloist ['səuləuɪst] *n* Solist(in) *m(f)*

soluble ['sɔljubl] *adj* (*substance*) löslich; (*problem*) (auf)lösbar

solution [sə'luːʃən] *n* (*also fig*) Lösung *f*; (*of mystery*) Erklärung *f*

solve [sɔlv] *vt* (auf)lösen

solvent ['sɔlvənt] *adj* (*FIN*) zahlungsfähig ♦ *n* (*CHEM*) Lösungsmittel *nt*; (*phrases*) etwa 10

sombre ['sɔmbə*] (*US* **somber**) *adj* düster

KEYWORD

---

some [sʌm] *adj* **1** (*a certain amount or number of*) einige; (*a few*) ein paar; (*with singular nouns*) etwas; some tea/biscuits etwas Tee/ein paar Plätzchen; I've got some money, but not much ich habe ein bißchen Geld, aber nicht viel

2 (*certain: in contrasts*) manche(r, s); some people say that ... manche Leute sagen, daß ...

3 (*unspecified*) irgendein(e); some woman was asking for you da hat eine Frau nach Ihnen gefragt; some day eines Tages; some day next week irgendwann nächste Woche

♦ *pron* **1** (*a certain number*) einige; have you got some? haben Sie welche?

2 (*a certain amount*) etwas; I've read some of the book ich habe das Buch teilweise gelesen

♦ *adv*: some 10 people etwa 10 Leute

somebody ['sʌmbədɪ] *pron* = **someone**

somehow ['sʌmhau] *adv* (*in some way, for some reason*) irgendwie

someone ['sʌmwʌn] *pron* jemand; (*direct obj*) jemand(en); (*indirect obj*) jemandem

someplace ['sʌmpleɪs] (*US*) *adv* = **somewhere**

somersault ['sʌməsɔːlt] *n* Salto *m* ♦ *vi* einen Salto machen

something ['sʌmθɪŋ] *pron* etwas

sometime ['sʌmtaɪm] *adv* (*irgend*)einmal

sometimes ['sʌmtaɪmz] *adv* manchmal

somewhat ['sʌmwɔt] *adv* etwas

somewhere ['sʌmwɛə*] *adv* irgendwo; (*to a place*) irgendwohin; ~ **else** irgendwo anders

son [sʌn] *n* Sohn *m*

sonar ['səunɑː*] *n* Echolot *nt*

song [sɔŋ] *n* Lied *nt*; **sonic boom** *n* Überschallknall *m*

son-in-law ['sʌnɪnlɔː] *n* Schwiegersohn *m*

sonny ['sʌnɪ] (*inf*) *n* Kleine(r) *m*

soon [suːn] *adv* bald; ~ **afterwards** kurz danach; ~**er** (*time*) früher; (*for preference*) lieber; ~**er or later** früher oder später

soot [sut] *n* Ruß *m*

soothe [suːð] *vt* (*person*) beruhigen; (*pain*) lindern

sophisticated [sə'fɪstɪkeɪtɪd] *adj* (*person*) kultiviert; (*machinery*) hochentwickelt

sophomore ['sɔfəmɔː*] (*US*) *n* College-Student *m* im 2. Jahr

soporific [sɔpə'rɪfɪk] *adj* einschläfernd

sopping ['sɔpɪŋ] *adj* patschnaß

soppy ['sɔpɪ] (*inf*) *adj* schmalzig

soprano [sə'prɑːnəu] *n* Sopran *m*

sorcerer ['sɔːsərə*] *n* Hexenmeister *m*

sordid ['sɔːdɪd] *adj* erbärmlich

sore [sɔː*] *adj* schmerzend; (*point*) wund ♦ *n* Wunde *f*; ~**ly** *adv* (*tempted*) stark, sehr

sorrow ['sɔrəu] *n* Kummer *m*, Leid *nt*; ~**ful** *adj* sorgenvoll

sorry ['sɒrɪ] *adj* traurig, erbärmlich; ~! Entschuldigung!; **to feel ~ for sb** jdn bemitleiden; **I feel ~ for him** er tut mir leid; ~? (*pardon*) wie bitte?

sort [sɔːt] *n* Art *f*, Sorte *f* ♦ *vt* (*also*: ~ **out**: *papers*) sortieren; (: *problems*) sichten, in Ordnung bringen; ~**ing office** *n* Sortierstelle *f*

SOS *n* SOS *nt*

so-so ['səʊ'səʊ] *adv* so (-so) la-la

sought [sɔːt] *pt, pp of* **seek**

soul [səʊl] *n* Seele *f*; (*music*) Soul *m*; ~**-destroying** *adj* trostlos; ~**ful** *adj* seelenvoll

sound [saʊnd] *adj* (*healthy*) gesund; (*safe*) sicher; (*sensible*) vernünftig; (*theory*) stichhaltig; (*thorough*) tüchtig, gehörig ♦ *adv*: **to be ~ asleep** fest schlafen ♦ *n* (*noise*) Geräusch *nt*, Laut *m*; (GEOG) Sund *m* ♦ *vt* erschallen lassen; (*alarm*) (Alarm) schlagen; (MED) abhorchen ♦ *vi* (*make a ~*) schallen, tönen; (*seem*) klingen; **to ~ like** sich anhören wie; ~ **out** *vt* (*opinion*) erforschen; (*person*) auf den Zahn fühlen +*dat*; ~ **barrier** *n* Schallmauer *f*; ~ **effects** *npl* Toneffekte *pl*; ~**ing** *n* (NAUT *etc*) Lotung *f*; ~**ly** *adv* (*sleep*) fest; (*beat*) tüchtig; ~**proof** *adj* (*room*) schalldicht; ~**track** *n* Tonstreifen *m*; (*music*) Filmmusik *f*

soup [suːp] *n* Suppe *f*; **in the ~** (*inf*) in der Tinte; ~ **plate** *n* Suppenteller *m*; ~**spoon** *n* Suppenlöffel *m*

sour ['saʊə*] *adj* (*also fig*) sauer; **it's ~ grapes** (*fig*) die Trauben hängen zu hoch

source [sɔːs] *n* (*also fig*) Quelle *f*

south [saʊθ] *n* Süden *m* ♦ *adj* Süd-, südlich ♦ *adv* nach Süden, südwärts; **S~ Africa** *n* Südafrika *nt*; **S~ African** *adj* südafrikanisch ♦ *n* Südafrikaner(in) *m(f)*; **S~ America** *n* Südamerika *nt*; **S~ American** *adj* südamerikanisch ♦ *n* Südamerikaner(in) *m(f)*; ~**-east** *n* Südosten *m*; ~**erly** ['sʌðəlɪ] *adj* südlich; ~**ern** ['sʌðən] *adj* südlich, Süd-; **S~ Pole** *n*

Südpol *m*; ~**ward(s)** *adv* südwärts, nach Süden; ~**-west** *n* Südwesten *m*

souvenir [suːvə'nɪə*] *n* Souvenir *nt*

sovereign ['sɒvrɪn] *n* (*ruler*) Herrscher(in) *m(f)* ♦ *adj* (*independent*) souverän

soviet ['səʊvɪət] *adj* sowjetisch; **the S~ Union** die Sowjetunion

sow¹ [saʊ] *n* Sau *f*

sow² [səʊ] (*pt* **sowed**, *pp* **sown**) *vt* (*also fig*) säen

soya ['sɔɪə] (US **soy**) *n*: ~ **bean** Sojabohne *f*; ~ **sauce** Sojasauce *f*

spa [spɑː] *n* (*place*) Kurort *m*

space [speɪs] *n* Platz *m*, Raum *m*; (*universe*) Weltraum *m*, All *nt*; (*length of time*) Abstand *m* ♦ *vt* (*also*: ~ **out**) verteilen; ~**craft** *n* Raumschiff *nt*; ~**man** (*irreg*) *n* Raumfahrer *m*; ~ **ship** *n* Raumschiff *nt*

spacing *n* Abstand *m*; (*also*: ~ **out**) Verteilung *f*

spacious ['speɪʃəs] *adj* geräumig, weit

spade [speɪd] *n* Spaten *m*; ~**s** *npl* (CARDS) Pik *nt*

Spain [speɪn] *n* Spanien *nt*

span [spæn] *n* Spanne *f*; (*of bridge etc*) Spannweite *f* ♦ *vt* überspannen

Spaniard ['spænjəd] *n* Spanier(in) *m(f)*

Spanish ['spænɪʃ] *adj* spanisch ♦ *n* (LING) Spanisch *nt*; **the ~** *npl* (*people*) die Spanier *pl*

spank [spæŋk] *vt* verhauen, versohlen

spanner ['spænə*] (BRIT) *n* Schraubenschlüssel *m*

spar [spɑː] *n* (NAUT) Sparren *m* ♦ *vi* (BOXING) einen Sparring machen

spare [speə*] *adj* Ersatz- ♦ *n* = **spare part** ♦ *vt* (*lives, feelings*) verschonen; (*trouble*) ersparen; **to ~** (*surplus*) übrig; ~ **part** *n* Ersatzteil *nt*; ~ **time** *n* Freizeit *f*; ~ **wheel** *n* (AUT) Reserverreifen *m*

sparing ['speərɪŋ] *adj*: **to be ~ with** geizen mit; ~**ly** *adv* sparsam; (*eat*, *spend etc*) in Maßen

spark [spɑːk] *n* Funken *m*; ~**(ing) plug** *n* Zündkerze *f*

sparkle [ˈspɑːkl] *n* Funkeln *nt*; *(gaiety)* Schwung *m* ♦ *vi* funkeln

sparkling [ˈspɑːklɪŋ] *adj* funkelnd; *(wine)* Schaum-; *(mineral water)* mit Kohlensäure; *(conversation)* spritzig, geistreich

sparrow [ˈspærəʊ] *n* Spatz *m*

sparse [spɑːs] *adj* spärlich

spasm [ˈspæzəm] *n* (MED) Krampf *m*; *(fig)* Anfall *m*; ~**odic** [spæzˈmɔdɪk] *adj* (fig) sprunghaft

spat [spæt] *pt, pp of* **spit**

spate [speɪt] *n (fig)* Flut *f*, Schwall *m*; **in** ~ *(river)* angeschwollen

spatter [ˈspætə*] *vt* bespritzen, verspritzen

spatula [ˈspætjʊlə] *n* Spatel *m*

spawn [spɔːn] *vi* laichen ♦ *n* Laich *m*

speak [spiːk] *(pt* **spoke**, *pp* **spoken)** *vt* sprechen, reden; *(truth)* sagen; *(language)* sprechen ♦ *vi*: **to** ~ **(to)** sprechen (mit *or* zu); **to** ~ **to sb of** *or* **about sth** mit jdm über etw *acc* sprechen; ~ **up!** sprich lauter!; ~**er** *n* Sprecher(in) *m(f)*, Redner(in) *m(f)*; *(loudspeaker)* Lautsprecher *m*; *(POL)*: **the S**~**er** der Vorsitzende des Parlaments *(BRIT)* or des Kongresses *(US)*

spear [spɪə*] *n* Speer *m* ♦ *vt* aufspießen; ~**head** *vt (attack etc)* anführen

spec [spek] *(inf)* *n*: **on** ~ auf gut Glück

special [ˈspeʃəl] *adj* besondere(r, s); ~**ist** *n (TECH)* Fachmann *m*; *(MED)* Facharzt *m* Fachärztin *f*; ~**ity** [speʃiˈælɪti] *n* Spezialität *f*; *(study)* Spezialgebiet *nt*; ~**ize** *vi*: **to** ~**ize (in)** sich spezialisieren (auf *+acc*); ~**ly** *adv* besonders; *(explicitly)* extra

species [ˈspiːʃiːz] *n* Art *f*

specific [spəˈsɪfɪk] *adj* spezifisch; ~**ally** *adv* spezifisch

specification [spesɪfɪˈkeɪʃən] *n* Angabe *f*; *(stipulation)* Bedingung *f*; ~**s** *npl (TECH)* technische Daten *pl*

specify [ˈspesɪfaɪ] *vt* genau angeben

specimen [ˈspesɪmɪn] *n* Probe *f*

speck [spek] *n* Fleckchen *nt*

speckled [ˈspekld] *adj* gesprenkelt

specs [speks] *(inf)* *npl* Brille *f*

spectacle [ˈspektəkl] *n* Schauspiel *nt*; ~**s** *npl (glasses)* Brille *f*

spectacular [spekˈtækjʊlə*] *adj* sensationell; *(success etc)* spektakulär

spectator [spekˈteɪtə*] *n* Zuschauer(in) *m(f)*

spectre [ˈspektə*] *(US* **specter)** *n* Geist *m*, Gespenst *nt*

speculate [ˈspekjʊleɪt] *vi* spekulieren

speech [spiːtʃ] *n* Sprache *f*; *(address)* Rede *f*; *(manner of speaking)* Sprechweise *f*; ~**less** *adj* sprachlos

speed [spiːd] *n* Geschwindigkeit *f*; *(gear)* Gang *m* ♦ *vi (JUR)* zu schnell fahren; **at full** *or* **top** ~ mit Höchstgeschwindigkeit; ~ **up** *vt* beschleunigen ♦ *vi* schneller werden; schneller fahren; ~**boat** *n* Schnellboot *nt*; ~**ily** *adv* schleunigst; ~**ing** *n* Geschwindigkeitsüberschreitung *f*; ~ **limit** *n* Geschwindigkeitsbegrenzung *f*; ~**ometer** [spɪˈdɔmɪtə*] *n* Tachometer *m*; ~**way** *n (bike racing)* Motorradrennstrecke *f*; ~**y** *adj* schnell

spell [spel] *(pt, pp* **spelt** *(BRIT)* or ~**ed)** *n (magic)* Bann *m*; *(period of time)* Zeitlang *f* ♦ *vt* buchstabieren; *(imply)* bedeuten; **to cast a** ~ **on sb** jdn verzaubern; ~**bound** *adj* (wie) gebannt; ~**ing** *n* Rechtschreibung *f*

spelt [spelt] *(BRIT)* *pt, pp of* **spell**

spend [spend] *(pt, pp* **spent)** *vt (money)* ausgeben; *(time)* verbringen; ~**thrift** *n* Verschwender(in) *m(f)*

spent [spent] *pt, pp of* **spend**

sperm [spɜːm] *n (BIOL)* Samenflüssigkeit *f*

spew [spjuː] *vt (er)*brechen

sphere [sfɪə*] *n (globe)* Kugel *f*; *(fig)* Sphäre *f*, Gebiet *nt*

spherical [ˈsferɪkəl] *adj* kugelförmig

spice [spaɪs] *n* Gewürz *nt* ♦ *vt* würzen

spick-and-span [ˈspɪkənˈspæn] *adj* blitzblank

spicy ['spaɪsɪ] adj (food) stark gewürzt; (fig) pikant

spider ['spaɪdə*] n Spinne f

spike [spaɪk] n Dorn m, Spitze f

spill [spɪl] (pt, pp spilt or ~ed) vt verschütten ♦ vi sich ergießen; ~ **over** vi überlaufen; (fig) sich ausbreiten

spilt [spɪlt] pt, pp of spill

spin [spɪn] (pt, pp spun) n (trip in car) Spazierfahrt f; (AVIAT) (Ab)trudeln nt; (on ball) Drall m ♦ vt (thread) spinnen; (like top) (herum)wirbeln ♦ vi sich drehen; ~ **out** vt in die Länge ziehen

spinach ['spɪnɪtʃ] n Spinat m

spinal ['spaɪnl] adj Rückgrat-; ~**cord** n Rückenmark nt

spindly ['spɪndlɪ] adj spindeldürr

spin-dryer ['spɪn'draɪə*] (BRIT) n Wäscheschleuder f

spine [spaɪn] n Rückgrat nt; (thorn) Stachel m; ~**less** adj (also fig) rückgratlos

spinning ['spɪnɪŋ] n Spinnen nt; ~**top** n Kreisel m; ~**wheel** n Spinnrad nt

spin-off ['spɪnɒf] n Nebenprodukt nt

spinster ['spɪnstə*] n unverheiratete Frau f; (pej) alte Jungfer f

spiral ['spaɪərl] n Spirale f ♦ adj spiralförmig; (movement etc) in Spiralen ♦ vi sich (hoch)winden; ~ **staircase** n Wendeltreppe f

spire [spaɪə*] n Turm m

spirit ['spɪrɪt] n Geist m; (humour, mood) Stimmung f; (courage) Mut m; (verve) Elan m; (alcohol) Alkohol m; ~**s** npl (drink) Spirituosen pl; **in good** ~**s** gut aufgelegt; ~**ed** adj beherzt; ~ **level** n Wasserwaage f

spiritual ['spɪrɪtjʊəl] adj geistig, seelisch; (REL) geistlich ♦ n Spiritual nt

spit [spɪt] (pt, pp spat) n (for roasting) (Brat)spieß m; (saliva) Spucke f ♦ vi spucken; (rain) sprühen; (make a sound) zischen; (cat) fauchen

spite [spaɪt] n Gehässigkeit f ♦ vt kränken; **in** ~ **of** trotz; ~**ful** adj gehässig

spittle ['spɪtl] n Speichel m, Spucke f

splash [splæʃ] n Spritzer m; (of colour) (Farb)fleck m ♦ vt bespritzen ♦ vi spritzen

spleen [spli:n] n (ANAT) Milz f

splendid ['splendɪd] adj glänzend

splendour ['splendə*] (US **splendor**) n Pracht f

splint [splɪnt] n Schiene f

splinter ['splɪntə*] n Splitter m ♦ vi (zer)splittern

split [splɪt] (pt, pp split) n Spalte f; (fig) Spaltung f; (division) Trennung f ♦ vt spalten ♦ vi (divide) reißen; ~ **up** vi sich trennen

splutter ['splʌtə*] vi stottern

spoil [spɔɪl] (pt, pp spoilt or ~ed) vt verderben; (child) verwöhnen; ~**s** npl Beute f; ~ **sport** n Spielverderber m; **spoilt** [spɔɪlt] pt, pp of spoil

spoke [spəʊk] pt speak ♦ n Speiche f

spoken ['spəʊkn] pp of speak

spokesman ['spəʊksmən] (irreg) n Sprecher m

spokeswoman ['spəʊkswʊmən] (irreg) n Sprecherin f

sponge [spʌndʒ] n Schwamm m ♦ vt abwaschen ♦ vi: **to** ~ **on** auf Kosten leben +gen; ~ **bag** (BRIT) n Kulturbeutel m; ~ **cake** n Rührkuchen m

sponsor ['spɒnsə*] n Sponsor m ♦ vt fördern; (in finance) finanzieren; (public) Schirmherrschaft f

spontaneous [spɒn'teɪnɪəs] adj spontan

spooky ['spu:kɪ] (inf) adj gespenstisch

spool [spu:l] n Spule f, Rolle f

spoon [spu:n] n Löffel m; ~**feed** (irreg) vt mit dem Löffel füttern; (fig) hochpäppeln; ~**ful** n Löffel(voll) m

sport [spɔ:t] n Sport m; (person) feine(r) Kerl m; ~**ing** adj sportlich, fair; **to give sb a** ~**ing chance** jdm eine faire Chance geben;

jacket (US) n = sports jacket; **~s car** n Sportwagen m; **~s coat** n Sportjackett nt; **~sman** (irreg) n Sportler m; **~smanship** n Sportlichkeit f; **~swear** n Sportkleidung f; **~swoman** (irreg) n Sportlerin f; **~y** adj sportlich

spot [spɔt] n Punkt m; (dirty) Fleck(en) m; (place) Stelle f; (MED) Pickel m ♦ vt erspähen; (mistake) bemerken; **on the ~** an Ort und Stelle; (at once) auf der Stelle; **~ check** n Stichprobe f; **~less** adj fleckenlos; **~light** n Scheinwerferlicht nt; (lamp) Scheinwerfer m; **~ted** adj gefleckt; **~ty** adj (face) pickelig

spouse [spauz] n Gatte m/Gattin f

spout [spaut] n (of pot) Tülle f; (jet) Wasserstrahl m ♦ vi speien

sprain [spreɪn] n Verrenkung f ♦ vt verrenken

sprang [spræŋ] pt of spring

sprawl [sprɔːl] vi sich strecken

spray [spreɪ] n Spray m f; (off sea) Gischt f; (of flowers) Zweig m ♦ vt besprühen, sprayen

spread [spred] (pt, pp spread) n (extent) Verbreitung f; (inf: meal) Schmaus m; (for bread) Aufstrich m ♦ vt ausbreiten; (scatter) verbreiten; (butter) streichen ♦ vi sich ausbreiten; **~-eagled** ['spred:i:gld] adj: **to be ~-eagled** alle viere von sich strecken

spree [spriː] n (shopping) Einkaufsbummel m; **to go on a ~** einen draufmachen

sprightly ['spraɪtlɪ] adj munter, lebhaft

spring [sprɪŋ] (pt sprang, pp sprung) n (leap) Sprung m; (metal) Feder f; (season) Frühling m; (water) Quelle f ♦ vi (leap) springen; **~ up** (problem) auftauchen; **~board** n Sprungbrett nt; **~-clean** n (also: **~-cleaning**) Frühjahrsputz m; **~time** n Frühling m; **~y** adj federnd, elastisch

sprinkle ['sprɪŋkl] vt (salt) streuen;

(liquid) sprenkeln; **to ~ water on, to ~ with water** mit Wasser besprengen

sprinkler ['sprɪŋklə*] n (for lawn) Sprenger m; (for fire fighting) Sprinkler m

sprint [sprɪnt] n (race) Sprint m ♦ vi (gen: run fast) rennen; (SPORT) sprinten

sprite [spraɪt] n Elfe f; Kobold m

sprout [spraut] vi sprießen; **~s** npl (also: Brussels **~s**) Rosenkohl m

spruce [spruːs] n Fichte f ♦ adj schmuck, adrett

sprung [sprʌŋ] pp of spring

spry [spraɪ] adj flink, rege

spun [spʌn] pt, pp of spin

spur [spɜː*] n Sporn m; (fig) Ansporn m ♦ vt (also: **~ on**: fig) anspornen; **on the ~ of the moment** spontan

spurious ['spjuəriəs] adj falsch

spurn [spɜːn] vt verschmähen

spurt [spɜːt] n (jet) Strahl m; (acceleration) Spurt m ♦ vi (liquid) schießen

spy [spaɪ] n Spion(in) m(f) ♦ vi spionieren ♦ vt erspähen; **~ing** n Spionage f

sq. abbr = square

squabble ['skwɔbl] n Zank m ♦ vi sich zanken

squad [skwɔd] n (MIL) Abteilung f; (POLICE) Kommando nt

squadron ['skwɔdrən] n (cavalry) Schwadron f; (NAUT) Geschwader nt; (air force) Staffel f

squalid ['skwɔlɪd] adj verkommen

squall [skwɔːl] n Bö f, Windstoß m

squalor ['skwɔlə*] n Verwahrlosung f

squander ['skwɔndə*] vt verschwenden

square [skweə*] n Quadrat nt; (open space) Platz m; (instrument) Winkel m; (inf: person) Spießer m ♦ adj viereckig; (inf: ideas, tastes) spießig ♦ vt (arrange) ausmachen; (MATH) ins Quadrat erheben ♦ vi (agree) übereinstimmen; **all ~** quitt; **a ~ meal** eine ordentliche Mahlzeit; **2 metres ~** 2 Meter im Quadrat; **1 ~**

metre 1 Quadratmeter; **~ly** adv
fest, gerade

squash [skwɔʃ] n (BRIT: drink) Saft
m; (game) Squash nt ♦ vt zerquetschen

squat [skwɔt] adj untersetzt ♦ vi
hocken; **~ter** n Hausbesetzer m

squawk [skwɔ:k] vi kreischen

squeak [skwi:k] vi quiek(s)en;
(spring, door etc) quietschen

squeal [skwi:l] vi schrill schreien

squeamish [ˈskwi:mɪʃ] adj empfindlich

squeeze [skwi:z] n (POL) Geld-
knappheit f ♦ vt pressen, drücken;
(orange) auspressen; **~ out** vt aus-
quetschen

squelch [skweltʃ] vi platschen

squib [skwɪb] n Knallfrosch m

squid [skwɪd] n Tintenfisch m

squiggle [ˈskwɪgl] n Schnörkel m

squint [skwɪnt] vi schielen ♦ n: to
have a **~** schielen; to **~ at** sb/sth
nach jdm/etw schielen

squire [ˈskwaɪə*] (BRIT) n Gutsherr
m

squirm [skwɜ:m] vi sich winden

squirrel [ˈskwɪrəl] n Eichhörnchen nt

squirt [skwɜ:t] vt, vi spritzen

Sr abbr (= senior) sen.

St abbr (= saint) hl., St.; (= street)
Str.

stab [stæb] n (blow) Stich m; (inf:
try) Versuch m ♦ vt erstechen

stabilize [ˈsteɪbəlaɪz] vt stabilisieren
♦ vi sich stabilisieren

stable [ˈsteɪbl] adj stabil ♦ n Stall m

stack [stæk] n Stapel m ♦ vt stapeln

stadium [ˈsteɪdɪəm] n Stadion nt

staff [stɑ:f] n (stick, MIL) Stab m;
(personnel) Personal nt; (BRIT:
SCH) Lehrkräfte pl ♦ vt (with people) besetzen

stag [stæg] n Hirsch m

stage [steɪdʒ] n Bühne f; (of journey) Etappe f; (degree) Stufe f;
(point) Stadium nt ♦ vt (put on) aufführen; (simulate) inszenieren;
(demonstration) veranstalten; **in
~s** etappenweise; **~coach** n Postkut-

sche f; **~ door** n Bühneneingang m;
~ manager n Intendant m

stagger [ˈstægə*] vi wanken, taumeln
♦ vt (amaze) verblüffen; (hours)
staffeln; **~ing** adj unglaublich

stagnant [ˈstægnənt] adj stagnie-
rend; (water) stehend

stagnate [stægˈneɪt] vi stagnieren

stag party n Männerabend m (vom
Bräutigam vor der Hochzeit gegeben)

staid [steɪd] adj gesetzt

stain [steɪn] n Fleck m ♦ vt beflecken; **~ed glass window** buntes
Glasfenster nt; **~less** adj (steel)
rostfrei; **~ remover** n Fleckentfer-
ner m

stair [stɛə*] n (Treppen)stufe f; **~s**
npl (flight of steps) Treppe f; **~case**
n Treppenhaus nt, Treppe f; **~way** n
Treppenaufgang m

stake [steɪk] n (post) Pfahl m; (money) Einsatz m ♦ vt (bet: money) setzen; to be at **~** auf dem Spiel stehen

stale [steɪl] adj alt; (bread) alt-
backen

stalemate [ˈsteɪlmeɪt] n (CHESS)
Patt nt; (fig) Stillstand m

stalk [stɔ:k] n Stengel m, Stiel m ♦
vt (game) jagen; **~ off** vi abstolzie-
ren

stall [stɔ:l] n (in stable) Stand m, Box
f; (in market) (Verkaufs)stand m ♦
vt (AUT) abwürgen ♦ vi stehenbleiben; (fig) Ausflüchte machen; **~s** npl
(BRIT: THEAT) Parkett nt

stallion [ˈstælɪən] n Zuchthengst m

stalwart [ˈstɔ:lwət] n treue(r) Anhänger m

stamina [ˈstæmɪnə] n Durchhaltevermögen nt, Zähigkeit f

stammer [ˈstæmə*] n Stottern nt ♦
vt, vi stottern, stammeln

stamp [stæmp] n Briefmarke f; (for
document) Stempel m ♦ vi stampfen
♦ vt (mark) stempeln; (mail) frankieren; (foot) stampfen mit; **~ album** n Briefmarkenalbum nt; **~ col-
lecting** n Briefmarkensammeln nt

stampede [stæmˈpi:d] n panische
Flucht f

stance [stæns] n Haltung f

stand [stænd] (pt, pp **stood**) n (for objects) Gestell nt; (seats) Tribüne f ♦ vi stehen; (rise) aufstehen; (decision) feststehen ♦ vt setzen, stellen; (endure) aushalten; (person) ausstehen; (nonsense) dulden; **to make a** ~ Widerstand leisten; **to** ~ **for parliament** (BRIT) für das Parlament kandidieren; ~ **by** vi (be ready) bereitstehen ♦ vt fus (opinion) treu bleiben +dat; ~ **down** vi (withdraw) zurücktreten; ~ **for** vt fus (signify) stehen für; (permit, tolerate) hinnehmen; ~ **in for** vt fus einspringen für; ~ **out** vi (be prominent) hervorstechen; ~ **up** vi (rise) aufstehen; ~ **up for** vt fus (defend) eintreten für; ~ **up to** vt fus: **to** ~ **up to sth** einer Sache dat gewachsen sein; **to** ~ **up to sb** sich jdm gegenüber behaupten

standard [ˈstændəd] n (measure) Norm f; (flag) Fahne f ♦ adj (size etc) Normal-; ~s npl (morals) Maßstäbe pl; ~**ize** vt vereinheitlichen; ~**lamp** (BRIT) n Stehlampe f; ~ **of living** n Lebensstandard m

stand-by [ˈstændbaɪ] n Reserve f; **to be on** ~ in Bereitschaft sein; ~ **ticket** n (AVIAT) Standby-Ticket nt

stand-in [ˈstændɪn] n Ersatz m

standing [ˈstændɪŋ] adj (erect) stehend; (permanent) ständig; (invitation) offen ♦ n (duration) Dauer f; (reputation) Ansehen nt; **of many years'** ~ langjährig; ~ **order** (BRIT) n (at bank) Dauerauftrag m; ~ **orders** npl (MIL) Vorschrift f; ~ **room** n Stehplatz m

stand-offish [stændˈɒfɪʃ] adj zurückhaltend, sehr reserviert

standpoint [ˈstændpɔɪnt] n Standpunkt m

standstill [ˈstændstɪl] n: **to be at a** ~ stillstehen; **to come to a** ~ zum Stillstand kommen

stank [stæŋk] pt of **stink**

staple [ˈsteɪpl] n (in paper) Heftklammer f; (article) Haupterzeugnis nt ♦ adj Grund-, Haupt- ♦ vt (fest)klammern; ~**r** n Heftmaschine f

star [stɑ:*] n Stern m; (person) Star m ♦ vi die Hauptrolle spielen ♦ vt: **to** ~**ring** ... in der Hauptrolle/den Hauptrollen ...

starboard [ˈstɑ:bəd] n Steuerbord nt

starch [stɑ:tʃ] n Stärke f

stardom [ˈstɑ:dəm] n Berühmtheit f

stare [stɛə*] n starre(r) Blick m ♦ vi: **to** ~ **at** starren auf +acc, anstarren

starfish [ˈstɑ:fɪʃ] n Seestern m

stark [stɑ:k] adj öde ♦ adv: ~ **naked** splitternackt

starling [ˈstɑ:lɪŋ] n Star m

starry [ˈstɑ:rɪ] adj Sternen-; ~-**eyed** adj (innocent) blauäugig

start [stɑ:t] n Anfang m; (SPORT) Start m; (lead) Vorsprung m ♦ vt in Gang setzen; (car) anlassen ♦ vi anfangen; (car) anspringen; (on journey) aufbrechen; (SPORT) starten; (with fright) zusammenfahren; **to** ~ **doing** or **to do sth** anfangen, etw zu tun; ~ **off** vi anfangen; (begin moving) losgehen, losfahren; ~ **up** vi beginnen; (startled) erschrecken ♦ vt beginnen; (car) anlassen; (engine) starten; ~**er** n (AUT) Anlasser m; (for race) Starter m; (BRIT: COOK) Vorspeise f; ~**ing point** n Ausgangspunkt m

startle [ˈstɑ:tl] vt erschrecken

startling [ˈstɑ:tlɪŋ] adj erschreckend

starvation [stɑ:ˈveɪʃən] n Verhungern nt

starve [stɑ:v] vi verhungern ♦ vt verhungern lassen; **I'm starving** ich sterbe vor Hunger

state [steɪt] n (condition) Zustand m; (POL) Staat m ♦ vt erklären; (facts) angeben; **the S~s** (USA) die Staaten; **to be in a** ~ durchdrehen; ~**ly** adj würdevoll; ~**ment** n Aussage f; (POL) Erklärung f; ~**sman** (irreg) n Staatsmann m

static [ˈstætɪk] n (also: ~ **electricity**) Reibungselektrizität f

station [ˈsteɪʃən] n (RAIL etc) Bahnhof m; (police etc) Wache f; (in society) Stand m ♦ vt parkend

stationary ['steɪʃənərɪ] adj stillstehend; (car) parkend

stationer ['steɪʃənə*] n Schreibwarenhändler m; **~'s** n (shop) Schreibwarengeschäft nt; **~y** n Schreibwaren pl

station master n Bahnhofsvorsteher m

station wagon n Kombiwagen m

statistics [stə'tɪstɪks] n Statistik f

statue ['stætjuː] n Statue f

stature ['stætʃə*] n Größe f

status ['steɪtəs] n Status m

statute ['stætjuːt] n Gesetz nt

statutory ['stætjʊtərɪ] adj gesetzlich

staunch [stɔːntʃ] adj standhaft

stave [steɪv] n (MUS) Notenlinien pl ♦ vt: to **~ off** (threat) abwenden; (attack) abwehren

stay [steɪ] n Aufenthalt m ♦ vi bleiben; (reside) wohnen; to **~ put** an Ort und Stelle bleiben; to **~ the night** übernachten; **~ behind** vi zurückbleiben; **~ in** vi (at home) zu Hause bleiben; **~ on** vi (continue) länger bleiben; **~ out** vi (of house) wegbleiben; **~ up** vi (at night) aufbleiben; **~ing power** n Durchhaltevermögen nt

stead [sted] n: in sb's **~** an jds Stelle dat; to **stand sb in good ~** jdm zugute kommen

steadfast ['stedfəst] adj standhaft, treu

steadily ['stedɪlɪ] adv stetig, regelmäßig

steady ['stedɪ] adj (firm) fest, stabil; (regular) gleichmäßig; (reliable) beständig; (hand) ruhig; (job, boyfriend) fest ♦ vt festigen; to **~ o.s. on/against** sth sich stützen auf/gegen etw acc

steak [steɪk] n Steak nt; (fish) Filet nt

steal [stiːl] (pt stole, pp stolen) vt stehlen ♦ vi stehlen; (go stealthily) sich stehlen

stealth [stelθ] n Heimlichkeit f; **~y**

steam [stiːm] n Dampf m ♦ vt (COOK) im Dampfbad erhitzen ♦ vi dampfen; **~ engine** n Dampfmaschine f; **~er** n Dampfer m; **~roller** n Dampfwalze f; **~ship** n = steamer; **~y** adj dampfig

steel [stiːl] n Stahl m ♦ adj Stahl-; (fig) stählern; **~works** n Stahlwerke pl

steep [stiːp] adj steil; (price) gepfeffert ♦ vt einweichen

steeple ['stiːpl] n Kirchturm m; **~chase** n Hindernisrennen nt

steer [stɪə*] vt, vi steuern; (car etc) lenken; **~ing** n (AUT) Steuerung f; **~ing wheel** n Steuer- or Lenkrad nt

stellar ['stelə*] adj Stern(en)-

stem [stem] n Stiel m ♦ vt aufhalten; **~ from** vt fus abstammen von

stench [stentʃ] n Gestank m

stencil ['stensl] n Schablone f ♦ vt (auf)drucken

stenographer [ste'nɒgrəfə*] (US) n Stenograph(in) m(f)

step [step] n Schritt m; (stair) Stufe f ♦ vi treten, schreiten; **~s** npl (BRIT) = stepladder; to take **~s** Schritte unternehmen; **in/out of (with)** im/nicht im Gleichklang (mit); **~ down** vi (fig) abtreten; **~ off** vt fus aussteigen aus; **~ up** vt steigern; **~brother** n Stiefbruder m; **~daughter** n Stieftochter f; **~father** n Stiefvater m; **~ladder** n Trittleiter f; **~mother** n Stiefmutter f; **~ping stone** n Stein m; (fig) Sprungbrett nt; **~sister** n Stiefschwester f; **~son** n Stiefsohn m

stereo ['stɪərɪəʊ] n Stereoanlage f ♦ adj (also: **~phonic**) stereophonisch

stereotype ['stɪərɪətaɪp] n Prototyp m; (fig) Klischee nt ♦ vt stereotypieren; (fig) stereotyp machen

sterile ['steraɪl] adj steril; (person) unfruchtbar

sterling ['stɜːlɪŋ] adj (FIN) Sterling-; (character) gediegen ♦ n (ECON) das Pfund Sterling; **a pound ~** ein Pfund Sterling

stern [stə:n] adj streng ♦ n Heck nt, Achterschiff nt

stew [stju:] n Eintopf m ♦ vt, vi schmoren

steward ['stjuəd] n Steward m; **~ess** n Stewardess f

stick [stɪk] (pt, pp stuck) n Stock m; (of chalk etc) Stück nt ♦ vt (stab) stechen; (fix) stecken; (put) stellen; (gum) (an)kleben; (inf: tolerate) vertragen ♦ vi (stop) steckenbleiben; (get stuck) klemmen; (hold fast) kleben, haften; **~ out** vi (project) hervorstehen; **~ up** vi (project) in die Höhe stehen; **~ up for** vt fus (defend) eintreten für; **~er** n Aufkleber m; **~ing plaster** n Heftpflaster nt

stickler ['stɪklə*] n: **~ (for)** Pedant m (in +acc)

stick-up ['stɪkʌp] (inf) n (Raub)überfall m

sticky ['stɪkɪ] adj klebrig; (atmosphere) stickig

stiff [stɪf] adj steif; (difficult) hart; (paste) dick; (drink) stark; **~en** vt versteifen, (ver)stärken ♦ vi sich versteifen

stifle ['staɪfl] vt unterdrücken

stifling ['staɪflɪŋ] adj drückend

stigma ['stɪgmə] (pl BOT, MED, REL **~ta**; fig **~s**) n Stigma nt

stigmata ['stɪgmətə] npl of **stigma**

stile [staɪl] n Steige f

stiletto [stɪ'letəʊ] (pl also: **~ heel**) n Pfennigabsatz m

still [stɪl] adj still ♦ adv (immer) noch; (anyhow) immerhin; **~born** adj totgeboren; **~ life** n Stilleben nt

stilt [stɪlt] n Stelze f

stilted ['stɪltɪd] adj gestelzt

stimulate ['stɪmjʊleɪt] vt anregen, stimulieren

stimuli ['stɪmjʊlaɪ] npl of **stimulus**

stimulus ['stɪmjʊləs] (pl **-li**) n Anregung f, Reiz m

sting [stɪŋ] (pt, pp stung) n Stich m; (organ) Stachel m ♦ vi stechen; (on skin) brennen ♦ vt stechen

stingy ['stɪndʒɪ] adj geizig, knauserig

stink [stɪŋk] (pt stank, pp stunk) n

Gestank m ♦ vi stinken; **~ing** adj widerlich

stint [stɪnt] n Pensum nt; (period) Betätigung f ♦ vi knausern; **to do one's ~** seine Arbeit tun; (share) seinen Teil beitragen

stipulate ['stɪpjʊleɪt] vt festsetzen

stir [stə:*] n Bewegung f; (COOK) Rühren nt; (sensation) Aufsehen nt ♦ vt (um)rühren ♦ vi sich rühren; **~ up** vt (mob) aufhetzen; (mixture) umrühren; (dust) aufwirbeln

stirrup ['stɪrəp] n Steigbügel m

stitch [stɪtʃ] n (with needle) Stich m; (MED) Faden m; (of knitting) Masche f; (pain) Stich m ♦ vt nähen

stoat [stəʊt] n Wiesel nt

stock [stɒk] n Vorrat m; (COMM) (Waren)lager nt; (live~) Vieh nt; (COOK) Brühe f; (FIN) Grundkapital nt ♦ adj stets vorrätig; (standard) Normal- ♦ vt (in shop) führen; **~s** npl (FIN) Aktien pl; in/out of **~** vorrätig/nicht vorrätig; **to take ~ of** (fig) Bilanz ziehen aus; **~s and shares** Effekten pl; **~ up** vi: **to ~ up (with)** Reserven anlegen (von)

stockbroker ['stɒkbrəʊkə*] n Börsenmakler m

stock cube n Brühwürfel m

stock exchange n Börse f

stocking ['stɒkɪŋ] n Strumpf m

stockist ['stɒkɪst] n Händler m

stock: **~ market** n Börse f; **~ phrase** n Standardsatz m; **~pile** n Vorrat m ♦ vt aufstapeln; **~taking** (BRIT) n (COMM) Inventur f, Bestandsaufnahme f

stocky ['stɒkɪ] adj untersetzt

stodgy ['stɒdʒɪ] adj pampig; (fig) trocken

stoke [stəʊk] vt schüren

stole [stəʊl] pt of **steal** ♦ n Stola f

stolen ['stəʊlən] pp of **steal**

stolid ['stɒlɪd] adj stur

stomach ['stʌmək] n Bauch m, Magen m ♦ vt vertragen; **~-ache** n Magen- or Bauchschmerzen pl

stone [stəʊn] n Stein m; (BRIT:

weight) Gewichtseinheit *f* = 6.35 kg ♦
vt (olive) entkernen; *(kill)* steinigen;
~-cold *adj* eiskalt; **~-deaf** *adj* stock-
taub; **~work** *n* Mauerwerk *nt*

stony ['stəʊnɪ] *adj* steinig

stood [stʊd] *pt, pp* of **stand**

stool [stuːl] *n* Hocker *m*

stoop [stuːp] *vi* sich bücken

stop [stɒp] *n* Halt *m*; *(bus ~)* Haltestelle *f*; *(punctuation)* Punkt *m* ♦ *vt*
anhalten; *(bring to and)* aufhören
(mit) *(bring to end)*, lens lassen ♦ *vi*
aufhören; *(clock)* stehenbleiben; *(remain)* bleiben; **to ~ doing sth** aufhören, etw zu tun; **to ~ dead** innehalten; **~ off** *vi* kurz haltmachen;
~ up *vt (hole)* zustopfen, verstopfen;
~gap *n* Notlösung *f*; **~lights** *npl*
(AUT) Bremslichter *pl*; **~over** *n (on
journey)* Zwischenaufenthalt *m*

stoppage ['stɒpɪdʒ] *n* (An)halten *nt*;
(traffic) Verkehrsstockung *f*; *(strike)*
Arbeitseinstellung *f*

stopper ['stɒpə*] *n* Propfen *m*,
Stöpsel *m*

stop press *n* letzte Meldung *f*

stopwatch ['stɒpwɒtʃ] *n* Stoppuhr *f*

storage ['stɔːrɪdʒ] *n* Lagerung *f*; **~
heater** *n* (Nachtstrom)speicherofen
m

store [stɔː*] *n* Vorrat *m*; *(place)* Lager
nt, Warenhaus *nt*; *(BRIT: large
shop)* Kaufhaus *nt*; *(US)* Laden *m* ♦
vt lagern; **~s** *npl (supplies)* Vorräte
pl; **~ up** *vt* sich eindecken mit;
~room *n* Lagerraum *m*, Vorrats-
raum *m*

storey ['stɔːrɪ] *(US* **story**) *n* Stock *m*

stork [stɔːk] *n* Storch *m*

storm [stɔːm] *n (also fig)* Sturm *m* ♦
vt, vi stürmen; **~y** *adj* stürmisch

story ['stɔːrɪ] *n* Geschichte *f*; *(lie)*
Märchen *nt*; *(US)* = **storey**; **~book**
n Geschichtenbuch *nt*; **~teller** *n* Ge-
schichtenerzähler *m*

stout [staʊt] *adj (bold)* tapfer; *(fat)*
beleibt ♦ *n* Starkbier *nt*; *(also: sweet
~)* ≈ Malzbier *f*

stove [stəʊv] *n (Koch)*herd *m*; *(for
heating)* Ofen *m*

stow [stəʊ] *vt* verstauen; **~away** *n*
blinde(r) Passagier *m*

straddle ['strædl] *vt (horse, fence)*
rittlings sitzen auf +dat; *(fig)*
überbrücken

straggle ['strægl] *vi (branches etc)*
wuchern; *(people)* nachhinken; **~r** *n*
Nachzügler *m*; **straggly** *adj (hair)*
zottig

straight [streɪt] *adj* gerade; *(honest)* offen, ehrlich; *(drink)* pur ♦ *adv
(direct)* direkt, geradewegs; **to put or
get sth ~** etw in Ordnung bringen;
~away *adv* sofort; **~ off** sofort; **~en
(up)** *vt (also: ~en out)* gerade machen; *(fig)*
klarstellen; **~faced** *adv* ohne die
Miene zu verziehen ♦ *adj*: **to be ~-
faced** keine Miene verziehen; **~for-
ward** *adj* einfach, unkompliziert

strain [streɪn] *n* Belastung *f*; *(streak,
trace)* Zug *m*; *(of music)* Fetzen *m*
♦ *vt* überanstrengen; *(stretch)* anspannen; *(muscle)* zerren; *(filter)*
(durch)seihen ♦ *vi* sich anstrengen;
~ed *adj (laugh)* gezwungen; *(relations)* gespannt; **~er** *n* Sieb *nt*

strait [streɪt] *n* Straße *f*, Meerenge *f*;
~jacket *n* Zwangsjacke *f*; **~laced**
adj engherzig, streng

strand [strænd] *n (of hair)* Strähne *f*;
(also fig) Faden *m*; **~ed** *adj (also
fig)* gestrandet

strange [streɪndʒ] *adj* fremd; *(unusual)* seltsam; **~r** *n* Fremde(r) *mf*

strangle ['stræŋgl] *vt* erwürgen;
~hold *n (fig)* Umklammerung *f*

strap [stræp] *n* Riemen *m*; *(on
clothes)* Träger *m* ♦ *vt (fasten)* fest-
schnallen

strapping ['stræpɪŋ] *adj* stramm

strata ['strɑːtə] *npl* of **stratum**

stratagem ['strætədʒəm] *n* (Kriegs)-
list *f*

strategic [strə'tiːdʒɪk] *adj* strate-
gisch

strategy ['strætədʒɪ] *n (fig)* Strategie
f

stratum ['strɑːtəm] *(pl* **-ta**) *n* Schicht
f

straw [strɔː] *n* Stroh *nt*; *(single stalk*

drinking ~) Strohhalm m; **that's the last ~!** das ist der Gipfel!

strawberry ['strɔ:bəri] n Erdbeere f

stray [strei] adj (animal) verirrt; (thought) zufällig ♦ vi herumstreunen

streak ['stri:k] n Streifen m; (in character) Einschlag m; (in hair) Strähne f ♦ vt streifen ♦ vi zucken; (move quickly) flitzen; ~ **of bad luck** Pechsträhne f; ~**y** adj gestreift; (bacon) durchwachsen

stream [stri:m] n (brook) Bach m; (fig) Strom m ♦ vt (SCH) in (Leistungs)gruppen einteilen ♦ vi strömen; **to ~ in/out** hinein-/hinausströmen

streamer ['stri:mə*] n (flag) Wimpel m; (of paper) Luftschlange f

streamlined ['stri:mlaınd] adj stromlinienförmig; (effective) rationell

street [stri:t] n Straße f ♦ adj Straßen-; ~**car** (US) n Straßenbahn f; ~ **lamp** n Straßenlaterne f; ~ **plan** n Stadtplan m; ~**wise** (inf) adj: **to be ~wise** wissen, wie es lang geht

strength [streŋθ] n (also fig) Stärke f; Kraft f; ~**en** vt (ver)stärken

strenuous ['strenjuəs] adj anstrengend

stress [stres] n Druck m; (mental) Streß m; (GRAM) Betonung f ♦ vt betonen

stretch [stretʃ] n Strecke f ♦ vt ausdehnen, strecken ♦ vi sich erstrecken; (person) sich strecken; ~ **out** vi sich ausstrecken ♦ vt ausstrecken

stretcher ['stretʃə*] n Tragbahre f

strewn [stru:n] adj: ~ **with** übersät mit

stricken ['strikən] adj (person) ergriffen; (city, country) heimgesucht; ~ **with** (arthritis, disease) leidend unter +dat

strict [strikt] adj (exact) genau; (severe) streng; ~**ly** adv streng, genau

stridden ['stridn] pp of **stride**

stride [straid] (pt **strode**, pp **stridden**) n lange(r) Schritt m ♦ vi schreiten

strident ['straidənt] adj schneidend, durchdringend

strife [straif] n Streit m

strike [straik] (pt, pp **struck**) n Streik m; (attack) Schlag m ♦ vt (hit) schlagen; (collide) stoßen gegen; (come to mind) einfallen +dat; (stand out) auffallen +dat; (find) finden ♦ vi (stop work) streiken; (attack) zuschlagen; (clock) schlagen; **on** ~ (workers) im Streik; **to ~ a match** ein Streichholz anzünden; ~ **down** vt (lay low) niederschlagen; ~ **out** vt (cross out) ausstreichen; ~ **up** vt (music) anstimmen; (friendship) schließen; ~**r** n Streikende(r) mf

striking ['straikiŋ] adj auffallend

string [striŋ] (pt, pp **strung**) n Schnur f; (row) Reihe f; (MUS) Saite f ♦ vt: **to ~ together** aneinanderreihen ♦ vi: **to ~ out** sich verteilen; **the ~s** npl (MUS) die Streichinstrumente pl; **to pull ~s** (fig) Fäden ziehen; ~ **bean** n grüne Bohne f; ~(**ed**) **instrument** n (MUS) Saiteninstrument nt

stringent ['strindʒənt] adj streng

strip [strip] n Streifen m ♦ vt (uncover) abstreifen, abziehen; (clothes) ausziehen; (TECH) auseinandernehmen ♦ vi (undress) sich ausziehen; ~ **cartoon** n Bildserie f

stripe [straip] n Streifen m; ~**d** adj gestreift

strip lighting n Neonlicht nt

stripper ['stripə*] n Stripteasetänzerin f

strive [straiv] (pt **strove**, pp **striven**) vi: **to ~ (for)** streben (nach)

strode [strəud] pt of **stride**

stroke [strəuk] n Schlag m; (SWIMMING, ROWING) Stoß m; (TECH) Hub m; (MED) Schlaganfall m; (caress) Streicheln nt ♦ vt streicheln; **at a ~** mit einem Schlag

stroll [strəul] n Spaziergang m ♦ vi

schlendern; **~er** (US) n (pushchair) Sportwagen m ♦

strong [stroŋ] adj stark; (firm) fest; they are 50 ~ sie sind 50 Mann stark; **~box** n Kassette f; **~hold** n Hochburg f; **~ly** adv stark; **~room** n Tresor m

strove [strəuv] pt of strive

struck [strʌk] pt, pp of strike

structure ['strʌktʃə*] n Struktur f, Aufbau m; (building) Bau m

struggle ['strʌgl] n Kampf m ♦ vi (fight) kämpfen

strum [strʌm] vt (guitar) klimpern auf +dat

strung [strʌŋ] pt, pp of string

strut [strʌt] n Strebe f, Stütze f ♦ vi stolzieren

stub [stʌb] n Stummel m; (of cigarette) Kippe f ♦ vt: to ~ one's toe sich dat den Zeh anstoßen; **~ out** vt ausdrücken

stubble ['stʌbl] n Stoppel f

stubborn ['stʌbən] adj hartnäckig

stucco ['stʌkəu] n Stuck m

stuck [stʌk] pt, pp of stick ♦ adj (jammed) klemmend; **~-up** adj hochnäsig

stud [stʌd] n (button) Kragenknopf m; (place) Gestüt nt ♦ vt (fig): **~ded with** übersät mit

student ['stju:dənt] n Student(in) m(f); (US) Student(in) m(f), Schüler(in) m(f) ♦ adj Studenten-; **~ driver** (US) n Fahrschüler(in) m(f)

studio ['stju:diəu] n Studio nt; (for artist) Atelier nt; **~ apartment** (US) n Appartement nt; **~ flat** n Appartement nt

studious ['stju:diəs] adj lernbegierig

study ['stʌdɪ] n Studium nt; (investigation) Studium nt, Untersuchung f; (room) Arbeitszimmer nt; (essay etc) Studie f ♦ vt studieren; (face) erforschen; (evidence) prüfen ♦ vi studieren

stuff [stʌf] n Stoff m; (inf) Zeug nt ♦ vt stopfen, füllen; (animal) ausstopfen; **~ing** n Füllung f; **~y** adj (room) schwül; (person) spießig

stumble ['stʌmbl] vi stolpern; to ~ across (fig) zufällig stoßen auf +acc

stumbling block ['stʌmblɪŋ-] n Hindernis nt

stump [stʌmp] n Stumpf m ♦ vt umwerfen

stun [stʌn] vt betäuben; (shock) niederschmettern

stung [stʌŋ] pt, pp of sting

stunk [stʌŋk] pp of stink

stunning ['stʌnɪŋ] adj betäubend; (news) überwältigend, umwerfend

stunt [stʌnt] n Kunststück nt, Trick m

stunted adj verkümmert

stuntman (irreg) n Stuntman m

stupefy ['stju:pɪfaɪ] vt betäuben; (by news) bestürzen

stupendous [stju'pendəs] adj erstaunlich, enorm

stupid ['stju:pɪd] adj dumm; **~ity** [stju'pɪdɪtɪ] n Dummheit f

stupor ['stju:pə*] n Betäubung f

sturdy ['stɜ:dɪ] adj kräftig, robust

stutter ['stʌtə*] n Stottern nt ♦ vi stottern

sty [staɪ] n Schweinestall m

stye [staɪ] n Gerstenkorn nt

style [staɪl] n Stil m; (fashion) Mode f

stylish ['staɪlɪʃ] adj modisch

stylist ['staɪlɪst] n (hair ~) Friseur m, Friseuse f

stylus ['staɪləs] n (Grammophon-) nadel f

suave [swɑ:v] adj zuvorkommend

sub... prefix Unter...; **~conscious** adj unterbewußt ♦ n: **the ~con-scious** das Unterbewußte; **~contract** vt (vertraglich) untervermitteln; **~divide** vt unterteilen

subdue [səb'dju:] vt unterwerfen; **~d** adj (lighting) gedämpft; (person) still

subject [n 'sʌbdʒɪkt, vb səb'dʒɛkt] n (of kingdom) Untertan m; (citizen) Staatsangehörige/r m/f; (topic) Thema nt; (SCH) Fach nt; (GRAM) Subjekt nt ♦ adj: to be ~ to unterworfen sein +dat; (exposed) ausgesetzt sein +dat (subdue) unterwerfen; (expose) aussetzen; ~**ive** [səb'dʒektɪv] adj subjektiv; ~ **matter** n Thema nt

subjugate ['sʌbdʒʊgeɪt] vt unterjochen

subjunctive [səb'dʒʌŋktɪv] adj Konjunktiv- ♦ n Konjunktiv m

sublet ['sʌb'let] (irreg: like let) vt untervermieten

sublime [sə'blaɪm] adj erhaben

submachine gun ['sʌbmə'ʃiːn-] n Maschinenpistole f

submarine [sʌbmə'riːn] n Unterseeboot nt, U-Boot nt

submerge [səb'mɜːdʒ] vt untertauchen; (flood) überschwemmen ♦ vi untertauchen

submission [səb'mɪʃən] n (obedience) Gehorsam m; (claim) Behauptung f; (of plan) Unterbreitung f

submissive [səb'mɪsɪv] adj demütig, unterwürfig (pej)

submit [səb'mɪt] vt behaupten; (plan) unterbreiten ♦ vi (give in) sich ergeben

subnormal ['sʌb'nɔːməl] adj minderbegabt

subordinate [sə'bɔːdɪnət] adj untergeordnet ♦ n Untergebene(r) mf

subpoena [sə'piːnə] n Vorladung f ♦ vt vorladen

subscribe [səb'skraɪb] vi: to ~ to (view etc) unterstützen; (newspaper) abonnieren; ~**r** n (to periodical) Abonnent m; (TEL) Telefonteilnehmer m

subscription [səb'skrɪpʃən] n Abonnement nt; (money subscribed) (Mitglieds)beitrag m

subsequent ['sʌbsɪkwənt] adj folgend, später; ~**ly** adv später

subside [səb'saɪd] vi sich senken; ~**nce** [səb'saɪdəns] n Senkung f

subsidiary [səb'sɪdɪərɪ] adj Neben- ♦ n (company) Tochtergesellschaft f

subsidize ['sʌbsɪdaɪz] vt subventionieren

subsidy ['sʌbsɪdɪ] n Subvention f

subsistence [səb'sɪstəns] n Unterhalt m

substance ['sʌbstəns] n Substanz f

substantial [səb'stænʃəl] adj (strong) fest, kräftig; (important) wesentlich; ~**ly** adv erheblich

substantiate [səb'stænʃɪeɪt] vt begründen, belegen

substitute ['sʌbstɪtjuːt] n Ersatz m ♦ vt ersetzen

substitution [sʌbstɪ'tjuːʃən] n Ersetzung f

subterfuge ['sʌbtəfjuːdʒ] n Vorwand m; (trick) Trick m

subterranean [sʌbtə'reɪnɪən] adj unterirdisch

subtitle ['sʌbtaɪtl] n Untertitel m

subtle ['sʌtl] adj fein; ~**ty** n Feinheit f

subtotal ['sʌb'təʊtl] n Zwischensumme f

subtract [səb'trækt] vt abziehen; ~**ion** [səb'trækʃən] n Abziehen nt, Subtraktion f

suburb ['sʌbɜːb] n Vorort m; the ~**s** die Außenbezirke pl; ~**an** [sə'bɜːbən] adj Vorort(s)-, Stadtrand-; ~**ia** [sə'bɜːbɪə] n Vorstadt f

subversive [sʌb'vɜːsɪv] adj subversiv

subway ['sʌbweɪ] n (US) U-Bahn f; (BRIT) Unterführung f

succeed [sək'siːd] vi (person) erfolgreich sein, Erfolg haben; (plan etc also) gelingen ♦ vt (nach)folgen +dat; he ~**ed in doing it** es gelang ihm, es zu tun; ~**ing** adj (nach)folgend

success [sək'ses] n Erfolg m; to be ~**ful** (in doing sth) Erfolg haben (bei etw); ~**ful** adj erfolgreich; ~**fully** adv erfolgreich

succession [sək'seʃən] n (Aufeinander)folge f; (to throne) Nachfolge f

successive [sək'sesɪv] adj aufeinanderfolgend

successor [sək'sesə*] n Nachfolger(in) m(f)

succinct [sək'sɪŋkt] adj knapp

succulent ['sʌkjʊlənt] adj saftig

succumb [sə'kʌm] vi: to ~ (to) erliegen (+dat); (yield) nachgeben

(+dat)

such [sʌtʃ] adj solche(r, s); ~ a book so ein Buch; ~ books solche Bücher; ~ courage so ein Mut; ~ a long trip so eine lange Reise; ~ a lot of so viel(e); ~ as wie; a noise ~ as to ein derartiger Lärm, daß; as ~ an sich; ~-and-such a time/town die und die Zeit/Stadt

suck [sʌk] vt saugen; (ice cream etc) lutschen; ~er n (inf) n Idiot m

suction [ˈsʌkʃən] n Saugkraft f

sudden [ˈsʌdn] adj plötzlich; all of a ~ auf einmal; ~ly adv plötzlich

suds [sʌdz] npl Seifenlauge f; (lather) Seifenschaum m

sue [suː] vt verklagen

suede [sweid] n Wildleder nt

suet [suit] n Nierenfett nt

Suez [ˈsuːiz] n: the ~ Canal der Suezkanal

suffer [ˈsʌfə*] vt (er)leiden ♦ vi leiden; ~er n Leidende(r) mf; ~ing n Leiden nt

suffice [səˈfaɪs] vi genügen

sufficient [səˈfɪʃnt] adj ausreichend; ~ly adv ausreichend

suffix [ˈsʌfɪks] n Nachsilbe f

suffocate [ˈsʌfəkeɪt] vt, vi ersticken

suffrage [ˈsʌfrɪdʒ] n Wahlrecht nt

suffused [səˈfjuːzd] adj: to be ~ with sth von etw erfüllt sein

sugar [ˈʃʊgə*] n Zucker m ♦ vt zuckern; ~ beet n Zuckerrübe f; ~ cane n Zuckerrohr nt; ~y adj süß

suggest [səˈdʒest] vt vorschlagen; (show) schließen lassen auf +acc; ~ion [səˈdʒestʃən] n Vorschlag m; ~ive adj anregend; (indecent) zweideutig

suicide [ˈsuːɪsaɪd] n Selbstmord m; to commit ~ Selbstmord begehen

suit [suit] n Anzug m; (CARDS) Farbe f ♦ vt passen +dat; (clothes) stehen +dat; well ~ed (well matched: couple) gut zusammenpassend; ~able adj geeignet, passend; ~ably adv passend, angemessen

suitcase [ˈsuːtkeɪs] n (Hand)koffer m

suite [swiːt] n (of rooms) Zimmer-

flucht f; (of furniture) Einrichtung f; (MUS) Suite f

suitor [ˈsuːtə*] n (JUR) Kläger(in) m(f)

sulfur [ˈsʌlfə*] (US) n = sulphur

sulk [sʌlk] vi schmollen; ~y adj schmollend

sullen [ˈsʌlən] adj mürrisch

sulphur [ˈsʌlfə*] (US sulfur) n Schwefel m

sultana [sʌlˈtɑːnə] n (fruit) Sultanine f

sultry [ˈsʌltrɪ] adj schwül

sum [sʌm] n Summe f; (money) Betrag m, Summe f; (arithmetic) Rechenaufgabe f; ~ up vt, vi zusammenfassen

summarize [ˈsʌməraɪz] vt kurz zusammenfassen

summary [ˈsʌmərɪ] n Zusammenfassung f ♦ adj (justice) kurzerhand erteilt

summer [ˈsʌmə*] n Sommer m ♦ adj Sommer-; ~house n (in garden) Gartenhaus nt; ~time n Sommerzeit f

summit [ˈsʌmɪt] n Gipfel m; ~ (conference) n Gipfelkonferenz f

summon [ˈsʌmən] vt herbeirufen; (JUR) vorladen; (gather up) aufbringen; ~s (JUR) n Vorladung f ♦ vt vorladen

sump [sʌmp] (BRIT) n (AUT) Ölwanne f

sumptuous [ˈsʌmptjʊəs] adj prächtig

sun [sʌn] n Sonne f; ~bathe vi sich sonnen; ~burn n Sonnenbrand m

Sunday [ˈsʌndeɪ] n Sonntag m; ~ school n Sonntagsschule f

sundial [ˈsʌndaɪəl] n Sonnenuhr f

sundown [ˈsʌndaʊn] n Sonnenuntergang m

sundry [ˈsʌndrɪ] adj verschieden; all and ~ alle; **sundries** npl (miscellaneous items) Verschiedene(s) nt

sunflower [ˈsʌnflaʊə*] n Sonnenblume f

sung [sʌŋ] pp of sing

brille f

sunk [sʌŋk] pp of **sink**

sun: **~light** ['sʌnlaɪt] n Sonnenlicht nt; **~lit** ['sʌnlɪt] adj sonnenbeschienen; **~ny** ['sʌnɪ] adj sonnig; **~rise** ['sʌnraɪz] n Sonnenaufgang m; **~set** ['sʌnsɛt] n Sonnenuntergang m; **~shade** ['sʌnʃeɪd] n Sonnenschirm m; **~shine** ['sʌnʃaɪn] n Sonnenschein m; **~stroke** ['sʌnstrəʊk] n Hitzschlag m; **~tan** ['sʌntæn] n (Sonnen)bräune f; **~tan oil** n Sonnenöl nt

super ['su:pə*] (inf) adj prima, klasse

superannuation ['su:pərænjʊ'eɪʃən] n Pension f

superb [su:'pə:b] adj ausgezeichnet, hervorragend

supercilious [su:pə'sɪlɪəs] adj herablassend

superficial [su:pə'fɪʃəl] adj oberflächlich

superfluous [sʊ'pə:flʊəs] adj überflüssig

superhuman [su:pə'hju:mən] adj (effort) übermenschlich

superimpose ['su:pərɪm'pəʊz] vt übereinanderlegen

superintendent [su:pərɪn'tɛndənt] n Polizeichef m

superior [sʊ'pɪərɪə*] adj überlegen; (better) besser ♦ n Vorgesetzte(r) mf; **~ity** [sʊpɪərɪ'ɒrɪtɪ] n Überlegenheit f

superlative [su:'pə:lətɪv] n überragend

superman ['su:pəmæn] (irreg) n Übermensch m

supermarket ['su:pəma:kɪt] n Supermarkt m

supernatural [su:pə'nætʃərəl] adj übernatürlich

superpower ['su:pəpaʊə*] n Weltmacht f

supersede [su:pə'si:d] vt ersetzen

supersonic ['su:pə'sɒnɪk] adj Überschall-

superstition [su:pə'stɪʃən] n Aberglaube m

superstitious [su:pə'stɪʃəs] adj abergläubisch

supervise ['su:pəvaɪz] vt beaufsichtigen, kontrollieren

supervision [su:pə'vɪʒən] n Aufsicht f

supervisor ['su:pəvaɪzə*] n Aufsichtsperson f; **~y** adj Aufsichts-

supine ['su:paɪn] adj auf dem Rücken liegend

supper ['sʌpə*] n Abendessen nt

supplant [sə'plɑ:nt] vt (person, thing) ersetzen

supple ['sʌpl] adj geschmeidig

supplement [n 'sʌplɪmənt, vb sʌplɪ'mɛnt] n Ergänzung f; (in book) Nachtrag m ♦ vt ergänzen; **~ary** [sʌplɪ'mɛntərɪ] adj ergänzend

supplier [sə'plaɪə*] n Lieferant m

supplies [sə'plaɪz] npl (food) Vorräte pl; (MIL) Nachschub m

supply [sə'plaɪ] vt liefern ♦ n Vorrat m; (supplying) Lieferung f ♦ adj (teacher etc) Aushilfs-; see also **supplies**

support [sə'pɔ:t] n Unterstützung f, (TECH) Stütze f ♦ vt (hold up) stützen, tragen; (provide for) ernähren; (be in favour of) unterstützen; **~er** n Anhänger(in) m(f)

suppose [sə'pəʊz] vt, vi annehmen; to be **~d** to do sth etw tun sollen; **~dly** [sə'pəʊzɪdlɪ] adv angeblich

supposing [sə'pəʊzɪŋ] conj angenommen

supposition [sʌpə'zɪʃən] n Voraussetzung f

suppress [sə'prɛs] vt unterdrücken; **~ion** [sə'prɛʃən] n Unterdrückung f

supremacy [sʊ'prɛməsɪ] n Vorherrschaft f, Oberhoheit f

supreme [sʊ'pri:m] adj oberste(r, s), höchste(r, s)

surcharge ['sə:tʃɑ:dʒ] n Zuschlag m

sure [ʃʊə*] adj sicher, gewiß; **~!** (of course) klar!; to make **~** of sth/ that sich einer Sache gen vergewissern, sich vergewissern, daß; **~ enough** (with past) tatsächlich; (with future) ganz bestimmt; **~footed** adj sicher (auf den Füßen)

~ly adv (certainly) sicherlich, gewiß; **~ly** it's wrong das ist doch wohl falsch

surety ['ʃʊərətɪ] n Sicherheit f; (person) Bürge m

surf [sɜ:f] n Brandung f

surface ['sɜ:fɪs] n Oberfläche f ♦ vt (roadway) teeren ♦ vi auftauchen; ~**mail** n gewöhnliche Post f

surfboard ['sɜ:fbɔ:d] n Wellenreiterbrett nt

surfeit ['sɜ:fɪt] n Übermaß nt

surfing ['sɜ:fɪŋ] n Wellenreiten nt

surge [sɜ:dʒ] n Woge f ♦ vi wogen

surgeon ['sɜ:dʒən] n Chirurg(in) m(f)

surgery ['sɜ:dʒərɪ] n (BRIT: place) Praxis f; (: time) Sprechstunde f; (treatment) Operation f; to undergo ~ operiert werden; ~**hours** (BRIT) npl Sprechstunden f

surgical ['sɜ:dʒɪkəl] adj chirurgisch; ~ **spirit** (BRIT) n Wundbenzin nt

surly ['sɜ:lɪ] adj verdrießlich, grob

surmount [sɜ:'maʊnt] vt überwinden

surname ['sɜ:neɪm] n Zuname m

surpass [sɜ:'pɑ:s] vt übertreffen

surplus ['sɜ:pləs] n Überschuß m ♦ adj überschüssig, Über(schuß)-

surprise [sə'praɪz] n Überraschung f ♦ vt überraschen

surprising [sə'praɪzɪŋ] adj überraschend; ~**ly** adv überraschend(erweise)

surrender [sə'rendə*] n Kapitulation f ♦ vi sich ergeben

surreptitious [sʌrəp'tɪʃəs] adj heimlich; (look also) verstohlen

surrogate ['sʌrəgɪt] n Ersatz m; ~ **mother** n Leihmutter f

surround [sə'raʊnd] vt umgeben; ~**ing** adj (countryside) umliegend; ~**ings** npl Umgebung f; (environment) Umwelt f

surveillance [sɜ:'veɪləns] n Überwachung f

survey [n 'sɜ:veɪ, vb sɜ:'veɪ] n Übersicht f ♦ vt überblicken; (land) vermessen; ~**or** [sə'veɪə*] n Land(ver)messer(in) m(f)

survival [sə'vaɪvəl] n Überleben nt

survive [sə'vaɪv] vt, vi überleben

survivor [sə'vaɪvə*] n Überlebende(r) mf

susceptible [sə'septəbl] adj: ~ (to) empfindlich (gegen); (charms etc) empfänglich (für)

suspect [adj 'sʌspekt, vb səs'pekt] n Verdächtige(r) mf ♦ adj verdächtig ♦ vt verdächtigen; (think) vermuten

suspend [səs'pend] vt verschieben; (from work) suspendieren; (hang up) aufhängen; (SPORT) sperren; ~**ed sentence** n (JUR) zur Bewährung ausgesetzte Strafe; ~**er belt** n Strumpf(halter)gürtel m; ~**ers** npl (BRIT) Strumpfhalter m; (: men's) Sockenhalter m; (US) Hosenträger m

suspense [səs'pens] n Spannung f

suspension [səs'penʃən] n (from work) Suspendierung f; (SPORT) Sperrung f; (AUT) Federung f; ~ **bridge** n Hängebrücke f

suspicion [səs'pɪʃən] n Mißtrauen nt; Verdacht m

suspicious [səs'pɪʃəs] adj mißtrauisch; (causing suspicion) verdächtig

sustain [səs'teɪn] vt (maintain) aufrechterhalten; (confirm) bestätigen; (JUR) anerkennen; (injury) davontragen; ~**able** adj (development, growth etc) aufrechtzuerhalten; ~**ed** adj (effort) anhaltend

sustenance ['sʌstɪnəns] n Nahrung f

swab [swɒb] n (MED) Tupfer m

swagger ['swægə*] vi stolzieren

swallow ['swɒləʊ] n (bird) Schwalbe f; (of food etc) Schluck m ♦ vt (ver)schlucken; ~ **up** vt verschlingen

swam [swæm] pt of **swim**

swamp [swɒmp] n Sumpf m ♦ vt überschwemmen

swan [swɒn] n Schwan m

swap [swɒp] n Tausch m ♦ vt: to ~ sth (for sth) etw (gegen etw) tauschen or eintauschen

swarm [swɔ:m] n Schwarm m ♦ vi:

to ~ or be ~ing with wimmeln von

swarthy ['swɔ:ðɪ] *adj* dunkel, braun

swastika ['swɒstɪkə] *n* Hakenkreuz *nt*

swat [swɒt] *vt* totschlagen

sway [sweɪ] *vi* schwanken; (*branches*) schaukeln, sich wiegen ♦ *vt* schwenken; (*influence*) beeinflussen

swear [swɛə*] (*pt* swore, *pp* sworn) *vi* (*promise*) schwören; (*curse*) fluchen; to ~ to sth schwören auf etw *acc*; ~**word** *n* Fluch *m*

sweat [swet] *n* Schweiß *m* ♦ *vi* schwitzen

sweater ['swetə*] *n* Pullover *m*

sweatshirt *n* Sweatshirt *nt*

sweaty ['swetɪ] *adj* verschwitzt

Swede [swi:d] *n* Schwede *m*, Schwedin *f*

swede [swi:d] (*BRIT*) *n* Steckrübe *f*

Sweden ['swi:dn] *n* Schweden *nt*

Swedish ['swi:dɪʃ] *adj* schwedisch ♦ *n* (*LING*) Schwedisch *nt*

sweep [swi:p] (*pt, pp* swept) *n* (*chimney* ~) Schornsteinfeger *m* ♦ *vt* fegen, kehren *vi* (*go quickly*) rauschen; ~ **away** *vt* wegfegen; ~ **past** *vi* vorbeisausen; ~ **up** *vt* zusammenkehren; ~**ing** *adj* (*gesture*) schwungvoll; (*statement*) verallgemeinernd

sweet [swi:t] *n* (*course*) Nachtisch *m*; (*candy*) Bonbon *nt* ♦ *adj* süß; ~**corn** *n* Zuckermais *m*; ~**en** *vt* süßen; (*fig*) versüßen; ~**heart** *n* Liebste(r) *mf*; ~**ness** *n* Süße *f*; ~**pea** *n* Gartenwicke *f*

swell [swel] (*pt* ~ed, *pp* swollen or ~ed) *n* Seegang *m* ♦ *adj* (*inf*) todschick ♦ *vt* (*numbers*) vermehren *vi* (*also*: ~ up) (an)schwellen; ~**ing** *n* Schwellung *f*

sweltering ['sweltərɪŋ] *adj* drückend

swept [swept] *pt, pp of* sweep

swerve [swɜ:v] *vi* ausscheren

swift [swɪft] *n* Mauersegler *m* ♦ *adj* geschwind, schnell, rasch; ~**ly** *adv* geschwind, schnell, rasch

swig [swɪg] *n* Zug *m*

swill [swɪl] *n* (*for pigs*) Schweinefutter *nt* ♦ *vt* spülen

swim [swɪm] (*pt* swam, *pp* swum) *n*: to go for a ~ schwimmen gehen ♦ *vi* schwimmen ♦ *vt* (*cross*) (durch)schwimmen; ~**mer** *n* Schwimmer(in) *m(f)*; ~**ming** *n* Schwimmen *nt*; ~**ming cap** *n* Badehaube *f*, Badekappe *f*; ~**ming costume** (*BRIT*) *n* Badeanzug *m*; ~**ming pool** *n* Schwimmbecken *nt*; (*private*) Swimmingpool *m*; ~**suit** *n* Badeanzug *m*

swindle ['swɪndl] *n* Schwindel *m*, Betrug *m* ♦ *vt* betrügen

swine [swaɪn] *n* (*also fig*) Schwein *nt*

swing [swɪŋ] (*pt, pp* swung) *n* (*child's*) Schaukel *f*; (*movement*) Schwung *m*; (*MUS*) Swing *m* ♦ *vt* schwingen ♦ *vi* schwingen, schaukeln; (*turn quickly*) schwenken; **in full** ~ in vollem Gange; ~ **bridge** *n* Drehbrücke *f*; ~ **door** (*BRIT*) *n* Schwingtür *f*

swingeing ['swɪndʒɪŋ] (*BRIT*) *adj* hart; (*taxation, cuts*) extrem

swinging door (*US*) *n* Schwingtür *f*

swipe [swaɪp] *n* Hieb *m* ♦ *vt* (*inf*: *hit*) hart schlagen; (: *steal*) klauen

swirl [swɜ:l] *vi* wirbeln

swish [swɪʃ] *adj* (*inf*: *smart*) schick ♦ *vi* zischen; (*grass, skirts*) rascheln

Swiss [swɪs] *adj* Schweizer, schweizerisch ♦ *n* Schweizer(in) *m(f)*; **the** ~ *npl* (*people*) die Schweizer *pl*

switch [swɪtʃ] *n* (*ELEC*) Schalter *m*; (*change*) Wechsel *m* ♦ *vt* (*ELEC*) schalten; (*change*) wechseln ♦ *vi* wechseln; ~ **off** *vt* ab- oder ausschalten; ~ **on** *vt* an- oder einschalten; ~**board** *n* Zentrale *f*; (*board*) Schaltbrett *nt*

Switzerland ['swɪtsələnd] *n* die Schweiz

swivel ['swɪvl] *vt* (*also*: ~ *round*) drehen ♦ *vi* sich drehen

swollen ['swəʊlən] *pp of* swell

swoon [swu:n] *vi* (*old*) in Ohnmacht fallen

swoop [swu:p] n Sturzflug m; (esp by police) Razzia f ♦ vi (also: ~ down) stürzen

swop [swɔp] = **swap**

sword [sɔːd] n Schwert nt; **~fish** n Schwertfisch m

swore [swɔː*] pt of **swear**

sworn [swɔːn] pp of **swear**

swot [swɔt] vt, vi pauken

swum [swʌm] pp of **swim**

swung [swʌŋ] pt, pp of **swing**

sycamore ['sɪkəmɔː*] n (US) Platane f; (BRIT) Bergahorn m

syllable ['sɪləbl] n Silbe f

syllabus ['sɪləbəs] n Lehrplan m

symbol ['sɪmbəl] n Symbol nt; **~ic(al)** [sɪm'bɒlɪk(əl)] adj symbolisch

symmetry ['sɪmɪtrɪ] n Symmetrie f

sympathetic [sɪmpə'θetɪk] adj mitfühlend

sympathize ['sɪmpəθaɪz] vi mitfühlen; **~r** n Mitfühlende(r) m(f); (POL) Sympathisant(in) m(f)

sympathy ['sɪmpəθɪ] n Mitleid nt, Mitgefühl nt; (condolence) Beileid nt; **with our deepest ~** mit tiefempfundenem Beileid

symphony ['sɪmfənɪ] n Sinfonie f

symposium [sɪm'pəʊzɪəm] n Tagung f

symptom ['sɪmptəm] n Symptom nt; **~atic** [sɪmptə'mætɪk] adj (fig): **~atic of** bezeichnend für

synagogue ['sɪnəgɒg] n Synagoge f

synchronize ['sɪŋkrənaɪz] vt synchronisieren ♦ vi gleichzeitig sein or ablaufen

syncopated ['sɪŋkəpeɪtɪd] adj synkopiert

syndicate ['sɪndɪkət] n Konsortium nt

synonym ['sɪnənɪm] n Synonym nt

synonymous [sɪ'nɒnɪməs] adj gleichbedeutend

synopsis [sɪ'nɒpsɪs] n Zusammenfassung f

syphon ['saɪfən] = **siphon**

Syria ['sɪrɪə] n Syrien nt

syringe [sɪ'rɪndʒ] n Spritze f

syrup ['sɪrəp] n Sirup m; (of sugar)

Melasse f

system ['sɪstəm] n System nt; **~atic** [sɪstə'mætɪk] adj systematisch; **~ disk** n (COMPUT) Systemdiskette f; **~s analyst** n Systemanalytiker(in) m(f)

T

ta [tɑː] (BRIT: inf) excl danke

tab [tæb] n Aufhänger m; (name ~) Schild nt; **to keep ~s on** (fig) genau im Auge behalten

tabby ['tæbɪ] n (also: ~ cat) getigerte Katze f

table ['teɪbl] n Tisch m; (list) Tabelle f ♦ vt (PARL: propose) vorlegen, einbringen; **to lay or set the ~** den Tisch decken; **~cloth** n Tischtuch nt; **~ of contents** n Inhaltsverzeichnis nt; **~ d'hôte** n Tagesmenü nt; **~ lamp** n Tischlampe f; **~mat** n Untersatz m; **~spoon** n Eßlöffel m; **~spoonful** n Eßlöffel(voll) m

tablet ['tæblət] n (MED) Tablette f; (for writing) Täfelchen nt

table tennis ['teɪbltenɪs] n Tischtennis nt

table wine ['teɪblwaɪn] n Tafelwein m

tabloid ['tæblɔɪd] n Zeitung f in kleinem Format; (pej) Boulevardzeitung f

tabulate ['tæbjuleɪt] vt tabellarisch ordnen

tacit ['tæsɪt] adj stillschweigend

taciturn ['tæsɪtɜːn] adj wortkarg

tack [tæk] n (small nail) Stift m; (US: thumb~) Reißzwecke f; (stitch) Heftstich m; (NAUT) Lavieren nt; (course) Kurs m ♦ vt (nail) nageln; (stitch) heften ♦ vi aufkreuzen

tackle ['tækl] n (for lifting) Flaschenzug m; (NAUT) Takelage f; (SPORT) Tackling n ♦ vt (deal with) anpacken, in Angriff nehmen; (person) festhalten; (player) angehen

tacky ['tækɪ] adj klebrig

tact [tækt] n Takt m; **~ful** adj taktvoll

voll
tactical ['tæktɪkəl] *adj* taktisch
tactics ['tæktɪks] *npl* Taktik *f*
tactless ['tæktlɪs] *adj* taktlos
tadpole ['tædpəʊl] *n* Kaulquappe *f*
taffy ['tæfɪ] (US) *n* Sahnebonbon *nt*
tag [tæg] *n* (*label*) Schild *nt*, Anhänger *m*; (*maker's name*) Etikett *nt*; (*phrase*) Floskel *f*; ~ **along** *vi* mitkommen

tail [teɪl] *n* Schwanz *m*; (*of list*) Schluß *m* ♦ *vt* folgen +*dat*; ~ **away** *or* **off** *vi* abfallen, schwinden; ~**back** (*BRIT*) *n* (*AUT*) (Rück)stau *m*; ~**coat** *n* Frack *m*; ~ **end** *n* Schluß *m*, Ende *nt*; ~**gate** *n* (*AUT*) Heckklappe *f*

tailor ['teɪlə*] *n* Schneider *m*; ~**ing** *n* Schneidern *nt*; ~**-made** *adj* maßgeschneidert; (*fig*): ~**-made for sb** jdm wie auf den Leib geschnitten
tailwind ['teɪlwɪnd] *n* Rückenwind *m*
tainted ['teɪntɪd] *adj* verdorben

take [teɪk] (*pt* **took**, *pp* **taken**) *vt* nehmen; (*trip, exam, PHOT*) machen; (*capture: person*) fassen; (: *town; also COMM, FIN*) einnehmen; (*carry to a place*) bringen; (*get for o.s.*) sich *dat* nehmen; (*gain, obtain*) bekommen; (*put up with*) hinnehmen; (*respond to*) aufnehmen; (*interpret*) auffassen; (*assume*) annehmen; (*contain*) Platz haben für; (*GRAM*) stehen mit; **to ~ sth from sb** jdm etw wegnehmen; **to ~ sth from sth** (*MATH: subtract*) etw von etw abziehen; (*extract, quotation*) etw einer Sache *dat* entnehmen; ~ **after** *vt fus* ähnlich sein +*dat*; ~ **apart** *vt* auseinandernehmen; ~ **away** *vt* (*remove*) wegnehmen; (*carry off*) wegbringen; ~ **back** *vt* (*return*) zurückbringen; (*retract*) zurücknehmen; ~ **down** *vt* (*pull down*) abreißen; (*write down*) aufschreiben; ~ **in** *vt* (*deceive*) hereinlegen; (*include*) einschließen; ~ **off** *vi* (*plane*) starten ♦ *vt* (*remove*) wegnehmen; (*clothing*) ausziehen; (*imitate*) nachmachen; ~

on *vt* (*undertake*) übernehmen; (*engage*) einstellen; (*opponent*) antreten gegen; ~ **out** *vt* (*girl, dog*) ausführen; (*extract*) herausnehmen; (*insurance*) abschließen; (*licence*) sich *dat* geben lassen; (*book*) ausleihen; (*remove*) entfernen; **to ~ sth out of sth** (*drawer, pocket etc*) etw aus etw herausnehmen; ~ **over** *vt* übernehmen ♦ *vi*: **to ~ over from sb** jdn ablösen; **to ~** *vt fus* (*like*) mögen; (*adopt as practice*) sich *dat* angewöhnen; ~ **up** *vt* (*raise*) aufnehmen; (*dress etc*) kürzer machen; (*occupy*) in Anspruch nehmen; (*engage in*) sich befassen mit; ~**away** *adj* zum Mitnehmen; ~**home pay** *n* Nettolohn *m*; ~**n** ['teɪkn] *pp of* take; ~**off** *n* (*AVIAT*) Start *m*; (*imitation*) Nachahmung *f*; ~**out** (*US*) *adj* = takeaway; ~**over** *n* (*COMM*) Übernahme *f*

takings ['teɪkɪŋz] *npl* (*COMM*) Einnahmen *pl*
talc [tælk] *n* (*also: talcum powder*) Talkumpuder *m*
tale [teɪl] *n* Geschichte *f*, Erzählung *f*; **to tell ~s** (*fig: lie*) Geschichten erfinden
talent ['tælənt] *n* Talent *nt*; ~**ed** *adj* begabt
talk [tɔːk] *n* (*conversation*) Gespräch *nt*; (*rumour*) Gerede *nt*; (*speech*) Vortrag *m* ♦ *vi* sprechen, reden; ~**s** *pl* (*POL etc*) Gespräche *pl*; **to ~ about** sprechen von +*dat* or über +*acc*; **to ~ sb into doing sth** jdn überreden, etw zu tun; **to ~ sb out of doing sth** jdm ausreden, etw zu tun; **to ~ shop** fachsimpeln; ~ **over** *vt* besprechen; ~**ative** *adj* gesprächig
tall [tɔːl] *adj* groß; (*building*) hoch; **to be 1 m 80 ~** 1,80 m groß sein; ~**boy** (*BRIT*) *n* Kommode *f*; ~ **story** *n* übertriebene Geschichte *f*
tally ['tælɪ] *n* Abrechnung *f* ♦ *vi* übereinstimmen
talon ['tælən] *n* Kralle *f*
tame [teɪm] *adj* zahm; (*fig*) fade

tamper ['tæmpə*] vi: to ~ with herumpfuschen an +dat

tampon ['tæmpɔn] n Tampon m

tan [tæn] n (on skin) (Sonnen)bräune f; (colour) Gelbbraun nt ♦ adj (gelb)braun ♦ vt bräunen; (skins) gerben ♦ vi braun werden

tang [tæŋ] n Schärfe f

tangent ['tændʒənt] n Tangente f; to go off at a ~ (fig) vom Thema abkommen

tangerine [tændʒə'ri:n] n Mandarine f

tangible ['tændʒəbl] adj greifbar

tangle ['tæŋgl] n Durcheinander nt; (trouble) Schwierigkeiten pl; to get in(to) a ~ sich verheddern

tank [tæŋk] n (container) Tank m, Behälter m; (MIL) Panzer m

tanker ['tæŋkə*] n (ship) Tanker m; (vehicle) Tankwagen m

tanned [tænd] adj (skin) gebräunt

tantalizing ['tæntəlaɪzɪŋ] adj verlockend; (annoying) quälend

tantamount ['tæntəmaunt] adj: ~ to gleichbedeutend mit

tantrum ['tæntrəm] n Wutanfall m

tap [tæp] n (gentle blow) Klopfen nt ♦ vt (strike) klopfen; (supply) anzapfen; (telephone) abhören; on ~ (fig: resources) zur Hand; ~-dancing ['tæpdɑ:nsɪŋ] n Steppen nt

tape [teɪp] n Band nt; (magnetic) (Ton)band nt; (adhesive) Klebstreifen m ♦ vt (record) aufnehmen; ~ measure n Maßband nt

taper ['teɪpə*] n (dünne) Wachskerze f ♦ vi spitz zulaufen

tape recorder n Tonbandgerät nt

tapestry ['tæpɪstrɪ] n Wandteppich m

tar [tɑ:*] n Teer m

target ['tɑ:gɪt] n Ziel nt; (board) Zielscheibe f

tariff ['tærɪf] n (duty paid) Zoll m; (list) Tarif m

tarmac [tɑ:mæk] n (AVIAT) Rollfeld nt

tarnish ['tɑ:nɪʃ] vt matt machen; (fig) beflecken

tarpaulin [tɑ:'pɔ:lɪn] n Plane f

tarragon ['tærəgən] n Estragon m

tart [tɑ:t] n (Obst)torte f; (inf) Nutte f ♦ adj scharf; ~ up (inf) vt aufmachen (inf); (person) auftakeln (inf)

tartan ['tɑ:tən] n Schottenkaro m ♦ adj mit Schottenkaro

tartar ['tɑ:tə*] n Zahnstein m; ~(e) sauce n Remouladensoße f

task [tɑ:sk] n Aufgabe f; to take sb to ~ sich dat jdn vornehmen; ~ force n Sondertrupp m

tassel ['tæsl] n Quaste f

taste [teɪst] n Geschmack m; (sense) Geschmackssinn m; (small quantity) Kostprobe f; (liking) Vorliebe f ♦ vt schmecken; (try) probieren ♦ vi schmecken; can I have a ~ of this wine? kann ich diesen Wein probieren?; to have a ~ for stw etw mögen; in good/bad ~ geschmackvoll/geschmacklos; you can ~ the garlic (in it) man kann den Knoblauch herausschmecken; to ~ of sth nach einer Sache schmecken; ~ful adj geschmackvoll; ~less adj (insipid) fade; (in bad ~) geschmacklos

tasty ['teɪstɪ] adj schmackhaft

tattered ['tætəd] adj = in tatters

tatters ['tætəz] npl: in ~ in Fetzen

tattoo [tə'tu:] n (MIL) Zapfenstreich m; (on skin) Tätowierung f ♦ vt tätowieren

tatty ['tætɪ] adj (BRIT: inf) adj schäbig

taught [tɔ:t] pt, pp of teach

taunt [tɔ:nt] n höhnische Bemerkung f ♦ vt verhöhnen

Taurus ['tɔ:rəs] n Stier m

taut [tɔ:t] adj straff

tawdry ['tɔ:drɪ] adj (bunt und) billig

tawny ['tɔ:nɪ] adj gelbbraun

tax [tæks] n Steuer f ♦ vt besteuern; (strain) strapazieren; (strength) angreifen; ~able adj (income) steuerpflichtig; ~ation n (AUT) Kraftfahrzeugsteuerplakette f; ~ evasion n Steuerhinterziehung f

~-**free** adj steuerfrei

taxi ['tæksɪ] n Taxi nt ♦ vi (plane) rollen; ~ **driver** n Taxifahrer m; ~ **rank** (BRIT) n Taxistand m; ~ **stand** n Taxistand m

tax ['tæks]: ~**payer** n Steuerzahler m; ~ **relief** n Steuerermäßigung f; ~ **return** n Steuererklärung f

TB n abbr (= tuberculosis) Tb f, Tbc f

tea [ti:] n Tee m; (meal) (frühes) Abendessen nt; ~ **high** ~ (BRIT) Abendessen nt; ~ **bag** n Teebeutel m; ~ **break** (BRIT) n Teepause f

teach [ti:tʃ] (pt, pp taught) vt lehren, unterrichten; (SCH) lehren, unterrichten; (show): to ~ **sb sth** jdm etw beibringen ♦ vi lehren, unterrichten; ~**er** n Lehrer(in) m(f); ~**ing** n (~er's work) Unterricht m; (doctrine) Lehre f

tea: ~ **cosy** n Teewärmer m; ~**cup** n Teetasse f; ~ **leaves** npl Teeblätter pl

team [ti:m] n Team nt; (SPORT) Mannschaft f; (animals) Gespann nt

teamwork n Gemeinschaftsarbeit f, Teamarbeit f

teapot ['ti:pot] n Teekanne f

tear¹ [tɛə*] (pt tore, pp torn) n Riß m ♦ vt zerreißen; (muscle) zerren ♦ vi (zer)reißen; (rush) rasen; **tear along** n (rush) entlangrasen; **tear up** vt (sheet of paper etc) zerreißen

tear² [tɪə*] n Träne f

tearful ['tɪəful] adj weinend; (voice) weinerlich

tear gas ['tɪəgæs] n Tränengas nt

tearoom ['ti:rum] n Teestube f

tease [ti:z] n Hänsler m ♦ vt necken

tea set n Teeservice nt

teaspoon ['ti:spu:n] n Teelöffel m

teat [ti:t] n (of woman) Brustwarze f; (of animal) Zitze f; (of bottle) Sauger m

tea time n (in the afternoon) Teestunde f; (mealtime) Abendessen nt

tea towel n Geschirrtuch nt

technical ['teknɪkəl] adj technisch; (knowledge, terms) Fach-; ~**ity** [teknɪˈkælɪtɪ] n technische Einzelheit f; (JUR) Formsache f; ~**ly** adv technisch; (speak) spezialisiert; (fig) genau genommen

technician [tekˈnɪʃən] n Techniker m

technique [tekˈni:k] n Technik f

technological [teknəˈlɒdʒɪkəl] adj technologisch

technology [tekˈnɒlədʒɪ] n Technologie f

teddy (bear) ['tedɪ(bɛə*)] n Teddybär m

tedious ['ti:dɪəs] adj langweilig, ermüdend

tee [ti:] n (GOLF) Abschlagstelle f; (object) Tee nt

teem [ti:m] vi (swarm): to ~ (with) wimmeln (von); **it is** ~**ing (with rain)** es gießt in Strömen

teenage ['ti:neɪdʒ] adj (fashions etc) Teenager-, jugendlich; ~**r** n Teenager m, Jugendliche(r) mf

teens [ti:nz] npl Teenageralter nt

tee-shirt ['ti:ʃɜ:t] n T-Shirt nt

teeter ['ti:tə*] vi schwanken

teeth [ti:θ] npl of **tooth**

teethe [ti:ð] vi zahnen

teething ring ['ti:ðɪŋ-] n Beißring m

teething troubles ['ti:ðɪŋ-] npl (fig) Kinderkrankheiten pl

teetotal ['ti:'təutl] adj abstinent

telecommunications ['telɪkəmju:nɪˈkeɪʃənz] npl Fernmeldewesen nt

telegram ['telɪɡræm] n Telegramm nt

telegraph ['telɪgrɑ:f] n Telegraph m

telephone ['telɪfəun] n Telefon nt, Fernsprecher m ♦ vt anrufen; (message) telefonisch mitteilen; **to be on the** ~ (talking) telefonieren; (possessing phone) Telefon haben; ~ **booth** n Telefonzelle f; ~ **box** (BRIT) n Telefonzelle f; ~ **call** n Telefongespräch nt, Anruf m; ~ **directory** n Telefonbuch nt; ~ **number** n Telefonnummer f

telephonist [tə'lefənɪst] (BRIT) n Telefonist(in) m(f)

telephoto lens ['telɪfəʊtəʊ'lenz] n Teleobjektiv nt

telescope ['telɪskəʊp] n Teleskop nt, Fernrohr nt ♦ vi ineinanderschieben

televise ['telɪvaɪz] vt durch das Fernsehen übertragen

television ['telɪvɪʒən] n Fernsehen nt; on ~ im Fernsehen; ~ (set) n Fernsehapparat m, Fernseher m

telex ['teleks] n Telex nt ♦ vt per Telex schicken

tell [tel] (pt, pp told) vt (story) erzählen; (secret) ausplaudern; (say, make known) sagen; (distinguish) erkennen; (be sure) wissen ♦ vi (talk) sprechen; (be sure) wissen; (divulge) es verraten; (have effect) sich auswirken; to ~ sb to do sth jdm sagen, daß er etw tun soll; to ~ sth of sth to sb jdm etw von etw ~ sb by sth jdn an etw dat erkennen; to ~ sth from etw unterscheiden von; to ~ of sth von etw sprechen; ~ off vt: to ~ sb off jdn ausschimpfen; ~er n Kassenbeamte(r) m/f; ~ing adj verräterisch; (blow) hart; ~tale adj verräterisch

telly ['telɪ] (BRIT: inf) n (= television) TV nt

temerity [tɪ'merɪtɪ] n (Toll)kühnheit f

temp [temp] n abbr (= temporary) Aushilfssekretärin f; ♦ vi als Aushilfskraft arbeiten

temper ['tempə*] n (disposition) Temperament nt; (anger) Zorn m ♦ vt (tone down) mildern; (metal) härten; to be in a (bad) ~ wütend sein; to lose one's ~ die Beherrschung verlieren

temperament ['temprəmənt] n Temperament nt; ~al [temprə'mentl] adj (moody) launisch

temperance ['tempərəns] n Mäßigung f; (abstinence) Enthaltsamkeit f

temperate ['tempərət] adj gemäßigt

temperature ['tempritʃə*] n Tempe-

ratur f; (MED: high ~) Fieber nt; to have or run a ~ Fieber haben

template ['templɪt] n Schablone f

temple ['templ] n Tempel m; (ANAT) Schläfe f

temporal ['tempərəl] adj (of time) zeitlich; (worldly) irdisch, weltlich

temporarily ['tempərərɪlɪ] adv zeitweilig, vorübergehend

temporary ['tempərərɪ] adj vorläufig; (road, building) provisorisch

tempt [tempt] vt (persuade) verleiten; (attract) reizen, (ver)locken; to ~ sb into doing sth jdn dazu verleiten, etw zu tun; ~ation n Versuchung f; (temp'teɪʃən] n Versuchung f; ~ing adj (person) verführerisch; (object, situation) verlockend

ten [ten] num zehn

tenable ['tenəbl] adj haltbar

tenacious [tə'neɪʃəs] adj zäh, hartnäckig

tenacity [tə'næsɪtɪ] n Zähigkeit f, Hartnäckigkeit f

tenancy ['tenənsɪ] n Mietverhältnis nt

tenant ['tenənt] n Mieter m; (of larger property) Pächter m

tend [tend] vt (look after) sich kümmern um ♦ vi: to ~ to do etw gewöhnlich tun

tendency ['tendənsɪ] n Tendenz f; (of person) Tendenz f, Neigung f

tender ['tendə*] adj zart; (loving) zärtlich ♦ n (COMM: offer) Kostenanschlag m ♦ vt (an)bieten; (resignation) einreichen; ~ness n Zartheit f; (being loving) Zärtlichkeit f

tendon ['tendən] n Sehne f

tenement ['tenɪmənt] n Mietshaus nt

tenet ['tenət] n Lehre f

tennis ['tenɪs] n Tennis nt; ~ ball n Tennisball m; ~ court n Tennisplatz m; ~ player n Tennisspieler(in) m(f); ~ racket n Tennisschläger m; ~ shoes npl Tennisschuhe pl

tenor ['tenə*] n Tenor m

tenpin bowling ['tenpɪn-] n Bowling nt

tense [tens] *adj* angespannt ♦ *n* Zeitform *f*

tension ['tenʃən] *n* Spannung *f*

tent [tent] *n* Zelt *nt*

tentacle ['tentəkl] *n* Fühler *m*; (*of sea animals*) Fangarm *m*

tentative ['tentətɪv] *adj* (*movement*) unsicher; (*offer*) Probe-; (*arrangement*) vorläufig; (*suggestion*) unverbindlich; **~ly** *adv* versuchsweise; (*try, move*) vorsichtig

tenterhooks ['tentəhʊks] *npl*: **to be on ~** auf die Folter gespannt sein

tenth [tenθ] *num* zehnte(r, s)

tent peg *n* Hering *m*

tent pole *n* Zeltstange *f*

tenuous ['tenjʊəs] *adj* schwach

tenure ['tenjʊə*] *n* (*of land*) Besitz *m*; (*of office*) Amtszeit *f*

tepid ['tepɪd] *adj* lauwarm

term [tɜːm] *n* (*period of time*) Zeit(raum *m*) *f*; (*limit*) Frist *f*; (*SCH*) Quartal *nt*; (*UNIV*) Trimester *nt*; (*expression*) Ausdruck *m* ♦ *vt* (*be*)nennen; **~s** *npl* (*conditions*) Bedingungen *pl*; **in the short/long ~** auf kurze/lange Sicht; **to be on good ~s with** sb gut mit jdm auskommen; **to come to ~s with** (*person*) sich einigen mit; (*problem*) sich abfinden mit

terminal ['tɜːmɪnl] *n* (*BRIT: also*: **coach ~**) Endstation *f*; (*AVIAT*) Terminal *m*; (*COMPUT*) Terminal *nt* or *m* ♦ *adj* Schluß-; (*MED*) unheilbar

terminate ['tɜːmɪneɪt] *vt* beenden ♦ *vi* enden, aufhören

terminus ['tɜːmɪnəs] (*pl* **termini**) *n* Endstation *f*

terrace ['terəs] *n* (*BRIT: row of houses*) Häuserreihe *f*; (*in garden etc*) Terrasse *f*; **the ~s** (*BRIT: SPORT*) die Ränge; **~d** *adj* (*garden*) terrassenförmig angelegt; (*house*) Reihen-

terrain [te'reɪn] *n* Terrain *nt*, Gelände *nt*

terrible ['terəbl] *adj* schrecklich, entsetzlich, fürchterlich

terribly ['terəblɪ] *adv* fürchterlich

terrific [tə'rɪfɪk] *adj* unwahrscheinlich; **~!** klasse!

terrify ['terɪfaɪ] *vt* erschrecken

territorial [terɪ'tɔːrɪəl] *adj* Gebiets-, territorial

territory ['terɪtərɪ] *n* Gebiet *nt*

terror ['terə*] *n* Schrecken *m*; (*POL*) Terror *m*; **~ist** *n* Terrorist(in) *f(m)*; **~ize** *vt* terrorisieren

terse [tɜːs] *adj* knapp, kurz, bündig

test [test] *n* Probe *f*; (*examination*) Prüfung *f*; (*PSYCH, TECH*) Test *m* ♦ *vt* prüfen; (*PSYCH*) testen

testicle ['testɪkl] *n* (*ANAT*) Hoden *m*

testify ['testɪfaɪ] *vi* aussagen; **to ~ to sth** etw bezeugen

testimony ['testɪmənɪ] *n* (*JUR*) Zeugenaussage *f*; (*fig*) Zeugnis *nt*

test match *n* (*SPORT*) Länderkampf *m*

test tube *n* Reagenzglas *nt*

testy ['testɪ] *adj* gereizt; reizbar

tetanus ['tetənəs] *n* Wundstarrkrampf *m*, Tetanus *m*

tetchy ['tetʃɪ] *adj* empfindlich

tether ['teðə*] *vt* anbinden ♦ *n*: **at the end of one's ~** völlig am Ende

text [tekst] *n* Text *m*; (*of document*) Wortlaut *m*; **~book** *n* Lehrbuch *nt*

textiles ['tekstaɪlz] *npl* Textilien *pl*

texture ['tekstʃə*] *n* Beschaffenheit *f*

Thai [taɪ] *adj* thailändisch ♦ *n* Thailänder(in) *m(f)*; (*LING*) Thailändisch *nt*; **~land** *n* Thailand *nt*

Thames [temz] *n*: **the ~** die Themse

than [ðæn, ðən] *prep* (*in comparisons*) als

thank [θæŋk] *vt* danken +*dat*; **you've him to ~ for your success** Sie haben Ihren Erfolg ihm zu verdanken; **~ you (very much)** danke (vielmals), danke schön; **~ful** *adj* dankbar; **~less** *adj* undankbar; **~s** *npl* Dank *m* ♦ *excl* danke!; **~s to** *prep* +*gen*; **T~sgiving (Day)** (*US*) *n* Thanksgiving Day *m*

that [ðæt] *adj* (*demonstrative*: *pl* **those**) der/die/das; jene(r, s) one das da

♦ *pron* **1** (*demonstrative: pl* those) das; who's/what's that? wer ist da/ was ist das?; is that you? bist du das?; that's what he said genau das hat er gesagt; what happened after that? was passierte danach?; that is das heißt

2 (*relative: subj*) der/die/das, die; (: *direct obj*) den/die/das, die; (: *indirect obj*) dem/der/dem, denen; all (that) I have alles, was ich habe

3 (*relative: of time*): the day (that) an dem Tag, als; the winter (that) he came in der im Winter, in dem er kam

♦ *conj* daß; he thought that I was ill er dachte, daß ich krank sei, er dachte, ich sei krank

♦ *adv* (*demonstrative*) so; I can't work that much ich kann nicht so viel arbeiten

thatched [θætʃt] *adj* strohgedeckt; (*cottage*) mit Strohdach

thaw [θɔː] *n* Tauwetter *nt* ♦ *vi* tauen; (*frozen foods, fig: people*) auftauen ♦ *vt* (auf)tauen lassen

─────────────
KEYWORD
─────────────

the [ðiː, ðə] *def art* **1** der/die/das; to play the piano/violin Klavier/Geige spielen; I'm going to the butcher's/the cinema ich gehe zum Fleischer/ins Kino; Elizabeth the First Elisabeth die Erste

2 (*+ adj to form noun*) das, die; the rich and the poor die Reichen und die Armen

3 (*in comparisons*): the more he works the more he earns je mehr er arbeitet, desto mehr verdient er

theatre ['θɪətə*] (*US* **theater**) *n* Theater *nt*; (*for lectures etc*) Saal *m*; (*MED*) Operationssaal *m*; **~goer** *n* Theaterbesucher(in) *m(f)*

theatrical [θɪ'ætrɪkəl] *adj* Theater-; (*career*) Schauspieler-; (*showy*) theatralisch

theft [θeft] *n* Diebstahl *m*

their [ðɛə*] *adj* ihr; *see also* **my**; **~s** *pron* ihre(r, s); *see also* **mine**

them [ðɛm, ðəm] *pron* (*acc*) sie; (*dat*) ihnen; *see also* **me**

theme [θiːm] *n* Thema *nt*; (*MUS*) Motiv *nt*; **~ park** *n* (thematisch gestalteter) Freizeitpark *m*; **~ song** *n* Titelmusik *f*

themselves [ðəm'sɛlvz] *pl pron* (*reflexive*) sich (selbst); (*emphatic*) selbst; *see also* **oneself**

then [ðɛn] *adv* (*at that time*) damals; (*next*) dann ♦ *conj* also, folglich; (*furthermore*) ferner ♦ *adj* damalig; from ~ on von da an; by ~ bis dahin; the ~ president der damalige Präsident

theology [θɪ'ɒlədʒɪ] *n* Theologie *f*

theoretical [θɪə'rɛtɪkəl] *adj* theoretisch; **~ly** *adv* theoretisch

theory ['θɪərɪ] *n* Theorie *f*

therapist ['θɛrəpɪst] *n* Therapeut(in) *m(f)*

therapy ['θɛrəpɪ] *n* Therapie *f*

─────────────
KEYWORD
─────────────

there [ðɛə*] *adv* **1**: there is, there are *es or* da ist/sind; (*there exists/ exist also*) es gibt; there are 3 of them (*people, things*) es gibt 3 davon; there has been an accident da war ein Unfall

2 (*referring to place*) da, dort; (*with vb of movement*) dahin, dorthin; put it in/on there leg es dahinein/ dorthinauf

3: there, there (*esp to child*) na, na

thereabouts [ðɛərə'baʊts] *adv* (*place*) dort in der Nähe, dort irgendwo; (*amount*): 20 *or* ~ ungefähr 20

thereafter [ðɛər'ɑːftə*] *adv* danach

thereby [ðɛə'baɪ] *adv* dadurch, damit

therefore ['ðɛəfɔː*] *adv* deshalb, daher

there's ['ðɛəz] = **there is**; **there has**

thermometer [θə'mɒmɪtə*] *n* Thermometer nt

Thermos ['θɜːməs] ® n Thermosflasche f

thesaurus [θɪ'sɔːrəs] n Synonymwörterbuch nt

these [ðiːz] pron, adj (pl) diese

theses ['θiːsiːz] npl of thesis

thesis ['θiːsɪs] n (for discussion) These f; (UNIV) Dissertation f, Doktorarbeit f

they [ðeɪ] pl pron sie; (people in general) man; ~ say that ... (it is said that) es wird gesagt, daß ...; = they had; they would they shall; they will they are they have

thick [θɪk] adj dick; (forest) dicht; (liquid) dickflüssig; (slow, stupid) dumm, schwer von Begriff ♦ n: in the ~ of mitten in +dat; it's 20 cm ~ es ist 20 cm dick or stark; ~en vi (fog) dichter werden ♦ vt (sauce etc) verdicken; ~ness n Dicke f; Dichte f; Dickflüssigkeit f; ~set adj untersetzt; ~skinned adj dickhäutig

thief [θiːf] (pl thieves) n Dieb(in) m(f)

thieves [θiːvz] npl of thief

thieving ['θiːvɪŋ] n Stehlen nt ♦ adj diebisch

thigh [θaɪ] n Oberschenkel m

thimble ['θɪmbl] n Fingerhut m

thin [θɪn] adj dünn; (person) dünn, mager; (excuse) schwach ♦ vt: to ~ (down) (sauce, paint) verdünnen

thing [θɪŋ] n Ding nt; (affair) Sache f; my ~s meine Sachen pl; the best ~ would be to ... das beste wäre, ...; how are ~s? wie geht's?

think [θɪŋk] (pt, pp thought) vt, vi denken; what did you ~ of them? was halten Sie von ihnen?; to ~ about sth/sb nachdenken über etw/jdn; I'll ~ about it ich überlege es mir; to ~ of doing sth vorhaben or beabsichtigen, etw zu tun; I ~ so/not ich glaube (schon)/glaube nicht; to ~ well of sb viel von jdm halten; ~ over vt überdenken; ~ up vt sich dat ausdenken; ~ tank n Expertengruppe f

thinly ['θɪnlɪ] adv dünn; (disguised) kaum

third [θɜːd] adj dritte(r, s) ♦ n (person) Dritte(r) mf; (part) Drittel nt; ~ly adv drittens; ~ party insurance (BRIT) n Haftpflichtversicherung f; ~-rate adj minderwertig; the T~ World n die Dritte Welt f

thirst [θɜːst] n (also fig) Durst m; ~y adj (person) durstig; (work) durstig machend; to be ~y Durst haben

thirteen ['θɜː'tiːn] num dreizehn

thirty ['θɜːtɪ] num dreißig

this [ðɪs] adj (demonstrative: pl these) diese(r, s); this evening heute abend; this one diese(r, s) (da) ♦ pron (demonstrative: pl these) dies, das; who/what is this? wer/was ist das?; this is where I live hier wohne ich; this is what he said das hat er gesagt; this is Mr Brown (in introductions/photo) dies ist Mr Brown; (on telephone) hier ist Mr Brown ♦ adv (demonstrative): this high/long etc so groß/lang etc

thistle ['θɪsl] n Distel f

thorn [θɔːn] n Dorn m; ~y adj dornig; (problem) schwierig

thorough ['θʌrə] adj gründlich; ~bred n Vollblut nt ♦ adj reinrassig, Vollblut-; ~fare n Straße f; "no ~fare" „Durchfahrt verboten"; ~ly adv gründlich; (extremely) äußerst

those [ðəʊz] pl pron die (da), jene ♦ adj die, jene

though [ðəʊ] conj obwohl ♦ adv trotzdem

thought [θɔːt] pt, pp of think ♦ n (idea) Gedanke m; (thinking) Denken nt, Denkvermögen nt; ~ful adj (thinking) gedankenvoll, nachdenklich; (kind) rücksichtsvoll, aufmerksam; ~less adj gedankenlos, unbesonnen; (unkind) rücksichtslos

thousand ['θaʊzənd] num tausend; two ~ zweitausend; ~s of Tausende (von); ~**th** adj tausendste(r, s)

thrash [θræʃ] vt verdreschen (fig) (vernichtend) schlagen; ~ **about** vi um sich schlagen; ~ **out** vt ausdiskutieren

thread [θred] n Faden m, Garn nt; (on screw) Gewinde nt; (in story) Faden m ♦ vt (needle) einfädeln; ~**bare** adj (also fig) fadenscheinig

threat [θret] n Drohung f; (danger) Gefahr f; ~**en** vt bedrohen ♦ vi drohen; to ~**en sb with sth** jdm etw androhen

three [θriː] num drei; ~**-dimensional** adj dreidimensional; ~**-piece suit** n dreiteilige(r) Anzug m; ~**-piece suite** n dreiteilige Polstergarnitur f; ~**-wheeler** n Dreiradwagen m

thresh [θreʃ] vi, vt dreschen

threshold [ˈθreʃhəuld] n Schwelle f

threw [θruː] pt of throw

thrift [θrɪft] n Sparsamkeit f; ~**y** adj sparsam

thrill [θrɪl] n Reiz m, Erregung f ♦ vt begeistern, packen; to be ~**ed** with (gift etc) sich unheimlich freuen über +acc; ~**er** n Krimi m; ~**ing** adj spannend; (news) aufregend

thrive [θraɪv] (pt ~**d**, throve, pp ~**d**, thriven) vi: to ~ (on) gedeihen (bei); thriven [ˈθrɪvn] pp of thrive

thriving [ˈθraɪvɪŋ] adj blühend

throat [θrəut] n Hals m, Kehle f; to have a sore ~ Halsschmerzen haben

throb [θrɒb] n Pochen nt ♦ vi klopfen, pochen

throes [θrəuz] npl: in the ~ of mitten in +dat

throng [θrɒŋ] n (Menschen)schar f ♦ vt sich drängen in +dat

throttle [ˈθrɒtl] n Gashebel m ♦ vt erdrosseln

through [θruː] prep durch; (time) während +gen; (because of) aus, durch ♦ adv durch ♦ adj (ticket, train) durchgehend; (finished) fertig; to put sb ~ (to) (TEL) eine Verbindung haben mit; (have finished) fertig

sein; no ~ way (BRIT) Sackgasse f; ~**out** [θruˈaut] prep (place) überall in +dat; (time) während +gen ♦ adv überall; die ganze Zeit

throve [θrəuv] pt of thrive

throw [θrəu] (pt threw, pp thrown) n Wurf m ♦ vt werfen; to ~ **a party** eine Party geben; to ~ **away** vt wegwerfen; (waste) verschwenden; (money) verschwenden; ~ **off** vt abwerfen; (pursuer) abschütteln; ~ **out** vt hinauswerfen; (rubbish) wegwerfen; (plan) verwerfen; ~ **up** vt, vi (vomit) speien; ~**away** adj Wegwerf-; ~**in** n Einwurf m; **thrown** [θrəun] pp of throw

thru [θruː] (US) = through

thrush [θrʌʃ] n Drossel f

thrust [θrʌst] (pt, pp thrust) n (TECH) Schubkraft f ♦ vt, vi (push) stoßen

thud [θʌd] n dumpfe(r) (Auf)schlag m

thug [θʌg] n Schlägertyp m

thumb [θʌm] n Daumen m ♦ vt (book) durchblättern; to ~ **a lift** per Anhalter fahren (wollen); ~**tack** (US) n Reißzwecke f

thump [θʌmp] n (blow) Schlag m; (noise) Bums m ♦ vt schlagen auf +acc ♦ vt hämmern, pochen ♦ vt schlagen auf +acc

thunder [ˈθʌndə*] n Donner m ♦ vi donnern; (train etc) to ~ **past** vorbeidonnern ♦ vt brüllen; ~**bolt** n Blitz m; ~**clap** n Donnerschlag m; ~**storm** n Gewitter nt, Unwetter nt; ~**y** adj gewitterschwül

Thursday [ˈθɜːzdeɪ] n Donnerstag m

thus [ðʌs] adv (in this way) so; (therefore) somit, also, folglich

thwart [θwɔːt] vt vereiteln, durchkreuzen; (person) hindern

thyme [taɪm] n Thymian m

thyroid [ˈθaɪrɔɪd] n Schilddrüse f

tiara [tɪˈɑːrə] n Diadem nt; (of pope) Tiara nt

tic [tɪk] n Tick m

tick [tɪk] n (sound) Ticken nt; (mark) Häkchen n ♦ vi ticken ♦ vt abhaken; **in a** ~ (BRIT: inf) sofort;

off vt abhaken; (person) ausschimpfen; ~ **over** vi (engine) im Leerlauf laufen; (fig) auf Sparflamme laufen

ticket ['tɪkɪt] n (for travel) Fahrkarte f; (for entrance) (Eintritts)karte f; (price ~) Preisschild nt; (luggage ~) (Gepäck)schein m; (raffle ~) Los nt; (parking ~) Strafzettel m; (in car park) Parkschein m; ~ **collector** n Fahrkartenkontrolleur m; ~ **office** n (RAIL etc) Fahrkartenschalter m; (THEAT etc) Kasse f

tickle ['tɪkl] n Kitzeln nt ♦ vt kitzeln; (amuse) amüsieren

ticklish ['tɪklɪʃ] adj (also fig) kitzlig

tidal ['taɪdl] adj Flut-, Tide-; ~ **wave** n Flutwelle f

tidbit ['tɪdbɪt] (US) n Leckerbissen m

tiddlywinks ['tɪdlɪwɪŋks] n Floh(hüpf)spiel nt

tide [taɪd] n Gezeiten pl; high/low ~ Flut f/Ebbe f

tidy ['taɪdɪ] adj ordentlich ♦ vt aufräumen, in Ordnung bringen

tie [taɪ] n (BRIT: neck) Kravatte f, Schlips m; (sth connecting) Band nt; (SPORT) Unentschieden nt ♦ vt (fasten, restrict) binden ♦ vi (SPORT) unentschieden spielen; (in competition) punktgleich sein; **to** ~ **in a bow** zur Schleife binden; **to** ~ **a knot in sth** einen Knoten in etw acc machen; ~ **down** vt festbinden; **to** ~ **sb down to jdn** binden an +acc; ~ **up** vt (dog) anleinen; (parcel) verschnüren; (boat) festmachen; (person) fesseln; **to be** ~**d up** (busy) beschäftigt sein

tier [tɪə*] n Rang m; (of cake) Etage f

tiff [tɪf] n Krach m

tiger ['taɪgə*] n Tiger m

tight [taɪt] adj (close) eng, knapp; (schedule) gedrängt; (firm) fest; (control) streng; (stretched) stramm, angespannt; (inf: drunk) blau, stramm ♦ adv (squeeze) fest; ~**en** vt anziehen, anspannen; (restrictions) verschärfen ♦ vi sich spannen; ~**-fisted** adj knauserig; ~**ly** adv eng;

fest; (stretched) straff; ~**-rope** n Seil nt; ~**s** npl (esp BRIT) Strumpfhose f

tile [taɪl] n (on roof) Dachziegel m; (on wall or floor) Fliese f; ~**d** adj (roof) gedeckt, Ziegel-; (floor, wall) mit Fliesen belegt

till [tɪl] n Kasse f ♦ vt bestellen ♦ prep, conj = **until**

tiller ['tɪlə*] n Ruderpinne f

tilt [tɪlt] vt kippen, neigen ♦ vi sich neigen

timber ['tɪmbə*] n Holz nt; (trees) Baumbestand m

time [taɪm] n Zeit f; (occasion) Mal nt; (rhythm) Takt m ♦ vt zur rechten Zeit tun, zeitlich einrichten; (SPORT) stoppen; **in 2 weeks'** ~ in 2 Wochen; **a long** ~ lange; **for the** ~ **being** vorläufig; **4 at a** ~ zu jeweils 4; **from** ~ **to** ~ gelegentlich; **to have a good** ~ sich amüsieren; **in** ~ (soon enough) rechtzeitig; (after some ~) mit der Zeit; (MUS) im Takt; **in no** ~ im Handumdrehen; **any** ~ jederzeit; **on** ~ pünktlich, rechtzeitig; **five** ~ **5** fünfmal 5; **what** ~ **is it?** wieviel Uhr ist es?, wie spät ist es?; **at** ~**s** manchmal; ~ **bomb** n Zeitbombe f; ~**less** adj (beauty) zeitlos; ~ **limit** n Frist f; ~**ly** adj rechtzeitig; günstig; ~ **off** n freie Zeit f; ~**r** n (~ switch) in kitchen) Schaltuhr f; ~ **scale** n Zeitspanne f; ~**-share** adj Time-sharing-; ~ **switch** (BRIT) n Zeitschalter m; ~**table** n Fahrplan m; (SCH) Stundenplan m; ~ **zone** n Zeitzone f

timid ['tɪmɪd] adj ängstlich, schüchtern

timing ['taɪmɪŋ] n Wahl f des richtigen Zeitpunkts, Timing nt; (AUT) Einstellung f

timpani ['tɪmpənɪ] npl Kesselpauken pl

tin [tɪn] n (metal) Blech nt; (BRIT: can) Büchse f, (BRIT: can) Dose f; ~**foil** n Stanniolpapier nt

tinge [tɪndʒ] n (colour) Färbung f, (fig) Anflug m ♦ vt färben; ~**d with**

mit einer Spur von

tingle ['tɪŋgl] n Prickeln nt ♦ vi prickeln

tinker ['tɪŋkə*] n Kesselflicker m; ~ **with** vt fus herumpfuschen an +dat

tinkle ['tɪŋkl] vi klingeln

tinned [tɪnd] (BRIT) adj (food) Dosen-, Büchsen-

tin opener ['-əupnə*] (BRIT) n Dosen- or Büchsenöffner m

tinsel ['tɪnsl] n Rauschgold nt

tint [tɪnt] n Farbton m; (slight colour) Anflug m; (hair) Tönung f; ~**ed** adj getönt

tiny ['taɪnɪ] adj winzig

tip [tɪp] n (pointed end) Spitze f; (money) Trinkgeld nt; (hint) Wink m, Tip m ♦ vt (slant) kippen; (hat) antippen; (~ over) umkippen; (waiter) ein Trinkgeld geben +dat; ~**-off** n Hinweis m, Tip m; ~**ped** (BRIT) adj (cigarette) Filter-

tipsy ['tɪpsɪ] adj beschwipst

tiptoe ['tɪptəu] n: on ~ auf Zehenspitzen

tiptop ['tɪp'tɒp] adj: in ~ condition tipptopp, erstklassig

tire [taɪə*] n (US) = tyre ♦ vt, vi ermüden, müde machen/werden; ~**d** adj müde; to be ~**d** of sth etw satt haben; ~**less** adj unermüdlich; ~**lessly** adv unermüdlich; ~**some** adj lästig

tiring ['taɪərɪŋ] adj ermüdend

tissue ['tɪʃuː] n Gewebe nt; (paper handkerchief) Papiertaschentuch nt; ~ **paper** n Seidenpapier nt

tit [tɪt] n (bird) Meise f; ~ **for tat** wie du mir, so ich dir

titbit ['tɪtbɪt] (US tidbit) n Leckerbissen m

titillate ['tɪtɪleɪt] vt kitzeln

titivate ['tɪtɪveɪt] vt schniegeln

title ['taɪtl] n Titel m; ~ **deed** n Eigentumsurkunde f; ~ **role** n Hauptrolle f

titter ['tɪtə*] vi kichern

titular ['tɪtjʊlə*] adj (in name only) nominell

TM abbr (= trademark) Wz

to [tuː, tə] prep 1 (direction) zu, nach; I go to France/school ich gehe nach Frankreich/zur Schule; to the left nach links

2 (as far as) bis

3 (with expressions of time) vor; a quarter to 5 Viertel vor 5

4 (for, of) für; secretary to the director Sekretärin des Directors

5 (expressing indirect object): to give sth to sb jdm etw geben; to talk to sb mit jdm sprechen; I sold it to a friend ich habe es einem Freund verkauft

6 (in relation to) zu; 30 miles to the gallon 30 Meilen pro Gallone

7 (purpose, result): to my surprise zu meiner Überraschung

♦ with vb 1 (infin): to go/eat gehen/essen; to want to do sth etw tun wollen; to try/start to do sth versuchen/anfangen, etw zu tun; he has a lot to lose er hat viel zu verlieren

2 (with vb omitted): I don't want to ich will (es) nicht

3 (purpose, result) um; I did it to help you ich tat es, um dir zu helfen

4 (after adj etc): ready to use gebrauchsfertig; too old/young to ... zu alt/jung, um ... zu ...

♦ adv: push/pull the door to die Tür zuschieben/zuziehen

toad [təud] n Kröte f; ~**stool** n Giftpilz m

toast [təust] n (bread) Toast m; (drinking) Trinkspruch m ♦ vt trinken auf +acc; (bread) toasten; (warm) wärmen; ~**er** n Toaster m

tobacco [tə'bækəu] n Tabak m; ~**nist** [tə'bækənɪst] n Tabakhändler m; ~**nist's (shop)** n Tabakladen m

toboggan [tə'bɒgən] n (Rodel)schlitten m

today [tə'deɪ] adv heute; (at the present time) heutzutage

toddler ['tɒdlə*] n Kleinkind nt

toddy ['tɔdɪ] n (Whisky)grog m

to-do [tə'duː] n Theater nt

toe [təu] n Zehe f; (of sock, shoe) Spitze f ♦ vt: to ~ the line (fig) sich einfügen; ~nail n Zehennagel m

toffee ['tɔfɪ] n Sahnebonbon nt; ~apple (BRIT) n kandierte(r) Apfel m

together [tə'geðə*] adv zusammen; (at the same time) gleichzeitig; ~with zusammen mit; gleichzeitig mit; ~ness n (company) Beisammensein n

toil [tɔɪl] n harte Arbeit f, Plackerei f ♦ vi sich abmühen, sich plagen

toilet ['tɔɪlət] n Toilette f ♦ cpd Toiletten-; ~ bag n Waschbeutel m; ~ paper n Toilettenpapier nt; ~ries ['tɔɪlətrɪz] npl Toilettenartikel pl; ~roll n Rolle f Toilettenpapier; ~water n Toilettenwasser nt

token ['təukən] n Zeichen nt; (gift ~) Gutschein m; book/record ~ (BRIT) Bücher-/Plattengutschein m

Tokyo ['təukjəu] n Tokio nt

told [təuld] pt, pp of tell

tolerable ['tɔlərəbl] (bearable) erträglich; (fairly good) leidlich

tolerant ['tɔlərnt] adj: be ~ (of) vertragen +acc

tolerate ['tɔləreɪt] vt dulden; (noise) ertragen

toll [təul] n Gebühr f ♦ vi (bell) läuten

tomato [tə'mɑːtəu] (pl ~es) n Tomate f

tomb [tuːm] n Grab(mal) nt

tomboy ['tɔmbɔɪ] n Wildfang m

tombstone ['tuːmstəun] n Grabstein m

tomcat ['tɔmkæt] n Kater m

tomorrow [tə'mɔrəu] n Morgen nt ♦ adv morgen; **the day after** ~ übermorgen; ~ **morning** morgen früh; **a week** ~ morgen in einer Woche

ton [tʌn] n Tonne f (BRIT = 1016kg; US = 907kg); (NAUT: also: register ~) Registertonne f; ~s of (inf) Unmenge von

tone [təun] n Ton m; ~ **down** vt

(criticism ...
ours) ...
bringen; ...
(fig ...

tongs [tɔŋz ...
Lockenstab ...

tongue [tʌŋ ...
Sprache f; wi...
haft; ~-tied ...
~-twister n Zu...

tonic ['tɔnɪk] n (...ED) Stärkungsmittel nt; (drink) Tonic n

tonight [tə'naɪt] adv heute abend

tonsil ['tɔnsl] n Mandel f; ~**litis** [tɔnsɪ'laɪtɪs] n Mandelentzündung f

too [tuː] adv zu; (also) auch; ~ **bad!** Pech!; ~ **many** zu viele

took [tuk] pt of take

tool [tuːl] n (also fig) Werkzeug nt; ~**box** n Werkzeugkasten m

toot [tuːt] n Hupen nt ♦ vi tuten; (AUT) hupen

tooth [tuːθ] (pl **teeth**) n Zahn m; ~**ache** n Zahnschmerzen pl, Zahnweh nt; ~**brush** n Zahnbürste f; ~**paste** n Zahnpasta f; ~**pick** n Zahnstocher m

top [tɔp] n Spitze f; (of mountain) Gipfel m; (of tree) Wipfel m; (toy) Kreisel m; (~ gear) vierte(r)/fünfte(r) Gang m ♦ adj oberste(r, s) ♦ vt (list) an erster Stelle stehen auf +dat; **on** ~ **of** oben auf +dat; **from** ~ **to bottom** von oben bis unten; ~ **off** (US) vt auffüllen; ~ **up** vt auffüllen; ~ **floor** n oberste(s) Stockwerk nt; ~ **hat** n Zylinder m; ~-**heavy** adj kopflastig

topic ['tɔpɪk] n Thema nt, Gesprächsgegenstand m; ~**al** adj aktuell

topless ['tɔpləs] adj (bather etc) oben ohne

top-level ['tɔp'levl] adj auf höchster Ebene

topmost ['tɔpməust] adj oberste(r, s)

topple ['tɔpl] vt, vi stürzen, kippen

top-secret ['tɔp'siːkrɪt] adj streng geheim

...ops'tɜːvɪ] adv durch-
...tʃ] n (BRIT: ELEC) Ta-
...ampe f; (with flame) Fackel f
..e [tɔːʳ] pt of tear¹

...rment [n 'tɔːment, vb tɔː'ment] n
Qual f ♦ vt (distress) quälen
torn [tɔːn] pp of tear¹ ♦ adj hin- und
hergerissen
torrent ['tɔrənt] n Sturzbach m; ~**ial**
[tə'renʃəl] adj wolkenbruchartig
torrid ['tɔrɪd] adj heiß
tortoise ['tɔːtəs] n Schildkröte f;
~**shell** ['tɔːtəʃel] n Schildpatt m
tortuous ['tɔːtjuəs] adj gewunden
torture ['tɔːtʃəʳ] n Folter f ♦ vt fol-
tern
Tory ['tɔːrɪ] (BRIT) n (POL) Tory m
♦ adj Tory-, konservativ
toss [tɔs] vt schleudern; to ~ a coin
or to ~ up for sth etw mit einer
Münze entscheiden; to ~ and turn
(in bed) sich hin und her werfen
tot [tɔt] n (small quantity) bißchen
nt; (small child) Knirps m
total ['təutl] n Gesamtheit f; (money)
Endsumme f ♦ adj Gesamt-, total ♦
vt (add up) zusammenzählen; (a-
mount to) sich belaufen auf
totalitarian [təutælɪ'tɛərɪən] adj to-
talitär
totally ['təutəlɪ] adv total
totter ['tɔtəʳ] vi wanken, schwanken
touch [tʌtʃ] n Berührung f; (sense of
feeling) Tastsinn m ♦ vt (feel) berühren; (come against) leicht anstoßen; (emotionally) rühren; a ~ of
(fig) eine Spur von; to get in ~
with sb sich mit jdm in Verbindung
setzen; to lose ~ (friends) Kontakt
verlieren; ~ **on** vt fus (topic) berühren ♦ vt, erwähnen; ~ **up** vt
(paint) auffrischen; ~**-and-go** adj
riskant, knapp; ~**down** n Landen nt,
Niedergehen nt; ~**ed** adj (moved)
gerührt; ~**ing** adj rührend; ~**line** n
Seitenlinie f; ~**sensitive screen** n
(COMPUT) berührungsempfindlicher
Bildschirm m; ~**y** adj empfindlich,
reizbar

tough [tʌf] adj zäh; (difficult)
schwierig ♦ n Schläger(typ) m; ~**en**
vt zäh machen; (make strong) abhärten
toupee ['tuːpeɪ] n Toupet nt
tour [tuəʳ] n Tour f ♦ vi umherreisen; (THEAT) auf Tour sein; auf
Tour gehen; ~**ing** n Umherreisen nt;
(THEAT) Tournee f
tourism ['tuərɪzm] n Fremdenver-
kehr m, Tourismus m
tourist ['tuərɪst] n Tourist(in) m(f) ♦
cpd (class) Touristen-; ~ **office** n
Verkehrsamt nt
tournament ['tuənəmənt] n Tour-
nier nt
tousled ['tauzld] adj zerzaust
tout [taut] vi: to ~ for auf Kunden-
fang gehen für ♦ n: ticket ~ Kun-
denschlepper(in) m(f)
tow [təu] vt (ab)schleppen; **on**
(BRIT) or **in** (US) ~ (AUT) im
Schlepp
toward(s) [tə'wɔːd(z)] prep (with
time) gegen; (in direction of) nach
towel ['tauəl] n Handtuch nt; ~**ing**
n (fabric) Frottee m or nt; ~ **rack**
(US) n Handtuchstange f; ~ **rail**
n Handtuchstange f
tower ['tauəʳ] n Turm m; ~ **block**
(BRIT) n Hochhaus nt; ~**ing** adj
hochragend
town [taun] n Stadt f; to go to ~
(fig) sich ins Zeug legen; ~ **centre** n
Stadtzentrum nt; ~ **clerk** n Stadt-
direktor m; ~ **council** n Stadtrat m;
~ **hall** n Rathaus nt; ~ **plan** n
Stadtplan m; ~ **planning** n
Stadtplanung f
towrope ['təurəup] n Abschlepptau
nt
tow truck (US) n (breakdown lorry) Abschleppwagen m
toxic ['tɔksɪk] adj giftig, Gift-
toy [tɔɪ] n Spielzeug nt; ~ **with** vt
fus spielen mit; ~**shop** n Spielwaren-
geschäft nt
trace [treɪs] n Spur f ♦ vt (follow a
course) nachspüren +dat; (find out)
aufspüren; (copy) durchpausen; **tra-**

cing paper n Pauspapier nt

track [træk] n (mark) Spur f; (path)
Weg m; (race-) Rennbahn f;
(RAIL) Gleis nt ♦ vt verfolgen; to
keep ~ of sb jdn im Auge behalten;
~ down vt aufspüren; ~**suit** n Trainingsanzug m

tract [trækt] n (of land) Gebiet nt;
(booklet) Traktat nt

traction ['trækʃən] n (power) Zugkraft f; (AUT: grip) Bodenhaftung f;
(MED): in ~ im Streckverband

trade [treɪd] n (commerce) Handel
m; (business) Geschäft nt, Gewerbe
nt; (people) Geschäftsleute pl; (skilled manual work) Handwerk nt ♦ vi:
to ~ (in) handeln (mit) ♦ vt tauschen; ~ in vt in Zahlung geben; ~
fair n Messe nt; ~**in price** n Preis
m, zu dem eine in Zahlung genommen
wird; ~**mark** n Warenzeichen nt; ~
name n Handelsbezeichnung f; ~r n
Händler m; ~**sman** (irreg) n (shopkeeper) Geschäftsmann m; (workman) Handwerker m; (delivery man)
Lieferant m; ~ **union** n Gewerkschaft f; ~**unionist** n Gewerkschaftler(in) m(f)

trading ['treɪdɪŋ] n Handel m; ~ **estate** (BRIT) n Industriegelände nt

tradition [trə'dɪʃən] n Tradition f;
~**al** adj traditionell, herkömmlich

traffic ['træfɪk] n Verkehr m; (esp in
drugs): ~ (in) Handel m (mit) ♦ vi:
to ~ in (esp drugs) handeln mit; ~
circle (US) n Kreisverkehr m; ~ **jam**
n Verkehrsstauung f; ~ **lights** npl
Verkehrsampel f; ~ **warden** n ≈
Verkehrspolizist m (ohne amtliche
Befugnisse), Politesse f (ohne amtliche Befugnisse)

tragedy ['trædʒədɪ] n Tragödie f

tragic ['trædʒɪk] adj tragisch

trail [treɪl] n (track) Spur f; (of
smoke) Rauchfahne f; (of dust)
Staubwolke f; (road) Pfad m, Weg m
♦ vt (animal) verfolgen; (person)
folgen +dat; (drag) schleppen ♦ vi
(hang loosely) schleifen; (plants)
sich ranken; (be behind) hinterher

hinken; (SPORT) weit zurückliegen;
(walk) zuckeln; ~ **behind** vi zurückbleiben; ~**er** n Anhänger m;
(US: caravan) Wohnwagen m; (for
film) Vorschau f; ~ **truck** (US) n
Sattelschlepper m

train [treɪn] n Zug m; (of dress)
Schleppe f; (series) Folge f ♦ vt
(teach: person) ausbilden; (: animal) abrichten; (: mind) schulen;
(SPORT) trainieren; (aim) richten ♦
vi (exercise) trainieren; (study) ausgebildet werden; ~ of thought Gedankengang m; to ~ sth on (aim)
etw richten auf +acc; ~**ed** adj (eye)
geschult; (person, voice) ausgebildet;
~**ee** [treɪ'niː] n Lehrling m; Praktikant(in) m(f); ~**er** n (SPORT) Trainer m; Ausbilder m; ~**ing** n (for occupation) Ausbildung f; (SPORT)
Training nt; **in** ~**ing** im Training;
~**ing college** n Pädagogische Hochschule f, Lehrerseminar nt; ~**ing
shoes** npl Turnschuhe pl

traipse [treɪps] vi latschen

trait [treɪ(t)] n Zug m, Merkmal nt

traitor ['treɪtə*] n Verräter m

trajectory [trə'dʒɛktərɪ] n Flugbahn
f

tram [træm] (BRIT) n (also: ~car)
Straßenbahn f

tramp [træmp] n Landstreicher m ♦
vi (walk heavily) stampfen, stapfen;
(travel on foot) wandern

trample ['træmpl] vt (nieder)trampeln ♦ vi herumtrampeln;
to ~ (underfoot) herumtrampeln
auf +dat

tranquil ['træŋkwɪl] adj ruhig, friedlich; ~**lity** (US ~**ity**) n Ruhe f; ~**lizer** (US ~**izer**) n Beruhigungsmittel
nt

transact [træn'zækt] vt abwickeln;
~**ion** [træn'zækʃən] n Abwicklung f;
(piece of business) Geschäft nt,
Transaktion f

transcend [træn'send] vt übersteigen

transcript ['trænskrɪpt] n Abschrift f,
Kopie f; (JUR) Protokoll nt; ~**ion**
[træn'skrɪpʃən] n Transkription f

(product) Abschrift f

transfer [n 'trænsfə*, vt træns'fə:*] n (~ring) Übertragung f; (of business) Umzug m; (being ~red) Versetzung f; (design) Abziehbild nt; (SPORT) Transfer m ♦ vt (business) verlegen; (person) versetzen; (prisoner) überführen; (drawing) übertragen; (money) überweisen; **to ~ the charges** (BRIT: TEL) ein R-Gespräch führen

transform [træns'fɔ:m] vt umwandeln; **~ation** [trænsfə'meiʃən] n Umwandlung f, Verwandlung f; **~er** n (ELEC) Transformator m

transfusion [træns'fju:ʒən] n Blutübertragung f, Transfusion f

transient ['trænziənt] adj kurz(lebig)

transistor [træn'zistə*] n (ELEC) Transistor m; (radio) Transistorradio nt

transit ['trænzit] n: **in ~** unterwegs

transition [træn'ziʃən] n Übergang m; **~al** adj Übergangs-

transit lounge n (at airport etc) Warteraum m

transitory ['trænzitəri] adj vorübergehend

translate [trænz'leit] vt, vi übersetzen

translation [trænz'leiʃən] n Übersetzung f

translator [trænz'leitə*] n Übersetzer(in) m(f)

transmission [trænz'miʃən] n (of information) Übermittlung f; (ELEC, MED, TV) Übertragung f; (AUT) Getriebe nt

transmit [trænz'mit] vt (message) übermitteln; (ELEC, MED, TV) übertragen; **~ter** n Sender m

transparency [træns'pεərənsi] n Durchsichtigkeit f; (BRIT: PHOT) Dia(positiv) nt

transparent [træns'pærənt] adj durchsichtig; (fig) offenkundig

transpire [træns'paiə*] vi (turn out) sich herausstellen; (happen) passieren

transplant [vb træns'plɑ:nt, n 'trænsplɑ:nt] vt umpflanzen; (MED, also fig: person) verpflanzen ♦ n

(MED) Transplantation f; (organ) Transplantat nt

transport [n 'trænspɔ:t, vb træns'pɔ:t] n Transport m, Beförderung f ♦ vt befördern; transportieren; **means of ~** Transportmittel nt; **~ation** [trænspɔ:'teiʃən] n Transport m, Beförderung f; (means) Beförderungsmittel nt; (cost) Transportkosten pl; **~ café** (BRIT) n Fernfahrerlokal nt

transverse ['trænzvə:s] adj Quer-; (position) horizontal; (engine) querliegend

trap [træp] n Falle f; (carriage) zweirädrige(r) Einspänner m; (inf: mouth) Klappe f ♦ vt fangen; (person) in eine Falle locken; **~door** n Falltür f

trappings ['træpiŋz] npl Aufmachung f

trash [træʃ] n (rubbish) Plunder m; (nonsense) Mist m; **~ can** (US) n Mülleimer m

traumatic [trɔ:'mætik] adj traumatisch

travel ['trævl] n Reisen nt ♦ vi reisen ♦ vt (distance) zurücklegen; (country) bereisen; **~s** npl (journeys) Reisen pl; **~ agency** n Reisebüro nt; **~ agent** n Reisebürokaufmann(frau) m(f); **~ler** (US **~er**) n Reisende(r) m; **~ler's cheque** (US **~er's check**) n Reisescheck m; **~ling** (US **~ing**) n Reisen nt; **~ sickness** n Reisekrankheit f

trawler n (NAUT, FISHING) Fischdampfer m, Trawler m

tray [trei] n (tea ~) Tablett nt; (receptacle) Schale f; (for mail) Ablage f

treacherous ['tretʃərəs] adj verräterisch; (road) tückisch

treachery ['tretʃəri] n Verrat m

treacle ['tri:kl] n Sirup m, Melasse f

tread [tred] (pt trod, pp trodden) n Schritt m, Tritt m; (of stair) Stufe f; (on tyre) Profil nt ♦ vi treten; **~ on** vt fus treten auf +acc

treason ['triːzn] n Verrat m

treasure ['treʒə*] n Schatz m ♦ vt schätzen

treasurer ['treʒərə*] n Kassenverwalter m, Schatzmeister m

treasury ['treʒərɪ] n (POL) Finanzministerium nt

treat [triːt] n besondere Freude f ♦ vt (deal with) behandeln; to ~ sb to sth jdm ein Vergnügen spendieren

treatise ['triːtɪz] n Abhandlung f

treatment ['triːtmənt] n Behandlung f

treaty ['triːtɪ] n Vertrag m

treble ['trebl] adj dreifach ♦ vt verdreifachen; ~ **clef** n Violinschlüssel m

tree [triː] n Baum m; ~ **trunk** n Baumstamm m

trek [trek] n Treck m, Zug m; (inf) anstrengender Weg m ♦ vi trecken

trellis ['trelɪs] n Gitter nt; (for gardening) Spalier nt

tremble ['trembl] vi zittern; (ground) beben

trembling ['tremblɪŋ] n Zittern nt ♦ adj zitternd

tremendous [trə'mendəs] adj gewaltig, kolossal; (inf: very good) prima

tremor ['tremə*] n Zittern nt; (of earth) Beben nt

trench [trentʃ] n Graben m; (MIL) Schützengraben m

trend [trend] n Tendenz f; ~**y** (inf) adj modisch

trepidation [trepɪ'deɪʃən] n Beklommenheit f

trespass ['trespəs] vi: to ~ on widerrechtlich betreten; "no ~ing" „Betreten verboten"

tress [tres] n Locke f

trestle ['tresl] n Bock m; ~ **table** n Klapptisch m

trial ['traɪəl] n (JUR) Prozeß m; (test) Versuch m, Probe f; (hardship) Prüfung f; by ~ **and error** durch Ausprobieren

triangle ['traɪæŋgl] n Dreieck nt; (MUS) Triangel f

triangular [traɪ'æŋgjʊlə*] adj dreieckig

tribal ['traɪbəl] adj Stammes-

tribe [traɪb] n Stamm m; ~**sman** (irreg) n Stammesangehörige(r) m

tribulation [trɪbjʊ'leɪʃən] n Not f, Mühsal f

tribunal [traɪ'bjuːnl] n Gericht nt; (inquiry) Untersuchungsausschuß m

tributary ['trɪbjʊtərɪ] n Nebenfluß m

tribute ['trɪbjuːt] n (admiration) Zeichen nt der Hochachtung; to pay ~ to sb/sth jdm/einer Sache Tribut zollen

trick [trɪk] n Trick m; (CARDS) Stich m ♦ vt überlisten, beschwindeln; to play a ~ on sb jdm einen Streich spielen; that should do the ~ das müßte eigentlich klappen; ~**ery** n Tricks pl

trickle ['trɪkl] n Tröpfeln nt; (small river) Rinnsal nt ♦ vi tröpfeln; (seep) sickern

tricky ['trɪkɪ] adj (problem) schwierig; (situation) kitzlig

tricycle ['traɪsɪkl] n Dreirad nt

trifle ['traɪfl] n Kleinigkeit f; (COOK) Trifle m ♦ adv: a ~ ... ein bißchen ...

trifling ['traɪflɪŋ] adj geringfügig

trigger ['trɪgə*] n Drücker m; ~ **off** vt auslösen

trim [trɪm] adj gepflegt; (figure) schlank ♦ n (state) Verfassung f; (embellishment, on car) Verzierung f ♦ vt (clip) schneiden; (trees) stutzen; (decorate) besetzen; (sails) trimmen; ~**mings** npl (decorations) Verzierung f, Verzierungen pl; (extras) Zubehör nt

Trinity ['trɪnɪtɪ] n: the ~ die Dreieinigkeit f

trinket ['trɪŋkɪt] n kleine(s) Schmuckstück nt

trip [trɪp] n (kurze) Reise f; (outing) Ausflug m; (stumble) Stolpern nt ♦ vi (walk quickly) trippeln; (stumble) stolpern; on a ~ auf Reisen; ~ **up** vi stolpern; (fig) stolpern, einen Fehler machen ♦ vt zu Fall bringen; (fig) hereinlegen

tripe [traɪp] n (food) Kutteln pl; (rubbish) Mist m

triple ['trɪpl] adj dreifach

triplets ['trɪplɪts] npl Drillinge pl

triplicate ['trɪplɪkət] n: **in ~** in dreifacher Ausfertigung

tripod ['traɪpɔd] n (PHOT) Stativ nt

trite [traɪt] adj banal

triumph ['traɪʌmf] n Triumph m ♦ vi: **to ~ (over)** triumphieren (über +acc); **~ant** [traɪ'ʌmfənt] adj triumphierend

trivia ['trɪvɪə] npl Trivialitäten pl

trivial ['trɪvɪəl] adj gering(fügig), trivial

trod [trɔd] pt of tread; **~den** ['trɔdn] pp of tread

trolley ['trɔlɪ] n Handwagen m; (in shop) Einkaufswagen; (for luggage) Kofferkuli m; (table) Teewagen m; **~ bus** n Oberleitungsbus m, Obus m

trombone [trɔm'bəʊn] n Posaune f

troop [truːp] n Schar f; (MIL) Trupp m; **~s** npl Truppen pl; **~ in/out** vi hinein-/hinausströmen; **~ing the colour** n (ceremony) Fahnenparade f

trophy ['trəʊfɪ] n Trophäe f

tropic ['trɔpɪk] n Wendekreis m; **~al** adj tropisch

trot [trɔt] n Trott m ♦ vi trotten; **on the ~** (BRIT: fig: inf) in einer Tour

trouble ['trʌbl] n (problems) Ärger m; (worry) Sorge f; (in country, industry) Unruhen pl; (effort) Mühe f; (MED): **stomach ~** Magenbeschwerden pl ♦ vt (disturb) stören; **~s** npl (POL etc) Unruhen pl; **to ~ to do sth** sich bemühen, etw zu tun; **to be in ~** Probleme or Ärger haben; **to go to the ~ of doing sth** sich die Mühe machen, etw zu tun; **what's the ~?** was ist los?; (to sick person) wo fehlt's?; **~d** adj (person) beunruhigt; (country) geplagt; **~-free** adj sorglos; **~maker** n Unruhestifter m; **~shooter** n Vermittler m; **~some** adj lästig, unangenehm; (child) schwierig

trough [trɔf] n (vessel) Trog m; (channel) Rinne f, Kanal m; (MET)

Tief nt

trounce [traʊns] vt (esp SPORT) vernichtend schlagen

trousers ['traʊzəz] npl Hose f

trout [traʊt] n Forelle f

trowel ['traʊəl] n Kelle f

truant ['truːənt] n: **to play ~** (BRIT) (die Schule) schwänzen

truce [truːs] n Waffenstillstand m

truck [trʌk] n Lastwagen m; (RAIL) offene(r) Güterwagen m; **~ driver** n Lastwagenfahrer m; **~ farm** (US) n Gemüsegärtnerei f

truculent ['trʌkjʊlənt] adj trotzig

trudge [trʌdʒ] vi sich (mühselig) dahinschleppen

true [truː] adj (exact) wahr; (genuine) echt; (friend) treu

truffle ['trʌfl] n Trüffel f or m

truly ['truːlɪ] adv wirklich; **yours ~** Ihr sehr ergebener

trump [trʌmp] n (CARDS) Trumpf m; **~ed-up** adj erfunden

trumpet ['trʌmpɪt] n Trompete f

truncheon ['trʌntʃən] n Gummiknüppel m

trundle ['trʌndl] vt schieben ♦ vi: **to ~ along** entlangrollen

trunk [trʌŋk] n (of tree) (Baum)stamm m; (ANAT) Rumpf m; (box) Truhe f, Überseekoffer m; (of elephant) Rüssel m; (US: AUT) Kofferraum m; **~s** npl (also: swimming ~s) Badehose f

truss [trʌs] n (MED) Bruchband nt ♦ vt (also: ~ up) fesseln

trust [trʌst] n (confidence) Vertrauen nt; (for property etc) Treuhandvermögen nt ♦ vt (rely on) vertrauen +dat (acc), sich verlassen auf +acc; (hope) hoffen; (entrust): **to ~ sth to sb** jdm etw anvertrauen; **~ed** adj treu; **~ee** [trʌs'tiː] n Vermögensverwalter m; **~ful** adj vertrauensvoll; **~ing** adj vertrauensvoll; **~worthy** adj vertrauenswürdig; (account) glaubwürdig

truth [truːθ, pl truːðz] n Wahrheit f; **~ful** adj ehrlich

try [traɪ] n Versuch m ♦ vt (attempt)

versuchen; (test) (aus)probieren; (JUR: person) unter Anklage stellen; (: case) verhandeln; (courage, patience) auf die Probe stellen ♦ vi (make effort) versuchen, sich bemühen; **to have a ~** es versuchen; **to ~ to do sth** versuchen, etw zu tun; **~ on** vt (dress) anprobieren; (hat) aufprobieren; **~ out** vt ausprobieren; **~ing** adj schwierig

T-shirt ['ti:ʃɜːt] n T-shirt nt

T-square ['tiːskweə*] n Reißschiene f

tub [tʌb] n Wanne f, Kübel m; (for margarine etc) Becher m

tubby ['tʌbɪ] adj rundlich

tube [tjuːb] n (pipe) Röhre f, Rohr nt; (for toothpaste etc) Tube f; (in London) U-Bahn f; (AUT: for tyre) Schlauch m; **~ station** n (in London) U-Bahnstation f

tubing ['tjuːbɪŋ] n Schlauch m

tubular ['tjuːbjʊlə*] adj röhrenförmig

TUC (BRIT) n abbr = Trades Union Congress

tuck [tʌk] n (fold) Falte f, Einschlag m ♦ vt (put) stecken; (gather) fälteln, einschlagen; **~ away** vt wegstecken; **~ in** vt hineinstecken; (blanket etc) feststecken; (person) zudecken ♦ vi (eat) hineinhauen, zulangen; **~ up** vt (child) warm zudecken; **~ shop** n Süßwarenladen m

Tuesday ['tjuːzdɪ] n Dienstag m

tuft [tʌft] n Büschel m

tug [tʌg] n (jerk) Zerren nt, Ruck m; (NAUT) Schleppdampfer m ♦ vt, vi zerren, ziehen; (boat) schleppen; **~-of-war** f n Tauziehen nt

tuition [tjuːˈɪʃən] n (BRIT) Unterricht m; (: private ~) Privatunterricht m; (US: school fees) Schulgeld nt

tulip ['tjuːlɪp] n Tulpe f

tumble ['tʌmbl] n (fall) Sturz m ♦ vi fallen, stürzen; **to ~ to** vt fus kapieren; **~down** adj baufällig; **~ dryer** (BRIT) n Trockner m; **~r** ['tʌmblə*] n (glass) Trinkglas nt

tummy ['tʌmɪ] n (inf) Bauch m

tumour ['tjuːmə*] n (US tumor) n Ge-

schwulst f, Tumor m

tumultuous [tjuːˈmʌltjʊəs] adj (welcome, applause etc) stürmisch

tuna ['tjuːnə] n Thunfisch m

tune [tjuːn] n Melodie f ♦ vt (MUS) stimmen; (AUT) richtig einstellen; **to sing in ~/out of ~** richtig/falsch singen; **to be out of ~ with** nicht harmonieren mit; **~ in** vi einschalten; **~ up** vi (MUS) stimmen; **~ful** adj melodisch; **~r** n (person) (Instrumenten)stimmer m; (part of radio) Tuner m; **piano ~r** Klavierstimmer(in) m(f)

tunic ['tjuːnɪk] n Waffenrock m; (loose garment) lange Bluse f

tuning ['tjuːnɪŋ] n (RAD, AUT) Einstellen nt; (MUS) Stimmen nt; **~ fork** n Stimmgabel f

Tunisia [tjuːˈnɪzɪə] n Tunesien nt

tunnel ['tʌnl] n Tunnel m, Unterführung f ♦ vi einen Tunnel anlegen

turbulent ['tɜːbjʊlənt] adj stürmisch

tureen [tjʊˈriːn] n Terrine f

turf [tɜːf] n Rasen m; (piece) Sode f ♦ vt mit Grassoden belegen; **~ out** (inf) vt rauswerfen

turgid ['tɜːdʒɪd] adj geschwollen

Turk [tɜːk] n Türke m, Türkin f

Turkey ['tɜːkɪ] n Türkei f

turkey ['tɜːkɪ] n Puter m, Truthahn m

Turkish ['tɜːkɪʃ] adj türkisch ♦ n (LING) Türkisch nt

turmoil ['tɜːmɔɪl] n Aufruhr m, Tumult m

turn [tɜːn] n (rotation) (Um)drehung f; (performance) (Programm)nummer f; (MED) Schock m ♦ vt (rotate) drehen; (change position of) umdrehen, wenden; (page) umblättern; (transform): **to ~ sth into sth** etw in etw acc verwandeln; (direct) zuwenden ♦ vi (rotate) sich drehen; (change direction: in car) abbiegen; (: wind) drehen; **~ round** umdrehen, wenden; (become) werden; (leaves) sich verfärben; (milk) sauer werden; (weather) umschlagen; **to do sb a good ~** jdm et-

was Gutes tun; **it's your ~** du bist
dran *or* an der Reihe; **in ~, by ~s**
abwechselnd; **to take ~s** sich abwechseln; **it gave me quite a ~**
das hat mich schön erschreckt; **"no
left ~"** (AUT) "Linksabbiegen verboten"; **~ away** vi sich abwenden;
~ back vt umdrehen; (person) zurückschicken; (clock) zurückstellen
♦ vi umkehren; **~ down** vt (refuse)
ablehnen; (fold down) umschlagen;
~ in vi (to bed) ins Bett gehen ♦
vt (fold inwards) einwärts biegen; **~
off** vi abbiegen ♦ vt ausschalten;
(tap) zudrehen; (machine, electricity) abstellen; **~ on** vt (light) einschalten, einschalten; (tap) aufdrehen; (machine) anstellen; **~ out** vt
(prove to be) sich erweisen; (people)
sich entwickeln ♦ vt (light) ausschalten; (gas) abstellen; (produce) produzieren; **how did the cake ~ out?**
wie ist der Kuchen geworden?; **~
round** vi (person, vehicle) sich herumdrehen; (rotate) sich drehen; **~
up** vi auftauchen; (happen) passieren, sich ereignen ♦ vt (collar) hoch-
klappen, hochstellen; (nose)
rümpfen; (increase: radio) lauter
stellen; (: heat) höher drehen; **~ing
point** n Wendepunkt m

turnip ['tɜːnɪp] n Steckrübe f

turnout ['tɜːnaʊt] n (Besucher)zahl
f; (COMM) Produktion f

turnover ['tɜːnəʊvə*] n Umsatz m;
(of staff) Wechsel m

turnpike ['tɜːnpaɪk] (US) n ge-
bührenpflichtige Straße f

turnstile ['tɜːnstaɪl] n Drehkreuz nt

turntable ['tɜːnteɪbl] n (of record
player) Plattenteller m; (RAIL)
Drehscheibe f

turn-up ['tɜːnʌp] (BRIT) n (on trousers) Aufschlag m

turpentine ['tɜːpəntaɪn] n Terpentin
nt

turquoise ['tɜːkwɔɪz] n (gem) Türkis
m; (colour) Türkis nt ♦ adj
türkisfarben

turret ['tʌrɪt] n Turm m

turtle ['tɜːtl] n Schildkröte f; **~ neck
(sweater)** n Pullover m mit Schild-
krötkragen m

tusk [tʌsk] n Stoßzahn m

tussle ['tʌsl] n Balgerei f

tutor ['tjuːtə*] n (teacher) Privatleh-
rer m; (college instructor) Tutor m;
~ial [tjuː'tɔːrɪəl] n (UNIV) Kollo-
quium nt, Seminarübung f

tuxedo [tʌk'siːdəʊ] (US) n Smoking
m

TV ['tiː'viː] n abbr (= television) TV
nt

twang [twæŋ] n scharfe(r) Ton m;
(of voice) Näseln nt

tweezers ['twiːzəz] npl Pinzette f

twelfth [twelfθ] adj zwölfte(r, s)

twelve [twelv] num zwölf; **at ~
o'clock** um 12 Uhr; (midday) um 12 Uhr; (midnight) um Null Uhr

twentieth ['twentɪɪθ] adj zwanzig-
ste(r, s)

twenty ['twentɪ] num zwanzig

twice [twaɪs] adv zweimal; **~ as
much** doppelt soviel

twiddle ['twɪdl] vt, vi: **to ~ (with)**
sth an etw dat herumdrehen; **to ~
one's thumbs** (fig) Däumchen drehen

twig [twɪg] n dünne(r) Zweig m ♦ vt
(inf) kapieren, merken

twilight ['twaɪlaɪt] n Zwielicht nt

twin [twɪn] n Zwilling m ♦ adj
Zwillings-; (very similar) Doppel-
♦ vt (towns) zu Partnerstädten machen; **~-bedded room** n Zimmer nt
mit zwei Einzelbetten

twine [twaɪn] n Bindfaden m ♦ vi
(plants) sich ranken

twinge [twɪndʒ] n stechende(r)
Schmerz m, Stechen nt

twinkle ['twɪŋkl] n Funkeln nt, Blitzen nt ♦ vi funkeln

twirl [twɜːl] n Wirbel m ♦ vt, vi (herum)wirbeln

twist [twɪst] n (/) Drehung f;
(bend) Kurve f ♦ vt (turn) drehen;
(make crooked) verbiegen; (distort)
verdrehen ♦ vi (wind) sich winden

(*curve*) sich winden

twit [twɪt] (*inf*) n Idiot m

twitch [twɪtʃ] n Zucken nt ♦ vi zucken

two [tu:] num zwei; **to put ~ and ~ together** seine Schlüsse ziehen; **~door** adj zweitürig; **~faced** adj falsch; **~fold** adj, adv zweifach, doppelt; **to increase ~fold** verdoppeln; **~piece** n **~piece (suit)** n Zweiteiler m; **~piece (swimsuit)** n zweiteilige(r) Badeanzug m; **~seater** n (plane, car) Zweisitzer m; **~some** n Paar nt; **~way** adj (traffic) Gegen-

tycoon [taɪˈkuːn] n (business) ~ (Industrie)magnat m

type [taɪp] n Typ m, Art f; (PRINT) Type f ♦ vt, vi maschineschreiben, tippen; **~cast** adj (THEAT, TV) auf eine Rolle festgelegt; **~face** n Schrift f; **~script** n maschinegeschriebene(r) Text m; **~writer** n Schreibmaschine f; **~written** adj maschinegeschrieben

typhoid [ˈtaɪfɔɪd] n Typhus m

typical [ˈtɪpɪkl] adj: ~ (**of**) typisch (für)

typify [ˈtɪpɪfaɪ] vt typisch sein für

typing [ˈtaɪpɪŋ] n Maschineschreiben nt

typist [ˈtaɪpɪst] n Maschineschreiber(in) m(f), Tippse f (inf)

tyrant [ˈtaɪərnt] n Tyrann m

tyre [taɪə*] (US **tire**) n Reifen m; **~ pressure** n Reifendruck m

U

U-bend [ˈjuːˈbend] n (in pipe) U-Bogen m

ubiquitous [juːˈbɪkwɪtəs] adj überall zu findend; allgegenwärtig

udder [ˈʌdə*] n Euter nt

UFO [ˈjuːfəʊ] n abbr (= unidentified flying object) UFO nt

ugh [əːh] excl hu

ugliness [ˈʌɡlɪnɪs] n Häßlichkeit f

ugly [ˈʌɡlɪ] adj häßlich; (bad) böse, schlimm

UK n abbr = United Kingdom

ulcer [ˈʌlsə*] n Geschwür nt

Ulster [ˈʌlstə*] n Ulster nt

ulterior [ʌlˈtɪərɪə*] adj: ~ **motive** Hintergedanke m

ultimate [ˈʌltɪmət] adj äußerste(r, s), allerletzte(r, s); **~ly** adv schließlich, letzten Endes

ultrasound [ˈʌltrəˈsaʊnd] n (MED) Ultraschall m

umbilical cord [ʌmˈbɪlɪkl] n Nabelschnur f

umbrella [ʌmˈbrelə] n Schirm m

umpire [ˈʌmpaɪə*] n Schiedsrichter m ♦ vt, vi schiedsrichtern

umpteenth [ʌmpˈtiːnθ] (inf) num zig; **for the ~ time** zum X-ten Mal

UN n abbr = United Nations

unable [ʌnˈeɪbl] adj: **to be ~ to do sth** etw nicht tun können

unaccompanied [ˈʌnəˈkʌmpənɪd] adj ohne Begleitung

unaccountably [ˈʌnəˈkaʊntəblɪ] adv unerklärlich

unaccustomed [ˈʌnəˈkʌstəmd] adj nicht gewöhnt; (unusual) ungewohnt; **~ to** nicht gewöhnt an +acc

unanimous [juːˈnænɪməs] adj einmütig; (vote) einstimmig; **~ly** adv einmütig; einstimmig

unarmed [ʌnˈɑːmd] adj unbewaffnet

unashamed [ˈʌnəˈʃeɪmd] adj schamlos

unassuming [ˈʌnəˈsjuːmɪŋ] adj bescheiden

unattached [ˈʌnəˈtætʃt] adj ungebunden

unattended [ˈʌnəˈtendɪd] adj (person) unbeaufsichtigt; (thing) unbewacht

unauthorized [ʌnˈɔːθəraɪzd] adj unbefugt

unavoidable [ˈʌnəˈvɔɪdəbl] adj unvermeidlich

unaware [ˈʌnəˈwɛə*] adj: **to be ~ of sth** sich dat einer Sache gen nicht bewußt sein; **~s** adv unversehens

unbalanced [ʌnˈbælənst] adj unausgeglichen; (mentally) gestört

unbearable [ʌn'bɛərəbl] *adj* unerträglich

unbeatable ['ʌn'bi:təbl] *adj* unschlagbar

unbeknown(st) ['ʌnbɪ'nəʊn(st)] *adv*: ~ to me ohne mein Wissen

unbelievable [ʌnbɪ'li:vəbl] *adj* unglaublich

unbend ['ʌn'bend] (*irreg: like* bend) *vt* geradebiegen ♦ *vi* aus sich herausgehen

unbias(s)ed [ʌn'baɪəst] *adj* unparteiisch

unbreakable [ʌn'breɪkəbl] *adj* unzerbrechlich

unbridled [ʌn'braɪdld] *adj* ungezügelt

unbroken ['ʌn'brəʊkən] *adj* (*period*) ununterbrochen; (*spirit*) ungebrochen; (*record*) unübertroffen

unburden [ʌn'bɜ:dn] *vt*: to ~ o.s. (jdm) sein Herz ausschütten

unbutton ['ʌn'bʌtn] *vt* aufknöpfen

uncalled-for [ʌn'kɔ:ldfɔ:*] *adj* unnötig

uncanny [ʌn'kænɪ] *adj* unheimlich

unceasing [ʌn'si:sɪŋ] *adj* unaufhörlich

unceremonious [ʌnserɪ'məʊnɪəs] *adj* (*abrupt, rude*) brüsk; (*exit, departure*) überstürzt

uncertain [ʌn'sɜ:tn] *adj* unsicher; (*doubtful*) ungewiß; (*unreliable*) unbeständig; (*vague*) undeutlich, vag(e); ~ty *n* Ungewißheit *f*

unchanged ['ʌn'tʃeɪndʒd] *adj* unverändert

unchecked ['ʌn'tʃekt] *adj* ungeprüft; (*not stopped: advance*) ungehindert

uncivilized ['ʌn'sɪvɪlaɪzd] *adj* unzivilisiert

uncle ['ʌŋkl] *n* Onkel *m*

uncomfortable [ʌn'kʌmfətəbl] *adj* unbequem, ungemütlich

uncommon [ʌn'kɒmən] *adj* ungewöhnlich; (*outstanding*) außergewöhnlich

uncompromising [ʌn'kɒmprəmaɪzɪŋ] *adj* kompromißlos, unnachgiebig

unconcerned [ʌnkən'sɜ:nd] *adj* unbekümmert; (*indifferent*) gleichgültig

unconditional ['ʌnkən'dɪʃənl] *adj* bedingungslos

uncongenial ['ʌnkən'dʒi:nɪəl] *adj* unangenehm

unconscious [ʌn'kɒnʃəs] *adj* (*MED*) bewußtlos; (*not meant*) unbeabsichtigt ♦ *n*: the ~ das Unbewußte; ~**ly** *adv* unbewußt

uncontrollable [ʌnkən'trəʊləbl] *adj* unkontrollierbar, unbändig

unconventional [ʌnkən'venʃənl] *adj* unkonventionell

uncouth [ʌn'ku:θ] *adj* grob

uncover [ʌn'kʌvə*] *vt* aufdecken

undecided ['ʌndɪ'saɪdɪd] *adj* unschlüssig

undeniable [ʌndɪ'naɪəbl] *adj* unleugbar

under ['ʌndə*] *prep* unter ♦ *adv* darunter; ~ there da drunter; ~ repair in Reparatur; ~**age** [ʌndər'eɪdʒ] *adj* minderjährig

undercarriage ['ʌndəkærɪdʒ] (*BRIT*) *n* (*AVIAT*) Fahrgestell *nt*

undercharge [ʌndə'tʃɑ:dʒ] *vt*: to ~ sb jdm zu wenig berechnen

underclothes ['ʌndəkləʊðz] *npl* Unterwäsche *f*

undercoat ['ʌndəkəʊt] *n* (*paint*) Grundierung *f*

undercover ['ʌndəkʌvə*] *adj* Geheim-

undercurrent ['ʌndəkʌrənt] *n* Unterströmung *f*

undercut ['ʌndəkʌt] (*irreg: like* cut) *vt* unterbieten

underdeveloped ['ʌndədɪ'veləpt] *adj* Entwicklungs-, unterentwickelt

underdog ['ʌndədɒg] *n* Unterlegene(r) *mf*

underdone ['ʌndə'dʌn] *adj* (*COOK*) nicht gar, nicht durchgebraten

underestimate ['ʌndər'estɪmeɪt] *vt* unterschätzen

underexposed ['ʌndərɪks'pəʊzd]

adj unterbelichtet

underfed [ˈʌndəˈfed] *adj* unterernährt

underfoot [ˈʌndəˈfut] *adv* am Boden

undergo [ˈʌndəˈgəu] (*irreg: like* go) *vt* (*experience*) durchmachen; (*operation*, *test*) sich unterziehen +*dat*

undergraduate [ˈʌndəˈgrædjuət] *n* Student *m(f)*

underground [ˈʌndəgraund] *n* U-Bahn *f* ♦ *adj* Untergrund-

undergrowth [ˈʌndəgrəuθ] *n* Gestrüpp *nt*, Unterholz *nt*

underhand(ed) [ˈʌndəˈhænd(id)] *adj* hinterhältig

underlie [ʌndəˈlai] (*irreg: like* lie) *vt* (*form the basis of*) zugrundeliegen +*dat*

underline [ʌndəˈlain] *vt* unterstreichen; (*emphasize*) betonen

underling [ˈʌndəliŋ] *n* Handlanger *m*

undermine [ʌndəˈmain] *vt* untergraben

underneath [ʌndəˈniːθ] *adv* darunter ♦ *prep* unter

underpaid [ˈʌndəˈpeid] *adj* unterbezahlt

underpants [ˈʌndəpænts] *npl* Unterhose *f*

underpass [ˈʌndəpɑːs] (*BRIT*) *n* Unterführung *f*

underprivileged [ˈʌndəˈprivilidʒd] *adj* benachteiligt, unterprivilegiert

underrate [ˈʌndəˈreit] *vt* unterschätzen

undershirt [ˈʌndəʃɜːt] (*US*) *n* Unterhemd *nt*

undershorts [ˈʌndəʃɔːts] (*US*) *npl* Unterhose *f*

underside [ˈʌndəsaid] *n* Unterseite *f*

underskirt [ˈʌndəskɜːt] (*BRIT*) *n* Unterrock *m*

understand [ʌndəˈstænd] (*irreg: like* stand) *vi*, *vt* verstehen; I ~ that ... ich habe gehört, daß ...; am I to ~ that ...? soll das (etwa) heißen, daß ...; what do you ~ by that? was verstehen Sie darunter?; it is understood that ... es wurde vereinbart, daß ...; to make o.s. understood sich verständlich machen; is that understood? ist das klar?; ~able *adj* verständlich; ~ing *n* Verständnis *nt* ♦ *adj* verständnisvoll

understatement [ˈʌndəsteitmənt] *n* (*quality*) Untertreibung *f*; that's an ~! das ist untertrieben!

understood [ʌndəˈstud] *pt*, *pp of* **understand** ♦ *adj* klar; (*implied*) angenommen

understudy [ˈʌndəstʌdi] *n* Ersatz(schau)spieler(in) *m(f)*

undertake [ʌndəˈteik] (*irreg: like* take) *vt* unternehmen ♦ *vi*: to ~ to do sth sich verpflichten, etw zu tun

undertaker [ˈʌndəteikə*] *n* Leichenbestatter *m*

undertaking [ʌndəˈteikiŋ] *n* (*enterprise*) Unternehmen *nt*; (*promise*) Verpflichtung *f*

undertone [ˈʌndətəun] *n*: in an ~ mit gedämpfter Stimme

underwater [ˈʌndəˈwɔːtə*] *adv* unter Wasser ♦ *adj* Unterwasser-

underwear [ˈʌndəwɛə*] *n* Unterwäsche *f*

underworld [ˈʌndəwɜːld] *n* (*of crime*) Unterwelt *f*

underwriter [ˈʌndəraitə*] *n* Assekurant *m*

undesirable [ʌndiˈzaiərəbl] *adj* unerwünscht

undies [ˈʌndiz] (*inf*) *npl* (Damen)unterwäsche *f*

undisputed [ˈʌndisˈpjuːtid] *adj* unbestritten

undo [ʌnˈduː] (*irreg: like* do) *vt* (*unfasten*) öffnen, aufmachen; (*work*) zunichte machen; ~ing *n* Verderben *nt*

undoubted [ʌnˈdautid] *adj* unbezweifelt; ~ly *adv* zweifellos, ohne Zweifel

undress [ʌnˈdres] *vi* ausziehen ♦ *vi* sich ausziehen

undue [ʌnˈdjuː] *adj* übermäßig

undulating [ˈʌndjuleitiŋ] *adj* wellenförmig; (*country*) wellig

unduly [ʌnˈdjuːli] *adv* übermäßig

unearth [ʌnˈɜːθ] *vt* (*dig up*) ausgraben; (discover) ans Licht bringen

unearthly [ʌnˈɜːθlɪ] adj (hour) nachtschlafen

uneasy [ʌnˈiːzɪ] adj (worried) unruhig; (feeling) ungut

uneconomic(al) [ˈʌniːkəˈnɒmɪk(əl)] adj unwirtschaftlich

uneducated [ʌnˈedjʊkeɪtɪd] adj ungebildet

unemployed [ʌnɪmˈplɔɪd] adj arbeitslos ♦ npl: **the ~** die Arbeitslosen pl

unemployment [ʌnɪmˈplɔɪmənt] n Arbeitslosigkeit f

unending [ʌnˈendɪŋ] adj endlos

unerring [ʌnˈɜːrɪŋ] adj unfehlbar

uneven [ʌnˈiːvən] adj (surface) uneben; (quality) ungleichmäßig

unexpected [ʌnɪkˈspektɪd] adj unerwartet; **~ly** adv unerwartet

unfailing [ʌnˈfeɪlɪŋ] adj nie versagend

unfair [ʌnˈfeə*] adj ungerecht, unfair

unfaithful [ʌnˈfeɪθfʊl] adj untreu

unfamiliar [ʌnfəˈmɪlɪə*] adj ungewohnt; (person, subject) unbekannt; **to be ~ with** nicht kennen +acc, nicht vertraut sein mit

unfashionable [ʌnˈfæʃnəbl] adj unmodern; (area, hotel etc) nicht in Mode

unfasten [ʌnˈfɑːsn] vt öffnen, aufmachen

unfavourable [ʌnˈfeɪvərəbl] (US unfavorable) adj ungünstig

unfeeling [ʌnˈfiːlɪŋ] adj gefühllos, kalt

unfinished [ʌnˈfɪnɪʃt] adj unvollendet

unfit [ʌnˈfɪt] adj ungeeignet; (in bad health) nicht fit; **~ for sth** zu or für etw ungeeignet

unfold [ʌnˈfəʊld] vt entfalten; (paper) auseinanderfalten ♦ vi (develop) sich entfalten

unforeseen [ʌnfɔːˈsiːn] adj unvorhergesehen

unforgettable [ʌnfəˈgetəbl] adj unvergeßlich

unforgivable [ʌnfəˈgɪvəbl] adj un-

verzeihlich

unfortunate [ʌnˈfɔːtʃnət] adj unglücklich, bedauerlich; **~ly** adv leider

unfounded [ʌnˈfaʊndɪd] adj unbegründet

unfriendly [ʌnˈfrendlɪ] adj unfreundlich

ungainly [ʌnˈgeɪnlɪ] adj linkisch

ungodly [ʌnˈgɒdlɪ] adj (hour) nachtschlafend; (row) heillos

ungrateful [ʌnˈgreɪtfʊl] adj undankbar

unhappiness [ʌnˈhæpɪnəs] n Unglück nt, Unglückseligkeit f

unhappy [ʌnˈhæpɪ] adj unglücklich; **~ with** (arrangements etc) unzufrieden mit

unharmed [ʌnˈhɑːmd] adj wohlbehalten, unversehrt

unhealthy [ʌnˈhelθɪ] adj ungesund

unheard-of [ʌnˈhɜːdɒv] adj unerhört

unhurt [ʌnˈhɜːt] adj unverletzt

unidentified [ʌnaɪˈdentɪfaɪd] adj unbekannt, nicht identifiziert

uniform [ˈjuːnɪfɔːm] n Uniform f ♦ adj einheitlich; **~ity** [juːnɪˈfɔːmɪtɪ] n Einheitlichkeit f

unify [ˈjuːnɪfaɪ] vt vereinigen

unilateral [juːnɪˈlætərəl] adj einseitig

uninhabited [ʌnɪnˈhæbɪtɪd] adj unbewohnt

unintentional [ʌnɪnˈtenʃənl] adj unabsichtlich

union [ˈjuːnjən] n (uniting) Vereinigung f; (alliance) Bund m, Union f; (trade ~) Gewerkschaft f; **U~** Jack n Union Jack m

unique [juːˈniːk] adj einzig(artig)

unison [ˈjuːnɪzn] n Einstimmigkeit f; **in ~** einstimmig

unit [ˈjuːnɪt] n Einheit f; **kitchen ~** Küchenelement nt

unite [juːˈnaɪt] vt vereinigen ♦ vi sich vereinigen; **~d** adj vereinigt; (together) vereint; **U~d Kingdom** n Vereinigte(s) Königreich nt; **U~d Nations (Organization)** n Vereinte Nationen pl; **U~d States (of Ameri-**

ca) *n* Vereinigte Staaten *pl* (von Amerika)

unit trust (*BRIT*) *n* Treuhandgesellschaft *f*

unity ['juːnɪtɪ] *n* Einheit *f*; (*agreement*) Einigkeit *f*

universal [juːnɪ'vɜːsəl] *adj* allgemein

universe ['juːnɪvɜːs] *n* (Welt) *all nt*

university [juːnɪ'vɜːsɪtɪ] *n* Universität *f*

unjust [ʌn'dʒʌst] *adj* ungerecht

unkempt [ʌn'kempt] *adj* ungepflegt

unkind [ʌn'kaɪnd] *adj* unfreundlich

unknown [ʌn'nəʊn] *adj*: ~ (to sb) (jdm) unbekannt

unlawful [ʌn'lɔːfʊl] *adj* illegal

unleaded *adj* (*petrol*) bleifrei, unverbleit; I use ~ ich fahre bleifrei

unleash [ʌn'liːʃ] *vt* entfesseln

unless [ən'les] *conj* wenn nicht, es sei denn; ~ he comes es sei denn, er kommt; ~ otherwise stated sofern nicht anders angegeben

unlike [ʌn'laɪk] *adj* unähnlich ♦ *prep* im Gegensatz zu

unlikely [ʌn'laɪklɪ] *adj* (*not likely*) unwahrscheinlich (*unexpected: combination etc*), merkwürdig

unlimited [ʌn'lɪmɪtɪd] *adj* unbegrenzt

unlisted [ʌn'lɪstɪd] (*US*) *adj* nicht im Telefonbuch stehend

unload [ʌn'ləʊd] *vt* entladen

unlock [ʌn'lɒk] *vt* aufschließen

unlucky [ʌn'lʌkɪ] *adj* unglücklich; (*person*) unglückselig; to be ~ Pech haben

unmarried [ʌn'mærɪd] *adj* unverheiratet, ledig

unmask [ʌn'mɑːsk] *vt* entlarven

unmistakable [ʌnmɪs'teɪkəbl] *adj* unverkennbar

unmitigated [ʌn'mɪtɪgeɪtɪd] *adj* ungemildert, ganz

unnatural [ʌn'nætʃrəl] *adj* unnatürlich

unnecessary [ʌn'nesəsərɪ] *adj* unnötig

unnoticed [ʌn'nəʊtɪst] *adj*: to go ~ unbemerkt bleiben

UNO ['juːnəʊ] *n abbr* = United Nations Organization

unobtainable [ʌnəb'teɪnəbl] *adj*: this number is ~ kein Anschluß unter dieser Nummer

unobtrusive [ʌnəb'truːsɪv] *adj* unauffällig

unofficial [ʌnə'fɪʃl] *adj* inoffiziell

unpack [ʌn'pæk] *vt, vi* auspacken

unpalatable [ʌn'pælətbl] *adj* (*truth*) bitter

unparalleled [ʌn'pærəleld] *adj* beispiellos

unpleasant [ʌn'pleznt] *adj* unangenehm

unplug [ʌn'plʌg] *vt* den Stecker herausziehen von

unpopular [ʌn'pɒpjʊlə*] *adj* (*person*) unbeliebt; (*decision etc*) unpopulär

unprecedented [ʌn'presɪdəntɪd] *adj* beispiellos

unpredictable [ʌnprɪ'dɪktəbl] *adj* unvorhersehbar; (*weather, person*) unberechenbar

unprofessional [ʌnprə'feʃənl] *adj* unprofessionell

unqualified [ʌn'kwɒlɪfaɪd] *adj* (*success*) uneingeschränkt, voll; (*person*) unqualifiziert

unquestionably [ʌn'kwestʃənəblɪ] *adv* fraglos

unravel [ʌn'rævl] *vt* (*disentangle*) ausfasern, entwirren; (*solve*) lösen

unreal [ʌn'rɪəl] *adj* unwirklich

unrealistic [ʌnrɪə'lɪstɪk] *adj* unrealistisch

unreasonable [ʌn'riːznəbl] *adj* unvernünftig; (*demand*) übertrieben

unrelated [ʌnrɪ'leɪtɪd] *adj* ohne Beziehung; (*family*) nicht verwandt

unrelenting [ʌnrɪ'lentɪŋ] *adj* unerbittlich

unreliable [ʌnrɪ'laɪəbl] *adj* unzuverlässig

unremitting [ʌnrɪ'mɪtɪŋ] *adj* (*efforts, attempts*) unermüdlich

unreservedly [ʌnrɪ'zɜːvɪdlɪ] *adv* offen; (*believe, trust*) uneingeschränkt; (*cry*) rückhaltlos

unrest [ˈʌnˈrest] n (discontent) Unruhe f; (fighting) Unruhen pl

unroll [ˈʌnˈrəul] vt aufrollen

unruly [ˈʌnˈruːlɪ] adj (child) undiszipliniert; schwer lenkbar

unsafe [ˈʌnˈseif] adj nicht sicher

unsaid [ˈʌnˈsed] adj: to leave sth ~ etw ungesagt lassen

unsatisfactory [ˈʌnsætɪsˈfæktərɪ] adj unbefriedigend; unzulänglich

unsavoury, (US **unsavory**) [ˈʌnˈseivərɪ] adj (fig) widerwärtig

unscathed [ˈʌnˈskeiðd] adj unversehrt

unscrew [ˈʌnˈskruː] vt aufschrauben

unscrupulous [ˈʌnˈskruːpjuləs] adj skrupellos

unsettled [ˈʌnˈsetld] adj (person) rastlos; (weather) wechselhaft

unshaven [ˈʌnˈʃeivn] adj unrasiert

unsightly [ˈʌnˈsaitlɪ] adj unansehnlich

unskilled [ˈʌnˈskild] adj ungelernt

unspeakable [ˈʌnˈspiːkəbl] adj (joy) unsagbar; (crime) scheußlich

unstable [ˈʌnˈsteibl] adj instabil; (mentally) labil

unsteady [ˈʌnˈstedɪ] adj unsicher; (growth) unregelmäßig

unstuck [ˈʌnˈstʌk] adj: to come ~ sich lösen; (fig) ins Wasser fallen

unsuccessful [ˈʌnsəkˈsesful] adj erfolglos

unsuitable [ˈʌnˈsuːtəbl] adj unpassend

unsure [ˈʌnˈʃuə*] adj (uncertain) unsicher; to be ~ of o.s. unsicher sein

unsuspecting [ˈʌnsəsˈpektiŋ] adj nichtsahnend

unsympathetic [ˈʌnsimpəˈθetik] adj gefühllos; (response) abweisend; (unlikeable) unsympathisch

untapped [ˈʌnˈtæpt] adj (resources) ungenützt

unthinkable [ʌnˈθiŋkəbl] adj unvorstellbar

untidy [ʌnˈtaidɪ] adj unordentlich

untie [ʌnˈtai] vt aufschnüren

until [ənˈtil] prep, conj bis; ~ he comes bis er kommt; ~ then bis

dann; ~ now bis jetzt

untimely [ʌnˈtaimlɪ] adj (death) vorzeitig

untold [ˈʌnˈtəuld] adj unermeßlich

untoward [ʌntəˈwɔːd] adj widrig

untranslatable [ʌntrænzˈleitəbl] adj unübersetzbar

unused [ˈʌnˈjuːzd] adj unbenutzt

unusual [ʌnˈjuːʒuəl] adj ungewöhnlich

unveil [ʌnˈveil] vt enthüllen

unwavering [ʌnˈweivəriŋ] adj standhaft, unerschütterlich

unwelcome [ʌnˈwelkəm] adj (at a bad time) unwillkommen; (unpleasant) unerfreulich

unwell [ʌnˈwel] adj: to feel or be ~ sich nicht wohl fühlen

unwieldy [ʌnˈwiːldɪ] adj sperrig

unwilling [ˈʌnˈwiliŋ] adj: to be ~ to do sth nicht bereit sein, etw zu tun; ~ly adv widerwillig

unwind [ʌnˈwaind] (irreg: like wind²) vt abwickeln ♦ vi (relax) sich entspannen

unwise [ʌnˈwaiz] adj unklug

unwitting [ʌnˈwitiŋ] adj unwissentlich

unworkable [ʌnˈwɜːkəbl] adj (plan) undurchführbar

unworthy [ʌnˈwɜːðɪ] adj (person): ~ (of sth) (einer Sache gen) nicht wert

unwrap [ˈʌnˈræp] vt auspacken

unwritten [ˈʌnˈritn] adj ungeschrieben

KEYWORD

up [ʌp] prep: to be up sth oben auf etw dat sein; to go up sth (auf) etw acc hinauf gehen; go up that road gehen Sie die Straße hinauf
♦ adv 1 (upwards, higher) oben; put it up a bit higher stell es etwas weiter nach oben; up there da oben, dort oben; up above hoch oben
2: to be up (out of bed) auf sein; (prices, level) gestiegen sein; (building, tent) stehen
3: up to (as far as) bis; up to now

bis jetzt

4: to be up to (*depending on*) das hängt von dir ab; (*equal to*): he's not up to it (*job, task etc*) er ist dem nicht gewachsen; (*inf*: be doing: showing disapproval, suspicion): what is he up to? was führt er im Schilde?; it's not up to me to decide die Entscheidung liegt nicht bei mir; his work is not up to the required standard seine Arbeit entspricht nicht dem geforderten Niveau ♦ *n*: ups and downs (*in life, career*) Höhen und Tiefen *pl*

up-and-coming [ʌpənd'kʌmɪŋ] *adj* aufstrebend

upbringing ['ʌpbrɪŋɪŋ] *n* Erziehung *f*

update [ʌp'deɪt] *vt* auf den neuesten Stand bringen

upgrade [ʌp'greɪd] *vt* höher einstufen

upheaval [ʌp'hi:vəl] *n* Umbruch *m*

uphill ['ʌp'hɪl] *adj* ansteigend; (*fig*) mühsam ♦ *adv*: to go ~ bergauf gehen/fahren

uphold [ʌp'həʊld] (*irreg*: *like* hold) *vt* unterstützen

upholstery [ʌp'həʊlstərɪ] *n* Polster *nt*; Polsterung *f*

upkeep ['ʌpkiːp] *n* Instandhaltung *f*

upon [ə'pɔn] *prep* auf

upper ['ʌpə*] *n* (*on shoe*) Oberleder *nt* ♦ *adj* obere(r, s), höhere(r, s); to have the ~ hand die Oberhand haben; ~-class *adj* vornehm; ~most *adj* oberste(r, s), höchste(r, s); what was ~most in my mind hat mich in erster Linie beschäftigt

upright ['ʌpraɪt] *adj* aufrecht

uprising ['ʌpraɪzɪŋ] *n* Aufstand *m*

uproar ['ʌprɔ:*] *n* Aufruhr *m*

uproot [ʌp'ruːt] *vt* ausreißen

upset [*n* 'ʌpset, *vb, adj* ʌp'set] (*irreg*: *like* set) *n* Aufregung *f* ♦ *vt* (*overturn*) umwerfen; (*disturb*) aufregen, bestürzen; (*plans*) durcheinanderbringen ♦ *adj* (*person*) aufgeregt; (*stomach*) verdorben

upshot ['ʌpʃɔt] *n* (End)ergebnis *nt*

upside-down ['ʌpsaɪd'daʊn] *adv* verkehrt herum; (*fig*) drunter und drüber

upstairs ['ʌp'steəz] *adv* oben; (*go*) nach oben ♦ *adj* (*room*) obere(r, s), Ober- ♦ *n* obere(s) Stockwerk *nt*

upstart ['ʌpstaːt] *n* Emporkömmling *m*

upstream ['ʌp'striːm] *adv* stromaufwärts

uptake ['ʌpteɪk] *n*: to be quick on the ~ schnell begreifen; to be slow on the ~ schwer von Begriff sein

uptight [ʌp'taɪt] (*inf*) *adj* (*nervous*) nervös; (*inhibited*) verklemmt

up-to-date ['ʌptə'deɪt] *adj* (*clothes*) modisch, modern; (*information*) neueste(r, s)

upturn ['ʌptɜːn] *n* Aufschwung *m*

upward ['ʌpwəd] *adj* nach oben gerichtet; ~(s) *adv* aufwärts

uranium [juə'reɪnɪəm] *n* Uran *nt*

urban ['ɜːbən] *adj* städtisch, Stadt-

urbane [ɜː'beɪn] *adj* höflich

urchin ['ɜːtʃɪn] *n* (*boy*) Schlingel *m*; (*sea* ~) Seeigel *m*

urge [ɜːdʒ] *n* Drang *m* ♦ *vt*: to ~ sb to do sth jdn (dazu) drängen, etw zu tun

urgency ['ɜːdʒənsɪ] *n* Dringlichkeit *f*

urgent ['ɜːdʒənt] *adj* dringend

urinal ['juərɪnl] *n* (*MED*) Urinflasche *f*; (*public*) Pissoir *nt*

urinate ['juərɪneɪt] *vi* urinieren

urine ['juərɪn] *n* Urin *m*, Harn *m*

urn [ɜːn] *n* Urne *f*; (*tea* ~) Teemaschine *f*

us [ʌs] *pron* uns; *see also* me

US *n abbr* = United States

USA *n abbr* = United States of America

usage ['juːzɪdʒ] *n* Gebrauch *m*; (*esp LING*) Sprachgebrauch *m*

use [*n* juːs, *vb* juːz] *n* (*employment*) Gebrauch *m*; (*point*) Zweck *m* ♦ *vt* gebrauchen; in ~ in Gebrauch; out of ~ außer Gebrauch; to be of ~ nützlich sein; it's no ~ es hat keinen Zweck; what's the ~? was soll's?

~d to (*accustomed to*) gewöhnt an +*acc*; **she ~d to live here** (*formerly*) sie hat früher mal hier gewohnt; **~ up** vt aufbrauchen, verbrauchen; **~d** adj (*car*) Gebraucht-; **~ful** adj nützlich; **~fulness** n Nützlichkeit f; **~less** adj nutzlos, unnütz; **~r** n Benutzer m; **~r-friendly** adj (*comput*) benutzerfreundlich

usher ['ʌʃə*] n Platzanweiser m
usherette [ʌʃə'rɛt] n Platzanweiserin f
usual ['juːʒəl] adj gewöhnlich, üblich; **as ~** wie üblich; **~ly** adv gewöhnlich
usurp [juːˈzɜːp] vt an sich reißen
utensil [juːˈtɛnsl] n Gerät nt; **kitchen ~s** Küchengeräte pl
uterus ['juːtərəs] n Gebärmutter f
utilitarian [juːtɪlɪˈtɛərɪən] adj Nützlichkeits-
utility [juːˈtɪlɪtɪ] n (*usefulness*) Nützlichkeit f; (*also: public ~*) öffentliche(r) Versorgungsbetrieb m; **~ room** n Hauswirtschaftsraum m
utilize ['juːtɪlaɪz] vt benützen
utmost ['ʌtməʊst] adj äußerste(r, s) ♦ n **to do one's ~** sein möglichstes tun
utter ['ʌtə*] adj äußerste(r, s), höchste(r, s), völlig ♦ vt äußern, aussprechen; **~ance** n Äußerung f; **~ly** adv äußerst, absolut, völlig
U-turn ['juːˈtɜːn] n (*AUT*) Kehrtwendung f

V

v. abbr = verse; **v** abbr; versus; volt; (= *vide*) siehe
vacancy ['veɪkənsɪ] n (*BRIT: job*) offene Stelle f; (*room*) freie(s) Zimmer nt
vacant ['veɪkənt] adj leer; (*unoccupied*) frei; (*house*) leerstehend, unbewohnt; (*stupid*) (gedanken)leer; **~ lot** (*US*) n unbebaute(s) Grundstück nt
vacate [vəˈkeɪt] vt (*seat*) frei ma-

chen; (*room*) räumen
vacation [vəˈkeɪʃən] n Ferien pl, Urlaub m; **~ist** (*US*) n Ferienreisende(r) mf
vaccinate ['væksɪneɪt] vt impfen
vaccine ['væksiːn] n Impfstoff m
vacuum ['vækjʊm] n Vakuum nt; **~ bottle** (*US*) n Thermosflasche f; **~ cleaner** n Staubsauger m; **~ flask** (*BRIT*) n Thermosflasche f; **~-packed** adj vakuumversiegelt
vagina [vəˈdʒaɪnə] n Scheide f
vagrant ['veɪɡrənt] n Landstreicher m
vague [veɪɡ] adj vag(e); (*absent-minded*) geistesabwesend; **~ly** adv unbestimmt, vage
vain [veɪn] adj eitel; (*attempt*) vergeblich; **in ~** vergebens, umsonst
valentine ['væləntaɪn] n (*also: ~ card*) Valentinsgruß m
valet ['væleɪ] n Kammerdiener m
valiant ['væliənt] adj tapfer
valid ['vælɪd] adj gültig; (*argument*) stichhaltig; (*objection*) berechtigt; **~ity** [vəˈlɪdɪtɪ] n Gültigkeit f
valley ['vælɪ] n Tal nt
valour ['vælə*] (*US* **valor**) n Tapferkeit f
valuable ['væljʊəbl] adj wertvoll; (*time*) kostbar; **~s** npl Wertsachen pl
valuation [væljʊˈeɪʃən] n (*FIN*) Schätzung f; Beurteilung f
value ['væljuː] n Wert m; (*usefulness*) Nutzen m ♦ vt (*prize*) (hoch)schätzen, werthalten; (*estimate*) schätzen; **~ added tax** (*BRIT*) n Mehrwertsteuer f; **~d** adj geschätzt
valve [vælv] n Ventil nt; (*BIOL*) Klappe f; (*RAD*) Röhre f
van [væn] n Lieferwagen m; (*BRIT: RAIL*) Waggon m
vandal ['vændl] n Rowdy m
vandalism ['vændəlɪzəm] n mutwillige Beschädigung f
vandalize ['vændəlaɪz] vt mutwillig beschädigen
vanguard ['vænɡɑːd] n (*fig*) Spitze f

vanilla [vəˈnɪlə] *n* Vanille *f*; ~ **ice cream** *n* Vanilleeis *nt*

vanish [ˈvænɪʃ] *vi* verschwinden

vanity [ˈvænɪtɪ] *n* Eitelkeit *f*; ~ **case** *n* Schminkkoffer *m*

vantage [ˈvɑːntɪdʒ] *n*: ~ **point** gute(r) Aussichtspunkt *m*

vapour [ˈveɪpəʳ] (*US* **vapor**) *n* (*mist*) Dunst *m*; (*gas*) Dampf *m*

variable [ˈvɛərɪəbl] *adj* wechselhaft, veränderlich; (*speed, height*) regulierbar

variance [ˈvɛərɪəns] *n*: to be at ~ (with) nicht übereinstimmen (mit)

variation [vɛərɪˈeɪʃən] *n* Variation *f*; (*of temperature, prices*) Schwankung *f*

varicose [ˈværɪkəʊs] *adj*: ~ **veins** Krampfadern *pl*

varied [ˈvɛərɪd] *adj* unterschiedlich; (*life*) abwechslungsreich

variety [vəˈraɪətɪ] *n* (*difference*) Abwechslung *f*; (*varied collection*) Vielfalt *f*; (*COMM*) Auswahl *f*; (*sort*) Sorte *f*, Art *f*; ~ **show** *n* Varieté *nt*

various [ˈvɛərɪəs] *adj* verschieden; (*several*) mehrere

varnish [ˈvɑːnɪʃ] *n* Lack *m*; (*on pottery*) Glasur *f* ♦ *vt* lackieren

vary [ˈvɛərɪ] *vt* (*alter*) verändern; (*give variety to*) abwechslungsreicher gestalten ♦ *vi* sich (ver)ändern; (*prices*) schwanken; (*weather*) unterschiedlich sein

vase [vɑːz] *n* Vase *f*

Vaseline [ˈvæsɪliːn] (®) *n* Vaseline *f*

vast [vɑːst] *adj* weit, groß, riesig

VAT [væt] *n abbr* = **value added tax**) MwSt *f*

vat [væt] *n* große(s) Faß *nt*

vault [vɔːlt] *n* (*of roof*) Gewölbe *nt*; (*tomb*) Gruft *f*; (*in bank*) Tresorraum *m*; (*leap*) Sprung *m* ♦ *vt* (*also:* ~ **over**) überspringen

vaunted [ˈvɔːntɪd] *adj*: **much-vaunted** vielgerühmt

VCR *n abbr* = **video cassette recorder**

VD *n abbr* = **venereal disease**

VDU *n abbr* = **visual display unit**

veal [viːl] *n* Kalbfleisch *nt*

veer [vɪəʳ] *vi* sich drehen; (*of car*) ausscheren

vegetable [ˈvedʒətəbl] *n* Gemüse *nt* ♦ *adj* Gemüse-; ~**s** *npl* (*CULIN*) Gemüse *nt*

vegetarian [vedʒɪˈtɛərɪən] *n* Vegetarier(in) *m(f)* ♦ *adj* vegetarisch

vegetate [ˈvedʒɪteɪt] *vi* (dahin)vegetieren

vehemence [ˈviːɪməns] *n* Heftigkeit *f*

vehement [ˈviːɪmənt] *adj* heftig

vehicle [ˈviːɪkl] *n* Fahrzeug *nt*; (*fig*) Mittel *nt*

veil [veɪl] *n* (*also fig*) Schleier *m* ♦ *vt* verschleiern

vein [veɪn] *n* Ader *f*; (*mood*) Stimmung *f*

velocity [vɪˈlɒsɪtɪ] *n* Geschwindigkeit *f*

velvet [ˈvelvɪt] *n* Samt *m* ♦ *adj* Samt-

vendetta [venˈdetə] *n* Fehde *f*; (*in family*) Blutrache *f*

vending machine [ˈvendɪŋ-] *n* Automat *m*

vendor [ˈvendɔːʳ] *n* Verkäufer *m*

veneer [vəˈnɪəʳ] *n* Furnier(holz) *nt*; (*fig*) äußere(r) Anstrich *m*

venereal disease [vɪˈnɪərɪəl-] *n* Geschlechtskrankheit *f*

Venetian blind [vɪˈniːʃən-] *n* Jalousie *f*

vengeance [ˈvendʒəns] *n* Rache *f*; **with a ~** gewaltig

venison [ˈvenɪsn] *n* Reh(fleisch) *nt*

venom [ˈvenəm] *n* Gift *nt*

vent [vent] *n* Öffnung *f*; (*in coat*) Schlitz *m*; (*fig*) Ventil *nt* ♦ *vt* (*emotion*) abreagieren

ventilate [ˈventɪleɪt] *vt* belüften

ventilator [ˈventɪleɪtəʳ] *n* Ventilator *m*

ventriloquist [venˈtrɪləkwɪst] *n* Bauchredner *m*

venture [ˈventʃəʳ] *n* Unternehmung *f*, Projekt *nt* ♦ *vt* wagen; (*life*) aufs Spiel setzen ♦ *vi* sich wagen

venue [ˈvenjuː] *n* Schauplatz *m*

verb [vɜːb] n Zeitwort nt, Verb nt; **~al** adj (spoken) mündlich; (translation) wörtlich; **~ally** adv mündlich

verbatim [vɜːˈbeɪtɪm] adv Wort für Wort ♦ adj wortwörtlich

verbose [vɜːˈbəʊs] adj wortreich

verdict [ˈvɜːdɪkt] n Urteil nt

verge [vɜːdʒ] n (BRIT) Rand m ♦ vi: to ~ on grenzen an +acc; "soft ~s" (BRIT: AUT) „Seitenstreifen nicht befahrbar"; on the ~ of doing sth im Begriff, etw zu tun

verify [ˈverɪfaɪ] vt (über)prüfen; (confirm) bestätigen; (theory) beweisen

veritable [ˈverɪtəbl] adj wirklich, echt

vermin [ˈvɜːmɪn] npl Ungeziefer nt

vermouth [ˈvɜːməθ] n Wermut m

vernacular [vəˈnækjʊlə*] n Landessprache f

versatile [ˈvɜːsətaɪl] adj vielseitig

versatility [vɜːsəˈtɪlɪtɪ] n Vielseitigkeit f

verse [vɜːs] n (poetry) Poesie f, (stanza) Strophe f; (of Bible) Vers m; in ~ in Versform

versed [vɜːst] adj: (well-)versed in bewandert in +dat, beschlagen in +dat

version [ˈvɜːʃən] n Version f; (of car) Modell nt

versus [ˈvɜːsəs] prep gegen

vertebrate [ˈvɜːtɪbrət] n (animal) Wirbel~

vertical [ˈvɜːtɪkəl] adj senkrecht

vertigo [ˈvɜːtɪɡəʊ] n Schwindel m

verve [vɜːv] n Schwung m

very [ˈverɪ] adv sehr ♦ adj (extreme) äußerste(r, s); the ~ book which genau das Buch, welches; the ~ last der/die/das allerletzte; at the ~ least allerwenigstens; ~ much sehr

vessel [ˈvesl] n (ship) Schiff nt; (container) Gefäß nt

vest [vest] n (BRIT) Unterhemd nt; (US: waistcoat) Weste f; **~ed interests** npl finanzielle Beteiligung f; (people) finanziell Beteiligte pl; (fig) persönliche(s) Interesse nt

vestige [ˈvestɪdʒ] n Spur f

vestry [ˈvestrɪ] n Sakristei f

vet [vet] n abbr (= veterinary surgeon) Tierarzt m/-ärztin f ♦ vt genau prüfen

veteran [ˈvetərn] n Veteran(in) m(f)

veterinarian [vetrɪˈnɛərɪən] (US) n Tierarzt m/-ärztin f

veterinary [ˈvetrɪnərɪ] adj Veterinär~; ~ **surgeon** (BRIT) n Tierarzt m/-ärztin f

veto [ˈviːtəʊ] (pl ~es) n Veto nt ♦ vt sein Veto einlegen gegen

vex [veks] vt ärgern; **~ed** adj verärgert; **~ed question** umstrittene Frage f

VHF abbr (= very high frequency) UKW f

via [ˈvaɪə] prep über +acc

viable [ˈvaɪəbl] adj (plan) durchführbar; (company) rentabel

vibrant [ˈvaɪbrənt] adj (lively) lebhaft; (bright) leuchtend; (full of emotion: voice) bebend

vibrate [vaɪˈbreɪt] vi zittern, beben; (machine, string) vibrieren

vibration [vaɪˈbreɪʃən] n Schwingung f; (of machine) Vibrieren nt

vicar [ˈvɪkə*] n Pfarrer m; **~age** n Pfarrhaus nt

vicarious [vɪˈkɛərɪəs] adj nachempfunden

vice [vaɪs] n (evil) Laster nt; (TECH) Schraubstock m

vice-chairman n stellvertretende(r) Vorsitzende(r) m

vice-president n Vizepräsident m

vice squad n ≈ Sittenpolizei f

vice versa [ˈvaɪsɪˈvɜːsə] adv umgekehrt

vicinity [vɪˈsɪnɪtɪ] n Umgebung f; (closeness) Nähe f

vicious [ˈvɪʃəs] adj gemein, böse; ~ **circle** n Teufelskreis m

victim [ˈvɪktɪm] n Opfer nt; **~ize** vt benachteiligen

victor [ˈvɪktə*] n Sieger m

Victorian [vɪkˈtɔːrɪən] adj viktorianisch; (fig) (sitten)streng

victorious [vɪkˈtɔːrɪəs] adj siegreich

victory ['vɪktərɪ] n Sieg m

video ['vɪdɪəʊ] adj Fernseh-, Bild- ♦ n (~ film) Video m; (also: ~ cassette) Videokassette f; (: ~ cassette recorder) Videorekorder m; ~ tape n Videoband nt

vie [vaɪ] vi wetteifern

Vienna [vɪ'enə] n Wien nt

view [vjuː] n (sight) Sicht f, Blick m; (scene) Aussicht f; (opinion) Ansicht f; (intention) Absicht f ♦ vt (situation) betrachten; (house) besichtigen; **to have sth in** ~ etw beabsichtigen; **on** ~ ausgestellt; **in** ~ **of** wegen +gen, angesichts +gen; ~**er** n (~finder) Sucher m; (TV) Fernsehzuschauer(in) m(f); ~**finder** n Sucher m; (PHOT: small projector) Sucher m; ~**point** n Standpunkt m

vigil ['vɪdʒɪl] n (Nacht)wache f; ~**ance** n Wachsamkeit f; ~**ant** adj wachsam

vigorous ['vɪgərəs] adj kräftig; (protest) energisch, heftig; ~**ly** adv kräftig; energisch, heftig

vile [vaɪl] adj (mean) gemein; (foul) abscheulich

vilify ['vɪlɪfaɪ] vt verleumden

villa ['vɪlə] n Villa f

village ['vɪlɪdʒ] n Dorf nt; ~**r** n Dorfbewohner(in) m(f)

villain ['vɪlən] n Schurke m

vindicate ['vɪndɪkeɪt] vt rechtfertigen

vindictive [vɪn'dɪktɪv] adj nachtragend, rachsüchtig

vine [vaɪn] n Rebstock m, Rebe f

vinegar ['vɪnɪgə*] n Essig m

vineyard ['vɪnjəd] n Weinberg m

vintage ['vɪntɪdʒ] n (of wine) Jahrgang m; ~ **wine** n edle(r) Wein m

viola [vɪ'əʊlə] n Bratsche f

violate ['vaɪəleɪt] vt (law) übertreten; (rights, rule, neutrality) verletzen; (sanctity, woman) schänden

violation [vaɪə'leɪʃən] n Verletzung f; Übertretung f

violence ['vaɪələns] n (force) Heftigkeit f; (brutality) Gewalttätigkeit f

violent ['vaɪələnt] adj (strong) heftig; (brutal) gewalttätig, brutal; (contrast) kraß; (death) gewaltsam

violet ['vaɪələt] n Veilchen nt ♦ adj veilchenblau, violett

violin [vaɪə'lɪn] n Geige f, Violine f; ~**ist** n Geiger(in) m(f)

VIP n abbr (= very important person) VIP m

virgin ['vɜːdʒɪn] n Jungfrau f ♦ adj jungfräulich, unberührt; ~**ity** [vɜː'dʒɪnɪtɪ] n Unschuld f

Virgo ['vɜːgəʊ] n Jungfrau f

virile ['vɪraɪl] adj männlich

virility [vɪ'rɪlɪtɪ] n Männlichkeit f

virtually ['vɜːtjʊəlɪ] adv praktisch, fast

virtual reality n (COMPUT) virtuelle Realität f

virtue ['vɜːtjuː] n (moral goodness) Tugend f; (good quality) Vorteil m, Vorzug m; **by** ~ **of** aufgrund +gen

virtuous ['vɜːtjʊəs] adj tugendhaft

virulent ['vɪrjʊlənt] adj (poisonous) bösartig; (bitter) scharf, geharnischt

virus ['vaɪərəs] n (also: COMPUT) Virus m

visa ['viːzə] n Visum nt

vis-à-vis ['viːzəviː] prep gegenüber

viscous ['vɪskəs] adj zähflüssig

visibility [vɪzɪ'bɪlɪtɪ] n (MET) Sicht(weite) f

visible ['vɪzəbl] adj sichtbar

visibly ['vɪzəblɪ] adv sichtlich

vision ['vɪʒən] n (ability) Sehvermögen nt; (foresight) Weitblick m; (in dream, image) Vision f

visit ['vɪzɪt] n Besuch m ♦ vt besuchen; (town, country) fahren nach; ~**ing** adj (professor) Gast-; ~**ing hours** npl (in hospital etc) Besuchszeiten pl; ~**or** n (in house) Besucher(in) m(f); (in hotel) Gast m

visor ['vaɪzə*] n Visier nt; (on cap) Schirm m; (AUT) Blende f

vista ['vɪstə] n Aussicht f

visual ['vɪzjʊəl] adj Seh-, visuell; ~ **aid** n Anschauungsmaterial nt; ~ **display unit** n Bildschirm(gerät nt) m; ~**ize** ['vɪzjʊəlaɪz] vt sich +dat vorstellen

vital ['vaɪtl] adj (important) unerläßlich; (necessary for life) Lebens-, lebenswichtig; (lively) vital; **~ity** [vaɪ'tælɪtɪ] n Vitalität f; **~ly** adv: **~ important** äußerst wichtig; **~ statistics** npl (fig) Maße pl

vitamin ['vɪtəmɪn] n Vitamin nt

vivacious [vɪ'veɪʃəs] adj lebhaft

vivid ['vɪvɪd] adj (graphic) lebendig; (memory) lebhaft; (bright) leuchtend; **~ly** adv lebendig; lebhaft; leuchtend

V-neck ['viː'nek] n V-Ausschnitt m

vocabulary [vəʊ'kæbjʊlərɪ] n Wortschatz m, Vokabular nt

vocal ['vəʊkəl] adj Vokal-, Gesang-; (fig) lautstark; **~ cords** npl Stimmbänder pl

vocation [vəʊ'keɪʃən] n (calling) Berufung f; **~al** adj Berufs-

vociferous [vəʊ'sɪfərəs] adj lautstark

vodka ['vɒdkə] n Wodka m

vogue [vəʊg] n Mode f

voice [vɔɪs] n Stimme f; (fig) Mitspracherecht nt ♦ vt äußern

void [vɔɪd] n Leere f ♦ adj (invalid) nichtig, ungültig; (empty): **~ of** ohne, bar +gen; see **null**

volatile ['vɒlətaɪl] adj (gas) flüchtig; (person) impulsiv; (situation) brisant

volcano [vɒl'keɪnəʊ] n Vulkan m

volition [vəʊ'lɪʃən] n Wille m; **of one's own ~** aus freiem Willen

volley ['vɒlɪ] n (of guns) Salve f; (of stones) Hagel m; (of words) Schwall m; (tennis) Flugball m; **~ball** n Volleyball m

volt [vəʊlt] n Volt nt; **~age** n (Volt)spannung f

voluble ['vɒljʊbl] adj redselig

volume ['vɒljuːm] n (book) Band m; (size) Umfang m; (space) Rauminhalt m; (of sound) Lautstärke f

voluminous [vəˈluːmɪnəs] adj üppig; (clothes) wallend; (correspondence, notes) umfangreich

voluntarily ['vɒləntrɪlɪ] adv freiwillig

voluntary ['vɒləntərɪ] adj freiwillig

volunteer [vɒlən'tɪə*] n Freiwillige(r) mf ♦ vi sich freiwillig melden; **to ~ to do sth** sich anbieten, etw zu tun

voluptuous [vəˈlʌptjʊəs] adj sinnlich

vomit ['vɒmɪt] n Erbrochene(s) nt ♦ vt spucken ♦ vi sich übergeben

vote [vəʊt] n Stimme f; (ballot) Abstimmung f; (result) Abstimmungsergebnis nt; (franchise) Wahlrecht nt ♦ vi, vt wählen; **~ of thanks** n Dankesworte pl; **~r** n Wähler(in) m(f)

voting ['vəʊtɪŋ] n Wahl f

voucher ['vaʊtʃə*] n Gutschein m

vouch for [vaʊtʃ-] vt bürgen für

vow [vaʊ] n Versprechen nt; (REL) Gelübde nt ♦ vt geloben

vowel ['vaʊəl] n Vokal m

voyage ['vɔɪɪdʒ] n Reise f

vulgar ['vʌlgə*] adj (rude) vulgär; (of common people) allgemein, Volks-; **~ity** [vʌl'gærɪtɪ] n Vulgarität f

vulnerable ['vʌlnərəbl] adj (easily injured) verwundbar; (sensitive) verletzlich

vulture ['vʌltʃə*] n Geier m

W

wad [wɒd] n (bundle) Bündel nt; (of paper) Stoß m; (of money) Packen m

waddle ['wɒdl] vi watscheln

wade [weɪd] vi: **to ~ through** waten durch

wafer ['weɪfə*] n Waffel f; (REL) Hostie f; (COMPUT) Wafer f

waffle ['wɒfl] n Waffel f; (inf: empty talk) Geschwafel nt ♦ vi schwafeln

waft [wɑːft] vt, vi wehen

wag [wæg] vt (tail) wedeln mit ♦ vi wedeln

wage [weɪdʒ] n (also: **~s**) (Arbeits)lohn m ♦ vt: **to ~ war** Krieg führen; **~ earner** n Lohnempfänger(in) m(f); **~ packet** n Lohntüte f

wager ['weɪdʒə*] n Wette f ♦ vt, vi

wetten

waggle ['wægl] vt (tail) wedeln mit ♦ vi wedeln

wag(g)on ['wægən] n (horse-drawn) Fuhrwerk nt; (US: AUT) Wagen m; (BRIT: RAIL) Waggon m

wail [weɪl] n Wehgeschrei nt ♦ vi wehklagen, jammern

waist [weɪst] n Taille f; ~coat (BRIT) n Weste f; ~line n Taille f

wait [weɪt] n Wartezeit f ♦ vi warten; to lie in ~ for sb jdm auflauern; I can't ~ to see him n kann's kaum erwarten, ihn zu sehen; "no ~ing" (BRIT: AUT) „Halteverbot"; ~ behind vi zurückbleiben; ~ for vt fus warten auf +acc; ~ on vt fus bedienen; ~er n Kellner m; ~ing list n Warteliste f; ~ing room n (MED) Wartezimmer nt; (RAIL) Wartesaal m; ~ress n Kellnerin f

waive [weɪv] vt verzichten auf +acc

wake [weɪk] (pt woke ~d, pp woken) vt wecken ♦ vi (also: ~ up) aufwachen ♦ n (NAUT) Kielwasser nt; (for dead) Totenwache f; to ~ up to (fig) sich bewußt werden +gen

waken ['weɪkən] vt aufwecken

Wales [weɪlz] n Wales nt

walk [wɔːk] n Spaziergang m; (gait) Gang m; (route) Weg m ♦ vi gehen; (stroll) spazierengehen; (longer) wandern; ~s of life Sphären pl; a 10-minute ~ 10 Minuten zu Fuß; to ~ out on sb (inf) jdn sitzenlassen; ~er n Spaziergänger m; (hiker) Wanderer m; ~ie-talkie ['wɔːkɪ'tɔːkɪ] n tragbare(s) Sprechfunkgerät nt; ~ing n Gehen nt; (hiking) Wandern nt ♦ adj Wander-; ~ing shoes npl Wanderschuhe pl; ~ing stick n Spazierstock m; ~out n Streik m; ~over (inf) n leichte(r) Sieg m; ~way n Fußweg m

wall [wɔːl] n (inside) Wand f; (outside) Mauer f; to go to the ~ auf Mauern umgehen

wallet ['wɒlɪt] n Brieftasche f

wallflower ['wɔːlflaʊə*] n Goldlack m; to be a ~ (fig) ein Mauerblümchen sein

wallop ['wɒləp] (inf) vt schlagen, verprügeln

wallow ['wɒləʊ] vi sich wälzen

wallpaper ['wɔːlpeɪpə*] n Tapete f

wally ['wɒlɪ] (inf) n Idiot m

walnut ['wɔːlnʌt] n Walnuß f

walrus ['wɔːlrəs] n Walroß nt

waltz [wɔːlts] n Walzer m ♦ vi Walzer tanzen

wan [wɒn] adj bleich

wand [wɒnd] n (also: magic ~) Zauberstab m

wander ['wɒndə*] vi (roam) (herum)wandern; (fig) abschweifen

wane [weɪn] vi abnehmen; (fig) schwinden

wangle ['wæŋgl] (BRIT: inf) vt: to ~ sth etw richtig hindrehen

want [wɒnt] n (lack) Mangel m ♦ vt (need) brauchen; (desire) wollen; (lack) nicht haben; ~s npl (needs) Bedürfnisse pl; for ~ of aus Mangel an +dat; mangels +gen; to ~ to do sth etw tun wollen; to ~ sb to do sth wollen, daß jd etw tut; ~ed adj (criminal etc) gesucht; "cook ~" (in advertisements) „Koch/Köchin gesucht"; ~ing adj: to be found ~ing sich als unzulänglich erweisen

wanton ['wɒntən] adj mutwillig, zügellos

war [wɔː*] n Krieg m; to make ~ Krieg führen

ward [wɔːd] n (in hospital) Station f; (of city) Bezirk m; (child) Mündel nt; ~ off vt abwenden, abwehren

warden ['wɔːdn] n (guard) Wächter m, Aufseher m; (BRIT: in youth hostel) Herbergsvater m; (UNIV) Heimleiter m; (BRIT: also: traffic ~) Verkehrspolizist m, ~ Politesse f

warder ['wɔːdə*] (BRIT) n Gefängniswärter m

wardrobe ['wɔːdrəʊb] n Kleiderschrank m; (clothes) Garderobe f

warehouse ['wɛəhaʊs] n Lagerhaus nt

wares [wɛəz] npl Ware f

warfare ['wɔːfeə*] n Krieg m;
Kriegsführung f

warhead ['wɔːhed] n Sprengkopf m

warily ['wɛərɪlɪ] adv vorsichtig

warlike ['wɔːlaɪk] adj kriegerisch

warm [wɔːm] adj warm; (welcome)
herzlich ♦ vt, u wärmen; I'm ~ mir
ist warm; it's ~ es ist warm; ~
vt aufwärmen ♦ vi warm werden;
~-hearted adj warmherzig; ~ly adv
warm; herzlich; ~th n Wärme f;
Herzlichkeit f

warn [wɔːn] vt: to ~ (of or
against) warnen (vor +dat); ~ing n
Warnung f; without ~ing unerwartet; ~ing light n Warnlicht nt; ~ing
triangle n (AUT) Warndreieck nt

warp [wɔːp] vt verziehen; ~ed adj ge-
wellig; (fig) pervers

warrant ['wɔrənt] n (for arrest)
Haftbefehl m

warranty ['wɔrəntɪ] n Garantie f

warren ['wɔrən] n Labyrinth nt

warrior ['wɔrɪə*] n Krieger m

Warsaw ['wɔːsɔː] n Warschau nt

warship ['wɔːʃɪp] n Kriegsschiff nt

wart [wɔːt] n Warze f

wartime ['wɔːtaɪm] n Krieg m

was [wɔz, wəz] pt of **be**

wash [wɔʃ] n Wäsche f ♦ vt waschen; (dishes) abwaschen ♦ vi sich
waschen; (do ~ing) waschen; to
have a ~ sich waschen; ~ away vt
abwaschen, wegspülen; ~ off vt abwaschen; ~ up vi (BRIT) spülen;
(US) sich waschen; ~able adj
waschbar; ~basin n Waschbecken
nt; ~ bowl (US) n Waschbecken nt;
~ cloth (US) n (face cloth) Waschlappen m; ~er n (TECH) Dichtungsring m; (machine) Waschmaschine f; ~ing n Wäsche f; ~ing
machine n Waschmaschine f; ~ing
powder (BRIT) n Waschpulver nt

Washington n Washington nt

wash: ~ing-up n Abwasch m;
~ing-up liquid n Spülmittel nt; ~
out (inf) n (event) Reinfall m; (person) Niete f; ~room n Waschraum

m

wasn't ['wɔznt] = was not

wasp [wɔsp] n Wespe f

wastage ['weɪstɪdʒ] n Verlust m;
natural ~ Verschleiß m

waste [weɪst] n (wasting) Verschwendung f; (what is wasted) Abfall m ♦ adj (useless) überschüssig,
Abfall- ♦ vt (object) verschwenden;
(time, life) vergeuden ♦ vi: to ~
away verfallen; ~s npl (land) Einöde f; ~ **disposal unit** (BRIT) n
Müllschlucker m; ~ful adj verschwenderisch; (process) aufwendig;
~ **ground** (BRIT) n unbebaute(s)
Grundstück nt; ~land n Ödland nt;
~paper basket n Papierkorb m;
~ **pipe** n Abflußrohr nt

watch [wɔtʃ] n Wache f; (for time)
Uhr f ♦ vt ansehen; (observe) beobachten; (be careful of) aufpassen auf
+acc; (guard) bewachen ♦ vi zusehen; **to be on the ~** (for sth) (auf
etw acc) aufpassen; to ~ TV fernsehen; to ~ **sb doing sth** jdm bei etw
zuschauen; ~ **out** vi Ausschau halten; (be careful) aufpassen; ~ **out!**
paß auf!; ~dog n Wachthund m;
(fig) Wächter m; ~ful adj wachsam;
~maker n Uhrmacher m; ~man n
(also: night ~) (Nacht)-
wächter m; ~strap n Uhrarmband
nt

water ['wɔːtə*] n Wasser nt ♦ vt
(be)gießen; (river) bewässern;
(horses) tränken ♦ vi (eye) tränen;
~s npl (of sea, river etc) Gewässer
nt; ~ **down** vt verwässern; ~ **closet**
(BRIT) n (Wasser)klosett nt;
~colour (US watercolor) n (painting) Aquarell nt; (paint) Wasserfarbe
f; ~cress n (Brunnen)kresse f; ~fall
n Wasserfall m; ~ **heater** n Heiß-
wassergerät nt; ~ing can n Gießkanne f; ~ **level** n Wasserstand m; ~lily
n Seerose f; ~line n Wasserlinie f;
~logged adj (ground) voll Wasser,
(wood) mit Wasser vollgesogen; ~
main n Haupt(wasser)leitung f;
~mark n Wasserzeichen nt; (on

wall) Wasserstandsmarke f; **~melon** n Wassermelone f; **~polo** n Wasserball(spiel) nt; **~proof** adj wasserdicht; **~shed** n Wasserscheide f; **~skiing** n Wasserschilaufen nt; **~tank** n Wassertank m; **~tight** adj wasserdicht; **~way** n Wasserweg m; **~works** npl Wasserwerk nt; **~y** adj wäss(e)rig

watt [wɔt] n Watt nt

wave [weɪv] n Welle f; (with hand) Winken nt ♦ vt (move to and fro) schwenken; (hand, flag) winken mit; (hair) wellen ♦ vi (person) winken; (flag) wehen; **~length** n (also fig) Wellenlänge f

waver ['weɪvə*] vi schwanken

wavy ['weɪvɪ] adj wellig

wax [wæks] n Wachs f; (sealing ~) Siegellack m; (in ear) Ohrenschmalz nt ♦ vt (floor) (ein)wachsen ♦ vi (moon) zunehmen; **~works** npl Wachsfigurenkabinett nt

way [weɪ] n Weg m; (method) Art und Weise f; (direction) Richtung f; (habit) Gewohnheit f; (distance) Entfernung f; (condition) Zustand m; **which ~?** - **this** ~ welche Richtung? - hier entlang; **on the ~** (en route) unterwegs; **to be in the ~** im Weg sein; **to go out of one's ~ to do sth** sich besonders anstrengen, um etw zu tun; **to lose one's ~** sich verirren; **"give ~"** (BRIT: AUT) „Vorfahrt achten!"; **in a ~** in gewisser Weise; **by the ~** übrigens; **in some ~s** in gewisser Hinsicht; **"~ in"** (BRIT) „Eingang"; **"~ out"** (BRIT) „Ausgang"

waylay [weɪ'leɪ] (irreg: like lay) vt auflauern +dat

wayward ['weɪwəd] adj eigensinnig

W.C. (BRIT) n WC nt

we [wiː] pl pron wir

weak [wiːk] adj schwach; **~en** vt schwächen ♦ vi schwächer werden; **~ling** n Schwächling m; **~ness** n Schwäche f

wealth [welθ] n Reichtum m; (abundance) Fülle f; **~y** adj reich

wean [wiːn] vt entwöhnen

weapon ['wepən] n Waffe f

wear [wɛə*] (pt wore, pp worn) n (clothing): **sports/baby ~** Sport-/Babykleidung f; (use) Verschleiß m ♦ vt (have on) tragen; (smile etc) haben; (use) abnutzen ♦ vi (last) halten; (become old) (sich) verschleißen; **evening ~** Abendkleidung f; **~ and tear** Verschleiß m; **~ away** vt verbrauchen ♦ vi schwinden; **~ down** vt (people) zermürben; **~ off** vi sich verlieren; **~ out** vt verschleißen; (person) erschöpfen

weary ['wɪərɪ] adj müde ♦ vt ermüden ♦ vi überdrüssig werden

weasel ['wiːzl] n Wiesel nt

weather ['weðə*] n Wetter nt ♦ vt verwittern lassen; (resist) überstehen; **under the ~** (fig: ill) angeschlagen (inf); **~-beaten** adj verwittert; **~cock** n Wetterhahn m; **~ forecast** n Wettervorhersage f; **~vane** n Wetterfahne f

weave [wiːv] (pt wove, pp woven) vt weben; **~r** n Weber(in) m(f); **weaving** n (craft) Webkunst f

web [web] n Netz nt; (membrane) Schwimmhaut f

wed [wed] (pt, pp wedded) vt heiraten ♦ n: **the newly-weds** npl die Frischvermählten pl

we'd [wiːd] = we had; we would

wedding ['wedɪŋ] n Hochzeit f; **silver/golden ~ anniversary** Silberhochzeit f/Goldene Hochzeit f; **~ day** n Hochzeitstag m; **~ dress** n Hochzeitskleid nt; **~ present** n Hochzeitsgeschenk nt; **~ ring** n Trauring m, Ehering m

wedge [wedʒ] n Keil m; (of cheese etc) Stück nt ♦ vt (fasten) festklemmen; (pack tightly) einkeilen

wedlock ['wedlɔk] n Ehe f

Wednesday ['wenzdeɪ] n Mittwoch m

wee [wiː] (SCOTTISH) adj klein, winzig

weed [wiːd] n Unkraut nt ♦ vt jäten;

~killer n Unkrautvertilgungsmittel nt; **~y** adj (person) schmächtig

week [wiːk] n Woche f; **a ~ today/ on Friday** heute/Freitag in einer Woche; **~day** n Wochentag m; **~end** n Wochenende nt; **~ly** adj wöchentlich; (wages, magazine) Wochen- ♦ adv wöchentlich

weep [wiːp] (pt, pp wept) vi weinen; **~ing willow** n Trauerweide f

weigh [wei] vt, vi wiegen; **to ~ anchor** den Anker lichten; **~ down** vt niederdrücken; **~ up** vt abschätzen

weight [weit] n Gewicht nt; **to lose/ put on ~** abnehmen/zunehmen; **~ing** n (allowance) Zulage f; **~lifter** n Gewichtheber m; **~y** adj (heavy) gewichtig; (important) schwerwiegend

weir [wiə*] n (Stau)wehr nt

weird [wiəd] adj seltsam

welcome [ˈwelkəm] n Willkommen nt, Empfang m ♦ vt begrüßen; **thank you - you're ~!** danke - nichts zu danken

welder [ˈweldə*] n (person) Schweißer(in) m(f)

welding [ˈweldiŋ] n Schweißen nt

welfare [ˈwelfeə*] n Wohl nt; (social) Fürsorge f; **~ state** n Wohlfahrtsstaat m; **~ work** n Fürsorge f

well [wel] n Brunnen m; (oil ~) Quelle f ♦ adj (in good health) gesund ♦ adv gut ♦ excl nun!, na schön!; **I'm ~** es geht mir gut; **get ~ soon!** gute Besserung!; **as ~** auch; **as ~ as** sowohl als auch; **~ done!** gut gemacht!; **to do ~** (person) gut zurechtkommen; (business) gut gehen; **~ up** vi emporsteigen; (fig) aufsteigen

we'll [wiːl] = we will; = we shall

well: **~-behaved** [ˈwelbiˈheivd] adj wohlerzogen; **~-being** [ˈwelbiːiŋ] n Wohl nt; **~-built** [ˈwelˈbilt] adj kräftig gebaut; **~-deserved** [ˈweldiˈzɜːvd] adj wohlverdient; **~-dressed** [ˈwelˈdrest] adj gut gekleidet; **~-heeled** [ˈwelˈhiːld] (inf) adj (wealthy) gut gepolstert

wellingtons [ˈweliŋtənz] npl (also: wellington boots) Gummistiefel pl

well: **~-known** [ˈwelˈnəun] adj bekannt; **~-mannered** [ˈwelˈmænəd] adj wohlerzogen; **~-meaning** [ˈwelˈmiːniŋ] adj (person) wohlmeinend; (action) gutgemeint; **~-off** [ˈwelˈɔf] adj gut situiert; **~-read** [ˈwelˈred] adj (sehr) belesen; **~-to-do** [ˈweltəˈduː] adj wohlhabend; **~-wisher** n Gönner m

Welsh [welʃ] adj walisisch ♦ n (LING) Walisisch nt; **the ~** npl (people) die Waliser pl; **~man/woman** (irreg) n Waliser/in m(f); **~ rarebit** n überbackene Käseschnitte m

went [went] pt of go

wept [wept] pt, pp of weep

were [wɜː*] pt pl of be

we're [wiə*] = we are

weren't [wɜːnt] = were not

west [west] n Westen m ♦ adj West-, westlich ♦ adv westwärts, nach Westen; **the W~** der Westen; **W~ Country** (BRIT) n der Südwesten Englands; **~erly** adj westlich; **~ern** adj westlich, West- ♦ n (CINE) Western m; **W~ Indian** adj westindisch ♦ n Westindier(in) m(f); **W~ Indies** npl Westindische Inseln pl; **~ward(s)** adv westwärts

wet [wet] adj naß; **to get ~** naß werden; **"~ paint"** „frisch gestrichen"; **~ blanket** n (fig) Triefel m; **~ suit** n Taucheranzug m

we've [wiːv] = we have

whack [wæk] n Schlag m ♦ vt schlagen

whale [weil] n Wal m

wharf [wɔːf] n Kai m

wharves [wɔːvz] npl of wharf

what [wɔt] adj **1** (in direct/indirect questions) welche(r, s), was für ein(e); **what size is it?** welche Größe ist das?

2 (in exclamations) was für ein(e); **what a mess!** was für ein Durcheinander!

♦ pron (interrogative/relative) was; **what are you doing?** was machst du gerade?; **what are you talking about?** wovon reden Sie?; **what is it called?** wie heißt das?; **what about ...?** wie wär's mit ...?; **I saw what you did** ich habe gesehen, was du gemacht hast

♦ excl (disbelieving) wie, was; **what, no coffee!** wie, kein Kaffee?; **I've crashed the car – what!** ich hatte einen Autounfall – was!

whatever [wɒt'evə*] adj: ~ **book** welches Buch auch immer ♦ pron: **do ~ is necessary** tu, was (immer auch) nötig ist; ~ **happens** egal, was passiert; **nothing ~** überhaupt or absolut gar nichts; **do ~ you want** tu, was (immer) du (auch) möchtest; **no reason ~ or whatsoever** überhaupt or absolut kein Grund

whatsoever [wɒtsəuevə*] adj = **whatever**

wheat [wiːt] n Weizen m; ~ **germ** n Weizenkeim m

wheedle [wiːdl] vt: **to ~ sb into doing sth** jdn dazu überreden, etw zu tun; **to ~ sth out of sb** jdm etw abluchsen

wheel [wiːl] n Rad nt; (steering ~) Lenkrad nt; (disc) Scheibe f ♦ vt schieben; ~**barrow** n Schubkarren m; ~**chair** n Rollstuhl m; ~ **clamp** n (AUT) Parkkralle f

wheeze [wiːz] vi keuchen

KEYWORD

when [wen] adv wann

♦ conj **1** (at, during, after the time that) wenn; (with past reference) als; **she was reading when I came in** sie las, als ich hereinkam; **be careful when you cross the road** seien Sie vorsichtig, wenn Sie über die Straße gehen

2 (on, at which) als; **on the day when I met him** an dem Tag, an dem ich ihn traf

3 (whereas) wo ... doch

whenever [wen'evə*] adv wann (auch) immer; (any time) wenn ♦ adv (every time that) jedesmal wenn

where [weə*] adv (place) wo; (direction) wohin; ~ **from** woher; **this is ~ ...** hier ... ; ~**abouts** ['weərə'bauts] adv wo ♦ n Aufenthaltsort m; **nobody knows his ~abouts** niemand weiß, wo er ist; ~**as** [weər'æz] conj während, wo ... doch; ~**by** pron woran, wodurch, womit, wovon; ~**upon** conj woraufhin, wonach; (at beginning of sentence) daraufhin

wherever [weər'evə*] adv wo (immer)

wherewithal ['weərwɪðɔːl] n nötige (Geld)mittel pl

whet [wet] vt (appetite) anregen

whether ['weðə*] conj ob; **I don't know ~ to accept or not** ich weiß nicht, ob ich es annehmen soll oder nicht; ~ **you go or not** ob du gehst oder nicht; **it's doubtful/unclear ~ ...** es ist zweifelhaft/nicht klar ob ...

KEYWORD

which [wɪtʃ] adj **1** (interrogative: direct, indirect) welche(r, s); **which one?** welche(r, s)?

2: in which case in diesem Fall; **by which time** zu dieser Zeit

♦ pron **1** (interrogative) welche(r, s); (of people also) wer

2 (relative) der/die/das; (referring to people) was; **the apple which you ate/which is on the table** der Apfel, den du gegessen hast/der auf dem Tisch liegt; **he said he saw her, which is true** er sagte, er habe sie gesehen, was auch stimmt

whichever [wɪtʃ'evə*] adj welche(r, s) auch immer; (no matter which) ganz gleich welche(r, s); ~ **book you take** welches Buch du auch nimmst; ~ **car you prefer** egal, welches Auto du vorziehst

whiff [wɪf] n Hauch m

while [waɪl] n Weile f ♦ conj während; **for a ~** eine Zeitlang; **~ away** vt (time) sich dat vertreiben

whim [wɪm] n Laune f

whimper [ˈwɪmpəʳ] n Wimmern nt ♦ vi wimmern

whimsical [ˈwɪmzɪkəl] adj launisch

whine [waɪn] n Gewinsel nt, Gejammer nt ♦ vi heulen, winseln

whip [wɪp] n Peitsche f; (POL) Fraktionsführer m ♦ vt (beat) peitschen; (snatch) reißen; **~ped cream** n Schlagsahne f; **~round** (BRIT: inf) n Geldsammlung f

whirl [wɜːl] n Wirbel m ♦ vt, vi (her-um)wirbeln; **~pool** n Wirbel m; **~wind** n Wirbelwind m

whirr [wɜːʳ] vi schwirren, surren

whisk [wɪsk] n Schneebesen m ♦ vt (cream etc) schlagen; **to ~ sb away** or **off** mit jdm davon sausen

whisker [ˈwɪskəʳ] n: **~s** (of animal) Barthaare pl; (of man) Backenbart m

whisky [ˈwɪskɪ] n (US, IRISH **whiskey**) n Whisky m

whisper [ˈwɪspəʳ] n Flüstern nt ♦ vt, vi flüstern

whistle [ˈwɪsl] n Pfiff m; (instrument) Pfeife f ♦ vt, vi pfeifen

white [waɪt] n Weiß nt; (of egg) Eiweiß nt ♦ adj weiß; **~ coffee** (BRIT) n Kaffee m mit Milch; **~collar worker** n Angestellte(r) m; **~ elephant** n (fig) Fehlinvestition f; **~ lie** n Notlüge f; **~ paper** n (POL) Weißbuch nt; **~wash** n (paint) Tünche f; (fig) Ehrenrettung f ♦ vt weißen, tünchen; (fig) reinwaschen

whiting [ˈwaɪtɪŋ] n Weißfisch m

Whitsun [ˈwɪtsn] n Pfingsten nt

whittle [ˈwɪtl] vt: **~ away** or **down** stutzen, verringern

whizz [wɪz] vi: **to ~ past** or **by** vorbeizischen, vorbeischwirren; **~ kid** (inf) n Kanone f

KEYWORD

who [huː] pron **1** (interrogative)

wer; (acc) wen; (dat) wem; **who is it?**, **who's there?** wer ist da?

2 (relative) der/die/das; **the man/woman who spoke to me** der Mann/die Frau, der/die mit mir sprach

whodu(n)nit [huːˈdʌnɪt] (inf) n Krimi m

whoever [huːˈevəʳ] pron wer/wer/wem auch immer; (no matter who) ganz gleich wer/wen/wem

whole [həʊl] adj ganz ♦ n Ganze(s) nt; **the ~ of the town** die ganze Stadt; **on the ~** im großen und ganzen; **as a ~** im großen und ganzen; **~hearted** adj rückhaltlos; **~heartedly** adv von ganzem Herzen; **~meal** adj (bread, flour) Vollkorn-; **~sale** n Großhandel m ♦ adj (trade) Großhandels-; (destruction) Massen-; **~saler** n Großhändler m; **~some** adj bekömmlich, gesund; **~wheat** adj = wholemeal

wholly [ˈhəʊlɪ] adv ganz, völlig

KEYWORD

whom [huːm] pron **1** (interrogative: acc) wen; (: dat) wem; **whom did you see?** wen haben Sie gesehen?; **to whom did you give it?** wem haben Sie es gegeben?

2 (relative: acc) den/die/das; (: dat) dem/der/dem; **the man whom I saw/to whom I spoke** der Mann, den ich sah/mit dem ich sprach

whooping cough [ˈhuːpɪŋ-] n Keuchhusten m

whore [hɔːʳ] n Hure f

whose [huːz] adj **1** (possessive: interrogative) wessen; (: relative) dessen; (after f and pl) deren ♦ pron wessen; **~ book is this?**, **~ is this book?** wessen Buch ist dies?; **~ is this?** wem gehört das?

KEYWORD

why [waɪ] adv warum, weshalb ♦ conj warum, weshalb; **that's not**

why I'm **here** ich bin nicht deswegen hier; **that's the reason why** deshalb

♦ *excl (expressing surprise, shock, annoyance)* na so was; *(explaining)* also dann; **why, it's you!** na so was, du bist es!

wick [wɪk] n Docht m
wicked ['wɪkɪd] adj böse
wicker ['wɪkə*] n *(also:* ~**work)** Korbgeflecht n
wicket ['wɪkɪt] n Tor nt, Dreistab m
wide [waɪd] adj breit; weit; *(in firing)* daneben ♦ adv: **to open ~** weit öffnen; **to shoot ~** daneben schießen; ~**angle lens** n Weitwinkelobjektiv nt; ~**awake** adj hellwach; ~**ly** adv weit; *(known)* allgemein; ~**n** vt erweitern; **to open** adj weit geöffnet; ~**spread** adj weitverbreitet
widow ['wɪdəʊ] n Witwe f; ~**ed** adj verwitwet; ~**er** n Witwer m
width [wɪdθ] n Breite f, Weite f
wield [wiːld] vt schwingen, handhaben
wife [waɪf] *(pl* **wives)** n (Ehe)frau f, Gattin f
wig [wɪg] n Perücke f
wiggle ['wɪgl] n Wackeln nt ♦ vt wackeln mit ♦ vi wackeln
wild [waɪld] adj wild; *(violent)* heftig; *(plan, idea)* verrückt; ~**erness** ['wɪldənɪs] n Wildnis f, Wüste f; ~ **goose chase** n *(fig)* fruchtlose(s) Unternehmen n; ~**life** n Tierwelt f; ~**ly** adv wild, ungestüm; *(exaggerated)* irrsinnig; ~**s** npl: **the** ~**s** die Wildnis f
wilful ['wɪlfʊl] *(US* **willful)** adj *(intended)* vorsätzlich; *(obstinate)* eigensinnig

will [wɪl] aux vb 1 *(forming future tense)* werden; **I will finish it tomorrow** ich mache es morgen zu Ende
2 *(in conjectures, predictions)* he

will or **he'll be there by now** er dürfte jetzt da sein; **that will be the postman** das wird der Postbote sein
3 *(in commands, requests, offers)*: **will you be quiet!** sei endlich still!; **will you help me?** hilfst du mir?; **will you have a cup of tea?** trinken Sie eine Tasse Tee?; **I won't put up with it!** das lasse ich mir nicht gefallen!

♦ vt wollen

♦ n Wille m; *(JUR)* Testament nt

willing ['wɪlɪŋ] adj gewillt, bereit; ~**ly** adv bereitwillig, gern; ~**ness** n (Bereit)willigkeit f
willow ['wɪləʊ] n Weide f
willpower ['wɪlpaʊə*] n Willenskraft f
willy-nilly ['wɪlɪ'nɪlɪ] adv einfach so
wilt [wɪlt] vi (ver)welken
wily ['waɪlɪ] adj gerissen
win [wɪn] *(pt, pp* **won)** n Sieg m ♦ vt, vi gewinnen; **to ~ sb over** or **round** jdn überzeugen or dazu bringen
wince [wɪns] n Zusammenzucken nt ♦ vi zusammenzucken
winch [wɪntʃ] n Winde f
wind¹ [wɪnd] n Wind m; *(MED)* Blähungen pl
wind² [waɪnd] *(pt, pp* **wound)** vt *(rope)* winden; *(bandage)* wickeln ♦ vi *(turn)* sich winden; ~ **up** vt *(clock)* aufziehen; *(debate)* (ab)schließen
windfall ['wɪndfɔːl] n unverhoffte(r) Glücksfall m
winding ['waɪndɪŋ] adj *(road)* gewunden
wind instrument ['wɪndɪnstrʊmənt] n Blasinstrument nt
windmill ['wɪndmɪl] n Windmühle f
window ['wɪndəʊ] n Fenster nt; ~ **box** n Blumenkasten m; ~ **cleaner** n Fensterputzer m; ~ **envelope** n Fensterbriefumschlag m; ~ **ledge** n Fenstersims m; ~ **pane** n Fensterscheibe f; ~**sill** n Fensterbank f
windpipe ['wɪndpaɪp] n Luftröhre f

wind power n windenergie f
windscreen ['wındskriːn] (BRIT) n
Windschutzscheibe f; ~ **washer** n
Scheibenwaschanlage f; ~ **wiper** n
Scheibenwischer m
windshield ['wındʃiːld] (US) n =
windscreen
windswept ['wındswept] adj vom
Wind gepeitscht; (person) zerzaust
windy ['wındı] adj windig
wine [waın] n Wein m; ~ **cellar** n
Weinkeller m; ~ **glass** n Weinglas nt;
~ **list** n Weinkarte f; ~ **merchant** n
Weinhändler m; ~ **tasting** n Wein-
probe f; ~ **waiter** n Weinkellner m
wing [wıŋ] n Flügel m; (MIL) Gruppe f; ~s npl (THEAT) Seitenkulisse
f; ~**er** n (SPORT) Flügelstürmer m
wink [wıŋk] n Zwinkern nt ♦ vi zwinkern, blinzeln
winner ['wınə*] n Gewinner m,
(SPORT) Sieger m
winning ['wınıŋ] adj (team) siegreich, Sieger-; (goal) entscheidend;
~ **post** n Ziel nt; ~**s** npl Gewinn m
winter ['wıntə*] n Winter m ♦ adj
(clothes) Winter- ♦ vi überwintern;
~ **sports** npl Wintersport m
wintry ['wıntrı] adj Winter-, winter-
lich
wipe [waıp] n: to give sth a ~ etw
(ab)wischen ♦ vt wischen; ~ **off** vt
abwischen; ~ **out** vt (debt) tilgen;
(destroy) auslöschen; ~ **up** vt aufwischen
wire [waıə*] n Draht m; (telegram)
Telegramm nt ♦ vt telegrafieren; to
~ **sb** jdm telegrafieren
wireless ['waıəlıs] (BRIT) n Ra-
dio(apparat) nt
wiring ['waıərıŋ] n elektrische Leitungen pl
wiry ['waıərı] adj drahtig
wisdom ['wızdəm] n Weisheit f; (of
decision) Klugheit f; ~ **tooth** n Weis-
heitszahn m
wise [waız] adj klug, weise ♦ suffix:
timewise zeitlich gesehen
wisecrack n Witzelei f
wish [wıʃ] n Wunsch m ♦ vt

wünschen; best ~es (on birthday
etc) alles Gute; (on letter) herz-
liche Grüße; to ~ **sb** goodbye jdn
verabschieden; he ~ed me well er
wünschte mir Glück; to ~ **to do sth**
etw tun wollen; to ~ **for** vt fus sich auf
wünschen; ~**ful thinking** n Wunsch-
denken nt
wishy-washy ['wıʃı'wɒʃı] (inf) adj
(colour) verwaschen; (ideas, argument) verschwommen
wisp [wısp] n (Haar)strähne f; (of
smoke) Wölkchen nt
wistful ['wıstful] adj sehnsüchtig
wit [wıt] n (also: ~**s**) Verstand m no
pl; (amusing ideas) Witz m; (person)
Witzbold m
witch [wıtʃ] n Hexe f; ~**craft** n He-
xerei f

KEYWORD

with [wıð, wıθ] prep **1** (accompanying, in the company of) mit; wir
stayed **with friends** wir
übernachteten bei Freunden; **I'll be
with you in a minute** ich bin sofort da; **I'm not
with you** (I don't understand) das
verstehe ich nicht; **to be with it**
(inf: up-to-date) auf dem laufenden
sein; (: alert) (voll) da sein (inf)
2 (descriptive, indicating manner
etc) mit; **the man with the grey
hat** der Mann mit dem grauen Hut;
red with anger rot vor Wut

withdraw [wıθ'drɔː] (irreg: like
draw) vt zurückziehen; (money) abheben; (remark) zurücknehmen ♦ vi
sich zurückziehen; ~**al** n Zu-
rückziehung f; Abheben nt; Zu-
rücknahme f; ~**n** adj (person) verschlossen
wither ['wıðə*] vi (ver)welken
withhold [wıθ'həuld] (irreg: like
hold) vt: to ~ **sth (from sb)** (jdm)
etw vorenthalten
within [wıð'ın] prep innerhalb +gen
♦ adv innen; ~ **sight of** in Sichtwei-
te von; ~ **the week** innerhalb dieser

Woche; ~ **a mile of** weniger als eine Meile von

without [wɪð'aʊt] prep ohne; ~ **speaking/sleeping** etc ohne zu sprechen/schlafen etc

withstand [wɪθ'stænd] n (irreg: like **stand**) vt widerstehen +dat

witness ['wɪtnəs] n Zeuge m, Zeugin f ♦ vt (see) sehen, miterleben; (document) beglaubigen; ~ **box** n Zeugenstand m; ~ **stand** (US) n Zeugenstand m

witticism ['wɪtɪsɪzəm] n witzige Bemerkung f

witty ['wɪtɪ] adj witzig, geistreich

wives [waɪvz] pl of **wife**

wizard ['wɪzəd] n Zauberer m

wk abbr = **week**

wobble ['wɒbl] vi wackeln

woe [wəʊ] n Kummer m

woke [wəʊk] pt of **wake**

woken ['wəʊkən] pp of **wake**

woman ['wʊmən] n (pl **women**) n Frau f; ~ **doctor** n Ärztin f; ~**ly** adj weiblich

womb [wuːm] n Gebärmutter f

women ['wɪmɪn] npl of **woman**; ~'s **lib** (inf) n Frauenrechtsbewegung f

won [wʌn] pt, pp of **win**

wonder ['wʌndə*] n (marvel) Wunder nt; (surprise) Staunen nt, Verwunderung f ♦ vi sich wundern ♦ vt: I ~ **whether** ... ich frage mich, ob ...; it's no ~ **that** es ist kein Wunder, daß; **to** ~ **at** sich wundern über +acc; **to** ~ **about** sich Gedanken machen über +acc; ~**ful** adj wunderbar, herrlich; ~**fully** adv wunderbar

won't [wəʊnt] = **will not**

woo [wuː] vt (woman) den Hof machen +dat, umwerben; (audience etc) umwerben

wood [wʊd] n Holz nt; (forest) Wald m; ~ **carving** n Holzschnitzerei f; ~**ed** adj bewaldet; ~**en** adj (also fig) hölzern; ~**pecker** n Specht m; ~**wind** n Blasinstrumente pl; ~**work** n Holzwerk nt; (craft) Holzarbeiten pl; ~**worm** n Holzwurm m

wool [wʊl] n Wolle f; **to pull the** ~

over sb's eyes (fig) jdm Sand in die Augen streuen; ~**len** (US **woolen**) adj Woll-; ~**lens** npl Wollsachen pl; ~**ly** (US **wooly**) adj wollig; (fig) schwammig

word [wɜːd] n Wort nt; (news) Bescheid m ♦ vt formulieren; **in other** ~s anders gesagt; **to break/keep one's** ~ sein Wort brechen/halten; ~**ing** n Wortlaut m; ~ **processing** n Textverarbeitung f; ~ **processor** n Textverarbeitungsgerät nt

wore [wɔː*] pt of **wear**

work [wɜːk] n Arbeit f; (ART, LITER) Werk nt ♦ vi arbeiten; (machine) funktionieren; (medicine) wirken; (succeed) klappen; ~s n sg (BRIT: factory) Fabrik f, Werk nt ♦ npl (of watch) Werk nt; **to be out of** ~ arbeitslos sein; **in** ~**ing order** in betriebsfähigem Zustand; ~ **loose** vi sich lockern; ~ **on** vi weiterarbeiten ♦ vt fus (be engaged in) arbeiten an +dat; (influence) bearbeiten; ~ **out** vi (sum) aufgehen; (plan) klappen ♦ vt (problem) lösen; (plan) ausarbeiten; **it** ~s **out at £100** das gibt or macht £100; ~ **up** vt: **to get** ~**ed up** sich aufregen; ~**able** adj (soil) bearbeitbar; (plan) ausführbar; ~**aholic** [wɜːkə'hɒlɪk] n Arbeitssüchtige(r) m/f; ~**er** n Arbeiter(in) m/f; ~**force** n Arbeiterschaft f; ~**ing class** n Arbeiterklasse f; ~**ing-class** adj Arbeiter-; ~**man** (irreg) n Arbeiter m; ~**manship** n Arbeit f, Ausführung f; ~**sheet** n Arbeitsblatt nt; ~**shop** n Werkstatt f; ~ **station** n Arbeitsplatz m; ~-**to-rule** (BRIT) n Dienst m nach Vorschrift

world [wɜːld] n Welt f; **to think the** ~ **of sb** große Stücke auf jdn halten; ~**ly** adj weltlich, irdisch; ~-**wide** adj weltweit

worm [wɜːm] n Wurm m

worn [wɔːn] pp of **wear** ♦ adj (clothes) abgetragen; ~-**out** adj (object) abgenutzt; (person) völlig erschöpft

worried ['wʌrɪd] adj besorgt, beunru-

higt
worry ['wʌrɪ] n Sorge f ♦ vt beunruhigen ♦ vi (feel uneasy) sich sorgen, sich dat Gedanken machen; ~**ing** adj beunruhigend

worse [wɜːs] adj schlechter, schlimmer ♦ adv schlimmer, ärger ♦ n Schlimmere(s) nt, Schlechtere(s) nt; **a change for the ~** eine Verschlechterung; ~**n** vt verschlimmern ♦ vi sich verschlechtern; ~ **off** adj (fig) schlechter dran

worship ['wɜːʃɪp] n Verehrung f ♦ vt anbeten; **Your W~** (BRIT: to mayor) Herr/Frau Bürgermeister (: to judge) Euer Ehren

worst [wɜːst] adj schlimmste(r, s), schlechteste(r, s) ♦ adv am schlimmsten, am ärgsten ♦ n Schlimmste(s) nt, Ärgste(s) nt; **at ~** schlimmstenfalls

worsted ['wʊstɪd] n Kammgarn nt

worth [wɜːθ] n Wert m ♦ adj wert; **it's ~** es ist lohnt sich; **to be ~ one's while (to do sth)** die Mühe wert sein (, etw zu tun); ~**less** adj wertlos; (person) nichtsnutzig; ~**while** adj lohnend, der Mühe wert

worthy [wɜːðɪ] adj wert, würdig

KEYWORD

would [wʊd] aux vb **1** (conditional tense): **if you asked him he would do it** wenn du ihn fragtest, würde er es tun; **if you had asked him he would have done it** wenn du ihn gefragt hättest, hätte er es getan

2 (in offers, invitations, requests): **would you like a biscuit?** möchten Sie ein Plätzchen?; **would you ask him to come in?** würden Sie ihn bitte hineinbitten?

3 (in indirect speech): **I said I would do it** ich sagte, ich würde es tun

4 (emphatic): **it WOULD have to snow today!** es mußte ja ausgerechnet heute schneien!

5 (insistence): **she wouldn't behave** sie wollte sich partout nicht an-

ständig benehmen

6 (conjecture): **it would have been midnight** es mag ungefähr Mitternacht gewesen sein; **it would seem so** es sieht wohl so aus

7 (indicating habit): **he would go there on Mondays** er ging jeden Montag dorthin

would-be ['wʊdbɪ] (pej) adj Möchtegern-

wouldn't ['wʊdnt] = would not

wound¹ [wuːnd] n (also fig) Wunde f ♦ vt verwunden, verletzen (also fig)

wound² [waʊnd] (pt, pp) of **wind**

wove [wəʊv] pt of **weave**; ~**n** ['wəʊvən] pp of **weave**

wrangle ['ræŋgl] n Streit m ♦ vi sich zanken

wrap [ræp] n (stole) Schal m ♦ vt einwickeln; ~ **up** vt einwickeln; (deal) abschließen; ~ **up** vt Umschlag m, Schutzhülle f; ~**ping paper** n Einwickelpapier nt

wrath [rɒθ] n Zorn m

wreak [riːk] vt (havoc) anrichten; (vengeance) üben

wreath [riːθ, pl riːðz] n Kranz m

wreck [rek] n (ship) Wrack nt; (sth ruined) Ruine f ♦ vt zerstören; ~**age** n Trümmer pl

wren [ren] n Zaunkönig m

wrench [rentʃ] n (spanner) Schraubenschlüssel m; (twist) Ruck m ♦ vt reißen, zerren; **to ~ sth from sb** jdm etw entreißen or entwinden

wrestle ['resl] vi: **to ~ (with sb)** (mit jdm) ringen; ~**r** n Ringer(in) m(f); **wrestling** n Ringen nt

wretched ['retʃɪd] adj (hovel) elend; (inf) verflixt; **I feel ~** mir ist elend

wriggle ['rɪgl] n Schlängeln nt ♦ vi sich winden

wring [rɪŋ] (pt, pp wrung) vt wringen

wrinkle ['rɪŋkl] n Falte f, Runzel f ♦ vt runzeln ♦ vi sich runzeln; (material) knittern

wrist [rɪst] n Handgelenk nt; ~**watch** n Armbanduhr f

writ [rɪt] n gerichtliche(r) Befehl m

write [raɪt] (pt **wrote**, pp **written**) vt, vi schreiben; ~ **down** vt aufschreiben; ~ **off** vt (dismiss) abschreiben; ~ **out** vt (essay) abschreiben; (cheque) ausstellen; ~ **up** vt schreiben; **~-off** n: it is a ~-off das kann man abschreiben; **~r** n Schriftsteller m

writhe [raɪð] vi sich winden

writing ['raɪtɪŋ] n (act) Schreiben nt; (hand-) (Hand)schrift f; in ~ schriftlich; ~ **paper** n Schreibpapier nt

written ['rɪtn] pp of **write**

wrong [rɒŋ] adj (incorrect) falsch; (morally) unrecht ♦ n Unrecht nt ♦ vt Unrecht tun +dat; he was ~ in doing that es war nicht recht von ihm, das zu tun; **you are** ~ **about that, you've got it** ~ da hast du unrecht; **to be in the** ~ im Unrecht sein; **what's** ~ **with your leg?** was ist mit deinem Bein los?; **to go** ~ (plan) schiefgehen; (person) einen Fehler machen; **~ful** adj unrechtmäßig; **~ly** adv falsch; (accuse) zu Unrecht

wrote [rəʊt] pt of **write**

wrought [rɔːt] adj: ~ **iron** Schmiedeeisen nt

wrung [rʌŋ] pt, pp of **wring**

wry [raɪ] adj ironisch

wt. abbr = **weight**

X

Xmas ['eksməs] n abbr = **Christmas**

X-ray ['eksreɪ] n Röntgenaufnahme f ♦ vt röntgen; **~s** npl Röntgenstrahlen pl

xylophone ['zaɪləfəʊn] n Xylophon n

Y

yacht [jɒt] n Jacht f; **~ing** n (Sport)segeln nt; **~sman** n Sportsegler m

Yank [jæŋk] (inf) n Ami m

yap [jæp] vi (dog) kläffen

yard [jɑːd] n Hof m; (measure) (englische) Elle f, Yard nt (0,91 m); **~stick** n (fig) Maßstab m

yarn [jɑːn] n (thread) Garn nt; (story) (Seemanns)garn nt

yawn [jɔːn] n Gähnen nt ♦ vi gähnen; **~ing** adj (gap) gähnend

yd. abbr = **yard(s)**

yeah [jɛə] (inf) adv ja

year [jɪə] n Jahr nt; **to be 8 ~s old** acht Jahre alt sein; **an eight-year-old child** ein achtjähriges Kind; **~ly** adj, adv jährlich

yearn [jɜːn] vi: **to ~ (for)** sich sehnen (nach); **~ing** n Verlangen nt, Sehnsucht f

yeast [jiːst] n Hefe f

yell [jel] n gellende(r) Schrei m ♦ vi laut schreien

yellow ['jeləʊ] adj gelb ♦ n Gelb nt

yelp [jelp] n Gekläff nt ♦ vi kläffen

yeoman ['jəʊmən] (irreg) n: **Y~ of the Guard** Leibgardist m

yes [jes] adv ja ♦ n Ja nt, Jawort nt; **to say ~** ja sagen; **to answer ~** mit Ja antworten

yesterday ['jestədeɪ] adv gestern ♦ n Gestern nt; **~ morning/evening** gestern morgen/abend; **all day ~** gestern den ganzen Tag; **the day before ~** vorgestern

yet [jet] adv noch; (in question) schon; (up to now) bis jetzt ♦ conj doch, dennoch; **it is not finished ~** es ist noch nicht fertig; **the best ~** das bisher beste; **as ~** bis jetzt; (in past) bis dahin

yew [juː] n Eibe f

yield [jiːld] n Ertrag m ♦ vt (result, crop) hervorbringen; (interest, profit) abwerfen; (concede) abtreten ♦ vi nachgeben; (MIL) sich ergeben; **"~"** (US: AUT) „Vorfahrt gewähren"

YMCA n abbr (= Young Men's Christian Association) CVJM m

yoga ['jəʊgə] n Joga m

yoghourt ['jɒgət] n Joghurt m

yog(h)urt ['jɒgət] n = yoghourt

yoke [jəʊk] n (also fig) Joch nt

yolk [jəʊk] n Eidotter m, Eigelb nt

yonder ['jɒndə*] adv dort drüben, da drüben ♦ adj jene(r, s) dort

---

KEYWORD

you [juː] pron 1 (subj, in comparisons: German familiar form: sg) du; (: pl) ihr; (in letters also) Du, Ihr; (: German polite form) Sie; **you** Germans ihr Deutschen; **she's younger than you** sie ist jünger als du/Sie

2 (direct object, after prep +acc: German familiar form: sg) dich; (: pl) euch; (in letters also) Dich, Euch; (: German polite form) Sie; **I know you** ich kenne dich/euch/Sie

3 (indirect object, after prep +dat: German familiar form: sg) dir; (: pl) euch; (in letters also) Dir, Euch; (: German polite form) Ihnen; **I gave it to you** ich gab es dir/euch/Ihnen

4 (impers: one: subj) man; (: direct object) einen; (: indirect object) einem; **fresh air does you good** frische Luft tut gut

you'd [juːd] = you had; you would

you'll [juːl] = you will; you shall

young [jʌŋ] adj jung ♦ npl: **the ~** die Jungen pl; **~ish** adj ziemlich jung; **~ster** n Junge m, junge(r) Bursche m, junges Mädchen nt

your ['jɔː*] adj (familiar: sg) dein; (: pl) euer, eure pl; (polite) Ihr; see also my

you're ['jʊə*] = you are

yours [jɔːz] pron (familiar: sg) deine(r, s); (: pl) eure(r, s); (polite) Ihre(r, s); see also mine

yourself [jɔː'self] pron (emphatic) selbst; (familiar: sg: acc) dich (selbst); (: dat) dir (selbst); (: pl) euch (selbst); (polite) sich (selbst); see also oneself

youth [juːθ, pl juːðz] n Jugend f;

(young man) junge(r) Mann m; **~s** npl (young people) Jugendliche pl; **~ club** n Jugendzentrum nt; **~ful** adj jugendlich; **~ hostel** n Jugendherberge f

you've [juːv] = you have

YTS (BRIT) n abbr (= Youth Training Scheme) staatliches Förderprogramm für arbeitslose Jugendliche

Yugoslav ['juːgəʊ'slɑːv] adj jugoslawisch ♦ n Jugoslawe m, Jugoslawin f

Yugoslavia ['juːgəʊ'slɑːvɪə] n Jugoslawien nt

yuppie ['jʌpɪ] (inf) n Yuppie m ♦ adj yuppiehaft, Yuppie-

YWCA n abbr (= Young Women's Christian Association) CVJF m

Z

zany ['zeɪnɪ] adj (ideas, sense of humour) verrückt

zap [zæp] vt (COMPUT) löschen

zeal [ziːl] n Eifer m; **~ous** ['zeləs] adj eifrig

zebra ['ziːbrə] n Zebra nt; **~ crossing** (BRIT) n Zebrastreifen m

zero ['zɪərəʊ] n Null f; (on scale) Nullpunkt m

zest [zest] n Begeisterung f

zigzag ['zɪgzæg] n Zickzack m

zip [zɪp] n Reißverschluß m ♦ vt (also: **~ up**) den Reißverschluß zumachen +gen; **~ code** (US) n Postleitzahl f; **~ fastener** n Reißverschluß m; **~per** (esp US) n Reißverschluß m

zodiac ['zəʊdɪæk] n Tierkreis m

zombie ['zɒmbɪ] n: **like a ~** (fig) wie im Tran

zoo [zuː] n Zoo m

zoology [zəʊ'ɒlədʒɪ] n Zoologie f

zoom [zuːm] vi: **to ~** past vorbeisausen; **~ lens** n Zoomobjektiv nt

zucchini [zuː'kiːnɪ] (US) npl Zucchini pl

GERMAN IRREGULAR VERBS
*with 'sein'

infinitive	present indicative (2nd, 3rd sg.)	imperfect	past participle
aufschrecken*	schrickst auf, schrickt auf	schrak or schreckte auf	aufgeschreckt
ausbedingen	bedingst aus, bedingt aus	bedang or bedingte aus	ausbedungen
backen	bäckst, bäckt	backte or buk	gebacken
befehlen	befiehlst, befiehlt	befahl	befohlen
beginnen	beginnst, beginnt	begann	begonnen
beißen	beißt, beißt	biß	gebissen
bergen	birgst, birgt	barg	geborgen
bersten*	birst, birst	barst	geborsten
bescheißen*	bescheißt, bescheißt	beschiß	beschissen
bewegen	bewegst, bewegt	bewog	bewogen
biegen	biegst, biegt	bog	gebogen
bieten	bietest, bietet	bot	geboten
binden	bindest, bindet	band	gebunden
bitten	bittest, bittet	bat	gebeten
blasen	bläst, bläst	blies	geblasen
bleiben*	bleibst, bleibt	blieb	geblieben
braten	brätst, brät	briet	gebraten
brechen*	brichst, bricht	brach	gebrochen
brennen	brennst, brennt	brannte	gebrannt
bringen	bringst, bringt	brachte	gebracht
denken	denkst, denkt	dachte	gedacht
dreschen	drisch(e)st, drischt	drasch	gedroschen
dringen*	dringst, dringt	drang	gedrungen
dürfen	darfst, darf	durfte	gedurft
empfehlen	empfiehlst, empfiehlt	empfahl	empfohlen
erbleichen*	erbleichst, erbleicht	erbleichte	erblichen
erlöschen*	erlischst, erlischt	erlosch	erloschen
erschrecken*	erschrickst, erschrickt	erschrak	erschrocken
essen	ißt, ißt	aß	gegessen
fahren*	fährst, fährt	fuhr	gefahren
fallen*	fällst, fällt	fiel	gefallen
fangen	fängst, fängt	fing	gefangen
fechten	fichtst, ficht	focht	gefochten
finden	findest, findet	fand	gefunden
flechten	flichtst, flicht	flocht	geflochten
fliegen*	fliegst, fliegt	flog	geflogen

315

infinitive	present indicative (2nd, 3rd sing.)	imperfect	past participle
fliehen*	fliehst, flieht	floh	geflohen
fließen*	fließt, fließt	floß	geflossen
fressen	frißt, frißt	fraß	gefressen
frieren	frierst, friert	fror	gefroren
gären*	gärst, gärt	gor	gegoren
gebären*	gebierst, gebiert	gebar	geboren
geben	gibst, gibt	gab	gegeben
gedeihen*	gedeihst, gedeiht	gedieh	gediehen
gehen*	gehst, geht	ging	gegangen
gelingen*	——, gelingt	gelang	gelungen
gelten	giltst, gilt	galt	gegolten
genesen*	gene(se)st, genest	genas	genesen
genießen	genießt, genießt	genoß	genossen
geraten*	gerätst, gerät	geriet	geraten
geschehen*	——, geschieht	geschah	geschehen
gewinnen	gewinnst, gewinnt	gewann	gewonnen
gießen	gießt, gießt	goß	gegossen
gleichen	gleichst, gleicht	glich	geglichen
gleiten*	gleitest, gleitet	glitt	geglitten
glimmen	glimmst, glimmt	glomm	geglommen
graben	gräbst, gräbt	grub	gegraben
greifen	greifst, greift	griff	gegriffen
haben	hast, hat	hatte	gehabt
halten	hältst, hält	hielt	gehalten
hängen	hängst, hängt	hing	gehangen
hauen	haust, haut	haute	gehauen
heben	hebst, hebt	hob	gehoben
heißen	heißt, heißt	hieß	geheißen
helfen	hilfst, hilft	half	geholfen
kennen	kennst, kennt	kannte	gekannt
klimmen*	klimmst, klimmt	klomm	geklommen
klingen	klingst, klingt	klang	geklungen
kneifen	kneifst, kneift	kniff	gekniffen
kommen*	kommst, kommt	kam	gekommen
können	kannst, kann	konnte	gekonnt
kriechen*	kriechst, kriecht	kroch	gekrochen
laden	lädst, lädt	lud	geladen
lassen	läßt, läßt	ließ	gelassen
laufen*	läufst, läuft	lief	gelaufen
leiden	leidest, leidet	litt	gelitten
leihen	leihst, leiht	lieh	geliehen
lesen	liest, liest	las	gelesen

infinitive	present indicative (2nd, 3rd sing.)	imperfect	past participle
liegen*	liegst, liegt	lag	gelegen
lügen	lügst, lügt	log	gelogen
mahlen	mahlst, mahlt	mahlte	gemahlen
meiden	meidest, meidet	mied	gemieden
melken	melkst, melkt	melkte	gemolken
messen	mißt, mißt	maß	gemessen
mißlingen	——, mißlingt	mißlang	mißlungen
mögen	magst, mag	mochte	gemocht
müssen	mußt, muß	mußte	gemußt
nehmen	nimmst, nimmt	nahm	genommen
nennen	nennst, nennt	nannte	genannt
pfeifen	pfeifst, pfeift	pfiff	gepfiffen
preisen	preist, preist	pries	gepriesen
quellen*	quillst, quillt	quoll	gequollen
raten	rätst, rät	riet	geraten
reiben	reibst, reibt	rieb	gerieben
reißen*	reißt, reißt	riß	gerissen
reiten*	reitest, reitet	ritt	geritten
rennen*	rennst, rennt	rannte	gerannt
riechen	riechst, riecht	roch	gerochen
ringen	ringst, ringt	rang	gerungen
rinnen*	rinnst, rinnt	rann	geronnen
rufen	rufst, ruft	rief	gerufen
salzen	salzt, salzt	salzte	gesalzen
saufen	säufst, säuft	soff	gesoffen
saugen	saugst, saugt	sog	gesogen
schaffen	schaffst, schafft	schuf	geschaffen
scheiden	scheidest, scheidet	schied	geschieden
scheinen	scheinst, scheint	schien	geschienen
schelten	schiltst, schilt	schalt	gescholten
scheren	scherst, schert	schor	geschoren
schieben	schiebst, schiebt	schob	geschoben
schießen	schießt, schießt	schoß	geschossen
schinden	schindest, schindet	schindete	geschunden
schlafen	schläfst, schläft	schlief	geschlafen
schlagen	schlägst, schlägt	schlug	geschlagen
schleichen*	schleichst, schleicht	schlich	geschlichen
schleifen	schleifst, schleift	schliff	geschliffen
schließen	schließt, schließt	schloß	geschlossen
schlingen	schlingst, schlingt	schlang	geschlungen
schmeißen	schmeißt, schmeißt	schmiß	geschmissen
schmelzen*	schmilzt, schmilzt	schmolz	geschmolzen
schneiden	schneidest, schneidet	schnitt	geschnitten

infinitive	present indicative (2nd, 3rd sing.)	imperfect	past participle
schreiben	schreibst, schreibt	schrieb	geschrieben
schreien	schreist, schreit	schrie	geschrie(e)n
schreiten	schreitest, schreitet	schritt	geschritten
schweigen	schweigst, schweigt	schwieg	geschwiegen
schwellen*	schwillst, schwillt	schwoll	geschwollen
schwimmen*	schwimmst, schwimmt	schwamm	geschwommen
schwinden*	schwindest, schwindet	schwand	geschwunden
schwingen	schwingst, schwingt	schwang	geschwungen
schwören	schwörst, schwört	schwor	geschworen
sehen	siehst, sieht	sah	gesehen
sein*	bist, ist	war	gewesen
senden	sendest, sendet	sandte	gesandt
singen	singst, singt	sang	gesungen
sinken*	sinkst, sinkt	sank	gesunken
sinnen	sinnst, sinnt	sann	gesonnen
sitzen*	sitzt, sitzt	saß	gesessen
sollen	sollst, soll	sollte	gesollt
speien	speist, speit	spie	gespie(e)n
spinnen	spinnst, spinnt	spann	gesponnen
sprechen	sprichst, spricht	sprach	gesprochen
sprießen*	sprießt, sprießt	sproß	gesprossen
springen*	springst, springt	sprang	gesprungen
stechen	stichst, sticht	stach	gestochen
stecken	steckst, steckt	steckte or stak	gesteckt
stehen	stehst, steht	stand	gestanden
stehlen	stiehlst, stiehlt	stahl	gestohlen
steigen*	steigst, steigt	stieg	gestiegen
sterben*	stirbst, stirbt	starb	gestorben
stinken	stinkst, stinkt	stank	gestunken
stoßen*	stößt, stößt	stieß	gestoßen
streichen	streichst, streicht	strich	gestrichen
streiten*	streitest, streitet	stritt	gestritten
tragen	trägst, trägt	trug	getragen
treffen	triffst, trifft	traf	getroffen
treiben*	treibst, treibt	trieb	getrieben
treten*	trittst, tritt	trat	getreten
trinken	trinkst, trinkt	trank	getrunken
trügen	trügst, trügt	trog	getrogen
tun	tust, tut	tat	getan
verderben*	verdirbst, verdirbt	verdarb	verdorben
verdrießen	verdrießt, verdrießt	verdroß	verdrossen

infinitive	present indicative (2nd, 3rd sing.)	imperfect	past participle
vergessen	vergißt, vergißt	vergaß	vergessen
verlieren	verlierst, verliert	verlor	verloren
verschleißen	verschleißt, verschleißt	verschliß	verschlissen
wachsen*	wächst, wächst	wuchs	gewachsen
wägen	wägst, wägt	wog	gewogen
waschen	wäschst, wäscht	wusch	gewaschen
weben	webst, webt	webte *or* wob	gewoben
weichen*	weichst, weicht	wich	gewichen
weisen	weist, weist	wies	gewiesen
wenden	wendest, wendet	wandte	gewandt
werben	wirbst, wirbt	warb	geworben
werden*	wirst, wird	wurde	geworden
werfen	wirfst, wirft	warf	geworfen
wiegen	wiegst, wiegt	wog	gewogen
winden	windest, windet	wand	gewunden
wissen	weißt, weiß	wußte	gewußt
wollen	willst, will	wollte	gewollt
wringen	wringst, wringt	wrang	gewrungen
zeihen	zeihst, zeiht	zieh	geziehen
ziehen*	ziehst, zieht	zog	gezogen
zwingen	zwingst, zwingt	zwang	gezwungen

UNREGELMÄSSIGE ENGLISCHE VERBEN

present	pt	pp	present	pt	pp
arise	arose	arisen	dig	dug	dug
awake	awoke	awaked	do (3rd	did	done
be (am, is,was,	were	been	person;		
are;			he/she/it/		
being)			does)		
bear	bore	born(e)	draw	drew	drawn
beat	beat	beaten	dream	dreamed,	dreamed,
become	became	become		dreamt	dreamt
begin	began	begun	drink	drank	drunk
behold	beheld	beheld	drive	drove	driven
bend	bent	bent	dwell	dwelt	dwelt
beset	beset	beset	eat	ate	eaten
bet	bet,	bet,	fall	fell	fallen
	betted	betted	feed	fed	fed
bid	bid,	bid,	feel	felt	felt
	bade	bidden	fight	fought	fought
bind	bound	bound	find	found	found
bite	bit	bitten	flee	fled	fled
bleed	bled	bled	fling	flung	flung
blow	blew	blown	fly (flies)	flew	flown
break	broke	broken	forbid	forbade	forbidden
breed	bred	bred	forecast	forecast	forecast
bring	brought	brought	forget	forgot	forgotten
build	built	built	forgive	forgave	forgiven
burn	burnt,	burnt,	forsake	forsook	forsaken
	burned	burned	freeze	froze	frozen
burst	burst	burst	get	got	got, (US)
buy	bought	bought			gotten
can	could	(been	give	gave	given
		able)	go (goes)	went	gone
cast	cast	cast	grind	ground	ground
catch	caught	caught	grow	grew	grown
choose	chose	chosen	hang	hung,	hung,
cling	clung	clung		hanged	hanged
come	came	come	have (has;	had	had
cost	cost	cost	having)		
creep	crept	crept	hear	heard	heard
cut	cut	cut	hide	hid	hidden
deal	dealt	dealt	hit	hit	hit

present	pt	pp	present	pt	pp
hold	held	held	**sell**	sold	sold
hurt	hurt	hurt	**send**	sent	sent
keep	kept	kept	**set**	set	set
kneel	knelt,	knelt,	**shake**	shook	shaken
	kneeled	kneeled	**shall**	should	—
know	knew	known	**shear**	sheared	shorn,
lay	laid	laid			sheared
lead	led	led	**shed**	shed	shed
lean	leant,	leant,	**shine**	shone	shone
	leaned	leaned	**shoot**	shot	shot
leap	leapt,	leapt,	**show**	showed	shown
	leaped	leaped	**shrink**	shrank	shrunk
learn	learnt,	learnt,	**shut**	shut	shut
	learned	learned	**sing**	sang	sung
leave	left	left	**sink**	sank	sunk
lend	lent	lent	**sit**	sat	sat
let	let	let	**slay**	slew	slain
lie (lying)	lay	lain	**sleep**	slept	slept
light	lit,	lit,	**slide**	slid	slid
	lighted	lighted	**sling**	slung	slung
lose	lost	lost	**slit**	slit	slit
make	made	made	**smell**	smelt,	smelt,
may	might	—		smelled	smelled
mean	meant	meant	**sow**	sowed	sown,
meet	met	met			sowed
mistake	mistook	mistaken	**speak**	spoke	spoken
mow	mowed	mown,	**speed**	sped,	sped,
		mowed		speeded	speeded
must	(had to)	(had to)	**spell**	spelt,	spelt,
pay	paid	paid		spelled	spelled
put	put	put	**spend**	spent	spent
quit	quit,	quit,	**spill**	spilt,	spilt,
	quitted	quitted		spilled	spilled
read	read	read	**spin**	spun	spun
rid	rid	rid	**spit**	spat	spat
ride	rode	ridden	**split**	split	split
ring	rang	rung	**spoil**	spoiled,	spoiled,
rise	rose	risen		spoilt	spoilt
run	ran	run	**spread**	spread	spread
saw	sawed	sawn	**spring**	sprang	sprung
say	said	said	**stand**	stood	stood
see	saw	seen	**steal**	stole	stolen
seek	sought	sought	**stick**	stuck	stuck

present	pt	pp	present	pt	pp
sting	stung	stung	think	thought	thought
stink	stank	stunk	throw	threw	thrown
stride	strode	stridden	thrust	thrust	thrust
strike	struck	struck, stricken	tread	trod	trodden
			wake	woke, waked	woken, waked
strive	strove	striven			
swear	swore	sworn	wear	wore	worn
sweep	swept	swept	weave	wove, weaved	woven, weaved
swell	swelled	swollen, swelled	wed	wedded, wed	wedded, wed
swim	swam	swum			
swing	swung	swung	weep	wept	wept
take	took	taken	win	won	won
teach	taught	taught	wind	wound	wound
tear	tore	torn	wring	wrung	wrung
tell	told	told	write	wrote	written

NUMMER

NUMBERS

ein(s)	1	one	
zwei	2	two	
drei	3	three	
vier	4	four	
fünf	5	five	
sechs	6	six	
sieben	7	seven	
acht	8	eight	
neun	9	nine	
zehn	10	ten	
elf	11	eleven	
zwölf	12	twelve	
dreizehn	13	thirteen	
vierzehn	14	fourteen	
fünfzehn	15	fifteen	
sechzehn	16	sixteen	
siebzehn	17	seventeen	
achtzehn	18	eighteen	
neunzehn	19	nineteen	
zwanzig	20	twenty	
einundzwanzig	21	twenty-one	
zweiundzwanzig	22	twenty-two	
dreißig	30	thirty	
vierzig	40	forty	
fünfzig	50	fifty	
sechzig	60	sixty	
siebzig	70	seventy	
achtzig	80	eighty	
neunzig	90	ninety	
hundert	100	a hundred	
hunderteins	101	a hundred and one	
zweihundert	200	two hundred	
zweihunderteins	201	two hundred and one	
dreihundert	300	three hundred	
dreihunderteins	301	three hundred and one	
tausend	1000	a thousand	
tausend(und)eins	1001	a thousand and one	
fünftausend	5000	five thousand	
eine Million	1000000	a million	
erste(r,s)	1.	first	1st
zweite(r,s)	2.	second	2nd
dritte(r,s)	3.	third	3rd
vierte(r,s)	4.	fourth	4th
fünfte(r,s)	5.	fifth	5th
sechste(r,s)	6.	sixth	6th

siebte(r,s)	7.	seventh	7th	
achte(r,s)	8.	eighth	8th	
neunte(r,s)	9.	ninth	9th	
zehnte(r,s)	10.	tenth	10th	
elfte(r,s)	11.	eleventh	11th	
zwölfte(r,s)	12.	twelfth	12th	
dreizehnte(r,s)	13.	thirteenth	13th	
vierzehnte(r,s)	14.	fourteenth	14th	
fünfzehnte(r,s)	15.	fifteenth	15th	
sechzehnte(r,s)	16.	sixteenth	16th	
siebzehnte(r,s)	17.	seventeenth	17th	
achtzehnte(r,s)	18.	eighteenth	18th	
neunzehnte(r,s)	19.	nineteenth	19th	
zwanzigste(r,s)	20.	twentieth	20th	
einundzwanzigste(r,s)	21.	twenty-first	21st	
dreißigste(r,s)	30.	thirtieth	30th	
hundertste(r,s)	100.	hundredth	100th	
hunderterste(r, s)	101.	hundred-and-first	101st	
tausendste(r,s)	1000.	thousandth	1000th	

Bruche usw.

Fractions etc.

ein Halb	½	a half	
ein Drittel	⅓	a third	
ein Viertel	¼	a quarter	
ein Fünftel	⅕	a fifth	
null Komma fünf	0,5	(nought) point five	0.5
drei Komma vier	3,4	three point four	3.4
sechs Komma acht neun	6,89	six point eight nine	6.89
zehn Prozent	10%	ten per cent	
hundert Prozent	100%	a hundred per cent	

Beispiele

Examples

er wohnt in Nummer 10	he lives at number 10
es steht in Kapitel 7	it's in chapter 7
auf Seite 7	on page 7
er wohnt im 7. Stock	he lives on the 7th floor
er wurde 7.	he came in 7th
im Maßstab eins zu zwanzigtausend	scale one to twenty thousand

UHRZEIT	THE TIME
wieviel Uhr ist es?, wie spät ist es?	*what time is it?*
es ist …	*it's …*
Mitternacht, zwölf Uhr nachts	midnight, twelve p.m.
ein Uhr (morgens *or* früh)	one o'clock (in the morning), one (a.m.)
fünf nach eins, ein Uhr fünf	five past one
zehn nach eins, ein Uhr zehn	ten past one
viertel nach eins, ein Uhr fünfzehn	a quarter past one, one fifteen
fünf vor halb zwei, ein Uhr fünfundzwanzig	twenty-five past one, one twenty-five
halb zwei, ein Uhr dreißig	half past one, one thirty
fünf nach halb zwei, ein Uhr fünfunddreißig	twenty-five to two, one thirty-five
zwanzig vor zwei, ein Uhr vierzig	twenty to two, one forty
viertel vor zwei, ein Uhr fünfundvierzig	a quarter to two, one forty-five
zehn vor zwei, ein Uhr fünfzig	ten to two, one fifty
zwölf Uhr (mittags), Mittag	twelve o'clock, midday, noon
halb eins (mittags *or* nachmittags), zwölf Uhr dreißig	half past twelve, twelve thirty (p.m.)
zwei Uhr (nachmittags)	two o'clock (in the afternoon), two (p.m.)
halb acht (abends)	half past seven (in the evening), seven thirty (p.m.)
um wieviel Uhr?	*at what time?*
um Mitternacht	at midnight
um sieben Uhr	at seven o'clock
...anzig Minuten	in twenty minutes
...hn Minuten	fifteen minutes ago

in zwan

vor fünfze